D0753520

INTRODUCTION TO PSYCHOLINGUISTICS

MATTHEW J. TRAXLER

INTRODUCTION TO PSYCHOLINGUISTICS

UNDERSTANDING LANGUAGE SCIENCE

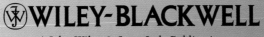

WILEY-BLACKWELL

A John Wiley & Sons, Ltd., Publication

This edition first published 2012

Blackwell Publishing was acquired by John Wiley & Sons in February 2007. Blackwell's publishing program has been merged with Wiley's global Scientific, Technical, and Medical business to form Wiley-Blackwell.

Registered Office
John Wiley & Sons Ltd, The Atrium, Southern Gate, Chichester, West Sussex, PO19 8SQ, UK

Editorial Offices
350 Main Street, Malden, MA 02148-5020, USA
9600 Garsington Road, Oxford, OX4 2DQ, UK
The Atrium, Southern Gate, Chichester, West Sussex, PO19 8SQ, UK

For details of our global editorial offices, for customer services, and for information about how to apply for permission to reuse the copyright material in this book please see our website at www.wiley.com/wiley-blackwell.

Library of Congress Cataloging-in-Publication Data is available for this title.

ISBN 9781405198622

A catalogue record for this book is available from the British Library.

This book is published in the following electronic formats: ePDFs [ISBN 9781444344325]; Wiley Online Library [ISBN 9781444344592]; ePub [ISBN 9781444344578]; mobi [ISBN 9781444344585].

Set in 10/12pt Minion Pro by SPi Publisher Services, Pondicherry, India

2 2012

CONTENTS

3 WORD PROCESSING 79

4 SENTENCE PROCESSING 141

5 DISCOURSE PROCESSING 187

ILLUSTRATIONS

Figures

Plates

Plates fall between pages 266 and 267.

ACKNOWLEDGMENTS

The author and publisher gratefully acknowledge the permission granted to reproduce the copyright material in this book:

Figure 1.1 From Terrace, H. S., Pettitto, L. A., Sanders, R. J., & Bever, T. G. (1979). Can an ape create a sentence? *Science, 206,* 891–902, used by permission of the American Association for the Advancement of Science.

Figure 2.1 From Levelt, W. J. M., Roelofs, A., & Meyer, A. S. (1999). A theory of lexical access in speech production. *Behavioral and Brain Sciences, 22,* 1–75, used by permission of Cambridge University Press.

Figure 2.2 From Arieh, Y., & Algom, D. (2002). Processing picture–word stimuli: The contingent nature of picture and of word superiority. *Journal of Experimental Psychology: Learning, Memory, and Cognition, 28,* 221–232, used by permission of the American Psychological Association.

Figure 2.3 From Dell, G. S., Schwartz, M. F., Martin, N., Saffran, E. M., & Gagnon, D. A. (1997). Lexical access in normal and aphasic speakers *Psychological Review, 104,* 801–838, used by permission of the American Psychological Association.

Figure 2.4 From the *American Journal of Psychology*, copyright 1952 by the Board of Trustees of the University of Illinois. Used with permission of the author and the University of Illinois Press.

Figure 2.5 From the *American Journal of Psychology*, copyright 1952 by the Board of Trustees of the University of Illinois. Used with permission of the author and the University of Illinois Press.

Figure 2.6 From Liberman, A. M., Cooper, F. S., Shankweiler, D. P., & Studdert-Kennedy, M. (1967). Perception of the speech code. *Psychological Review, 74,* 431–461, used by permission of the American Psychological Association.

Figure 2.7 From Whalen, D. H., & Liberman, A. M. (1987). Speech perception takes precedence over nonspeech perception. *Science, 237,* 169–171, used by permission of the American Association for the Advancement of Science.

Figure 2.8a © Eric Isselée/iStockphoto.com.

Figure 2.8b © Sergiy Goruppa/iStockphoto.com.

Figure 3.1 Created by Matthew Traxler.

Figure 3.2 Created by Matthew Traxler.

Figure 3.3 Created by Matthew Traxler.

Figure 3.4 From Rhodes, S. M., & Donaldson, D. I. (2008). Association and not semantic relationships elicit the N400 effect: Electrophysiological evidence from an explicit language comprehension task. *Psychophysiology, 45,* 50–59, used with permission of Wiley-Blackwell publishing.

Figure 3.5 From Nelson, D. L., Bennett, D. J., Gee, N. R., Schreiber, T. A., & McKinney, V. M. (1993). Implicit memory: Effects of network size and interconnectivity on cued recall. *Journal of Experimental Psychology: Learning, Memory, & Cognition, 19,* 747–764.

Figure 3.6	Created by Matthew Traxler.
Figure 3.7	Created by Matthew Traxler.
Figure 3.8	From Tucker, M., & Ellis, R. (2001). The potentiation of grasp types during visual object categorization. *Visual Cognition, 8,* 769–800, used with permission of Taylor & Francis.
Figure 3.9	From Pulvermüller, F., Hauk, O., Nikulin, V. V., & Ilmoniemi, R. (2005). Functional links between motor and language systems. *European Journal of Neuroscience, 21,* 793–797, used with permission of John Wiley & Sons.
Plate 2	From Hauk, O., Johnsrude, I., & Pulvermuller, F. (2004). Somatotopic representation of action words in human motor and premotor cortex. *Neuron, 41,* 301–307. Used with permission of Elsevier.
Plate 3	From Saygin, A. P., Wilson, S. M., Dronkers, N. F., & Bates, E. (2004). Action comprehension in aphasia: Linguistic and non-linguistic deficits and their lesion correlates. *Neuropsychologia, 42,* 1788–1804. Used with permission of Elsevier.
Figure 3.10	Created by Matthew Traxler.
Figure 3.11	From Morton, J. (1969). Interaction of information in word recognition. *Psychological Review, 76,* 165–178. Used with permission of the American Psychological Association.
Figure 3.12	From McClelland, J. L., & Rumelhart, D. E. (1981). An interactive activation model of context effects in letter perception: Part 1. An account of basic findings. *Psychological Review, 88,* 375–407. Used with permission of the American Psychological Association.
Figure 3.13	From McClelland, J. L., & Rumelhart, D. E. (1981). An interactive activation model of context effects in letter perception: Part 1. An account of basic findings. *Psychological Review, 88,* 375–407. Used with permission of the American Psychological Association.
Figure 3.14	From Elman, J. L. (2004) An alternative view of the mental lexicon. *Trends in Cognitive Sciences, 8,* 301–306. Used with permission of Elsevier.
Plate 4	From Vandenberghe, R., Price, C., Wise, R., Josephs, O., & Frackowiak, R. S. J. (1996). *Nature, 383,* 254–256. Used with permission of Nature Publishing Group.
Plate 5	From Martin, A., Wiggs, C. L., Ungerleider, L. G., & Haxby, J. V. (1996). Neural correlates of category-specific knowledge. *Nature, 379,* 649–652. Used with permission of Nature Publishing Group.
Figure 3.15	From Posner, M. I., Petersen, S. E., Fox, P. T., & Raichle, M. E. (1988). Localization of cognitive operations in the human brain. *Science, 240,* 1627–1631, used by permission of the American Association for the Advancement of Science.
Figure 3.16	From Price, C. J., Moore, C. J., Humphreys, G. W., & Wise, R. J. S. (1997). Segregating semantic from phonological processes during reading. *Journal of Cognitive Neuroscience, 9,* 727–733. Used with permission of MIT Press.
Plate 6	From Goldberg, R. F., Perfetti, C. A., Fiez, J. A., & Schneider, W. (2007). Selective retrieval of abstract semantic knowledge in left prefrontal cortex. *The Journal of Neuroscience, 27,* 3790–3798. Used with permission of the Society for Neuroscience.
Figure 3.17	From Cohen, L., Lehéricy, S., Chochon, F., Lemer, C., Rivaud, S., & Dehaene, S. (2002). Language-specific tuning of visual cortex? Functional properties of the visual word form area. *Brain, 125,* 1054–1069. Used with permission of Oxford University Press.

Plate 7 From Damasio, H., Grabowski, T. J., Tranel, D., Hichwa, R. D., & Damasio, A. R. (1996). A neural basis for lexical retrieval. *Nature, 380,* 499–505. Used with permission of Nature Publishing Group.

Figure 4.1 Created by Matthew Traxler.

Figure 4.2 From Tanenhaus, M. K., Spivey-Knowlton, M. J., Eberhard, K. M., & Sedivy, J. C. (1995). Integration of visual and linguistic information in spoken language comprehension. *Science, 268,* 1632–1634, used by permission of the American Association for the Advancement of Science.

Figure 4.3 Created by Matthew Traxler.

Figure 5.1 From Bransford, J. D., & Johnson, M. K. (1972). Contextual prerequisites for understanding: Some investigations of comprehension and recall. *Journal of Verbal Learning and Verbal Behavior, 11,* 717–726. Used with permission of Elsevier.

Figure 5.2 Created by Matthew Traxler.

Figure 5.3 Originally published in Kintsch, W., Welsch, D., Schmalhofer, F., & Zimny, S. (1990). Sentence memory: A theoretical analysis. *Journal of Memory and Language, 29,* 133–159, reprinted with permission of Elsevier.

Figure 5.4 Gernsbacher, M. A., & Faust, M. E. (1991). The mechanism of suppression: A component of general comprehension skill. *Journal of Experimental Psychology: Learning, Memory, and Cognition, 17,* 245–262.

Plate 8 From Ferstl, E. C., Rinck, M., & Von Cramon, D. Y. (2005). Emotional and temporal aspects of situation model processing during text comprehension: An event-related fMRI study. *Journal of Cognitive Neuroscience, 17,* 724–739. Used with permission of MIT Press.

Figure 5.5 From Münte, T. F., Schiltz, K., & Kutas, M. (1998). When temporal terms belie conceptual order. *Nature, 395,* 71–73. Used with permission of Nature Publishing Group.

Figure 5.6 From Suh, S., & Trabasso, T. (1993). Inferences during reading: Converging evidence from discourse analysis, talk-aloud protocols, and recognition priming. *Journal of Memory and Language, 32,* 279–300. Used with permission of John Wiley and Sons.

Figure 5.7 From Robertson, D. A., Gernsbacher, M. A., Guidotti, S. J., Robertson, R. W., Irwin, W., Mock, B. J., & Campana, M. E. (2000). Functional neuroanatomy of the cognitive process of mapping during discourse comprehension. *Psychological Science, 11,* 255–260. Used with permission of John Wiley and Sons.

Figure 5.8 From Mason, R. A., & Just, M. A. (2004). How the brain processes causal inferences in text: A theoretical account of generation and integration component processes utilizing both cerebral hemispheres. *Psychological Science, 15,* 1–7. Used with permission of Sage Publishing.

Figure 5.9 From Mason, R. A., & Just, M. A. (2004). How the brain processes causal inferences in text: A theoretical account of generation and integration component processes utilizing both cerebral hemispheres. *Psychological Science, 15,* 1–7. Used with permission of Sage Publishing.

Plate 9 Originally appeared in Jung-Beeman, M., Bowden, E. M., Haberman, J., Frymiare, J. L., Arambel-Liu, S., Greenblatt, R., Reber, P. J., & Kounios, J. (2004). Neural activity observed in people solving verbal problems with insight. *Public Library of Science – Biology, 2,* 500–510, reprinted with permission of Sage Publishing.

Plate 10 From Virtue, S., Haberman, J., Clancy, Z., Parrish, T., & Beeman, MJ. (2006). Neural activity of inferences during story comprehension. *Brain Research, 1084,* 104–114. Used with permission of Elsevier.

Plate 11 From St. George, M., Kutas, M., Martinez, A., & Sereno, M. I. (1999). Semantic integration in reading: Engagement of the right hemisphere during discourse processing. *Brain, 122,* 1317–1325. Used with permission of Oxford University Press.

Plate 12 From St. George, M., Kutas, M., Martinez, A., & Sereno, M. I. (1999). Semantic integration in reading: Engagement of the right hemisphere during discourse processing. *Brain, 122,* 1317–1325. Used with permission of Oxford University Press.

Plate 13 From Kuperberg, G. R., Lakshmanan, B. M., Caplan, D. N., & Holcomb, P. J. (2006). Making sense of discourse: An fMRI study of causal inferencing across sentences. *Neuroimage, 33,* 343–361. Used with permission of Elsevier.

Plate 14 From Kuperberg, G. R., Lakshmanan, B. M., Caplan, D. N., & Holcomb, P. J. (2006). Making sense of discourse: An fMRI study of causal inferencing across sentences. *Neuroimage, 33,* 343–361. Used with permission of Elsevier.

Figure 6.1 Created by Matthew Traxler.

Figure 6.2 From Järvikivi, J., van Gompel, R. P. G., Hyöna, J., & Bertram, R. (2005). Ambiguous pronoun resolution. *Psychological Science, 16,* 260–264. Used with permission of John Wiley and Sons.

Plate 15 From Bottini, G., Corcoran, R., Sterzi, R., Paulescu, E., Schenone, P., Scarpa, P., Frackowiak, R. S. J., & Frith, C. D. (1994). The role of right hemisphere in the interpretation of figurative aspects of language: A positron emission tomography study. *Brain, 117,* 1241–1253. Used with permission of Oxford University Press.

Plate 16 From Rapp, A. M., Leube, D. T., Erb, M., Grodd, W., & Kircher, T. T. J. (2004). Neural correlates of metaphor processing. *Cognitive Brain Research, 20,* 395–402. Used with permission of Elsevier.

Plate 17 From Mashal, N., Faust, M., Hendler, T., & Jung-Beeman, M. (2007). An fMRI investigation of the neural correlates underlying the processing of novel metaphoric expressions. Brain and Language, *100,* 115–126. Used with permission of Elsevier.

Figure 8.1 From Brown, P. M., & Dell, G. S. (1987). Adapting production to comprehension: The explicit mention of instruments. *Cognitive Psychology, 19,* 441–472. Used with permission of Elsevier.

Figure 8.2 From Wardlow-Lane, L., & Ferreira, V. S. (2008). Speaker-external versus speaker-internal forces on utterance form: Do cognitive demands override threats to referential success? *Journal of Experimental Psychology: Learning, Memory, and Cognition, 34,* 1466–1481. Used by permission of the American Psychological Association.

Figure 8.3 From Keysar, B., Barr, D. J., Balin, J. A., & Brauner, J. S. (2000). Taking perspective in conversation: The role of mutual knowledge in comprehension. *Psychological Science, 11,* 32–38. Used with permission of John Wiley and Sons

Figure 9.1 From Saffran, J. R. (2003). Statistical language learning: Mechanisms and constraints. *Current Directions in Psychological Science, 12,* 110–114. Used with permission of John Wiley and Sons.

Figure 9.2 From Saffran, J. R., Pollak, S. D., Seibel, R. L., & Shkolnik, A. (2007). Dog is a dog is a dog: Infant rule learning is not specific to language. *Cognition, 105,* 669–680. Used with permission of Elsevier.

Figure 9.3 From Yuan, S., & Fisher, C. (2009). "Really? She blicked the baby?" Two-year-olds learn combinatorial facts about verbs by listening. *Psychological Science, 20,* 619–626. Used with permission of Sage Publications.

Figure 10.1 Created by Matthew Traxler.

Figure 10.2 Created by Matthew Traxler.

Figure 10.3 From Reichle, E. D., Pollatsek, A., & Rayner, K. (2006). E-Z Reader: A cognitive-control, serial-attention model of eye-movement behavior during reading. *Cognitive Systems Research, 7,* 4–22. Used with permission of Elsevier.

Figure 10.4 From Engbert, R., Nuthmann, A., Richter, E. M., & Kliegl, R. (2005). SWIFT: A dynamical model of saccade generation during reading. *Psychological Review, 112,* 777–813. Used by permission of the American Psychological Association.

Figure 10.5 © Universal Images Group Limited/Alamy.

Figure 10.6 From Perfetti, C. A., Liu, Y., Fiez, J., Nelson, J., Bolger, D. J., & Tan, L. (2007). Reading in two writing systems: Accommodation and assimilation of the brain's reading network. *Bilingualism: Language and Cognition, 10,* 131–146. Used with permission of Cambridge University Press.

Figure 10.7 From Coltheart, M., Rastle, K., Perry, C., Langdon, R., & Ziegler, J. (2001). DRC: A dual route cascaded model of visual word recognition and reading aloud. *Psychological Review, 108,* 204–256. Used with permission of the American Psychological Association.

Figure 10.8 From Seidenberg, M. S., & McClelland, J. L. (1989). A distributed, developmental model of word recognition and naming. *Psychological Review, 96,* 523–568. Used with permission of the American Psychological Association.

Figure 10.9 Created by Matthew Traxler.

Plate 18 From Dietz, N. A. E., Jones, K. M., Gareau, L., Zeffiro, T. A., & Eden, G. F. (2005). Phonological decoding involves left posterior fusiform gyrus. *Human Brain Mapping, 26,* 81–93. Used with permission of John Wiley and Sons.

Figure 10.10 From Bailey, C. E., Manis, F. R., Pedersen, W. C., & Seidenberg, M. S. (2004). Variation among developmental dyslexics: Evidence from a printed-word-learning task. *Journal of Experimental Child Psychology, 87,* 125–154. Used with permission of Elsevier.

Figure 11.1 Created by Matthew Traxler.

Figure 11.2 Created by Matthew Traxler.

Figure 11.3 © Bev McConnell/iStockphoto.

Figure 11.4 From Green, D. W. (1998). Mental control of the bilingual lexico-semantic system. *Bilingualism: Language and Cognition, 1,* 67–81. Used with permission of Cambridge University Press.

Figure 11.5 From Bialystok, E., Craik, F. I. M., Klein, R., & Viswanathan, M. (2004). Bilingualism, aging, and cognitive control: Evidence from the Simon task. *Psychology and Aging, 19,* 290–303. Used with permission of the American Psychological Association.

Figure 12.1 Fingerspelling chart, layout and design copyright © 2007, William Vicars, sign language resources at Lifeprint.com.

Figure 12.2	From Emmorey, K., Grabowski, T., McCullough, S., Damasio, H., Ponto, L. L. B., Hichwa, R. D., & Bellugi, U. (2003). Neural systems underlying lexical retrieval for sign language. *Neuropsychologia, 41,* 83–95. Used with permission of Taylor and Francis.
Figure 12.3	From Corina, D. P., Kritchevsky, M., & Bellugi, U. (1996). Visual language processing and unilateral neglect: Evidence from American Sign Language. *Cognitive Neuropsychology, 13,* 321–356. Used with permission of Taylor and Francis.
Figure 12.4	From Poizner, H., Newkirk, D., Bellugi, U., & Klima, E. S. (1981). Representation of inflected signs from American Sign Language in short-term memory. *Memory & Cognition, 9,* 121–131. Used with permission of Elsevier.
Figure 12.5	From Singleton, J. L., & Newport, E. L. (2004). When learners surpass their models: The acquisition of American Sign Language from inconsistent input. *Cognitive Psychology, 49,* 370–407. Used with permission of Elsevier.
Plate 19	From Neville, H. J., Bavelier, D., Corina, D., Rauschecker, J., Karni, A., Lalwani, A., Braun, A., Clark, V., Jezzard, P., & Turner, R. (1998). Cerebral organization for language in deaf and hearing subjects: Biological constraints and effects of experience *Proceedings of the National Academy of Sciences, 95,* 922–929. Reprinted with permission of National Academy of Sciences, U.S.A., Copyright 1998.
Figure 12.6	From Hickok, G., Bellugi, U., & Klima, E. S. (1998a). The neural organization of language: Evidence from sign language aphasia. *Trends in Cognitive Sciences, 2,* 129–136. Used with permission of Elsevier.
Figure 13.1	From Dronkers, N. F., Plaisant, O., Iba-Zizen, M. T., & Cabanis, E.A. (2007). Paul Broca's historic cases: High resolution MR imaging of the brains of Leborgne and Lelong. *Brain, 130,* 1432–1441. Used with permission of Oxford University Press.
Plate 20	From Catani, M., Jones, D. K., and ffytche, D. H. (2005). Perisylvian language networks of the human brain. *Annals of Neurology, 57,* 8–16. Used with permission of John Wiley and Sons.
Figure 13.4	Image © Sovereign, ISM/Science Photo Library.
Plate 21	From Dronkers, N. F., Wilkins D. P., Van Valin R. D., Redfern B. B., & Jaeger, J. J. (2004). Lesion analysis of the brain areas involved in language comprehension. *Cognition, 92,* 145–77. Used with permission of Elsevier.
Figure 13.5	From Grodzinsky, Y., Piñango, M. M., Zurif, E., & Drai, D. (1999). The critical role of group studies in neuropsychology: Comprehension regularities in Broca's aphasia. *Brain and Language, 67,* 134–147. Used with permission of Elsevier.
Figure 14.1	From Homae, F., Watanabe, H., Nakano, T., Asakawa, K., & Taga, G. (2006). The right hemisphere of sleeping infant perceives sentential prosody. *Neuroscience Research, 54,* 276–280. Used with permission of Elsevier.
Figure 14.2	From Burgess, C., & Simpson, G. B. (1988). Cerebral hemispheric mechanisms in the retrieval of ambiguous word meanings. *Brain and Language, 33,* 86–103. Used with permission of Elsevier.

Every effort has been made to trace copyright holders and to obtain their permission for the use of copyright material. The publisher apologizes for any errors or omissions in the above list and would be grateful if notified of any corrections that should be incorporated in future reprints or editions of this book.

PREFACE

The last time I wrote a preface, I killed a guy. Well, I didn't actually kill him. I just said he was dead even though he isn't. (Sorry Eno!) One of my major goals in writing this preface is not to kill anyone who isn't already dead. My other major goal is to use the word "shenanigans."

I learned two things from my previous preface-writing experience. Lesson 1: Sometimes, people read the preface. In this case, it was Gerard Kempen, who was kind enough to interrogate me about my error while I was in the middle of hosting a major scientific conference. Gerard, if you're reading this: I promise not to kill anyone this time. Lesson 2: It stinks to screw up in a very public way. It's much better to screw up in private.

In the light of lesson 2, my editors and I have taken special care to ensure that the contents of this book are as accurate as possible at the time of printing. We have been assisted in this endeavor by a number of highly talented and thoughtful reviewers, to whom I am profoundly grateful. These reviewers include Chuck Clifton and several anonymous experts, all of whom are wise in the ways of language. Mark Seidenberg answered e-mails at all hours of the day and provided timely advice and guidance at critical junctures in the drafting process. Judy Kroll was also very generous with advice and pointers to useful information. It goes without saying that I am responsible for any errors or omissions that remain.

Before I started working on this book, I spent a long time teaching language and reflecting on disappointing teaching evaluations. Like many professors, and amateur mechanics everywhere, I blamed my tools. In particular, I blamed the textbooks that I was using. I decided that the only solution was to write my own book, and this is the result. I hope that the book presents language in a coherent way that is accessible to the average student. If it doesn't, I'm going to have to write another book.

Language scientists have discovered a lot of great things about the way the mind works. (We are the Kevin McHales of cognitive science. We score a quiet 20 points off the bench every game, but the flashy guys with the robots and the mirror neurons get all the headlines.) The field has developed strong momentum since I started observing it mumble mumble years ago, so this is an exciting time to be learning about language. I hope that the book conveys some of that excitement.

No book is the work of any one person. I am very grateful to my current and former editors at Wiley-Blackwell, especially Christine Cardone, who is a deep fountain of advice and encouragement. Anna Oxbury also deserves special mention for diligent copyediting and numerous suggestions of ways to improve the copy. Matt Bennett and Nicole Benevenia have also been wonderful.

I am also thankful to all the magnificent teachers and mentors that I have been fortunate to learn from over the years. Randy Fletcher gave me a great start doing research at the University of Minnesota. Morton Ann Gernsbacher showed me what it means to work (no one can match her—don't even try). Martin Pickering taught me how sentences work. Don Foss rescued me from being a fly-fishing guide in Colorado. Most days, that's a good thing. Thanks, Don.

I am also grateful to my students and colleagues at the University of California, Davis. Megan Zirnstein and Kristen Tooley deserve special mention for keeping me on my toes.

Finally, I am most deeply grateful for the continuing support of my whole family, but especially Rose and Tina. They put up with a lot of shenanigans.

Davis, California

An Introduction to Language Science

The rules aren't the ones we were taught in school.

IVAN SAG

One of my favorite language scientists is Daniel L. Everett, a former evangelical Christian missionary who has spent more than 30 years living among and studying the *Pirahã* (pronounced "pee-da-HAN"), a group of about 300 hunter-gatherers, who live alongside a river in a largely unspoiled and remote part of the Amazon rain forest. Everett went there originally to learn the Pirahã language so that he could translate the Bible and spread the gospel to the Pirahã. To do so, he had to overcome the heat, tropical diseases, jaguars, hostile traders, gigantic anacondas,[1] biting insects, snakes that drop from the ceiling, electric eels, piranhas, caimans,[2] a tiny fish that tries to swim up any unguarded body cavity,[3] and much more. You can read about his adventures in the autobiographical book *Don't Sleep, There Are Snakes*. More importantly, for our purposes, you can read about what he discovered about the language that the Pirahã speak, and the ways that it differs from languages that citizens of industrialized nations are more familiar with. It turns out that Everett's research touches on some of the biggest, most general, and most difficult questions that language scientists have attempted to tackle. What does it mean to know a language? How do languages work? Where do they come from? What made languages take their current form(s)? How is language related to thought? Are thought and language identical? This chapter examines these questions, too, not because they have clear answers (most of them do not), but because taking a run at

Introduction to Psycholinguistics: Understanding Language Science, First Edition.
Matthew J. Traxler.

these questions can give us a deeper appreciation of what language is, how it got to be that way, and how our language abilities fit in with other cognitive (thinking) skills.

Part of Everett's research addresses one of the most fundamental questions in language science: What is language? What does it mean to know a language? This is the kind of *essentialist* question that *psycholinguists* (psychologists who study the mental and neural processes as well as the behaviors associated with language) tend to avoid whenever possible (Stanovich, 2009). However, the precise definition of language and a description of its component features greatly concerns researchers who want to know what mental abilities you need to use language, which of those abilities are used for language but not other kinds of cognitive tasks, and whether non-human animals share some or all of our ability to produce and understand language (Everett, 2005, 2007; Hauser, Chomsky, & Fitch, 2002; Jackendoff & Pinker, 2005; Pinker, 1994; Pinker & Bloom, 1990; Pinker & Jackendoff, 2005; Talmy, 2009).

Language Characteristics

Descriptions of language often appeal to Charles Hockett's (1960) design features. Let's focus on a subset of these features, because some of his proposed design features are not necessary for language (e.g., using the vocal channel for sending and receiving messages—sign language users do just fine without it), while others are not specific to language (e.g., cultural transmission—learning to make perogies or knit sweaters is also culturally transmitted). A set of central, possibly necessary, design features could include the following: *semanticity*, *arbitrariness*, *discreteness*, *displacement*, *duality of patterning*, and *generativity*. Let's consider each of these in turn.

Semanticity refers to the idea that language can communicate meaning, and that specific signals can be assigned specific meanings. This occurs at multiple levels in languages, as individual words can be assigned particular meanings, and so can longer expressions that contain more than one word.

Arbitrariness refers to the fact that there is no necessary relationship between actual objects or events in the world and the symbols that a language uses to represent those objects or events. For example, the word that goes with an object need not resemble the real object in any way. One result of arbitrariness is that names for objects can be completely different across languages (*koshka*, *gato*, *chat*, *neko*, and *mao* are all words for *cat*). The name could be changed as long as everyone agreed, and the name change would not affect the ability to express the concept in the language. Tomorrow, we English speakers could all start calling cats "lerps," and as long as everyone agreed, this would work just fine. Sometimes, people point to *onomatopoeia* (words like "moo" and "oink") in English as an example of a non-arbitrary relationship between sound and meaning. Sometimes people argue that the words for large objects have deep-sounding vowels made with the vocal cavity opened up to be big (*ocean*, *tower*), while words for small objects have high-sounding vowels with the vocal cavity closed down to be small (*pin*, *bitsy*). But *onomatopoeia* is not as systematic as people assume (the Dutch equivalent of "oink" is "knorr-knorr"), and there are plenty of counterexamples to the "big concept—big vowel" hypothesis (e.g., *infinity*).

Discreteness refers to the idea that components of the language are organized into a set of distinct categories, with clear-cut boundaries between different categories. For example, every speech sound in English is perceived as belonging to one of about 40 phoneme categories (e.g., a sound is either a /p/ or a /b/; it's either a /t/ or a /d/). For Pirahã speakers, every speech sound made by another Pirahã speaker will be recognized as one of 11 phonemes.[4] Think of how many different speakers a language has, how different all of their voices are, how their speech can vary from occasion to occasion in how fast they talk, whether they speak clearly or not, and so on. Despite all of the vast differences between speakers, and differences within speakers over time, people who speak the same language will fit every sound made by every speaker into one of the available categories.

Displacement refers to a language's ability to convey information about events happening out of sight of the speaker (*spatial displacement*), about events that happened before the moment when the person speaks, and events that have not yet taken place as the person is speaking (*temporal displacement*). Different languages accomplish displacement in different ways. English has a system of auxiliary verbs (e.g., *will, was, were, had*) and affixes (e.g., *pre-* in *predates*; *-ed* in *dated*) to signal when an event occurred relative to the moment of speaking or relative to other events. Other languages, such as Mandarin, lack these kinds of *tense markers*, but use other means, such as adverbial expressions, to achieve the same means (so you would say the equivalent of, "Yesterday, the man goes" rather than "The man went"). Displacement is a ubiquitous feature of human languages, although the degree and scope of displacement may be more limited in some languages than others (Everett, 2008), but it is largely or completely absent in animal communication systems. Primates may call to one another to signal the presence of predators or food, as will bees, but these behaviors have more the flavor of a reflex, rather than being the result of a controlled, intentional desire to convey information (Tomasello, 2007).

Duality of patterning refers to the fact that we simultaneously perceive language stimuli in different ways; for example, as a collection of phonemes and as a set of words. The word *wasp* consists of four basic speech sounds or *phonemes* – /w/, /o/, /s/, and /p/. Normally, we "see through" the phonemes and the individual word-sounds to the meaning that a speaker is trying to convey, but each of these kinds of patterns, speech sounds (phonemes) and words, can be detected if we decide to pay attention to the form of the speaker's message, rather than its meaning.

Finally, *generativity* refers to the fact that languages have a fixed number of symbols, but a very large and potentially infinite number of messages that can be created by combining those symbols in different patterns. English has about 40 phonemes, but those 40 phonemes can be combined in an infinite number of ways. Similarly, the average high school graduate knows the meanings of about 50,000 different words, but can combine those words in new patterns to produce an unlimited number of meanings.

Language scientists agree that all of the preceding characterize human languages, but they do not all agree on other aspects of language. Many of these disagreements revolve around a component of language called *grammar* (or *syntax* by some theorists). At a very basic level, languages provide us the means to associate sounds with meanings (Hauser et al., 2002). Other animals are also able to associate arbitrary sounds with objects in the environment, similar to the way people associate sounds and meanings. Vervet monkeys make one kind of call when they see an airborne predator, and a different kind of call when they see a predator on the ground; and they respond in the appropriate way depending on which call they hear. If it's an eagle call, they dive into the bushes. If it's a leopard call, they head up into the trees. Vervets lack the capacity to combine sets of calls into longer messages (but see below for evidence that some apes have this ability). If vervets had a system of rules that enabled them to combine calls into more complex messages (e.g., "look at the size of that leopard!"), we would say that they have a *grammar*.

Grammar is one of the two chief components of a language. The other is the *lexicon*, the part of long-term memory that stores information about words (Sag, Wasow, & Bender, 2003). Languages need both of these components so that speakers can formulate messages that express *propositions* (statements of who did what to whom, roughly). To create such messages, a speaker searches for symbols in the lexicon that match the concepts that she wishes to convey. The grammar tells her how to combine the symbols to create the appropriate signals (speech sounds) that will transmit her message to a listener.

Before we go any further, we need to get straight a common misunderstanding of the word *grammar*. When people hear "grammar," they often think of "grammar school" or the system of rules that your 8th grade English teacher tried to get you to memorize so that you could speak and write standard English. Like me, you probably failed to internalize many of your 8th grade English teacher's lessons. This is partly because 8th grade English is unbearably boring and partly because the principles that your 8th grade teacher was trying to foist on you are completely arbitrary and artificial. For example, Mrs Heidemann tried to get me to believe that you cannot end a sentence with a preposition.[5] But then, there's this kid whose dad always reads him the same story at bedtime. One night, when dad turned up with the same old horrible book, the kid said, *Hey, Dad! What did you bring that book that I didn't want to be read to out of up for?* Five prepositions at the end, perfectly interpretable.[6] Mrs Heidemann was trying to teach me *prescriptive grammar*. Prescriptive grammars are collections of artificial rules. If you follow the grammar teacher's prescription (like you follow a doctor's prescription), your language will sound like that used by members of the upper class in England's home counties.

The vast majority of language scientists are not interested in prescriptive grammar. The kind of grammar we are interested in is *descriptive grammar*, which is the set of rules or principles that governs the way people use language "in the wild." That is, how people naturally and normally think and behave. Here is an example of a descriptive rule of grammar: "Each clause can only have one main verb." You already know this rule, even though nobody, not even Mrs Heidemann, ever tried to teach it to you. As a result, you would never say, *Mrs Heidemann brewed drank the coffee*. Similarly, English descriptive grammar says, "Put verbs in the middle, not at the beginning of sentences." Again, you already know this rule, because you never say things like *Drank the coffee Mrs Heidemann*. So when this book talks about grammar, remember that it is talking about descriptive (the natural kind) not prescriptive grammar, the Mrs Heidemann kind. Language scientists who study grammar greatly prefer studying descriptive grammar because most of us are interested in the human mind and, as Ivan Sag and colleagues noted (2003, p. 42), "A theory of grammar is a theory about the mental representation of linguistic knowledge."

Descriptive grammars explain why language takes the form that it does. Steven Pinker and Ray Jackendoff (2005) suggest that grammars regulate the combination of symbols into messages in three crucial ways. First, the grammar determines the order that symbols appear in expressions. In English, adjectives come before nouns (*red wine*). In French, the adjectives mostly come after the nouns (*vin rouge*), with a few exceptions (e.g., *grand dame*, "great woman"). Second, the grammar dictates different kinds of *agreement*. Agreement means that certain words in a sentence must appear in a specific form because of the presence of another word in the sentence. In English, we have number agreement (*girls like* but not *girls likes* or *girl like*, as in *Girls like books* but not *Girls likes books*). Other languages have other kinds of agreement, such as Spanish *gender* agreement (*el toro* not *la toro*). Finally, the grammar determines *case marking*, where words must appear in particular forms depending on what grammatical functions they fulfill. English has lost most of its case marking, but it still has some in its system of pronouns (*He left* not *Him left*; *I like him* but not *I like he*). Russian has tons of case marking, as nouns and other words appear in different forms depending on what role they play in the sentence (e.g., vodka changes to vodku as the noun moves from subject to object; Водка здесь *Vodka zdes'* "Here is the vodka," but not Водку здесь *Vodku zdes'*; Я пил водку *Ya pil vodku* "I drank vodka," but not Я пил водка *Ya pil vodka*).

To figure out what rules of grammar people actually carry around in their heads with them, linguists spend a great deal of time and effort observing people speaking spontaneously and recording the details of how they combine words into longer expressions. They then take these records and try to determine why words appear in specific parts of phrases and sentences, and why they appear in particular forms. This type of analysis allows them to deduce the rules behind the patterns that appear in transcripts of speech. When this type of analysis is done on English, it leads to a number of conclusions about English grammar. For example, English is a *subject-verb-object* language. In declarative statements, the grammatical *subject* of the sentence, which is normally the focus of attention or the topic of the discourse, appears at the beginning of the sentence. The verb appears in the middle. The grammatical *object*, which normally is the thing that is acted upon, comes last. Other languages order these elements in different ways. Japanese, for example, puts its verbs at the end. Languages like Russian have free word order and make much greater use than English of different versions of nouns to express who is initiating the action and who is being acted upon. To figure out which system a language has, you actually have to go out and watch people use the language. Sometimes, doing that produces big surprises.

Based on observations of English and other languages, Chomsky and his colleagues have proposed that *recursion* is a core property of the grammars of all languages (Fitch, Hauser, & Chomsky, 2005; Hauser et al., 2002). Further, based on a detailed analysis of human language and animal communication systems, they proposed that recursion is the *only* property that is specific to human language. "The narrow language faculty includes recursion and this is the only uniquely human component of the faculty of language" (Hauser et al., 2002, p. 1569). Chomsky's team proposes that all other properties of language are either shared with non-language thought processes or with non-human communication systems. What are they talking about and why does it matter? *Recursion* is defined as "the ability to place one component inside another component of the same type." So, where language is concerned, recursion could happen if you could place one phrase inside another phrase of the same type or one sentence inside another sentence.[7]

English allows us to place one sentence inside another sentence. Here's a sentence:

Tom likes beans.

We can place that sentence inside another sentence:

Susan thinks (X)   (where X is a sentence)

The result would be:

Susan thinks Tom likes beans.

The degree to which this sort of recursion can go on is essentially infinite, and is limited only by the speaker's ability and willingness to continue:

John knows Dave believes Jenny hopes Carol recognizes Bob realizes … Susan thinks Tom likes beans.

Thus, recursion is one of the characteristics that gives language the property of *discrete infinity*, the ability to generate infinite messages (even infinitely long messages) from finite means.

Most of the languages that have been studied do have recursion, but there does appear to be at least one exception: Pirahã (Everett, 2005, 2008). In English, recursion is often used to create expressions that modify or change the meaning of one of the elements of the sentence. For example, to take the word *nails* and give it a more specific meaning, we could use an *object relative clause* such as *that Dan bought*, as in

Hand me the nails <u>that Dan bought</u>.

In this sentence, the relative clause *that Dan bought* (which could be glossed as "Dan bought the nails") is contained within a larger noun phrase: *the nails (that Dan bought (the nails))*. So the relative clause is nested within a larger phrase, kind of like a stack of bowls. Pirahã expresses the same meaning in a much different form, one that does not involve recursion. To express the meaning that goes with "Hand me the nails that Dan bought," a Pirahã speaker would say the equivalent of:

> Give me the nails. Dan bought those very nails. They are the same. (Everett, 2008, p. 227).

In this case, none of the expressions are contained within other expressions of the same type. Pirahã even appears to lack a very simple form of recursion that happens when you use a *coordinate structure* to put two noun phrases together, as in *Dan and Ted went to Brazil* (E. Gibson, personal communication). In *Dan and Ted*, you have an overarching noun phrase (of the form *NP and NP*) that contains two separate noun phrases (*Dan*, *Ted*). To express a meaning like this, a Pirahã speaker would say the equivalent of, "Dan went to Brazil. Ted went to Brazil." Instead of having a stack of bowls, Pirahã has the linguistic equivalent of a string of pearls. All of the statements are connected to each other in an important way, but none of them is contained within any of the others. If recursion does not occur in Pirahã language, which is still definitely a language on a par with other languages in its ability to convey meaning, then recursion is not a necessary characteristic of human languages, despite the fact that most of them have it anyway.

Why does Pirahã lack recursion? Everett's (2008) answer is that Pirahã lacks recursion because recursion introduces statements into a language that do not make direct assertions about the world. When you say, *Give me the nails that Dan bought*, that statement *presupposes* that it is true that Dan bought the nails, but it does not say so outright. In Pirahã, each of the individual sentences is a direct statement or assertion about the world. "Give me the nails" is a command equivalent to "I want the nails" (an assertion about the speaker's mental state). "Dan bought the nails" is a direct assertion of fact, again expressing the speaker's mental state ("I know Dan bought those nails"). "They are the same" is a further statement of fact. Everett describes the Pirahã as being a very literal-minded people. They have no creation myths. They do not tell fictional stories. They do not believe assertions made by others about past events unless the speaker has direct knowledge of the events, or knows someone who does. As a result, they are very resistant to conversion to Christianity, or any other faith that requires belief in things unseen. Everett argues that these cultural principles determine the form of Pirahã grammar. Specifically, because the Pirahã place great store in first-hand knowledge, sentences in the language must be assertions. Nested statements, like relative clauses, require presuppositions (rather than assertions) and are therefore ruled out. If Everett is right about this, then Pirahã grammar is shaped by Pirahã culture. The form their language takes is shaped by their cultural values and the way they relate to one another socially. If this is so, then Everett's study of Pirahã grammar would overturn much of the received wisdom on where grammars come from and why they take the form they do. Which leads us to …

Grammar, Language Origins, and Non-Human Communication Systems

Many language scientists are concerned with the precise definition of language and with detailed descriptions of the grammars of different languages because having those two things nailed down can help us understand how humans think and how we compare with other living creatures around us. One of the most basic questions that we might like to answer is: Why do humans have language? That question motivates research on the emergence of language abilities in the human evolutionary line as well as research on the language abilities of non-human animals. Figuring out how language abilities developed in the human evolutionary line requires us to analyze the language abilities of ancestors long dead. We need to understand how we are similar to and different from evolutionary ancestors in terms of both language and non-language characteristics. The major obstacle in this line of research is that we have no way of directly observing either the behavior of these ancestors or their nervous systems. As a result, researchers are forced to draw inferences from the fossil record and from artifacts found along with fossil remains. Understanding how we relate to other living animals is potentially easier, because we have living specimens to study. But there are complex issues here as well, some of which are addressed below.

There are two main, overarching ideas about how modern human language abilities emerged from evolutionary ancestors who lacked language, and the same ideas can be used to describe our relationship to living, non-human close relatives (e.g., chimpanzees, bonobos, gorillas, and other primates). These two ideas can be captured by the concepts *continuity* and *discontinuity* (Lenneberg, 1967; Lieberman, 2000; Penn, Holyoak, & Povinelli, 2008). According to the continuity hypothesis, modern human language is quantitatively different from precursor mental abilities, but it is not different in kind or in quality from more basic communication systems. According to the continuity hypothesis, human language abilities are closely related to pre-existing communicative abilities and represent a relatively modest upgrade from those abilities. One advantage of this approach is that we can apply general ideas about adaptation and natural selection to the development of human language, the same way we apply those ideas to other characteristics of humans. The discontinuity hypothesis, by contrast, proposes that some aspects of modern human language abilities represent a clean break from the past, that our language abilities are qualitatively different from more basic communication systems, either in our evolutionary ancestors or in living, non-human animal communication systems. That is, humans possess communication abilities that do not exist in other, more primitive systems. One of the challenges for discontinuity theorists is to identify language abilities that exist in humans but not other species (or in our ancestors), and to explain how the gap between human language abilities and more primitive communication systems was crossed. Let's consider the evolution of human language abilities within our direct ancestors after considering the language abilities of other living modern species (e.g., chimps, dolphins, monkeys).

Research on communication abilities in apes

There are no data which prove that other apes are unable to communicate linguistically.
E. SUE SAVAGE-RUMBAUGH

Studies of how animals communicate can help test ideas related to the continuity hypothesis. As Lenneberg (1967, p. 228) puts it, "[If human] forms of communication ... descended from primitive animal forms of communication, [then] a study of the latter is likely to disclose that there is indeed a straight line of evolution of this feature." Apes and monkeys provide useful comparisons to humans because some apes, such as chimpanzees, are closely related biologically to humans. Monkeys and apes are also highly intelligent, which makes them good candidates to share some of the complex abilities that are involved in producing and understanding language. For example, understanding language requires a listener to recognize the meaning or semantic force of an utterance. It turns out that analogous abilities are present in some species of monkeys. Diana monkeys make different calls for aerial predators and ground predators, as do other species of monkeys (Zuberbühler, 2003; Zuberbühler, Cheney, & Seyfarth, 1999). Are the calls just blindly, instinctively elicited by the sight of the predator, or do monkeys actually assign some meaning to the different calls? If you play to a Diana monkey a recording of another Diana monkey making an alarm call that goes with an aerial predator, like an eagle, and then follow that up with the sound that the eagle itself makes, the Diana monkeys are not surprised. At least, they don't act surprised when the "eagle" monkey call is followed by a stimulus associated with the actual eagle itself. By contrast, if you play the Diana monkey alarm call for "eagle" and then play the sound of a jaguar growling, the little guys go bonkers. It's as if they know "the eagle monkey sound *means* there's an eagle around." So, even though the sound of an eagle is much different than the sound of the "eagle" warning call, behaviorally, Diana monkeys treat the two as equivalent. This ability to treat an arbitrary sound as a "pointer" to an object in the environment is very similar to what people do when they associate an arbitrary collection of sounds (a word) with something else (a concept).

Apes may also make different vocalizations to point to different objects besides predators. For instance, one captive ape (called Kanzi) produces slightly different vocalizations in different contexts. When Kanzi's trainers commented on or asked about bananas, grapes, or juice, Kanzi would often include some kind of vocalization in his response. When those vocal responses were subjected to an acoustic analysis, the vocal response in each context was slightly different (Tagliatela, Savage-Rumbaugh, & Baker, 2003). While it would be premature to say that Kanzi has his own spoken "words" for grape, banana, and juice, the ability to produce different vocal responses in different circumstances is a necessary precursor to spoken language, because spoken language requires us to make different sounds when referring to different concepts.

A number of researchers have attempted to teach language to chimpanzees. The idea was to find out whether human language ability was determined by genetics, or whether it was the result of immersion in cultures where language use was constantly present. If chimps could learn to use language, then human language abilities could not be solely caused by human genetics. In the early days, a chimp named Vicki was trained to make vocal responses to receive rewards. Vicki was never very good at this, primarily because the chimp vocal apparatus is not well configured to make speech sounds, and because chimps do not have good voluntary control over vocalizations (Gardner & Gardner, 1969; Lieberman, 2000). After they figured this out, researchers began to train chimps to use gestures to communicate. Two of the most famous of these animals were Nim Chimpsky and Washoe. Because chimps have much greater voluntary control over gesturing than vocalization, chimps have been much more successful mastering aspects of gestural communication. Members of other species, such as the mountain gorilla Koko, have also learned to communicate in this way (Gardner & Gardner, 1975; Jensvold & Gardner, 2000).

It turns out that when apes learn to sign, they talk mostly about food (see Table 1.1). This makes sense, as chimps like Nim and Washoe were taught to sign using operant conditioning techniques, according to which the chimps were given treats when they produced target behaviors (Premack, 1990). However, according to their human companions, Washoe and Nim's signing went beyond the boundaries of their operant training and showed some of the characteristics of human languages. In one famous example, Washoe was said to make the signs "water" and "bird" to describe a duck that had landed on a pond in her enclosure (Fouts, 1975). This could reflect a generative use of previously learned symbols. That is, Washoe could have been combining signs that were learned to label other concepts in order to label a new concept, the same way you could combine old words to create a new meaning. Similar claims are made regarding bonobos (a species closely related to chimps). Kanzi was credited by his trainers with rudimentary grammatical knowledge on the basis of producing

Table 1.1 The ten most frequent three-sign sequences by Nim Chimpsky (adapted from Terrace et al., 1979, p. 894)

Signs	Frequency
play me Nim	81
eat me Nim	48
eat Nim eat	46
tickle me Nim	44
grape eat Nim	37
banana Nim eat	33
Nim me eat	22
banana eat Nim	26
eat me eat	22
me Nim eat	21

two-symbol strings such as "M&M grape" and "potato oil." However, it is also possible that apes just make signs in a sequence, and are not making the monkey equivalent of compound words. An ape could sign "water" and "bird" in succession, without necessarily intending to apply the combination to refer to the duck.

Chimps were also claimed to have mastered some aspects of grammar, including the ability to interpret *wh-questions* (e.g., *Who is that? What is that?*; Gardner & Gardner, 1975). They are also claimed to observe the basics of word order by producing signs that express specific kinds of meanings in specific places in multi-sign sequences (Terrace, Pettitto, Sanders, & Bever, 1979).[8] For example, when Nim the chimp produced the sign "more" in combination with any other sign, he was much more likely to place the sign "more" first (as in *more banana*) than to use the reverse order (*banana more*). Terrace and colleagues concluded that Nim must have had an internal rule that he applied when constructing sequences of signs containing "more" ("more X" roughly, where X could be replaced by any sign for an object). Similarly, *give X* appeared far more frequently than *X give*. This kind of grammatical knowledge is a vital component of some human languages, including English.

It is sometimes difficult to decide what caused an ape to produce a particular sequence of signs. If you wish to believe that apes have language abilities similar to human children (and for similar reasons), then you would view the following conversation as being highly coherent (from Jensvold & Gardner, 2000):

Washoe: fruit gimme
Trainer: Who funny?
Washoe: Roger
Trainer: Where cat?
Washoe: Roger gimme.
Trainer: Where cat?
Washoe: Gimme

Figure 1.1 Nim Chimpsky signs "me," "hug," and "cat" to his trainer as an increasingly worried tabby (*Felis catus*) looks on (from Terrace et al., 1979, p. 892)

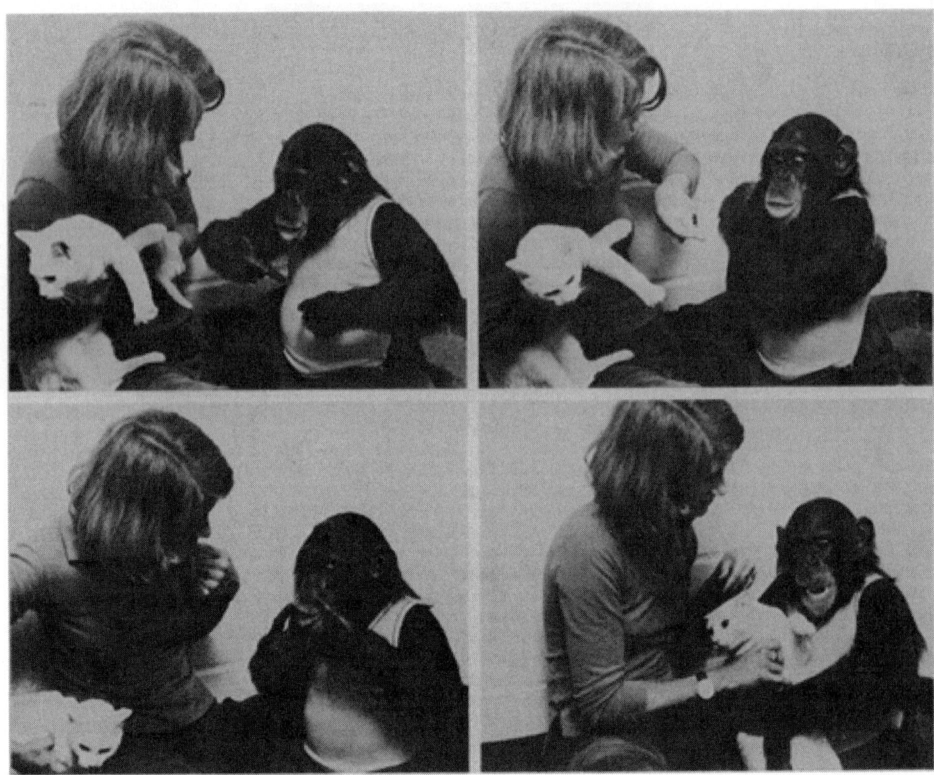

The response to the trainer's first question (Who funny?) could express the idea that the chimp has heard and understood the question, thought about possible answers, and selected Roger as an appropriate funny person. But a skeptical observer might argue that the rest of the exchange casts doubt on this interpretation of Washoe's behavior. Washoe seems to be focused on fruit throughout (perhaps because Washoe has received fruit on previous occasions after producing similar behavior). So the sign "Roger" after "who funny" could just be a false start for the expression "Roger gimme," which could be paraphrased as "Roger give me fruit." In which case, the whole exchange appears to take the form of two ships passing in the night, rather than a coherent conversation.

Operant conditioning techniques succeeded in getting chimps to produce signs, and other training techniques have also been successful in both chimps and the closely related species, bonobo. Sue Savage-Rumbaugh and her colleagues pioneered observational learning techniques as an alternative to operant conditioning (Brakke & Savage-Rumbaugh, 1996a, b; Lyn, Greenfield, & Savage-Rumbaugh, 2006; Lyn & Savage-Rumbaugh, 2000; Savage-Rumbaugh & Fields, 2000; Sevcik & Savage-Rumbaugh, 1994; Shanker, Savage-Rumbaugh, & Taylor, 1999; Tagliatela et al., 2003; Williams & Savage-Rumbaugh, 1997). In observational learning contexts, an animal is exposed to humans who are modeling language behaviors, such as gesturing. The animal may choose to repeat or imitate some of these behaviors, but is not rewarded with food for doing so.

Savage-Rumbaugh adopted a framework that appeals to three main factors to explain why animals (including humans) have whatever communicative abilities they enjoy: biological characteristics of the species (*phylogeny*), maturational characteristics of the individual (*ontogeny*), and culture or environment. Any, or more likely all, of these features can determine how much skill an individual will have producing and understanding language (e.g., humans are better than fish at using language, 12-year-old humans are better than 12-month-olds, and children in highly interactive households are likely to have greater language abilities than children from less interactive households). Savage-Rumbaugh proposed that some of the limitations in chimp language abilities observed in early studies of non-human communication could have resulted from the fact that training in language started relatively late in the life of individual chimps, the kind of language environment that the chimps were exposed to, and/or the chimp's genetic or biological characteristics.

In an attempt to gather further evidence regarding these possibilities, Savage-Rumbaugh raised a chimp named *Panpanzee* and a bonobo named *Panbanisha*, starting when they were infants, in a language-rich environment. Chimpanzees are the closest species to humans. The last common ancestor of humans and chimpanzees lived between about 5 million and 8 million years ago. Bonobos are physically similar to chimpanzees, although bonobos are a bit smaller on average. Bonobos as a group also have social characteristics that distinguish them from chimpanzees. They tend to show less intra-species aggression and are less dominated by male members of the species.[9] Despite the physical similarities, the two species are biologically distinct. By testing both a chimpanzee and a bonobo, Savage-Rumbaugh could hold environmental factors constant while observing change over time (ontogeny) and differences across the two species (phylogeny). If the two animals acquired the same degree of language skill, this would suggest that cultural or environmental factors have the greatest influence on their language development. Differences between them would most likely reflect phylogenetic biological differences between the two species. Differences in skill over time would most likely reflect ontogenetic or maturational factors.

Rather than reward the developing apes with food in return for signing, adult caregivers modeled language behaviors for the apes.

> *Caregivers communicated to [the apes] with spoken English and visuographic symbols called "lexigrams." The visual symbols were printed on a card, and the animals could point to various symbols that were associated with different concepts. During their training, the apes were exposed to spoken English (which they were not able to emulate), gestures (which they could copy), and lexigrams (which they were also able to use). Because the rearing paradigm stressed observational learning [learning by watching] and emphasized the young apes' language comprehension, [apes] were encouraged to attend to these communications but were not required to produce the symbols themselves in order to receive food or other reward. (Brakke & Savage-Rumbaugh, 1996b, p. 363)*

By comparing how much her chimp and her bonobo learned to how much operant-trained chimps learned in previous studies, Savage-Rumbaugh could estimate the effects of cultural/environmental factors on language learning in apes.

Over the course of the study, which lasted for just under four years, the apes developed communication skills using both gesture and the lexigrams (Brakke & Savage-Rumbaugh, 1996a, b). Communication via gesture developed before attempts to use lexigrams in both apes, and the chimpanzee continued to rely exclusively on gesture for a whole year after the bonobo had started to use lexigrams. Panpanzee the chimp did appear to imitate her trainers' use of the lexigrams, but she did not use them spontaneously. Panpanzee appeared more likely than Panbanisha the bonobo to combine using the lexigrams with gesturing throughout the study period, and the chimp was about 50% more likely to combine gesturing and pointing to lexigrams when she interacted with her trainers. Overall, the chimp produced fewer "words" during the study period. Because the chimp and the bonobo were both reared using the same methods, under essentially identical environmental conditions, differences between the chimp and the bonobo are not likely to result from differences in the environment, but could be caused by biological/genetic differences between the species.[10]

Savage-Rumbaugh reports that, among the animals exposed to enriched language environments from infancy, four have acquired receptive vocabularies of 500 words or more, with productive vocabularies of 150 words or more. Further, she reports that bonobos raised in a language-enriched environment (including Kanzi and his half-sister Mulika) appear to use symbols more spontaneously than chimps raised under operant-learning conditions (who tend to sign mostly in human-initiated exchanges). If so, the immersion methods that Savage-Rumbaugh used to teach her animals may be responsible for the greater spontaneity of their signing behavior.

"Monkeys don't talk"

Chimpanzee signing should not be labeled linguistic.
ESTEBAN RIVAS

Keep your stinking paws off me, you damned, dirty ape.
CHARLTON HESTON, *PLANET OF THE APES*

Some researchers interpret ape signing behavior as being highly consistent with the linguistic behavior of young children, but in some ways, the behavior of signing apes differs greatly from the language-related behavior of young children. First and foremost, the acquisition of language-related (or language-like) behaviors in apes varies widely from one animal to the next. In contrast to children, who universally acquire a native language given normal brain function, a stable environment, and exposure to a model, some apes acquire the ability to interpret symbols and use them to communicate, and some do not, even when they are exposed to the same models (see, e.g., the difference between Kanzi and Matata; Sevcik & Savage-Rumbaugh, 1994). This fact, by itself, could indicate that apes are using different mechanisms than humans to acquire language skills. Furthermore, children do much more than copy the behaviors of their adult caregivers. Children actively experiment with the language (as when infants babble) and develop knowledge of the sound system of language before they begin to produce their first words (analogous to ape signs or lexigrams). Such prelinguistic babbling behavior has not been reported in apes, suggesting that the mechanisms of acquisition and development are different in humans than in apes.

The acquisition and use of grammar also appears to work differently in children than in apes. When children produce multi-word utterances, their longer utterances contain elements of their shorter utterances, but they also contain new elements. Repetition of elements within utterances is almost unheard of in child language, but it is common in the signing of apes. For example, some of Nim's sign sequences include expressions like "eat Nim eat Nim," and "banana me eat banana" (Terrace et al., 1979, p. 894). In fact, repetition appears to be a major mechanism contributing to Nim's (and other chimps') longer utterances (e.g., "give orange me give eat orange me eat orange give me eat orange give me you," Terrace et al., 1979, p. 895; Rivas, 2005). Repetition occurs in over 90% of some apes' (e.g., Koko's) signing behavior. These repetitious sequences resemble the "superstitious" behaviors produced by pigeons, dogs, and college undergraduates when there is a contingency between behavior and reward, but when the delivery of a reward is delayed (Bruner & Revusky, 1961). Imagine that Washoe gets rewarded for producing signs. Imagine that some time elapses between the time when Washoe makes a sign and the time when he gets his reward. During that interval, additional signs may be produced. Washoe may come to "believe" that a sequence, rather than a particular sign, caused the reward to appear. Alternatively, intermittent reinforcement increases the rate of behaviors in animals generally, so if apes are reinforced on a variable schedule, they will tend to produce longer and longer sets of signs, not because they have acquired more complex grammatical rules, but simply because external rewards delivered on variable schedules draw more behaviors out of animals.[11]

Critical observers of ape language studies have also suggested that the way apes use signs is different from the way humans use words (Rivas, 2005; Seidenberg & Pettito, 1987; Tomasello, 2007). Humans use words to express *intentions* (ideas behind or motivations for speaking), while apes' use of symbols seems much shallower and less intentional. Humans also commonly use words to draw attention to objects or events in the environment, or to comment on those objects and events. Apes most commonly make signs in order to get something. To put it in more neutral terms, most ape signs are associated with objects (fruit, juice, M&Ms) and actions (tickling, chasing) that are rewarding to apes. As Tomasello (2007, p. 152) notes, "Most if not all ape gestures are imperative, intended to influence the behavior of others directly, whereas many human gestures are used for declarative or informative purposes." It is difficult, therefore, to determine the extent to which apes' signing behavior is maintained by extrinsic reward, and how much reflects an intention to communicate particular thoughts. This orientation toward reward appears to be present even in apes who were trained using observational methods. For example, although Kanzi the bonobo was trained using observational learning methods, rather than direct operant reward, his pattern of sign use closely matches that of apes that were trained using more traditional operant conditioning techniques. As many as 96% of Kanzi's signs can be interpreted as requests (Greenfield & Savage-Rumbaugh, 1990), consistent with the idea that much of his signing behavior is maintained by reward or the prospect of reward. Brakke and Savage-Rumbaugh (1996b, p. 365) report similar patterns of request-like behavior for the chimp *Panpanzee* and the bonobo *Panbanisha*, who were reared in a similar fashion to Kanzi.[12]

Apes also appear to apply such grammatical rules as they may have much less consistently than humans. For example, although Washoe signs "more X" far more often than he signs "X more," the difference is not as high as it should be if he were truly applying a grammatical rule. In languages like English, when a grammatical rule is in place, the related behavior is almost 100% consistent. An English-speaking child would *always* say, *I want more juice*, and would never say, *I want juice more*. There are limited exceptions to consistent application of grammatical rules, but these typically occur when the grammar offers two or more ways to express the same idea. For example, you can say, *Give Mary more juice* (which is called a *ditransitive* sentence) or you could say the equivalent *Give more juice to Mary* (which is called a *dative* sentence). An individual speaker may flip back and forth between these two options, but that is because that individual has two grammatical rules for how to form sentences involving the transfer of objects from one person to another (*X verb Y to Z*, and *X verb Z Y*, roughly). Different rules get triggered on different occasions, but once a rule gets triggered, it is followed to the letter (so you would never get a sentence like *Give to more juice Mary* or *John Mary give more juice*).[13] More recent research shows that, although non-human primates can learn some of the patterns characteristic of human language grammars, other patterns appear to be beyond their grasp (Hauser, Newport, & Aslin, 2001; Newport, Hauser, Spaepen, & Aslin, 2004; Ramus, Hauser, Miller, Morris, & Mehler, 2000).

Apes and people also differ greatly in the way they take turns during interactions. In dialogue, different cultures differ somewhat in the degree to which one speaker's utterances will overlap with another's, but interruptions are relatively infrequent (they certainly do happen, but the interruption is often marked as such by the interrupter). Apes interrupt people all of the time, usually to ask them for food (Terrace et al., 1979). This ubiquity of interruptions suggests that one of the prerequisites for full-blown language to emerge is the ability of individuals to engage in impulse control. If individuals in a communicative exchange are not able to control the impulse to vocalize, that is to coordinate their verbal behavior with other members of the group, the result is a cacophony of overlapping sounds, making it difficult or impossible for any individual to be heard over the general din (think of a seal colony, or the internet).

To summarize, although apes display some behaviors that humans do, including producing signs to refer to specific objects and events, there are substantial differences between the ways humans and apes use language (although see Lieberman, 2000, for a vigorous defense of similarities between ape and human language abilities). Whether you view these differences as being fatal to the continuity hypothesis depends on how you view the relationship between ape language abilities and human language abilities. If you view the ape abilities as being more primitive versions of the human abilities, then the continuity hypothesis wins. If you view the differences between humans and apes as being so great that human behaviors must be generated by an entirely different set of mental processes, then the discontinuity hypothesis wins.

Language origins

Studying ape communication is a way to investigate why humans have the language abilities that they enjoy. Abilities that apes demonstrate are likely to have been present in the last common ancestor of apes and humans. It is possible, but less likely, that shared abilities of humans and apes developed independently after the two species split between 5 and 8 million years ago. Other means to study language origins involve comparing modern humans to our evolutionary ancestors. By assessing human ancestors' physical features and artifacts, theorists can develop ideas about how and when modern language abilities emerged. Much of this work is speculative, because the critical evidence needed to discriminate between different theories is unavailable. As with research that compares living humans and living apes, much of the theorizing in the evolutionary approach to language origins revolves around the concepts of continuity and discontinuity. Continuity theory views modern humans' language abilities as reflecting modifications of abilities that existed in our ancestors. Discontinuity theory views modern humans' language abilities as being distinct and separate from our ancestors' abilities.

One thing that all language scientists agree on is that the human capacity for speech is an *adaptation*, in the Darwinian sense. An adaptation is a characteristic of a species that has been selected for and maintained by environmental factors. That is, at some point in the past, there was variability within the species such that some individuals had more of the relevant characteristic than others did. Those individuals who had more of the characteristic were more likely to survive and reproduce (they were biologically more fit), and so individuals without the characteristic in question became scarcer and scarcer in the population until their numbers declined to zero. Speech is viewed as an adaptation in part because of its obvious advantages—it allows for the near instantaneous sharing of complex knowledge across individuals and the coordination of joint activities—but also in part because of its less obvious disadvantages (Aitchison, 2000; Darwin, 1859/1979). To produce a wide range of speech sounds, the larynx needs to be deeper in the throat in humans than it is in other species (including in our close relatives, chimpanzees and bonobos). As a result of its position deep in the throat, humans are not able to close off their airway when they eat. That makes it more likely that humans will choke to death accidentally. According to the Centers for Disease Control, about 150 children in the United States die each year from foreign objects lodging in their windpipes. Other animals do not choke as frequently as people do, because they can close off their airways when they eat. The fact that the descended larynx persists is evidence that this characteristic is maintained because of its selective advantages, in spite of its potential drawbacks.

It is generally agreed that modern language abilities, most specifically the ability to produce spoken language, would not have been possible without two modern human characteristics: (a) A vocal apparatus that allows for the production of a variety of distinct speech sounds (phonemes); and (b) The ability to exert a high degree of very fine control over that vocal apparatus (Lieberman, 2000; MacLarnon & Hewitt, 1999).

When, exactly, did modern language emerge? We can only speculate. Because our ancestors lacked the kind of control necessary for speech (and if we discount the possibility that language was developed as a gestural system before it was developed as a vocal system; see Falk 2004, and replies therein; Hewes, 1973), it is likely that complex, modern language emerged some time during the last 200,000 to 70,000 years. While it is possible that the same processes caused language to appear at the same time as other features of *Homo sapiens*, it is also possible that the cultural and artistic revolution that occurred approximately 50,000 years ago coincided with the emergence of fully modern languages.

Philip Lieberman (2000) argues that human ancestors (e.g., *Homo erectus*) had the ability to speak, although their speech would not have been as refined as modern humans' speech. This conclusion is based on reasoning about why the human vocal tract has the shape it does. Lieberman notes that to produce vowel sounds such as /i/ (as in *meet*) and /u/ (as in *you*), the space above the larynx in the throat has to be about the same length as the horizontal space between the top of the throat and the mouth opening. For natural selection to produce and maintain this configuration, Lieberman argues, some rudimentary speech abilities must have been present beforehand. Natural selection could then have favored individuals who had physical characteristics that allowed them to produce a wider range of vowel sounds. Unless some rudimentary speech abilities were present prior to the advent of *Homo sapiens*, a lowered larynx, and the accompanying ability to produce more vowel sounds, would have to be the result of a massive and incredibly lucky mutation, rather than gradual evolution by natural selection.

Other researchers view speech as being absent until the advent of *Homo sapiens*. Speaking is an exercise in controlled exhalation. Rather than breathing out smoothly in one continuous motion, speaking requires us to rapidly change the flow of air out of the lungs in order to control fine aspects of speech, such as how much emphasis or stress (*accent*) we place on each word and syllable.[14] MacLarnon and Hewitt argue that speech could not have been present in our ancestors, because, like modern apes, our evolutionary ancestors lacked the ability to exert this fine degree of control, as evidenced by the relatively small diameter of the nerves that lead from the brain to the relevant upper-torso and throat muscles (MacLarnon & Hewitt, 1999). When early *Homo sapiens* fossils were compared to *Australopithecus afarensis*, *Homo erectus*, and *Neanderthal* specimens, only early *Homo sapiens* had the kinds of nerve tracts that are associated with modern humans. This enhancement of breathing control not only increases the range of speech sounds that people can produce, it also increases the absolute amount of time they can speak without stopping to catch their breath. Non-human vocalizations in primates are limited to about 5 seconds. Humans can go on for upwards of 10 seconds without stopping for breath.[15]

The fossil record shows that human ancestors before *Homo sapiens* emerged, between about 70,000 and 200,000 years ago, had some of the cultural and physical characteristics of modern humans, including making tools and cooking food. If we assume that modern language emerged sometime during the *Homo sapiens* era, then it would be nice to know why it emerged then, and not before. One possibility is that a general increase in brain size relative to body weight in *Homo sapiens* led to an increase in general intelligence, and this increase in general intelligence triggered a language revolution. On this account, big brain comes first and language emerges later. This hypothesis leaves a number of questions unanswered, however, such as, what was that big brain doing before language emerged? If the answer is "not that much," then why was large brain size maintained in the species (especially when you consider that the brain demands a huge proportion of the body's resources)? And if language is an optional feature of big, *sapiens* brains, why is it a universal characteristic among all living humans? Also, why do some groups of humans who have smaller sized brains nonetheless have fully developed language abilities?

Another line of thought starts with the idea that word-like units had to be present before more complex sequences of words emerged (Aitchison, 2000). Before you begin to use words, you have to appreciate the idea that sounds can be associated with objects, the *naming insight*. But where did that naming insight develop? One possibility is that it was an extension of more primitive verbal systems. Non-human primates already have some aspects of semantics (meaning) in their call systems, using alarm calls to activate knowledge of particular kinds of animals, rather than treating them as mere noise. Candidates for the first word-like units in human languages include noises imitating predators or prey, grunting noises made in concert with physical exertion, or the equivalents of lip-smacks and hooting that apes make as greetings. The theory is that you would need some number of such *proto-words* before the language could develop a system of speech sounds, and you need a system of speech sounds before you could synthesize a larger set of words to express a wider range of concepts. Unfortunately, no existing data indicate which, if any, of these candidates gave rise to the first words. It is likely, however, that once the naming insight took hold, that the stock of words would have expanded rapidly.

The next step in language evolution could have been the development of something approximating a modern pidgin. Pidgins develop when adult speakers of different languages are placed in circumstances that require them to communicate (Bickerton, 1988). Pidgins are generally simpler than full-blown languages, with a restricted vocabulary and rudimentary grammar. For example, the following expressions are used in *Tok Pisin*, a pidgin used in Papua New Guinea (Aitchison, 2000, p. 124):

han bilong diwai	"branch of a tree"
han bilong pik	"front legs of a pig"
han bilong pisin	"bird's wing"

In a creole (a language that emerges from the combination of two or more pre-existing languages) or another kind of full-blown language, we would expect concepts such as branch, legs, and wings to have shorter names; and the language would not depend upon the extension of one term *hand* to cover a wide variety of objects (although there may be advantages to making the similarity between hands, branches, legs, and wings explicit). Pidgins tend to lack the grammatical features of true languages, including markers for past and present tense on verbs, number agreement between subjects and verbs, sets of distinct prepositions (*on*, *of*, *below*, etc.), and case marking (e.g., changes in the form of nouns depending on their position within a sentence or their semantic role). Thus, pidgins represent an intermediate form between having no grammar at all, and having the kind of complex grammar that is characteristic of all true languages.

Some theorists suggest that grammar is the only thing that distinguishes human language abilities from those of our ancestors and those of our living relatives (e.g., the apes). If so, where did grammar come from? One possibility is suggested by the language bioprogram hypothesis (Bickerton, 1988; Lenneberg, 1967; Pinker, 1994). According to the language bioprogram hypothesis, human genetics creates the mental equivalent of the heart, stomach, lungs, or other organ. Like the heart, which depends on other organs for support, the language organ relies on other mental abilities for support. But also like the heart, which specializes in taking deoxygenated blood from the body, passing it to the lungs, and recirculating oxygenated blood back to the body, the language organ also specializes. In particular, it specializes in building the hierarchical, symbolic representations that underlie the ability to speak and the ability to understand speech. Is there any evidence that genetics contributes to human language abilities, and grammar in particular? (And remember, we're talking about *real*, descriptive grammar, not Mrs Heidemann's prescriptive grammar.)

Evidence for a genetic origin of grammar comes from two chief sources:[16] Studies of *creoles* (full-blown languages that develop out of pidgins) and studies of genetic anomalies that are associated with language disorders. If genetics contributes to our language abilities, then we would expect fully grammatical language to develop in children, whether they are exposed to a fully grammatical model language or not. Some studies have detected just such a pattern (Bickerton, 1988). In these studies, children who grow up listening to their parents speak pidgin appear to spontaneously add grammatical markers, such as case, tense, and agreement features, and wind up speaking a version of the language that is qualitatively different from the pidgin that their parents speak. Some of this research has been criticized because it relied on retrospective (historical) reports of elderly people talking about events from their childhood and because the individuals in question were being exposed to fully grammatical languages when their parents spoke their native language at home. However, more recent work on Nicaraguan Sign Language (LSN) is less subject to these criticisms (Emmorey, 2002; Senghas & Coppola, 2001).

In Nicaragua before the Sandinista revolution, children who were deaf tended to grow up isolated from one another and the vast majority were born to parents who could hear and speak, but could not sign. Thus, deaf children did not have a sign language model to follow. Most of them developed systems of "home sign," idiosyncratic systems of gesture that allowed them to communicate with their caregivers and families. Starting in 1977, a central school for the deaf was established, which brought together deaf children from all over the country for the first time in Nicaragua. Children were taught officially using oral methods (speaking and lip-reading training), but they communicated with each other in their spare time using gestures. Early on, the deaf children's system of gestures developed a standard, shared vocabulary, but the system lacked many of the grammatical features of full-blown sign languages. However, as younger children were added to the mix, they spontaneously added grammatical features found in other sign languages. This was accomplished even though the deaf children were not exposed to an adult language model. One way to explain this phenomenon is to propose that children's genetic heritage provides them with the mental tools they need to "invent" a grammatical system, as well as the drive to implement such a system if it is not already present in their environment.

Studies of individuals with *selective language impairment* (SLI) also suggest a genetic contribution to language abilities (Enard et al., 2002; Gopnik, 1990; 1994; Gopnik & Crago, 1991). One set of studies focused on a particular family living in England (the *KE family*). Half of the members of this family appear to be entirely normal in their general intelligence and their language abilities. The other half of the family also appear to have essentially normal intellectual abilities, but they have a number of problems producing and understanding language. For example, the affected members of the family have difficulty with past tense endings on verbs. They are likely to speak sentences such as "Yesterday he walks," or "After thinking about it for a while, she finally jump and fell." In writing sentences, the affected individuals do produce the correct tense endings some of the time, but generally this happens in response to explicit instruction on individual verbs. That is, they do not appear to apply the general rule "To make the past tense, add *-ed* to the end." Other verb-related markers are also not applied, or applied incorrectly (as in "Carol is cry in the church."). Affected individuals also have problems making plural nouns out of singular nouns. In the *wug test*, people are given nonsense words, like *wug*, and *zat*, and are asked to make them plural. "Here is one zat. Now there are two ______." When asked to fill in the blank, one family member said, "zacko." Genetic testing revealed that the affected members of the family all have an unusual form of the *FOXP2* gene, while the unaffected members have the more common form (Lai, Fisher, Hurst, Vargha-Khadem, & Monaco, 2001).

Although the deficit shown in the KE family has been attributed to grammar, specifically, some researchers favor an explanation under which the family suffers from a more general problem planning and executing sequences of behaviors (Vargha-Khadem et al., 1998; Watkins, Dronkers, & Vargha-Khadem, 2002). This latter interpretation helps explain why affected family members have difficulty moving facial muscles on command as well as problems repeating single words clearly. So, either the gene is directly responsible for instilling some aspects of grammar as an innate feature of human cognitive abilities (as per the genetic bioprogram hypothesis; Bickerton, 1988; Pinker, 1994) or the gene affects those parts of the brain which normally are involved in planning sequences of behavior, and our language production and comprehension processes normally tap into those resources as we speak and interpret language.

Language and Thought

The throat motor segment thus becomes the controlling segment of the body.
J. B. WATSON

You may have had the experience that when you are thinking about something or planning some kind of activity that you have a voice in your head, probably sounding much like your own voice, that is talking to you about whatever it is you are thinking about. This inner monologue is such a common experience when you are thinking that you might believe that "talking to yourself" and thinking are one and the same thing. You would be in good company if you thought this was how cognition worked, as the famed behaviorists J. B. Watson and B. F. Skinner both advocated versions of this idea (Skinner, 1957; Watson, 1924). Watson asked and answered the question in this way (1924, pp. 341, 347): "Do we think only in words, that is, in verbal motor contractions? My own answer has been: Yes ... 'thinking' is largely sub-vocal talking." However, since Watson's time, plenty of evidence has accumulated to show that thinking and language are separate, though linked, abilities.

The beginning of the end for Watson's theory of language and thought came in 1947, when medical doctors strapped a healthy 34-year-old research volunteer to a gurney in Salt Lake City and injected him with curare (Smith, Brown, Toman, & Goodman, 1947; see Table 1.2). Curare paralyzes the muscles of the body completely, including the *pharyngeal* (throat) muscles that Watson believed were critical for thought processes. About four minutes after the curare injection was completed, the research volunteer lost the ability to speak because his throat muscles could no longer move. Despite the loss of speech, the volunteer could still perceive everything that was happening around him. After he recovered, the volunteer reported that he was "clear as a bell" during the entire time he was paralyzed. In addition, during the time that he could not speak, the volunteer answered yes-or-no questions by moving muscles that had not yet become completely paralyzed, including his eyebrow and eyelid muscles. His answers to these questions were "entirely correct." Based on the events during the experiment, and on the volunteer's subsequent description of his experience, Smith's research team concluded that de-activating the speech muscles had no effect on the volunteer's ability to perceive, think about, or remember, the events that occurred during total muscular paralysis.

The curare results are fatal for Watson's idea that thinking and moving the throat muscles, whether overtly or covertly, are the same thing, but he could still be right if "talking to

Table 1.2 Some of the events reported during muscular paralysis caused by curare injection (from Smith et al., 1947, pp. 1–14)

2:11 PM:	Curare injection administered over 15 minutes.*
2:20:	Speech no longer possible. Can hear distinctly. Still able to nod head and move hands.
2:22:	Subject reports by movement of head that the experience is not unpleasant.
2:26:	Ability to comprehend and answer questions accurately is indicated by correctness of replies when inquiries are restated in the negative or double negative.
2:45:	Subject now unable to signal response to inquiries due to complete paralysis.
2:48:	Eyelids manually opened. Subject stated upon recovery that he was "clear as a bell" all this period.
4:50	Subject is able to sit up on edge of bed. Complete subjective report dictated.

*All events are direct quotes or paraphrases of the original report.

yourself" (without moving any muscles) is the same thing as thinking. But this alternative hypothesis also has major problems. First, individuals who have lost the ability to speak or understand language are nonetheless able to think. In these cases, the problem is not paralyzed muscles, it is the inability to produce the inner monologue at all. One such case involved a French-speaking monk, "Brother John," who experienced periodic failures to speak or to understand spoken or written language as the result of epileptic seizures (Lecours & Joanette, 1980). Brother John's epileptic episodes could last as little as a few minutes or as long as several hours. During the worst parts of these episodes, Brother John was incapable of speaking coherently and often of writing as well, but that did not destroy his ability to think. Subjectively, Brother John reported that his ability to produce inner monologue was also incapacitated during his seizures. However, during his episodes, he continued to recognize familiar objects, he was capable of handling complex tools, carrying out instructions that he had received before the epileptic seizure began (including instructions to alert researchers that he was having a major spell and to record his speech during the spell on a tape recorder), and performing short and long multiplication and division. During longer episodes, Brother John would sometimes sleep, but he often times stayed fully conscious (although feeling poorly) throughout these spells. Further, like the curare volunteer, Brother John could remember events that happened while his language abilities were incapacitated and talk about them afterwards in detail. During one major episode that happened while he was traveling across Europe by train, Brother John got off at the correct stop, found a hotel, checked in, and ordered a meal (he just pointed to the menu to order). As Brother John himself reported, "I could think clearly within my inner self but, when it came to [silently] talking to myself, I experienced difficulty finding my words" (Lecours & Joanette, 1980, p. 10).

Cases such as Brother John's show that you do not need language in order to think (where thinking is defined as the ability to reason, plan, make decisions, and respond appropriately to complex environmental stimuli). Other cases show that you do not need to think particularly well in order to use language. Two such examples are found in individuals with Williams syndrome and in "Christopher," an autistic person who has a remarkable capacity to learn foreign languages.

Williams syndrome is a disorder that results in abnormal brain structure and functioning as well as mental retardation (Lightwood, 1952; Williams, Barratt-Boyes, & Lowe, 1961). Severe mental limitations do not cripple the ability to use language among people who have Williams syndrome. One woman with Williams syndrome is unable to do basic arithmetic calculations or retrieve a small set of objects on request. She can, however, talk up a storm, as in the following:

> *I love listening to music. I like a little bit of Beethoven, but I especially like Mozart and Chopin and Bach. I like the way they develop their music—it's very light, it's very airy, and it's very cheerful music. I find Beethoven depressing. (Finn, 1991, p. 54)*

As Karmiloff-Smith and colleagues (1998, p. 343) note, "Some aspects of language seem relatively spared, whereas many non-linguistic functions, such as spatial cognition, number planning, and problem solving are severely impaired." This does not mean that the language abilities of people with Williams syndrome are normal. They appear to respond differently to some aspects of meaning (semantics) and language structure (syntax) than normal individuals. However, the important thing is that the language abilities of people with Williams syndrome are more sophisticated than you would expect based on their overall levels of intelligence and based on comparisons to other kinds of mentally retarded people, including those with Down syndrome whose language abilities are highly impaired (Reilly, Klima, & Bellugi, 1990; Thomas et al., 2001; Tyler et al., 1997; but see Tomasello, 1995). Ursula Bellugi, who has contributed greatly to the study of both Williams syndrome and sign language, summarizes the situation like this (Losh, Bellugi, Reilly, & Anderson, 2000, pp. 268–269):

> *adolescents with Williams syndrome perform far better than age and IQ-matched children with Down syndrome on a wide variety of language tasks ... The spontaneous language of adults and adolescents with WMS has been characterized as fluent and generally grammatically well formed, although not without occasional errors.*

"Christopher" is the pseudonym for an autistic person who, despite being unable to look after himself, has managed to learn 13 foreign languages (Smith & Tsimpli, 1995; Tsimpli & Smith, 1999). However, as with Williams syndrome, Christopher's language abilities are not entirely normal. He has difficulty understanding non-literal language, including metaphors (e.g., *The race horse flew around the track*) and irony (e.g., saying *That felt good!* after you stub your toe), as well as jokes and rhetorical questions. But that's not important right now. What is important is that Christopher's language skills *overall* are far beyond what one would expect based on his general level of cognitive function. In fact, his ability to learn foreign languages is far beyond what one would expect even if he were highly intelligent.

These examples show that you do not need language to think (Brother John); and that you can have sophisticated language skills despite poor functioning in non-language thought domains (Christopher, Williams syndrome). This pattern is what scientists call a *double dissociation*, which happens when you can fill in all four cells of a two-by-two matrix. In our matrix, we have (non-language) thought processes on one side and language ability on the other. If you could only have good language and good thought at the same time, and poor language and poor thought at the same time, that would strongly suggest that language and thought depend on one another, and could even be the same thing. But because you can have one without the other, this means that they are at least partially separate and are not the same thing. Thus, the weaker version of Watson's "speech is thought" hypothesis, that inner monologue and thinking are the same, is falsified as well.

Whorf, linguistic determinism, and linguistic relativity

Although language and thought are not identical, that does not mean that they cannot influence each other. One of language's chief purposes is to express our thoughts; and the language we speak may also affect the way we think about and perceive the world. Before we had Commander Worf from Star Trek, psycholinguists, linguists, and philosophers looked to Benjamin Lee Whorf for inspiration. Whorf and his linguistics advisor, Edward Sapir, developed the idea that the language we speak influences the way we think. Their theory goes by different names, but let's call it *linguistic determinism*, which helps to highlight the idea that language drives thought, that the way we think is determined by the language we speak. This attitude is exhibited in social norms against using racist or sexist terms or expressions, the idea being that eliminating such expressions from the language will make the accompanying thoughts less likely to occur in people who hear the language. If a language lacks terms that refer in a derogatory way to classes of people, it will be difficult for speakers of that language to express those thoughts, so they will express other, more acceptable thoughts instead.

One of Whorf's chief motivations in proposing linguistic determinism was an analysis of Eskimo-language vocabulary.[17] Possibly based on Franz Boas' (1911) analysis of Eskimo, Whorf concluded that, where English has a single word *snow*, Eskimo languages have multiple words. Why does Eskimo have multiple words, where English has one? Whorf argued that Eskimos had more words for snow because they carved up the concept "snow" into multiple, distinct subconcepts, assigning a different word to each different subconcept. They would do this for the same reason that, if you have more than one child, you give them each a different name. You conceive of them as being separate individuals, and it would be unthinkable to call them all by the same name. But linguistic determinism really says more than this. It says that if your language has many words for snow, you will be able to perceive differences between different kinds of snow that people whose language lacks those distinctions will *not* be able to see. That is, because you speak Eskimo, you see more different kinds of snow. Because I speak English, I cannot see the differences that you can.

In a devastating[18] critique, Geoffrey Pullum, a linguist from Edinburgh, Scotland, knocked down two pillars of linguistic determinism: the contents of Eskimo vocabulary and the relationship between vocabulary and perception (Pullum, 1989; see also Martin, 1986). First, Eskimo languages do *not* appear to have more words for snow than English does.[19] As Martin (p. 422) notes, "Eskimo has about as much differentiation as English does for 'snow' at the mono-lexemic [single-word] level: *snow* and *flake*. That these roots and others may be modified to reflect semantic distinctions not present in English is a result of gross features of Eskimo morphology [word form] and syntax [language structure] and not of lexicon [vocabulary]." Pullum's analysis agrees with Martin's. He notes, "C. W. Schultz-Lorentzen's *Dictionary of the West Greenlandic Eskimo Language* (1927) gives just two possibly relevant roots: *qanik*, meaning 'snow in the air' or 'snowflake', and *aput*, meaning 'snow on the ground'" (Pullum, 1989, p. 280). If Eskimo and English carve up the universe of snow into roughly the same number and kinds of categories, then language cannot be the source of any differences in the way speakers of Eskimo languages (Aleuts, Inuits, and Yupik) and speakers of other languages perceive the world. But even more seriously for linguistic determinism, there is no actual evidence one way or the other regarding the abilities of Eskimo-speakers and members of other language groups to perceive differences between different kinds of snow. We don't know for a fact that Aleuts, Inuits, and Yupik people have better or more sophisticated snow perception than the average New Yorker. Even if we assume that Eskimos have more words for snow, this language difference has not been shown to lead to a difference in perception. Both parts of linguistic determinism are in trouble.

Whorf provided no evidence that different groups of people perceive the world differently. Subsequent to Whorf, a number of researchers looked for evidence that speakers of different languages perceive the world in similar ways. They found some degree of success in the areas of emotion and color perception (Berlin & Kay, 1969; Ekman, Sorenson, & Friesen, 1969; Hardin & Maffi, 1997; Huang et al., 2009; Kay & Maffi, 2000; Lenneberg & Roberts, 1956). In studies of emotion perception, people all over the world, from both industrialized and primitive cultures, recognize the same basic emotions in pictures that show happiness, anger, and disgust. Different languages also characterize emotion using similar terminology, organized in analogous ways. Languages can have as few as two terms for emotions, and if they have only two, they will be the equivalents of *anger* and *guilt* (Hupka, Lenton, & Hutchison, 1999). The next terms that will appear will be *amusement, alarm, adoration*, and *depression*. Languages that have more terms than these six will have all six. That is, no language has a word for *lonely* but not a word for *guilt*. Similar perception of emotional expressions (in pictures) and a consistent organization of emotional vocabulary across languages both point toward a shared conceptualization of human emotion across cultures, despite vast differences in both language and culture across speakers of different languages.

Color perception and color words work similarly to emotion. Most languages have seven or fewer basic color terms (Kay & Maffi, 1999). Languages that have only two color terms will have rough equivalents to the English words *black* and *white*.[20] The next term to appear will be *red*, followed by *yellow*, *green*, or both yellow and green. After that group, *blue*, *brown*, *purple*, *pink*, *orange*, and *gray* show up. No language has a term for orange that does not also have a term for red, just as no language has a term for *confused* unless it also has a word for *happy*. These similarities in color classification may reflect the fact that all people (minus the color-blind) have the same underlying physical mechanisms and processes for color perception. We all have three cone types that react to light, and these three cone types are connected into neural systems that place dark in opposition to light, yellow in opposition to blue, and green in opposition to red (Goldstein, 2006). Given identical anatomy and physiology across language groups, it is not surprising that we all perceive color in similar, if not identical, ways. Thus, in at least two areas of perception, the language a person speaks does not appear to dictate the way that person perceives the world.

As a result of concerns like those raised by Pullum, as well as studies showing that speakers of different languages perceive the world similarly, many language scientists have viewed linguistic determinism as being dead on arrival (see, e.g., Pinker, 1994). Many of them would argue that language serves thought, rather than dictating to it. If we ask the question, what is language good for? one of the most obvious answers is that language allows us to communicate our thoughts to other people. That being the case, we would expect language to adapt to the needs of thought, rather than the other way around. If an individual or a culture discovers something new to say, the language will expand to fit the new idea (as opposed to preventing the new idea from being hatched, as the Whorfian hypothesis suggests). This anti-Whorfian position does enjoy a certain degree of support from the vocabularies of different languages, and different subcultures within individual languages. For example, the class of words that refer to objects and events (*open class*) changes rapidly in cultures where there is rapid technological or social changes (such as most Western cultures). The word *internet* did not exist when I was in college, mumble mumble years ago. The word *Google* did not exist 10 years ago. When it first came into the language, it was a noun referring to a particular web-browser. Soon after, it became a verb that meant "to search the internet for information." In this case, technological, cultural, and social developments caused the language to change. Thought drove language. But did language also drive thought? Certainly. If you hear people saying "Google," you are going to want to know what they mean. You are likely to engage with other speakers of your language until this new concept becomes clear to you. Members of subcultures, such as birdwatchers or dog breeders, have many specialist terms that make their communication more efficient, but there is no reason to believe that you need to know the names for different types of birds before you can perceive the differences between them—a bufflehead looks different than a pintail no matter what they're called.

Whorf makes a comeback

The claim that the language or languages we learn determine the ways we think is clearly untenable. But it does not necessarily follow that language is merely a code system which neither affects the process by which thinking proceeds nor the nature of the thoughts manipulated in that process.
ALFRED BLOOM

On the other hand, having the term *bufflehead* in your vocabulary certainly makes communication more efficient. I can say, "Today, I am hunting the wily bufflehead," rather than saying, "Today, I am hunting a small, mostly black waterfowl, with yellow eyes and a crest." If my language does not have a ready-made word for a concept, perhaps my thought processes will be channeled toward concepts that are easily expressible (Hunt & Agnoli, 1991). Alternatively, if my language has a ready-made word for a concept, I am more likely to be reminded of that concept as it appears in conversation. I am also less likely to be distracted or otherwise prevented from attending to a particular concept when my language has a ready-made label for that concept, compared to when reference to the concept has to be built up from other concepts that my language has labels for. Or, as Alfred Bloom puts it (1984, p. 276), "Indirect elicitation is likely to leave the hearer or reader more vulnerable to the effects of distracting complexities which may simply interfere with his/her ability to arrive at the intended concept."

Linguistic determinism—the idea that the language you speak strongly limits the thoughts you are capable of thinking—has fallen out of favor in psychology and linguistics, but the idea that language affects thinking in less drastic ways has actually gained traction in the last decade or so. Many theorists now believe that language can affect non-linguistic (non-language) perceptual and thought processes, so that speakers of one language may perform differently than speakers of other languages on a variety of perceptual and cognitive tasks. Chinese offers two such examples: counting skill and counterfactual reasoning.[21] Consider counting skill first.

Different languages express numbers in different ways, so language could influence the way children in a given culture acquire number concepts (Hunt & Agnoli, 1991; Miller & Stigler, 1987). Chinese number words differ from English and some other languages (e.g., Russian) because the number words for 11–19 are more transparent in Chinese than in English. In particular, Chinese number words for the teens are the equivalent of "ten-one," "ten-two," "ten-three" and so forth. This makes the relationship between the teens and the single digits more obvious than equivalent English terms, such as *twelve*. As a result, children who speak Chinese learn to count through the teens faster than children who speak English. This greater accuracy at producing number words leads to greater accuracy when children are given sets of objects and are asked to say how many objects are in the set. Chinese-speaking children performed this task more accurately than their English-speaking peers, largely because they made very few errors in producing number words while counting up the objects. One way to interpret these results is to propose that the Chinese language makes certain relationships more obvious (that numbers come in groups of ten; that there's a relationship between different numbers that end in the word "one"), and making those relationships more obvious makes the counting system easier to learn.[22]

Pirahã offers a potentially more dramatic case of number terminology affecting cognitive abilities (Everett, 2008; Frank, Everett, Fedorenko, & Gibson, 2008; Gelman & Gallistel, 2004; Gordon, 2004). Pirahã has no words that correspond to Arabic numerals (*one*, *two*, *three*, etc.). The terms that they do have for quantifying objects (*hói*, *hoí*, and *baágiso*; the little accent marks indicate vowels pronounced with a high tone) appear to be relational terms along the lines of "fewer" and "more."[23] The lack of number words in the language does not prevent Pirahã speakers from perceiving that different sets of objects have different quantities of individual objects. Pirahã are able to match sets of different objects, such as spools of thread and balloons, based on the number of objects in each set. However, the lack of number terms does appear to affect Pirahã speakers' ability to remember the exact quantity of different sets of items. If, for example, a number of objects is placed in a can, and objects are drawn from the can one at a time, Pirahã speakers are likely to make errors when they are asked to indicate when the can is empty. The likelihood of these errors increases as the number of objects in the can increases. So, when the task involves the direct perception of the objects involved, and does not require any type of memory, Pirahã do as well as anyone else. But when memory for objects is required, Pirahã speakers are at a disadvantage. Results like these may favor a "weak" form of linguistic determinism. Language does not affect perception directly, but language allows speakers to encode knowledge in a form that is relatively easy to maintain (it's easier to remember the sound "eight" than it is to maintain a picture in your head of exactly eight objects).

Despite their superior arithmetic abilities, it's not all sunshine and light for speakers of Chinese. They may have more difficulty than English speakers with *counterfactual* statements, again potentially because of characteristics of the Chinese language. Counterfactual statements are ways to express things that might have been, but did not happen. Chen, Chiu, Roese, Tam, and Lau (2006) define them this way, "Counterfactuals are thoughts of what might have been, of how the past might have turned out differently." Counterfactual reasoning is a useful tool in reasoning about events. Considering what might have happened had we acted differently is an important aspect of avoiding similar mistakes in the future (as in *Scary Movie III*, when the character Sayaman says, "I'm sorry about that night. If I hadn't fallen asleep for that exact 20 minutes. If I hadn't drank that exact whole bottle of Jaegermeister …"). English has direct means of expressing counterfactuals (If x, … would y …), but Chinese does not. According to Bloom, Chinese counterfactuals are expressed using less direct means (1984, p. 276):

> *A Chinese speaker might state explicitly "John did not take linguistics" and then follow that statement by the past implicational statement "If he did, then he was excited about it" and the remark would again be accorded a counterfactual interpretation—i.e., be interpreted as roughly equivalent to the English, *"If he had taken linguistics, he would have been excited about it."*

In tests of counterfactual reasoning on English-speakers and (Taiwanese) Chinese-speakers, Bloom showed that, while about three quarters of the English-speakers were willing to accept a counterfactual statement, only about one quarter of the Chinese-speakers were willing to do so. Bloom attributed these results to the way counterfactual statements need to be expressed in Chinese (as in "If all circles are large and if this small triangle 'Δ' is a circle, is the triangle large?" instead of "If all circles are large, and if this small triangle were a circle, would it be large?") Bloom reports that Chinese-speakers were somewhat perturbed by his questions, "Chinese speakers tended to wonder, 'How can all circles be large? How can a triangle be a circle? What are you talking about?'" Thus, the forms that the two languages provide appear to make some aspects of reasoning more straightforward for speakers of English compared to speakers of Chinese. Other cross-cultural differences may influence the kind of alternative scenarios that Chinese-speaking individuals think of when they reason counterfactually. Chen and colleagues' (2006) research suggests that cultures influence the kind of counterfactual scenarios individuals build. For example, Chinese-speakers who are unlucky in love may be more likely to think up counterfactuals that involve deleting something they did (*negative* counterfactual), rather than adding something more to what they did (*positive* counterfactual).[24]

More recent research provides evidence that some aspects of color perception may not be present universally in the human species, contrary to claims made by members of the universalist school, such as Berlin and Kay. One recent study tested the ability of different groups of speakers to discriminate (notice the difference between) different shades of the color blue (Winawer et al., 2007). Why blue? Because Russian, but not English, draws a mandatory distinction between different shades of blue. In English, we can call royal blue, robin's egg blue, powder blue, sky blue, and midnight blue all "blue." While plain old "blue" is less specific than any of these other terms, it is not *wrong* to call any of them blue. Russian works differently. Russian draws a mandatory distinction between light shades of blue, such as robin's egg blue and true blue (a tip of the cap to my Scottish friends), and dark shades of blue, such as royal blue. Lighter shades of blue are called голубой ("goluboy"). Darker shades of blue are called синий ("siniy"). It is wrong if you are speaking Russian to call powder blue "siniy" or to call royal blue "goluboy." As a result, when a Russian-speaker wishes to communicate about a blue-colored object, she must decide before she speaks whether the object falls into the light blue or dark blue category. Because color (hue) is a continuously varying characteristic, Russian speakers must impose a categorical organization on the world of blue things in order to talk about them. Different Russian speakers have slightly different boundaries between the "goluboy" and "siniy" categories, but they all make the distinction.

Does this language-imposed need to carve up blue into subcategories affect the way Russian speakers perceive the color blue? Some recent data suggest that it does (Winawer et al., 2007). In a set of experiments, two groups of speakers were tested. One group consisted of Russian speakers, while the other group consisted of English speakers. Russian and English speakers were given a card that had three colored squares printed on it, with one square on top, and two squares next to one another below that. The speakers' task was simply to say which of the two bottom squares was the same color as the top square. Sometimes, all three squares came from the same side of the "goluboy"/"siniy" border—all were light blue or all were dark blue. Sometimes, two squares came from the same side of the border, while the third square came from the opposite side. If language has *no* effect on perception, then Russian speakers should function just like English speakers on the judgment task. If everyone sees blue the same way, then everyone should respond the same way on the task. But if language imposes organization on the way we perceive the world, then Russian speakers should behave differently than English speakers. More specifically, Russian speakers should find the task easier when one of the squares is light blue and the others are dark blue, or when one of the squares is dark blue and the others are light blue. It should be harder for Russians to do the task if all of the squares come from the same side of the border. Why? The idea is that language forces Russians to categorize all of the shades of blue that they see. Because this categorization is automatic, it happens very quickly, and automatically categorizing one thing as "siniy" and another thing as "goluboy" should help you decide very quickly that the two things are different. By contrast, English speakers should not care what shades of blue they have, because they are all categorized as "blue." Consistent with the linguistic determinism hypothesis, Russians were faster and more accurate judging the squares in the case where some of the colors were on opposite sides of the "siniy"/"goluboy" boundary. Russians had a harder time judging the squares when all of the colors were "siniy" or when all of the colors were "goluboy." For the English speakers, it didn't matter. They were just as fast and just as accurate no matter what assortment of colors appeared on the cards.[25]

In previous experiments, researchers had shown that people can remember a particular color better if their language has a specific term for that color. These experiments were intended to show an effect of language on color perception and categorization, as per the Whorfian hypothesis. However, Pinker (1994) and others have criticized these experiments on the following grounds: They do not show that different languages cause people to perceive or categorize the world differently. Instead, they show that, if your language has a word for a color, you remember the word rather than the color, because verbal information is more stable and durable than visual information. However, Winawer and colleagues' study is not vulnerable to this kind of criticism, because it involved a direct perception task with little or no memory involved. Thus, the most likely explanation for the Russian speakers' performance is that a lifetime of using Russian to talk about blue things has caused them to develop a habit of noticing the difference between lighter blue and darker blue objects—their language has compelled them to attend to an aspect of the environment that speakers of other languages tend to ignore most of the time. So, it is not that Russians enjoy super-human vision or super-human judgment abilities. Instead, years of practice have sharpened their skills at classifying one segment of the color spectrum.

Similar kinds of effects can be found in individuals who use sign language (Emmorey, 2002; see also Chapter 12). Karen Emmorey notes that fluent signers perform better on a variety of *visuospatial* tasks than individuals who communicate via spoken language. Visuospatial tasks involve using your visual abilities to construct a representation of objects in space, their movement trajectories, and their positions relative to one another. Examples of such tasks include apparent motion perception, face recognition and discrimination, mental imagery, and mental rotation. Apparent motion happens when stationary objects, such as lights on a theater sign (or marquee), come on in a sequence that makes it appear as though they are moving. (Movies, too, are made up of a series of still pictures which, when shown at a high rate, produce the illusion of smooth movement.) If non-signers see static pictures of an individual in two different poses, and they perceive apparent motion, they perceive that body parts move in straight lines from one position to the next, no matter what. However, if the apparent body motion mimics a sign-language expression involving motion along a curved path, deaf signers will perceive that body parts moved along a curved path, as opposed to a straight one. Thus, knowledge from the sign language appears to influence visual perception, at least when the visual information by itself does not unambiguously indicate how the body actually moved.

Signed languages use facial expressions to convey certain aspects of meaning, so signers must pay careful attention to each other's faces to accurately interpret their conversational partners' intended meanings. As with Russians paying attention to shades of blue, interpreting sign languages makes signers more sensitive to slight differences in facial expressions. In one kind of face-perception test, the *Benton Test of Face Recognition*, people look at a face head on, and they also look at pictures of the same person taken from other angles. The task is to decide which of the alternative pictures matches the head-on picture. Signing children and adults are better at this task than age-matched non-signing children and adults. Other tasks involving face perception and memory also show an advantage for signers over non-signers.

Mental rotation tasks have a long and glorious history as the metaphorical equivalent of shock troops in the Cognitive Revolution.[26] In such tasks, participants look at two complex geometric figures and decide as quickly as possible whether the two figures are identical, or whether they are mirror images of one another. Non-signing, hearing participants take longer to do the task as the degree of rotation of the two figures increases. Two figures shown at the same orientation are judged most quickly. Two figures shown rotated 180 degrees relative to one another are judged more slowly. Signers, by contrast, respond to the figures at about the same speed no matter how they are oriented to one another, and they are faster overall than non-signers. Emmorey suggests that the superior spatial abilities of signers are the result of the need to mentally re-orient signs during comprehension in order to keep track of who did what to whom.

To summarize, research on the relationship between language and thought shows that the way your language works does not change the way you perceive the world—that is, it does not give you super-human perceptual abilities that other people can not have unless they speak your language—but it may make some cognitive tasks easier. Tasks can be made easier if your language motivates you to pay attention to particular perceptual features of the world (as in color naming) or gives you practice performing specific kinds of mental processes (like mental rotation or facial expression recognition).

A Description of the Language-Processing System

The rest of the book discusses mental processes that are involved in producing and understanding language. In the following chapters, language is treated as a set of mental mechanisms and processes operating largely independently of other cognitive systems. That is, the book seeks to explain how and why language is produced and understood. To do so, it breaks language abilities down into major subcomponents and examines each subcomponent individually. This treatment of language follows from the *modularity* tradition (Fodor, 1983). Fodor proposed that language was a mental module, which he defined as a mental ability that is *domain specific*, *genetically determined*, with a *distinct neural structure*, and *computationally autonomous* (Fodor, 1983, p. 21). Let's not worry about genetically determined for now. *Domain-specific* means that a mental processing unit deals with some kinds of information, but not others. For example, the visual system responds to light but not to sound. *Distinct neural structure* means that particular brain regions are associated with specific computations. For example, basic visual processing takes place in the visual cortex; more complicated visual processing takes place in other brain areas. *Computationally autonomous* means that a mental processing mechanism does its job independent of what is happening simultaneously in other processing mechanisms (this feature sometimes goes by the name *encapsulation*). While there are substantial disagreements about the extent to which language processing satisfies Fodor's conditions, treating different aspects of language processing as though they were independent, modular processes helps break down a hugely complex system into more manageable chunks (just keep in mind that the whole system needs to work together in a coordinated fashion to produce and understand language). So what modules or subcomponents might the language system have? It is easier to deal with this question by describing production and comprehension separately, starting with production.

The production system starts with conceptual knowledge and ends with a set of speech sounds. The first potential subcomponent of the production system is a set of processes that takes activated conceptual knowledge and uses it to activate related word knowledge in the mental lexicon (see Chapter 2). Once a set of candidate word representations has been activated, they need to be placed in a specific order—conceptual knowledge is not linear, but speech is, because you can only pronounce one word at a time. Once words have been placed in a particular order, they need to be *inflected*. That is, they need to be given the appropriate *phonological form*. For example, an English speaker would use a different form of the verb *kick* depending on whether the event took place before or after the utterance. So, part of the production mechanism has to keep track of what the ordering conventions of the language are, and how the *morphological* (word form) *system* works, so that the right word appears in the right form in the right place. Once the details of the utterance have been worked out, the speech production system has to work out a plan to move the actual vocal apparatus, including a plan that will make some of the elements of the utterance louder than others (*accent*) as well as modulating the tone and tempo of the utterance (*prosody*). Each of these subcomponent processes (conceptual–lexical mapping, ordering and inflection, and articulation) could be controlled by a different module, although this is not logically necessary, and some evidence suggests that processes taking place within the speech production system do not meet Fodor's criteria for modular processes (a fuller discussion awaits in Chapter 2). Nonetheless, to understand how speech production works, it is helpful to consider different subparts of the system separately, so that is how we will proceed.

The comprehension system starts with a set of speech sounds (phonemes, syllables, and words) and maps them to a set of concepts or meanings. As with production, it is useful to chop the comprehension process into bits and consider each separately, as though each one was a module (even the components of comprehension may *not* match Fodor's definition of modules). Speech perception kicks off the comprehension process, and it is considered as a separate stage in Chapter 2. The first goal of speech perception is to identify the words that appear in the input. This process of *lexical access* is considered in Chapter 3. Once you have identified a set of words, you need to figure out how they are organized and how they relate to one another. This *parsing* process is considered as a separate set of mental events in Chapter 4. Once you have more than one sentence to work with, you need to figure out how those sentences relate to one another. Processes at this level are considered in Chapters 5 and 6. Often times, speakers express themselves using metaphors or other forms of non-literal language. The processes you use to interpret these kinds of expression are taken up in Chapter 7.

Although comprehension and production are normally treated as independent topics, much of the time when we are engaged in language processing, we are simultaneously trying to understand what someone is saying and planning what we are going to say next. In fact, most of our language input comes during dialogue. Issues that arise when speakers and listeners interact in dialogue are taken up in Chapter 8.

Chapter 9 considers how language abilities develop in individual children, with a special emphasis on word learning.

Chapters 1–9 represent the "core" topics in the study of language, but there is truly outstanding research going on in other areas as well. These "supplemental" areas are tackled in chapters 10–14. Many teachers and researchers consider some or all of the topics covered in these latter chapters as belonging at the center of the study of language, and there is really nothing wrong with that.

Summary and Conclusions

This chapter has introduced some of the fundamental properties of language and attempted to address where language comes from. Language is a form of communication that is used to transfer information between individuals who speak the language, as well as serving other functions, such as social bonding. While language is a form of communication, it has special properties that are not present in other forms of communication, including semanticity, arbitrariness, discreteness, displacement, generativity, and duality of patterning. Languages are also distinguished from other communication systems by *grammar*, the set of rules or principles that determines how the symbols of the language can be combined, and how meanings are assigned to combinations of symbols. Grammar is a powerful device that allows language users to generate an infinite number of messages from a finite number of symbols.

Much of the research in language science attempts to answer questions relating to how modern languages came to take their current form. On the one hand, some theories propose that grammar and language are the product of gradual evolution from closely related communication systems (the *continuity* hypothesis). Other theories propose that modern human language represents a clean break from ancestral communication systems and the communication systems of our closest living relatives, the great apes. Continuity proponents point toward the sophisticated communication skills of apes, like Kanzi and Nim Chimpsky, and conclude that complex speech skills were present in human ancestors, such as *Homo erectus*. Discontinuity proponents argue that ape language skills are qualitatively different from and inferior to human language abilities. Although they are in the odd position of arguing simultaneously that grammar is genetically determined but that it is not the result of natural selection, and although it is not currently clear how genes could install components of grammar in the human mind, discontinuity proponents can point to evidence from creoles and individuals with specific language impairment to bolster their claims about a genetic contribution to modern language abilities. Finally, research on the relationship between language and thought paints a somewhat complicated picture. Whorf appears to be wrong in his claim that language dictates perception, and that individuals who speak different languages have qualitatively different perceptual abilities; but he does appear to be right in claiming that the language you speak can influence how easy it is for you to accomplish certain cognitive tasks, such as discriminating different colors or keeping track of large sets of objects.

TEST YOURSELF

1. What are the main characteristics that all languages have in common?
2. Give an example of a descriptive rule of grammar. Give an example of a prescriptive rule.
3. Describe three aspects of form that grammars govern. Give an example of each.
4. Give an example of recursion. Describe evidence suggesting that some languages lack recursion.
5. How do the *continuity* and *discontinuity* hypotheses differ? What evidence can you present for each hypothesis? Is there any evidence that calls either of them into question? Which hypothesis do you favor and why?
6. What kind of linguistic skills do non-human primates have? Should we think of them as "knowing language"?
7. What evidence do we have that modern human languages resulted from adaptation and natural selection? When did modern languages first appear? What are the major factors that caused human language abilities to diverge from non-human primates?
8. What is the relationship between language and thought? Describe evidence suggesting that general thinking abilities and language involve distinct sets of mental skills. Describe evidence suggesting that language influences the way humans think. Are there some things that you can't do if your language lacks the proper vocabulary?

THINK ABOUT IT

1. The chapter presented some of the characteristics that all natural languages have. (What are they?) Can you think of any other characteristics that should be added to the list?
2. Imagine you are observing a new species of primate in the wild. What behaviors would you have to observe to conclude that the new species was using a language?
3. Some languages (e.g., Spanish, Russian) require speakers to decide the gender of a noun (masculine, feminine, and neuter) before they speak. Other languages (e.g., English, Persian) do not. Do you think cultures whose languages have a grammatical gender system are likely to be more sexist than languages that do not? Why or why not?

Notes

1 A kind of snake that crushes its prey to death.
2 Similar to alligators and crocodiles.
3 *Especially* those ones.
4 Ten if it's a female speaker. You might think that Pirahã is inferior to English because it has fewer phonemes, and more is better. If so, Hmong, with its 80 phonemes would be twice as good as English. But drawing that sort of conclusion would be a mistake. Having more phonemes has some advantages. For example, languages with more phonemes can have shorter words, because a larger inventory of phonemes makes it easier to distinguish one word from another. But a simplified inventory of speech sounds allows for greater flexibility in pronunciation, especially when tones (pitch) are used to discriminate different words. As a result of having a relatively small phoneme inventory, Pirahã can be hummed, sung, whistled, and shouted over distances that normally cause phonological information to be severely degraded (Everett, 2008). Silbo-Gomero is another whistled language, but its scope appears to be more limited than Pirahã (Carreiras, Lopez, Rivero, & Corina, 2005).
5 With apologies to Mrs Heidemann, who was doing her best to help us learn stuff.
6 A better joke, whose punch line is "Where's the library at _____" is, sadly, unprintable.
7 It would also happen if you could place one phoneme within another phoneme, one syllable inside another syllable, or one word inside another word, but none of these are possible. You can put one story inside another story, as in flashbacks in narratives.
8 Some studies of bottlenose dolphins have produced evidence that the animals pay attention to symbol order when interpreting multi-symbol statements (Herman, Richards, & Wolz, 1984). However, Premack's analysis of these studies suggests that the dolphins' behavior reflects general-purpose cognition, rather than any language-specific process (Premack, 1985).
9 And they have a lot more sex than chimps do—or people, for that matter.
10 Although idiosyncratic characteristics of the individual animals cannot be ruled out. Such differences have been observed between animals of the same species. Kanzi's mother was largely unsuccessful learning to communicate using lexigrams. Kanzi, her offspring, learned spontaneously by watching his mother interact with her trainers. Of course, similar differences in verbal ability are widespread within groups of humans. While every normal individual learns his or her native language to a degree that allows him or her to communicate effectively with others, some people have larger vocabularies than others, some speak more fluently than others, and some are better at learning second or third languages than others.
11 Recent reports of chimps signing for non-food items (Russell et al., 2005), tools specifically, could simply reflect an instance of *chaining*. The apes need the tool to get the food reward. Similarly, reports of intentional communication based on chimps' perseverative signing after being given half a banana (Leavens, Russell, & Hopkins, 2005) could represent a kind of discriminative learning. If the chimps in question are rewarded for signing on a schedule with intervals between successive rewards, then both maintaining signing prior to reward and cessation of signing immediately after reward could be driven by the schedule, rather than the apes' internal intentional state.
12 Although they did occasionally produce signs for objects that they did not want. For example, they would make the sign for "dog" when a dog was barking in the distance.

13 As with some of the other effects reported in Terrace et al. (1979) a more recent corpus analysis of chimp signing failed to find any consistency at all in the way chimps order signs in multi-sign utterances (Rivas, 2005).
14 "The subtlety of control required of the intercostal muscles during human speech makes demands of the same order as those that are made on the small muscles of the hand" (MacLarnon and Hewitt, 1999, p. 350).
15 By contrast, tongue enervation is fairly similar between modern humans and our ancestors from as long as 300,000 years ago (MacLarnon & Hewitt, 1999).
16 The study of neglected and "feral" children, such as Genie (Curtiss, 1977), constitutes a third line.
17 Ignore for the moment that Eskimo is an umbrella term that covers distinct language groups, Aleut, Inuit, and Yupik, with different dialects spoken within the language groups.
18 And very funny.
19 Where "word" is defined as root morphemes; see Chapter 3.
20 See Saunders and van Brakel (1997) and Saunders (2000) for an opposing view.
21 Conceptualizing time may be a third (Boroditsky, 2001), although the underlying mental processes mapping space and time may be fundamentally non-linguistic (Cassanto & Boroditsky, 2008).
22 Other interpretations are possible, such as that Chinese culture places greater emphasis on arithmetic earlier in life, and so children in that culture practice those skills more. Such an interpretation is supported by research showing that older Americans and older Chinese-speakers have comparable arithmetic and mathematical skills (Geary, Salthouse, Chen, & Fan, 1996). If language alone drove differences between Chinese and English speakers, those advantages should have been just as apparent in older speakers as in younger ones.
23 Some people are worried that the Pirahã lose track of their children because their language does not offer a means of counting heads. But the Pirahã, like people everywhere, recognize their children as individuals rather than objects to be counted.
24 See Au, 1983, 1992, for a vigorously argued dissent, although the disagreement may hinge on whether Au's subjects were monolingual enough in Chinese (see also Gilovich et al., 2003).
25 Both groups had an easier time when the wavelength difference between the comparisons was large than when it was smaller; and the beneficial effects of the linguistic distinction between "siniy" and "goluboy" were greatest for the Russian speakers when the discrimination task was at its most difficult, that is, when the wavelength difference between the squares was smallest.
26 Viva la revolución

References

Aitchison, J. (2000). *The seeds of speech.* Cambridge, England: Cambridge University Press.

Au, K. (1983). Chinese and English counterfactuals: The Sapir–Whorf hypothesis revisited. *Cognition, 15,* 155–187.

Au, K. (1992). Cross-linguistic research on language and cognition: Methodological challenges. In H. Chen, & O. Tzeng (Eds.), *Advances in psychology: Vol. 90. Language processing in Chinese,* (pp. 367–381). Oxford, England: North-Holland.

Berlin, B., & Kay, P. (1969). *Basic color terms: Their universality and evolution.* Berkeley, CA: University of California Press.

Bickerton, D. (1988). Creole languages and the bioprogram. In F. J. Newmeyer (Ed.), *Linguistics: The Cambridge survey: Vol. 2* (pp. 285–301). Cambridge, England: Cambridge University Press.

Bloom, A. (1984). Caution—The words you use may affect what you say: A response to Au. *Cognition, 17,* 275–287.

Boas, F. (1911). *The mind of primitive man.* New York: Collier.

Boroditsky, L. (2001). Does language shape thought? Mandarin and English speakers' conceptions of time. *Cognitive Psychology, 43,* 1–22.

Brakke, K. E., & Savage-Rumbaugh, E. S. (1996a). The development of language skills in *Pan,* I: Comprehension. *Language & Communication, 15,* 121–148.

Brakke, K. E., & Savage-Rumbaugh, E. S. (1996b). The development of language skills in *Pan,* II: Production. *Language & Communication, 16,* 361–380.

Bruner, A., & Revusky, S. H. (1961). Collateral behavior in humans. *Journal of Experimental Analysis of Behavior, 4,* 349–350.

Carreiras, M., Lopez, J., Rivero, F., & Corina, D. (2005). Neural processing of a whistled language. *Nature, 433,* 31–32.

Cassanto, D., & Boroditsky, L. (2008). Time in the mind: Using space to think about time. *Cognition, 106,* 579–593.

Chen, J., Chiu, C., Roese, N. J., Tam, K., & Lau, I. (2006). Culture and counterfactuals: On the importance of life domains. *Journal of Cross-Cultural Psychology, 37,* 75–84.

Curtiss, S. (1977). *Genie: A psycholinguistic study of a modern-day "Wild Child."* San Diego, CA: Academic Press.

Darwin, C. (1859/1979). *The origin of species.* New York: Hill and Wang.

Ekman, P., Sorenson, E. R., & Friesen, W. V. (1969). Pan-cultural elements in facial displays of emotion. *Science, 164,* 86–88.

Emmorey, K. (2002). *Language, cognition, and the brain: Insights from sign language research.* Mahwah, NJ: Erlbaum.

Enard, W., Przeworski, M., Fisher, S. E., Lai, C. S. L., Wiebe, V., Kitano, T. et al. (2002). Molecular evolution of FOXP2, a gene involved in speech and language. *Nature, 418,* 869–872.

Everett, D. L. (2005). Cultural constraints on grammar and cognition in Pirahã. *Current Anthropology,* 46, 621–646.

Everett, D. L. (2007). Challenging Chomskyan linguistics: The case of Pirahã. *Human Development, 50,* 297–299.

Everett, D. L. (2008). *Don't sleep, there are snakes.* New York: Random House.

Falk, D. (2004). Prelinguistic evolution in early hominids: Whence motherese? *Behavioral and Brain Sciences, 27,* 491–451.

Finn, R. (1991). Different minds. *Discover, 12,* 54.

Fitch, W. T., Hauser, M. D., & Chomsky, N. (2005). The evolution of the language faculty: Clarifications and implications. *Cognition, 97,* 179–210.

Fodor, J. A. (1983). *The modularity of mind.* Cambridge, MA: MIT Press.

Fouts, R. S. (1975). Capacities for language in the great apes. In R. H. Tuttle (Ed.), *Socioecology and psychology of primates* (pp. 371–390). The Hague/Paris: Mouton Publishers.

Frank, M. C., Everett, D. L., Fedorenko, E., & Gibson, E. (2008). Number as a cognitive technology: Evidence from Pirahã language and cognition. *Cognition, 108,* 819–824.

Gardner, B. T., & Gardner, R. A. (1975). Evidence for sentence constituents in the early utterances of child and chimpanzee. *Journal of Experimental Psychology, 104,* 244–267.

Gardner, R. A., & Gardner, B. T. (1969). Teaching sign language to a Chimpanzee. *Science, 165,* 664–672.

Geary, D. C., Salthouse, T. A., Chen, G., & Fan, L. (1996). Are East Asian versus American differences in arithmetical ability a recent phenomenon? *Developmental Psychology, 32,* 254–262.

Gelman, R., & Gallistel, C. R. (2004). Language and the origin of numerical concepts. *Science, 306,* 441–443.

Gilovich, T., Wang, R. F., Regan, D., & Nishina, S. (2003). Regrets of action and inaction across cultures. *Journal of Cross-Cultural Psychology, 34,* 61–71.

Goldstein, E. B. (2006). *Sensation and perception.* New York: Wadsworth.

Gopnik, M. (1990). Feature-blind grammar and dysphasia. *Nature, 344,* 715.

Gopnik, M. (1994). Impairments of tense in a familial language disorder. *Journal of Neurolinguistics, 8,* 109–133.

Gopnik, M., & Crago, M. B. (1991). Familial aggregation of a developmental disorder. *Cognition, 39,* 1–50.

Gordon, P. (2004). Numerical cognition without words: Evidence from Amazonia. *Science, 306,* 496–499.

Greenfield, P. M., & Savage-Rumbaugh, E. S. (1990). Grammatical combination in *Pan paniscus*: Processes of learning and invention in the evolution and development of language. In S. T. Parker & K. R. Gibson (Eds.), *Language and intelligence in monkeys and apes: Comparative developmental perspectives* (pp. 540–578). Cambridge, England: Cambridge University Press.

Hardin, C. L., & Maffi, L. (1997). *Color categories in thought and language.* Cambridge, England: Cambridge University Press.

Hauser, M. D., Newport, E. L., & Aslin, R. N. (2001). Segmentation of the speech stream in a non-human primate: Statistical learning in cotton-top tamarins. *Cognition, 78,* B53–B64.

Hauser, M. D., Chomsky, N., & Fitch, W. T. (2002). The faculty of language: What is it, who has it, and how did it evolve? *Science, 298,* 1569–1579.

Herman, L. M., Richards, D. G., & Wolz, J. P. (1984). Comprehension of sentences by bottlenose dolphins. *Cognition, 16,* 129–219.

Hewes, G. W. (1973). Primate communication and the gestural origin of language. *Current Anthropology, 14,* 5–24.

Hockett, C. F. (1960). The origin of speech. *Scientific American, 203,* 88–96.

Huang, J., Fan, J., He, W., Yu, S., Yeow, C., Sun, G., et al. (2009). Could intensity ratings of Matsumoto and Ekman's JACFEE pictures delineate basic emotions? A principal component analysis in Chinese university students. *Personality and Individual Differences, 46,* 331–335.

Hunt, E., & Agnoli, F. (1991). The Whorffian hypothesis: A cognitive psychology perspective. *Psychological Review, 98,* 377–389.

Hupka, R. B., Lenton, A. P., & Hutchison, K. A. (1999). Universal development of emotion categories in natural language. *Journal of Personality and Social Psychology, 77,* 247–278.

Jackendoff, R., & Pinker, S. (2005). The nature of the language faculty and its implications for evolution of language. *Cognition, 97,* 211–225.

Jensvold, M. L. A., & Gardner, R. A. (2000). Interactive use of sign language by cross-fostered chimpanzees (*Pan troglodytes*). *Journal of Comparative Psychology, 114,* 335–346.

Karmiloff-Smith, A., Tyler, L. K., Voice, K., Sims, K., Udwin, O., Howlin, P., et al. (1998). Linguistic dissociations in Williams syndrome: Evaluating receptive syntax in on-line and off-line tasks. *Neuropsychologia, 36,* 343–351.

Kay, P., & Maffi, L. (1999). Color appearance and the emergence and evolution of basic color lexicons. *American Anthropologist, 101,* 743–760.

Kay, P., & Maffi, L. (2000). Color appearance and the emergence and evolution of basic color lexicons. *American Anthropologist, 101,* 743–760.

Lai, C. S., Fisher, S. E., Hurst, J. A., Vargha-Khadem, F., & Monaco, A. P. (2001). A novel forkhead-domain gene is mutated in a severe speech and language disorder. *Nature, 413,* 519–523.

Leavens, D. A., Russell, J. L., & Hopkins, W. D. (2005). Intentionality as measured in the persistence and elaboration of communication by Chimpanzees (*Pan troglodytes*). *Child Development*, 76, 291–306.

Lecours, A., & Joanette, Y. (1980). Linguistic and other psychological aspects of paroxysmal aphasia. *Brain & Language, 10,* 1–23.

Lenneberg, E. H. (1967). *Biological foundations of language*. Malabar, FL: Krieger.

Lenneberg, E. H. & Roberts, J. M. (1956). *The language of experience: A study in methodology*. Indiana University Publications in Anthropology and Linguistics Memoir 13: supplement to *International Journal of American Linguistics, 22,* 2. Baltimore: Waverly Press.

Lieberman, P. (2000). *Human language and our reptilian brain*. Cambridge, MA: Harvard University Press.

Lightwood, R. (1952). Idiopathic hypercalcaemia with failure to thrive. *Proceedings of the Royal Society of Medicine, 45,* 401–410.

Losh, M., Bellugi, U., Reilly, J., & Anderson, D. (2000). Narrative as a social engagement tool: The excessive use of evaluation in narratives from children with Williams syndrome. *Narrative Inquiry, 10,* 265–290.

Lyn, H., & Savage-Rumbaugh, E. S. (2000). Observational word learning in two bonobos (*Pan paniscus*): Ostensive and non-ostensive contexts. *Language & Communication, 20,* 255–273.

Lyn, H., Greenfield, P., & Savage-Rumbaugh. S. (2006). The development of representational play in chimpanzees and bonobos: Evolutionary implications, pretense, and the role of interspecies communication. *Cognitive Development, 21,* 199–213.

MacLarnon, A. M., & Hewitt, G. P. (1999). The evolution of human speech: The role of enhanced breathing control. *American Journal of Physical Anthropology, 109,* 341–363.

Martin, L. (1986). Eskimo words for snow: A case study in the genesis and decay of an anthropological example. *American Anthropologist, 88,* 418–423.

Miller, K. F., & Stigler, J. W. (1987). Counting in Chinese: Cultural variation in a basic cognitive skill. *Cognitive Development, 2,* 279–305.

Newport, E. L., Hauser, M. D., Spaepen, G., & Aslin, R. N. (2004). Learning at a distance II: Statistical learning of non-adjacent dependencies in a non-human primate. *Cognitive Psychology, 49,* 85–117.

Penn, D. C., Holyoak, K. J., & Povinelli, D. J. (2008). Darwin's mistake: Explaining the discontinuity between human and nonhuman minds. *Behavioral and Brain Sciences, 31,* 109–178.

Pinker, S. (1994). *The language instinct.* New York: Harper.

Pinker, S., & Bloom, P. (1990). Natural language and natural selection. *Behavioral and Brain Sciences, 13,* 707–784.

Pinker, S., & Jackendoff, R. (2005). The faculty of language: What's special about it? *Cognition, 95,* 201–236.

Premack, D. (1985). "Gavagai!" or the future history of the animal language controversy. *Cognition, 19,* 207–296.

Premack, D. (1990). Words: What are they, and do animals have them? *Cognition, 37,* 197–212.

Pullum, G. K. (1989). The great Eskimo vocabulary hoax. *Natural Language and Linguistic Theory, 7,* 275–281.

Ramus, F., Hauser, M. D., Miller, C., Morris, D., & Mehler, J. (2000). Language discrimination by human newborns and by cotton-top tamarin monkeys. *Science, 288,* 349–351.

Reilly, J., Klima, E. S., & Bellugi, U. (1990). Once more with feeling: Affect and language in atypical populations. *Development and Psychopathology, 2,* 367–391.

Rivas, E. (2005). Recent use of signs by Chimpanzees (*Pan troglodytes*) in interactions with humans. *Journal of Comparative Psychology, 119,* 404–417.

Russell, J. L., Braccini, S., Buehler, N., Kachin, M. J., Schapiro, S. J., & Hopkins, W. D. (2005). Chimpanzee (*Pan troglodytes*) intentional communication is not contingent upon food. *Animal Cognition, 8,* 263–272.

Sag, I., Wasow, T., & Bender, E. M. (2003). *Syntactic theory: A formal introduction.* Stanford, CA: Center for the Study of Language and Information.

Saunders, B. A. C. (2000). Revisiting basic color terms. *Journal of the Royal Anthropological Institute, 6,* 81–99.

Saunders, B. A. C., & van Brakel, J. (1997). Are there nontrivial constraints on colour categorization? *Behavioral and Brain Sciences, 20,* 167–228.

Savage-Rumbaugh, E. S., & Fields, W. M. (2000). Linguistic, cultural, and cognitive capacities of bonobos. *Culture & Psychology, 6,* 131–153.

Seidenberg, M. S., & Petitto, L. A. (1987). Communication, symbolic communication, and language: Comment on Savage-Rumbaugh, McDonald, Sevcik, Hopkins, and Rupert (1986). *Journal of Experimental Psychology: General, 116,* 279–287.

Senghas, A., & Coppola, M. (2001). Children creating a language: How Nicaraguan Sign Language acquired a spatial grammar. *Psychological Science, 12,* 323–328.

Sevcik, R. A., & Savage-Rumbaugh, E. S. (1994). Language comprehension and use by great apes. *Language & Communication, 14,* 37–58.

Shanker, S. G., Savage-Rumbaugh, E. S., & Taylor, T. J. (1999). Kanzi: A new beginning. *Animal Learning & Behavior, 27,* 24–25.

Skinner, B. F. (1957). *Verbal behavior.* Acton, MA: Compton.

Smith, N., & Tsimpli, I. (1995). *The mind of a savant: Language learning and modularity.* Oxford, England: Blackwell.

Smith, S. M., Brown, H. O., Toman, J. E. P., & Goodman, L. S. (1947). The lack of cerebral effects of d-tubercurarine. *Anesthesiology, 8,* 1–14.

Stanovich, K. E. (2009). *How to think straight about psychology* (9th ed.). New York: Allyn & Bacon.

Tagliatela, J. P., Savage-Rumbaugh, S., & Baker, L. A. (2003). Vocal production by a language-competent *Pan paniscus. International Journal of Primatology, 24,* 1–7.

Talmy, L. (2009, December). *How language structures concepts.* Paper presented to the International Conference on Language and Cognition: State of the Art. Centre for Behavioral and Cognitive Sciences, Allahabad University. Allahabad, India.

Terrace, H. S., Pettitto, L. A., Sanders, R. J., & Bever, T. G. (1979). Can an ape create a sentence? *Science, 206,* 891–902.

Thomas, M. S. C., Grant, J., Barham, Z., Gsödl, M., Laing, E., Lakusta, L., et al. (2001). Past tense formation in Williams syndrome. *Language and Cognitive Processes, 16,* 143–176.

Tomasello, M. (1995). Language is not an instinct. *Cognitive Development, 10,* 131–156.

Tomasello, M. (2007). If they're so good at grammar, then why don't they talk? Hints from apes' and humans' use of gestures. *Language Learning and Development, 3,* 133–156.

Tsimpli, I., & Smith, N. (1999). Modules and quasi-modules: Language and theory of mind in a polyglot savant. *Learning and Individual Differences, 10,* 193–215.

Tyler, L. K, Karmiloff-Smith, A., Voice, J. K., Stevens, T., Grant, J., Udwin, O., et al. (1997). Do individuals with Williams syndrome have bizarre semantics? Evidence for lexical organization using an on-line task. *Cortex, 33,* 515–527.

Vargha-Khadem, F., Watkins, K. E., Price, C. J., Ashburner, J., Alcock, K. J., Connely, A., et al. (1998). Neural basis of an inherited speech and language disorder. *Proceedings of the National Academy of Science, 95,* 12695–12700.

Watkins, K. E., Dronkers, N. F., & Vargha-Khadem, F. (2002). Behavioural analysis of an inheristed speech and language disorder: Comparison with acquired aphasia, *Brain, 125,* 454–464.

Watson, J. B. (1924). The place of kinesthetic, visceral, and laryngeal organization in thinking. *Psychological Review, 31,* 339–347.

Williams, J. C. P., Barratt-Boyes, B. G., & Lowe, J. B. (1961). Supravalvular aortic stenosis. *Circulation, 24,* 1311–1318.

Williams, K. E., & Savage-Rumbaugh, E. S. (1997). Comprehension skills of language-competent and non-language-competent apes. *Language & Communication, 17,* 301–317.

Winawer, J., Witthoft, N., Frank, M. C., Wu, L., Wade, A. R., & Boroditsky, L. (2007). Russian blues reveal effects of language on color discrimination. *Proceedings of the National Academy of Science, 104,* 7780–7785.

Zuberbühler, K. (2003). Referential signaling in non-human primates: Cognitive precursors and limitations for the evolution of language. In P. J. B. Slater, J. S. Rosenblatt, C. T. Snowdon, T. J. Roper, & M. Naguib (Eds.), *Advances in the study of behavior: vol. 33* (pp. 265–307). San Diego, CA: Academic Press.

Zuberbühler, K., Cheney, D. L., & Seyfarth, R. M. (1999). Conceptual semantics in a nonhuman primate. *Journal of Comparative Psychology, 113,* 33–42.

Speech Production and Comprehension

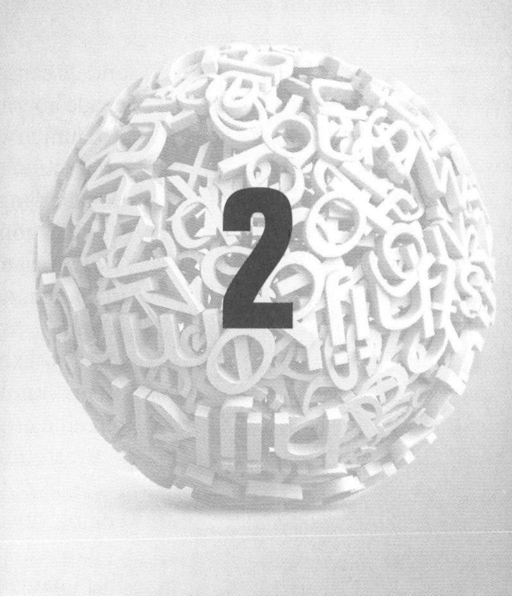

People don't just turn into a Scotsman for no reason at all.

GRAHAM CHAPMAN

In the Monty Python television series, one episode presented a sketch in which the entire population of England, women and children included, turned into Scotsmen. ("The over-crowding was pitiful. Three men to a caber.")[1] In the skit, space aliens from the planet Skyron did the dirty work. Strangely, in the real world, there is a neurological syndrome that can turn you into a Scotsman. Well, you don't literally turn into a Scotsman, but you do end up talking like a Scotsman. That is, you can acquire an accent that sounds Scottish as the result of experiencing brain damage. One such adult patient spoke English with a London accent (southern English) before her injury, but after suffering a stroke "three native Scottish speakers reported that her post-stroke accent did sound Scottish to them" (Dankovičová et al., 2001, p. 213). Other kinds of accent changes have also been reported: English to Spanish or Norwegian; Belgian Dutch to French and Moroccan; Norwegian to German (caused, ironically, by injury from German shrapnel; Moen, 2000). This neurological condition is called, appropriately, *foreign accent syndrome*. It is rare, but dozens of cases have been documented starting in the early 1900s. Why do people acquire foreign-sounding accents? It has to do with the way brain injury changes the mental and motor processes that are involved in speech production (talking). One of the chief goals of this chapter is to describe these planning and output processes. (The other is to describe how speech sounds are perceived.) Let's return to foreign accent syndrome

Introduction to Psycholinguistics: Understanding Language Science, First Edition.
Matthew J. Traxler.

and its causes once you have a bit of speech production theory under your belt. Then we'll tackle how a brain injury can turn you into a Scotsman, or at least make you sound like one.

Human communication occurs most frequently via speech, so understanding speech production (talking) and comprehension lays the foundation for an understanding of human language abilities. Contemporary theories of speech production take as their starting point the moment in time where the speaker has an idea she wishes to convey. Thus, they focus primarily on how speakers convert ideas into a form that can be expressed in speech, and take for granted that speakers have ideas to convey. (A separate branch of cognitive psychology focuses on how people come up with ideas, and how people select ideas to express; see, e.g., Goldstein, 2007). While the basic process of speech planning seems simple—you have an idea, you pick words to express the idea, you say the words—research on speech planning and production shows that the mental processes that intervene between thinking of an idea and producing the physical movements that create speech are quite complex. One of the main goals of this chapter is to describe some of the hidden complexity of the speech production system.

Once a speaker has decided what to say and how to say it, she produces a set of behaviors that change her immediate physical environment, chiefly by creating a pattern of sound waves—an *acoustic signal*—that is available to listeners. The listener's chief task is to somehow analyze the acoustic signal so that the speaker's intended meaning can be recovered. This, too, seems like a simple task. The listener recognizes the words that the speaker produced, matches those words to concepts, and, hey presto! understands what the speaker meant to say. However, acoustic analysis of speech shows that the sound waves that speakers produce are wickedly complex and that, just as in speech production, there is a great deal of mental work that needs to be done after sound waves hit the ear drum before the listener can recover the speaker's intended meaning. This chapter will explain why analyzing the physical properties of speech is tricky and review current theories that try to explain how listeners overcome obstacles created by the peculiar acoustic properties of speech.

Speech Production

To explain how speech is produced, a theory must describe the mental representations that support the translation between ideas, which are mentally represented in a non-language form, and the mental plans that cause muscles to move.[2] After all, speech requires physical action—a process called *articulation*. In fact, speech is more complicated than many other physical actions that we perform, because speech requires exquisitely tight control over more than 100 muscles moving simultaneously (Meister, Wilson, Deblieck, Wu, & Iacoboni, 2007). Theories of speech production try to answer questions like: Once you have an idea that you wish to convey, what steps must you take to retrieve the linguistic representations you need to express your idea? How do you organize those representations? How do you translate those representations into a form that the motor system can use to generate the actual, physical gestures that create speech sounds?

Speech production requires at least three kinds of mental operations (Griffin & Ferreira, 2006). First, you have to think of something to say. The processes that accomplish that are called *conceptualization*. Once you have something to say, you must figure out a good way to express that idea given the tools that your language provides. This type of processing is called *formulation*. Finally, you need to actually move your muscles to make a sound wave that a listener can perceive. These processes are called *articulation*.

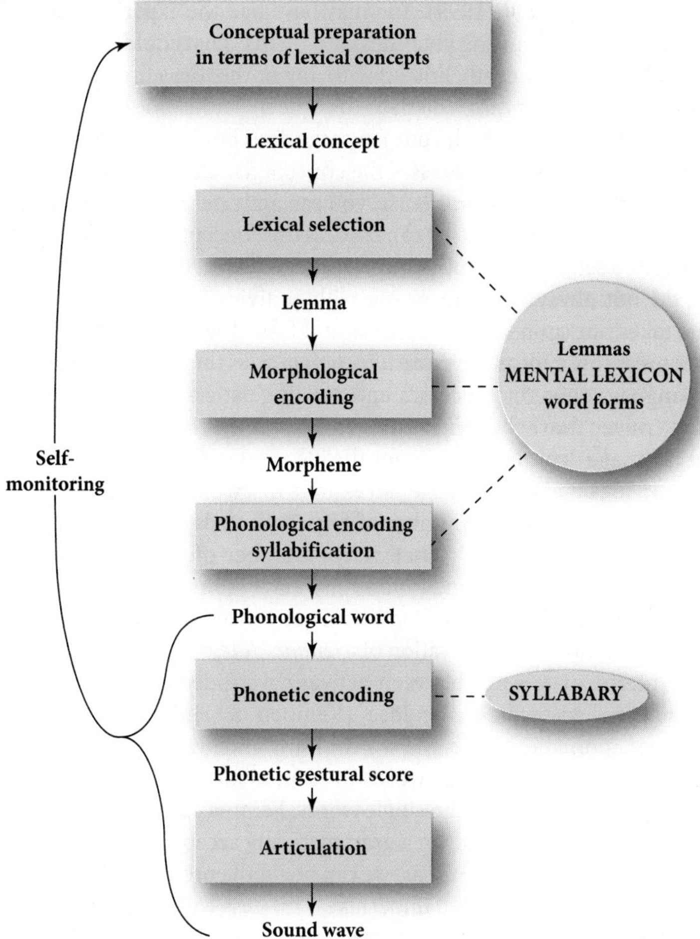

Figure 2.1 A schematic of Levelt and colleagues' speech production model (Levelt et al., 1999, p. 3)

One influential approach to speech production is Willem Levelt's production theory, which has been adapted as a mathematical model called WEAVER++ (Jescheniak & Levelt, 1994; Levelt, 1989; Levelt, Roelofs, & Meyer, 1999; Roelofs, Özdemir, & Levelt, 2007). An overview of the WEAVER production system appears in Figure 2.1. Take a moment to have a look at it, but don't panic! Let's break it down, step by step. The first really important thing to realize about speech production is that activating an idea does *not* automatically lead to activation of the speech sounds you need to express the idea. That is, thinking of the concept "cat" does not automatically lead to activation of the speech sounds /k/, /a/, and /t/. One of the goals of WEAVER++ is to describe the intermediate steps between activating an idea and activating the sounds that you need to express the idea. Speech production is viewed as involving a sequence of mental processes. Each mental process accomplishes a subgoal, and the output of one mental process provides the information needed for the next mental process.

Each box in the model in Figure 2.1 indicates a kind of mental process. For example, "conceptual preparation in terms of lexical concepts" boils down to this: Choose the idea(s) that you want to express, but make sure that your idea lines up with words that you have in your language. The output of this process, a *lexical concept*, is an idea for which your language has a label (Levelt et al., 1999). You may have had the experience where you have an idea, but you have trouble putting your idea into words. That could happen because your (non-linguistic) idea does not neatly line up with any of the ideas for which your language has a pre-existing word. In that case, you need to come up with some combination of lexical concepts to express the idea for which your language does not have a single term. Here is an example: English has a word that expresses the concept *female horse*. That word is *mare*. If you want to express the concept *female horse*, you can activate the lexical concept *mare*. But English does not have a single word that can express the concept *female elephant*. To express that idea, you need to select and combine two different lexical concepts (female, elephant). Because ideas do not always line up neatly with individual words, we need a stage of processing that takes our (non-linguistic) ideas and finds the lexical (linguistic) forms that we can use to express those ideas. The *lexicalization process* therefore serves as the interface between non-language thought processes and the linguistic systems that produce verbal expressions that convey those thoughts.

When your language does have a word for the idea you wish to express, the activation of a *lexical concept*, an idea that the language can express in a word, will lead to *lexical selection*. Often times, a language will have a number of different words that are close in meaning to the idea that you wish to express. In that case, a number of different representations in memory will become activated, and you must have some means to choose which representation will be selected for production. That process is lexical selection, and the outcome of lexical selection is the activation of a *lemma*. A *lemma* is a mental representation that reflects an intermediate stage between activating an idea and activating the speech sounds that you need to express the idea (Kempen & Huijbers, 1983). The lemma incorporates information about what the word means and *syntactic* information that you need to combine that word with other words to express more complex ideas. Most of the time, we speak in sentences, rather than single words. Lemmas provide the information that we need to speak a sequence of words in a grammatically acceptable way.

Once we have activated a set of lemmas, we can begin the process of activating the sound codes that we need to speak. First, we undertake a process called *morphological encoding*. Morphemes are basic units of language representation. They are the language equivalent of atoms in physics. Atoms are basic units and building blocks of matter; morphemes are basic units and building blocks of meaning in a language. Morphological processing is important because words appear in different forms depending on aspects of their meanings as well as grammatical aspects of the sentences in which they appear. Levelt (1989, p. 182) provides a good example. He notes that each word we know has a *morphological specification* that tells us how the word behaves when it is placed in a sentence. The morphological specification for the word *eat* includes, "that it is a root form (i.e., it is not further analyzable into constituent morphemes), that its third-person present tense inflection is *eats*, and that its past-tense inflection is *ate*." So, if we are talking about an event in the past, we will use a past-tense form of the verb *eat* (i.e., *ate*, *was eating*, or *had eaten*). If two people are performing an action at the moment you are speaking, you say *eat*, but if only one person is performing the action, you say *eats* (*They eat*; *He eats*). The form of the word, its morphological specification (*ate* vs. *was eating* vs. *eat* vs. *eats*), changes depending on what precise role the lemma is playing in the sentence.

Having selected a set of morphemes to produce, morphological encoding activates the speech sounds (phonemes) we need to plan the articulatory movements that will create the speech signal. The speech sounds you produce depend on the morphemes that you activate, so you have to have the right set of morphemes activated, and you have to arrange them in the right sequence, before you can activate the speech sounds.

To sketch the production process so far: Concepts point you to lemmas. Lemmas point you to the morphological information you need to combine lemmas into larger phrases.

Morphological encoding points you to the speech sounds (phonemes) you need to express specific sets of lemmas in specific forms.

Having the right set of morphemes activated in the right sequence gets us a step closer to moving our speech muscles, but it does not get us all the way home. Once you have the morphemes slotted into the right positions you can activate the individual speech sounds (*phonemes*), but speaking involves more than just saying a sequence of phonemes. In contemporary speech production theory, the lemma represents abstract information about a word, such as its grammatical class, its meaning, and the way it may combine with other lemmas; while what we normally think of as a word (the collection of sounds) is referred to as a *lexeme*. To produce the lexeme, we need to activate a set of phonemes (speech sounds) and organize them into groups for production.

Evidence for the lexeme as a psychologically real level of representation comes from studies involving the production of *homophones* (Jescheniak & Levelt, 1994; Jescheniak, Meyer, & Levelt, 2003). A homophone is a word that has more than one meaning. A lexeme like /but/ has two spellings (*butt* and *but*) and more than one distinct meaning. In English, the *but* version of the lexeme occurs very frequently, whereas the *butt* version (as in *I was often the butt of her sick practical jokes*) occurs very rarely. According to current production models (Dell, 1986; Levelt et al., 1999), both the *but* version and the *butt* version activate the same lexeme, because the lexeme represents how the word is pronounced, and both versions of /but/ are pronounced the same way. If so, lexemes should experience the *frequency inheritance* effect. That is, if a word has a high-frequency twin (*but* is the high-frequency twin of *butt*), you should produce the low-frequency version (*butt*) about as fast as you produce the high-frequency version (*but*), because the overall lexeme frequency is high. By contrast, if a word has two versions, but both are low frequency, then it should take a relatively long time to respond to the word (*flecks* and *flex* for example, are both low-frequency forms). Experiments involving picture naming provide evidence for frequency inheritance, as do experiments involving translation from one language to another. In both cases, low-frequency versions of words are produced quickly if they have a higher-frequency twin (i.e., if the frequency of their lexeme is high). Thus, the time it takes you to produce a word is not based solely on how frequently that word's meaning is used. Instead, it depends partly on how often you use a particular collection of sounds (a lexeme).

When we speak, we do not simply emit a string of phonemes. Those phonemes need to be organized into larger units, because, when we speak, we speak in syllables. Producing each syllable requires a coordinated set of actions, and each set of coordinated actions needs to be planned. Before we start to speak, we need to figure out which speech sounds (phonemes) we need, but we also need to figure out how to map the set of activated phonemes onto a set of syllables. This latter process is called *syllabification*.[3] Syllabification involves two subcomponent processes: activating a *metrical structure* and inserting individual speech sounds (phonemes) into positions in the metrical structure. The metrical structure consists of a set of syllable-sized units. In addition to specifying the number of syllables that you need, the metrical structure indicates the relative emphasis or loudness (*accent*) that each syllable should receive. The word *banana*, for example, has an accent on the second syllable. The word *Panama* has accent on the first syllable. So, the metrical structure for *banana* would be represented as "σ σ′ σ," and the metrical structure for *Panama* would be represented as "σ′ σ σ." Each σ symbol stands for a syllable, and the ′ mark indicates which syllable in the string should be accented. Once the metrical structure has been laid down, individual phonemes can be inserted into positions within each syllable.

Evidence that syllabification is a real mental process that intervenes between morphological processing and articulation can be found in studies of the way people speak. For example, consider the word *escorting* (Levelt et al., 1999, p. 5). It has two morphemes, the root *escort*, and the suffix *-ing*. When people actually speak the word *escorting*, they usually produce it in three segments, which sound something like, "ess," "core," and "ting" (*ess-core-ting*, rather than *ess-cort-ing*). That means that the syllabification processes in production have placed the /t/ phoneme together with the *-ing* morpheme, rather than with the root morpheme *escort*. So, we do not simply activate morphemes, activate the phonemes that go with each morpheme, and produce them in sequence. Instead, after the morphemes are activated, we calculate the best way to organize the sequence of phonemes into syllables, and it is the syllables that actually serve as the basis of production. That is true, even when the processes responsible for calculating syllables lump together phonemes from different words. If you were going to speak a sentence that included the phrase *He will escort us*, you would most likely take the /t/ phoneme from the word *escort* and stick it into a syllable along with the word *us*. So, you would actually say something that sounds like "es-core-tuss" (rather than "es-cort-us"). So, while we need morphemes and words to plan what to say, speech does not simply involve activating the speech sounds in individual words. Instead, the speech planning system activates a set of morphemes or words, and then it figures out the best way to organize those morphemes and words into a set of syllables. Sometimes the syllables respect morpheme and word boundaries, but often times they do not. In Levelt and Wheeldon's words (1994, p. 243), "Speakers do not concatenate citation forms of words, but create rhythmic, pronounceable metrical structures that largely ignore lexical word boundaries."[4]

The output of the syllabification process is a set of *phonological words*. In the WEAVER++ model, a phonological word is a set of syllables that is produced as a single unit. So, while "escort" and "us" are two different lemmas and two different words, when they are actually spoken, they come out as a single phonological word, /ess-core-tuss/. According to the WEAVER++ model, you can begin to speak as soon as you have activated all of the syllables in a given phonological word. Further evidence that we speak in phonological words, rather than in morphemes and (lexical) words, comes from colloquial (informal) speech and dialects. If you live in America, you probably find the comedian Jeff Foxworthy endlessly entertaining. One of Foxworthy's comedy bits involves an utterance that is pronounced *wichadidja*. *Wichadidja* is a phonological word that is composed of four lexical words, *With*, *you*, *did*, and *you*, as in *You didn't bring your varmint gun wichadidja?* If people spoke in lexical words ("dictionary" words or *citation forms*), expressions like *wichadidja* would not exist.

While you may plan each utterance by activating a number of lemmas and morphemes simultaneously, you plan the actual speech movements (*articulation*) one phonological word at a time. And you plan the movements you need to produce each phonological word one syllable at a time, in a "left-to-right" fashion. That is, you activate the phonemes for the syllable that you will need first (e.g., "ess" in *escort us*) before you activate phonemes for syllables that you will need later on. Evidence for left-to-right activation of phonemes in phonological words comes from studies involving *phoneme monitoring* in picture-naming experiments. In these experiments, people look at a picture and try to say a word that describes the picture as quickly as possible. So, if you were looking at a picture of a floppy, furry animal, you should say *rabbit* as quickly as possible. In a secondary task, you would be given a target phoneme and would be asked to press a button as quickly as possible if the target phoneme occurred in the picture's name. So, if you were asked to monitor the target phonemes /r/ or /b/, you should press the button when you see the picture of the floppy-eared animal. If you were asked to monitor the target phoneme /k/, you should refrain from responding. People can do this phoneme-monitoring task very accurately, and they respond a little bit faster if the target phoneme comes from the beginning of the word than if the target phoneme comes from the middle or the end of the word (Wheeldon & Levelt, 1995).

To summarize how the WEAVER++ model works, production begins with a set of ideas that the speaker wishes to express. In the next step, those ideas are tied to lexical concepts, because the language may have specific words for some of the ideas, but may require combinations of words to express other ideas. After a set of lexical concepts has been activated, lemmas that correspond to those lexical concepts become activated. Activating lemmas provides information about the morphological properties of words, including information about how words can be combined. After a set of morphemes has been activated and organized into a sequence, the speech sounds (phonemes) that are required can be activated and placed in a sequence. Phonological encoding involves the activation of a metrical structure and syllabification (organizing a set of phonemes into syllable-sized groups, whether the specific phonemes come from the same morpheme and word, or not). The outcome of this process is a set of phonological words consisting of a sequence of syllable-sized frames. During phonetic encoding, the speech production system consults a set of stored representations of specific syllables. The system activates the appropriate syllable representations and places them in the appropriate positions in the frame. This representation is used by the motor system to create a *phonetic gestural score*, which is the representation used by the motor system to plan the actual muscle movements (articulation) that will create sounds that the listener will perceive as speech.

Evidence supporting models of speech production like the WEAVER++ model can be found in three kinds of studies: Speech errors, tip-of-the-tongue experiences, and reaction time studies involving picture naming, which often use a version of the picture–word interference task. Mathematical modeling using computer programs to simulate what happens in speech errors, tip-of-the-tongue experiences and picture-naming experiments is also used to test ideas about how information flows through the speech production system.

Speech errors

The analysis of speech errors has a long and glorious history in psychology in general and psycholinguistics in particular. Sigmund Freud viewed speech errors as a window into the unconscious mind. He believed that speech errors revealed our true inner thoughts—thoughts that we suppressed in order to be polite. Modern psycholinguistic theories view speech errors as reflecting breakdowns in various components of the speech production process (Dell, 1986; Garrett, 1975; 1980; Levelt, 1983; Levelt et al., 1999; Postma, 2000). We can use speech errors to inform our understanding of speech production processes because speech errors are *not* random. In particular, *slips of the tongue* occur in systematic patterns, and those patterns can be related back to aspects of the speech production process. As Dell (1986, p. 286) notes, "Slips of the tongue can be seen as products of the productivity of language. A slip is an unintended novelty. Word errors create syntactic novelties; morphemic errors create novel words; and sound errors create novel, but phonologically legal, combinations of sounds."

Each of these different kinds of errors provides information about how different components of the production system work. For instance, people sometimes substitute one word for another when they are speaking. If people are placed under time pressure, and they are asked to name a picture of a cat, they will sometimes say *rat* or *dog*. This type of *semantic substitution* error likely reflects the *conceptual preparation* or *lexical selection* component of the speech production process. Semantic substitutions could reflect conceptual preparation if an individual mistakenly focuses on the wrong (non-linguistic) concept. Alternatively, semantic substitutions can reflect the way (non-linguistic) concepts are related to one another, and how the activation of (non-linguistic) concepts is tied to activation of lemmas (Dell, Schwartz, Martin, Saffran, & Gagnon, 1997; Levelt et al., 1999; Nooteboom, 1973). According to WEAVER++, concepts are stored in long-term memory in networks or collections of concepts. Within these networks, concepts that have similar meanings are connected to one another. As a result, when you think of the concept "cat," activation will spread to, or spill over onto, closely related concepts, such as "rat" and "dog." In order to select the correct lemma, you need to ignore related concepts in order to focus on the *target* concept (e.g., "cat"). Semantic substitutions can also reflect lemma-selection errors (rather than concept selection errors), because activating a (non-linguistic) concept will feed activation to lemmas that are associated with that concept. So, activating the "cat" concept will activate associated concepts ("rat" and "dog"), and those associated concepts will activate associated lemmas. When it comes time for the speaker to choose a lemma for further processing, she will choose the target lemma (*cat*) most of the time, but every once in a while, she may be fooled because alternative lemmas for *rat* and *dog* will also be activated. These kinds of behaviors are classified as speech errors, or "slips of the tongue," because people clearly did not use the commonly accepted term for the picture, even though they do know the appropriate term (as evidenced by frequent self-corrections in this kind of study).

Other types of speech errors may reflect breakdowns in other components of the speech production system. Sometimes, the correct set of phonemes is produced, but some phonemes appear in the wrong positions in the utterance. These *sound exchanges* are thought to reflect a stage of processing after a set of lemmas and morphemes has been activated, but before an articulatory plan (plan to move the speech muscles) has been compiled. In a sound exchange, you might be hoping to say, *big feet*, but instead you say *fig beet*. These kind of errors can be elicited in the lab by putting experimental subjects under time pressure. Researchers set up the experiment so that subjects get used to producing a specific pattern of sounds, and then they switch the pattern (Baars & Motley, 1974). Subjects might be asked to say, *bid meek*, *bud muck*, and *big men*, all of which have a /b/ in the first position in the first syllable and an /m/ in the first position in the second syllable. Then, right after that, subjects might have to say, *mad back*. About 10% of the time, subjects make an error and say, *bad mack* or *bad back*.[5] (Try this with your friends! See whether you can make them produce sound exchange errors.)

Sound exchange errors almost always occur when sounds are exchanged between words in the same phrase, and the vast majority involve movement of only a single phoneme from each word (Nooteboom, 1969). So, you are more likely to say *That guy has fig beet*, where the two target words are in the same noun phrase, than you are to say, *These beet are really fig* (Target: *These feet are really big*), where one word appears in a subject noun phrase and the other appears as part of the following verb phrase. In addition, sound exchanges almost always respect the *positional constraint*. That is, when sounds trade places, they almost always come from the same part of the word, usually the first phoneme. You would almost never say *tig feeb* by mistake, as this error would violate the positional constraint.

In Dell's (1986) production model, the positional constraint reflects the way individual phonemes are activated and inserted into *frames* (syllable-length mental representations, possibly, as in Levelt's model). According to the model, a number of frames can be activated simultaneously, so when you are planning for *big feet*, you activate two syllable frames, and you activate the phonemes you need to fill in those frames. Each of those phonemes is marked with an *order tag*, which tells the production system which phoneme comes first, which comes second, and so on. Because two syllable frames are activated simultaneously, and two phonemes that have "first" order tags are also activated simultaneously, sometimes the production system will confuse the two, and select the wrong phoneme for each of the two available "first" phoneme slots. Normally, the activation levels of the two "first" phonemes will differ at different points in time (generally, the /b/ phoneme will have more activation early in the planning process and the /f/ phoneme will have more activation later), and so mistakes will be relatively rare. But sometimes, if the activation levels of the two "first" phonemes are close enough, they will get reversed. Most errors respect the positional constraint, because the production system will not jam a phoneme with a "first" positional tag into the slot labeled "last," and vice versa. Further, most sound exchanges involve two phonemes from the same phrase. This suggests that the articulatory plan is built for no more than one phrase at a time.

A similar set of assumptions, that the production process generates a set of labeled slots and that activated units have tags that match available slots, also explains why people sometimes produce *word exchange* errors. A word exchange happens when a word that should have appeared in one position is produced in a different position. You might want to say, *My girlfriend plays the piano*, but say, *My piano plays the girlfriend* by mistake. In that case, *girlfriend* and *piano* participated in a word exchange. The majority of word exchange errors respect the *category* constraint (Dell, 1986; Postma, 2000). *Category* refers approximately to parts of speech, such as *noun*, *verb*, *adjective*, and so on. Most of the time, when two words participate in an exchange, they come from the same category (hence, *category* constraint). According to frame-and-slot models (e.g., Garrett, 1975; Mackay, 1972), speech involves a degree of advance planning. Rather than planning a word at a time, we can lay out the frame for an entire clause or sentence as we are looking for a particular set of words and the precise forms we need to produce those words. This frame consists of a set of slots (places for individual words to go), and each slot is labeled for the kind of word that has to appear there (noun, verb, adjective, and so on). As with sound exchange errors, word exchanges happen when more than one candidate is activated simultaneously, more than one candidate has the same tag (e.g., noun), and the production system assigns the wrong candidate to an open slot. Because the slots are labeled, however, the production system does not get the categories wrong. Verbs do not appear in noun slots; nouns do not appear in preposition slots; prepositions do not appear in verb slots.

Access interruptus: Tip-of-the-tongue experiences

Overt speech errors provide us with insights into the way the speech production system operates, but they are not the only game in town. *Tip-of-the-tongue experiences* also provide us with evidence about speech production. A tip-of-the-tongue experience (TOT for short) happens when you are trying to retrieve a word, you have a strong subjective impression that you know the word, but you are temporarily unable to consciously recall and pronounce the word. According to contemporary production theories (e.g., Dell, 1986; Levelt et al., 1999; Roelofs et al., 2007), TOT states occur when you have accessed the correct lemma, but you have been unable to fully activate the phonological information that goes along with that lemma. TOT experiences are taken as evidence for the distinction between semantic (meaning) activation and phonological (sound) activation that plays a role in all current accounts of speech production.[6] But why not simply view TOT experiences as evidence for the failure of meaning-related semantic processes? Why view TOT experiences as reflecting the temporary failure of phonological processes? A variety of results point to phonological encoding, rather than semantic processes, as being the culprit (Brown, 1991; Brown & McNeill, 1966; Rubin, 1975).

But first, how do language scientists study the TOT? There are a number of ways to do this (Brown, 1991). Sometimes, researchers ask people to carry around a diary and record all of their TOT experiences in a given time period (a few weeks or months, usually). Those kinds of studies indicate that people experience TOTs about once or twice a week, with the frequency of TOT experiences increasing as people get older. Another way to induce TOT experiences is to provide people with the definitions of rare, but familiar, words. For example, can you think of the words that go with the following definitions?

1. The first name of the character "Scrooge" in Charles Dickens' *A Christmas Carol.*
2. A small boat of the Far East, propelled by a single oar over the stern and provided with a roofing of mats.
3. A secretion of the sperm whale intestine used to make perfume; an ingredient in the perfume sent by Dr Hannibal Lecter to FBI agent Clarice Starling in the movie *Hannibal.*
4. A one-word name for a person who collects stamps. (Spoiler Alert: The answers appear in note 7.[7])

For fun, see how many of your friends can come up with the appropriate terms, and find out whether any of them experience a TOT. The interesting question is not whether they know the word. The interesting question is, if they know the word, are they able to access the appropriate sounds straight away, or do they experience a TOT? This method of measuring TOT experiences is called *prospecting*. If you test a large enough group of people, many of them will report having a TOT experience when they try to think of the words that go with the preceding definitions. By asking about detailed aspects of the experience, researchers can figure out how much information people have about the target word (Do they really know it? Can they think of any of the sounds in the word? How many syllables does it have?), they can determine whether the retrieval failure is temporary, and they can pinpoint the source of the problem.

TOT experiences do not reflect failures of semantic activation or lemma retrieval because people who are experiencing a TOT are able to predict accurately how likely it is that they will be able to come up with the correct word in the near future (Nelson, 1984). If the correct meaning were *not* activated much of the time during the TOT experience, then people would not be able to predict their own future successful retrieval of the target word. People can activate the correct lemma during a TOT experience, but do they activate any phonological (sound) information at all? The evidence suggests that they do. People who are experiencing a TOT state are likely to report the correct number of syllables in the (temporarily inaccessible) word, they are likely to correctly report the first phoneme in the word, and when asked to produce similar words to the target, they mostly come up with words that sound like the target word (Lovelace, 1987). People experiencing a TOT are more likely to accurately report the first and last letters in the target word, and less likely to accurately report letters from the middle, suggesting that substantial information about the overall form of the word as well as its component sounds are activated during the TOT experience. The likelihood of a TOT experience may reflect the strength of the relationship between the conceptual, lemma, and phonological levels of representation. Words that we encounter infrequently are more likely to produce TOT experiences than words that we encounter more frequently, so we will have associated sound and meaning less often for words that produce TOTs. About 40% of laboratory-induced TOTs are resolved within a few seconds or a few minutes of the onset of the TOT, which further supports the idea that TOTs reflect temporary failure of phonological activation, rather than some other aspect of the production process.

Picture naming and picture–word interference studies

Picture-naming studies provide evidence about speech production because they offer a window into a very basic aspect of speech: How do you find the word you need to express a concept, and how do you activate the sounds that make up the word? Early studies in picture

Figure 2.2 An example stimulus from a picture–word interference experiment (from Arieh & Algom, 2002, p. 222)

recognition and picture naming showed that people activate different concepts at about the same speed, but concepts that were used less frequently in speech or writing led to longer response times (Oldfield & Wingfield 1965; Wingfield, 1968). In these experiments, participants looked at pictures and performed one of two tasks. In one task, they simply stated whether they had seen the object before (recognition test). In the other, they named the object in the picture. There were very small differences in the amount of time it took people to recognize less familiar versus more familiar objects. There were much larger differences in the amount of time it took people to name less familiar versus more familiar objects. Thus, the amount of time it takes people to plan a spoken response appears to be affected more by how often they produce the collection of sounds that labels a concept, and less by how often they think about a specific concept.

Additional research addresses how concepts are organized and how they are related to one another in long-term memory. The way concepts are organized can affect how easy it is to retrieve the specific concept you need in a particular situation. Do you activate just the concept you need right when you need it? Or do you need to sift through a set of activated concepts before you can select the one you need? Picture-naming research suggests that concepts do compete with one another for selection during the process of speech production (Dell et al., 1997; Garrett, 1975; Griffin & Ferreira, 2006).[8] In experiments that use the *picture–word interference* task, participants look at pictures that have words printed on top of them (see Figure 2.2). Experimenters can manipulate the relationship between the picture and the word. Sometimes, the word refers to the object in the picture (the *identity* condition). The identity condition leads to faster naming responses, most likely because both the word and the picture stimulus point toward the same lexeme. So the target sounds are activated by two different sources. Sometimes, the word refers to an object related to the object in the picture (the *semantic* condition). Other times, the word refers to an object whose name is similar to the object in the picture (the *phonological* condition). For instance, if the picture were of a house, the word might be *mouse* in the phonological condition. The question these kinds of experiments address is: How will presentation of a potentially competing stimulus affect access to and production of the picture name? In general, the *semantic* condition produces interference effects: People are slower to name pictures when the overlapping word has a meaning similar to the object in the picture (Cutting & Ferreira, 1999).[9] However, when the overlapping word has a similar-sounding name to the picture, people name the object in the picture faster. Because the semantic (meaning) relationship between the word and the picture produces one pattern (it slows people down), while the phonological (sound) relationship between the word and the picture produces another pattern (it speeds people up), picture–word interference experiments reinforce the distinction between conceptual/semantic activation processes and phonological encoding processes in speech production. These two aspects of speech production appear to be controlled by semi-independent processors (semi-independent because the sounds you activate depend on the concepts you activate).[10]

The spreading activation model of speech production

Production models like WEAVER++ describe a set of mental representations that is involved in speaking—concepts, lemmas, lexemes, syllabified metrical representations, gestural scores—and many researchers in production agree that those representations, or a similar collection, underlie spoken language. However, WEAVER++ also assumes a specific kind of information flow as people go from activated concepts to activated lemmas to activated sets of syllabified phonemes. In particular, the model assumes a strict *feed forward* pattern of activation and no mutually inhibitory links between representations at a given level of representation (*mutual inhibition* means that as one mental representation gains activation it sends signals that reduce the activation of other representations). According to WEAVER++, production begins with a set of activated concepts, which leads to activation of a set of lemmas. Before phonological (sound) information can be activated, one of those lemmas must be selected for further processing. No matter how many lemmas are activated, and no matter how much activation any alternative lemmas enjoy, the phonological encoding system only works on the one lemma that gets selected. WEAVER++ falls within the *feed forward* class of processing models because information only moves in one direction in the system, from concepts to lemmas to lexemes to phonemes. But the system does not allow activation to feed back in the opposite direction. Lexemes may not feed back and influence the activation of lemmas, and lemmas may not feed back and influence the activation of concepts. According to this account, the occasional semantic substitution error happens because a target concept activates related concepts, which activate their associated lemmas, so sometimes the wrong lemma gets selected.

But this is not the only explanation for semantic substitution errors. Accounts like Gary Dell's *spreading activation* model of speech production differ from the WEAVER++ model primarily in proposing a different kind of information flow throughout the speech production system (Dell, 1986; Dell et al., 1997). According to Dell, information is allowed to flow both in a feed forward direction (as in WEAVER++) and in a feedback direction (opposite to WEAVER++). However, unlike WEAVER++, in the spreading activation account, activation is allowed to *cascade* through the system. In WEAVER, selection has to take place at one level of the system before activation starts to build up at the next. No phonemes get activated until lemma selection is complete. In the spreading activation account, by contrast, as soon as activity begins at one level, activation spreads to the next level. Thus, selection does not necessarily occur at one level before activity is seen at the next. The spreading activation model also assumes feedback between levels of representation. So, if the lemma for *cat* gains some activation, it will feed back to the concept layer and reinforce activation of the "cat" conceptual representation. If the phonological information associated with the pronunciation /kat/ begins to be activated, it will feed back and reinforce the activation of the "cat" lemma.

Proposing that information flows both forwards and backwards through the language production system in a cascade helps to explain a number of things that happen when people speak. For example, feedback connections from the phonological (sound) processors to the lemma (abstract word form) level help explain the *lexical bias* effect. The lexical bias effect refers to the fact that, when people produce sound exchange errors, more often than not, the thing that they actually produce is a real word. If speech errors simply reflected random errors in the phonological units, there is no reason why sound exchange errors would result in an actual word being produced. If errors were purely based on hiccups in phonological output processes, then you would be just as likely to get an error such as *bnip* or *tlip* or just random gibberish as any other kind of error. However, real speech errors almost never violate *phonotactic constraints* (rules about how phonemes can be combined) and they create real words more often than they should purely by chance (an error such as

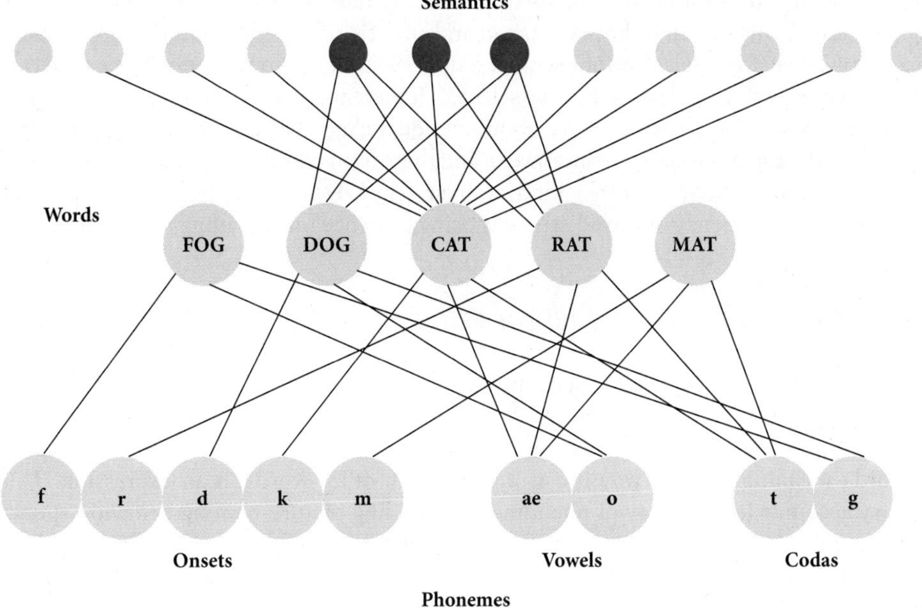

Figure 2.3 Representation of an interactive, spreading activation model for speech production (from Dell et al., 1997, p. 805)

slip in place of the target *blip* is far more likely than *tlip* or *blep*). Likewise, a speaker is more likely to make an error by reversing the beginnings of *big feet* than *big horse*. In the former case, *fig* and *beet* are both words. In the latter case, neither *hig* nor *borse* is a word.

Interactive spreading activation accounts (e.g., Dell, 1986; Dell et al., 1997) explain the lexical bias effect by appealing to feed-forward and feedback links between lemmas and phonological output mechanisms. Figure 2.3 shows how these two subprocessors might be connected (Dell et al., 1997, p. 805). In this kind of model, phonological activation begins as soon as lemmas ("words" in this diagram) begin to be activated, but before a final candidate has been chosen. As individual phonemes begin to be activated, they send feedback to the lemmas that they are connected to, increasing the activation of the lemmas. Because real words have representations at the lemma level, and non-words do not, it is likely that mistaken activation among the phonemes will reinforce the activation of a word that sounds like the intended target word. It is less likely that a non-word error will result, because any set of phonemes that would lead to a non-word being produced will not enjoy any reinforcing activation from the lemma level. Thus, on average, sets of phonemes that produce non-words will be less activated than sets of phonemes that produce real words.

Interactive activation accounts also help to explain *mixed errors*. In a mixed error, the word that a person produces by mistake is related in both meaning and sound to the intended word. So, a person is more likely to say *lobster* by mistake when they mean to say *oyster* than they are to say *octopus*, because *lobster* both sounds like and has a similar meaning to the target. Further, these types of mixed errors occur more frequently than they should if errors were purely random (Baars, Motley, & MacKay, 1975; Dell & Reich, 1981; Levelt et al., 1991). Spreading activation accounts of speech production view the relatively high likelihood of mixed errors as resulting from cascading activation and feedback processes between levels. Thinking about *oysters* will activate semantically related items, such as *lobsters* and *octopi*, which will lead to activation of the *oyster* lemma, but also *lobster* and *octopus* lemmas. Activating the *oyster*, *lobster*, and *octopus* lemmas will cause feed-forward activation of the sounds that make up those words. Because the *ster* set of phonemes is being driven by both the target and an active competitor lemma, those sounds are highly likely to be selected for eventual output. Sounds that occur only in the target, or only in a competitor, are less likely to be selected. If there were *no* cascading activation, then either *octopus* or *lobster* would have about an equal chance of out-competing the target (*oyster*) at the conceptual and lemma layers, and there is no reason why mixed errors should be more common than any other kind of error. Thus, Dell and colleagues interpret the relatively high frequency of mixed errors as being evidence for cascading activation.[11]

Potential limitations of lemma theory

Both WEAVER++ and spreading activation style models propose that language production processes tap into a level of representation equivalent to the lemma. The lemma is viewed as a pre-phonological (pre-sound) mental representation that captures information about a word's meaning and the way it can interact with other words in an expression. This theory accounts for a variety of phenomena, including picture-naming behavior, speech errors, and tip-of-the-tongue experiences. However, not everyone is a big fan of lemma theory as it is currently described. For instance, Alfonso Caramazza argues that lemma theory does not do a very good job dealing with evidence from patients with brain damage.

Brain damage can lead to language production difficulties, and different types of damage can lead to different patterns of difficulties (Caramazza, 1997). Caramazza begins with the observation that if the lemma is a necessary level of representation in production, then brain damage that affects the set of lemma representations should have consistent effects on people's ability to produce language, whether they are speaking or writing. Lemmas are thought to represent grammatical information associated with specific words. So if the lemmas are damaged, grammatical aspects of production should be affected. In fact, there are patients who have difficulty with just some types of words. Some patients have difficulty with *content* words (semantically rich words like *cat*, *table*, and *Hannibal Lecter*) but little difficulty with *function words* (semantically "light" grammatical markers like *the*, *of*, and *was*). Lemma theory would explain a patient like that by proposing that the lemmas for content words are selectively damaged, while lemmas representing function words are intact. But, as Caramazza notes, there are patients who have the opposite pattern of deficits, depending on how they are producing a given word. One pattern of problems can occur in speech, while the opposite pattern can occur in written language production, *within the same patient*. A given patient could have trouble with function words (but not content words) in writing, and trouble with content words (but not function words) while speaking. If both processes tap into the same set of lemmas, it should not be possible for this pattern of problems to appear. If the spoken production problem for content words is based on broken content-word lemmas, then the same problem should occur in written language production.

Further evidence against the lemma hypothesis comes from semantic substitution errors in brain-damaged patients. Some patients when asked to name pictures out loud will consistently use the wrong word. For example, one patient consistently said the word *dish* when asked to name a picture of a cook. When the same patient was asked to write (rather than say) the name of the picture, she wrote *forks*. These errors were not random, as the patient consistently produced one word (*dish*) while speaking, and the other (*forks*) while writing. Caramazza proposes that the solution to the problem lies in having two separate sources of word-form information, one for spoken language and one for written language. He proposes further that grammatical information is stored separately from lemma representations, as this can account for different patterns of function-word and content-word deficits within the same patient that depend on whether the patient is speaking or writing.

Self-monitoring and self-repair

Speakers make errors sometimes when they talk, but they also succeed in expressing their meaning much of the time, despite the complexity that speech production involves. Speakers can monitor their own output to fix mistakes after they happen (*self-repair*), but they also deploy mental machinery internal to the speech production system to prevent internal, temporary problems from creating overt errors in the output. Evidence for internal, pre-output monitoring comes from studies showing that when speakers make an error, they can replace the incorrect word with the correct one with almost no time elapsing between the error and the correction. Because it takes upwards of half a second to prepare a spoken response for a concept, "instant repair" means that both the monitoring and the repair planning must take place as the error-ful response is being produced. As Postma (2000, p. 105), notes, "There is ample evidence that speakers are capable of anticipating forthcoming mistakes, i.e., that they can inspect their speech programs prior to articulation … Speakers in a number of cases react without delay to an overt error. In addition, the correction is executed without further waiting (suggesting it must have been ready before the interruption was made." Incredibly, these internal monitoring processes are able to assess whether an error will lead to an embarrassing result, and both the galvanic skin response (a measure of how much resistance the skin offers to electrical current) and the likelihood of particular kinds of errors both reflect the operations of an internal monitoring system (Hartsuiker & Kolk, 2001; Levelt, 1983; Motley, Baars, & Camden, 1983; Motley, Camden, & Baars, 1982; Wheeldon & Levelt, 1995). If you were asked to produce the phrase *tool kits*, and you committed a sound exchange error, the result could be embarrassing. (Think what would happen if you went to the hardware store and tried to say, *Could I grab one of your tool kits?* and made a sound exchange error.) Sound exchange errors under those circumstances are less likely than sound exchanges that do not produce taboo words. Also, when participants are placed under time pressure, their galvanic skin response is higher for stimuli such as *tool kits* than pairs of words that do not produce taboo words when the initial sounds are exchanged, such as *pool kits*.[12]

Although some aspects of self-monitoring are carried out before overt production, they do not come for free. The ability to self-monitor depends on there being sufficient mental resources available to carry out both speech planning processes and the monitoring itself. Further, there is a trade-off between speech planning and speech monitoring. The more mental resources you dedicate to speech planning, the less there is left over for self-monitoring. Error detection is more robust at the ends of phrases and clauses, because the great majority of the utterance has already been planned and the planning load is at its lowest level (Blackmer & Mitton, 1991; Postma, 2000).

Articulation

The ultimate goal of speech planning as laid out in accounts like WEAVER++ and Dell's spreading activation model is to make the speech muscles move to produce sound. This process is called *articulation*. To speak, we configure our *vocal tract*, which consists of everything from the vocal folds upwards and outwards to our lips and noses. Articulation is both the end-point of speech planning and production and the starting point for speech comprehension. Some accounts of articulation in production classify speech sounds (phonemes) according to the way the articulators move (Browman & Goldstein, 1989, 1990, 1991). The articulators include the lips, the tongue tip, tongue body, the velum (the part of the soft palate toward the back of your mouth), and the glottis (a structure in your throat that houses the vocal folds). These different articulators can be moved semi-independently to perturb or stop the flow of air coming out of your lungs. These disturbances of the smooth flow of air set up vibrations which are modified by the movement of the articulators and create the sound waves that characterize human speech.

According to the articulatory phonology theory, the outcome of the speech planning process is a gestural score, which creates a *contrastive gesture*—a gesture that creates a noticeable difference between the current speech signal (sound) and other signals that the language employs. The *gestural score* tells the articulators how to move. More specifically, it tells the motor system to "(1) [move] a particular set of articulators; (2) toward a location in the vocal tract where a constriction occurs; (3) with a specific degree of constriction; and (4) … in a characteristic dynamic manner" (Pardo & Remez, 2006, p. 217). The movement of the articulators produces a set of speech sounds (phonemes) that can be classified according to their *place of articulation*, *manner of articulation*, and *voicing*. English, for instance, has six stop consonants (/k/, /g/, /t/, /d/, /p/, /b/) that differ in place of articulation. /p/ and /b/ are *labial* because they are made by pressing the lips together. /t/ and /d/ are *dental* or *alveolar* stops because they involve stopping the flow of air behind the teeth (rather than behind the lips or elsewhere). /k/ and /g/ are velar because they involve stopping the flow of air with the back of the tongue pressed up against the velum. Each of the three gestures (lips together, tongue against teeth, tongue against velum) can be accompanied by vibration of the vocal folds or not. Simultaneous release of air with vocal fold vibration leads to a *voiced* stop (as in /b/, /d/, and /g/). A delay between releasing the pent-up air and the beginning (onset) of vocal fold vibration leads to an *unvoiced* stop (as in /p/, /t/, and /k/). Manner of articulation refers to how much the flow of air is disturbed. Maximum blockage of the air flow leads to a stop consonant, squeezing the air flow without stopping it leads to a *fricative* (as in /z/ and /sh/ sounds), while keeping the air flowing relatively freely creates vowel sounds.

Savvy observers of language will have noticed that we do not produce isolated phonemes. We produce whole gangs of them when we talk, with an average of about one phoneme every 100 milliseconds in conversational speech. (Much higher rates can be obtained if you really try.) Because we produce many phonemes in a short period of time, we have to figure out ways to transition from producing one to the next smoothly and efficiently. To do that, we *coarticulate*. That is, the gestures for one phoneme overlap in time with the gestures for the preceding and following phoneme.[13] Coarticulation affects both the production and the perception of speech. For example, the way you move your articulators for the phoneme /p/ changes depending on which phoneme needs to come next. Say the word *pool*. Now say the word *pan*. Think about how your lips are placed just *before* you say the word. (Repeat as necessary until you notice the difference between how your lips are positioned before each word. Use a mirror or, better still, ask a friend to help.)

***

Intermission while you practice *pool* and *pan*.

***

Seriously. Try it.

***

You should notice that, before you start to say the word *pool*, your lips are in a rounded shape and they stick out a little bit. Before you say *pan*, your lips are drawn slightly back and are not rounded. Why the difference? It's a function of what phoneme comes next. The "oo" sound in pool is a rounded vowel. It's also a vowel that has a relatively low tone. When you round your lips, that matches the rounded nature of the vowel. Poking your lips out lengthens the resonant chamber formed by your vocal tract, which lowers the *fundamental frequency* (the lowest of the steady-state vibrations that makes up the sound wave), and makes the "oo" have a nice, deep tone. The rounded, poking-out characteristics of the "oo" vowel are anticipated by the speech planning process, and so they assign some aspects of the vowel (roundness, poking-out-ness) to the preceding consonant gesture. The "a" sound in *pan* is a *back vowel*, because it is formed by a constriction of the air toward the back of your mouth. To anticipate that movement, the speech planning system programs a flattened out, slightly drawn back version of the preceding /p/ phoneme.

Coarticulation not only affects the way you shape your articulators when you speak different combinations of phonemes, it also affects the sound waves that are produced as you speak them (Liberman & Mattingly, 1985). Before we explore the effects of coarticulation on the sound waves that occur when you speak, let's take a brief detour into the physical, acoustic characteristics of speech sounds.

Moving the articulators is a physical event that, like many other physical events, creates sound waves that travel through the air. Therefore speech, like other forms of sound, can be treated as a physical, acoustic signal. Acoustic signals, however complex, can be analyzed with respect to two properties: frequency and amplitude (Goldstein, 2006). All acoustic signals are created when an acoustic medium (air, normally, but wood, water, steel, and other substances can also be used) is subjected to physical forces that alternately compress it (make it more dense) and rarify it (make it less dense). One episode of compression and rarefaction is referred to as a *cycle*, and the amount of time it takes to complete a cycle determines the *frequency* of the sound wave. More cycles in a given period means higher frequency; fewer cycles means a lower frequency. The standard measure of frequency in acoustics is Hertz (Hz), which is the number of cycles per second. We subjectively experience differences in frequency as differences in *pitch*. High-pitched sounds (Minnie Mouse's voice, tea kettles whistling) result from high-frequency vibrations. Low-pitched sounds (foghorns, the roar of the surf) result from low-frequency vibrations. Amplitude refers to the change in pressure between the peak and the minimum pressures in the sound wave. We experience increases in amplitude as increases in volume or loudness. The standard measure of amplitude is Decibels (dB). High-amplitude sounds are loud; low-amplitude sounds are quiet.

Foreign Accent Syndrome Revisited

It's time to cash in your newly acquired knowledge of speech production. Foreign accent syndrome (FAS) occurs when "speech takes on characteristics normally associated with a dialect that is not [one's] own, or it resembles the performance of a non-native speaker of the language" (Moen, 2000, p. 5). Standard explanations of FAS appeal to theoretical models like Pim Levelt's and Gary Dell's to explain why people can develop foreign-sounding accents after brain injury (Blumstein, Alexander, Ryalls, Katz, & Dworetzky, 1987; Kurowski, Blumstein, & Alexander, 1996; Mariën, Verhoeven, Wackenier, Engelborghs, & De Deyn, 2009). Speech sounds are created when articulators are moved toward specific targets at specific velocities creating specific degrees of closure with specific timing of voicing. Before these motor movements begin, there has to be a gestural score that specifies how and when the articulators are going to move. To create this gestural score, speakers have to undertake syllabification to divide the planned output into syllable-sized chunks. Once the output is syllabified, speakers have to craft a prosodic contour that extends over multiple syllables. A foreign-sounding accent can arise because the prosodic contour is disrupted, because the process of syllabification is disrupted, or if the articulation of individual phonemes is disrupted. For example, some patients with FAS show smaller than normal changes in pitch when they ask questions, abnormal patterns of accents (LOUDER vs. softer words and syllables), abnormal lengthening of vowels, and abnormal pausing. All of these could result from problems computing a prosodic contour. In addition, the long pauses between utterances suggest that patients are having some difficulty coming up with an articulatory plan or gestural score. Problems articulating individual phonemes may also contribute to the foreign flavor of the patient's speech. In some cases, speech sounds that should be articulated toward the back of the mouth are produced by closing off the air flow at more anterior (forward) locations. Patients may add or delete phonemes, especially from consonant clusters (e.g., *spl*, *rtr*) because they have difficulty making individual gestures. Syllabification may also be affected, as some patients produce syllables more like isolated units. *Escort us* might be produced more like "*Ess*," "*cort*," "*us*," than the usual way with the "t" syllabified with the "us." So, different aspects of speech planning (syllabification, prosody) and the (mis)execution of specific speech gestures can turn you into a Scotsman.

Speech Perception

I can't understand a word you've said the whole time.
RICKY BOBBY

Take a moment to look at Figure 2.4, which provides a visual representation of the sound waves produced when someone says, *to catch pink salmon* (Cooper, Delattre, Liberman, Borst, & Gerstman, 1952; Liberman, Delattre, & Cooper, 1952). The name for graphs like those shown in Figure 2.4 is *sound spectrogram*.[14] Frequency (in Hz) is represented on the *y*-axis, and time is represented on the *x*-axis. Consider first the top half of the figure, which represents real speech. The dark areas of the graph represent frequencies at which sound energy is present in the signal. Going vertically, there are alternating bands of sound energy (represented as dark patches) and bands where no sound energy is present (represented as light patches). Over time, the pattern of energy changes. For instance, there is a lot of activity in the low-frequency part of the spectrum when someone is saying the /a/ in *catch*, and again when the /a/ sound in *salmon* is produced. But when the /ch/ sound in *catch* and the /s/ sound in *salmon* are produced, there is very little energy in the low-frequency range, and much more energy at higher frequencies.

Now have a look a the bottom half of Figure 2.4. You will notice that the range of frequencies is the same as in the top half. But you will also notice that the pattern of dark and light patches is much simpler. Liberman and colleagues (1952) painted the pattern in the bottom of Figure 2.4 by hand and ran it through a machine they called the *pattern playback machine* (see Figure 2.5). The pattern playback machine converted the pattern of light and dark in the artificial, hand-painted spectrogram into a set of sound waves. Liberman and colleagues discovered that they could greatly simplify the pattern of energy in the sound wave without destroying the perceiver's ability to recognize the phonological content of the stimulus. That is, when they pushed the pattern in the bottom of Figure 2.5 through the pattern playback machine, their subjects reported that it sounded like *to catch pink salmon*. Thus, while the full pattern of energy represented in the top of Figure 2.4 may

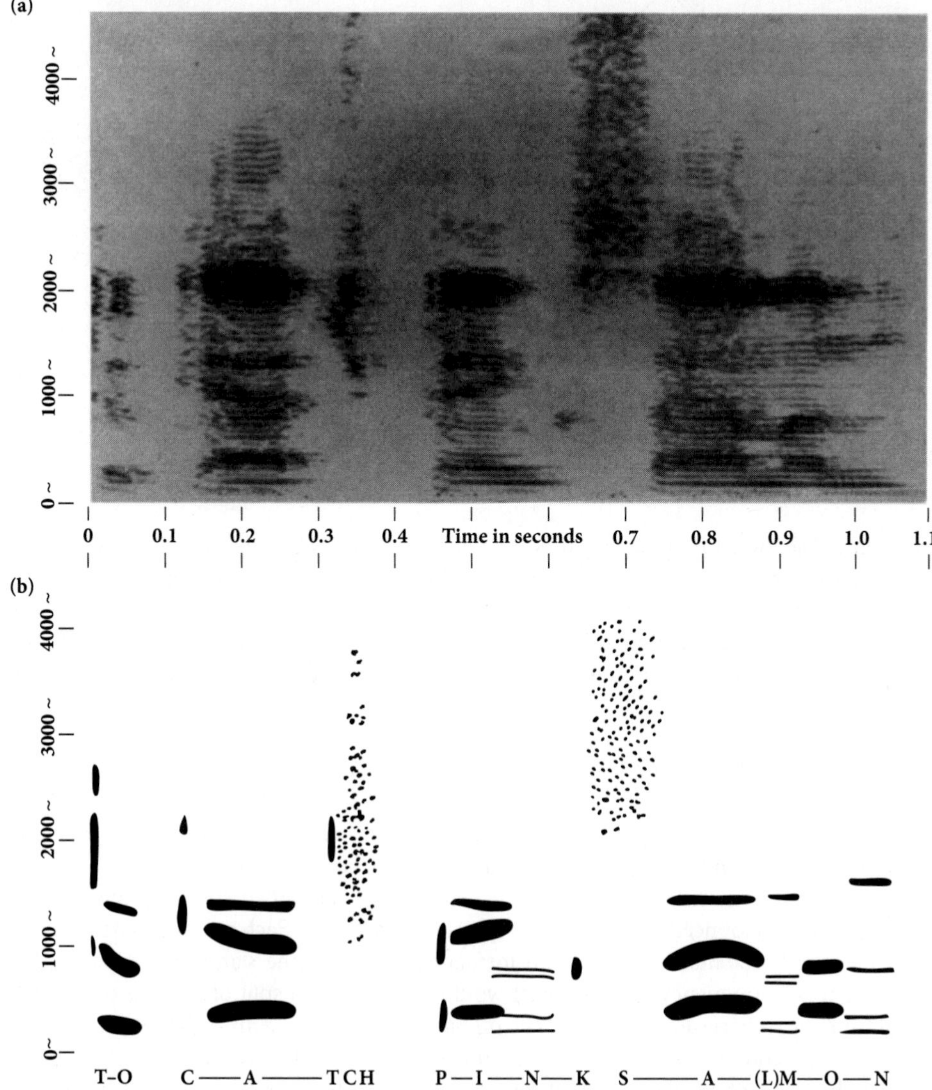

Figure 2.4 Sound spectrograms of the phrase *to catch pink salmon* created from real (top) and simplified, artificial speech (bottom) (from Liberman etal., 1952, p. 498)

be necessary for the speech to sound fully natural, or for the listener to recognize whose voice created the signal, the stripped-down, simplified version at the bottom of Figure 2.4 carried all of the information necessary for people to perceive the phonemes that the signal was meant to convey (see also Remez, Rubin, Berns, Pardo, & Lang, 1994).

Liberman and colleagues (1952; Cooper et al., 1952) proposed that the phonological content of speech could be described in terms of *formants* and *formant transitions*. Formants are steady-state, stable patterns of vibrations, as in the /a/ and /u/ sounds in *to catch pink salmon*, and in fact formants are associated with vowel sounds in general. Formant transitions consist of short bursts of sounds, which often coincide with rapid increases or decreases in frequency. Fricatives, such as the /s/ in *salmon* appear as random patterns of energy spread across a broad frequency range (a bit like the white noise that you hear when you are between radio stations). Each speech sound is made up of a set of formants and/or formant transitions. The formants and transitions are classified according to their average

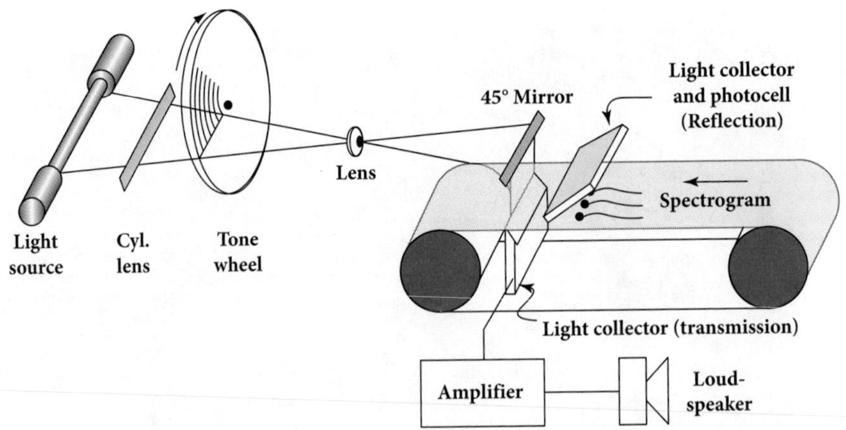

Figure 2.5 The pattern playback machine (from Liberman, Delattre, & Cooper, 1952, p. 501)

frequency. The lowest frequency component of a phoneme is the first formant (for vowels) or first formant transition (for consonants). The next highest component is the second formant, or formant transition, and so on. Initially, speech researchers believed that they would be able to find a unique acoustic pattern for each phoneme, but they rapidly discovered that reality is more complicated than that. Which brings us back to coarticulation.

Coarticulation effects on speech perception

As noted previously, the way you move your articulators when you produce a given phoneme changes depending on the context in which the phoneme occurs. Figure 2.6 (from Liberman, Cooper, Shankweiler, & Studdert-Kennedy, 1967) shows simplified spectrograms for two syllables, /di/ (pronounced "dee") and /du/ (pronounced "doo"). Each syllable consists of two formants (the horizontal bars) and two formant transitions (the slanty bars representing rapid changes in frequency). Notice what would happen if you split off the /d/ part of the signal from the /i/ part (on the left) and the /u/ part (on the right). Although the two /d/ parts of the syllables sound exactly the same when they are followed by two different vowels (/i/ and /u/) the actual physical signals that correspond to the /d/ phonemes are very different. In the /di/ syllable, the /d/ part of the signal consists of two formant transitions, and both of them are characterized by rapid increases in frequency over time (the bars for the two formant transitions both slant upwards to the right). Now notice the pattern for the /d/ sound in the /du/ syllable. Not only is the frequency of the second formant transition much lower for /du/ when compared to /di/, but instead of increasing in frequency over time (slanting up and to the right) it decreases in frequency over time (slanting down and to the right). Despite large differences in the actual, acoustic signal, when the two patterns are played in the context of a following vowel sound, both acoustic signals are perceived as being the same—they both sound like /d/. But something different happens if you play just the formant transitions, without the rest of the syllable—without the formants that make up the vowel sounds. When the two formant transitions are played separately from the rest of the syllable, and separately from each other, people hear them as being different sounds. They both sound like whistles or chirps, but the /d/ sound from the /di/ syllable sounds like a rising whistle, and the /d/ sound from the /du/ syllable sounds like a lower-pitched falling whistle. Liberman and colleagues (1967, p. 435) summarize these findings thus: "What is perceived as the same phoneme is cued, in different contexts, by features that are vastly different in acoustic terms."

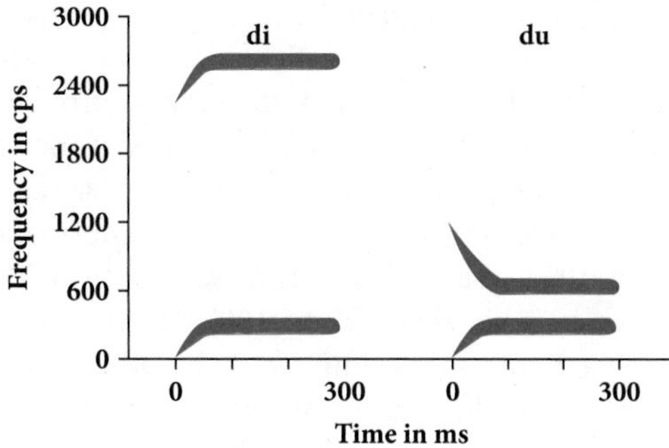

Figure 2.6 Artificial spectrogram for the syllables /di/ and /du/ (from Liberman et al., 1967, p. 79)

A couple of important things are happening here. First, when you produce a /d/ sound, the way you make the /d/ sound and its physical form is different when the /d/ sound is followed by different vowels (that's coarticulation). Second, despite the differences in the way you make the /d/ sound and the actual physical properties of the sound waves, you perceive the two signals as being the same phoneme (this is a form of *perceptual constancy*—different physical patterns are perceived as being the same). Finally, your perceiving the two signals as being the same does not reflect insensitivity or inability to detect a difference between the formant transitions. When the two transitions are presented in isolation, you hear them as being different sounds.

Another aspect of coarticulation concerns the way speech sounds are spread out over time. When we write down speech, one letter occupies one position, the next letter occupies a separate, following position, and so on. But in speech, there are no clean breaks between phonemes, and the acoustic parts of one phoneme may overlap partially or entirely with other phonemes. Carol Fowler likens phonemes to Easter eggs, and describes speech production as being like pushing Easter eggs through a set of rollers that squish them all together. As Liberman and Mattingly note (1985, p. 4), "the movements for gestures implied by a single symbol (phoneme) are typically not simultaneous, and the movements implied by successive symbols often overlap extensively." The listener is therefore faced with the task of going through the mass of squished-up eggs and rebuilding the original set of Easter eggs.

In one way, though, this "smearing" of information about a phoneme throughout an extended period of time can be beneficial, as demonstrated by the perception of *silent center vowels* (Liberman & Whalen, 2000). Silent center vowels are perceived when researchers edit a recording to remove part of the acoustic signal for an utterance. For example, they might erase the middle portion of the acoustic signal for *bag*. When you say the word *bag*, coarticulation means that information about the vowel starts to show up as you are pronouncing the /b/, and continues through production of the /g/ sound. When the middle part is erased, the word does not sound entirely normal, but people still correctly identify which phoneme was present in the original utterance (i.e., they hear something that sounds like *bag*, rather than something that sounds like *big*, *bug*, or *bog*). So, as long as the preceding and the following consonants carry information that results from coarticulation, listeners can accurately identify the missing vowel sound.

Evidence for coarticulation effects on speech perception also comes from studies involving *cross-spliced stimuli*. These are kind of like "Franken-stimuli," where parts of one spoken word have been chopped off and bolted onto a different word (like parts of different bodies were put together to make Frankenstein's monster). More specifically, single-syllable words can be divided into *onsets* (the "burst" of sound that starts the syllable, like the /p/ in *pink* or the /pr/ in *press*) and *codas* (the end of the syllable). The coda includes the vowel and the final consonant or consonant cluster. Coarticulation means that the way the burst is pronounced depends on the coda, and the way the coda is pronounced depends on the burst. The two place constraints on each other, but the way the burst is perceived has stronger effects on the way the coda is perceived than vice versa (i.e., the information that arrives first has a greater effect on perception than the information that arrives later; Gaskell & Marslen-Wilson, 1997; Marslen-Wilson & Warren, 1994; Martin & Brunell, 1982; Streeter & Nigro, 1979; Warren & Marslen-Wilson, 1987, 1988). If two syllables are recorded, and the end of one is spliced onto the beginning of the other, people are more likely to misperceive the coda as matching the original unspliced version that the burst came from. That is, the word *job* is likely to be misperceived as *jog* if the *jo* part came from a recording of the word *jog*. Also, if the /g/ and /b/ phonemes are presented without their initial bursts, people are likely to mistake them for one another. Thus, eliminating information that comes from coarticulation makes the perceiver's job harder, suggesting that listeners routinely use information that appears "early" or "late" (where "early" means that the information appears during the articulation of a preceding phoneme, and "late" means that the information spills over into articulation of a following phoneme) to help identify which phoneme the speaker actually intended to produce.

Paradoxically, while coarticulated signals help the listener identify the phonemes that the speaker intended to produce, coarticulation is a major factor that makes it difficult to formally analyze the acoustic properties of speech. Ideally, we would like to know how acoustic signals line up with phonemes. In a simple world, there would be a one-to-one relationship between acoustic signals and phonemes. That way, if you had a phoneme, you would know what acoustic signal to produce. Likewise, if you had an acoustic signal, you would know what phoneme to look up (because there would only be one matching candidate in your long-term memory). Unfortunately, coarticulation as well as intra- and inter-speaker variability renders this simple system unworkable. As Liberman and Mattingly (1985 p. 12) note, "There is simply no way to define a phonetic category in purely acoustic terms." But if the speech signal can be decoded and its component phonemes identified (it can be and they are), there must be some way to untie the knot. The next sections will summarize the chief contenders for explaining how acoustic signals are analyzed so that people can recover the sets of phonemes they express. The *motor theory* of speech perception and the *general acoustic* approach represent two viable alternatives that are the focus of speech perception research today (Diehl, Lotto, & Holt, 2004; Kluender & Kiefte, 2006; Pardo & Remez, 2006).

The motor theory of speech perception

The motor theory of speech perception proposes that gestures, rather than sounds, represent the fundamental unit of mental representation in speech (Cooper et al., 1952; Liberman et al., 1952; Liberman, Delattre, Cooper, & Gerstman, 1954; Liberman et al., 1967; Liberman & Mattingly, 1985; Liberman & Whalen, 2000; see also Fowler, 1986, 2008; Galantucci, Fowler, & Turvey, 2006).[15] That is, when you speak, you attempt to move your articulators to particular places in specific ways. Each of these movements constitutes a gesture. The motor part of the speech production system takes the sequence of words you want to say and comes up with a *gestural score* (movement plan) that tells your articulators how to move. According to the theory, if you can figure out what gestures created a speech signal, you can figure out what the gestural plan was, which takes you back to the sequence of syllables or words that went into the gestural plan in the first place. So by knowing what the gestures are, you can tell what the set of words was that produced that set of gestures.

Going back to the /di/ versus /du/ example of coarticulation, the "core" part of that gesture is tapping the tip of your tongue against the back of your teeth (or your alveolar ridge, possibly). Other parts of the gesture, lip position for example, are affected by coarticulation (flat lips for /di/, poking-out, rounded lips for /du/), but the core component of the gesture is the same regardless of the phonological context. Thus, rather than trying to map acoustic signals directly to phonemes, Alvin Liberman and his colleagues proposed that we map acoustic signals to the gestures that produced them, because there is a closer relationship between gestures and phonemes than there is between acoustic signals and phonemes. In their words (Liberman et al., 1952, p. 513), "The relation between perception and articulation will be considerably simpler (more nearly direct) than the relation between perception and acoustic stimulus." Further, "Perceived similarities (and differences) will correspond more closely to the articulatory than the acoustic similarities among the sounds." Thus, differences between two acoustic signals will not cause you to perceive two different phonemes as long as the gestures that created those two different acoustic signals are the same.

Motor theory also seeks to explain how a person can perceive an acoustic stimulus as a phoneme in one context (e.g., the formant transitions in Figure 2.6) but as a chirp or a buzz in another context. To explain that, motor theory proposes that speech perception is accomplished by a naturally selected *module* (Fodor, 1983). This speech perception module monitors incoming acoustic stimulation and reacts strongly when the signal contains the characteristic complex patterns that make up speech. When the speech module recognizes an incoming stimulus as speech, it *preempts* other auditory processing systems, preventing their output from entering consciousness. So, while non-speech sounds are analyzed according to basic properties of frequency, amplitude, and timbre, and while we are able to perceive those characteristics of non-speech sounds accurately, when the speech module latches onto an acoustic stimulus, it prevents the kind of *spectral analysis* (figuring out the pattern of frequencies and amplitudes in a stimulus) that general auditory processing mechanisms normally carry out for non-speech auditory stimuli (Liberman & Mattingly, 1985, 1989; Liberman & Whalen, 2000). This *principle of preemption* explains why formant transitions are perceived as chirps or high-pitched whistles when played in isolation, but as phonemes when played in the context of other speech sounds. When transitions are played in isolation, they are not recognized as speech, so the spectral analysis dominates perception, and they sound like chirps. "When transitions of the second formant … are presented in isolation, we hear them as we should expect to—that is, as pitch glides or as differently pitched 'chirps.' But when they are embedded in synthetic syllables, we hear unique linguistic events, [bæ], [dæ], [gæ], which cannot be analyzed in auditory terms" (Mattingly, Liberman, Syrdal, & Halwes, 1971, p. 132).

This preemption of normal auditory perceptual processes for speech stimuli can lead to *duplex perception* under special, controlled laboratory conditions (Liberman & Mattingly, 1989; Whalen & Liberman, 1987). To create their experimental stimuli, researchers constructed artificial speech stimuli that sounded like /da/ or /ga/ depending on whether the second formant transition decreased in frequency over time (/da/) or increased (/ga/). Next, they edited the stimuli to create separate signals for the transition and the rest of the syllable, which they called the *base* (see Figure 2.7). They played the two parts of the stimulus over headphones, with the transition going in one ear and the base going in the other. The question was, how would people perceive the stimulus? Would chopping up the stimulus make it sound like gibberish? Or would it still be perceived as speech? It turned out that people perceived two different things at the same time. At the ear that the transition was played into, people perceived a high-pitched chirp or whistle. But at the same time, they perceived the original syllable, just as if the entire, intact stimulus had been presented.[16]

Liberman and colleagues argued that simultaneously perceiving the transition in two ways—as a chirp and as a phoneme—reflected the simultaneous operation of the speech

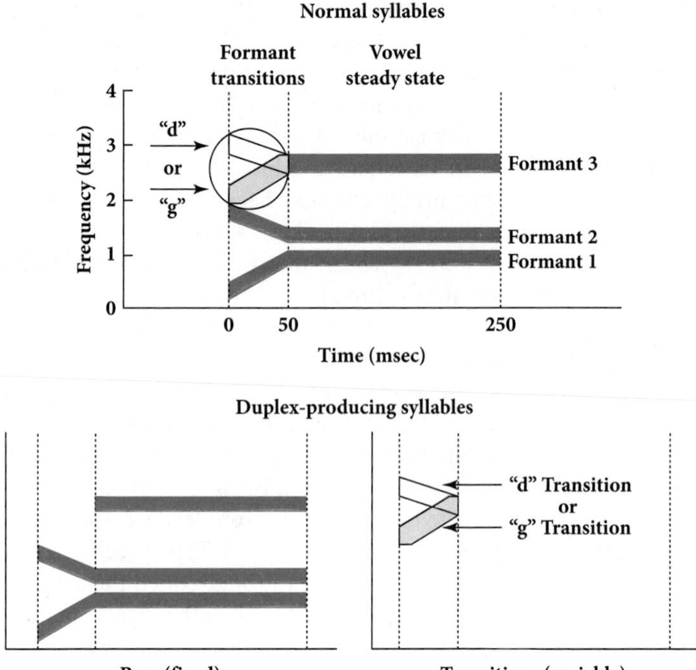

Figure 2.7 Simplified acoustic stimuli that are perceived as /da/ or /ga/ (from Whalen & Liberman, 1987). Researchers edited the stimuli so that a formant transition would be played to one ear, while the "base" (the rest of the signal) was played to the other ear. People perceived the stimulus as consisting of a "whistle" or a "chirp" at one ear and the complete syllable (/da/ or /ga/, depending on which formant transition was played) at the other ear.

perception module and general-purpose auditory processing mechanisms. Duplex perception happened because the auditory system could not treat the transition and base as coming from the same source (because two different sounds were played into two different ears). Because the auditory system recognized two different sources, it had to do something with the transition that it would not normally do. That is, it had to analyze it for the frequencies it contained, and the result was hearing it as a "chirp." But simultaneously, the speech processing module recognized a familiar pattern of transitions and formants. As a result, the auditory system reflexively integrated the transition and base, and produced the experience of hearing a unified syllable, despite the fact that it was working with two spatially distinct stimuli. In the early days of duplex perception research, speech was the only kind of stimulus known to produce such effects, which was taken as evidence that speech was "special" and subject to its own principles, separate from other kinds of auditory stimuli.

According to the motor theory, *categorical perception* is another product of the speech perception module. Categorical perception happens when a wide variety of physically distinct stimuli are perceived as belonging to one of a fixed (usually fairly small) set of categories. For example, every vocal tract is different from every other vocal tract. As a result, the sound waves that come out of your mouth when you say *pink* are different than the sound waves that come out of my mouth when I say *pink*, and those two stimuli are different than the sound waves that come out of Arnold Schwarzenegger's mouth when he says *pink*. Nonetheless, your phonological perception system is blind to the physical differences, and perceives all of those signals as containing an instance of the category /p/. You may notice that your voice has slightly (or greatly) different qualities than Arnold Schwarzenegger's, but you categorize the speech sounds he makes the same way you categorize your own or anybody else's. All of those different noises map to the same set of about 40 phonemes (in English). In addition, although the acoustic properties of speech stimuli can vary across a wide range, your perception does not change in little bitty steps, with each little bitty change in the acoustic signal. You are insensitive to some kinds of variation in the speech signal, but when the speech signal changes enough, you perceive that change as the difference between one phoneme and another (Liberman, Harris, Hoffman, & Griffith, 1957). An example may help to illustrate.

Recall that the difference between some stop consonants and others is whether they are voiced or not. The difference between /b/ and /p/ for example, is that the /b/ is voiced while the /p/ is not. Other than voicing, the two phonemes are essentially identical. They are both *labial plosives*, meaning that you make them by closing your lips, allowing air pressure to build up behind your lip-dam, and then releasing that pressure suddenly, creating a burst of air that rushes out of your mouth. The difference between the two phonemes has to do with the timing of the burst and the vocal fold vibrations that create voicing. For the /b/ sound, the vocal folds begin vibrating while your lips are closed or just after. (That's for English speakers. Spanish speakers actually start their vocal folds vibrating before the burst for voiced stop consonants.) For the /p/ sound, there is a delay between the burst and the point in time when the vocal folds begin to vibrate. The amount of time that elapses between the burst and vocal fold vibration is called *voice onset time*. Voice onset time is a variable that can take any value whatsoever, so it is said to be a continuous variable.[17] You could have a voice onset time of 0 milliseconds (or *ms*; which is one thousandth of a second), 0.5 ms, 1.895 ms, 20 ms, 50.22293 ms, or any other value you can think of. But even though voice onset time can vary continuously in this way, we do not perceive much of that variation. For example, you cannot generally hear the difference between a voice onset time of 2 ms and 7 ms, or between 7 ms and 15 ms. Instead, you map a range of voice onset times onto the same percept. Those different acoustic signals are treated as *allophones*—different signals that are perceived as being the same phoneme. You experience a range of short voice onset times as the /b/ phoneme; and you perceive a range of long voice onset times as the /p/ phoneme. However, something interesting happens at around 20 ms voice onset time. At values less than that, you perceive the acoustic signal as being the /b/ phoneme; at longer values than that, you perceive the signal as being the /p/ phoneme. (And so do babies! Eimas, Siqueland, Jusczyk, & Vigorito, 1971). Further, your ability to discriminate between different acoustic signals depends on whether two signals come from the same side of the voice onset time "border" or whether they come from opposite sides. If two stimuli come from the same side of the border (with voice onset times of, say, 10 and 17 ms), you have a lot of trouble hearing the difference. But if two stimuli having the same absolute difference in voice onset time come from opposite sides of the border (17 and 24 ms, say), you have a much greater chance of hearing the difference. Liberman argued that this categorical perception of speech sounds provided further evidence that the speech perception system was special and different from the auditory perception processes that dealt with non-speech sounds.

The McGurk effect: Visual gestures affect speech perception

According to the motor theory of speech perception, understanding speech requires you to figure out which gestures created a given acoustic signal. Because figuring out the gestures is the primary goal of the speech perception system, you might expect that system to use any sort of information that could help identify the gestures. While acoustic stimuli offer cues to what those gestures are, other perceptual systems could possibly help out, and if they can, motor theory says that the speech perception system will take advantage of them. In fact, two non-auditory perceptual systems—vision and touch—have been shown to affect speech perception. The most famous demonstration of *multi-modal speech perception* is the McGurk effect (Kerzel & Bekkering, 2000; McGurk & MacDonald, 1976). The McGurk effect happens when people watch a video of a person talking, but the audio portion of the tape has been altered. For example, the video might show a person saying *ga*, but the audio signal is of a person saying *ba*. What people actually perceive is someone saying, *da*. If the visual information is removed (when an individual shuts his eyes, for example), the auditory information is accurately perceived and the person hears *ba*. (You can experience the McGurk effect yourself by typing "McGurk effect" into your favorite web-browser and following the links to any of several demonstrations of the effect.) The McGurk effect is incredibly robust: It happens even when people are fully warned that the auditory and visual information do not match; and it happens even if you try to pay close attention to the auditory information and ignore the visual (unless you look away or close your eyes). It happens when real words are used rather than nonsense syllables (Dekle, Fowler, & Funnell, 1992). It happens even if the auditory and visual information is processed only by one of the brain's two hemispheres (Baynes, Funnell, & Fowler, 1994).

The McGurk effect happens because your speech perception system combines visual and auditory information when perceiving speech, rather than relying on auditory information alone. Of course, the auditory information by itself is sufficient for perception to occur (otherwise, we would not be able to communicate over the phone), but the McGurk effect shows that visual information influences speech perception when that visual information is available. The McGurk effect is an example of multi-modal perception because two *sensory modalities*, hearing and vision, contribute to the subjective experience of the stimulus (two modes of perception, therefore multi-modal perception).

The vision–hearing combination is not the only way to alter speech perception. There is a more "icky" (Carol Fowler's term; Fowler, 2008) way to create another variant of the standard McGurk effect. In this alternative method, information from touch (*haptic* perception) is combined with auditory information to change the way people perceive a spoken syllable (Fowler & Dekle, 1991). This kind of speech perception occurs outside the laboratory from time to time in a specialized mode called *tadoma*. Helen Keller and other hearing- and vision-impaired individuals have learned to speak by using their sense of touch to feel the articulatory movements involved in speech. In the lab, haptic perception has been used to investigate the limits of multi-modal speech perception. According to the motor theory, information about speech gestures should be useful, regardless of the source, auditory or otherwise. That being the case, information about articulatory gestures that is gathered via the perceiver's sense of touch should affect speech perception, similar to the way visual information does. To find out whether that happens, Carol Fowler had experimental participants feel her lips while they listened to a recording of a female speaker (also CF) speaking a variety of syllables. Blindfolded and gloved,[18] experimental participants heard the syllable /ga/ over a speaker (or over headphones in a separate experiment) while CF simultaneously (silently) mouthed the syllable /ba/. As a result, the experimental participant felt the articulatory gestures appropriate to one syllable, but heard the acoustic signal appropriate to a different syllable. As in the visual version of the McGurk effect, what participants actually perceived was a compromise between the auditory signal and the haptic (touch) signal. Instead of perceiving the spoken syllable /ga/, or the felt syllable /ba/, they heard the "hybrid" syllable /da/. Just as in the visual McGurk effect, speech perception was influenced by input from two perceptual modalities.

Motor theory explains both versions of the McGurk effect, the visual one and the haptic one, as stemming from the same basic process. The goal of the speech perception system is not a spectral analysis of the auditory input. Rather, it is figuring out what set of gestures created the auditory signal in the first place. Motor theory straightforwardly handles visual and haptic effects on speech perception by arguing that both vision and touch can contribute information that helps the perceiver figure out what gesture the speaker made. Under natural conditions, the visual, touch, and auditory information will all line up perfectly, meaning that secondary sources of information (non-auditory sources, that is) will be perfectly valid cues. While speech perception does not absolutely require visual or haptic input, those sources can certainly be useful. Think about what you do in a noisy bar when the background noise makes it hard to hear your conversational partner. Odds are, you look at her mouth. Why? Because the visual information helps to supplement the noisy and degraded auditory input. Why is that useful? According to motor theory, the visual information is useful because what you are really trying to do is figure out what speech gestures your partner is making. That's useful, because figuring out the gestures leads you back to the gestural score, figuring out the gestural score leads you back to the phonemes, and figuring out the phonemes gets you back to the message.

Mirror neurons: The motor theory enjoys a renaissance

Motor theory has been enjoying a renaissance recently sparked off by new evidence about monkey neurons (Gallese, Fadiga, Fogassi, & Rizzolatti, 1996; Gentilucci & Corballis, 2006; Kohler et al., 2002; Rizzolatti & Arbib, 1998). More specifically, researchers working on Macaque monkeys (*Macaca nemestina*) discovered neurons in a part of the monkey's frontal lobes that responded when a monkey performed a particular action, when the monkey watched someone else perform that action, or when the monkey heard a sound associated with that action. These neurons were called *mirror neurons*. The existence of mirror neurons in monkeys was established by invasive single-cell recording techniques. Similar experiments in humans are ethically impossible, and so the existence of the human equivalent of Macaca mirror neurons remains a hypothesis, rather than an established fact.

The part of the brain where mirror neurons were found in monkeys is called *area F5*, which bears some resemblance to a part of the human brain that is important for language processing, *Broca's area* (see Chapter 13). Neuroimaging and research involving direct recording from neurons in Broca's area (part of the frontal lobes of the brain in the left hemisphere) both show that it participates in speech perception (Sahin, Pinker, Cash, Schomer, & Halgren, 2009; St. Heim, Opitz, & Friederici, 2003). The researchers who discovered mirror neurons proposed that mirror neurons could be the neurological mechanism that the motor theory of speech perception requires. That is, mirror neurons in Broca's area could fire when an individual produces a particular set of phonemes. The same mirror neurons would fire when the same individual heard those same phonemes, providing a bridge between speaking and listening. (Keep in mind, this all presupposes that mirror neurons exist in human brains, which has not been demonstrated at the time of writing.)

Although it is not possible (yet) to record from single human neurons, other kinds of experiments have been conducted to try to find evidence for the participation of the human motor cortex in speech perception. The experimental logic is as follows: Motor theory says that accessing representations of specific speech gestures underlies speech perception. Those representations of speech gestures must be stored in the parts of the brain that control articulatory movements. The parts of the brain that control articulation are the motor cortex in the frontal lobes of the brain and the adjacent premotor cortex. Put that all together and it means that, according to motor theory, you should activate the motor cortex when you perceive speech. Proponents of mirror neurons argue that mirror neurons are the neural (brain) mechanism that establishes the link between heard speech and motor representations that underlie speech production. Mirror neurons have recently been found in the monkey equivalent of the motor cortex (they have also been found in the monkey equivalent of the human premotor cortex and in the monkey equivalent of the parietal lobes). Proponents of mirror neurons view evidence that the motor cortex responds to speech as supporting their view of speech perception. Some mirror neuron enthusiasts argue further that mirror neurons play a role in speech perception in modern humans because our speech production and perception processes evolved from an older manual gesture system (Gentilucci & Corballis, 2006).[19]

Although mirror neurons have not been found in humans, proponents of the mirror neuron hypothesis have used slightly less direct ways to find evidence for the involvement of motor and premotor cortices in speech perception. This evidence comes in two distinct forms: neuroimaging data and *transcranial magnetic stimulation* (TMS) studies (Benson et al., 2001; Binder et al., 1997; Capelletti, Fregni, Shapiro, Pascual-Leone, & Caramazza, 2008; Fadiga, Craighero, Buccino, & Rizzolatti, 2002; Gow & Segawa, 2009; McNealy, Mazziotta, & Dapretto, 2006; Meister et al., 2007; Pulvermüller et al., 2006; Sato, Tremblay, & Gracco, 2009; St. Heim et al., 2003; Watkins, Strafella, & Paus, 2003). In Pulvermüller and colleagues' study, participants listened to syllables that resulted from bilabial stops (/pa/, /ba/) or alveolar stops (/ta/, /da/) on *listening* trials. On *silent production* trials, participants imagined themselves making those sounds. Measurements of their brains' activity were gathered using functional magnetic resonance imaging (fMRI). Listening to speech caused substantial brain activity in the superior (top) parts of the temporal lobes on both sides of the participants' brains (which correspond to primary and secondary auditory receiving areas), but it also caused a lot of brain activity in the motor cortex in the experimental participants' frontal lobes. Further, brain activity in the motor cortex depended on what kind of speech sounds the participants were listening to. If they were listening to a bilabial stop syllable, activity was observed in one part of motor cortex. If they were listening to an alveolar stop syllable, activity was observed in a different part of the motor cortex. The brain areas that responded when participants listened to speech were similar to the brain areas that responded when participants imagined saying the same syllables. That is, listening to or imagining saying the syllable /ba/ was correlated with brain activity in one part of the motor cortex. Listening to or imagining saying /ta/ was correlated with brain activity in a different part of the motor cortex. Motor theory explains these results by arguing that the same brain areas that produce speech are involved in perceiving it. Hearing or saying /ba/ activates the same part of motor cortex because listening to /ba/ activates stored representations that are involved in moving the lips. Hearing or producing /da/ activates a different part of the motor cortex from /ba/, because tongue movements (involved in producing /da/) rely on motor representations that are stored in a different part of the motor cortex. Other neuroimaging studies also show activity in the frontal lobes when people listen to speech, although some studies find frontal lobe activity only when the experimental participants have to explicitly compare different syllables or phonemes (so the frontal lobe activity may be related to the process of comparing speech sounds rather than the act of perceiving those speech sounds in the first place; Buchanan et al., 2000; Newman & Twieg, 2001; Scott, McGettigan, & Eisner, 2009; Zatorre, Evans, Meyer, & Gjedde, 1992).[20]

TMS experiments have also been used to bolster the motor theory of speech perception (Fadiga et al., 2002; Meister et al., 2007; Watkins et al., 2003). In this kind of experiment, a strong magnetic field is created right next to an experimental participant's head. The magnetic field interferes temporarily with the normal functioning of neurons in the cortex just below the magnetic coil. Magnetic stimulation can alter an individual's behavior on various cognitive tasks, and the results of stimulation can be measured by neural responses at other locations on the body. For example, magnetic stimulation of parts of the motor cortex can lead to increases in neural activity in the muscles of the hand and fingers. These enhanced responses are called *motor-evoked potentials*. When TMS was applied to participants' motor cortex in one study, participants were less able to tell the difference (*discriminate*) between two similar phonemes.[21] Further, when people listen to speech sounds that involve tongue movements, and have TMS applied to the parts of motor cortex that control the tongue, increased motor-evoked potentials are observed in the participants' tongue muscles. When TMS is applied elsewhere, or when the speech sounds do not involve tongue movements, motor-evoked potentials measured at the tongue are no different than normal. Motor-evoked potentials at the tongue are also obtained when TMS is applied and people watch videos of other people talking (Watkins et al., 2003). All of these experiments show that the motor cortex generates neural activity in response to speech, consistent with the motor theory of speech perception.

The mirror neuron theory of speech perception jumps the shark

And then it gets a little bit crazy. If you ask the average psycholinguist or neurolinguist[22] whether the parts of the motor cortex that control leg movements should be involved in speech perception, they tend to say things like "No," "No way," or "Huh?" However, the same kinds of TMS manipulations that lead to motor-evoked potentials in the tongue muscles also produce motor-evoked potentials in the leg muscles (Liuzzi et al., 2008). It makes sense, from the motor theory perspective, that TMS should lead to activity in the tongue muscles when we listen to speech, because motor theory says the representations we need to figure out the speech gestures reside in the motor cortex (the mirror neuron variant of motor theory makes the same claim). But how much sense does it make to say that perceptual representations for speech perception reside in the leg-control part of the motor cortex? The authors of the leg study concluded that speech perception depends on "an extended action–language network, also including the leg motor circuits" (Liuzzi et al., 2008, p. 2825). They propose a link between non-verbal gesture and speech gestures, and a further link between leg movements (which do not play a major role in human communication, despite claims to the contrary) and manual (hand and arm) gestures (which do).

Instead of taking the leg results as strong evidence for motor theory, the disinterested observer might actually use these results to call into question the entire TMS/motor-evoked potential research enterprise. If your experimental technique produces a thoroughly anomalous result, it might just be possible that there is something wrong with that technique as a research tool. On the other hand, widespread activity in motor cortex in response to speech would make sense, if listening to speech triggers circuits that people use to prepare behavioral responses, which could include a variety of both verbal and non-verbal movements (Scott et al., 2009). Alternatively, motor neurons might respond to speech because they are involved in a monitoring and correction circuit. When we speak, we monitor it for errors (see above). When an individual's own speech is electronically altered as it is being produced, that individual will alter their spoken output to compensate for the electronic changes in less than 150 milliseconds (Tourville, Reilly, & Guenther, 2007; see also Okada & Hickok, 2006). Neuroimaging shows that this feedback loop involves groups of both posterior, temporal lobe neurons, and neurons in the frontal lobes. So, activity in motor cortex could involve neural circuits that normally respond to speech perception processes (that are carried out elsewhere in the brain), by dynamically adjusting speech output. Alternatively, one way to verify that you have heard a speech sound correctly would be to covertly produce your own version of the speech sound and compare the two examples. This would account for motor activation during speech perception—it would reflect self-generation of phonemes for comparison to the input.

Other problems for mirror neuron/motor theory

Motor theory has faced a number of challenges besides some odd results in the TMS research (Hickok, 2008; Lotto, Hickok, & Holt, 2009). Some challenges to motor theory are rooted in the strong connection it makes between perception and production (based on the idea that perception involves the activation of motor representations of specific speech gestures). Infants, for example, are fully capable of perceiving the differences between many different speech sounds, despite the fact that they are thoroughly incapable of producing those speech sounds (Eimas et al., 1971; see Chapter 9). To account for this result, we either have to conclude that infants are born with an innate set of speech–motor representations (and are incapable of making the appropriate gestures only because they have not yet learned to control their articulators well enough) or that having a set of speech–motor representations is not necessary to perceive phonemes.

Additional experimental observations have also cast doubt on whether speech–motor representations are necessary for speech perception. No one would suggest, for example, that non-human animals have a supply of speech–motor representations, especially if those animals are incapable of producing anything that sounds like human speech. Two such animals are Japanese quail and chinchillas (see Figure 2.8). Japanese quail and chinchillas, once they are trained to respond to one class of speech sounds, and refrain from responding to another class, will demonstrate aspects of speech perception that resemble human performance. More specifically, both kinds of animal show categorical perception of speech, and both show compensation for coarticulation (Diehl et al, 2004; Kluender, Diehl, & Killeen, 1987; Kluender & Kiefte, 2006; Kuhl & Miller, 1975).[23] Since these animals lack the human articulatory apparatus, they cannot have speech–motor representations. Because they respond to aspects of speech very much like humans do, motor theory's claim that speech–motor representations are necessary for speech perception is seriously threatened.

Quail and chinchillas show that aspects of speech perception are not limited to human perceivers. Other research shows that duplex perception and categorical perception are not limited to speech perception. Sounds other than speech, such as slamming doors, produce duplex perception when the original signals are edited so that two parts of the acoustic signal are played to different ears. Sounds other than speech, such as the sound a violin makes when it is bowed versus plucked, show categorical shifts in perception. When a violin string is plucked, there is a burst, a brief delay, and then the onset of steady-state vibration (comparable to the burst and vocal fold vibration in speech signals that are perceived as stop consonants). When the same violin string is played with a bow, the vibration and burst begin nearly simultaneously. When violin sounds are edited to vary the lag between the burst and the onset of vibration, short lags are perceived as bowed sounds, but there is a sudden change to perceiving the sound as a string being plucked when the burst–vibration lag gets longer. Both of these effects run contrary to the motor theory's claim that these aspects of speech perception are the result of a specially tuned processing module (Kluender & Kiefte, 2006; Lotto et al., 2009). If categorical and duplex perception were the result of a special speech processing module, they would occur only for speech sounds.

Figure 2.8 Japanese Quail (left) and Chinchilla (right). They perceive differences between different phonemes, they look good, and they taste good.

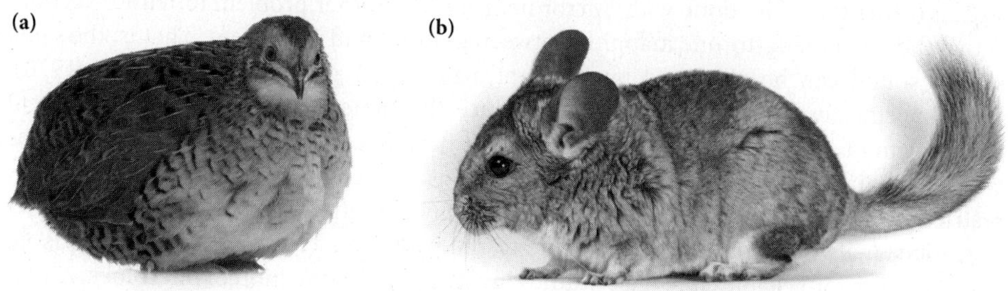

Research with aphasic patients (patients who have a variety of language-related problems as the result of brain damage) casts further doubt on the motor theory. A century and a half ago, Paul Broca and Carl Wernicke showed that some brain-damaged patients could understand speech, but not produce it, while other patients could produce fluent speech, but could not understand it (see Chapter 13). Two patients (Messrs Leborgne and Lelong), both of whom could understand speech, had extensive damage in the frontal lobes of their brains, specifically in the part of their brains that corresponds to area F5 in *Macaca* (where mirror neurons are located in monkeys). The existence of clear dissociations between speech perception and speech production provides strong evidence that intact motor representations are not necessary for perceiving speech. Although the kinds of language disorders that result from brain damage are complex, and not all cases neatly fit into the "broken perception" or "broken production" categories, numerous cases that show the selective impairment of either perception or production (but not both) have been described (see Caplan & Hildebrandt, 1988; note that subtle comprehension impairments have been shown in patients in the "broken production" category, but these involve syntax rather than phonology). If speech perception requires access to intact motor representations, then brain damage that impairs spoken language output should also impair spoken language perception, but this pattern does not appear much of the time.

A motor or mirror neuron advocate might argue that the damage in the reported cases is not extensive enough to wipe out the speech–motor representations, or that *unilateral* damage (limited to one side of the brain) does not wipe out all of the relevant motor representations. However, even with both motor cortices (the one in the left hemisphere and the one in the right hemisphere of the brain) thoroughly damaged, at least some patients can still understand speech quite well (Caltagirone, 1984). The motor theory of speech perception claims that speech is understood because listeners can use the incoming acoustic signal to activate representations of the physical motions that created it. Because the motor (muscle movement) representations are thought to be stored in the parts of the brain that control movement (i.e., the motor and premotor cortices in the frontal lobes), motor theory predicts that damage to those frontal regions should produce significant problems with speech perception. After all, if you understand speech by activating motor representations (which allows you to tell which gestures created the acoustic signal), and if those motor representations are stored in a particular part of the brain, then damaging those parts of the brain should cause problems understanding speech, because you can no longer find the motor representations you need.[24]

Motor theory and mirror neuron theory have been criticized because they do not indicate how acoustic signals allow listeners to figure out which gestures produced those signals (other than, "it's done with mirror neurons"). Another problem for either account is that there is a many-to-one mapping between gestures and phonemes. That is, the same speech sound can be produced by different articulatory gestures (MacNeilage, 1970). More specifically, different people can produce the same phoneme by using different configurations of the vocal tract. Because the vocal tract offers a number of locations where the air flow can be restricted, and because different combinations of air-flow restriction have the same (or nearly the same) physical effect, they wind up producing acoustic signals that are indistinguishable to the perceiver. That means that there is no single gesture for syllables like /ga/. Studies involving the production of bite-block vowels also show that very different gestures can lead to the same or nearly the same acoustic signal, and perception of the same set of phonemes (Gay, Lindblom, & Lubker, 1981). In this kind of experiment, speakers hold an object between their teeth and attempt to say a given syllable. When they do, the way they move their articulators is different than normal, but the acoustic signal that comes out can be very close to the normal one. Motor theory can account for this set of facts in one of two ways. It could propose that more than one speech–motor representation goes with a given phoneme. But that would complicate the representation of speech sounds, and the perceiver could wind up needing separate sets of speech–motor representations for each speaker. Alternatively, motor theory could propose that there is a single set of "ideal" or "prototype" speech–motor representations, and that an acoustic analysis of the speech signal determines which of these "ideal" gestures most closely matches the acoustic input, but that would violate the spirit and letter of the motor theory.

The general auditory approach to speech perception

The general auditory (GA) approach to speech perception starts with the assumption that speech perception is not special (Diehl & Kluender, 1989; Diehl, Walsh, & Kluender, 1991; Diehl et al., 2004; Kluender & Kiefte, 2006; Pardo & Remez, 2006). Instead, "speech sounds are perceived using the same mechanisms of audition and perceptual learning that have evolved in humans … to handle other classes of environmental sounds" (Diehl et al., 2004, p. 154). Researchers in this tradition look for consistent patterns in the acoustic signal for speech that appear whenever particular speech properties are present. Further, they seek to explain commonalities in the way different people and even different species react to aspects of speech. For example, some studies have looked at the way people and animals respond to *voicing contrasts* (the difference between unvoiced consonants like /p/ and voiced consonants like /b/). These studies suggest that our ability to perceive voicing is related to fundamental properties of the auditory system. We can tell whether two sounds occurred simultaneously if they begin more than 20 ms apart. If two sounds are presented starting within about 20 ms of each other, we will perceive them as being simultaneous in time. If one starts more than 20 ms before the other, we perceive them as occurring in a sequence, one before the other. The voicing boundary for people and quail sits right at that same point. If vocal fold vibration starts within 20 ms of the burst, we perceive the phoneme as voiced. But if there's more than a 20 ms gap between the burst and vocal fold vibration, we perceive an unvoiced stop. Thus, this aspect of phonological perception could be based on a fundamental property of auditory perception, rather than the peculiarities of the gestures that go into voiced and unvoiced stop consonants.

Because the acoustic signals created by speech are tremendously complex, the general acoustic approach, as it stands, does not offer an explanation of the full range of human (or animal) speech perception abilities. Its chief advantages lie in its ability to explain common characteristics of human and non-human speech perception, as well as common properties of human speech and non-speech perception. Because the general auditory approach is not committed to gestures as the fundamental unit of phonological representation, it is not vulnerable to many of the criticisms leveled at the motor theory.

The *fuzzy logical model of speech perception* (FLMP), one of the better known approaches within the general auditory tradition, incorporates the idea that there is a single set of "ideal" or "prototype" representations of speech sounds, as determined by their acoustic characteristics (Massaro & Chen, 2008; Massaro & Oden, 1995; Oden & Massaro, 1978; see also Movellan & McClelland, 2001). According to FLMP, speech perception reflects the outcomes of two kinds of processes: *bottom up* and *top down*. Bottom-up processes are those mental operations that analyze the acoustic properties of a given speech stimulus. These bottom-up processes activate a set of potentially matching phonological representations. Stored representations of phonemes are activated to the degree that they are similar to acoustic properties in the speech stimulus; more similar phonemes attain higher degrees of activation, less similar phonemes attain lower degrees of activation. Top-down processes are those mental operations that use information in long-term memory to try to select the best possible candidate from among the set of candidates activated by the bottom-up processes. This may be especially important when the bottom-up information is ambiguous or degraded. For example, when the /n/ phoneme precedes the /b/ sound (as in *lean bacon*), often times coarticulation makes the /n/ phoneme come out sounding more like an /m/. When someone listens to *lean bacon*, bottom-up processes will activate both the prototype /n/ phoneme and the prototype /m/ phoneme, because the actual /n/ part of the signal will be intermediate between the two prototypes. According to the FLMP, our knowledge that *lean bacon* is a likely expression in English should cause us to favor the /n/ interpretation, because there is no such expression as "leam bacon." However, if the /n/ sound were in a non-word, such as *pleam bacon*, a listener would be more likely to pick the /m/ interpretation, because the competing /n/ sound would not receive any support from "top-down" processes. This effect, the tendency to perceive ambiguous speech stimuli as real words if possible, is known as the *Ganong* effect, after its discoverer, William Ganong (1980).

FLMP also offers a mechanism that can produce *phonemic restoration effects* (Bashford, Riener, & Warren, 1992; Bashford & Warren, 1987; Bashford, Warren, & Brown, 1996; Miller & Isard, 1963; Samuel, 1981, 1996; Sivonen, Maess, Lattner, and Friederici, 2006; Warren, 1970). Phonemic restoration happens when speech stimuli are edited to create gaps. For instance, you might record the word *legislators*, and delete the middle "s" sound. When you play that stimulus with the "s" deleted, people often times notice that there is a gap in the word, and it sounds funny. However, if you insert a noise, like the sound of someone coughing, or even white noise, people experience *phonemic restoration*—they hear the word as if the middle "s" sound were present, as if someone had pronounced *legislators* perfectly. If you put your specially edited word in the middle of a sentence, as in *It wasn't until midnight that the legi(cough)lators finished the bill*, people again hear the word *legislators* as if it had been pronounced perfectly, with the middle "s" sound in its normal place, and they hear the cough as if it happened just before or just after the edited word. (People hear *It wasn't until midnight that the (cough) legislators finished the bill.*) These phonemic restoration effects are stronger for longer words than shorter words, and they are stronger for sentences that are grammatical and make sense than sentences that are ungrammatical or don't make sense. Further, the specific phoneme that is restored can depend on the meaning of the sentence that the edited word appears in. For example, if you hear *The wagon lost its (cough)eel*, you will most likely hear the phoneme /w/ in place of the cough. But if you hear *The circus has a trained (cough)eel*, you will most likely hear the phoneme /s/. Research involving *evoked response potentials* (ERPs) that are created when groups of neurons fire in response to a stimulus show that the nervous system does register the presence of the cough noise very soon after it appears in the stimulus (within about 200 ms).

All of these results suggest that a variety of possible sources of top-down information affect the way the acoustic signal is perceived. Further, they suggest that perception of speech involves analyzing the signal itself as well as biasing the results of this analysis based on how well different candidate phonological interpretations fit in with other aspects of the message. These other aspects could include whether the phonological interpretation results in a real word or not (as in *lean* vs. *leam*), whether the semantic interpretation of the sentence makes sense (as in *I saw them kiss* vs. *I saw them dish*), and how intact the top-down information is (a poorly constructed sentence is less likely to make up for a degraded acoustic signal).

Summary and Conclusions

Speaking requires you to have an idea and it requires you to move your articulators. Sounds simple, but there are a lot of steps you have to take after you have an idea and before it makes it into the world as a set of sound waves. You have to find the right lexicalized concepts in your language, you have to activate the lemma representations that correspond to those lexicalized concepts. Having done that, you have to find the right forms for those lemmas, which involves both morphological and syntactic processing. One you have activated the right set of morphemes and have arranged them in a series, you can start activating sounds that will express your idea. Activating sound codes entails a set of processes that lead to syllabification, where specific activated speech sounds are assigned to specific positions in specific syllables. Having accomplished that much, the syllabified representation is turned over to the motor system, which creates a gestural score that your motor control systems use to signal over 100 muscles that are involved in speech. The final outcome of that process is a set of muscle movements that drive the articulators, which perturb the flow of air coming out of your body and create the characteristic patterns that we perceive as speech.

Understanding speech requires that you register the acoustic pattern created by the movement of the articulators and use it to recover the speaker's intended meaning. Sounds simple, but there are a lot of steps you have to take after you register the presence of a speech stimulus before you can figure out what it means. Coarticulation makes the analysis of the speech signal especially challenging, because there are no clear temporal breaks that signal where one phoneme ends and the next one begins, and because the gestures used to produce a phoneme are affected by the preceding and following phonemes. Because the articulators are moving simultaneously, and because the precise nature of the movements for a given phoneme depend on both the preceding and the following phonemes, there is no one-to-one relationship between acoustic signals and phonemes. Motor theory, and its mirror neuron variant, propose that we "see through" the complexity of the acoustic characteristics of speech by using the speech signal to activate representations of the movements (gestures) that created the speech signal. Motor theory advocates propose that speech perception is carried about by a specially functioning and dedicated processing module. According to motor theory, this module leads to special properties of speech perception, including duplex and categorical perception. Mirror neuron advocates point to parts of monkey brains that respond when the monkey makes a gesture (e.g., grasping an object) or sees someone else make the same gesture. Mirror neurons are seen as the vital bridge between perception and production that the motor theory requires.

Critics of motor theory, on the other hand, have shown that speech perception is not "special" as defined by motor theory. Non-human animals, like Japanese quail and chinchillas, perceive aspects of speech much the same way humans do; and humans experience duplex and categorical perception for non-speech sounds. As an alternative to motor theory, some accounts propose that general-purpose auditory processing mechanisms are deployed for speech. The general auditory approach can explain why non-human animals perceive some kinds of phonemes, and why speech has some of the characteristics that it has—such as having perceptual boundaries at specific voice onset times. The fuzzy logical model of speech perception falls within this tradition. It proposes that both signal analysis and stored information influence the perception of any given speech stimulus. Such interactions of bottom-up and top-down information are demonstrated by phenomena like the Ganong effect and different kinds of phonemic restoration. However, the general auditory approach does not yet constitute a complete theory of speech perception, and so speech perception continues to be actively and intensively researched by language scientists.

TEST YOURSELF

1. What kinds of mental processes do speakers go through prior to articulation?
2. According to the WEAVER++ model, what kinds of representations do speakers activate before they speak? What evidence supports the psychological reality of models such as WEAVER++? What observations suggest that aspects of the WEAVER++ system may not be present in human speakers?
3. Describe the difference between a concept and a lexicalized concept. What roles do each of them play in speech production?
4. What kinds of errors do people make when they speak? What do the errors tell us about the speakers' mental processes?
5. Describe similarities and differences between Gary Dell's spreading activation model and the WEAVER++ model of speech production. What evidence favors each account?
6. Describe the tip-of-the tongue phenomenon. What kinds of words are most likely to produce a TOT and why?
7. How is speech perceived according to Liberman's motor theory? What is coarticulation and what role does it play in the theory? What is the McGurk effect and what does it tell us about speech perception? Why do some people believe that motor neurons provide the physical/neural basis for speech perception? Is there anything wrong with the mirror neuron hypothesis?
8. What are the chief theoretical alternatives to motor theory? Why might one prefer these alternatives?

THINK ABOUT IT

1. Try to induce tip-of-the tongue states. Design an experiment (for example, you could compare different kinds of words). Use the definitions from the tip-of-the tongue section (above) or come up with some of your own. Test your classmates or your friends. How often are you able to induce TOT states? Do some kinds of words work better than others? Are your results consistent with the experimental results?
2. Take some time to listen to conversations around you. When two people are conversing, are there similarities in what the two partners say or how they say it? What do you think accounts for these similarities?
3. Find a quiet place to work, a partner, and a pencil. Sit so that you and your partner can hear each other but not see each other. Have your partner speak a short list of words, like *pencil, box, toaster, walnut, camera*, and *thing*. Flip a coin before saying each word. If the coin comes up "heads," speak the word while holding the pencil between your teeth. (This is kind of like doing a bite-block production experiment.) See if you can hear when your partner has the pencil in her mouth. Which kinds of speech sounds are most affected by the pencil? See if you can figure out why. See if you can determine what cues you are using to figure out when your partner is using a pencil.

Notes

1 Caber (n.): A very large wooden log that is thrown in contests of strength.
2 To be truly complete, the theory would also have to explain how the articulatory apparatus is controlled, but that is a conceptually separate topic. Most theories of speech production are satisfied to let the motor system deal with the actual movements, although some evidence suggests that articulator movement in speech is programmed dynamically each time speech is produced, rather than being controlled by an inventory of pre-compiled gestural plans. For example, speakers can produce acoustic signals that are within the range of normal variation even if their vocal apparatus is significantly perturbed by bite-blocks or other mechanical methods (e.g., Gay et al., 1981).
3 The process is called resyllabification in some accounts of speech production, but this seems to imply an initial stage of processing in which syllables are tied to individual words and then reorganized, which may not be accurate.
4 Syllable frequency effects also suggest that they are a psychologically real representational unit that participates in production (Levelt & Wheeldon, 1994).
5 At parties, we used to play a profane version of this experiment called "fuzzy duck–ducky fuzz". Oh, the laughter we enjoyed. Good times.
6 See also Moss, McCormick, & Tyler, 1997, for evidence of semantic over phonological priority in lexical access.
7 Ebenezer, sampan, ambergris, philatelist.
8 The precise mechanism that produces "competition" effects is still under investigation. Some accounts favor mutual inhibition within the conceptual and lemma levels (e.g., Dell et al., 1997), while others favor non-inhibitory processes in networks where multiple sources can feed activation to different candidates (e.g., Roelofs, Meyer, & Levelt, 1996).
9 Facilitatory and inhibitory effects depend on the precise timing of the onset of the target picture and the word. Interested readers may wish to consult Griffin & Ferreira (2006) and Levelt (1989).
10 And vice versa in interactive accounts like Dell's spreading activation model (Dell, 1986; Dell et al., 1997) and related accounts (e.g., Cooper & Ferreira, 1999).
11 But see Roelofs et al. (1996) for a strictly feed-forward, serial-selection model that can produce mixed errors as well as the lexical bias.

12 In another study, Motley and colleagues showed that slips of the tongue that led to sexually suggestive statements were more frequent when experimental participants were in a sexually charged frame of mind (Motley & Baars, 1979). Participants made more pain-related slips of the tongue when they expected to receive an electric shock.
13 Alvin Liberman, the founder of the modern study of speech perception, argued that we are specially adapted by evolution for just this purpose—to produce and understand coarticulated speech. Otherwise, he argues, we could only talk as fast as we can spell (i.e., really slowly), and communication would suffer.
14 Other names also appear in the literature, including sonogram, sonograph, and spectrograph. This chapter follows Liberman and uses spectrogram.
15 Fowler's direct realist perspective offers a different theory of perception within the motor theory tradition. The chief difference between the two approaches is that the most current version of Liberman's motor theory treats prototype "intended gestures" as being the fundamental units of speech perception, while Fowler believes that the fundamental units are the actual speech gestures that speakers produce (see, e.g., Fowler, 2008).
16 In another version of the experiment, the two parts of the stimulus were both played to both ears, but the relative loudness of each component was manipulated. The elided transition began to affect perception at intensities below the detection threshold for the transition when presented in isolation, and produced duplex perception when the intensity of the transition was about 20 dB greater than the base. Liberman and colleagues view both of these effects—sub-threshold effects on phonological perception and duplex perception with large intensity differences between transition and base—as evidence for modular speech processing.
17 Other examples of perceptual variables that can vary continuously are hue in vision (related to color perception) or saturation in gustation (which can lead to gradual changes in taste perception).
18 It would have been much ickier without the gloves.
19 Of course, there is no direct evidence for this hypothesis and these authors have not ruled out the equally likely possibility that modern speech evolved from more primitive systems of vocal signals (e.g., alarm calls rather than manual gestures).
20 But note that while fMRI and other imaging studies also find frontal activity correlated with phoneme comparison and judgment tasks, they often do not find frontal activity for speech perception tasks that do not involve comparison and judgment. Thus, frontal activations may reflect perceptual processes, but they might also reflect working memory processes, executive function, attention, or other subcomponent processes involved in phonological comparisons.
21 See Hickok (2008) for a wide-ranging critique of the mirror neuron theory of action understanding.
22 And I have …
23 Pinker (1994) objects to these findings because, he argues, the animals require thousands of training trials, while human infants require few or none. But this criticism is really misplaced. While the animals may require many trials to learn the experimental procedure (that they get rewarded for particular behaviors under particular contingencies), they do not, in fact, need thousands of trials to respond appropriately to a given stimulus after this basic training. While the animals are trained on a specific set of training stimuli, their ability to discriminate phonemes and to compensate for coarticulation generalizes to novel stimuli (that they were not exposed to during the basic training period; see, e.g., Kluender & Kiefte, 2006).
24 Of course, it is always possible that there are multiple sets of motor representations for speech gestures, stored in multiple parts of the brain (just as monkeys have multiple somatotopic maps), but motor theory clearly associates speech perception with motor representations stored in the motor strip and adjacent premotor areas.

References

Arieh, Y., & Algom, D. (2002). Processing picture-word stimuli: The contingent nature of picture and of word superiority. *Journal of Experimental Psychology: Learning, Memory, and Cognition, 28,* 221–232.

Baars, B. J., & Motley, M. T. (1974). Spoonerisms: Experimental elicitation of human speech errors. *JSAS Catalog of Selected Documents in Psychology, 4,* 118.

Baars, B. J., Motley, M. T., & MacKay, D. (1975). Output editing for lexical status from artificially elicited slips of the tongue. *Journal of Verbal Learning and Verbal Behavior, 14,* 382–391.

Bashford, J. A., Jr., Riener, K. R., & Warren, R. M. (1992). Increasing the intelligibility of speech through multiple phonemic restorations. *Perception and Psychophysics, 51,* 211–217.

Bashford, J. A., Jr., & Warren, R. M. (1987). Multiple phonemic restorations follow the rules for auditory induction. *Perception and Psychophysics, 42,* 114–121.

Bashford, J. A., Jr., Warren, R. M., & Brown, C. A. (1996). Use of speech-modulated noise adds strong "bottom-up" cues for phonemic restoration. *Perception and Psychophysics, 58,* 342–350.

Baynes, K., Funnell, M. G., & Fowler, C. A. (1994). Hemispheric contributions to the integration of visual and auditory information in speech perception. *Perception and Psychophysics, 55,* 633–641.

Benson, R. R., Whalen, D. H., Richardson, M., Swainson, B., Clark, V. P., Lai, S., et al. (2001). Parametrically dissociating speech and nonspeech perception in the brain using fMRI. *Brain & Language, 78,* 364–396.

Binder, J. R., Frost, J. A., Hammeke, T. A., Cox, R. W., Rao, S. M., & Prieto, T. (1997). Human brain language areas identified by functional magnetic resonance imaging. *The Journal of Neuroscience, 17,* 353–362.

Blackmer, E. R., & Mitton, J. L. (1991). Theories of monitoring and timing of repairs in spontaneous speech. *Cognition, 39,* 173–194.

Blumstein, S. E., Alexander, M. P., Ryalls, J. H., Katz, W., & Dworetzky, B. (1987). On the nature of foreign accent syndrome: A case study. *Brain & Language, 31,* 215–244.

Brown, A. S. (1991). A review of tip-of-the-tongue experience. *Psychological Bulletin, 109,* 204–223.

Brown, A. S., & McNeill, D. (1966). The "tip of the tongue" phenomenon. *Journal of Verbal Learning and Verbal Behavior, 5,* 325–337.

Browman, C. P., & Goldstein, L. (1989). Articulatory gestures as phonological units. *Phonology, 6,* 201–251.

Browman, C. P., & Goldstein, L. (1990). Representation and reality: Physical systems and phonological structure. *Journal of Phonetics, 18,* 411–424.

Browman, C. P., & Goldstein, L. (1991). Gestural structures: Distinctiveness, phonological processes and historical change. In I. G. Mattingly & M. Studdert-Kennedy (Eds.), *Modularity and the motor theory of speech perception: Proceedings of a conference to honor Alvin M. Liberman* (pp. 313–338). Hillsdale, NJ: Erlbaum.

Buchanan, T. W., Lutz, K., Mirzazade, S., Specht, K., Shah, N. J., Zilles, K., et al. (2000). Recognition of emotional prosody and verbal components of spoken language: An fMRI study. *Cognitive Brain Research, 9,* 227–238.

Caltagirone, V. G. (1984). Speech suppression without aphasia after bilateral perisylvian softenings (bilateral rolandic operculum damage). *Italian Journal of Neurological Science, 5,* 77–83.

Caplan, D., & Hildebrandt, N. (1988). *Disorders of syntactic comprehension.* Cambridge, MA: MIT Press.

Cappelletti, M., Fregni, F., Shapiro, K., Pascual-Leone, A., & Caramazza, A. (2008). Processing nouns and verbs in the left frontal cortex: A transcranial magnetic stimulation study. *Journal of Cognitive Neuroscience, 20,* 707–720.

Caramazza, A. (1997). How many levels of processing are there in lexical access? *Cognitive Neuropsychology, 14,* 177–208.

Cooper, C. J., & Ferreira, V. S. (1999). Semantic and phonological information flow in the production lexicon. *Journal of Experimental Psychology: Learning, Memory, and Cognition, 25,* 318–344.

Cooper, F. S., Delattre, P. C., Liberman, A. M., Borst, J. M., & Gerstman, L. J. (1952). Some experiments on the perception of synthetic speech sounds. *The Journal of the Acoustical Society of America, 24,* 597–606.

Cutting, J. C., & Ferreira, V. S. (1999). Semantic and phonological information flow in the production lexicon. *Journal of Experimental Psychology: Learning, Memory, and Cognition, 25,* 318–344.

Dankovičová, J., Gurd, J. M., Marshall, J. C., MacMahon, M. K. C., Stuart-Smith, J., Coleman, J. S., et al. (2001). Aspects of non-native pronunciation in a case of altered accent following stroke (Foreign Accent Syndrome). *Clinical Linguistics and Phonetics, 15,* 195–218.

Dekle, D. J., Fowler, C. A., & Funnell, M. G. (1992). Audiovisual integration in perception of real words. *Perception and Psychophysics, 51,* 355–362.

Dell, G. S. (1986). A spreading-activation theory of retrieval in sentence production. *Psychological Review, 93,* 283–321.

Dell, G. S., & Reich, P. A. (1981). Stages in sentence production: An analysis of speech error data. *Journal of Verbal Learning and Verbal Behavior, 20,* 611–629.

Dell, G. S., Schwartz, M. F., Martin, N., Saffran, E. M., & Gagnon, D. A. (1997). Lexical access in normal and aphasic speakers. *Psychological Review, 104,* 801–838.

Diehl, R. L., & Kluender, K. R. (1989). On the objects of speech perception. *Ecological Psychology, 1,* 121–144.

Diehl, R. L., Lotto, A. J., & Holt, L. L. (2004). Speech perception. *Annual Review of Psychology, 55,* 149–179.

Diehl, R. L., Walsh, M. A., & Kluender, K. R. (1991). On the interpretability of speech/nonspeech comparisons: A reply to Fowler. *Journal of the Acoustical Society of America, 89,* 2905–2909.

Eimas, P. D., Siqueland, E. R., Jusczyk, P., & Vigorito, J. (1971). Speech perception in infants. *Science, 171,* 303–306.

Fadiga, L., Craighero, L., Buccino, G., & Rizzolatti, G. (2002). Speech listening specifically modulates the excitability of tongue muscles: A TMS study. *European Journal of Neuroscience, 15,* 399–402.

Fodor, J. (1983). *Modularity of mind.* Cambridge, MA: MIT Press.

Fowler, C. A. (1986). An event approach to the study of speech perception from a direct-realist perspective. *Journal of Phonetics, 14,* 3–28.

Fowler, C. A. (2008). The FLMP STMPed. *Psychonomic Bulletin & Review, 15,* 458–462.

Fowler, C. A., & Dekle, D. J. (1991). Listening with eye and hand: Cross-modal contributions to speech perception. *Journal of Experimental Psychology: Human Perception and Performance, 17,* 816–828.

Galantucci, B., Fowler, C. A., & Turvey, M. T. (2006). The motor theory of speech perception reviewed. *Psychonomic Bulletin & Review, 13,* 361–377.

Gallese, V., Fadiga, L., Fogassi, L., & Rizolatti, G. (1996). Action recognition in the premotor cortex. *Brain, 119,* 593–609.

Ganong, W. F., III (1980). Phonetic categorization in auditory word perception. *Journal of Experimental Psychology: Human Perception and Performance, 6,* 110–125.

Garrett, M. F. (1975). The analysis of sentence production. In G. Bower (Ed.), *Psychology of learning and motivation* (pp. 133–177). New York: Academic Press.

Garrett, M. F. (1980). Levels of processing in sentence production. In B. Butterworth (Ed.), *Language production, Vol. 1* (pp. 177–220). London, England: Academic Press.

Gaskell, M. G., & Marslen-Wilson, W. D. (1997). Integrating form and meaning: A distributed model of speech perception. *Language and Cognitive Processes, 12,* 613–656.

Gay, T., Lindblom, B., & Lubker, J. (1981). Production of bite-block vowels: Acoustic equivalence by selective compensation. *Journal of the Acoustical Society of America, 69,* 802–810.

Gentilucci, M., & Corballis, M. C. (2006). From manual gesture to speech: A gradual transition. *Neuroscience and Biobehavioral Reviews, 30,* 949–960.

Goldstein, E. B. (2006). *Sensation and perception.* New York: Wadsworth.

Goldstein, E. B. (2007). *Cognitive psychology.* New York: Wadsworth.

Gow, D. W., Jr., & Segawa, J. A. (2009). Articulatory mediation of speech perception: A causal analysis of multi-modal imaging data. *Cognition, 110,* 222–236.

Griffin, Z. M., & Ferreira, V. S. (2006). Properties of spoken language production. In M. J. Traxler and M. A. Gernsbacher (Eds.), *The handbook of psycholinguistics* (2nd ed., pp. 21–59). Amsterdam, The Netherlands: Elsevier.

Hartsuiker, R. J., & Kolk, H. H. J. (2001). Error monitoring in speech production: A computational test of the perceptual loop theory. *Cognitive Psychology, 42,* 113–157.

Hickok, G. (2008). Eight problems for the mirror neuron theory of action understanding in monkeys and humans. *Journal of Cognitive Neuroscience, 21,* 1229–1243.

Jescheniak, J. D., & Levelt, W. J. M. (1994). Word frequency effects in speech production: Retrieval of syntactic information and of phonological form. *Journal of Experimental Psychology: Learning, Memory, and Cognition, 20,* 824–843.

Jescheniak, J. D., Meyer, A. S., & Levelt, W. J. M. (2003). Specific-word frequency is not all that counts in speech production: Comments on Caramazza, Costa et al. (2001) and new experimental data. *Journal of Experimental Psychology: Learning, Memory, and Cognition, 29,* 432–438.

Kempen, G., & Huijbers, P. (1983). The lexicalization process in sentence production and naming: Indirect election of words. *Cognition, 14,* 185–209.

Kerzel, D., & Bekkering, H. (2000). Motor activation from visible speech: Evidence from stimulus response compatibility. *Journal of Experimental Psychology: Human Perception and Performance, 26,* 634–647.

Kluender, K. R., Diehl, R. L., & Killeen, P. R. (1987). Japanese quail can learn phonetic categories. *Science, 237,* 1195–1197.

Kluender, K. R., & Kiefte, M. (2006). Speech perception within a biologically realistic information-theoretic framework. In M. J. Traxler & M. A. Gernsbacher (Eds.), *The handbook of psycholinguistics* (2nd ed., pp. 153–200). Amsterdam, The Netherlands: Elsevier.

Kohler, E., Keysers, C., Umilta, A., Fogassi, L., Gallese, V., & Rizzolatti, G. (2002). Hearing sounds, understanding actions: Action representation in mirror neurons. *Science, 297,* 846–848.

Kuhl, P. K., & Miller, J. D. (1975). Speech perception by the chinchilla: Voiced–voiceless distinctions in alveolar plosive consonants. *Science, 190,* 69–72.

Kurowski, K., Blumstein, S. E., & Alexander, M. (1996). The foreign accent syndrome: A reconsideration. *Brain & Language, 54,* 1–25.

Levelt, W. J. M. (1983). Monitoring and self-repair in speech. *Cognition, 14,* 41–104.

Levelt, W. J. M. (1989). *Speaking: From intention to articulation.* Cambridge, MA: MIT Press.

Levelt, W. J. M. (1994). Do speakers have access to a mental syllabary? *Cognition, 50,* 239–269.

Levelt, W. J. M., Roelofs, A., & Meyer, A. S. (1999). A theory of lexical access in speech production. *Behavioral and Brain Sciences, 22,* 1–75.

Levelt, W.J. M., Schriefers, H., Vorberg, D., Meyer, A. S., Pechmann, T., & Havinga, J. (1991). The time course of lexical access in speech production: A study in picture naming. *Psychological Review, 98,* 122–142.

Levelt, W. J. M., & Wheeldon, L. (1994). Do speakers have access to a mental syllabary? *Cognition, 50,* 239–269.

Liberman, A. M., Cooper, F. S., Shankweiler, D. P., & Studdert-Kennedy, M. (1967). Perception of the speech code. *Psychological Review, 74,* 431–461.

Liberman, A. M., Delattre, P., & Cooper, F. S. (1952). The role of selected stimulus-variables in the perception of unvoiced stop consonants. *The American Journal of Psychology, 65,* 497–516.

Liberman, A. M., Delattre, P. C., Cooper, F. S., & Gerstman, L. J. (1954). The role of consonant–vowel transitions in the perception of the stop and nasal consonants. *Psychological Monographs, 68,* 1–13.

Liberman, A. M., Delattre, P. C., Gerstman, L. J., & Cooper, F. S. (1956). Tempo of frequency change as a cue for distinguishing classes of speech sounds. *Journal of Experimental Psychology, 52,* 127–137.

Liberman, A. M., Harris, K. S., Hoffman, H. S., & Griffith, B. C. (1957). The discrimination of speech sounds within and across phoneme boundaries. *Journal of Experimental Psychology, 54,* 358–368.

Liberman, A. M., & Mattingly, I. G. (1985). The motor theory of speech perception revisited. *Cognition, 21,* 1–36.

Liberman, A. M., & Mattingly, I. G. (1989). A specialization for speech perception. *Science, 243,* 489–494.

Liberman, A. M., & Whalen, D. H. (2000). On the relation of speech to language. *Trends in Cognitive Sciences, 4,* 187–196.

Liuzzi, G., Ellger, T., Flöel, A., Breitenstein, C., Jansen, A., & Knecht, S. (2008). Walking the talk: Speech activates the leg motor cortex. *Neuropsychologia, 46,* 2824–2830.

Lotto, A. J., Hickok, G. S., & Holt, L. L. (2009). Reflections on mirror neurons and speech perception. *Trends in Cognitive Sciences, 13,* 110–114.

Lovelace, E. (1987). Attributes that come to mind in the TOT state. *Bulletin of the Psychonomic Society, 25,* 370–372.

Mackay, D. (1972). The structure of words and syllables: Evidence from errors in speech. *Cognitive Psychology, 86,* 210–227.

MacNeilage, P. F. (1970). Motor control of serial ordering of speech. *Psychological Review, 62,* 615–625.

Mariën, P., Verhoeven, J., Wackenier, P., Engelborghs, S., & De Deyn, P. P. (2009). Foreign accent syndrome as a developmental motor speech disorder. *Cortex, 45,* 870–878.

Marslen-Wilson, W. D., & Warren, P. (1994). Levels of representation and process in lexical access. *Psychological Review, 101,* 653–675.

Martin, J. G., & Brunell, H. T. (1982). Perception of anticipatory coarticulation effects in vowel–stop consonant–vowel sequences. *Journal of Experimental Psychology: Human Perception and Performance, 15,* 576–585.

Massaro, D. W., & Chen, T. H. (2008). The motor theory of speech perception revisited. *Psychonomic Bulletin & Review, 15,* 453–457.

Massaro, D. W., & Oden, G. C. (1995). Independence of lexical context and phonological information in speech perception. *Journal of Experimental Psychology: Learning, Memory, and Cognition, 21,* 1053–1064.

Mattingly, I. G., Liberman, A. M., Syrdal, A. K., & Halwes, T. (1971). Discrimination in speech and nonspeech modes. *Cognitive Psychology, 2,* 131–157.

McGurk, H., & MacDonald, J. (1976). Hearing lips and seeing voices. *Nature, 264,* 746–747.

McNealy, K., Mazziotta, J. C., & Dapretto, M. (2006). Cracking the language code: Neural mechanisms underlying speech parsing. *The Journal of Neuroscience, 26,* 7629–7639.

Meister, I. G., Wilson, S. M., Deblieck, C., Wu, A. D., & Iacoboni, M. (2007). The essential role of premotor cortex in speech perception. *Current Biology, 17,* 1692–1696.

Miller, G. A., & Isard, S. (1963). Some perceptual consequences of linguistic rules. *Journal of Verbal Learning and Verbal Behavior, 2,* 217–228.

Moen, I. (2000). Foreign accent syndrome: A review of contemporary explanations. *Aphasiology, 14,* 5–15.

Moss, H. E., McCormick, S. F., & Tyler, L. K. (1997). The time course of activation of semantic information during spoken word recognition. *Language and Cognitive Processes, 12,* 695–731.

Motley, M. T., & Baars, B. J. (1979). Effects of cognitive set upon laboratory induced verbal (Freudian) slips. *Journal of Speech & Hearing Research, 22,* 421–432.

Motley, M. T., Baars, B. J., & Camden, C. T. (1983). Formulation hypotheses revisited: A reply to Stemberger. *Journal of Psycholinguistic Research, 12,* 561–566.

Motley, M. T., Camden, C. T., & Baars, B. J. (1982). Covert formulation and editing of anomalies in speech production: Evidence from experimentally elicited slips of the tongue. *Journal of Verbal Learning and Verbal Behavior, 21,* 578–594.

Movellan, J. R., & McClelland, J. L. (2001). The Morton–Massaro law of information integration: Implications for models of perception. *Psychological Review, 108,* 113–148.

Nelson, T. O. (1984). A comparison of current measures of the accuracy of feeling-of-knowing predictions. *Psychological Bulletin, 95,* 109–133.

Newman, S. D., & Twieg, D. (2001). Differences in auditory processing of words and pseudowords: An fMRI study. *Human Brain Mapping, 14,* 39–47.

Nooteboom, S. G. (1969). The tongue slips into patterns. In A. G. Schiarone, A. J. van Essen, & A. A. Van Raad (Eds.), *Leyden studies in linguistics and phonetics* (pp. 114–132). The Hague: Mouton.

Nooteboom, S. (1973). The tongue slips into patterns. In V. Fromkin (Ed.), *Speech errors as linguistic evidence* (pp. 144–156). The Hague, Netherlands: Mouton.

Oden, G. C., & Massaro, D. W. (1978). Integration of featural information in speech perception. *Psychological Review, 85,* 172–191.

Okada, K., & Hickok, G. (2006). Left posterior auditory-related cortices participate in both speech perception and speech production: Neural overlap revealed by fMRI. *Brain & Language, 98,* 112–117.

Oldfield, R. C., & Wingfield, A. (1965). Response latencies in naming objects. *The Quarterly Journal of Experimental Psychology, 17,* 273–281.

Pardo, J. S., & Remez, R. E. (2006). The perception of speech. In M. J. Traxler & M. A. Gernsbacher (Eds.), *The handbook of psycholinguistics* (2nd ed., pp. 201–248). Amsterdam, The Netherlands: Elsevier.

Pinker, S. (1994). *The language instinct.* New York: Harper.

Postma, A. (2000). Detection of errors during speech production: A review of speech monitoring models. *Cognition, 77,* 97–131.

Pulvermüller, F., Huss, M., Kheriff, F., del Prado Martin, F. M., Hauk, O., & Shtyrov, Y. (2006). Motor cortex maps articulatory features of speech sounds. *Proceedings of the National Academy of Sciences, 103,* 7865–7870.

Remez, R. E., Rubin, P. E., Berns, S. M., Pardo, J. S., & Lang, J. M. (1994). On the perceptual organization of speech. *Psychological Review, 101,* 129–156.

Rizzolatti, G., & Arbib, M. A. (1998). Language within our grasp. *Trends in Neurosciences, 21,* 188–194.

Roelofs, A., Meyer, A. S., & Levelt, W. J. M. (1996). Interaction between semantic and orthographic factors in conceptually driven naming: Comment on Starreveld and La Heij (1995). *Journal of Experimental Psychology: Learning, Memory, and Cognition, 22,* 246–251.

Roelofs, A., Özdemir, R., & Levelt, W. J. M. (2007). Influences of spoken word planning on speech recognition. *Journal of Experimental Psychology: Learning, Memory, and Cognition, 33,* 900–913.

Rubin, D. C. (1975). Within word structure in the tip-of-the-tongue phenomenon. *Journal of Verbal Learning and Verbal Behavior, 14,* 392–397.

Sahin, N. T., Pinker, S., Cash, S. S., Schomer, D., & Halgren, E. (2009). Sequential processing of lexical, grammatical, and phonological information within Broca's area. *Science, 326,* 445–449.

Samuel, A. G. (1981). Phonemic restoration: Insights from a new methodology. *Journal of Experimental Psychology: General, 110,* 474–494.

Samuel, A. G. (1996). Does lexical information influence the perceptual restoration of phonemes? *Journal of Experimental Psychology: General, 125,* 28–51.

Sato, M., Tremblay, P., & Gracco, V. L. (2009). A mediating role of the premotor cortex in phoneme segmentation. *Brain & Language, 111,* 1–7.

Scott, S. K., McGettigan, C., & Eisner, F. (2009). A little more conversation, a little less action: Candidate roles for the motor cortex in speech perception. *Nature Reviews: Neuroscience, 10,* 295–302.

Sivonen, P., Maess, B., Lattner, S., & Friederici, A. D. (2006). Phonemic restoration in a sentence context: Evidence from early and late ERP effects. *Brain Research, 1121,* 177–189.

St. Heim, B., Opitz, K., & Friederici, A. D. (2003). Phonological processing during language production: fMRI evidence for a shared production–comprehension network. *Cognitive Brain Research, 16,* 285–296.

Streeter, L. A., & Nigro, G. N. (1979). The role of medial consonant transitions in word perception. *Journal of the Acoustical Society of America, 65,* 1533–1541.

Tourville, J. A., Reilly, K. J., & Guenther, F. H. (2007). Neural mechanisms underlying auditory feedback control of speech. *Neuroimage, 39,* 1429–1443.

Warren, P., & Marslen-Wilson, W. D. (1987). Continuous uptake of acoustic cues in spoken word-recognition. *Perception and Psychophysics, 41,* 262–275.

Warren, P., & Marslen-Wilson, W. D. (1988). Cues to lexical choice: Discriminating place and voice. *Perception and Psychophysics, 43,* 21–30.

Warren, R. M. (1970). Perceptual restoration of missing speech sounds. *Science, 167,* 392–393.

Watkins, K. E., Strafella, A. P., & Paus, T. (2003). Seeing and hearing speech excites the motor system involved in speech production. *Neuropsychologia, 41,* 989–994.

Whalen, D. H., & Liberman, A. M. (1987). Speech perception takes precedence over nonspeech perception. *Science, 237,* 169–171.

Wheeldon, L. R., & Levelt, W. J. M. (1995). Monitoring and the time course of phonological encoding. *Journal of Memory and Language, 34,* 311–334.

Wingfield, A. (1968). Effects of frequency on identification and naming of objects. *American Journal of Psychology, 81,* 226–234.

Zatorre, R. J., Evans, A. C., Meyer, E., & Gjedde, A. (1992). Lateralization of phonetic and pitch discrimination in speech processing. *Science, 256,* 846–849.

Word Processing

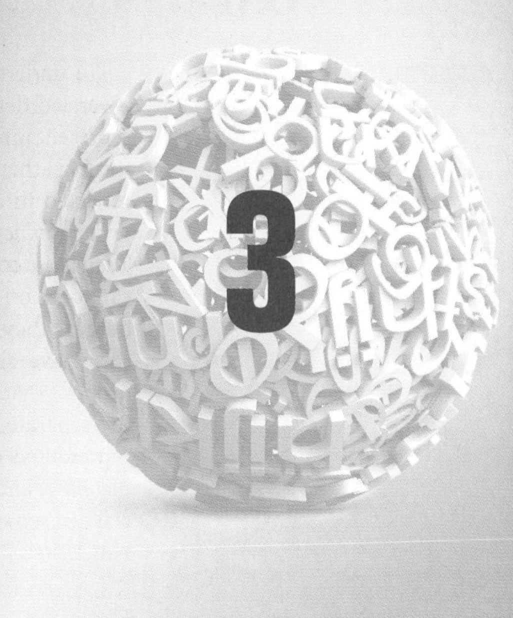

Polysynthetic languages go overboard … packing whole English sentences into a single word, as in Cayuga Ę̨skakhehǫna'táyę̨thwahs, *"I will plant potatoes for them again."*

NICHOLAS EVANS AND STEPHEN LEVINSON

One principle that guides traditional linguistic theories is that language consists of two components, a *lexicon* that captures information about words, their components and their meanings, and a grammar that lays out the principles governing how words can be combined into phrases and sentences. As the example above shows, this distinction between words and longer expressions generated by a grammar is not always as neat and tidy as it is in English. However, a great deal of word-processing theory has been built on the basis of English and other *analytic* languages, and a great deal can be learned by reviewing this research. So, let's put aside for the time being questions relating to more complex (but still very interesting) alternative systems.

This chapter will focus on the mental lexicon, what information it contains, and how that information is accessed and used in real time as people are trying to understand utterances. Big questions about words in language science include: How do we mentally represent word forms? How are those representations organized? How are word meanings represented in the mind? When we hear or see a word, how do we go about searching our memories for a matching form? What parts of the brain are involved in storing and accessing word meanings and what are the neural events that support word processing?

Introduction to Psycholinguistics: Understanding Language Science, First Edition.
Matthew J. Traxler.

To understand how words are represented and processed, we need to subject them to several different kinds of analysis. Separate kinds of analyses are required because we represent information about words in at least two distinct ways. First, we mentally represent the *form* that words take, the way they sound and the way they look. The way they sound is reflected in a *phonetic* or *phonological* code, and the way they look is represented in an *orthographic* code. We also represent the meaning that words convey, which is referred to as a *semantic* coding system. When we talk about how word representations are organized, we can focus on different kinds of mental representation. Words may be related to one another because they sound similar (gave–cave), because they look similar (wow–mow), or because they have similar meanings (horse–donkey). Prominent accounts of word processing propose that word forms are represented in *lexical networks* and word meanings are stored in a separate, but linked, *semantic memory* or *conceptual store*. To understand how words are represented and processed, we have to be clear whether we are talking about *form* or *meaning*, and we have to recognize that the mind represents these attributes in different ways in separate, but linked systems (Balota, Yap, & Cortese, 2006; Collins & Loftus, 1975; Hutchison, 2003; McClelland & Rumelhart, 1985).

The Anatomy of a Word: How We Mentally Represent Word Form

The analysis of word form starts with an analysis of subcomponents. Words are made up of parts. In the same way that we can analyze molecules as being made up of different kinds of atoms, and we can analyze atoms as being made up of different kinds of particles, so we can divide words up into their subcomponent parts. Different psychological and linguistic theories emphasize different aspects of words, and different theories make different claims about which parts of words have the biggest impact on mental processes that activate stored information about words, but classical linguistic theories regarding those parts provide a good way to organize our thinking about words.

Classical linguistic approaches to word form representation view words as involving a hierarchical arrangement of components. In speech, the lowest level of organization is the phonetic feature. Phonetic features, like place and manner of articulation, combine to produce the next level of organization, the phoneme. Phonemes can be combined to make up *bigrams* (pairs of phonemes) and *trigrams* (triplets), or we can think of combinations of phonemes as composing *syllables*, consonant–vowel (CV) or consonant–vowel–consonant (CVC) combinations. (CV and CVC combinations result from the fact that when we talk, we alternately open and close our jaws, starting and stopping the flow of air—we literally flap our jaws when we speak). Syllables themselves can be divided into *onsets* (the initial CV combination, like *spa* in *spam*) and *rimes* (the ending VC combination, like *am* in *spam*).

One or more speech sounds can combine to produce a *morpheme*—defined as the smallest unit in a language that can be assigned a meaning. One or more morphemes can be combined to produce a word. *Cat*, for instance, is a *monomorphemic* ("one morpheme") word because there is only one morpheme that makes up the word. Languages also combine morphemes to produce *polymorphemic* ("more than one morpheme") words, as in the compound word *blackboard* (some languages, like, Turkish, Finnish, and German are prolific combiners of morphemes).[1] Languages also provide ways of changing the flavor of a word meaning. We can alter the meaning of cat (a *singular* noun, used to refer to one animal) by adding a *bound morpheme*, *-s*, resulting in the polymorphemic word *cats* (a *plural* noun, used to refer to more than one animal).

Lexical Semantics

The whole point of having words in the language is that words can convey meaning from speaker to listener. How is that accomplished? To begin the discussion, we have to discriminate between two different definitions of the term *meaning*. When we talk about word meanings, we can differentiate between *sense* and *reference* (Jackendoff, 1983). *Sense* refers approximately to dictionary-like or encyclopedic knowledge that we have about words. So, for example, the word *cat* maps on to information about generic form and function. When we hear *cat* we can access the information that cats are mammals, they have fur, they are kept as pets, and so forth. When we hear *knife*, we think of metal objects used for cutting things. *Reference* is another form of meaning that words are involved in. When we use words to refer to people, objects, or ideas the words themselves have senses, but their specific meaning in a given context depends on what the words point to—what they *refer* to.

Consider the situation depicted in Figure 3.1. This mini-universe consists of two objects. If someone wants to direct your attention to one of the objects, she needs to craft an utterance that refers to that object. There is a very large (possibly infinite) number of different expressions one could use to point to either object. Each of these different expressions will have a different sense. Let's say our speaker chooses to refer to one of the objects as *The dark orange one*. The sense of the words *dark orange* helps the listener pick out the object on the left. So, the speaker could also have said, *The one on the left*. That expression picks out the same object as *the dark orange one* did, so it has the same referent, and in that way the two expressions "mean" the same thing—both expressions direct your attention toward the same object. But the two expressions have different senses—being dark orange is not the same thing as being on the left—and so the two expressions "mean" different things at the level of sense. Different expressions that have the same sense can have different referents in different contexts. If our speaker said, *The bigger one* in the context of Figure 3.1, that would point to the dark orange object. But if she said the same thing in the context of Figure 3.2, that would point to the pale orange object. We can talk about the meaning of a word by referring to the sense of the word; and we can talk about the meaning of a word by focusing on what the word refers to. Chapter 6 discusses reference in some detail, so this chapter will deal exclusively with the *sense* meaning of words. When this chapter talks about *semantics* or meaning, think "sense."

So how are word meanings (*senses*, that is) represented in the mental lexicon? And what research tools are appropriate to investigating word representations? One approach to investigating word meaning relies on introspection—thinking about word meanings and drawing conclusions from subjective experience. It seems plausible, based on introspection, that entries in the mental lexicon are close analogs to dictionary entries. If so, the lexical representation of a given word would incorporate information about its grammatical function (what category does it belong to, *verb*, *noun*, *adjective*, etc.), which determines how it can combine with other words (adverbs go with verbs, adjectives with nouns). Using

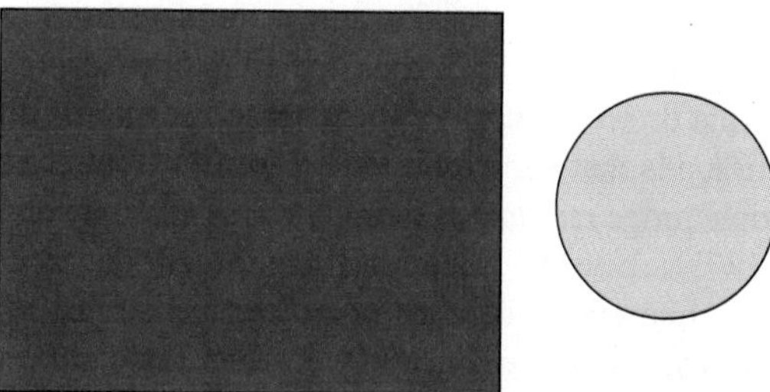

Figure 3.1 A two-object universe.

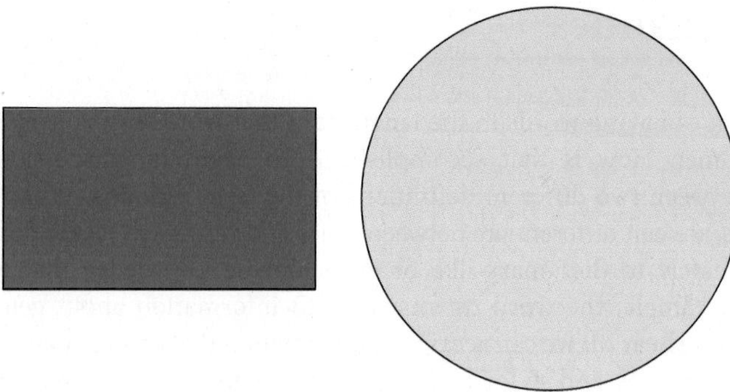

Figure 3.2 Another two-object universe.

words in this sense involves the assumption that individual words refer to *types*—that the core meaning of a word is a pointer to a completely interchangeable set of objects in the world (Gabora, Rosch, & Aerts, 2008). Each individual example of a category is a *token*. So, *team* is a type, and *Yankees*, *Twins*, and *Mudhens* are tokens of that type.[2]

If word meanings are types, how do we represent types? We could represent a given type by making a list of defining, necessary, or core characteristics. Some words seem to be easily represented by a small number of core, necessary features. "Bachelor," for example, seems to be well represented by combining the concepts "human," "adult," "male," and "unmarried." However, this apparent simplicity may be misleading. How about the concept "cat"? We could use its core features (e.g., "cat" = "cute and furry killing machine"). But we know an awful lot more than that about cats (they have claws, they see well at night, they cough up hairballs, they don't make good doorstops, you can't use them to iron your clothes, etc., etc.). The question then becomes, of all of the millions of things one could include in the dictionary entry under the word *cat*, which things get put in and which things get left out? Does the meaning of *cat* include the fact that it can breathe? Does it include the fact that it is larger than a tomato and smaller than an automobile? Probably not. But where do you draw the line? Which properties are prestored in long-term memory, and which are derived "on the fly"? What we really need to store to represent the meaning of the word *cat* is just its core or essential properties—those things that make up the essence of "cat" and that discriminate between cats and other kinds of things. In which case, we might store just features like "mammal, feline, pet, makes purring sound" and perhaps a visual image of a prototypical cat. This approach runs into trouble very quickly, however, as many fairly easy to understand concepts do not have consistent, core properties across different versions of the concept. Even apparently simple concepts like "bachelor" run into trouble (Pinker, 1994). Are monks bachelors? Not really, but they certainly are human, adult, male, and unmarried. The concept described by the word *game* is fairly common, and different activities are fairly easy to categorize as games, but there does not appear to be a single feature or combination of features that is consistent across all of the things we identify as being a game (Gabora et al., 2008; Murphy & Medin, 1985). So, if the concept "game" does not have any necessary or common features, what do we list under properties in the mental dictionary entry for the word *game*? Another issue is that some referents seem to be better examples of a category than others. Most people judge *red hair* as being a worse example of the word *red* than *fire engine red* (Rosch, 1973). If word meanings are based on types made up of fully interchangeable tokens, then every instance of *red* should be just as good as every other instance of *red*. But real words and the concepts they refer to do not seem to have necessary, core, or defining features (some tokens are better than others), and many categories are a bit "fuzzy" or vague—it is not clear where exactly one category stops and another one begins.

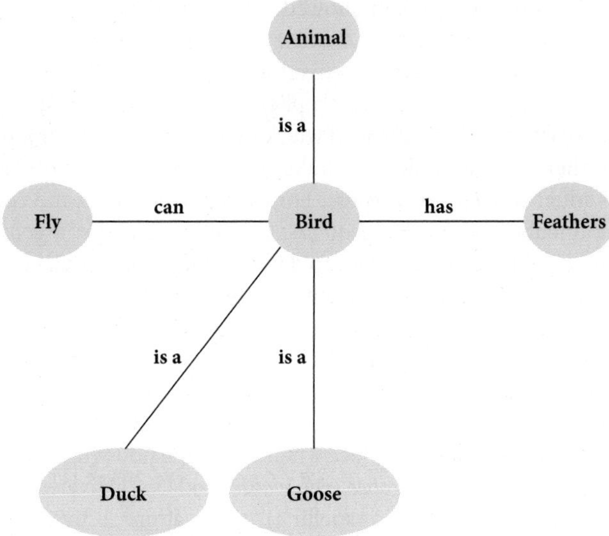

Figure 3.3 A piece of a semantic network.

These are the kinds of problems that have led many language scientists to abandon the "defining" or "core" features approach to lexical semantics. Until someone comes up with a much better categorization scheme, dictionary-definition-like entries do not seem to be a good way of explaining how word meanings are represented in the mental lexicon.

One way to sidestep problems associated with the dictionary entry theory of semantics is to operationalize word meanings as reflecting collections of associated concepts. According to this type of account, a word meaning is defined as "whatever comes to mind when someone says the word." This approach, exemplified by *semantic network* theory (Collins & Loftus, 1975; Collins & Quillian, 1972; see also Rips, Shoben & Smith, 1973; Smith, Shoben, & Rips, 1974), has been the dominant theory in artificial intelligence approaches to semantics for the past 30 years (see Ober & Shenaut, 2006, for a review; related approaches include Ken McRae's feature-based semantic nets; McRae & Boisvert, 1998; McRae, Cree, Seidenberg, & McNorgan, 2005; McRae, de Sa, & Seidenberg, 1997). The goal of semantic network theory is to explain how word meanings are encoded in the mental lexicon and to explain certain patterns of behavior that people exhibit when responding to words.

Semantic network theory proposes that a word's meaning is represented by a set of *nodes* and the *links* between them (as in Figure 3.3). The nodes represent concepts whose meaning the network is trying to capture, and the links represent relationships between concepts. For example, the concept *goose* would be represented as an address in memory (a node) connected to other addresses in memory by different kinds of links. One of the important kinds of links in semantic network theory is the "*is a*" type. The *is a* link encodes relationships between general categories and the concepts that fall within the category. So, *goose* would be connected to the *waterfowl* node with a unidirectional *is a* link (representing the concept that *a goose is a waterfowl*). The *waterfowl* category node could be connected to many different instances (*duck*, *goose*, *coot*, *swan*, *seagull*, and so forth), and could in turn be connected to a superordinate category node, like *bird*, with yet another *is a* link. According to this view, subordinate concepts, like *goose*, inherit the properties of superordinate nodes via transitive inference (a goose is a waterfowl, a waterfowl is a bird, therefore a goose is a bird). This means that there is no need to directly connect the specific concept *goose* to the more general concept *bird*, and this helps conserve memory resources.

In early work, Collins and Quillian showed that statements such as *A canary can fly* primed responses to statements such as *A canary is a bird*. The explanation for this effect was that reading *A canary can fly* caused activation to spread from *canary is a bird* to *a bird can fly*. So hearing *A canary can fly* entails implicitly activating the relationship *a canary is a bird*, and that property is already activated when subjects read *a canary is a bird* (Collins & Quillian, 1970). Other kinds of nodes and links are used to represent other properties and attributes of individual concepts, like *goose*. For example, *has* links and *can* links connect concepts to components (a *goose has feathers*, *a beak*, and *wings*; a *goose can fly*). The meaning of a word, on this account, is captured by the pattern of activated nodes and links. The meaning of *goose* is based on the concepts that goose is connected to, and the kinds of links that form the connections.

The idea of *spreading activation* is used to explain how information represented in the semantic network is accessed, and why words that are related to one another facilitate access to one another (Collins & Loftus, 1975; Posner & Snyder, 1975). Spreading activation is a hypothetical mental process that takes place when one of the nodes in the semantic network is activated. So, if someone says, *goose*, the *goose* node is activated by the matching phonological (sound) or orthographic (spelling) information. Activation from the *goose* node then spreads to nodes that are connected to it. So, activating *goose* causes activation to spread to the superordinate node, *bird*, and to the attributes connected to *bird*, *has wings*, *has feathers*, and *can fly*. Spreading activation has two important properties: (a) It is automatic. It happens very fast and we can not control it. (b) It diminishes the further it has to go. Like ripples in a pond, nodes that are directly connected to *goose* are strongly and quickly activated when you see or hear *goose*; and more distantly connected nodes are less strongly and less quickly activated, and beyond a couple of degrees of separation, no changes in activation should occur.

The two proposed properties of spreading activation help explain how people respond during *priming* tasks. *Priming* occurs when presenting one stimulus at time 1 helps people respond to another stimulus at time 2. In classic work on word processing, people respond faster in *lexical decision* and *naming* experiments when a target word like *duck* is preceded by a related word like *goose*, compared to a control condition where *duck* is preceded by an unrelated word like *horse* (Meyer & Schvaneveldt, 1971, 1976; Moss, Ostrin, Tyler, & Marslen-Wilson, 1995). This kind of priming is referred to as *semantic priming*. Semantic network theory explains semantic priming as resulting from the spread of activation in the

A number of experimental tasks are used to investigate word processing. Two of the most common ones are *lexical decision* and *naming*. In the lexical decision task, people are presented with lists of stimuli, either auditorily or visually on a computer screen. Some of the stimuli are real words, like *cat*, *dog*, *bachelor*, and some are not, like *wat*, *rog*, and *lachenor*. The individual's task is to indicate, as quickly as possible, whether the stimulus is a word or not. The idea is that, if you have an entry in your mental dictionary that corresponds to the stimulus, you will say "yes," otherwise you will say "no," and the amount of time it takes you to respond is an index of how easy it was to access the word's entry in the lexicon. *Naming* also (usually) involves lists of words, but it is not necessary to present non-words, and you respond by saying the word out loud as quickly as you can. Here again, the idea is that the amount of time it takes you to say the target word measures how long it takes you to access the lexicon and find the word you are trying to say (see Balota et al., 2006; Potts, Keenan, & Golding, 1988).

semantic network. Because *duck* and *goose* have many attributes in common, activating one of the concepts necessarily leads to substantial activation in the set of properties that makes up the meaning of the other concept. So, if you hear *goose*, you activate *waterfowl*, *bird*, *feathers*, and *can fly*. When you subsequently hear *duck*, those pre-activated concepts support the naming or lexical decision response (you have to wait for a shorter period of time for the network to activate the parts of the network that represent the concept *duck*). When you hear the prime word *horse*, activation spreads to closely connected nodes, but activation dies away before it reaches the part of the network that represents concepts related to *duck*. So, when you hear *horse* before the target word *duck*, the pattern of activation representing the meaning of the word *duck* starts from zero (or *normal resting activation*), it takes the network longer to activate the appropriate bits, and your behavioral response is correspondingly slower. Faster response time to primed words is also associated with decreased neural activity when a target word is preceded by a related prime word compared to when it is preceded by an unrelated word (e.g., Kuperberg, Lakshmanan, Greve, & West, 2008; Rissman, Eliassen, & Blumstein, 2003; Wagner, Desmond, Demb, Glover, & Gabrieli, 1997).

Spreading activation is thought to diminish substantially beyond one or two links in the network. Evidence for this comes from *mediated priming* studies involving pairs of words like *lion–stripes*. The word *lion* is related to the word *stripes* through the mediating word *tiger* (*lion* is associated with *tiger*, *tiger* is associated with *stripes*). When you hear *lion*, activation spreads to *tiger*. When *tiger* gets activated, it should cause activation to spread to *stripes*. If so, then *lion* should prime your response to the word *stripes*. In fact, hearing or reading the word *lion* does lead to a small priming effect for the word *stripes*, so activation does spread beyond directly connected concepts (such as *lion* and *tiger*). But if activation can spread beyond immediately connected nodes, what prevents activation from spreading all over the network? If it did, nearly everything in the network would be activated every time you heard any word.[3] According to semantic network theory, what prevents activation spreading all over the network is that the total amount of activation that can be spread is limited. So, nodes directly connected to the prime word are strongly activated, but less directly connected nodes are less strongly activated, with activation diminishing with increasing distance in the network. And, in fact, *lion* primes *stripes* much less than it primes the directly related word *tiger*, as predicted by diminishing spread of activation with distance (Balota & Lorch, 1986; de Groot, 1983; McNamara & Altarriba, 1988).

The hypothetical mental process of spreading activation is thought to be automatic, and behavioral evidence suggests that word-to-word associations are activated quickly, without conscious effort, and outside of our control. In Jim Neely's (1977) study, people were told to expect a particular kind of word after they heard a category label. The category label might be something like *body part*, but the subjects were told that words referring to birds would follow the cue *body part*. If people can control the activation of concepts, then they should focus their attention on birds immediately after they hear or see the cue *body part*. If people can control the spread of activation, concepts related to *body part* (like *arm*, *leg*, *hand*) should not be primed, and members of the expected category *birds* should be primed. When Neely tested people's responses to expected (bird) targets immediately after the cue *body part*, there was no priming. But the unexpected, body part names (*arm*, *leg*, *hand*) were primed. If a delay (a couple hundred milliseconds) intervened between the time when the cue (*body part*) appeared and the expected target appeared, then priming for bird names did occur. Neely explained this by proposing that, when people get the cue (*body part*) they strategically think up a short list of bird names that they might hear. It takes time to come up with this list, so there is no priming for birds right away, but later on when the list has been generated, there is a good chance that the target word will be on the generated list, and this speeds up the response. The pattern of response (immediate, fast reaction to body parts;

delayed priming of bird names) is consistent with two processes: fast, automatic activation spreading from the cue to related concepts and slower, non-automatic (strategic) attention shift to a short list of likely bird names. The existence of fast, automatic spreading activation and a slower strategic modulation of word activation levels is also supported by data showing that some aphasic patients appear to have intact automatic priming, but impaired strategic priming. In experiments with short lags between primes and targets, these aphasic patients show normal levels of priming, but at longer lags, no priming is observed (Hagoort, 1997; Ostrin & Tyler, 1993).

According to semantic network theory, words are related to one another by virtue of having links to shared nodes. *Duck* and *goose* both connect to the *bird* node, the *feathers* node, and so forth. Two words can prime one another because they have similar representations due to shared nodes. This leads to the kinds of priming effects described above and also influences what happens to semantic knowledge when the brain is damaged (e.g., Moss, Tyler, Durrant-Peatfield, and Bunn, 1998). Two words can also be related to one another, whether they share nodes or not, if the two words co-occur in the language. So *police* and *jail* will prime one another, not because police officers resemble jails or vice versa, but because the two words appear together often, and so the presence of one of the pair may be used to predict the appearance of the other in the near future (as in classical conditioning theory; Skinner, 1957). One of the challenges in word-processing research is to determine whether priming effects (like *duck–goose* priming) result from sharing nodes in a network, which is the classical view of semantic priming, or whether priming occurs simply because words co-occur, whether they share features of meaning (like *doctor–nurse*) or not (like *police–jail*). Although the degree of priming that is observed in an experiment depends critically on what kinds of tasks are used and how stimuli are displayed, robust priming is observed for pairs of words that are associated with one another (Moss et al., 1995; Perea & Gotor, 1997; Shelton & Martin, 1992). Priming is harder to detect when pairs of words share elements of meaning, but are not associated, especially when the semantic relationship consists of belonging to the same general category (like *animal* or *clothing*). So, although *pig* and *horse* come from the same category (*animal*, or even more specifically *farm animal*), the priming between *horse* and *pig* is more fragile than between pairs of words that have an associative relationship (like *dog* and *cat*).[4]

There is an ongoing discussion in language science about whether purely semantic relationships (*horse–pig*) produce priming effects in tasks that tap automatic meaning activation, but there is a growing consensus that associative priming and semantic priming are governed by different mechanisms. Recent ERP evidence supports this conclusion. Sinéad Rhodes and David Donaldson (2008) conducted an experiment where they showed subjects pairs of words that were only associatively related (fountain–pen), semantically and associatively related (dog–cat), only semantically associated (bread–cereal), or unrelated (beard–tower). They found that the purely semantically related pairs evoked a neural response in the brain that was the same as the response evoked by unrelated pairs of words. Associatively related pairs decreased the magnitude of the N400 effect,[5] whether the pairs also had a semantic relationship or not (see Figure 3.4). Recent behavioral and neuropsychological studies also suggest that people respond differently to association than they do to semantic relatedness. People respond to association more quickly than they respond to semantic relatedness (Perea & Rosa, 2002). Alzheimer's dementia patients also show priming for associatively related words, but not for semantically related pairs like *bread–cereal* that are not otherwise associated (Glosser & Friedman, 1991; Glosser, Grugan, Friedman, Lee, & Grossman, 1998; Ober, Shenaut, & Reed, 1995).

Concepts that co-occur more often in real life can become more strongly connected in the semantic network. As Perea and Rosa (2002, p. 189) explain, "the terms for things frequently connected in experience become themselves connected in the mental lexicon."

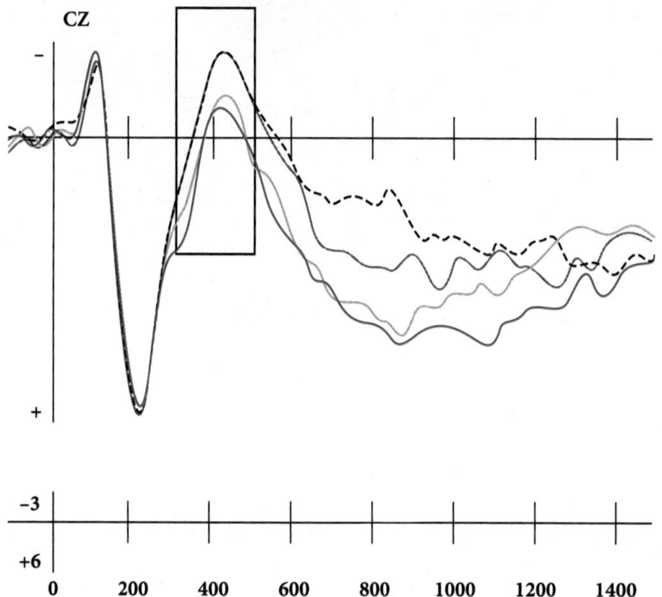

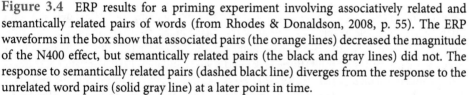

Figure 3.4 ERP results for a priming experiment involving associatively related and semantically related pairs of words (from Rhodes & Donaldson, 2008, p. 55). The ERP waveforms in the box show that associated pairs (the orange lines) decreased the magnitude of the N400 effect, but semantically related pairs (the black and gray lines) did not. The response to semantically related pairs (dashed black line) diverges from the response to the unrelated word pairs (solid gray line) at a later point in time.

These patterns of connectivity between different words have been shown to affect how easy it is to remember words. *Connectivity* reflects how many words are associated with a specific target word, and how many connections are shared between that set of words (see Figure 3.5). Some words have few associates, and those associates have few connections between them. Those words have *low connectivity. High connectivity* words have more associates, and those associates have more connections between them. In Figure 3.5, *dog* is low in connectivity and *dinner* is high. High connectivity words are easier to remember than low connectivity words in both cued and free recall (Nelson, Bennett, Gee, Schreiber, & McKinney, 1993; see also Breedin, Saffran, & Schwartz, 1998; Mirman & Magnuson, 2008). High connectivity words also produce different patterns of brain activity in the temporal lobes than low connectivity words (Pexman, Hargreaves, Edwards, Henry, & Goodyear, 2007; Wible et al., 2006). Thus, the structure of the associations in semantic memory affects the degree to which processing one word facilitates processing of a subsequent word, memory for individual words, and the brain's response to different words.

Associationist accounts of word meaning: HAL and LSA

Whether "pure" automatic semantic priming exists or not, associative relations seem to play a powerful role in how people respond to words, which suggests that associative relations

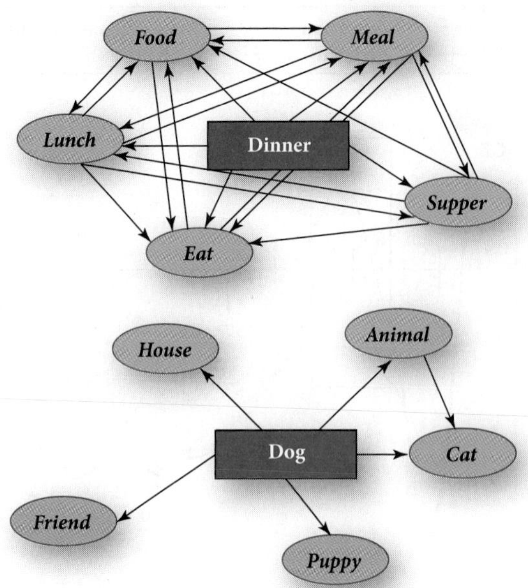

Figure 3.5 Connectivity for *dinner* and *dog* (from Nelson et al., 1993, p. 748)

are encoded in the lexical representation of word form, meaning, or both. There are some mathematical models of semantic memory that place great emphasis on pure association, the extent to which words co-occur in utterances, and propose that this is the basis upon which word meanings are built (Burgess & Lund, 1997; Landauer, 1999; Landauer & Dumais, 1997; Landauer, Foltz, & Laham, 1998; Lund & Burgess, 1996). Two prominent models of this type have been developed in the past decade or so, Burgess and Lund's *Hyperspace Analog to Language (HAL)*[6] and Landauer and Dumais' *Latent Semantic Analysis (LSA)*. (You can explore how LSA works for yourself at http://lsa.colorado.edu.) According to HAL and LSA, a word's meaning is determined by the words that it appears with. If two words appear together more than they appear with other words, then the meanings of those two words are highly related. To determine whether two words are related in this way, HAL and LSA both depend on *corpora*,[7] which are large collections of utterances, which ideally reflect random, representative samples of the utterances that appear in the language as a whole. HAL's corpus included over 200 million words that were taken from USENET, an internet resource that has chat groups on a wide range of topics. HAL tracks 70,000 different words and uses its corpus data to determine how likely it is that each word will appear in the same utterance as each other word. For each word pair, HAL assigns a co-occurrence value based on how close the two words are, up to a distance of 10 words. Words that appear adjacent to one another get a score of 10. Words that are separated by one word get a score of 9, and so forth. At the end of this process, HAL has a 70,000 by 70,000 matrix that reflects word-to-word co-occurrence. A word's meaning is defined as the pattern of values in each of the cells in the matrix for each word. So each word has 140,000 numbers assigned to it, and the pattern of numbers, the *vector*, is the word's meaning.

LSA's original corpus included almost five million words that were taken from an encyclopedia. LSA divided its corpus into 30,000 episodes, and assessed the number of times each one of 60,000 words appeared in each episode. LSA, like HAL, starts with a matrix. But unlike HAL, LSA assesses the relationship between a word and a number of contexts or episodes, rather than directly measuring co-occurrence between different words. In LSA, a word that appears many times in episodes 1 and 29,000 would get a high number in those two cells. Once the cell values have been assigned, LSA subjects them to a form of factor analysis that captures commonalities in patterns of co-occurrences between words and episodes. Instead of 30,000 individual values being assigned to each word, factor analysis reduces the number of values to about 300. Similar to HAL, a word's meaning is represented in LSA as a pattern of values (a vector) across the 300 dimensions.

HAL and LSA use different methods to assess the degree to which words co-occur, but they have in common the ideas that semantic representations incorporate a large number of dimensions (hundreds, in fact) and that word meanings can be described as vectors across those large numbers of dimensions. HAL has been used successfully to model priming effects in lexical decision (Lund, Burgess, & Atchley, 1995) as well as how people categorize words (Burgess & Lund, 1997). LSA has successfully modeled judgments of semantic similarity (saying whether two words are synonyms or not), aspects of children's vocabulary development (Landauer & Dumais, 1997), and judgments about the quality of text summaries (Kintsch et al., 2000; León, Olmos, & Escudero, 2006). A similar high-dimensional model of word meanings has been used successfully to predict which brain regions will become most activated in response to a particular word (Mitchell et al., 2008).

One of the advantages of high-dimensional co-occurrence approaches to semantics is that they avoid some of the problems associated with the feature-based approach to word meaning. We can ask people to list features of objects, and we can use those lists of features to predict reaction times and similarity judgments. On this account, semantic similarity is a function of the number of overlapping semantic features—words with more features in common have more similar meanings. But there is (currently) no objective way to decide whether the mental representation of a word actually includes all and only the features that people list when we ask them to introspect about words, and feature-based representational theories can always be modified to include new features in the face of unexpected experimental results, which makes such accounts difficult to falsify (Buchanan, Westbury, & Burgess, 2001). LSA and HAL get around the problem of subjectivity in feature descriptions by doing away with subjective feature descriptions altogether. Their methods of calculating semantic similarity are entirely objective and, hence, replicable and falsifiable.

The symbol grounding problem

Although HAL and LSA make good predictions for similarity judgments and some aspects of categorization, some language scientists are not comfortable with the idea that meaning depends entirely on word-to-word associations, whether based on simple co-occurrence or mathematically transformed co-occurrence. The chief among these objections also applies to semantic network theory. As explained by Art Glenberg and others (e.g., Glenberg & Robertson, 2000; Harnad, 1990; Zwaan & Rapp, 2006), co-occurrence and association are not sufficient, by themselves, to describe word meanings, because associationist approaches like HAL and LSA merely describe mappings, albeit highly complex mappings, between symbols. Unless those symbols are *grounded* in some set of representations outside the symbol system, the symbols cannot be assigned any meaning.

There are different versions of this position. One of them is John Searle's *Chinese Room* argument (Searle, 1980). Searle asks you to imagine being an English speaker in a small room with two slots in it, a rule book, and a stack of cards that have Chinese characters printed on them. You speak no Chinese and you do not know the meanings of any Chinese characters, but you do have a rule book that tells you what to do. When a Chinese character comes in one slot, you consult the rule book which tells you to pick some other characters out of your stack and push them out the other slot. If you have the correct rule book, you can respond perfectly appropriately, and your behavior would be entirely compatible with a

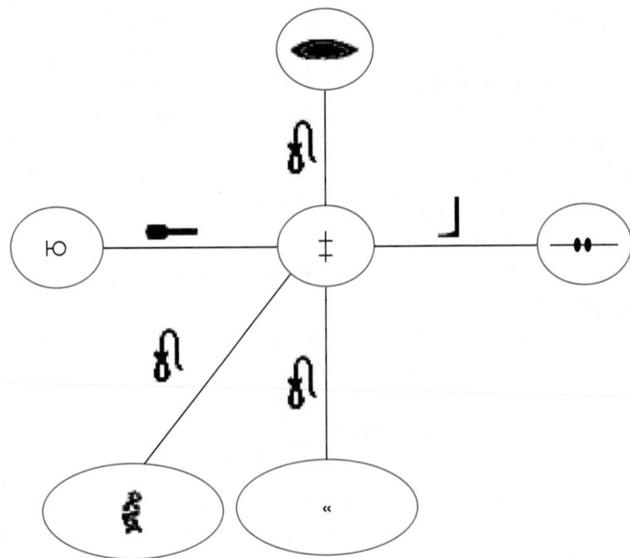

Figure 3.6 A hypothetical "semantic" network.

native speaker of Chinese. So, if the characters coming in said "two plus two equals?", you could consult the rule book, and it would tell you to pick out the character that goes with "four." People from the outside would think that whoever is in the box understands every statement perfectly. But actually, you do not understand anything, you are just responding to symbols based on what the rule book says you should do. So, you can respond to symbols, but to you, those symbols have no meaning. The symbols could just as well have been, "Ю," "₣," "◙," and "‡," and your response (as dictated by the rule book) could have been "«." Until we *ground* those symbols in something other than more symbols, they have no semantic content, and hence no meaning.

Here's another way of looking at the *grounding* problem. Let's go back to our semantic network model for a moment. According to semantic network theory, the meaning of *goose* is based on a pattern of activation among a group of nodes associated with *goose* via links in the network. We understand what the *goose* node represents by seeing what nodes it is connected to, and what kinds of links connect the different nodes. But how do we understand the nodes that are connected to *goose*? We understand the meaning of those nodes by seeing what nodes they are connected to, and what kinds of links connect the different nodes. But how do we understand *those* nodes? By seeing what nodes they are connected to … you get the idea.[8] The argument is equivalent to the *Chinese Room* case. Unless the symbols in the semantic network (or primitive feature network or high-dimensional-analog-to-language network) are connected to something other than abstract symbols, they can have no meanings. We might as well replace the labels in the semantic network with those in Figure 3.6. Or (as Art Glenberg put it many years ago), those in Figure 3.7.

Embodied semantics

How can the grounding problem be solved? One answer that has been gaining steam in the recent past is the *embodiment* or *embodied semantics* approach to meaning. Embodied semantics argues that abstract symbols or groups of symbols, like words, carry meaning because those symbols are tied to representations outside of the (traditionally defined) linguistic system. Specifically, words are tied to representations that we build using our

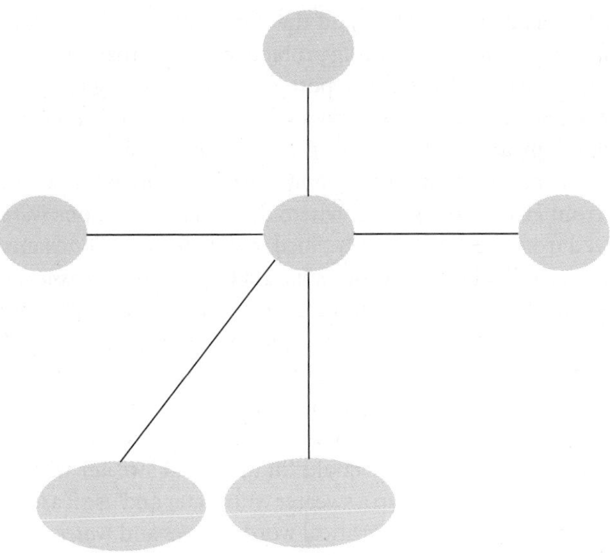

Figure 3.7 Another hypothetical "semantic" network.

perceptual apparatus (our five senses: vision, hearing, touch, taste, and smell). In that way, words do not just activate patterns of abstract symbols, words evoke perceptual experiences with real-world objects. When someone says *cat*, you do not just "think" "Ю ₣ ◙ ‡", you model the features of actual cats using the same apparatus that you use to perceive a real-live, flesh-and-blood kitty. Glenberg and Robertson (2000) refer to this principle as the *indexical hypothesis.*

According to the indexical hypothesis, establishing a word's meaning requires three processes. First, the word must be tied or *indexed* to actual objects in the world or analog representations of those objects in the mind (the *projected world* in Jackendoff's, 1983, terminology; see also Zwaan, Madden, Yaxley, & Aveyard, 2004). *Analog* representations are contrasted with *abstract* representations, in that analog representations carry some of the features of the actual object itself (Kosslyn, 1973; Stevens & Coupe, 1978). For example, a picture of a horse is an analog representation of a horse. The same information can be captured in an *abstract* way in a JPG file as a sequence of zeroes and ones. Glenberg refers to the analog mental representations of real-world objects as *perceptual symbols*, which implies that people have the ability to mentally manipulate these symbols as appropriate in the context that the utterance provides (Barsalou, 1999). In the second step, people "use the indexed object or perceptual symbol to derive affordances" (Glenberg & Robertson, 2000, p. 384). The idea of *affordances* comes from the work of J. J. Gibson, a prominent theoretician and researcher in the area of perception. *Affordances* are determined by the interaction of our perceptual abilities and the physical characteristics of our bodies and the physical properties of objects in the world. For example, what makes a chair a chair is that the combination of our bodies' physical properties and the chair's physical properties allows us to use the chair for sitting—the chair *affords* sitting. (Chairs' physical properties provide other affordances as well. A chair can be used for self-defense in a bar fight. It can be used to raise the body and retrieve snacks from the high shelf, and so forth.) The third process in creating meaning from utterances is to *mesh* or combine the affordances of the different indexed objects and characters in the utterance. When we interpret utterances, we index words to real-world objects by activating perceptual symbols, and the combinations of perceptual symbols determine what actions are available, how objects and actors might interact, and therefore what events are possible or likely.

The embodied semantics approach, and the indexical hypothesis in particular, offer a potential solution to the symbol grounding problem, but does that mean that the hypothesis is actually correct? We can evaluate the hypothesis by contrasting predictions made by the indexical hypothesis with predictions generated from the high-dimension co-occurrence approaches to word meaning. To do so, Glenberg and Robertson (2000) constructed scenarios where critical objects were *not* good fits to the context based on co-occurrence metrics derived from HAL and LSA, but where the described actions *were* consistent with affordances derived from the situation described in the scenario. For example, subjects read this context sentence (Glenberg & Robertson, 2000, p. 385): *Marissa forgot to bring her pillow on her camping trip.* Subjects would then read one of two continuations. One of the continuations included a word that matched the affordances generated by the situation; and the other continuation did not. The afforded continuation was, *As a substitute for her pillow, she filled up an old sweater with* ***leaves****.* The non-afforded continuation was, *As a substitute for her pillow, she filled up an old sweater with* ***water****. Leaves* matches the affordances of the described situation (because you really could fill up an old sweater with leaves), but *water* does not (because you really can't fill up a sweater with water and use it as a pillow). Critically, the LSA association values for the two critical words, *leaves* and *water*, in the context of the preceding text are the same. According to LSA, both continuations are equally meaningful and good. When people were asked to judge the plausibility of the two continuations, though, they rated the afforded continuation as being much better than the non-afforded continuation. In this case, the indexical hypothesis, but not the high-dimensional symbol association approach, accurately predicted how people would judge the meaning of the sentences.

Since the original work on the indexical hypothesis was published, a number of other studies have pointed toward a relationship between the linguistic–semantic system and perceptual and motor systems that have been traditionally viewed as outside the language system. The indexical hypothesis, and related approaches, view the perceptual and motor systems as providing some of the machinery that creates meaning within the linguistic system. But apart from off-line judgment tasks like Glenberg and Robertson's (2000), is there any evidence that the semantic system and these other perceptual and motor systems are linked? In fact, there is growing evidence that they are.

In one study, participants made plausibility judgments (i.e., "Yes or no, does this statement make sense?") after reading statements like *He opened the drawer*, and *He closed the drawer* (Glenberg & Kaschak, 2002). The experimenters manipulated whether subjects responded by moving their hand away from their body to press a key, or instead moved their hand toward their own body. In some conditions, the sentences implied motion toward the body (opening a drawer means you pull the drawer towards yourself) or away from the body (closing a drawer indicates motion away from yourself). The subjects' answers could be made with a body movement that was either the same as the motion implied by the sentence (move your hand away from yourself to answer "yes"; the sentence says *He closed the drawer*), or the subjects could answer with a body movement that was opposite to that indicated in the sentence (move your hand away to answer "yes" to *He opened the drawer*). In this experiment, subjects' responses were faster when the motion undertaken to answer the question matched the motion indicated by the sentence. Why did this happen? According to the embodied semantics position, people understand the meaning of expressions like *open/close the drawer* by indexing the words to perceptual symbols (mental models of the objects), and then mentally simulating the action indicated by the sentence. To mentally simulate the action in the sentence, you use the same motor system that you use to move your actual body. So, your physical response to the question uses the same resource that you use to figure out the meaning of the sentence—the motor system. If word meanings were based on arbitrary and abstract networks of symbols, there is no reason why language

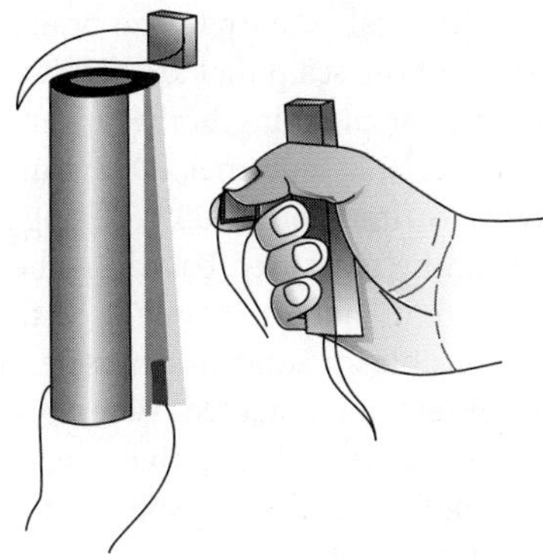

Figure 3.8 The input device used by Tucker & Ellis (2001, p. 776). Power grip responses were made with the larger component. Precision grip responses were made with the smaller component.

should have any effect on your body movements. If meaning is governed entirely by abstract symbol systems, you should respond just as quickly no matter what direction you need to move your hand.

Early work on the relationship between motor and semantic/conceptual systems revealed that responses to a word speeded up when people's hands were shaped like they would be if they were actually using the named object, such as a pen or a knife (Klatzky, Pellegrino, McCloskey, & Doherty, 1989; see also Lieberman, 2000; Setola & Reilly, 2005). Thus, action in the motor system can facilitate response to a word. Additional work in this line provides further evidence that individual word meanings and motor responses interact (Tucker & Ellis, 2001, 2004; see also Buccino et al., 2005; Zwaan & Taylor, 2006). One kind of study capitalizes on the fact that we interact with some objects using a *precision* grip—like pens, silverware, and buttons. We interact with other objects using a *power* grip—like hammers, baseball bats, and shovels. Figure 3.8 shows a device that Tucker and Ellis invented to record subjects' responses when they were showed words or pictures of objects. A power grip was used to trigger the larger of the two components, and a precision grip was used to trigger the smaller one. The subjects' task was to read words presented one by one on a computer screen and judge as quickly as possible whether the object was natural or man-made (this is a kind of *semantic categorization* task). Half of the participants made their response by using a power grip, and half made their response by using a precision grip. Subjects in the power-grip response condition responded faster to words describing power-grip objects, like rakes and shovels, and slower to words describing precision grip objects, like pens and forks. Subjects in the precision-grip response condition showed the opposite pattern, responding faster to pens and forks and slower to baseball bats and shovels. Further experimental evidence showed that the word–motor connection goes in the other direction as well—word processing has an effect on the motor system. When people make a motor movement at the same time as they are reading an action-related word, motor movements are slowed down. But if people read the same words *before* they begin moving, movements are speeded up (Boulenger et al., 2006). These results can be explained if we assume that part of a word's meaning includes a mental simulation of the object, and that these mental simulations involve modeling how you typically move as you interact with the object.

The word–action compatibility effects just described suggest a close relationship between a system of meanings and the motor system that we use to move ourselves around and interact with objects in the world. The results of some ERP experiments and *transcranial magnetic stimulation* (TMS) experiments support this view as well. In ERP studies that endeavor to locate the source of electrical activity in the brain, the strongest response to action–word stimuli occurs at parts of the scalp that are directly over the motor strip—the part of the brain that is responsible for planning body movements (Hauk, Johnsrude, & Pülvermüller, 2004; Pulvermüller, Harle, & Hummel, 2001; Pulvermüller, Lutzenberger, & Preissl, 1999; Pulvermüller, Shtyrov, & Ilmoniemi, 2005).[9] Using a technique similar to ERP, *motor evoked potentials* (MEPs) can be measured based on the activity at *neuromuscular junctions*—the places where efferent nerves connect with skeletal muscle tissue. Neuromuscular junctions are responsible for activating muscles in response to signals from the brain, which is how body movements are executed. When people listen to sentences that describe hand-related actions (like sewing), MEP activity measured above hand muscles decreases, but foot muscles are unaffected. When people listen to sentences about foot-related actions, the opposite pattern occurs (Buccino et al., 2005). Finally, when Parkinson's dementia patients were tested, they showed reduced priming for action-related words but normal priming for other kinds of words when they were *not* taking medication that improves motor function. When the patients were on medication that boosts motor function, the differences in amount of priming between action words and non-action words disappeared (Boulenger et al., 2008).

In TMS experiments, a powerful magnetic field is generated very close to the scalp (see Plate 1), which can induce electrical activity in populations of neurons directly beneath the TMS device. TMS-induced neural activity can facilitate the mental processes that are involved in information processing (perhaps by synchronizing neural activity in a population of neurons involved in the task), and so TMS can be used to assess the extent to which different parts of the brain are involved in different aspects of language processing. In one such TMS study, people made lexical decisions in response to words that were related either to arm movements or leg movements (Pulvermüller, Hauk, Nikulin, & Illmoniemi, 2005). The words were presented in writing on a computer screen and 100 ms after the words appeared on the computer screen, TMS was applied either over parts of the motor cortex involved in hand movements or parts involved in leg movements. In a control condition, *sham* (fake) TMS was applied to make sure that any effects were not due to demand characteristics of the experimental task. As illustrated in Figure 3.9, TMS speeded lexical decisions to words related to the part of the body controlled by the part of motor cortex that was stimulated. When arm areas were stimulated, lexical decisions to arm-related words were made more quickly.

Semantic processing of words is thought to be strongly left lateralized, and in this study TMS affected responses to words when it was applied over the left hemisphere, but not when it was applied over the right. Sham (fake) stimulation also had no effect, which rules out demand characteristics as the source of the reaction-time effects. Other TMS studies produced comparable results. For example, Oliveri and colleagues used TMS to show that motor cortex responds more strongly to action-related nouns and verbs (*the axe, to bite*) than to nouns and verbs that do not have specific associated actions (*the cloud, to belong*) (Oliveri et al., 2004).

fMRI investigations of the relationship between word processing and the motor system have capitalized on the fact that the motor system is organized such that different parts of the brain are responsible for controlling different parts of the body. In the motor strip, the parts of the brain that control hand movements are distinct from the parts of the brain that control leg movements, face movement is controlled by different brain regions than arm movement, and so on. If there is a close connection between the linguistic–semantic system and the motor system, and if the semantic system "borrows" parts of the motor system to instantiate the meanings of particular words, then different kinds of words should produce different patterns of activation in the motor system. When fMRI was used to determine where activity in the brain occurred in response to words that refer to movements of

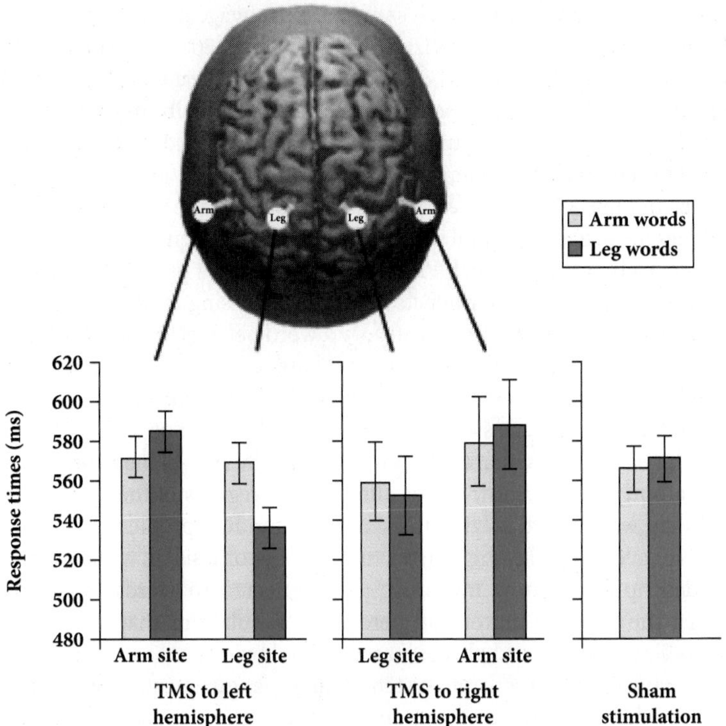

Figure 3.9 TMS and lexical decisions (from Pulvermüller, Hauk, Nikulin, & Ilmoniemi, 2005, p. 795). The top picture shows where TMS was applied in the left and right hemispheres. Response times on the lexical decision task appear below the brain. Left-hemisphere stimulation affected lexical decision latencies, but right-hemisphere stimulation did not. In the left hemisphere, arm words were responded to more quickly following TMS over the part of the motor cortex that controls arm movements. A similar effect was observed for leg-related words after leg-area stimulation. Sham TMS had no effect.

the face (*smile*), arm (*throw*), or leg (*walk*), increased activity was observed in "classical" language areas, like *Wernicke's* area (at the junction of the parietal, occipital, and temporal lobes in the left hemisphere) and *Broca's* area (in the left frontal lobe, just in front of the motor strip) (Hauk et al., 2004), but increased activity was observed in other brain areas as well. The neural response to words referring to body movements was compared to brain activity that occurred when subjects actually moved the corresponding body part (see Plate 2). The striking result here is that words related to actions led to increased neural activity in the same parts of the brain that became active when subjects actually moved the corresponding body part. This result is consistent with the embodied semantics view that word processing involves the activation of perceptual–motor representations. Listening to sentences describing face, arm, and leg actions produces a similar pattern of activation, with areas of motor and premotor cortex activated to different degrees by face-, arm-, and leg-related action sentences (Tettamanti et al., 2005). Reading sentences has comparable effects. The parts of the brain that become active when a person views an action also become active when the same person reads a sentence describing the corresponding action (Aziz-Zadeh, Wilson, Rizzolatti, & Iacoboni, 2006).

Some scientists believe that the neural basis for the kinds of mental simulation proposed by the embodied semantics approach involves *mirror neurons* in addition to motor system. Mirror neurons become active when monkeys engage in an action—like grasping a cup—and they also become active when monkeys watch someone else engage in the same action (Gallese & Lakoff, 2005; Rizzolatti & Arbib, 1998; Rizzolatti & Craighero, 2004). The logic of this approach is strengthened by the fact that the part of the monkey's brain that is analogous to Broca's area, a part of the frontal lobe classically associated with speech, contains mirror neurons (Buccino et al., 2005). The idea is that the linguistic–semantic system also drives these mirror neurons and uses them to represent the meaning of words that describe objects and actions. On this account, perceiving the word *hammer* triggers a response in the mirror neuron system that closely resembles the pattern of neural response that happens when we use a hammer ourselves or watch someone else use a hammer. Recent research in word processing shows that merely observing a hand shape has similar effects on word processing as actually making the hand shape, in particular on identifying what category a word belongs to (as in Klatzky et al., 1989; Vainio, Symes, Ellis, Tucker, & Ottoboni, 2008). These results are consistent with the mirror neuron hypothesis in that observation appears to have similar effects on the interaction between the motor and language systems as real action does.

Although the embodied semantics approach, and the mirror neuron hypothesis, do a good job explaining why and how words affect motor regions of the brain and vice versa, and it goes a long way toward solving the symbol grounding problem, not everyone views embodiment in general, and the mirror neuron hypothesis in particular, as being a satisfactory description of how meanings are connected to words. Some theorists are concerned that the kinds of motor and perceptual simulations that seem to occur when people process action words and phrases (as indicated by response–language compatibility effects) may be governed by a separate system than the language interpretation system, and/or that such simulations may be an optional component of language interpretation (e.g., Oliveri et al., 2004). Other researchers propose that mental simulation is a by-product of processing words, and is not strictly necessary to represent word meanings. Other approaches view activation of the motor system by words to be the result of a kind of spreading activation between a "disembodied" semantic system that is linked to separately functioning cognitive systems for perception and action (Mahon & Carmazza, 2008). Finally, some people argue that the existence of mirror neurons in humans has not been conclusively demonstrated (Gernsbacher, 2009), and that the mirror neuron hpothesis cannot explain why damage to Broca's area does not lead to comprehension deficits (Corina & Knapp, 2006; see also Lotto, Hickok, & Holt, 2008).

If motor simulation of actions is an inevitable consequence of word processing, then neural activity in the motor system should be observed whenever people process action-related words. If motor simulation is an optional by-product of word processing, then neural activity in the motor system may occur after some word-processing tasks but not others. Tomasino and colleagues tested this possibility in a recent TMS study (Tomasino, Fink, Sparing, Dafotakis, & Weiss, 2008). Tomasino and colleagues zapped their subjects with TMS pulses while they were processing action words. They manipulated the lag between presenting the word and applying a TMS pulse as well as the task that their subjects carried out. When participants were engaged in an explicit visual imagery task (subjects were asked to imagine themselves performing the action denoted by a target word and say whether the action required wrist rotation), TMS facilitated the response, and then only when the TMS pulse was delivered about 90 ms after the target word. Other tasks with the same target words, silent reading and frequency judgment, were not affected by the TMS pulses. So, previous positive findings in TMS studies may reflect an optional element of visual imagery, rather than reflecting the necessary consequences of word processing. Additionally, different types of language may evoke motor representations to different degrees. For example, figurative language (such as metaphors; see Chapter 7) may not evoke spatial models in the same way that literal language does (Bergen, Lindsay, Matlock, & Narayanan, 2007), which calls into question the universality of perceptual simulation in word processing.

Although some neuropsychological data support the integration of linguistic and (traditionally defined) non-linguistic systems for action comprehension (e.g., Saygin, Wilson, Dronkers, & Bates, 2004, see Plate 3), neuropsychological data from patients with brain damage can also be used to argue that the semantics of action words does not depend on perceptual–motor representations. First, lesions in motor cortex are not always followed by problems recognizing and understanding action words (De Renzi & di Pellegrino, 1995; Saygin et al., 2004). When Saygin and colleagues measured the relationship between lesion location and degree of impairment on different tasks, they found some regions of the brain that caused impairment for reading of action-related words, but that did not associate with impairment for perceiving those actions. Other regions correlated with impairment of action perception, but not reading about actions. This suggests a separation between the linguistic–semantic system and the visual–perceptual system, contra the embodied semantics position. Saygin and colleagues therefore suggested (p. 1799) that, "There was no overall correlation between patients' deficits in the two domains [visual perception and reading], suggesting that the deficits observed in the comprehension of pantomimed actions and comprehension of actions through reading are not tightly coupled processes."[10] Negri and colleagues (2007) also showed that knowledge of how to produce actions and the knowledge necessary to recognize actions do not always go together. Some people can recognize actions that they are not able to produce because of brain damage in the motor area. This calls into question the idea that using the motor cortex to mentally simulate actions is a necessary component of recognizing and understanding actions (see also Mahon & Caramazza, 2005).

To summarize, the semantic network model is still the standard theory of lexical semantics. Connections between words and the process of automatic spreading activation help explain why different patterns of priming occur for different kinds of words across a variety of experimental tasks. HAL and LSA propose that the structure of the associations in the semantic network capture the essence of word meanings, but that position does not offer an answer to the symbol grounding problem. Embodied semantics and perceptual simulation offer a potential answer to the symbol grounding problem, and there is a growing body of experimental evidence that indicates a relationship between word processing and parts of the brain that are responsible for perceptual and motor processes.

Lexical Access

Most models of lexical access do not actually deal with activation of meaning.
GARETH GASKELL AND WILLIAM MARSLEN-WILSON (2002, p. 261)

Lexical access refers to the set of mental representations and processes that are involved in identifying which specific words we are hearing (during spoken word processing) or seeing (during visual word processing). Recognizing words leads to the activation of semantic information, but models of lexical access typically deal specifically with the activation of word *form* information (stored representations of how words sound or what they look like), with the activation of semantic information being treated as a consequence of the activation of form. The recognition of familiar words during spoken language processing is so automatic and seemingly effortless, that many people think that there is really nothing there to explain. For many people, but certainly not all, reading seems similarly effortless. This apparent ease and automaticity obscures the fact that lexical access involves complex mental operations and, despite its apparent simplicity, considerable debate continues among language scientists about which exact properties of words are involved in lexical access, what exact mental mechanisms take part, and how the entire process is organized.

One of the principles of spoken word processing that constrains all theories of lexical access is that people are able to identify spoken words really amazingly quickly. In seminal work in this area, William Marslen-Wilson (1973) employed a *shadowing task* to estimate how much time it took people to identify words. In the shadowing task, subjects listen to recorded speech and they try to repeat (or shadow) as quickly as possible the words that they hear. As Marslen-Wilson notes (p. 522), spoken language delivers about 5 syllables per second (at an average speaking rate of 158 words per minute). Some of Marslen-Wilson's subjects, the *fast shadowers*, were able to repeat the stream of words at a lag of as little as 250 ms (a quarter of a second), which means that they were following along not much more than a syllable behind the input. When Marslen-Wilson analyzed the kinds of errors that people made, he found that they were not random, nor did they consist of mere pronunciation difficulties. Instead, when people made errors, the incorrect words that they produced were fully compatible with the semantic and syntactic content of the preceding context. Out of 132 errors where subjects replaced or added words, only three violated syntactic constraints on acceptable continuations. This means that fast shadowers were able to perform lexical access very fast indeed, and that higher order aspects of the speech stream—minimally, its syntactic form—were computed within a few hundred milliseconds of the word's onset. Findings like these show that speech processing and lexical access from spoken words are highly *incremental*—the speech stream is segmented into words, and higher order relationships between words are represented before major clause or sentence boundaries are encountered. So, to explain lexical access of spoken words, the very least we need is a system that can identify individual words very quickly.

Additional evidence for very fast lexical access comes from *word monitoring* and *gating* tasks (Grosjean, 1980; Marslen-Wilson, 1987; Marslen-Wilson & Tyler, 1980). Word monitoring involves listening to utterances and responding as quickly as possible when a specific target word appears in the input. The *gating* task involves listening to short snippets of the beginnings (*onsets*) of words. The subject's task is to say what word is present in the stimulus. The length of the snippet is increased by small increments (25 or 50 ms) until the subject can correctly say what word the snippet belongs to. The length of the snippet serves as an estimate of how much *bottom-up* information (auditory stimulation) the subject requires to identify the word. These different tasks all provide roughly the same estimate of the amount of input it takes for people to identity spoken words. For one- and two-syllable words in the context of a spoken sentence, the average is about 200 ms worth of input (a fith of a second; Marslen-Wilson, 1973, 1985; Marslen-Wilson & Tyler, 1975; Seidenberg & Tanenhaus, 1979); it takes about another 100 ms of input before people can recognize isolated words.

As noted earlier, word forms can be divided up and analyzed according to their subcomponents. Spoken words can be divided into phonemes, which can be further divided into phonetic features. We can also view words as being made up of syllables, which in turn are composed of sets of phonemes. Words can also be thought of as being made up of organized *sublexical* ("below the level of the word") units of meaning called morphemes. Different theories of lexical access make different claims about which of these units affect the process of recognizing specific words from spoken input. Some theories propose that phonetic features, but not phonemes, play a role. Some theories propose that phonetic features, phonemes, and word-level representations all play a role. Some theories propose that word meanings themselves play a role in lexical access. To organize the discussion, this section starts with first-generation accounts including John Morton's *logogen*[11] and the *frequency ordered serial bin-search* models (Clarke & Morton, 1983; Jackson & Morton, 1984; Morton, 1969; Taft & Forster, 1975). Then it turns to second-generation accounts, such as the original version of the *COHORT* and TRACE models.

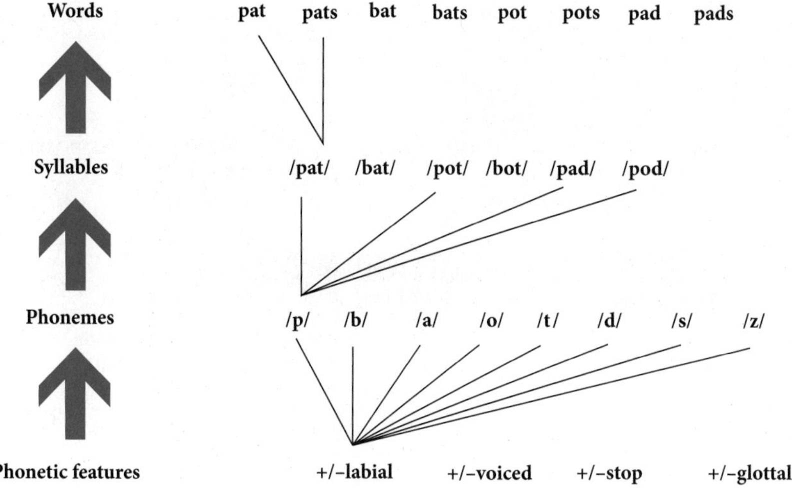

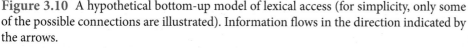

Figure 3.10 A hypothetical bottom-up model of lexical access (for simplicity, only some of the possible connections are illustrated). Information flows in the direction indicated by the arrows.

Finally, it discusses third-generation accounts, such as the *distributed cohort model* and Jeff Elman's *Simple Recurrent Network* approach (an offspring of models like *TRACE*).

All of these accounts have a common goal: They try to explain how people take inputs from the auditory or the visual system and match those inputs to stored representations of word form. To explain how that is done, a theory of lexical access has to say how the mind organizes the input—what characteristics or features it perceives in the input—and how it connects those characteristics to word form representations. As a starting point, consider this *default model* of lexical access. Words are made up of parts. Some of those parts (e.g., phonetic features) are more basic than others (e.g., syllables). We could have a model of lexical access that says: take a segment of speech, start by identifying the most basic units (e.g., phonetic features), combine those features to find more complex units (e.g., phonemes), combine those features to find even more complex units (e.g., syllables) and then use those units to find stored words that have matching forms. This is called a *bottom-up* processing system, because information flow in the system starts with more basic units, which are conceived of as being at the bottom of a hierarchy like the one in Figure 3.10, and proceeds upwards through more and more complex units. Information could flow from higher level representations to lower level ones, which is called *top-down* processing. Models of lexical access differ from one another in terms of the kinds of representations that they believe participate in lexical acess as well as the way information flows throughout the system.

First-generation models

First-generation models of lexical access were based on artificial-intelligence style analyses of the problem of recognizing words from spoken input. John Morton's *logogen model* is a bottom-up driven system that takes spoken or visual input and uses it to activate previously stored word form representations (Morton, 1969). The heart of the logogen model was a set of processing units that would receive input from either spoken or written modalities, and would fire when their excitatory inputs exceeded some criterion level or *threshold.* As Morton notes (p. 165): "The logogen is a device which accepts information from the

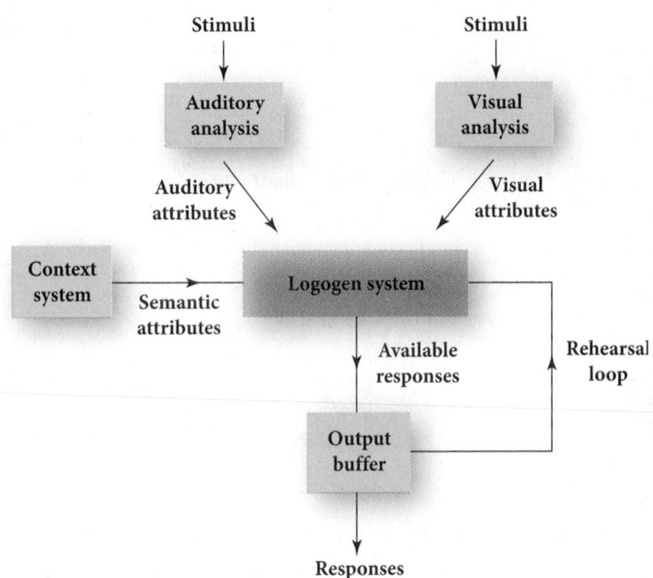

Figure 3.11 A schematic of the information flow in John Morton's (1969) *logogen* model.

sensory analysis mechanisms concerning the properties of linguistic stimuli and from context producing mechanisms. When the logogen has accumulated more than a certain amount of information, a response (in the present case the response of a single word) is made available." Max Coltheart and his colleagues describe the logogen system in this way (Coltheart, Rastle, Perry, & Langdon, 2001, p. 209), "*Logogens* are evidence-collecting devices with thresholds. Evidence is collected from visual or auditory input, and when the amount of evidence collected by a word's logogen exceeds that logogen's threshold, information about that word in the cognitive system (e.g., its meaning) is accessed."

Each word in a person's vocabulary is represented by a logogen, so words are recognized when the activation levels of their corresponding logogen exceed some threshold. What has to happen in order for a logogen to have its activation raised above threshold? In Morton's system, logogens could receive inputs from either spoken words (subject to auditory analysis), written words (subject to visual analysis), or preceding context (which would activate logogens based on semantic attributes). Normally, input would come from either the auditory or visual systems, and not both at once, but it is certainly possible that both auditory and visual evidence could be present simultaneously (as in reading along while someone speaks). The semantic input mechanism allows for context to influence the amount of time it takes to recognize a word. Context words that are semantically related to an individual logogen will raise the activation of the logogen before the listener gets direct perceptual evidence that the corresponding word is actually present in the input. The logogen system operates on these three kinds of inputs and, when individual logogens became activated at a level above their thresholds, they send signals to an output buffer (see Figure 3.11). Unless new input continues to activate the logogen, a decay function returns its activation to baseline levels within about one second. Once a logogen has been triggered or activated, its threshold for activation is temporarily lowered. As a result, less evidence is needed in the acoustic and visual input channels to reactivate the logogen. This mechanism can account for repetition priming effects—it is easier to recognize a word the second time you see it than the first because the activation threshold is lower the second time around.

The logogen model makes two key assumptions. First, it assumes that information flow is strictly bottom-up. Auditory and visual processing units affect the activation of logogens, but logogens do not affect the activation levels of the auditory and visual processing units that feed into the logogen. Second, it assumes that there are no direct connections between and among the logogens themselves. As a result, the activation level of one logogen does not affect the activation of any of the other logogens.

The logogen theory is an important one in psycholinguistics, because it was one of the first attempts to mathematically model (and therefore explain) how people respond to words. The model was successful on a number of dimensions. First, it had been known for a long time that word frequency affects a variety of behaviors. Words that occur frequently in a language are easier to process than words that appear less frequently. Why should this be the case? Morton suggested that repeated exposure to high-frequency words lowers the threshold for activation in the logogens that represent those high-frequency words. So less external evidence ("bottom-up" input) is required before you can recognize a high-frequency word, and therefore you respond faster to high-frequency words than to low-frequency words. This may also help explain why high-frequency words tend to be shorter than lower frequency words (as per *Zipf's Law*; Zipf, 1949). Shorter words pack less phonological and/or orthographic information than longer words, but this does not make them harder to recognize and process, because more frequent exposure lowers their activation. The model also helps explain why high-frequency words are easier to recognize than low-frequency words when they have been degraded by noise. Noise in the signal decreases the quality of the bottom-up input, but high-frequency words don't need as much bottom-up input, so they are recognized even in noisy environments.

MORPHOLOGY AND LEXICAL ACCESS

The logogen model was the first one to mathematically model the mental processes involved in lexical access (word form recognition), but was followed up shortly by other models. One of the most prominent subsequent models was Ken Forster and Marcus Taft's *frequency ordered bin search* (FOBS) model (Forster, 1989; Forster & Bednall, 1976; Taft & Forster, 1975). Like logogen, FOBS proposed that word form representations were activated by bottom-up input from the auditory system. According to Taft and Forster's model, lexical access involves people using auditory (or visual) cues to search their long-term memories for a matching stimulus. This search process is organized so that people do not need to search the entire lexicon every time they need to look up a word. Instead, lexical (word form) representations are organized into *bins*. The bins are organized according to word frequency. High-frequency words are at the "front" of the bin and are searched first; lower frequency words are stored toward the "back" of the bin and are searched later. When you encounter an auditory stimulus, that opens up a bin (kind of like opening up a file drawer), and you search through the bin looking for an entry that matches the stimulus, starting with the most frequent item in the bin, then the next most frequent, and so on until you have searched the entire bin. The search process ends when you find an item in the bin that matches the stimulus. This kind of search is called *self-terminating* (the process stops itself when it succeeds), so you don't keep searching the bins for an additional match after you have found one good candidate. One last important characteristic of the model is that words are organized in the bins according to shared *roots*. To define what a shared root is, and why it might be important, we need to discuss a bit of *morphology*.

The FOBS account proposes that *morphemes* are an important level of representation in lexical access, so we need to know what a morpheme is. Morphemes are defined as the smallest unit of language that can be assigned an independent meaning. Words are made up of one or more morphemes. The basic morpheme in a word is its *root*, or *root morpheme* (sometimes called a *stem*). *Board* is a *monomorphemic* word, because it cannot be decomposed into smaller units of meaning. So the root morpheme for *board* is the same as the word itself. *Blackboard* is a *polymorphemic* word, because it can be decomposed into smaller units. Specifically, it contains the morphemes *black* and *board*, each of which has a meaning of its own, and each of which contributes to the meaning of the word as a whole. Which of the morphemes in *blackboard* is the root? While some linguistic theories would argue that *board* is the root (because a *blackboard* is a kind of a *board*, not a kind of *black*), the FOBS account proposes that *black* is the root, because speech processing gives priority to information coming first, and in speech, we hear the morpheme *black* before we hear the morpheme *board*.

The category *morpheme* can itself be divided into subcategories. Polymorphemic words are made up of a *root* and one or more *affixes*. (Compound words are special because they are made up by combining two or more *root* morphemes.) *Affixes* can be *prefixes* that come before the root, *suffixes* that come after the root, or *infixes* that divide a root into two parts, one of which comes before the infix, and one of which comes after. Standard American English does not have any infixes;[12] Arabic has many. Affixes make up the class of *bound* morphemes (as opposed to *free* morphemes), because they can not appear by themselves (whereas free morphemes can). Affixes come in different flavors, as well. *Inflectional morphemes* change the flavor of a word's meaning; and *derivational morphemes* change the syntactic category that a word belongs to. So, we can change the flavor of the word *cat* without changing its core meaning or its syntactic category by adding the bound-morpheme, -*s*. We can change the tense of a verb by adding inflectional morphemes like -*ed* or -*ing* (e.g., *bake, baked, baking*). If we want to change the *category* of a word, we can add derivational morphemes like -*ly* or -*tion*. So, we can take a verb like *confuse* and change it to a noun with the -*tion* derivational morpheme—*confuse* becomes *confusion*. We can change the verb to an adjective with the -*ing* derivational morpheme—*confuse* becomes *confusing*. We can stack morphemes end to end to change from a noun to an adjective and back to a noun again—*truth* (n.) becomes *truthy* (adj.) becomes *truthiness* (n.). So, the morphological system in English is one of the properties that contributes to the productivity or generativity of the system. We can combine old morphemes in new ways to come up with new meanings.[13]

So what do morphemes have to do with lexical access? It depends on how you think word representations are organized, and what you think happens when people encounter a polymorphemic word. The FOBS model says that lexical representations are organized into bins, and each bin is built around a root. All of the variants of *dog* are listed under a bin, and *dog* is the base entry.[14] So, *dog, dogs, dogged, dogpile*, and *dog-tired* are all represented in the same bin. Any time you encounter the root *dog*, you search through the *dog* bin looking for a matching entry. Alert readers will have noted that there are many versions of *dog* that are not identical to the label on the bin (*dog*). What happens when the stimulus does not match the label on the bin? According to the FOBS model, the incoming stimulus has to be analyzed according to its root, because the root is what gets the listener access to the correct bin. Whenever a listener encounters a polymorphemic word (*dogs, dogpile, dogaphobia*), the first thing the listener needs to do is figure out what the root is. Therefore, the first step in lexical access is *morphological decomposition*—the incoming stimulus needs to be broken down into parts that correspond to individual morphemes before the root can be identified. A word like *dogs* is analyzed as being made up of the root morpheme *dog* and the plural inflectional suffix -*s*.

Is there any evidence that suggests that lexical access involves morphological decomposition? Such evidence comes in various forms. First, as noted previously, people respond more quickly to frequent words than infrequent words. But it's actually a bit more complicated than that, because we can measure frequency in different ways. We could assign frequency estimates to an entire word, regardless of how many morphemes it contains.

We could look at a corpus and count up every time the word *dogs* appears in exactly that form. We could count up the number of times that *cats* appears in precisely that form. In that case we would be measuring *surface frequency*—how often the exact word occurs. But the words *dogs* and *cats* are both related to other words that share the same root morpheme. We could decide to ignore minor differences in surface form and instead concentrate on how often the family of related words appears. If so, we would treat *dog*, *dogs*, *dog-tired*, and *dogpile* as being a single large class, and we would count up the number of times any member of the class appears in the corpus. In that case, we would be measuring *root* frequency—how often the shared word root appears in the language. Those two ways of counting frequency can come up with very different estimates. For example, perhaps the exact word *dog* appears very often, but *do-pile* appears very infrequently. If we base our frequency estimate on surface frequency, *dogpile* is very infrequent. But if we use root frequency instead, *dogpile* is very frequent, because it is in the class of words that share the root *dog*, which appears fairly often.

If we use these different frequency estimates (surface frequency and root frequency) to predict how long it will take people to respond on a reaction time task, root frequency makes better predictions than surface frequency does. A word that has a low surface frequency will be responded to quickly if its root frequency is high (Bradley, 1979; Taft, 1979, 1994). This outcome is predicted by an account like FOBS that says that word forms are accessed via their roots, and not by models like logogen where each individual word form has a separate entry in the mental lexicon.

Further evidence for the morphological decomposition hypothesis comes from priming studies involving words with real and *pseudo-affixes*. Many polymorphemic words are created when derivational affixes are added to a root. So, we can take the verb *grow* and turn it into a noun by adding the derivational suffix *-er*. A *grower* is someone who *grows* things. There are a lot of words that end in *-er* and have a similar syllabic structure to *grower*, but that are not real polymorphemic words. For example, *sister* looks a bit like *grower*. They both end in *-er* and they both have a single syllable that precedes *-er*. According to the FOBS model, we have to get rid of the affixes before we can identify the root. So, anything that looks or sounds like it has a suffix is going to be treated like it really does have a suffix, even when it doesn't. Even though *sister* is a monomorphemic word, the lexical access process breaks it down into a *pseudo-* (fake) *root*, *sist*, and a *pseudo-suffix*, *-er*. After the *affix stripping* process has had a turn at breaking down *sister* into a root and a suffix, the lexical access system will try to find a bin that matches the pseudo-root *sist*. This process will fail, because there is no root morpheme in English that matches the input *sist*. In that case, the lexical access system will have to re-search the lexicon using the entire word *sister*. This extra process should take extra time, therefore the affix stripping hypothesis predicts that *pseudo-suffixed* words (like *sister*) should take longer to process than words that have a real suffix (like *grower*). This prediction has been confirmed in a number of reaction time studies—people do have a harder time recognizing pseudo-suffixed words than words with real suffixes (Lima, 1987; Smith & Sterling, 1982; Taft, 1981). People also have more trouble rejecting pseudo-words that are made up of a prefix (e.g., *de*) and a real root morpheme (e.g., *juvenate*) than a comparable pseudo-word that contains a prefix and a non-root (e.g., pertoire). This suggests that morphological decomposition successfully accesses a bin in the *dejuvenate* case, and people are able to rule out *dejuvenate* as a real word only after the entire bin has been fully searched (Taft & Forster, 1975). Morphological structure may also play a role in word learning. When people are exposed to novel words that are made up of real morphemes, such as *genvive* (related to the morpheme *vive*, as in *revive*) they rate that stimulus as being a better English word and they recognize it better than an equally complex stimulus that does not incorporate a familiar root (such as *gencule*) (Dorfman, 1994, 1999).

FOBS is also consistent with experiments showing that words that are related via a shared morpheme prime one another (Drews & Zwitserlood, 1995; Emmorey, 1989; Stanners, Neiser, & Painton, 1979; see also Deutsch, Frost, Pelleg, Pollatsek, & Rayner, 2003).[15] In these priming experiments, the targets are root words, like *honest*, and the prime words are either identical to the target (*honest*) or a prefixed version of the target (e.g., *dishonest*). To control for possible effects at other levels, like letter overlap, in another condition the target would be a word like *son* and the prime would be a word that had many of the same letters, like *arson* (but the two words do *not* share a root morpheme, because *arson* is not a kind of *son*). In these experiments, equivalent priming occurred when the prime was either identical to the target (e.g., *honest–honest*), or contained the target as a root (as in the *dishonest–honest* case). No priming was observed for words that only had overlapping letters (the *arson–son* case). These effects are compatible with FOBS, because prefixed words like *dishonest* are accessed via their roots. So, processing the word *dishonest* entails activating the representation of the root morpheme *honest*. If *honest* is presented right after *dishonest*, its lexical entry should be more activated than normal, which speeds up the response. Similar effects occur for words with suffixes, so a prime word like *departure* speeds responses to targets like *depart* when both prime and target words are presented in spoken form or written form, or when the prime is presented in one form and the target in another (Frost, Forster, & Deutsch, 1997; Marslen-Wilson & Tyler, 1997; Marslen-Wilson, Tyler, Waksler, & Older, 1994).

Masked priming experiments also support a role for morphemes in lexical access. In masked priming studies, the prime word is presented followed by a pattern that covers the place where the prime was. Masking the prime stimulus prevents the visual system from taking up additional information about the prime word once the mask is displayed. Primes can be presented for very short amounts of time—as little as 43 ms, less than a twentieth of a second. When prime exposure duration is manipulated—some primes are shown for a very short time before being masked, some primes are shown for longer—different patterns of priming occur for semantic and morphological primes. At very short prime exposure durations, semantic priming (*doctor–nurse*) does not occur, but it is very robust at longer prime exposure durations. The opposite pattern happens for morphological primes. At very short prime exposure durations, morphological priming (*apartment–apart*) is robust, but that priming effect disappears at longer prime exposure durations (Rastle, Davis, Marslen-Wilson, & Tyler, 2000). Results like these indicate that morphological priming effects, such as those that happen when *dishonest* is used to prime *honest*, do not reflect semantic overlap between the meaning of *dishonest* and the meaning of *honest*. Likewise, orthographic (letter) overlap does not account for priming in morphologically related pairs (if it did, *apartment* should prime *apart*, because all of the letters in *apart* are also in *apartment*). This suggest that morphological representations and processes play a unique role in lexical access, separate from semantic, phonological and orthographic effects, as suggested by FOBS. Neuroimaging data also support a unique role for morphemes in lexical processing, because prime–target word pairs that share a root morpheme are associated with decreased neural activity in the left inferior frontal lobe (Bozic, Marslen-Wilson, Stamatakis, Davis, & Tyler, 2007), while other kinds of prime–target pairs are not.

To summarize, the FOBS model proposes that word form representations are organized into bins. The set of bins is organized according to root frequency, and entries within the bins are organized according to surface frequency. This architecture explains why words with more frequent roots are processed faster than words with less frequent roots, and it can explain smaller effects of surface frequency. The model also explains why words that have pseudo-affixes are more difficult to process as a class than equally long and frequent words that have real affixes.

TRACE

The trace model of lexical access differs from previous models in that, rather than having a serial, bottom-up, architecture, the model is highly *interactive*. In serial, bottom-up systems, activation of processing units is determined solely by stimulation provided by the input. The activation of one processing unit in a bottom-up system does not directly affect the activation of other processing units at the same level of the system. For example, an activated phoneme unit does not change the activation of other phoneme units. Activation at higher levels of a bottom-up processing system does *not* affect activation at lower levels of the system. Phonemes affect the activations of word units, but word units do *not* affect activation in the units that represent phonemes. By constrast, interactive processing systems have connections between processing units that allow units within the same level to affect one another, and that allow processing units at higher levels of the system to affect units at lower levels. Figure 3.12 gives a schematic view of the processing architecture in the TRACE model of lexical access (McClelland & Elman, 1986; McClelland & Rumelhart, 1981; Rumelhart & McClelland, 1982). The basic organization of processing units and information flow appears in the top part of the figure. A more detailed view of the way processing units are connected to one another appears at the bottom.

The top part of Figure 3.12 shows that TRACE can take either visual or auditory input. The most basic unit of analysis is visual features (short lines at different orientations, curves, angles) and acoustic features (basic components of sound in the speech stream). The bottom part of the figure shows how different processing units are connected to one another. This diagram shows how the system is organized for visual word processing (it's a little easier to conceptualize than phonetic features). The input to the system is *features*—short lines at different orientations in this case. These visual features are connected to letter representations. The equivalent in spoken word processing would be phonemes. All of the connections between features and letters (and phonemes) are excitatory, and the letter and phoneme levels do *not* feed back to the feature level.

The TRACE model assumes that activation is *cascaded*. Cascaded activation contrasts with *threshold activation*. In the logogen model, *threshold activation* means that a processing unit (e.g., a logogen) sits quietly until input causes its activation to exceed some threshold value. In a system that uses cascaded activation, units receiving input begin to send output as soon as any activation at all comes in from other units. Using cascaded activation, visual features in TRACE start to send activation forward as soon as they begin to be identified, so letter-level processing units start to become active soon after feature-level processing units start to become active. That means that letter representations start to become activated as soon as any visual feature has been identified, and you do not need to perceive all of the features of a letter before you start to activate letter-level processing units. Notice also that individual features are connected to more than one letter-processing unit. The horizontal line visual feature has excitatory connections to the letters "A", "T", "G", and "S"; and an inhibitory connection to the letter "N." When a horizontal visual feature is detected in the input, all four of those letters increase their activation, and the letter "N" decreases in activation. If four different letters are activated, how does the system decide which letter it is actually seeing? Notice that within the layer of units representing letters (and phonemes), *all* of the connections are inhibitory. This means that when a letter-processing unit starts to get activated by the bottom-up input from the features, it will try to decrease the activation of the other letters that it is connected to. This pattern of connections leads to *lateral inhibition*—processing units within a layer of units in the network try to reduce or inhibit each other's levels of activation. This makes sense, because a feature can be only part of one

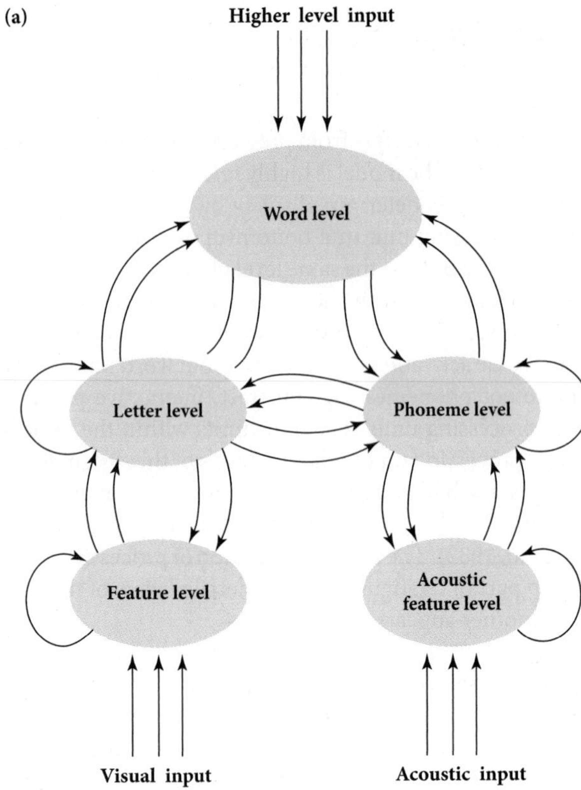

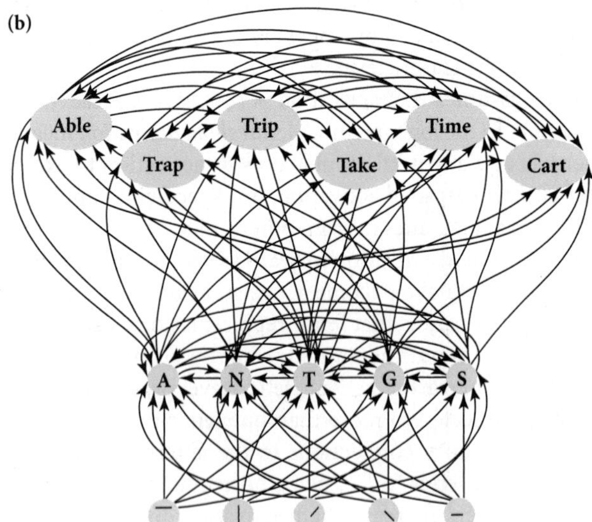

Figure 3.12 The TRACE model of lexical access (McClelland & Rumelhart, 1981, pp. 378, 380). The top part shows the basic architecture. Connections with arrows at the end indicate excitatory influences; connections with round ends indicate inhibitory influences.

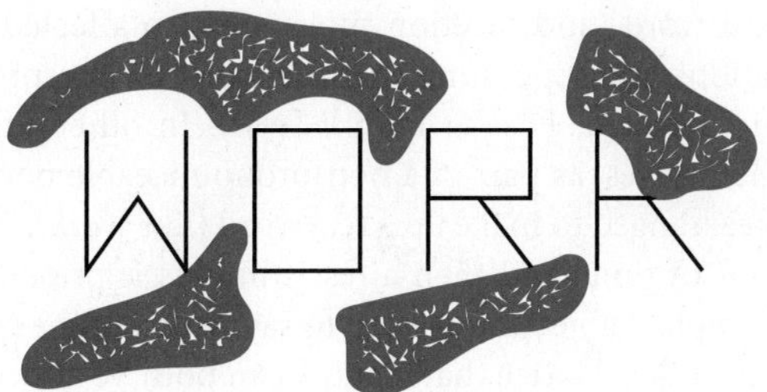

Figure 3.13 An example of degraded input that TRACE is good at processing.

letter. So, if the feature comes from the letter "t," the representation of the letter "t" should try to inhibit other possibly competing candidates. After the bottom-up input has been received, inhibitory connections within a processing layer cause different letter representations to compete with one another, and the letter with the most support from the bottom-up features will eventually "win" the competition—its activation will increase and it will inhibit competing letter representations until eventually there is only one candidate left standing.

Letter representations have a slightly more complex relationship with word form representations. Letters have excitatory inputs to the words they are components of, and inhibitory connections to words that they are *not* components of. Activating the letter "A" will excite the words *able* and *trap*, and it will inhibit the word *time*. Letters have excitatory and inhibitory feedback connections from the word layer as well. This means that, as a word starts to become activated, it will feed excitation or inhibition back to the letter level. So, if the word *able* starts to get activation from the letter "A," it will start to activate its other component letters, "B," "L," and "E," via excitatory *top-down* feedback connections, possibly before those letter representations have been activated by bottom-up input. Simultaneously, activity at the word level for *able* will inhibit letter-level representations that are not present in *able*. This is one of the properties of trace that allow it to deal with degraded input, like that shown in Figure 3.13. A strictly bottom-up system would not be able to identify the right-most letter in Figure 3.13, because it could just as easily be an "R" as a "K," and so a strictly bottom-up system might not be able to correctly identify the word as *work*. However, in the TRACE model, the intact letters "W," "O," and "R" would activate the word form representations "WORK", "WORD," and "WORM", which would feed activation back to the letter level, and the combination of top-down and bottom-up activation from the remaining intact features would eventually cause activation of the "k" letter representation to exceed possible competitors.

TRACE also offers a good explanation of the *word superiority* effect. The word superiority effect refers to a class of behaviors indicating that we have an easier time recognizing and processing letters and phonemes when they appear in the context of a word than when they appear by themselves or in the context of a string of letters that does not make up a real word. The greater ease of processing letters and phonemes in the context of a word can be demonstrated in a number of different ways. In the 1800s, Erdmann and Dodge (Erdmann & Dodge, 1898, in Balota et al., 2006) showed that people could read a word containing up to 22 letters in the same amount of time it took them to identify 4 or 5 individual letters when those letters were not part of a real word. Other demonstrations of the word superiority effect come from phoneme and letter monitoring experiments (Foss & Swinney, 1973; Johnston & McClelland, 1973; Reicher, 1969; Savin & Bever, 1970; Wheeler, 1970; the phoneme restoration effects discussed in Chapter 2 also represent a form of word superiority).[16] In these experiments, subjects are given a target phoneme, like /s/, they listen to recorded speech, and they press a key as quickly as possible when they detect the presence of the target phoneme. Reaction times are faster when the target phonemes appear as part of a real word (and reaction times are also affected by how frequent the word-level representations are, suggesting that the word form representation is accessed *before* the phoneme is detected; Foss & Blank, 1980). In other experiments, letters are presented either by themselves, as part of a non-pronounceable non-word (like *owrk*), or with the same letters rearranged to make up a real word (like *work*). The stimuli are flashed for a very brief amount of time, and then a test stimulus is presented consisting of two letters, *d* and *k*, for example. Subjects are asked to say which of the two letters appeared in the briefly presented stimulus. Notice that *d* and *k* can both be added to *wor* to make up a word, which eliminates guessing as a strategy for improving accuracy on the task when real words were presented. Despite this handicap, subjects were more accurate at identifying letters when the briefly presented stimulus was a word than in the other conditions. So, activating a word-level form representation helps people identify individual letters. This can be explained by the TRACE model by proposing that activation of word-level form representations strengthens the activation of letter-level representations via excitatory feedback as well as inhibition of possible competing letters that are not part of the activated word-level representation. McClelland and Rumelhart explain the word superiority effect on letter detection in this way (1981, p. 389): "the reason letters in words fare better than letters in nonwords is that they benefit from feedback that can drive them to higher activation levels."

To summarize the important properties of the TRACE model: It is a highly interactive system. Bottom-up input, top-down feedback, and lateral inhibition combine to determine how much activation any given unit in the network enjoys. The TRACE model explains how and why we can deal with degraded input. The network computes the best fit to the degraded stimulus by simultaneously assessing multiple levels of representation, and a good fit at one level can compensate for a bad fit at another level. Finally, TRACE explains why letters in whole words are easier to perceive than individual letters by themselves. Feedback from the word layer boosts the activation of lower level letter representations.

COHORT

The COHORT model is another prominent second-generation account of lexical access (Marslen-Wilson, 1987, 1989; Marslen-Wilson & Welsh, 1978). The COHORT model was developed specifically to explain lexical access for spoken words. The COHORT model views the process of lexical access as involving three kinds of processes: *activation* (or *contact*), *selection*, and *integration*. During the initial *activation* or *contact* phase of processing, multiple word form representations are activated in response to the auditory stimulus. COHORT views contact as being influenced only by bottom-up auditory information, and not by contextual information, and so activation in COHORT is referred to as an *autonomous* process—it is affected by auditory stimulation but not by other potentially relevant cognitive processes. As a result, stored representations of words that do not fit into the evolving context are activated anyway as long as they match the acoustic properties of the word stimulus. *Selection* involves sorting through the activated word form representations to find the one that best matches the auditory stimulus. COHORT says that selection depends on the bottom-up stimulus, because bottom-up information activates word candidates, but it also depends on context. Words that fit better into the context will have an advantage over words that do not fit, especially in cases where the bottom-up input is ambiguous between two or more stored word candidates. *Integration* happens when the features of the selected word are incorporated into the evolving representation of the entire utterance. During integration, properties of the selected word—its grammatical class and meaning—are evaluated with respect to how well they fit with the preceding context. Because COHORT deals with spoken input, it views lexical access and the activation of word form as resulting from a continuous evaluation of the similarity between the auditory stimulus and stored word form representations based on auditory properties. COHORT also views the process of lexical access as being radically incremental. Word representations are activated as soon as the initial sounds in the acoustic stimulus have been perceived, and it is possible for people to identify individual words in the speech stream *before* they hear the entire word.[17]

COHORT is called COHORT because the process of lexical access starts with a contact phase in which all words that match the perceived acoustic profile are activated. So within about 100–150 ms of the onset of a word, a whole group of matching candidate word forms become more available or accessible than usual. This group of activated word forms is called a *cohort*.[18] After this initial activation phase, the lexical access mechanism continues to check the list of activated candidates against further input from the speech stream, and it eliminates candidates that no longer match the input. Simultaneously, it checks the characteristics of each member of the activated cohort against requirements imposed by the context—the correct target word has to have the right syntactic (structural) and semantic (meaning) properties to continue being activated.

One advantage of the COHORT model is that it makes very specific predictions about when, exactly, a word can be recognized and its meaning accessed. COHORT says that word recognition depends on reducing the set of activated words to the one that matches the acoustic input. The point where the COHORT is reduced to a sole survivor is called the *recognition point* (Marslen-Wilson, 1987). A word like *trespass*, can be recognized well before the end of the word, because there are no other words besides *trespass* that are consistent with the onset *tresp* (Marslen-Wilson & Tyler, 1980).[19] COHORT allows for minor adjustments to the recognition point based on semantic or syntactic requirements imposed by context. Words that are highly predictable in context may be recognized a bit faster than less predictable words. According to COHORT, word recognition is *contingent* on two factors: First, there has to be positive evidence for the presence of the word (e.g., the input *tres* provides clues that the word *trespass* is the matching word target). Second, the input has to rule out the presence of other words (e.g., the onset *tr* rules out the possibility that the matching word target is *tap*, *top*, *table*, or any other word that does not begin with *tr*). So, the word *trespass* can be recognized "early" (before the end of the word) only if lexical access includes a mechanism that knows when all other possibilities have been eliminated.

What evidence supports the prediction that multiple word candidates are activated early in lexical access, shortly after you hear a word's onset? In a cross-modal priming experiment, participants listened to words like *captain* and *captive* that have the same onset (up to the *t* sound in the middle of the word). Visual probe words were presented either "early" in the word (at or before the *t* sound) or later in the word (during the final *-ain* or *-ive* syllable). When the probe word was presented early, two words were still compatible with the input so far (*capt* could continue and become either *captain* or *captive*). When the probe word was presented later, only one of the word candidates was still compatible with the auditory input. The target words were semantically related to one of the two meanings. The target word *ship* was presented, because it is related to *captain*. Alternatively, the target word *guard* was presented, because it is related to *captive*. The question was: Which target words would be primed by the auditory stimulus? If COHORT is correct, and word onsets activate all of the entries related to the auditory stimulus, then both *ship* and *guard* should be primed at the "early" probe point. At the "late" probe point, which comes after the recognition point, only one of the probe words should be primed. More specifically, priming should be observed only for the probe word whose meaning is associated with the surviving word candidate. This is exactly the pattern of priming that subjects experienced. Early in the word, both *ship* and *guard* were primed. Later on, only the matching meaning was primed (Marslen-Wilson & Zwitserlood, 1989). So, if people heard *capti*, and the probe word appeared simultaneously with the *i* sound, only the target word *guard* was primed, and not *ship*. When these ambiguous spoken word onsets (*capt-*) were embedded in spoken sentences that made one meaning much more likely than the other, priming was still observed for both *ship* and *guard*, which suggests that context was not able to "turn off" or prevent access to the contextually inappropriate word (Zwitserlood, 1989). So, as Marslen-Wilson explains (1987, p. 89), "No contextual pre-selection is permitted, and context cannot prevent the accessing and activation of contextually inappropriate word candidates."[20]

How does COHORT compare to TRACE? They differ with respect to how word form representations become activated. TRACE views word form activation as resulting from a process of competition and mutual inhibition. COHORT views word form activation as reflecting a massively parallel process without competition until the selection phase. The two accounts therefore make different predictions about what will happen as multiple word candidates become activated. According to TRACE, more activated word candidates are associated with less activation being gained by any one candidate, and greater competition between candidates. Because COHORT allows for unlimited parallel activation of word candidates, the number of activated candidates does not affect the speed with which the correct candidate is identified. To test this aspect of the models, Marslen-Wilson manipulated word onsets in a non-word detection task. Specifically, some of his stimuli were still consistent with many words at the point right before new auditory information rendered them non-words. Other stimuli were consistent with very few words right before new auditory information rendered them non-words. Presumably, to recognize that the stimulus is a non-word, people have to search through the set of activated candidate words to find a match. If words compete with one another, or if people search through the list in a serial fashion (as in FOBS), then the non-word judgments should take longer for bigger sets, and less time for smaller sets. However, reaction time data indicated that non-word judgments were made equally quickly, no matter how big the set of matching candidates was.

COHORT and TRACE also differ with respect to how similarity between the stimulus and stored word forms affects processing. TRACE relies on global similarity match to determine how active a stored word form becomes. So, it does not matter where a slight mismatch occurs in a word, at the beginning or the end. As long as the overall stimulus is close to the stored representation, the stored representation will become active. In COHORT, word onsets are critical, because word onsets determine which representations will make it into the cohort, and which will be left out. As a result, mismatches at the beginnings of words should have greater effects than mismatches at the ends of words. According to TRACE, activation of word nodes will be a function of similarity (*bone* and *pone* will both lead to similar patterns of activation in the network). As a result, words that share offsets should prime each other's meanings (because presenting *pone* activates the similar entry *bone*). The prediction, then, is that if you hear *pone*, you should respond faster to words associated with *bone*, like *arm*, *broken*, and *shin*. However, offset-matching primes are almost completely ineffective, suggesting that word onsets really do set the stage for lexical access (Marslen-Wilson & Zwitserlood, 1989; see also Allopenna, Magnuson, & Tanenhaus, 1998; McQueen & Viebahn, 2007).

What evidence supports the psychological reality of recognition points? In one-syllable (*monosyllable*) words, the recognition point and the end of the word are one and the same, but for many multi-syllable (*polysyllable*) words, the recognition point comes well before the end of the word. The COHORT model says that words are recognized when the acoustic stimulus reaches the recognition point. So people can recognize words and access their meanings without having to wait until the very end of the word. Some experiments involve phoneme monitoring. Recall that phoneme monitoring speed is affected by word frequency, suggesting that word identification precedes the monitoring response (Foss & Blank, 1981). It turns out that phoneme monitoring speed is strongly correlated with the recognition point. Words that have early recognition points lead to faster phoneme monitoring times than words that have later recognition points (Marslen-Wilson, 1984), whether the words are presented in isolation or as part of an extended utterance (Tyler & Wessels, 1983). Non-word detection time also depends on when, exactly, the non-word stimulus diverges from real words that share the same onset. A non-word like *trenkitude* can be identified as a non-word faster than an equally long non-word like *cathedruke,* because *trenkitude* becomes a non-word sooner than *cathedruke*. The only English word with the same onset as *trenkitude* are *trench*, *trend*, and slight variations thereof (e.g., *trendy*), so *trenkitude* becomes a non-word at the *k*. *Cathedruke* has a potential word match, *cathedral*, up to the *dr*, and so becomes a non-word later. When people engage in non-word detection experiments, they respond faster to words like *trenkitude* than equally long non-words like *cathedruke*, which provides further evidence for the special status afforded to recognition points in the COHORT model. Both *cathedruke* and *trenkitude* provide bottom-up, positive evidence for real words, and so both should lead to roughly equivalent activation of word targets under both the logogen and FOBS models.[21] Plus, the FOBS and logogen processing systems might have to wait until the entire stimulus has been perceived before they can be certain that no logogen will fire or no bin will match the input. Thus, these models do not provide strong justification for why non-word detection times should differ between *cathedruke* and *trenkitude*.

The available evidence suggests that words are identified very quickly, and that the bottom-up information that is present at the point in time when words are identified often is not sufficient, by itself, to pick out one single word (Marslen-Wilson, 1987). One estimate is that 200 ms of spoken input is compatible, on average, with about 40 different words. This also is bad news for models, like FOBS, that say that word identification is based on an autonomous search process based on purely bottom-up information, because it appears that lexical access is well under way before a unique root morpheme can be identified. Another piece of bad news for FOBS is that lower frequency words affect recognition points as much as higher frequency words do. According to models like FOBS, higher frequency entries are searched before lower frequency entries are. So, if a word has a lower frequency competitor, this should not affect how quickly that word is accessed. However, COHORT makes a different prediction. According to COHORT, word candidates are activated based on their match to the initial sequence of sounds in the acoustic input, regardless of how frequent the word candidate is. So, if a higher frequency target word, like *rap*, has a lower frequency cohort member, like *rapture*, it will be recognized slower than an equivalent high-frequency word that does *not* have a lower frequency competitor. In fact, response times in a variety of tasks involving spoken words depend on the recognition point, independent of the frequency of the actual target word (Marslen-Wilson, 1987).

Activating multiple candidate words and continuously evaluating the goodness of fit between the acoustic input and the activated candidate set, as proposed by COHORT, confers a number of benefits to the listener. First, activating multiple candidates ensures that the correct word will be available for selection and further processing. Second, continuously evaluating the fit between the stimulus and the set of activated candidates ensures that the correct candidate will be selected as soon as the bottom-up input discriminates the correct target from similar competitors. These characteristics therefore maximize the speed and accuracy of the lexical access mechanism.

The original version of the COHORT model did not have an explicit account of word frequency effects, but this shortcoming was repaired in follow-on versions of the model.

After it was established that frequency did affect word recognition times, independent of where the recognition point was, COHORT was modified to include different rise times in the level of activation for higher frequency and lower frequency word forms. This is essentially equivalent to the logogen model's move of lowering thresholds for higher frequency word forms. So the revised COHORT model, like the TRACE model, does not view word form activation as all-or-none. Instead, word forms can have no activation, a little activation, or lots of activation (consistent with behavioral evidence for early effects of frequency; Cleland, Gaskell, Quinlan, & Tamminen, 2006; Dahan & Gaskell, 2007). For instance, if people are shown an array of objects, and they listen to a word that has an ambiguous onset, like *bell* (because the *be* part is consistent with a wide variety of words, *bell, bed, bet, bend*, etc.), they look more often and more quickly at a picture that goes with a high-frequency word than a picture that goes with a lower frequency word (Dahan, Magnuson, & Tanenhaus, 2001). Responses to high-frequency visual word targets are also more facilitated by an auditory prime than low-frequency targets (e.g., the high-frequency word *feel* is more primed when people hear the onset sounds *fee*; and the low-frequency word *robe* is less primed when people hear the onset sounds *roe*; Marslen-Wilson, 1990). To account for these kinds of effects, "Elements are not simply switched on or off as the sensory and contextual information accumulates, until a single candidate is left standing. Instead, the outcome and the timing of the recognition process will reflect the differential levels of activation of successful and unsuccessful candidates" (Marslen-Wilson, 1987, p. 93).

The revised COHORT model also alters its view of the input representation (Lahiri & Marslen-Wilson, 1991; Marslen-Wilson & Warren, 1994). The original version of COHORT, logogen, FOBS, and TRACE all assume that a level of phonological processing units mediates between acoustic–phonetic features and word representations. That is, acoustic features activate phoneme nodes, and then phoneme nodes activate words. This information flow can produce catastrophic failure, however, if the bottom-up input is miscategorized, and the wrong phone is identified. To solve this problem, COHORT suggests that acoustic–phonetic features are directly connected to word-level representations (and that phoneme identification is a by-product of activating word forms). That way, words that have similar acoustic–phonetic features will be activated. For example, *bat*, which has a voiced labial stop at its onset, would be partially activated when someone said *pat*, which has a de-voiced labial stop at its onset.

The direct mapping of phonetic features to word form representations also helps explain other *sublexical* (below the level of the word) effects on lexical access. Many English words contain *onset embedded* words. The word *lightning* starts with *light*. The word *hamster* starts with *ham*, which is a word by itself. However, it turns out that the string *ham* is pronounced slightly differently when it is a word all by itself compared to when it is just the first syllable of a bigger word. Specifically, *ham* has a longer duration, it sounds more like *haaaaam*, when it is spoken as an independent word (as in *This haaaaam tastes really good*) than when it is produced as part of a bigger word (as in *This hamster tastes really good*). These differences in pronunciation are detected by the auditory lexical access system fast enough to bias activation toward the matching word candidate. So the short word *ham* becomes more active when *ham* is pronounced with a longer duration (*haaaaam*); and the longer word *hamster* becomes more active when *ham* is pronounced with a shorter duration (Davis, Marslen-Wilson, & Gaskell, 2002; Salverda, Dahan, & McQueen, 2003; Salverda et al., 2007; Shatzman & McQueen, 2006). Other sublexical properties, like where the stress occurs, can also affect how rapidly individual word candidates become active (e.g., you pronounce *record* differently when it is a verb versus when it is a noun, but subtle differences in stress patterns also occur for stand-alone words like *ham* and the same segments that are embedded in larger words; McQueen, Norris, & Cutler, 1994).

Third-generation models: Distributed features and distributed cohort

DISTRIBUTED FEATURE MODELS

The parallel distributed processing enterprise continued to grow and develop with the invention of newer and more advanced mathematical models of lexical access. For example, Jeff Elman's *simple recurrent network* (SRN) model assumed that words were represented as a pattern of neural activity across a multi-layered network. As shown in Figure 3.14, the

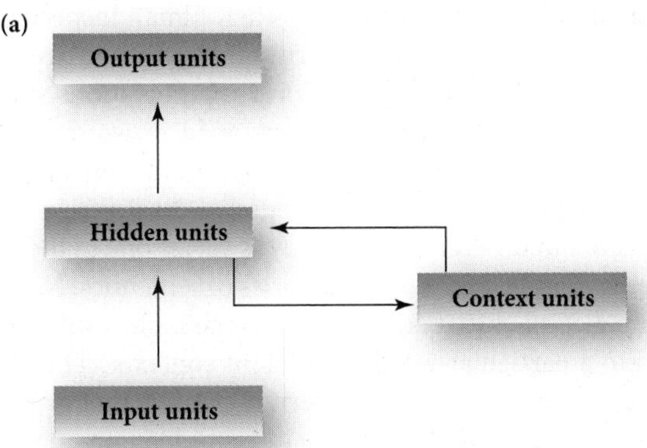

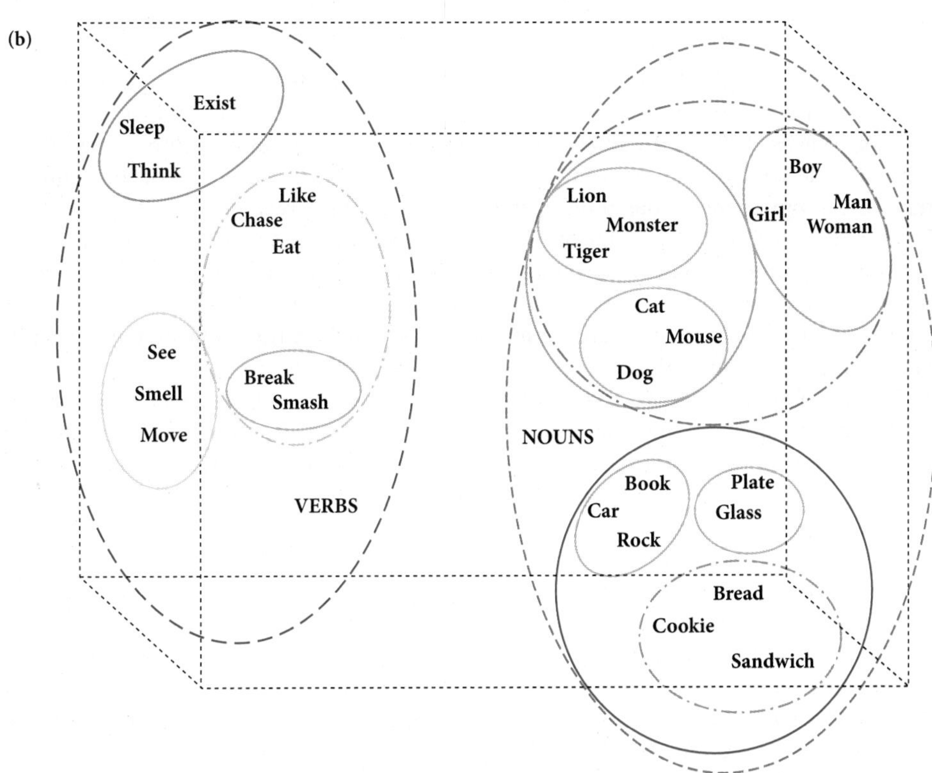

Figure 3.14 A schematic of Elman's (2004, p. 203) simple recurrent network model of auditory word processing. Top: The architecture of the network. Bottom: The semantic space that emerged after the model was trained.

SRN model adapted TRACE's three-layered network and added to it a set of context units. The job of the context units was to store a copy of the activations in the hidden units between processing cycles. In this way, the network would respond not just to the current state of the input units, but also to recent events, as reflected in the activity of the context units. The explicit task that the network performed was to predict the upcoming word in an utterance. Before training, the network's connection weights were randomized, and then it processed a set of sentences one word at a time. As each word was encountered, the network tried to predict what the next word would be. When it made errors, the connection weights throughout the network were changed so that its output would more closely match the desired output the next time around. In this system, word identities can be represented as a pattern of activation among the hidden units. When Elman inspected these patterns after the network was trained, he found that the patterns split neatly into two classes, corresponding to nouns and verbs. Within each class, the word representations subdivided further into subclasses, with similar representations being assigned to words that we would judge as being close in meaning (see Figure 3.14, bottom). The model further subdivided individual word representations (e.g., *book*), by producing slightly different patterns of activation when the word appeared in different contexts. This solves one of the sticky problems faced by the "dictionary entry" and feature-based theories of semantics. Namely, how do you have enough entries in the dictionary to take care of all of the slightly different shades of meaning that you can assign to a particular word in different contexts? The SRN model solves this problem by letting context influence the pattern of activity that occurs in the network, so the representation of the word *ball* (the activity in the hidden units) will be slightly different in a baseball context and a playground context.

DISTRIBUTED COHORT MODEL

The distributed COHORT model (DCM) borrows some of its architectural features from parallel distributed processing models like Elman's distributed feature model (Gaskell & Marslen-Wilson, 1997, 2001, 2002). DCM takes phonetic features as its input, runs them through a hidden layer of processing units, which is also connected to a set of context units that store a copy of the hidden units' pattern of activation between processing cycles (as in Elman's SRN). The system uses the output of the hidden units to activate two further groups of processing units, one of which represents phonological word forms and one of which represents word meanings ("lexical semantics"). In this model, acoustic stimuli activate phonetic feature units, which activate hidden units, which in turn activate semantic and phonological word form units

DCM proposes that auditory/phonological information is represented in one set of processing units, while semantic information is represented in another set of processing units. But rather than information flowing from acoustic to phonetic to word form to meaning, as in the default model, auditory information is conceived of as being directly and simultaneously connected to both stored phonological codes and stored semantic (meaning) codes. Thus, each word in your vocabulary is represented simultaneously as a vector in a phonological space and as a vector in a semantic space. You recognize a word when the pattern of activity in the phonological and semantic units stabilizes and settles into the pattern that corresponds to that word. Because auditory information for phonologically related words is similar, different words that contain the same sounds will activate similar patterns of activation within the phonological units. Because word meanings are arbitrarily and essentially randomly connected to auditory information, different words with similar sounds will activate different, randomly assorted parts of the semantic space.

The simultaneous activation of phonological and semantic units has a number of consequences for word recognition and activation of meaning. In the initial moments of lexical access, when the onsets of words are heard, processing units in both the phonological and semantic spaces become activated. Activation in the phonological space will be coherent and mutually reinforcing because words with the same onset will share aspects of phonological representation. Activation in the semantic space will represent a blend of different semantic patterns. That is, the initial pattern of activation in the semantic network does not correspond to any of the stable states that represent individual word meanings. The pattern of activity in the semantic nodes therefore does not correspond to any familiar word meaning.

One of the things that the DCM is good at is explaining how *coarticulation* affects word recognition and lexical access. As you recall from Chapter 2, coarticulation changes the way phonemes are produced. A phoneme that is normally produced with the tongue touching the alveolar ridge, such as the /n/ sound can be pronounced like an /m/ if the following phoneme is going to be a bilabial stop like the /b/ sound. So, the /n/ in *lean* will be pronounced as an /m/ sound in the context of *lean bacon* (*lean* will be pronounced as if it were *leam*). Although this is an example of coarticulation that crosses a word boundary, similar effects occur within words. The way you pronounce the /o/ sound in *job* is slightly different than the way you pronounce the /o/ sound in *jog*—the phoneme that follows the /o/ sound "pulls" the articulators away from their normal places and toward the place where the /b/ and /g/ phonemes are normally produced (the front and the back of the mouth, respectively). DCM captures these coarticulation effects by representing the /o/ sound in *jog* with a slightly different pattern in the phonological units than the /o/ sound in *job*.

In normal speech, the /o/ sound in *jog* will always be a little bit different than the /o/ sound in *job*, and the speech recognition system can use these differences to predict the phoneme that will follow. But what happens if there is a mismatch between the /o/ sound and the next phoneme? According to the default model, phoneme identification precedes lexical access, the /o/ sounds in *jog* and *job* will both be identified as /o/, so if the /o/ in *jog* is spliced into the word *job*, that should not cause any problems at all. But according to DCM, cross-splicing vowels that are pronounced in different ways in different contexts will be a problem, because the pattern of activation in the phonological units that results from this kind of cross-splicing will not match the pattern of activation that normally occurs. In fact, people have a hard time responding to cross-spliced stimuli when both of the segments of the cross-spliced stimulus come from real words (Dahan, Magnuson, Tanenhaus, & Hogan, 2001; Gaskell, Quinlan, Tamminen, & Cleland, 2008; Marslen-Wilson & Warren, 1994; Streeter & Nigro, 1979).[22] When DCM is used to model people's responses to cross-spliced stimuli with sublexical mismatch between vowels and adjacent consonants, it accurately predicts reaction times on both lexical decision and phoneme monitoring tasks (Gaskell & Marslen-Wilson, 1997).

DCM also has a good explanation for what happens to word perception when coarticulation and assimilation change the way people pronounce words, like *lean* and *run*. The velar consonant /n/ gets pronounced like an /m/ when it is followed by a bilabial stop consonant (e.g., /b/ and /p/), because the bilabial stop "pulls" the articulators away from their usual or canonical positions. How do people perceive these "altered" pronunciations? It depends on whether the changed stimulus closely matches a word that you already know, and it also depends on whether you hear the "altered" stimulus in isolation or in the context of an extended utterance. When the word *lean* is followed by a word beginning with a bilabial stop, it is pronounced like *leam* (Gaskell & Snoeren, 2008). So, *leam* could be stored in the lexicon as an alternative pronunciation of *lean*, in which case people should perceive *leam* as *lean*. But when *leam* is presented in isolation people perceive it as *leam*. When the same token is embedded in an extended utterance, with a bilabial stop following the coarticulated /m/ sound, they perceive the word as being *lean*. Sometimes coarticulation produces another real word, as when coarticulated *run* turns into *rum*. When the coarticulated *rum* token is presented in isolation, people perceive it as being the word *rum*. When the coarticulated *rum* token is presented in an extended utterance followed by a bilabial stop, people are more likely to perceive it as the word *run*, than if *rum* is presented all by itself (Gaskell & Marslen-Wilson, 2001), and this effect is stronger when the preceding sentence context favors the *exercise* meaning over the *drinking* meaning. DCM can explain these context effects on perception by invoking the semantic portion of the network. When the bottom-up acoustic information favors two lexical entries about equally, and the pattern of phonological activation is intermediate between /m/ and /n/, the candidate that produces the better match in the semantic side "wins" the competition and ends up being selected.

DCM is also good at explaining why words with multiple meanings are harder to process than words with multiple related senses (Rodd, Gaskell, & Marslen-Wilson, 2004). Words with multiple meanings, like *bark* (as in *tree bark* and *Does your dog bark? The ancient mariner crossed the sea in a bark*) lead to less coherent activation in the semantic part of the network; and words with multiple senses, like *twist* (as in *Give the handle a twist, Can you do the twist? Oliver has gone round the twist*) lead to a more coherent pattern of activation. (Elman's SRN makes similar claims with respect to different flavors of meaning for words like *ball.*)

DCM differs from the original COHORT model in that DCM places less emphasis on word beginnings as a critical element in lexical access. Part of the motivation for this is experiments that show that non-word primes can activate word form representations that differ in onset (*dob* and *tob* will both prime the word *bob*; Connine, Blasko, & Titone, 1993), as long as the altered phoneme shares some features with the original phoneme.

Lexical Ambiguity Resolution

So far, we have been assuming that each word in the input has one and only one matching representation in the lexicon, and only one meaning. This is not true. Many words have more than one meaning. The word *bank*, for example, can refer to a place where you keep your money or it can refer to a place next to a river where you go fishing. According to some estimates, over 40% of the words that you hear in English have more than one meaning (and this does not include the temporary ambiguities that happen when you hear words with onset-embedded words in them, like *ham* in *hamster*; Gernsbacher, 1990). So what happens when you hear or read a word that has more than one meaning? Do you go straight to the contextually appropriate or correct meaning? Or do you have to sort through incorrect or contextually inappropriate meanings before you get to the correct one?

According to the *exclusive access* hypothesis, you can use cues from the context to immediately select the correct meaning of an ambiguous word like *bank*. When you hear or see the word *bank* you access only one meaning. If you are listening to a story about money, you access the financial institution meaning; and if the story is about fishing, you access the river-related meaning instead. But as we saw before, early events in word processing seem to involve activation of multiple candidates pretty much all the time. If visual and acoustic stimuli activate multiple word forms that they are associated with, maybe word forms simultaneously activate multiple meanings that they are associated with. This latter hypothesis is called the *exhaustive access* account. Exhaustive access says that you activate all of the meanings that are associated with an individual word like *bank*, even though only one of those meanings will be appropriate in any given situation.[23]

The exclusive and exhaustive access accounts were first tested in a series of priming experiments (Swinney, 1979; Onifer & Swinney, 1981; Seidenberg, Tanenhaus, Leiman, & Bienkowski, 1982). In these experiments, ambiguous words like *bug* were embedded in contexts that made one of their meanings more appropriate than the other. For example, the sentence might be, *The spy swept the room looking for concealed bugs*, in which case the "listening device" meaning of *bug* would be appropriate. In another case, the context sentence might be, *The cook picked up a bag of flour in the kitchen and saw the bugs.* In that case, the correct meaning would be the "insect" version. To assess which meanings subjects accessed, their responses to words associated with the different meanings were measured. If people access the "listening device" meaning of *bug,* then they should respond faster to the target word *listen* than to an unrelated control word. If people access the "insect" meaning of *bug,* then they should respond faster to the target word *insect* than to an unrelated control word. So after people heard the word *bugs,* they responded as quickly as possible to a test word flashed up on a computer screen. The test word could be related to one or the other meaning of the word *bug,* or it could be unrelated. The difference in response time between related and control words provides an index of how activated the related word meanings were. Hearing the word *bugs* made people respond faster to target words related to either of its meanings, no matter which meaning was appropriate in context. These results are more compatible with the exhaustive access hypothesis, and they are incompatible with the exclusive access hypothesis. People do not appear to select only the right meaning. Both contextually appropriate meanings and inappropriate meanings are activated when people hear an ambiguous word like *bugs.*

If appropriate and inappropriate meanings are both activated when we hear an ambiguous word, how do we ever figure out the correct meaning of an utterance? If the "insect" meaning gets activated in a "listening device" context, why don't we interpret the utterance as referring to insects rather than listening devices? The answer is that context does affect meaning selection eventually, even though it does not appear to prevent incorrect meanings from being activated in the first place. In follow-on experiments investigating meaning selection for ambiguous words, experimenters manipulated the amount of time that elapsed between the ambiguous word and presentation of the target word. The amount of time that passes between presentation of the ambiguous word and presentation of the target is called *stimulus offset asynchrony* (or SOA). In some studies, target words are presented immediately after the ambiguous word in some conditions, and they are presented at longer SOAs in other conditions. Different patterns of results are observed at different SOAs in experiments looking at ambiguous word processing. If target words are presented immediately after the ambiguous word, all of a word's associated meanings are primed. But if you wait until 250–500 ms after the ambiguous word to present the target word, you get a different pattern of results. At longer SOAs, only meanings that are appropriate in context are primed. This means that, although all of the meanings of *bugs* are activated when you hear the word, context causes you to deactivate or suppress the inappropriate meaning after a short period of time. Thus, your long-term representation for the utterance will contain only the appropriate meanings, and your interpretation will not be cluttered with inappropriate meanings.

Does context influence meaning selection for ambiguous words?

To explain how context influences meaning selection in ambiguous word processing, we need to introduce the idea of *meaning dominance.* Many words have multiple meanings, but those meanings are not all created equal. Some meanings occur more frequently than others. For example, the "metal ore" meaning of *tin* (as in *This can is made out of tin*) is far more frequent in American English than the "container" meaning of *tin* (as in *I bought a tin of beans.*) So, *tin* is like *bugs,* in that they both have more than one meaning. But *tin* is unlike *bugs* in that one of its meanings occurs more often than the other. This property of ambiguous words is referred to as *meaning dominance.* Some ambiguous words have one frequent (*dominant*) meaning, and other less frequent (*subordinate*) meanings. Let's call this kind of word a *biased* ambiguous word. Other ambiguous words have two roughly equally frequent meanings. Let's call this kind of word a *balanced* ambiguous word. It turns out that different kinds of ambiguous words, biased and balanced, have different effects on people's behavior, and these differences reflect different underlying meaning-access processes.

When balanced ambiguous words are presented in a neutral context, they behave like *bugs* did—both meanings are activated simultaneously to roughly the same extent. That can be demonstrated in experiments involving eye tracking. In an eye-tracking experiment, people read texts—sentences, in this case—and their eye movements are recorded. Because eye movements are linked to the mental processes involved in interpreting the text (Rayner, 1998; Rayner & Pollatsek, 1989, 2006), we can estimate how much difficulty people have interpreting a given piece of text by measuring how long they look at that piece of text. When people read balanced ambiguous words in a sentence, *The woman saw the bugs …* they fixate those words longer than matched control words that have only one meaning. When people read biased words, like *tin*, a different pattern emerges. People read biased words just as quickly as matched unambiguous control words, suggesting that they are only activating one meaning. Note that in these cases, the context that comes before the balanced ambiguous word does not indicate which meaning is appropriate. These are called *neutral* contexts. But we can change the context so that it favors one or the other of the word's meanings. For example, we could change the context so that it favors the "insect" meaning of *bugs*, as in *What crawled out from under the sink was a bunch of bugs.*

This kind of biasing context has different effects depending on whether the critical word is balanced (*bugs*) or biased (*tin*). Biasing contexts cause balanced ambiguous words to be processed as quickly as matched unambiguous words. So you read *bugs* just as quickly as a word with only one meaning when the preceding context points you toward one of its meanings (Duffy, Henderson, & Morris, 1989; Rayner & Duffy, 1987; see also Tabossi, Colombo, & Job, 1987, and Tabossi & Zardon, 1993, who found a similar pattern of results in a set of priming experiments). Biasing contexts have different effects on biased ambiguous words, depending on whether the dominant or subordinate meaning is appropriate. If the context makes the dominant meaning appropriate (e.g., *The miners went under the mountain to look for* ***tin***), the ambiguous word is processed just as quickly as a matched control word that has only one meaning (e.g., *The miners went under the mountain to look for* ***gold***). But if the biasing context points toward the infrequent meaning of a biased ambiguous word (*The miners went to the store and saw that they had beans in a tin*), it takes people a long time to read the word *tin*, suggesting that they are having a hard time accessing its subordinate (less frequent) meaning. A recent neuroimaging experiment showed that the same factors of meaning dominance (balanced versus biased) and context (supporting the dominant or subordinate meaning of a biased ambiguous word) affected the neural response to sentences containing ambiguous words (Mason & Just, 2007).

Balanced ambiguous words are read slowly in neutral contexts (suggesting exhaustive access to all of their meanings) and quickly in biasing contexts (suggesting that biasing context helps people select an appropriate meaning of a balanced ambiguous word). Biased ambiguous words are read quickly in neutral contexts (suggesting rapid access to one meaning), quickly when biasing context points toward the dominant meaning, and slowly when biasing context points toward the subordinate meaning. This pattern of response inspired the *reordered access theory* (Duffy et al., 1989; Rayner & Duffy, 1987). According to *reordered access*, access to word meanings is influenced by two interacting factors. The first factor is meaning dominance—more frequent meanings will be easier to access than infrequent meanings. When you encounter a word, the bottom-up input activates all of the semantic representations associated with the word. Word representations are organized as in the TRACE model, so that when more than one representation is activated by a word, the activated representations compete with one another. Biased ambiguous words are easy to process because the dominant meaning wins the competition quickly. Balanced ambiguous words are more difficult to process because the two competing representations are more evenly matched, and it takes longer for competition to select a winner. The second factor that influences meaning selection is the context that a word appears in. When context and meaning dominance both favor the frequent meaning of an ambiguous word, competition between multiple activated word meanings is short-lived—the dominant meaning wins the competition very quickly. When context favors the less frequent meaning, its activation is raised to the point where it becomes an effective competitor with the more dominant meaning. As a result, the subordinate meaning can be selected when context favors it, but it takes more time for the subordinate meaning to beat down the more frequent dominant meaning.

The Neural Basis of Lexical Representation and Lexical Access

Investigating what happens when people experience brain damage (*neuropsychological* approaches) and measuring activity in the intact brain (*neurophysiological* and *neuroimaging* approaches) are great ways to study how word meanings are organized in the brain and how the brain performs the processes required for lexical access. Neuropsychological approaches have demonstrated that knowledge of concepts and knowledge about word forms are handled by quasi-independent systems in the brain. That is, people can have intact knowledge of concepts, without being able to recover information about the word forms that refer to those concepts and vice versa (e.g., Damasio, Grabowski, Tranel, Hichwa, & Damasio, 1996; Tranel, Logan, Frank, & Damasio, 1997). Neuroimaging experiments support a shared semantic system for words and pictures, but some brain areas respond more to words than pictures, and vice versa (Vandenberghe, Price, Wise, Josephs, & Frackowiak, 1996; Wagner et al., 1997). When subjects judged the similarity between word meanings or pictures, both kinds of stimuli activated a network of left-hemisphere brain areas including the superior occipital cortex, the inferior (bottom) temporal lobes and the inferior frontal lobes (see Plate 4, top). Word-specific activity was observed in a region of the left hemisphere in the superior temporal and medial (toward the center of the brain) anterior (front) temporal lobes (Plate 4, middle), as well as in the frontal cortex. Pictures selectively activated a region near the left superior temporal sulcus (Plate 4, bottom).

In the normally functioning brain, non-linguistic conceptual knowledge and linguistic knowledge about words somehow combine to produce meaning when words are heard or read. How is this done? And where is it done? Answering where word meanings are stored in the brain and how the brain activates those meanings in response to auditory and visual stimulation runs into immediate complications when you consider that there are many different ways to classify words at many different levels of abstraction (open class vs. closed class, noun vs. verb, animate vs. inanimate, regular vs. exception, high frequency vs. low frequency, animal vs. vegetable vs. mineral, and on and on and on). So you should not be surprised to learn that, although widespread left-lateralized brain activity occurs when people listen to or read words, the specific pattern of brain activity reflects an interaction of word and task properties (Booth et al., 2003; Friederici, Opitz, & von Cramon, 2000; Posner & Raichle, 1994). Brain responses that depend on word properties can be observed in both neuropsychological and neuroimaging studies. Some aphasic patients appear to have greater difficulty retrieving information about verbs than about nouns, and others have the opposite problem (Caramazza & Hillis, 1991; Damasio & Tranel, 1993). These differences in the ability to retrieve words happen even when the two versions are nearly identical, as

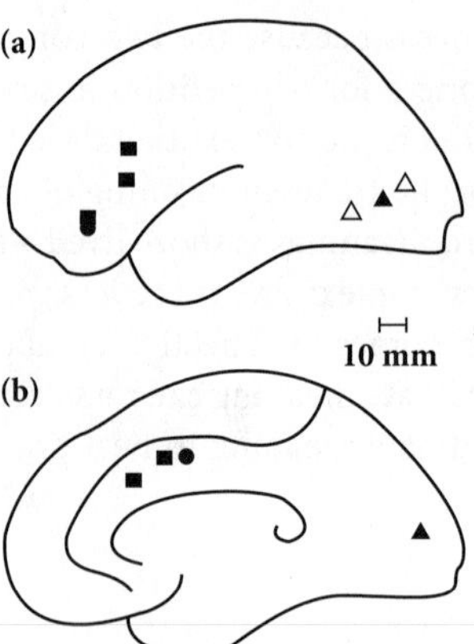

Figure 3.15 Results from PET neuroimaging experiments (Posner, Petersen, Fox, & Raichle, 1988, p. 1630). Triangles indicate greater neural activity when participants passively looked at words, compared to a fixation cross baseline condition (solid black shapes indicate left-hemisphere activity, open shapes indicate right-hemisphere activity). Squares indicate areas with greater activity in the action-generation task versus repeating nouns out loud. Circles indicate areas with greater activity during the dangerous animals task than passive viewing of nouns.

in the noun–verb pair *a crack* and *to crack*, and may be more severe for words that are less semantically complex, despite their greater frequency in the language (Breedin et al., 1998).

Different kinds of words appear to activate different brain areas, potentially reflecting differences in the way the brain represents the concepts the words refer to. In a landmark PET study, Alex Martin and colleagues showed pictures of animals and tools and had participants say the names of the pictured object silently to themselves (Martin et al., 1996).[24] Different patterns of activation in the brain were observed for animals and tools. Greater activity was observed in occipital regions when naming animals, and greater activity was observed in inferior frontal regions when naming tools (see Plate 5).[25] Other ERP and imaging studies have shown that words referring to *concrete* entities (like *cat*, *dog*, and *table*) produce different patterns of neural response than function words (like *between*, *because*, and *where*; Nobre & McCarthy, 1994; Nobre, Price, Turner, & Friston, 1997).

Neuroimaging and neuropsychological studies also show that the brain areas involved in processing a word differ depending on what kind of task people are doing when they encounter the word. When people are asked to generate the action that goes with a noun like *hammer*, activity is focused in the anterior cingulate gyrus, the left inferior frontal lobes, and the right cerebellum (Petersen, Fox, Posner, Mintun, & Raichle, 1989; Posner et al., 1988; Posner & Raichle, 1994). In seminal PET imaging studies, Mike Posner and colleagues measured the brain's response to sets of nouns under different task conditions that he hoped would engage different brain regions. In one condition, brain activity during passive perception of words was compared to a fixation-cross baseline (that is, subjects just looked at an "X" on the screen during the baseline task). In the *dangerous animals* condition, participants would view a list of nouns and decide whether each one represented a dangerous animal or not (this is a type of *semantic categorization* task). In the *action generation* task, participants viewed each noun (e.g., *hammer*) and said an action that a person would undertake with that object (e.g., *pound*). Passively viewing words and not doing anything with them led to greater activity in the occipital lobes in both cerebral hemispheres. Tasks that tapped semantic features (dangerousness) or associations (between nouns and actions) produced left-lateralized activation in the frontal lobes (see Figure 3.15).

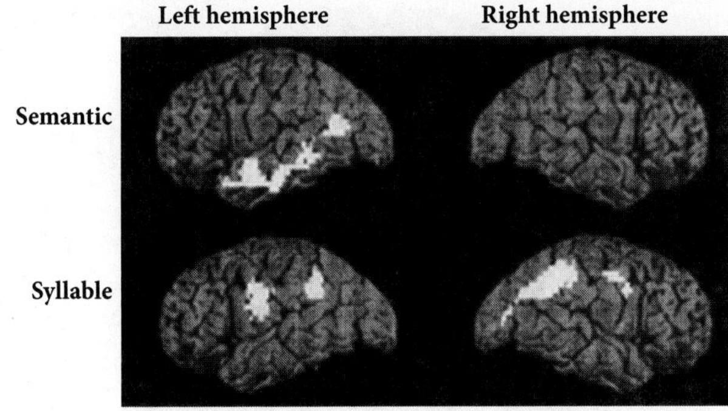

Figure 3.16 PET data showing the neural response to a semantic judgment task (top) and a phonological judgment task (bottom) (Price et al., 1997, p. 729)

Different patterns of brain activity are also observed between tasks that focus on the semantic properties of words in contrast to their phonological properties. PET data showed significant neural activity throughout substantial parts of the left temporal lobe in response to semantic judgments, and bilateral (both sides of the brain) activation in more dorsal (toward the top) areas in response to judgments about how words sound (Price, Moore, Humphreys, & Wise, 1997; see Figure 3.16). Other neuroimaging experiments also indicate that left prefrontal involvement in semantic processing tasks differs across different tasks involving the same words (Goldberg, Perfetti, Fiez, & Schneider, 2007). Questions that tapped abstract, verbally acquired knowledge about animals led to stronger activation of left frontal regions than questions that tapped more concrete, directly observable properties of animals, even though the different kinds of questions were equally difficult to answer (see Plate 6; see also Bright, Moss, Longe, Stamatakis, & Tyler, 2006; Demb et al., 1995).[26] Different regions of the left prefrontal cortex also appear to be involved in tasks that tap semantic versus phonological knowledge associated with individual words. Some subregions are more activated when participants judge whether two words have similar meanings, while other subregions are more activated when participants judge whether two words rhyme (Heim et al., 2005; Roskies, Fiez, Balota, Raichle, & Petersen, 2001; see also Mainy et al., 2008). Transcranial magnetic stimulation results also suggest an anterior–semantic, posterior–phonological organization of the left inferior frontal region (Gough, Nobre, & Devlin, 2005). Other studies have shown differences in brain activity in the left inferior frontal lobe occurring in response to lexical decision and verb-generation tasks (Frith, Friston, Liddle, & Frackowiak, 1991).

Keeping in mind that the precise pattern of brain activity that is associated with a word depends on characteristics of the individual word and the task that the person is engaged in, word processing tasks generally activate a network of left-hemisphere regions. Right-hemisphere activity is also seen in some circumstances, especially for processing of words referring to abstract concepts (Kiehl et al., 1999), but greater neural activity in word processing tasks normally occurs in the left hemisphere.

Processing models assume a separate set of input representations for auditory and visual word processing (e.g., Coltheart et al., 2001; McClelland & Elman, 1986; McClelland & Rumelhart, 1981), and this division is reflected in different patterns of activity in spoken and visual word processing. Auditory input more strongly activates Wernicke's area (near the junction of the occipital, temporal, and parietal lobes); and visual input may not activate this area at all (Howard et al., 1992; Petersen, Fox, Posner, Mintun, & Raichle, 1988). Brain regions involved in auditory word processing include the superior temporal lobes bilaterally. These regions are involved in analyzing the acoustic and phonetic properties of the input

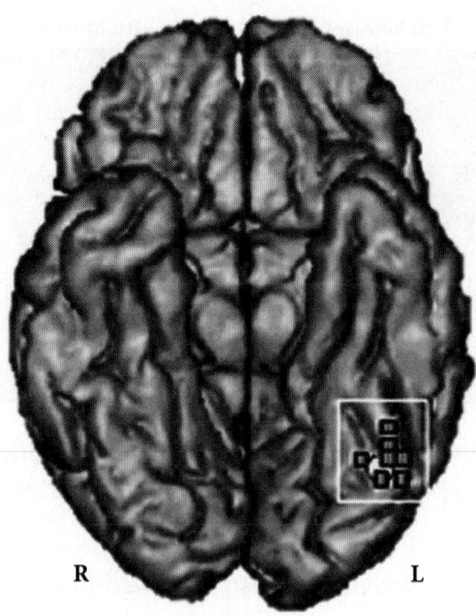

Figure 3.17 The visual word form area (from Cohen et al., 2002, p. 1060). The left hemisphere appears on the right side of the figure.

(Kluender & Kiefte, 2006; Scott, Blank, Rosen, & Wise, 2000). Some theorists suggest that a portion of the superior (top) posterior (toward the back) temporal lobe in the left hemisphere contains a *phonological word form area* that is responsible for mapping acoustic information onto stored representations of individual words (e.g., Friederici, 2002).

Basic visual processing of written words is conducted by portions of the *striate* ("stripey") and *extrastriate visual cortex* in the occipital lobes in both hemispheres (these areas also respond to other complex visual stimuli). Further input processing of written words is associated with activity in the *visual word form area*, an area in the left hemisphere anterior (toward the front) to basic visual processing areas that is near other *perisylvian* cortical regions that are thought to be involved in phonological and semantic processes (Cohen et al., 2002; Dehaene, Le Clec'H, Poline, Le Bihan, & Cohen, 2002; McCandliss, Cohen, & Dehaene, 2003; Nobre, Allison, & McCarthy, 1994). This area responds to pronounceable letter strings, but not to spoken words or word-like stimuli; and it does not respond to complex visual stimuli other than words. Figure 3.17 displays the location of the visual word form area.[27]

When a stimulus has activated auditory or visual input codes, additional neural activity will reflect access to aspects of the words' semantic and syntactic properties, and the integration of these features into a representation of the ongoing discourse. At some point, this activity will not depend on whether the word was heard or read, and so it will reflect modality-independent information associated with the word in question. Such *post-lexical* processes are associated with widespread left-lateralized neural activity spread across regions in the anterior occipital cortex forward through inferior parietal lobes, the medial and inferior temporal lobes, the temporal poles, and the inferior frontal lobes (Friederici et al., 2000; Howard et al., 1992). However, only a small portion of this activity appears to be task independent. Activity in the inferior (bottom) temporal lobe and frontal lobes appears to increase when tasks focus on semantic (as opposed to syntactic or visual features) of words. Activity in the superior temporal lobes appears to be more related to phonological analysis, which has led some theorists to propose a neural organization scheme in which dorsal (toward the top) brain areas are involved in phonological and motor analysis of speech input, while middle areas are involved in syntactic–relational information, and ventral (toward the bottom) areas are involved in retrieval of semantic information (Shalom & Poeppel, 2008; Thompson-Schill, Aguirre, D'Esposito, & Farah, 1999).

Similarly, the brain may be organized along the posterior–anterior dimension, with more posterior regions involved in retrieval of more basic features and more anterior areas involved in processing complex combinations of features and other relational information (Noppeney et al., 2007; Randall, Moss, Rodd, Greer, & Tyler, 2004). This approach is supported by neuropsychological studies showing dissociations between verbs and nouns. Problems dealing with verbs are more associated with frontal lobe damage, while problems dealing with nouns referring to concrete entities is associated more with temporal lobe damage (Caramazza & Hillis, 1991). An alternative hypothesis proposes that the poster–anterior organization may reflect a functional–perceptual distinction, as stimuli relating to tools (defined by their functions) appear to activate posterior brain regions more strongly than stimuli relating to animals (which are distinguished more by what they look like than what they're good for; Tranel, Grabowski, Lyon, & Damasio, 2005), whether those stimuli are conveyed as words, pictures, or as sounds associated with objects (like *moo* for cow, or a snipping sound for scissors).

Hanna Damasio and her colleagues tested over 100 brain-damaged patients and correlated their performance on tasks involving the names of tools, animals, and people (Damasio et al., 1996). By mapping the locations of brain lesions and comparing lesion location with performance for different kinds of words, Damasio's group found that brain damage in posterior areas of the left temporal lobe correlated with deficits on tools, damage to adjacent more anterior regions was correlated with deficits on animals, and damage to the temporal pole was correlated with deficits on people (see Plate 7). These data could be interpreted as showing that different concepts are represented by different underlying neural systems. But critically, the vast majority of Damasio's patients could define concepts that they could not name. So, a patient might respond to a picture of a skunk by saying, "Oh, that animal makes a terrible smell if you get too close to it; it is black and white, and gets squashed on the road by cars sometimes" (Damasio et al., 1996, p. 499). So the patient's problem is not that they lack knowledge about the concept; rather there is something that prevents them from coming up with the name even though they can access aspects of the concept's meaning. As a result, Damasio and colleagues suggest that the temporal regions affected by their patients' lesions are responsible for *intermediary processes* that provide the links between distributed conceptual knowledge and phonological word form knowledge that is supported by language areas in the superior temporal lobe and the temporal–parietal–occipital junction. That is, the different regions of the temporal lobe are not storing localized conceptual representations. Instead,

> *when the concept of a given tool is evoked (based on the activation of several regions which support pertinent conceptual knowledge) … an intermediary region becomes active and promotes (in the appropriate sensorimotor structures) the explicit representation of phonemic knowledge pertaining to the word form which denotes the given tool. When a concept from another category is evoked, that of a particular person for example, a different intermediary region is engaged. (Damasio et al., 1996, pp. 503–504)*

How are word meanings represented in the brain?

One of the enduring controversies in language science relates to how word meanings are represented in the brain, and a good way to get into this debate is to look at the phenomenon of *category-specific* semantic deficits. Category-specific semantic deficits happen when an individual has difficulty understanding the meanings of some types of words but not others. In particular, there seems to be a distinction between the processing of words that refer to natural kinds (animals, plants, and foods) and artificial or man-made objects (tools, buildings, and objects). The existence of category-specific deficits has been used to argue for localized semantic representations or separate semantic systems for living and non-living things (e.g., Caramazza & Hillis, 1991; Pinker, 1994). According to the *localizationist* theories, semantic memory has been divided into separate categories by natural selection, because those categories represent biologically important domains. That conceptual division is reflected in a physical division of different kinds of concepts in different physical locations in the brain. So, if a lesion strikes the area that is responsible for representing conceptual knowledge of tools, an individual with that kind of damage will not be able to comprehend or produce words relating to those lost concepts. Other concepts may be completely spared, however, because they are physically instantiated in an undamaged region of the brain.

The localizationist approach contrasts with the distributed representation approach. According to the distributed representation approach, concepts are represented as coordinated patterns of activity across a wide variety of brain regions. In this kind of account, word representations can be thought of as a kind of *Hebbian cell assembly* (e.g., Pulvermüller, 1999). Hebb was a theorist who was active in memory research at the dawn of the cognitive revolution. He argued that concepts (and other kinds of long-term memories) consisted of linked groups of neurons. Groups of neurons are tied together with excitatory connections so that any time one of the members of the group becomes active, all of the other members of the group also become active. In this way, a simple retrieval cue could activate a rich and complex array of knowledge. You can think of a word as a retrieval cue that activates a sub-assembly representing the word's form, and the concepts and associations that become activated when you hear the word reflect the other components of a Hebbian cell assembly. How do Hebbian cell assemblies form in the brain? According to Pulvermüller (1999), such assemblies form when different groups of neurons are active at the same time. For word learning, this happens when neurons that respond to the sound of a word fire at the same time as other neurons that are responsible for representing perceptual (visual, tactile, auditory, etc.) and functional (what do you do with the object?) properties of the object. Once these associations are formed, you can access the sound when the perceptual and functional properties are activated (by direct experience or recollection); and the sound will similarly activate perceptual and functional representations associated with the name (as in the embodied semantics account). The fundamental claim is that word representations reflect neurally distributed groups of neurons that fire together when one subcomponent of the cell assembly becomes activated.

The idea that different kinds of words are represented in different parts of the brain has been investigated by looking at how word knowledge breaks down following brain damage and by neurophysiological and neuroimaging studies of normally functioning individuals. At first blush, the existence of category-specific deficits in semantic knowledge and word processing would seem to favor localization over distributed representations. Localized representations offer a quick and efficient explanation for why one category would go away but others would not, and one of the hallmarks of distributed systems is graceful and gradual reduction in function following damage. However, a detailed look at the available evidence and a fresh look at the organization of semantic memory provides a major boost to the distributed representations position.

First, consider that the loss of knowledge of living things is more common than loss of knowledge of artificial kinds. Better preservation of knowledge about artificial kinds than natural kinds can be demonstrated in *confrontation naming* (patients try to say the word that goes with a pictured animal or object), *category fluency* (patients try to give as many

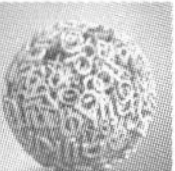

DEFINITIONS OF LIVING AND NON-LIVING THINGS PROVIDED BY PATIENTS WITH A CATEGORY-SPECIFIC DEFICIT FOR LIVING THINGS

Patient RC
Bee—"Bees are animals. And I've forgotten what they look like. But they're two-eyed, similar to humans. Two eyes of a see-through. Or a hearing, of—two ears. Of a mouth—of an eating, drinking."

Bike—"Bikes are two-wheeled, some are four-wheeled—of a learning of, of a learning for children ... or a two in the centr-ish, in the two on either side on the back, of a balance, of a get a go, of a p ... of a, I don't know what it's called ... of a pedalling, of a pedalling and a steering and a four-wheeled as a start of a learn."

(Moss et al., 1998, p. 304)

Patient JBR
Snail—"An insect animal."

Briefcase—"Small case used by students to carry papers."
(Warrington & Shallice, 1984; in Saffran & Schwartz, 1994, pp. 513–514)

examples as possible of a given category, like *plant*, or *animal*), and *definition* tasks (patients try to give a definition for a word). The box above provides some example definition task responses from patients with category-specific deficits for living things. These patients typically have damage to inferior and anterior portions of the temporal lobes (Saffran & Schwartz, 1994). Deficits for tools are associated with damage to posterior portions of the temporal lobes, and the portion of the parietal lobe near the occipital–temporal junction (Damasio et al., 1996). Worse performance for non-living than for living categories is generally observed only in patients with the most severe semantic deficits (Moss et al., 1998). The localizationist/separate systems position explains why knowledge of living and non-living things can differ, but it does not explain why deficits occur for living things more often than non-living things.

Second, consider that the degradation of semantic knowledge is not all-or-nothing. Some information about the impaired category is preserved, and patients do better on some tasks than others, depending on how much detailed knowledge is required to do the task, independent of whether the task taps into knowledge of living or non-living concepts. Bright and his colleagues (Bright et al., 2006) used a technique similar to Bates and colleagues' voxel-based lesion symptom mapping technique (VLSM) to investigate the relationship between conceptual knowledge, word processing, and the brain. In this study, patients with brain damage in different parts of the brain performed tasks that involved different types of words—natural kinds (like *cat*, *horse*) and artifacts (like *hammer*, *automobile*). The researchers measured the neural response to different kinds of objects and different kinds of information-processing tasks using fMRI. As in VLSM, the researchers measured where the peak response in the brain occurred, they assessed how well patients did on the different kinds of objects and tasks, and they correlated the neural response with accuracy on the different tasks. Patients with greater signal intensity in the anterior (front) part of the temporal lobes did better on tasks involving natural kinds, when those tasks called for judgments about the fine details that you would need to know to discriminate between different concepts (e.g., *Do cats have whiskers? Do dogs bark?*). Questions that tapped shared features (*Do cats have legs? Do dogs have fur?*) were *not* associated with greater signal intensity in the anterior temporal lobes. If knowledge of natural kinds was supported in general by a neural network located in the anterior temporal lobes, both kinds of questions should have led to similar signal intensities in that brain region. Thus, these results are more compatible with a distributed account of semantic knowledge, with increasingly complex features and combinations of features supported by more anterior regions, but without a dissociation between living and non-living categories in terms of where in the brain associated information is stored.

Thomas Grabowski and colleagues' (2001) PET neuroimaging study involving famous landmarks and people also creates problems for the localizationist account of semantic representation. According to the localizationist account, concepts from different categories (e.g., animals, tools) are represented in different regions of the brain and accessed by different neural systems. The perceptual–functional approach argues instead that left-hemisphere semantic processing regions are organized along the posterior–anterior axis such that functional and more general features are represented more posteriorly, and more complex combinations of features are represented more anteriorly. According to the localizationist account, pictures of landmarks (e.g., The Washington Monument, The Hubert H. Humphrey Metrodome, Carhenge) and people should activate different brain regions than pictures of famous people. According to the perceptual–functional approach, discriminating between landmarks and people both involve assessing fine-grained details, and so discriminating landmarks and people should both depend on more anterior regions, such as the temporal pole. In Grabowski and colleagues' PET study, unique landmarks and famous people both activated the left temporal pole and no differences in neural activity in any brain region were found between the famous landmarks and famous people conditions. These data are straightforwardly compatible with the perceptual–functional approach, but pose problems for accounts that propose separate localized representations for living and non-living categories. Other neuroimaging studies have also shown that the same brain regions become activated by words in different conceptual categories (Chao, Weisberg, & Martin, 2002).

Category-specific deficits can be explained in a localizationist framework by proposing that certain concepts are represented at particular places in the brain, and the semantic system is organized so that similar concepts are represented in nearby locations in the brain. So a lesion that wipes out the "cat" concept is likely to wipe out similar concepts as well, but may spare semantically dissimilar concepts. The *correlated features approach* makes different representational assumptions, and offers a different way to explain category-specific deficits. According to the correlated features approach, semantic/conceptual knowledge is represented in distributed neural networks. Because semantic representations are distributed, you can't point to a place in the brain and say, "That is where the concept 'cat' is stored."

The assumption of distributed knowledge has two major consequences. First, when you hear the word *cat* or think about cats, a wide variety of brain regions become activated, each of which may be responding to different aspects of the meaning of *cat*. This approach is similar to Pulvermüller's (1999) cell assemblies approach and other distributed representation and processing theories. Second, the same large, distributed network of brain regions is responsible for all of our semantic/conceptual knowledge. So, knowledge about cats and other natural kinds is stored and activated by the same distributed system that is responsible for our knowledge about tools and other non-natural kinds. But if knowledge about animals and tools is spread all over the brain, and if knowledge about cats is handled by the same system that handles knowledge about hammers, how can we have a problem with just animals or with just tools?

The answer may be in the structure of the concepts themselves (Moss et al., 1998). Concepts consist of different kinds of features. Some features are *correlated* and some are *distinctive*. Correlated features are shared by many individual examples within a category. Distinctive features are those properties that make the difference between being one thing and being another. Living things have properties that tend to be highly correlated, and differences between different kinds of living things depend on minor differences in very specific (distinctive) attributes. As a result, if you know one thing about an animal, a lot of other properties are highly likely. If you know that something has eyes, it's almost certain that it has a mouth, a nose, lungs, four limbs, ears, and so forth. To tell the difference between different animals, you need detailed knowledge about subsets of properties. Does it have stripes and whiskers? Then it might be a tiger. Does it have stripes and a mane? Then it might be a zebra. By contrast, non-living things are more likely to have un-correlated properties—knowing one thing about a non-living thing does not make prediction of its other properties very easy. Non-living things are also more likely to have multiple distinguishing features than living things. If you know an object has a handle, that does not allow you to predict whether it will have a bowl at the end of the handle, a flat head, or a point. But if you know that the rest of the object has a sharp edge, you are very likely to be dealing with a knife and not a hammer. Patients with category-specific deficits have more trouble with properties that discriminate between concepts that have many correlated features; and they have little trouble dealing with *common* features that occur across many different examples within a category. If someone has a specific deficit about animals, and you ask them about the properties that animals have in common (eyes, ears, legs, etc.), their performance is normal or near normal. If instead, you ask about *distinctive features*, they have a big problem. Patients like RC (reported in Moss et al., 1998; see also Bunn, Tyler, & Moss, 1998) could provide numerous shared features of animals, but not for artifacts. For artifacts, RC was able to provide distinctive features but not shared properties.

Neuroimaging data from patients with a category-specific deficit reinforce the idea that these deficits result from a general inability to deal with distinctive features generally, rather than a particular kind of concept (e.g., living vs. non-living). In Peter Bright and colleagues' (2006; see also Devlin et al., 2002) study, fMRI was used to image brain activity in patients with category-specific deficits. While they were being scanned, they answered questions about pictures of living and non-living objects. The non-living objects included vehicles, which are an interesting case, because they have many correlated features (e.g., engine, steering wheel, tires, seats, and so forth), and the features that distinguish them tend to be highly idiosyncratic (all sedans look alike to someone who drives a truck and vice versa). So in terms of feature structure, vehicles are a lot like animals. In the fMRI experiment, some of the questions asked about shared properties (*Does it have tires? Does it have eyes?*) and some asked about distinctive properties (*Does it have claws? Does it have a peace-symbol on the hood?*). The idea was to find out if the patients had trouble with living versus non-living things and whether brain activity and question responses differed between animals and vehicles. If instead the feature structure drives subjects' performance, then the patients should do worse on distinctive feature questions than on shared feature questions, whether the targets were living or non-living. The fMRI results indicated that patients who did better on the distinctive feature questions had more activity near the temporal pole in the left hemisphere, whether the questions were about living or non-living things. This result is straightforwardly compatible with the concept structure hypothesis, and is not readily explained by the localizationist position. The concept structure hypothesis can also explain why category-specific deficits for living things are observed more commonly than category-specific deficits for non-living things. Specifically, the concept structure hypothesis suggests that the trick to discriminating living things is to pick out the few, highly specific discriminating features from among the larger number of highly correlated common features. This places greater burdens on a unified semantic processing system that handles both living and non-living kinds (Moss & Tyler, 2003).

Summary and Conclusions

The study of word representations and the processes that we use to activate and use stored knowledge relating to words is one of the most important enterprises in language science. Words can be represented in many different ways at many different levels of abstraction, and the way these representations are organized and connected to one another can affect the way different words are processed. An important distinction in the study of words is the difference between form and meaning. Theories of lexical access, such as logogen, TRACE, and COHORT, are primarily concerned with the representation and activation of word form information. Research in this area has shown that feature- and morpheme-level representations are an important component of the lexical access process. Although many viable models continue to be researched, and they differ in many fine details, there is general consensus that lexical access involves activation of multiple candidates and competition between them for selection. Research on lexical semantics focuses around the construct of networks of associations between words and the concepts they refer to. While we need some mechanism to tie systems of symbols to something other than symbols, associations within the lexical–symbol system appear to affect how people respond to words, and may play an important role in how new word meanings are acquired. The study of word–brain relationships indicates that word form and semantic representations are supported by widespread, left-lateralized networks; and the particular pattern of activity that occurs in response to a word depends on aspects of the word's form, its meaning, and the task that the individual is performing when the word is encountered. In terms of lexical semantics, although some categories of meaning are more vulnerable to brain damage than others, the available evidence favors the hypothesis that a single, distributed system is responsible for storing knowledge about word meanings.

TEST YOURSELF

1. What components go together to make a word?
2. What do we mean by *meaning*? How are different meanings of the word *meaning* related?
3. How are word senses represented in long-term memory? How closely do meanings resemble dictionary definitions? How can meanings be represented in associationist networks?
4. Describe the embodied semantics hypothesis and contrast it with associationist semantics. What evidence favors each approach to lexical semantics? What role do mirror neurons play in embodied semantics?
5. Describe and contrast the logogen, FOBS, TRACE, and COHORT models of lexical access. What observations can each model account for or explain? Describe research findings that could be problematic for each account.

6. Describe the role that morphemes play in lexical access. What do priming experiments involving the manpulation of morphemes tell us about lexical access?
7. Compare the distributed cohort model to Elman's simple recurrent network model. What evidence supports each model?
8. How are ambiguous words processed?
9. What parts of the brain are involved in storing and activating information about words?
10. What is a category deficit? How do you get one? What's the best explanation for category deficit?

THINK ABOUT IT

1. Find a newspaper article. Have a contest to see how many semantically ambiguous words you and your friends can find in the article. See if you can re-write the first paragraph of the story so that it has no ambiguous words. Why do you think natural languages have ambiguous words? What are the advantages and disadvantages?

Notes

1 Hyöna & Pollatsek (1998, p. 1612) provide the following example from Finnish of people chaining morphemes to make new words: "*lumi* = snow, *lumipallo* = snowball, *lumipallosota* = snowball fight, *lumipallosotatantere* = snowball fight field."

2 *Team* itself can be a token of a more general category, like *organization* (*team, company, army*). *Type* and *token* are used differently in the speech production literature. There, *token* is often used to refer to a single instance of a spoken word; *type* is used to refer to the abstract representation of the word that presumably comes into play every time an individual produces that word.

3 ... and *Kevin Bacon* would activate every name you know.

4 Which are associated because they appear together in common idioms like "It was raining cats and dogs," "They fought like cats and dogs," and because they appear together in a wide variety of scenarios.

5 Every word that you encounter affects your brain waves. One component of that response is an increase in negative voltage measured at the scalp that peaks about 400 ms after you hear a word. Some words cause a large peak. Some cause a smaller peak. Generally, words that make more sense in a given context produce smaller N400 effects.

6 Named after the homicidal computer in Stanley Kubrick's film *2001: A Space Odyssey*.

7 Corpora is the plural form of *corpus*, which is Latin for *body*.

8 The "foreign translator" argument is similar. As described by Glenberg & Robertson (2000, pp. 381–382), "You just landed in an airport in a foreign country and ... you do not speak the local language. As you disembark, you notice a sign printed in the foreign language (whose words are arbitrary abstract symbols to you). Your only resource is a dictionary printed in that language; that is, the dictionary consists of other arbitrary abstract symbols. You use the dictionary to look up the first word in the sign, but you don't know the meaning of any of the words in the definition. So, you look up the first word in the definition, but you don't know the meaning of the words in that definition, and so on. Obviously, no matter how many words you look up, that is, no matter how many structural relations you determine among the arbitrary abstract symbols, you will never figure out the meaning of any of the words."

9 These kinds of ERP results need to be approached with some degree of caution because (a) the way current propagates through body tissues means that the source of the electrical activity is not necessarily directly beneath the electrode that records the response; and (b) source-modeling is an inexact science (T. Y. Swaab, personal communication).

10 Saygin and colleagues (2004) did find different patterns of reading–perception deficit correlations in different subgroups of patients, classified based on the severity of their aphasic symptoms. They concluded on the basis of perception–reading deficit correlations within mildly impaired aphasics that there may be a common neural substrate for linguistic and non-linguistic action comprehension. They also suggested that their data support the embodied view of semantics, despite the fact that some of their strongest lesion–deficit correlations occurred for areas that are not considered to be part of the mirror neuron system.

11 From *logos*—"word" and *genus*—"birth" (Morton, 1969, p. 165).

12 But see Pinker, 1994, *The Language Instinct*, for a four-letter word that gets used as an infix in colloquial English.

13 Obligatory cute kid story: When Rose was about 3 years old, she showed me a picture in one of her books and said, "This is an impostosaurus. It's a dinosaur that pretends to be a different dinosaur." The derivation is: Start with *impostor*. Strip off the *-er* suffix. Take *dinosaur*. Strip off the *-saur* suffix. Combine the two, add the *-us* suffix that goes with dinosaur species names. Pretty slick for a 3-year-old.

14 The revised COHORT model makes a similar claim, but only words with a semantic relationship are listed under a single lexical entry. So, *departure, departed, and departing* are stored together under the morphologically and semantically related *depart* root morpheme; but *apartment* and *apart* are stored separately, despite the fact that they both contain the common root morpheme *apart* (Marslen-Wilson et al., 1994).

15 Word identification in natural reading also appears to benefit from morpheme overlap between words. Word repetition and morpheme overlap had similar effects on eye movements shortly after test words were fixated. It is possible that morphological effects are stronger in languages that have richer morphological systems than English (Deutsch et al., 2003).

16 Foss & Swinney (1973) demonstrated that people could detect the presence of a two-syllable word *faster* than they could detect the first syllable that those words contained. So the word superiority effect extends to larger units of analysis than letters and phonemes.

17 One estimate suggests that 60% of English words become uniquely identifiable before their final phoneme (Luce, 1986).

18 In ancient Rome, large military units were divided into smaller groups of soldiers called "cohorts."

19 With the exception of strongly related inflectional variants like *trespasses*, *trespassed*, trespassing, and so forth.

20 Multiple activation and limited interaction with context also occur in experimental situations where subjects are learning new vocabulary that refers to actions involving novel objects. Visual world data suggest that word-onset competitors are attended to more often than other kinds of distracting stimuli, and context that restricts the possible range of referents reduces, but does not eliminate, those competition effects (Revill, Tanenhaus, & Aslin, 2008).

21 Logogen also does not have a straightforward means of dealing with non-word stimuli, as non-words will not be represented by logogens (Marslen-Wilson, 1987).

22 Although the effect of sublexical mismatch has been claimed to be evidence against the TRACE model, more recent behavioral and modeling efforts have shown that specific versions of TRACE are capable of producing the correct pattern of coarticlatory mismatch effects (see Dahan et al., 2001). Such mismatch effects are still bad news for strictly bottom-up accounts like logogen.

23 Exception: Puns.

24 See Caplan (2009) for an alternative interpretation of this experiment.

25 Martin et al. (1996) checked for error rates by performing additional scans while subjects made an overt response, but these data could not be included in the brain activity analyses due to contamination by motor system activity involved in the speech response. Possible visual differences between tools and animals were controlled in a further experiment where subjects responded to silhouettes rather than line drawings; the brain activity results were the same.

26 One perplexing issue that confronts language scientists is this: Neuroimaging data suggest that frontal lobe structures play a role in the activation and use of semantic information during production and comprehension, but many patients with frontal lobe damage do not appear to have problems performing tasks that require access to semantic information, like category judgments (e.g., Damasio, et al., 1996; Price et al., 1997). One possibility is that frontal regions participate in "effortful retrieval, maintenance, and/or control of semantic information, whereas long-term storage of the conceptual and semantic knowledge is dependent on posterior regions" (Fiez, 1997, p. 81; see also Thompson-Schill, D'Esposito, Aguirre, & Farah, 1997).

27 There is an ongoing debate about the visual word form area. The basic question is whether the visual word form area is involved in tasks that are not related to word processing (see Schlaggar & McCandliss, 2007).

References

Allopenna, P. D., Magnuson, J. S., & Tanenhaus, M. K. (1998). Tracking the time course of spoken word recognition using eye movements: Evidence for continuous mapping models. *Journal of Memory and Language, 38,* 419–439.

Aziz-Zadeh, L., Wilson, S. M., Rizzolatti, G., & Iacoboni, M. (2006). Congruent embodied representations for visually presented actions and linguistic phrases describing actions. *Current Biology, 16,* 1818–1823.

Balota, D. A., & Lorch, R. F. (1986). Depth of automatic spreading activation: Mediated priming effects in pronunciation but not in lexical decision. *Journal of Experimental Psychology: Learning, Memory, and Cognition, 12,* 336–345.

Balota, D. A., Yap, M. J., & Cortese, M. J. (2006). Visual world recognition: The journey from features to meaning (a travel update). In M. J. Traxler & M. A. Gernsbacher, *The handbook of psycholinguistics* (2nd ed., pp. 285–375). Amsterdam, The Netherlands: Elsevier.

Barsalou, L. W. (1999). Perceptual symbol systems. *Behavioral and Brain Sciences, 22,* 577–660.

Bergen, B. K., Lindsay, S., Matlock, T., & Narayanan, S. (2007). Spatial and linguistic aspects of visual imagery in sentence comprehension. *Cognitive Science, 31,* 733–764.

Booth, J. R., Burman, D. D., Meyer, J. R., Gitelman, D. R., Parrish, T. B., & Mesulam, M. M. (2003). Relation between brain activation and lexical performance. *Human Brain Mapping, 19,* 155–169.

Boulenger, V., Mechtouff, L., Thobois, S., Broussolle, E., Jeannerod, M., & Nazir, T. A., (2008). Word processing in Parkinson's Disease is impaired for action verbs but not for concrete nouns. *Neuropsychologia, 46,* 743–756.

Boulenger, V., Roy, A. C., Paulignan, Y., Deprez, V., Jeannerod, M., & Nazir, T. A. (2006). Cross-talk between language processes and overt motor behavior in the first 200 ms of processing. *Journal of Cognitive Neuroscience, 18,* 1607–1615.

Bozic, M., Marslen-Wilson, W. D., Stamatakis, E. A., Davis, M. H., & Tyler, L. K. (2007). Differentiating morphology, form, and meaning: Neural correlates of morphological complexity. *Journal of Cognitive Neuroscience, 19,* 1464–1475.

Bradley, D. (1979). Lexical representations of derivational relations. In M. Aranoff & M. Kean (Eds.), *Juncture* (pp. 37–55). Cambridge, MA: MIT Press.

Breedin, S. D., Saffran, E. M., & Schwartz, M. F. (1998). Semantic factors in verb retrieval: An effect of complexity. *Brain & Language, 63,* 1–31.

Bright, P., Moss, H. E., Longe, O., Stamatakis, E. A., & Tyler, L. K. (2006). Conceptual structure modulates anteromedial temporal involvement in processing verbally presented object properties. *Cerebral Cortex, 17,* 1066–1073.

Buccino, G., Riggio, L., Melli, G., Binkofski, F., Gallese, V., & Rizzolatti, G. (2005). Listening to action-related sentences modulates the activity of the motor system: A combined TMS and behavioral study. *Cognitive Brain Research, 24,* 355–363.

Buchanan, L., Westbury, C., & Burgess, C. (2001). Characterizing semantic space: Neighborhood effects in words recognition. *Psychonomic Bulletin & Review, 8,* 531–544.

Bunn, E. M., Tyler, L. K., & Moss, H. E. (1998). Category-specific semantic deficits: The role of familiarity and property type reexamined. *Neuropsychology, 12,* 367–379.

Burgess, C., & Lund, K. (1997). Modelling parsing constraints with high-dimensional context space. *Language and Cognitive Processes, 12,* 177–210.

Caplan, D. (2009). Experimental design and interpretation of functional neuroimaging studies of cognitive processes. *Human Brain Mapping, 30,* 59–77.

Caramazza, A., & Hillis, A. E. 1991. Lexical organization of nouns and verbs in the brain. *Nature, 349,* 788–790.

Chao, L. L., Weisberg, J., & Martin, A. (2002). Experience-dependent modulation of category-related brain activity. *Cerebral Cortex, 12,* 545–551.

Clarke, R., & Morton, J. (1983). Cross modality facilitation in tachistoscopic word recognition. *The Quarterly Journal of Experimental Psychology, 35A,* 76–96.

Cleland, A. A., Gaskell, M. G., Quinlan, P. T., & Tamminen, J. (2006). Frequency effects in spoken and visual word recognition: Evidence from dual-task methodologies. *Journal of Experimental Psychology: Human Perception and Performance, 32,* 104–119.

Cohen, L., Lehéricy, S., Chochon, F., Lemer, C., Rivaud, S., & Dehaene, S. (2002). Language-specific tuning of visual cortex? Functional properties of the visual word form area. *Brain, 125,* 1054–1069.

Collins, A. M., & Loftus, E. F. (1975). A spreading-activation theory of semantic processing. *Psychological Review, 82,* 407–428.

Collins, A. M., & Quillian, M. R. (1970). Facilitating retrieval from semantic memory: The effect of repeating part of an inference. In A. F. Sanders (Ed.), *Attention and Performance: vol. 3* (pp. 304–314). Amsterdam, The Netherlands: North Holland.

Collins, A. M., & Quillian, M. R. (1972). How to make a language user. In E. Tulving & W. Donaldson (Eds.), *Organization of Memory* (pp. 309–351). New York: Academic Press.

Coltheart, M., Rastle, K., Perry, C., & Langdon, R. (2001). DRC: A dual route cascaded model of visual word recognition and reading aloud. *Psychological Review, 108,* 204–256.

Connine, C. M., Blasko, D. G., & Titone, D. (1993). Do the beginnings of spoken words have a special status in auditory word recognition? *Journal of Memory and Language, 32,* 193–210.

Corina, D. P., & Knapp, H. (2006). Sign language processing and the mirror neuron system. *Cortex, 42,* 529–539.

Dahan, D., & Gaskell, M. G. (2007). The temporal dynamics of ambiguity resolution: Evidence from spoken-word recognition. *Journal of Memory and Language, 57,* 483–501.

Dahan, D., Magnuson, J. S., & Tanenhaus, M. K. (2001). Time course of frequency effects in spoken-word recognition: Evidence from eye movements. *Cognitive Psychology, 42,* 317–367.

Dahan, D., Magnuson, J. S., Tanenhaus, M. K., & Hogan, E. M. (2001). Subcategorical mismatches and the time course of lexical access: Evidence for lexical competition. *Language and Cognitive Processes, 16,* 507–534.

Damasio, H., Grabowski, T. J., Tranel, D., Hichwa, R. D., & Damasio, A. R. (1996). A neural basis for lexical retrieval. *Nature, 380,* 499–505.

Damasio, A. R., & Tranel, D. 1993. Nouns and verbs are retrieved with differently distributed neural systems. *Proceedings of the National Academy of Science, 90,* 4957–4960.

Davis, M. H., Marslen-Wilson, W. D., & Gaskell, M. G. (2002). Leading up the lexical garden path: Segmentation and ambiguity in spoken word recognition. *Journal of Experimental Psychology: Human Perception and Performance, 28,* 218–244.

De Groot, A. M. B. (1983). The range of automatic spreading activation in word priming. *Journal of Verbal Learning and Verbal Behavior, 22,* 417–436.

Dehaene, S., Le Clec'H, G., Poline, J., Le Bihan, D., & Cohen, L. (2002). The visual word form area: A prelexical representation of visual words in the fusiform gyrus. *Neuroreport, 13,* 321–325.

Demb, J. B., Desmond, J. E., Wagner, A. D., Vaidya, C. J., Glover, G. H., & Gabrieli, J. D. E. (1995). Semantic encoding and retrieval in the left inferior prefrontal cortex: A functional MRI study of task difficulty and process specificity. *Journal of Neuroscience, 15,* 5870–5878.

De Renzi, E., & di Pellegrino, G. (1995). Sparing of verbs and preserved, but ineffectual reading in a patient with impaired word production. *Cortex, 31,* 619–636.

Deutsch, A., Frost, R., Pelleg, S., Pollatsek, A., & Rayner, K. (2003). Early morphological effects in reading: Evidence from parafoveal preview benefit in Hebrew. *Psychonomic Bulletin & Review, 10,* 415–422.

Devlin, J. T., Russell, R. P., Davis, M. H., Price, C. J., Moss, H. E., Fadili, M. J., et al. (2002). Is there an anatomical basis for category-specificity? Semantic memory studies in PET and fMRI. *Neuropsychologia, 40,* 54–75.

Dorfman, J. (1994). Sublexical components in implicit memory for novel words. *Journal of Experimental Psychology: Learning, Memory, and Cognition, 20,* 1108–1125.

Dorfman, J. (1999). Unitization of sublexical components in implicit memory for novel words. *Psychological Science, 10,* 387–392.

Drews, E., & Zwitserlood, P. (1995). Morphological and orthographic similarity in visual word recognition. *Journal of Experimental Psychology: Human Perception and Performance, 21,* 1098–1116.

Duffy, S. A., Henderson, J. M., & Morris, R. K. (1989). Semantic facilitation of lexical access during sentence processing. *Journal of Experimental Psychology: Learning, Memory, and Cognition, 15,* 791–801.

Erdmann, B., & Dodge, R. (1898). *Psychologische Untersuchungen über das Lesen*. Halle, Germany: M. Niemeyer.

Elman, J. L. (2004). An alternative view of the mental lexicon. *Trends in Cognitive Sciences, 8,* 301–306.

Emmorey, K. D. (1989). Auditory morphological priming in the lexicon. *Language and Cognitive Processes, 4,* 73–92.

Fiez, J. A. (1997). Phonology, semantics, and the role of the left inferior prefrontal cortex. *Human Brain Mapping, 5,* 79–83.

Forster, K. I. (1989). Basic issues in lexical processing. In W. D. Marslen-Wilson (Ed.), *Lexical representation and process* (pp. 75–107). Cambridge, MA: MIT Press.

Forster, K. I., & Bednall, E. S. (1976). Terminating and exhaustive search in lexical access. *Memory & Cognition, 4,* 53–61.

Foss, D. J., & Blank, M. A. (1980). Identifying the speech codes. *Cognitive Psychology, 12,* 1–31.

Foss, D. J., & Swinney, D. A. (1973). On the psychological reality of the phoneme: Perception, identification, and consciousness. *Journal of Verbal Learning and Verbal Behavior, 12,* 246–257.

Friederici, A. D. (2002). Towards a neural basis of auditory sentence processing. *Trends in Cognitive Science, 6,* 78–84.

Friederici, A. D., Opitz, B., & von Cramon, D. Y. (2000). Segregating semantic and syntactic aspects of processing in the human brain: An fMRI investigation of different word types. *Cerebral Cortex, 10,* 698–705.

Frith, C. D., Friston, K. J., Liddle, P. F., & Frackowiak, R. S. J. (1991). A PET study of word finding. *Neuropsychologia, 29,* 1137–1148.

Frost, R., Forster, K. I., & Deutsch, A. (1997). What can we learn from the morphology of Hebrew? A masked-priming investigation of morphological representation. *Journal of Experimental Psychology: Learning, Memory, and Cognition, 23,* 829–856.

Gabora, L., Rosch, E., & Aerts, D. (2008). Toward an ecological theory of concepts. *Ecological Psychology, 20,* 84–116.

Gallese, V., & Lakoff, G. (2005). The brain's concepts: The role of the sensory-motor system in reason and language. *Cognitive Neuropsychology, 22,* 455–479.

Gaskell, M. G., & Marslen-Wilson, W. D. (1997). Integrating form and meaning: A distributed model of speech perception. *Language and Cognitive Processes, 12,* 613–656.

Gaskell, M. G., & Marslen-Wilson, W. D. (2001). Lexical ambiguity resolution and spoken word recognition: Bridging the gap. *Journal of Memory and Language, 44,* 325–349.

Gaskell, M. G., & Marslen-Wilson, W. D. (2002). Representation and competition in the perception of spoken words. *Cognitive Psychology, 45,* 220–266.

Gaskell, M. G., Quinlan, P. T., Tamminen, J., & Cleland, A. A. (2008). The nature of phoneme representation in spoken word recognition. *Journal of Experimental Psychology: General, 137,* 282–302.

Gaskell, M. G., & Snoeren, N. D. (2008). The impact of strong assimilation on the perception of connected speech. *Journal of Experimental Psychology: Human Perception and Performance, 34,* 1632–1647.

Gernsbacher, M. A. (1990). *The structure building framework.* Hillsdale, NJ: Erlbaum.

Gernsbacher, M.A. (2009, March). *Do psycholinguists believe that humans have mirror neurons?* Talk presented to the 22nd Annual CUNY Conference on Human Sentence Processing. Davis, CA.

Glenberg, A. M., & Kaschak, M. P. (2002). Grounding language in action. *Psychonomic Bulletin & Review, 9,* 558–565.

Glenberg, A. M., & Robertson, D. A. (2000). Symbol grounding and meaning: A comparison of high-dimensional and embodied theories of meaning. *Journal of Memory and Language, 43,* 379–401.

Glosser, G., & Friedman, R. B. (1991). Lexical but not semantic priming in Alzheimer's disease. *Psychology and Aging, 6,* 522–527.

Glosser, G., Grugan, P. K., Friedman, R. B., Lee, J. H., & Grossman (1998). Lexical, semantic, and associative priming in Alzheimer's disease. *Neuropsychology, 12,* 218–224.

Goldberg, R. F., Perfetti, C. A., Fiez, J. A., & Schneider, W. (2007). Selective retrieval of abstract semantic knowledge in left prefrontal cortex. *The Journal of Neuroscience, 27,* 3790–3798.

Gough, P. M, Nobre, A. C., & Devlin, J. T. (2005). Dissociating linguistic processes in the left inferior frontal cortex with transcranial magnetic stimulation. *The Journal of Neuroscience, 25,* 8010–8016.

Grabowski, T. J., Damasio, H., Tranel, D., Boles Ponto, L. L., Hichwa, R. D., & Damasio, A. R. (2001). A role for left temporal pole in the retrieval of words for unique entities. *Human Brain Mapping, 13,* 199–212.

Grosjean, F. (1980). Spoken word recognition processes and the gating paradigm. *Perception and Psychophysics, 28,* 267–283.

Hagoort, P. (1997). Semantic priming in Broca's aphasics at a short SOA: No support for an automatic access deficit. *Brain & Language, 56,* 287–300.

Harnad, S. (1990). The symbol grounding problem. *Physica D, 42,* 335–346.

Hauk, O., Johnsrude, I., & Pulvermüller, F. (2004). Somatotopic representation of action words in human motor and premotor cortex. *Neuron, 41,* 301–307.

Heim, S., Alter, K., Ischebeck, A. K., Amunts, K., Eickhoff, S. B., Mohlberg, H., et al. (2005). The role of left Brodmann's areas 44 and 45 in reading words and pseudowords. *Cognitive Brain Research, 25,* 982–993.

Howard, D., Patterson, K., Wise, R., Brown, W. D., Friston, K., Weiller, C., et al. (1992). The cortical localization of the lexicons. *Brain, 115,* 1769–1782.

Hutchison, K. A. (2003). Is semantic priming due to association strength or feature overlap? A microanalytic review. *Psychonomic Bulletin & Review, 10,* 785–813.

Hyöna, J., & Pollatsek, A. (1998). Reading Finnish compound words: Eye fixations are affected by component morphemes. *Journal of Experimental Psychology: Human Perception and Performance, 24,* 1612–1627.

Jackendoff, R. (1983). *Semantics and cognition*. Cambridge, MA: MIT Press.

Jackson, A., & Morton, J. (1984). Facilitation of auditory word recognition. *Memory & Cognition, 12,* 568–574.

Johnston, J. C., & McClelland, J. L. (1973). Visual factors in word perception. *Perception and Psychophysics, 14,* 365–370.

Kiehl, K. A., Liddle, P. F., Smith, A. M., Mendrek, A., Forster, B. B., & Hare, R. D. (1999). Neural pathways involved in the processing of concrete and abstract words. *Human Brain Mapping, 7,* 225–233.

Kintsch, E., Steinhart, D., Stahl, G., Matthews, C., Lamb, R., & the LSA Research Group (2000). Developing summarization skills through the use of LSA-based feedback. *Interactive Learning Environments, 8,* 87–109.

Klatzky, R. L., Pellegrino, J. W., McCloskey, B. P., & Doherty, S. (1989). Can you squeeze a tomato? The role of motor representations in semantic sensibility judgments. *Journal of Memory and Language, 28,* 56–77.

Kluender, K. R., & Kiefte, M. (2006). Speech perception within a biologically realistic information-theoretic framework. In M. J. Traxler & M. A. Gernsbacher (Eds.), *The handbook of psycholinguistics* (2nd ed., pp. 153–199). Amsterdam, The Netherlands: Elsevier.

Kosslyn, S. M. (1973). Scanning visual images: Some structural implications. *Perception and Psychophysics, 14,* 90–94.

Kuperberg, G. R., Lakshmanan, B. M., Greve, D. N., & West, W. C. (2008). Task and semantic relationship influence both the polarity and localization of hemodynamic modulation during lexico-semantic processing. *Human Brain Mapping, 29,* 544–561.

Lahiri, A., & Marslen-Wilson, W. D. (1991). The mental representation of lexical form: A phonological approach to the recognition lexicon. *Cognition, 38,* 245–294.

Landauer, T. K. (1999). Latent semantic analysis: A theory of the psychology of language and mind. *Discourse Processes, 27,* 303–310.

Landauer, T. K., & Dumais, S. T. (1997). A solution to Plato's problem: The latent semantic analysis theory of acquisition, induction, and representation of knowledge. *Psychological Review, 104,* 211–240.

Landauer, T. K., Foltz, P. W., & Laham, D. (1998). An introduction to latent semantic analysis. *Discourse Processes, 25,* 259–284.

León, J. A., Olmos, R., & Escudero, I. (2006). Assessing short summaries with human judgments procedure and latent semantic analysis in narrative and expository texts. *Behavior Research Methods, 38,* 616–627.

Lieberman, P. (2000). *Human language and our reptilian brain.* Cambridge, MA: Harvard University Press.

Lima, S. D. (1987). Morphological analysis in sentence reading. *Journal of Memory and Language, 26,* 84–99.

Lotto, A. J., Hickok, G. S., & Holt, L. L. (2008). Reflections on mirror neurons and speech perception. *Trends in Cognitive Sciences, 13,* 110–114.

Luce, P. A. (1986). A computational analysis of uniqueness points in auditory word recognition. *Perception and Psychophysics, 39,* 155–158.

Lund, K., & Burgess, C. (1996). Producing high-dimensional semantic spaces from lexical co-occurrence. *Behavior Research Methods, Instruments, & Computers, 28,* 203–208.

Lund, K., Burgess, C., & Atchley, R. A. (1995). Semantic and associative priming in high-dimensional space. In *Proceedings of the Cognitive Science Society* (pp. 660–665). Hillsdale, NJ: Erlbaum.

Mahon, B. Z., & Caramazza, A. (2005). The orchestration of the sensory-motor systems: Clues from neuropsychology. *Cognitive Neuropsychology, 22,* 480–494.

Mahon, B. Z., & Caramazza, A. (2008). A critical look at the embodied cognition hypothesis and a new proposal for grounding conceptual content. *Journal of Physiology–Paris, 102,* 59–70.

Mainy, N., Jung, J., Baciu, M., Kahane, P., Schoendorff, B., Minotti, L., et al. (2008). Cortical dynamics of word recognition. *Human Brain Mapping, 29,* 1215–1230.

Manis, F. R., Seidenberg, M. S., Doi, L. M., McBride-Chang, C. & Peterson, A. (1996). On the bases of two subtypes of developmental dyslexia. *Cognition, 58,* 157–195.

Marslen-Wilson, W. D. (1973). Linguistic structure and speech shadowing at very short latencies. *Nature, 244,* 522–523.

Marslen-Wilson, W. D. (1984). Function and process in spoken word recognition. In H. Bouma and D. G. Bouwhuis (Eds.), *Attention and performance, vol. 10. Control of language processes* (pp. 125–150). Mahwah, NJ: Erlbaum.

Marslen-Wilson, W. D. (1985). Speech shadowing and speech comprehension. *Speech Communication, 4,* 55–73.

Marslen-Wilson, W. D. (1987). Functional parallelism in spoken word recognition. *Cognition, 25,* 71–102.

Marslen-Wilson, W. D. (1989). Access and integration: Projecting sound onto meaning. In W. D. Marslen-Wilson (Ed.), *Lexical representation and process* (pp. 3–24). Cambridge, MA: MIT Press.

Marslen-Wilson, W. D. (1990). Activation, competition, and frequency in lexical access. In G. T. M. Altmann (Ed.), *Cognitive models of speech processing: Psycholinguistic and computational perspectives* (pp. 148–172). Cambridge, MA: MIT Press.

Marslen-Wilson, W. D., & Tyler, L. K. (1975). Processing structure of sentence perception. *Nature, 257,* 784–786.

Marslen-Wilson, W. D., & Tyler, L. K. (1980). The temporal structure of spoken language understanding. *Cognition, 8,* 1–71.

Marslen-Wilson, W. D., & Tyler, L. K. (1997). Dissociating types of mental computation. *Nature, 387,* 592–594.

Marslen-Wilson, W. D., Tyler, L. K., Waksler, R., & Older, L. (1994). Morphology and meaning in the English mental lexicon. *Psychological Review, 101,* 3–33.

Marslen-Wilson, W. D., & Warren, P. (1994). Levels of perceptual representation and process in lexical access: Words, phonemes, and features. *Psychological Review, 101,* 653–675.

Marslen-Wilson, W. D., & Welsh, A. (1978). Processing interactions and lexical access during word recognition in continuous speech. *Cognitive Psychology, 10,* 29–63.

Marslen-Wilson, W. D. & Zwitserlood, P. (1989). Accessing spoken words: The importance of word onsets. *Journal of Experimental Psychology: Human Perception and Performance, 15,* 576–585.

Martin, A., Wiggs, C. L., Ungerleider, L. G., & Haxby, J. V. (1996). Neural correlates of category-specific knowledge. *Nature, 379,* 649–652.

Mason, R. A., & Just, M. A. (2007). Lexical ambiguity in sentence comprehension. *Brain Research, 1146,* 115–127.

McCandliss, B., Cohen, L., & Dehaene, S. (2003). The visual word form area: Expertise for reading in the fusiform gyrus. *Trends in Cognitive Sciences, 7,* 293–299.

McClelland, J. L., & Elman, J. L. (1986). The TRACE model of speech perception. *Cognitive Psychology, 23,* 1–44.

McClelland, J. L., & Rumelhart, D. E. (1981). An interactive activation model of context effects in letter perception: Part 1. An account of basic findings. *Psychological Review, 88,* 375–407.

McClelland, J. L., & Rumelhart, D. E. (1985). Distributed memory and the representation of general and specific information. *Journal of Experimental Psychology: General, 114,* 159–188.

McNamara, T. P., & Altarriba, J. (1988). Depth of spreading activation revisited: Semantic mediated priming occurs in lexical decisions. *Journal of Memory and Language, 27,* 545–559.

McQueen, J. M., Norris, D., & Cutler, A. (1994). Competition in spoken word recognition: Spotting words in other words. *Journal of Experimental Psychology: Learning, Memory, and Cognition, 20,* 621–638.

McQueen, J. M., & Viebahn, M. C. (2007). Tracking recognition of spoken words by tracking looks to printed words. *The Quarterly Journal of Experimental Psychology, 60,* 661–671.

McRae, K., & Boisvert, S. (1998). Automatic semantic similarity priming. *Journal of Experimental Psychology: Learning, Memory, and Cognition, 24,* 558–572.

McRae, K., Cree, G. S., Seidenberg, M. S., & McNorgan, C. (2005). Semantic feature production norms for a large set of living and nonliving things. *Behavior Research Methods, 37,* 547–559.

McRae, K., de Sa, V. R., & Seidenberg, M. S. (1997). On the nature and scope of featural representations of word meaning. *Journal of Experimental Psychology: General, 126,* 99–130.

Meyer, D. E., & Schvaneveldt, R. W. (1971). Facilitation in recognizing pairs of words: Evidence of a dependence between retrieval operations. *Journal of Experimental Psychology, 90,* 227–234.

Meyer, D. E., & Schvaneveldt, R. W. (1976). Meaning, memory structure, and mental processes. *Science, 192,* 27–33.

Mirman, D., & Magnuson, J. S. (2008). Attractor dynamics and semantic neighborhood density: Processing is slowed by near neighbors and speeded by distant neighbors. *Journal of Experimental Psychology: Learning, Memory, and Cognition, 34,* 65–79.

Mitchell, T. M., Shinkareva, S. V., Carlson, A., Chang, K., Malave, V. L., Mason, R.A., et al. (2008). Predicting human brain activity associated with the meanings of nouns. *Science, 320,* 1191–1194.

Morton, J. (1969). Interaction of information in word recognition. *Psychological Review, 76,* 165–178.

Moss, H. E., Ostrin, R. K., Tyler, L. K., & Marslen-Wilson, W. D. (1995). Accessing different types of lexical semantic information: Evidence from priming. *Journal of Experimental Psychology: Learning, Memory, and Cognition, 21,* 863–883.

Moss, H. E., & Tyler, L. K. (2003). Weighing up the facts of category-specific semantic deficits. *Trends in Cognitive Sciences, 7,* 480–481.

Moss, H. E., Tyler, L. K., Durrant-Peatfield, M., & Bunn, E. M. (1998). "Two eyes of a see-through": Impaired and intact semantic knowledge in a case of selective deficit for living things. *Neurocase, 4,* 291–310.

Murphy, G. L., & Medin, D. L. (1985). The role of theories in conceptual coherence. *Psychological Review, 92,* 289–316.

Neely, J. H. (1977). Semantic priming and retrieval from lexical memory: Roles of inhibitionless spreading activation and limited-capacity attention. *Journal of Experimental Psychology: General, 106,* 226–254.

Negri, G. A. L., Rumiati, R. I., Zadini, A., Ukmar, M., Mahon, B. Z., & Caramazza, A. (2007). What is the role of motor simulation in action and object recognition? Evidence from apraxia. *Cognitive Neuropsychology, 24,* 795–816.

Nelson, D. L., Bennett, D. J., Gee, N. R., Schreiber, T. A., & McKinney, V. M. (1993). Implicit memory: Effects of network size and interconnectivity on cued recall. *Journal of Experimental Psychology: Learning, Memory, and Cognition, 19,* 747–764.

Nobre, A. C., Allison, T., & McCarthy, G. (1994). Word recognition in the human inferior temporal lobe. *Nature, 372,* 260–263.

Nobre, A. C., & McCarthy, G. (1994). Language-related ERPs: Scalp distributions and modulation by word type and semantic priming. *Journal of Cognitive Neuroscience, 6,* 233–255.

Nobre, A. C., Price, C. J., Turner, R., & Friston, K. (1997). Selective processing of nouns and function words in the human brain. *Neuroimage, 5,* 53.

Noppeney, U., Patterson, K., Tyler, L. K., Moss, H., Stamatakis, E. A., Bright, P., et al. (2007). Temporal lobe lesions and semantic impairment: A comparison of herpes simplex virus encephalitis and semantic dementia. *Brain, 130,* 1138–1147.

Ober, B. A., & Shenaut, G. K. (2006). Semantic memory. In M. J. Traxler & M. A. Gernsbacher, *The handbook of psycholinguistics* (2nd ed., pp. 403–453). Amsterdam, The Netherlands: Elsevier.

Ober, B. A., Shenaut, G. K., & Reed, B. R. (1995). Assessment of associative relations in Alzheimer's disease: Evidence for the preservation of semantic memory. *Aging and Cognition, 2,* 254–267.

Oliveri, M., Finocchiaro, A., Shapiro, K., Gangitano, M., Caramazza, A., & Pascual-Leone, A. (2004). All talk and no action: A transcranial magnetic stimulation study of motor cortex activation during action word production. *Journal of Cognitive Neuroscience, 16,* 374–381.

Onifer, W., & Swinney, D. A. (1981). Accessing lexical ambiguities during sentence comprehension: Effects of frequency of meaning and contextual bias. *Memory & Cognition, 9,* 225–236.

Ostrin, R. K., & Tyler L. K. (1993). Automatic access to lexical semantics in aphasia: Evidence from semantic and associative priming. *Brain & Language, 45,* 147–159.

Perea, M., & Gotor, A. (1997). Associative and semantic priming effects occur at very short SOAs in lexical decision and naming. *Cognition, 67,* 223–240.

Perea, M., & Rosa, E. (2002). The effects of associative and semantic priming in the lexical decision task. *Psychological Research, 66,* 180–194.

Petersen, S. E., Fox, P. T., Posner, M. I., Mintun, M., & Raichle, M. E. (1988). Positron emission tomographic studies of the cortical anatomy of single-word processing. *Nature, 331,* 585–589.

Petersen, S. E., Fox, P. T., Posner, M. I., Mintun, M., & Raichle, M. E. (1989). Positron emission tomographic studies of the processing of single words. *Journal of Cognitive Neuroscience, 1,* 153–170.

Pexman, P. M., Hargreaves, I. S., Edwards, J. D., Henry, L. C., & Goodyear, B. G. (2007). The neural consequences of semantic richness: When more comes to mind, less activation is observed. *Psychological Science, 18,* 401–406.

Pinker, S. (1994). *The language instinct*. New York: Harper.

Posner, M. I., Petersen, S. E., Fox, P. T., & Raichle, M. E. (1988). Localization of cognitive operations in the human brain. *Science, 240,* 1627–1631.

Posner, M. I., & Raichle, M. E. (1994). *Images of mind*. New York: Scientific American Books.

Posner, M. I., & Snyder, C. R. (1975). Attention and cognitive control. In R. L. Solso (Ed.), *Information processing and cognition* (pp. 55–85). Hillsdale, NJ: Erlbaum.

Potts, G. R., Keenan, J. M., & Golding, J. M. (1988). Assessing the occurrence of elaborative inferences: Lexical decision versus naming. *Journal of Memory and Language, 27,* 399–415.

Price, C. J., Moore, C. J., Humphreys, G. W., & Wise, R. J. S. (1997). Segregating semantic from phonological processes during reading. *Journal of Cognitive Neuroscience, 9,* 727–733.

Pulvermüller, F. (1999). Words in the brain's language. *Behavioral and Brain Sciences, 22,* 253–336.

Pulvermüller, F., Härle, M., & Hummel, F. (2001). Walking or talking? Behavioral and neurophysiological correlates of action verb processing. *Brain & Language, 78,* 143–168.

Pulvermüller, F., Hauk, O., Nikulin, V. V., & Ilmoniemi, R. (2005). Functional links between motor and language systems. *European Journal of Neuroscience, 21,* 793–797.

Pulvermüller, F., Lutzenberger, W., & Preissl, H. (1999). Nouns and verbs in the intact brain: Evidence from event-related potentials and high frequency cortical response. *Cerebral Cortex, 9,* 497–506.

Pulvermüller, F., Shtyrov, Y., & Ilmoniemi, R. (2005). Brain signatures of meaning access in action word recognition. *Journal of Cognitive Neuroscience, 17,* 884–892.

Randall, B., Moss, H. E., Rodd, J. M., Greer, M., & Tyler, L. K. (2004). Distinctiveness and correlation in conceptual structure: Behavioral and computational studies. *Journal of Experimental Psychology: Learning, Memory, and Cognition, 30,* 393–406.

Rastle, K., Davis, M. H., Marslen-Wilson, W. D., & Tyler, L. K. (2000). Morphological and semantic effects in visual word recognition: A time-course study. *Language and Cognitive Processes, 15,* 507–537.

Rayner, K. (1998). Eye movements in reading and information processing: Twenty years of research. *Psychological Bulletin, 124,* 372–422.

Rayner, K., & Duffy, S. A. (1987). Eye movements and lexical ambiguity. In J.K. O'Regan & A. Levy-Schoen, *Eye movements: From physiology to cognition* (521–529). New York: Elsevier.

Rayner, K., & Pollatsek, A. (1989). *The psychology of reading*. Mahwah, NJ: Erlbaum.

Rayner, K., & Pollatsek, A. (2006). Eye-movement control in reading. In M. J. Traxler & M. A. Gernsbacher (Eds.), *The handbook of psycholinguistics* (2nd ed., pp. 613–657). Amsterdam, The Netherlands: Elsevier.

Reicher, G. M. (1969). Perceptual recognition as a function of meaningfulness of stimulus material. *Journal of Experimental Psychology, 81,* 274–280.

Revill, K. P., Tanenhaus, M. K., & Aslin, R. N. (2008). Context and spoken word recognition in a novel lexicon. *Journal of Experimental Psychology: Learning, Memory, and Cognition, 34,* 1207–1223.

Rhodes, S. M., & Donaldson, D. I. (2008). Association and not semantic relationships elicit the N400 effect: Electrophysiological evidence from an explicit language comprehension task. *Psychophysiology, 45,* 50–59.

Rips, L. J., Shoben, E. J., & Smith, E. E. (1973). Semantic distance and the verification of semantic relations. *Journal of Verbal Learning & Verbal Behavior, 12,* 1–20.

Rissman, J., Eliassen, J. C., & Blumstein, S. E. (2003). An event-related fMRI investigation of implicit semantic priming. *Journal of Cognitive Neuroscience, 15,* 1160–1175.

Rizzolatti, G., & Arbib, M. A. (1998). Language within our grasp. *Trends in Neurosciences, 21,* 188–194.

Rizzolatti, G., & Craighero, L. (2004). The mirror-neuron system. *Annual Review of Neuroscience,* ***27,*** 169–192.

Rodd, J. M., Gaskell, M. G., & Marslen-Wilson, W. D. (2004). Modelling the effects of semantic ambiguity in word recognition. *Cognitive Science, 28,* 89–104.

Rosch, E. H. (1973). Natural categories. *Cognitive Psychology, 4,* 328–350.

Roskies, A. L., Fiez, J. A., Balota, D. A., Raichle, M. E., & Petersen, S. E. (2001). Task-dependent modulation of regions in the left inferior frontal cortex during semantic processing. *Journal of Cognitive Neuroscience, 13,* 829–843.

Rumelhart, D. E., & McClelland, J. L. (1982). An interactive activation model of context effects in letter perception: Part 2. The contextual enhancement effect and some tests and extensions of the model. *Psychological Review, 89,* 60–94.

Saffran, E. M., & Schwartz, M. F. (1994). Of cabbages and things: Semantic memory from a neuropsychological perspective: A tutorial review. In C. Umiltà & M. Moscovitch (Eds.), *Attention and performance: vol. 15. Conscious and nonconscious information processing* (pp. 507–536). Cambridge, MA: MIT Press.

Salverda, A. P., Dahan, D., & McQueen, J. M. (2003). The role of prosodic boundaries in the resolution of lexical embedding in speech comprehension. *Cognition, 90,* 51–89.

Salverda, A. P., Dahan, D., Tanenhaus, M. K., Crosswhite, K., Masharov, M., & McDonough, J. (2007). Effects of prosodically modulated sub-phonetic variation on lexical competition. *Cognition, 105,* 466–476.

Savin, H. B., & Bever, T. G. (1970). The nonperceptual reality of the phoneme. *Journal of Verbal Learning and Verbal Behavio*r, *9,* 295–302.

Saygin, A. P., Wilson, S. M., Dronkers, N. F., & Bates, E. (2004). Action comprehension in aphasia: Linguistic and non-linguistic deficits and their lesion correlates. N*europsychologia, 42,* 1788–1804.

Schlaggar, B. L., & McCandliss, B. D. (2007). Development of neural systems for reading. *Annual Review of Neuroscience, 30,* 475–503.

Scott, S. K., Blank, C. C., Rosen, S., & Wise, R. J. S. (2000). Identification of a pathway for intelligible speech in the left temporal lobe. *Brain, 123,* 2400–2406.

Searle, J. R. (1980). Minds, brains, and programs. *Behavioral and Brain Sciences, 3,* 417–457.

Seidenberg, M. S. & Tanenhaus, M. K. (1979). Orthographic effects on rhyme monitoring. *Journal of Experimental Psychology: Human Learning and Memory, 5,* 546–554.

Seidenberg, M. S., Tanenhaus, M. K., Leiman, J. M., & Bienkowski, M. (1982). Automatic access of the meanings of ambiguous words: Evidence from priming and eye fixations. *Memory & Cognition, 28,* 1098–1108.

Setola, P., & Reilly, R. G. (2005). Words in the brain's language: An experimental investigation. *Brain & Language, 94,* 251–259.

Shalom, D. B., & Poeppel, D. (2008). Functional anatomic models of language: Assembling the pieces. *The Neuroscientist, 14,* 119–127.

Shatzman, K. B., & McQueen, J. M. (2006). Prosodic knowledge affects the recognition of newly acquired words. *Psychological Science, 17,* 372–377.

Shelton, J. R., & Martin, R. C. (1992). How semantic is automatic semantic priming? *Journal of Experimental Psychology: Learning, Memory, and Cognition, 18,* 1191–1210.

Skinner, B. F. (1957). *Verbal behavior*. Acton, MA: Copley Publishing Group.

Smith, E. E., Shoben, E. J., & Rips, L. J. (1974). Structure and process in semantic memory: A featural model for semantic decisions. *Psychological Review, 81,* 214–241.

Smith, P. T., & Sterling, C. M. (1982). Factors affecting the perceived morphological structure of written words. *Journal of Verbal Learning and Verbal Behavior, 21,* 704–721.

Stanners, R. F., Neiser, J. J., & Painton, S. (1979). Memory representation for prefixed words. *Journal of Verbal Learning & Verbal Behavior, 18,* 733–743.

Stevens, A., & Coupe, P. (1978). Distortions in judged spatial relations. *Cognitive Psychology, 10,* 422–437.

Streeter, L. A., & Nigro, G. N. (1979). The role of medial consonant transitions in word perception. *Journal of the Acoustical Society of America, 65,* 1533–1541.

Swinney, D.A. (1979). Lexical access during sentence comprehension: (Re)consideration of context effects. *Journal of Verbal Learning and Verbal Behavior, 18,* 645–659.

Tabossi, P., Colombo, L., & Job, R. (1987). Accessing lexical ambiguity: Effects of context and dominance. *Psychological Research, 49,* 161–167.

Tabossi, P., & Zardon, F. (1993). Processing ambiguous words in context. *Journal of Memory and Language, 32,* 359–372.

Taft, M. (1979). Recognition of affixed words and the word frequency effect. *Memory & Cognition, 7,* 263–272.

Taft, M. (1981). Prefix stripping revisited. *Journal of Verbal Learning and Verbal Behavior, 20,* 289–297.

Taft, M. (1994). Interactive activation as a framework for understanding morphological processing. *Language and Cognitive Processes, 9,* 271–294.

Taft, M., & Forster, K. (1975). Lexical storage and retrieval for prefixed words. *Journal of Verbal Learning and Verbal Behavior, 14,* 638–647.

Tettamanti, M., Buccino, G., Saccuman, M. C., Gallese, V., Danna, M., Scifo, P., et al. (2005). Listening to action-related sentences activates fronto-parietal motor circuits. *Journal of Cognitive Neuroscience, 17,* 273–281.

Thompson-Schill, S. L., Aguirre, G. K., D'Esposito, M., & Farah, M. J. (1999). A neural basis for category and modality specific semantic knowledge. *Neuropsychologia, 37,* 671–676.

Thompson-Schill, S. L., D'Esposito, M., Aguirre, G. K., & Farah, M. J. (1997). Role of left inferior prefrontal cortex in retrieval of semantic knowledge: A reevaluation. *Proceedings of the National Academy of Science, 94,* 14792–14797.

Tomasino, B., Fink, G. R., Sparing, R., Dafotakis, M., & Weiss, P. H. (2008). Action verbs and the primary motor cortex: A comparative TMS study of silent reading, frequency judgments, and motor imagery. *Neuropsychologia, 46,* 1915–1926.

Tranel, D., Grabowski, T. J., Lyon, J., & Damasio, H. (2005). Naming the same entities from visual or from auditory stimulation engages similar regions of left inferotemporal cortices. *Journal of Cognitive Neuroscience, 17,* 1293–1305.

Tranel, D., Logan, C. G., Frank, R. J., & Damasio, A. R. (1997). Explaining category-related effects in the retrieval of conceptual and lexical knowledge for concrete entities: Operationalization and analysis of factors. *Neuropsychologia, 35,* 1329–1339.

Tucker, M., & Ellis, R. (2001). The potentiation of grasp types during visual object categorization. *Visual Cognition, 8,* 769–800.

Tucker, M., & Ellis, R. (2004). Action priming by briefly presented objects. *Acta Psychologica, 116,* 185–203.

Tyler, L. K., & Wessels, J. (1983). Quantifying contextual contributions to word-recognition processes. *Perception and Psychophysics, 34,* 409–420.

Vandenberghe, R., Price, C., Wise, R., Josephs, O., & Frackowiak, R. S. J. (1996). Functional anatomy of a common semantic system for words and pictures. *Nature, 383,* 254–256.

Vainio, L., Symes, E., Ellis, R., Tucker, M., & Ottoboni, G. (2008). On the relations between action planning, object identification, and motor representations of observed actions and objects. *Cognition, 108,* 444–465.

Wagner, A. D., Desmond, J. E., Demb, J. B., Glover, G. H., & Gabrieli, J. D. E. (1997). Semantic repetition priming for verbal and pictorial knowledge: A functional MRI study of left inferior prefrontal cortex. *Journal of Cognitive Neuroscience, 9,* 714–726.

Wheeler, D. D. (1970). Processes in word recognition. *Cognitive Psychology, 1,* 59–85.

Wible, C. G., Han, S. D., Spencer, M. H., Kubicki, M., Niznikiewicz, M. H., Jolesz, F. A., et al. (2006). Connectivity among semantic associates: An fMRI study of semantic priming. *Brain & Language, 97,* 294–305.

Zipf, G. K. (1949). *Human behavior and the principle of least effort.* New York: Hafner.

Zwaan, R. A., Madden, C. J., Yaxley, R. H., & Aveyard, M. E. (2004). Moving words: Dynamic representations in language comprehension. *Cognitive Science, 28,* 611–619.

Zwaan, R. A., & Rapp, D. N. (2006). Discourse comprehension. In M. J. Traxler & M. A. Gernsbacher (Eds.), *The handbook of psycholinguistics* (2nd ed., pp. 725–764). Amsterdam, The Netherlands: Elsevier.

Zwaan, R. A., & Taylor, L. J. (2006). Seeing, acting, understanding: Motor resonance in language comprehension. *Journal of Experimental Psychology: General, 135,* 1–11.

Zwitserlood, P. (1989). The locus of the effects of sentential-semantic context in spoken-word processing. *Cognition, 32,* 25–64.

Sentence Processing

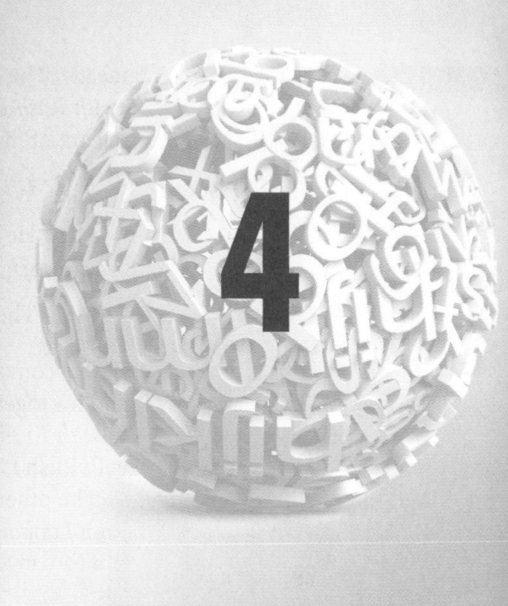

Time flies like an arrow. Fruit flies like a banana.

MARX

When people speak, they produce sequences of words. When people listen or read, they also deal with sequences of words. Speakers systematically organize those sequences of words into phrases, clauses, and sentences. When listeners try to comprehend those sequences, they have to determine how the sequence of words is organized, and use this information to recover the speaker's intended meaning. Thus, when language scientists study sentences, they are interested in how people organize words before and during speaking; and they are interested in what cues listeners use to figure out how words in sentences relate to one another, as those cues are vital in enabling listeners to recover the speaker's intended message. The study of *syntax* involves discovering the cues that languages provide that show how words in sentences relate to one another. The study of *syntactic parsing* involves discovering how comprehenders use those cues to determine how words in sentences relate to one another during the process of interpreting a sentence.

Here's an example of how the organization of words into phrases can affect meaning (see Pinker, 1994; see also Bever, 1970; Columbia Press, 1980):

(1) Dr. Phil discussed sex with Rush Limbaugh.

Listeners (and readers) could organize the words in this sentence in at least two distinct ways, and the way the sentence is organized determines what it

Introduction to Psycholinguistics: Understanding Language Science, First Edition.
Matthew J. Traxler.

means. The likely intended meaning happens when readers treat the *prepositional phrase* "*with Rush Limbaugh*" as being closely related to the verb *discussed*. This meaning would fall out of the following hypothetical conversation (Conversation 1):

You: Who did Dr. Phil have on his radio show this morning?
Me: He had Rush Limbaugh on the show.
You: What did they talk about?
Me: They talked about sex. Dr. Phil discussed sex with Rush Limbaugh.

In this conversation, the critical thing that the listener needs to do is to package *discussed* and *sex* together, as in *Dr. Phil (discussed sex)* and the listener needs to tie that whole thing to *with Rush Limbaugh*. We could paraphrase that meaning as, "Dr. Phil had a discussion with Rush Limbaugh; the discussion was about sex."

The other way to organize the sentence involves treating the prepositional phrase *with Rush Limbaugh* as being closely related to the noun *sex*. This other meaning would emerge from a conversation like this one (Conversation 2):

You: Who did Dr. Phil have sex with?
Me: Dr. Phil had sex with Rush Limbaugh.
You: I don't believe you.
Me: Really. He talked about it afterwards. Dr. Phil discussed sex with Rush Limbaugh.
You: !

If we wanted to draw a diagram that depicts the different ways that we could organize the words in *Dr. Phil discussed sex with Rush Limbaugh*, we could use a *phrase structure tree* (or *tree diagram*). Phrase structure trees can seem complicated, but they are really just a handy way of showing how words in sentences relate to one another.[1] Every sentence has to have a noun phrase and a verb phrase. So the top of our phrase structure tree will have an "S" (for *sentence*), and below that, we will have an "NP" for (*noun phrase*) and a "VP" (for *verb phrase*), like this:

(2)

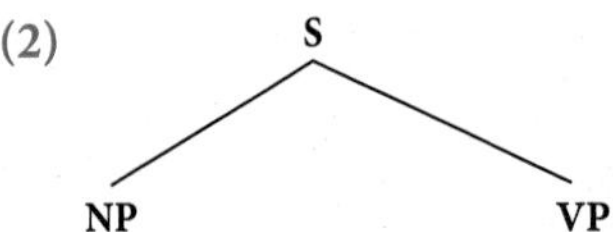

This part of the diagram shows that we have a sentence, and that the sentence consists of one noun phrase and one verb phrase. In a phrase structure tree, the labels, like NP, VP, and S, are called *nodes* and the connections between the different nodes form *branches*. The patterns of nodes and branches show how the words in the sentence are grouped together to form phrases and clauses.

In sentence (1), the leftmost noun phrase will consist of *Dr. Phil* no matter what meaning is assigned, so let's go ahead and add that to our tree below the NP node.

(3)

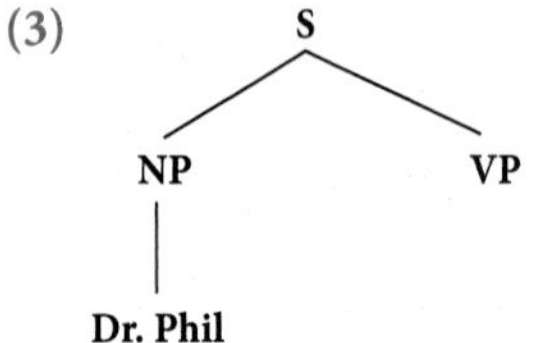

The important differences in the structure of sentence (1) all occur inside the VP node. The meaning that Conversation 1 expresses involves *with Rush Limbaugh* modifying the meaning of *discussed sex*. To express that relationship, we need to organize our VP node so that *with Rush Limbaugh* is assigned as a modifier of the verb *discussed*. We can do that by organizing the VP like this:

(4)

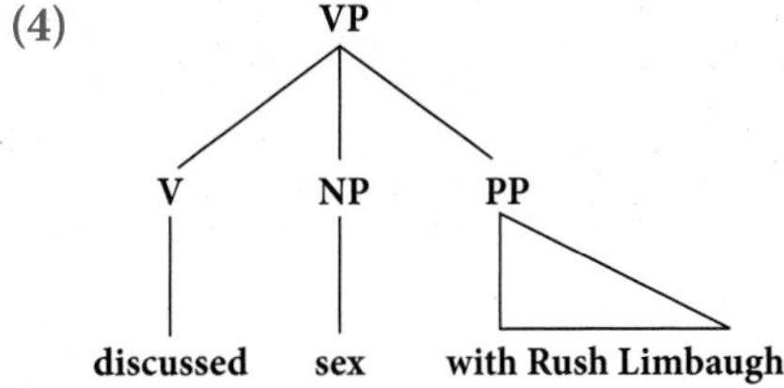

(The "PP" stands for *Prepositional Phrase*. Words like *with*, *of*, *in* and so forth are called prepositions.)

If we want to get the meaning in Conversation 2, we need to organize the VP differently. We need to put *with Rush Limbaugh* and *sex* together. We can do that using a structure like this one:

(5)

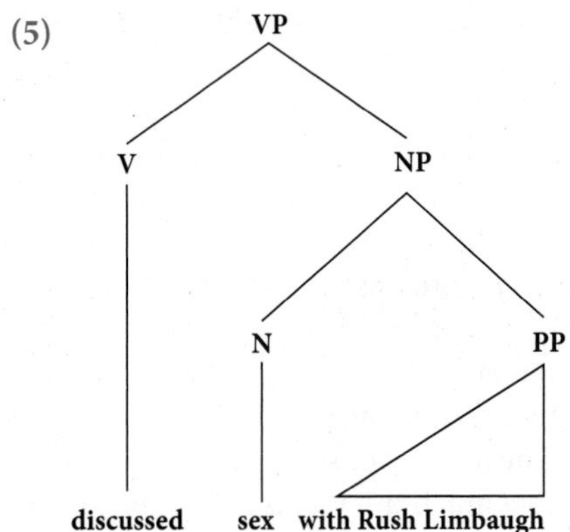

Now that we have our our VP diagrams sorted out, we can build two different trees, one that captures the meaning in Conversation 1 (6a) and one that captures the meaning in Conversation 2 (6b):

(6) a.

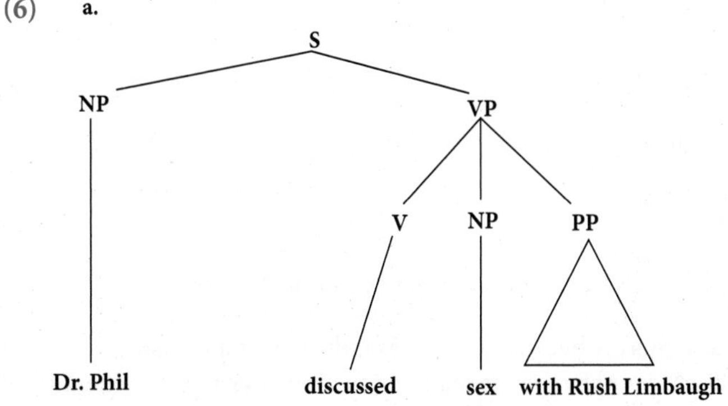

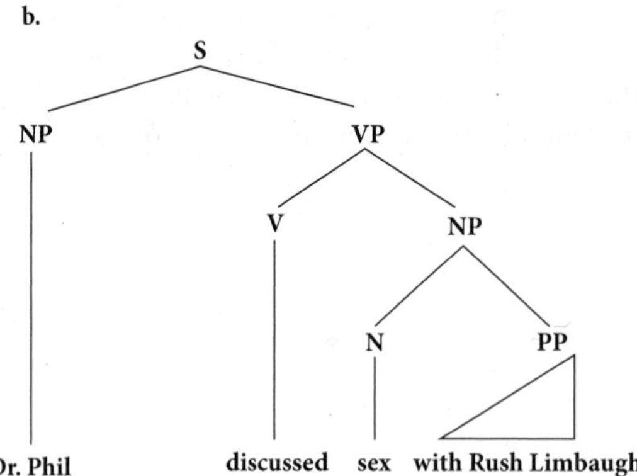

Although there is more to sentence processing than just figuring out which words go together to make phrases, language scientists have learned a great deal about the mental processes that people use to interpret sentences by studying *globally ambiguous* sentences like (1). Globally ambiguous sentences have sequences of words that can be organized in more than one way, and those different ways of organizing the sentence are all consistent with the grammar of the language. One basic question that language scientists have asked is, are ambiguous sentences like (1) harder to understand than less ambiguous sentences that express about the same meaning? In other words, does ambiguity impose processing costs on the listener (or reader)?

The short answer to this question is: Yes, ambiguity leads to longer reading times, lower comprehension accuracy, and different patterns of brain activity in comprehenders than unambiguous sentences that say the same thing (see, e.g., Frazier & Rayner, 1982; Kutas, van Petten, & Kluender, 2006; Trueswell, Tanenhaus, & Garnsey, 1994). The longer and more complicated answer to the question is: There are cases where ambiguity doesn't produce noticeable processing costs, and ultimately processing cost depends on a variety of factors, including what information the listener has just processed, and what contextual information is available (see Traxler & Tooley, 2007, for a review). Let's start with the straightforward cases and come back to the tricky ones later.

How do we know that ambiguous sentences impose processing costs on the listener or reader? One thing we can do is measure how much time it takes for someone to understand a sentence that is ambiguous, and compare that to how much time it takes for someone to understand a sentence that is unambiguous. Most of the time when language scientists do this, they are investigating sentences that are only *temporarily ambiguous*. Temporarily ambiguous sentences contain a sequence of words that can be configured in more than one way, but the sentence as a whole has only a single grammatically licensed or acceptable structure. (In fact, sentences like (1) that are completely ambiguous are very rare and may not be fully representative of sentences in general.)

Here's an example of a sentence that is temporarily ambiguous (from Frazier & Rayner, 1982; see also Adams, Clifton, & Mitchell, 1998; Ferreira & Clifton, 1986; van Gompel & Pickering, 2001):

(7) While Susan was dressing the baby played on the floor.

Compare (7) to the unambiguous (8):

(8) While Susan was dressing herself the baby played on the floor.

Sentence (7) is temporarily ambiguous because where, exactly, the first clause ends is not entirely clear. It could end after *the baby*, but it really ends after *dressing*. Listeners (and readers) need to figure out whether the noun phrase *the baby* is supposed to go with the preceding *Susan was dressing*, as in *Susan was dressing the baby*, or whether *the baby* starts a new clause, as in *Susan was dressing (herself) and the baby played on the floor*. In (8), the sentence is unambiguous because *herself* closes off the *subordinate clause* "*While Susan was dressing herself*" and there is no way to put *the baby* in that clause.

***

(Hey students: Impress your professor by asking about *prosody*! Some people do not like example (7), because, they say, if a person spoke sentence (7), they would put in a pause after the word *dressing* to indicate that the clause is over, and so the listener would *not* be in doubt about where the clause ends, and so sentence (7) really is *not* ambiguous when it is spoken. The short answer to that objection is: That's right. The longer answer is: It's more complicated than that. Speakers sometimes do include cues that help the listener organize the words into phrases, but they don't do that all the time. We will return to this topic later in the section on *prosody*.)

***

In sentence (7), listeners have to figure out whether the *baby* goes with *Susan was dressing* or starts up a new clause. Do they come up with the correct solution right away? Or do they make mistakes? Alternatively, in cases of uncertainly, do they delay making any decision until they have enough information to be certain that they are correct? We can find out by measuring processing load during critical parts of the sentence. In general, the longer it takes people to understand part of a sentence, the greater the processing load that part of the sentence imposes. So, which parts of sentence (7) are difficult to process?

When reading times for different parts of sentence (7) are measured, they show that there are no major increases in processing load during the ambiguous part. That is, reading times for *the baby* are about the same whether the sentence is ambiguous or not (Frazier & Rayner, 2002; Traxler, 2002, 2005). Readers get through *While Susan was dressing the baby* just as fast as the equivalent parts of the unambiguous sentence (8). So ambiguity, in and of itself, is not a huge burden on the listener or the reader. Where people *do* slow down is at the verb *played*. People have much more trouble processing *played* in sentence (7) than they do in sentence (8). Why is that? And what does it mean?

It means a couple of things. First, it means that listeners and readers are making decisions about how to organize words into phrases and clauses before they have enough information to be certain of making the correct decision. This means that, in sentence processing, just as in word processing, listeners and readers follow the *immediacy principle* and use an *incremental processing strategy* (Foss & Hakes, 1982; Just & Carpenter, 1980). The immediacy principle says that people do as much interpretive work as they can, based on partial information, and making possibly incorrect assumptions, rather than waiting until they have all the information they need to be certain of making the correct decision. Second, it means that making structural choices, by itself, is not very difficult to do. If it were, people should slow down at points of sentences where more interpretive possibilities were available to them, and this does not seem to be the case. Finally, it means that when people have a choice of different structures, they sometimes make the wrong choice. If they always made the correct choice, then there should be no problem processing any part of sentence (7). The fact that readers slow down at the verb *played* suggests that something special is happening at that point of the sentence. What might that be?

One explanation is that during the beginning of the sentence (*While Susan was dressing the baby*), listeners and readers treat *the baby* as the thing that is being dressed, they include *the baby* in the same clause as *Susan was dressing*, and this leads to processing problems shortly thereafter. To interpret the sentence that way, listeners need to build a structure like that shown in (9):

(9)

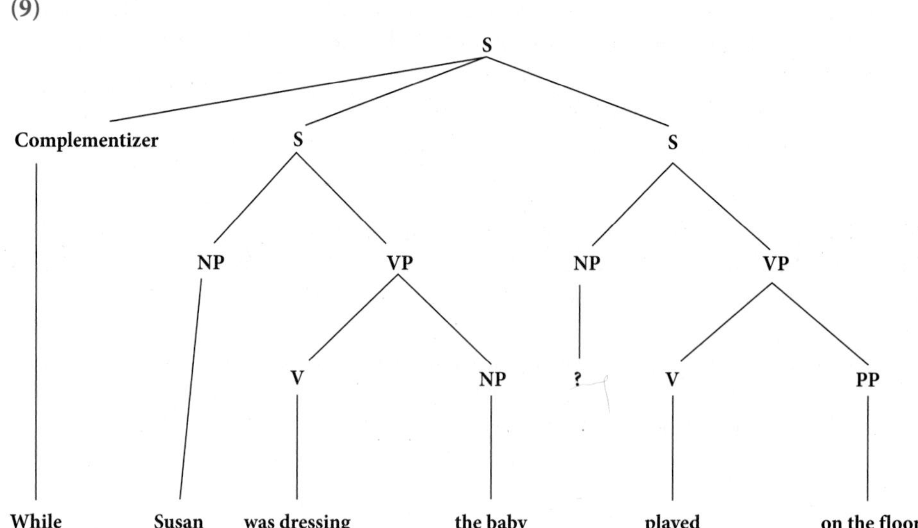

If the beginning of the sentence is packaged as shown in (9), then the verb *played* has no subject (the verb *was dressing* has, metaphorically, stolen *the baby* away from its rightful owner). If *the baby* is assigned or attached to the verb *was dressing*, there is no grammatically acceptable or legal way for the listener to incorporate the verb *played* into a single sentence with *While Susan was dressing the baby* … The solution to this dilemma is for the comprehender to undo her original structural commitments—in other words, to take *the baby* away from *was dressing* and give it back to its rightful owner *played*. To do that, comprehenders must adopt or build a syntactic structure like that shown in (10):

(10)

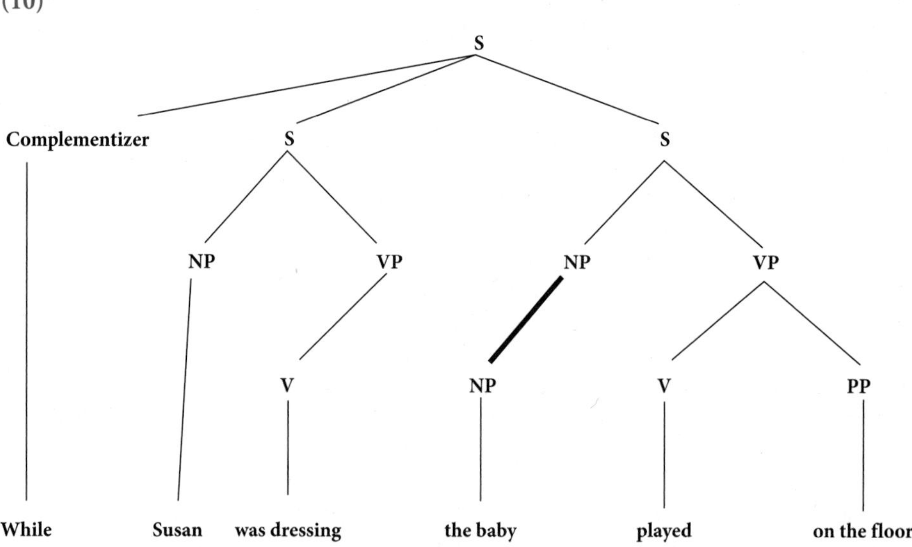

This correct structural configuration then leads to the correct meaning being assigned, Susan dressed (herself) and the baby played on the floor. Notice that baby-stealing is not possible in sentence (8), and so there is no need to do the mental work of disconnecting *dressing* and *the baby*, no need to un-make structural decisions, and no need to revise an incorrect structure. (*herself* fills the object role in (8) that *the baby* tries to fill in (7)).

Language scientists have investigated a wide variety of *garden path* sentences, and they have consistently found that sentences like (7), where listeners initially build one syntactic structure (e.g., (9)), and later replace that structure with another (e.g., (10)), are harder to understand (take longer and lead to more errors of interpretation) than equivalent sentences that are unambiguous (Altmann & Steedman, 1988; Britt, 1994; Ferreira & Clifton, 1986; Frazier & Rayner, 1982; Konieczny & Hemforth, 2000; Phillips, Kazanina, & Abada, 2005; Pickering & Traxler, 1998; Rayner, Carlson, & Frazier, 1983; Trueswell, Tanenhaus, & Kello, 1993). They have therefore spent a lot of time developing theories that explain how, exactly, people react to garden path sentences and what, exactly, makes them difficult to process.

To predict and explain which sentences will be particularly difficult to process, language scientists appeal to the concept of *syntactic parsing*. Syntactic parsing is a mental process or set of processes that takes sequences of words and organizes them into hierarchical structures(similar to those in the preceding diagrams). Note that the mental representations that the people build don't have to be literally "trees in the head." A number of equivalent representational schemes are possible, and ultimately the relevant structural information is physically represented as patterns of firings in large populations of neurons. (Some theories assume representations like the phrase structure trees above, and they don't worry about how neurons work at all; other theories are far more concerned about how populations of neurons respond to different sentences, and they do not worry about how, exactly, those sentences would be represented by tree diagrams.) The really important thing is that the parser determines how words in sentences relate to one another. The *syntactic structures*, and our diagrams, are just a way of keeping track of these relationships. A *syntactic parser*, or simply *parser*, is a mechanism that carries out processes that identify relationships between words in sentences. Many different sets of processes could accomplish the task of organizing sequences of words into hierarchical structures. Language scientists would like to find out which specific set of processes people actually use when they parse sentences. The next section of this chapter will explore some of these accounts, starting with Lyn Frazier's classic *garden path* theory.

Models of Parsing: Two-Stage Models

Sentences like (7) metaphorically lead you down the garden path and leave you stranded there so that you have to make your way back to the beginning and start over. So they are often called garden path sentences. The idea that listeners build the wrong structure for some temporarily ambiguous sentences (such as sentence (7)) while they are processing the ambiguous part, discover their error when they get to the *disambiguating* information (e.g., *played* in (7)), and then revise their initial syntactic (structural) and semantic (meaning) commitments, sits at the core of the garden path approach to sentence processing and interpretation (Frazier, 1979; 1987). Frazier's garden path theory is considered a *two-stage* model of syntactic parsing, because she proposes that syntactic parsing takes place in two distinct processing stages or steps. In the first stage, the incoming sequence of words is analyzed to determine what *categories* the words belong to (categories correspond to parts of speech, such as Noun, Verb, Preposition, and so on). Once the categories have been identified, the parser can build a syntactic structure for the sequence. Note that *no* other information besides word category information is used in the initial structure-building process. The parser does not care which particular words it is looking at—it only wants to know what categories are represented in the input. In the second stage of sentence

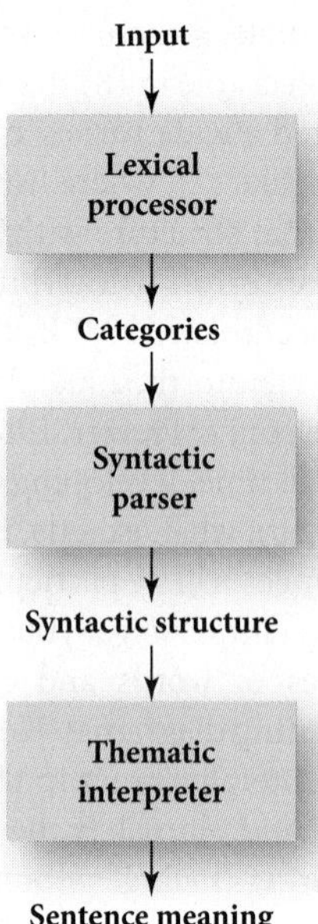

Figure 4.1 The garden path model of syntactic parsing.

interpretation, standard meaning is computed by applying semantic rules to the structured input. Next, let's look at the two proposed stages of processing in a bit more detail.

In the first stage, a lexical processor identifies the categories that are represented in the input, and its output is fed into the syntactic parsing mechanism (see Figure 4.1). If we feed the sentence *While Susan was dressing the baby played on the floor*, into the lexical processor, it will output this sequence of categories:

Conjunction–Noun–Verb–Determiner–Noun–Verb–Preposition–Determiner–Noun

The parser can build a syntactic structure for this string of categories without knowing what specific words are actually represented in the input. Once a syntactic structure has been built, the actual words in the sentence can be assigned positions in the tree (as in (10)), and the entire configuration can be sent to a *thematic interpreter*. The thematic interpreter's job is to apply a set of rules that assigns roles to each of the elements in the syntactic tree, based on their position in the tree and how they are connected to other words (for example, grammatical subjects are treated as being old or given information, and the system prefers to treat them as the initiator of the action described in the clause). If the thematic interpreter produces a meaning that makes sense, is consistent with the listener's prior knowledge or assumptions, and can be readily integrated with preceding sentences in the discourse, then the process of interpreting the sentence ends and the listener can move on to the next one. If the thematic interpreter produces a meaning that lacks one or more of these qualities, one remedy is to send a signal to the syntactic parser that prompts the parser to try to find an alternative structure for the sequence of words (and note that for the parser, unlike NASA, failure is always an option).

Garden path theory assumes that the parser begins to build a syntactic structure as soon as the lexical processor begins to deliver information about word categories. The thematic processor also appears to work on a word-by-word basis. That is, semantic interpretation does not wait until the end of a phrase or a clause—listeners monitor the meaning of utterances constantly as they are processing those utterances, and the process of interpretation will slow down or stop as soon as listeners detect either syntactic or semantic problems with the input. According to garden path theory, it is this rush to interpretation that sometimes leads people astray. Because structural and semantic decisions are made on a word-by-word basis, the parser is forced to choose between alternative structures when more than one structure is compatible with the input (rather than delaying a decision to collect more evidence). So the parser often chooses which structural option to pursue before it has definitive information about which structure is actually required. Sometimes the parser makes the correct decision, but, as we saw in example sentence (7), sometimes it does not. When the parser makes an incorrect decision, the structure that it built initially has to be undone, and processing is disrupted. Two important consequences follow from these assumptions: First, for garden path theory to work as a general theory of parsing, it needs to explain how people make choices when more than one syntactic structure is possible. Second, for garden path theory to work as a theory about how *people* parse sentences, there should be evidence that people have problems at just those points in sentences where garden path theory says structural reanalysis is taking place. (It is also possible that garden path theory could claim that the act of making a structural choice imposed processing costs, but as we noted before, there is little or no evidence that making structural decisions, by itself, leads to any significant processing load.)

So, according to garden path theory, how do people decide which structure to build when more than one structure is grammatically acceptable (or *licensed*) and consistent with the sequence of categories at a particular point in the sentence? First, garden path theory assumes that people can only build one syntactic structure at a time. That means that it represents a kind of *serial* processing system (as opposed to a *parallel* processing system, which could build more than one structure at a time). Second, garden path theory says that the overarching principle that the parser relies on is *simplicity*. That is, the parser seeks to build the least complicated structure that it can. Pursuing the simpler structure conveys two main benefits. First, simpler structures take less time to build than more complicated structures. Second, simpler structures place lower demands on cognitive resources like working memory than more complicated structures do, and reduced demands on working memory also translates into greater speed.

According to garden path theory, the parser pursues its structure-building goals and obeys the simplicity principle by deploying processing *heuristics*, basic rules that can be applied quickly and consistently, to make decisions about which structure to build at any given point. Heuristics have some advantages and some drawbacks. The main advantage is that decisions can be made very quickly on the basis of incomplete information—and people need to make sentence processing decisions quickly because language input arrives at a rate of about 200 words per minute in both speech and reading. The main disadvantage is that heuristics do not always lead to the correct solution. However, the occasional error that heuristics lead to, and the resulting delay in getting to the correct interpretation, is outweighed by the overall time savings that the heuristics provide.

The classic version of garden path theory proposes two heuristics: *late closure* and *minimal attachment*. Late closure says, **Do not postulate unnecessary structure. If possible, continue to work on the same phrase or clause as long as possible.** Minimal attachment says, **When more than one structure is licensed and consistent with the input, build the structure with the fewest nodes.** More recent variants of the garden path approach postulate additional principles, such as the *main assertion* preference, which says, **Given a choice between two structures, build the structure where the new elements relate to the main assertion of the sentence.** Let's look at how these three rules operate, starting with the late closure heuristic.

In sentence (7), when listeners get to the NP *the baby*, they can choose to attach it as part of the preceding clause, as in: [While Susan was dressing the baby …]. Alternatively, they can choose to close off the first clause right after *dressing*. In that case, the phrasal organization would look like this: [While Susan was dressing] [the baby . . .]. The late closure heuristic dictates that the first organization will be pursued, because doing so allows the parser to continue working on the same clause. Pursuing the second organization means that the parser has to start building a new clause before there is definitive evidence that the first clause really is finished. The actual structure of sentence (7) is incompatible with this initial choice, however, and so additional processing is needed to revise the structure. Sentence (8) is compatible with the parser's intial choice (the parser chooses to put *herself* in the first clause, which is correct), so no additional processing takes place. Hence, garden path theory predicts that sentence (7) should be harder to process than sentence (8), and that prediction has been confirmed in numerous experiments where people's reading times were measured (e.g., Frazier & Rayner, 1982; Pickering & van Gompel, 2002; Traxler, 2002, 2005). People consistently slow down in sentence (7) when they get to the main verb *played*, which is the point where the parser's initial structural assumptions are shown to be false.

To look at how minimal attachment works, let's look at a a sentence that is similar to sentence (1), but where semantic (meaning) information forces an interpretation like that diagrammed in (6b).

(11) The burglar blew up the safe with the rusty lock.

Here, semantic information forces people to adopt a structure like (6b), because safes can have rusty locks, but you can't use a rusty lock to blow up a safe. In a sentence like (12), people adopt a structure like (6a) because you can use dynamite to blow up a safe.

(12) The burglar blew up the safe with the dynamite.

Look at (6), and count the number of nodes that it takes to represent the intended meaning of sentence (11). Notice that (6a) has fewer nodes than (6b). Because minimal attachment says "build the tree with the fewest nodes," when people listen to sentence (11), they will build the structure where *rusty lock* is attached to *blew up* (rather than *safe*). According to garden path theory, when the structure in (6a) is sent to the thematic processor with the words in sentence (11), the thematic processor will generate an error message (because it does not make sense to use a rusty lock to blow up a safe). In sentence (12), the minimal attachment heuristic leads to the correct syntactic structure, and the thematic processor has no trouble because the parser's output places *dynamite* and *blew up* together, and it makes sense to use dynamite to blow something up. (Notice that the minimal attachment heuristic also leads to the preferred and non-libelous interpretation of *Dr. Phil discussed sex with Rush Limbaugh.*)

When researchers measured how long it took people to understand sentences like (11) and (12), they found that people took longer to understand sentences like (11) (Rayner, Carlson, & Frazier, 1983). Why is this? One possibility is that people really use the minimal attachment heuristic to make structural decisions. Because the structure that listeners have to build for sentence (11) is more complicated than the structure that they have to build for sentence (12), they initially adopt the simpler structure, and this leads to problems when the thematic interpreter really needs the more complicated structure (as it does when it processes sentence (11)). Thus, garden path theory provided two sets of predictions that were confirmed by observing people's behavior as they processed sentences.

Sometimes different sentence-processing heuristics pull listeners in different directions at the same time. For example, the *main assertion* heuristic operates in cases like (13) and (14):

(13) The young woman delivered the bread that she baked to the store today.
(14) The young woman baked the bread that she delivered to the store today.

The main assertion heuristic says, "When you have a choice of where to attach new information, attach it so that it goes with the sentence's main assertion." When listeners get to the prepositional phrase *to the store* in (13) and (14), they have to choose whether to attach that phrase to the main verb in the sentence (*delivered* in (13), *baked* in (14)) or to the more recently encountered verb (*baked* in (13), *delivered* in (14)). The second verb is inside a *relative clause*, which in turn is modifying (providing additional information about) the preceding noun *bread*. The main assertion of the sentence is provided by the main clause (*The young woman delivered the bread*), rather than the relative clause, which provides additional, elaborative information. As a result, the main assertion heuristic predicts that people will have less trouble with sentence (13) than sentence (14). (Can you work out why this should be so?) However, the late closure heuristic makes the opposite prediction. It says that, when listeners get to the prepositional phrase *to the store*, they are currently working on the relative clause (*bread that she baked/bread that she delivered*). As a result, late closure says that (14) should be easier than (13). (Again, see if you can work out why this is so.) In cases like this, garden path theory predicts that people will have no more trouble processing sentences like (13) than sentences like (14), because, while the main assertion heuristic motivates attaching the prepositional phrase to the first verb, this preference is canceled out by the late closure heuristic. That prediction has been confirmed by measuring people's reading times—reading times are equivalent for sentences like (13) and (14) (Traxler & Frazier, 2008).

What happens when the main assertion preference is deactivated? That happens when the prepositional phrase *to the store* appears in a *subordinate clause*, as it does in sentences (15) and (16):

(15) Before the young woman delivered the bread that she baked to the store today, the clerk stacked the shelves.
(16) Before the young woman baked the bread that she delivered to the store today, the clerk stacked the shelves.

In (15) and (16), the main assertion is *the clerk stacked the shelves*, and there is no gramatically licensed way to associate the prepositional phrase *to the store* with the main assertion. When the main assertion preference is deactivated in this way, garden path theory says that the late closure heuristic should dominate people's structural choices. As a result, the prepositional phrase *to the store* should be easier to process in sentences like (16) than sentences like (15), and this is the pattern that appears in people's reading times (Traxler & Frazier, 2008).

Findings like these suggest that the parser deploys heuristics in a flexible way. The specific heuristics that are used at any given point in time depend on the characteristics of the sentences that are being processed. So, to predict how people will react to any given sentence, we need to know what properties the sentence has (what kinds of phrases and clauses it contains) and we need to know what processing heuristics people will use for that kind of sentence. One of the advantages of garden path theory is that it makes fairly specific claims about both of these things, so it is testable and potentially falsifiable.

Models of Parsing: Constraint-Based Models

Now that we have surveyed the garden path model, it is time to explore some alternative theories. *Constraint-based* parsing models constitute the most prominent alternative to two-stage models (e.g., MacDonald, Pearlmutter, & Seidenberg, 1994; Spivey-Knowlton & Sedivy,

1995; Tanenhaus, Spivey-Knowlton, Eberhard, & Sedivy, 1995; Trueswell et al., 1993). There are two critical differences between the garden path and constraint-based models. The first is that, rather than building one structure at a time, constraint-based parsers are capable of pursuing multiple structural possibilities simultaneously. Constraint-based parsers often times adopt a parallel distributed processing/neural network architecture, similar to the one that the TRACE model of lexical processing is based on (e.g., Elman, 1994, 2004; Green & Mitchell, 2006; Rohde & Plaut, 1999; Spivey-Knowlton & Sedivy, 1995; Stevenson, 1994; St. John & McClelland, 1992; Tabor & Hutchins, 2004). Constraint-based parsers represent different aspects of sentences, including their syntactic structures, as patterns of activation spread across large numbers of interconnected processing units. These groups of processing units and the connections among them are intended to resemble the functioning of networks of neurons in the brain. As in the TRACE model, partial and incomplete information can lead to partial activation of multiple mental representations, so at any given point in a sentence, the neural network could have multiple syntactic structure representations partially activated. The system as a whole effectively ranks these structural hypotheses, with more activation being assigned to structures that are more likely given the input and less activation being assigned to structures that are less likely given the input. An implicit assumption in most constraint-based accounts is that syntactic structures compete for activation, similar to what happens at the level of word processing in accounts of lexical access like TRACE (the competition assumption is made explicit in some versions of constraint-based processing accounts). The second critical difference between the garden path and constraint-based parsers is that the garden path parser relies solely on word category information for its inputs, but constraint-based parsers can draw on a much wider variety of cues to decide what structures to build and the relative emphasis to place on each alternative structure. Finally, constraint-based parsers are often referred to as *one-stage* models because lexical, syntactic, and semantic processes are all viewed as taking place simultaneously (as opposed to lexical processing preceding syntactic processing preceding semantic processing, which is the general approach taken by two-stage models).

The following sections explain how constraint-based parsers work and describe evidence supporting the idea that human sentence parsing processes are affected by multiple sources of information in addition to category information.

Story context effects

To start with, let's look at a set of studies that caused big problems for the classic garden path theory (Altmann, Garnham, & Dennis, 1992; Altmann, Garnham, & Henstra, 1994; Altmann & Steedman, 1988; Crain & Steedman, 1985). Recall that the garden path parser only pays attention to word category information during its initial attempts to build a syntactic structure for a sentence. If that is true, then information that appears in preceding sentences should have *no* effect on the initial processing of a given sentence. Let's look at sentence (11)—*The burglar blew up the safe with the rusty lock*—again. When would someone want to say something like this? In particular, why add the information about the safe having a rusty lock? Usually, speakers would add this information because they want to distinguish between one safe (that has a rusty lock) from some other safe or set of safes (that do *not* have rusty locks). But when sentence (11) appears all by itself, listeners have no direct indication that there could be more than one safe. The sentence only mentions one safe, and the definite article *the* strongly implies that there really is only one possible safe (otherwise, the speaker would say *a safe*). So, whether the syntactic structure of sentence (11) is complicated or not, the sentence creates challenges for listeners. In particular, when listeners get to *rusty lock*, they need to revise some of their semantic assumptions. They have to change from assuming only a single safe to assuming at least two safes, and they have to assume that the implicitly introduced safe or safes do not have rusty locks. These semantic changes have to be made regardless of the syntactic structure that listeners initially build for the sentence.

If that is all true, can we do anything to make sentence (11) easier, without changing its syntactic structure? The answer is, yes we can. We could tell people ahead of time that there is more than one safe, using a mini-story like (17):

(17) The burglar was planning his next job. He knew that the warehouse had two safes. Although one was brand new from the factory, the other one had been sitting out in the rain for ten years. *The burglar blew up the safe with the rusty lock.*

What should happen if this mini-story ended with sentence (11)? According to garden path theory, sentence (11) should still be hard to process, because regardless of what happens in the mini-story, the syntactic structure that you need for sentence (11) is still complicated and hard to build. But according to the *referential context* acount (a specific version of constraint-based parsing theory), the parser can use contextual information to decide which syntactic structure it will favor at a given point in time. The referential context account says, "If you have a choice of structures, build the syntactic structure that is most consistent with your current semantic assumptions. If you have a choice of structures, build whichever one allows referring expressions to be unambiguous." This means that sometimes the parser will build a more complicated syntactic structure when a simpler one is licensed by the grammar and consistent with the input.

Sentence (11) starts by saying *The burglar blew up the safe* … As soon as listeners get to *the safe*, they try to figure out what *the safe* refers to. Notice that the context in the mini-story has introduced two safes—a new one and an old one. By itself, *the safe* could refer to either of these two safes. Thus, listeners need additional information to figure out which of the two safes the NP *the safe* is supposed to point to. If listeners attach *with the rusty lock* to *the safe*, that will create a phrase that is semantically unambiguous and that fits well with the preceding story context. If they build the simpler syntactic structure, *the safe* will remain ambiguous—it could refer to either of the safes introduced previously in the story. Referential theory predicts that, in the context of stories like (17), comprehenders will build the more complicated structure rather than the simpler one for sentences like (11). As a result, sentences like (11) should be very easy to process despite their complicated syntax when they appear in stories like (17). This prediction was confirmed when people's reading times were measured. When sentence (11) appeared by itself, people slowed down when they read *the rusty lock*. When sentence (11) appeared in the context of story (17), people did *not* slow down when they read *rusty lock*. Thus, contrary to what the garden path theory predicts, the parser does seem to pay attention to information that context makes available at least some of the time to make decisions about which syntactic structure to build for a new sentence.

Subcategory frequency effects

The garden path parser uses only word category information to make initial decisions about which syntactic structures it will build. But words can provide more information than that. For example, consider the verbs *took* and *put*. Both of these words belong to the same syntactic category—Verb. But, other than having different meanings, are the two verbs equivalent? One way to approach that question is to see what kinds of syntactic structures the two verbs can be part of. Let's start with *took*. Can *took* appear without anything following it?

(18) Dr. Phil took.

Most people would say that sentence (18) sounds odd. So let's mark it with an asterisk to show that it is odd.

*(18) Dr. Phil took.

What if we add a noun phrase (NP) after *took*?

(19) Dr. Phil took a nap.

Much better! So, we conclude that *took* is the kind of a verb that needs a *post-verbal argument*. Specifically, *took* needs to have a *direct object*, in this case *a nap*. In technical terms, we call verbs like *took* "*obligatorily transitive*" (transitive verbs take a post-verbal, direct-object argument).

How about *put*?

*(20) Dr. Phil put.

That's odd. How about (21)?

*(21) Dr. Phil put a book.

Still odd. How about (22)?

(22) Dr. Phil put a book on the shelf.

Fine. So, *took* and *put* are similar in that neither one can appear all by itself without anything coming after, but they are different in other ways. *Took* is fine with just a direct object, but *put* requires both a direct object and a goal. Thus, they are both in the category Verb, but they belong to different *subcategories*, because they have different requirements for different kinds of partners (sometimes called *arguments* or *complements*), and so different requirements for syntactic structures. (See if you can draw the structure for the VP when it has a direct object and when it has both a direct object and a PP goal argument. Ask your professor for help if you get stuck.)

Verbs like *took* and *put* are fairly picky about the kinds of complements they need and the kinds of syntactic structures they can appear in. Other verbs are more flexible. Consider the verb *was reading*. It can appear without any post-verbal arguments at all, as in (23), where it is *intransitive*:

(23) Dr. Phil was reading.

It can appear with a direct object, as in (24), where it is transitive:

(24) Dr. Phil was reading a story.

It can appear with a direct object and an *indirect object*, as in (25), and then it is *ditransitive*:

(25) Dr. Phil was reading a little girl a story.

So *was reading* has a number of subcategory possibilities, including intransitive, transitive, and ditransitive; and each of these subcategory possibilities is associated with a different syntactic structure. There are, in fact, many verbs that are flexible in this way. (See if you can think of a few.)

Constraint-based parsers differ from two-stage parsers like the garden path parser because constraint-based theory says that structural information is associated with individual words in the lexicon and this information influences which structural hypotheses will be pursued as sentences are being processed. In particular, a constraint-based parser will use subcategory information to determine which structural analysis to favor when more than one structure is consistent with the input. How does this work? Consider the following sentence fragment:

(26) The student saw the answer …

This fragment could continue

… to the last question.

In that case, *the answer* is the direct-object argument of *saw*, and the sentence should be structured as in (27).

(27)

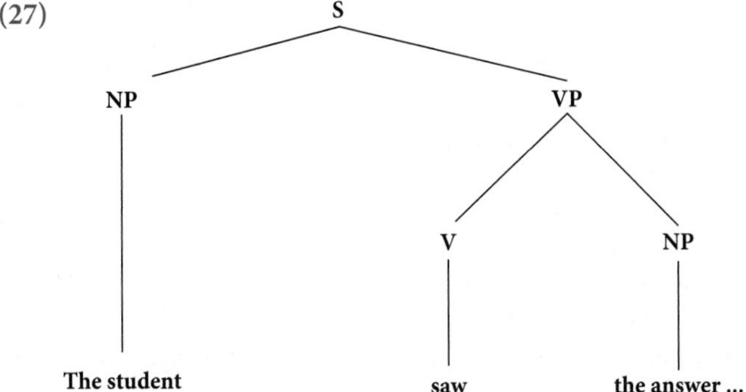

But in sentence (28)

(28) The student saw the answer …

continues with

… was in the back of the book.

In that case, *the answer* does not represent the direct object of *saw*. Instead, *the answer* is the subject of the verb *was*, and the sentence should be structured as in (29). In sentence (28), the part *the answer was in the back of the book* is called a *sentence complement. The answer was in the back of the book* is a sentence complement because it really is a sentence that could appear all by itself and because the whole thing is the post-verbal complement of *saw*.

(29)

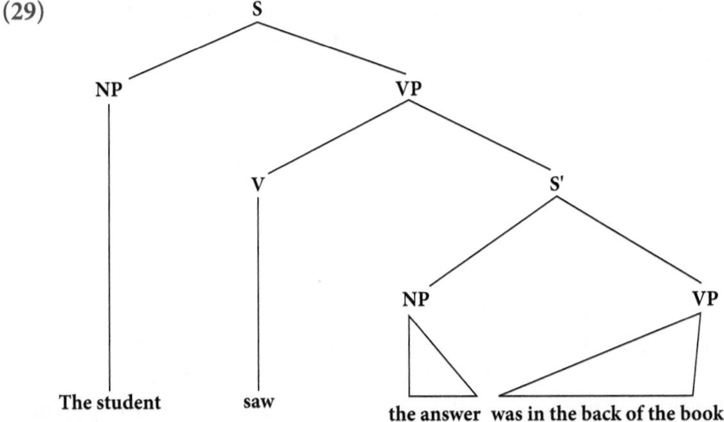

So, when comprehenders get to "the answer" in (26) and (27), they face a choice between the structures in (30):

(30)
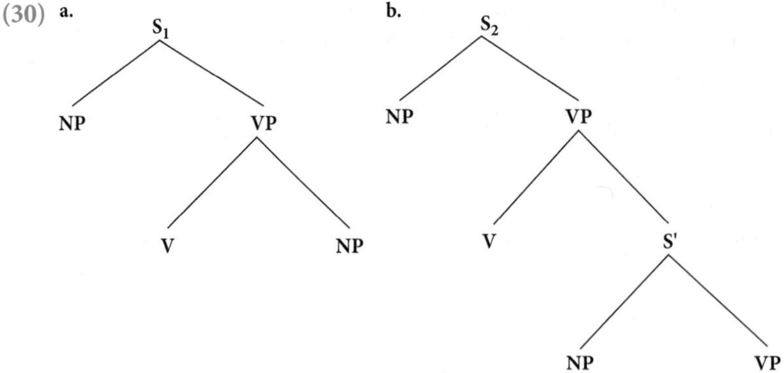

Garden path theory predicts that people should prefer the left-hand structure (a), because it is simpler than the right-hand structure (b) and because pursuing that structure allows comprehenders to continue working on the current VP. So garden path theory predicts that sentences like (28) should be harder to understand than sentences like (26), and this is true in general. Constraint-based theory also predicts that (28) should be harder than (26), but for a different reason. It turns out that both theories are correct in this instance—sentences like (28) really are harder to process than sentences like (26) (Frazier & Rayner, 1982; Pickering & Traxler, 1998).

Constraint-based theory assumes that people pay attention to *subcategory preference* information. Subcategory preference information reflects the likelihood that a given structure and a given verb go together. Consider the verb *saw* again. Suppose you know that 9 times out of 10 in the past *saw* was followed by a direct object (as in 26). Suppose that, after you heard *The student saw* but before you got the next word, someone would let you bet about what structure the sentence as a whole would have. Would you bet on direct object or on something else, sentence complement perhaps? If you bet (or predicted) that the next thing would be a direct object, you would be right in the long run 90% of the time (and you would become rich). Essentially, this is what the constraint-based parser does. It takes information about the past—e.g., the likelihood that a given structure will appear when a given verb appears—and uses it to predict the future. So, according to constraint-based theory, (28) is hard because the parser predicts that a direct object is coming, and so the parser assigns more weight to the syntactic structure that allows *saw* to have a direct object. When the sentence actually provides the input for a different structure (sentence complement in this case), the constraint-based parser has to change its mind. The constraint-based parser has been garden-pathed, not because it has used the wrong heuristics, but because sentence (28) goes against the general pattern that has occurred in the past.

Garden path theory and constraint-based parsing theory both make the same prediction for sentences (26) and (28), and they both provide an explanation for people's actual observed behavior. But garden path theory and constraint-based parsing theory do not always make identical predictions. They make opposite predictions for sentences like (31) and (32):

(31) Dr. Phil realized his goals early on.
(32) Dr. Phil realized his goals were out of reach.

The syntactic structures we need for (31) and (32) are the same structures that we need for the corresponding (26) and (28). In (31), *his goals* is the direct-object argument of *realized*, so it has the same structure as (26). In (32), *his goals* is the subject of a sentence complement (*his goals were out of reach*), so it has the same structure as (28). Garden path theory predicts that (32) should be harder than (31) (for the reasons laid out above), but constraint-based theory predicts that (32) should be just as easy to process as (31). Why is that?

According to constraint-based parsing theory, (32) should be just as easy as (31) because the subcategory information in (32) points readers toward the correct syntactic structure right away. Unlike the verb *saw*, *realized* appears with a sentence complement about 90% of the time. In the language at large, it is much more likely that someone would say *I realized I was late*, than something like *I realized a profit*. So, what happens when people hear *Dr. Phil realized …*? The constraint-based parser will predict that a sentence complement is coming and will favor the more complicated structure at that point. In effect, the parser will be well prepared to deal with the rest of sentence (32) because it is expecting the structure that actually appears. Hence, no structural revisions are necessary to deal with the complicated structure of the end of sentence (32).

***

(Hey students: Confound your professor by asking why (31) isn't harder to process than (32)! If your professor answers "the cost of the unlikely structure is balanced by the benefits of having a simple structure," give her a round of applause.)

***

So, across sentences (26)–(32), garden path theory predicts that (26) and (31) will be easy to process and (28) and (32) will be hard to process. By contrast, constraint-based parsing theory predicts that only sentence (28) will be hard to process, because the structure that the parser predicts is different from the structure that actually appears only in that case. Eye-tracking and self-paced reading experiments showed that only sentences like (28) cause comprehenders difficulty (Garnsey, Pearlmutter, Myers, & Lotocky, 1997; Trueswell et al., 1993). This can be explained if we assume that the parser keeps track of how often specific verbs go together with different syntactic struct ures and that it uses this information very quickly when it is making decisions about which structural options to pursue. Findings like these also support the idea that the parser is trying to anticipate which structures it is likely to encounter in the near future, and that subcategory information is one of the sources of information that the parser uses to make its predictions.

When comprehenders demonstrate sensitivity to subcategory preference information (the fact that some structures are easier to process than others when a sentence contains a particular verb), they are behaving in ways that are consistent with the *tuning hypothesis*. The tuning hypothesis says, "that structural ambiguities are resolved on the basis of stored records relating to the prevalence of the resolution of comparable ambiguities in the past" (Mitchell, Cuetos, Corley, & Brysbaert, 1995, p. 470; see also Bates & MacWhinney, 1987; Ford, Bresnan, & Kaplan, 1982; MacDonald et al., 1994). In other words, people keep track of how often they encounter different syntactic structures, and when they are uncertain about how a particular string of words should be structured, they use this stored information to rank the different possibilities. In the case of subcategory preference information, the frequencies of different structures are tied to specific words—verbs in this case. The next section will consider the possibility that frequencies are tied to more complicated configurations of words, rather than to individual words.

Cross-linguistic frequency data

So far, when considering parsing strategies and theories, the focus has been entirely on English. However, considerable work has been done in other languages that helps illuminate how people parse and interpret sentences. One line of *cross-linguistic research* (research that compares how different languages are processed) has focused on the extent to which structural preferences in different languages match the frequencies with which different structures occur in those languages. For example, Spanish speakers can use a relative clause to modify a preceding noun. Sentence (33) is globally ambiguous because the relative clause "who was standing on the balcony with her husband" could go with either "(female) servant" or "actress" (from Cuetos & Mitchell, 1988):

(33) Alguien disparo contra la criada de la actriz que esta ba en el balcon con su marido.

"Someone shot the (female) servant of the actress who was standing on the balcony with her (male) spouse."

(34) Alguien disparo contra el criado de la actriz que esta ba en el balcon con su marido.

"Someone shot the (male) servant of the actress who was standing on the balcony with her (male) spouse."

Sentence (34) is temporarily ambiguous because, although "who was standing on the balcony" could describe either "(male) servant" or "actress," the end of the relative clause ("with her spouse") ties the relative clause definitely to the second of the two nouns. For sentences like (33) and (34), English readers exhibit a preference to attach the relative clause to the second of the two nouns ("actress"), but Spanish speakers exhibit a preference to attach the relative clause to the first of the two nouns ("servant"; Carreiras & Clifton, 1993; 1999). French speakers also appear to prefer to attach the relative clause to the the first noun in equivalent French sentences, while Italians and Germans prefer the second (Cuetos, Mitchell, & Corley, 1996; Mitchell et al., 1995). Why should there be this difference in structural preferences across languages? One possibility is that the frequency with which the structures appear differs across languages. While attachment to the first noun appears to be the more frequent option in Spanish and French for sentences like (33) and (34), English and Italian appear to pattern the other way.

Although it would be possible to tie the likelihood of being modified to individual nouns, it appears that structural frequency information is being associated with larger elements—configurations of nouns. (For example, people are more likely to modify a noun like *thing* than a more specific noun like *apple*, and people almost never modify proper names. So you're far more likely to hear plain old *Dr. Phil* than *The Dr. Phil who is standing right over there talking about sex with Rush Limbaugh.*) The idea that frequencies are associated with groups of words is supported by the fact that near exact translations of the same sentences like (33) and (34) have been used in different languages, so the same nouns are represented in the different studies. If the structural preferences were associated with individual nouns, they should be pretty similar across languages.

Experimental outcomes for sentences like (33) and (34) appear to support the idea that frequent structures are easier to process than less frequent structures. This is compatible with constraint-based accounts' claims that people keep track of how often they encounter particular kinds of sentences, and that they lean toward structures they have encountered in the past when a new sentence can be structured in more than one way. However, there is a possible counter-example from Dutch. Marc Brysbaert and Don Mitchell measured Dutch speakers' eye movements while they read the Dutch equivalents of (33) and (34) (Brysbaert & Mitchell, 1996). The eye movements indicated that Dutch speakers had more trouble interpreting the test sentences when the relative clause went with the first noun than when it went with the second noun. But when researchers looked at a database of Dutch sentences (that came from newspaper and magazine articles), they found that relative clauses went with the first noun more often than they went with the second. So, the more frequent structure appeared to be more difficult to process, contrary to what constraint-based and other frequency dependent parsing theories would predict. However, when other researchers analyzed the test sentences and the sentences from the database, they found that semantic factors like animacy and concreteness were more important than position in determining where the modifying relative clauses should go (Desmet, De Baecke, Drieghe, Brysbaert, & Vonk, 2006). So, when more *fine-grained* information was taken into account, reading time could be predicted by detailed frequency information.

The cross-linguistic investigation of relative clause attachment raises a further important issue: How does the parser decide whether something is frequent or infrequent? If we just count all sentences, simple active voice sentences will be the most frequent (example active voice sentence: *John kissed Mary*). The parser should therefore favor the direct-object interpretation of any sentence that starts with a noun phrase and a verb phrase. But if we start counting up which structures go with an individual verb, then the parser should favor the sentence complement interpretation of any sentence that starts with a noun phrase followed by the verb *realized* followed by another noun. But if we start counting up the likelihood of specific verb–noun combinations, then the parser should switch back to favoring the direct-object interpretation of any sentence that starts with a noun, the verb *realized*, and the noun *goals*. Likewise, if we start factoring in animacy, then any sentence that starts with an inanimate noun should reduce the likelihood of a simple, active structure. This problem goes by the name *the grain size problem* (coined by Don Mitchell in an article in 1987). Languages offer us multiple levels of analysis (different *grains*), people can potentially keep track of statistics at any level of analysis, and the degree to which a structural alternative is preferred can differ at different grains. One solution to the grain size problem is to suggest that the parser does not keep any statistics at all (as some two-stage models claim). If the parser does not try to estimate likelihood, and instead bases its decisions on other criteria (like *simplicity* or *recency*), then there is no reason for us to worry that different frequencies apply at different grains. Another solution is to suggest that the parser keeps track of statistics at different grains, and that it combines data from different grains to arrive at an overall estimate of likelihood. So, in our example involving *realized*, the parser will give some weight to the fact that the most common structure in the language is subject-verb-object, it will also give some weight to the fact that the most likely structure for any sentence with the verb *realized* in it is the sentence complement structure, but if it gets *realized* followed by *goals*, the parser will pay attention to the fact that, at this very fine grain, *goals* is a really good direct object for *realized*, and will therefore boost the activation of the syntactic structure that goes with that interpretation.

Semantic effects

So far, we have seen how a constraint-based parser could use story context information and subcategory information to anticipate upcoming syntactic structure. Another source of information that the parser could rely on is the semantic (meaning) information associated with specific words in sentences (as in the *realized his goals* example). Again, this is a point where constraint-based theory differs from garden path theory, because garden path theory says that the parser ignores semantic information as it is making its initial structural decisions. To see how that works, let's look at a kind of sentence called a *reduced relative*:

(35) The defendant examined by the lawyer went to prison.

(35) is called a reduced relative because it contains a relative clause *examined by the lawyer* that modifies the meaning of the preceding NP *The defendant* ("Which defendant are we talking about?" "The one examined by the lawyer."). The sentence can be made easier to process if we introduce the relative clause with a *relativizer*. In (36) the relativizer *who* unambiguously marks the start of the relative clause.

(36) The defendant who was examined by the lawyer went to prison.

Numerous studies have shown that sentences like (35) are harder to process than sentences like (36) (e.g., Clifton et al., 2003; Ferreira & Clifton, 1986). Why is that? In general, reduced relatives are difficult to process because listeners have a hard time figuring out that they are dealing with a relative clause rather than something else. Why do they have trouble identifying the relative clause? One reason is that the beginning of the reduced relative clause looks like a regular old *main clause*. (Main clauses consist of the grammatical subject of the sentence, the main verb of the sentence, and the arguments and modifiers that go with the main verb. Subordinate and relative clauses provide additional information about the main clause or individual words that appear in the main clause.) So, while processing *The defendant examined ...* listeners might begin to build a syntactic structure that is appropriate for a main clause continuation. If so, they would be ill prepared to deal with the actual continuation in (35), but they would be well prepared if the sentence continued as in (37):

(37) The defendant examined the photographs.

The structural choices that the parser faces are represented in (38).

(38)

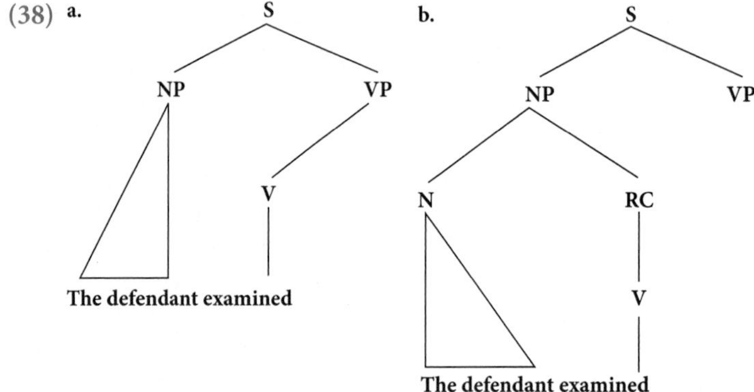

(38a) shows the structure that you need for the main clause interpretation. (38b) shows the structure that you need for the relative clause interpretation.

Notice that the structure in (38b) is more complicated than the structure in (38a), and so garden path theory predicts that people will prefer the structure in (38a)—the main clause structure. As a result, people should have trouble dealing with a sentence that requires the more complicated structure in (38b). Constraint-based parsing theory also predicts that the reduced relative clause in (35) will be hard to process, but for a different reason. Constraint-based theory says that the problem of figuring out that *examined* is part of a relative clause is made worse by the fact that *defendant* refers to a person, and people are very likely to *examine* things. That is, *defendant* falls in the category of *animate* things. *Animate* things, like people, animals, and fish, can move around, have goals, initiate actions, and so forth. *Inanimate* things, like rocks, trees, and houses, do not move around, do not have goals, and do not initiate actions. Most of the time, when a sentence starts with an animate entity, the animate entity is responsible for starting the action described in the sentence (as in 37).

The technical name for someone or something that starts an action is *agent* or *thematic agent* (Jackendoff, 1990). It is less likely that an animate entity that starts a sentence will be the recipient of an action that is initiated by someone else. The technical names for someone or something that is the target of an action are *theme*, *experiencer*, or *recipient*. (An exception to the general pattern of an animate initial noun being the agent occurs in *passive* sentences, like *The defendant was examined by the lawyer*. But here, the sentence provides abundant structural cues that clarify the *patient* status of the initial noun *defendant*. See if you can spot some of the cues that the passive provides.) So, according to constraint-based parsing theory, when people hear *The defendant examined …*, they know that *defendant* is animate, they assume that the animate *defendant* will initiate the action, and *examined* provides them with the action that the *defendant* is initiating. When they actually get *by the lawyer*, all of those assumptions need to be undone. *The defendant* isn't the initiator of the *examining* action, he's the recipient. *The defendant* isn't examining anything, he's being examined. On top of all of that semantic (meaning) revision, it turns out that the parser's structural assumptions were also wrong. Chaos! The poor listener has been garden-pathed in a major way and has to do a lot of work to clean up the mess.

***

(Hey students: An even more difficult reduced relative than sentence (35) is, *The editor played the tape was furious*. Astonish your professor by explaining to him why that one is harder than sentence (35).)

***

If semantics is the driving factor that turns reduced relatives into mental train wrecks, it should be possible to use semantic information to make sentences like (35) easier to process. How might we do that? Because the train wreck starts with assumptions about *the defendant*, we could start by triggering a different set of assumptions. We can do that by starting the sentence with an inanimate noun, like *evidence*, as in (39):

(39) The evidence examined by the lawyer was complicated.

Because *evidence* is inanimate, it is not a good agent and is highly unlikely to initiate the action in the sentence. But it is a really good thematic patient. So when listeners hear *The evidence examined …*, they should heavily discount the possibility that they are looking at a sentence with a main-clause structure like (37). So, the parser should immediately rule out the possibility that *examined* is the main verb of the sentence and it should choose a different structure right away. By using information about the meaning of the initial noun (is it animate or inanimate?), the parser can avoid building the wrong structure for the sentence. If this allows the parser to avoid making bad semantic and structural assumptions, then people should not have very much trouble processing sentences like (39). In fact, although there is some uncertainty about how quickly semantic information influences the structure-building process, sentences like (39) with inanimate initial nouns are easier to interpret than sentences like (35) with animate initial nouns—having an inanimate initial noun like *evidence* does reduce the overall processing difficulty that the reduced relative imposes on the comprehender (Clifton et al., 2003; Trueswell et al., 1994). (Researchers agree that animacy either helps comprehenders get to the right syntactic structure straight away, or it helps them dump a bad structure faster so that they can start building the right structure faster after building the wrong structure, or both.) Note that if the animacy experiments show that comprehenders use animacy to avoid building bad structure, then findings like these are problematic for garden path parsing theory. The garden path parser ignores semantics when it makes its structural decisions, so it should make the same structural choices for sentences with animate initial nouns and sentences with inanimate initial nouns.

Prosody

When people speak sentences, they produce sequences of words, and they modulate the speed, loudness, and pitch that they speak at depending on what roles the words are playing in the sentence. The speech information that identifies specific words is called *segmental* information (where a "segment" is any discrete unit that can be identifed, including phonemes, syllables, and words). The information that correlates with grammatical role and other discourse functions is called *suprasegmental* information ("suprasegmental" means the speech pattern extends across more than one segment), and this is normally what is referred to when language scientists use the term *prosody* (Speer & Blodgett, 2006). People who study prosody categorize speech patterns into two general classes. *Non-linguistic* prosody consists of those aspects of speech that provide cues to the speaker's general mental state. Is the speaker happy, angry, or depressed? The tone and tempo of the speaker's output will differ depending on how the speaker is feeling at the moment. *Linguistic* prosody consists of those aspects of speech that provide cues to how the words are organized into phrases and clauses. For example, stress—how loud particular speech segments are spoken—can indicate whether someone is speaking a compound noun or whether someone is speaking an adjective and a noun. If someone says *green HOUSE,* it is likely that they are talking about a house that's been painted green. If someone says *GREEN house*, they are probably talking about a place where you grow plants when it's too cold outside. Another example is the difference between statements and questions. Suppose someone says *John wants a hamburger* with a rising tone at the end. Normally, a speaker would use that prosodic cue to indicate uncertainty—the speaker is asking a question. If the speaker pronounces the same sentence with a falling tone at the end, that usually indicates that the speaker is making a statement—i.e., the speaker knows what John wants.

Prosody can provide cues that help the parser to construct the correct syntactic structures when the input is syntactically ambiguous. For example, consider sentence (40) (from Speer & Blodgett, 2006, p. 506):

(40) The professor said the student had on socks that did not match.

This sentence could be pronounced in different ways with pauses in different locations. Try speaking the sentence with a big pause after *said*, and no big pauses anywhere else. If you pronounce the sentence that way, who has the mismatched socks, the professor or the student? Now try speaking the sentence with two big pauses, one right before *said* and one right after *student*. Now it should be someone else who is having a bad socks day. Pauses are a good cue to phrase structure, because words that go together to make a phrase are usually pronounced together without any major pauses or breaks. This does not always happen, however, as sometimes speakers make mistakes or are dysfluent—real speech is full of false starts, "ums", "ahs", "you knows", and other verbal tics that can interfere with the clean packaging of prosodic cues and phrase structure. So, while prosodic cues can be very useful, they are not always available, and when they are, they are not always 100% valid. Therefore, one question language scientists have asked is: How much do listeners rely on prosody when they are making syntactic structure decisions? This section will review some of the studies that indicate that, when prosodic cues are available, listeners use them very quickly to choose between alternative structural possibilities.

Because naturally occurring speech has a lot of syntactic and prosodic properties that are not easy to control for in an experiment, language scientists often use carefully constructed utterances to test how listeners respond to prosodic cues. Using carefully planned and recorded speech allows them to control for nuisance variables. Researchers who study prosody have also created a very sophisticated analytical tool called the *ToBI* (Tones and Breaks Index) system that allows them to clearly identify the prosodic cues that are present in any given utterance. With these tools in hand, researchers can systematically manipulate the prosodic cues in sentences that are controlled with regard to their syntactic structures and meaning. They can then present their sentences to listeners in situations that allow them to carefully observe the listeners' behavior. Researchers draw inferences about how prosody affects the meaning assigned to globally ambiguous sentences and determine how quickly listeners combine prosodic and syntactic information as they interpret sentences.

Prosodic cues appear to strongly influence the interpretation of some sentences that have globally ambiguous syntactic structure. For example, consider sentence (41) (from Carlson, Clifton, & Frazier, 2001):

(41) Susie learned that Bill telephoned after John visited.

This sentence is globally ambiguous because *after John visited* could tell us when Susie learned something about Bill, in which case the phrase *after John visited* attaches to the verb *learned.* Alternatively, the phrase *after John visited* could tell us when Bill telephoned, in which case it attaches to *telephoned.* If there is a relatively large pause between *Bill* and *telephoned*, listeners are likely to judge that *after John visited* goes with *telephoned.* If there is a relatively large pause after *telephoned*, listeners are likely to judge that *after John visited* goes with *learned.*

Sentences like (41) are somewhat artificial, because they have been digitally altered, but similar effects occur under more natural circumstances. For example, researchers observed naive participants who came into the lab and took part in a game (Schafer, Speer, Warren, & White, 2000). The game involved game pieces that came in different shapes and colors. A "driver" instructed a "slider" how to move the pieces around the board. The trick was that the driver knew where the pieces were supposed to end up, but only the slider knew the location of bonuses (cookies) and penalties (ravenous goats). The driver and slider cooperated to earn points. The researchers elicited temporarily ambiguous sentences from the participants by giving them a list of scripted sentences that they could use to play the game, such as (42) and (43):

(42) When that moves the square should land in a good place.
(43) When that moves the square it should land in a good place.

Drivers spontaneously produced prosodic cues that helped to disambiguate the sentences (e.g., they would pause after *moves* when speaking sentences like (42) and after *square* in (43)). Next, the researchers deleted everything after the word *square* and played the truncated sentences to a new set of participants. These participants were asked to guess how the sentences would continue. They were able to accurately predict what ending the original speakers had used, and this indicates that the listeners were using prosodic information to choose between alternative syntactic structure possibilities.

Other research addresses the question of how quickly listeners use prosody to make structural decisions. One such study involved sentences like (44) and (45) (Kjelgaard & Speer, 1999; see also Snedeker & Trueswell, 2003):

(44) When Roger leaves the house <u>is</u> dark.
(45) When Roger leaves the house <u>it's</u> dark.

(44) is a garden path sentence very similar to (7). (45) is also temporarily ambiguous, but it is normally easier to process than (44), because the listener's syntactic assumptions match the structure that the sentence actually requires. We could help the listener deal with sentence (44) by inserting a big pause after the word *leaves* (try pronouncing the sentence that way). We could make things more difficult for the listener by pronouncing *leaves the house* all together without any pause between *leaves* and *the house*, and by putting in a big pause before *is* (try pronouncing the sentence that way—it will probably sound strange to you). (There are other prosodic cues that can help the listener deal with (44). Those cues

involve changing the average pitch of different parts of the utterance and the length or duration of the words in the utterance. (See Speer & Blodgett, 2006, for a more complete description.) The same prosodic changes can be made to sentences like (45). When the prosodic cues point listeners toward the correct syntactic structure, the prosody is said to be *cooperating*. When the prosodic cues point listeners toward the incorrect syntactic structure, it is said to be *conflicting*. Researchers can measure how hard it is to process sentences like (44) and (45) using a variety of experimental tasks. They can ask listeners to press a button when they have figured out what the sentence means after they hear it. Alternatively, they can ask listeners to respond to a visual target word after listening to most of the sentence. For example, listeners might be asked to name (speak) the word *is* after listening to *When Roger leaves the house*. If listeners have been building the correct syntactic structure for the beginning of the sentence, it should be easier to say *is* than if they have been building the wrong structure. The same predictions apply for sentence (45). Participants' behavior on both of these tasks showed that they used prosodic cues very quickly to make structural decisions in sentences like (44) and (45). Listeners pressed the "Got it" button faster when the sentences had cooperating prosody than when they had conflicting prosody; and they pronounced the syntactically disambiguating main verb (*is* or *it's*) faster for cooperating than conflicting prosody as well.

Visual context effects

Previously, we have seen that information in a story, and the way a new sentence fits into the story, can affect the structural choices that the parser makes. This section will review further evidence that syntactic parsing can be influenced by information from outside the language-processing system. Specifically, the information available in a visual scene can increase the parser's preference for a complex syntactic structure. To see how this works, consider sentence (46):

(46) The girl placed the apple on the towel in the box.

(46) is a garden path sentence because comprehenders interpret the first prepositional phrase (PP) *on the towel* as the goal of the placing action (i.e., they think that the girl put the apple on the towel). To interpret the sentence as it was intended, comprehenders have to attach the first PP to *the apple* (as in *Which apple did the girl place? The apple (that was) on the towel.*). In that case, *on the towel* is a *source* rather than a goal location. Garden path theory says that sentences like (46) are hard to process because the minimal attachment heuristic makes the parser adopt the wrong syntactic structure. Constraint-based parsing theory and referential theory say that sentences like (46) are hard to process because, when the sentence appears by itself, nothing tells the listener that there might be more than one apple, and so there is no obvious reason to treat *on the towel* as information that discriminates between the explicitly mentioned apple and some other set of un-mentioned apples. We have seen that mentioning more apples in a story context can make sentences like (46) easier to process, but is there any other kind of context that can have a similar effect?

To answer that question, Mike Tanenhaus and his colleagues conducted a study where they manipulated what listeners were looking at as they listened to and tried to understand sentences like (46) (Tanenhaus et al., 1995). This study used the *visual world* experimental method (or paradigm). In the visual world paradigm, participants wear an eye-tracking device that shows researchers where they are looking during an experiment. Real objects are placed on a table in front of the participant. Participants listen to sentences about these objects and they respond to the sentences by moving the objects around. The researchers

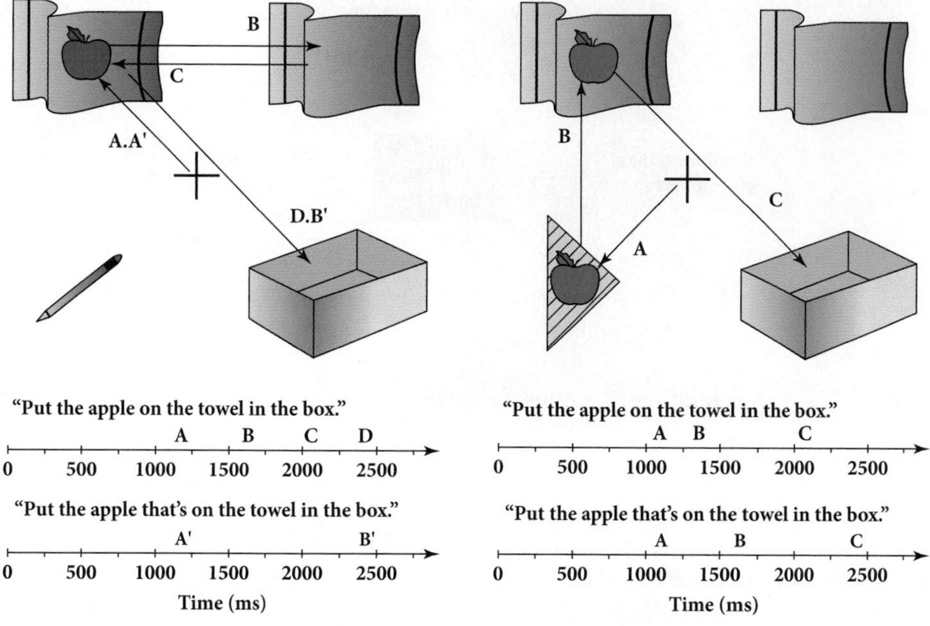

Figure 4.2 Sample visual displays and eye-movement patterns (from Tanenhaus et al., 1995)

can manipulate characteristics of both the visual display and the sentences to see what effect this has on participants' eye movements. By analyzing participants' eye movements, researchers can draw conclusions about how the participants interpreted the sentences.

For example, consider the displays in Figure 4.2. The left-hand display contains only a single apple, and that apple is on a towel. The left-hand display also has an empty towel and a box. The right-hand display contains two apples. One of the apples is on a napkin and the other apple is on a towel. There is also a towel with nothing on it. So both displays have an empty towel that could match up with the goal interpretation of *on the towel*. Because it has two apples, the right-hand display is the visual equivalent to the story that mentioned two safes. While participants looked at either the left-hand display (the one-apple display) or the right-hand display (the two-apple display), they listened to a sentence that said, *Put the apple on the towel in the box*. The critical thing that the researchers wanted to know was: Where did participants look when they heard *on the towel*? If participants interpreted *on the towel* (incorrectly) as the goal of *Put the apple*, then they should look at the empty towel. If they interpret *on the towel* (correctly) as modifying the meaning of *apple*, then they should look at the apple that is on the towel. So what happened in the experiment?

First, let's consider what happened when the visual display only had one apple (the left-hand side of Figure 4.2). When participants heard *on the towel* in *Put the apple on the towel* ..., they were more likely to look at the empty towel than the apple. So it looks like participants were interpreting *on the towel* (incorrectly) as a goal, rather than something that modified the meaning of *apple*. But something very different happened when the visual display had two apples (one on a towel and one on a napkin) and an empty towel. Under these conditions, when participants heard *on the towel*, they were more likely to look at the apple that was on the towel, rather than looking at the empty towel. So it looks like participants were (correctly) interpreting *on the towel* as going with *apple* when the visual display had two apples. That result is very similar to the story context experiment involving sentences like (11)—*The burlar blew up the safe with the rusty lock*. This new result goes beyond those

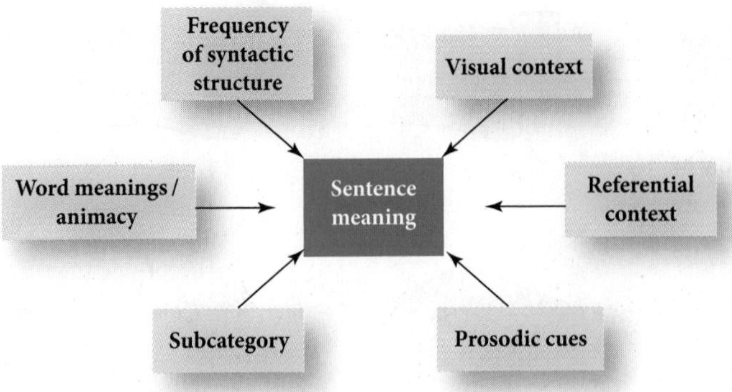

Figure 4.3 A constraint-based outlook on syntactic parsing.

previous ones, however, by showing that information from other modalities (i.e., vision) has a rapid effect on processes taking place within the language-processing system. When the display has two apples, the expression *the apple* by itself does not successfully refer to either apple. Under those conditions, participants were willing to build a more complicated syntactic structure so that they could attach *on the towel* as a modifier of the expression *the apple*, and in that case, the expression as a whole *the apple on the towel* successfully picked out one of the two apples in the display. So the way the syntactic parser functioned was affected by what was happening in the visual system.

Interim Summary

So far in this chapter, we have seen that sentence interpretation involves a parser that makes decisions about how words in sentences relate to one another. We have looked at two different processing mechanisms that have been proposed to explain how parsing takes place. The currently available experimental evidence shows that there are some aspects of people's behavior that are not fully compatible with the garden path theory. As a result, many researchers favor one of the constraint-based versions of sentence-processing theory. If one wanted to draw a picture to represent the main assumptions that constraint-based theory makes about sentence processing, it might look like Figure 4.3. The key points to take away are:

1. A constraint-based parser can activate multiple syntactic structures simultaneously.
2. It ranks different structures based on how much evidence is available for each in the input.
3. Evidence for a given structure and its accompanying semantic interpretation can come from multiple sources, including story context, visual context, subcategory information, and the semantic properties of specific words.

Argument Structure Hypothesis

One of the central claims that constraint-based theory makes about parsing is that structural information is tied to specific words in the lexicon. What does this structural information look like? Let's look at how structural information related to verbs might be represented.

One possibility is that our long-term memories contain information about phrase structure trees like those in (47) (MacDonald et al., 1994). For a verb like *was reading*, long-term memory would contain at least three phrase structure trees, one for the intransitive form, one for the transitive form, and one for the ditransitive form. But what about the dative form? Is that represented, too? If so, there would be a fourth tree, as in (48). And what if the dative form is supplemented by information about location? Do we need another tree for *was reading the book to the girl at the park*? If so, we need the structure in (49). What if we had something like this? *Dr. Phil was reading the book to the girl at the park next to the fire station that was built by generous pilgrims from Burkina Faso who liked to take long walks with their vicious pet lizards.* If we wanted to prestore all of the structure that goes with the verb, then we would need something like (50).

(47) ***"was reading"***

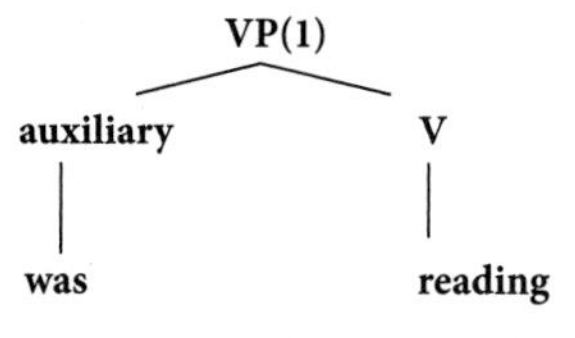

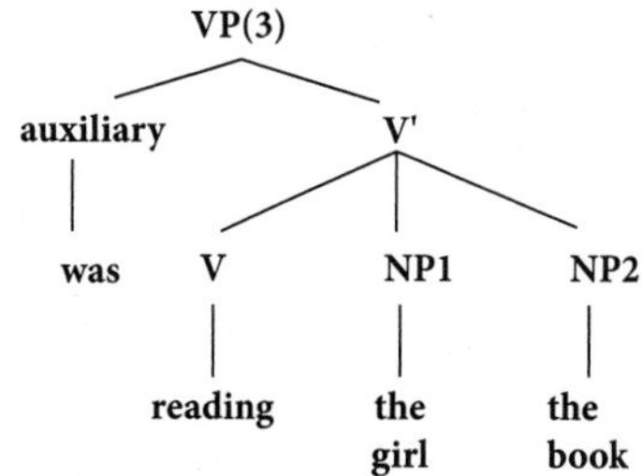

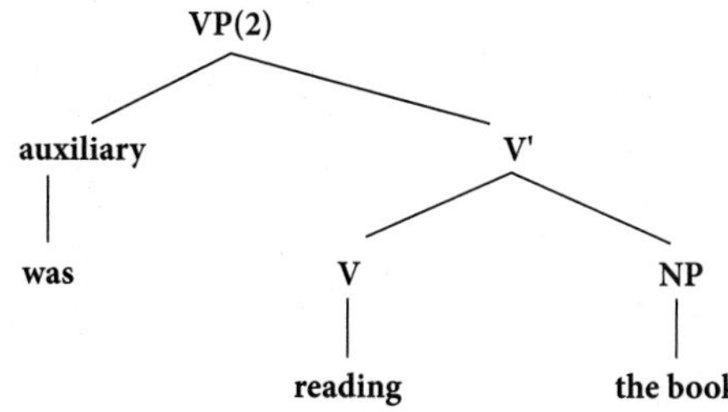

(48)

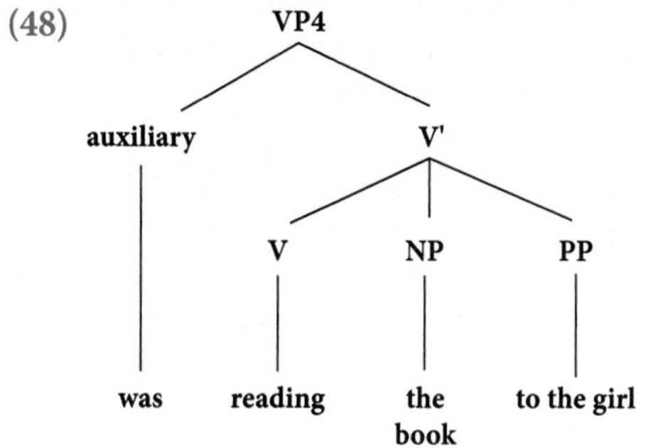

(49)

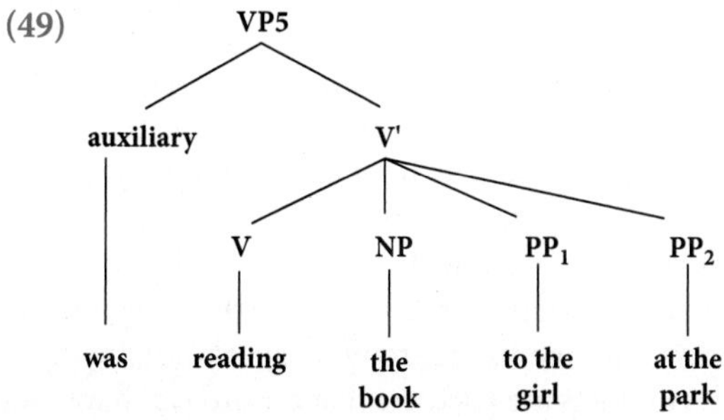

(50)

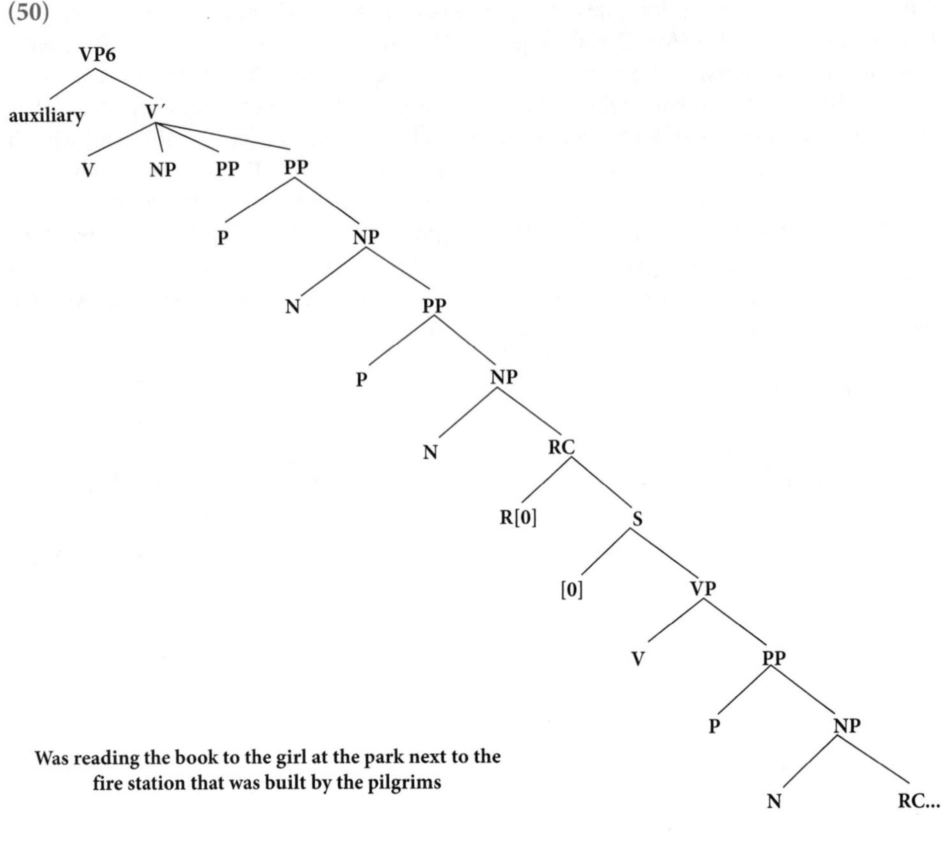

***

(Hey students: This doesn't even take into account the multiple structural ambiguities and alternative interpretations for the sentence in (50), such as the interpretation where the vicious pet lizards helped to build the fire station. See if you can draw the syntactic structure for that interpretation. If you can, show it to your professor and tell her you get an "A" for the course.)

***

What we really need is some set of principles or guidelines that allows us to avoid the psycholinguistic equivalent of *the leg-shaving problem*: Where do I stop? In leg-shaving, many people adopt the principle, "I stop below the knee." This principle requires us to decide where, exactly the knee is, and that can be somewhat ambiguous, but now we at least have a clear "stop" rule, and we can proceed even if we have only a rough idea where the knee is. Can we come up with a similar principle for verb-related syntactic structure? One possible stop rule for storing syntactic representations is the *argument structure* hypothesis (Boland & Blodgett, 2006; Boland & Boehm-Jernigan, 1998; Tutunjian & Boland, 2008). According to the argument structure hypothesis, structural information related to a verb's *arguments* is stored in the lexicon, and everything else is computed "on the fly." So, like figuring out where the knee is, we have to figure out what counts as an argument.

Linguists have spent considerable effort coming up with principles that support a distinction between *arguments* and *adjuncts*. Although there is not 100% agreement in linguistics about how to draw the distinction, arguments are (roughly speaking) linguistic partners that a word absolutely must have. Adjuncts are partners that a word can have, but does not need. Arguments are usually thought of as being elements of meaning that a word needs to express a complete thought. These elements of meaning are usually explicitly expressed in the sentence, but sometimes they can be omitted. For example, the verb *eating* is thought to require an object (you have to eat something in order to eat), but that semantic argument can be omitted from the actual spoken sentence if the speaker wishes to focus the listener's attention on the action, as in *Dr. Phil was eating* (Jackendoff, 2002).

Verbs can have between zero and four arguments. Verbs like *rained* and *snowed* have zero arguments (Jackendoff, 2002). Because languages require sentences to have grammatical subjects, speakers include a meaningless pronoun as a place-holder when they use zero-argument verbs in sentences, as in, *It rained. It snowed.* Verbs like *sneezed* have one argument, as in *Dr. Phil sneezed.* (The arguments are underlined in the examples.) Verbs like *devoured* have two arguments, as in *Dr. Phil devoured the sandwich.* (And in the case of *devoured* all of the arguments must be included in the actual spoken sentence. **Devoured the sandwich* and **Dr. Phil devoured* are both ungrammatical.) Verbs like *put* have three arguments (*Dr. Phil put the sandwich on the plate.*) Verbs like *bet* or *wagered* have four arguments—a bettor, an opponent, something that is being risked, and an event, as in *Dr. Phil bet Rush Limbaugh a sandwich that Big Brown would win the Kentucky Derby*. As far as we know, there are no 5-, 6-, or 57-argument verbs. (E-mail me if you can think of a counter-example.)

Given that the maximum number of arguments for a verb is four, the problem of storing structural possibilities for verbs is greatly simplified. Instead of having an infinite number of structures associated with each verb, we have between one and five. In the case of *was reading*, everything beyond the subject (*Dr. Phil*) and the direct object (*book*), is optional. The argument structure hypothesis would claim, therefore, that only two structural possibilities would be stored in long term memory and associated with *was reading*. So, when comprehenders access the verb form *was reading*, they would activate two associated syntactic structures, one that did not have a place for a post-verbal object, and one that did.

How is this information accessed and used during parsing? According to constraint-based parsing theory in general, and the argument structure hypothesis in particular, when listeners access the lexical representation of a verb like *was reading*, they immediately activate the associated structural information (kind of like what happens with spreading activation in semantic processing). The different structural possibilities are activated to the extent that they have appeared in the past with the verb in question. So, if *was reading* most often appeared with a direct and an indirect object, the ditransitive structure will be more active than the intransitive structure. If it appeared most often with just a direct object, then that structure will be more activated than any of the stored alternatives.

The *argument structure hypothesis* provides a somewhat more nuanced view of how argument-hood influences parsing. According to the argument structure hypothesis, argument frames and their corresponding syntactic structures are important because they determine how some elements of sentences are interpreted. For example, how should a comprehender interpret a prepositional phrase like *to Harry*? It could be interpreted as the goal of a transferring action, as in *The bully sent a threatening letter to Harry* (Boland & Blodgett, 2006, p. 386). But the prepositional phrase could be interpreted instead as a location, as in *The bully stapled a threatening letter to Harry* (Boland & Blodgett, 2006, p. 386). How does a comprehender know which interpretation to apply to the prepositional phrase? The argument structure hypothesis contends that the subcategory properties of the verb determine how the prepositional phrase is interpreted. When the lexical representation of the verb specifies a recipient or goal argument (e.g., *sent* specifies a recipient), then a prepositional phrase headed by *to* will be interpreted as that goal argument. When the verb does not specify a goal argument, prepositional phrases headed by *to* will be interpreted as locations.

Is there any evidence that suggests that the argument structure hypothesis accurately describes how syntactic information is represented in long-term memory? For starters, a growing body of evidence suggests that arguments are treated differently than adjuncts during sentence interpretation. For example, consider sentences (51) and (52) (from Clifton, Speer, & Abney, 1989):

(51) The saleswoman tried to interest the man in the wallet. (People interpret this as meaning she wanted him to buy the wallet; not that the man was inside the wallet.)
(52) The saleswoman interested the man in his fifties. (People interpret this as meaning that the man was between 50 and 60 years old; not that the saleswoman wanted the man to like being between 50 and 60 years old.)

In sentence (51), *in the wallet* is an argument of the verb *interested* because people have to be interested in something. (Contrast that with the verb sneezed. You don't have to sneeze anything, you just have to sneeze.) In (52), *in his fifties* is an adjunct of the noun *man* because, although we can always think or talk about how old the man is, we don't have to. But note that, until we figure out the exact meaning of *wallet* and *in his fifties*, and until we integrate those meanings with the preceding parts of the sentence, it is not clear whether we are dealing with an argument or an adjunct. According to some accounts of parsing, including the argument structure hypothesis, comprehenders have a general preference or bias to interpret incoming phrases as arguments. Given this assumption, comprehenders will try to treat both *in the wallet* and *in his fifties* as arguments of the verb *interested*. Since *wallet* makes more sense than *his fifties* as something to be interested in, comprehenders should take less time to process *wallet* than *his fifties*. Indeed, when reading times were used to measure processing load, comprehenders were able to process sentences like (51) faster than sentences like (52) (Clifton, Speer, & Abney, 1999; Speer & Clifton, 1998; see also Britt, 1994; Schutze & Gibson, 1999). So, people appear to process argument relations faster than non-argument (or *adjunct*) relations.

Other studies show that people are more satisfied with the outcome of the interpretive process when they can interpret phrases like *to Harry* as arguments as opposed to when they are forced to interpret those same phrases as adjuncts. For example, if people are ask to judge how natural sentences are, they rate sentences where the arguments are explicitly stated higher than sentences where adjuncts, but not arguments, are explicitly stated (Boland & Blodgett, 2006).

Other evidence for an effect of argument status on parsing and interpretation comes from studies showng that people infer a "missing" argument in cases where a verb requires an argument, but the argument is not explicitly included in the sentence (Koenig, Mauner, & Bienvenue, 2003; Mauner, Tanenhaus, & Carlson, 1995). For example, consider the difference between the simple past tense verb *sank* and the very closely related past perfective *was sunk*. If somebody says, *The ship sank*, there does not have to be an external agent. The sentence describes a change of state (the ship goes from floating on the top of the ocean to sitting on the bottom of the ocean), but the change of state can be internally caused by the ship itself (maybe the hull was very rusty and sprung a leak). However, if somebody says, *The ship was sunk*, that means that somebody or something other than the ship was responsible for the change in the ship's state. Do people process sentences like *The ship sank* differently than *The ship was sunk*? Gail Mauner and her colleagues showed that they do, in the following way: When people hear sentences like *The ship was sunk*, that need an agent but don't explicitly provide one, comprehenders immediately add or infer the presence of the unnamed external agent. So, they interpret the sentence with a missing argument as if it said, *The ship was sunk by somebody* ... If the sentence then continues with a *purpose clause*, for example, ... *to collect the insurance money*, that purpose clause is very easy to process, because comprehenders have already inferred that there's somebody involved in the sinking, and that somebody is available to provide the subject of the purpose clause. However, if the sentence starts *The ship sank* ... and continues ... *to collect the insurance money*, then comprehenders have a hard time processing the sentence. Why? Because the beginning of the sentence (*The ship sank* ...) does not require people to infer an agent, so there's nothing in the comprehender's representation of the sentence to connect up with the purpose clause ... *to collect the insurance money*. There's no one in the comprehender's mental representation who could serve as the person with the insurance fraud motive.

Limitations, Criticisms, and Some Alternative Parsing Theories

Although a considerable amount of experimental work in the past decade has produced results favorable to a variety of processing accounts that fall within the constraint-based sentence-processing framework, some people still prefer some version of a two-stage parsing theory. There are a number of reasons for this, but let's just focus on two of the main criticisms of the general constraint-based approach.

The first criticism is based on the suggestion that the parser may not always favor likely structures over less likely, but simpler structures (e.g., Clifton, Kennison, & Albrecht, 1997). For example, in sentences like (53), the less likely structure is simpler and adopting the less likely structure leads to a semantically odd interpretation:

(53) The athlete realized her shoes somehow got left on the bus.

The athlete realized her shoes is just weird. So if people interpret the beginning of sentence (53) as having a subject, a verb, and a direct object, they should slow down when they read the word *shoes*. But recall that *realized* hates direct objects and really likes sentence complements. If the parser uses this information immediately, then comprehenders should never consider *realized her shoes* as going together inside the same verb phrase. In that case, comprehenders should have no difficulty with (53), because they will correctly package *her shoes* together with *somehow got left on the bus* to make up a sentence complement. When sentences like (53) were used in an eye-movement experiment, readers did slow down at *shoes*, suggesting that they did consider the (incorrect) direct-object interpretation, which would mean that in this case they favored the simple structure over the likely structure (Pickering, Traxler, & Crocker, 2000).

The second criticism of the constraint-based approach relates to the absence of evidence that sentences with simple syntactic structures are ever hard to process. Let's return for a moment to the sentence *The burglar blew up the safe with the rusty lock*. According to the constraint-based referential theory of sentence processing, the right kind of story context will cause comprehenders to favor, assign more activation to, or have a bias toward, the more syntactically complex noun-modification interpretation. If that is the case, then when the structurally simple sentence appears in a context that supports the more complex structure, that should make the simple structure harder to process. To date, no such evidence has appeared. Researchers have looked for analogous effects in other sentence types, also without success so far (with one exception, Sedivy, 2002, Experiment 4). Consider, for example, the *main clause* construction in (54) (Binder, Duffy, & Rayner, 2001, p. 312):

(54) The criminal exiled his undependable partner and changed his identity.

Sentences like (54) can be embedded in a story where there are two different criminals. Similar to the *burglar blew up the safe* case, a two-criminal context should encourage comprehenders to favor the complex, reduced relative structure over the simple main clause one as people read the beginning of the sentence (*The criminal exiled* …). If context changes people's structural preferences in that way (and as predicted by a generic constraint-based account), then sentences like (54) should be harder to process when the story mentions two criminals than when it mentions only one. However, sentences like (54) appear to be relatively easy to process regardless of what information appears in preceding context.

Further criticisms of the constraint-based approach to parsing relate to the testability of various constraint-based proposals and the fact that some types of sentences do not seem to be very susceptible to context effects; interested readers should consult Pickering & van Gompel (2006), for further details; and MacDonald and Seidenberg (2006), for additional arguments in favor of constraints.

More recent theoretical developments in sentence processing have attempted to move beyond the older two-stage and constraint-based processing accounts, while retaining the best features of each approach. Let's briefly consider three of these more recent developments.

Construal

The *construal* account is essentially a refinement of the classic garden path parsing theory (Frazier & Clifton, 1996). Construal retains the idea that parsing occurs in discrete stages, but it adopts the idea that context can influence which structure the parser prefers and the idea that the parser can sometimes build multiple structures simultaneously. If that sounds a lot like a constraint-based parser to you, pat yourself on the back. But construal differs from the average constraint-based account in that there are a limited set of circumstances under which the parser will respond to contextual information or build syntactic structures in parallel. Most of the time, the construal parser will behave just like the garden path parser. In fact, it will even use the same *late closure* and *minimal attachment* heuristics to make definite decisions about which structural alternative to pursue. How does the parser decide which strategy to use?

To answer that, we need to think about different kinds of relationships between words. Construal says that dependencies between words can come in two flavors, primary relations and non-primary relations. *Primary relations* correspond roughly to *argument* relations as defined above. *Non-primary relations* correspond to everything else. All other things being equal, the parser prefers to treat incoming material as though it represents a primary relation. When the parser interprets an incoming word or set of words as representing a primary relation, it makes its structural decisions based on the standard garden path processing heuristics. But when the incoming material can't be interpreted as reflecting a primary relation, the parser will use a different strategy to deal with the material. In the first stage, the parser will *affiliate* the incoming material to the preceding sentence context. During this stage, the parser will simultaneously consider all possible attachment sites for the incoming material—effectively building multiple syntactic structures simultaneously. During a following stage of processing, the parser evaluates the different structural possibilities in light of the story context, sentence-level meaning, and other possibly "non-syntactic" sources of information.

To explore the construal parser in greater detail, consider sentences (55) and (56):

(55) The daughter of the colonel who had a black dress left the party.
(56) The daughter of the colonel who had a black mustache left the party.

In (55), people generally interpret the relative clause *who had a black dress* as going with *daughter* rather than *colonel*. In (56), they interpret the relative clause *who had a black mustache* as going with *colonel* rather than with *daughter*. Before you start writing an angry e-mail to my boss (her name is Debra): Of course, it is possible for a colonel to have a black dress. First, colonels can be female. Second, I'll bet you that some male colonels have black dresses in the back of their wardrobe. And yes, it is certainly possible for a colonel's daughter to have a black mustache. Despite these possibilities, most people automatically interpret the sentences in the way described above.

If comprehenders apply the late closure heuristic to parse (55) and (56), they should have an easier time processing (55) than (56). (See if you can work out why this should be the case.) But the construal account says that *who had a black dress* and *who had a mustache* are adjuncts of the preceding noun, and so represent non-primary relations. Under those conditions, the parser *affiliates* the relative clause to the preceding context and simultaneously looks for every place that the relative clause could attach. In (55) and (56), there are two possible hosts for the relative clause (*daughter* and *colonel*). In (55), the *daughter*-related structure works well given the meanings of all of the words involved, and in (56) the *colonel*-related structure works well. So, when it comes time to evaluate the different structural possibilities, there is always one good one. As a result, the construal account predicts no difference in difficulty between (55) and (56), and this is the pattern that actually occurs when participants' reading times are measured (Traxler, Pickering, & Clifton, 1998; for further evidence relating to the Construal account, see Frazier & Clifton, 1996.)

Race-based parsing

The *race-based* account represents a different refinement of the parallel processing approach to parsing (Traxler et al., 1998; van Gompel, Pickering, & Traxler, 2000). Like constraint-based parsers, the race-based account stipulates that the parser can build multiple syntactic structures in parallel. And like the garden path and construal accounts, the race-based approach to parsing advocates a two-stage process. In the first stage of processing, all structures that are licensed by the grammar accrue activation from the input. But rather than competing for a fixed pool of activation, syntactic structures race against each other. So, adding activation to one structural representation does not take away activation from any possible alternatives. According to this account, the first structure to exceed some threshold amount of activation is taken to represent the input and that structure is used as the basis for semantic interpretation.

Evidence for the race-based account comes from reading time experiments on sentences like (55), (56), and (57):

(57) The brother of the colonel who had a black mustache left the party.

Recall that readers had no preference for (55) or (56), both were equally easy to process. But now have a look at (57). In (57), *who had a black mustache* could go with either *brother* or *colonel*. So, in a race, it does not matter which structure gets to the threshold first. If *brother who had a black mustache* wins the race, you wind up with a sensible interpretation. The same thing happens if *colonel who had a black mustache* wins the race. But what about in (55) and (56)? If *colonel who had a black dress* wins, the reader will be puzzled. If *daughter who had a black mustache* wins the race, readers will be similarly puzzled. So, while readers do not have a preference either way between (55) and (56), that does not mean that the sentences are easy to process (although they are certainly easier than some very complex and tricky garden path sentences, like *The horse raced past the barn fell.*) The race-based parsing account says that, in (55) and (56), the winning structure will lead to a weird interpretation about half the time. So, on average, readers will have to reanalyze their initial structural and semantic interpretation about half the time. As a result, even though there is a very sensible interpretation for both (55) and (56), comprehenders will often arrive at the sensible interpretation only after they have built a structure that leads to a nonsensical interpretation.

To distinguish between construal's parallel affiliation and evaluation parsing process and a race, we need to compare (55) and (56) to (57). Construal predicts that they should all be equally easy. The race-based parsing account predicts that (57) will be easier than both (55) and (56). When people's eye movements were monitored as they read sentences like (55)–(57), sentences like (57) really did prove easier to process than (55) and (56). Analogous effects occurred in another sentence type (58)–(60), where minimal attachment is the relevant garden path processing heuristic:

(58) This morning, I shot an elephant in my pajamas. (minimal attachment)
(59) This morning, I shot an elephant with great big tusks. (non-minimal attachment)
(60) This morning, I shot a poacher with a rifle. (ambiguous)

Sentences like (58)–(60) are analogous to the *daughter of the colonel* sentences, because they involve a choice of places to attach a modifier (to a verb or to a noun), sometimes the attachment leads to a good interpretation, but sometimes it does not. In (60), both attachments lead to a good interpretation (you can use a rifle to shoot a poacher; a poacher can carry a rifle and get shot). So, no matter what attachment the comprehender opts for and builds for sentence (60), the result is sensible. In (58) and (59), half of the available attachments lead to bad interpretations (an elephant should not wearing my pajamas; I cannot use a big tusk to shoot something). So, the race-based parsing account predicts that (60) will be easier to process than the other two kinds of sentence once comprehenders get to the modifier (*with a rifle*, *in my pajamas*, *with great big tusks*). That prediction was verified by eye-movement data (van Gompel, Pickering, & Traxler, 2001).

Race-based parsing and constraint-based parsing both allow multiple syntactic structures to accrue activation simultaneously, but they differ in that activated structures try to inhibit or interfere with one another according to (some) constraint-based parsing accounts, but in a race-based architecture, alternative structures do not steal activation from one another—they increase or decrease their activation based on the cues available in the input. So, if one structure has a lot of activation, that does not prevent another structure from accruing activation as well. To distinguish between race-based and constraint-based parsing experimentally, it is important to find out whether syntactic structures do, in effect, compete with one another. Considerable mathematical modeling has been done showing that people's reading times can be predicted by neural-network models that incorporate competition between activated structures. These models tend to show that reading times are slowest at those points in a sentence where a previously low-ranked (or barely activated) structure suddenly needs to be promoted over a structure that previously enjoyed a high amount of activation (very similar to what happens in the processing of lexical ambiguity, reviewed in Chapter 3). These models also predict that if two structures are activated to about the same degree (say, two structures are both about 50% likely given the input at a certain point in the sentence), then comprehenders should slow down because two evenly matched competitors will take longer to sort out than when one competitor is much stronger than the other. So, what happens when two structural alternatives are about equally likely?

To find out, Roger van Gompel and his colleagues tested sentences like (61) and (62):

(61) I read that the bodyguard of the governor retiring after the troubles is very rich.
(62) I read quite recently that the governor retiring after the troubles is very rich.

In (61), the modifying expression *retiring after the troubles* could go with *bodyguard* or *governor*. Pretesting showed that people put the modifying expression with *bodyguard* about half the time, and with *governor* about half the time, suggesting that their structural preferences were pretty well balanced. In (62), there is only one place where the modifier could go (it goes with *governor*). If syntactic structures are activated in parallel (more than one at a time), and if they compete with one another for activation, then it should take people longer to read *retiring after the troubles* in (61), where there are two structures to compete, than in (62), where there is only one. When processing load was measured using eye tracking, however, readers were just as fast in (61) as they were in (62), suggesting that syntactic structures did not compete with one another (van Gompel, Pickering, Pearson, & Liversedge, 2005; see Green & Mitchell, 2006, for an alternative viewpoint).

Good-enough parsing

Fernanda Ferreira's *good-enough parsing* hypothesis represents a recent, more radical departure from the classical approaches to parsing and interpretation (Christianson, Williams, Zacks, & Ferreira, 2006; Ferreira, Bailey, & Ferraro, 2002; Ferreira, Christianson, & Hollingworth, 2001; Ferreira & Patson, 2007). Good-enough parsing starts by asking, "What good is parsing, anyway? Do we really need it?" The short answer to these questions is: Sometimes we don't need syntax and parsing at all. For example, if you know someone is communicating about cheese, a mouse, and an act of eating, you can be highly confident that after the event, the cheese is gone and the mouse is heavier, rather than the other way around. In this case, syntax provides cues that are redundant with the lexical information. The words by themselves tell you everything you need to know, and there is no need to compute syntactic structure to recover the speaker's intentions or the event that inspired the act of communication. In fact, there is some evidence that the lexical level can overpower the syntactic level when the two are placed in opposition. Consider, for example, the *passive* sentence (63):

(63) The mouse was eaten by the cheese.

This sentence sets up a conflict between the lexical–semantic content of the individual words and the sentence meaning that should be derived given standard assumptions about parsing and interpretation. If we transformed sentence (63) into an active form, we would get (64):

(64) The cheese ate the mouse.

But if we rely just on the lexical information, we would get the interpretation expressed by (65):

(65) The mouse ate the cheese.

One very basic question that researchers have addressed is: What meaning do people assign to sentences like (63)? If they build the correct syntactic structure for (63), they should come up with the interpretation in (64). If they just go with the lexical information and don't bother with doing a whole bunch of syntactic parsing, then they will probably come up with the (more sensible, but unlicensed) interpretation in (65). When people are given sentences like (63) and are asked to choose the best paraphrase or come up with an active sentence on their own that expresses the same meaning, many people come up with the sensible, rather than the grammatically licensed, interpretation. This suggests that people may not always compute syntactic relations between words in sentences or that, when the syntax and the lexical level disagree, people prefer to base their interpretation on default lexical–semantic associations. Either outcome would go against standard assumptions about how sentences are interpreted—that people look up words in the mental lexicon, structure the input, and use semantic rules to assign a standard meaning to the structured input.

Further evidence that people fail to construct the correct structure for some sentences comes from sentences like (66):

(66) While the hunter was stalking the deer drank from the puddle.

If participants parse this sentence correctly, they should not interpret the sentence to mean that the hunter was stalking the deer. But when participants were asked directly after reading the sentence, "Was the hunter stalking the deer?", they would very likely answer "yes." That is the result that one would expect if readers left *the deer* attached as the direct object of *was stalking*, but that structure is not licensed by the grammar. You may object that just because, under the correct parse, the sentence does not explicitly say that the hunter was stalking the deer, there is nothing in the sentence that directly contradicts that interpretation. To address that criticism, researchers ran an additional set of experiments using sentences like (67):

(67) While the hunter was stalking the deer in the zoo drank from the puddle.

Because it is very highly unlikely that a hunter would stalk an animal in a zoo, the correct syntactic structure should lead participants to an interpretation where the hunter is stalking something besides a deer. Nevertheless, when participants in this study were asked the same question, "Was the hunter stalking the deer?", they were likely to respond "Yes." How can that be?

According to the good-enough parsing hypothesis, comprehenders set a threshold for understanding. If the communicative context is high stakes and getting the meaning right is really important, comprehenders will allocate sufficient resources to build syntactic structures licensed by the grammar. Additionally, in those cases where the comprehender initially builds a faulty or incorrect syntactic structure, they will undertake the processes necessary to revise that structure, even if doing so is effortful and resource intensive. However, in most experimental contexts, the stakes are very low (for the participants, anyway), there are no consequences for failing to interpret, and the sentences tend to be tricky and abstract, and refer to little or any real-world content. Under those conditions, participants will do just enough syntactic processing to come up with some meaning. If the syntax is tricky, as it is in sentences like (66) and (67), and participants' thresholds for feeling like they understand is low, they may not recognize that there is a problem with the syntax—either because they are not actually parsing the input or because they are satisfied with a structure that is not licensed according to the standard grammar.

On top of inability or reluctance to build syntactic structure, comprehenders may be unwilling to abandon an interpretation just because the interpretation is not supported by a licensed parse. For example, it appears that participants in garden path experiments stick with their initial semantic interpretations, while simultaneously showing signs that they are undertaking syntactic revisions at least some of the time. For example, participants persist in thinking that the hunter was hunting deer in sentences like (66) and (67), even though the correct parse, especially of sentence (67) seems to rule out that interpretation. Other experimental evidence also suggests that comprehenders are less likely to successfully revise an initial interpretation when a change in syntactic structure entails a change in meaning (van Gompel, Pickering, Pearson, & Jacob, 2006). So, participants appear to maintain initial syntactic commitments when changing a syntactic structure involves changes in semantic interpretation as well.

One problem in distinguishing between the good-enough parsing account and alternative accounts is that we need to have a way to tell the difference between an error and a good-enough parse. If someone reads a sentence and comes up with the wrong meaning, is this because the system is designed to mis-parse the sentence (as assumed under the good-enough parsing account)? Or did they just make an error? In practice, these two possibilities are extremely hard to distinguish experimentally. So we will need more studies before we can choose whether some version of a determinate parser (like the garden path, constraint-based, and race-based parsers) or a good-enough parser more closely describes the mechanism that people actually carry around in their heads.

Parsing Long-Distance Dependencies

So far, we have been considering the processing of sentences where the words that go together to make phrases appear right next to one another as the sentences are produced. For example, in a simple active sentence like (68), the subject, verb, and direct object are all adjacent to one another.

(68) The girl chased the boy.

Thus, the relationships between the words in the sentence are classified as *local* dependencies. Many sentences have *long-distance* dependencies (sometimes called *non-local*, sometimes called *unbounded* dependencies), where the words that have close syntactic relationships appear in separate locations in the sentence. Sentence (69) has a meaning very similar to sentence (68), but instead of having all local dependencies, it has some long-distance dependencies.

(69) It was the boy whom the girl chased.

In sentence (69) *the boy* is the object argument of the verb *chased*, but rather than coming right after the verb (which is the normal pattern in English), *the boy* appears before the verb *chased*. As a result, *the boy* and *chased* together form a long-distance dependency. (See if you can think up some other examples of sentences where there are long-distance dependencies.)

Sentences like (68) and (69) are closely related in meaning, and according to some theories of sentence representation and interpretation, they have a common underlying syntactic representation. For example, Noam Chomsky's *gaps-and-traces* account says that people plan and produce sentences like (69) starting with a *canonical* form like the one that you would use to represent the syntax of sentence (68), see (70) (Chomsky, 1965, 1981). *Canonical* syntactic form corresponds to the simplest possible phrase structure that could be used to express the syntactic relationships between the words in a sentence. If we have two actors, a boy and a girl, and an action of chasing, the form in (70) is the simplest structure we could use to express the idea that the girl chased the boy.

(70)

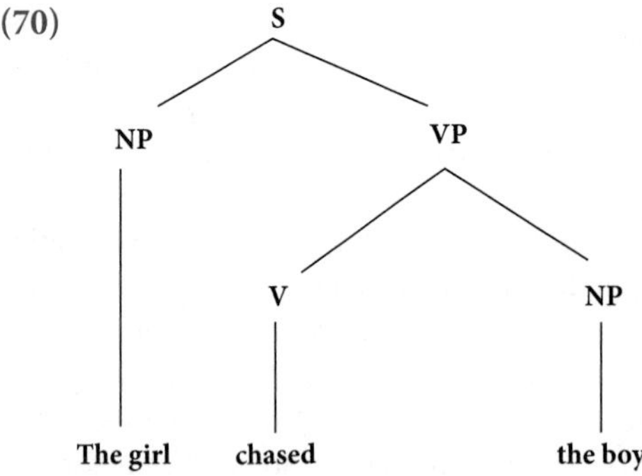

To produce the more complex sentence (69), the gaps-and-traces hypothesis says that people perform *transformations* on the canonical form. These transformations involve moving *the boy* out of its normal direct-object position following the verb *chased* into a position closer to the beginning of the sentence. (Speakers do this when they are trying to draw more attention to the recipient of the action.) Moving *the boy* out of the *chased* VP leaves a void in the syntactic structure of that clause. *Chased* needs a direct object, and because *boy* is no longer there to be the direct object, something has to happen, otherwise the structure would violate the grammar. What happens, according to gaps-and-traces theory, is that people insert a mental place-holder to take the place of the missing direct object. This mental place holder is called a *gap* or *gap site*. The resulting representation of the *chased* VP looks like the one in (71).

(71)

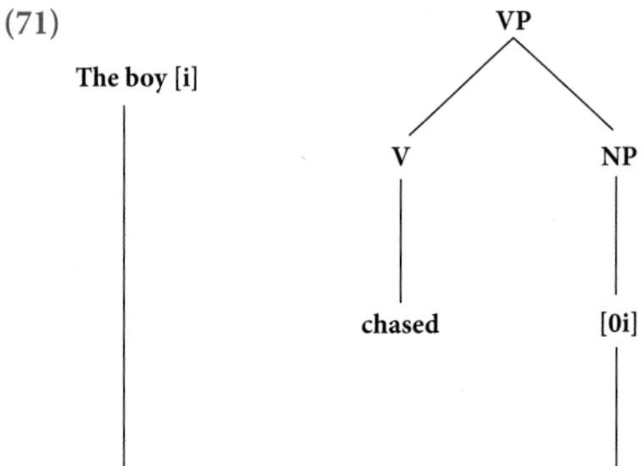

In sentences like (69), the noun phrase *the boy* is called a *filler* or *filler phrase*. According to some linguistic accounts, sentences where all the dependencies are local are parsed by associating words directly with one another. But long-distance dependencies are processed by associating fillers with gaps, rather than by associating fillers directly with the words that govern how they are to be interpreted. So, to parse a sentence like (69), people first identify the filler phrase *the boy. The boy* can be recognized as a filler because the phrase *It was …* often times precedes a displaced element like *the boy* (although sometimes it will be used in a simple declarative statement like *It was lunchtime.*) Having identified a filler phrase, people start looking for a place to put it. Right after the verb *chased*, they infer or posit a gap site—because *chased* is missing its direct object. They associate the filler phrase with the gap site and then they associate the gap site with the verb *chased*. Associating the filler phrase and the gap site establishes a "trace" (analogous to a mental pathway) between the filler and the gap site. Doing so allows people to recognize that the *boy* goes together with *chased*, the verb phrase with *chased* is complete, and interpretation can be completed.

Is there any evidence that gap-filling is a real psychological process? The short answer is "yes." Some experimental evidence comes from *cross-modal* priming and *cross-modal naming* experiments (Nicol & Pickering, 1993; Nicol & Swinney, 1989). In a *cross-modal* experiment, participants are exposed to language coming in from two different senses—hearing and vision—at different times. For example, people might listen to a sentence like (72):

(72) That's <u>the boy</u> that the people at the party liked [gap site] very much.

In (72), *the boy* is a filler phrase, and the gap site appears right after the verb *liked*. If gap filling is a real psychological process, something special should happen when people reach the gap site. To find out whether something special happens, researchers showed participants target words on a computer screen at different points in time as the participants were listening to sentences like (72). The researchers measured how long it took participants to respond to the visual target words. If the participants responded quickly, that suggests that information associated with the target words was particularly activated or accessible. If people responded more slowly, that suggests that information associated with the target words was less activated. According to the gaps-and-traces account, information about the filler phrase (*the boy*) should be particularly active and accessible right at the gap site. So, if you measured how long it takes people to respond to the filler word itself, people should respond especially quickly right after the verb *liked*. To test that prediction, researchers interrupted the spoken sentence right before the verb *liked* (where nothing special should be happening) and right after the verb *liked* (i.e., at the gap site, where something special should be happening), and presented a visual target word. Participants would have to respond to the target word by saying it out loud ("naming" it) as fast as they could. In the experiment, participants responded to target words like *the boy*, or semantically associated words (like *the girl*), faster after than before the verb *liked*. So it looks like something special did happen right where the gaps-and-traces account says it should.

Sentences like (72) only have one filler phrase and one possible gap site. Other sentences are more ambiguous. For example, sentence (73) has two places where the filler phrase could go (but it actually only goes in one of them, the second one):

(73) That's the boy that the girl liked [possible gap site] to ignore [actual gap site].

(See if you can think of a sentence that has three possible gap sites.) The possible gap site in (73) is sometimes called a *doubtful gap* because, although it could be the place where the filler goes, the filler does not have to go there (and in this case, it doesn't). How do people parse sentences with multiple possible gap sites? According to Janet Fodor's *active filler* strategy, the parser tries to put the filler into every possible gap site as soon as it locates one (Fodor, 1979, 1989). If that were the case, then people would routinely mis-parse sentences like (73). When they encountered the filler phrase *the boy*, they would start looking for a gap to put it in. There is a possible gap right after *liked*, because the verb liked can have a direct object (i.e., the sentence *could* have been the equivalent of *The girl liked the boy.*). But if the parser assigns *the boy* as the direct object of *liked*, there will be no room for the actual post-verbal complement of *liked*, the *infinitival* phrase *to ignore*. The active filler strategy therefore predicts that sentences like (73) are a kind of garden path sentence. People first put the filler in the wrong place (in the doubtful gap after *liked*.) When they hear *to ignore*, they know that this filler-gap assignment is incorrect, and they re-parse the sentence so that *the boy* is inside the infinitival phrase *to ignore* (and so people eventually interpret the sentence in the correct way, as meaning *The girl liked to ignore the boy*). In fact, sentences like (73) that have a doubtful gap in them are more difficult to process than equivalent unambiguous sentences when the first gap site is not the correct host for the filler phrase (Pickering & Traxler, 2001, 2003; Stowe, 1986).

Not all linguists and psycholinguists agree that gaps and traces are involved in the parsing of long-distance dependencies. Some theories of grammar do not include gaps as an element of their representational systems (e.g., *Head-Driven Phrase Structure Grammar*, or *HPSG*; see Sag, Wasow, & Bender, 2003). Some accounts of parsing also do away with the concept of a gap (Pickering & Barry, 1991, 1993). One such account, Martin Pickering and Guy Barry's *gap-free* parsing account, says that local dependencies and long-distance dependencies are handled in the same way: words are associated directly with one another. So, rather than finding a gap site, when the parser spots a filler phrase, it looks for a word that is missing one of its partners. For example, instead of associating a filler with a gap, and then associating the gap with a verb, the parser associates the filler directly with the verb. How can we decide whether the gaps-and-traces account or the gap-free account does a better job of describing what people actually do when they parse and interpret sentences?

The approach taken by some researchers is to look for sentences where the critical verb comes before the hypothetical gap site. If something special happens at the verb, that would suggest that the filler is associated directly with the verb. If nothing special happens before people get to the gap site, then that would suggest that the filler is associated with the gap, and *not* directly with the verb. In sentences like (74), the gap site comes well after the verb that goes with the filler:

(74) That's <u>the pistol</u> [filler] with which the killer shot the helpless man [**gap**] yesterday.

The gap site is after *man* in (74), because, if the sentence were "de-scrambled," it would say *The killer shot the helpless man with* ***the pistol*** *yesterday*. Does anything special happen at the verb? To find out, researchers compared reading times for sentences like (74) with reading times for sentences like (75):

(75) That's the pistol [filler] in which the killer shot the helpless man [**gap**] yesterday.

(75) differs from (74) by only a single word (*in* instead of *with*). Changing the preposition from *with* to *in* changes the meaning of the sentence so that (75) makes a lot less sense than (74). In particular, sentence (75) stops making sense at the verb *shot* if people immediately associate the filler phrase *the pistol* with the verb. If people wait until they get to the gap site after *man*, then they will not notice that (75) is odd until well after the verb *shot*. Normally, when a sentence stops making sense, processing load goes up as people try to diagnose what is wrong and correct the problem. So, researchers can use reading time to tell whether processing load has increased. When reading times for (74) are compared to reading times for (75), reading times for (75) are much longer starting at the verb *shot* (Pickering & Traxler 2001, 2003; Traxler & Pickering, 1996). Since the verb *shot* comes a long time before the hypothetical gap site, it looks like people associate the filler phrase directly with the verb, rather than with a gap. Results like these have motivated some theorists to say that gaps are not necessary, and so they prefer theories that say that syntactic structure representations do not include anything like a gap. An additional advantage of the gap-free approach is that we do not need special and different syntactic structure-building processes to handle long-distance dependencies. Both local and long-distance dependencies are parsed by associating words directly with one another.

Summary and Conclusions

Parsing is an important aspect of interpreting sentences. This chapter has reviewed evidence for and against two-stage and one-stage theories of human parsing processes. The available evidence suggests that the parser makes use of a wide variety of information very quickly as it is figuring out how words in sentences relate to one another. As a result, many researchers have adopted some version of the constraint-based processing framework to explain how parsing is accomplished. They view syntactic parsing as resulting from the operation of distributed neural networks. Alternative parsing accounts agree with some of the theoretical claims made by constraint-based advocates, such as simultaneous consideration of different syntactic structures, but without agreeing that current neural network models capture all of the key aspects of people's parsing processes. The chapter also described the difference between local and long-distance dependencies and showed that the direct-association hypothesis could explain how both local and long-distance dependencies are parsed and account for experimental results in each domain.

TEST YOURSELF

1. Describe the relationship between sentence structure and sentence meaning. How does the way that we organize words in sentences influence the meanings we assign to those sentences?
2. What do experiments in which reading times are measured tell us about the process of interpreting a sentence? What do these experiments have to say about incrementality and immediacy?
3. Describe a prominent two-stage account of sentence processing. What experimental evidence supports such an account?
4. What kinds of information can influence the process of building a syntactic structure for a sentence? Give examples of each kind of information.
5. Explain how constraint-based models differ from two-stage models. Describe experiments that support constraint-based models of sentence processing.
6. Describe the argument structure hypothesis. How does it compare to two-stage and constraint-based accounts. Why might a person believe in the argument structure hypothesis?
7. Describe two alternatives to both the two-stage and constraint-based accounts of sentence processing.
8. Describe how long-distance dependencies differ from local dependencies. Describe two accounts of long-distance dependency processing.

THINK ABOUT IT

1. Draw phrase-structure diagrams for the following sentences. (Hint: (c) may be better represented using a dependency diagram than a phrase-structure tree. Ask your professor for help if you get stuck.)
   a. Hungry monkeys ate tasty bananas.
   b. Bananas tasty monkeys hungry ate.
   c. Tasty bananas ate monkeys hungry.

What do you see when you compare the different kinds of sentences? Which one do you think would be easiest to produce or comprehend? (More hints: (a) is typical in English, (b) is more like Japanese, (c) is like Latin.)

2. Design an experiment to investigate how people respond to syntactically ambiguous sentences. Write some syntactically ambiguous sentences. Write some unambiguous sentences that mean the same thing. Ask your classmates or your friends to provide ratings for the sentences—how much do they like each one, or how much sense do they make, or how grammatical are they, or how hard are they to understand. Which dependent measures do you think will have different values for the ambiguous sentences compared to the unambiguous ones? Which measurements do you think will be the same for ambiguous and unambiguous sentences? What do you think accounts for these differences (or lack thereof)?

Note

1 Although some theorists contend that phrase structure representations apply universally, they may not be particularly good descriptions for languages that allow words from different phrases to be intermixed. These scrambling languages may be better described in terms of dependencies, rather than phrase structures (Evans & Levinson, 2009).

References

Adams, B. C., Clifton, C., Jr., & Mitchell, D. C. (1998). Lexical guidance in sentence processing. *Psychonomic Bulletin & Review, 5,* 265–270.

Altmann, G. T. M., Garnham, A., & Dennis, Y. (1992). Avoiding the garden path: Eye movements in context. *Journal of Memory and Language, 31,* 685–712.

Altmann, G. T. M., Garnham, A., & Henstra, J. A. (1994). Effects of syntax in human sentence parsing: Evidence against a structure-based proposal mechanism. *Journal of Experimental Psychology: Learning, Memory, and Cognition, 20,* 209–216.

Altmann, G. T. M., & Steedman, M. (1988). Interaction with context during human sentence processing. *Cognition, 30,* 191–238.

Bates, E., & MacWhinney, B. (1987). Competition, variation, and language learning. In B. MacWhinney (Ed.), *Mechanisms of language acquisition* (pp. 157–193). Hillsdale, NJ: Erlbaum.

Bever, T. G. (1970). The cognitive basis for linguistic structures. In JR. Hayes (Ed.), *Cognition and the development of language* (pp. 279–352). New York: Wiley.

Binder, K. S., Duffy, S. A., & Rayner, K. (2001). The effects of thematic fit and discourse context on syntactic ambiguity resolution. *Journal of Memory and Language, 44,* 297–324.

Boland, J. E., & Blodgett, A. (2006). Argument status and PP-attachment. *Journal of Psycholinguistic Research, 35,* 385–403.

Boland, J. E., & Boehm-Jernigan, H. (1998). Lexical constraints and prepositional phrase attachment. *Journal of Memory and Language, 39,* 684–719.

Britt, M. A. (1994). The interaction of referential ambiguity and argument structure in the parsing of prepositional phrases. *Journal of Memory and Language, 33,* 251–283.

Brysbaert, M., & Mitchell, D. C. (1996). Modifier attachment in sentence parsing: Evidence from Dutch. *The Quarterly Journal of Experimental Psychology, 49A,* 664–695.

Carlson, K., Clifton Jr., C., & Frazier, L. (2001). Prosodic boundaries in adjunct attachment. *Journal of Memory and Language, 16,* 58–81.

Carreiras, M., & Clifton Jr., C. (1993). Relative clause interpretation preferences in Spanish and English. *Language and Speech, 36,* 353–372.

Carreiras, M., & Clifton Jr., C. (1999). Another word on parsing relative clauses: Eyetracking evidence from Spanish and English. *Memory & Cognition, 27,* 826–833.

Chomsky, N. (1965). *Aspects of the theory of syntax.* Cambridge, MA: MIT Press.

Chomsky, N. (1981). *Lectures on government and binding.* Dordrecht, The Netherlands: Foris.

Christianson, K., Williams, G. C., Zacks, R. T., & Ferreira, F. (2006). Younger and older adults' "Good-Enough" interpretations of garden-path sentences. *Discourse Processes, 42,* 205–238.

Clifton, C., Jr., Kennison, S. M., & Albrecht, J. E. (1997). Reading the words *her, his, him*: Implications for parsing principles based on frequency and on structure. *Journal of Memory and Language, 36,* 276–292.

Clifton, C., Jr., Speer, S., & Abney, S. P. (1991). Parsing arguments: Phrase structure and argument structure as determinants of initial parsing decisions. *Journal of Memory and Language, 30,* 251–271.

Clifton, C., Traxler, M. J., Williams, R., Mohammed, M., Morris, R. K., & Rayner, K. (2003). The use of thematic role information in parsing: Syntactic processing autonomy revisited. *Journal of Memory and Language, 49,* 317–334.

Columbia Press (1980). *Squad helps dog bite victim.* New York: Doubleday.

Crain, S., & Steedman, M. (1985). On not being led up the garden path: The use of context by the psychological parser. In D. Dowty, L., Karttunen, & A. Zwicky (Eds.), *Natural language parsing: Psychological, computational, and theoretical perspectives.* Cambridge, England: Cambridge University Press.

Cuetos, F., & Mitchell, D. C. (1988). Cross-linguistic differences in parsing: Restrictions on the use of the late closure strategy in Spanish. *Cognition, 30,* 73–105.

Cuetos, F., Mitchell, D. C., & Corley, M. M. B. (1996). Parsing in different languages. In M. Carreiras, J. E. Garcia-Albea, & N. Sebastian-Galles (Eds.), *Language processing in Spanish* (pp. 145–187). Hillsdale, NJ: Erlbaum.

Desmet, T., De Baecke, C., Drieghe, D., Brysbaert, M., & Vonk, W. (2006). Relative clause attacment in Dutch: On-line comprehension corresponds to corpus frequencies when lexical variables are taken into account. *Language and Cognitive Processes, 21,* 454–485.

Elman, J. L. (1994). Implicit learning in neural networks: The importance of starting small. In C. Umilta & M. Moscovitch (Eds.), *Attention and performance: vol. 15. Conscious and nonconscious information processing* (pp. 861–888). Cambridge, MA: MIT Press.

Elman, J. L. (2004). An alternative view of the mental lexicon. *Trends in Cognitive Sciences, 8,* 301–306.

Evans, N., & Levinson, S. C. (2009). The myth of language universals: Language diversity and its importance for cognitive science. *Behavioral and Brain Sciences, 32,* 429–448.

Ferreira, F., Bailey, K. G. D., & Ferraro, V. (2002). Good-enough representations in language comprehension. *Current Directions in Psychological Science, 11,* 11–15.

Ferreira, F., Christianson, K., & Hollingworth, A. (2001). Misinterpretations of garden-path sentences: Implications for models of sentence processing and reanalysis. *Journal of Psycholinguistic Research, 30,* 3–20.

Ferreira, F., & Clifton, Jr., C. (1986). The independence of syntactic processing. *Journal of Memory and Language, 25,* 348–368.

Ferreira, F., & Patson, N. (2007). The good enough approach to language comprehension. *Language and Linguistics Compass, 1,* pp. 71–83.

Fodor, J. D. (1979). Parsing strategies and constraints on transformations. *Linguistic Inquiry, 9,* 427–473.

Fodor, J. D. (1989). Empty categories in sentence processing. *Language and Cognitive Processes, 4,* 155–209.

Ford, M., Bresnan, J. W., & Kaplan, R. M. (1982). A competence based theory of syntactic closure. In J. W. Bresnan (Ed.), *The mental representation of grammatical relations* (pp. 727–796). Cambridge, MA: MIT Press.

Foss, D. J., & Hakes, D. T. (1982). *Psycholinguistics: An introduction to the psychology of language.* Englewood Cliffs, NJ: Prentice Hall.

Frazier, L. (1979). *On comprehending sentences: Syntactic parsing strategies.* Ph.D. dissertation, University of Connecticut. West Bend, IN: Indiana University Linguistics Club.

Frazier, L. (1987). Sentence processing: A tutorial review. In M. Coltheart (Ed.), *Attention and performance 12: The psychology of reading* (pp. 559–586). Hillsdale, NJ: Erlbaum.

Frazier, L., & Clifton, Jr., C. (1996). *Construal.* Boston, MA: MIT Press.

Frazier, L., & Rayner, K. (1982). Making and correcting errors during sentence comprehension: Eye-movements in the analysis of structurally ambiguous sentences. *Cognitive Psychology, 14,* 178–210.

Garnsey, S. M., Pearlmutter, N. J., Myers, E., & Lotocky, M. A. (1997). The contributions of verb bias and plausbility to the comprehension of temporarily ambiguous sentences. *Journal of Memory and Language, 37,* 58–93.

Green, M. J., & Mitchell, D. C. (2006). Absence of real evidence against competition during syntactic ambiguity resolution. *Journal of Memory and Language, 55,* 1–17.

Jackendoff, R. (1990). *Semantic structures.* Boston, MA: MIT Press.

Jackendoff, R. (2002). *Foundations of language.* Oxford, England: Oxford University Press.

Just, M. A., & Carpenter, P. A. (1980). A theory of reading: From eye fixations to comprehension. *Psychological Review, 87,* 329–354.

Kjelgaard, M. M., & Speer, S. R. (1999). Prosodic facilitation and interference in the resolution of temporary syntactic closure ambiguity. *Journal of Memory and Language, 40,* 153–194.

Koenig, J. P., Mauner, G., & Bienvenue, B. (2003). Arguments for adjuncts. *Cognition, 89,* 67–103.

Konieczny, L., & Hemforth, B. (2000). Modifier attachment in German: Relative clauses and prepositional phrases. In A. Kennedy, R. Radach, D. Heller, & J. Pynte (Eds.), *Reading as a perceptual process* (pp. 517–527). Amsterdam, The Netherlands: Elsevier.

Kutas, M., van Petten, C., & Kluender, R. (2006). Psycholinguistics electrified. In M. J. Traxler & M. A. Gernsbacher (Eds.), *The handbook of psycholinguistics* (2nd ed., pp. 659–724). Amsterdam, The Netherlands: Elsevier.

MacDonald, M. C., Pearlmutter, N. J., & Seidenberg, M. S. (1994). Lexical nature of syntactic ambiguity resolution. *Psychological Review, 101,* 676–703.

MacDonald, M. C., & Seidenberg, M. (2006). Constraint satisfaction accounts of lexical and syntactic processing. In M. J. Traxler and M. A. Gernsbacher (Eds.), *The handbook of psycholinguistics* (2nd ed., pp. 581–612). Amsterdam, The Netherlands: Elsevier.

Mauner, G., Tanenhaus, M. K., & Carlson, G. N. (1995). Implicit arguments in sentence processing. *Journal of Memory and Language, 34,* 357–382.

Mitchell, D. C. (1987). Lexical guidance in human parsing: Locus and processing characteristics. In M. Coltheart (Ed.) *Attention and performance 12: The psychology of reading* (pp. 601–618). Hillsdale, NJ: Erlbaum.

Mitchell, D. C., Cuetos, F., Corley, M. M. B., & Brysbaert, M. (1995). Exposure-based models of human parsing: Evidence for the use of coarse-grained (nonlexical) statistical records. *Journal of Psycholinguistic Research, 24,* 469–488.

Nicol, J., & Pickering, M. J. (1993). Processing syntactically ambiguous sentences: Evidence from semantic priming. *Journal of Psycholinguistic Research, 22,* 207–237.

Nicol, J., & Swinney, D. (1989). The role of structure in coreference assignment during sentence comprehension. *Journal of Psycolinguistic Research, 18,* 5–19.

Phillips, C., Kazanina, N., & Abada, S. H. (2005). ERP effects on the processing of syntactic long-distance dependencies. *Cognitive Brain Research, 22,* 407–428.

Pickering, M. J., & Barry, G. (1991). Sentence processing without empty categories. *Language and Cognitive Processes, 6,* 229–259.

Pickering, M. J., & Barry, G. (1993). Dependency categorial grammar and coordination. *Linguistics, 31,* 855–902.

Pickering, M. J., & Traxler, M. J. (1998). Plausibility and recovery from garden paths: An eye-tracking study. *Journal of Experimental Psychology: Learning, Memory, and Cognition, 24,* 940–961.

Pickering, M. J., & Traxler, M. J. (2001). Strategies for processing unbounded dependencies: Lexical information and verb-argument assignment. *Journal of Experimental Psychology: Learning, Memory, and Cognition, 27,* 1401–1410.

Pickering, M. J., & Traxler, M. J. (2003). Evidence against the use of subcategorisation frequency in the processing of unbounded dependencies. *Language and Cognitive Processes, 18,* 469–503.

Pickering, M. J., Traxler, M. J., & Crocker, M. W. (2000). Ambiguity resolution in sentence processing: Evidence against frequency-based accounts. *Journal of Memory and Language, 43,* 447–475.

Pickering, M. J., & van Gompel, R. P. G. (2006). Syntactic Parsing. In M. J. Traxler and M. A. Gernsbacher (Eds.), *the handbook of psycholinguistics* (2nd ed., pp. 455–504). Amsterdam, The Netherlands: Elsevier.

Pinker, S. (1994). *The language instinct*. New York: Harper.

Rayner, K., Carlson, M., & Frazier, L. (1983). The interaction of syntax and semantics during sentence processing: Eye movements in the analysis of semantically biased sentences. *Journal of Verbal Learning and Verbal Behavior, 22,* 358–374.

Rohde, D. L. T., & Plaut, D. C. (1999). Language acquisition in the absence of explicit negative evidence: How important is starting small. *Cognition, 72,* 67–109.

Sag, I. A., Wasow, T., & Bender, E. M. (2003). *Syntactic theory: A formal introduction*. Palo Alto, CA: Stanford University Press.

Schafer, A. J., Speer, S. R., Waren, P., & White, S. D. (2000). Intonational disambiguation in sentence production and comprehension. *Journal of Psycholinguistic Research, 29,* 169–182.

Schutze, C. T., & Gibson, E. (1999). Argumenthood and English prepositional phrase attachment. *Journal of Memory and Language, 40,* 409–431.

Sedivy, J. C. (2002). Invoking discourse-based contrast sets and resolving syntactic ambiguities. *Journal of Memory and Language, 46,* 341–370.

Snedeker, J., & Trueswell, J. (2003). Using prosody to avoid ambiguity: Effects of speaker awareness and referential context. *Journal of Memory and Language, 48,* 103–130.

Speer, S., & Blodgett, A. (2006). Prosody. In M. J. Traxler & M. A. Gernsbacher (Eds.), *The handbook of psycholinguistics* (2nd ed., pp. 505–538). Amsterdam, The Netherlands: Elsevier.

Speer, S. R., & Clifton, C., Jr. (1998). Plausibility and argument structure in sentence comprehension. *Memory & Cognition, 26,* 965–978.

Spivey-Knowlton, M., & Sedivy, J. C. (1995). Resolving attachment ambiguities with multiple constraints. *Cognition, 55,* 227–267.

St. John, M. F., & McClelland, J. L. (1992). Parallel constraint satisfaction as a comprehension mechanism. In R. G. Reilly & N. E. Sharkey (Eds.), *Connectionist approaches to natural language processing* (pp. 97–136). Hillsdale, NJ: Erlbaum.

Stevenson, S. (1994). Competition and recency in a hybrid network model of syntactic disambiguation. *Journal of Psycholinguistic Research, 23,* 295–322.

Stowe, L. A. (1986). Parsing WH-constructions: Evidence for on-line gap location. *Language and Cognitive Processes, 1,* 227–245.

Tabor, W., & Hutchins, S. (2004). Evidence for self-organized sentence processing: Digging-in effects. *Journal of Experimental Psychology: Learning, Memory, and Cognition, 30,* 431–450.

Tanenhaus, M. K., Spivey-Knowlton, M. J., Eberhard, K. M., & Sedivy, J. C. (1995). Integration of visual and linguistic information in spoken language comprehension. *Science, 268,* 1632–1634.

Traxler, M. J. (2002). Plausibility and subcategorization preference in children's processing of temporarily ambiguous sentences: Evidence from self-paced reading. *Quarterly Journal of Experimental Psychology, 55A,* 75–96.

Traxler, M. J. (2005). Plausibility and verb subcategorization preference in temporarily ambiguous sentences. *Journal of Psycholinguistic Research, 34,* 1–30.

Traxler, M. J., & Frazier, L. (2008). The role of pragmatic principles in resolving attachment ambiguities: Evidence from eye-movements. *Memory & Cognition, 36,* 314–328.

Traxler, M. J., & Pickering, M. J. (1996). Plausibility and the processing of unbounded dependencies: An eye-tracking study. *Journal of Memory and Language, 35,* 454–475.

Traxler, M. J., Pickering, M. J., & Clifton Jr., C. (1998). Adjunct attachment is not a form of lexical ambiguity resolution. *Journal of Memory and Language, 39,* 558–592.

Traxler, M. J., & Tooley, K. M. (2007). Lexical mediation and context effects in parsing. *Brain Research, 1146,* 59–74.

Trueswell, J. C., Tanenhaus, M. K., & Garnsey, S. M. (1994). Semantic influences on parsing: Use of thematic role information in syntactic ambiguity resolution. *Journal of Memory and Language, 33,* 285–318.

Trueswell, J., Tanenhaus, M. K., & Kello, C. (1993). Verb-specific constraints in sentence processing: Separating effects of lexical preference from garden-paths. *Journal of Experimental Psychology: Learning, Memory, and Cognition, 19,* 528–553.

Tutunjian, D., & Boland, J. E., (2008). Do we need a distinction between arguments and adjuncts? Evidence from psycholinguistic studies of comprehension. *Language and Linguistics Compass, 1,* 631–646.

Van Gompel, R. P. G., & Pickering, M. (2001). Lexical guidance in sentence processing: A note on Adams, Clifton, and Mitchell. *Psychonomic Bulletin & Review, 8,* 851–857.

Van Gompel, R. P. G., Pickering, M. J., Pearson, J., & Jacob, G. (2006). The activation of inappropriate analyses in garden-path sentences: Evidence from structural priming. *Journal of Memory and Language, 55,* 335–362.

Van Gompel, R. P. G., Pickering, M. J., Pearson, J., & Liversedge, S. P. (2005). Evidence against competition during syntactic ambiguity resolution. *Journal of Memory and Language, 52,* 284–307.

Van Gompel, R. P. G., Pickering, M. J., & Traxler, M. J. (2000). Unrestricted race: A new model of syntactic ambiguity resolution. In A. Kennedy (Ed.), *Reading as a perceptual process* (pp. 621–648). Amsterdam, The Netherlands: Elsevier.

Van Gompel, R. P. G., Pickering, M. J., & Traxler, M. J. (2001). Reanalysis in sentence processing: Evidence against current constraint-based and two-stage models. *Journal of Memory and Language, 45,* 225–258.

Discourse Processing

5

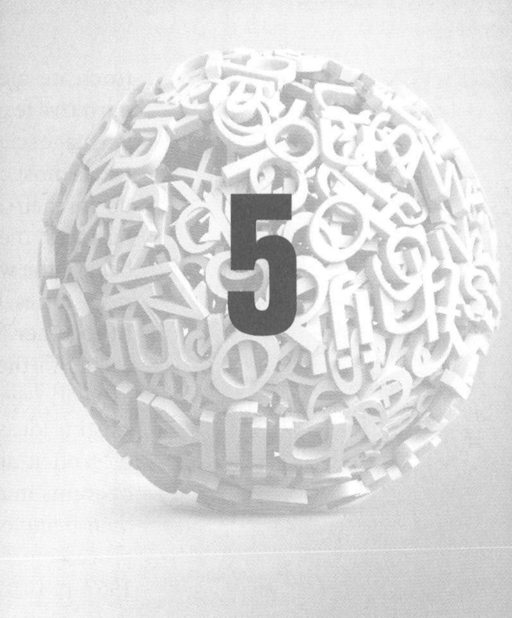

What makes us human is really our imaginations. I think we are probably not actually homo sapiens. *I think we are* Pan narens. *We are a chimpanzee that's good at telling stories.*

TERRY PRATCHETT

To interpret clauses and sentences, comprehenders engage in complex processes that produce intermediate products before a final interpretation is reached. During interpretation, comprehenders do a substantial amount of mental work to structure the input. So comprehenders do not treat sentences as mere lists of words. Comprehenders also engage in complex cognitive processing involving intermediate stages as they interpret *discourse*—interrelated sets of sentences—including *narratives* (stories) and *expository texts* (texts that try to explain how things work, like this one). This process of understanding involves building mental representations that capture features of the text itself (such as the exact words that it contains, the order in which words appear, and the syntactic structures that the speaker or author used), but the comprehender must do much more than this to figure out what the text is about. If the comprehender does not do this additional work and go beyond representing the text itself, her representations of the text will resemble an incoherent list of clauses and sentences, and she will not appreciate the ideas that the text conveys. This chapter focuses on describing the mental representations and processes that comprehenders bring to bear

Introduction to Psycholinguistics: Understanding Language Science, First Edition.
Matthew J. Traxler.

to create meaning while listening to or reading discourse. The chief focus will be on *narrative* texts (stories), because this is the area that has received the most attention from language scientists. This focus is not accidental, however, as the comprehension of narrative text is most closely related to the kind of *attributional* (explanatory) processing that people do in their daily lives (Singer, Graesser, & Trabasso, 1994). As people go about their business, they try to understand why and how events happen in the world, why people behave the way they do, and what is likely to happen in the future. Similarly, when people read stories, they try to figure out why events happen, how the different events in the story fit together, why characters do what they do, and why and how characters react to the events in the story. To do so, comprehenders combine information that is directly and explicitly signaled by the text with information that they supply themselves, including pre-existing ideas and knowledge about physical and psychological causation. This combination of explicit and implicit information helps comprehenders make sense of the sequence of events in the story, characters' actions, their emotional responses, and so forth. Rather than being a passive process, comprehension resembles other forms of active cognitive processing. "Seeing, hearing, and remembering are all acts of *construction*" (Neisser, 1967, p. 10).

Current approaches to discourse comprehension focus on four main aspects of processing. First, there are a whole set of processes that are responsible for identifying the exact content of the clauses and sentences that make up the text itself. Second, there are processes that connect the actual words in the text with the ideas, objects, or events that those words refer to (these are called *referential* processes). Third, there are processes that are responsible for connecting the different pieces of the text to one another (these are the processes that establish textual *cohesion* or *coherence*). Finally, there are processes that are responsible for building a representation of what the text is about (these are processes involved in building a *discourse representation* or *mental model*). A good way to describe these interrelated processes is to look at some current theories that seek to explain how extended texts are processed and interpreted. The next sections will review Walter Kintsch's *construction–integration theory* and related approaches, Morton Ann Gernsbacher's *structure building framework*, and Rolf Zwaan's *event indexing model.*

Construction–Integration Theory

Perhaps the best known and most widely studied theory of discourse comprehension is Walter Kintsch's *construction–integration theory* (Kintsch, 1988, 1998; Kintsch & van Dijk, 1978). The construction integration processing model represents a kind of *production* system, not because it has anything to do with speaking (although Kintsch has proposed that the model can be adapted as an account of spoken-language planning), but rather because the system is built like a particular kind of computer program—a production system. In a production system, the contents of an active memory buffer (short-term or working memory) are scanned. A set of if–then rules (or *productions*) is applied based on the contents of the active memory buffer. For example, one production rule might be: "If the contents of the memory buffer are empty, then input another unit of text." Another rule might be: "If two units of text in the working memory buffer have overlapping content, then connect those two units into one larger unit." Thus, the discourse processing system consists of a set of productions that manipulates the contents of working memory and builds coherent, structured mental representations that can be stored in a stable form in the comprehender's long-term memory.

The construction–integration production system interprets texts by building three distinct kinds of mental representations. The least abstract mental representation is the *surface model*, which is essentially a phrase structure tree that captures the exact words in the text, along with their syntactic relations. To build the second model, interface processes take the surface model as input, do some work on that input, and output a set of *propositions* that the surface model represents. The mental representation that describes the propositions represented by the text is called the *text-base*. The text-base is close to the verbatim form of the text itself, but it can include some information that was not explicitly mentioned in the text (some examples appear below), and it does not include information about the precise wording of the original text—so some surface information is lost as the construction–integration system builds the text-base representation. Finally, at the highest level of abstraction, the construction–integration theory proposes that comprehenders build a *situation model*. The situation model describes the ideas and/or events that the text is about. This is the ultimate goal of the construction–integration system, as it is with most comprehenders. People are usually not particularly interested in the exact wording of a text (unless the person in question is a proofreader, a poet, or a playwright). Normally, people read texts because they want to know what happened and why, and they are not particularly concerned about how, exactly, that knowledge is conveyed.

We have already spent a considerable amount of time discussing how words are identified and how sentences are parsed, so we don't need to spend additional time here discussing how the surface model is built. Just take your favorite parsing model and plug it in to do that job. Instead, let's take some time to think about propositions and the text-base level of representation.

The text-base representation consists of a set of connected *propositions*. Propositions are defined in two ways in construction–integration theory. The first definition of a proposition is, "a predicate and its arguments." Basically, that boils down to a verb (the predicate) and the role-players that go along with the verb (the arguments). So, in sentence (1)

(1) The customer wrote the company a complaint.

wrote is the predicate, *customer* is the subject/agent argument, *the company* is the indirect object/recipient argument, and *a complaint* is the direct object/theme argument. If we wanted to express that proposition in a convenient, generic notation form, it would look like this (Kintsch, 1994, p. 71):

Proposition 1: predicate [agent, recipient, theme]

The specific proposition in the preceding sentence could be represented in the following form:

Proposition 1: write [customer, company, complaint]

Propositions capture the action, state, or change of state that is being expressed in an utterance, and the arguments of the predicate indicate which characters or objects are involved in the action, as well as other information that elaborates on how the action is taking place. (Note that the definition of *argument* in Kintsch's construction–integration theory is different than the definition of *argument* that is more common in linguistic theories. According to Kintsch, all of the partners of the predicate count as arguments. According to linguistic theories, optional partners, like locations, the specific time that the action takes place, and so forth, would be called *adjuncts* rather than arguments.)

The other way that *proposition* is defined in construction–integration theory is, "The smallest unit of meaning that can be assigned a truth value." Anything smaller than that is a predicate or an argument. Anything bigger than that is a *macroproposition*. So, *wrote* is a predicate, and *wrote the company* is a predicate and one of its arguments. Neither is a proposition, because neither can be assigned a truth value. That is, it doesn't make sense to ask, "True or false: *wrote the company*?" But it does make sense to ask, "True or false: *The customer wrote the company*?" To answer that question, you would consult some representation of the real or an imaginary world, and the statement would either accurately describe the state of affairs in that world (i.e., it would be true) or it would not (i.e., it would be false).

Although the precise mental mechanisms that are involved in converting the surface form to a set of propositions have not been worked out, and there is considerable debate about the specifics of propositional representation (see, e.g., Kintsch, 1998; Perfetti & Britt, 1995), a number of experimental studies have supported the idea that propositions are a real element of comprehenders' mental representations of texts (van Dijk & Kintsch, 1983). In other words, propositions are *psychologically real*—there really are propositions in the head. For example, Ratcliff and McKoon (1978) used priming methods to find out how comprehenders' memories for texts are organized. There are a number of possibilities. It could be that comprehenders' memories are organized to capture pretty much the verbatim information that the text conveyed. In that case, we would expect that information that is nearby in the verbatim form of the text would be very tightly connected in the comprehender's memory of that text. So, for example, if you had a sentence like (2) (from Ratcliff & McKoon, 1978)

(2) The <u>geese</u> crossed the <u>horizon</u> as the <u>wind</u> shuffled the clouds.

the words *horizon* and *wind* are pretty close together, as they are separated by only two short function words. If the comprehender's memory of the sentence is based on remembering it as it appeared on the page, then *horizon* should be a pretty good retrieval cue for *wind* (and vice versa).

If we analyze sentence (2) as a set of propositions, however, we would make a different prediction. Sentence (2) represents two connected propositions, because there are two predicates, *crossed* and *shuffled*. If we built a propositional representation of sentence (2), we would have a *macroproposition* (a proposition that is itself made up of other propositions), and two *micropropositions* (propositions that combine to make up macropropositions). The macroproposition is:

as (Proposition 1, Proposition 2)

The micropropositions are:

Proposition 1: crossed [geese, the <u>horizon</u>]
Proposition 2: shuffled [the <u>wind</u>, the clouds]

Notice that the propositional representation of sentence (2) has *horizon* in one proposition, and *wind* in another. According to construction–integration theory, all of the elements of that go together to make a proposition should be more tightly connected in memory to each other than to anything else in the sentence. As a result, two words from the same proposition should make better retrieval cues than two words from different propositions. Those predictions can be tested by asking subjects to read sentences like (2), do a distractor task for a while, and then write down what they can remember about the sentences later on. On each trial, one of the words from the sentence will be used as a retrieval cue or reminder. So, before we ask the subject to remember sentence (2), we will give her a hint. The hint (retrieval cue) might be a word from proposition 1 (like *horizon*) or a word from proposition

2 (like *clouds*), and the dependent measure would be the likelihood that the participant will remember a word from the second proposition (like *wind*). Roger Ratcliff and Gail McKoon found that words that came from the same proposition were much better retrieval cues (participants were more likely to remember the target word) than words from different propositions, even when distance in the verbatim form was controlled. In other words, it does not help that much to be close to the target word in the verbatim form of the sentence unless the reminder word is also from the same proposition as the target word (see also Wanner, 1975; Weisberg, 1969).

Other studies using reaction time methods also support the psychological reality of propositions. If memory for texts is organized around propositions, which would mean that people extract propositions as they comprehend stories, then people should be able to access information from one proposition faster than information from two separate propositions. To test this hypothesis, Ratcliff and McKoon (1978) had people read pairs of unrelated sentences like (3) and (4):

(3) Geese crossed the horizon as the wind shuffled the clouds.
(4) The chauffeur jammed the clutch when he parked the truck.

They then had their participants perform a *probe recognition task*. In a probe recognition task, participants are presented with a list of words. Their task is to say as fast as possible, yes or no, whether each word appeared in a text that they had read previously. Unbeknownst to the participants, the list of words was organized so that sometimes a pair of adjacent words in the list was from the same proposition (e.g., *horizon* and *crossed*), sometimes the pair of words was from a different proposition, but the same sentence (e.g., *horizon* and *wind*), and sometimes the pair of words was from a different sentence (e.g., *horizon* and *clutch*). The dependent measure in a probe recognition study is how long it takes the participant to answer the yes-or-no question. If the representation of the test word is very active, or very accessible, people should respond very quickly; otherwise, they should be slow. In Ratcliff and McKoon's experiment, the first word in the pair serves as a retrieval cue. If the text is organized into propositions, then presenting the first word should activate other information from the same proposition more than it activates other information from the same sentence; and information from the same sentence should be more activated than information from a different sentence. This prediction was confirmed. Reading and responding to cue words like *horizon* caused participants to respond much faster to target words from the same proposition, the cue words had some effect (but not as big) on target words from the same sentence, and they had no effect at all on target words from the other sentence in the pair.

Other evidence for the psychological reality of propositions includes the fact that the number of words recalled from a sentence depends on the number of propositions in the sentence, when length is held constant (Forster, 1970). Error rates on recall tasks also depend on the number of propositions in the sentence. Errors increase geometrically as the number of propositions to be remembered increases, irrespective of the length of the text (Barshi, 1997; in Kintsch, 1998). Propositions tend to be recalled in an all-or-nothing fashion. That is, if any part of the proposition is recalled it is very highly likely that the entire proposition will be recalled (Goetz, Anderson, & Schallert, 1981). Overall reading time for a text depends on the number of propositions in the text, again when the number of words in different texts containing different numbers of propositions is held constant (Kintsch & Keenan, 1973). Finally, when people read stories, are given an individual word from the story, and are asked to say the first word that comes to mind (a form of *free association* test), the most likely response will be a word from the same proposition (Weisberg, 1969).

The final type of mental representation that people build while reading texts is the *situation model* (sometimes called a *mental model*, Johnson-Laird, 1983). The situation model is a mental simulation of the events in a story, and it captures a number of different features of the real or imaginary world that the text is about, including space, time, causality, and characters' emotional states. One way to appreciate the importance of the situation model is to see what happens to text processing when the situation model cannot be built. Read the following paragraph and see whether you can make sense of it (from Bransford & Johnson, 1972, p. 719; see also Johnson, Doll, Bransford, & Lapinski, 1974):

> *If the balloons popped, the sound wouldn't be able to carry since everything would be too far away from the correct floor. A closed window would also prevent the sound from carrying, since most buildings tend to be well insulated. Since the whole operation depends on a steady flow of electricity, a break in the middle of the wire would also cause problems. Of course, the fellow could shout, but the human voice is not loud enough to carry that far. An additional problem is that a string could break on the instrument. Then there could be no accompaniment to the message. It is clear that the best situation would involve less distance. Then there would be fewer potential problems. With face to face contact, the least number of things could go wrong.*

If you are like most people, you will find it very difficult to understand the preceding paragraph, even if you read it over several times. The main problem here is that it is nearly impossible to figure out what the paragraph is about. That is, it is impossible to build a model of the situation or context that the words in the paragraph refer to. What does the author mean by *problems*? What kind of problems? What kind of stringed instrument is the paragraph about? What do balloons have to do with it?

It turns out that when people listen to paragraphs like this, they view them as being incoherent, and their memory for the contents of the paragraph tends to be very poor (Bransford & Johnson, 1972). Now, read the paragraph again after looking at the picture in Figure 5.1. If you are like most people, you will find it much easier to make sense of the text after looking at the picture. Why the big difference? One answer is that, without the picture, it is impossible (or nearly so) to build a situation model that captures what the text is about, so your representation of the text lacks *global coherence*. Without an overarching situation model, it is difficult to figure out what the words in the paragraph refer to (so you have trouble establishing *reference*); and it is difficult to figure out how individual sentences in the paragraph relate to preceding and following sentences, so your representation of the text lacks *local coherence*. With the picture in mind, you can bring to bear all of your general world knowledge about instruments and the problems that are involved in trying to impress a dream woman. This allows you to establish reference (e.g., *instrument* refers to electric guitar), and you understand how and what kinds of *problems* might arise (if the balloons pop, the speaker will fall). So the situation model, which is where general world knowledge meets the specifics of the text itself, is a vital element of discourse comprehension.

Construction and integration

The ultimate goal of the construction–integration system is to build a situation model describing relevant aspects of what a text is about. The system builds a surface form representation, converts that to a text-base, and then builds a situation model that reflects the contents of the text-base combined with information from general world knowledge. How does this all take place? The construction–integration account proposes that discourse processing is divided into discrete *cycles*. This is because there are limits on the capacity of

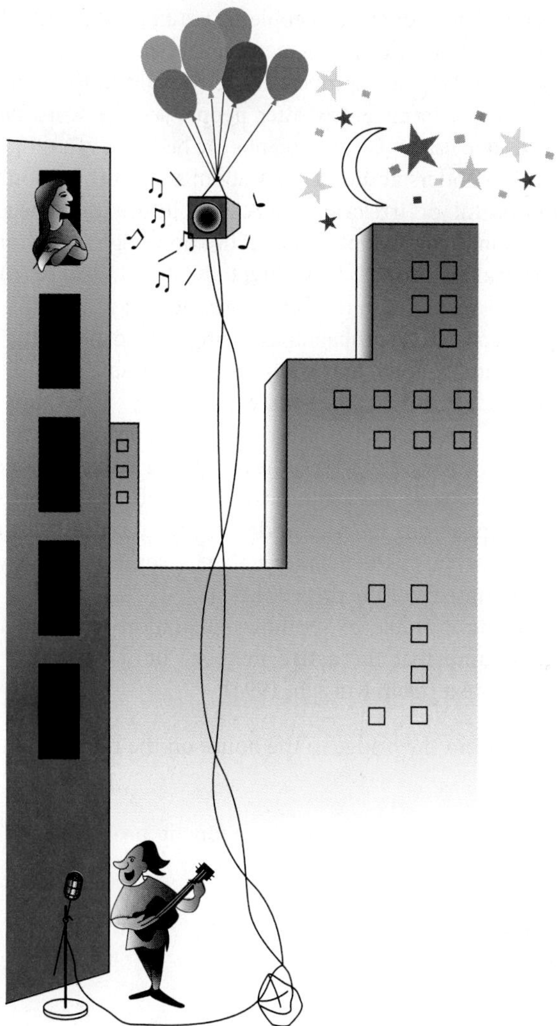

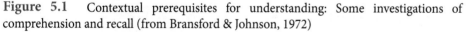

Figure 5.1 Contextual prerequisites for understanding: Some investigations of comprehension and recall (from Bransford & Johnson, 1972)

active or working memory, so only a small part of the text can be worked on at any given time. During any given processing cycle, only a small portion of the text is being worked on. Each processing cycle itself consists of different subcycles. The first of these subcycles is the *construction* phase; and the second is the *integration* phase.

In the construction phase, new text is brought into the system for processing. A surface form representation is built, propositions are extracted, and knowledge is activated to the degree that it is associated with the words in the text and the activated propositions. This knowledge activation phase is conceptualized as being largely or entirely automatic. That is, so long as the comprehender is paying attention and is trying to comprehend, she has little or no control over what information becomes active and available to the comprehension system. We have already seen that the semantic associates of ambiguous words become active, regardless of their relationship to the context of the sentences that they appear with (see Chapter 3). Construction–integration theory proposes similarly that general knowledge that is associated with the current contents of the active memory buffer also becomes activated automatically. So, for example, if people are reading a story about a musical concert and they see an unambiguous word like *piano*, all of the properties of *piano* become accessible (activated), whether those properties are relevant to the current context or not (but see Tabossi, 1988). So, immediately after people see the word *piano* they respond quickly to probe words like *heavy* (because pianos are heavy), even though that property is not particularly useful to understanding a story about a concert. It is only at later stages of processing that non-useful or irrelevant associated information becomes deactivated. Construction–integration theory adopts a model of knowledge activation very close to the TRACE account of lexical processing. According to Kintsch (1998, p. 76), "Meaning has to be constructed by activating nodes in the neighborhood of a word. This activation process is probabilistic, with activation probabilities being proportional to the strengths of connections among the nodes, and it may continue for a variable amount of time, spreading outward into the knowledge net from the source node."

Once knowledge has been activated promiscuously, constraint satisfaction processes reduce the pattern of activated nodes, so that the remaining activated nodes are most closely relevant to the overall context or theme of the text. These activated nodes are conceptualized as a set of activated propositions in the working memory buffer. During the *integration* phase of processing, the propositions that are active in working memory are connected to one another and to the contents of the preceding text.

Let's look at a specific example to see how integration works in the construction–integration system. Assume that the active memory buffer contains two propositions extracted from this mini-text (from Kintsch, 1994):

> John traveled by car from the bridge to the house on the hill. A train passed under the bridge.

If the first sentence were parsed into its component propositions, the propositional representation would look like this:

(P1) predicate: TRAVEL
agent: John
instrument: car
source: bridge
goal: house
modifier: on hill

If the second sentence were parsed into its component propositions, the propositional representation would look like this:

(P2) predicate: PASS
object: train
location: under bridge

With these two propositions active in the working memory buffer, the construction integration system now tries to find a way to *integrate* them, to build a representation that establishes a relationship between the two propositions. According to Kintsch, the production system applies an *argument overlap* strategy to integrate the propositions. The *argument overlap* strategy says, "When you have two propositions active in working memory, look for arguments in each proposition that represent the same concept. When you find overlapping arguments, use those arguments to tie the two propositions together."

In our example mini-text, the proposition extracted from the first sentence can be integrated with the proposition extracted from the second sentence, because they share the argument *bridge*. So what makes the two sentences fit together is that readers assume that the *bridge* that John started at is the same *bridge* that the train passed under. If readers do not make this assumption, then they will not be able to figure out how the first sentence relates to the second, their representation of the mini-text will be incoherent, and, if they remember both propositions, they will most likely remember the two as reflecting entirely separate and independent events.

In order for two propositions to be related or *integrated*, both propositions must be in an active state in the working memory buffer at the same time. However, given that working memory capacity is limited to about seven independent chunks of information (Baddeley, 1972; Miller, 1956), and given that the processes used to manipulate the contents of working memory also use up some of the available resources, only a small number of propositions can be active in working memory simultaneously. Sometimes, the comprehender will have a proposition that is active in working memory that does not relate to, and can not be integrated with, other active propositions in working memory. When this happens, comprehenders can search their long-term memory to try to find a proposition from earlier in the discourse that does relate to the "orphaned" new proposition. These *reinstatement searches* are sometimes needed to maintain coherence, but they are costly in terms of processing resources, as indicated by increased reading times at points in texts where incoming propositions cannot be directly related to immediately preceding text (Fletcher, 1981, 1986; Fletcher & Bloom, 1988; Fletcher, Hummel, & Marsolek, 1990). Sometimes, the reinstatement search will fail to supply an old proposition that can connect to the new proposition. In that case, the orphaned proposition will be purged from working memory. There is some chance that the proposition will be stored as an independent unit in long-term memory, but it is more likely that the proposition will simply be lost or forgotten. Purging propositions from working memory frees up capacity that will be needed for new propositions in the next processing cycle.

Once a text-base representation has been built and propositions have been integrated, comprehenders can update their situation model—their representation of what the text is about. As comprehenders update their situation models, they include information that is directly stated in the text, but they also use their general world knowledge to add information to the situation model that is not directly stated in the text. This process of *inference* can take many forms, and there is a debate about when and how different kinds of inferences are made (see below), but there is no question that inferred information is an important aspect of comprehenders' situation models. For example, texts do not always explicitly state how two different propositions are related, and comprehenders must supply the "missing" information themselves (or else their representation of the text will be incoherent). For example, consider this brief story from Haviland and Clark (1974):

> Mary unpacked some picnic supplies. The beer was warm.

To integrate these two sentences, the reader has to determine how they fit together. Because there is not any explicit overlap between the two sentences at the level of arguments, the comprehender needs to do some extra work to *bridge* the two sentences (so this kind of inference is called a *bridging* inference). In this case, the comprehender infers that *the beer* and *some picnic supplies* go together (because general world knowledge tells them that people often take beer along when they go on a picnic), and so the two sentences can be integrated on that basis. This process of inferencing takes time and uses up some of the available processing resources, however, and so *The beer was warm*, takes longer to read in the context of *picnic supplies* than it would if the preceding sentence explicitly mentioned *beer*. Generally speaking, researchers working on discourse processing agree that bridging inferences are made "on-line," during the process of discourse interpretation, and do not

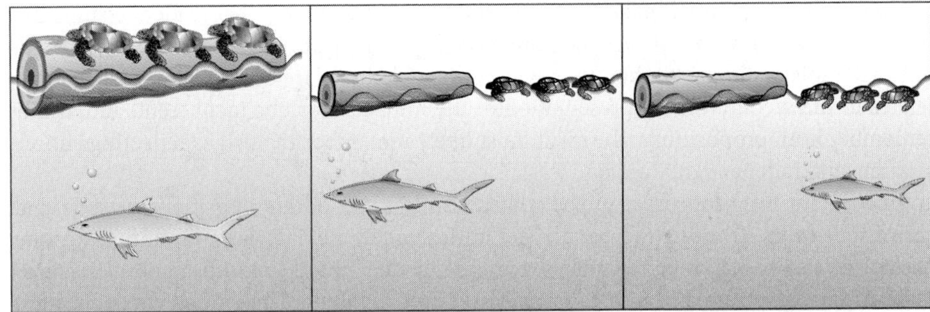

"Three turtles rested on a log and a fish swam beneath it/them." "Three turtles rested beside a log and a fish swam beneath it." "Three turtles rested beside a log and a fish swam beneath them."

Figure 5.2 Three turtles, a fish, and a log

depend on any kind of special strategy on the comprehender's part (e.g., Graesser, Singer, & Trabasso, 1994; McKoon & Ratcliff, 1992).

Previously, we reviewed evidence that propositions are a psychologically real aspect of comprehenders' mental representations of texts. But what about the other elements of the construction–integration representational scheme? Do we really need three levels of representation: the surface form, the textbase, and the situation model? Or can we just stop at propositions? There is, in fact, considerable evidence from studies of how people remember texts that supports the distinction between surface form, the text-base, and the situation model. These experiments also provide evidence that comprehenders construct all three kinds of mental representations when they process extended discourse.

The idea that we represent more than just the verbatim form of the text comes from classic memory studies from the early 1970s. These experiments provide evidence that, while the situation model is developed on the basis of the verbatim or surface form, there really are at least two different representations being built. In these studies, people read either sentence (5), (6), (7), or (8) (Bransford, Barclay, & Franks, 1972; see also Franks & Bransford, 1974; Johnson, Bransford, & Solomon, 1973):

(5) Three turtles rested on a log and a fish swam beneath them.
(6) Three turtles rested on a log and a fish swam beneath it.
(7) Three turtles rested beside a log and a fish swam beneath them.
(8) Three turtles rested beside a log and a fish swam beneath it.

They were told beforehand that their memories for the sentences would be tested later on. The participants' task was to try to memorize the sentences exactly as they were written. Notice that the meaning of sentences (5) and (6) is essentially the same, even though there is a slight difference in the wording of the two sentences (*them* in (5) is replaced by *it* in (6)). Both meanings are conveyed by the leftmost configuration of objects in Figure 5.2. The surface forms of sentences (7) and (8) are distinguished by the same small change in wording (*it* replaces *them*), but this small change in wording also changes the meaning. Sentence (7) goes with the middle configuration of objects in Figure 5.2, while sentence (8) goes with the rightmost configuration. If people remember the surface form of the sentences they read, then they should be equally accurate when asked to remember the exact wording of a sentence that they have previously read. So, after a short retention interval (a few minutes doing a distractor task), people were presented with pairs of sentences, one of which they had read, and one of which they had not, and they were asked to pick out the exact sentence that they had read. People were much less accurate picking between sentences

(5) and (6), which express the same meaning. They were much more accurate picking between sentences (7) and (8), which express different meanings. These findings indicate that the memory for surface form decays very rapidly (within a couple of minutes), but memory for meaning or gist is more durable. A person can identify the exact wording of a sentence she read previously if her situation model representation is consistent with only one of the available choices. But if two sentences convey the same meaning (i.e., they map onto the same situation model), a person has much more difficulty remembering which version she read, even when she tries to memorize the exact wording of the sentences.

More recent research shows that, in addition to representing spatial relations in their situation models, people also represent *temporal* relations, that is how events in a story are laid out in time (Rinck, Hähnel, & Becker, 2001). This experiment used the same study-test procedure as the classic Barclay experiments, but in addition to conveying spatial information, some of the test sentences conveyed temporal information. The test sentences (which were presented in German) described two events as occurring simultaneously, with a third event following, as in sentence (9):

(9) The piano was heard together with the harp and the soprano sang along with it.

In German, the feminine gender pronoun *ihr* ("it") can only refer to the harp. In half of the test sentences, the feminine pronoun *ihr* was replaced by the masculine pronoun *ihm*, which can only refer to the piano. But whether the pronoun refers to the harp or the piano, both versions map onto the same sequence of events (or the same "temporal model"). As was the case when to-be-memorized sentences referred to the same spatial model, subjects were not able to recognize which version (the one with *ihr* or the one with *ihm*) that they had actually studied when they were tested following a brief distractor task.

Further evidence for the independent existence of surface, text-base, and situation models come from studies of more lengthy texts. For example, consider the following brief paragraph (from Fletcher & Chrysler, 1990; see also Kintsch, Welsch, Schmalhofer, & Zimny, 1990):

> *George likes to flaunt his wealth by purchasing rare art treasures. He has a Persian rug worth as much as my car and it's the cheapest thing he owns. Last week he bought a French oil painting for $12,000 and an Indian necklace for $13,500. George says his wife was angry when she found out that the necklace cost more than the carpet. His most expensive "treasures" are a Ming vase and a Greek statue. The statue is the only thing he ever spent more than $50,000 for. It's hard to believe that the statue cost George more than five times what he paid for the beautiful Persian carpet.*

In Randy Fletcher and Sue Chrysler's study, participants read the preceding story. Later, they were asked to say whether test sentences had appeared verbatim in the story or not. The test sentences were designed to probe the surface form, the text-base, or the situation model. To test the surface form, the test sentence either contained the exact wording that had appeared in the text, or else one of the words was replaced by a synonym (e.g., *rug* in *He has a Persian rug worth more than my car* would be replaced with the word *carpet*). If participants correctly report that *He has a Persian carpet* is a new phrase that did not appear in the story, then they have an accurate surface form representation. To test the text-base, the set of propositions that the participants built from the text, the word *necklace* in *his wife was angry when she found out that the necklace cost more than the carpet* was replaced by the word *painting*. It is true (according to the story) that the painting cost more than the carpet, but that is not what the wife was angry about. So, if participants correctly reject the sentence with *painting* in place of *necklace*, they must have remembered the proposition *the wife was upset that the* <u>*necklace*</u> *cost more than the carpet*. Finally, to test the

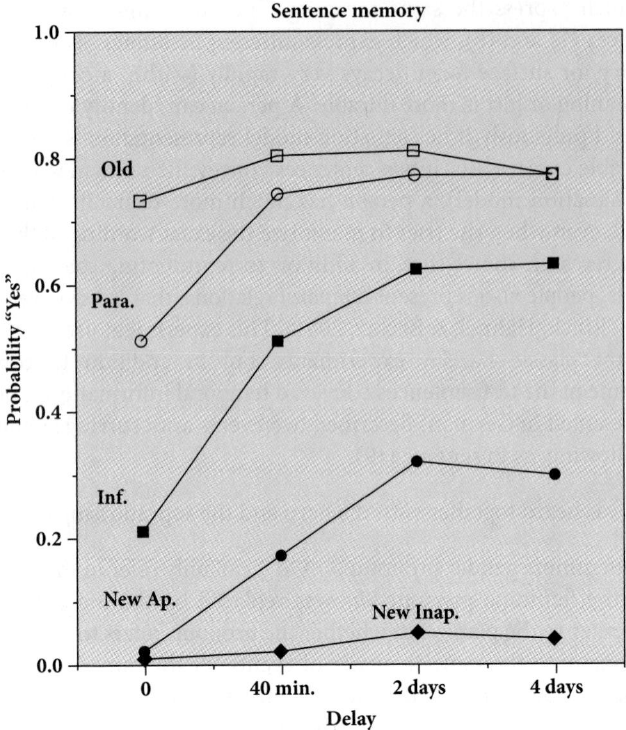

Figure 5.3 Recognition memory results from Kintsch et al. (1990)

situation model, the word *carpet* was replaced by the word *vase* to make the test sentence *his wife was angry that the necklace cost more than the vase*. If participants falsely recognize this last test sentence, this violates the correct situation model, because the vase is stated to be worth much more than the carpet. When participants' recognition memory was tested, they almost never made mistakes about the situation model, they sometimes made mistakes about the specific propositions that were in the story, and they frequently made mistakes about the specific wording of the story. Differences between the error rates for different kinds of questions shows that the questions were tapping into different kinds of mental representations.

Kintsch and his colleagues (1990) also found evidence for separate memory strengths for different kinds of text representations. In this study, participants read short paragraphs and, after varying retention intervals, judged whether test sentences were exactly the same as sentences they had read in stories previously. When the test sentences violated the situation model, participants almost never said they appeared in the stories, even after a delay of four days between reading the story and being tested (see Figure 5.3, the bottom line labeled "New inap." reflects how often participants false alarmed and said that a new sentence that violated the original situation model was really an old sentence from the original story). By contrast, participants were very likely to say "yes" to new sentences when the new sentences were paraphrases of sentences that had appeared in the stories, and this likelihood increased as the delay between initial reading and test increased (see Figure 5.3, the open circles labeled "Para." for "paraphrase"). This shows that the surface form representation is fairly weak and decays very rapidly. The "Inf." curve represents new test sentences that reflect information that was not directly stated in the original text, but could be inferred from it. (For example, if you read that *John sent Susan a love letter*, you might infer that John wanted to go on a date with Susan.) The graph shows that, immediately after reading the story, participants knew the difference between information that was explicitly stated in the story and inferences that they drew from the explicitly stated information. But as time elapsed, participants were more and more likely to "remember" that inferred information was directly stated in the original story. This kind of mistake is often called a "source memory" error by memory researchers, because although the information in the inference is accurate, people make mistakes about how they acquired the information (see, e.g., Jacoby, Woloshyn, & Kelley, 1989). Surface form, propositions, and the situation model are each represented separately and remembered for different lengths of time by people who read stories. The situation model is the strongest and longest lasting representation, the text-base is the next strongest, and the surface form is the weakest and shortest lived (but some surface information does survive, even over the long haul; Gernsbacher, 1985; Keenan, MacWhinney, & Mayhew, 1977).[1]

So, to summarize, the construction–integration production system builds three separate mental representations. The surface form model represents the exact words in the text and their syntactic relations. The text-base represents a set of connected propositions extracted from the surface form. The situation model includes information directly and explicitly stated in the text plus information that comprehenders supply themselves in the form of inferences. Text is processed in cycles. In each cycle, comprehenders input a few propositions' worth of text and knowledge associated with the inputted text becomes automatically activated. In the integration phase comprehenders connect new propositions to previously processed propositions, draw inferences, and update their situation models.

The Structure Building Framework

The *structure building framework* (Gernsbacher, 1990) is a theory of discourse processing that has influenced researchers for the past two decades. Like the construction–integration account, the structure building framework seeks to explain how comprehenders build mental representations of extended discourse. But while Kintsch's theory is largely restricted to spoken and written text, Morton Ann Gernsbacher's theory can be applied to the comprehension of both verbal and non-verbal materials (like picture stories). And while Kintsch's account explains discourse comprehension as being the product of special purpose discourse comprehension mechanisms, the structure building framework appeals to general purpose cognitive mechanisms to explain how discourse is interpreted and remembered. According to Gernsbacher, the processes that are responsible for discourse comprehension are also responsible for other cognitive tasks that may not be directly related to language. Some specifics will help illustrate these points.

The structure building framework proposes that general purpose cognitive mechanisms are responsible for discourse comprehension. To understand a story, comprehenders begin with the process of *laying a foundation*. The *foundation* is based on the information that arrives first, just as laying a foundation is the first thing that happens when you build a house. Two additional general processes, *mapping* and *shifting*, are used to continue building the structure once the foundation has been laid. The mapping process connects incoming information to the foundation as long as the incoming information is related to, or coheres with, the preceding information. If the new information is not related to the preceding information, comprehenders undertake the process of *shifting* to build a new *substructure*. Thus, the comprehenders' mental representation of a story, or any set of events with a coherent structure, consists of a foundation, plus an appropriate number of connected substructures. The story representation as a whole then, consists of "several branching substructures (Gernsbacher, 1995, p. 49)," with the branches terminating at the foundation.

According to the structure building framework, the metaphorical building blocks that comprehenders use to create their representations for stories consist of activated *memory nodes* (similar to the nodes in Collins and Quillian's semantic network theory; or propositions in Kintsch's construction–integration framework). When memory nodes become activated by a text, they send out processing signals. The processing signals that the memory nodes send out lead to either *enhancement* or *suppression* of other memory nodes. The enhancement mechanism increases the activation of memory nodes that are related to the input and the currently activated set of memory nodes. The suppression mechanism decreases the activation of memory nodes.

This fairly simple account can be used to explain a wide variety of experimental results. For example, if the process of laying a foundation is psychologically real, then we should see evidence that first-mentioned parts of texts are dealt with differently than later-arriving parts. One piece of evidence is that comprehenders take longer to process a given word if it appears as the first word in a sentence than if it appears later (Aaronson & Scarborough, 1976). People also process the first sentence in a paragraph more slowly than other sentences (Cirilo & Foss, 1980; Haberlandt, 1980). Similar effects occur for non-verbal materials. For example, when viewing a picture story, people spend more time looking at the first picture in the story than the other pictures (Gernsbacher, 1996). This slow-down would be expected if comprehenders are dedicating special effort to encoding the first-mentioned parts of a story or text (i.e., laying a foundation).

Given this extra effort at encoding, we might expect that information arriving first in a text should enjoy some kind of special status in the mental representation of the text, and it turns out that it does. This *advantage of first mention* has been demonstrated in experiments where people read or listen to sentences like (10) (Gernsbacher & Hargreaves, 1988; Gernsbacher, Hargreaves, & Beeman, 1989).

(10) Tina beat Lisa in the state tennis match.

After reading this sentence, people verify that the first-mentioned person (*Tina*) appeared in the sentence much faster than they verify that the second-mentioned person (*Lisa*) did, suggesting that in the comprehender's mental representation of sentence (10), the first-mentioned person enjoys a higher degree of activation. One might offer a counter-explanation to the advantage of first mention hypothesis by appealing to the fact that *Tina* is the grammatical subject of the sentence (a prominent and important syntactic position), but verification times for *Tina* are still faster than verification times for *Lisa* when both are part of a conjoined subject (as in *Tina and Lisa beat Susan and Marsha in the state tennis match*). Similarly, the semantic role that the individual characters play also does not override the advantage of first mention. In sentence (10), *Tina* is the subject of the sentence and she is also the thematic *agent* (do-er, or initiator) of the action. In (11), *Tina* is still the first-mentioned participant, but now she is the *patient* (do-ee, or recipient) of the action:

(11) *Tina* was beaten by *Lisa* in the state tennis match.

People still verify that *Tina* appeared in sentence (11) faster than they verify that *Lisa* was in sentence (11), suggesting again that people pay special attention to first-mentioned participants, whether the first-mentioned character is the initiator or recipient of the action described in the text.

Evidence for *mapping* and *shifting* processes can be found by looking at how textual cohesion and coherence affect processing and memory for texts. Mapping occurs when incoming information is highly related to the part of the text that is currently being processed. Shifting occurs when incoming information does not closely relate to the material currently being processed. Shifting should produce two effects. First, because the process of shifting takes up processing resources, comprehenders should slow down at points in a text where coherence breaks occur, because it takes more time for them to shift and start building a new substructure than it does to map the same information onto an ongoing substructure. Second, because shifting results in the construction of a new substructure, information from previous portions of the text should become less available after shifting has occurred. Both of these predictions enjoy support from experiments on text processing. The first prediction is verified by experiments showing that parts of texts that follow topic shifts are processed more slowly than texts that maintain the current topic (Mandler & Goodman, 1982).

Other experiments show that information becomes less available after the comprehender has shifted and started a new substructure. For example, clause structure determines how accessible concepts are after a sentence has been processed (Caplan, 1972). Sentences (12) and (13) each contain two substructures, each of which consists of a clause.

(12) Now that artists are working fewer hours, oil prints are rare.
(13) Now that artists are working in oil, prints are rare.

In (12), the word *oil* appears in the second clause (the second substructure). In (13), *oil* appears in the first clause (the first substructure). So, according to the mapping and shifting hypotheses, *oil* should be more accessible at the end of sentence (12), because it is part of the most recently constructed substructure, than at the end of the sentence (13), because there it is part of the first substructure and comprehenders will have shifted and built a new substructure after they read the word *oil*. Participants more quickly verified that the word *oil* appeared in the test sentence at the end of sentence (12) than at the end of sentence (13), consistent with the mapping and shifting hypotheses. Note that the word *oil* is followed by the exact same three words in both (12) and (13), so the pure effect of recency cannot explain this outcome.[2] Similar loss of information occurs at important boundaries in non-verbal picture stories (Gernsbacher, 1985). Participants are less able to remember the left-right orientation of pictures (a surface feature that does not affect meaning) from picture stories after they finish "reading" the story than while they are in the process of comprehending the story. Further, the process of shifting can help explain some of the differences between good and poor comprehenders. Comprehenders who score lower on tests of general verbal ability, such as the Verbal section of the SAT, are less able to access recently comprehended information, which might indicate that they shift and build new substructures more often than comprehenders who are better able to comprehend what they read (Gernsbacher, Varner, & Faust, 1990).

The hypothetical processes of enhancement and suppression have also been supported by research findings. *Enhancement* is viewed as an automatic process whereby knowledge that is related to the current text is activated rapidly, without conscious volition (as long as the comprehender is paying minimal attention), and proceeds in an uncontrolled fashion, at least initially. Findings from probe recognition experiments and reading time studies indicate that information is activated as people listen to or read stories, whether that information is relevant to the context or current topic of the discourse or not (e.g., Duffy, Henderson, & Morris, 1989; Onifer & Swinney, 1981; Rayner & Duffy, 1988; Seidenberg, Tanenhaus, Leiman, & Bienkowski, 1982; Swinney, 1979). For example, if comprehenders read sentence (14),

(14) The teacher has a lot of patience.

and they are asked to judge whether a target word is semantically related to the sentence, they have a hard time rejecting the word *hospital*. That is because when they see the word *patience*, they activate the phonologically related word *patients*, which is semantically related to the word *hospital* (Gernsbacher & Faust, 1991). So, even though the word *patients* has a completely different meaning than the word *patience*, the similarity in the way they sound creates an associative relationship, and this associative relationship means that we have to activate both meanings, even though we only need one.

This automatic, widespread activation of associated knowledge occurs very rapidly, within a few hundred milliseconds after a word is encountered, but if the comprehender is to end up with a coherent representation of what the text is about, this automatically activated but irrelevant information must be removed from the comprehender's representation of the discourse. That is where the process of *suppression* comes in. Suppression operates on those activated memory nodes that are not closely related to the topic or theme of the ongoing discourse. When the unrelated information is removed, the resulting discourse representation is less cluttered with irrelevant details, and hence more coherent. The process of suppression is conceptualized as a less automatic process than enhancement. It takes longer to work than enhancement does (e.g., Neely, 1977; Wiley, Mason, & Myers, 2001) and it is more variable across individuals. In fact, differences in suppression ability may underlie differences in people's ability to understand texts.

Differences between individuals in how well they are able to suppress irrelevant information have been demonstrated in a series of studies involving lexically ambiguous words like *spade*. As we saw in Chapter 3, reading or listening to words like *spade* leads to the automatic activation of all of the meanings related to the word. So, when readers see the word *spade*, they activate both the *playing card* meaning and the *shovel* meaning. This automatic activation of multiple meanings occurs even when the word *spade* appears in a context that makes only one of the meanings appropriate. In Sentence (15), only the *shovel* meaning of *spade* fits with the rest of the sentence:

(15) The gardener dug with the spade.

However, if the word *ace* is presented, and people are asked to judge whether its meaning is related to the preceding sentence, they take a long time to say "no", because the playing card meaning is activated by the word *spade*. To get rid of this irrelevant meaning, the mechanism of suppression starts to operate on the activated playing card meaning, and after a short period of time, a few hundred milliseconds, the "playing card" meaning of *spade* is no longer activated—it has been suppressed.

How does suppression work? Is it as automatic as enhancement? There are a number of reasons to think that suppression is not just a mirror image of enhancement. First, suppression takes a lot longer to work than enhancement does. Second, while knowledge activation (enhancement) occurs about the same way for everyone, not everyone is equally good at suppressing irrelevant information, and this appears to be a major contributor to differences in comprehension ability between different people (Gernsbacher, 1993; Gernsbacher & Faust, 1991; Gernsbacher et al., 1990). For example, Gernsbacher and her colleagues acquired Verbal SAT scores for a large sample of students at the University of Oregon (similar experiments have been done on Air Force recruits in basic training, who are about the same age as the college students). Verbal SAT scores give a pretty good indication of how well people are able to understand texts that they read, and there are considerable differences between the highest and lowest scoring people in the sample. This group of students was then asked to judge whether target words like *ace* were semantically related to a preceding sentence like (15), above. Figure 5.4 presents representative data from one of these experiments. The left-hand bars show that the *ace* meaning was highly activated for both good comprehenders (the dark bars) and poorer comprehenders (the light bars) immediately after the sentence. After a delay of one second (a very long time in language

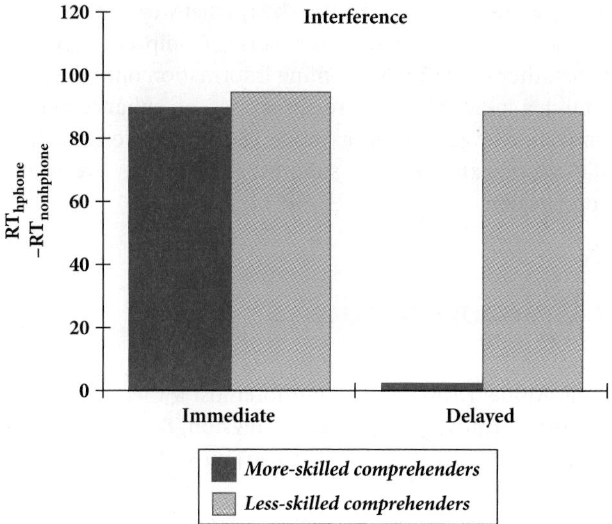

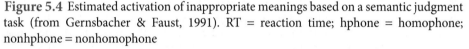

Figure 5.4 Estimated activation of inappropriate meanings based on a semantic judgment task (from Gernsbacher & Faust, 1991). RT = reaction time; hphone = homophone; nonhphone = nonhomophone

processing terms), the good comprehenders had suppressed the contextually inappropriate "playing card" meaning of *spade*, but the poor comprehenders still had that meaning activated (shown in the right-hand bars of Figure 5.4).

Further evidence for the non-automatic nature of the suppression process comes from studies like the Gernsbacher experiments, but using slightly different experimental tasks. One potential problem with the semantic judgment task used by Gernsbacher is that it can encourage participants in the experiment to think about different meanings of the test words and it requires an explicit, conscious judgment of how the sentence and the target word go together. Thus, people's responses might be influenced more by their decision-making processes than by processes involved in interpreting the text itself. To try to get around this problem, Debra Long and her colleagues manipulated the kind of task that participants engaged in, and they tried to find tasks that could be done on the basis of more automatic mental processes (Long, Seely, & Oppy, 1999). When Long and her colleagues used a naming task (which is thought to be relatively immune to strategic or controlled mental processes; McKoon, Ratcliff, & Ward, 1994; Potts, Keenan, & Golding, 1988), rather than a semantic judgment task, both better and poorer comprehenders showed the same pattern of meaning activations. Both groups showed a high degree of activation for contextually inappropriate meanings immediately after reading sentences like (15). Both groups appeared to suppress the contextually inappropriate meaning after a delay of 850 ms. The experimental task was changed to lexical decision in a second experiment and meaning judgment in a third. Performance on both lexical decision and meaning judgment is thought to reflect strategic mental processes. Under these conditions, less skilled comprehenders again appeared to keep the contextually inappropriate "playing card" meaning active even after significant delays, consistent with the original Gernsbacher results. Hence, it appears that less skilled comprehenders do have trouble suppressing contextually inappropriate meanings, and this deficit is especially apparent in tasks where performance requires comprehenders to manage conflict between different sources of information, such as an ambiguous word and the context it appears in, in order to produce a response.

To sum up, the structure building framework says that we use general purpose cognitive mechanisms to process and understand discourse. Comprehenders begin by laying a foundation, and then they either map incoming information onto the current structure, or they shift and build a new substructure. Processes of enhancement and suppression manipulate the activation levels of memory nodes. Shifting too often can lead to incoherent mental representations of texts. Failing to suppress activated but irrelevant information can also impair comprehension.

The Event Indexing Model

The Event Indexing Model (EIM) is first and foremost a theory about how people build situation models from narrative texts (Zwaan, Langston, & Graesser, 1995). According to the EIM, the purpose of the discourse comprehension system is to understand the "goals and actions of protagonists … and events that unfold in the real world or some fictional world" (Zwaan et al., 1995, p. 292; see also Zwaan & Rapp, 2006). To represent these story elements, five core aspects of stories are tracked, and each event in the story is indexed or tagged according to each of the five core features: The time frame over which the event occurs (*time*), the characters that are involved in the event (*protagonists*), the causal connection of the current event to preceding and following events (*causation*), the spatial location(s) where the events occur (*space*), and how the event relates to a protagonist's goals (*motivation*). Similar to the structure building framework, the EIM conceptualizes events as activated memory nodes, and the representation of a story consists of a set of memory nodes and the connections between them. Each memory node is coded for the five previously mentioned features, and as each new piece of the text is processed, it is evaluated as to how it relates to previously activated memory nodes. So, each time a new piece of text is processed, the comprehender updates the situation model to reflect the information provided by the text. Different pieces of text can require updating of different features of the event index.

Sometimes, new information in a text elaborates on the elements of a previously activated event node. But sometimes, new information indicates a break between the previously activated event and the new information. According to the EIM, if there is a discontinuity on one or more of the five features, the current event node is deactivated and a new node is activated. This process is similar to the *shifting* process in the structure building framework, and discontinuities in stories should produce measurable processing costs (because shifting to work on a new event node is more complicated than continuing to map incoming information onto a previously activated event node). So, one way to test the EIM is to see how people respond when a new piece of text creates a discontinuity between the activated memory node and the new information provided by the text. In fact, people do process parts of texts that create discontinuities slower than parts of texts that can be mapped directly onto a previously activated memory node (Zwaan, Magliano, & Graesser, 1995). For example, when the text explicitly signals a temporal discontinuity (e.g., it says, *A day later …*), concepts mentioned just before the discontinuity are less accessible than in an equivalent story that does not signal a temporal discontinuity (e.g., it says, *A moment later …*; Zwaan, 1996). Texts can indicate that currently described events are part of *flashbacks*, and so occurred a long time ago in the virtual world described by the text. When the recency of the flashback episode is manipulated (i.e., the text either says the flashback episode happened recently or a long time ago), information from episodes that is described as taking place a long time ago is less accessible than information that is described as happening more recently (Claus & Kelter, 2006; see also Kelter, Kaup, & Claus, 2006).

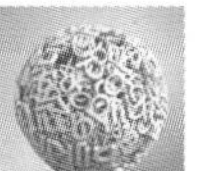

THE CZAR AND HIS DAUGHTERS (GRAESSER, 1981)

Once there was a Czar who had three lovely daughters. One day the three daughters went walking in the woods. They were enjoying themselves so much that they forgot the time and stayed too long. A dragon kidnapped the three daughters. As they were being dragged off, they cried for help. Three heroes heard their cries and set off to rescue the maidens. The heroes fought the dragon. Then the heroes returned the daughters to their palace. When the Czar heard of the rescue, he rewarded the heroes.

Another way to assess the EIM is to see how comprehenders organize and remember the events in texts. According to the EIM, parts of texts that have overlapping values in the event index should be connected together in the comprehender's mental representation of the story. For example, two sub-events that occur at the same time should be represented more closely than two sub-events that occur at different times. Take a minute to read the story "The Czar and His Daughters." Notice that the action of *dragging* takes place at the same time as *crying*. Normally, these two concepts would be unrelated—they are semantically very different, and people tend not to associate the two. But because the two events are connected by the temporal structure of the story, comprehenders should create a connection between *crying* and *dragging* when they read the story. By contrast, the actions of *walking* and *crying* are unrelated both in general terms (for the same reasons *crying* and *dragging* are unrelated), and the event structure of the story also does nothing to bring the two actions together. To test whether the story affects how people view the relationship between *crying* and *dragging*, Rolf Zwaan and his colleagues (Zwaan et al., 1995) asked people to read stories like "The Czar and His Daughters" and then to perform a categorization task. To perform the categorization task (also known as a *clustering* task), the subjects read a list of verbs and placed the verbs inside a set of boxes. The subjects were told to place two verbs in the same box if they thought the verbs "belonged together" (Zwaan et al., 1995, p. 294). Subjects who had read the story were far more likely to place *dragging* and *crying* in the same box than they were to place *walking* and *crying* together, but subjects who had *not* read the story were just as likely to place *walking* and *crying* together as they were to place *dragging* and *crying* together. Pairs of verbs that were related on the other event indexing dimensions (space, causation, entities, and goals) were also likely to be grouped together by subjects who had read the story and not by subjects who had not read the story. These results indicate that people use all five of the event indexing dimensions to organize their representations of stories.

Recent neuroimaging results also support separate indexing of different story characteristics (Ferstl, Rinck, & Von Cramon, 2005). Evelyln Ferstl and her colleagues manipulated whether words in a story conveyed temporal information (*Markus' train arrived at the station 20 minutes <u>before</u> Claudia's*) or emotional information (*Sarah couldn't remember that she had ever been so <u>sad</u>*; Ferstl et al., 2005, p. 726). Emotion-conveying words led to increased brain activity in posterior ventromedial prefrontal cortex (see the green-marked regions in Plate 8). Words that conveyed temporal information produced increased brain activity in a different set of brain regions (marked in yellow and red in Plate 8), including parts of the frontal and parietal cortices on both sides of the brain. Additional fMRI and positron emission tomography (PET) studies also suggest that different kinds of indexing processes are supported to different degrees by different networks of brain regions. Stories that call on people to infer characters' mental states produce different patterns of brain activity when compared to stories that require inferences about physical causes (Ferstl, Neumann, Bogler, & Von Cramon, 2008; Fletcher et al., 1995; Mason, Williams, Kana, Minshew, & Just, 2008).[3] Of course, when people understand a story, these different indexing dimensions are normally integrated into a coherent whole (Rapp & Taylor, 2004).

Modeling space, time, protagonists, and motivation

SPACE

The EIM proposes that we use our general perceptual apparatus to build situation models from texts. One of the main tasks that our perceptual apparatus does for us is modeling three-dimensional space, so that we can navigate through the world, pick out perceptual targets for detailed processing and evaluation, predict how objects will move, and so forth. It is not surprising, then, that spatial models are an important aspect of discourse understanding. To comprehend stories, we build an internal representation of the space that the events in stories take place in, and we track the movements of characters through this virtual space (e.g., Black, Turner, & Bower, 1979; Bower & Morrow, 1990; Bower & Rinck, 2001; Glenberg, Meyer, & Lindem, 1987; Morrow, Bower, & Greenspan, 1989; Morrow, Greenspan, & Bower, 1987; Rapp, Klug, & Taylor, 2006). Languages provide us with numerous ways to mark spatial relations (e.g., *over there, in, behind, next to, to the left*, and so forth). Although different languages have different ways of expressing spatial relationships (Choi, McDonough, Bowerman, & Mandler, 1999), spatial modeling is a general feature of discourse comprehension. Comprehenders assume that the information in stories will be consistent throughout with regards to the way space is described, and it is more difficult to process parts of texts that are inconsistent with previously inferred spatial relations than parts of texts that are consistent with previously inferred spatial relations (de Vega, 1995).

In some of the classic experiments on spatial modeling of texts from Gordon Bower's lab, research subjects start by memorizing the layout of a fictitious space (Bower & Morrow, 1990; Bower & Rinck, 2001; Morrow et al., 1987, 1989). Subjects continue to look at and memorize the layout until their accuracy on a test reaches a very high level. After they successfully memorize the layout of the imaginary building, including the locations of particular objects within the building, participants then listen to a story about a character moving through the memorized space. During the story, the research subjects are interrupted periodically by a visual target word on a computer screen. Their task is to react as quickly as possible to the word (by saying whether the object is present in the imaginary building, or by indicating whether the target on the computer screen is a word or not, or simply by naming the object). People's reaction time on the test depends on how far the main character is from the named object in the virtual, or imaginary space. If the main character in the story is close to the tested object, then people respond quickly. If the main character is distant from the tested object, then people respond more slowly. Findings like these indicate that people represent space in stories in an anological form, which means that their mental representation of space in stories preserves features of actual, three-dimensional, real-world space (as shown in the general mental representation literature in mental rotation and image scanning experiments; e.g., Kosslyn, 1973; Shepard & Metzler, 1971). So, people who listen to stories about a character moving through an imaginary space behave as though there is a "spotlight of attention" following the main character through the space. Objects that are in close proximity to the main character enjoy higher than normal activation because the comprehender's attention is focused on the main character, but attention is not limited to the main character (hence the spotlight metaphor).

One of the benefits of having a spotlight (rather than a laser beam) of attention is that objects that are likely to be mentioned in the near future enjoy a higher than normal degree of activation, and so comprehenders can access and integrate those concepts more quickly once they are mentioned.

One of the potential concerns about Bower's map task experiments is that subjects had to spend a considerable amount of time memorizing the layout of the spaces they would hear about later, and this is not a normal part of the way people experience language. People also sometimes object that the probe recognition task is unnatural. However, when stories refer to spaces that people are already familiar with (so they do not have to memorize anything special for the experiment), the same kinds of effects occur (Glenberg et al., 1987), whether activation of a concept is assessed by the probe recognition task or a naturalistic reading task. Objects that are in close virtual proximity to a currently focused character enjoy a higher degree of activation than objects that are further away from the currently focused character in the comprehenders' mental model of the situation.

TIME

Comprehenders model temporal relations in narratives by taking advantage of real-world knowledge and explicit cues in the discourse (e.g., de Vega, Robertson, Glenberg, Kaschak, & Rinck, 2004). Speakers and listeners share schematic knowledge about the temporal organization of commonly occurring events (e.g., eating food comes after ordering food at a restaurant), and this schematic organization affects the way people tell stories (Barsalou & Sewell, 1985). Comprehenders model time in stories by applying a default strategy, modified by the presence of explicit linguistic cues. The default strategy is to assume that events in the world occurred in the order that they were described in the story, but that default assumption can be overridden by schematic knowledge or by explicit cues in the discourse. If the information conveyed explicitly by the text activates a schema, comprehenders will assume that the events conform to the order specified by the schema, unless the text directly indicates something else. When there is no pre-existing schema, or the schema leaves the order of the events unspecified, comprehenders apply the *temporal iconicity* heuristic, and assume that the events occurred in the order they were mentioned in the story. So, if a story said, *Megan and Kristen ate lunch and walked to the park*, comprehenders assume that the event of eating happened before the event of walking. This *temporal iconicity* assumption frees speakers and writers from having to explicitly mark every event in a story with a time tag.

Speakers can decide to explicitly signal that events are described in a different order than they occurred using connectives like *before* and *after*, or using explicit time tags (e.g., *at noon, at twilight*). So, a speaker could say *Before Megan ate lunch, Kristen walked to the park.* However, when a text describes events in a different order than they happened, people take a little extra time to process that text (Mandler, 1986).[4] Violations of temporal iconicity also produce different patterns of neural activity, as indicated by ERP measures (Münte, Schiltz, & Kutas,1998; Figure 5.5). Münte's study showed that sentences that violate temporal iconicity (the *before* sentences) produce a greater negative deflection in the ERP signal than sentences that describe events in the same order that they happened (the *after* sentences). The size of the difference correlated with subjects' working memory capacity, so this supports the idea that comprehenders model the events in the order that they are described, but when temporal iconicity is violated, they have to mentally flip the order of the events. This flipping process uses up working memory resources.[5]

PROTAGONISTS

Stories are centered around characters, so it is not surprising that comprehenders include a wide variety of features of protagonists in their mental models in stories. Characters' mental states are modeled extensively as comprehenders process stories. So, for example,

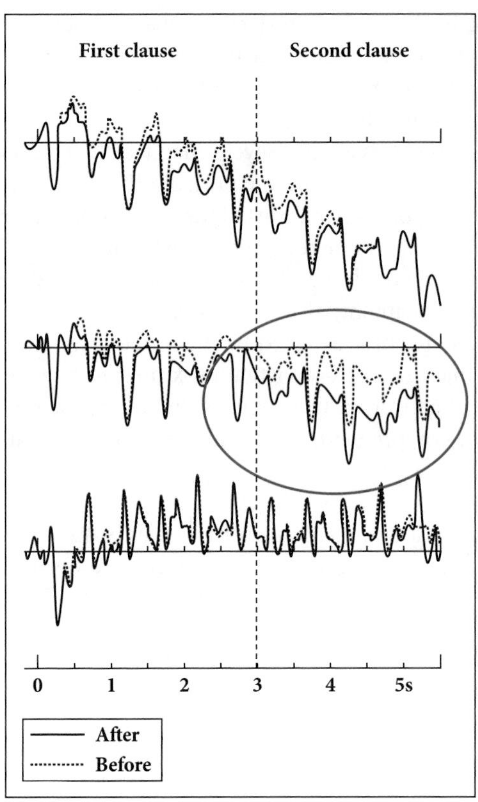

Figure 5.5 ERP data from Münte et al., 1998 (p. 71)
Test sentences: *After/before the scientist submitted the paper, the journal changed its policy.* The ERP signal in the circle shows increased negativity for the *before* sentences during processing of the second clause

in the Bower map-task experimental paradigm, objects that are in a room that a main character is *thinking* about enjoy a higher degree of activation and accessibility than other objects that may be associated with the virtual story space. This modeling of characters' mental states extends to modeling of their perceptual experiences. In other words, comprehenders adopt the visual perspective of characters in stories and view the virtual story world through their eyes. As a result, objects in the story that are out of the focused character's line of sight are less accessible to the story comprehender (are less activated in the story comprehender's situation model) than objects that are "visible" to the focused character, and comprehenders' reaction times to virtually occluded objects are slower than reaction times to objects that are visible from the focused character's perspective (Horton & Rapp, 2003).

Comprehenders also model character's emotional states, and use them to draw inferences about how characters will respond to events in stories (Gernsbacher, Goldsmith, & Robertson, 1992; Gernsbacher, Hallada, & Robertson, 1998; Gernsbacher & Robertson, 1992).[6] So, if you are reading a story about someone winning the state tennis match, you would be surprised and respond more slowly if that character were described later as being sad or depressed. Comprehenders also model aspects of characters' personalities, this information is accessible when the characters are mentioned, and may serve as the basis for inferencing. Have a look at the story about the character Carol (from Peracchi & O'Brien, 2004; p. 1046; see also Rapp, Gerrig, & Prentice, 2001):

Context Version 1:
Carol was known for her short temper and her tendency to act without thinking. She never thought about the consequences of her actions, so she often suffered negative repercussions.

Context Version 2:
Carol was known for her ability to peacefully settle any confrontation. She would never even think to solve her problems with physical violence.

Continuation:
Carol was fed up with her job waiting on tables. Customers were rude, the chef was impossibly demanding, and the manager had made a pass at her just that day. The last straw came when a rude man at one of her tables complained that the spaghetti she had just served was cold. As he became louder and nastier, she felt herself losing control. Without thinking of the consequences, she picked up the plate of spaghetti, and raised it above the rude man's head.

Test Word: *dump*

In Peracchi and O'Brien's experiment, comprehenders either read version 1 of the context or version 2 of the context before reading the continuation. The continuation describes a sorely trying day at the restaurant, and the question is whether comprehenders represent information about the focused character's personality, and use that information to predict how the story will turn out. When the target word *dump* was presented to readers after the sentence *She picked up the plate of spaghetti, and raised it above the rude man's head*, subjects responded to it faster if Carol had previously been described as having a short temper, but no faster than a control condition if she had previously been described as being calm and peaceful. So it appears as though comprehenders do model characters' personality traits, they activate those models when the character is mentioned in the text, and they use the modeled personality traits to predict how things will turn out in the story.

MOTIVATION

Another way comprehenders organize their representations of narrative texts is by keeping track of protagonists' (main characters') goals (Egidi & Gerrig, 2006; Singer & Halldorson, 1996; Singer, Halldorson, Lear, & Andrusiak, 1992; Singer & Richards, 2005; Suh & Trabasso, 1993; Trabasso & Suh, 1993; Trabasso, van den Broek, & Suh, 1989). Narratives frequently have a complex goal structure, and so information about characters' goals increases and decreases in accessibility as comprehenders process the narrative. Sometimes, goals are nested within goals. In Soyoung Suh and Tom Trabasso's seminal work on goal inferences, they presented people with stories that had complex goal structures. For example, a character called Jimmy wanted a new bike (first-mentioned and superordinate goal), so he tried to get a job (second-mentioned and subordinate goal). Half of the time (goal success condition), the superordinate goal was described as being satisfied (Jimmy's mom agrees to buy him a bike) before the subordinate goal was mentioned. The other half of the time, the superordinate goal was thwarted (Jimmy's mom does not agree to buy him a bike) before the subordinate goal was mentioned. When the superordinate goal is thwarted, presumably Jimmy still has that goal (at least, the text does not state that he has abandoned it). Under those conditions, the superordinate goal remains more active in the comprehender's mental representation of the story. This is demonstrated by the fact people mention the superordinate goal more in the goal failure condition when they are asked to talk out loud while reading the story (see Figure 5.6, "goal failure" condition). When the goal succeeds (Timmy's mom buys a bike), that superordinate goal becomes less active in comprehenders'

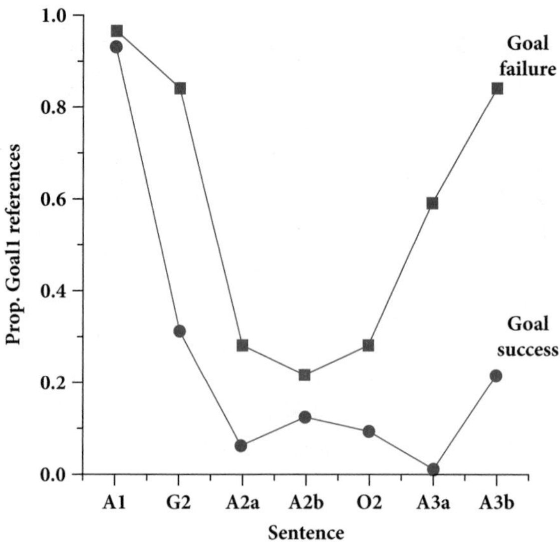

Figure 5.6 Goal failure and goal success (from Suh & Trabasso, 1993, p. 289)

representations of the story (see Figure 5.6, "goal success" condition). These activation differences are also reflected in differences in reaction times to goal-related target words between the goal failure and goal success conditions. Subjects respond to target words related to the superordinate goal faster in the goal failure condition (where the main character is still pursuing the goal) than in the goal success condition (where the main character has moved on and is now motivated by some other goal).

Comprehenders' ability to track goals in narratives is actually very sophisticated, as they appear to be able to track multiple goals of multiple characters, and do so to the extent that the characters are salient, prominent, or central to the narrative. Further, comprehenders are able to recognize when different characters' goals are in conflict (Magliano, Taylor, & Kim, 2005; Richards & Singer, 2001).

Causation, Cohesion, and Coherence in Discourse Encoding and Memory

The modeling of causal relations is an important aspect of the EIM, but it is also a core issue in discourse processing, interpretation, and memory more generally. More specifically, causal connections between propositions seem to be the glue that holds different parts of narratives together. Recall that, in reviewing the construction–integration theory, the notion of argument overlap was introduced. Argument overlap occurs when two adjacent pieces of text contain information that refers to the same object, character, or concept. When this occurs, two propositions can be linked together on the basis of this overlapping information. This kind of textual connection is sometimes referred to as *cohesion*—different parts of a text go together by virtue of having common elements that refer to the same thing in the world. Cohesion is one factor that can contribute to textual *coherence*—the notion that different parts of a text fit together somehow. Cohesion is an important element of the mental representation of extended discourse, but some researchers think that construction–integration's focus on cohesion as the prime factor that ties propositions together is a mistake. They note that there are things besides argument overlap that can tie propositions together and that texts that are highly cohesive are not always highly coherent. Consider, for example, the following paragraph:

> *It was a sunny day in the city on the hill. Hills are higher than valleys. The central valley contains a number of interesting museums. Museums often have antique weapons. Weapons of mass destruction are a threat to security. Linus' security blanket needs washing.*

If we asked people to judge whether the preceding paragraph was coherent, most of them would say it's pretty incoherent. This is so even though each proposition in the paragraph can be linked to the preceding proposition because of argument overlap. According to construction–integration theory, this paragraph should be rated as highly coherent, but it patently is not. What is missing from the preceding paragraph is any kind of causal structure. Although adjacent sentences refer to the same concepts, there is no other reason why one sentence follows the other. You could scramble the order of the sentences at random and the result would be nearly as coherent as the original.

Some researchers have therefore proposed that a critical element of discourse coherence and discourse understanding is the discovery of the causal structure of the story (Fletcher, 1986; Fletcher & Bloom, 1988; Fletcher et al., 1990; Trabasso & van den Broek, 1985; Trabasso et al., 1989; van den Broek & Trabasso, 1986). Rather than looking for overlapping arguments, readers analyze the statements in narrative according to two criteria:

1. Is this statement a cause of events that occur later in the story?
2. Is this statement a consequence of events that occurred earlier in the story?

To determine whether something is a cause, comprehenders apply the *necessity in the circumstances* heuristic (which is based on the causal analysis of the philosopher Hegel). The necessity in the circumstances heuristic says that "A causes B, if, in the circumstances of the story, B would not have occurred if A had not occurred, and if A is sufficient for B to occur." Let's look at an example (from Keenan, Baillet, & Brown, 1984):

> Timmy's brother punched him again and again. The next day Timmy's body was covered in bruises.

Event A (Timmy's brother punching him) is considered a cause for event B (Timmy having a lot of bruises the next day), because in the context of this mini-drama, being punched is enough all by itself for bruises to happen (it is sufficient), and absent some other named cause, event A is necessary for event B to occur (take away punching and the bruises also go away).

When people read or listen to stories, they are not so much concerned that adjacent units of texts (sentences, paragraphs, or episodes) have common arguments (although causally connected elements often will have common arguments, for example "Timmy" in the preceding mini story). What is important to comprehenders is to figure out *why* events follow one another in a given sequence, and discovering a causal relation answers the question of why event B followed event A in the story.

The importance of causal structure in the mental processing of texts can be demonstrated in a variety of ways. First, the propositional structure of texts can be described as a network of causal connections. Some of the propositions in a story will be on the central causal chain that runs from the first proposition in the story (*Once upon a time …*) to the last (*… and they lived happily ever after*). Other propositions will be on causal dead-ends or side-plots. In *Cinderella*, her wanting to go to the ball, the arrival of the fairy godmother, the loss of the glass slipper, and the eventual marriage to the handsome prince, are all on the central causal chain. Many of the versions of the Cinderella story do not bother to say what happens to the evil stepmother and stepsisters after Cinderella gets married. Those events are off the central causal chain and, no matter how they are resolved, they do not affect the central causal chain. As a result, if non-central events are explicitly included in the story, they are not remembered as well as more causally central elements (Fletcher, 1986; Fletcher & Bloom, 1988; Fletcher et al., 1990).

Second, causal connections between propositions in stories also provide a basis for maintaining information in an active state between processing cycles. According to the *leading edge* strategy (Kintsch, 1988, 1994), comprehenders connect propositions to one another based on argument overlap. So, when they are choosing propositions to maintain in working memory, they choose the most recently encountered propositions. Other accounts appeal to the importance of causal connections in narrative (e.g., Fletcher, 1986). According to the *current state strategy*, the discourse processing system looks for recently encountered propositions that have *antecedents* but no *consequences.* Antecedents are events in the preceding story that caused the proposition in question to happen. So, in the Timmy mini-story, *being punched* is the antecedent of *having bruises*; and *having bruises* is the consequence of *being punched.* In the Timmy mini-story, *Timmy's body was covered in bruises* is both the most recent proposition and the end of the causal chain. So, both the leading edge strategy and the current state strategy predict that this proposition will remain in working memory as a continuation of the Timmy story is being processed. In longer and more complex narratives, the most recently encountered proposition is not necessarily at the end of the causal chain. So, experimentally, it is possible to manipulate whether the final clause or sentence in a story meets the criteria of having antecedents but no consequences in the preceding text. According to the leading edge strategy, this will not matter, so long as a new proposition shares an argument with the most recently encountered proposition. According to the current state strategy, processing times should increase if the most recently encountered proposition does not provide a cause for an incoming, new proposition. When extended narrative texts are analyzed for their causal structure, and when causal structure and argument overlap are used to predict the amount of time it takes people to process and interpret different portions of the text, the current state strategy does a better job of predicting how long it takes people to read different parts of the text. In other words, causal structure, rather than argument overlap, appears to exert a bigger influence on how long it takes people to integrate different bits of narrative texts.

Further evidence against the leading edge strategy, according to which comprehenders link sentences based on associative links, comes from a reading time and memory study conducted by Wolfe and his colleagues (Wolfe, Magliano, & Larsen, 2005). They showed that that semantic (associative) relationships between sentences influenced processing time and memory only when the sentences did not share a clear causal relationship. The current state strategy also does a better job than the leading edge strategy in predicting how people will choose to continue a story (van den Broek, Linzie, Fletcher, & Marsolek, 2000). When given a choice between a more distant proposition that is at the end of the causal chain, and a more recent proposition that is not, speakers base story continuations on the more distant, but more causally central proposition.

The causal structure of a narrative affects how long it takes people to process incoming text, and this is probably because causal structure influences how easy it is to integrate adjacent elements of text. This factor influences the amount of time it takes to process incoming text, but it also affects the likelihood that comprehenders will remember how two pieces of text go together. This has been demonstrated in experiments that systematically varied how causally related adjacent elements of texts were. For example, consider the Timmy mini-story again (Keenan, et al., 1984; see also Duffy, Shinjo, & Myers, 1990; Myers, Shinjo, & Duffy, 1987):[7]

> Timmy's brother punched him again and again. The next day his body was covered in bruises. (High coherence)

These two sentences are highly coherent because they have a strong causal relationship. Timmy getting punched caused him to have bruises. It is possible to manipulate this relationship by replacing the first proposition. For instance, you could have:

> Timmy was riding his bicycle. The next day his body was covered in bruises. (Medium coherence)

These two events do not have the same tight causal relationship as the preceding version, but it is not too hard to connect them together. Riding a bicycle in and of itself does not cause people to have bruises. So the two sentences can not be integrated as easily as the version where the first sentence provides the cause for the second (as defined by Hegel, see above). Most people when they read this second version infer a plausible *bridging* event, such as *Timmy fell off his bicycle*. Falling off one's bicycle is a reasonable consequence of riding a bicycle, and it provides a reasonable cause for having bruises. So, while it takes longer to read this second mini-story (because you need to take time to make the bridging inference), comprehenders can build an integrated representation of the two explicitly mentioned events by inferring the presence of an unmentioned third event. Now, consider this third version of the Timmy story.

> Timmy went to his neighbor's house to play. The next day his body was covered in bruises. (Low coherence)

In this version, it is more difficult to figure out how the two events go together, and there is no clear path to a bridging inference. There are many events that could connect the two sentences, and none of them seems very highly likely or very extremely plausible. Were they playing tackle football? Did he get in a fight with his neighbor? Were they practicing tae kwan do with no pads? Did they get in a car accident? In the low coherence version, it will probably take comprehenders a long time to come up with a plausible way to relate the two events, they are likely to have lower confidence in the accuracy of their inferences, and they may fail to bridge the gap.

In fact, when participants are asked to read the second sentence in each pair (*The next day his body was covered in bruises*), their reading times are a straight line function of causal relatedness. The target sentence is read fastest in the highly coherent version, slower in the medium coherence version, and slowest of all in the low coherence version (Keenan et al., 1984). These differences in reading time likely reflect inferencing processes. No inference is needed in the highly coherent version, an obvious inference is available in the medium coherence version, and it takes a long time to come up with one of many non-obvious inferences in the low coherence version (and some additional time might be necessary to choose which inference to include in the integrated discourse representation). While coherence has a straightforward effect on processing time, it has a less straightforward effect on memory. If the first sentence is given to participants as a retrieval cue, and their task is to remember the target sentence (*The next day his body was covered in bruises*), the best recall is *not* in the highly coherent version, it is actually in the medium coherence version of the Timmy story. Across the three conditions, high coherence, medium coherence, low coherence, memory performance creates an upside-down-U-shaped pattern. Both the high and low coherence versions of the story lead to lower levels of recall than the medium coherence version.

There are likely two factors at work that determine recall performance. First, comprehenders may fail to build an integrated discourse representation at all in the low coherence version. That is, they fail to discover a connection between the two events during on-line interpretive processing, and so, if they store both events in long-term memory, they store them as independent, unrelated events. So, activating one event at test does not lead to any increased activation of the other event at test, because there is no connection between them in long-term memory.

The difference in recall performance between the high and medium coherence condition is most likely a function of *depth of processing*. Depth of processing refers to the fact that the more mental effort we put into processing a stimulus, the stronger our mental representation and memory of that stimulus will be (Craik & Tulving, 1975). Ironically, because the highly coherent pair of sentences does not require much effort to encode, it does not leave much of an impression in memory. By contrast, the moderately coherent pair requires a bit more effort in the form of a bridging inference, but the extra time and effort taken to connect the two sentences and the fact that we engage in a more active process to make the connection both contribute to a stronger integrated representation, and this leads to superior memory performance. In fact, it is possible to have people do more active processing on the highly coherent pairs, by asking them to mentally elaborate on the explicitly stated information. In Susan Duffy and colleagues' (1990) experiment, they made sure that some of their research subjects would elaborate on all of the sentence pairs by instructing them to write down a sentence that could "come between" the two critical sentences (Duffy et al., 1990, p. 30). The other subjects just read the sentences, as in the previous studies. Participants who read and elaborated on pairs of sentences recalled all of the target sentences equally well, whether the original sentence pair had been in the high, moderate, or low coherence condition. Further, in the elaboration condition, recall was just as good after 24 hours as it was if subjects were tested immediately after they read the sentences. This study shows that the way comprehenders approach the text has a big effect on how much they can remember later on. If they use a "deeper" encoding strategy, such as elaboration, memory is much stronger and lasts much longer, and this can overcome features of the text that make it either too coherent or too incoherent to leave a strong memory trace.

The Role of General World Knowledge in Discourse Processing

All current models of discourse processing and interpretation place great emphasis on the role that general world knowledge plays in the construction of coherent representations of texts. What form does this knowledge take and how is it applied as texts are being processed? General world knowledge can affect discourse processing in at least three distinct ways. First, we have knowledge about the way stories are typically structured, and these expectations affect the way we process and remember texts. Second, general world knowledge provides the information we need to make inferences that keep our representations of texts coherent. Third, general world knowledge affects the form and content of the situation models we build to represent what texts are about. Let's consider each of these ideas in turn.

First, because we are storytelling monkeys, we have had a great deal of exposure to narrative. But because different cultures put together narratives in different ways, our expectations for what kinds of events will occur in narratives, and how those events will be expressed, is heavily dependent on the kind of culture we are raised in. For example, Sir Frederic Bartlett (1932/1995) is still widely quoted in psycholinguistics because he showed that memory for texts depends largely upon the expectations and knowledge that comprehenders bring to the task as they are listening to or reading stories. In his landmark study, Bartlett had people read the story below, "War of the Ghosts," and then engage in a variety of re-production tasks.

> *One night two young men from Egulac went down to the river to hunt seals and while they were there it became foggy and calm. Then they heard war-cries, and they thought: "Maybe this is a war-party." They escaped to the shore, and hid behind a log. Now canoes came up, and they heard the noise of paddles, and saw one canoe coming up to them. There were five men in the canoe, and they said:*
>
> *"What do you think? We wish to take you along. We are going up the river to make war on the people."*
>
> *One of the young men said, "I have no arrows."*
>
> *"Arrows are in the canoe," they said.*
>
> *"I will not go along. I might be killed. My relatives do not know where I have gone. But you," he said, turning to the other, "may go with them."*
>
> *So one of the young men went, but the other returned home.*
>
> *And the warriors went on up the river to a town on the other side of Kalama. The people came down to the water and they began to fight, and many were killed. But presently the young man heard one of the warriors say, "Quick, let us go home: that Indian has been hit." Now he thought: "Oh, they are ghosts." He did not feel sick, but they said he had been shot.*
>
> *So the canoes went back to Egulac and the young man went ashore to his house and made a fire. And he told everybody and said: "Behold I accompanied the ghosts, and we went to fight. Many of our fellows were killed, and many of those who attacked us were killed. They said I was hit, and I did not feel sick."*
>
> *He told it all, and then he became quiet. When the sun rose he fell down. Something black came out of his mouth. His face became contorted. The people jumped up and cried.*
>
> *He was dead.*
>
> (Bartlett, 1932/1995)

One task involved a group of people each telling the story from memory to one other person in the group, who would then tell the story to a third person, and so on. The point of the experiment was to find out how close the final version of the story was to the original. Bartlett found that his subjects consistently changed the story as they retold it, in particular, "by adding statements about the characters' thoughts, motivations, intentions, and feelings" (Johnston, 2001, p. 355). Violating people's expectations about story structure influences their ability to remember the verbatim form of the story and elements of meaning, but it also affects how difficult texts are to process and interpret. When story constituents are moved away from the normal locations in stories, reading times slow down, both at the place where the moved constituent is taken from and the new place where it is inserted (Mandler & Goodman, 1982).

Mandler and Johnson (1977) developed an artificial intelligence approach to representing the contents of stories. They reasoned that stories have an internal structure the same way that phrases and sentences have an internal structure. When comprehenders encounter a new story, they use their knowledge of the typical story components and their relations to encode information from the new story. In Western narrative, we expect stories to begin with descriptions of characters and settings; and we expect to encounter a series of episodes that plays out in a temporal order roughly from oldest to most recent, and we expect the episodes to be coherent by virtue of having a causal structure—we expect later episodes to be directly or indirectly caused by the events taking place earlier in the story.[8] As a result, people's memories for stories will be biased in the direction of the typical story structure. When stories actually conform to the typical style, this bias does not lead to substantial differences between the actual story and people's memory for the story. But when the story differs substantially from the normal form (in that culture), as the "War of the Ghosts" tale does, then the way people remember the story will be much different than what the actual text of the story would dictate. This is because, when people read stories such as the "War of the Ghosts", which do not conform to the usual narrative form, they impose the typical narrative structure on the text itself, and so they find causal connections, and they infer particular motives for characters in the story, where none are explicitly stated.[9]

Story grammars represent one kind of *schema*—a structured, pre-existing package of knowledge related to a particular domain (story form, in this case)—but other kinds of schemas also play an important role in discourse comprehension. Stories frequently refer to common experiences, and speakers and writers depend upon comprehenders having knowledge about these common experiences, so that the comprehenders can "fill in the gaps" between pieces of information that are explicitly stated in the text itself. These knowledge schemas, thus, play an important role in inference generation (Schank, 1972; Schank & Abelson, 1977).[10] For example, if we are reading an episode about going to a restaurant, the author is not likely to mention typically occurring objects or characters, like waiters, cooks, tables, and silverware, unless these objects are critical to moving the plot forward or developing the characters. In fact, there is a fair amount of consistency between different individuals in the content and organization of their verbal reports about common events, like going to the doctor or eating at a restaurant (Bower, Black, & Turner, 1979). As a result, if you read

> Susan and Bill went into the restaurant, sat down, and ordered lunch.

This would make sense, because your schema for going to a restaurant contains the information that restaurants have chairs (to sit on) and that you can get food there, including lunch. Further, you would experience very little difficulty integrating the following

> Susan dropped <u>her fork</u>.

even though *fork* was not explicitly mentioned in the context. This is because your pre-existing knowledge schema for the typical objects and events in restaurants includes the information that when people sit down at a restaurant, they sit down at a table, and the table has silverware on it. Schemas also include knowledge about typical events that take place in a given context. And so we would not be surprised to read

> They paid the check and left.

even if the story did not explicitly mention that Susan and Bill finished eating and their waiter brought them a bill. If the specific restaurant in the story violated an aspect of the comprehender's restaurant schema, that would likely be mentioned by the writer (e.g., *Oddly, there was no silverware on the table*). In a similar way, schematic knowledge helps us appreciate when something interesting or unusual happens in the story. So, comprehenders would slow down and pay more attention if our restaurant story continued:

> When Susan bent down to pick up her fork, she saw a bomb ticking away under the next table.

If people did not deploy schematic knowledge while comprehending stories, writers would have to spend pages and pages filling in basic facts, storytelling would be much less efficient, and it would be more difficult to highlight the unusual (which is really the point of telling stories—what speakers and writers really want to do is convey *new* information).

Although world knowledge is normally described in a propositional or fact-based way, comprehenders bring more than that to the table when they are understanding discourse. In particular, people have moral and ethical beliefs that are somewhat independent of their storehouse of factual knowledge (although the facts we learn certainly do influence our moral and ethical judgments). It turns out that our moral and ethical beliefs do affect the way we interpret texts, and those effects can be observed even in the brain wave activity that occurs when people read or listen to texts (van Berkum, in press; van Berkum, Holleman, Nieuwland, Otten, & Murre, 2008).

Building Situation Models

Some accounts of discourse processing adopt the idea that texts can be treated as sets of instructions. The instructions tell the language processing system how to build a situation model. So, to understand how texts are processed, we need to understand what the instructions are, and how comprehenders use these instructions to build situation models. According to the *structure mapping and focus theory* (Sanford & Garrod, 1981, 1998, 2008), texts provide instructions that lead to the automatic activation of situation-specific background knowledge, and they lead comprehenders to focus their attention on specific parts of this background knowledge. One surprising aspect of this kind of account is that, if contextually inappropriate information is included in the verbatim form of the text, but that information is not in the focus of attention, readers will often fail to notice that there is anything strange about the texts. This phenomenon is frequently referred to as the *Moses illusion*, because of studies involving sentences like this (Barton & Sanford, 1993; Bredart & Modolo, 1988; Erickson & Mattson, 1981; Hannon & Daneman, 2001; van Oostendorp & de Mul, 1990):

> How many animals of each type did Moses take on the ark?

Of course, if you are familiar with the "great flood" story from the Bible, you know that it was Noah, and not Moses at all, who put the animals on the boat. But a high proportion of people who read questions like the preceding one fail to note the anomaly, and they go ahead and give the answer "two."

Similar effects occur in longer narratives as well. Barton and Sanford (1993) presented large groups of people with paragraphs about a plane crash, like this one:

> *There was a tourist flight travelling from Vienna to Barcelona. On the last leg of the journey, it developed engine trouble. Over the Pyrenees, the pilot started to lose control. The plane eventually crashed right on the border. Wreckage was equally strewn in France and Spain. The authorities were trying to decide where to bury the survivors.*
>
> *What is the solution to the problem?*

Many of their research subjects wrote solutions like:

> *They should be buried* in their home countries.

Of course, it's possible that participants who wrote answers like this really didn't notice that the paragraph used the word *survivors* rather than the word *deceased* in the critical final sentence. However, some people wrote answers like this:

The *survivors should be buried* where their relatives wish.

These kinds of findings indicate that, when participants start reading a story about a plane crash, they activate situationally relevant information (consistent with schema theory; Schank, 1977; Schank & Abelson, 1977), and they use that activated background knowledge to assign reference to subsequently encountered pieces of the text. When they get to the word *survivors*, they map that word to the activated portion of the background knowledge that corresponds to the concept *deceased* or *victims*, even though the stored lexical meaning of *survivor* is opposite to that of the schematically supplied concept *deceased*. On other words, the situation model has overpowered the lexical level of representation (in fact, comprehenders may have simply bypassed the lexicon and mapped the word *survivor* directly to an already activated portion of their situation models).

The Moses illusion shows that the situation model has the power to override semantic information tied to individual words. But when does this process take place, and how do lexical and contextual information interact to produce meaning? There is considerable evidence that discourse information places immediate constraints on interpretation, such that the "normal" meaning of individual words is never activated if the text is sufficiently constraining (as the Moses illusion texts seem to be) (Camblin, Gordon, & Swaab, 2007; Hess, Foss, & Carroll, 1995; Ledoux, Camblin, Swaab, & Gordon, 2006; van Berkum, Zwitserlood, Hagoort, & Brown, 2003). Normally you would read the sentence *The peanut was in love* much slower than the sentence *The peanut was salted*, and your brain wave activity would show a bigger N400 effect in response to *love* than to *salted*. However, if the discourse context introduces a kind of cartoon scenario where the peanut is portrayed as an animate, sentient being, the N400 effects are reversed. So, the discourse context has overridden the normal features associated with peanuts and replaced them with situation-specific features (Nieuwland & van Berkum, 2006).

Of course, some of the people in the Moses illusion studies do notice that things like burying survivors would be strange, and subsequent studies have shown that at least two factors contribute to the likelihood that an individual comprehender will experience the Moses illusion. First, if the anomalous word shares aspects of meaning with the intended word, the likelihood of experiencing a Moses illusion increases. For example, Moses and Noah are pretty close in meaning in many people's understanding of the terms—they are both older, male, bearded, serious Old Testament characters. When more distinctive characters are introduced into the scenario—Adam, for example—the strength of the Moses illusion is greatly reduced (van Oostendorp & de Mul, 1990). In terms of on-line processing, eye-tracking data show that people notice distinctively anomalous intruders—such as Adam in the Noah scenario—but less distinctively anomalous intruders such as Moses lead to no initial difficulty in the situation model building process. Later on, processing slows down a little. This slow-down probably reflects the mental processes used to assign a new, extended meaning to the intruding word (Stewart, Pickering, & Sturt, 2004).

Another way to reduce the Moses illusion and to make it more likely that comprehenders will detect the anomaly is to use linguistic cues to focus attention on the intruding item. Syntactic structures such as *clefts* (like 16) and *there-insertions* (like 17) offer ways to do this.

(16) It was Moses who took two of each kind of animal on the Ark.
(17) There was a guy called Moses who took two of each kind of animal on the Ark.

When attention is focused on Moses using these kinds of grammatical cues, subjects are more likely to notice that he does not fit in with the great flood scenario, and they are less likely to experience the Moses illusion.

Focusing constructions have effects on other aspects of situation model construction, as they help to regulate the degree of activation that is assigned to different parts of the situation model. Structure mapping and focus theory adopts a view of situation model construction under which characters in stories are represented by *tokens* (mental placeholders in the model), and other information in the stories is then mapped onto activated tokens. If a token has been focused, it is easier to map information onto that token. So, for example, it will be easier to map new information onto the token for *mayor* in sentence (18) than in sentence (19) (from Birch & Garnsey, 1995, p. 289; Birch, Albrecht, & Myers, 2000):

(18) It was the mayor who refused to answer a reporter's question.
(19) The mayor refused to answer a reporter's question.

Because the *it*-cleft is a more *marked* structure (it deviates from the norm, is less frequent, and has explicit cues that differentiate it from the norm), the concept *mayor* is more accessible after (18) than after (19), even though *mayor* is the first-encountered character in both cases, and is in the prominent *subject* syntactic position in (19) and the less prominent *object* position in the main clause in (18).[11] This difference in the *information structure* of the two sentences leads to differences in recognition and recall. Recall and recognition are better when a character is focused (*mayor* in (18)), than when it is not (*mayor* in (19) (Cutler & Fodor, 1979; Singer, 1976). People also spend more time looking at focused than unfocused parts of texts (Zimmer & Engelkamp, 1981), suggesting that they are making special efforts to encode focused concepts (which is also consistent with the structure-building process of laying a foundation). In recognition probe experiments, people respond faster to target words when those target words refer to focused tokens than unfocused tokens (Birch & Garnsey, 1995; Birch et al., 2000). All of these findings suggest that focused parts of text enjoy higher than normal levels of activation in the comprehender's situation model.

Languages provide other ways besides syntactic position to signal comprehenders to boost the activation of specific parts of their situation models. English has cues that signal comprehenders that particular concepts will be referred to in the future. These cues are called *cataphors*, and elements in a discourse that are *cataphorically marked* receive higher degrees of activation and are more resistant to having their activations reduced by other elements of the comprehender's situation model (Gernsbacher & Jescheniak, 1995; Jescheniak, 2000). For example, speakers can use loudness—*spoken stress*—to mark parts of the discourse that should be kept more available than normal. When the loudness of nouns in a spoken discourse was manipulated (as in the verbal equivalent of *Susan needed to buy an ASHTRAY* versus *Susan needed to buy an ashtray*), people respond to the probe word *ashtray* faster after they hear a sentence where *ashtray* is louder than when it is spoken at a lower volume. People also mark elements of a discourse that they will continue to talk about using the indefinite article *this* (even children do this; Wright & Givón, 1987). The indefinite *this* has a similar effect to spoken stress on the activation of concepts in a comprehender's situation model. When a concept is introduced with the indefinite *this* (as in *Susan needed to buy <u>this</u> ashtray* versus *Susan needed to buy <u>an</u> ashtray*), people respond to the probe word *ashtray* faster than if the concept were introduced with the more commonly encountered indefinite article *a*/*an* (Gernsbacher & Shroyer, 1989). Further, when concepts are introduced with these cataphoric devices, they resist being deactivated or suppressed when other concepts are introduced into the discourse. Normally, if speakers introduce a new topic, previously encountered information becomes less active or accessible. So, if *Susan saw an ashtray* was followed by *and then she found an end table*, normally the accessibility of *ashtray* would decrease after *end table* was introduced into the discourse. So, reaction time to the probe word *ashtray* generally increases after comprehenders process the words *end table.*[12] However, when *ashtray* is marked by spoken stress or the indefinite *this*, its activation level remains high even after comprehenders encountered *end table*, and so reaction times to the probe word *ashtray* remain fast.

Inferencing: Memory-Based Account of Discourse Processing: Minimalist vs. Constructionist Inferencing

Memory-based text processing accounts appeal to general memory processes to predict and explain how comprehenders will react to texts as they read them and how the texts will be remembered over the long term. General working memory functions lead to *primacy* and *recency* effects (Deese & Kaufman, 1957). Almost totally regardless of the kinds of stimuli people are exposed to, they remember stimuli at or near the beginning of the group better than later-occurring information (the *primacy effect*); and they remember stimuli at or near the end of the group better than information in the middle (the *recency* effect). Similar effects occur in discourse processing and memory. People remember the first character in a text better than characters that come later (which could reflect a kind of primacy effect); and, immediately after they finish processing a piece of text, recently encountered parts of the text are remembered better than earlier occurring parts of the text (a kind of recency effect) (e.g., Gernsbacher et al.,1989).

According to the memory-based approach, texts activate information from long-term memory by a process of *resonance* (as in Doug Hintzman's *Minerva* computational model of memory processing; Hintzman, 2001). Resonance activates information from long-term memory depending on how closely related the information conveyed by the text matches or is associated with the information stored in long-term memory. As Gerrig and McKoon (1998, p. 69) indicate, "the degree to which specific information in memory will be evoked depends on the strength of the association between the cue in short-term memory and the information in long-term memory." Further, knowledge activation occurs automatically (we can't control it) and the activation process is very dumb. It does not select information based on relevance, or interest, it just activates whatever information has an association of any kind to the bit of text that is being processed at the moment. As Kintsch notes (Kintsch, et al., 1990, p. 136),

> *Comprehension is simulated as a production system, the rules of which operate at various levels: some build propositions from the linguistic information provided by the text; some generate macropropositions; some retrieve knowledge from the comprehender's long-term memory that is related to the text, thus serving as mechanisms for elaboration and inference. All these rules share one general characteristic: they are weak, "dumb" rules that do not always achieve the desired results. In addition to what should have been constructed, these rules generate redundant, useless, and even contradictory material.*

The memory-based approach to discourse processing contrasts with other more "top-down" approaches, which assume that a reader's goals and "search for meaning" play a more active role in the construction of mental representations from texts (e.g., Singer et al., 1994).

One of the potential benefits of a fast, dumb knowledge-activation process is that when concepts, characters, or objects are explicitly mentioned in texts, they will already have had their activation and accessibility boosted by virtue of their associations with previously processed parts of the text (Gerrig & McKoon, 1998). This notion of *readiness* suggests that the fast, automatic activation of associated knowledge will speed discourse comprehension by simplifying the task of figuring out what the explicitly mentioned information refers to. Another benefit of memory-based text processing is that using a fast, dumb, associative mechanism limits the number of inferences that the reader will draw from any given text. Given the huge store of knowledge that comprehenders bring to the text interpretation process, an unconstrained inference process would result in massive numbers of inferences, most of which would not be relevant to either the author's intent or the comprehender's goals in reading the text. By limiting activation to only the information in long-term memory most closely associated with the set of propositions active in working memory, the information overload that unlimited inference entails can be avoided. An additional claim is that information explicitly provided by texts can activate associated information from long-term memory, even if the text does not directly refer to the associated information (McKoon, Gerrig, & Greene, 1996; see also Deese, 1959; Roediger & McDermott, 2000).

In the memory-based approach, information becomes activated when it is associated with the current state of the working memory system, and information decays or has its activation reduced unless it is refreshed by new information conveyed by the text. Information explicitly conveyed by a text can activate information from long-term memory because the explicitly conveyed information has a pre-existing association to information in long-term memory (i.e., words have standard meanings that can be accessed from the lexicon during discourse processing) and the text itself can set up new associations that are then stored as part of the long-term memory representation of the discourse. Evidence for this latter type of association comes from experiments on anaphoric reference. If *Susan* and *Jane* discuss a third character, *Ted*, an episode that brings Susan and Jane back together will increase Ted's activation level and make him more accessible (McKoon, et al., 1996; Gerrig & McKoon, 1998). As a result, subjects in experiments will respond to the word *Ted* faster and will be more capable of figuring out the connection between a pronoun and *Ted*. This reactivation of the third character happens even when the text only alludes to an episode involving him or her. The text does not have to explicitly mention the third character. Thus, reading this story has created a new set of associations in long-term memory between the characters that interacted, even indirectly, in the story.

One of the areas where memory-based text processing and other approaches diverge is in the area of inference generation. Specifically, accounts differ as to which kinds of inferences are drawn naturally by comprehenders as they are in the act of interpreting texts. The memory-based position says that very few inferences are drawn during the actual process of interpretation, and those inferences that are drawn are constructed by automated mental processes. This notion of *minimal inference* says that inferences will be drawn under only two limited conditions. First, inferences will be drawn if they are necessary to establish cohesion between adjacent parts of the text (two sentences, say). Second, inferences will be drawn if the inferences are based on "quickly and easily available" information (McKoon & Ratcliff, 1992, p. 441). So, in cases like those in the Keenan et al. "Timmy" experiments, causal inferences will be drawn because they are necessary for the information in the two sentences to be integrated into a coherent whole. But other kinds of inferences may not be drawn (see the box on p. 222 for some of the more common types of inferences). For example, if you read *The delicate vase fell off the high shelf*, and the text does not explicitly state what happened to the vase, you might infer that the vase broke. Similarly, if you read the sentence *The woman stirred her coffee*, you might infer that she used a spoon (rather than a fork or her fingers). According to the minimal inference hypothesis, none of these inferences are drawn, and so the associated information, *broke* for the causal inference and *spoon* for the instrument inference, would *not* become activated when you read *The delicate*

SOME KINDS OF INFERENCES

- *Causal*
  The delicate vase fell off the shelf. *Inference*: It broke.
- *Bridging*
  Timmy was riding his bike. He came home covered with scrapes and bruises. *Inference*: Timmy fell off his bike.
- *Instrument*
  The woman stirred her coffee. *Inference*: She used a spoon.
- *Elaborative*
  Dave ate four pounds of crab. *Inference*: Dave likes crab.
- *Goal*
  Susan left early for the birthday party. She stopped at the mall on the way. *Inference*: Susan wanted to buy a present.

vase fell off the high shelf and *The woman stirred her coffee*. You *would* make the inference *Timmy fell* in the bridging inference case, because that event (or one very much like it) is needed to tie the two sentences together.

A large number of experiments have tried to test exactly when people make different kinds of inferences when they read or listen to stories (see Zwaan, 2006, for a review). The general consensus is that bridging inferences are routinely drawn, elaborative inferences are rarely drawn, and causal and instrument inferences are drawn under very limited circumstances. For example, instrument inferences are drawn quickly if the instrument has been explicitly introduced previously in the discourse and the context selects very strongly for one particular instrument. Most people stir coffee with a spoon almost all of the time they stir coffee, so that context is highly constraining. Consistent with the minimal inference hypothesis, comprehenders appear to avoid drawing some inferences that they might reasonably draw.

This does not mean that the minimal inference hypothesis makes the correct prediction all of the time, however. For example, according to the minimal inference position, inferences will be drawn only if the information needed to draw the inference is readily available or the information is necessary to establish cohesion between adjacent elements in the text (that is to establish *local* coherence). However, some evidence suggests that comprehenders make inferences when the text is locally coherent—each adjacent element has a clear relation to the preceding and following elements—and the information needed for the inference is distant in the surface form, and so should not be quickly and easily available (Long, Golding, & Graesser, 1992; Singer et al., 1992; Singer et al., 1994).

Take a moment to read the following story (Goal inference story from Singer, 1993, in Singer et al., 1994, p. 432):

> *Valerie left early for the birthday party. She checked the contents of her purse. She backed out of the driveway. She headed north on the freeway. She exited at Antelope drive. She spent an hour shopping at the mall.*

[The control condition starts with the sentence: *Valerie left the birthday party early.*]
Because the story refers to Valerie in each sentence, the story is locally coherent throughout—each sentence can be related to the preceding and following sentences because of argument

overlap. Under these conditions, no inference is necessary to establish coherence. Nonetheless, when people read the final sentence *Valerie spent an hour shopping at the mall*, they very quickly verify the statement *Birthday parties involve presents* (and they do so faster than in the control condition, which makes the birthday party irrelevant to the rest of the story). Thus, it appears as though subjects in this study inferred Valerie's motive for shopping (i.e., she was looking for a birthday present). This outcome is problematic for the minimal inference position in two ways. First, no inferences should be drawn when the text is locally coherent. Second, by the time people reach the critical final sentence, the information necessary to make the goal inference (that there's a birthday party) should have been long gone from working memory.

There also appear to be individual differences in the extent to which comprehenders incorporate inferred information into their discourse representations, although knowledge activation processes appear to be fairly uniform across groups of better and poorer comprehenders (Long & Chong, 2001; Long, Oppy, & Seely, 1994; 1997). If minimal inference is taken as a universal inference-generation mechanism, it does not explain why some people make inferences while others do not. Because the empirical record provides partial support for both minimalist and constructionist positions, some authors advocate hybrid accounts that factor in both passive, dumb knowledge activation processes and more strategic, top-down inference generation processes (e.g., Long & Lea, 2005; van Den Broek, Rapp, & Kendeou, 2005).

The Neural Basis of Discourse Comprehension

Although scientific investigation of discourse processing is still in its early stages, considerable progress has been made in the last decade in understanding how the brain responds to connected discourse (see Ferstl, 2007; Ferstl et al., 2008, for reviews). In particular, the advent of brain imaging techniques like PET and fMRI has allowed researchers to investigate the links between brain activity and text properties in new ways, and this has led to new insights about how the brain is organized to process discourse.

Language scientists have known for a long time that more coherent text produces different brain wave activity than less coherent texts (Kutas, van Petten, & Kluender, 2006). For example, the initial words of sentences processed in isolation produce larger negative voltage at the scalp (reflected by the N400 ERP wave form) than the same words appearing as part of a connected narrative (Van Petten, 1995). Whether a word makes sense in the context provided by preceding text also modulates the size of the N400 wave form (van Berkum et al., 2003). Violations of background knowledge, whether acquired in the experimental session or brought in via general experience, are also reflected in brain wave activity as indexed by the N400 (Fischler, Childers, Achariyapaopan, & Perry, 1985; Hagoort, Hald, Bastiaansen, & Peterson, 2004; Van Berkum, Hagoort, & Brown, 1999). Notably, these N400 effects really are caused by the fit between the currently focused text and the linguistic and general knowledge context, and not by low-level word-to-word associations (Otten & Van Berkum, 2007). However, other ERP components may also be sensitive to changes in discourse coherence or plausibility. Using ERP methods, Petra Burkhardt tested pairs of sentences that can be easily mapped together on the basis of lexical (word–word) associations (*Yesterday a Ph.D. student was shot downtown. The press reported that the pistol was probably from army stocks;* Burkhardt, 2007, p. 1852) versus sentences that are more difficult to connect (*Yesterday a Ph.D. student was killed … the pistol…; Yesterday a Ph.D. student was*

Table 5.1 Indefinite and definite article conditions (from Robertson et al., 2000, p. 256)

Indefinite article condition	Definite article condition
A grandmother sat at a table.	The grandmother sat at the table.
A child played in a backyard.	The child played in the backyard.
A mother talked on a telephone.	The mother talked on the telephone.
A husband drove a tractor.	The husband drove the tractor.
A grandchild walked up to a door.	The grandchild walked up to the door.
A little boy pouted and acted bored.	The little boy pouted and acted bored.

found dead ... the pistol...). Burkhardt's study showed that the P600 component of the ERP signal increased as the difficulty of the coherence relationship increased.[13]

Some of the early work in brain imaging of discourse processing tried to find out how textual cohesion and coherence affects the brain's response to written text. One way to make a text more or less cohesive and coherent is to manipulate the kinds of *articles* that appear in the text. Generally, the *indefinite article* "*a*"/"*an*" introduces a new topic into the discourse, and so it indicates that there is a break between the new piece of text and what has come before. By contrast, the definite article *the* indicates that the following noun has already been introduced in the discourse context. As such, the definite article tells the comprehender that the new information is closely related to the preceding text, and, rather than preparing for a new concept, the comprehender should search the discourse representation and map the following noun onto a previously introduced referent. Thus, by manipulating whether an article is indefinite or definite, the author can make a text seem more or less cohesive or coherent (see the examples in Table 5.1). Notice how the right-hand definite article version seems more coherent. Part of this is because the definite article makes it easier to connect new sentences to previous ones (e.g., it's easier to map *the grandchild* and *the little boy* together than *a grandchild* and *a little boy*).

David Robertson and his colleagues were interested in finding out whether the brain responds differently to less coherent and more coherent text, so they manipulated the presence of definite articles (Robertson et al., 2000). So, they had people read sets of sentences with and without definite articles and used fMRI to assess which parts of the brain responded more strongly to the different kinds of stimuli.

Figure 5.7 shows that, compared to the definite article condition, the indefinite article condition produced more brain activity in the right hemisphere, but not in the left hemisphere. The black bars show that there were greater increases in blood flow to right-hemisphere regions during processing of the incoherent texts than during processing of the coherent texts. While the effect was in the same direction in the left hemisphere (the white bars), the difference between the two conditions was not statistically significant. Previously, the left hemisphere had been considered the dominant or sole contributor to processing the meaning of language input. This study was one of the first to indicate that right-hemisphere regions play a role in establishing coherence. In particular, the right hemisphere is far more activated when texts lack the cues that normally help comprehenders figure out how different parts of the text go together.[14]

Other brain imaging experiments have attempted to determine what role different parts of the brain play in establishing causal coherence in texts. Some of these studies have

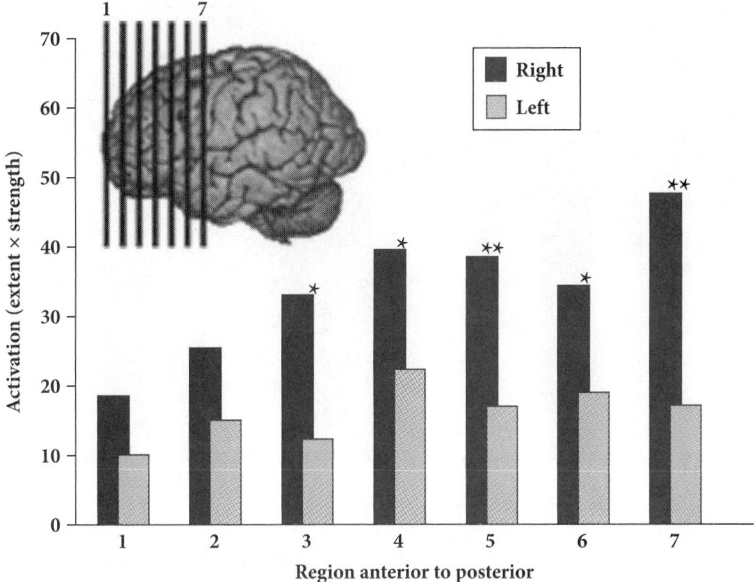

Figure 5.7 The effect of discourse cohesion on the brain's response to discourse (from Robertson et al., 2000, p. 259)

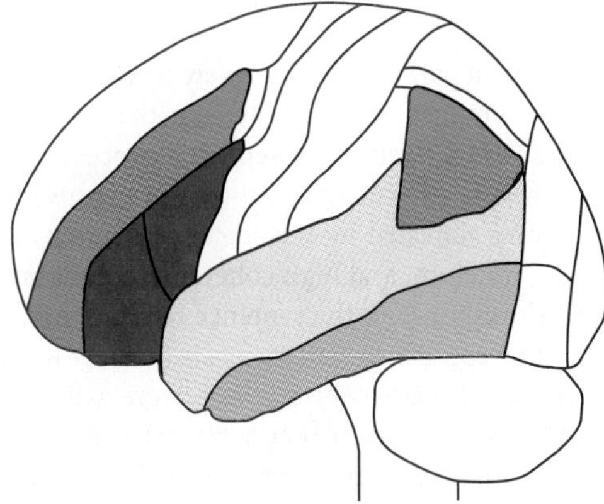

Figure 5.8 Brain regions that were analyzed by Mason & Just (2004, p. 4)

capitalized on a coherence manipulation that produced robust reaction time and memory effects in behavioral studies (Duffy et al., 1990; Keenan et al., 1984; Myers et al., 1987). Rob Mason and Marcel Just performed an fMRI study on sentence pairs like those in the "Timmy" experiments. To analyze their fMRI data, Mason and Just divided the brain into large regions (as shown in Figure 5.8; only the left hemisphere is shown, but Mason and Just analyzed data from both hemispheres). They divided each of these large regions into a set of small cube-shaped regions called voxels. Subjects had their brains scanned as they read highly related (*Timmy's brother punched him … his body was covered in bruises.*), moderately related (*Timmy rode his bike … bruises*), or distantly related pairs of sentences (*Timmy went to the neighbors' … bruises*). To see how the brain responded in each of these conditions, Mason and Just found voxels that had more blood flow in response to people reading the sentences as compared to when people just looked at a fixation cross on the computer screen. Figure 5.9 shows the outcome of this analysis.

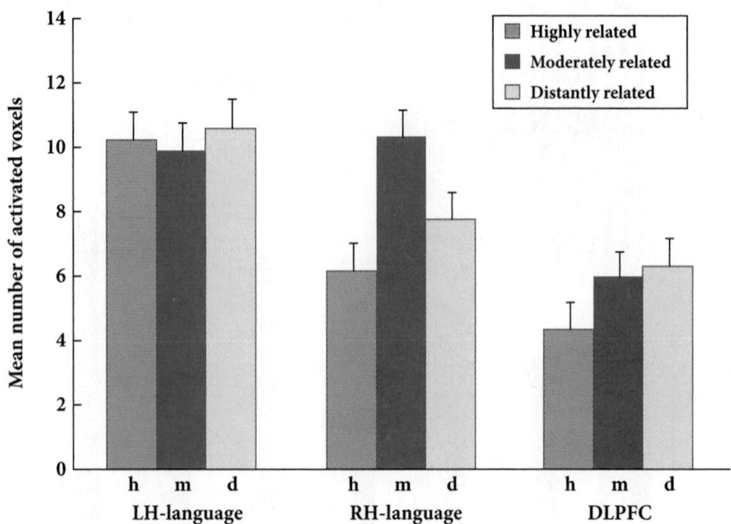

Figure 5.9 The average number of activated voxels in left-hemisphere brain regions (leftmost bars), right-hemisphere brain regions (middle bars) and the dorsolateral prefrontal cortex on both sides of the brain (from Mason & Just, 2004, p. 5). The striped bars show data from the highly related condition. The black bars show data from the moderately related condition. And the white bars show activity in the distantly related condition

To estimate how hard different parts of the brain were working in the different conditions (low, medium, and high coherence), they counted up the number of voxels that were activated (had greater blood flow during the sentence processing task than during the resting look-at-a-fixation-cross task). The leftmost bars in Figure 5.9 show that, in the left hemisphere, many voxels were activated by the sentence reading task, but there were no differences between the low, medium, and high coherence conditions. The next set of bars shows the right hemisphere's response to the sentence reading task. Here, the most voxels were activated by the medium-coherence sentence pair (*Timmy was riding his bike ... The next day his body was covered in bruises*). Fewer voxels were activated by the low and high coherence pairs. The rightmost bars show that a frontal part of the brain (dorsolateral prefrontal cortex, of DLPFC) had greater activation in the medium and low coherence conditions than in the high coherence condition. This part of the brain is thought to be involved when working memory resources are brought to bear on an information processing task, and so activation differences here probably reflect that working memory is needed to make bridging inferences (although the attempt to make a bridging inference may fail in the low coherence condition). The main thing to take away from Figure 5.9 is that, while the right hemisphere does respond differently to different degrees of coherence, the left hemisphere apparently does not (at least, there is no indication in this experiment that the left hemisphere cares whether pairs of sentences are related or not). Thus, one might conclude that, while the left hemisphere figures out what sentences mean, the right hemisphere is responsible for establishing coherence between sentences, or perhaps that the right hemisphere is responsible for drawing inferences.

The conclusion that the right hemisphere is responsible for drawing inferences is consistent with some recent research on the phenomenon of insight. Insight experiences happen when people are working on a problem, and just before they work out the solution, they get the feeling that they know what the solution is (these experiences are sometimes described as "Aha!" moments; Bowden & Beeman, 2003). As panel B in Plate 9 shows, the left hemisphere does not respond differently when people experience an "Aha!" moment of insight and when they do not (Jung-Beeman et al., 2004; see also Beeman & Bowden, 2000; Kounios et al., 2006). But, as Panel C shows, the right hemisphere shows greater neural activity when people have an insight that leads them to solve a problem.

A similar pattern of processing may take place during the generation of inferences. To generate an inference, comprehenders take the information from two adjacent parts of the text and use their background knowledge to come up with a way to connect them. One way to accomplish this, especially when there is no direct overlap between the arguments in two adjacent pieces of text, is to rely on more distant semantic relationships, which would be more likely to be activated in the right hemisphere than the left (Beeman, 1993; Beeman et al., 1994).

Both behavioral and neuroimaging data support the idea that the right hemisphere plays a role in inference generation. In behavioral experiments, semantic priming for target words related to the solution of an insight problem gets bigger as subjects' "Aha!" feelings increase (Bowden & Beeman, 2003). Also, *predictive inferences* appear to engage the right hemisphere more than the left (Beeman, Bowden, & Gernsbacher, 2000). Take, for instance, the sentence *The space shuttle sat on the ground, waiting for the signal.* This sentence might lead you to predict that there will be information forthcoming about the shuttle taking off. So, reading the sentence and making a predictive inference could lead to facilitated processing of the target word *launch* (Beeman et al., 2000, p. 311; Duffy, 1986). To see whether people draw this kind of inference, Mark Beeman and his colleagues presented target words like *launch* in the right visual hemifield. When this is done, the target word is processed first by the left hemisphere. The experiment showed that people processed *launch* no faster than an unrelated control word when the left hemisphere had the first shot at it. However, priming was observed when the word *launch* was presented in the left hemifield and was processed first by the right hemisphere. Similar methods have been used to test the maintenance of topic information (Faust, Barak, & Chiarello, 2006). When topic is manipulated by either having two sentences that refer to the same topic or referring to different topics, priming is observed for left visual field/right-hemisphere targets whether the target word is related to the first or second topic. However, priming in the RVF/left hemisphere is observed only when the target sentence is related to the most recently encountered meaning. These results suggest that the two hemispheres respond to topic information in different ways. The left hemisphere has more specific activation that delays more rapidly, and the right hemisphere has more diffuse activation that lasts longer (consistent with the *coarse coding hypothesis*, Beeman et al., 1994).

Neuroimaging experiments provide additional support. In one fMRI experiment investigating inference generation during the processing of fairly normal stories, greater activation was observed in the right hemisphere, in the right superior temporal lobe to be more exact, when the text supplied information that strongly implied a particular inference (Virtue, Haberman, Clancy, Parrish, & Beeman, 2006). Plate 10 shows areas of the right hemisphere that were more activated when the text implied, but did not explicitly state, a particular event. In that case, and given the degree of textual support for the inference, subjects were likely to infer the "missing" event. When processing of coherent stories is compared to processing of lists of unrelated sentences, substantial differences in activation are observed in the right hemisphere, which suggests that right-hemisphere regions play a role in establishing coherence (Vogeley et al., 2001). Finally, major differences in right-hemisphere activity happen when the ability to map text to a global theme is manipulated. Recall that in the Bransford and Johnson (1972) experiment, participants had a much easier time recalling story elements when elements of the story could be related to a specific scenario (like a young man serenading a young woman by using a set of floating speakers). Similar memory results are obtained when a title is used as the functional equivalent of the picture in the Bransford and Johnson paradigm. In one such study using neural imaging (fMRI) as the dependent measure, participants read paragraphs like this (St. George, Kutas, Martinez, & Sereno, 1999, p. 1318):

> This is very rewarding but tends to be quite expensive even if you own all that you need. The outfit does not really matter. One can get seriously injured without proper instruction even if it comes more naturally to some people than others. Some don't like the smell or the lack of control …

This paragraph makes a lot more sense if you know that the title is "Horseback Riding," because now referring expressions like *outfit* and *smell* can be tied to specific concepts and the entire paragraph can be related to a single, consistent theme. Plate 11 shows the results of an fMRI experiment. In the experiment, people read paragraphs like this one either without a title (where it would be hard to make sense) or with a title (where you could build a much more coherent discourse representation). Plate 12 is a little bit confusing, because the right side of the brain is shown on the left side of the graph. So, first find the right hemisphere. Then compare the amount of activation (the red part) when there is a title (the left-hand picture) versus when there is no title (the right-hand picture). Now look at the right-hand side of Plate 12, which shows the right-hemisphere response when there was a title (top) and when there was no title (bottom). Both figures show that the left-hemisphere activity is about the same whether there is a title or not, but the right hemisphere shows greater activity when the passage has no title and less activity when it does have a title. One way to explain these results is to suppose that the right hemisphere plays a special role in establishing textual coherence by mapping the different parts of the passage onto a central theme. When the passage lacks a title, this kind of processing is more difficult, and so the right hemisphere works harder.[15]

Although the right hemisphere does appear to play a role in inferencing and the establishment of coherence relations between different parts of texts, it would be a mistake to think that all inferencing takes place in the right hemisphere or that the right hemisphere is involved in every kind of inference. One of the earliest neuroimaging studies of auditory discourse processing showed that connected discourse led to greater activation in both the right and left temporal poles (the very frontmost part of the temporal lobes; Mazoyer et al., 1993). When topics are changed across sentence pairs (*Do you believe in angels? Yes, I like to go to camp*) versus kept the same (*Do you believe in angels? Yes, I have my own special angel*), both right- and left-hemisphere regions are activated, although relatively greater activity is observed in the right hemisphere, in both adults and children (Caplan & Dapretto, 2001; Dapretto, Lee, & Caplan, 2005). Additionally, data from patients with damage to the left prefrontal cortex show that they have difficulty establishing coherence relations between adjacent parts of texts, and they also had trouble drawing inferences that would help to maintain coherence (Zalla, Phipps, & Grafman, 2002; see also Ferstl, Guthke, & von Cramon, 2002).

The left hemisphere also appears to play a role in processing stories that involve character's thoughts, beliefs, and emotions. Stories that require people to infer the mental responses of the characters involved in the story are called *theory of mind stories*. When people read such stories, they draw conclusions about characters' thoughts and feelings (Gernsbacher et al., 1992; Gernsbacher et al., 1998). Processing of *theory of mind* stories has been compared to processing of stories that call for inferences about physical, but not mental, events. A theory of mind story might talk about character A getting character B fired (in which case, you might infer that character A responded by feeling guilty). A physical story might talk about a delicate vase falling from a high shelf (in which case, you might infer that the vase broke). When processing of theory of mind stories is compared to processing of physical stories, both of which require inferences, but different kinds of inferences, greater activation is seen in two parts of the left hemisphere (Fletcher et al.,

1995; Mason et al., 2008; see also Maguire, Frith, & Morris, 1999). One is the dorsomedial prefrontal cortex, or DMPC and a part of the cingulate cortex toward the rear of the brain.

The left hemisphere also appears to participate in causal inferencing. For example, although the right hemisphere does seem to respond to texts that call for predictive inferences (see above), behavioral data suggest that the left hemisphere is more responsive to texts that describe causal connections when those texts require a bridging inference. So, if people read, *The shuttle sat on the ground. Then the shuttle disappeared into space*, they bridge the gap between the two sentences by inferring that the shuttle was launched. Under these conditions, *launch* is processed faster than a control word when it is presented in the right visual field (i.e., to the left hemisphere), but not when it is presented in the left visual field (i.e., to the right hemisphere) (Beeman et al., 2000).[16]

Alert readers will have spotted the inconsistency between the Beeman group's results and the Mason and Just imaging data, where the right hemisphere but not the left appeared to respond to texts that differ in the degree of coherence (Beeman et al., 2000; Mason & Just, 2004). Fortunately, we have a more recent fMRI study that helps reconcile this inconsistency (Kuperberg, Lakshmanan, Caplan, & Holcomb, 2006). Gina Kuperberg and her colleagues tested three kinds of sentence pairs: high coherence, medium coherence, and low coherence. They increased the power of their experiment by adding more sentence pairs and by looking for more localized activity. Mason and Just averaged activity across large areas of the brain, and so they may have missed effects limited to smaller brain regions. Kuperberg's group also time-locked their fMRI measurements to just the second sentence in the pair, which is where the degree of coherence becomes apparent, rather than averaging neural activity across both the first and second sentences. Despite these changes, Kuperberg's group did partially replicate the Mason and Just findings. Specifically, they did find evidence that the right hemisphere worked harder when the two sentences were unrelated compared to when the two sentences were highly coherent (as shown in Plate 13). However, where the previous study failed to find different patterns of brain activity in the left hemisphere in the different coherence conditions, Kuperberg's study showed that there were many parts of both the right and left hemispheres that were more responsive to medium coherence sentence pairs than either high or low coherence sentence pairs. The yellow portions of Plate 14 show those parts of the brain that were more active during processing of the second sentence in the medium coherence pairs (compared to the high and low coherence pairs). Notice that there are substantial areas in both hemispheres that respond more strongly in the medium coherence condition.[17] Similarly, there are parts of the brain that are less responsive to the medium coherence stimuli (blue areas in Plate 14). So, Kuperberg's results reinforce the idea that, while the right hemisphere participates in inferencing and the construction of coherent discourse representations, a wide variety of left-hemisphere regions are also involved. In light of these results, it makes more sense to view inferencing and coherence as the outcome of a collaborative process between widely dispersed networks in both hemispheres of the brain, rather than being functions that are carried out in specific locations in the brain. (Kuperberg's study also helps illustrate how quickly brain imaging techniques and experimental design have progressed.)

Summary and Conclusions

This chapter has reviewed three prominent and complementary accounts of discourse processing: construction integration, the structure building framework, and the event indexing models. Each of them makes a unique contribution to our understanding of how people process and interpret narratives. The goal of processing narratives is to build a mental model of the situation described in the real or imaginary world that the story is about. To accomplish this, information that is associated with the explicitly stated contents of the story is combined the comprehender's general world knowledge. This process involves a high-fidelity, but short-lived representation of what the text actually says (the surface model), a more abstract representation that captures the propositions conveyed by the text (the text-base), and a long-lived situation model that incorporates inferences that the comprehender generates herself from the verbatim information in the text and her own store of world knowledge. Inferences, especially causal inferences, play an important role in filling in the gaps in stories when two adjacent elements of the text cannot be readily integrated. Finally, although neurophysiological (ERP) methods are well established in language science, sophisticated neuroimaging techniques have only recently been brought to bear to help us figure out how discourse interpretation processes are implemented in the brain. These newer imaging techniques have already revealed that right-hemisphere structures participate in discourse comprehension in ways that were unknown in the recent past. However, the available data do not support a clear division of labor between the two cerebral hemispheres. Discourse processing and interpretation rely on distributed networks of cooperating neural systems in both hemispheres.

TEST YOURSELF

1. Describe Kintsch's construction–integration account of discourse processing. What kinds of representations are involved? How are they related to one another? How are they built or activated?
2. What are *propositions* and what do they contribute to discourse comprehension? What is the relationship between surface form and propositions? What is the relationship between propositions and situation models? What evidence supports the psychological reality of propositions?
3. What do comprehenders remember after they read a story? Describe an experiment showing that some representations are more durable than others.
4. Describe Gernsbacher's structure building framework. In what ways does it resemble construction–integration? In what ways does it differ? Describe experiments that support the existence of mapping, shifting, enhancement, and suppression and explain how each process contributes to discourse comprehension.
5. What does Zwaan's event indexing model say about discourse processing? What kinds of information do comprehenders put in their mental models? What kinds of evidence support claims made by the event indexing model?
6. What does the causal chain hypothesis say about discourse comprehension? What happens when two adjacent parts of a text do not have an obvious causal connection?
7. Describe different kinds of inferences. What role do inferences play in discourse comprehension? When and how do comprehenders draw inferences?
8. Describe the structure mapping and focus account. How does it relate to the Moses illusion?
9. Which parts of the brain participate in discourse processing? What functions do the left and right hemispheres undertake?

THINK ABOUT IT

1. Find a novel, such as *Moby Dick* or *Roughing It.* Read the first two or three paragraphs. Write down the propositions that appear in each paragraph (in proposition notation form). Draw a diagram that shows how the propositions are related to one another. (Ask your professor for help if you get stuck.)
2. Design an experiment to test the effect of world knowledge on discourse comprehension. Write a story like the "balloon serenade" story. Give your friend a copy without a title and see how long it takes her to read it. Ask her to paraphrase the story or answer comprehension questions. Give another friend a copy with a title and see what happens. What makes one version easier to understand than the other?
3. Read your friend the "War of the Ghosts Story." Ask your friend to write down as much of the story as she can recall. Compare the original to your friend's version. Is there anything missing? Did she add in anything new? What accounts for differences between the original and your friend's version?

Notes

1 The way the situation model is organized also affects how information conveyed by texts is remembered. If comprehenders can build a unified situation model that relates the disparate concepts in a text into a single tight package, all of the information from the text will be roughly equally accessible from a given retrieval cue. However, if the information cannot be represented in a single, unified mental model, and multiple models must be built to accommodate the explicitly stated information, extra time is needed to retrieve information associated with particular retrieval cues (Radvansky, Spieler, & Zacks, 1993).

2 One might also object to this interpretation of the findings by noting that *oil* is in the subordinate clause in sentence (13), and is verified slower, and *oil* is in the main clause in (12), and is verified faster. However, because the order of main and subordinate clauses is flexible, the order of the main and subordinate clauses can be manipulated, and this has not been shown to modify the effects of first mention or the loss of accessibility caused when a new substructure is initiated (Carreiras, Gernsbacher, & Villa, 1995; Gernsbacher et al., 1989).

3 The specific brain regions include the left dorsomedial prefrontal cortex (dMPFC), the temporal poles on both sides of the brain, the left superior temporal gyrus, and the posterior cingulate cortex.

4 Causal relationships are immune to costs associated with the violation of iconicity, possibly because texts that describe causal relationships tap a pre-existing schema.

5 Zwaan and Yaxley (2003) present evidence that an iconicity effect also holds for spatial relations. People respond to target words faster when text is laid out the same way real objects are typically laid out. So, if the test item has the word *attic* printed above the word *basement*, people respond quickly. The same effect does *not* happen if the same two words are printed side by side.

6 There is some uncertainty as to how specific the emotions are that comprehenders attribute to characters (e.g., Gygax, Garnham, & Oakhill, 2004; Gygax, Oakhill, & Garnham, 2003; Gygax, Tapiero, & Caruzzo, 2007).

7 Recent ERP results also support separable effects of different kinds of coherence-establishing mental operations (Yang, Perfetti, & Schmalhofer, 2007). The N400 component indexes the difficulty of constructing a bridging inference, the P300 component indexes the creation of a referential co-indexing of two different but related expressions (e.g., *blew up* versus *exploded*), and the N200 component indexes direct mapping of two identical lexical items across a sentence boundary.

8 One of the notable aspects of postmodern Western literature is the degree to which it diverges from these norms. For example, James Joyce's novel *Ulysses* is famous as the first example of "stream of consciousness" narrative, which more or less preserves temporal order, but which severely violates the expectation of causal coherence. Kurt Vonnegut's novels, such as *Slaughterhouse 5*, have causal structure, but severely violate the

expectation of coherent temporal order, as signaled by one of the great opening sentences in twentieth-century literature: :Listen: Billy Pilgrim has come unstuck in time." But in folk tales and the kinds of stories we tell each other over the dinner table, these aspects of story grammar are more or less fully in place.

9 One of the phenomena that is claimed to support the psychological reality of story grammars and their use in real time to comprehend narrative is that elements that are higher in a story grammar representational hierarchy are remembered better than elements that are lower in the putative hierarchy. However, as far as the author is aware, these analyses have not been conducted when causal relatedness is controlled for. That is, it is not clear whether position in the story structure or position on the causal chain is the actual factor that accounts for the memorability of different parts of stories.

10 There is some uncertainty as to whether schematic knowledge is as structured as Bower et al., and Schank and Abelson described it. Some of the consistency in the way different people report the organization of events in typical episodes, like restaurant scenes and doctor visits, may be because the episodes are conveyed in story format (Mandler & Murphy, 1983). So, it's not clear whether the consistent structure of schemas is the result of structured knowledge, or structure imposed on amorphous knowledge by storytelling conventions. It's probably both.

11 Some accounts propose that clefting does not increase the activation of the focused concept. Rather, clefting helps make the concept that the clefted element refers to distinct from other concepts in the discourse. Hence, clefting raises the accessibility of the clefted element by making it more likely that memory retrieval processes will find the appropriate element when a referring expression is encountered (Foraker & McElree, 2007; see also Gordon, Hendrick, & Johnson, 2001).

12 There is some uncertainty about whether *ashtray*'s activation goes down because *end table* steals some of its activation, or whether *ashtray*'s activation is decreased by enhancement and suppression processes that operate independently on different elements of the discourse. Gernsbacher & Jescheniak (1995) argue that active suppression is a better explanation than competition or activation stealing, because activation estimates for a cataphorically marked expression remain the same when a second cataphorically marked element is introduced into the discourse.

13 The P600 is an effect that is observed in ERP experiments when comprehenders encounter difficulty interpreting a sentence. If a sentence is ungrammatical, it will cause greater positive voltage at the scalp approximately 600 ms after the point where the sentence stops being grammatical.

14 Ferstl and Von Cramon (2001) failed to find right-hemisphere activation for incohesive and incoherent texts, but their study involved pairs of sentences, rather than paragraphs.

15 Maguire et al. (1999) failed to find right-hemisphere activations in a PET imaging experiment that was very similar to the St. George et al. (1999) experiment. Instead, they found that coherence differences modulated activity in a set of left-hemisphere regions. A number of methodological differences, including spoken vs. written text, pictures vs. titles, whole-brain imaging vs. region-of-interest analysis, might account for the difference in outcomes.

16 The magnitude of these priming effects appears to be affected by how much constraint, or predictability, the text provides. The left-hemisphere response to bridging inferences appears to be limited when the text does not strongly predict one particular inference. The right hemisphere seems to activate inference-related concepts whether the text strongly predicts one outcome or not (Virtue, van den Broek, & Linderholm, 2006).

17 These areas include the ventrolateral prefrontal cortices bilaterally (dmPFC), the ventrolateral prefrontal cortex (vlPFC) in the left hemisphere, the angular gyrus/Wernicke's area in the left hemisphere, the inferior temporal lobe in the left hemisphere, and the anterior cingulate gyrus bilaterally.

References

Aaronson, D., & Scarborough, H. S. (1976). Performance theories for sentence coding: Some quantitative evidence. *Journal of Experimental Psychology: Human Perception and Performance, 2*, 56–70.

Baddeley, A. (1972). *Working memory*. Oxford, England: Oxford University Press.

Barsalou, L. W., & Sewell, D. R. (1985). Contrasting the representation of scripts and categories. *Journal of Memory and Language, 24*, 646–665.

Barshi, I. (1997). *Message length and misunderstandings in aviation communication: Linguistic properties and cognitive constraints*. Unpublished doctoral dissertation. Boulder, CO: University of Colorado.

Bartlett, F. C. (1932/1995). *Remembering: A study in experimental and social psychology*. New York: Cambridge University Press.

Barton, S. B., & Sanford, A. J. (1993). A case study of anomaly detection: Shallow semantic processing and cohesion establishment. *Memory & Cognition, 21*, 477–487.

Beeman, M. J. (1993). Semantic processing in the right hemisphere may contribute to drawing inferences from discourse. *Brain & Language, 44,* 80–120.

Beeman, M. J., & Bowden, E. M. (2000). The right hemisphere maintains solution-related activation for yet-to-be-solved problems. *Memory & Cognition, 28,* 1231–1241.

Beeman, M. J., Bowden, E. M., & Gernsbacher, M. A. (2000). Right and left hemisphere cooperation for drawing predictive and coherence inferences during normal story comprehension. *Brain & Language, 71,* 310–336.

Beeman, M. J., Friedman, R. B., Grafman, J., Perez, E., Diamond, S., & Lindsay, M. B. (1994). Summation priming and coarse semantic coding in the right hemisphere. *Journal of Cognitive Neuroscience, 6,* 26–45.

Birch, S. L., Albrecht, J. E., & Myers, J. L. (2000). Syntactic focusing structures influence discourse processing. *Discourse Processes, 30,* 285–304.

Birch, S. L., & Garnsey, S. M. (1995). The effect of focus on memory for words in sentences. *Journal of Memory and Language, 34,* 232–267.

Black, J. B., Turner, T. T., & Bower, G. H. (1979). Point of view in narrative comprehension, memory, and production. *Journal of Verbal Learning and Verbal Behavior, 18,* 187–198.

Bowden, E. M., & Beeman, M. J. (2003). Aha! Insight experience correlates with solution activation in the right hemisphere. *Psychonomic Bulletin & Review, 10,* 730–737.

Bower, G. H., Black, J. B., & Turner, T. J. (1979). Scripts in memory for text. *Cognitive Psychology, 11,* 177–220.

Bower, G. H., & Morrow, D. G. (1990). Mental models in narrative comprehension. *Science, 247,* 44–48.

Bower, G. H., & Rinck, M. (2001). Selecting one among many referents in spatial situation models. *Journal of Experimental Psychology: Learning, Memory, and Cognition, 27,* 81–98.

Bransford, J. D., Barclay, J. R., & Franks, J. J. (1972). Sentence memory: A constructive versus interpretive approach. *Cognitive Psychology, 3,* 193–209.

Bransford, J. D., & Johnson, M. K. (1972). Contextual prerequisites for understanding: Some investigations of comprehension and recall. *Journal of Verbal Learning and Verbal Behavior, 11,* 717–726.

Bredart, S., & Modolo, K. (1988). Moses strikes again: Focalization effects on a semantic illusion. *Acta Psychologica, 67,* 135–144.

Burkhardt, P. (2007). The P600 reflects cost of new information in discourse memory. *Cognitive Neuroscience and Neuropsychology, 18,* 1851–1854.

Camblin, C. C., Gordon, P. C., & Swaab, T. Y. (2007). The interplay of discourse congruence and lexical association during sentence processing: Evidence from ERPs and eye tracking. *Journal of Memory and Language, 56,* 103–128.

Caplan, D. (1972). Clause boundaries and recognition latencies for words in sentences. *Perception and Psychophysics, 12,* 73–76.

Caplan, R., & Dapretto, M. (2001). Making sense during conversation: An fMRI study. *Brain Imaging, 12,* 3625–3632.

Carreiras, M., Gernsbacher, M. A., & Villa, V. (1995). The advantage of first mention in Spanish. *Psychonomic Bulletin & Review, 2,* 125–129.

Choi, S., McDonough, L., Bowerman, M., & Mandler, J. M. (1999). Early sensitivity to language-specific spatial categories in English and Korean. *Cognitive Development, 14,* 241–268.

Cirilo, R. K., & Foss, D. J. (1980). Text structure and reading time for sentences. *Journal of Verbal Learning and Verbal Behavior, 19,* 96–109.

Claus, B., & Kelter, S. (2006). Comprehending narratives containing flashbacks: Evidence for temporally organized representations. *Journal of Experimental Psychology: Learning, Memory, and Cognition, 32,* 1031–1044.

Craik, F. I., & Tulving, E. (1975). Depth of processing and the retention of words in episodic memory. *Journal of Experimental Psychology, 104,* 268–294.

Cutler, A., & Fodor, J. A. (1979). Semantic focus and sentence comprehension. *Cognition, 7,* 49–59.

Dapretto, M., Lee, S. S., & Caplan, R. (2005). A functional magnetic resonance imaging study of discourse coherence in typically developing children. *Brain Imaging, 16,* 1661–1665.

Deese, J. (1959). On the prediction of occurrence of particular verbal intrusions in immediate recall. *Journal of Experimental Psychology, 58,* 17–22.

Deese, J., & Kaufman, R. A. (1957). Serial effects in recall of unorganized and sequentially organized verbal material. *Journal of Experimental Psychology, 54,* 180–187.

De Vega, M. (1995). Backward updating of mental models during continuous reading of narratives. *Journal of Experimental Psychology: Learning, Memory, and Cognition, 21,* 373–385.

De Vega, M., Robertson, D. A., Glenberg, A. M., Kaschak, M. P., & Rinck, M. (2004). On doing two things at once: Temporal constraints on actions in language comprehension. *Memory & Cognition, 32,* 1033–1043.

Duffy, S.A. (1986). Role of expectations in sentence integration. *Journal of Experimental Psychology: Learning, Memory, and Cognition, 12,* 208–219.

Duffy, S. A., Henderson, J. M., & Morris, R. K. (1989). Semantic facilitation of lexical access during sentence processing. *Journal of Experimental Psychology: Learning, Memory, and Cognition, 15,* 791–801.

Duffy, S. A., Shinjo, M., & Myers, J. L. (1990). The effect of encoding task on memory for sentence pairs varying in causal relatedness. *Journal of Memory and Language, 29,* 27–42.

Egidi, G., & Gerrig, R. J. (2006). Readers' experiences of characters' goals and actions. *Journal of Experimental Psychology: Learning, Memory, and Cognition, 32,* 1322–1329.

Erickson, T. D., & Mattson, M. E. (1981). From words to meaning: A semantic illusion. *Journal of Verbal Learning and Verbal Behavior, 20,* 540–551.

Faust, M., Barak, O., & Chiarello, C. (2006). The effects of multiple script priming on word recognition by the two cerebral hemispheres: Implications for discourse processing. *Brain & Language, 99,* 247–257.

Ferstl, E. C. (2007). The functional neuroanatomy of text comprehension: What's the story so far? In F. Schmalhofer & C. A. Perfetti (Eds.), *Higher level language processes in the brain* (pp. 53–102). Mahwah, NJ: Erlbaum.

Ferstl, E. C., Guthke, T., & von Cramon, D. Y. (2002). Text comprehension after brain injury: Left prefrontal lesions affect inference processes. *Neuropsychology, 16,* 292–308.

Ferstl, E. C., Neumann, J., Bogler, C., & Von Cramon, D. Y. (2008). The extended language network: A meta-analysis of neuroimaging studies on text comprehension. *Human Brain Mapping, 29,* 581–593.

Ferstl, E. C., Rinck, M., & Von Cramon, D. Y. (2005). Emotional and temporal aspects of situation model processing during text comprehension: An event-related fMRI study. *Journal of Cognitive Neuroscience, 17,* 724–739.

Ferstl, E. C., & Von Cramon, D. Y. (2001). The role of coherence and cohesion in text comprehension: An event-related fMRI study. *Cognitive Brain Research, 11,* 325–340.

Fischler, I., Childers, D. G., Achariyapaopan, T., & Perry, N. W. (1985). Brain potentials during sentence verification: Automatic aspects of comprehension. *Biological Psychology, 21,* 83–105.

Fletcher, C. R. (1981). Short-term memory processes in text comprehension. *Journal of Verbal Learning and Verbal Behavior, 20,* 564–574.

Fletcher, C. R. (1986). Strategies for the allocation of short-term memory during comprehension. *Journal of Memory and Language, 25,* 43–58.

Fletcher, C. R., & Bloom, C. P. (1988). Causal reasoning in the comprehension of simple narrative texts. *Journal of Memory and Language, 27,* 235–244.

Fletcher, C. R., & Chrysler, S. (1990). Surface forms, textbases, and situation models: Recognition memory for three types of textual information. *Discourse Processes, 13,* 175–190.

Fletcher, C. R., Happe, F., Frith, U., Baker, S.C., Dolan, R.J., Frackowiak, R.S.J., et al. (1995). Other minds in the brain: A functional imaging study of "theory of mind" in story comprehension. *Cognition, 57,* 109–128.

Fletcher, C. R., Hummel, J. E., & Marsolek, C. J. (1990). Causality and the allocation of attention during comprehension. *Journal of Experimental Psychology: Learning, Memory, and Cognition, 16,* 233–240.

Foraker, S., & McElree, B. D. (2007). The role of prominence in pronoun resolution: Active versus passive representations. *Journal of Memory and Language, 56,* 357–383.

Forster, K. (1970). Visual perception on rapidly presented word sequences of varying complexity. *Perception and Psychophysics, 8,* 215–221.

Franks, J. J., & Bransford, J. D. (1974). Memory for syntactic form as a function of semantic context. *Journal of Experimental Psychology, 103,* 1037–1039.

Gernsbacher, M. A. (1985). Surface information loss in comprehension. *Cognitive Psychology, 17,* 324–363.
Gernsbacher, M. A. (1990). *Language comprehension as structure building*. Mahwah, NJ: Erlbaum.
Gernsbacher, M. A. (1993). Less skilled readers have less efficient suppression mechanisms. *Psychological Science, 4,* 294–298.
Gernsbacher, M. A. (1995). The mechanisms of suppression and enhancement in comprehension. *Canadian Psychology/Psychologie Canadienne, 36,* 49–50.
Gernsbacher, M. A. (1996). The structure-building framework: What it is. What it might also be, and why. In B. K. Britton & A. E. Graesser (Eds.), *Models of understanding text* (pp. 289–312). Mahwah, NJ: Erlbaum.
Gernsbacher, M. A., & Faust, M. E. (1991). The mechanism of suppression: A component of general comprehension skill. *Journal of Experimental Psychology: Learning, Memory, and Cognition, 17,* 245–262.
Gernsbacher, M. A., Goldsmith, H. H., & Robertson, R. W. (1992). Do readers mentally represent characters' emotional states? *Cognition and Emotion, 6,* 89–111.
Gernsbacher, M. A., Hallada, B. M., & Robertson, R. W. (1998). How automatically do readers infer fictional characters' emotional states? *Scientific Studies of Reading, 2,* 271–300.
Gernsbacher, M. A., & Hargreaves, D. J. (1988). Accessing sentence participants: The advantage of first mention. *Journal of Memory and Language, 27,* 699–717.
Gernsbacher, M. A., Hargreaves, D. J., & Beeman, M. (1989). Building and accessing clausal representations: The advantage of first mention versus the advantage of clause recency. *Journal of Memory and Language, 28,* 735–755.
Gernsbacher, M. A., & Jescheniak, J. D. (1995). Cataphoric devices in spoken discourse. *Cognitive Psychology, 29,* 24–58.
Gernsbacher, M. A., & Robertson, R. W. (1992). Knowledge activation versus sentence mapping when representing fictional characters' emotional states. *Language and Cognitive Processes, 7,* 353–371.
Gernsbacher, M. A., & Shroyer, S. (1989). The cataphoric use of the indefinite *this* in spoken narratives. *Memory & Cognition, 17,* 536–540.
Gernsbacher, M. A., Varner, K. R., & Faust, M. E. (1990). Investigating individual differences in general comprehension skill. *Journal of Experimental Psychology: Learning, Memory, and Cognition, 16,* 430–445.
Gerrig, R. J., & McKoon, G. (1998). The readiness is all: The functionality of memory-based text processing. *Discourse Processes, 26,* 67–86.
Glanzer, M., & Cunitz, A. R. (1966). Two storage mechanisms in free recall. *Journal of Verbal Learning and Verbal Behavior, 5,* 351–360.
Glenberg, A. M., Meyer, M., & Lindem, K. (1987). Mental models contribute to foregrounding during text comprehension. *Journal of Memory and Language, 26,* 69–83.
Goetz, E. T., Anderson, R. C., & Schallert, D. L. (1981). The representation of sentences in memory. *Journal of Verbal Learning and Verbal Behavior, 20,* 369–385.
Gordon, P. C., Hendrick, R., & Johnson, M. (2001). Memory interference during language processing. *Journal of Experimental Psychology: Learning, Memory, and Cognition, 27,* 1411–1423.
Graesser, A. C. (1981). *Prose comprehension beyond the word.* New York: Springer.
Graesser, A. C., Singer, M., & Trabasso, T. (1994). Constructing inferences during text comprehension. *Psychological Review, 101,* 371–395.
Gygax, P., Garnham, A., & Oakhill, J. (2004). Inferring characters' emotional states: Can readers infer specific emotions? *Language and Cognitive Processes, 19,* 613–638.
Gygax, P., Oakhill, J., & Garnham, A. (2003). The representation of characters' emotional responses: Do readers infer specific emotions? *Cognition and Emotion, 17,* 413–428.
Gygax, P., Tapiero, I., & Caruzzo, E. (2007). Emotion inferences during reading comprehension: What evidence can the self-paced reading paradigm provide? *Discourse Processes, 44,* 33–50.
Haberlandt, K. (1980). Story grammar and reading time of story constituent. *Poetics, 9,* 99–118.
Hagoort, P., Hald, L., Bastiaansen, M., & Petersson, K. M. (2004). Integration of word meaning and world knowledge in language comprehension. *Science, 304,* 438–441.
Hannon, B., & Daneman, M. (2001). Susceptibility to semantic illusions: An individual differences perspective. *Memory & Cognition, 29,* 449–462.

Haviland, S. E., & Clark, H. H. (1974). What's new? Acquiring new information as a process in comprehension. *Journal of Verbal Learning and Verbal Behavior, 13,* 512–521.

Hess, D. J., Foss, D. J., & Carroll, P. (1995). Effects of global and local context on lexical processing during language comprehension. *Journal of Experimental Psychology: General, 124,* 62–82.

Hintzman, D. L. (2001). Similarity, global matching, and judgments of frequency. *Memory & Cognition, 29,* 547–556.

Horton, W. S., & Rapp, D. N. (2003). Out of sight, out of mind: Occlusion and the accessibility of information in narrative comprehension. *Psychonomic Bulletin & Review, 10,* 104–109.

Jacoby, L. L., Woloshyn, V., & Kelley, C. (1989). Becoming famous without being recognized: Unconscious influences of memory produced by dividing attention. *Journal of Experimental Psychology: General, 118,* 115–125.

Jescheniak, J. (2000). The cataphoric use of spoken stress in narratives. *Psychological Research, 63,* 14–21.

Johnson, M. K., Bransford, J. D., & Solomon, S. K. (1973). Memory for tacit implications of sentences. *Journal of Experimental Psychology, 98,* 203–205.

Johnson, M. K., Doll, T. J., Bransford, J. D., & Lapinski, R. H. (1974). Context effects in sentence memory. *Journal of Experimental Psychology, 103,* 358–360.

Johnson-Laird, P. N. (1983). *Mental models.* Cambridge, MA: Harvard University Press.

Johnston, E. B. (2001). The repeated reproduction of Bartlett's *Remembering. History of Psychology, 4,* 341–366.

Jung-Beeman, M., Bowden, E. M., Haberman, J., Frymiare, J. L., Arambel-Liu, S., Greenblatt, R., et al. (2004). Neural activity observed in people solving verbal problems with insight. *Public Library of Science – Biology, 2,* 500–510.

Keenan, J. M., Bailet, S. D., & Brown, P. (1984). The effects of causal cohesion on comprehension and memory. *Journal of Verbal Learning and Verbal Behavior, 23,* 115–126.

Keenan, J. M., MacWhinney, B., & Mayhew, D. (1977). Pragmatics in memory: A study of natural conversation. *Journal of Verbal Learning and Verbal Behavior, 16,* 549–560.

Kelter, S., Kaup, B., & Claus, B. (2006). Representing a described sequence of events: A dynamic view of narrative comprehension. *Journal of Experimental Psychology: Learning, Memory, and Cognition, 30,* 451–464.

Kintsch, W. (1988). The use of knowledge in discourse processing: A construction–integration model. *Psychological Review, 95,* 163–182.

Kintsch, W. (1994). Discourse processes. In G. d'Ydewalle, P. Eelen, & P. Bertelson (Eds.), *International perspectives on psychological science: Vol. 2. The state of the art* (pp. 135–155). Hillsdale, NJ: Erlbaum.

Kintsch, W. (1998). *Comprehension: A paradigm for cognition.* Cambridge, England: Cambridge University Press.

Kintsch, W., & Keenan, J. (1973). Reading rate and retention as a function of the number of propositions in the base structure of sentences. *Cognitive Psychology, 5,* 257–279.

Kintsch, W., & van Dijk, T. A. (1978). Towards a model of text comprehension and production. *Psychological Review, 85,* 363–394.

Kintsch, W., Welsch, D., Schmalhofer, F., & Zimny, S. (1990). Sentence memory: A theoretical analysis. *Journal of Memory and Language, 29,* 133–159.

Kosslyn, S. M. (1973). Scanning visual images: Some structural implications. *Perception and Psychophysics, 14,* 90–94.

Kounios, J., Frymiare, J. L., Bowden, E. M., Fleck, J. I., Subramaniam, K., Parrish, T. B., et al. (2006). The prepared mind: Neural activity prior to problem presentation predicts subsequent solution by sudden insight. *Psychological Science, 17,* 882–890.

Kuperberg, G. R., Lakshmanan, B. M., Caplan, D. N., & Holcomb, P. J. (2006). Making sense of discourse: An fMRI study of causal inferencing across sentences. *Neuroimage, 33,* 343–361.

Kutas, M., van Petten, C., & Kluender, R. (2006). Psycholinguistics electrified II (1994–2005). In M. J. Traxler & M. A. Gernsbacher (Eds.), *The handbook of psycholinguistics* (2nd ed., pp. 725–764). Amsterdam, The Netherlands: Elsevier.

Ledoux, K., Camblin, C. C., Swaab, T. Y., & Gordon, P. C. (2006). Reading words in discourse: The modulation of lexical priming effects by message-level context. *Behavioral and Cognitive Neuroscience Reviews, 5,* 107–127.

Long, D. L., & Chong, J. L. (2001). Comprehension skill and global coherence: A paradoxical picture of poor comprehenders' abilities. *Journal of Experimental Psychology: Learning, Memory, and Cognition, 27,* 1424–1429.

Long, D. L., Golding, J. M., & Graesser, A. C. (1992). A test of the on-line status of goal-related inferences. *Journal of Memory and Language, 31,* 634–647.

Long, D. L., & Lea, R. B. (2005). Have we been searching for meaning in all the wrong places? Defining the "search after meaning" principle in comprehension. *Discourse Processes, 39,* 279–298.

Long, D. L., Oppy, B. J., & Seely, M. R. (1994). Individual differences in the time course of inferential processing. *Journal of Experimental Psychology: Learning, Memory, and Cognition, 20,* 1456–1470.

Long, D. L., Oppy, B. J., & Seely, M. R. (1997). Individual differences in readers' sentence- and text-level representations. *Journal of Memory and Language, 36,* 129–145.

Long, D. L., Seely, M. R., & Oppy, B. J. (1999). The strategic nature of less skilled readers' suppression problems. *Discourse Processes, 27,* 281–302.

Magliano, J. P., Taylor, H. A., & Kim, H-J. J. (2005). When goals collide: Monitoring the goals of multiple characters. *Memory & Cognition, 33,* 1357–1367.

Maguire, E. A., Frith, C. D., & Morris, R. G. M. (1999). The functional neuroanatomy of comprehension and memory: The importance of prior knowledge. *Brain: A Journal of Neurology, 122,* 1839–1850.

Mandler, J. M. (1986). On the comprehension of temporal order. *Language and Cognitive Processes, 1,* 309–320.

Mandler, J. M., & Goodman, M. S. (1982). On the psychological validity of story structure. *Journal of Verbal Learning and Verbal Behavior, 21,* 507–523.

Mandler, J. M., & Johnson, N. S. (1977). Remembrance of things parsed: Story structure and recall. *Cognitive Psychology, 9,* 111–151.

Mandler, J. M., & Murphy, C. M. (1983). Subjective judgments of script structure. *Journal of Experimental Psychology Learning, Memory, and Cognition, 9,* 534–543.

Mason, R. A., & Just, M. A. (2004). How the brain processes causal inferences in text: A theoretical account of generation and integration component processes utilizing both cerebral hemispheres. *Psychological Science, 15,* 1–7.

Mason, R. A., Williams, D. L., Kana, R. K., Minshew, N., & Just, M. A. (2008). Theory of mind disruption and recruitment of the right hemisphere during narrative comprehension in autism. *Neuropsychologia, 46,* 269–280.

Mazoyer, B. M., Tzourio, N., Frak, V., Syrota, A., Murayama, N., Levrier, O., et al. (1993). The cortical representation of speech. *Journal of Cognitive Neuroscience, 5,* 467–479.

McKoon, G., Gerrig, R. J., & Greene, S. B. (1996). Pronoun resolution without pronouns: Some consequences of memory-based text processing. *Journal of Experimental Psychology: Learning, Memory, and Cognition, 22,* 919–932.

McKoon, G., & Ratcliff, R. (1992). Inference during reading. *Psychological Review, 99,* 440–466.

McKoon, G., Ratcliff, R., & Ward, G. (1994). Testing theories of language processing: An empirical investigation of the on-line lexical decision task. *Journal of Experimental Psychology: Learning, Memory, and Cognition, 20,* 1219–1228.

Miller, G. (1956). The magic number seven plus or minus two: Some limits on our capacity for processing information. *Psychological Review, 63,* 81–97.

Morrow, D. G., Bower, G. H., & Greenspan, S. L. (1989). Updating situation models during narrative comprehension. *Journal of Memory and Language, 28,* 292–312.

Morrow, D. G., Greenspan, S. L., & Bower, G. H. (1987). Accessibility and situation models in narrative comprehension. *Journal of Memory and Language, 26,* 165–18.

Münte, T. F., Schiltz, K., & Kutas, M. (1998). When temporal terms belie conceptual order. *Nature, 395,* 71–73.

Myers, J. L., Shinjo, M., & Duffy, S. A. (1987). Degree of causal relatedness and memory. *Journal of Memory and Language, 26,* 453–465.

Neely, J. H. (1977). Semantic priming and retrieval from lexical memory: Roles of inhibitionless spreading activation and limited-capacity attention. *Journal of Experimental Psychology: General, 106,* 226–254.

Neisser, U. (1967). *Cognitive psychology*. New York: Appleton-Century-Crofts.

Nieuwland, M. S., & van Berkum, J. J. A. (2006). When peanuts fall in love: N400 evidence for the power of discourse. *Journal of Cognitive Neuroscience, 18,* 1098–1111.

Onifer, W., & Swinney, D. A. (1981). Accessing lexical ambiguities during sentence comprehension: Effects of frequency of meaning and contextual bias. *Memory & Cognition, 9,* 225–236.

Otten, M. & Van Berkum, J. J. A. (2007). What makes a discourse constraining? Comparing the effects of discourse message and scenario fit on the discourse-dependent N400 effect. *Brain Research, 1153,* 166–177.

Perfetti, C. A., & Britt, M. A. (1995). Where do propositions come from? In C. A. Weaver, S. Mannes, & C. R. Fletcher (Eds.), *Discourse comprehension: Essays in honor of Walter Kintsch* (pp. 11–34). Hillsdale, NJ: Erlbaum.

Peracchi, K. A., & O'Brien, E. (2004). Character profiles and the activation of predictive inferences. *Memory & Cognition, 32,* 1044–1052.

Potts, G. R., Keenan, J. M., & Golding, J. M. (1988). Assessing the occurrence of elaborative inferences: Lexical decision versus naming. *Journal of Memory and Language, 27,* 399–415.

Pratchett, T. (2007). *The Hogfather*. Santa Monica, CA: Genius Entertainment.

Radvansky, G. A., Spieler, D. H., & Zacks, R. T. (1993). Mental model organization. *Journal of Experimental Psychology: Learning, Memory, and Cognition, 19,* 95–114.

Rapp, D. N., Gerrig, R. J., & Prentice, D. A. (2001). Readers' trait-based models of characters in narrative comprehension. *Journal of Memory and Language, 45,* 737–750.

Rapp, D. N., Klug, J. L., & Taylor, H. A. (2006). Character movement and the representation of space during narrative comprehension. *Memory & Cognition, 34,* 1206–1220.

Rapp, D. N., & Taylor, H. A. (2004). Interactive dimensions in the construction of mental representations for text. *Journal of Experimental Psychology: Learning, Memory, and Cognition, 30,* 988–1001.

Ratcliff, R., & McKoon, G. (1978). Priming in item recognition: Evidence for the propositional structure of sentences. *Journal of Verbal Learning & Verbal Behavior, 17,* 403–417.

Rayner, K., & Duffy, S. A. (1988). On-line comprehension processes and eye movements during reading. In M. Daneman, G. E. Mackinnon, & W. T. Garry (Eds.), *Reading research: Advances in theory and practice* (pp. 13–66). San Diego, CA: Academic.

Richards, E., & Singer, M. (2001). Representation of complex goal structures in narrative comprehension. *Discourse Processes, 31,* 111–135.

Rinck, M., Hähnel, A., & Becker, G. (2001). Using temporal information to construct, update, and retrieve situation models of narratives. *Journal of Experimental Psychology: Learning, Memory, and Cognition, 27,* 67–80.

Robertson, D. A., Gernsbacher, M. A., Guidotti, S. J., Robertson, R. W., Irwin, W., Mock, B. J., et al. (2000). Functional neuroanatomy of the cognitive process of mapping during discourse comprehension. *Psychological Science, 11,* 255–260.

Roediger, H. L., III, & McDermott, K. B. (2000). Tricks of memory. *Current Directions in Psychological Science, 9,* 123–127.

St. George, M., Kutas, M., Martinez, A., & Sereno, M. I. (1999). Semantic integration in reading: Engagement of the right hemisphere during discourse processing. *Brain, 122,* 1317–1325.

Sanford, A. J., & Garrod, S. C. (1981). *Understanding written language*. Chichester, England: John Wiley & Sons, Ltd.

Sanford, A. J., & Garrod, S. C. (1998). The role of scenario mapping in text comprehension. *Discourse Processes, 26,* 159–190.

Sanford, A. J., & Garrod, S. C. (2008). Memory-based approaches and beyond. *Discourse Processes, 39,* 205–224.

Schank, R. C. (1972). Conceptual dependency: A theory of natural language understanding. *Cognitive Psychology, 3,* 552–631.

Schank, R. C., & Abelson, R. P. (1977). *Scripts, plans, goals and understanding: An inquiry into human knowledge structures*. Oxford, England: Lawrence Erlbaum.

Seidenberg, M. S., Tanenhaus, M. K., Leiman, J. M., & Bienkowski, M. (1982). Automatic access of the meanings of ambiguous words in context: Some limitations of knowledge-based processing. *Cognitive Psychology, 14,* 489–537.

Shepard, R. N., & Metzler, J. (1971). Mental rotation of three-dimensional objects. *Science, 171,* 701–703.

Singer, M. (1976). Thematic structure and the integration of linguistic information. *Journal of Verbal Learning and Verbal Behavior, 15,* 549–558.

Singer, M., Graesser, A. C., & Trabasso, T. (1994). Minimal or global inference during reading. *Journal of Memory and Language, 33,* 421–441.

Singer, M., & Halldorson, M. (1996). Constructing and validating motive bridging inferences. *Cognitive Psychology, 30,* 1–38.

Singer, M., Halldorson, M., Lear, J. C., & Andrusiak, P. (1992). Validation of causal bridging inferences in discourse understanding. *Journal of Memory and Language, 31,* 507–524.

Singer, M., & Richards, E. (2005). Representing complex narrative goal structures: Competing memory-based and situational influences. *Discourse Processes, 39,* 189–204.

Stewart, A. J., Pickering, M. J., & Sturt, P. (2004). Using eye movements during reading as an implicit measure of the acceptability of brand extensions. *Applied Cognitive Psychology, 18,* 697–709.

Suh, S., & Trabasso, T. (1993). Inferences during reading: Converging evidence from discourse analysis, talk-aloud protocols, and recognition priming. *Journal of Memory and Language, 32,* 279–300.

Swinney, D. A. (1979). Lexical access during sentence comprehension: (Re)consideration of context effects. *Journal of Verbal Learning and Verbal Behavior, 18,* 645–659.

Tabossi, P. (1988). Effects of context on the immediate interpretation of unambiguous nouns. *Journal of Experimental Psychology: Learning, Memory, and Cognition, 14,* 153–162.

Trabasso, T., & Suh, S. (1993). Understanding text: Achieving explanatory coherence through on-line inferences and mental operations in working memory. *Discourse Processes, 16,* 3–34.

Trabasso, T., & van den Broek, P. (1985). Causal thinking and the representation of narrative events. *Journal of Memory and Language, 24,* 612–630.

Trabasso, T., van den Broek, P., & Suh, S. Y. (1989). Logical necessity and transitivity of causal relations in stories. *Discourse Processes, 12,* 1–25.

Van Berkum, J. J. A. (in press). The neuropragmatics of "simple" utterance comprehension: An ERP review. In U. Sauerland & K. Yatsushiro (Eds.), *Semantic and pragmatics: From experiment to theory*. New York: Palgrave MacMillan.

Van Berkum, J. J. A., Hagoort, P., & Brown, C. M. (1999). Semantic integration in sentences and discourse: Evidence from the N400. *Journal of Cognitive Neuroscience, 11,* 657–671.

Van Berkum, J. J. A., Holleman, B., Nieuwland, M. S., Otten, M., & Murre, J. (2008). *Right or wrong? The brain's fast response to moral statements*. Manuscript submitted for publication.

Van Berkum, J. J. A., Zwitserlood, P., Hagoort, P., & Brown, C. M. (2003). When and how do listeners relate a sentence to the wider discourse? Evidence from the N400 effect. *Cognitive Brain Research, 17,* 701–718.

Van den Broek, P., Linzie, B., Fletcher, C. R., & Marsolek, C. J. (2000). The role of causal discourse structure in narrative writing. *Memory & Cognition, 28,* 711–721.

Van den Broek, P., Rapp, D. N., & Kendeou, P. (2005). Integrating memory-based and constructionist processes in accounts of reading comprehension. *Discourse Processes, 39,* 299–316.

Van Dijk, T. A., & Kintsch, W. (1983). *Strategies of discourse comprehension*. New York: Academic.

Van den Broek, P., & Trabasso, T. (1986). Causal networks versus goal hierarchies in summarizing text. *Discourse Processes, 9,* 1–15.

Van Oostendoorp, H., & de Mul, S. (1990). Moses beats Adam: A semantic relatedness effect on a semantic illusion. *Acta Psychologica, 74,* 35–46.

Van Petten, C. (1995). Words and sentences: Event related brain potential measures. *Psychophysiology, 32,* 511–525.

Virtue, S., Haberman, J., Clancy, Z., Parrish, T., & Beeman, M. J. (2006). Neural activity of inferences during story comprehension. *Brain Research, 1084,* 104–114.

Virtue, S., van den Broek, P., & Linderholm, T. (2006). Hemispheric processing of inferences: The effects of textual constraint and working memory capacity. *Memory & Cognition, 34,* 1341–1354.

Vogeley, K., Bussfeld, P., Newen, A., Herrmann, S., Happe, F., Falkai, P., et al. (2001). Mind reading: Neural mechanisms of theory of mind and self-perspective. *Neuroimage, 14,* 170–181.

Wanner, E. (1975). *On remembering, forgetting, and understanding sentences*. The Hague, The Netherlands: Mouton.

Weisberg, P. (1969). Sentence processing assessed through intrasentence word associations. *Journal of Experimental Psychology, 82,* 332–338.

Wiley, J., Mason, R. A., & Myers, J. L. (2001). Accessibility of potential referents following categorical anaphors. *Journal of Experimental Psychology, 27,* 1238–1249.

Wolfe, M. B. W., Magliano, J. P., & Larsen, B. (2005). Causal and semantic relatedness in discourse understanding and representation. *Discourse Processes, 39,* 165–187.

Wright, S., & Givón, T. (1987). The pragmatics of indefinite reference: Quantified text-based studies. *Studies in Language, 11,* 1–33.

Yang, C. L., Perfetti, C. A., & Schmalhofer, F. (2007). Event-related potential indicators of text integration across sentence boundaries. *Journal of Experimental Psychology: Learning, Memory, and Cognition, 33,* 55–89.

Zalla, T., Phipps, M., & Grafman, J. (2002). Story processing in patients with damage to the prefrontal cortex. *Cortex, 38,* 215–231.

Zimmer, H. D., & Engelkamp, J. (1981). The given–new structure of cleft sentences and their influence on picture viewing. *Psychological Research, 43,* 375–389.

Zwaan, R. A. (1996). Processing narrative time shifts. *Journal of Experimental Psychology: Learning, Memory, and Cognition, 22,* 1196–1207.

Zwaan, R. A. (2006). Discourse Processing. In M. J. Traxler & M. A. Gernsbacher (Eds.), *The handbook of psycholinguistics* (2nd ed., pp. 725–764). Amsterdam, The Netherlands: Elsevier.

Zwaan, R. A., Langston, M. C., & Graesser, A. C. (1995). The construction of situation models in narrative comprehension: An event-indexing model. *Psychological Science, 6,* 292–297.

Zwaan, R. A., Magliano, J. P., & Graesser, A. C. (1995). Dimensions of situation model construction in narrative comprehension. *Journal of Experimental Psychology: Learning, Memory, and Cognition, 21,* 386–397.

Zwaan, R. A., & Rapp, D. N. (2006). Discourse comprehension. In M. J. Traxler & M. A. Gernsbacher (Eds.), *The handbook of psycholinguistics* (2nd ed., pp. 725–764). Amsterdam, The Netherlands: Elsevier.

Zwaan, R. A., & Yaxley, R. H. (2003). Spatial iconicity affects semantic relatedness judgments. *Psychonomic Bulletin & Review, 10,* 954–958.

Reference

Speakers introduce characters, objects, and concepts into a discourse, and then refer back to those same characters, objects, and concepts to provide new information about them and to elaborate their meanings.[1] A listener therefore must recognize when a new utterance or phrase refers back to a previously introduced discourse element. If she fails to do this, her representation of the discourse will resemble a list of unrelated statements, rather than a coherent package that relates concepts to one another in a sensible way. Referential processing is therefore one of the major mechanisms that contributes to discourse coherence. This chapter focuses on the mental operations that establish *reference*, processes that enable listeners to connect new portions of a discourse to previously introduced portions.

Because speakers can choose from a variety of different kinds of referring expressions, and because a particular referring expression can refer to more than one concept, establishing *co-reference*—deciding that two different expressions refer to the same thing—can be tricky. Take, for example, Steve Miller's classic song "The Joker."[2]

Some people call me the space cowboy
Some call me the gangster of love
Some people call me Maurice

In the song, Steve Miller informs us that people call him by different names (*space cowboy, gangster of love, and Maurice*).[3] These three expressions have different meanings and fall into different classes of referring expressions. *Space cowboy* and *gangster of love* are *explicit noun phrases* (or *full-NPs*) and *Maurice* is a *proper name*. These three expressions also have different *senses*. If you look up *cowboy* and *gangster* in the dictionary, they will have different

Introduction to Psycholinguistics: Understanding Language Science, First Edition.
Matthew J. Traxler.

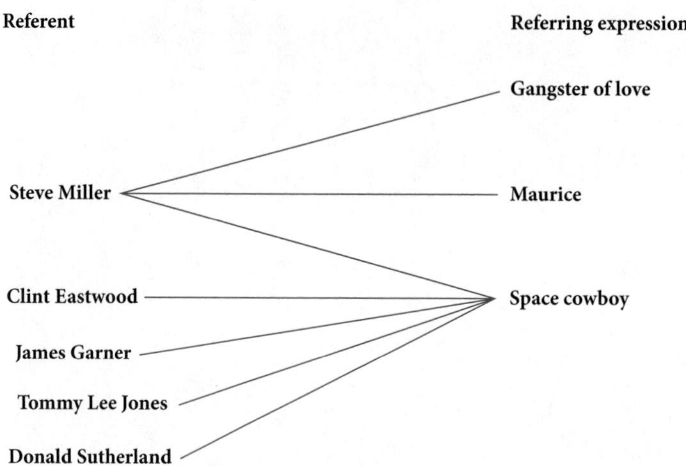

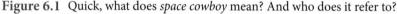

Figure 6.1 Quick, what does *space cowboy* mean? And who does it refer to?

definitions; and so they have different meanings in terms of their senses. But in terms of reference, because all three terms are connected to *Steve Miller*, they all have the same meaning, because they all have the same *referent*. This example shows that the same referent (*Steve Miller*, in this case), can be referred to by any number of different *referring expressions*.

There are multiple mappings in the other direction as well. Consider the expression *Space cowboy. Space cowboy* could refer to *Steve Miller* (because he says so), but it could also refer to *Clint Eastwood*, *James Garner*, *Tommy Lee Jones*, or *Donald Sutherland*, because each of those actors appeared in the 2000 movie entitled *Space Cowboys* in the role of an aging astronaut (referred to as a "space cowboy"). Most types of referring expression, with the possible exception of proper names like *Clint Eastwood*, are multiply ambiguous in this way:[4] A given expression can refer to more than one thing, and a given thing can be referred to by more than one referring expression (as diagrammed in Figure 6.1). Thus, speaking involves making choices between different kinds of referring expressions; and interpreting referring expressions in discourse represents an exercise in ambiguity resolution. (When a speaker says *space cowboy*, which musician or actor is she referring to, or is she applying that label to a new individual?)

Because the same referring expression can apply to multiple concepts, comprehenders must do more than look up the dictionary meaning of the referring expression (its sense) to discover its contextual meaning (its reference). Theories of discourse processing and reference suggest that comprehenders represent the meaning of a discourse by building a *situation model* (or *discourse model*) that contains *tokens* (mental place-holders) for characters, objects, and concepts previously introduced by the speaker. To interpret a referring expression, comprehenders use the referring expression as a retrieval cue to activate information previously encountered in the discourse (or to search the lexicon and general knowledge if the referring expression does not connect to information previously introduced in the discourse). If the referring expression successfully reactivates information previously encountered in the discourse, the comprehender may be able to connect the referring expression to one of the tokens previously introduced into the situation model (additional subtleties will be addressed below). The referring expression is called an *anaphor* and the token to which the anaphor refers is the *antecedent*. When the comprehender successfully identifies the token that goes with an anaphor, she has established *co-reference*. If the comprehender fails to identify a previously established token to go with an anaphor, she has two basic options: She can introduce a new token into the current situation model or she can build an entirely separate model. This second option leads to the least coherent discourse representation, as the comprehender is treating the new information as being completely unconnected with the previous information (e.g., Klin, Guzmán, Weingartner, & Ralano, 2006).

Because anaphors are often ambiguous, establishing co-reference can be thought of as a kind of inference process (see Haviland & Clark, 1974). Consider this example:

(1) Steve wanted to buy his son a gift for his birthday. He went to the pet store and bought a puppy. He was delighted with the gift.

This mini-story has several expressions that could be taken as anaphors referring back to previously introduced referents. Consider the two uses of *his* in the first sentence. Most people would interpret the first use of *his* as referring back to *Steve*, but you would most likely interpret the second *his* as referring to *Steve's son. His son* does not *have* to refer to *Steve's son*, but most people would interpret it that way, because the gender features of *his* match the gender features of a recently introduced, prominent character in the discourse (*Steve*). Comprehenders *can* choose to interpret *his* as referring to a character that has not been explicitly mentioned in the discourse (maybe the speaker is pointing at Steve's friend when she says *his son*, in which case *his* would refer to Steve's friend, and not to Steve). Recent neuroimaging and neurophysiological research shows that listeners do sometimes make this kind of choice, especially when the gender features of the pronoun fail to pick out a specific referent, but also that attaching the anaphor to a referent outside the current sentence in this way leads to sustained processing costs (Nieuwland, Petersson, & van Berkum, 2007; Nieuwland & van Berkum, 2008; see Callahan, 2008, and van Berkum, in press, for recent reviews of ERP research on anaphora).

Full-noun-phrase (*full-NP*) anaphors like *the gift* also require acts of inference to incorporate into the situation model. Most readers would conclude fairly quickly that the noun phrase *the gift* and *a puppy* are one and the same, but this is not logically necessary—it would just be pragmatically strange for the speaker to introduce the gift with the definite article *the* without having previously introduced something that *the gift* could refer to. The pronoun *he* in the final sentence could refer to *Steve* or to *Steve's son* or, in special circumstances, somebody besides either of those two.[5] This example shows that, even in a very short discourse that is subjectively really easy to understand, your referential processing system is working hard behind the scenes to deliver a sensible interpretation.

Given that speakers have a range of choices of forms for anaphors, and given that comprehenders have a range of choices of how to interpret a given anaphor, how do comprehenders successfully associate anaphors with referents? The answer is that the form of the anaphor and the current state of the discourse representation both contribute by providing cues that comprehenders can use to *co-index* (mentally connect) anaphors and referents. The interpretation of an individual anaphor reflects the complex interplay of factors associated with the anaphor and factors associated with possible referents. Although interpretation depends on how anaphors interact with possible referents, let's start by considering characteristics of referents separately from characteristics of anaphors. Let's hold off on the discussion of how the two interact for just a bit.

Characteristics of Referents That Make Co-Reference Easier

Although the ease with which listeners can figure out which referent an anaphor refers to depends on characteristics of both the referent and the anaphor, researchers have identified characteristics of each that individually contribute to referential success or failure. One major characteristic of referents that facilitates anaphoric reference is *focus*. Focus is defined in very specific ways in theories such as Sanford and Garrod's *scenario mapping and focus* framework, and Grosz and colleagues' *centering theory* (see below), but, roughly speaking, you can think of the *focus* of a discourse as being the topic (what the discourse is about), the most important, and/or the most salient element in the discourse at a specific moment in time. (Focus shifts over time as new concepts are introduced and as different aspects of previously introduced concepts are highlighted.) All other things being equal, it is easier to establish co-reference with a focused antecedent than a non-focused antecedent. Further, focus is a matter of degree rather than an either/or proposition. The focused element can stand out only a little bit from other, non-focused elements of the discourse, or the focused element can be really super-focused and be very distinct from other elements of the discourse. Language offers a number of ways to heighten the focus on a particular referent. For example, *syntactic position* can affect the degree of focus. Syntactic subjects, such as *Steve* in sentence (1) are more focused than words in other syntactic positions, such as direct objects (e.g., *a gift* in (1)) or *prepositional objects* (e.g., *his birthday* in (1)) (Gordon & Hendrick, 1997; Gordon & Scearce, 1995). As a result, listeners have less difficulty resolving an anaphor that refers back to a syntactic subject (with the exceptions noted below) than an anaphor that refers back to words in non-syntactic-subject positions.

There are some cases, however, where unusual syntactic structure and unusual word orders can make a given element even more focused than it would be if it appeared in subject position in a common subject–verb–object sentence. Syntactic structures, such as *it-clefts* and *there-insertions* lead to greater focus than the default subject–verb–object syntactic form, as in examples (2) and (3):

(2) It was John who stole the money. (Compare to *John stole the money.*)
(3) There was a banker who stole a bunch of money. (Compare to *A banker stole a bunch of money.*)

When speakers use *it*-clefts and *there*-insertions to introduce a referent (e.g., *John, a banker*), listeners are more likely to produce an utterance that refers to *John/the banker* than in contexts with non-clefted syntactic structure (e.g., *John stole the money/A banker stole a bunch of money*). Listeners also respond more quickly to an anaphor that refers to the focus of the clefted or *there*-inserted element (Almor, 1999; Almor & Eimas, 2008; Birch, Albrecht, & Myers, 2000; Birch & Garnsey, 1995; Fletcher, 1984; Morris & Folk, 1998). Both the production and the comprehension effects suggest that using a cleft or a *there*-insertion enhances the activation of the focused element, making it stand out more from possible alternative referents. This heightened prominence in the listener's mental representation of the utterance makes it easier for the listener to use the focused element in a continuation sentence or retrieve the focused element when an anaphor refers to it.

Position in a sentence can also have an effect independent of the syntactic structure of the sentence. All other things being equal, the entity that the speaker mentions first will be more prominent than anything that the speaker mentions later in the sentence. As a result, it is easier to refer to the first-mentioned participant than to any of the other participants, independent of what kind of syntactic structure the speaker used. If a sentence introduces more than one possible referent, the first-mentioned referent will enjoy a more prominent position in the listener's representation of the discourse. For example, *Pam* is the first-mentioned referent in each of the following sentences (adapted from Gernsbacher, 1989; Gernsbacher & Hargreaves, 1988):

(4) Ann beat Pam in the state tennis match.
(5) It was Ann who beat Pam in the state tennis match.
(6) According to Ann, Pam was a terrible loser.

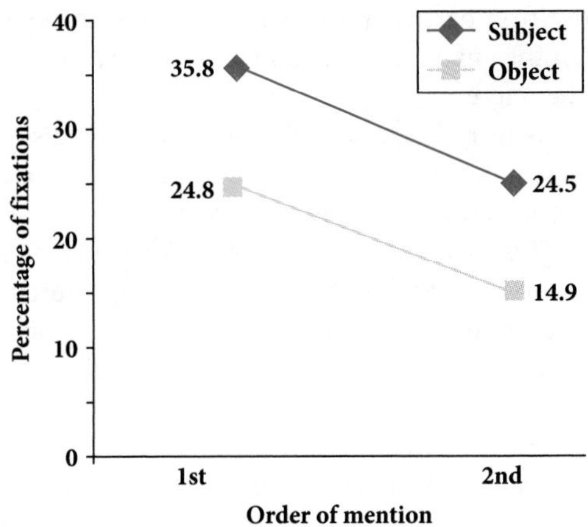

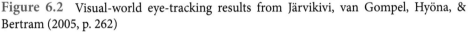

Figure 6.2 Visual-world eye-tracking results from Järvikivi, van Gompel, Hyöna, & Bertram (2005, p. 262)

In each of these sentences, *Ann* is the first-mentioned participant and *Pam* is second. In (4), *Ann* is also the syntactic subject of the main clause in the sentence, but in (5) and (6), *Ann is* not the main-clause subject. In (5) *Ann* is the object of the verb *was*; in (6) *Ann* is a prepositional object, and *Pam* is the main-clause subject. If a subsequent sentence uses the pronoun *she*, participants tend to interpret the pronoun as going with *Ann*, the first-mentioned participant, regardless of the syntactic structure of the sentence and the syntactic position (e.g., subject vs. object vs. prepositional object) that *Ann* occupies. Thus, the first-mentioned participant is the most accessible referent and is the easiest target for an anaphor to hit.[6]

Eye movement behavior can index how activated different potential referents are, and such behavior shows that both syntactic position and order of mention affect the relative activation of different potential referents. To establish these facts, Järvikivi and his colleagues (Järvikivi et al., 2005) used a visual world paradigm involving spoken sentences in Finnish. In Finnish, word order is less constrained than English, so syntactic objects can go before syntactic subjects some of the time. It's as if the speaker said,

> ***Pam (object)*** *beat in the state tennis match* ***Ann (subject).***[7] ***She …***
> (meaning *Ann beat Pam in the state tennis match.*)

In the visual world experiment, pictures of famous people were used as referents and the experimenters measured where people looked when they heard pronoun such as *she*. Presumably, they would look at the most highly activated referent when they heard the pronoun. The results of the experiment showed that both order of mention and syntactic position (syntactic subject versus object) affected the way listeners interpreted the anaphor. Figure 6.2 represents the results of the experiment. Anaphors led to more fixations on pictures of subjects (e.g., *Ann*) than objects (e.g., *Pam*), but they also led to more fixations on the first-mentioned participant (e.g., *Pam*) than the second-mentioned participant (e.g., *Ann*). When the subject appeared first, it had the most fixations. When the subject appeared second, it attracted the same amount of fixations as the (first-mentioned) object. When the object appeared first, it had about the same amount of fixations as the (second-mentioned) subject. Second-mentioned objects attracted the fewest fixations. These data indicate that both subject/object status and order-of-mention affected how activated different possible referents were. Participants found it easier to attach the anaphor to the first-mentioned participant, whether the first participant was a subject or an object. They also found it relatively easier to attach the anaphor to the syntactic subject, so both factors affected how easy it was to identify the referent.

The way the referent is introduced into the discourse can also affect how focused or salient the referent is, which in turn affects how easy it is to refer back to that entity. When speakers want to emphasize an entity, they can use stress (loudness) or they can use an indefinite article (e.g., ***This guy*** *walks into a bar with a parrot on his shoulder* ... *vs.* ***A guy*** ...). People are more likely to continue the story by referring to *guy* when he has been introduced with the indefinite *this* than the indefinite article *a*. Probe-recognition times are also faster when *guy* is introduced with the indefinite *this*, and the level of activation for *this guy* makes its referent more resistant to interference from other concepts than *a guy* (Gernsbacher & Jescheniak, 1995).

The position of the referent in the larger discourse structure (structure above the level of individual sentences) also affects how easy or difficult it is to establish co-reference. All other things being equal, anaphors make contact with referents more easily for more recently mentioned referents. Anaphors are harder to interpret as the distance between the anaphor and the referent increases (Givón, 1983; O'Brien, 1987). Pronouns and full-NP anaphors can be resolved fairly easily if a referent appeared within one clause prior to the anaphor. Anaphoric reference becomes much more difficult if the referent appeared more than one clause before the anaphor (Clark & Sengul, 1979). Clark and Sengul explain effects like these by appealing to a special memory buffer. In their words (p. 35), "the last clause processed grants the entities it mentions a privileged place in working memory. They are ready to be referred to by nouns and pronouns." So one reason why focused referents are easier to refer to may involve a special part of working memory that is used to keep track of the most important, topical, or relevant part of the discourse (but more about this later).

Semantic factors associated with the referent word also influence how easy it is to refer to the referent with an anaphor. All other things being equal, it is easier to refer to a more typical member of a category using either a pronoun or a full-NP anaphor that refers to a general category. Consider the following pair of sentences:

(7) The <u>ostrich</u> lived in the zoo and **it/the bird** was very docile.
(8) The <u>pigeon</u> lived in the zoo and **it/the bird** was very docile.

Pigeon is a typical example of the category *bird*, while *ostrich* represents an unusual or atypical example of the category. Subjects read the second half of sentences such as (7) (*it/the bird was very docile*) slower than the equivalent part of sentences that resemble (8) (Garnham, 1989; Garrod & Sanford, 1977; Sanford, Garrod, & Boyle, 1977, but see Almor, 1999).[8] When listeners encounter the anaphor *it* or *the bird*, they must reactivate the referent that the anaphor refers to. Because *pigeon* has more features that are typical of the category *bird*, *bird* serves as a better memory retrieval cue for *pigeon* than *ostrich*.

Properties of the discourse model also make reference to specific discourse tokens easier or more difficult. Discourse often sets up a spatial model—a representation of the physical space in which objects reside and actors carry out their actions. Within such stories, comprehenders track the movements of main and secondary characters, and they tend to pay closest attention to whichever character is currently in focus (with an additional default preference to pay attention to the main character; Morrow, 1985; Morrow, Bower, & Greenspan, 1989; Rinck & Bower, 1995; see also Dutke, 2003). However, because attention "spills over" from the focused character, objects that are in close virtual proximity can enjoy an increase in activation or focus compared to their normal resting levels. This can facilitate reference to those "close" objects, even when they have not been explicitly mentioned in the text. In experiments where people either memorize the layout of a building or read stories about familiar spaces, the amount of time it takes them to respond to probe words representing objects in the story is essentially a straight line function of spatial distance between the main character and the probed object in the "virtual world" represented by the comprehender's discourse model. Such effects extend beyond probe-word experiments, however, as they are also observed in experiments where subjects merely read passages that mention objects that are either close to or far away from the focused character's location in the virtual story space. Referring expressions are read faster when the referent objects are close to the main character (where "close" is defined as distance in the virtual space defined by the reader's mental model of the story). Referring expressions are read more slowly when the referent objects are further away from the main character (see also Glenberg, Meyer, & Lindem, 1987).

In addition to conveying information about spatial relations, discourse also conveys information about time (*temporal information*) either explicitly (by specifically saying that *x* amount of time has passed) or implicitly (because comprehenders know how long different events usually last). A session of Congress lasts longer than a house party. A house party lasts longer than making a sandwich. The temporal structure of a narrative can change the degree of focus on characters mentioned in the narrative (Ditman, Holcomb, & Kuperberg, 2008; Speer & Zacks, 2005; see also Zwaan, Langston, & Graesser, 1995). Specifically, characters become less accessible after an explicit or implied event boundary, and becoming less accessible makes it harder for comprehenders to connect an anaphor to the antecedent character. In behavioral experiments, this translates to increased processing time for anaphors when the appropriate referent was last mentioned prior to an event boundary. In ERP experiments, temporal shifts lead to increased amplitude (size) of the N400 effect (which can measure how difficult it is to integrate new parts of texts with older parts); and some evidence suggests that, rather than being all or none, the brain's response to temporal shifts is graded. Longer time shifts produce the biggest increase in the N400 effect, medium-sized time shifts produce smaller increases in the N400 effect, and the shortest time shifts produce the smallest N400 effects (Ditman et al., 2008). So, if a subject heard, *Dave and Susan went to school before* ***the session of Congress/the house party/making a sandwich.*** *After the session of Congress/the house party/making a sandwich,* ***he****...*, it would be hardest to identify the referent for *he* in the *Congress* version, and easiest in the *sandwich* version.

The comprehender's situation model also keeps track of the current status of the various characters introduced in the text, and situation model status can affect whether a given antecedent is accessible and available for anaphoric reference (Nieuwland, Otten, & van Berkum, 2007; van Berkum, Brown, & Hagoort, 1999). For example, a story might introduce two characters, both of whom are female. Under these circumstances, referring to one of the females with the very non-explicit pronoun *she* would be infelicitous (as in ****Two girls*** *went to the store and* ***she*** ...). Using the non-specific full-NP *the girl* as an anaphor would be just as bad in this context. However, sometimes a story will have two female characters, but one of them is not part of the current event because the character is located in part of the virtual story space where she cannot interact with the focused characters. Consider the following mini-story (adapted from Van Berkum et al., 1999):

> David had told the **two girls** to clean up their room before lunch time. But one of the girls had stayed upstairs in bed all morning and the other had gone downtown and had not returned. When David went upstairs, he told ***the girl*** ...

Although this story introduces two girls, which could make reference with the full-NP *the girl* infelicitous (bad), the ERP response to *the girl* in stories similar to this one is very similar to the response when only one girl has been introduced into the story. The ERP response to *the girl* in this kind of story is also very different than in stories where two girls have been introduced and both have been maintained in focus. This latter situation produces a sustained increase in negative voltage (lasting several hundred milliseconds), and has been given the label the *nREF* effect.

Discourse can also bring one character into focus and push another one out without explicitly saying that one character has gone off somewhere. This can be accomplished by manipulating properties of the verb in a sentence that introduces two characters. Consider the sentence fragments in (9) and (10):

(9) Susan praised Rick because …
(10) Susan apologized to Rick because …

Most people would continue sentence (9) by saying something about Rick. By contrast, most people would continue sentence (10) by saying something about Susan. The reason for this is that the word *because* strongly suggests that the following clause will provide the reason or cause for the action in the first clause (Traxler, Bybee, & Pickering, 1997; Traxler, Sanford, Aked, & Moxey, 1997) and the verb in the first clause strongly implies that one character really caused the action to happen (Garvey & Caramazza, 1974). So, normally *Susan* would praise *Rick* because *Rick* did something good, and so *Rick* is the more direct cause of the praising action. Normally, *Susan* would apologize to *Rick* because of something that she did, not because of something *Rick* did (although the opposite is certainly possible, maybe Susan apologized to Rick because he pulled a gun on her; maybe Susan praised Rick because she was in a really good mood, not because of anything particularly praiseworthy that Rick did).

Verbs like *blame* and *apologize* are said to carry information about *implicit causality* because, although they do not come right out and say it, the verbs imply that one of the characters and not the other is the root cause of the action. *Praise* picks out its object as its cause; *apologize* picks out the syntactic subject. Because understanding narrative involves discovering the causes for the events described in the narrative, implicit causality verbs have the effect of increasing the degree of focus on the implicit cause (*Rick* in (9), *Susan* in (10)). As a result, it is easier for an anaphor to refer to *Rick* in (9) than in (10). In (9) implicit causality information from the verb helps *Rick* compete for selection with *Susan*, even though *Susan* is in the more prominent (subject) syntactic position. Although accounts differ as to when and why, exactly, implicit causality affects focus and anaphoric reference, language scientists generally agree that implicit causality does affect how difficult it is for anaphoric expressions to refer to the characters involved in the event that the sentence describes (Garnham, Traxler, Oakhill, & Gernsbacher, 1996; Guerry, Gimenes, Caplan, & Rigalleau, 2006; Long & Deley, 2000; McDonald & MacWhinney, 1995; Van Berkum, Koornneef, Otten, & Nieuwland, 2007).

General world knowledge—an individual's storehouse of facts about the world and the way things work—can also play a role in making anaphoric reference to specific referents easier or more difficult. The effects of general world knowledge, in combination with the state of the discourse model, can be observed in the acceptability of reference with *definite* and *indefinite articles* (Hawkins, 1978, 1991). Definite articles include the closed-class function word *the*, and contrast with indefinite articles, such as *a/an*. According to Hawkins' (1991) analysis, definite and indefinite articles are in *complementary distribution*. They behave like Clark Kent and Superman. You never see Clark Kent in the same place and time where you see Superman, and vice versa. Definite articles most often are used with noun phrases that refer back to previously introduced referents; whereas speakers typically use indefinite articles to refer to concepts that are being introduced into the discourse for the first time. However, the use of definite and indefinite articles interacts with general world knowledge in the following way: If a previously introduced concept has the appropriate knowledge structure, a definite article can be used to refer to a newly introduced concept. For example, if a speaker wanted to introduce the concept *engine*, normally *engine* would have to be preceded by an indefinite article (e.g., *an engine*). But if the speaker has previously talked about *a car*, then the definite article *the* is *licensed* (i.e., the speaker can use it). So, if the speaker says, *John got in his car*, she can go on to say ***the engine** started right away*, using the definite article. This is because everyone knows that cars have exactly one engine, and mentioning *car* suffices to make its unique *engine* available in the discourse representation (it's as if the speaker had said *John got in his car, which has an engine*; only the speaker does not have to point out the obvious; listeners' world knowledge will supply the "missing" information).[9] The speaker can then use the definite article to point back to the implicitly introduced *engine* and the listener can readily find the referent for the definite description *the engine* (Garrod & Sanford, 1981). Having a single, unique engine also rules out using the indefinite article in this case. Even though *engine* has not been mentioned, and normally speakers introduce previously unmentioned entities with *in*definite articles, it would be strange to say

(11) *John got in his car. An engine started right away.* (Unless the engine that started is in a completely different car than John's.)

Indefinite articles can pick out subsets of previously introduced discourse entities, if doing so is licensed by general world knowledge. A speaker can say, *I went to a wedding last weekend* and *a bridesmaid fell into the koi pond*, because unlike cars and engines, weddings often have more than one bridesmaid. In this case *the bridesmaid* would sound strange, unless the speaker has previously established that the wedding only had one bridesmaid.

General world knowledge also affects whether *unheralded pronouns* (or unheralded anaphors more generally) can be used to establish links to concepts implicitly introduced previously in the discourse. An *unheralded pronoun* is a pronoun that refers to a concept that has not been explicitly introduced by the speaker. Normally, using a pronoun without a previously introduced referent is problematic, as in the use of the unheralded *she* in the following:

*?**She** picked up her bags and Susan went to the airport.*

But world knowledge can implicitly introduce a referent that the unheralded pronoun can refer to. If someone at your college said *I went to the football game on Saturday*, you could use an unheralded pronoun in the question *Did **they** win?* and it is highly likely that your partner would correctly infer that *they* refers to the home team.

To summarize, a number of factors associated with referents makes resolving anaphors easier or more difficult. Syntactic position, narrative structure above the sentence level, semantic properties of referents, properties of the discourse, and the organization of world knowledge all affect how easy it is to use an anaphor to pick out a particular referent. The next section summarizes some of the properties of anaphors that also make reference easier or more difficult.

Characteristics of Anaphors That Make Co-Reference Easier

As mentioned previously, anaphors come in different flavors. Zero anaphors are the least explicit and can be used felicitously only in contexts where only a single, prominent entity is in the focus of attention, which normally occurs when the anaphor is produced soon after the antecedent, as in *John went to the store and (zero anaphor) bought some milk.* Proper names are the most explicit anaphor form, they can be used when many words intervene between the anaphor and the antecedent, and they can be used in the face of multiple possible competitors, as in *Clint, Donald, James, and Tommy Lee went to the store this morning after they finished shooting the last scene of the blockbuster film "Space Cowboys" and* ***Clint*** *bought some milk*. All other things being equal, a more explicit anaphor will make establishing co-reference easier. In sentences where explicit name anaphors are felicitous (see below), explicit names lead to the shortest probe-reaction and reading times and they have the greatest impact on possible competitors (Gernsbacher, 1989). Consider these sentences (adapted from Gernsbacher, 1989):

(12) Ann beat Steve in the state tennis match and she/Ann celebrated all night long.
(13) Ann beat Steve in the state tennis match and he/Steve cried all night long.

Here, there are two possible antecedents, *Ann* and *Steve*, that differ in gender (one is female, one is male). The activation levels of the possible antecedents, *Ann* and *Steve* can be estimated using probe-reaction methods at different points in the sentence—before and after the anaphor, and at the end of the sentence.[10] Probe-reaction methods show that pronouns have weak effects on the relative activation of possible antecedents (e.g., reaction time to the probe-word *Ann* is about the same just before and just after the pronoun *she*). But using the names rather than the pronouns as anaphors has more powerful effects. Activation levels of the antecedent increase sharply when a name is used as the anaphor, and activation levels of the competing referent decrease sharply (reaction time to *Steve* increases dramatically when *Ann*, rather than *she*, is the anaphor; and the same pattern holds for *Ann* when *Steve* is used as the anaphor). Similar results have been found for full-NP anaphors when words that are semantically associated with the antecedent are probed, rather than the antecedent itself (Greene, McKoon, & Ratcliff, 1992; see also Chang, 1980; Corbett & Chang, 1983; MacDonald & MacWhinney, 1990). In one set of experiments, a context sentence introduced a referent, such as *burglar*, that was subsequently referred to with a full-NP anaphor (e.g., *criminal*; Dell, McKoon & Ratcliff, 1983). Activation for the antecedent *burglar* was assessed by comparing reaction time to words that had been introduced in the same proposition as *burglar* to random control words. Subjects responded more quickly to concepts associated with the antecedent after the antecedent had been reinstated in working memory by the full-NP anaphor (see also Nicol & Swinney, 1989). Less powerful effects are associated with less explicit anaphors.

Anaphors also come with *lexical features*, such as gender and number that can help pick out an antecedent from among possible competitors. English has an impoverished gender marking system compared to other languages, such as Russian, French and Spanish. In English only human and a subset of animate nouns are reliably marked for gender.[11] Nonetheless, English pronouns (and other languages' pronouns as well) carry lexical features that do discriminate between males and females, between singular and plural referents, and between animate and inanimate referents. When gender, number, or animacy features of the anaphor match only one possible referent, resolving the anaphor is easier than in cases where the lexical features of the anaphor match more than one possible antecedent. Such effects may reflect the use of lexical features to restrict the set of possible referents that become reactivated in response to the anaphor, but the prevailing opinion amongst language scientists appears to be that anaphors automatically reactivate potential antecedents, even antecedents whose features clash with the lexical features of the anaphor.

According to *memory-based processing* approaches, an anaphor causes potential antecedents to quickly *resonate* (like a tuning fork can cause piano strings to resonate). This resonance process has all the hallmarks of an automatic process—it is fast, occurs outside of conscious control, and is dumb. Studies of anaphor resolution in contexts where there are no possible matching antecedents show that people very quickly determine when an anaphor cannot be resolved (i.e., it has no matching referent in memory; Cook, Myers, & O'Brien, 2005; Glucksberg & McCloskey, 1981; Nieuwland & van Berkum, 2008). Memory-based processing explains such effects as representing the rapid effects of the *resonance* process. The anaphor (like a tuning fork) sends a signal simultaneously to the contents of working (active) memory and long-term memory. In cases where there is no matching antecedent at all (or where the activation triggered by the resonance process is divided among too many possible antecedents), nothing in memory will resonate strongly enough to the anaphor to be considered as a possible antecedent. Under those circumstances, the listener may very well conclude that the anaphoric expression is really introducing a new discourse entity.

The "dumb" part of the resonance process can be demonstrated in experiments where antecedents that should not be considered, because they are in positions where they cannot co-refer, nonetheless compete for selection with the correct antecedent (Almor, 1999; Badecker & Straub, 2002; Kennison, 2003; Sturt, 2003). Similarly, mismatch of lexical features between anaphors and antecedents does not appear to stop the mismatching antecedents from resonating. However, lexical features are used to quickly weed out potential antecedents that mismatch the anaphor with respect to number, gender or animacy (as in *memory-based* processing approaches, Cook et al., 2005; Foraker & McElree, 2007; Greene et al., 1992; Klin et al., 2006; Myers & O'Brien, 1998; O'Brien, 1987; see also Hintzman, 2001; but see Arnold, Eisenband, Brown-Schmidt, & Trueswell, 2000; Osterhout, Bersick, & McLaughlin, 1997). Reading and probe-reaction times are slower when the lexical features of an anaphor match both the features of a structurally accessible antecedent and a structurally inaccessible antecedent—the referential processing system treats the anaphor as if it were ambiguous. Response times are faster when the features of the structurally inaccessible antecedent also clash with the features of the anaphor. Resonance processes also appear to reactivate individual features of antecedents in circumstances where people fail to fully establish the link between the anaphor and its antecedent (Klin et al., 2006).

So, rather than being all-or-none, and rather than being carried out in a single undifferentiated process, resolving an anaphor involves a two-stage process. In the first stage, the anaphor serves as a retrieval cue, which causes information in memory to resonate (become more active). If no information in memory strongly resonates, comprehenders quickly realize that the anaphor fails to co-refer with an antecedent. In cases where information does resonate strongly, comprehenders carry out a second stage of processing in which they evaluate the characteristics of the resonating information, and they choose to connect the anaphor to the resonating information that most closely matches the lexical, syntactic, and pragmatic requirements of the anaphoric expression. This process is easier when only one potential antecedent matches the anaphor's features (Garnham & Oakhill, 1985). The process of resolving co-reference is more difficult when some features of the potential antecedent match the anaphor, but others do not (as when syntactic prominence favors one potential antecedent, but the gender features favor another).

The Relationship between an Anaphor and Possible Referents Affects Anaphor Resolution

Anaphor resolution requires the listener to use features of the anaphor to search memory for the referent whose lexical and discourse features are most closely aligned with the cues that the anaphor provides. Referring expressions differ along a dimension of explicitness, and research employing continuation methods, where subjects read a fragment of text and produce an utterance that reflects what they think will happen next, show that the form of the anaphor reflects how salient or prominent the referent is in the discourse model. More salient or prominent antecedents are referred to with less explicit anaphors (pronouns or zero anaphors). Less salient or prominent antecedents are referred to with more explicit anaphors (full-NPs or proper names). Given that speakers tend to produce different kinds of anaphoric expressions for more versus less salient antecedents, it should be possible for listeners to make use of the explicitness of the anaphor to figure out what the anaphor refers to, and in fact, this is what they appear to do. Consider the following:

> Steve gave his son a gift and **he** …

Because the speaker used a non-explicit anaphor, and because *Steve* is the most prominent player in the discourse, listeners will prefer to interpret *he* as co-referential with *Steve*, even though this is not logically necessary. For example, if the preceding fragment continued

> … thanked him profusely …

the pronoun **he** would most likely refer to the *son* and not to *Steve*. So, perhaps the speaker should have said

> … and the son thanked Steve profusely …

in order to avoid confusion.

If pronouns are very ambiguous and proper names are far less ambiguous, and if proper names more powerfully reduce the activity of possible competitors, why don't speakers just stick to proper names, or better yet, serial numbers? Like this:

> Rocky$_{\text{Inmate\#112111}}$ was talking to Buster$_{\text{Inmate\#112222}}$. Buster$_{\text{Inmate\#112222}}$ traded some cigarettes$_{\text{(Cigs\#555555)}}$ with Jethro$_{\text{Inmate \#113333}}$, but Rocky$_{\text{Inmate \#112111}}$ stole the cigarettes$_{\text{(Cigs\#555555)}}$ right away.

Including the full name, rank, and serial number eliminates any possibility of mis-assigning the anaphor to the wrong referent.

The answer comes in two parts. First, in normal circumstances, lexical, discourse, and pragmatic cues provide enough information to enable the listener to uniquely identify a referent for each anaphor. Second, perhaps more importantly, using a more explicit anaphor, such as a proper name, when a less explicit anaphor is possible, creates problems for the listener (Almor, 1999; Gordon, Grosz, & Gilliom, 1993; Grosz & Sidner, 1986; Gundel, Hedberg, & Zacharski, 1993). Compare the following sets of sentences:

(14) Steve bought a puppy. Steve brought the puppy home. Steve gave the puppy to Steve's son.

(15) Steve bought a puppy. He brought it home. He gave it to his son.

In (14), the proper name *Steve* appears repeatedly, which should make figuring out who *Steve* refers to fairly easy (they're all the same, right?). In (15), the pronoun *he* appears instead of Steve in the second and third sentences, which should complicate the process of determining that *he* in the second and third sentences co-refers with *Steve* (because *he* could refer to *Steve, the puppy* if it's male, or someone not yet mentioned). But despite the greater ambiguity of *he* relative to *Steve*, raters blind to the purpose of the study prefer the sequence in (15) to the sequence in (14), they take less time to comprehend the sequence in (15) than (14), and their brain wave activity indicates that they have less trouble integrating the second and third sentences with the first in (15) compared to (14) (Camblin, Ledoux, Boudewyn, Gordon, & Swaab, 2006; Garnham, Oakhill, & Cain, 1997; Gordon & Hendrick, 1997; Ledoux, Gordon, Camblin, & Swaab, 2007; Swaab, Camblin, & Gordon, 2004). The greater processing difficulty that sometimes accompanies proper name and full-NP anaphors (as compared to pronoun anaphors) is called the *repeated name penalty* and it shows that more explicit anaphors are not always better than less explicit anaphors. Recent functional imaging (fMRI) research further indicates that the brain response to proper name anaphors differs from the response to less explicit forms (Almor, Smith, Bonilha, Fridriksson, & Rorden, 2007).

Why is a more explicit anaphor sometimes worse than a less explicit anaphor? A detailed answer will wait until we consider some detailed theories of how co-reference is established, but the core issue is that, in sequences like (14), the characteristics of the anaphor (in particular its very explicit nature) are incompatible with the current state of the discourse model. We use explicit proper name anaphors to pick out either very weakly activated antecedents or to select from among a set of more than one highly activated antecedents. If we use an explicit form when there is only one highly activated possible referent, the listener might wonder why we are providing more information than required (a violation of the Gricean maxim of *quantity*). Alternatively, the listener may assume that the repeated name refers to a new discourse entity and therefore take extra time to set up a new token for that new entity. Further, because the new and old tokens have the same name (e.g., *Steve*), the listener will have difficulty keeping the two representations separate (leading to *similarity based interference*, e.g., Gordon, Hendrick, & Johnson, 2001).

Binding Theory

The relative positions of referents and anaphors in a syntactic structure interact with specific anaphor forms to determine whether an anaphor can refer to a specific previously introduced entity. One linguistic theory that seeks to explain how different kinds of anaphors can refer to particular antecedents in particular syntactic positions is *binding theory* (Chomsky, 1981, 1986; see Gordon & Hendrick, 1997, 1998 for very readable descriptions of the theory). Chomsky divides anaphors into three categories, which correspond to regular pronouns such as *he*, *she*, *him*, and *her*, *reflexive pronouns* such as *himself* and *herself*, and *R-expressions*, which include proper names. He suggests that different types of anaphors[12] are in *complementary distribution*, where distribution is defined across syntactic positions in sentences. For example, reflexive pronouns like *himself* and *herself* must pick out an antecedent that is in the same clause of the sentence. So, while (16) is acceptable, (17) is not:

(16) Jane$_{(i)}$ saw herself$_{(i)}$ in the mirror.
(17) *Jane$_{(i)}$ thought that Tom saw herself$_{(i)}$ in the mirror.

(The little $_{(i)}$ markers are meant to indicate which referent the anaphor refers to.) If a speaker wants to express the idea that *Tom saw Jane* in the mirror in (17), the speaker would have to use a regular pronoun (e.g., *her*) or the proper name (e.g., *Jane*), as in (18):

(18) Jane$_{(i)}$ thought that Tom saw <u>her</u>$_{(i)}$/<u>Jane</u>$_{(i)}$ in the mirror.

Compared to reflexives and what they can refer to, the opposite pattern holds for regular pronouns, like *him* and *her*. These kinds of anaphors may not refer to an antecedent in the same clause; they must refer to an antecedent in a different clause than the one they appear in. As a result, (19) is acceptable, but (20) is not:

(19) Tina$_{(i)}$ was sick and she$_{(i)}$ spent a week in bed.
(20) *Tina$_{(i)}$ saw her$_{(i)}$ and she$_{(i)}$ spent a week in bed.

In (20) *her* may not refer to *Tina* (*She* saw *Tina's brother*, likewise cannot be interpreted as meaning *Tina saw Tina's brother*). Chomsky says that this is because, in the syntactic structure of sentence (20), the noun phrase containing Tina *c-commands* the phrase that contains the pronoun *her* (in Chomsky's system, if the structural node immediately above *Tina* includes the phrase that the pronoun *her* appears in, the NP that contains *Tina* is said to *c-command* the NP containing the pronoun *her*). Pronouns like *he*, *she*, *him*, and *her* are said to be *free*, because they can refer to antecedents outside their immediate syntactic environment (e.g., their own clause). Reflexives like *himself* and *herself* are not free, because they must find their antecedents within the same clause. Chomsky developed three basic rules that explain how different kinds of anaphors are distributed in different syntactic environments, and these are called Principles A–C (see Chomsky, 1981, p. 188).

Principle A says that a reflexive must be bound (has to have an antecedent) in the same clause.
Principle B says that regular pronouns may not refer to an antecedent in the same local syntactic structure (clause, roughly).
Principle C says that R-expressions (e.g., proper names) also cannot have an antecedent that is in a c-command relationship with the phrase that contains the R-expression.

The chief support for this theory comes from trained linguists' intuitions about what is acceptable and what is not.

Recently, Chomsky's binding theory has been subjected to testing by language scientists who deployed a variety of judgment and behavioral measurements (Badecker & Straub, 2002; Clifton, Kennison, & Albrecht, 1997; Gordon & Hendrick, 1997, 1998; Gordon & Scearce, 1995; Kennison, 2003; Nicol & Swinney, 1989; Sturt, 2003; Yang, Gordon, Hendrick, & Hue, 2003; Yang, Gordon, Hendrick, Wu, & Chou, 2001). Testing theories about linguistic representation and processing faces some of the same challenges that arise in the testing of new medical and pharmaceutical treatments. Namely, if the researcher has prior beliefs about what the outcome of the study *should* be, this may taint data collection and analysis in more or less subtle ways. Usually, the researcher winds up paying more attention to evidence that favors the preferred hypothesis and less attention to evidence that contradicts the preferred hypothesis. Using intuitive judgments as the main or sole basis of theory testing is therefore a scientifically risky proposition.

To get around this problem, Peter C. Gordon and Randall Hendrick (1997) had naive raters (college students) who were fluent speakers of English judge the acceptability of different kinds of anaphors in different kinds of syntactic environments. Specifically, they tested whether reflexive pronouns could refer to antecedents within or outside their "home" clause. They also tested whether regular pronouns could refer to antecedents in similarly distributed positions. In addition, they tested the conditions under which repeated name reference was acceptable in different syntactic environments; and they manipulated whether an antecedent was focused (as in a sentence with an *it*-cleft) or unfocused (as in a regular subject–verb–object sentence). Together, raters' opinions about whether specific antecedent–anaphor relationships were acceptable should tell us whether naive, fluent speakers use rules such as Principles A–C to make and evaluate connections between anaphors and antecedents. This study does not suffer from the "self-fulfilling prophecy" problem because naive raters did not know what theories were being tested nor how their behavior should look according to binding theory.

College students' ratings were very consistent with Principles A and B. They hated sentences such as *John thought that Susan injured himself*, and they liked sentences such as *John thought that Susan injured herself* (Principle A). They hated sentences such as *She called Susan* if *she* and *Susan* were supposed to refer to the same person, but they liked *Susan called before she came over* (Principle B). Principle C did not fare so well. Gordon and Hendrick found that the acceptability of repeated name anaphors was strongly dependent on the focus status of the potential antecedent (unfocused antecedents were greatly preferred to focused antecedents). Because binding theory does not incorporate psychological focus as a governing principle, it cannot account for such effects.[13] Principle C also implies that a name anaphor should be an acceptable way to refer back to a previously introduced referent, as long as the referent does not c-command the anaphor. So, sequences such as *John$_{(i)}$ said that John$_{(i)}$ would win* (Gordon & Hendrick, 1997, p. 338) should be perfectly fine, but raters who do not already believe in binding theory judge expressions like that as being marginally acceptable at best.

Behavioral experiments involving eye tracking and self-paced reading have also cast doubt on Principle C (Badecker & Straub, 2002; Kennison, 2003; Sturt, 2003; but see Clifton et al., 1997; Nicol & Swinney, 1989). The general approach taken in these experiments is to place a referent in a syntactic position where it should be "invisible" to an anaphor, because one of the principles in binding theory says that an antecedent in that position cannot co-refer with an anaphor in another position. In a mini-discourse such as (21), the reflexive pronoun *himself* can co-refer with *surgeon* but *not* with *Jonathan* or *Jennifer*.

(21) Jonathan/Jennifer was pretty worried at the hospital. He/She remembered that the surgeon had pricked himself with a used syringe needle.

Experiments like these can test binding theory because binding theory says that manipulating the initial character (*Jonathan* vs. *Jennifer*) should have no effect on processing the reflexive pronoun *himself*. This is because binding constraints should prevent the reader from ever considering *Jonathan* or *Jennifer* as being the antecedent that goes with the reflexive pronoun. Nonetheless, different labs using different reading time measures on different subject populations have found that the status of the "inaccessible" referent (*Jonathan*, *Jennifer*) does affect how difficult it is to figure out who the reflexive *himself* refers to (as indicated by how long it takes people to read the reflexive pronoun and the material that follows). When *Jonathan* appears in the "inaccessible" position, readers spend more time reading the reflexive pronoun and the following material compared to when the gender-mismatching antecedent *Jennifer* appears in that position. This result is straightforwardly *in*compatible with binding theory, but it is consistent with memory-based resonance approaches to anaphoric reference. According to resonance theory, all potential antecedents in the story resonate to the reflexive pronoun (even the ones that have a different gender). So, even though syntax may rule out *Jonathan* as co-referring with *himself*, *Jonathan* still resonates after people read the reflexive pronoun *himself*, and so *Jonathan* has to be weeded out as a referent in a later evaluative stage. Experiments like these suggest that binding constraints may help in referent selection, but they do not serve as an initial "filter" that prevents the referential processing systems from considering antecedents based on their relative positions in syntactic structures.

Psycholinguistic Theories of Anaphoric Reference

Having described some of the characteristics of antecedents and anaphors and how antecedents and anaphors interact, let's turn to some theories that have attempted to incorporate judgment and behavioral data in their explanations of how people respond to anaphors. In particular, let's look at the *focus mapping framework*, *centering theory*, and the *information load hypothesis* in turn.

The memory focus model

Simon Garrod and Tony Sanford were among the first researchers to suggest that resolving anaphoric expressions (i.e., connecting anaphors to antecedents) involves a two-stage process (Garrod, Freudenthal, & Boyle, 1984; Garrod & Sanford, 1983; Garrod & Terras, 2000). They called the first stage of processing *bonding* and the second stage *binding*. The first stage of the focus mapping system involves the activation of potential antecedents and the second stage involves evaluating the activated potential antecedents for the degree of fit with the anaphor (similar to the memory-based/resonance approaches outlined previously). The memory focus model deals with salience/prominence effects by proposing that the contents of memory can be divided into a set of entities that are in *explicit focus* and a further set of entities that are in *implicit focus*. Explicit focus includes those discourse entities that are active in working memory and are immediately available to be referred to. Implicit focus includes discourse entities that enjoy a relatively high degree of activation in long-term memory, by virtue of being mentioned previously in the discourse or by being strongly associated with the current contents of working memory (as in the *car–engine* example, (11) on p. **249**). The contents of explicit and implicit focus change over time. Entities can enter explicit focus if the speaker names those characters, objects, or concepts. Entities can also enter (or re-enter) explicit focus when they are referred to by an anaphor. An entity can remain in explicit focus so long as the entity is re-mentioned or remains the topic of the discourse. An entity can slip into implicit focus, and eventually out of implicit focus, if the speaker does not refresh the trace of the entity by mentioning it. The memory focus model helps explain why different kinds of anaphors are used in different circumstances—antecedents in explicit focus will lead to the least explicit anaphors (pronouns, zero anaphors), while antecedents in implicit focus or out of focus will require more explicit forms (full-NPs, names). The model also explains why reading times for the same referring expressions are different when the antecedent has been focused versus de-focused (Garrod et al., 1994). The model's stipulation of two-stage bonding and binding is consistent with eye-tracking results showing that early responses to anaphoric expressions (including full-NPs) are dominated by prestored lexical features, while later responses are dominated by the degree of fit between the anaphoric expression and the characteristics of the situation that the text describes (Garrod & Terras, 2000).

Centering theory

Centering theory, like the memory focus model, also makes some specific claims about how discourse is represented in the mind of the listener, and how the form of the discourse representation influences anaphoric reference (Gordon et al., 1993; Gordon & Hendrick, 1998; Gordon & Scearce, 1995; Grosz & Sidner, 1986). Specifically, centering theory suggests that each expression in a discourse contains two kinds of *centers*: a single *backward-looking center*, and a set of *forward-looking centers*. The backward-looking center provides the means of connecting the current expression with previous expressions. The forward-looking centers provide a set of concepts that future expressions can connect to. Consider the mini-story in (22) (from Tim Dorsey's *Florida Roadkill*):

(22) Serge slapped a fifty-pack of hundred-dollar bills on the glass display case. Without even showing his false driver's license, Serge walked out the door with TEC-9 and MAC-10 burp guns, two Peacemakers, three hunting rifles, scopes, and Sharon's kevlar ensemble.

The first sentence provides a number of concepts that could be picked up by the following sentence: *Serge, a fifty-pack of hundred-dollar bills, the glass display case.* The following sentence has a backward-looking center, *Serge*, that maps to the subject (and first-mentioned entity) in the preceding sentence. The second sentence in turn, offers its own set of forward looking centers: *Serge* (again), *(Serge's) false driver's license, the door, TEC-9 burp gun, MAC-10 burp gun, two Peacemakers, three hunting rifles, scopes, Sharon, Sharon's kevlar ensemble.* In fact, the story continues in the following sentence with *Serge* as its backward-looking center, maintaining *Serge* in a prominent position in the discourse.[14] So, while there is only one backward-looking center per expression, there can be any number of forward-looking centers, and these forward-looking centers will be ranked in the listener's mental representation according to their prominence in the discourse. All other things being equal, syntactic subjects will be more prominent than words in other syntactic positions. Degree of focus can be manipulated as described previously. All other things being equal, it will be easier for a backward-looking center to make contact with the most prominent forward-looking center than with less prominent forward-looking centers, which is consistent with the experimental evidence outlined above.

According to centering theory, listeners maintain a coherent discourse representation by connecting each new backward-looking center to one of the forward-looking centers in the preceding discourse. This process is facilitated when the form of the referring expression is appropriate given the prominence of the forward-looking center to which the referring expression should attach. As suggested by Grosz and colleagues and other theorists (e.g., Garrod and Sanford, 1983), because pronouns carry so little semantic information of their own (little beyond number and gender),they strongly signal that their meaning should be determined via connections with the preceding discourse. As a result, pronouns serve as instructions to the discourse-processing system that say, in effect, "search the discourse representation for something to connect to." More explicit referring forms, full-NPs and names for example, carry much more semantic information of their own (compare, e.g., *him* to *space cowboy*). As a result, according to centering theory, explicit referring forms do not instruct the discourse-processing mechanism to perform a memory search. Instead, explicitly referring forms instruct the listener to introduce a new discourse entity into the situation model. Only after the new entity has been introduced into the discourse representation will the listener attempt to integrate the information associated with the new referent with information that was previously entered into the situation model.

Centering theory can help explain a number of phenomena related to referential processing. First, centering theory predicts that the form of the referring expression should vary with the prominence of the antecedent, which is correct. Centering theory also predicts that pronouns that refer to prominent entities should be easier to understand than pronouns that refer to less prominent entities, which is also correct. Finally, centering theory offers a straightforward explanation for why repeated names can lead to processing difficulty. In sequences like (23), based on (14) above,

(23) Steve bought a puppy. Steve brought the puppy home. Steve gave the puppy to Steve's son.

Steve is the most prominent forward-looking center in the first sentence. As such, centering theory suggests that if the backward-looking center of the following sentence is to make direct contact with *Steve*, it should use a pronoun (because a pronoun instructs the processor to search the discourse representation for a matching center, *not* to introduce a new entity into the discourse; see also Ariel, 1990; Gundel et al., 1993). In (23), because the second sentence includes the proper name *Steve*, the first thing the listener does is set up a new token in the discourse representation (call it *Steve-#2*). This prevents the listener from immediately recognizing the relationship between the first and second sentences, and it means that the listener must engage in additional inferential processing to establish the link between *Steve-#2* and the *Steve* that was mentioned in the first sentence (Gordon & Hendrick, 1998). Repeating names, as in (23) also leads to a different pattern of brain response than using more felicitous pronouns, as demonstrated by a recent fMRI study by Amit Almor and colleagues (2007; see also Nieuwland et al., 2007).

When the referent of a proper name is less prominent in the discourse representation, a different set of problems arises, which changes the relative benefits and costs of proper names and pronouns. Consider the sequence in (24):

(24) The puppy was the best gift that Steve gave to his son David at his eleventh birthday, which was held at John's house. **He* played with it all afternoon.

Here, a pronoun is a really bad choice, because there are too many possible referents, and if *He* is supposed to refer to *Steve*, *Steve* is in a very non-prominent position. In this case, the costs associated with the proper name (introducing a new referent and then engaging in processes to establish equivalence with a previously introduced entity) are outweighed by the benefits of having stronger cues to the identity of the referent, so the proper name, not the pronoun, is the preferred form.

One potential drawback of centering theory is that it suggests that the most prominent forward-looking center is held in a special memory buffer, which makes it especially easy to refer to with a pronoun in a subsequent sentence. According to Stephani Foraker and Brian McElree (2007), entities that are held in focal attention in this way are identified more quickly than entities that do not enjoy focal attention. They predicted, therefore, that if a focused discourse entity in a mini-story really was placed in a special buffer, then subjects should respond to pronouns that refer to the focused entity faster than pronouns that refer to non-focused entities from the same sentence. However, when they used speed–accuracy tradeoff (SAT) methods to measure how long it took people to co-index anaphors and antecedents under different conditions, they found that focused and non-focused entities were accessed at the same speed.[15] The difference between focused and non-focused referents was that readers were more successful at retrieving the focused than the non-focused referents. But when they did succeed in retrieving focused and non-focused referents, they did so equally quickly for both kinds.

Informational load hypothesis

The *informational load hypothesis* (ILH) was formulated to address some very detailed aspects of listeners' behavior as they processed sentences containing anaphoric expressions (Almor, 1999; see also Almor & Eimas, 2008; Almor, Kempler, MacDonald, Anderson, & Tyler, 1999; Almor et al., 2007). Like centering theory, the ILH proposes that different kinds of referring expressions are more acceptable in some contexts than in others. Specifically, the information conveyed by the anaphor must be appropriate to the context that the anaphor appears in. Some referring expressions convey little or no information (e.g., the pronoun *it*), some convey more information than that (e.g., a full-NP such as *the bird*), and some convey a large amount of fairly specific information (e.g., full-NPs such as *the ostrich* and *the ostrich that is standing over there with its head in the sand*). The amount of information that is carried by the referring expression itself is referred to as its *informational load* (hence the name for the hypothesis).[16] At the center of the ILH is the idea that speakers should include enough information in their referring expressions so that listeners can identify the referent, but no more than is absolutely necessary (again, in line with Grice's principle of *quantity*). When there is a mismatch between the information required to establish co-reference and the information contained in the referring expression, listeners engage in unnecessary inference processes to try to figure out why the speaker is being so long-winded.

Information load can help explain why some sequences of antecedents and referring expressions are easier to understand than others. Consider the sequences in (25) and (26):

(25) The robin laid an egg. The bird sat on the egg until it hatched.
(26) The bird laid an egg. The robin sat on the egg until it hatched.

Sequences like (25) are easier to understand than sequences like (26) (e.g., Garrod & Sanford, 1977). The ILH explains the difference between (25) and (26) by appealing to the informational load carried by the referring expression in the second sentence. Because *bird* is less specific than *robin*, *bird* carries little or no new information, and so the listener treats it more like a regular old pronoun—i.e., the listener rapidly attempts to find a matching element in the previous discourse (which is not too hard, because the potential referent *robin* is sitting in a prominent position in the discourse representation). By contrast, the referring expression *robin* in the second sentence of (26) does carry some new information, because it is more specific than the alternative expression *bird*. As a result, listeners are more likely to treat *the robin* in (25) the way they treat a proper name. That is, their initial reflex will be to create a new token in their discourse representation that corresponds to *robin*, and only later will they attempt to integrate *robin* with *bird*. So (26) involves greater manipulation of the discourse representation and a later attempt to integrate the two sentences, leading to greater reading times for (26) compared to (25).

The ILH differs from other accounts of referential processing by proposing that focus critically affects the way more specific (e.g., *robin*) and more general referring expressions (e.g., *bird*) are handled by processes involved in co-reference. Like other theories, the ILH predicts that non-explicit anaphors will work better the more focused or prominent the antecedent is. Likewise, both the ILH and other theories (e.g., centering theory) predict that repeated name or repeated full-NP anaphors should be easier to process when their antecedent is un-focused (evidence supporting this claim appears above). Unlike other theories, however, the ILH says that processing difficulty depends on both focus on the antecedent and the amount of new information that the anaphor carries (its informational load). The interaction of focus and information load means that some anaphors that refer to strange or atypical category members should be processed faster than anaphors that refer to more common or typical category members, but only if the antecedent is focused (which would reverse the normal pattern that occurs with un-focused antecedents; see Garrod & Sanford, 1977). Let's say we converted Garrod & Sanford's ostrich–bird sentences into highly focused versions like this:

(27) What the girl saw was the ostrich. The bird …
(28) What the girl saw was the robin. The bird …

Reading time experiments confirmed the ILH's predictions about focus, typicality, and the informational load associated with the anaphors. Specifically, reading time data showed that sequences such as (27) were easier to understand than sequences such as (28).

Summary and Conclusions

This chapter has reviewed prominent linguistic and psycholinguistic theories of referential processing. Referential processing involves the intersection of general memory processes and discourse, syntactic, and lexical processing. Anaphoric expressions cause potential antecedents in the active discourse representation and long-term memory to resonate, which makes them available as targets for co-reference assignment. Discourse representations include sets of entities that vary in the degree of focus or prominence. The degree of focus interacts with the form of the referring expression, such that focused antecedents are easier to connect to less explicit anaphors and less focused antecedents are easier to connect to more explicit anaphors. Focus is, in turn, affected by syntactic, discourse, and pragmatic factors (e.g., syntactic subjects are more prominent than syntactic objects; first-mentioned entities are more prominent than later-mentioned entities; and entities marked by pragmatic operators such as spoken stress are more prominent than non-marked entities). Thus, while it is possible to isolate individual variables in specific experiments, and doing so can reveal important characteristics of referential processing, under normal everyday circumstances, listeners weigh a multitude of interacting influences as they undertake the referential processes that allow them to build coherent discourse representations.

TEST YOURSELF

1. Describe the process of establishing co-reference. Discuss some of the factors that complicate the process. How are co-referential processes related to inference-generating processes?
2. How many different kinds of anaphors are there? Why do we have so many? When do the different kinds of anaphors get used? What makes some anaphors easier to process than others? What characteristics of anaphors matter? How do characteristics of the antecedent affect co-reference?
3. Describe implicit causality and explain how it affects co-reference.
4. Why is it weird to say, "The pastor conducted the wedding ceremony and a bride looked beautiful?"
5. When is it a bad idea to use a highly specific/explicit anaphor and why?
6. What does binding theory say about co-reference? Describe experimental results that cast doubt on some aspects of binding theory.
7. Compare and contrast the memory focus model, centering theory, and the informational load hypothesis.

THINK ABOUT IT

1. Sponsor a contest. See who can come up with the most ways of referring to a common object in under 1 minute.

Notes

1 You may freely substitute *writer* for *speaker* and *reader* for *listener* throughout this chapter, unless otherwise noted.
2 The classic demonstration in linguistics and pyscholinguistics of the difference between sense and reference involves the expressions *morning star* and *evening star*, which have different senses, but the same referent. They are both names for the planet Venus. This footnote was included at the request of my good friend and colleague, Dr. Tamara Swaab.
3 Also, "Joker," "Smoker," and "Midnight Toker."
4 Although proper names can be ambiguous in certain contexts, as illustrated by Monty Python's "Bruce" sketch.
5 See if you can work out what some of those special circumstances might be.
6 But see Dopkins and Ngo (2005) for an alternative interpretation of order-of-mention results and Peter C. Gordon and colleagues' (Gordon, Hendrick, & Ledoux-Foster, 2000) study for a general indictment of the kinds of experiments that produced evidence for order-of-mention effects.
7 In Finnish, case marking on the critical nouns unambiguously indicates what syntactic role (subject or object) each noun plays in the sentence. English has a deeply impoverished case-marking system, so interested readers are encouraged to consult Järvikivi et al. (2005) and Hyöna (in press) for tutorials on Finnish case marking and its effects on sentence processing.
8 Typicality effects have been shown to interact with degree of focus (Almor, 1999).
9 Hawkins (1991) points out further that the definite article is only appropriate for unique entities within pragmatically defined sets, which also play a role in quantification. So we can say *My great uncle Al left a leg in France in World War I,** meaning he left one of his two legs in France; but we can't say *My great uncle Al left some legs in France* because the indefinite *some* implies "more than one, but not all of the set defined by the head." (*True story. Uncle Al insisted that other wounded soldiers be treated first, and it cost him the leg.)

   Garrod and Sanford (1983) refer to felicitous unheralded pronouns as *situational anaphors* and argue that they can be used when they refer to a discourse entity whose existence is necessarily or strongly implied in the situation that the text describes.
10 Again, keeping in mind the caveats highlighted by Gordon and colleagues.
11 A very small subset of inanimate nouns, like ships, are gender marked, as in John Masefield's poem "Sea Fever," "I must down to the seas again, and all I ask is a tall ship and a star to steer her by …"
12 Chomsky's terminology uses the terms *pronoun* and *anaphor* to discriminate between regular pronouns and reflexives and reciprocals, but I will stick with the terminology that is more common in psycholinguistics (*pronoun* vs. *reflexive pronoun*), rather than introducing an additional ambiguity to the term *anaphor*. Thus, the terminology in this section will be consistent with the terminology that has been used throughout the rest of the chapter.
13 Binding theory is also silent about the fact that pronouns such as *he* are preferentially interpreted as referring to sentential subjects in contexts where reference to subject and object are equally acceptable, as in *John told Bill that he deserved the prize* (Gordon & Hendrick, 1997, p. 333).
14 For the curious, the passage can be found on page 164 of *Florida Roadkill*, and the continuation sentence is: *He picked up a muzzle suppressor and the dealer showed him how to make it an operational silencer—"It's your Constitutional right."* See if you can work out what the forward-looking centers in this continuation sentence are.
15 See Chapter 7 for a detailed description of SAT experimental methods.
16 The technical specification of informational load is given in Almor (1999, pp. 751–752) as follows: "Informational load of an anaphor P, given an antecedent N, is a monotonic increasing function of the C-difference between the anaphor and the antecedent," where C-difference is a measure of semantic similarity between the anaphor and the antecedent.

References

Almor, A. (1999). Noun-phrase anaphora and focus: The informational load hypothesis. *Psychological Review, 106,* 748–765.

Almor, A., & Eimas, P. D. (2008). Focus and noun phrase anaphors in spoken language comprehension. *Language and Cognitive Processes, 23,* 201–225.

Almor, A., Kempler, D., MacDonald, M. C., Andersen, E. S., & Tyler, L. K. (1999). Why do Alzheimer patients have difficulty with pronouns? Working memory, semantics, and reference in comprehension and production in Alzheimer's disease. *Brain & Language, 67,* 202–227.

Almor, A., Smith, D. V., Bonilha, L., Fridriksson, J., & Rorden, C. (2007). What is in a name? Spatial brain circuits are used to track discourse referents. *Brain Imaging, 18,* 1215–1219.

Ariel, M. (1990). *Accessing noun-phrase antecedents.* London, UK: Routledge.

Arnold, J. E., Eisenband, J. G., Brown-Schmidt, S., & Trueswell, J. C. (2000). The rapid use of gender information: Evidence of the time course of pronoun resolution. *Cognition, 76,* B13–B26.

Badecker, W., & Straub, K. (2002). The processing role of structural constraints on the interpretation of pronouns and anaphors. *Journal of Experimental Psychology: Learning, Memory, and Cognition, 28,* 748–769.

Birch, S. L., Albrecht, J. E., & Myers, J. L. (2000). Syntactic focusing structures influence discourse processing. *Discourse Processes, 30,* 285–304.

Birch, S. L., & Garnsey, S. M. (1995). The effect of focus on memory for words in sentences. *Journal of Memory and Language, 34,* 232–267.

Callahan, S. M. (2008). Processing anaphoric expressions: Insights from electrophysiological studies. *Journal of Neurolinguistics, 21,* 231–266.

Camblin, C. C., Ledoux, K., Boudewyn, M., Gordon, P. C., & Swaab, T. Y. (2006). Processing new and repeated names: Effects of coreference on repetition priming with speech and fast RSVP. *Brain Research, 1146,* 172–184.

Chang, F. R. (1980). Active memory processes in visual sentence comprehension: Clause effects and pronominal reference. *Memory & Cognition, 8,* 58–64.

Chomsky, N. (1981). *Lectures on government and binding: The Pisa lectures.* Berlin, Germany: Mouton de Gruyter.

Chomsky, N. (1986). *Knowledge of language: Its nature, origin, and use.* New York: Praeger.

Clark, H. H., & Sengul, C. J. (1979). In search of referents for nouns and pronouns. *Memory & Cognition, 7,* 35–41.

Clifton, C., Jr., Kennison, S. M., & Albrecht, J. E. (1997). Reading the words *her, his, him*: Implications for parsing principles based on frequency and on structure. *Journal of Memory and Language, 36,* 276–292.

Cook, A. E., Myers, J. L., & O'Brien, E. J. (2005). Processing an anaphor when there is no antecedent. *Discourse Processes, 39,* 101–120.

Corbett, A. T., & Chang, F. R. (1983). Pronoun disambiguation: Accessing potential antecedents. *Memory & Cognition, 11,* 283–294.

Dell, G. S., McKoon, G., & Ratcliff, R. (1983). The activation of antecedent information during the processing of anaphoric reference in reading. *Journal of Verbal Learning and Verbal Behavior, 22,* 121–132.

Ditman, T., Holcomb, P. J., & Kuperberg, G. R. (2008). Time travel through language: Temporal shifts rapidly decrease information accessibility during reading. *Psychonomic Bulletin & Review, 15,* 750–756.

Dopkins, S., & Ngo, C. T. (2005). The role of recognition memory in anaphor identification. *Journal of Memory and Language, 53,* 186–203.

Dutke, S. (2003). Anaphor resolution as a function of spatial distance and priming: Exploring the spatial distance effect in situation models. *Experimental Psychology, 50,* 270–284.

Fletcher, C. R. (1984). Markedness and topic continuity in discourse processing. *Journal of Verbal Learning and Verbal Behavior, 23,* 487–493.

Foraker, S., & McElree, B. (2007). The role of prominence in pronoun resolution: Active versus passive representations. *Journal of Memory and Language, 56,* 357–383.

Garnham, A. (1989). Integrating information in text comprehension: The interpretation of anaphoric noun phrases. In G. N. Carlson & M. K. Tanenhaus (Eds.), *Linguistic structure in language processing* (pp. 359–399). Dordrecht, The Netherlands: Kluwer.

Garnham, A., & Oakhill, J. (1985). On-line resolution of anaphoric pronouns: Effects of inference making and verb semantics. *British Journal of Psychology, 76,* 385–393.

Garnham, A., & Oakhill, J., & Cain, K. (1997). The interpretation of anaphoric noun phrases: Time course, and effects of overspecificity. *The Quarterly Journal of Experimental Psychology, 50A,* 149–162.

Garnham, A., Traxler, M. J., Oakhill, J., & Gernsbacher, M. A. (1996). The locus of implicit causality effects in comprehension. *Journal of Memory and Language, 35,* 517–543.

Garrod, S., Freudenthal, D., & Boyle, E. (1994). The role of different types of anaphor in the on-line resolution of sentences in a discourse. *Journal of Memory and Language, 33,* 39–68.

Garrod, S., & Sanford, A. J. (1977). Interpreting anaphoric relations: The integration of semantic information while reading. *Journal of Verbal Learning and Verbal Behavior, 16,* 77–90.

Garrod, S., & Sanford, A. J. (1981). Bridging inferences and the extended domain of reference. In J. Long, & A. Baddeley (Eds.) *Attention and performance 9* (pp. 331–346). Hillsdale, NJ: Erlbaum.

Garrod, S., & Sanford, A. J. (1983). The mental representation of discourse in a focused system: Implications for the interpretation of anaphoric noun-phrases. *Journal of Semantics, 1,* 21–41.

Garrod, S., & Terras, M. (2000). The contribution of lexical and situational knowledge to resolving discourse roles: Bonding and resolution. *Journal of Memory and Language, 42,* 526–544.

Garvey, C., & Caramazza, A. (1974). Implicit causality in verbs. *Linguistic Inquiry, 5,* 459–464.

Gernsbacher, M. A. (1989). *The structure building framework.* Hillsdale, NJ: Erlbaum.

Gernsbacher, M. A., & Hargreaves, D. J. (1988). Accessing sentence participants: The advantage of first mention. *Journal of Memory and Language, 27,* 699–717.

Gernsbacher, M. A., & Jescheniak, J. D. (1995). Cataphoric devices in spoken discourse. *Cognitive Psychology, 29,* 24–58.

Givón, T. (1983). *Topic continuity in discourse: A quantitative cross-language study.* New York: John Benjamins.

Glenberg, A. M., Meyer, M., & Lindem, K. (1987). Mental models contribute to foregrounding during text comprehension. *Journal of Memory and Language, 26,* 69–83.

Glucksberg, S., & McCloskey, M. (1981). Decisions about ignorance: Knowing that you don't know. *Journal of Experimental Psychology: Human Learning and Memory, 7,* 311–325.

Gordon, P. C., Grosz, B. J., & Gilliom, L. A. (1993). Pronouns, names, and the centering of attention in discourse. *Cognitive Science, 17,* 311–347.

Gordon, P. C., & Hendrick, R. (1997). Intuitive knowledge of linguistic co-reference. *Cognition, 62,* 325–370.

Gordon, P. C., & Hendrick, R. (1998). The representation and processing of coreference in discourse. *Cognitive Science: A Multidisciplinary Journal, 22,* 389–424.

Gordon, P. C., & Hendrick, R., & Johnson, M. (2001). Memory interference during language processing. *Journal of Experimental Psychology: Learning, Memory, and Cognition, 27,* 1411–1423.

Gordon, P. C., & Hendrick, R., & Ledoux-Foster, K. (2000). Language comprehension and probe-list memory. *Journal of Experimental Psychology: Learning, Memory and Cognition, 26,* 766–775.

Gordon, P. C., & Scearce, K. A. (1995). Pronominalization and discourse coherence, discourse structure and pronoun interpretation. *Memory & Cognition, 23,* 313–323.

Greene, S. B., McKoon, G., & Ratcliff, R. (1992). Pronoun resolution and discourse models. *Journal of Experimental Psychology: Learning, Memory, and Cognition, 18,* 266–283.

Grosz, B. J., & Sidner, C. L. (1986). Attention, intentions, and the structure of discourse. *Computational Linguistics, 12,* 175–204.

Guerry, M., Gimenes, M., Caplan, D., & Rigalleau, F. (2006). How long does it take to find a cause? An online investigation of implicit causality in sentence production. *The Quarterly Journal of Experimental Psychology, 59,* 1535–1555.

Gundel, J. K., Hedberg, N., & Zacharski, R. (1993). Cognitive status and the form of referring expressions in discourse. *Language, 69,* 274–307.

Haviland, S. E., & Clark, H. H. (1974). What's new? Acquiring new information as a process in comprehension. *Journal of Verbal Learning and Verbal Behavior, 13,* 512–521.

Hawkins, J. A. (1978). *Definiteness and indefiniteness: A study in reference and grammaticality prediction.* London: Croome Helm.

Hawkins, J. A. (1991). On (in)definite articles: Implicatures and (un)grammaticality prediction. *Journal of Linguistics, 27,* 405–442.

Hintzman, D. L. (2001). Similarity, global matching, and judgments of frequency. *Memory & Cognition, 29,* 547–556.

Hyöna, J. (in press). Sentence processing in Finnish. *Language and Linguistics Compass.*

Järvikivi, J., van Gompel, R. P. G., Hyöna, J., & Bertram, R. (2005). Ambiguous pronoun resolution. *Psychological Science, 16,* 260–264.

Kennison, S. M. (2003). Comprehending the pronouns *her*, *him*, and *his*: Implications for theories of referential processing. *Journal of Memory and Language, 49,* 335–352.

Klin, C. M., Guzmán, A. E., Weingartner, K. M., & Ralano, A. S. (2006). When anaphor resolution fails: Partial encoding of anaphoric inferences. *Journal of Memory and Language, 54,* 131–143.

Ledoux, K., Gordon, P. C., Camblin, C. C., & Swaab, T. Y. (2007). Coreference and lexical repetition: Mechanisms of discourse integration. *Memory & Cognition, 35,* 801–815.

Long, D. L., & Deley, L. (2000). Implicit causality and discourse focus: The interaction of text and reader characteristics in pronoun resolution. *Journal of Memory and Language, 42,* 545–570.

McDonald, J. L., & MacWhinney, B. (1995). The time course of anaphor resolution: Effects of implicit verb causality and gender. *Journal of Memory and Language, 34,* 543–566.

MacDonald, M. C., & MacWhinney, B. (1990). Measuring inhibition and facilitation from pronouns. *Journal of Memory and Language, 29,* 469–492.

Morris, R. K., & Folk, J. R. (1998). Focus as a contextual priming mechanism in reading. *Memory & Cognition, 26,* 1313–1322.

Morrow, D. G. (1985). Prominent characters and events organize narrative understanding. *Journal of Memory and Language, 24,* 390–404.

Morrow, D. G., Bower, G. H., & Greenspan, S. L. (1989). Updating situation models during narrative comprehension. *Journal of Memory and Language, 28,* 292–312.

Myers, J. L., & O'Brien, E. J. (1998). Accessing the discourse representation during reading. *Discourse Processes, 26,* 131–157.

Nicol, J. & Swinney, D. (1989). The role of structure in co-reference assignment during sentence comprehension. *Journal of Psycholinguistic Research, 18,* 5–20.

Nieuwland, M. S., Otten, M., & van Berkum, J. J. A. (2007). Who are you talking about? Tracking discourse-level referential processing with event-related brain potentials. *Journal of Cognitive Neuroscience, 19,* 228–236.

Nieuwland, M. S., Petersson, K. M., & van Berkum, J. J. A. (2007). On sense and reference: Examining the functional neuroanatomy of referential processing. *Neuroimage, 37,* 993–1004.

Nieuwland, M. S., & van Berkum, J. J. A. (2008). The interplay between semantic and referential aspects of anaphoric noun phrase resolution: Evidence from ERPs. *Brain & Language, 106,* 119–131.

O'Brien, E. J. (1987). Antecedent search processes and the structure of text. *Journal of Experimental Psychology: Learning, Memory, and Cognition, 13,* 278–290.

Osterhout, L., Bersick, M., & McLaughlin, J. (1997). Brain potentials reflect violations of gender stereotypes. *Memory & Cognition, 25,* 273–285.

Rinck, M., & Bower, G. H. (1995). Anaphora resolution and the focus of attention in situation models. *Journal of Memory and Language, 34,* 110–131.

Sanford, A. J, Garrod, S., & Boyle, J. M. (1977). An independence of mechanisms in the origins of reading and classification related semantic distance effects. *Memory & Cognition, 5,* 214–220.

Speer, N. K., & Zacks, J. M. (2005). Temporal changes as event boundaries: Processing and memory consequences of narrative time shifts. *Journal of Memory and Language, 53,* 125–140.

Sturt, P. (2003). The time-course of the application of binding constraints in reference resolution. *Journal of Memory and Language, 48,* 542–562.

Swaab, T. Y., Camblin, C. C., & Gordon, P. C. (2004). Electrophysiological evidence for reversed lexical repetition effects in language processing. *Journal of Cognitive Neuroscience, 16,* 715–726.

Traxler, M. J., Bybee, M. D., & Pickering, M. J. (1997). Influence of connectives on language comprehension: Eye-tracking evidence for incremental interpretation. *Quarterly Journal of Experimental Psychology A, 50,* 481–497.

Traxler, M. J., Sanford, A. J., Aked, J. P., & Moxey, L. M. (1997). Processing causal and diagnostic statements in discourse. *Journal of Experimental Psychology: Learning, Memory, and Cognition, 23,* 88–101.

Van Berkum, J. J. A. (in press). The neuropragmatics of "simple" utterance comprehension: An ERP review. In U. Sauerland & K. Yatsushiro (Eds.), *Semantics and pragmatics: From experiment to theory*. Basingstoke, England: Palgrave MacMillan.

Van Berkum, J. J. A., Brown, C. M., & Hagoort, P. (1999). Early referential context effects in sentence processing: Evidence from event-related potentials. *Journal of Memory and Language, 41,* 147–182.

Van Berkum, J. J. A., Koornneef, A. W., Otten, M., & Nieuwland, M. S. (2007). Establishing reference in language comprehension: An electrophysiological perspective. *Brain Research, 1146,* 158–171.

Yang, C. L., Gordon, P. C., Hendrick, R., & Hue, C. W. (2003). Constraining the comprehension of pronominal expressions in Chinese. *Cognition, 86,* 283–315.

Yang, C. L., Gordon, P. C., Hendrick, R., Wu, J. T., & Chou, T. L. (2001). The processing of coreference for reduced expressions in discourse integration. *Journal of Psycholinguistic Research, 30,* 21–35.

Zwaan, R. A., Langston, M. C., & Graesser, A. C. (1995). The construction of situation models in narrative comprehension: An event-indexing model. *Psychological Science, 6,* 292–297.

Plate 1 Transcranial Magnetic Stimulation (TMS) (from the National Institute of Neurological Disorders and Stroke: http://intra.ninds.nih.gov/Research.asp?People_ID=196)

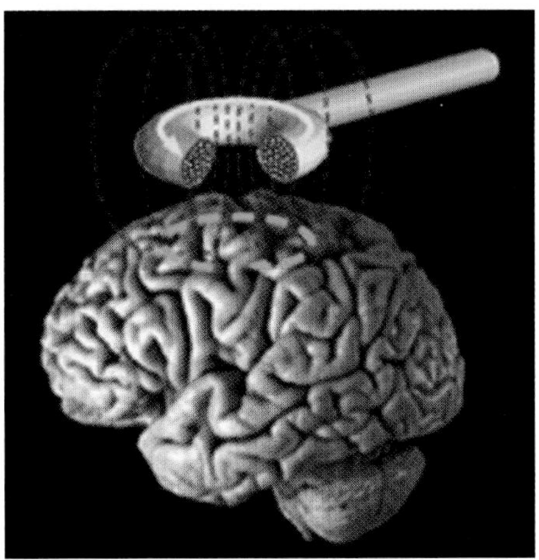

Plate 2 Patterns of neural activity in response to actual body movements (left side) and words referring to face (*smile*), arm (*throw*), and leg (*walk*) actions (right side) (Hauk, Johnsrude, & Pülvermüller, 2004, p. 304). Neural activity related to face movement appears in green, finger and arms movement in red, and foot and leg movement in blue.

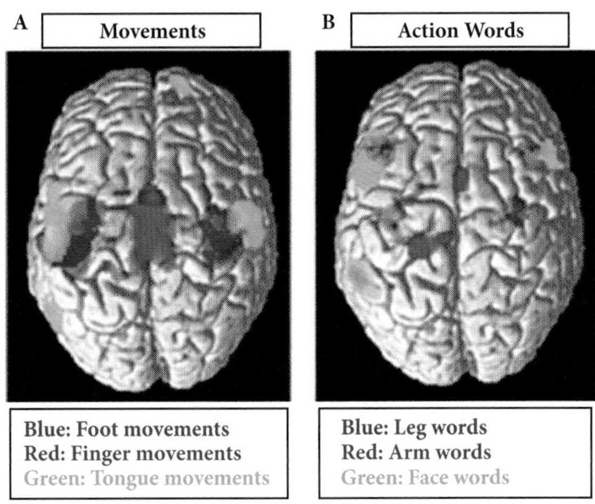

Plate 3 Voxel-based lesion–symptom mapping (VLSM) results for non-linguistic tasks (top) and reading comprehension (bottom) (from Saygin, Wilson, Dronkers, & Bates, 2004, p. 1797). Deficits in action perception are more strongly correlated with damage to frontal regions. Deficits in reading about actions are more strongly correlated with more posterior regions.

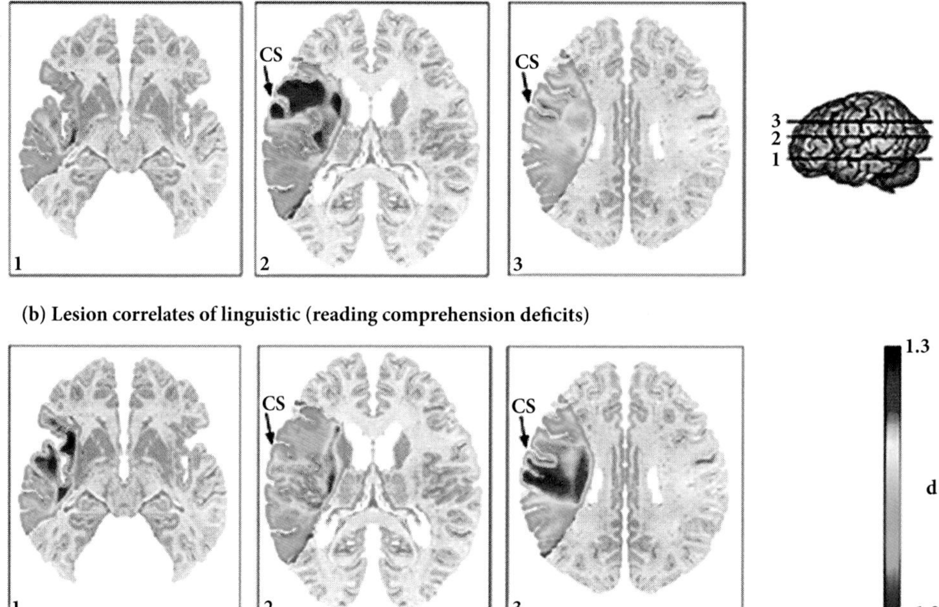

Plate 4 PET imaging data (from Vandenberghe, Price, Wise, Josephs, & Frackowiak, 1996, p. 255). Subjects performed similarity judgments on words or pictures. Top: common areas that were activated for both words and pictures. Middle: areas that were activated for words but not pictures. Bottom: areas that were activated for pictures but not words.

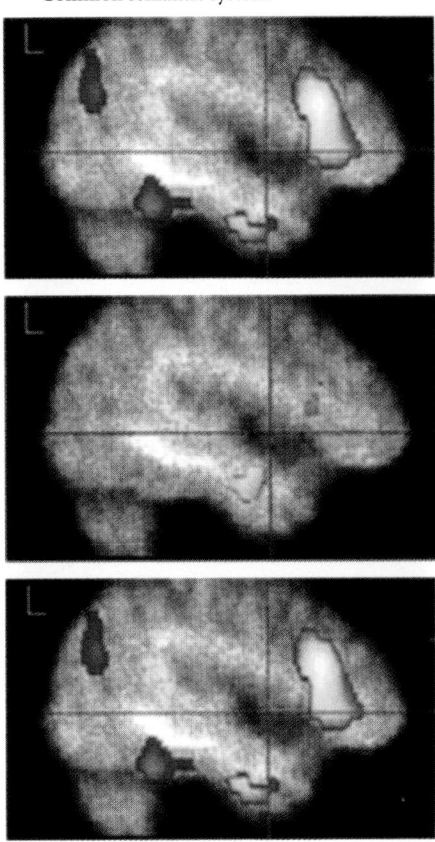

Plate 5 PET neuroimaging results from Martin, Wiggs, Ungerleider, & Haxby (1996, p. 651). The top half shows greater occipital lobe activity during covert naming of animals versus tools. The bottom half shows greater inferior frontal lobe activity during covert naming of tools versus animals.

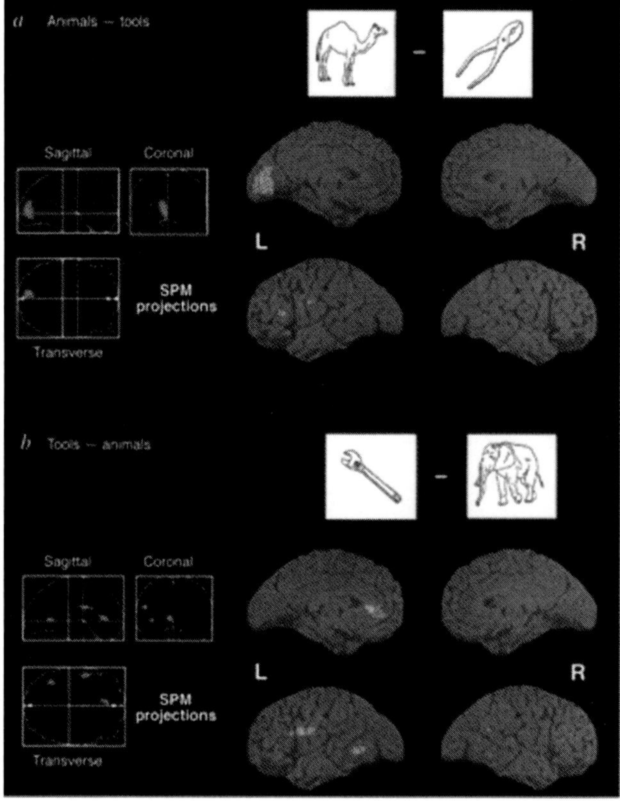

Plate 6 fMRI data showing greater left-lateralized frontal activity for questions tapping abstract versus perceptual properties of animals (shown in orange; Goldberg, Perfetti, Fiez, & Schneider, 2007, p. 3796). Questions that tapped visual features of animals led to increased activity in right parietal lobe (dark blue).

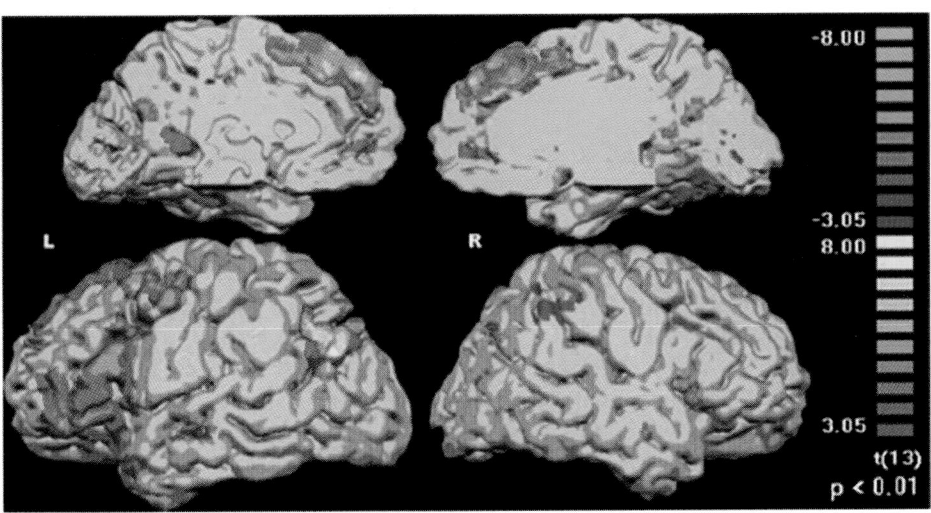

Plate 7 Lesion–performance correlations from Damasio, Grabowski, Tranel, Hichwa, & Damasio (1996, p. 501)

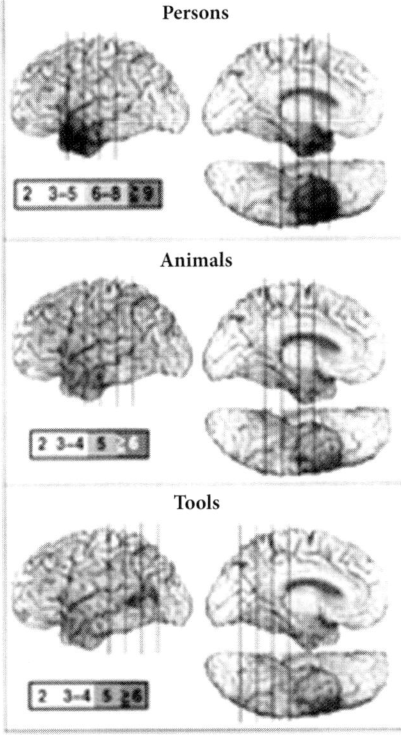

Plate 8 fMRI results comparing response to chronological (green) and emotional (yellow and red) information in stories (Ferstl, Rinck, & Von Cramon, 2005, p. 728)

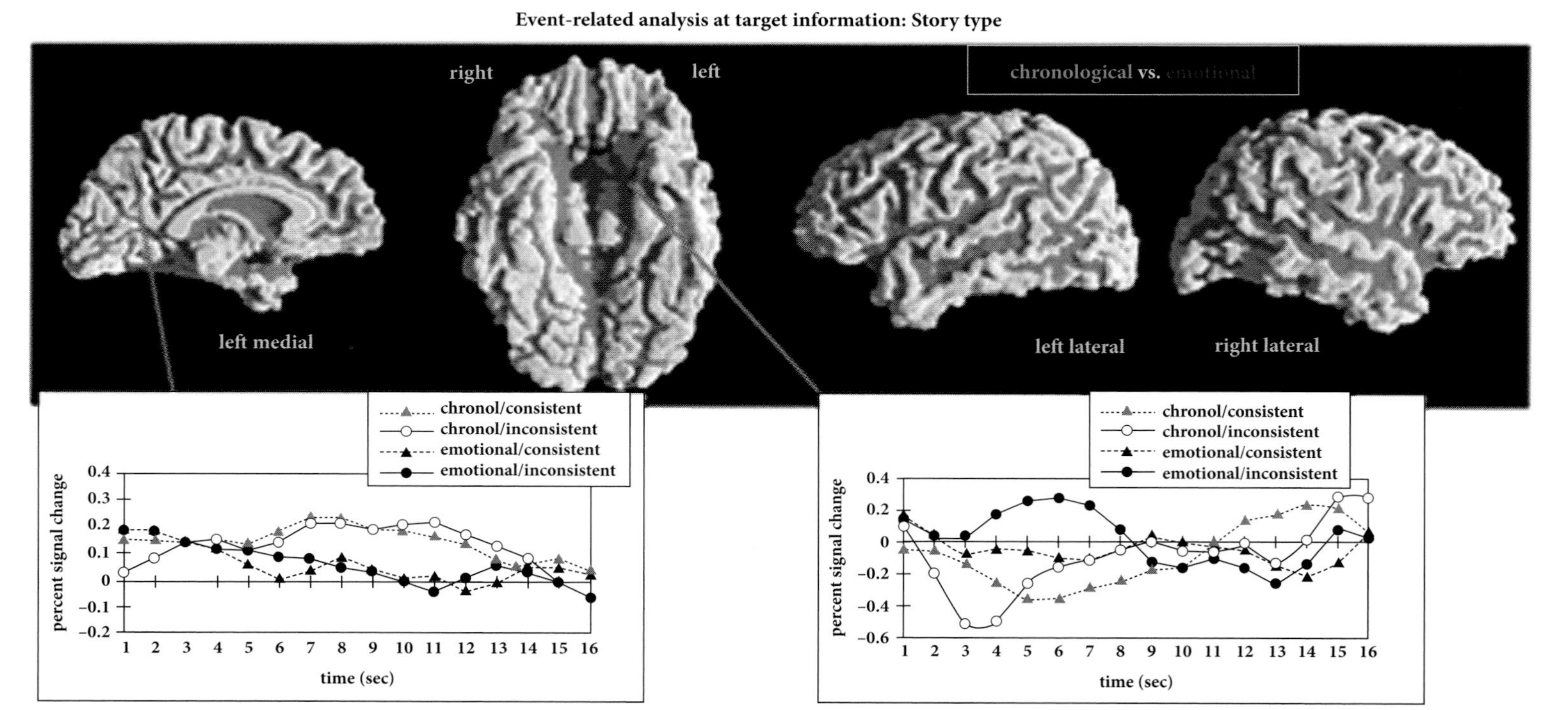

Plate 9 Brain activity during an insight-inducing problem-solving task (from Jung-Beeman et al., 2004)

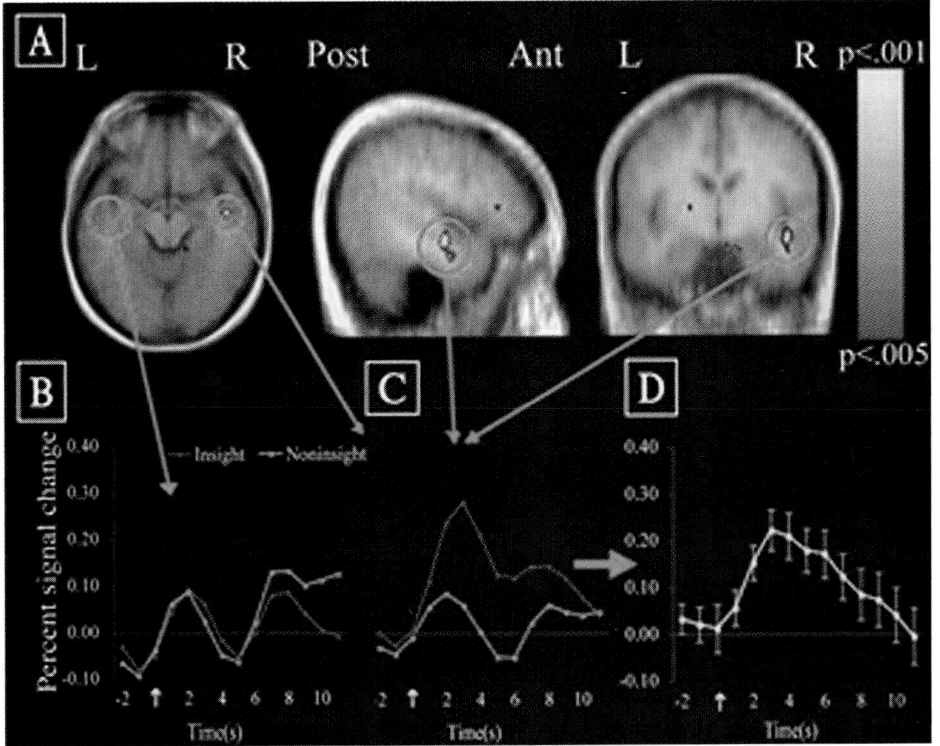

Plate 10 fMRI results from Virtue, Haberman, Clancy, Parrish, & Beeman (2006, p. 107). The areas in yellow and red, primarily in the right superior temporal lobe, showed greater activity when the text implied, rather than explicitly stated, that the focused character engaged in an action.

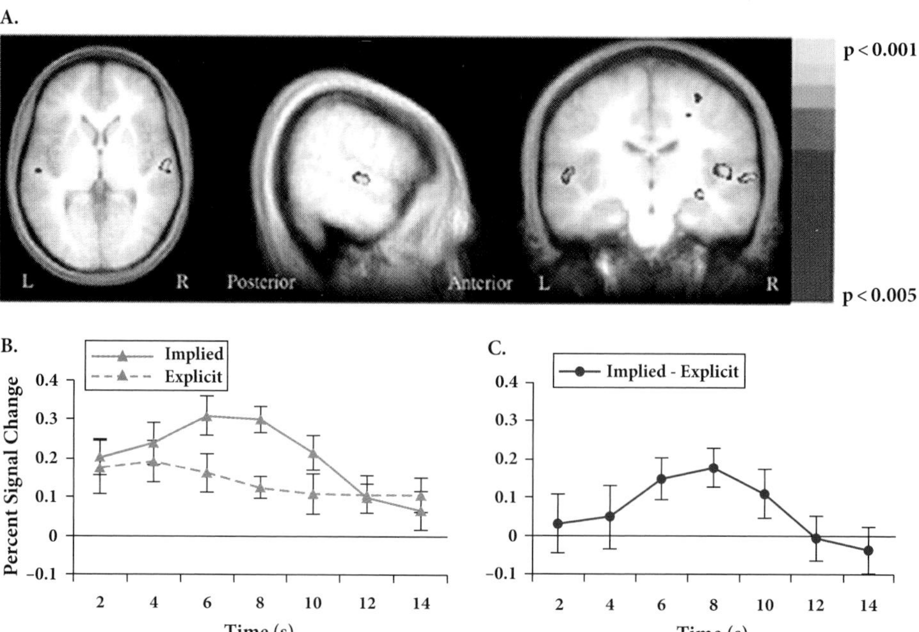

Plate 11 fMRI activation results from St. George, Kutas, Martinez, & Sereno (1999, p. 1320). The *right* hemisphere is pictured on the *left* hand side of the picture.

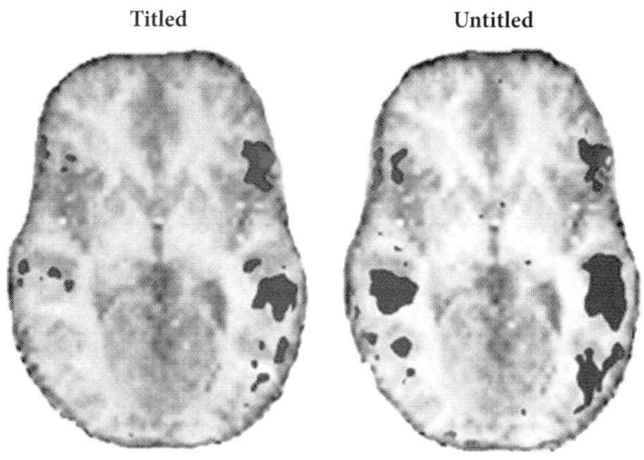

Plate 12 Whole-brain image of titled (top) vs. untitled (bottom) stories from St. George, Kutas, Martinez, & Sereno (1999, p. 1322)

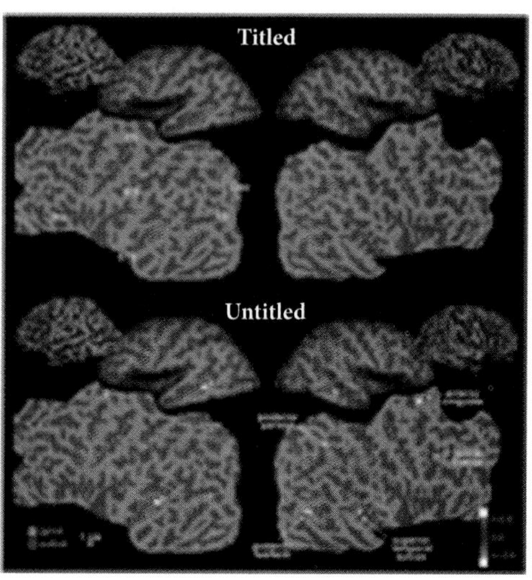

Plate 13 Right-hemisphere brain activity is greater for unrelated pairs of sentences than for closely related pairs of sentences (from Kuperberg, Lakshmanan, Caplan, & Holcomb, 2006, p. 357)

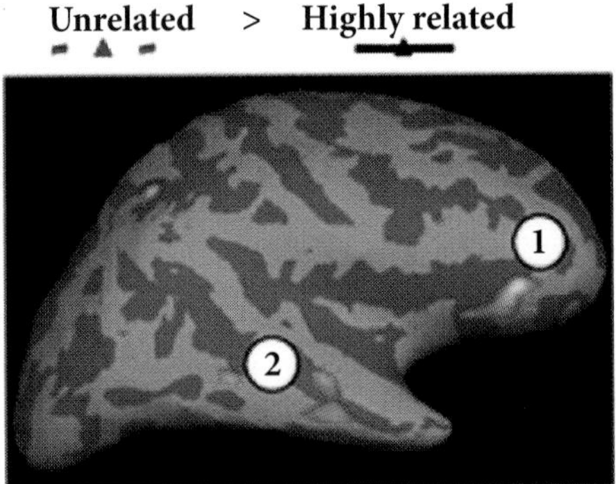

Plate 14 The brain responds differently to highly coherent versus incoherent stories. This is true of both the left hemisphere and the right hemisphere. Areas of the brain that respond more strongly to moderately coherent stories than to either highly coherent and incoherent stories are marked in yellow (from Kuperberg, Lakshmanan, Caplan, & Holcomb, 2006, p. 354)

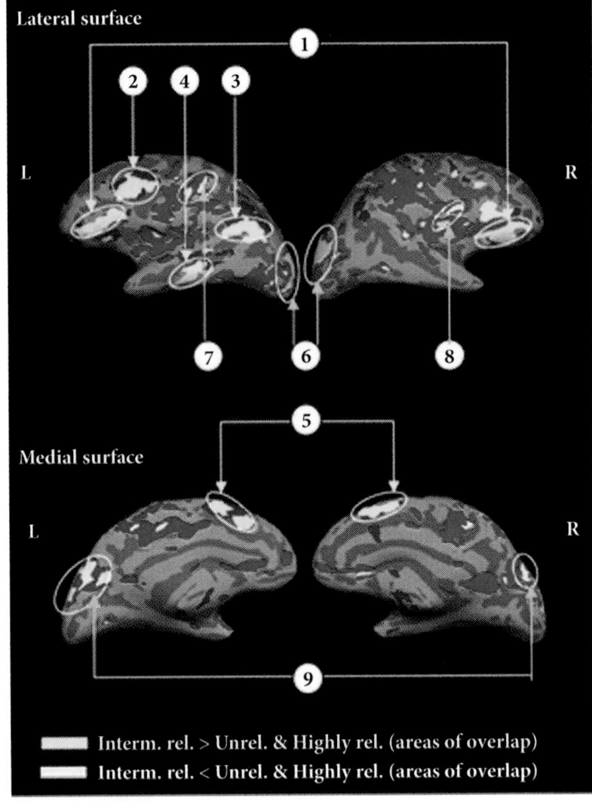

Plate 15 PET results from Bottini et al. (1994, p. 1246). The scans indicate greater blood flow in right-hemisphere brain regions for metaphoric sentences compared to literal sentences. The left-hand brains show the right hemisphere. The top brains show the medial (middle) surface of the brain. The bottom brains show the lateral (outside) surfaces.

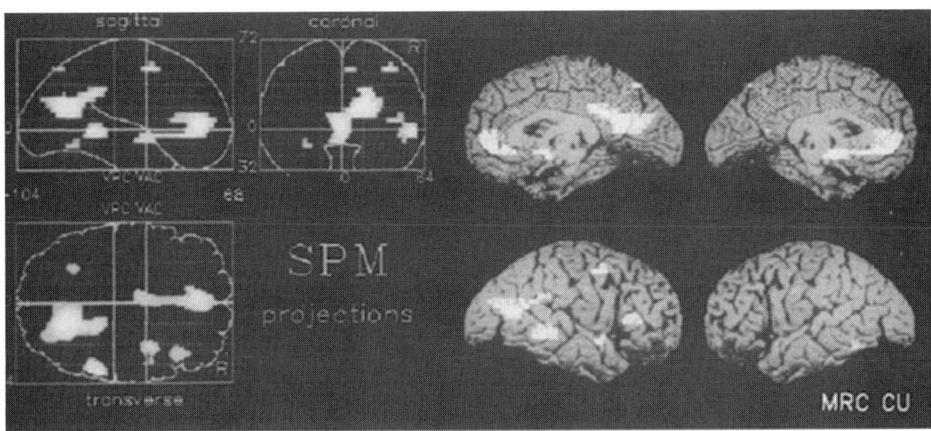

Plate 16 fMRI results from Rapp, Leube, Erb, Grodd & Kircher (2004, p. 399). Metaphoric sentences produced greater neural response in the left hemisphere when compared with literal sentences. No differences based on sentence type (literal vs. metaphoric) were observed in the right hemisphere. (Compare Plate 16 to Plate 15. The clash of data could hardly be more extreme.)

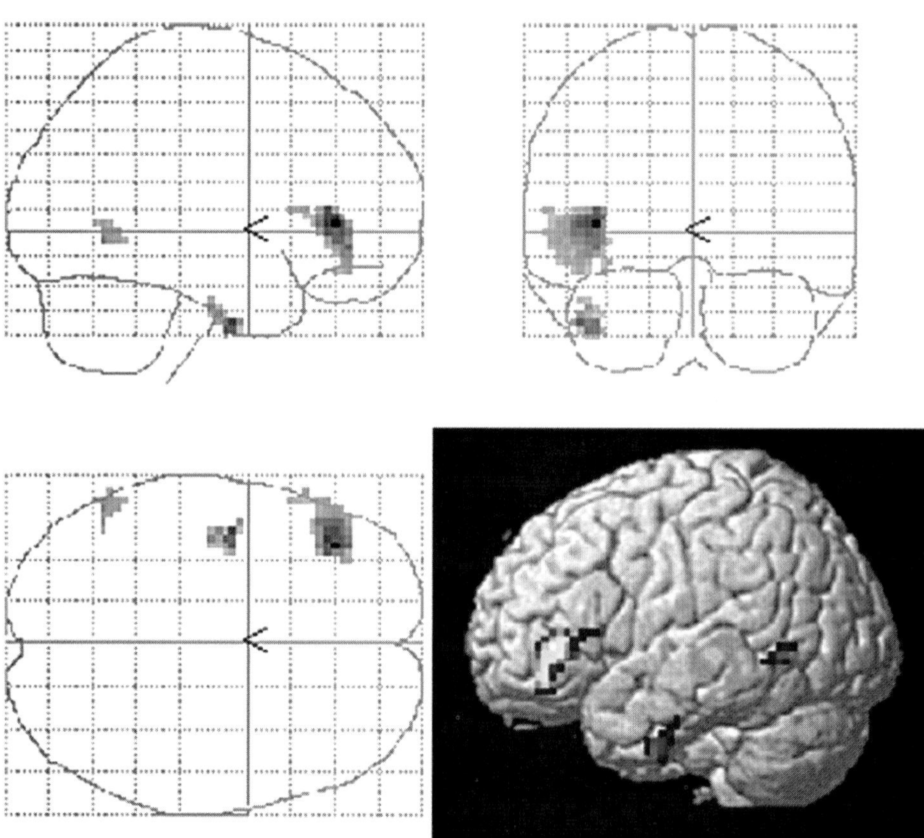

Plate 17 fMRI results from Mashal, Faust, Hendler, & Jung-Beeman (2007, p. 123). The orange areas represent parts of the brain that responded with greater activity to novel metaphors compared to conventional/familiar metaphors. The circled area is the right homologue of (counterpart to) Wernicke's area.

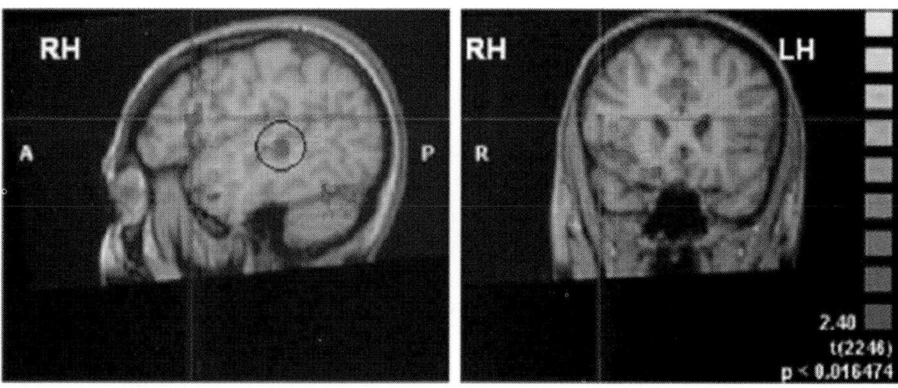

Plate 18 Neuroimaging data from Dietz, Jones, Gareau, Zeffiro, & Eden (2005, pp. 86, 88). Left: A comparison of neural activity for novel pseudo-words (left) and familiar words (right). Right: Activity associated with real word reading subtracted from activity in pseudo-word reading. The left hemisphere is shown on the right; the right hemisphere is shown on the left.

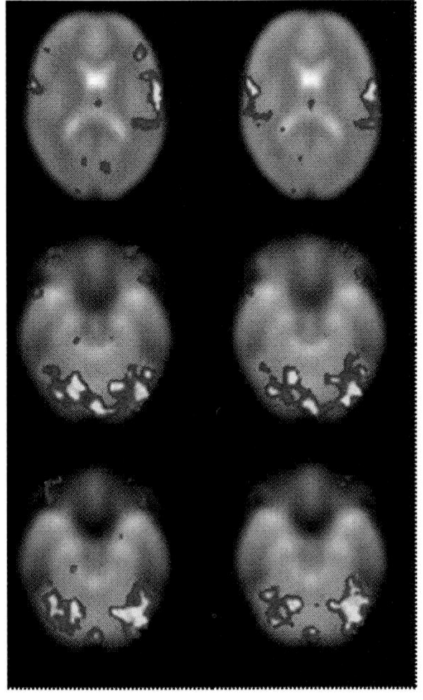

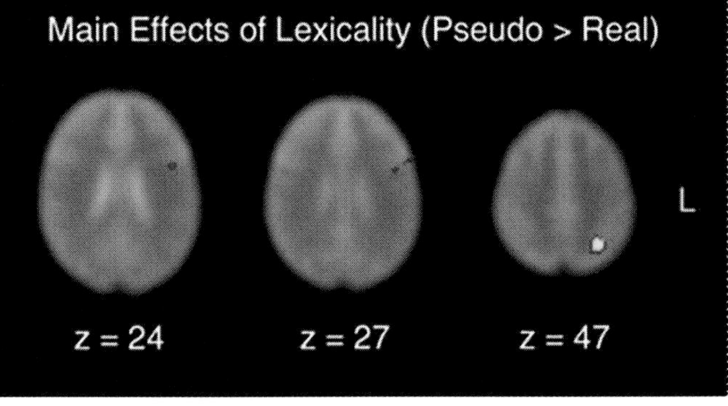

Plate 19 Brain response to viewing ASL sentences (from Neville et al., 1998, p. 924). The graph shows the difference between the brain's response to meaningless and meaningful ASL gestures. The left hemisphere appears on the left hand side. The right hemisphere appears on the right. The top two pictures are of hearing people who do not know sign language. Unsurprisingly, their brain's response to meaningless and meaningful signs is the same. The middle pictures show that deaf signers activate both hemispheres to a greater extent when seeing meaningful signs. The bottom pictures show that hearing signers have a bilateral response to meaningful signs as well, but they do not activate all of the right-hemisphere regions that deaf signers do. Red means very large difference in activation between meaningful and meaningless signs. Yellow means small, but still significant, difference in activation.

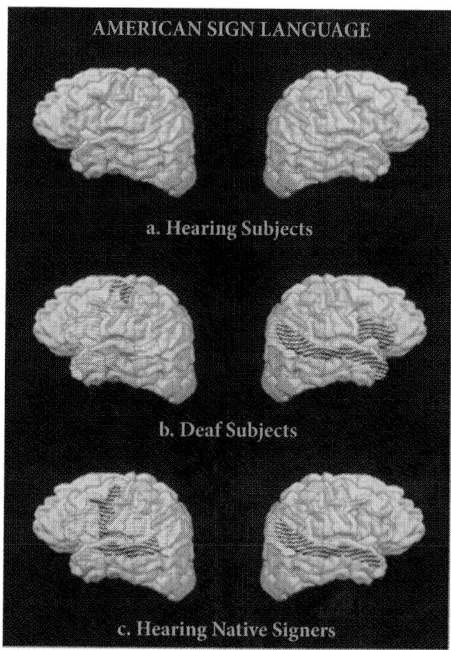

Plate 20 The arcuate fasciculus (from Catani, Jones, and ffytche, 2005)

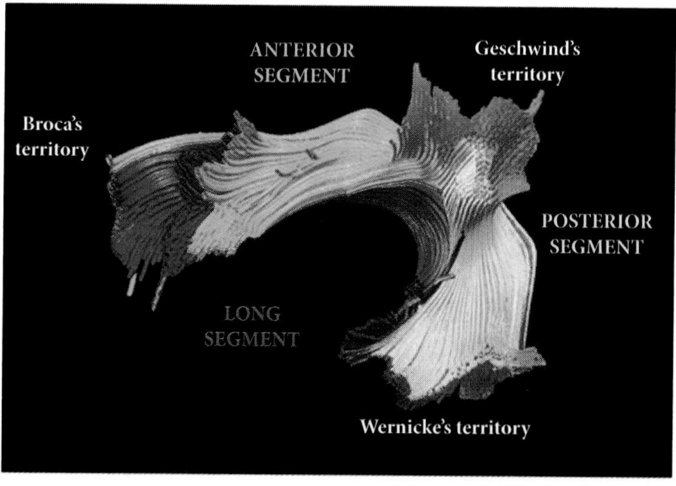

Plate 21 VLSM plot of positive t-values obtained by comparing patients with and without lesions at each voxel on the CYCLE-R sentence comprehension measure

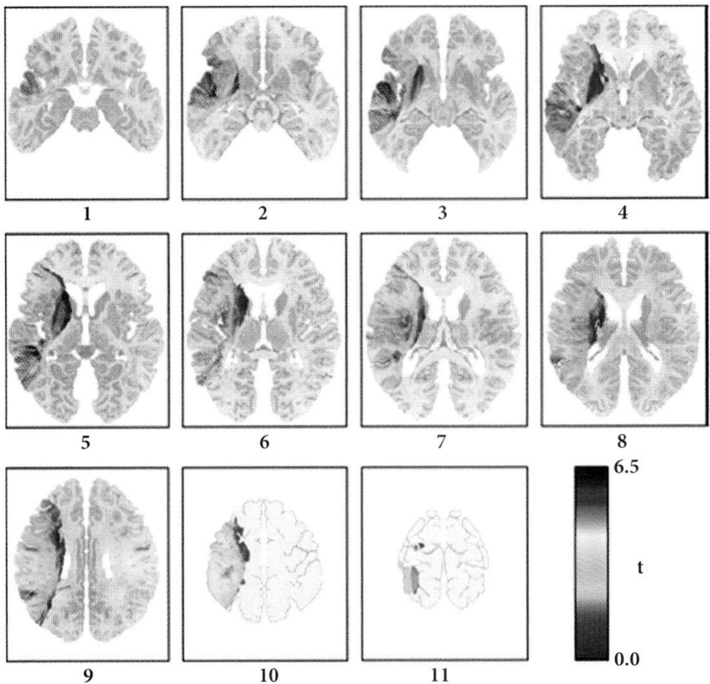

Non-Literal Language Processing

7

Thus far, we have been treating language as though there was a straightforward relationship between what the speaker said and what the speaker meant. But consider the following expressions:

Can you open the door?
He's a real stud.
The stop light went from green to red.

What do these expressions have in common? What they have in common is that what they say (the *standard* or *literal meaning*) and what they mean (*the speaker* or *intended meaning*) are different. Compare *Can you open the door?* to *Can you bench press 200 pounds?* On the surface, these two expressions look very similar, but they are interpreted in very different ways. Most people would interpret the first as a polite way of saying, *I want you to open the door*. Most people would interpret the second differently, not as a polite way of asking someone to lift 200 pounds, but rather as a direct request for information about how strong the addressee is. If a speaker wanted to do the polite request form of the bench-pressing question, they would most likely say something like, *Please bench press 200 pounds. I would like to watch*. Similarly, under all but the most limited circumstances, *He's a real stud* does not imply that the speaker thinks the subject is a male horse. Instead, the speaker is expressing the opinion that the subject possesses the qualities of a virile, strong male. But doesn't *The stop light went from green to red*, mean exactly that "The stop light went from green to red"? The tricky thing here is to think carefully about the basic meaning of the verb *went*. *Went* is the past tense form of the verb *go*, whose default, literal meaning expresses motion from one place to another. So, you might say, *The plane went from Los Angeles to Sacramento* to express

Introduction to Psycholinguistics: Understanding Language Science, First Edition.
Matthew J. Traxler.

motion of the plane along a pathway. But stop lights don't move along a pathway. They are stationary. What actually happened is that one light stopped shining right before another light started shining.[1] Nothing moved, but we still use a *verb of motion* to describe the event. In all three of these cases, we are dealing with *non-literal* language, because there is a difference between the standard meaning, based on the way the words in the expression are normally interpreted, and the meaning a listener actually assigns to the utterance. Non-literal language creates a number of challenges for the language comprehension system, because the relationship between what is said and what is meant is not always easy or straightforward for the listener to discover. This chapter reviews different types of non-literal language, explains why non-literal expressions create challenges for any interpretation system, and describes different theories about how non-literal language is processed and interpreted.

Types of Non-Literal Language

Non-literal language comes in several different forms. There are *indirect requests*, like *Can you open the door? Do you have the time? Would you pass the salt?* (which contrast with direct requests or commands: *Open the door! Tell me the time!*) There are *idioms* like, *Dave kicked the bucket*, and *Kathy spilled the beans*. There are different kinds of *metaphors*, like, *Susan flew down the street on her bicycle* and *That lecture was a sleeping pill*. There is *irony* and *sarcasm*, such as when your friend says *Now that was exciting*, after the sleeping pill lecture. All of these forms have in common the characteristic that what the speaker said, the *literal meaning*, is different than the interpretation that the speaker wants you to formulate, the *speaker meaning*. Because what is said is different from the intended meaning, non-literal language requires the listener to draw *pragmatic inferences*, by combining information about the speaker, the context in which the expression is produced, and the literal content of the utterance to answer the questions: What meaning does the speaker wish to convey (what is on the speaker's mind)? Why did the speaker produce that utterance in this context?

How are these pragmatic inferences drawn so that the listener can see beyond the literal meaning to the speaker meaning? Answering this question entails solving two related problems. First, how do you know that the speaker does not intend a literal meaning? That is, how do you spot when the speaker is using non-literal, rather than literal, language? This is sometimes called the *recognition* problem (Stern, 2000). Second, when the speaker meaning differs from the literal meaning, how does the listener compute the non-literal meaning? Let's start with the recognition problem first.

The Standard Pragmatic View

Figurative language has traditionally been considered derivative from and more complex than ostensibly straightforward literal language.
SAM GLUCKSBERG

The *standard pragmatic view* assumes that computing literal meaning is the core function in language interpretation (Clark & Lucy, 1975; Glucksberg, 1998; Searle, 1979). According to this view, when people hear a metaphoric expression, the first interpretation that the language comprehension system comes up with will be the one that is most closely connected to tangible objects and the directly perceivable world. If someone says, *Deb's a real tiger*, the standard pragmatic view says that you will interpret the expression as if it meant *Deb is a true example of a feline predator, usually orange-brown colored with black stripes, whose current range is limited to parts of south Asia and eastern Siberia.* Of course, normal people will *not* interpret *Deb's a real tiger* in this way—they will quickly come up with a more sensible interpretation. Nonetheless, the standard pragmatic view of non-literal language interpretation argues that the literal meaning is computed and at least temporarily considered as the intended meaning of the expression, even though that initial interpretation is later discarded in favor of a more sensible one (e.g., *Deb has an energetic and fierce personality.*) In this way, the standard pragmatic view resembles the *garden path theory* of syntactic parsing (see Chapter 4). Both argue for an initial stage of interpretation that works for many expressions, followed by a second stage of interpretation involving re-analysis and re-interpretation for expressions that do not fit the normal pattern. According to the standard pragmatic view of non-literal language interpretation, the reanalysis process involves computing an alternative meaning, rather than an alternative syntactic structure. The standard pragmatic view adopts this posture because, as Glucksberg explains, non-literal meanings are viewed as being more mysterious and complex than literal meanings. Consequently, as suggested by Colston & Gibbs (2002, p. 58), "Under ([the] standard pragmatic view, understanding any non-literal utterance requires that listeners analyze a sentence's literal meaning before other figurative meanings can be derived." Given the posture that literal meanings are computed first, how and why are metaphoric meanings ever discovered? Given that every expression can be interpreted literally (people really can kick the bucket, there really could be a Siberian tiger named "Deb" in your local zoo), how do people discover that the speaker or writer intended a non-literal meaning?

According to the standard pragmatic view, solving the recognition problem involves computing the literal meaning and checking whether the literal meaning makes sense in context (Clark & Lucy, 1975; Miller, 1979; Searle, 1979; Stern, 2000). So, the listener first computes the literal meaning, and then attempts to integrate that meaning with the linguistic and social context. The listener will engage in further pragmatic inferencing and non-literal interpretation only if the literal meaning is deficient in some way. The question then becomes: How does the listener know whether the literal interpretation is deficient? One way would be to simply check whether the literal interpretation is true or false. If, as the Barenaked Ladies say, *You can be my Yoko Ono*, that must be literally false. There is only one Yoko Ono, and you are not her. If *You can be my Yoko Ono* is obviously false, then the listener will be motivated to answer the question: Why did the speaker say something that is obviously false? Sometimes, this conflict between the truth conditions imposed by the world and the information content of the utterance can be resolved by adopting a metaphoric interpretation. You are not literally Yoko Ono, but you can have some of the properties that Yoko Ono exemplifies. If you really do have some of the properties that Yoko Ono exemplifies, then the meaning assigned to that utterance is no longer false, and you have simultaneously discovered a true interpretation and the reason why the speaker said *You can be my Yoko Ono*. The speaker is expressing an opinion that you possess some of the qualities that Yoko Ono possesses, which could be true.

This solution of the recognition problem runs into trouble fairly quickly, however. The reason why is because many literally true expressions are assigned a non-literal meaning (Glucksberg & Keysar, 1990; Glucksberg, Keysar, & McGlone, 1992; Stern, 2000). When George Harrison of the Beatles says, *I'm not the wreck of the Hesperus*, that is literally true. But Harrison is not rejecting a literal comparison of himself and a shipwreck, he is rejecting one metaphoric comparison in favor of a more apt metaphoric comparison (and so the next line of the song is, *Feel more like the Wall of China*). Here's another example: *John is a real Marine*, is literally true if John is in the Marine Corps. Nonetheless, most people would adopt a non-literal interpretation of that expression, along the lines of *John is a really good, exemplary, or skilled Marine*. Similarly, the expression *My wife is an animal* is literally true. But a non-literal meaning, along the lines of *My wife behaves in an unpredictable and uncivilized way*, will be preferred over the literal interpretation. So, literal falsehood is not a necessary precondition for an utterance to be assigned a non-literal meaning. What we need, then, is a theory that does not require utterances to be literally false before they are assigned a non-literal interpretation.

If literal falsehood is not sufficient to classify an utterance as non-literal, how can we know when a non-literal meaning is intended? There are, in fact, a number of other criteria that could be applied. As Stern (2000, p. 3) explains, an utterance could be considered deficient if its literal meaning is, "grammatically deviant, semantically anomalous, explicitly or implicitly self-contradictory, conceptually absurd, nonsensical … pragmatically inappropriate, obviously false, or so obviously true that no one would have reason to utter [it]." According to the standard pragmatic view, the listener will consider a non-literal interpretation when the literal meaning lacks one or more of the characteristics that make utterances fit into their contexts. For instance, if you were at a party, and an attractive stranger said, *Can you get me a beer?* you wouldn't just say, *Yes* (which is the appropriate response to a literal request for information). You would go and fetch a beer. On the other hand, if the same attractive stranger said, *Can you bench press 200 pounds?* You might very well say, *Yes I can, by cracky! Come by the gym tomorrow and I'll show you.* According to the standard pragmatic view, the indirect question *Can you get me a beer?* violates the normal conversational rules (as laid out by philosophers like H. Paul Grice, 1989) because people at parties generally obviously have the physical ability to fetch beer. The indirect request is therefore deviant, because the answer to the question (on its literal interpretation) is so obvious that there is no reason why any sane person would ask it. The listener can repair the situation, however, by reinterpreting the "deviant" utterance as a (non-literal) indirect request. By contrast, most people at parties do not obviously have the physical ability to lift very heavy weights, and so *Can you bench press 200 pounds?*, which has the same form as *Can you get me a beer?* is not considered deviant, and is therefore interpreted as a literal request for information.

A literal interpretation of an utterance may be rejected in favor of a non-literal meaning if the literal interpretation is false (as in *Deb is a real tiger*) or if the literal interpretation violates one or more of the characteristics of "normal" utterances. What are the characteristics of "normal" utterances, and where do they come from? One general theory that explains why utterances are "normal" or "abnormal" is Grice's (1989) theory of *conversational maxims*. A conversational maxim is a rule or guideline that applies to things people say while having a conversation. Grice starts with the idea that participants in a conversation try to cooperate with one another in order to expand the pool of shared knowledge (see also Clark, 1996; Glucksberg & Keysar, 1990; Wilkes-Gibbs & Clark, 1992). Engaging in this cooperative activity involves following other rules (maxims) as well. These include the maxims of *quality*, *quantity*, *manner*, and *relation*. The maxim of *quality* specifies that you should tell the truth; your utterances should be literally true. We don't like it when people lie to us. The maxim of *quantity* specifies that your utterances should provide new information. So you should not simply repeat information that is already in *common ground* (knowledge that is shared, and known to be shared, between the participants in the conversation). We get annoyed when we have to listen to the same story over and over again, or when someone repeats themselves unnecessarily, or belabors a point long after we have already figured out the thrust of their argument, or tries our patience by sticking to a settled topic, or doesn't tell us anything that we don't already know. The maxim of *manner* specifies that your utterances should be clear and unambiguous. You should convey information as plainly and directly as possible, so that your utterance does not have multiple possible interpretations. The maxim of *relation* specifies that your utterance should contribute to or continue the current topic of discussion, unless you explicitly introduce a new topic. So, if we are talking about baseball, my next utterance should be on the topic of baseball unless I say something like, *Enough baseball, let's talk about me now.*

Indirect requests such as *Can you get me a beer?* can violate the maxim of quantity. It is obvious from my appearance that I am physically capable of retrieving beer, so uttering that question does not provide me with an obvious means of moving the conversation forward *if* it is interpreted as a literal request for information. Metaphoric expressions also commonly violate one or more of the Gricean conversational maxims. If someone says to you, *My wife is an animal,* the literal interpretation will violate at least the maxims of quantity and relation, and possibly quality and manner. If you intended to use the literal meaning of *animal,* saying that your wife is an animal does not provide any new information (by definition, a wife must be a female human, and humans are a type of animal), so the utterance violates the maxim of quantity (*add new information*). It would be like saying, *My wife has lungs and skin, My wife has eyelids,* or *My wife is female.* Likewise, if the topic of conversation is one's spouse or one's relatives, it is hard to see how the information that someone is an animal relates to the general topic. Therefore the utterance violates the maxim of relation (*stick to the topic*). So, while literal falsehood may not be a sufficient test for non-literal intentions, Gricean violation could be. If so, solving the recognition problem involves (a) computing the literal meaning of a given expression; and (b) checking that literal meaning against the requirements imposed by Gricean maxims.

Whether the appropriate standard is literal falsehood or Gricean violation, the standard pragmatic view argues that we attempt a non-literal interpretation only after first computing and testing a literal interpretation against the preceding context. This solution to the recognition problem, then, naturally leads to a set of processing assumptions under which literal meaning is the default, and non-literal meaning is optional. One prediction that follows is that people, when listening to non-literal language, will only compute the intended non-literal meaning after they compute and reject the (unintended) literal meaning. But is it true that literal meanings are always computed first?

A large and growing body of experimental evidence shows that non-literal meanings are computed as fast as literal meanings. Ray Gibbs assessed the interpretation of indirect requests, such as *Can you open the window* (Gibbs, 1983), to see whether the direct, literal meaning was computed before the non-literal meaning. In a reaction time experimental task, participants read either literal (e.g., *I would like you to open the window*), direct requests or non-literal, indirect requests (e.g., *Can you open the window?*). The participants' task was to judge, as quickly as possible, whether paraphrases expressed the same meaning as the direct or indirect requests. Gibbs measured how long it took people to judge the paraphrases, on the assumption that this judgment could be done only after an interpretation of the direct and indirect requests had been computed. If literal meanings are computed before non-literal meanings, then paraphrase judgment times should be shorter in the direct request condition than in the *in*direct request condition. (Because the paraphrases were the same across the literal and non-literal conditions, the amount of time it took the subjects to interpret the paraphrases should not have influenced the outcome of the experiment.) If non-literal meanings are computed only when literal meaning is computed and found deficient, then paraphrase judgment should take longer in the indirect request condition than in the direct request condition. Gibbs found that paraphrase judgment times were the same across conditions, showing that his subjects interpreted the indirect requests just as quickly as the direct requests. In a related study, participants were asked to paraphrase literal and metaphoric expressions (Harris, 1976). The amount of time it took participants to start paraphrasing (*paraphrase initiation time*) was measured, on the assumption that paraphrases could be initiated only after a meaning was computed. Paraphrase initiation times were the same for literal and metaphoric expressions, indicating that both literal and non-literal expressions were computed at about the same speed. In another experiment using a sentence categorization task, subjects were able to identify and classify metaphoric expressions as quickly as they identified literal statements (Pollio, Fabrizi, Sills, & Smith, 1984).

Data from other experiments also support the idea that non-literal meanings can be computed as quickly as literal meanings. In Blasko and Connine's (1993) study, participants were presented with novel metaphoric expressions, such as *indecision is a whirlpool.* The question was whether the literal meaning of the final word *whirlpool* would be accessed before a non-literal or metaphoric meaning. The literal meaning of *whirlpool* is a mass of water that is circling and creating a depression in the surface of a body of water. To see whether people were thinking of that literal meaning, participants heard the phrase *indecision is a whirlpool* and responded to the visually presented target word *water.* In the context of *indecision is a whirlpool*, the metaphoric meaning of *whirlpool* doesn't really have anything to do with water. Instead, the metaphoric meaning is something like *When people are indecisive, their thinking goes around in a circle, and they act confused.* To see whether people were thinking of that non-literal meaning, subjects responded to the target word *confusion* after hearing the phrase *indecision is a whirlpool.* If literal meanings are computed faster than non-literal meanings, then subjects should respond to the literal-related target word *water* faster than the non-literal-related target word *confusion.* In fact, people responded to target words related to non-literal meanings (e.g., *confusion*) just as fast as they responded to target words related to literal meanings (e.g., *water*); and both kinds of target words were responded to faster than control words that were totally unrelated to any meaning of the expression *indecision is a whirlpool.* These results therefore support the idea that non-literal meanings are computed just as quickly as literal meanings.

McElree and Nordlie (1999) applied an unusual but highly effective experimental technique, speed–accuracy tradeoff (SAT), to find out how quickly literal and metaphoric meanings were computed. SAT provides a very accurate way of measuring when, exactly, different kinds of information become available and start to influence a person's behavior (see the box on p. 273 for a summary of how it works). McElree and Nordlie had people read literal and non-literal expressions and used SAT to measure how quickly people could understand the different kinds of expressions. The SAT results for literal and non-literal expressions were virtually identical, showing that non-literal meanings were computed just as quickly as literal meanings.

The previously summarized studies might all be viewed as involving unusual circumstances, and so you might want to discount their support for simultaneous computation of literal and non-literal meaning. Normally, when we encounter expressions in language, we are not asked to judge paraphrases, respond to target words that pop up separately from the main conversation, or respond on somebody else's deadline. Fortunately, there are more naturalistic methods that point toward the same conclusions. In a sentence-by-sentence reading study, participants read target sentences like (1) (Ortony, 1979):

(1) The sheep followed their leader over the cliff.

Sentence (1) can be interpreted as referring to real flesh-and-blood farm animals and a real geological feature, but it can also be interpreted in non-literal terms. If sentence (1) followed sentence (2), it should be assigned a non-literal interpretation:

(2) The investors looked to the Wall Street banker for advice.
(1) The sheep followed their leader over the cliff.

SPEED–ACCURACY TRADEOFF (SAT)

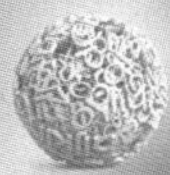

In most reaction time experiments, participants respond at their own speed. They are often encouraged to respond as quickly as possible without making errors, but it is still up to each individual subject to decide how to weigh these two criteria. Some subjects respond very quickly, before they are really ready, and they make a lot of errors. Data from that kind of subject is often discarded before the data from a study are analyzed. Some subjects respond more slowly, only after they are really, really sure that they have the right response ready, and they usually make very few errors. Many subjects with this profile are commonly included in published studies. If too many such subjects wind up in the analyzed data, the results may overestimate the amount of time it takes to complete an information processing task. As a result, one problem in interpreting many reaction time studies is that we do not know to what extent participants were trading extra time for increased accuracy, or decreased accuracy for greater speed. The speed–accuracy tradeoff (SAT) paradigm solves this problem. It does so by preventing subjects from trading speed for accuracy. Instead, subjects are trained to respond before a set, fixed deadline. If the deadline is very long, subjects' accuracy is very high. If the deadline is very short, subjects' accuracy will be very low. At intermediate deadlines, subjects' accuracy will be greater than zero, but less than perfect. By testing a set of subjects on many hundreds—sometimes thousands—of trials with different deadlines, experimenters can see when subjects' accuracy diverges from chance performance. At the point in time where subjects' performance becomes better than chance, the source of information that was manipulated must have been available to influence the subjects' behavior before that point (see McElree & Griffith, 1995, 1998; McElree & Nordlie, 1999; McElree, Pylkkännen, Pickering, & Traxler, 2006).

In the context of sentence (2), *sheep* refers to *investors*, *their leader* refers to *the Wall Street banker*, and *the cliff* refers to a sharp drop in the value of investments. So, to interpret sentence (1) in the context of sentence (2), people have to assign non-literal meanings to a number of the words in sentence (1). That condition was contrasted with a condition in which the literal meanings of the same words were called for, which is what happened when sentence (1) followed sentence (3):

(3) The animals were grazing on the hillside.
(1) The sheep followed their leader over the cliff.

Ortony measured how long it took people to read sentence (1) when it followed sentence (2), the *non-literal* condition, and when sentence (1) followed sentence (3), the *literal* condition. If literal meanings are computed faster than non-literal meanings, then reading times for sentence (1) should have been shorter in the literal condition than in the non-literal condition. In fact, subjects in this experiment read sentences like (1) just as quickly in the non-literal condition as in the literal condition. These results offer further evidence that non-literal meanings are computed just as quickly as literal meanings. Other eye-tracking studies looked at processing of individual words or phrases within sentences, rather than whole-sentence reading time (Inhoff, 1984; Shinjo & Myers, 1987), and also found equal reading times for components with literal meanings and components with non-literal meanings. Because reading is a highly practiced and very natural task for most adults (and especially the college students who served as subjects in these experiments), these studies are not subject to the "naturalness" criticism that might be applied to some of the other investigations of non-literal language processing, and they reach the same conclusions.

On balance, research on non-literal language processing shows that the "literal first" assumption of the standard pragmatic view cannot be correct. The standard pragmatic view also views non-literal interpretation as being optional in contexts where the literal interpretation fits reasonably well with the preceding context. However, research using a semantic version of the Stroop task shows that non-literal interpretation is obligatory, not optional, even in contexts where the literal interpretation would suit the comprehender's needs (Glucksberg, 1998; 2003; Glucksberg, Gildea, & Bookin, 1982; Keysar, 1989; Stroop, 1935; see also Kazmerski, Blasko, & Dessalegn, 2003; Wolff & Gentner, 2000). In the Stroop task, color names are printed in ink that does not match the color name. So, the word *blue* is printed in red ink. The subject's task is to say the name of the color of the ink, and ignore what the word says. So, you look at the word *blue* printed in red ink, and you have to say *red*, rather than *blue*. Subjects experience great difficulty ignoring the color name *blue*, so they are slow to say the ink color *red*, and they tend to make errors. This kind of task shows that access to the color name *blue* occurs automatically when people look at the word *blue*. Are non-literal meanings also automatically computed or accessed? To find out, people read statements that were literally false, but had a good non-literal interpretation. In a context where *Keith* is described as an adult who acts in an immature way, the statement *Keith is a baby* is literally false, but has a good non-literal interpretation. People who read statements such as this had the task of identifying statements that were literally true. In that task, the correct response to the statement *Keith is a baby* is to say "false." This task resembles the Stroop task, in that automatic access to the good metaphorical meaning could make the subjects' job harder, because the good metaphorical interpretation makes it harder for them to say that the sentence is untrue. Even though the task is to look for literal meaning only, if the metaphoric meaning is plausible, and if the metaphoric meaning is computed automatically, then people will have a hard time rejecting *Keith is a baby*, the same way they have trouble rejecting the response *blue* when the word *blue* is printed in red ink. In fact, people had much greater difficulty rejecting metaphorically "true" statements like *Keith is a baby* than equivalent literally and metaphorically "false" statements, such as, *Keith is a banana*. So, in the context of a task where literal meaning was sufficient (people could do the judgment task without ever computing non-literal meaning), people nonetheless automatically computed the non-literal meaning.

The preceding experiments show that the standard pragmatic view has two major things wrong with it. First, non-literal meanings become available to the listener as quickly as literal meanings do.[2] The assumption that literal meanings are computed first is not supported by the experimental data. Second, the standard pragmatic view says that computation of non-literal meanings is optional and undertaken only when the literal meaning is problematic in a given context. However, experiments like Glucksberg and colleagues' show that non-literal meanings are computed automatically in contexts where the literal meaning is entirely sufficient for the task at hand. Results like these have persuaded many language scientists to adopt an alternative theory under which literal and non-literal meanings are computed in parallel (e.g., Swinney & Cutler, 1979). Simultaneous computation of literal and non-literal meaning is consistent with the experimental results showing that both kinds of meanings are computed equally quickly and that non-literal meaning is computed whether the literal meaning is true or false. So, interpreting non-literal meanings is like interpreting words with multiple meanings (see Chapter 3). In both cases, multiple meanings are automatically activated and subsequently assessed against the requirements imposed by context, with the most compatible meaning eventually being selected as "*the*" interpretation of the ambiguous expression. We will explore the multiple meanings associated with non-literal expressions and how the system might go about selecting one contextually appropriate meaning after we discuss a bit more about one specific kind of non-literal expression: metaphor.

Metaphor

A metaphor allows us to indicate a relationship between two elements. The first element is the *topic* and the second element is the *vehicle*. The topic is the focus of the conversation; it is what the discourse is about (Ortony, 1975). The vehicle is some concept or exemplar that we are using to comment on the topic. In the expression, *Nicole Kidman is bad medicine*, *Nicole Kidman* is the topic and *bad medicine* is the vehicle. Of course, the expression is *not* intended to be interpreted as saying that Nicole Kidman is a pharmaceutical product that comes in bottles and has harmful side effects. Instead, the non-literal speaker meaning is something like, *Nicole Kidman is dangerous and can make you feel really bad.*[3] This expression is in the commonly occurring *A is B* form frequently used to express metaphoric meanings. Note that metaphors of this type are subject to the recognition problem, because literal category inclusion statements also take the form *A is B*, as in *Copper is a metal*, and *Dogs are mammals*. How do we solve the recognition problem for metaphors? This is not an easy question to answer in the abstract, but when we have a metaphoric comparison involving topic *A* and vehicle *B*, *A* and *B* are in some unusual relation to one another. As Greg Murphy (1996, p. 175) explains, in reference to the metaphoric expression *Lee is a block of ice:*

> *In order for a sentence to be perceived as metaphoric, the vehicle cannot apply in a straightforward way to the topic. For example,* Lee is an attorney *does not ... require any special ground for its interpretation. The usual, familiar meaning of* attorney *specifies a person with a particular profession, and since* Lee *is the name of a person, there is no inconsistency in calling* Lee *an attorney. However,* block of ice *literally means the solid, frozen state of the substance H_2O, and since a person is typically neither H_2O nor frozen, this predicate cannot be applied to Lee in a straightforward way. There must be some kind of mapping from the usual meaning of this phrase to the conveyed, nonliteral meaning.*

The *A is B* form is one kind of metaphor, called an *attributive metaphor* (Glucksberg & Keysar, 1990). When you use that kind of expression, you are asserting that some attributes (properties, characteristics, or features) of the vehicle apply to the topic. Sometimes, we use *single-word metaphors*, as in the expression *The girl* <u>*flew*</u> *down the hill on her bicycle*. In this case, the verb *flew* is not used in its default sense, as indicating motion through the air, but rather in a metaphoric sense that implies very rapid motion on the ground. We can also use *relational metaphors*, which you are familiar with from your experience with standardized tests like the ACT and the SAT. Relational metaphors take the form: *A is to B as C is to D* (or the shorthand *A:B::C:D*). If you picked up an article about the Iraq war, you might read, *George Bush considered Saddam Hussein the Hitler of the Middle East*. This is actually a nifty rhetorical device, because it sets up an implicit relationship between George Bush and an unmentioned third person (besides Saddam Hussein). See if you can work out what that relationship might be and who the unmentioned third person is (see endnote 4 for the spoiler).[4] The reason why the rhetorical device is so nifty is because George Bush is getting you to associate him with a positive model without explicitly saying, *I am just like this very famous hero person.*

One important question about metaphors is: How do we figure out what meaning we should apply to metaphors? A related question is: Do we have special semantic interpretation processes that we use for metaphors, but not for literal expressions? According to the *comparison* school of thought (e.g., Bottini et al., 1994; Fogelin, 1988; Ortony, 1979; Tversky, 1977), people interpret metaphors by mentally converting them to similes. Similes are like metaphors, in that they both have a topic and a vehicle; but similes are unlike metaphors in that they have an extra word (*like*, usually), and that extra word makes it explicit that two things are being compared. So, similes take the form, *A is like B* (or *A resembles B*, or *A is similar to B*). We can use similes to point out that two things have shared characteristics. You could say, *Copper is like tin*, *Baseball is like cricket*, or *Mexico is like Spain*. These are considered literal comparisons, because the default meanings of the topic and vehicle are involved in the comparison. Copper is like tin, because the default meanings for both include the information that they are metals, fairly common, dug out of the ground, only a little bit shiny, and so forth. Baseball and cricket both involve teams of players, balls, bats, grass fields, and so on. When we use a metaphor, such as *Nicole Kidman is bad medicine*, perhaps we interpret that expression by mentally converting it to a simile, of the form *Nicole Kidman is* <u>*like*</u> *bad medicine*. If that were the case, then after mentally converting the metaphor to a simile, we could apply the same processes to evaluate the metaphoric relationship between Nicole Kidman and bad medicine as we use to evaluate the literal relationship between copper and tin. The advantage of this approach is that we need only a bare minimum of special-purpose interpretive machinery for metaphors—the only special-purpose mental process is the one that turns metaphors into similes, and there the conversion is as simple as changing *is* to *is like*. In fact, this last point bears repeating. The comparison approach to metaphor comprehension asserts that the meaning of a metaphor is discovered by converting it to a simile, and the meaning stays the same before and after the conversion—the two expressions convey the same meaning. The only thing that changes between a metaphor and a simile is how the expression is worded.

Although the conversion-to-simile view of metaphor interpretation has the advantage of being simple and straightforward, it may not be able to account for the full range of facts about similes and metaphors. In fact, a closer examination of literal comparisons and metaphoric comparisons quickly turns up substantial differences between the two. One difference is that literal comparisons are generally *reversible*, but metaphoric comparisons are not. Most of the time, it does not matter which element appears in which order in a literal comparison, the basis of comparison between the two elements stays the same, and the overall semantic force of the statement also remains the same. *Copper is like tin* is essentially equivalent to *Tin is like copper*. There is no strong basis for preferring one version over the other, except perhaps if one of the two elements is made topical. So you might prefer to say *Baseball is like cricket*, if your English friend asked you to explain the rules of baseball. But you might prefer the opposite *Cricket is like baseball* if cricket were the topic of conversation. Many metaphors are not reversible in this way. You can say *Nicole Kidman is bad medicine*, but you can't say *Bad medicine is Nicole Kidman*. Some metaphors are reversible, but the meaning of the expression changes when it is reversed (unlike the similes, where the meaning of the expression as a whole remains essentially unchanged). For instance, if you said, My *surgeon is a butcher* the *grounds of comparison*, the relationship that connects *surgeon* to *butcher*, is that the surgeon is a bad surgeon (he chops up meat willy-nilly, like a butcher). If you reverse the topic and the vehicle, you get *My butcher is a surgeon*, which implies that the butcher is highly skilled. The same thing applies if these metaphors were converted to similes (*My surgeon is like a butcher*; *My butcher is like a surgeon*). So, there is something fundamentally different in literal comparisons and metaphors. Literal comparisons have more stable grounds for comparison and so the elements can be reversed; metaphors call on different grounds for comparison depending on the precise nature of the topic and vehicle and are therefore not generally reversible.

The conversion-to-simile view of metaphor interpretation also predicts that metaphoric expressions will take longer to interpret than similes that express the same relationship between topic and vehicle (because there is an extra conversion step necessary to comprehend metaphors). However, reaction time studies have shown that, under some circumstances, similes take *longer* to understand than equivalent metaphors (Glucksberg, 1998, 2003). It appears that metaphors can be interpreted without mentally converting them to similes.

To interpret metaphoric expressions, the listener must discover the grounds of comparison that the speaker is using to connect the topic to the vehicle. How do listeners accomplish this feat? The *property matching hypothesis* explains why and how similes and metaphors communicate relationships between topics and vehicles (Johnson & Malgady, 1979; Malgady & Johnson, 1980; Miller, 1979; Ortony, 1979; Tversky, 1977). According to the property matching hypothesis, interpreting similes and metaphors depends on finding properties of the topic that are identical to properties that the vehicle has. The advantage of this approach is that property matching can be used to interpret both literal comparisons and metaphoric ones, so it does away with the need for any special interpretation processes that apply only to metaphors. To interpret literal comparisons, such as *a dog is a mammal*, you find properties that you know go with the vehicle *mammal*, such as *has fur*, *has mammary glands*, *bears its young live*, and you see whether there are matching properties listed under the entry *dog*. When you find matching properties, you highlight them to draw attention to the fact that they are shared between the topic and vehicle. You do the same thing for metaphors. When you hear, *Nicole Kidman is bad medicine*, you find properties of the vehicle (*dangerous*, *makes people feel bad*) and you look for the same properties under the entry *Nicole Kidman*. The same process can be used whether the comparison is based on the metaphor form *A is B* or the simile form, *A is like B*. Another advantage of the property matching hypothesis is that it can explain why some metaphors just don't make sense. If no shared properties can be found for the topic and vehicle, then the metaphor will not make sense. So, if someone said, *billboards are like pears* (or *billboards are pears*), that would sound strange. According to the property matching hypothesis, *billboards are like pears* sounds strange because there are no properties that *pears* and *billboards* have in common, and so there are no grounds for comparison.

The *salience imbalance* hypothesis (Johnson & Malgady, 1979; Tourangeau & Sternberg, 1981) is a refined version of the property matching hypothesis. This hypothesis attempts to explain why speakers choose the metaphor (*A is B*) form sometimes and the simile (*A is like B*) form other times when highlighting relationships between topics and vehicles. Specifically, the salience imbalance hypothesis proposes that literal comparisons, of the form *A is like B*, will be used when the grounds of comparison involve properties that are salient in both the topic and the vehicle. Metaphors, of the *A is B* form, are used when the topic and vehicle share properties, but the grounds of comparison involve properties that are obscure in the topic, but highly salient in the vehicle. According to the salience imbalance hypothesis, we use *copper is like tin*, because being a metal, being mined, being useful in manufactured products, and being only a little bit shiny are salient properties of both copper and tin. That is, if we asked people to list properties of copper and tin, *metal*, *mined*, and *sort of shiny*, would appear high on the list for both copper and tin. The topic and vehicle in a metaphor, by contrast, produce different lists of properties, with different characteristics appearing in very different orders for the topic and vehicle. If, for instance, you were asked to list the properties of *Nicole Kidman*, you would most likely include *actress, dancer, Australian, cute and sassy, performed brilliantly opposite Will Ferrell in*

"Bewitched" near the top of the list and *heart-breaker, makes people feel bad* somewhere down near the bottom. Suppose you were then asked to list the properties of *bad medicine*. Right at the top would be properties such as, *dangerous* and *makes people feel bad*. So, *makes people feel bad* is a highly salient property of *bad medicine*, where salience is operationalized as position on the list. (Properties that are listed early are salient because, presumably, they come to mind easily.) When someone says, *Nicole Kidman is bad medicine, bad medicine* has salient properties (*dangerous, comes in bottles, makes people feel bad*) that match non-salient properties of Nicole Kidman (and *comes in bottles* can be ruled out as part of the grounds of comparison, because no such property will be found under the *Nicole Kidman* entry). By putting *Nicole Kidman* and *bad medicine* together, the speaker is promoting one or more low-salience features of Nicole Kidman into much higher and more salient positions in the mental representation of the topic. In this way, metaphoric comparisons make the listener think about the familiar in a new way, by reordering the salience of different properties associated with the topic, which contributes to the rhetorical force of the metaphoric expression.

Although property matching, like the conversion-to-simile view has the advantage of explaining how literal and metaphoric comparisons are interpreted, and why speakers would prefer a simile in one instance and a metaphor an another, the property matching hypothesis has trouble explaining the full range of metaphoric expressions. One problem is that the property matching hypothesis predicts that that the grounds of comparison in metaphors should involve low-salience properties of the topic and high-salience properties of the vehicle, but sometimes metaphors that are easy to interpret involve properties that are *low* in salience in both the topic and the vehicle. Consider sentence (4) (from Glucksberg & Keysar, 1990):

(4) The senator was an old fox who could outwit the reporters every time.

What is the grounds of comparison here? It must be that the senator is *clever* or *wily*. If you asked people to list properties of the word *senator*, you would get a list that included *politician, powerful, distinguished*, and so on. If you asked people to list properties of *fox*, you would get a list that included *furry, bushy tailed, hunted with dogs, can't be trusted to guard the hen-house*, and so on. *Clever* would be found way down near the bottom of properties listed in response to both *senator* and *fox*, if that property appeared at all. According to the salience imbalance hypothesis, sentence (4) should be a lousy metaphor, but people actually rate that sentence as being a good or *apt* metaphor. So an imbalance between the salience of a property in the topic and vehicle is not a necessary precondition for a good metaphor.

Even worse for the property matching view, some really good metaphors involve topics and vehicles that have zero shared properties. One standard metaphor is *No man is an island*. You could ask people to list the properties of *man* and *island* as long as you like, and it is unlikely that you will find any shared properties besides the fact that both *man* and *island* are *things* or *nouns* (and neither of those is involved in the grounds of comparison for *No man is an island*). Metaphors of the form *no man is an island* illustrate the principle that metaphors can be used to assign brand new properties to the topic, rather than merely highlighting existing, low-salience properties. Currently, the property matching hypothesis does not have any way to accommodate this phenomenon, even though *attribute introducing metaphors*, such as *the mind is a computer*, have played central roles in both common and scientific advances in knowledge. As Bowdle and Gentner (2005, p. 194), explain, " The computer metaphor of mind was not informative because it simply highlighted certain well-known aspects of the mind that were also true of computers but rather because it promoted a transfer of knowledge from the domain of computers to that of minds. Feature-matching models provide no mechanism for the projection of such distinctive (vehicle) properties."

A further problem with the comparison view is that metaphor and simile versions of a comparison do not always convey the same meaning because meaning does not always survive the conversion process. Literal similes cannot be translated into class inclusion statements at all. You can't convert *copper is like tin* into *copper is tin* (Glucksberg & Keysar, 1990). Likewise, many metaphors cannot be converted to similes and retain their meaning. Consider the expression, *My lawyer is a well-paid shark* (Bowdle & Gentner, 2005; Glucksberg & Haught, 2006a, 2006b). People assign expressions like that high aptness ratings (they think it is a good metaphor). But that expression does not fare so well when it is converted to a simile. People assign much lower aptness ratings to the simile version *My lawyer is <u>like</u> a well-paid shark* than they assign to the metaphor version. So metaphor and simile forms do not have equivalent meanings, and that goes against the comparison and mental-conversion-to-simile views of metaphor interpretation. As Glucksberg and Haught explain (2006a, p. 376), "If metaphors cannot always be paraphrased as similes, then metaphors cannot, in principle, be understood in terms of their corresponding similes, and vice versa. This means that comparison theories of metaphor comprehension, which rest on the assumption that metaphors and similes are equivalent, are fundamentally flawed."

Class inclusion and dual reference

The *class inclusion* hypothesis of metaphor interpretation provides an alternative to the conversion-to-simile and property matching views (Glucksberg, 1998, 2003; Glucksberg & Keysar, 1990; Glucksberg & Haught, 2006a, 2006b; Glucksberg, McGlone, & Manfredi, 1997). According to the class inclusion view of metaphor interpretation, all expressions, literal and non-literal, of the form *A is B* are interpreted as asserting that the topic (*A*) is a member of the category represented by the vehicle (*B*). This works equally well for both literal and metaphoric comparisons. A speaker can say, *A dog is a mammal*, and you can understand that by recognizing that *dog* is a member of the category *mammal*, and therefore inherits the characteristics of members of that category. Non-literal metaphoric expressions can be interpreted in a similar fashion. When I say, *Nicole Kidman is bad medicine*, *bad medicine* is a prototype for the ad hoc category *things that are surprisingly dangerous and bad for you*. If someone says, *Kyle is a pop-up ad*, you can interpret that by placing *Kyle* in the category that *pop-up ad* exemplifies—unexpected, mildly annoying things that temporarily stop you from doing whatever it is you're doing. The class inclusion hypothesis has the advantage of providing a unified explanation for how metaphoric and literal statements are interpreted, and it avoids some of the pitfalls of the comparison and mental-conversion-to-simile approaches.

The class inclusion view also has the advantage of explaining how and why people respond to metaphors and similes, and why there is a difference between metaphors and similes. To do so, it requires one auxiliary assumption. Namely, metaphoric expressions involve *dual reference* (a bit like ambiguous words), while literally interpreted similes and class inclusion statements involve only a single mapping between the topic and the vehicle. According to the dual reference hypothesis, when you see a statement of the form *My lawyer is a shark*, you think of a literal, flesh and blood, cartilaginous fish and you simultaneously think about an ad hoc category of dangerous and aggressive animals (which could also include, lions, tigers, and bears; as in *My lawyer is a lion/tiger/bear*). *Shark*, in this case, refers to both a *basic-level* concept (a real shark) and a *superordinate category* that the shark exemplifies, or is a prototypical member of. The simile version, *The lawyer is <u>like</u> a shark*, makes reference to just the basic level, literal *shark* and *not* to the superordinate category.

So, unlike the metaphoric expression, the simile version invites the question, *The lawyer is like a shark in what way?* The fact that metaphoric expressions involve dual reference and similes involve single reference means that you can do some things with metaphoric expressions that you cannot do with similes. Because *My lawyer is a shark* simultaneously refers to a real shark and a category of dangerous things, you can use a modifier, like *well-paid* to modify shark, as in (5) (Glucksberg & Haught, 2006a, p. 368):

(5) My lawyer is a well-paid shark.
(6) *My lawyer is like a well-paid shark.

The simile version in (6), by comparison, seems a bit odd. This is because in the simile version, *shark* refers to the literal shark, and its reference does not extend to the superordinate ad hoc category *dangerous things.* Since real, live, swimming sharks don't draw paychecks, it does not make sense to say *well-paid (literal) shark*, and the expression as a whole seems weird. This sense of weirdness was confirmed in an experiment where subjects were asked to rate the quality of expressions such as (5) and (6). Subjects rated modified metaphoric expressions like (5) higher than modified simile expressions like (6). Subjects also read expressions like (5) faster than expression like (6), even when adjustments were made to account for the extra word in (6).

Further evidence that metaphoric expressions of the form *A is B* are interpreted as class inclusion statements that call to mind superordinate categories comes from priming experiments (Glucksberg, Manfredi, & McGlone, 1997). Participants' reading times were measured for metaphoric expressions such as *My lawyer is a shark.* That target sentence could be preceded by a neutral control sentence or by a sentence that focused participants' attention on the literal meaning of the word *shark.* An example of a literal-focusing prime sentence would be *Sharks can swim.* The prime sentence *Sharks can swim* draws participants' attention toward the literal meaning of shark, and away from the superordinate category *dangerous animals.* Under those conditions, participants had a harder time understanding the metaphoric expression *My lawyer is a shark*, which requires them to establish a connection between the topic (*lawyer*) and the superordinate category (*dangerous animals*).

The basic version of the category inclusion hypothesis explains how a relationship is established between metaphorical topics and vehicles, but it does not explain how the same vehicle can point to different superordinate categories for different topics. For example, as Bowdle and Gentner (2005) point out, the vehicle *snowflake* can point to one superordinate category when the topic is *a child* and another category when the topic is *youth.* In the metaphoric expression *a child is a snowflake*, the metaphoric interpretation is that *every child is unique* (no two snowflakes are identical). In the metaphoric expression, *youth is a snowflake*, the metaphoric interpretation is that *youth is fleeting* (snowflakes melt easily). To explain how the same vehicle can induce different superordinate categories, Glucksberg and his colleagues (Glucksberg, Manfredi, & McGlone, 1997) developed a version of the category inclusion hypothesis under which the vehicle makes a set of superordinate categories available for interpretation, and characteristics of the topic point the reader toward the appropriate one. In that case, the topic and vehicle both impose constraints on interpretation, as opposed to the vehicle being the sole factor that influences the choice of superordinate category information. Because expressions such as *a child is a snowflake* and *youth is a snowflake* are equally easy to understand, Glucksberg and colleagues proposed that vehicles activate multiple superordinate categories in parallel. If superordinate categories were accessed one at a time, one of those metaphors should be easier to understand than the other.

The class inclusion hypothesis of metaphor interpretation closely aligns the processing and interpretation of metaphoric and literal comparisons. Glucksberg therefore joins a growing group of language scientists who view metaphor as a normal, mainstream part of human language use, rather than being a special class that needs special interpretive machinery and processes. In fact, rather than being rare and unusual, metaphors are produced frequently in the course of normal discourse. Speakers produce about six metaphors (about four "frozen" and two "novel" metaphors) per minute of speaking time, or about one every 10 seconds (Pollio, Barlow, Fine, & Pollio, 1977).

Conceptual mapping and meaning

The standard pragmatic view proposes that metaphoric expressions are special and different from "normal," common literal expressions. The experimental evidence reviewed above suggests that a number of assumptions that follow from the standard pragmatic view may not be correct. In light of this experimental evidence, a number of philosophers and language scientists have attempted to formulate new ideas about how metaphoric language fits into language use as a whole. One idea that has gained popularity in recent years is the *conceptual mapping* hypothesis (Gibbs, 1994; Lakoff & Johnson, 1980a, 1980b). First, the conceptual mapping hypothesis minimizes the distinction between metaphoric and literal language. Hence, philosophers, linguists, and psychologists who subscribe to the conceptual mapping hypothesis view metaphors as being a ubiquitous feature of normal discourse, and not particularly special (e.g., Giora, 2007; Lakoff, 1987; Pinker, 1994). According to this view, much of the language that we view as literal is really based on implicit metaphors (as in the stoplight example at the beginning of this chapter). Second, the conceptual mapping view suggests that much of our understanding of normal, everyday words is based on discovering or highlighting links between different domains. So, normal, literal words like *argument, love*, and *anger* are understood because they bring to mind other concepts, such as *war, journey*, and *heated fluid in a container*. This connection of different domains when we think about a concept such as *argument* allows us to use expressions like *his criticism was right on target, she attacked every one of my strong points, my barely adequate psychic defenses crumbled in the face of her logical blitzkrieg*. According to the conceptual mapping view, we can talk about arguments as war because the way we think about arguments, the way they are mentally defined, is based on connecting aspects of the process of arguing to analogous aspects of the process of fighting a war.

The conceptual mapping hypothesis comes in a *strong* form and a *weak* form. According to the strong form, unless a word refers to a directly perceivable concept (like *red*), the word will be defined and understood because of its metaphoric relationship to some other, more basic domain. As Murphy explains (1996, p. 178), "In a real sense, then, one does not really understand an argument—one only understands war, and the understanding of arguments is parasitic on this concept." In particular, certain *fundamental metaphors* are the basis of many commonly used expressions. These fundamental metaphors include *space and movement*, as well as *force, agency, and causation*. According to a *strong* form of the *conceptual mapping hypothesis*, all utterances other than those that directly express fundamental metaphors are interpreted by activating a fundamental metaphor and drawing connections (mapping) between the more complex domain and the fundamental metaphor (the *source domain*). So, when you interpret the utterance *The meeting <u>went</u> from 3 to 4 o'clock*, you use the fundamental metaphor *space and movement* to understand that the meeting had an extended duration in time. According to the theory, you create a mental space that (virtually) includes a straight line that represents time. That line is marked with a point representing the beginning of the meeting and another point marking the end of the meeting. So extended duration in time is understood with reference to distance in space, with greater distances corresponding to greater amounts of time. You can also use space and movement to understand financial transactions. If someone said, *When the old man died, the inheritance went to John*, you mentally conceptualize the acquisition of wealth by John as an object (*the inheritance*) that moved through space from a starting location (*the old man*) to a goal location (*John*). We use the fundamental metaphor of *force, agency, and causation* to understand seemingly literal expressions like *Evelina is polite to Ted*, and to understand how the meaning of that expression differs from expressions with very similar meanings, such as *Evelina is civil to Ted* (Pinker, 1994). The difference between *civil* and *polite* in terms of the *force, agency, and causation* metaphor is that the force that causes Evelina to be polite is internal to Evelina, while being *civil* involves a metaphoric situation where there are two forces in opposition, an internal force that is driving Evelina to be mean to Ted and an external force that is preventing her from doing so.

According to the *weak form* of the conceptual mapping hypothesis, underlying metaphors are not necessary and do not necessarily make up all of a concept's definition, but they are nonetheless routinely called to mind when words are used. So, although the domain *war* does not define the total meaning of the word *argument*, concepts directly related to *war* will become activated when we talk about arguments. Under this formulation, *argument* has its own definition and its own set of relationships between its component concepts, but the way those components are related to one another is influenced by the *war* metaphor. Because the *argument is war* metaphor is commonly used to talk about arguments, the way you mentally define and talk about arguments is shifted to become more similar to the way you mentally define and think about war.

Linguists like George Lakoff also contend that implicit metaphors play a powerful role in political discourse (e.g., Lakoff, 2002, 2008). For instance, when a politician talks about *tax relief*, that situates the concept of taxation inside a medical metaphor. Within that metaphorical realm, taxes are equivalent to disease that causes pain. The appropriate response to pain in the medical context is to remove the cause of the pain, and the person who removes that pain is a hero. By saying *tax relief*, a politician can implicitly activate the medical disease metaphor, get you to think of taxation as disease that causes pain, and consider the politician who removes the cause of the pain as the heroic doctor or nurse. According to Lakoff, listeners' attitudes can easily be influenced by implicit metaphors, with substantial benefits accruing to politicians who have mastered the use of metaphor.

Although the conceptual mapping hypothesis has gained popularity, it is not without its critics (Keysar, Shen, Glucksberg, & Horton, 2000; Murphy, 1996). The strong version of conceptual mapping has been criticized because metaphoric mappings do not appear to be necessary for a concept to be understood, and it may not be possible to work out the correct mappings between different domains without resorting to scientifically unacceptable assumptions. The fact that children may have a well-developed understanding of *anger* well before they develop an understanding of the physics involved in fluid dynamics calls into question the necessity of metaphoric mappings to understand anger.[5] The conceptual mapping hypothesis also does not explain why some aspects of source domains are included in metaphoric understanding, while others are not. In the *argument is war* mapping, attacking and defending forces, terrain, and methods of attack are used in expressions that utilize the metaphor, but chains of command, logistics, and uniforms, all of which are present in real, literal war situations, never appear in metaphoric comparisons of argument and war. Some of the aspects of the source domain (*war*) will be useful in describing, defining, or thinking about the target concept (*argument*), but many will not. The question then, is, how does the mind know which aspects of the source domain to use to define the target? Unless there is a little person in your mind (a *homunculus*) who already knows how arguments relate to wars, it may be impossible for just the right set of mappings to emerge.

Critics of both the strong and weak forms of the conceptual mapping hypothesis also object to the circular nature of some of the evidence mustered in support of the theory. To provide evidence for the conceptual mapping theory, proponents point out commonly used expressions (*I was crushed*, *She shattered my defenses*, and so on) and then formulate a metaphoric relation that is common across those commonly used expressions (e.g., *argument is war*). Then they provide further examples of commonly used expressions to confirm that people think about arguments by referring to concepts directly related to war. The problem is that the outcome predicted by the theory is the same as the observations that were used to generate the hypothesis in the first place. Ideally, we would like our theories to predict observations not yet obtained. As Keysar and colleagues (2000, p. 577) explain, "Using only linguistic evidence for deep connections between language and thought is circular … How do we know that people think of happy and sad in terms of up and down? Because people talk about happy and sad using words such as up and down. Why do people use expressions such as *his spirits rose*? Because people think of happy in terms of UP. Clearly, these arguments are circular and provide no substantive support for the [concept mapping hypothesis]."[6] Further, while there may be close mappings between aspects of the concept argument and aspects of the concept war, and while people may agree that war provides a number of terms that are useful in talking and thinking about arguments, it is always possible that argument and war are represented separately, and that people recognize the connections between them only after they have been made explicit. Even though the connections between argument and war may seem very compelling, war may still not serve as the fundamental basis of the way we define the word *argument*.

Some critics have also challenged the conceptual mapping hypothesis' assumption that words can have only a single literal meaning. According to conceptual mapping, we would interpret the words, *arm*, *leg*, *back*, and *seat*, when they refer to parts of a chair by mapping those terms onto the source domain *human body*. There is no logical reason, however, why the same word could not be used to refer literally to a part of a chair and, separately, to a part of the body (just as we re-use words like *bank* to literally refer to the side of a river and a place to keep money).

A final problem with the conceptual mapping hypothesis is that it does not say what should happen when a target concept, is related to several different metaphors. For example, *argument*, besides being metaphorically related to the *war* is also related to *building* (as in, *that argument needs buttressing, you're on a shaky foundation*), *container* (*she unpacked her claims about metaphor*), and *journey* (*I couldn't follow her line of reasoning, she left me behind when she started talking about idioms*). If a concept already has a definition (*argument is war*), why does it need a second (or third or fourth)? Worse still, some concepts with connections to multiple metaphoric domains inherit contradictory characteristics from different metaphors. As Murphy (1996) explains, *love* is conceptualized as a *journey* in which the participants cooperate to achieve a common goal, and simultaneously as a *valuable commodity* involved in a commercial exchange where the participants are in direct competition in pursuit of different goals.

The structural similarity view

To overcome some of the limitations of the conceptual mapping view, Murphy (1996) proposed the structural similarity view, which is similar to Dedre Gentner's (1983) *structure mapping* view. According to these accounts, all concepts are directly represented. For instance, there is a defined concept "argument" that is represented separately from a separate defined concept of "war." This formulation solves the homunculus problem associated with the conceptual mapping view. There is no need to propose a little person who makes sure that inappropriate relationships are filtered out when a source domain is used to define another concept. As Murphy (p. 187) proposes, "No one infers that guns are used in arguments, because one already knows that they are not." The structure mapping view proposes that concepts can be related to one another on the basis of similarity, but that similarity does not make one concept "parasitic" on another. So, we can understand love as a journey, as insanity, as a valuable commodity, and as a number of other things by sequentially relating love to each of these other domains. We can then appreciate similarities between the experience of love and other kinds of experiences, without having self-contradictory elements within the definition of the term *love* itself (as when *journey* and *valuable commodity* suggest both cooperation and competition).[7]

The career of metaphor hypothesis

The career of metaphor hypothesis represents a hybrid of the comparison and class inclusion views of metaphor interpretation (Bowdle & Gentner, 2005). According to this hypothesis, metaphors (metaphorically) have careers, like people have careers. When you start your career, you normally do the kinds of dirty jobs that nobody else wants to do, but as you progress, your duties and your behaviors change. Likewise, the way metaphors behave and the way they are interpreted change as the metaphor goes from being novel (new) to being frozen (old). According to the career of metaphor hypothesis, in the beginning, when a metaphorical expression is first coined, the metaphor is understood by a process of comparison and property matching. But as the metaphor becomes widely used and familiar, comprehenders shift to a category inclusion mode of processing, as proposed by Glucksberg and colleagues. As Bowdle and Gentner explain, "as metaphors are conventionalized, there is a shift in mode of processing from comparison to categorization" (p. 194). They note that words commonly used in metaphors, such as *roadblock*, or *bottleneck*, started out referring to concrete, real, directly perceivable objects. When people started noticing similarities between some other situation (like a problem at work) and the object referred to literally by words like *roadblock* or *bottleneck*, they would say, *Wow, this problem at work is just like a roadblock*, or *That darned xerox machine is acting like a bottleneck on our project*. At this stage of the expression's career, the critical words *roadblock* and *bottleneck* refer to their literal, directly perceivable real-world concepts. After the metaphoric comparison comes to be commonly used, people drop the *like* and just say, *That problem is a roadblock*. At this stage, the critical words' meaning is based on dual reference (as in the category inclusion hypothesis), with *roadblock* and *bottleneck* standing for the category *things that stop you from getting where you want to go/things that slow down a process*.

The chief evidence in favor of the career of metaphor hypothesis takes the form of aptness ratings for novel versus familiar metaphoric expressions. According to Bowdle and Gentner (2005), novel metaphors are interpreted via a process of comparison, as described in the conversion-to-simile approach. Older, more established metaphors are treated as in the category inclusion hypothesis, with dual reference and assignment of superordinate category properties of the vehicle to the topic. If new metaphoric expressions are mentally converted to similes, then subjects who are given a choice between a simile (*A is like B*) and a category inclusion statement (*A is B*) should prefer the simile form for novel comparisons (because it saves them a step in processing). If established metaphors are treated as category inclusion statements, then the opposite pattern should hold. For established metaphors, participants should prefer the category inclusion form over the simile form. Bowdle and Gentner presented subjects with both novel metaphors (e.g., *dancers are butterflies*) and established metaphors (e.g., *problems are roadblocks*) in both the category inclusion (*A is B*) form and the simile (*A is like B*) forms. As predicted by the career of metaphor hypothesis, people preferred the simile form for novel metaphors, but they preferred the category inclusion form for established metaphors. Comprehension times for novel metaphoric comparisons were also shorter when they were expressed in simile form than when they were expressed in category inclusion form.

One potential problem with this line of reasoning is that novel metaphors can be less apt, or less meaningful, than more established metaphors. Novel metaphors survive to become established metaphors, presumably, because they are successful at conveying some useful bit of meaning. Perhaps people prefer the simile form, not because an utterance is novel, but because the utterance is not a particularly apt metaphor. Perhaps people prefer the category inclusion form over the simile form because the statement in question effectively and efficiently taps a superordinate category, and using the simile form un-aptly focuses attention on the literal, basic category level rather than the more meaningful superordinate category level. To test that hypothesis Sam Glucksberg and Catrinel Haught (2006a, 2006b) presented people with novel and established metaphors that were equated for aptness ratings. Novel metaphors were rated as equally good and were read and comprehended equally quickly, whether they were expressed in category inclusion form (e.g., *My lawyer is an old shark*) or simile form (e.g., *My lawyer is like an old shark*). Further, some of the *novel* metaphors were rated as being better when they were expressed in category inclusion form than when they were expressed in simile form, which poses a problem for the career of metaphor hypothesis.

Why Metaphor?

Metaphor is pervasive in everyday life, not just in language but in thought and action. Our ordinary conceptual system, in terms of which we both think and act, is fundamentally metaphorical in nature.
LAKOFF AND JOHNSON

Metaphors are necessary and not just nice.
ANDREW ORTONY [8]

The following conversation between Stephen Colbert (SC), conservative television commentator, and Elizabeth Alexander (EA), Inaugural Poet and Yale University professor, took place on January 21, 2009[9] (emphases mine):

SC: Let's talk about meaning for a second, OK? Metaphors, OK? *What's the difference between a metaphor and a lie?* Because, you know, "I am the sun. You are the moon." That's a lie, you're not the moon. I'm not the sun, okay? What's the difference between a metaphor and a lie?

EA: Well, that was both a metaphor and a lie. So, the two are not necessarily exclusive. *A metaphor is a way of using language where you make a comparison to let people understand something as it relates to something else*, and that's how we use the language to increase meaning.

SC: *Well, why not just say what you mean, instead of dressing things up in all this flowery language* like, you know, the great romantic poets, you know "Shall I compare thee to a summer's day?" Why not just say "You are hot, let's *do* it"?

There are at least three good answers to Colbert's question.[10] The first has to do with pragmatics and the social nature of speech. The second and third have to do with communicative efficiency. First, although we can just come right out and say what we are thinking in a very direct way, that can be risky in many social situations. You don't always want your boss to know what you think. So you can either lie, try to escape the conversation, or produce an utterance with some kind of double meaning, like a metaphor.[11] The risk to one's ego and well-being grows exponentially when the topic is love. The problem with using very direct language in affairs of the heart is the crushing loss of face that can result when a direct approach is rejected. So, instead of saying, *You are hot, let's do it* you might say, *If you're not doing anything Saturday night, I know a great little restaurant.* That way, if the indirect approach fails, there is no loss of face, because there was no direct request for a romantic date, and the approacher can act as if nothing important just happened. If you say, *You are hot and I would like you to go on a date with me*, and the answer is *no*, there is no easy way to put a positive spin on that.

The second reason why you might choose a metaphor over a more literal form is because metaphors can pack a huge amount of complex meaning into a very small, very tight package. The Barenaked Ladies could have said, *It would not bother me if you accompanied me everywhere all the time, even if you irritated all of my friends and co-workers, made it much more difficult for me to do my job, and therefore caused my friends and co-workers to abandon me, reduced my artistic output and lowered my earnings.* Instead, they just say, *You can be my Yoko Ono.* Assuming that you have the background knowledge about Yoko Ono's relationship with John Lennon, which played a major role in breaking up the Beatles, you can easily map the novel situation onto the familiar situation without having to have the entire list of inferences made explicit for you. (Pop quiz: If you know someone who is your Yoko Ono, who are you, according to the metaphor?[12])

Third, good, apt metaphors help the listener make sense of the new information that the speaker wishes to convey. The resulting interpretation is therefore likely to be more accurate and more memorable. The benefit of apt metaphors is a result of mappings between a new and unfamiliar domain to an older, more familiar, and better understood domain. Comprehenders can use the well-understood older domain to organize their understanding of the new information, and the information associated with the older domain can also serve as retrieval cues for the new information. This is a tried-and-true strategy for teachers and fiction writers, as exemplified by the *Futurama* episode "Where no Fan has Gone Before":

> **Fry:** Well, usually on [*Star Trek*] someone would come up with a complicated plan then explain it with a simple analogy.

For instance, when they try to defeat the bad guy, Mellvar, the plan is first described without a helpful metaphor:

> **Leela:** If we can re-route engine power through the primary weapons and reconfigure them to Melllvar's frequency, that should overload his electro-quantum structure.

Because the average person has zero chance of understanding that, the scriptwriter provides a helpful metaphor:

> **Bender Bending Rodriguez:** Like putting too much air in a balloon!

Which is easily understood.

> **Fry:** Of course! It's so simple!

Laboratory research confirms the value of good metaphors. Subjects who read texts that use metaphoric expressions comprehended and remembered those texts better than texts where more literal expressions were used to convey the same information (Albritton,

McKoon, & Gerrig, 1995). In one such study, participants read an expository text that described attempts to reduce crime. Two groups of participants were tested. One of the groups read a text that was based on the metaphor *crime is disease*. The other group of participants read a more literal version of the same text. So, in the *crime is disease* version, the text might say, *The sources of crime were diagnosed. Officials desperately sought a cure.* The more literal version said, *The sources of crime were studied. Officials desperately sought a solution.* After the participants were done reading the text, they were asked to complete a surprise memory test. Subjects were asked to recall individual sentences from the text, and the preceding sentence was used as a recall cue. If you were a subject in the study, you would be given the recall cue, *The sources of crime were diagnosed* (from the metaphor version) or the cue *The sources of crime were studied* (from the literal version), and your task would be to recall the sentence that followed. Participants in the study performed better on the memory test when they had read the *crime is disease* metaphor version than when they had read the more literal version. Being able to map the novel domain (the causes of crime) onto a more familiar domain (disease) allowed participants to build a more coherent and more tightly interconnected mental representation of the expository text, which led to better comprehension and recall. So, when you want someone to understand something better, it helps to provide them with an apt metaphor. Using an apt metaphor is lighting a candle in the darkness.

Metonymy and Underspecification

Metaphors of the form *A* is *B* are fairly obvious and apparent uses of non-literal language, but there are non-literal forms that are not quite so obvious that nonetheless turn up frequently and have to be dealt with in our everyday experience of language comprehension. One such form is *metonymy* (pronounced me-*ta*-na-mee). *Metonymy* or *metonymic expressions* occur when a word that normally refers to one thing is used to refer to something else that bears a relationship to that word. An example will help illustrate. When someone says, *I spent the weekend reading Dickens*, *Dickens* is used as a metonym, and the expression as a whole is an example of *metonymy*. Contrast *I read Dickens* to *In 1870, my great-great granny on my mother's side met Dickens*. In this latter case, *Dickens* is being used to refer to the literal human being Charles Dickens. So, names like *Dickens* can be interpreted in at least two ways. They can be interpreted as referring to real live, literal people, or they can refer to products created by those real live, literal people. This creates a challenge for the language interpretation system. If Dickens were interpreted literally in the expression *I read Dickens*, that should result in people getting very confused. You can't, after all, literally read a human being the way you literally read a book, by turning pages and moving your eyes, and so forth. But people don't get confused. Why is that? And how does the language-processing system know which interpretation to apply when either the literal or metonymic meanings of Dickens could be appropriate at any given point?

Steven Frisson and Martin Pickering have come up with a theory that explains how metonymic expressions are interpreted (Frisson & Pickering, 1999, 2001, 2007; McElree, Frisson, & Pickering, 2006; see also Frazier & Rayner, 1990). Their theory deals with *producer-for-product* metonymies (*I read Dickens*), but also with other types, such as place-for-event metonymies, as in *The students protested after Vietnam* (compare to more literal *The students protested in* Vietnam), place-for-institution metonymies, as in *I talked to the convent yesterday* (compare to the more literal *I talked at the convent yesterday*), and controller-for-controlled metonymies, as in *Saddam Hussein invaded Kuwait* (compare to the more literal *Saddam Hussein went surfing in Kuwait*). The interpretation of metonymies poses the same kinds of challenges that the interpretation of other metaphors does. The listener has to solve the recognition problem as well as determining the relationship between the literal meaning and the metonymic meaning. As with metaphoric expressions, listeners could apply a *literal meaning first* strategy, whereby they access the literal meaning of the critical element (*Dickens, Vietnam, the convent*) and attempt to integrate that meaning with the context, proceeding to a non-literal metonymic meaning only when the initial integration process fails. Alternatively, listeners could adopt a *metonymic meaning first* strategy, whereby they bypass the literal meaning in favor of the non-literal metonymic meaning. Finally, listeners could attempt to compute both the literal and metonymic meanings at the same time, in parallel.

If listeners adopted the literal-first strategy, then metonymic expressions like *My great-great grandmother read Dickens* should be harder to understand than literal expressions like *My great-great grandmother dated Dickens.* If listeners adopted the metonymic-first strategy, then literal expressions should be harder to understand than metonymic expressions. If both meanings are computed in parallel, then the two kinds of expression should be equally easy to understand. Of course, it is possible that familiar metonymic words, such as *Vietnam*, may come to have two related senses stored in the mental lexicon, one that relates to the physical location, and one that relates to the famous event that took place in that physical location, the Vietnam war. If so, metonymous words like *Vietnam* and *Dickens* may behave like *polysemous words* (words that have two or more unrelated meanings), in that processing a metonymous word may involve the simultaneous activation of multiple meanings. If so, metonymous words like *Vietnam* and *Dickens* should be harder to process that equivalent words that have just one stored meaning.

These predictions were tested in a series of eye-tracking experiments by Frisson and his colleagues (Frisson & Pickering, 1999, 2001, 2007; McElree et al., 2006). They monitored subjects' eye movements as they read sentences containing different kinds of expressions. Some of the expressions were familiar metonymic words, such as *Vietnam* and *Dickens.* Some of the expressions had unfamiliar metonymic uses, such as *during Finland.* Some of the sentences required readers to access the metonymic meanings, as in *The students protested during Vietnam* (for the familiar metonymy) and *The students protested during Finland.* Some of the sentences required readers to access the literal meaning, as in *The students visited Vietnam* and *The students visited Finland.* The eye-movement data showed that subjects had a relatively hard time understanding the unfamiliar metonymic expressions (*The students protested during Finland*). Reading times on the critical word *Finland* were longer than the comparable familiar metonymy *Vietnam.* More importantly, familiar metonymic expressions were processed just as quickly as their literal counterparts. So, the metonymic expression *The students protested during Vietnam* was just as easy to process as the literal expression *The students visited Vietnam.* The results therefore indicate that processing difficulty for metonymic expressions is not determined by the fact that the expression is non-literal rather than literal. Instead, what made expressions in this experiment easy or difficult to process was whether or not the reader could access a familiar meaning.

Frisson and Pickering suggest that the processing of metonymic expressions is best understood as a form of *semantic underspecification. Semantic* underspecification means that, rather than activating a predefined, detailed sense of a word like *Dickens*, when you hear *Dickens* in the context of *I read Dickens*, you initially activate a wide field of concepts associated with *Dickens*, and you subsequently narrow that field to tailor the interpretation to the specific context that *Dickens* appears in (Frisson and Pickering refer to this latter process as the *homing-in stage*). As they explain (Frisson & Pickering, 1999, p. 1379), "One abstract, underspecified meaning of a word with a familiar metonymic sense and a literal sense is initially activated. This meaning is … the same for both senses. Hence, no extra processing is predicted for either sense." Apart from doing a good job incorporating the reaction time results, philosophical considerations also favor the underspecification account. Underspecification helps explain why familiar literal and metonymic expressions are processed equally quickly—the initial underspecified interpretation is compatible with both the literal and non-literal meanings. The underspecification hypothesis also helps deal with the fact that *Dickens* could refer to any of a large number of associated concepts—all of the books by Dickens, a specific title by Dickens, a specific copy of a specific title by Dickens, a statue of Dickens, a picture of Dickens, and on and on. If we had to activate just a single sense of *Dickens*, it is likely that we would have to engage in a lot of repair processing a lot of the time.

Idioms and Frozen Metaphors

There exists a huge dump of worn out metaphors which have lost all evocative power and are merely used because they save people the trouble of inventing phrases for themselves.
GEORGE ORWELL

Idioms are expressions in language that make use of ordinary words that have conventional meanings, but when you put the words together in a phrase, the meaning of the utterance is much greater than the sum of the parts. *Screw the pooch* was a commonly used English idiom during the past decade, and its meaning "to blunder" or "to make a mistake" does not transparently relate to any of the individual words in the expression (e.g., Gibbs, Nayak, & Cutting, 1990; Jackendoff, 1995). Idioms of this type are called *non-decomposable*, because they cannot be broken down into parts smaller than the whole expression. They contrast with *decomposable* idioms, which can be broken down into subparts, each of which can be related to a component of the idiom's definition. *Spill the beans*, as an example, can be broken down into the verb by itself, which maps on to *tell*, and *the beans* which maps on to *secrets*. Because individual words in idioms do not refer to their normal or default meanings, idiom comprehension poses a challenge to the language comprehension system. Somehow, the system must recognize that words are not being used in their normal sense, and it must recover the meaning that is generally assigned to the idiom as a whole. How does the comprehension system accomplish these tasks?

The classical view of idiom comprehension views idioms as being long words that are analyzed and interpreted as wholes (Chomsky, 1980, Katz, 1973). These accounts view idioms as being essentially "dead metaphors," which were once analyzed like other novel metaphoric expressions, but which over time have become conventionalized and associated with fixed, stored meanings, similar to other words in your vocabulary. As Gibbs, Nayak, and Cutting (1989, p. 576) explain, "This view suggests that the figurative meanings of idiomatic phrases are directly stipulated in the mental lexicon much like the meaning of an individual word is listed in a dictionary." According to this view, listeners do *not* access the meanings of individual words within the idiomatic expression as the idiom is being comprehended. Instead, the expression as a whole triggers lexical access for the idiomatic meaning, bypassing the normal syntactic and semantic analysis of the idiom's individual parts. Research on the processing and interpretation of idioms has led to a more nuanced, view, however.

According to the more recent *idiom decomposition* account of idiom comprehension, the way an idiom is processed and interpreted depends on specific details of the idiom (e.g., Gibbs, 1980, 1986; Gibbs et al., 1989; Gibbs & Nayak, 1991; Nayak & Gibbs, 1990). For instance, idioms can differ in terms of their *decomposability*—whether individual words in the idiom are associated with individual aspects of its meanings. Idioms such as *spill the beans* and *pop the question* are viewed as *decomposable*, because individual words can be tied to specific parts of the idiomatic meaning (e.g., *spill* = *tell*, *beans* = *secret*; *pop* = ask (suddenly), *question* = *marriage proposal*). The category of decomposable idioms can be further subdivided into *normally* and *abnormally* decomposable subcategories. *Lay down the law* is viewed as normally decomposable, because there is a semantic relationship between the conventional meanings of its component words and their idiomatic meanings (*law* = *rules*; the standard meanings of *law* and *rule* are similar). *Spill the beans* is viewed as abnormally decomposable, because the normal definitions of *beans* and *secrets* are semantically unrelated. Non-decomposable idioms such as *screw the pooch* (blunder) and *bury the hatchet* (make peace) cannot be analyzed into subparts that map directly to some subpart of the idiomatic meaning.

Decomposable idioms (e.g., *spill the beans*) and non-decomposable idioms (e.g., *screw the pooch*) behave differently along a couple of dimensions. First, decomposable idioms are more *syntactically flexible* than non-decomposable idioms (Gibbs et al., 1989; Gibbs & Nayak, 1989). This means that, if you rearrange the parts of a decomposable idiom, you are less likely to interfere with the idiomatic meaning than if you rearrange the parts of a non-decomposable idiom. So, if someone says, *the question was popped by Ted*, you are likely to view that as having an idiomatic meaning (*propose marriage*). But if someone said, *the pooch was screwed by Ted*, that is far less likely to retain its idiomatic meaning (*blunder*) and is more likely to be assigned a more conventional meaning (e.g., *Ted cheated the pooch*). Decomposable idioms are also more likely to be *lexically flexible* than non-decomposable idioms. This means that you can replace individual words in the idiom with other words, and still retain the idiomatic meaning. So, you can change the decomposable idiom *button your lip* to *fasten your lip*, *button your gob*, or (for our Scottish friends) *hush a gob*, without losing the idiomatic meaning ("be quiet"). There are also differences in the amount of time it takes people to process and interpret decomposable and non-decomposable idioms (Gibbs et al., 1989; Gibbs & Gonzales, 1985). People can process and understand decomposable idioms faster than non-decomposable idioms. Gibbs suggests that this speed advantage for decomposable idioms means that listeners process words in the idiom individually and assign them individual meanings while building up an interpretation of the idiom as a whole (contrary to the classic "dead metaphor" view; Chomsky, 1980; Katz, 1973). As Gibbs and colleagues (1989, p. 587, explain), "When an idiom is decomposable subjects can assign independent meanings to its individual parts and will quickly recognize how these meaningful parts combined to form the overall figurative interpretation of the phrase."

This line of research therefore challenges the idea that idiomatic expressions are treated as unanalyzable wholes. Additional research suggests that the conventional meanings of individual words can contribute to the meaning of idioms, even for non-decomposable idioms. For example Gibbs and colleagues note that, although the origin of non-decomposable idioms may be lost or obscure, there are often reasons why particular words and phrases take on the meanings they convey in contemporary language. For example, Hamblin and Gibbs (1999, p. 35) explain the origin of the phrase *kick the bucket*:

> *[It] originally came from one method of slaughtering hogs where hogs were tied by their feet on a wooden frame, called a "buquet" in French and then had their throats cut with a knife. People commented that, when the hogs died, they "kicked the buquet" ... Soon enough, people simply talked about dying for animals and human beings as "kicking the buquet" ... using one salient part of a scene to refer to the entire complex situation.*

Why does the expression contain the verb *kick*? Originally because of a literal, directly perceived sequence of events that involved kicking. But later, new situations could be

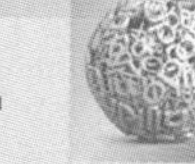

CONSISTENT CONTEXT FOR *CHEW THE FAT*

Joan and Sally are best friends. They have been confiding in each other for years. Every Thursday, they meet for coffee and talk. They often talk for hours while catching up on each others' lives. "You start," said Joan. "Tell me about what has been going on." Later, Joan told her husband about the conversation with Sally. *"We chewed the fat."*

INCONSISTENT CONTEXT FOR *CHEW THE FAT*

Joan and Sally are co-workers. Joan overheard some important news as she walked by the boardroom. Their office branch was going to be closing permanently. Joan saw Sally a little while later. "Have you heard the news?" Joan asked. "We might be losing our jobs." Later, Joan told her husband about the conversation with Sally. *"We chewed the fat."*

(Hamblin and Gibbs, 1999)

mapped onto the conventional scenario. Critically, the idiom *kicked the bucket* still conveys the idea of a sudden event, because the action of kicking is itself a sudden event. To show that individual elements of idioms still carry the meaning associated with individual words, Gibbs and colleagues presented subjects with idioms such as *kicked the bucket* (which implies a quick action) and *chewed the fat* (which implies a slower action). These idioms were presented in contexts that were either consistent with the type of action conveyed by the verb (*kicked* or *chewed*) or inconsistent with the type of action conveyed by the verb. So, idioms sometimes appeared in context that implied a fast action when the idiom itself implied a slow action, and vice versa, as in the example in the box above. People viewed the consistent versions as being more sensible than the inconsistent versions, which suggests that they had greater difficulty integrating the meaning associated with the idiom, in particular the fast or slow action indicated by the verb, when the context and idiom pointed towards different kinds of actions.

One of the shortcomings of research on idioms is that the vast majority of it has been conducted on English, and there on a restricted range of idiomatic expressions (Kreuz & Graesser, 1991). As a result, conclusions that have been drawn may not reflect universal properties of listeners, and they may reflect idiosyncratic properties of the restricted range of idioms tested in previous studies. Patrizia Tabossi and her colleagues tested Italian speakers' responses to a wide range of idiomatic expressions, and found evidence that may be incompatible with the idiom decomposition hypothesis, as formulated by Gibbs and colleagues (Tabossi, Fanari, & Wolf, 2008). They argued that the idiom decomposition hypothesis makes assumptions that may not hold up under closer scrutiny. First, it assumes that idiomatic expressions convey one specific meaning, and that meaning is captured by one specific literal paraphrase (e.g., *pop the question* equals exactly *propose marriage*, not *ask someone to marry suddenly*, or *kneel and suddenly ask "Will you marry me?"*).[13] Further, it assumes that people generally agree on how the individual parts of idioms connect to individual parts of their meanings. This assumption is based on inter-rater agreement for the kinds of idioms that have been tested in English (about 40 idioms in all). Tabossi and her colleagues noted that languages generally have many more than 40 idiomatic expressions, and she set about testing whether the idiom decomposition assumptions held for much larger samples of idioms. To do so, she had naive Italian raters assess Italian idioms (e.g., *tirare la caretta/pull the two-wheel cart*, "live a difficult life"; *essere al fresco/be at the fresh*, "be in jail"; *prendere un granchio/take a crab*; "make a blunder"). More specifically, subjects judged whether the idioms were decomposable, and, if so, whether they were normally or abnormally decomposable (as in the earlier studies by Gibbs and colleagues). The results showed that subjects did *not* agree on the choice of whether an idiom should be considered decomposable or, for those idioms that got the highest overall decomposable ratings, which ones were normally versus abnormally decomposable. Recall that the idiom decomposition hypothesis predicts that decomposable idioms should be more syntactically flexible than non-decomposable idioms. When Tabossi and colleagues tested their different kinds of idioms, they found that each type was about equally affected by different kinds of syntactic changes. Tabossi and colleagues also failed to find a speed advantage for any kind of idiom relative to the others (see also Titone & Connine, 1999), although they did replicate previous findings showing that the non-literal meanings of familiar idioms became available faster than their literal meanings (as expressed in literal paraphrases of the idioms). They concluded, therefore, that only a very restricted range of idioms behave in regular ways, as Gibbs' idiom decomposition hypothesis predicts.

Results like these have motivated researchers like Tabossi and Christina Cacciari to propose the *configuration hypothesis* to explain how idioms are represented in long-term memory and comprehended on-line (Cacciari, Padovani, & Corradini, 2007; Cacciari & Tabossi, 1988; Tabossi, Fanari, & Wolf, 2005; Tabossi et al., 2008). In their view, "idioms are mentally represented as configurations of lexical items without any separate representation in the lexicon" (Cacciari et al., 2007, p. 419). So, there is no prestored phrase-length item that corresponds to the idiom. Instead, the words that make up an idiom are processed in the normal way until the listener has received enough information that the idiom can be recognized as being a familiar configuration of words, or until it is highly likely that the string of words will be completed as a familiar idiom (so, listeners can anticipate the presence of an idiom before the entire idiom is heard; Titone & Connine, 1994). According to this view, idioms have a recognition point just like words do (see Chapter 3). As a result, idioms that are highly predictable in context, or that have earlier recognition points (perhaps because they are less syntactically flexible or non-decomposable), are processed more quickly than less predictable idioms; and idioms that have earlier recognition points are processed and understood more quickly than idioms that have later recognition points.

Embodiment and the Interpretation of Non-Literal Language

Gibbs also argues that embodiment and mental simulation play an important role in metaphor interpretation (Gibbs, 2003; Gibbs & Colston, 1995; Lakoff & Johnson, 1980a). This conclusion is based on metaphoric expressions that call upon our experience with physical bodies and physical processes that operate on those bodies. For example, the way we talk about emotion frequently evokes the metaphor *emotion is liquid in a container*. In studies where people are asked to talk about their emotional experiences, they often times use terms that refer literally to liquids and physical processes. One student who was asked to talk about *anger*, spontaneously produced the following (Gibbs, 2003, p. 5, my emphases), "At first, anger *burns* in my chest … the anger just *boiled* inside me. I wanted to grab my boyfriend by his shirt, pin him up against the wall and yell at him for being so stupid … Simply telling him that I was upset made my anger *fizzle out* a little. As we talked, my anger *melted* away." Conventional expressions such as, *blow your stack, flip your lid, get hot under the collar*, *blow off steam* and *explode* are also commonly used to express the concept and experience of *anger*. This underlying physical metaphor can color our understanding and experience of emotions like anger. Cognitive linguists, like Ray Gibbs, refer to the physical processes associated with liquids, heat, and containers, as the *source domain*. They suggest that understanding complex domains like emotion involves mappings between the source domain (heated fluids) and the target domain (emotion).

When you adopt the *anger is heated fluid in a closed container* metaphor, a number of conclusions logically follow. First, the fluid will increase in pressure as more heat is applied. Second, when the container fails, it will do so suddenly. Third, the container will fail without anyone consciously willing or wanting it to fail, so the response is essentially beyond anyone's control. When Gibbs (1992, 2003) assessed people's understanding of anger and their understanding of the physics of heated fluids and containers, he found them to be characterized in similar ways. Further, when people read idiomatic expressions such as *John blew his stack* they responded faster to subsequent target words, such as *heat*, that expressed part of the physical characteristics of the source domain. So, when we hear idiomatic expressions, they appear to automatically activate knowledge of the source domain, and we understand that when someone *blows their top* or *flips their lid*, they did not mean to do so (just as a pressurized container does not willfully explode, it just explodes).[14] As with word meanings, idiomatic expressions and visuomotor representations also appear to be connected (Wilson & Gibbs, 2007). When participants engage in body actions like swallowing, grasping, and chewing, they respond faster to idiomatic expressions like *he swallowed his pride*, *she grasped the truth*, and *they chewed on the idea*. If understanding idioms involved only the manipulation of abstract mental symbols, there is no particular reason why engaging in body actions should facilitate their interpretation.

The Neural Basis of Non-Literal Language Interpretation

Neurophysiological (ERP) and neuroimaging (fMRI, PET) experiments show that different networks of brain areas respond differently to literal and non-literal language (e.g., Bottini et al., 1994; Coulson & van Petten, 2002; Eviatar & Just, 2006). These studies supplement data from studies of patients with lesions (brain damage), who may have selective deficits in understanding or producing either literal or non-literal language (e.g., Brownell, 1984; Brownell & Stringfellow, 1999; Winner & Gardner, 1977). Early research on brain-damaged patients suggested that the right hemisphere of the brain might play a special role in the interpretation of non-literal speech. Patients with right-hemisphere damage were less able than patients with left-hemisphere damage in matching verbal metaphors (e.g., *he had a heavy heart*) with pictures that described either the non-literal meaning (e.g., a picture of a sad man) or pictures that described the literal meaning (e.g., a man carrying around a large, heavy heart). Subsequent studies (e.g., Brownell, Simpson, Bihrle, & Potter, 1990), suggested that right-hemisphere patients' problem was really with the picture-matching task, however, rather than metaphoric language per se (people with right-hemisphere brain damage often exhibit problems dealing with visuospatial information, as indicated by syndromes like *neglect*, where people have problems perceiving and imagining the left half of the visual world). When the task was changed from picture matching to giving a verbal definition of non-literal expressions, patients with right-hemisphere damage performed much better, indicating that they did know the meanings of many non-literal expressions. So, right-hemisphere damage does not inevitably produce profound impairment of figurative language understanding (see Thoma & Daum, 2006, for a review).

The patient data do not provide a firm basis for making inferences about right-hemisphere contributions to non-literal language processing. As a result, researchers have turned to neurophysiological and neuroimaging studies of healthy individuals to find out how the brain responds to non-literal language. Unfortunately, these studies do not provide a unified, coherent view about how the brain responds to non-literal language. Let's consider a couple of the prominent theories that relate brain function to the interpretation of non-literal language. One major idea, the *right hemisphere hypothesis*, proposes that, while the left hemisphere dominates the process of analyzing and interpreting literal language, the right hemisphere dominates the process of analyzing and interpreting non-literal language. This hypothesis received support from the early work on brain-damaged patients as well as the very first neuroimaging research on metaphor comprehension (Bottini et al., 1994). In Bottini and colleagues' study, six individuals had their cerebral blood flow measured as they read sentences that expressed novel metaphoric meanings (e.g., *The investors were squirrels collecting nuts*) or literal meanings (e.g., *The boy used stones as paperweights*). After they read each sentence, participants judged whether it made sense on its literal reading (in which case, the response to the metaphoric sentences should be *no*, while the response to the literal sentences should be *yes*). When blood flow changes in response to metaphoric sentences were compared to blood flow changes in response to literal sentences, a number of right-hemisphere regions showed greater response to the metaphoric sentences (compared to the literal), but no left-hemisphere regions showed similar greater response to metaphoric sentences (see Plate 15). These data were interpreted as showing that the right hemisphere was especially activated by metaphoric language, consistent with the right hemisphere hypothesis.

Subsequent imaging studies have not supported the right hemisphere hypothesis, however. A couple of fMRI experiments by Alexander Rapp and colleagues (Rapp, Leube, Erb, Grodd & Kircher, 2004, 2007) involved processing of sentences that conveyed relational metaphors in the *An a is a b* form, as in *Die Worte des Liebhabers sind Harfenklänge* ("The lover's words are harp sounds"); or literal category inclusion statements, as in *Die worte des Liebhabers sind Lügen* ("The lover's words are lies"). After reading the sentences, participants' judged whether the sentence conveyed a positive or negative message. As shown in Plate 16, when metaphoric sentences were compared to literal sentences, greater activity was observed in the left hemisphere for the metaphoric sentences, but no differences occurred in the right hemisphere. Additional fMRI experiments by Eviatar and Just (2006), Stringaris and colleagues (Stringaris, Medford, Giampietro, Brammer, & David, 2007), and Shibata and colleagues (Shibata, Abe, Terao, & Miyamoto, 2007) all involved sentences as stimuli, contrasts of metaphoric with literal materials, and fMRI measurement methods. They differed with respect to the tasks that subjects performed after reading the stimuli—some experiments involved categorizing the stimuli as metaphoric or literal, some involved a version of the go/no-go paradigm where participants made an overt response only for sentences that were nonsensical. Despite differences in language (Japanese vs. English vs. German), and differences in the secondary task, all of these studies showed greater left-hemisphere activation for metaphoric stimuli compared to literal stimuli, and little or no difference in the right hemisphere for different sentence types. In fact, the study on Japanese (Shibata et al., 2007) showed greater right-hemisphere activity for literal sentences than for metaphoric sentences, which runs directly counter to the right hemisphere hypothesis.

This mixed bag of neuroimaging results has motivated some researchers to try to formulate alternatives to the right hemisphere hypothesis. One such approach is Giora's *graded salience hypothesis* (e.g., Giora, 2003). According to graded salience, differences between the right and left hemisphere are by-products of the kinds of lexical coding that are undertaken by each hemisphere. As suggested by the coarse-coding hypothesis (Beeman, 1998), right-hemisphere lexical representations are more diffuse and have fuzzier boundaries than left-hemisphere lexical representations. As a result, when lexical representations get activated in the right hemisphere, they are more likely to weakly connect to distantly related concepts. This makes right-hemisphere lexical representations well suited to discovering and highlighting the kinds of distant semantic connections that are important in the understanding of novel metaphors. By contrast, the left hemisphere contains more sharply defined lexical representations, and it activates a narrower range of associations in response to individual words. This makes the left hemisphere good at cleanly and sharply activating prestored semantic relationships, which is ideal for the processing of conventional, familiar, well-worn metaphors. The net result, according to graded salience, is that the left hemisphere is good at activating the *salient* meaning of an expression, while the right hemisphere is better at activating *non-salient* meanings. What makes something salient can be a function of frequency (more frequent meanings are more salient), conventionality (more conventional meanings are more salient), or literality (more literal meanings, everything else being equal, are more salient). Critically, the non-literal meaning of an expression can be more salient than the literal meaning, if the non-literal meaning is more frequent. This is just what happens with frozen or familiar metaphors such as *iron fist*, *paper tiger*, and *bad medicine* (now that you've read this chapter). So, the left hemisphere should deal with salient meanings, including familiar metaphors, while the right hemisphere will play a bigger role in the processing of non-salient meanings, including novel, *un*familiar metaphors.

The graded salience hypothesis receives some support from fMRI experiments on metaphor processing and recent transcranial-magnetic stimulation (TMS) experiments. Two fMRI studies by Mashal and colleagues (Mashal, Faust, & Hendler, 2005; Mashal, Faust, Hendler, & Jung-Beeman, 2007; see also Ferstl, Neumann, Bogler, & von Cramon, 2008) involved pairs of words that, when taken together, indicate either a literal (e.g., *paper napkin*) or metaphoric (e.g., *paper tiger*) interpretation. Subjects read each pair of words and then made an explicit judgment about them. Specifically, they judged whether the pair were literally related, metaphorically related, or unrelated. All of the stimuli were pretested to see whether they fit into one of four categories: literal, novel metaphors, conventional (familiar) metaphors, or unrelated. The critical comparison was between the novel and conventional metaphor stimuli. According to the right hemisphere hypothesis, both novel and conventional metaphors should fire up the right hemisphere. But according to the graded salience hypothesis, only the novel metaphors should fire up the right hemisphere, because their metaphoric meanings will be less salient than their literal meanings. For the conventional/familiar metaphors, their non-literal meanings will be more salient than their literal meanings, so the left hemisphere should play the biggest role in their interpretation. As shown in Plate 17, novel metaphors produced greater response than conventional/familiar metaphors in the right hemisphere, as predicted by graded salience. In particular, greater activity was observed in the right posterior superior temporal sulcus and the right inferior frontal gyrus. Novel metaphors also produced greater activity in the left inferior frontal gyrus, an area that was also activated by sentences in the metaphor condition in other fMRI studies (see above).

Pobric and colleagues (Pobric, Mashal, Faust, & Lavidor, 2008) applied a strong magnetic field as people processed word pairs like those used in Mashal and colleagues' (2005, 2007) experiments. As reviewed in Chapters 2 and 3, TMS temporarily disrupts the activity of populations of neurons directly beneath the point where the TMS is applied. If the right and left hemispheres process different kinds of metaphors in different ways, as suggested by the graded salience hypothesis, then zapping the left and right hemispheres should have different consequences for people who are reading novel and conventional metaphors. So, in this TMS study, subjects read literal word-pairs (*paper napkin*), familiar metaphors (*paper tiger*), novel metaphors (*pearl tears*), or unrelated words (*frog napalm*). When subjects had their right hemispheres zapped with TMS, they had increased difficulty processing the novel metaphors, but the other kinds of expressions were unaffected. Zapping the left hemisphere interfered with conventional/familiar metaphors, but not the other types of expressions. These data are the first known demonstration of a causal relationship between hemispheric function and metaphor-processing ability. Messing with the right or left hemisphere did *not* have a global effect on language processing, nor did it affect metaphoric language globally. Rather, the effects were restricted to particular kinds of metaphoric expressions. Specifically, TMS interfered with the processing of novel metaphors when it was applied over the right hemisphere, but not the left. This result is most compatible with the graded salience hypothesis, and is additional bad news for the right hemisphere hypothesis.

Researchers have also used the *visual hemifield priming paradigm* to study how the two hemispheres respond to non-literal language. In the visual hemifield priming paradigm, target words are displayed in either the left visual hemifield (to the left of the spot the subject is looking at or *fixating*) or the right visual hemifield (to the right of the spot thesubject is looking at). When words are displayed off-center in this way, the image of the word is processed either in the left occipital lobe (if the word is displayed to the right of fixation) or in the right occipital lobe (if the word is displayed to the left of fixation). Although the two cerebral hemispheres share information (via the *corpus callosum*, a thick band of fibers that runs horizontally between the two hemispheres), presenting words off-center means that the early response to the target word will predominantly reflect activity in the directly stimulated hemisphere. Researchers can manipulate aspects of the context to force either a literal or a non-literal interpretation of the target word. In the word–word version of the visual hemifield priming paradigm, word pairs induce either a figurative (*stinging insult*) or literal (*stinging bee*) interpretation of the two-word compound. In a sentence version of the task, sentence context determines whether the target word should be assigned a literal or non-literal meaning. In a study by Anaki and colleagues (Anaki, Faust, & Kravetz, 1998) that used the word–word version of the task, only metaphoric meanings were primed in the right hemisphere (people responded faster to *insult* compared to an unrelated control word after the prime word *stinging*; *bee* was not primed in either the literal or control conditions). As with the neuroimaging results, however, the visual hemifield priming paradigm does not always show a right-hemisphere advantage for non-literal meanings. In follow-on studies using the word–word version (Kacinik & Chiarello, 2003) and the sentence version of visual hemifield priming (Faust & Weisper, 2000; Kacinik & Chiarello, 2007), both hemispheres showed priming for both literal and non-literal meanings, and sometimes the left hemisphere showed bigger priming effects than the right hemisphere for non-literal meanings (contra the right hemisphere hypothesis).

ERP (evoked response potential) results have been similarly mixed. Using literal word pairs (e.g., *ripe fruit*) and metaphoric word pairs (e.g., *conscience storm*), Arzouan and colleagues (Arzouan, Goldstein, & Faust, 2007) showed that the N400 component was larger for novel metaphors, next largest for familiar metaphors (e.g., *iron fist*), and smallest for literal expressions. They also showed that the N400 was largest over the right side of the brain, which they interpreted as indicating that the brain regions that gave rise to the N400 effects were in the right half of the brain (but, as indicated previously, these kinds of assumptions are shaky when we are dealing with ERP data). Another recent ERP study using the sentence version of visual hemifield priming produced a different outcome.

It showed that the brain's electrical response to literal and metaphoric meanings was about the same in both hemispheres (although the results did confirm that metaphoric sentences produced a greater N400 effect than literal sentences in both hemispheres; see also Blasko & Kazmerski, 2006; Kazmerski et al., 2003; Tartter, Gomes, Dubrovsky, Molholm, & Stewart, 2002).

At this point, you may be thinking: What is the point?! Why summarize all this research when nobody seems to have figured how the brain processes non-literal language? The answer is that, despite mixed results, all of these studies will be important in establishing how the brain responds to non-literal language. Further, as the neuroimaging study of non-literal language is still in its infancy, it is not surprising that debates and clashes of data continue. This is true in almost all young fields of inquiry, where disagreements and conflicting data are the rule rather than the exception. But that does not mean that progress cannot be made. In non-literal language research, progress will depend on how effective researchers are at addressing these conflicting experimental results. For example, future research will have to address how the type of stimuli affects the neural response. Studies that have supported the graded salience hypothesis have tended to use word pairs, while studies that have shown left-hemisphere involvement in novel metaphor processing have tended to use sentences, rather than word pairs. Future studies should systematically contrast word pairs and sentences, as well as novel and familiar metaphors, among other things. Stay tuned! We are sure to see more good work on neural processing and metaphor in the near future.

Summary and Conclusions

In this chapter, we have looked at strengths and (mostly) weaknesses of the *standard pragmatic view* of non-literal language processing. Although different neural networks appear to be involved to different degrees in the comprehension and production of literal and non-literal language, interpretation of non-literal language does not wait for the failure of literal interpretation. Instead, non-literal meanings appear to be directly accessible for large classes of non-literal expressions. Considerable theorizing and research has gone into understanding how metaphors are understood. *Comparison* views of metaphor interpretation, and especially the *salience imbalance* version, do not account very well for a number of aspects of metaphor interpretation. As a result, many language scientists prefer a version of the *class inclusion hypothesis* (Glucksberg, 1998; Glucksberg & Keysar, 1990; Glucksberg & McGlone, 1999). Class inclusion helps to unify the processing of both literal and metaphoric language by proposing that relational metaphors and literal class inclusion statements are interpreted in the same way. Specifically, the topic is asserted to be a member of the category exemplified by the vehicle. Other theorists, including Gibbs (e.g., 1994), have attempted to close the gap between literal and non-literal language processing in the area of idiom comprehension. According to Gibbs, components of idioms retain some of their standard meanings, and this shows up in the way idiomatic meanings fit into their contexts. Other accounts, such as Cacciari and Tabossi's, draw parallels between the processing of regular words and idioms by proposing that both involve multiple meaning activation prior to a recognition point, after which a single stored meaning is rapidly accessed and assigned to the idiomatic expression. Research on the neural basis of language is still in its infancy and is, as a result, what Berkeley Breathed might call "higgledy piggledy." But there is certainly hope there, however, as researchers have some well-articulated theories to work from and what Jeff Spicoli would surely call an "ultimate set of tools."

TEST YOURSELF

1. Try to talk to someone for five minutes without using non-literal language. Count how many times you slip up and use a metaphor.
2. Take the following idioms, classify them as decomposable or non-decomposable. Rearrange the order of the words in some way. Ask a friend to rate whether the idiomatic meaning is preserved. See if you can predict differences between different kinds of idioms.

   barking up the wrong tree
   a chip on your shoulder
   a piece of cake
   pulling my leg
   shaving his cow
   give him the slip

Notes

1 *Before* is itself a spatial metaphor that we use to talk about time. If you stand *before* a judge, that means you are in front of the judge (as opposed to being behind him).
2 In fact, the non-literal interpretations of some familiar idiomatic expressions may be recovered more quickly than their literal meanings (Gibbs, 1980, 1986).
3 Especially if you are Tom Cruise, although he appears to be doing well these days.
4 Spoiler: If Saddam Hussein is Hitler, and George Bush is Saddam Hussein's arch-rival, then George Bush is either Franklin Delano Roosevelt or Winston Churchill, because FDR and Churchill were Hitler's arch-rivals. Hussein:Hitler::Bush:FDR/Churchill.
5 Gibbs might suggest that the understanding of anger as fluid in a container is based on direct experience of our own internal bodily fluids (as in Gibbs, 2001; Gibbs, Lima, & Francozo, 2004), rather than perceptual experience with other kinds of fluids and containers outside the body. He claims (2001, p. 6), "Under stress, people experience the feeling of their bodily fluids becoming heated." Personally, I have never experienced the sensations that he attributes to fluids in the body in association with the experience of anger, and even if I did, there is no way for me to tell whether you have had the same subjective experience as me. Further, if we did have those subjective experiences, they could easily be influenced by culturally transmitted expectations, by the very expressions (*he flipped his lid, she boiled over*) that the subjective experiences are meant to give rise to.
6 Recent attempts have been made to muster evidence for the conceptual mapping hypothesis that do not depend on collecting examples of utterances that instantiate the metaphor in question (e.g., Teuscher, McQuire, Collins, & Coulson, 2008). The author's view of this evidence is that it offers weak support at best for the strong form of the conceptual mapping hypothesis. Stay tuned.
7 Gibbs responds that complex metaphoric relations, such as that that links *argument* and *war*, can be built up by combining more basic, primitive metaphoric domains (Gibbs, at al., 2004). For example, the *arguments are buildings* metaphor consists of a combination of two more primitive metaphors, *persisting is staying upright* and *structure is physical structure*. However, as with the conceptual mapping hypothesis more generally, it is incumbent on the proponents of such theories to explain how just the right combinations of primitive metaphors can emerge without a homunculus.
8 Quotation brazenly stolen from Bowdle & Gentner (2005, p. 193).
9 Available at www.comedycentral.com/colbertreport/full-episodes/index.jhtml?episodeId=216591.
10 Ignore for the moment that *You are hot* is an attributional metaphor.
11 As in Monty Python's "splunge" sketch (Python, 1998).
12 You are John Lennon, and you were fabulous on "Live in New York City."
13 Gibbs and colleagues also tend to assign very minimalist standard interpretations to idiomatic expressions. For example, *flip your lid* is assigned the meaning *become angry*, which probably does not match the

meaning that people actually assign to that idiom, viz *become extremely angry very suddenly and uncontrollably* (Kreuz & Graesser, 1991). If people are assumed to have these more complex understandings of idiomatic expressions, then much of the evidence in favor of the idiom decomposition hypothesis evaporates. For example, the fact that people do not like the expression *flipped his lid* in the context of a scenario where someone is slowly becoming angry could just mean that the conventional meaning of the idiom ("suddenly become angry") does not fit, the same way the literal expression *he smiled a big smile and laughed* would not fit.

14 One of the problems that anger management counselors have to overcome is people's idea that, like pressurized containers, they cannot control and therefore do not bear responsibility for their outbursts.

References

Albritton, D., McKoon, G., & Gerrig, R. (1995). Metaphor-based schemas and text comprehension: Making connections through conceptual metaphor. *Journal of Experimental Psychology: Learning, Memory, and Cognition, 21,* 612–625.

Anaki, D., Faust, M., & Kravetz, S. (1998). Cerebral hemispheric asymmetries in processing lexical metaphors. *Neuropsychologia, 36,* 691–700.

Arzouan, Y., Goldstein, A., & Faust, M. (2007). Brainwaves are stethoscopes: ERP correlates of novel metaphor comprehension. *Brain Research, 1160,* 69–81.

Beeman, M. (1998). Coarse semantic coding and discourse comprehension. In M. Beeman & C. Chiarello (Eds.), *Right hemisphere language comprehension: Perspectives from cognitive neuroscience* (pp. 255–284). Mahwah, NJ: Erlbaum.

Blasko, D. G., & Connine, C. M. (1993). Effects of familiarity and aptness on metaphor processing. *Journal of Experimental Psychology: Learning, Memory, and Cognition, 19,* 295–308.

Blasko, D. G., & Kazmerski, V. A. (2006). ERP correlates of individual differences in the comprehension of nonliteral language. *Metaphor and Symbol, 21,* 267–284.

Bottini, G., Corcoran, R., Sterzi, R., Paulescu, E., Schenone, P., Scarpa, P., Frackowiak, R. S. J., & Frith, C. D. (1994). The role of right hemisphere in the interpretation of figurative aspects of language: A positron emission tomography study. *Brain, 117,* 1241–1253.

Bowdle, B. F., & Gentner, D. (2005). The career of metaphor. *Psychological Review, 112,* 193–216.

Brownell, H. (1984). Sensitivity to lexical denotation and connotation in brain damaged patients. *Brain & Language, 22,* 253–264.

Brownell, H. H., Simpson, T. L., Bihrle, A. M., & Potter, H. H. (1990). Appreciation of metaphoric alternative word meanings by left and right brain-damaged patients. *Neuropsychologia, 28,* 375–383.

Brownell, H., & Stringfellow, A. (1999). Making requests: Illustrations of how right-hemisphere brain damage can affect discourse production. *Brain & Language, 68,* 442–465.

Cacciari, C., Padovani, R., & Corradini, P. (2007). Exploring the relationship between individuals' speed of processing and their comprehension of spoken idioms. *European Journal of Cognitive Psychology, 19,* 417–445.

Cacciari, C., & Tabossi, P. (1988). The comprehension of idioms. *Journal of Memory and Language, 27,* 668–683.

Chomsky, N. (1980). *Rules and representations.* New York: Columbia University Press.

Clark, H. H. (1996). *Using language.* Cambridge, England: Cambridge University Press.

Clark, H. H., & Lucy, P. (1975). Understanding what is meant from what is said: A study in conversationally conveyed requests. *Journal of Verbal Learning and Verbal Behavior, 14,* 56–72.

Colston, H. L., & Gibbs, R. W., Jr. (2002). Are irony and metaphor understood differently? *Metaphor and Symbol, 17,* 57–80.

Coulson, S., & van Petten, C. (2002). A special role for the right hemisphere in metaphor comprehension? ERP evidence from hemifield presentation. *Brain Research, 1146,* 128–145.

Eviatar, Z., & Just, M. A. (2006). Brain correlates of discourse processing: An fMRI investigation of irony and conventional metaphor comprehension. *Neuropsychologia, 44,* 2348–2359.

Faust, M., & Weisper, S. (2000). Understanding metaphoric sentences in the two cerebral hemispheres. *Brain and Cognition, 43,* 186–191.

Ferstl, E. C., Neumann, J., Bogler, C., & von Cramon, D. Y. (2008). The extended language network: A meta-analysis of neuroimaging studies on text comprehension. *Human Brain Mapping, 29,* 581–593.

Fogelin, R. J. (1988). *Figuratively speaking.* New Haven: Yale University Press.

Frazier, L., & Rayner, K. (1990). Taking on semantic commitments: Processing multiple meanings vs. multiple senses. *Journal of Memory and Language, 29,* 181–200.

Frisson, S., & Pickering, M. J. (1999). The processing of metonymy: Evidence from eye movements. *Journal of Experimental Psychology: Learning, Memory, and Cognition, 25,* 1366–1383.

Frisson, S., & Pickering, M. J. (2001). Obtaining a figurative interpretation of a word: Support for underspecification. *Metaphor and Symbol, 16,* 149–171.

Frisson, S., & Pickering, M. J. (2007). The processing of familiar and novel senses of a word: Why reading Dickens is easy but reading Needham can be hard. *Language and Cognitive Processes, 22,* 595–613.

Gentner, D. (1983). Structure mapping: A theoretical framework for analogy. *Cognitive Science, 7,* 155–170.

Gibbs, R. W., Jr. (1980). Spilling the beans on understanding and memory for idioms. *Memory & Cognition, 8,* 449–456.

Gibbs, R. W. (1983). Do people always process the literal meanings of indirect requests? *Journal of Experimental Psychology: Learning, Memory, and Cognition, 9,* 524–533.

Gibbs, R. W., Jr. (1986). Skating on thin ice: Literal meaning and understanding idioms in conversation. *Memory & Cognition, 14,* 149–156.

Gibbs, R. W., Jr. (1992). Why do idioms mean what they do? *Journal of Memory and Language, 31,* 485–506.

Gibbs, R. W., Jr. (1994). *The poetics of mind.* Cambridge, England: Cambridge University Press.

Gibbs, R. W., Jr. (2001). Evaluating contemporary models of figurative language understanding. *Metaphor and Symbol, 16,* 317–333.

Gibbs, R. W., Jr. (2003). Embodied experience and linguistic meaning. *Brain & Language, 84,* 1–15.

Gibbs, R. W., Jr., & Colston, H. L. (1995). The cognitive psychological reality of image schemas and their transformations. *Cognitive Linguistics, 6,* 347–378.

Gibbs, R. W., Jr., & Gonzales, G. (1985). Syntactic frozenness in processing and remembering idioms. *Cognition, 20,* 243–259.

Gibbs, R. W., Jr., Lima, P. L. C., & Francozo, E. (2004) Metaphor is grounded in embodied experience. *Journal of Pragmatics, 36,* 1189–1210.

Gibbs, R. W., Jr., & Nayak, N. P. (1991). Why idioms mean what they do. *Journal of Experimental Psychology: General, 120,* 93–95.

Gibbs, R. W., Nayak, N. P., & Cutting, C. (1989). How to kick the bucket and not decompose: Analyzability and idiom processing. *Journal of Memory and Language, 28,* 576–593.

Gibbs, R. W., Jr., Nayak, N. P., & Cutting, C. (1990). Taking on semantic commitments: Processing multiple meanings vs. multiple senses. *Journal of Memory and Language, 29,* 181–200.

Giora, R. (2003). *On our mind: Salience, context, and figurative language.* New York: Oxford University Press.

Giora, R. (2007). Is metaphor special? *Brain & Language, 100,* 111–114.

Glucksberg, S. (1998). Understanding metaphors. *Current Directions in Psychological Science, 7,* 39–43.

Glucksberg, S. (2003). The psycholinguistics of metaphor. *Trends in Cognitive Sciences, 7,* 92–96.

Glucksberg, S., Gildea, P., & Bookin, H. (1982). On understanding nonliteral speech: Can people ignore metaphors? *Journal of Verbal Learning and Verbal Behavior, 21,* 85–98.

Glucksberg, S., & Haught, C. (2006a). On the relation between metaphor and simile: When comparison fails. *Mind and Language, 21,* 360–378.

Glucksberg, S., & Haught, C. (2006b). Can Florida become *like* the next Florida? When metaphoric comparisons fail. *Psychological Science, 17,* 935–938.

Glucksberg, S., & Keysar, B. (1990). Understanding metaphorical comparisons: Beyond similarity. *Psychological Review, 97,* 3–18.

Glucksberg, S., Keysar, B., & McGlone, M. S. (1992). Metaphor understanding and accessing conceptual schema. *Psychological Review, 99,* 578–581.

Glucksberg, S., & McGlone, M. S. (1999). When love is not a journey: What metaphors mean. *Journal of Pragmatics, 31,* 1541–1558.

Glucksberg, S., Manfredi, D. A., & McGlone, M. S. (1997). Metaphor comprehension: How metaphors create new categories. In T. B. Ward, S. M. Smith, & J. Vaid (Eds.), *Creative thought: An investigation of conceptual structures and processes* (pp. 327–350). Washington, DC: American Psychological Association.

Glucksberg, S., McGlone, M. S., & Manfredi, D. (1997). Property attribution in metaphor comprehension. *Journal of Memory and Language, 36,* 50–67.

Grice, H. P. (1989). *Studies in the way of words.* Cambridge, MA: Harvard University Press.

Hamblin, J. L., & Gibbs, R. W., Jr. (1999). Why you can't kick the bucket as you slowly die: Verbs in idiom comprehension. *Journal of Psycholinguistic Research, 28,* 25–39.

Harris, R. (1976). Comprehension of metaphors: A test of the two-stage processing model. *Bulletin of the Psychonomics Society, 8,* 312–314.

Inhoff, A. W. (1984). Two stages of word processing during eye fixations in the reading of prose. *Journal of Verbal Learning & Verbal Behavior, 23,* 612–624.

Jackendoff, R. (1995). The boundaries of the lexicon. In M. Everaert, E. J. van der Linden, A. Schenk, & R. Schroeder (Eds.), *Idioms: Structural and psychological perspectives* (pp. 133–165). Hillsdale, NJ: Erlbaum.

Johnson, M. G., & Malgady, R. G. (1979). Some cognitive aspects of figurative language: Association and metaphor. *Journal of Psycholinguistic Research, 8,* 249–265.

Kacinik, N. A., & Chiarello, C. (2003). An investigation of hemisphere differences for moderately imageable words across high and low image contexts. *Brain and Cognition, 53,* 239–242.

Kacinik, N. A., & Chiarello, C. (2007). Understanding metaphors: Is the right hemisphere uniquely involved? *Brain & Language, 100,* 188–207.

Katz, J. (1973). Compositionality, idiomaticity, and lexical substitution. In S. Anderson & P. Kiparsky (Eds.), *A festschrift for Morris Halle* (pp. 357–376). New York: Holt, Rinehart, & Winston.

Kazmerski, V., Blasko, D., & Dessalegn, B. (2003). ERP and behavioral evidence of individual differences in metaphor comprehension. *Memory & Cognition, 31,* 673–689.

Keysar, B. (1989). On the functional equivalence of literal and metaphoric interpretations in discourse. *Journal of Memory and Language, 28,* 275–285.

Keysar, B., Shen, Y., Glucksberg, S., & Horton, W. S. (2000). Conventional language: How metaphorical is it? *Journal of Memory and Language, 43,* 576–593.

Kreuz, R. J., & Graesser, A. C. (1991). Aspects of idiom comprehension: Comment on Nayak and Gibbs. *Journal of Experimental Psychology: General, 120,* 90–92.

Lakoff, G. (1987). *Women, fire, and dangerous things: What categories reveal about the mind.* Chicago, IL: University of Chicago Press.

Lakoff, G. (2002). *Moral politics: How liberals and conservatives think.* Chicago, IL: University of Chicago Press.

Lakoff, G. (2008). *The political mind: Why you can't understand 21st-century American politics with an 18th-century brain.* New York: Viking.

Lakoff, G., & Johnson, M. (1980a). The metaphorical structure of the human conceptual system. *Cognitive Science, 4,* 195–208.

Lakoff, G., & Johnson, M. (1980b). *Metaphors we live by.* Chicago: University of Chicago Press.

Malgady, R. G., & Johnson, M. G. (1980). Measurement of figurative language: Semantic feature models of comprehension and appreciation. In R. P. Honeck & R. R. Hoffman (Eds.), *Cognition and figurative language* (pp. 239–258). Hillsdale, NJ: Erlbaum.

Mashal, N., Faust, M., & Hendler, T. (2005). The role of right hemisphere in processing nonsalient metaphorical meanings: Application of principal components analysis to fMRI data. *Neuropsychologia, 43,* 2084–2100.

Mashal, N., Faust, M., Hendler, T., & Jung-Beeman, M. (2007). An fMRI investigation of the neural correlates underlying the processing of novel metaphoric expressions. *Brain & Language, 100,* 115–126.

McElree, B., Frisson, S., & Pickering, M.J. (2006). Deferred interpretations: Why starting Dickens is taxing but reading Dickens isn't. *Cognitive Science, 30,* 181–192.

McElree, B., & Griffith, T. (1995). Syntactic and thematic processing in sentence comprehension: Evidence for a temporal dissociation. *Journal of Experimental Psychology: Learning, Memory, and Cognition, 21,* 134–157.

McElree, B., & Griffith, T. (1998). Structural and lexical constraints on filling gaps during sentence comprehension: A time-course analysis. *Journal of Experimental Psychology: Learning, Memory, and Cognition, 24,* 432–460.

McElree, B., & Nordlie, J. (1999). Literal and figurative interpretations are computed in equal time. *Psychonomic Bulletin & Review, 6,* 486–494.

McElree, B., Pylkkänen, L., Pickering, M. J., & Traxler, M. J. (2006). A time course analysis of enriched composition. *Psychonomic Bulletin & Review, 13,* 53–59.

Miller, G. A. (1979). Images and models: Similes and metaphors. In A. Ortony (Ed.), *Metaphor and thought* (pp. 357–400). Cambridge, England: Cambridge University Press.

Murphy, G. L (1996). On metaphoric representation. *Cognition, 60,* 99–108.

Nayak, N. P., & Gibbs, R. W., Jr. (1990). Conceptual knowledge in the interpretation of idioms. *Journal of Experimental Psychology, 119,* 315–330.

Ortony, A. (1975). Why metaphors are necessary and not just nice. *Educational Theory, 25,* 45–53.

Ortony, A. (1979). Beyond literal similarity. *Psychological Review, 86,* 161–180.

Pinker, S. (1994). *The language instinct.* New York: Harper.

Pobric, G., Mashal, N., Faust, M., & Lavidor, M. (2008). The role of the right cerebral hemisphere in processing novel metaphoric expressions: A transcranial magnetic stimulation study. *Journal of Cognitive Neuroscience, 20,* 170–181.

Pollio, H., Barlow, J., Fine, H., & Pollio, M. (1977). *Psychology and the poetics of growth: Figurative language in psychotherapy and education.* Hillsdale, NJ: Erlbaum.

Pollio, H. R., Fabrizi, M. S., Sills, A., & Smith, M. K. (1984). Need metaphoric comprehension take longer than literal comprehension? *Journal of Psycholinguistic Research, 13,* 195–214.

Python, M. (1998). *The complete Monty Python: Vo. 1 and Vol. 2.* New York: Methuen.

Rapp, A. M., Leube, D. T., Erb, M., Grodd, W., & Kircher, T. T. J. (2004). Neural correlates of metaphor processing. *Cognitive Brain Research, 20,* 395–402.

Rapp, A. M., Leube, D. T., Erb, M., Grodd, W., & Kircher, T. T. J. (2007). Laterality in metaphor processing: Lack of evidence from functional magnetic resonance imaging for the right hemisphere theory. *Brain & Language, 100,* 142–149.

Searle, J. (1979). Meaning and use. *Studies in Linguistics and Philosophy, 3,* 181–197.

Shibata, M., Abe, J., Terao, A., & Miyamoto, T. (2007). Neural bases of metaphor comprehension: An fMRI study. *Cognitive Studies: Bulletin of the Japanese Cognitive Science Society, 14,* 339–354.

Shinjo, M., & Myers, J. L. (1987). The role of context in metaphor comprehension. *Journal of Memory and Language, 26,* 226–241.

Stern, J. (2000). *Metaphor in context.* Cambridge, MA: MIT Press.

Stringaris, A. K., Medford, N. C., Giampietro, V., Brammer, M. J., & David, A. S. (2007). Deriving meaning: Distinct neural mechanisms for metaphoric, literal, and non-meaningful sentences. *Brain & Language, 100,* 150–162.

Stroop, J. R. (1935). Studies of interference in serial verbal reactions. *Journal of Experimental Psychology, 18,* 643–662.

Swinney, D., & Cutler, A. (1979). The access and processing of idiomatic expressions. *Journal of Verbal Learning and Verbal Behavior, 18,* 523–534.

Tabossi, P., Fanari, R., & Wolf, K. (2005). Spoken idiom recognition: Meaning retrieval and word expectancy. *Journal of Psycholinguistic Research, 34,* 465–495.

Tabossi, P., Fanari, R., & Wolf, K. (2008). Processing idiomatic expressions: Effects of semantic compositionality. *Journal of Experimental Psychology: Learning, Memory, and Cognition, 34,* 313–327.

Tartter, V. C., Gomes, H., Dumbrovsky, B., Molholm, S., & Stewart, R. V. (2002). Novel metaphors appear anomalous at least momentarily: Evidence from N400. *Brain & Language, 80,* 488–509.

Teuscher, U., McQuire, M., Collins, J., & Coulson, S. (2008). Congruity effects in time and space: Behavioral and ERP measures. *Cognitive Science, 32,* 563–578.

Thoma, P., & Daum, I. (2006). Neurocognitive mechanisms of figurative language processing: Evidence from clinical dysfunctions. *Neuroscience and Biobehavioral Reviews, 30,* 1182–1205.

Titone, D. A., & Connine, C. M. (1994). Comprehension of idiomatic expressions: Effects of predictability and literality. *Journal of Experimental Psychology: Learning, Memory, and Cognition, 20,* 1126–1138.

Titone, D. A., & Connine, C. M. (1999). On the compositional and noncompositional nature of idiomatic expressions. *Journal of Pragmatics, 31,* 1655–1674.

Tourangeau, R., & Sternberg, R. J. (1981). Aptness in metaphor. *Cognitive Psychology, 13,* 27–55.

Tversky, A. (1977). Features of similarity. *Psychological Review, 85,* 327–352.

Wilkes-Gibbs, D., & Clark, H. H. (1992). Coordinating beliefs in conversation. *Journal of Memory and Language, 31,* 183–194.

Wilson, N. L., & Gibbs, R. W., Jr. (2007). Real and imagined body movement primes metaphor comprehension. *Cognitive Science, 31,* 721–731.

Winner, E., & Gardner, H. (1977). The comprehension of metaphor in brain-damaged patients. *Brain, 100,* 719–727.

Wolff, P., & Gentner, D. (2000). Evidence for role-neutral initial processing of metaphors. *Journal of Experimental Psychology: Learning, Memory, and Cognition, 26,* 529–541.

Dialogue

Korean Air had a big problem (Kirk, 2002). Their planes were dropping out of the sky like ducks during hunting season. They had the worst safety record of any major airline. Worried company executives ordered a top-to-bottom review of company policies and practices to find out what was causing all the crashes. An obvious culprit would be faulty aircraft or bad maintenace practices. But their review showed that Korean Air's aircraft were well maintained and mechanically sound. So what was the problem? It turned out that the way members of the flight crew talked to one another was a major contributing factor in several air disasters. As with many airlines, Korean Air co-pilots were generally junior to the pilots they flew with. Co-pilots' responsibilities included, among other things, helping the pilot monitor the flight instruments and communicating with the pilot when a problem occurred, including when the pilot might be making an error flying the plane. But in the wider Korean culture, younger people treat older people with great deference and respect, and this social norm influences the way younger and older people talk to one another. Younger people tend to defer to older people and feel uncomfortable challenging their judgment or pointing out when they are about to fly a jet into the side of a mountain. In the air, co-pilots were waiting too long to point out pilot errors, and when they did voice their concerns, their communication style, influenced by a lifetime of cultural conditioning, made it more difficult for pilots to realize when something was seriously wrong. To correct this problem, pilots and co-pilots had to re-learn how to talk to one another. Pilots needed to learn to pay closer attention when co-pilots voiced their opinions, and co-pilots had to learn to be more direct and assertive when communicating with pilots. After instituting these and other changes, Korean Air's safety record improved and they stopped losing planes.

Introduction to Psycholinguistics: Understanding Language Science, First Edition.
Matthew J. Traxler.

Most of the time when communication goes awry, the result is mere confusion or hurt feelings. But as the Korean Air example shows, miscommunication in some contexts can be deadly (see also Whalen, Zimmerman, & Whalen, 1988). Studying dialogue can provide us with insights that help us understand factors that contribute to successful communication as well as factors that prevent effective communication. Studying dialogue is challenging because we have to take into account the joint and separate actions of two individuals, both of whom contribute to the conversation. Participants in conversation speak and listen, and an individual's comprehension and production processes overlap in time. Communication occurs via the words that participants speak, the *main channel*, but it also occurs via gestures and other forms of *backchannel* signals (such as head-nodding, *m-hmm* noises, and facial gestures) that listeners emit to indicate how well they are understanding what the speaker is saying (or at least, how well they think they are understanding the speaker). Because dialogue involves (at least) two participants, it helps to separate out the "speaker" and "listener" roles as we consider the factors that influence the behavior of speakers and listeners in a dialogue. But keep in mind that treating the speaker and listener roles as separate is really a matter of convenience.

This chapter reviews major theories of dialogue, all of which seek to predict and explain how speakers and listeners cooperate to exchange thoughts, beliefs, and information in conversation. The chapter begins with an overview of Paul Grice's ideas about the rules that speakers follow when crafting utterances. Next, it takes up Herb Clark's ideas about how speakers and listeners cooperate to expand the amount of information that they hold in common. Third, it considers how much weight speakers give to listeners' needs while they are planning and producing utterances (whether speakers are *cooperative* or *egocentric*). It also considers whether listeners pay attention to speakers' knowledge when they interpret speakers' statements (or whether listeners, too, are egocentric).

Gricean Maxims

When people converse, they use words in combinations to express ideas. But whether a contribution in a conversation makes sense depends on more than just the meanings of the individual words and the literal meaning of the combination of words. For example, it makes perfect sense in isolation to say, *Susan has nice hair*, and the normal force of that statement would be something like "the hair on Susan's head is attractive" or "most people would like to have hair like Susan's." But what if that statement were set in a particular context, say the context of a letter of recommendation? Let's say Susan is applying for a job and her former boss writes:

> Dear Potential Employer, I encourage you to hire Susan. Susan has nice hair.
> Sincerely, Susan's Former Boss.

Most likely, the reader will understand the propositional content of the statement ("Susan's hair = good'). But even though the reader can understand what the boss said, that reader will also think that something is seriously wrong with the statement. Even though the statement makes sense on its own, the boss should not have written that in that specific context. Normally, a letter of recommendation should discuss the candidate's qualifications for the position, personal qualities that would make her a good employee, and so forth. Because good hair does not qualify Susan for a job (unless it's some kind of hair modeling job), the statement lacks relevance, and therefore constitutes a faulty or flawed contribution in that situation.

H. Paul Grice, a philosopher of language who analyzed conversations and exchanges like the one sketched above, developed a theory to explain how people formulate statements when they converse or participate in written exchanges (Grice, 1989). His principles or rules of conversation are known as *Gricean maxims*. These principles are not hard-and-fast, absolute prescriptions for verbal behavior (unlike some principles of grammar, which are rarely or never violated). Instead, they are a set of guidelines that speakers normally adhere to, but sometimes ignore. However, when speakers ignore one of the Gricean Maxims, there is usually a reason why they do so. In Susan's letter of recommendation, the fact that her boss was only willing to comment on her hair probably tells us that Susan wasn't a very good employee. That is, the boss violated the principle that says "be relevant." In this case, what's relevant to the exchange is how good a worker Susan is. Because the boss does not comment on Susan's work habits, the obvious inference is that there isn't much good to say about them.[1]

Grice proposed that conversational principles should be organized in a hierarchy. The *cooperative principle* stands at the top of the hierarchy, and other principles are organized below that. According to Grice, the overarching goal of conversation is the exchange of information, and to do that speakers design their utterances to help the listener acquire information. That is, speakers cooperate with listeners whose goal is to learn something new. In Grice's terms (1989, p. 26), the cooperative principle directs speakers to, "Make your conversational contribution such as is required at the stage at which is occurs, by the accepted purpose or direction of the talk exchange in which you are engaged." Speakers most often cooperate, although sometimes they lie or purposely seek to confuse or baffle their listeners. To cooperate with listeners, speakers need to take into account listeners' presuppositions, beliefs, and knowledge. For example, if both partners in a conversation know that a person called Bob is very tired, it makes sense to say, *Bob succeeded in keeping his eyes open*. But if a listener thinks or knows that Bob is alert and chipper, then that same statement makes little or no sense. The speaker should choose the expression *Bob succeeded in keeping his eyes open*, only if the speaker believes the listener thinks Bob is tired. To be cooperative, therefore, the speaker must have and use knowledge about the listener's mental state.

When speakers cooperate with listeners, they follow a number of additional principles that determine whether their statements are well-formed and contextually appropriate. The main principles are those of *quantity*, *quality*, *relation*, and *manner*. Grice's *principle of quantity* says (1989, p. 26), "1. Make your contribution as informative as is required (for the current purposes of the exchange). 2. Do not make your contribution more informative than is required." Saying too little is costly, although it can be amusing, as when Graham Chapman addresses the question of how to rid the world of all known diseases (Python, 1990, p. 63):

> *Well, first become a doctor and discover a marvelous cure for something, and then, when the medical profession really starts to take notice of you, you can jolly well tell them what to do and make sure they get everything right so there'll never be any diseases ever again.*

Saying too much can also be costly. If someone asks you, *How do I get downtown from here?* you do *not* say, *Walk to your car, place your hand on the door handle. Raise the door handle until the door opens. Move your body so that you are sitting behind the steering wheel*… This violation of quantity is costly because it delays communication of information that meets the listener's needs and clutters the listener's representation of the discourse with irrelevant detail.

Grice's *principle of quality* says: "Try to make your contribution one that is true … 1. Do not say what you believe to be false. 2. Do not say that for which you lack adequate evidence" (1989, p. 27). So, speakers should not lie or just make stuff up.

According to the *principle of relation*, a speaker's contributions should be relevant to the current topic of conversation. According to Grice, listeners who assume that speakers are following the principle of relation can successfully interpret potentially ambiguous statements. Grice (p. 89) provides the word *grass* as an example. If the topic of conversation is about landscaping, and the speaker says *This is really good grass*, the principle of relation dictates that the intended meaning has to do with the stuff that grows on the front lawns of houses in American suburbia. However, in the context of a late-night debate about national drug control policy, the principle of relation should cause listeners to favor the "marijuana" meaning of *grass*. It would be weird if your lawn guy started talking about marijuana. It would be equally weird if lawn care sprang up during a discussion of drug policy.

The Gricean *principle of manner*, says (p. 27), "Be perspicuous" (that is, clear in expression or statement[2]). To be perspicuous, a speaker should: "1. Avoid obscurity of expression. 2. Avoid ambiguity. 3. Be brief (avoid unnecessary prolixity). 4. Be orderly." Style manuals, such as Strunk and White, provide further detailed advice about how to achieve the Gricean ideal of manner.

Taken as a whole, Grice's maxims provide us with a recipe for accomplishing two separate, but vital, communicative functions. On the one hand, they illustrate factors that speakers should take into account to craft effective statements. On the other hand, they provide listeners with clues that enable them to draw inferences that go beyond the literal content of a speaker's statements. However, Grice seemingly never intended his principles to serve as a theory of how speech is actually planned under the time pressures that limit speakers' performance in real conversation, and, in fact, some aspects of real conversation appear inconsistent with Grice's principles.[3] Subsequent theorizing in psycholinguistics has attempted to deal with some of these shortcomings. While Gricean principles are still recognized as a description of ideal speech planning and inference in dialogue, more recent accounts try to accommodate a wider range of phenomena that occur in real dialogues. Let's now turn to some of these additional phenomena.

Dialogue is Interactive

The opportunity for interaction is one of the main factors that distinguishes dialogue from monologue.[4] Classical approaches to dialogue (e.g., Cherry, 1956), however, view each participant in a dialogue as operating independently, somewhat like chess players. In chess, you think and then you make a move. Then I think for a bit and make a move. Then you think some more and make another move. Each move depends on the move that precedes it, but the decisions that get made are made by each individual thinking and acting alone. A similar process in dialogue would start with me saying something and you listening. When I'm done, you say something and I listen. We go back and forth, each taking turns to speak. As Martin Pickering and Simon Garrod note (2004, p. 170), the classic view of dialogue "simply involves chunks of monologue stuck together." However, in real dialogue, moves are not strictly sequential—the beginning of one person's speech often overlaps with the end of someone else's turn—and significant portions of the dialogue are created by partners interacting, cooperating, and collaborating on the content of the dialogue (Clark, 1996; Garrod & Pickering, 2004; Stivers et al., 2009). Further, rather than consisting of a series of one-off statements, dialogue is built up from multi-turn exchanges, as in the following example (Bangerter & Clark, 2003, p. 212; see also Clark & Schaefer, 1989). In this case, a director is attempting to tell a listener how to put together a set of Lego blocks to make a specific figure (* marks indicate where the two participants were speaking simultaneously).

A1: Okay. Um let's see. So we need a yellow two by two. Okay and that's going to fit on the right side of the blue block.

B1: M-hm.

A2: So that half of it oh yeah on one row of the right side of the blue block.

B2: Okay *so half of it's pointing to the right.

A3: *So half of it is pointing off to the right. Yeah.

B3: Got it.

In this case, speaker A's chief goal is to get listener B to put together two Lego blocks in a particular way. According to the classical theory of dialogue, speaker A would think about how to describe the arrangement of Legos, produce a statement that communicates that arrangement, and the listener would decipher the speaker's statement in order to recover the information it conveyed. However, the transcript shows something more complex than that taking place. Speaker A breaks the superordinate goal into sub-goals and begins by conveying one of them (statement A1). Listener B signals acceptance of the first part of the message (statement B1). In statement A2, the speaker begins to convey the rest of the instruction, catches herself half way through, and re-formulates her message. At that point, listener B helps out by elaborating on the information given in statement A2, which speaker A simultaneously verifies by saying almost exactly the same thing in statement A3. The ability of listener B to help out speaker A indicates that listener B is actively anticipating where the dialogue is likely to go, suggesting both incredibly rapid interpretation of speaker A's previous statement as well as a highly accurate understanding of the speaker's point of view. The listener verifies the content of the entire exchange by saying *Got it* (B3), providing the speaker with concrete evidence that her attempts to communicate have succeeded. Examples like these illustrate that, rather than being a sort of "ballistic," "all-or-nothing" activity, involving independent moves by independent players, dialogue involves a great deal of collaboration and joint, cooperative activity. Contrary to the maxims of manner and quality, speakers produce tentative descriptions before they have fully worked out all the details of their messages or determined the most effective way to express their ideas. Listeners are not passive. They actively anticipate how the conversation will evolve, and they provide speakers with explicit evidence of their understanding via both *backchannel* responses (head nods, *mhmmmm* noises) and main channel responses. (*What? Speak up, sonny! Got it.*)

Common Ground

Dialogues from the Lego task, and others like it, show that speakers do not always craft perfectly Gricean utterances. Sometimes, speakers lack the information they need to be perfectly informative, clear, concise, and helpful. Sometimes, they have the information but do not have enough time to fully evaluate it before they begin to speak. Despite violating Gricean principles of dialogue, speakers routinely manage to communicate effectively with listeners in face-to-face exchanges. This high level of communicative success is enabled largely by opportunities for cooperation and collaboration that interactive dialogue provides. Herb Clark and his colleagues have spent considerable effort building a theory of dialogue that attempts to capture the interactive nature of the communicative process (Clark, 1996; Clark & Schaefer, 1987; Schober & Clark, 1989; Wilkes-Gibbs & Clark, 1992). According to Clark and colleagues, the main goal in conversation is for partners to establish and expand *common ground*. "Common ground" sounds an awful lot like "common knowledge," or "shared knowledge," but it is really something different. "Common knowledge" or "shared knowledge" implies that two people know the same thing. But two people can know the same thing without having any awareness that the knowledge is shared. Common ground is a kind of shared knowledge, but common ground requires something extra: Both of the people in an exchange have to explicitly recognize that the knowledge is shared. So, "common *knowledge*" is "shared knowledge," but common *ground* is "mutually recognized common knowledge." Because of its emphasis on common ground, Clark's theory is sometimes referred to as *common ground theory*, or the *common ground theory* of dialogue.

According to Clark's common ground theory, successful communication takes place when two people expand the amount of common ground that they share. This approach helps to explain why contributions to dialogue normally consist of more than just single statements (as in the Lego example above). Because the goal of conversation is to expand common ground, and because the contents of common ground must be acknowledged by each conversational partner, speakers require some kind of evidence that each of their statements have succeeded in adding to common ground.[5] So, rather than just producing a sequence of statements, speakers in dialogues use information that is already in common ground to formulate statements, and they collaborate with their partners until both of them believe that communication has succeeded (Clark & Wilkes-Gibbs, 1986; Wilkes-Gibbs & Clark, 1992). Evidence of understanding can take a variety of forms, from implicit acceptance through back-channel responses (*mhmmmm*) to explicit statements of acceptance (*Got it*) (Bard et al., 2007).

Common ground theory helps explain how partners in dialogue choose particular expressions to refer to specific concepts, and how referring expressions evolve over the course of multiple exchanges between conversational partners. Early in an exchange, conversational partners will often negotiate about how to refer to something, and they will each make several individual contributions to the conversation as they craft and agree upon a particular referring expression. In a task where one person tries to describe an abstract picture to another, you might see an exchange like this the first time the two try to accomplish the task (from Wilkes-Gibbs & Clark, 1992, p. 184):

A: Okay the next one is … resembles someone that looks like they're trying to climb stairs. There's two feet, one is way above the other, and …

B: And there's a, there's a, a diamond on the right side, on a slant?

A: Yeah.

B: Got it.

A: Like, kind of looks like it's off the back.

B: Right, I got it.

But if the two are asked to do the same task, with the same pictures, a few more times, they will eventually refer to the same picture like this:

A: Uh, the next one is the person climbing the stairs.

B: OK.

And then like this:

A: Stair climber.

B: OK.

In the original exchange, the partners had to verify that they were looking at the same picture. In the second exchange, the speaker used part of the description from the first exchange (*someone that looks like they're trying to climb stairs*) to identify the picture, but can shorten the description because a reference to someone climbing the stairs has already been established in common ground (so the description becomes *person climbing the stairs*). In the final exchange, the description becomes shorter still. Participants in dialogue routinely craft referring statements by collaborating and verifying mutual understanding, and once those referring statements have been established, both participants in the dialogue can use them without further elaboration (see also Barr & Keysar, 2002; Carletta, Garrod, & Fraser-Krauss, 1998; Fay, Garrod, & Carletta, 2000). Further, if speakers violate the "referential pacts" that they negotiated previously with a specific listener (e.g., if speaker A in the previous exchange had suddenly started calling the *stair climber* the *diamond lady*), listeners experience some difficulty figuring out what the new term refers to (Metzing & Brennan, 2003). Thus, because prior exchanges establish information in common ground, a fuller description of the physical appearance of the picture is unnecessary, and communication becomes more efficient.

Because different pairs of conversational partners have different common ground, speakers need to pay attention to who, exactly, they are speaking to so that they can craft optimally effective messages. If I assume that a particular piece of knowledge is in common ground with a listener, but that knowledge is not actually in common ground, my attempt to communicate is likely to fail. However, once you and I have established common ground, we can exploit that resource to communicate more effectively with one another *and* to keep information out of the hands of people who overhear our conversation (Clark & Schaefer, 1987; see also Schober & Clark, 1989). In experiments involving pairs of friends conversing with one another, the conversational partners took advantage of personal experiences to craft referring expressions that unfamiliar third persons had difficulty interpreting. In these experiments, pairs of friends were asked to describe common landmarks from their university campus (such as a central fountain). Because pairs of friends had private experiences related to those landmarks, and those private experiences were part of the common ground between them, they could use those experiences (e.g., *This is where I put your teddy bear*) rather than the publicly available labels for the landmarks. While there was some "leakage" of private information, pairs of friends enjoyed great success concealing the true identity of the landmarks when they were instructed to do so (compared to when they were simply asked to describe the landmarks, without any reference to possible third parties). This success in communicating to each other and concealing information from third parties happened because two friends could take advantage of common ground that they shared. The third party failed to understand much of the conversation because the third party lacked the crucial knowledge supplied by common ground.

Common ground theory further offers a fresh perspective on a couple of old questions in dialogue research: How do people decide when it's time to take a turn in conversation? And why do speakers go *uhhhhhhhhhh*? According to one influential analysis of turn-taking behavior in conversation (Sacks, Schegloff, & Jefferson, 1974), who gets to talk when is determined by a set of "soft" constraints (as opposed to hard-and-fast rules), which, in combination, influence when people start and stop speaking during conversation. For example, in a group discussion, the person who is speaking now can influence who will speak next by looking at one specific person. The person that the speaker looks at is most likely to take the next turn (although someone else certainly can jump in). Likewise, a speaker is likely to look off into space if she plans to continue to speak for a while, but she will look at someone if she thinks her turn is coming to an end. Another rule specifies that overlap between speakers must be minimized—in most cultures, conversations are carried out by one person speaking while everyone else listens (Stivers et al., 2009). But if the speaker cannot immediately think of what to say next, and therefore pauses in the middle of her turn, someone else could jump in and cut her off before she has said what she wanted to say.

One theory of why speakers go *ummmmmmmm* is that they are trying to eliminate pauses in their speech, and thereby hold the floor until they have said what they want to say. Speakers can perform a similar trick by lengthening the pronunciation of function words, for example by pronouncing the word *the* as *theeeeee* or *a* as *uhhhhhhhhhh* when they want to hold the floor as they are trying to think of what to say next. So, in classical theories of dialogue, sounds like *uhhhhhhhh* and *theeeee* are called *filled pauses*. Alternatively, *theeeee* and *uhhhhhhhh* have been viewed as simple production errors. (Strong evidence against the "*uhhhhhhhh* as error" hypothesis comes from the fact that drunk people say *uhhhhhhhh* less than sober people. That's because they care less about making sense, much less holding the floor; Christenfeld & Creager, 1996.)

According to Clark and colleagues, however, (Brennan & Williams, 1995; Clark & Fox Tree, 2002; Fox Tree, 2001; Fox Tree & Clark, 1997), *theeeee* and *uhhhhhhhh* are conventional words in and of themselves, just like *cat* and *house*. Just like other words, speakers have control over when they produce *theeeee* and *uhhhhhhhh*, and these words serve to place particular concepts into common ground. Specifically, *theeeee* and *uhhhhhhhh* place into common ground knowledge that the speaker is experiencing an "upcoming delay (in speech planning) worthy of comment" (Clark & Fox Tree, 2002, p. 73). To provide evidence for that claim, Clark and colleagues can point to samples of naturally occurring speech containing instances of people saying *theeeee* and *uhhhhhhhh*. In these speech samples, speakers actually produce different versions of *uhhhhhhhh*, a short version (more like *um*) and a long version (*uhhhhhhhh*). In the speech samples, *um* is usually followed by a short pause, while *uhhhhhhhh* is followed by a longer pause. Because *um* appears before short pauses and *uhhhhhhhh* before long pauses, it must be the case that speakers have the ability to anticipate how long the pause is going to be (otherwise, the distribution of *um* and *uhhhhhhhh* would be random). Further, if *theeeee* and *uhhhhhhhh* are real words, then listeners should go beyond the speaker's explicit statement and draw inferences when *theeeee* and *uhhhhhhhh* appear in a statement. One inference that listeners draw from the long version (*uhhhhhhhh*) is that speakers are experiencing trouble recovering a word from memory. Under those circumstances, listeners are more likely to jump in and help complete the speaker's statement, and they are more likely to pay attention to unfamiliar objects in a visual display (Arnold, Hudson Kam, & Tanenhaus, 2007; Arnold, Tanenhaus, Altmann, & Fagnano, 2004).

Audience Design

Herb Clark's *common ground* approach proposes that speakers in dialogues commit significant mental resources to modeling their listeners' knowledge states, specifically by keeping track of the information that the speaker has in common ground with specific listeners. Speakers then use this knowledge to plan statements so that their listeners have the best possible chance of understanding them, for example, by using referring expressions that have been negotiated previously. Clark's theory of dialogue, therefore, incorporates the idea that speakers routinely engage in *audience design*: They take special pains to adapt what they say to meet the listener's specific needs. This does not mean that speakers consciously evaluate every possible way to craft their message. Speakers certainly *can* engage in painstaking, conscious deliberations, because deciding what to say and how to say it are under some degree of conscious control. But Clark's theory says that knowledge of the listener's needs can be rapidly and accurately deduced from a representation of common ground, and this can be done outside of conscious awareness and control. In fact, because speakers are under considerable time pressure during normal conversations, there may not be enough time for painstaking, exhaustive analysis, and so production processes may rely largely upon rapid, relatively automatic processes.

In general, speakers *do* appear to make some adjustments depending on who they are speaking to: Bilingual speakers can change languages. We talk differently to babies than to adults. If someone appears to be from out of town, we give more detailed directions than if they appear to be from the same city as us. In a noisy environment, we talk louder so the listener can hear better. These adjustments reflect a kind of *macro-audience design* where speakers make a decision at one point and apply that decision over an extended period of time. The common ground approach, and others like it, propose that speakers engage in a more *micro* style of audience design, where they are continuously making small adjustments based on moment-to-moment changes in the listener's knowledge, attentional state, and needs (Hanna, Tanenhaus, & Trueswell, 2003; Levelt, 1983). While there is general agreement that speakers can and do make macro-level adjustment when they speak, there is considerably less agreement about the extent to which speakers make *micro*-level adjustments.

Other theories of how speakers plan utterances view speakers as being more *egocentric* (Ferreira & Dell, 2000; Horton & Gerrig, 2005a, 2005b; Horton & Spieler, 2007; Keysar & Henly, 2002). That is, rather than dedicating mental resources to modeling listener's knowledge and tailoring utterances to meet the listener's specific needs, speakers' utterances are driven more by *availability*. The principle of availability says that speakers will produce whatever is easiest for them to produce, even when what is easy for speakers to say may be more difficult for listeners to understand. Information that is highly active, salient, or *available* to speakers will be easiest to produce, and so that information will show up in utterances. If that information is unhelpful to a listener, the speaker and listener will engage in a process of negotiation and repair to get communication back on track (as in the *common ground* approach). Accounts such as Keysar and colleagues' *monitoring and adjustment* hypothesis fall within the *egocentric production* class of theories, because they propose that speakers ignore listeners' knowledge and needs during initial utterance planning. However, speakers do monitor their own utterances, as well as feedback from listeners, and can adjust their messages based on the outcome of the monitoring process. But, any such statements will appear relatively late and speakers are likely to produce utterances that are sub-optimal from the listener's perspective some of the time.

It's important to study whether speakers in dialogue behave egocentrically or whether they design their utterances for their listeners, because determining the extent to which speakers behave egocentrically can help us figure out which theory of dialogue is the right one. As a result, researchers have spent considerable effort investigating whether speakers are egocentric. Dialogue research has enjoyed an upsurge of interest in the past decade or so, in part because advances in head-mounted eye-tracking technology have opened up new avenues of research. These experiments sometimes involve a real participant and a *confederate*, or *stooge*—someone who is working directly for the experimenter and is following a tightly controlled script. Having a stooge in the experiment helps experimenters get control over the *exuberant responsing* problem in dialogue. That is, people in dialogues can say whatever they want, whenever they want to, and this makes it hard to get control over variables that researchers might be interested in testing. Having a stooge means that researchers can present specific utterances at specific times, and they can then see how real participants react. Other experiments involve pairs of real participants, none of whom works for the experimenter. These latter experiments have the advantage of providing genuine feedback and interaction, at the cost of losing some of the experimental control that stooges provide.

If speakers engage in (micro-level) audience design, then they should avoid producing utterances that may cause difficulty for their listeners when an alternative is available to them. Syntactically ambiguous utterances are often difficult for people to understand. At least, they are more difficult to understand than equivalent *un*ambiguous utterances (see Chapter 4). If speakers take their listeners' needs into account when they are planning what to say, they should avoid syntactically ambiguous utterances. That being the case, speakers should be more likely to say something like (1a) than (1b):

(1) a. I knew the coach and his sister would arrive late.
 b. I knew <u>that</u> the coach and his sister would arrive late.

Inserting the optional word *that* in (1b) renders the sentence unambiguous, and sentences like (1b) really are a little easier to understand than ambiguous sentences like (1a). Vic Ferreira and Gary Dell tested whether speakers avoid ambiguous expressions by having participants read sentences such as (1a) and (1b) (Ferreira & Dell, 2000).[6] Later on, they repeated them back from memory (see also Arnold, Wasow, Asudeh, & Alrenga, 2004; Ferreira, Slevc, & Rogers, 2005; Haywood, Pickering, & Branigan, 2005; Keysar & Henly, 2002; Kraljic & Brennan, 2005; but see also Lockridge & Brennan, 2002). The question was whether speakers would add the optional word *that*, which would indicate that they were trying to make their sentences less ambiguous and therefore easier to understand. In this experiment, speakers did sometimes include the optional word *that*, but they did so to the same degree whether the word *that* was necessary to render the sentence unambiguous or not (sometimes, other cues meant that the sentence was already unambiguous, even without the word *that*). So, speakers did not appear to avoid ambiguity, and many of their utterances were, in fact, ambiguous. When speakers did use optional words that *could* make the sentence unambiguous, they did so just as much when the sentence was already unambiguous as they did when adding the word *that* could actually help out a listener. What really determined whether speakers used the word *that* was how hard it was for them to access the next word (e.g., *coach*). If a word had been recently encountered or was otherwise made highly salient, speakers left out the word *that* when they produced the sentence. Ferreira and Dell concluded that speakers use optional words such as *that*, not because they make life easier for listeners, but because they make life easier for speakers. When speakers are searching memory for the next word to say, and when that search is going a little bit slow, speakers can insert the highly frequent, closed-class, function word *that* to buy themselves just a little bit of extra time. (As Vic Ferreira once said, saying *that* is a fancy way of going *uhhhhhhhh* …)

Dialogue offers speakers other ways to engage in audience design besides using optional function words. When speakers are describing events, they make choices about how much detail to include (see Gricean maxim of *quantity*, above). If speakers engage in audience design, they should include information that will be difficult or impossible for their listeners to infer, but they should omit or neglect to mention information that is obvious or that would be fairly easy for listeners to infer. Is this how speakers really behave? To find out, Paula Brown and Gary Dell asked speakers to repeat short stories such as (2). The stories either mentioned a typical instrument (knife) or an unusual instrument (ice pick) (Brown & Dell, 1987, p. 444):

(2) The robber hid behind the door and when the man entered the kitchen he stabbed him in the back. He wiped the blood off the {knife/ice pick} and rummaged through the drawers. Later police investigators found his fingerprints all over the {knife/ice pick} and had no trouble catching him.

The participants' task was to read and retell the story from memory. If speakers engage in audience design, they should mention the ice pick more often than they mention the knife, because listeners are unlikely to infer that a strange instrument was used to stab the victim in the story. However, speakers might mention the ice pick more often simply because it is

(a)

(b)

Figure 8.1 Picture depicting "weird" ice pick instrument (left) or no instrument (right; the control condition) (from Brown & Dell, 1987, p. 453)

weird to stab someone with an ice pick, even more weird than stabbing them with a knife, and people in general tend to pay more attention to weird things than normal things.[7] *Ice pick* should be more salient and more memorable to the speakers themselves. So, rather than including *ice pick* when they retell the story because it helps listeners, speakers might mention *ice pick* just because it sticks in their mind. In fact, speakers do mention weird instruments like ice picks more than they mention normal instruments like knives, but this does not, by itself, tell us what causes speakers to behave this way.

To find out which of the hypotheses—audience design or salience—better explains why speakers mention weird instruments, speakers and (confederate) listeners viewed pictures such as the one in Figure 8.1 as the speakers repeated the stories. In the control condition, no instrument appeared in the picture. Having the picture present for both the speaker and the listener establishes a kind of common ground. When the left-hand picture is used, both the speaker and the listener know that an ice pick will be relevant to the story even before the speaker begins to tell the story, so the ice pick is part of the common ground. When the right-hand picture is used, only the speaker knows that an ice pick will be relevant to the story. So the ice pick is part of the speaker's privileged ground. If common ground is used by speakers to design their utterances, they should be more likely to mention the ice pick when the picture fails to provide the necessary information. In fact, speakers were just as likely to mention the ice pick when the listener was looking at the left-hand (ice pick) picture as when the listener was looking at the right-hand picture. So, rather than mentioning the ice pick because listeners needed that verbal information to understand the story, speakers mentioned the ice pick just because it is a strange and attention-grabbing element of the story. In other words, speakers in this experiment were behaving egocentrically.

Egocentric production

Three may keep a secret if two of them are dead.
BENJAMIN FRANKLIN

In the preceding example, mentioning the ice pick when the listener already knows about the ice pick (by virtue of having a picture) does not help listeners understand the story, but it certainly does not hurt anything. So, speakers are mildly violating Grice's maxim of quantity, but the cost that this violation creates for speakers and listeners is really very small. There are other circumstances, however, where failing to engage in audience design can impose costs on the speaker. When failing to take the listener's knowledge into account creates problems for the speaker, we would expect speakers to make special efforts to engage in audience design. Consider a situation where you have a big secret. Let's say you're a waiter and someone ordered orange juice. Let's say you found something in the orange juice, but you're running short, so you decide to serve it anyway. If you want a nice tip, what you do *not* want to do is alert the customer to any possible problems with the orange juice. So you should say something like *Here is your orange juice*, or just *Here you go*. But if you are thinking about what you just found in the orange juice, if that really captured your attention, you might actually say, *There's nothing wrong with this orange juice.*[8] If that happened, then the salience of your private thoughts would have trumped your desire to form an utterance that would improve your chances of getting a nice tip. Of greater theoretical interest, saying *There's nothing wrong with this orange juice*, suggests that (a) the waiter recognizes that there's a need to conceal some information in privileged ground, (b) he's making some attempt to keep that information privileged (i.e., he's at least trying to engage in audience design), but that (c) the pressures of his own internal thought process have caused him to produce an utterance that reveals that privileged information (i.e., that his attempt at audience design has failed).

This kind of egocentric production has also been observed in the laboratory under more controlled conditions (Wardlow-Lane & Ferreira, 2008; Wardlow-Lane, Groisman, & Ferreira, 2006). In studies investigating "leakage" of privileged information, speakers are asked to describe a target shape so that a listener can identify the target. As shown in Figure 8.2, speakers and listeners viewed a display where some objects could be seen by both, but one object was visible only to the speaker. In Clark's terms, the object visible only to the speaker was in *privileged ground*. To test whether audience design or salience had a stronger influence on speakers' behavior, the experimenters placed audience design and salience into

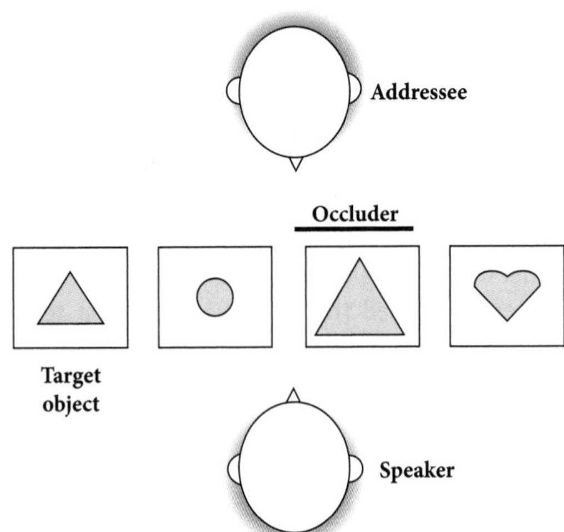

Figure 8.2 Experimental set-up from Wardlow-Lane et al. (2006, p. 274). The "occluder" prevents the listener ("addressee") from seeing one of the objects. The speaker's job is to get the listener to identify the target object, without being able to guess what is behind the occluder.

conflict. The experimental task required speakers to describe one of the mutually visible objects (the *target*), so that the listener could identify it. On some of the trials, the object in privileged ground was the same shape as the target object. The tricky part was that the speakers were supposed to keep the identity of the privileged object a secret. If the speaker engaged in audience design, that is if she considered only the objects that were in common ground (everything except the occluded object), then she would realize that the listener could see only three shapes, and the three shapes were unique (e.g., a triangle (target), a circle, and a heart). Thus, a speaker could get the listener to identify the target simply by saying, *Pick the triangle*. Note, however, that from the speaker's own perspective, *Pick the triangle* is ambiguous, because both the target object and the privileged object meet that description (they are both triangles). So, if the speaker designs an utterance taking into account only her own perspective, and not the listener's, she might very well say, *Pick the small triangle*. However, as soon as the speaker uses an adjective (*small*) to modify her description of the object, that should set off a chain of inferences in the listener. That chain might go something like this:

> I can only see one triangle. The speaker just said *Pick the small triangle*. If there's a small triangle, there must also be another, bigger triangle. Therefore, the object behind the occluder is a triangle.

So, when the speaker fails to take the listener's perspective into account, when she fails to engage in audience design, she will make mistakes (because the speaker's task is to keep the secret information secret). In this experiment, speakers frequently included adjectives (e.g., *small*) when describing the target objects, and they were *more* likely to do so when they were instructed to keep the occluded object secret. Thus, when the experimenters drew attention to the occluded object, the salience of the object to the speaker overcame speaker's abilities to engage in audience design. Experiments like these provide further evidence that the state of speakers' internal mental representations, in particular the degree to which specific concepts are attentionally focused or accessible, substantially affects production processes and may short-circuit speakers' attempts to design utterances for particular listeners.

Effects of Listeners' Perspective-Taking on Comprehension

Recall that one of the effects of common ground is to restrict the number of things that a speaker and listener will consider when they determine what a referring expression means (technically speaking, keeping common ground in mind "restricts the domain of reference"). While there are an infinite number of possible kings (King Henry V, Good King Wenceslas, Burger King™, etc.), if you are at an Elvis impersonator convention and someone says *The King*, it can only mean one thing. At the Elvis convention, the meaning of *The King* is effectively unambiguous because the common ground available to all of the attendees dictates that there is only one meaning that would be relevant. However, just because the final interpretation is clear does not mean that listeners automatically access that meaning right away. One of the questions in dialogue research is: How quickly does common ground restrict the domain of reference? Does common ground automatically and immediately render referring expressions like *The King* unambiguous? Or do participants in conversations need to go through a process of disambiguating referring expressions, the same way they go through a process of disambiguating words like *bank*, and *mint* that have more than one

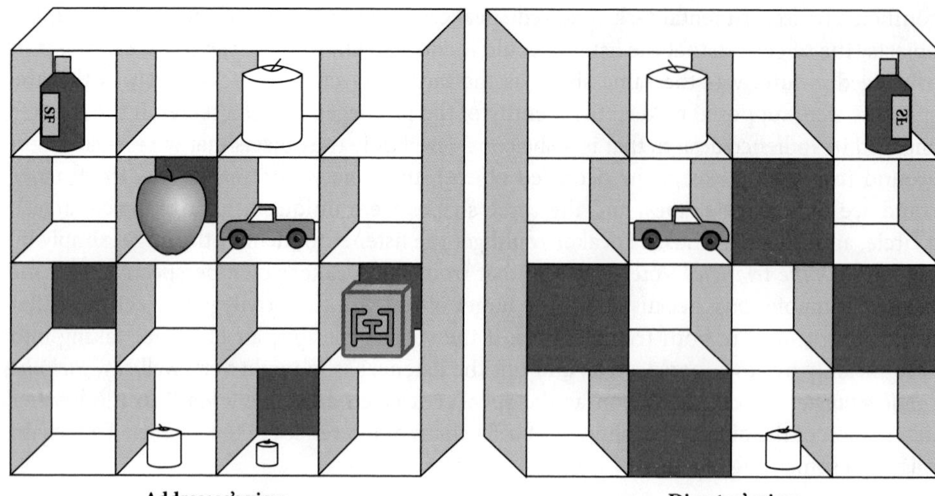

Figure 8.3 Examples of grids from Keysar, Barr, Balin, & Brauner (2000, p. 33). The listener's (addressee's) view is shown on the left. The director's view is on the right. Note that some of the objects were visible to both participants (e.g., the truck), but some were visible only to the listener (e.g., the apple, the block, and the smallest of the three candles).

meaning? Another way to frame that question is to look at it through the prism of common ground versus egocentric styles of processing. If listeners engage in egocentric processing when they interpret speakers' statements, then they may come up with meanings that the speaker did not intend. By contrast, if speakers make use of common ground when they plan their statements, and listeners also keep track of what concepts are included in common ground, then listeners should immediately interpret speakers' statements as the speakers intended.

Some experiments provide dramatic evidence in favor of the egocentric listener hypothesis (Keysar et al., 2000; Keysar, Barr, Balin, & Paek, 1998; Wu & Keysar, 2007). In these experiments, a speaker described objects to a listener and asked the listener to move the objects around a vertical grid (see Figure 8.3 for an example). The speaker sat on one side of the grid, while the listener sat on the other. To manipulate privileged and common ground, some of the objects were visible to both participants, but some were visible only to the listener. In Figure 8.3, the speaker could see a bottle, a truck, and two candles. Importantly, the listener could see *three* candles, the two that were visible to the speaker, plus another one. The very smallest candle, therefore, was in the listener's privileged ground, and was definitely *not* a part of the common ground. (In this case, common ground is defined as the set of objects that are visible to both the speaker and the listener.) The question that Boaz Keysar and his colleagues asked was: "If the speaker says *Pick up the small candle*, what will the listener do?" The listener's behavior depends on whether the listener consults common ground before she decides what the term *the small candle* refers to. If the listener consults common ground (if common ground restricts the domain of reference), she will find only two candles there (the one on the top row, and the bigger of the two candles on the bottom row). If those two candles make up the *contrast set* (the total set of objects that can be referred to with the term *candle*), then the term *the small candle* should be interpreted as meaning the left-most candle on the bottom row in Figure 8.3. But what if the listener ignores common ground? If the listener ignores common ground, then there are going to be three candles in the contrast set. That is, the set of potential referents for *candle* will include even the very tiny candle that the speaker cannot see. As a result, an egocentric listener—one who ignores common ground—will interpret *the small candle* as meaning the smallest one the listener can see (i.e., the rightmost candle in Figure 8.3).

In this experiment (Keysar et al., 2000), listeners wore a head-mounted eye-tracker so that the experimenters would know where listeners were looking as they listened to instructions such as *Pick up the small candle*, spoken by the confederate. Because there is a reasonably tight linkage between what people are thinking about and where they are looking (Tanenhaus, Spivey-Knowlton, Eberhard, & Sedivy, 1995), researchers can deduce which meaning listeners assigned to *the small candle* by checking where they look when they hear the word *candle*.[9] If listeners look at or pick up the very smallest candle in their display (the one that speakers cannot see), this would mean that they are ignoring common ground while they are figuring out what the expression *the small candle* refers to. In fact, listeners in this experiment and others like it, frequently looked at the very smallest candle, and sometimes they picked it up and moved it, before they looked at the correct candle: Listeners behaved egocentrically.

In an even more extreme version of the "candle" experiment, let's call it the "tape in a bag" experiment, listeners interacted with a confederate speaker (Keysar, Lin, & Barr, 2003). The task was very similar to the "candle" experiment in that listeners responded to instructions spoken by the confederate. A critical aspect of this study was that, on some trials, without the knowledge of the speaker, the listener hid an object inside a paper bag. For example, the listener hid a roll of Scotch Tape™ inside a paper lunch bag. Then, they placed the paper bag (with the tape hidden inside it), on a grid just like the grid in the "candle" experiment. The grid contained other objects, including a cassette tape. The vital question in this experiment was: How will listeners react when the speaker says, *Move the tape*. If listeners consider common ground when interpreting *tape*, then *tape* can only refer to the mutually visible cassette tape. But hiding the Scotch Tape in the bag makes that potential referent very highly salient to listeners. Egocentric pressures might therefore cause listeners to think of Scotch Tape when a speaker says *tape*, even though there is no way that the speaker can know what is inside the bag. In fact, listeners' overt behavior (the object that they reached for when they heard the word *tape*) as well as their eye movements (they tended to look at the paper bag when they heard *tape*) both indicated that listeners ignored common ground, and used their own egocentric perspective to interpret speakers' statements (see also Epley, Morewedge, & Keysar, 2004).

Results from experiments like these indicate that common ground failed to restrict the domain of reference—listeners thought that speakers were using the expression *the small candle* to tell them about a candle that only the listener could see (see also Epley, Keysar, van Boven, & Gilovich, 2004; Keysar et al., 1998). Listeners do tend to come up with the correct interpretation of *small candle* eventually, but they frequently think of the wrong candle before they identify the correct candle, so Keysar and colleagues argue in favor of a two-stage account of reference in dialogue. In the first stage, listeners take into account all of the information that is available to them, with more attention being devoted to salient concepts, and less attention being devoted to less salient concepts. At a later point in time, listeners can consult a representation of common ground to verify whether their egocentrically computed interpretation is likely to be correct. In cases like the candle experiment, consulting common ground will indicate to listeners that their initial interpretation is likely to be mistaken (because the speaker could not refer to an object that the speaker does not know about), and so the listener will come up with a revised interpretation that relies more on common ground than on egocentric sources of information. This aspect of Keysar and colleagues' account is known as the *perspective adjustment model*, which highlights the idea that listeners start out interpreting expressions based on their own egocentric perspective, and then make adjustments to that interpretation when they detect differences between their own perspective and the speaker's perspective.[10] The idea that adjustment away from your own perspective takes time receives support from experiments showing that listeners become more egocentric in their interpretations the less time they have to interpret referring expressions (i.e., when they have to come up with an interpretation before an artificial deadline; Epley, Keysar, et al., 2004).

The preceding experiments suggest that listeners often interpret speakers' statements from an egocentric point of view, and take into account common ground with the speaker only after a delay. However, additional studies indicate that egocentric interpretation is not an inevitable and unavoidable aspect of dialogue. Cultural characteristics appear to affect the extent to which listeners engage in egocentric interpretation (Wu & Keysar, 2007). In experiments that compare American college students to exchange students from more collectivist cultures,[11] students from collectivist cultures behaved as though they consulted common ground very early during the process of interpreting speakers' statements. When they participated in the "tape in a bag" experiment, students from collectivist cultures rarely looked at the paper bag, and they never attempted to pick up or move the bag when the speaker said *move the tape*. Some studies of American adults and children also indicate that listeners do sometimes consult common ground fairly quickly to determine what speakers are referring to (Brown-Schmidt, Gunlogson, & Tananhaus, 2008; Brown-Schmidt & Tanenhaus, 2008; Hanna et al., 2003; Hanna & Tanenhaus, 2004; Nadig & Sedivy, 2002). For example, in a task where a listener collaborated with a confederate speaker in a cooking task, listeners flexibly expanded or contracted the domain of reference depending on whether the speaker's hands were empty or full. When the speaker's hands were full, which meant that the speaker could not reach objects in front of her, listeners would consider objects in front of the speaker as potential referents for ambiguous expressions (e.g., *pick up the salt* when there were two salt shakers, one in front of the speaker and one in front of the listener). When the speaker's hands were empty, listeners would only consider objects that were in front of themselves. Mood also appears to affect the degree to which comprehenders engage in egocentric processing (Converse, Lin, Keysar, & Epley, 2008). People who are in a sad mental state appear to be less egocentric than people who are happy. Based on these kinds of results, some researchers believe that interpreting references in dialogue results from the weighting and evaluation of multiple sources of information simultaneously. According to *constraint-based accounts*, egocentrically available information is one source of information that can influence a listener, common ground is another source, but neither source automatically has a bigger influence on interpretation.

Summary and Conclusions

Dialogue is more than just chunks of monologue bolted together. Participants in dialogue simultaneously play the roles of speaker and listener—we monitor our own speech to make sure it comes out right and we plan what we are going to say next while we listen to other people speak. Although real dialogue often deviates from the ideals laid out by philosophers such as Paul Grice, and although real dialogue can be much harder to capture in the lab than monologue production or comprehension processes, dialogue follows lawful and consistent principles that we can discover via careful analysis. So, while speakers are not always optimally cooperative, perspicacious, and relevant, there are often good reasons why their behavior deviates from the ideal. Savvy listeners can capitalize on these deviations from the standard to read between the lines and accurately picture the speakers' true thoughts. More contemporary approaches to dialogue attempt to capture that interactive nature of the activity, and describe how interaction leads to expanded common ground and mutual knowledge. These interactive accounts capture features of dialogue that "serial monologue" accounts miss, such as why speakers are so heavily dependent on feedback, as well as helping explain how people manage turn-taking behavior. The common ground approach to dialogue naturally incorporates the concept of audience design to explain how and why speakers make particular choices as they craft their contributions and how and why listeners develop specific interpretations of those contributions. While a substantial body of evidence suggests that, at the micro-level, speakers are often driven more by internal needs and pressures than by optimal attention to their listeners' needs, speakers do appear to routinely adjust at more macro-levels (and some recent experiments suggests that speakers can fine-tune their utterances at least some of the time). Likewise, considerable research efforts have been dedicated to listeners' processing of speakers' utterances in dialogue. Much of this research supports the idea that listeners are egocentric, at least during the early stages of comprehension, but some studies have shown that listeners adjust relatively quickly to specific knowledge about speakers. Further research will be required to identify factors that determine how and when listeners are able to overcome their own egocentric perspective to more quickly and accurately interpret a speaker's intended meaning.

TEST YOURSELF

1. Describe Paul Grice's conversational maxims and explain how they influence the way dialogues unfold. Why might Grice's ideas fail to explain some aspects of real conversations?
2. How do partners in a dialogue establish, maintain, and expand common ground?
3. How egocentric are speakers and listeners during dialogue. Describe experimental results that support or challenge egocentricity.
4. Why do speakers go *ummmm* and *ah* during conversation?
5. Explain the concept of "audience design," give an example, and describe experimetnal results that suggest speakers engage in audience design during conversation. Describe experimental results that suggest that they don't.

THINK ABOUT IT

1. Can you hold a dialogue with a partner who is *not* following Grice's maxim of cooperation? Why or why not? What would such a dialogue look like?

Notes

1 Of course, the boss could simply come out and say, *Susan was a bad worker. Don't hire her*. Maybe the boss is trying to be polite ("If you can't say something good, don't say anything at all"). Maybe the boss is trying to avoid a lawsuit for defamation or slander.

2 Grice is a major violator of his own principles.

3 Research also calls into question the extent to which listeners expect speakers to be cooperative. Listeners appear to prefer consistent referring expressions, even in contexts where being consistent entails being less than optimally cooperative (Shintel & Keysar, 2007).

4 Grice never really considered how interaction and feedback might influence a speaker's behavior in dialogue. Grice argued that speakers craft utterances to produce a particular response in a target audience, but he does not talk about how speakers might react to specific feedback from that target audience. In his view, either the speaker would succeed in crafting an utterance or not. The listener played no active role in shaping a speaker's contribution.

5 Of course, different communicative situations involve different opportunities for interaction and grounding, and so speakers can adjust the extent to which they rely on feedback during utterance planning and execution. Written communication offers no opportunity for immediate feedback, a lecture offers some opportunity to sample the audience's response, while dialogue offers a multitude of immediate cues to communicative success. Speakers can continue to produce statements in the absence of feedback, but the likelihood of expanding common ground diminishes with diminishing feedback.

6 In Haywood et al.'s (2005) experiments, naive participants were more likely to produce a disambiguating *that* when a confederate had just produced one and when a visual display provided a context in which an utterance lacking the word *that* would be ambiguous. Because no time-course information is available from that study, it is not clear whether visual context led to relatively immediate effects on production, or whether speakers engaged in some amount of self-monitoring, which could lead to increased detection of potential problems in cases where the visual context created an ambiguity of reference.

7 That's why you get wall-to-wall TV coverage of things like Falcon the Balloon Boy.

8 This really happened.

9 They can also check to see which objects listeners actually reach for and/or move. The results are the same whichever measure you prefer: Listeners frequently move the very smallest candle, the one that speakers cannot see.

10 In many cases, the speaker's and listener's perspectives will be tightly aligned, and so no adjustment will be necessary. In cases where the speaker's and listener's perspectives are different, feedback and collaboration can repair the misalignment.

11 *Collectivist* cultures place relatively greater emphasis on social relationships and group membership. *Individualist* cultures place relatively greater emphasis on independence and a sense of the self separate from others.

References

Arnold, J. E., Hudson Kam, C. L., & Tanenhaus, M. K. (2007). If you say *Thee uh* you are describing something hard: The on-line attribution of disfluency during reference comprehension. *Journal of Experimental Psychology: Learning, Memory, and Cognition, 33,* 914–930.

Arnold, J. E., Tanenhaus, M. K., Altmann, R. J., & Fagnano, M. (2004). The old and thee, uh, new: Disfluency and reference resolution. *Psychological Science, 15,* 578–582.

Arnold, J. E., Wasow, T., Asudeh, A., & Alrenga, P. (2004). Avoiding attachment ambiguities: The role of constituent ordering. *Journal of Memory and Language, 51,* 55–70.

Bangerter, A., & Clark, H. H. (2003). Navigating joint projects with dialogue. *Cognitive Science, 27,* 195–225.

Bard, E. G., Anderson, A. H., Chen, Y., Nicholson, H. B. M., Havard, C., & Dalzel-Job, S. (2007). Let's you do that: Sharing the cognitive burdens of dialogue. *Journal of Memory and Language, 57,* 616–641.

Barr, D. J., & Keysar, B. (2002). Anchoring comprehension in linguistic precedents. *Journal of Memory and Language, 46,* 391–418.

Brennan, S. E., & Williams, M. (1995). The feeling of another's knowing: Prosody and filled pauses as cues to listeners about the metacognitive states of speakers. *Journal of Memory and Language, 34,* 383–398.

Brown, P. M., & Dell, G. S. (1987). Adapting production to comprehension: The explicit mention of instruments. *Cognitive Psychology, 19,* 441–472.

Brown-Schmidt, S., Gunlogson, C., & Tanenhaus, M. K. (2008). Addressees distinguish shared from private information when interpreting questions during interactive conversation. *Cognition, 107,* 1122–1134.

Brown-Schmidt, S., & Tanenhaus, M. K. (2008). Real-time investigation of referential domains in unscripted conversation: A targeted language game approach. *Cognitive Science, 32,* 643–684.

Carletta, J., Garrod, S., & Fraser-Krauss, H. (1998). Placement of authority and communication patterns in workplace groups. *Small Group Research, 29,* 531–559.

Cherry, E. C. (1956). *On human communication.* Cambridge, MA: MIT Press.

Christenfeld, N., & Creager, B. (1996). Anxiety, alcohol, aphasia, and *ums. Journal of Personality and Social Psychology, 70,* 451–460.

Clark, H. H. (1996). *Using language.* Cambridge, England: Cambridge University Press.

Clark, H. H., & Fox Tree, J. E. (2002). Using *uh* and *um* in spontaneous speaking. *Cognition, 84,* 73–111.

Clark, H. H., & Schaefer, E. F. (1987). Collaborating on contributions to conversations. *Language and Cognitive Processes, 2,* 19–41.

Clark, H. H., & Schaefer, E. F. (1989). Contributing to discourse. *Cognitive Science, 13,* 259–294.

Clark, H. H., & Wilkes-Gibbs, D. (1986). Referring as a collaborative process. *Cognition, 22,* 1–39.

Converse, B. A., Lin, S., Keysar, B., & Epley, N. (2008). In the mood to get over yourself: Mood affects theory of mind use. *Emotion, 8,* 725–730.

Epley, N., Keysar, B., van Boven, L., & Gilovich, T. (2004). Perspective taking as egocentric anchoring and adjustment. *Journal of Personality and Social Psychology, 87,* 327–339.

Epley, N., Morewedge, C. K., & Keysar, B. (2004). Perspective taking in children and adults: Equivalent egocentrism but differential correction. *Journal of Experimental Social Psychology, 40,* 760–768.

Fay, N., Garrod, S., & Carletta, J. (2000). Group discussion as interactive dialogue or as serial monologue. *Psychological Science, 11,* 481–486.

Ferreira, V. S., & Dell, G. S. (2000). Effect of ambiguity and lexical availability on syntactic and lexical production. *Cognitive Psychology, 40,* 296–340.

Ferreira, V. S., Slevc, L. R., & Rogers, E. S. (2005). How do speakers avoid ambiguous linguistic expressions? *Cognition, 96,* 263–284.

Fox Tree, J. E. (2001). Listeners' uses of *um* and *uh* in speech comprehension. *Memory & Cognition, 29,* 320–326.

Fox Tree, J. E., & Clark, H. H. (1997). Pronouncing "the" as "thee" to signal problems in speaking. *Cognition, 62,* 151–167.

Garrod, S., & Pickering, M. J. (2004). Why is conversation so easy? *Trends in Cognitive Sciences, 18,* 8–11.

Grice, P. (1989). *Studies in the way of words.* Cambridge, MA: Harvard University Press.

Hanna, J. E., & Tanenhaus, M. K. (2004). Pragmatic effects on reference resolution in a collaborative task: Evidence from eye movements. *Cognitive Science, 28,* 105–115.

Hanna, J. E., Tanenhaus, M. K., & Trueswell, J. C. (2003). The effects of common ground and perspective on domains of referential interpretation. *Journal of Memory and Language, 49,* 43–61.

Haywood, S. L., Pickering, M. J., & Branigan, H. P. (2005). Do speakers avoid ambiguities during dialogue? *Psychological Science, 16,* 362–366.

Horton, W. S., & Gerrig, R. J. (2005a). The impact of memory demands on audience design during language production. *Cognition, 96,* 127–142.

Horton, W. S., & Gerrig, R. J. (2005b). Conversational common ground and memory processes in language production. *Discourse Processes, 40,* 1–35.

Horton, W. S., & Spieler, D. H. (2007). Age-related differences in communication and audience design. *Psychology and Aging, 22,* 281–290.

Keysar, B., Barr, D. J., Balin, J. A., & Brauner, J. S. (2000). Taking perspective in conversation: The role of mutual knowledge in comprehension. *Psychological Science, 11,* 32–38.

Keysar, B., Barr, D. J., Balin, J. A., & Paek, T. S. (1998). Definite reference and mutual knowledge: Process models of common ground in comprehension. *Journal of Memory and Language, 39,* 1–20.

Keysar, B., & Henly, A. S. (2002). Speakers' overestimation of their effectiveness. *Psychological Science, 13,* 207–212.

Keysar, B., Lin, S., & Barr, D. J. (2003). Limits on theory of mind use in adults. *Cognition, 89,* 25–41.

Kirk, D. (2002, March 26). New standards mean Korean Air is coming off many "shun" lists. *New York Times.*

Kraljic, T., & Brennan, S. E. (2005). Prosodic disambiguation of syntactic structure: For the speaker or for the addressee? *Cognitive Psychology, 50,* 194–231.

Levelt, W. J. M. (1983). Monitoring and self-repair in speech. *Cognition, 14,* 41–104.

Lockridge, C. B., & Brennan, S. E. (2002). Addressees' needs influence speakers' early syntactic choices. *Psychonomic Bulletin & Review, 9,* 550–557.

Metzing, C., & Brennan, S. E. (2003). When conceptual pacts are broken: Partner-specific effects on the comprehension of referring expressions. *Journal of Memory and Language, 49,* 201–213.

Nadig, A. S., & Sedivy, J. C. (2002). Evidence of perspective-taking constraints in children's on-line reference resolution. *Psychological Science, 13,* 329–336.

Pickering, M. J., & Garrod, S. C. (2004). Toward a mechanistic psychology of dialogue. *Behavioral and Brain Sciences, 27,* 169–226.

Python, M. (1990). *Just the Words: Vol. 2.* London, England: Methuen, Mandarin.

Sacks, H., Schegloff, E. A., & Jefferson, G. (1974). A simplest systematics for the organization of turn-taking for conversation. *Language, 50,* 696–735.

Schober, M. F., & Clark, H. H. (1989). Understanding by addressees and overhearers. *Cognitive Psychology, 21,* 211–232.

Shintel, H., & Keysar, B. (2007). You said it before and you'll say it again: Expectations of consistency in communication. *Journal of Experimental Psychology: Learning, Memory, and Cognition, 33,* 357–369.

Stivers, T., Enfield, N. J., Brown, P., Englert, C., Hayashi, M., Heinemann, T., et al. (2009). Universals and cultural variation in turn-taking in conversation. *Proceedings of the National Academy of Sciences, 106,* 10587–10592.

Tanenhaus, M. K., Spivey-Knowlton, M. J., Eberhard, K., & Sedivy, J. C. (1995). Integration of visual and linguistic information in spoken language comprehension. *Science, 268,* 1632–1634.

Wardlow-Lane, L., & Ferreira, V. S. (2008). Speaker-external versus speaker-internal forces on utterance form: Do cognitive demands override threats to referential success? *Journal of Experimental Psychology: Learning, Memory, and Cognition, 34,* 1466–1481.

Wardlow-Lane, L., Groisman, M., & Ferreira, V.S. (2006). Don't talk about pink elephants! *Psychological Science, 17,* 273–277.

Whalen, J., Zimmerman, D. H., & Whalen, M. R. (1988). When words fail: A single case analysis. *Social Problems, 35,* 335–362.

Wilkes-Gibbs, D., & Clark, H. H. (1992). Coordinating beliefs in conversation. *Journal of Memory and Language, 31,* 183–194.

Wu, S., & Keysar, B. (2007). The effect of culture on perspective taking. *Psychological Science, 18,* 600–606.

Language Development in Infancy and Early Childhood

Babies are like people, only smaller.

PROBABLY STEVEN PINKER

The vast majority of children learn the language that their parents and peers speak without special instruction, threat, or reward. Children sometimes experience difficulty mastering the details of how words are pronounced, in which case they may need speech therapy to help them overcome these problems, but unless children have particular forms of genetic defect, such as those that result in *Down Syndrome* or *Specific Language Impairment*, they will achieve a high degree of skill understanding and producing language. The apparent ease with which children spontaneously acquire these abilities disguises the extraordinary challenges that they face in mastering language and the difficult problems they overcome in the process. This chapter details these challenges and problems and reviews studies that give us hints about the strategies children use to master language.

Prenatal Learning

Classical behaviorist approaches to learning (e.g., Skinner, 1957) viewed children as a *tabula rasa* ("blank slate"). The child's experience fills up the slate with knowledge about everything, including language. While children have general-purpose learning mechanisms, they are born knowing nothing

Introduction to Psycholinguistics: Understanding Language Science, First Edition.
Matthew J. Traxler.

about the world in which they will function. Behaviorists in the classical period subscribed to the hypothesis that *babies are dumb*.

More recent research in child development has shown that, rather than being blank slates, young infants have an innate appreciation of important aspects of the world, including important principles of visual perception such as occlusion, the physical properties of objects and substances, and numbers (Aguiar & Baillargeon, 1999; Hespos, Ferry, & Rips, 2009; Izard, Sann, Spelke, & Streri, 2009). In light of these newer findings, many cognitive and developmental psychologists subscribe to the *babies are smart* hypothesis, and many language scientists are now engaged in trying to find out just how smart babies are with respect to language skills.

Nativist approaches to language (e.g., Lenneberg, 1967) view language abilities as resulting from adaptation and natural selection. Researchers operating in this tradition have proposed that, when babies are born, they do not possess knowledge of a specific language—no one is born speaking French or Italian—but they do have innate learning mechanisms that allow the child to figure out how the adult language works. So, any child raised in France or Italy will wind up speaking French or Italian (e.g., Chomsky, 1981; Pinker, 1984, 1994b). "There is a special cognitive faculty for learning and using language" (Pinker, 1984, p. 33). These learning mechanisms cause the child to pay attention to specific aspects of her environment and to organize her perceptions in ways that lead to a uniform understanding of the adult language system. Thus, the nativist position falls within the smart-baby tradition, in that it views the infant as being born with certain kinds of knowledge already in place (more about this later).

Just because young infants appear to have knowledge about number, occlusion, and some principles of physics, that does not automatically mean that they have comparable knowledge about language. Whether children are born with knowledge of language, therefore, needs to be investigated. If we can determine what kinds of language-related knowledge infants and small children have at different points in time, that will help us decide whether that knowledge was gained as the result of experience (as the behaviorists claim) or whether that knowledge was gained by associating perceptual experiences with pre-existing knowledge structures (as the nativists claim).

One problem in discriminating between the behaviorist and nativist positions arises because learning can start before birth. Just because a baby is born with a particular kind of knowledge, that does not mean that the knowledge is *innate* (if by *innate knowledge*, we mean *instinctive*, *self-generated*, or *not caused by experience*). For example, newborn infants are able to tell the difference between recordings of someone speaking their native language, the language that their parents speak, and the same person speaking a different language. At two days old, children of French-speaking parents can detect when a bilingual female speaker is speaking French and when the same speaker is speaking Russian (Mehler, Jusczyk, Labertz, & Halsted, 1988). They prefer to listen to French, their native language, rather than Russian. Does that mean that knowledge of French is innate? Of course not. French people speak French because they are exposed to French-speaking models, not because they have "French language" genes. An alternative hypothesis says that French babies learn what French sounds like after one day of experience with French, most of which they spend asleep. But that, too, is highly unlikely. There is a third possibility, however, one that involves learning before birth—*prenatal* learning. How might this prenatal learning happen?

The fetus' auditory system is capable of perceiving environmental input in the third trimester of pregnancy, the last 90 days or so. Pregnancies normally last for about nine months. During that period of time, environmental sounds reach the fetus' ears and are processed by the developing auditory system. The fetus is encased in a sack of amniotic fluid and insulated from the outside world by the mother's body. Because the mother's voice is generated in and propagated through the mother's body, it is, on average, the loudest thing the fetus is exposed to. (When babies are born, they show a strong preference for their mother's voice compared to other female voices, but not their father's compared to other male voices. This is probably because, from the fetus' perspective, mom's voice is a lot louder than dad's before birth. DeCasper & Fifer, 1980.) The amniotic fluid and maternal tissue act as a filter that reduces the amplitude (loudness) of environmental sounds that originate outside of the mother. Low-frequency sounds (bass range) are less affected as they pass from the air, through the mother, to the fetus. The amplitude of high-frequency (treble range) sounds is greatly reduced. The speech sounds that make one phoneme different from another, and therefore make one word different from another, are mostly carried in the high-frequency portion of the *acoustic signal* (or sound wave; see Chapter 2). As a result, fetuses are not exposed to those parts of the speech signal that would enable them to start learning words. However, prosodic characteristics of speech (relative loudness or *accent*, fundamental frequency, tempo, pauses, and so forth) are largely carried by the lower frequency components of the acoustic signal, and so they *are* available to the fetus.

Thus, a third-trimester fetus has a functioning perceptual system that can take advantage of auditory stimuli that are present in the intra-uterine environment. Specifically, the fetus is exposed to auditory stimuli that provide the basic outline for the prosodic features of the fetus' native language. As we will see shortly, prosodic features can help the child identify important components of the speech signal, and a fetus that learns something about the prosody of her native language will gain substantial benefits when it comes time to learn her first language. But do fetuses respond to prosodic information? And do they retain any memory of their prenatal experience after being born? How could we find out?

Babies suck

Not figuratively! Babies are truly wonderful and will restore your faith in humanity if you spend any length of time with them. Babies suck quite literally. It is one of the few things they can do really well when they are born. Babies suck to eat, but they also engage in *nonnutritive sucking* in between feeding times. It turns out that you can train even newborn infants to suck hard by rewarding them for doing so. The *high-amplitude sucking* (HAS) research technique takes advantage of this fact. In high-amplitude sucking experiments, babies, even newborn infants as young as two days old, are connected to a device called a *pressure transducer* that measures how much pressure babies exert when they suck, and how often they suck. A pacifier (artificial nipple) with a very small hole in the end is inserted into the baby's mouth. During a baseline period, the machine measures how hard and how often the baby sucks when no stimulus is presented. The measurement of how hard the baby sucks is referred to as *amplitude* (higher amplitude means the baby exerts more pressure). Then, during a training period, the baby is rewarded with an *appetitive stimulus* (something the baby likes), such as the sound of her mother's voice, when she exerts more sucking pressure than the average amount, or sometimes when the baby sucks faster than normal.[1] When the baby's sucking amplitude drops back down to baseline, the baby is said to have *habituated* to the stimulus. The baby is acting as though she is bored with the stimulus. The more a baby likes the stimulus, the longer she will produce high-amplitude sucks to keep the stimulus going. If two different stimuli are played, you can figure out which one the baby prefers by seeing how long she is willing to keep her sucking amplitude high. You can also use this technique to find out whether an infant can tell the difference between two stimuli. If you play a stimulus to a baby long enough, the baby will habituate and her sucking amplitude will drop to baseline. If you change the stimulus at that point, and baby notices the change, she will *dis-habituate*. That is, her sucking amplitude will increase until she gets tired of the new stimulus. If she does not notice the difference between the old and the new stimulus, and she treats them as being identical, her sucking amplitude will stay low when you change from the original stimulus to a new one.

HAS experiments have been used to investigate the way prenatal exposure to speech affects fetuses and newborn infants (DeCasper, Lecanuet, Busnel, Granier-Deferre, & Maugeais, 1994; DeCasper & Spence, 1986; Krueger, Holditch-Davis, Quint, & DeCasper, 2004). In one set of studies, pregnant mothers recited a short story (such as *The Cat in the Hat*) two times a day every day during the last six weeks of their pregnancies. During this training period, fetuses had the opportunity to become familiar with one particular story. After the babies were born, they were tested using a version of the HAS technique. This testing period was completed before the babies were 2 ½ days old (the youngest infants were 44 *hours* old). All of the test babies listened to the familiar story (e.g., *Cat in the Hat*) as well as a new story read by the same person. Some of the babies were tested with recordings of their own mothers reading a familiar story, but half of the babies listened to a recording of an unfamiliar female reading the familiar story. If babies learned anything about the familiar story and retained that information over time, then they should behave differently when they heard the familiar story compared to when they heard the new, unfamiliar story.

No matter who read the story, the baby's own mother or somebody else, newborn infants worked harder to hear the familiar story than they did when the unfamiliar story served as the reinforcer. These results show that fetuses did learn something about language from their environment prior to being born. Because high-frequency information was filtered out of the acoustic stimulus during the training phase (before the babies were born), the babies' preference could not be based on the specific words in the familiar story. Similarly, because babies preferred the familiar story no matter who read the story, their behavior during testing could not reflect a preference for one specific voice (i.e., the mother's). So, what caused the newborn infants to prefer the familiar story over the unfamiliar one? The most likely cause is the prosodic cues available in the speech signal. Although prenatal fetuses could not hear the specific words in the story, prosodic information, including alternating patterns of loud and soft sounds, patterns of high and low tones, pauses, and so forth, would have been available. Those patterns are consistent enough across speakers that babies could detect the familiar prosodic pattern, even when the story was read by someone other than their own mother. These results show, then, that fetuses do respond to prosodic cues, and that they retain information about prosodic patterns. Therefore, prenatal learning of prosodic features could lay the foundation for further language learning after the infant is born.

Could it be possible that babies actually experience very rapid learning after birth? Could the preceding experimental results reflect a form of super-fast acquisition? It's unlikely, given that baby's exposure to the familiar story occurred only before birth, but additional experiments really lay this issue to rest (DeCasper et al., 1994; Krueger et al., 2004). These studies also used a study-test design, similar to the original DeCasper and Spence experiment. But instead of waiting for babies to be born, the researchers tested them while they were still inside their mothers. This prenatal testing took advantage of another fact about fetus physiology: In the last trimester, the fetus' heart rate changes when they process acoustic information. Specifically, the onset of an acoustic stimulus causes the heart rate to slow down (*cardiac deceleration*). Fetuses also respond to a change in the acoustic stimulus with cardiac deceleration (Lecanuet, Granier-Deferre, & Busnel, 1988). If fetuses fail to notice when one acoustic stimulus is replaced by another, then there should be no change in heart rate. Thus, heart rate can be used to test whether fetuses can spot the difference between two stimuli.

Taking advantage of infants' heart rate response to different stimuli, researchers assessed how third-trimester fetuses responded to recorded speech. In one such study, mothers recited brief nursery rhymes three times a day while their fetuses were in a quiet (*quiescent*) state. This training period lasted for about a month. Then, while the fetuses' heart rate was measured, they listened to a recording of a different female reading either the same nursery rhyme or a new, unfamiliar nursery rhyme. Fetuses showed greater cardiac deceleration for the familiar rhyme as compared to the new rhyme, and these effects were larger for older fetuses than for younger ones (most likely reflecting maturation of the nervous system). These results definitely rule out the "super-fast post-birth" learning hypothesis. Thus, fetuses learn and retain information about speech before they are born. Most likely, they learn about and remember the prosodic qualities of speech.

The reality of prenatal learning complicates the debate between the nativists and the behaviorists. Nativists have relied on abilities that appear in very young infants to argue for the existence of instincts or innate (presumably genetically driven) abilities. If an ability appears in a newborn infant, before that infant has had much exposure to the environment, then it is unlikely that the infant's behavior reflects learning based on exposure to the environment. If babies were born knowing how to ride a bicycle, we would have to consider the possibility that their genetic endowment wired their brains in just the right way to produce that ability. Similarly, if babies were born knowing something about how language works, we would have to consider the possibility that those abilities result from genetically driven neural organization. However, because we know that fetuses learn, we have to rule out prenatal learning before we conclude that abilities present in newborns reflect a genetically driven brain mechanism. In the case of voice preference (newborns prefer their own mother's voice over others), language preference (newborns prefer their native language over others), and story preference (newborns prefer familiar speech patterns over unfamiliar ones), prenatal learning because of exposure to specific stimuli suffices to explain the results, and appeals to innate, genetically driven, language-specific mechanisms are unnecessary. However, ruling out innate sources of these preferences does not rule out all innate knowledge. It just means that learning from the environment has to be considered an alternative hypothesis any time anyone appeals to innate knowledge to explain some aspect of an infant's behavior.

Infant Perception and Categorization of Phonemes

Infants learn about their first language by listening to people talk. To learn their first language, infants need to solve a number of different puzzles. They have to figure out which speech sounds (phonemes) occur in the language, and which do not. They have to figure out how those phonemes go together to make words. They have to figure out the relationship between words and meanings. They have to figure out how words go together to make sentences. They have to do all of this without any direct instruction. In the remainder of the chapter, we'll consider how infant speech perception relates to adults', how infants figure out the sound system of their native language, how they identify words in the speech signal, how they assign meanings to words, and how they figure out the grammar and syntax of their native language. Let's start with infant speech perception.

Phonemes constitute the building blocks of words in the baby's new language. Thus, one basic task that the infant must solve is to figure out how the inventory of speech sounds is organized—which differences between different sounds matter, and which can be safely ignored. This task is more complicated than it might seem at first. One complicating factor is that, although different speech sounds may have physical similarities, no two speech sounds are identical. For example, every speaker's voice is unique because of physical differences between different vocal tracts. Some speakers have higher pitched voices than others, so their speech sounds will contain relatively more high-frequency energy. Some people speak faster than others, so their speech sounds unfold differently in time. Despite these differences between different speech sounds, adults "shoehorn" widely diverse acoustic signals into a fixed number of categories (about 40 in English). Adults are so good at this, that we do not normally notice differences between sounds that belong to the same category, even though detailed physical analysis shows that those sounds have different physical properties.

It turns out that, in some ways, very young infants respond to speech sounds very much like adults do. For instance, studies of infants show that they experience categorical perception, just like adults. Using a variant of the HAS technique, Eimas and colleagues (Eimas, Siqueland, Jusczyk, & Vigorito, 1971) presented 1- and 4-month-old infants a syllable (i.e., /ba/) that has a short *voice onset time* (or VOT, the amount of time that elapses between the very beginning of the speech sound and the time when the vocal folds start to vibrate). After infants habituated to that syllable (as evidenced by a reduction in how fast they sucked on their pacifiers), the original stimulus /ba/ was replaced by one of two other stimuli. Sometimes, the syllable was replaced by another stimulus with another short VOT. Adults would perceive both of these stimuli as being /ba/, despite the fact that the two stimuli had slightly different VOTs. Sometimes, the original stimulus would be replaced by another stimulus that had a long VOT. Adults would perceive the second stimulus as being /pa/, rather than /ba/. The question was, would infants notice the change in stimuli when the two came from the same category (as defined by adults' perception of the two)? And would they notice the change when the two stimuli came from different categories (again as defined by adults' perception)? When the original and replacement stimuli both had relatively short VOTs, infants treated the two as being identical. That is, after they habituated to the original stimulus, their rate of high-amplitude sucking stayed the same when the short VOT stimulus was replaced by another short VOT stimulus. But when a long VOT stimulus replaced a short VOT stimulus, babies noticed the change, as evidenced by an increase in high-amplitude sucking just after the new stimulus replaced the old one. The results of this study suggested that infants, like adults, treat speech sounds as belonging to discrete categories. When two speech sounds had similar voice onset properties, infants treat them as being identical, even though the two sounds had different physical properties (different VOTs). When two speech sounds come from categories that adults perceive as separate (such as /ba/ versus /pa), infants also perceive these sounds as being separate.

Findings like these have been used by nativists to support the claim that *speech is special*. That is, they claim that humans perceive speech sounds using specialized mechanisms, possibly genetically determined (rather than learned), and that people treat speech differently than other kinds of sounds (e.g., Eimas et al., 1971; Liberman, Cooper, Shankweiler, & Studdert-Kennedy, 1967; Pardo & Remez, 2006). This claim has been challenged by researchers who note that other species besides humans treat speech sounds as categorical (Kluender & Kiefte, 2006)[2] and that people perceive non-speech sounds categorically as well. Because chinchillas and Japanese quail can be trained to categorize speech sounds similar to the way people do, it is hard to defend the idea that people perceive speech sounds categorically because they are uniquely adapted to have special speech-processing mechanisms. If categorical perception results from a special-purpose speech-processing system, we have to assume that chinchillas and quail have the same special system, which doesn't make sense because chinchillas and quail gain no benefit from categorizing speech sounds.

Categorical perception of non-speech sounds has been demonstrated in experiments using synthesized sounds (Cutting & Rosner, 1974; Jusczyk, Pisoni, Walley, & Murray, 1980; Jusczyk, Rosner, Cutting, Foard, & Smith, 1977). These synthesized sounds mimic some of the characteristics of musical instruments. For example, plucking a string on a violin creates the equivalent of longer VOT because there is a lag between the onset of the sound and the point in time where the violin string starts to vibrate in a steady state. When synthetic sounds that mimic the properties of naturally occurring non-speech sounds are played to adults and 2-month-old infants, both adults and infants perceive physically different stimuli as belonging to the same category. Stimuli with short lags between sound onset and steady-state vibration are perceived as sounding like someone dragging a bow across a string. Stimuli with longer lags between sound onset and steady-state vibration are perceived as sounding like someone plucking a string. As the lag between onset and vibration changes from short to long, there is an abrupt transition in the way the sound is perceived. At one lag, the sound is perceived as a "bowed" sound. At a very slightly longer lag, perception changes to "plucked." Because infants treat both speech and non-speech sounds as belonging to discrete categories, and because small changes in the physical characteristics of both speech and non-speech sounds can lead to large and abrupt changes in the way infants perceive those sounds, we can either conclude that children are born with two very similar "special" mechanisms, one that applies to speech sounds and one that applies to non-speech sounds, or we can conclude that categorical perception of speech results from a more general, "non-special" sound-processing system. The principle of parsimony (assume the simplest possible story) favors the latter explanation. So, while categorical perception may be the product of a biologically determined perceptual mechanism, the mechanism that produces categorical perception does not seem to have been selected for in humans specifically because it gives children an advantage in processing speech sounds.

Categorical perception of speech cannot be used as evidence for a genetically determined speech-processing mechanism (because other sounds produce categorical perceptions and because other animals besides humans perceive speech categorically). However, other evidence points toward a genetic basis for some aspects of speech processing. In particular, infants appear to have an innate (unlearned) preference to listen to speech (or attend to language-related gestures; Jusczyk, 1997; Jusczyk & Bertoncini, 1988; Krentz & Corina, 2008; and particular kinds of speech are more attractive than others; Cooper & Aslin, 1990).

Because some aspects of speech processing (e.g., categorical perception) appear to reflect general-purpose perceptual mechanisms, while other aspects appear to be innate (e.g., preference to listen to speech), Jusczyk and Bertoncini argue in favor of an *innately guided* learning process to explain how children acquire their first language. The innate part of the innately guided process is twofold. First, the infant has an instinct (innate drive) to pay attention to specific aspects of the environment, speech sounds in particular, and to undertake especially detailed processing of speech sounds. The initial state of the innate learning system must be general enough that the system can learn any possible human language. If the initial state were too narrowly focused, then the child might be born into a community with a language that fell outside the preset state of the learning mechanism. To ensure that the mechanism is capable of learning any human language, "The infant is innately prewired with broad categories that may develop in one of several different directions" (Jusczyk & Bertoncini, 1988, p. 233). The learning part happens when the infant is exposed to a specific language, and this exposure causes the child to move from the initial state, with little knowledge specific to the language, to the adult state, with fully developed phonological, lexical, morphological, and syntactic knowledge. To determine whether this account is plausible, we could look for evidence that young infants have broad speech categories and that those categories become refined as the child is exposed to one specific language.

Evidence for broad pre-existing categories can be found in studies of phonological processing in newborn and very young infants. For infants to be able to learn any human language, they must be capable of identifying important distinctions between different speech sounds (phonemes). A child could be genetically prewired to recognize specific *phonological contrasts* (differences between speech sounds, such as the characteristics that make the /p/ sound different than the /b/ sound). But this prewiring would be unnecessary if the adult language did not make use of that distinction. English, for example, does not make use of *aspiration* (whether a burst of air comes out while a phoneme is being produced),[3] but Hindi does. So, while aspiration or the lack thereof does not create a meaningful difference in English phonology, it does in Hindi. Similarly, adult Japanese speakers do not hear the difference between the *liquid* phonemes /r/ and /l/, because that distinction is not meaningful in Japanese. English adults do hear the difference, because that phonological contrast is meaningful (*rag* is different than *lag*). It is less harmful to be born being able to perceive a non-helpful contrast (such as the aspiration contrast in English). Being born with such a non-functional contrast may cause you to believe that there are two speech sounds in your native language when there is only one, but that will not prevent you from learning differences between different words. However, if you are born with phonological categories that blur or eliminate the difference between two different phonemes, then you will not be able to learn some words (you would treat *rag* and *lag* as being the same word).

Evidence from infant speech perception studies suggests that infants are born with the ability to recognize most phonological contrasts (Streeter, 1976; Werker, Gilbert, Humphrey, & Tees, 1981; Werker & Tees, 1983, 2002; see also Dehaene-Lambertz & Dehaene, 1994). Very young infants have the ability to detect the difference between phonemes even when they have had no opportunity whatsoever to hear the difference. In the Kikuyu language, there is only a single labial stop consonant (roughly equivalent to the English consonant /b/). *No* corresponding Kikuyu consonant differs from /b/ only in VOT. So, Kikuyu speakers do not have a labial stop consonant comparable to English /p/. Because there is no distinction between /b/ and /p/ in Kikuyu, children reared in a Kikuyu-speaking environment do not have the opportunity to learn that distinction via exposure to naturally occurring language. However, when 2-month old infants were tested on stimuli that were the English equivalents of /b/ and /p/, they could detect the difference. Kikuyu infants in a HAS experiment listened longest to the phoneme /b/, which did sound like a phoneme that they would have heard before (this reflects a kind of familiarity preference that is often observed in infant language studies). The infants dishabituated to two different phonemes with longer VOTs than the preferred stimulus. They listened longer to the two long-VOT stimuli than they did when the same stimulus was presented before and after the change point. Similar results have been obtained for 7-month-old infants of English-speaking parents tested on Hindi aspirated/non-aspirated phoneme contrasts, and for 6-month-old infants of English-speaking parents tested on contrasts that are present in Thompson (a language used by First Nations British Columbia residents). In all of these cases, infants perceive contrasts between phonemes that do not exist in their native language, that they have not had the opportunity to learn via exposure, and that adult speakers of those languages are incapable of perceiving. Results like these are consistent with the idea that children are born with a categorical organization of phonology that enables them to detect contrasts that may or may not be important in their native language. Because infants are sensitive to a huge variety of phonological contrasts, infants never face the problem of having too few phonological categories, and any contrast that is important in the adult version of the language can be preserved. The main problem infants need to solve, then, is to figure out which of the multitude of possible contrasts actually do matter, and to organize their phonological categories so that different versions of the same phoneme are mapped together into the same category (while still maintaining distinctions between speech sounds that really do represent different phonemes).

Experimental data show that the way infants organize phonological categories, and therefore the way they respond to speech stimuli, changes dramatically in the first year of life. Infants' ability to perceive non-native phonological contrasts is greatly reduced by their first birthday, and the way they respond to native language phonological contrasts also changes (Kuhl et al., 2006; Jusczyk, 1997; Werker & Tees, 1983; 2002). Thus, exposure to language in the environment appears to reinforce some phonological contrasts while eliminating others. How is that accomplished? Some theorists suggest that phonological *prototypes* emerge from the infants' experience (Kuhl, Williams, Lacerda, Stevens, & Lindblom, 1992). These prototypes represent a kind of perceptual average of specific instances of a given phoneme.[4] The idea is that the infant is exposed to many repeated instances of a given phoneme, because different speakers are all providing input to the infant, and because the same speaker will pronounce a given phoneme differently on different occasions. By mapping phonemes together on the basis of physical or perceptual similarity, and by treating the "average" as a perceptual "magnet," the infant learns to de-emphasize minor variations in pronunciation and to super-emphasize larger variations. This leads to sharper distinctions between phoneme categories that are used *contrastively* (changing the sound changes the meaning of the word it appears in). Additionally, phoneme contrasts that are not meaningful will eventually drop out of the system of phonological representations, because different versions (such as aspirated versus non-aspirated /p/) will all be attracted to the same perceptual "magnet." To test this possibility, researchers have looked at phoneme prototypes in different languages. For instance, Swedish and English both have phonemes that sound like "ee," but there are minor variations in pronunciation across the two languages so that the English "ee" has a different prototype than the Swedish "ee." When 6-month-old Swedish and English infants were exposed to minor variations from each prototype, they responded to those minor variations in different ways. Swedish infants treated minor variations of the Swedish prototype as being the same phoneme, but they treated equally minor variations of the English prototype as being completely different phonemes. English infants did the same thing, just in reverse. They treated minor variations from the English prototype as being the same as the prototype; equally minor variations from the Swedish prototype led to big changes in the infants' response.

Solving the Segmentation Problem

To learn their first language, infants need to figure out where the words are. They need to accomplish that task even though fluent speech does not often provide them with unambiguous indications of where words begin and end (Cutler, 1996; Jusczyk, 1997). Babies rarely hear a single word spoken in isolation. Only about 10% of the words young infants hear are spoken without any other words in the same utterance (with different mothers producing as few as 5% or as much as 17% of their total infant-directed output as isolated words; Brent & Siskind, 2001; Fernald & Morikawa, 1993). In experimental situations where mothers are asked explicitly to teach new words to their children, the frequency of isolated words in the mother's speech is still a relatively low 28% (Woodward & Aslin, 1990, in Jusczyk & Aslin, 1995). Nonetheless, some researchers (e.g., Bortfeld, Morgan, Golinkoff, & Rathbun, 2005; Brent & Siskind, 2001) hypothesize that infants learn some words by hearing them spoken in isolation. Many of the child's first 50 spoken words are those that have been heard in isolation, and the more often a word occurs in isolation, the more likely it is that this word will occur among those first 50 words. Further, based on extended naturalistic observation, care-takers appear to produce between about 6 and 60 isolated words per hour of interaction with small infants. Thus, it is at least plausible to

Figure 9.1 Sonogram of the question *Where are the silences between words?* (from Saffran, 2003, p. 111). Note that there are no silent gaps between words in the signal

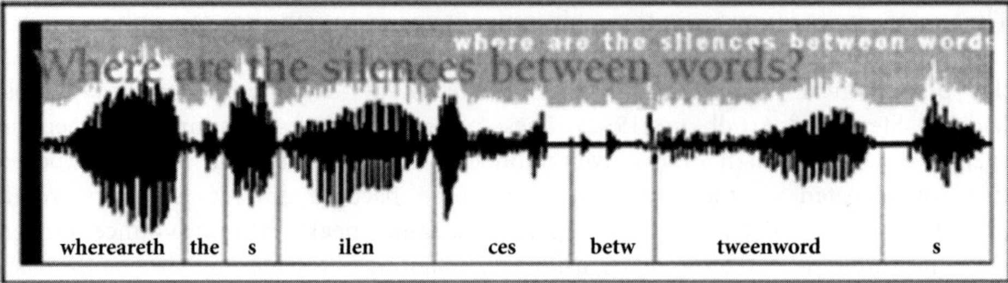

think that at least some words enter the child's vocabulary because the child has heard that word spoken all by itself on a number of different occasions. However, infants appear to learn some words that they have never heard spoken in isolation, and some studies suggest that embedding a word in a fluent string of connected speech can actually help infants to learn that word, rather than hinder them (Fernald & Hurtado, 2006; Saffran, 2001). Because infants learn some words that they hear only as part of longer utterances, either they have an innate ability to identify individual words heard amongst other words in fluent speech, or they must develop this ability via experience.

If you have ever listened to an unfamiliar foreign language, you will have an idea of how difficult it is to identify individual words in fluent streams of speech. Figure 9.1 shows that the places where people perceive boundaries between words do not correspond to silent parts of the speech signal. Speech does not have the equivalent of the white space in between words that helps us identify individual words when we read, so babies cannot rely on silence marking the beginnings and ends of words. Natural speech, therefore, presents infants (and anyone else unfamiliar with the language) with the *segmentation problem*: The message consists of collections of words, but the speech signal does not provide obvious cues as to where one word ends and the next one starts. Before an infant can start to learn words, that is to identify collections of sounds that make up a word and then associate meanings with those collections of sounds, the infant must *segment* the stream of speech, mentally chopping it up into word-sized chunks.

Experimental evidence suggests that the ability to segment speech into word-sized chunks does not appear until the infant is 6–7½ months old (Bortfeld et al., 2005; Jusczyk & Aslin, 1995; Jusczyk & Hohne, 1997). Evidence for young infants' segmentation ability comes from the *conditioned head turn* procedure. In this procedure, babies are seated on a caregiver's lap in front of an apparatus that has a central light and two additional lights, one on the baby's left and one of the baby's right. The central light is flashed to gain the baby's attention, and then one of the side lights is flashed. When the baby looks at the side light, sound is played through a speaker located adjacent to the side light. When the baby looks away from the side light for more than a couple of seconds, the sound is turned off and the trial is terminated. Experimenters can use this procedure to determine whether babies learn anything from prior exposure to a stimulus. During a training period, infants are exposed to some stimulus, such as an isolated word. Then, during the test period infants hear the familiar word or a novel, unfamiliar control word. If the baby can remember the familiar word, and if they can tell the difference between the familiar and the novel, unfamiliar word, then they should spend more time looking and listening when the familiar word is played than when the unfamiliar word is played. Young infants often display a preference for the familiar stimulus, looking and listening longer in that condition, but sometimes they show an opposite preference for novel stimuli. At 6 months of age, infants who are familiarized with a word by being exposed to that word spoken in isolation (by itself) do *not* listen longer to short sentences containing the familiar word. However, by 7½ months, infants who undergo the same training procedure *do* listen longer to short sentences that contain familiar words than sentences that contain unfamiliar words.[5] Result such as these show that 7½-month-old infants do remember something about the familiar word and that they are able to recognize that familiar word when it is part of a continuous stream of fluent speech. Thus, 7-½-month-olds have begun to solve the segmentation problem.

The fact that older infants but not younger infants show evidence of segmentation ability suggests that this ability is not innate, and is instead built from the infants' experience listening to the native language. If segmentation ability is not innate, there must be some pre-existing abilities (*precursors*) that the infant capitalizes on to develop segmentation ability. Researchers have identified two major classes of precursors that may provide the tools that infants need to solve the segmentation problem: Prosodic cues and *phonotactic knowledge* (phonotactic knowledge refers to the patterns of phonemes that occur in the language, see below; Cutler & Norris, 1988; Gerken & Aslin, 2005; Jusczyk, 1997; Morgan & Demuth, 1996).

Prosody can support segmentation of the speech signal because prosodic features correlate with word boundaries. Although this correspondence is not perfect, it may be consistent enough for infants to start identifying candidate words from the speech signal. The *prosodic bootstrapping* hypothesis proposes that infants pay attention to prosodic features of their native language, and that they use those features to identify candidate words.[6] Prosody is plausible as the entry point to segmentation because newborn infants can detect the difference between native and non-native utterances on the basis of prosodic differences, and because infants as young as 2 months old can detect differences between prosodic patterns, even when the phonological content of two utterances is identical, or nearly so (Hohne & Jusczyk, 1994). In the study, 2-month-old infants listened to someone saying *nitrates* or *night rates* (if you say those two things, and listen carefully, you may be able to hear slight differences in the way you pronounce them), which have the same phonological content, but different prosodic qualities. When infants habituated to (or got bored with) one of the utterances, they dishabituated when the other one was played.

Although young infants are sensitive to differences in prosody between different utterances, it takes them some time to learn about some of the basic prosodic patterns that occur frequently in their native language. For example, about 90% of the *bisyllabic* (two-syllable) words in English have a *trochaic stress pattern* (Jusczyk, Houston, & Newsome, 1999). In trochaic stress, the first syllable is spoken a little bit louder than the second syllable. The English words *cookie*, *baby*, and *bottle* all have trochaic stress (try pronouncing them with the second syllable louder than the first—that will sound strange). Some English words have *iambic stress*, where the second syllable is louder than the first. *Guitar*, *debate*, and *pursuit*, all have iambic stress. If babies pay attention to stress, and if they assume that a stressed syllable is an important unit in the language, they will be able to identify the beginnings of many words in the language by assuming that a stressed syllable is the beginning (or *onset*) of a word.[7] Researchers have labeled this version of prosodic bootstrapping the *metrical segmentation strategy*.

Young infants may not be sensitive at all to differences in stress patterns between different utterances (Weber, Hahne, Friedrich, & Friederici, 2004). When 4-month-old infants were presented with a speech stimulus consisting of a series of iambic words, with an occasional trochaic word inserted into the list, their brain wave activity was the same for words with different stress patterns. But older infants (5 months old) appeared to detect the different stress patterns. Their brain waves changed when they heard a trochaic (strong–weak stress) word that was preceded and followed by several iambic words.[8] Thus, sensitivity to stress patterns emerges over time in young infants, and is not part of the infants' innate package of language-learning tools. This makes sense if you believe that innate language skills must be broad enough to enable the infant to learn any language that she is exposed to. Different languages have different stress patterns. The iambic stress pattern is more common in French, for example, than the trochaic stress pattern. Thus, little French babies would need to deploy the opposite strategy and assume that *un*stressed syllables are word onsets in order to successfully apply the prosodic stress hypothesis. Infants may be born with a predisposition to listen to speech and pay attention to prosodic features in speech, but it would be counterproductive for them to be born with a specific version of the metrical segmentation strategy prewired. French babies would be disadvantaged if they were innately wired to assume that stressed syllables appear at the beginnings of words. English babies would be disadvantaged if they were innately wired to assume that words begin with unstressed syllables. The most likely theory, then, is that infants take some time to determine the dominant stress pattern in their native language before they start relying on stress patterns to form hypotheses about where words begin.

By 7½ months of age, infants who hear short sentences containing words with trochaic stress recognize those trochaic words when they are later tested using the conditioned head turn procedure (Jusczyk et al., 1999). Thus, 7½-month-old infants appear to use the dominant stress pattern in English (strong–weak) to hypothesize about where words begin. Infants appear to apply the metrical segmentation strategy even to samples of languages that they have not been exposed to before. For example, Houston and colleagues (Houston, Jusczyk, Kiujpers, Coolen, & Cutler, 2000) showed that 9-month-old infants from English-speaking families used the metrical segmentation strategy to identify candidate words in Dutch sentences. This is possible because Dutch has the same predominant trochaic stress pattern that English has. Having picked up the prevailing stress pattern in their native language, 9-month-olds behave as though they believe that stress pattern will apply to all kinds of speech, even if they are unfamiliar with the details of the new language.

Of course, the metrical segmentation strategy will not always succeed because many words that infants hear will have the opposite stress pattern. If a two-syllable word starts with a weak syllable instead of a strong one, then infants who apply the "strong syllable equals word onset" strategy will mis-segment speech that contains iambic words. So, for example, if an infant hears *My guiTAR is out of tune* (where TAR indicates a stressed syllable), she may extract the sequence *taris* and try to treat that like a word. In fact, experiments on 7½-month-old infants suggest that they make exactly this kind of mistake when they listen to short sentences containing iambic (weak–strong) words. They treat *TARis* as though it were a word. However, when 10½-month-old infants were tested, they were able to recognize iambic words, such as *guitar* after listening to short sentences containing iambic words. These results suggest that younger infants rely more heavily on the metrical segmentation strategy than older infants do, and that older infants rely on cues other than stress patterns to segment iambic words (otherwise, they would continue to treat *taris* as a word). What information might cause infants to shift away from exclusively relying on the metrical segmentation (strong = initial) strategy?

Two sources of information should be available to 10-month-old infants. First, they will have begun to build up a vocabulary based on the metrical segmentation strategy. They can use familiar trochaic words as "landmarks" to identify segments of speech for further analysis. So, if an iambic word is sandwiched between words that have stressed syllables (e.g., *JENny's guiTAR is LOVEly*), the metrical segmentation strategy is not going to come up with a neat way to carve up the utterance, and infants may start looking for an alternative. In fact, infants as young as 6 months old can identify new words (words they have not heard before) when those words appear immediately after a word that the child already knows. If the child knows the word *mommy* (as many 6-month-olds do), and if they hear the utterance *mommy's cup* (where *cup* is a word that the child does not yet know), they will recognize the word *cup* as being familiar in a subsequent testing phase (Bortfeld et al., 2005; see also Tincoff & Jusczyk, 1999).

In their search for a way to supplement the metrical segmentation strategy, older infants may begin to incorporate *phonotactic information* in their search for word boundaries. Phonotactic information refers to the patterns or combinations of phonemes that occur in different parts of words in a given language. For example, the phonotactic properties of English prevent a word from starting with the consonant cluster /gd/. But that kind of cluster is fine in Polish (e.g., *Gdansk*). Likewise, English words cannot end with /spl/, but they can begin that way (as in *splatter*, *splendid*, and *split*). Infants who notice where different combinations of phonemes occur in utterances can develop phonotactic knowledge that can help them segment speech. For example, a child who knows that words can start with /spl/ but cannot end with /spl/ will have an advantage when segmenting the utterance *This place is dirty*. Instead of treating it as *Thispl ace is dirty* (because no words end in /spl/), they are more likely to hypothesize a boundary between the /s/ and the /pl/.[9] Likewise, a child would not segment *bigdog*, as *bi gdog*, or as *bigd og*, because the sequence /gd/ does not occur at either the beginning or the end of any English words. Sensitivity to the phonotactic properties of the native language appears to emerge between 7½ and 9 months of age. For example, younger infants do not have a preference for listening to native language speech, but by 9 months of age, children do prefer to hear their native language instead of a prosodically similar foreign language. English and Dutch have similar prosodic systems, and Dutch babies do not care whether they are hearing Dutch or English until they get to be about 9 months old, at which point they prefer Dutch (Jusczyk, Friederici, Wessels, Svenkerud, & Jusczyk, 1993). Prosodic features of Dutch cannot account for this preference (because they are very similar to English), so the preference that emerges at 9 months most likely reflects details of the phonological/phonotactic system of Dutch. Further evidence that 9-month-old infants know about their native-language phonotactic system comes from experiments showing that children prefer to listen to pseudo-words (fake words) whose phoneme sequences occur often in their native language rather than pseudo-words whose phoneme sequences occur rarely in their native language (Jusczyk, Luce, & Charles-Luce, 1994). Younger infants did not show a preference either way, suggesting that knowledge of the native-language phonotactic system is not fully developed until somewhat later.

Phonotactic knowledge can support infants' ability to segment speech and identify individual words. But if infants do not know where the words begin and end, how do they ever learn that particular sequences of sounds are more common at the beginning of the word than the end, or that particular sequences of sounds are not possible at the beginning of a word? Where does phonotactic knowledge come from? One possibility is that infants begin to learn the phonotactic system by paying attention to the beginnings and ends of entire utterances. The beginning of an entire utterance has to be the beginning of a word, and the end of an utterance has to be the end of a word. By attending to the front and back end of utterances, infants can learn about the way phonemes are distributed in different parts of words. When mathematical modeling is used to simulate the development of word segmentation ability, the models "learn"[10] much more quickly when they are told where utterances in the training set begin and end (Christiansen, Allen, & Seidenberg, 1998). Infants may also use prosodic stress to learn about syllable onsets and offsets, by giving special attention to stressed syllables. Infants who are just learning to speak tend to reproduce accented (stressed) than unaccented (or unstressed) syllables, independent of the semantic content those syllables convey. In languages where root morphemes are stressed, children produce root morphemes before they produce other types. In languages where derivational or inflectional morphemes are stressed, children tend to produce those first (Pye, 1983).

Infant-directed speech

If you spend any time around infants, you will notice that when a baby shows up, adults turn into soppy, blithering idiots.[11] Babies have that effect on us. When we talk to infants, the way we speak changes radically.[12] The pitch of our voice increases. We speak in shorter sentences. We speak more clearly and distinctly, and we vary our pitch and our loudness much more than we do when we speak to adults. This collection of strange speech properties goes by the name *infant-directed speech* (IDS), *child-directed speech*, or *motherese*,[13] and it is the object of study of very serious, tough-minded language scientists. Why do adults use this special style of speaking when they address infants? One reason is that babies like it. Newborn infants prefer to hear the sound of a female voice speaking motherese over the same voice speaking adult-directed speech, and it helps infants stay in a good mood (Cooper & Aslin, 1990; 1994; Werker & McLeod, 1989). Beyond mood effects, IDS may help infants solve the segmentation problem. Because IDS has exaggerated prosodic features, IDS may provide clearer indications of important boundaries between words, phrases, and clauses. Further, IDS utterances are relatively short, which lightens the memory load that utterances impose on infants. Critical topic words also tend to appear in highly prominent positions within IDS utterances, often at the end, and topic words tend to be marked with special prosodic features (Fernald & Mazzie, 1991). IDS utterances also engage infants' attention, boosting even further the salience of speech stimuli that infants appear to have an innate drive to attend to.

Although not all cultures have infant-directed speech (Quiché Mayan appears to be one that does not; Pye, 1983), infants appear to benefit when adults use IDS while speaking to them (Liu, Kuhl, & Tsao, 2003; Thiessen, Hill, & Saffran, 2005). Infants aged 6 months to 1 year whose mothers spoke more clearly, as measured by physical differences between different vowel sounds, demonstrated superior ability to discriminate between similar sounding words. Thus, exposure to more clearly enunciated IDS appears to instill in infants the phonological contrasts that are important in their native language. In one direct test of segmentation skill, infants (6½–8½ months old) exposed to IDS outperformed infants who were exposed to adult-directed versions of the exact same test materials (Thiessen et al., 2005). In addition, studies of depressed mothers show that their infants lag behind their peers in speech-processing ability (at least through the early stages of speech segmentation and word learning; Kaplan, Bachorowski, Smoski, & Hudenko, 2002). The core problem in this instance appears to be that depressed mothers' speech does not contain the prosodic features that help support the infants' positive affect, mark important boundaries in the speech stream, and emphasize key elements. While infants of depressed mothers have difficulty learning new words when listening to their own mothers' speech, these same infants perform at about the same level as their peers (infants of non-depressed mothers) when they listened to another infant's non-depressed mother speak. Thus, the problem is not that infants of depressed mothers cannot learn, the problem is that the input they are getting lacks the IDS-related cues that could support and facilitate their learning.[14] To sum up, research on infant-directed speech indicates that, although IDS may not be necessary for children to learn their first language, it helps them master some aspects of speech comprehension and word learning, and it certainly does no harm. And it's fun.

PRACTICAL ADVICE CORNER

You may become a parent one day. If you don't become a parent yourself, you may know someone who becomes a parent. If so, you might be interested in whether parents' behavior influences a child's language development. The short answer is that, yes, parents have a great deal of influence on the course of a child's language development (Fernald, Perfors, & Marchman, 2006; Fernald, Swingley, & Pinto, 2001; Hurtado, Marchman, & Fernald, 2007; Marchman & Fernald, 2008; Pan, Rowe, Singer, & Snow, 2005; Swingley, Pinto, & Fernald, 1999; Tsao, Liu, & Kuhl, 2004). Very young infants treat words as perceptual wholes, and they sometimes fail to discriminate between two similar sounding words. However, by the age of 24 months, most infants have become very efficient and very accurate at recognizing familiar words. Like adults, 24-month-old children process familiar words incrementally. That is, they can recognize a familiar word before the entire word has been spoken. However, some babies are better at this than others. What makes the difference is the size of the baby's vocabulary and the speed with which the baby can process incoming speech. Further, these two abilities are in a symbiotic relationship of sorts: The more words the child knows, the faster she can recognize familiar words; The faster she can recognize familiar words, the more resources she has left over to pay attention to and learn from other parts of the speech signal. Further, these differences have long-term, cumulative effects. Children who are faster at recognizing familiar words at 6 months old have bigger vocabularies at 24 months old than children who are slower at recognizing familiar words at 6 months old. Speed of speech perception predicts long-term growth of both comprehension and production. This relationship holds in the United States both for middle- and upper-middle-class children learning English and for lower- and lower-middle-class children learning Spanish. Differences between fast and slow processors can be explained largely as a kind of practice effect. The more language infants hear, the more efficient they get at recognizing familiar words; and the more efficient they get at recognizing familiar words, the more they can learn about new words. Differences in processing efficiency between different infants can also be attributed in part to how much adults talk to them, and there are vast differences between and within different socio-economic groups in the amount of speech that gets directed toward infants. Maternal education also appears to matter a great deal. Independent of socio-economic status, mothers with more formal education speak more to their children than mothers with less formal education. Bottom line: Talk to babies. They will thank you later.

Statistical Learning and Speech Segmentation

Infants may make use of prosodic features to identify boundaries between words in fluent speech, but a recently developed alternative, the *statistical learning* approach, suggests that speech segmentation skill has little or nothing to do with the metrical segmentation strategy or other forms of prosodic bootstrapping (Saffran, 2001, 2003; Saffran, Aslin, & Newport, 1996; Thiessen & Saffran, 2003; see McMurray & Hollich, 2009). According to the statistical learning approach, infants notice patterns in complex stimuli and use those patterns to analyze speech stimuli and identify important subcomponents, including words. As Saffran (2003, p. 110) notes, "Infants can rapidly capitalize on the statistical properties of their language environments, including the distributions of sounds in words ... to discover important components of language structure." How might this work for learning words?

Saffran and colleagues (e.g., Saffran, et al.,1996; Saffran, 2001, 2003) note that, in English, some syllables are highly predictable from other syllables. Consider the word *pretty*. It has two syllables that sound like "pri" (/prI/ in the English phonetic alphabet) and "tee" (/ti/ in the phonetic alphabet). In infant directed speech, /ti/ follows /prI/ about 80% of the time (it's not clear what percentage of the time /ti/ is preceded by /prI/, but if a baby hears /prI/, it will very likely hear /ti/ right away).[15] The syllable /ti/, however, provides very little information about what syllable will come next. Just about anything could come after *pretty* (*baby*, *doggie*, *mommy*, *apple*, …), so there is no way the baby can predict what comes after /ti/. Notice that there's a clear difference in probabilities here that an infant could exploit to help figure out how the language works. If the likelihood of /ti/ given /prɪ/ is very high, maybe those two syllables should be considered as a package. Think of it this way: If you have a male friend, and every time you see your male friend, he is with the same female, you might soon deduce that those two are boyfriend and girlfriend, and you might start to think of them as a couple (kind of like Brangelina).[16] If, on the other hand, you have two other friends, but you never see them together at the same time, you would not assume that they are a couple. So, if some pairs of syllables co-occur more than others, an infant might start to think that the co-occurring syllables make up a word (e.g., *pretty*), and syllables that do not co-occur, or do so rarely, do not go together to make a word. If so, babies could use co-occurrence information to segment the speech stream, identifying words by treating high-probability pairs of syllables as words and low-probability pairs as separate.

Evidence that babies are capable of detecting patterns in syllables comes from experiments where babies listen to an artificial "mini-language" during a training phase, and get tested on what they learned later on (Saffran et al., 1996; Saffran, 2001, 2002; see Mirman, Magnuson, Graf-Estes, & Dixon, 2008, for similar experiments on adults). The mini-languages are made up of sets of nonsense syllables, such as *jik*, *pel*, and *rud*. The languages are designed such that some syllables always occur immediately after others. So if the infant hears *jik*, she always hears *pel* next. Other combinations of syllables occur much less frequently. For example, *rud* might appear immediately after *pel* a third of the time, but the other two thirds of the time, different syllables, such as *mib* and *lum*, would follow *pel*. This set of rules is used to create long strings of syllables, such as *jik pel rud neb jik pel mib vot loke hep jik pel lum*. A synthesizer, rather than a human speaker, generates the strings of syllables so *no* prosodic cues indicate where any word boundaries might be. So, the only information that the infant has to work with is the *transitional probability* between different syllables—the likelihood that one syllable will be followed by another. When infants are tested using a version of the conditioned head turn procedure, they listen for different amounts of time to pairs of syllables that are "words" in the language than pairs of syllables that have lower transitional probabilities (and therefore are not "words" in the language). The results are about the same when infants are exposed to real words from an unfamiliar real language, so English-learning babies recognize Italian words when they are exposed to a version of mini-Italian where pairs of syllables from real words have high transitional probability, and pairs of syllables that cross word boundaries have low transitional probability (Pelucchi, Hay, & Saffran, 2009).

Experiments such as these demonstrate that infants are capable of picking up statistical information present in the speech stream and using that information to segment the stream, even when there are no prosodic cues such as accent, changes in pitch, or pauses to help them identify individual parts of the speech stream that could be words. Further studies indicate that older infants (17–18 months old) can learn about phonotactic patterns by paying attention to statistical cues (Chambers, Onishi, & Fisher, 2003). They can also learn to associate high-probability pairs of syllables with pictures of unfamiliar objects (Graf-Estes, Evans, Alibaldi, & Saffran, 2007), which suggests that infants are treating the segments that they identify as being word-like, rather than just as interesting snippets of sound.

Figure 9.2 Patterns of dogs used to train and test 7-month-old infants (from Saffran, Pollak, Seibel, & Shkolnik, 2007, pp. 671–672)

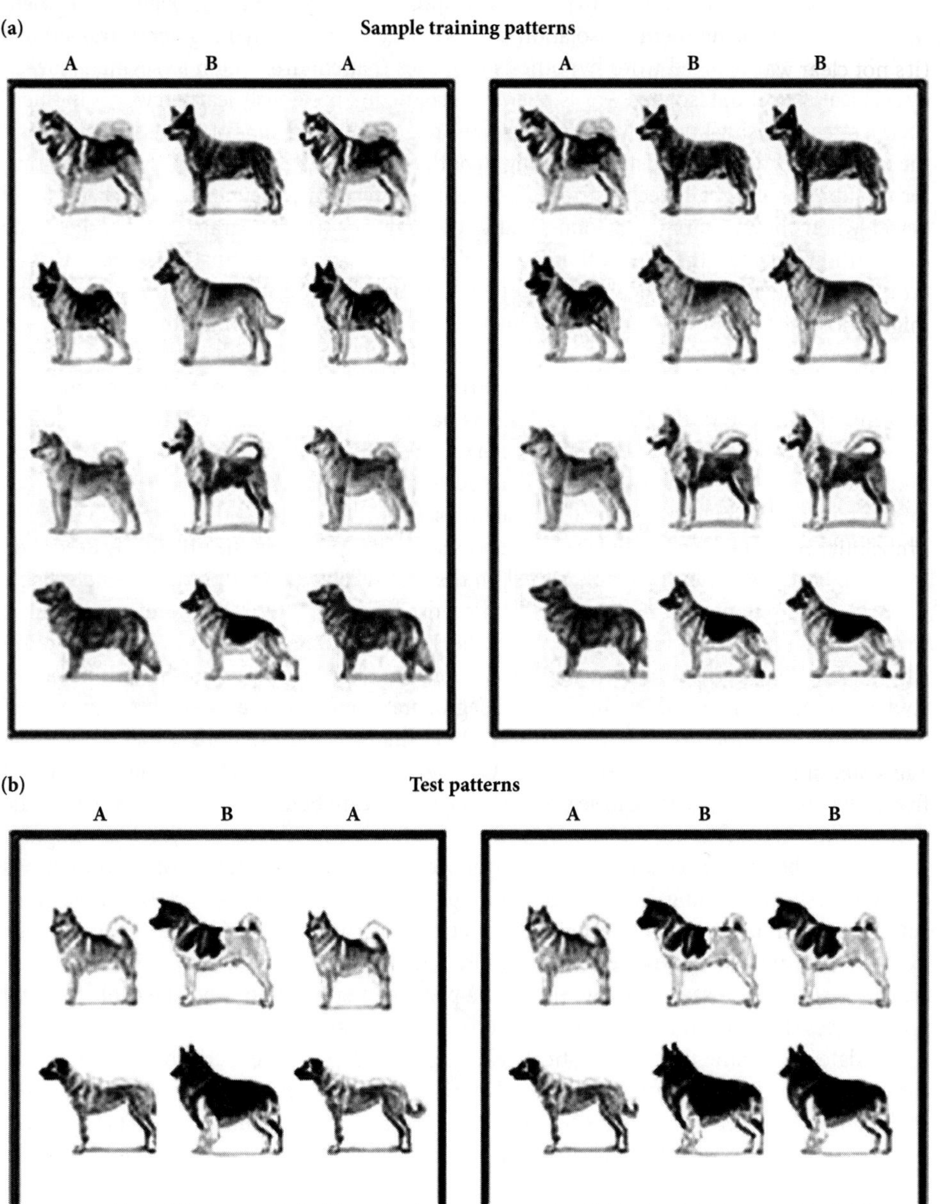

Further, statistical learning may be the result of a general-purpose learning mechanism in children. They can learn simple correspondences between visual stimuli (e.g., pictures of dogs), as in Figure 9.2. When children are exposed to sets of pictures based on the ABA pattern (e.g., Husky, German Shepherd, Husky), they spent more time looking at a novel AAB pattern (e.g., Dachshund, Dachshund, Labrador). The existence of statistical learning for both language and non-language visual stimuli could indicate that general-purpose learning mechanisms, rather than innate, genetically determined, language-specific learning mechanisms, are responsible for speech segmentation and word learning.

Language scientists seeking to explain how infants "break into" the speech stream want to know which cue or cues infants use first to begin solving the segmentation problem. The metrical segmentation strategy hypothesis proposes that children can begin to segment words without hearing them in isolation, and without knowing anything about transitional probabilities. The isolated word hypothesis proposes that children begin to segment speech by first learning about isolated words, then by recognizing previously learned words in fluent speech streams, using known words to detect the beginnings and ends of words that surround the familiar words. The statistical learning hypothesis suggests that none of this is necessary for infants to segment speech. Instead, infants pay attention to sequences of syllables and detect when the appearance of one syllable depends on the appearance of another. The competition between these hypotheses has triggered the psycholinguistic equivalent of an arms race, or a race to the beginning. Researchers have been testing younger and younger infants to try to figure out which cues infants rely on at the very beginning. In one such study, researchers provided both prosodic cues and transitional probability cues to word boundaries in an artificial mini-language (Thiessen & Saffran, 2003). In some of the stimuli, the prosodic cues mirrored those in English (i.e., the stress pattern was trochaic, strong–weak). In other stimuli, the prosodic cues were the opposite of the prevailing pattern in English. The transition probabilities between syllables were the same across the two sets. Younger (6½–7-month-old) infants paid attention to transitional probabilities, but were not influenced by prosodic cues. These infants listened for less time to sequences such as *jikpel* (from the previously described mini-language), whether the emphasis fell on the first syllable (*JIKpel*) or the second syllable (*jikPEL*). Older infants (8½–9 months old) showed a different pattern. They preferred familiar words (as defined by transitional probabilities) that had the trochaic (STRONG–weak) pattern, but that preference switched for iambic (weak–STRONG) words. In this study, younger infants appeared to base their segmentation choices entirely on transitional probabilities, and not prosodic information. Older infants appeared to base their choices on a mixture of prosodic and statistical cues. On the basis of these results, we might conclude that infants use statistical cues to segment the speech stream before they start to use prosodic cues, and therefore that the statistical learning hypothesis wins the race to the beginning.

However, before we declare the contest over, we should consider some possible limitations of the statistical learning hypothesis. To judge the contest, let's apply two simple tests: sufficiency and necessity. The sufficiency criterion says that, if you use a particular strategy by itself, that will be enough by itself to solve the segmentation problem. The necessity criteria is stronger. It says that you *must* use a particular strategy to solve the problem (and presupposes that the strategy is sufficient to solve the problem).

To date, experiments on statistical learning in infants have been based on highly simplified mini-languages with very rigid statistical properties. For example, transitional probabilities between syllables are set to 1.0 for "words" in the language, and .33 for pairs of syllables that cut across "word" boundaries.[17] Natural languages have a much wider range of transitional probabilities between syllables, the vast majority of which are far lower than 1.0. Researchers have used mathematical models to simulate learning of natural languages, using samples of real infant-directed speech to train the simulated learner (Yang, 2004). When the model has to rely on transitional probabilities alone, it fails to segment speech accurately. However, when the model makes two simple assumptions about prosody—that each word has a single stressed syllable, and that the prevailing pattern for bisyllables is trochaic (STRONG–weak)—the model is about as accurate in its segmentation decisions as 7½-month-old infants. This result casts doubt on whether the statistical learning strategy is sufficient for infants to learn how to segment naturally occurring speech (and if the strategy is not sufficient, it can not be necessary either).

The modeling work by itself is suggestive, but what we really need are controlled experiments with infants exposed to unfamiliar speech streams that contain a range of transitional probabilities that closely match those that occur in natural speech. Such studies have not yet been conducted. Some experimental work, however, suggests that substantial exposure (10 hours) to a language that has an unfamiliar prosodic pattern does not enable infants to segment the speech (Jusczyk, 1997). Because infants do segment unfamiliar speech that has a familiar prosodic pattern (e.g., English and Dutch) after minimal exposure, but do not segment a language with an unfamiliar prosodic structure (e.g., English and Mandarin), this also suggests that prosody, rather than statistical information, is responsible. The pattern of transitional probabilities in Dutch syllables *might be* higher than in Mandarin (a possibility that has not yet been addressed in the literature), otherwise, it is tempting to think that, at least for 9–10-month-old infants, the availability of prosodic cues make a bigger difference to their word segmentation ability than the availability of information about how likely one syllable is given another, at least when probabilistic information approximates what is available in natural speech.

Other studies suggest that statistical learning may not be necessary for segmentation to occur. (To be fair, the outcomes of statistical learning experiments suggest that other strategies may also be unnecessary for infants to segment speech, at least when transitional probabilities between syllables in words are high.) The isolated word and metrical segmentation strategies appear to be sufficient for the successful identification of at least some words in fluent speech. Further, the cross-language segmentation experiments reviewed above (Houston et al., 2000) indicate that infants do not need to know which syllables go together frequently in a language before they can identify words in that language. As Houston and colleagues (2000, p. 507), note, "The ability to extract familiar words from fluent speech is not dependent on familiarity with the phonetic structure of the input." Even some of the statistical learning experiments suggest that high transitional probabilities are not necessary for learners to identify important components of artificial mini-languages (Saffran, 2002). In some experiments, there is little difference in performance between learners who are exposed to mini-languages with high transitional probabilities and learners who are exposed to mini-languages with much lower transitional probabilities. In other experiments (e.g., Mirman et al., 2008, Experiment 1), learners appear to segment "words" composed of low-probability sequences of syllables (with transitional probabilities of .33) before they segment "words" composed of high-probability sequences (with transitional probabilities of 1.0).

Interim Summary

Can infants learn new words by hearing them spoken in isolation? It appears that they can. Can infants learn new words by paying attention to prosodic patterns in the language? It appears that they can. Can children detect statistical regularities in the language and use them to identify important components of the language? It appears that they can. Unless we assume babies are dumb, there is no reason to believe that they are incapable of taking advantage of whatever information speakers make available to them. Thus, the safest bet is to conclude that infants rely on a variety of cues to solve the segmentation problem. This conclusion is reinforced by testing on real infants, and mathematical modeling of the learning process also points to the benefits of paying attention to multiple cues. When a neural network seeks to accurately identify words in fluent, child-directed speech, the network is much more accurate when it uses multiple cues (Christiansen et al., 1998). One cue by itself may be unhelpful, but the value of that same cue can rise dramatically when it is combined with other cues. Infants, like good scientists, appear to be flexible, pragmatic learners rather than dogmatic followers of a single, narrow strategy. Babies are smart, so if a cue is available, there is a good chance that they will figure out a way to make use of that cue to help them learn.

Learning Word Meanings

Children start to produce words at about the age of 12 months ... if we stick to the more conservative estimate of 60,000, (this) equates to about 10 new words a day up until the end of high school.

PAUL BLOOM, *HOW CHILDREN LEARN THE MEANINGS OF WORDS*

Children are highly efficient word learners. As Paul Bloom notes (2000, p. 26), "They achieve this feat without any explicit training or feedback." Segmenting fluent speech into word-sized chunks of sound gets infants going on the road to mastering their first language, but before they can start to communicate effectively, they need to associate concepts with packages of sound (words) that they pull out of the speech stream. Children as old as 14 months who are still trying to master the phonological system of their native language have difficulty associating sounds and meanings, but children get better at learning words the longer they spend learning the language and the more skill they develop at discriminating between similar speech sounds (Fisher, Hunt, & Chambers, 2001; Mills et al., 2004; Stager & Werker, 1997). It takes most infants about 18 months to learn their first 50 words (as measured by how many different words they say in daily life), but after that children experience a *word spurt*, during which time the rate at which children learn new word meanings increases dramatically (McMurray, 2007). What is most amazing about children's word-learning abilities is that they are able to deduce new word meanings simply by hearing the word used a couple of times. Older children can deduce a word's meaning after hearing it used only once.

To accomplish these amazing feats of deduction, infants must overcome a set of serious challenges. One big obstacle that confronts infants is the *poverty of the stimulus* problem (Brown, 1957; Quine, 1960). *Poverty of the stimulus* as it applies to word learning refers to the fact that the environment does not provide the information that the child needs to identify one, and only one possible meaning for a word. Quine asks you to imagine traveling to a distant, foreign land that has rabbits in it. One morning, you and your local guide encounter a rabbit running across the path. You point at the rabbit and say *What's that?* The local guide says, *gavagai*. You might *assume* that *gavagai* means "rabbit," but your assumption could be wrong. The guide might really be saying "furry," or "long ears," or "mammal," or "lagomorph," or "above ground," or "running," or "anything with its back towards us," or "not a snake," or "that sucker's fast," or "tastes great," or "less filling." Maybe the guide is just saying, "What?" Briefly, there is nothing in the environment that rules in or rules out any particular interpretation of the utterance *gavagai*. This issue is highlighted in an urban legend (probably false) that describes the way the word *kangaroo* entered the English language. According to this legend, some of the first English people traveling in the Australian outback encountered kangaroos and asked their aboriginal guides *What's that?* The guides said *kangaroo*, which in their language means "I don't know."

So what is the poor infant to do? Folk theories of language acquisition, and also behaviorist theories, assume that children learn word meanings by playing a language game, sometimes called *point-and-say* (Bloom, 2000; Clark, 2009; Skinner, 1957).[18] In the point-and-say method, the parent points at something and makes a noise, like *bunny!* The child sees the object that is being pointed at and associates the noise with the object. Indeed, nouns in young children's vocabularies tend to refer to concrete objects, like dogs, cats, and balls, that could be the object of the point-and-say game (Brown, 1957). However, as Quine's analysis shows us, pointing and speaking, by themselves, do not provide enough information for the child to deduce the speaker's intended meaning. Before a child can learn word meanings, she has to somehow narrow down the range of possible meanings. Even if the infant somehow comes up with a successful strategy for object names, many of the words that the child needs to learn do not refer to discrete objects. For words such as *milk* and *plastic* (substances), or *thought* (a process), there is no object that someone could point to. Further, some of the earliest words that children produce are social interaction terms like *hi*, and *bye-bye* that also lack corresponding objects. How do infants learn those? Finally, if point-and-say were the primary word-learning mechanism, we would expect blind children to be horribly disadvantaged when it comes to learning word meanings, but they learn at about the same rate as other children (Landau & Gleitman, 1985).

What about labels for actions, like verbs? The point-and-say hypothesis supposes that children learn words because they simultaneously see an object and hear a label. But people rarely label an action while they are doing it (Fisher, Gleitman, & Gleitman, 1991; Gleitman & Gleitman, 1997). People don't say, *I'm drinking* while they are drinking. They don't say, *I'm closing the door now*, while they are closing a door. Action verbs such as *chase* and *flee* are especially tricky, because every event of *chasing* is also an example of a *fleeing* event. Every time someone chases, something flees, and vice versa (Fisher et al., 1991; Gleitman and Gleitman, 1997). If someone points to a scene while an action of chasing (and fleeing) is going on, and says *blicket*, how does the child know whether to interpret *blicket* as *chase* or *flee*? Both are going on at the same time, and the meaning of the word *blicket* depends on the point of view of the person speaking about the event, not on the point of view of the child observing the event. Considerable research in language development has been devoted to figuring out exactly how children narrow their search for word meanings and arrive at a set of meanings that very closely match the standard meanings used by everyone who knows the language. To understand how this trick is done, we have to start by abandoning the idea that point-and-say is the only, or even the most important, strategy that children use to learn what words mean. What are the alternatives?

Let's start by trying to solve the poverty of the stimulus problem so that the infant can start to build up a set of word meanings. One way to solve poverty of the stimulus is to propose that children have innate categories, such as *noun* and *verb*, which they seek to populate with specific words from their native language. According to this *genetically guided learning* hypothesis, infants populate those categories with specific words by attending to salient bits of speech and trying them out as nouns or verbs (Pinker, 1984, 1994b, 1996). This approach eliminates many of the possible interpretations of *gavagai* (those involving actions or complex relationships), but it does not get the child all the way home. For example, even if the child only considers object labels as meanings, *gavagai* could mean *animal*, *mammal*, *rodent*, or *rabbit*. Or gavagai could be a proper name for that specific bunny, equivalent to *Flopsy* or *Peter*. To solve that problem, the child could store each instance of *gavagai*, as well as an episodic memory of the context when the word was spoken. That way, if *gavagai* occurs when the child sees a dog, cat, and horse, the *rabbit* and *Flopsy* interpretations are ruled out, and something like *animal* or *mammal* becomes more likely.

Alternatives to the genetically guided learning hypothesis appeal to general-purpose learning and memory skills. According to approaches such as these, children have a general ability to pick up and remember linguistically conveyed information (Markson & Bloom, 1997; see also Swingley & Fernald, 2002), rather than a special mechanism that just does word learning. Research on learning and memory shows that both children and adults appear to have better recall for arbitrary information when that information is conveyed in language than by other means. For example, children and adults in Markson and Bloom's study were exposed to a set of objects. For one of the objects, they were told either that its name was *koba* or that it was given to the experimenter by her uncle. Both of these facts about the object are arbitrary, and both are conveyed using language. A different set of subjects were shown the same set of objects, and the experimenter placed a sticker on one of the objects (but did *not* name it or say where it came from). Up to one month later, children and adults in the two linguistically conveyed knowledge conditions (the *koba* and uncle conditions) were able to remember which object the arbitrary knowledge was associated with. However, people in the sticker condition could not remember which object was associated with the sticker. This result could indicate that learning new words uses the same mental equipment as learning new arbitrary facts conveyed by language, and that learning word meanings does not depend on a special-purpose word-learning mechanism. The explanation of why, exactly, language is more effective than other methods of conveying arbitrary information requires further investigation, however.

To overcome the poverty of the stimulus, infants could begin by assuming the most general possible interpretation of a new word (i.e., a new word would be treated as though it applied to everything, kind of like the word *thing*). Alternatively, the child could assume that a new word applied only to the specific object that the child was attending to when the word was spoken (i.e., a new word would be treated as a proper name, like *Flopsy* or *Evelina*). It appears that children use neither of these strategies. Instead, infants appear to have a pre-existing bias to treat new labels like *gavagai* as names for *basic level* categories (Masur, 1997). When people are asked to name objects, they tend to come up with labels that are not too specific and not too general, but that are just right to discriminate between different kinds of objects and to include a wide variety of examples of the concept (Rosch & Mervis, 1975). These "just right" labels are known as *basic level* terms, to discriminate them from *superordinate* and *subordinate level* words. If you see a picture such as one of those in Figure 9.2a or b, and you are asked to say what the picture shows, you will use a basic-level name like *dog*, rather than a subordinate-level name, like *Poodle*, or a *superordinate* category label, like *mammal* or *animal.*[19] Infants (and adults) also have a pre-existing bias to treat novel words as labels for entire objects, rather than parts of the objects, substances, colors, or other features of the object (Markman & Hutchinson, 1984). So if you and an infant are looking at Flopsy, and someone says, *Gavagai!*, both you and the infant are likely to assume that *gavagai* is a word that applies to the whole shebang (not just part of the thing), and also that the word is a basic-level term referring to the category of things that physically resemble Flopsy.

Children sometimes misconstrue the meanings of new words. When children learn a new word, they tend to *extend* that term by using it as a label for physically similar objects, especially those that have a similar shape (Markson, Diesendruck, & Bloom, 2008).[20] Sometimes, children *overextend* basic-level terms, by using a word like *bunny* to refer to all small, furry creatures, including cats and dogs. When they overextend, they apply a known label to a category for which competent adult speakers use a different label.[21] Children also sometimes *underextend* terms. In that case, the child fails to use a familiar label for other members of the same category. Bloom (2000) reports a child who, for a time, believed that only cars that he could see through his front window could be called *car*. All other cars were called something else. Another child reportedly interpreted *shoe* as referring only to the members of one set of shoes in one particular closet. While these types of errors represent a small minority of children's word output, they offer further evidence that Quine was on to something when he suggested that lining up sounds and meanings is not a trivial problem.

While children sometimes misconstrue the meanings of novel words, all normal children eventually come to understand words about the same way everyone else does. To achieve this feat, children apply some further strategies that allow them to identify and refine word meanings. These strategies include the *mutual exclusivity assumption* and the related *principle of contrast* (Clark, 2009; Markman & Wachtel, 1988). *Mutual exclusivity* involves the assumption that no two words in the language have exactly the same meaning.

So, if a child already knows the name of a concept, she will reject a second label as referring to the same concept. Children can use this principle to figure out the meanings of new words, because applying the principle of contrast rules out possible meanings. If you already know that *gavagai* means "rabbit," and your guide points at a rabbit and says, *blicket*, you will not assume that *gavagai* and *blicket* are synonyms. Instead, you will consider the possibility that *blicket* refers to a salient part of the rabbit (its ears, perhaps) or a type of rabbit or some other salient property of rabbits (that they're cute, maybe). In the lab, children who are taught two new names while attending to an unfamiliar object interpret the first name as referring to the entire object and the second name as referring to a salient part of the object. For somewhat older children (3–4 years old), parents often provide an explicit contrast when introducing children to new words that label parts of an object (Saylor, Sabbagh, & Baldwin, 2002). So, an adult might point to Flopsy and say, *See the bunny? These are his ears*. Children do not need such explicit instruction, however, as they appear to spontaneously apply the principle of contrast to deduce meanings for subcomponents of objects (e.g., *ears*) and substances that objects are made out of (e.g., *wood, naugahyde, duck tape*).

The principle of contrast also helps children learn how to organize words when more than one label can apply to a given concept (Clark, 2009). The principle of contrast, like the mutual exclusivity assumption, says that two labels should not apply to the same object, but if they do, there must be some difference in meaning between the two labels. For example, the words *dog*, *mammal*, and *animal* can all appropriately apply to the same mutt, but they do not mean the same thing. The choice of which exact term a speaker uses reflects the speaker's stance towards the named object and particular concepts that the speaker wishes to highlight. If the speaker chooses the word *mammal*, she may wish to draw attention to the similarity between Fido and physically diverse members of the mammal category. If she uses *dog*, she may wish to draw attention to differences between Fido and other kinds of pets. If a child lacked the principle of contrast, the child could assume that the words *dog*, *mammal*, and *animal*, are interchangeable. Further, nobody would ever correct the child if she said *mammal* when looking at Fido. (At least, it would be really strange if somebody said, *No, that's a dog, not a mammal.*) Worse still, without the principle of contrast, the child might assume that new words were just synonyms of words the child already knows. Of course, children do not make this kind of mistake. In the lab, children apply the principle of contrast to pick up new word meanings very rapidly (Markman & Wachtel, 1988). When children are shown a familiar object (e.g., a spoon) and an unfamiliar object (e.g., a whisk), and someone uses a novel word, as in *bring me the fendle*, children pick up the unfamiliar object, which indicates they have associated the new word with the unfamiliar object. It is as if children think, "Here are two objects. I know that one of them is called *spoon*. I don't know what the other one is called. I need to get the *fendle*. Because the spoon is called *spoon*, and *fendle* is different than *spoon*, *fendle* must be the name of the new object."

Because learning word meanings involves associating sounds and concepts, children cannot learn the meanings of words until they have some appreciation of the concepts that the words refer to. Thus, the kinds of thoughts that the child can entertain should have some effect on the way the child learns new words. Children's perceptual systems carve the world into discrete objects, and they have intuitive notions about how these objects should behave (Aguiar & Baillargeon, 1999; Hespos et al., 2009). Given that children have substantial knowledge about objects early on, we might expect them to learn names for objects before they learn names for other kinds of concepts. Since object names are primarily or exclusively nouns, we should expect infants to learn nouns before they learn other types of words, including verbs which generally convey information about relationships between objects or relationships between objects and events. Some researchers, therefore, believe that early word-learners should show a *noun bias* (a tendency to learn nouns before other kinds of words) regardless of the way adults speak to them. Characteristics of English make nouns relatively prominent in infant-directed speech. In other languages, including Italian, Japanese, and Chinese, nouns tend to be much less frequent, and they appear in less prominent places in infant-directed speech (Caselli, Casadio, & Bates, 1999). Does this difference in the relative frequency of nouns and verbs lead to differences in the rate at which infants in different cultures learn nouns and verbs? If concepts precede word learning, noun bias should apply to Italian, Japanese, and Chinese, just as it does to English. If the frequency with which words occur in prominent positions drives word learning, then infants in different cultures should learn nouns and verbs at different rates. Some studies do suggest that, in languages where verbs are more salient than nouns in IDS, infants learn verbs at an elevated rate compared to nouns (Fernald & Morikawa, 1993; Tardif, Gelman, & Xu, 1999; Tardif, Shatz, & Naigles, 1997). However, studies that show faster verb than noun learning tend to use short-term observation and a limited range of tasks that seek to elicit spoken word production. Studies that use naturalistic observation or parental report tend to show greater consistency across languages in the relative proportions of nouns and verbs early on in toddlers' vocabularies. Large-scale cross-linguistic studies on different languages that emphasize nouns and verbs to different degrees show that nouns make up a greater percentage of infants' and toddlers' early vocabulary than verbs (Bornstein et al., 2004). While more work needs to be done to settle the question definitively, it appears as though noun bias could be a general property of early word-learning, and so the idea that conceptual development leads vocabulary development is still plausible.[22]

Learning words also involves deducing that people intend to refer to concepts when they speak, that is, that people have *referential intent*. Knowing that other people have thoughts that differ from yours, and that they might wish to convey their thoughts to you, is part of your *theory of mind*. Some children, including children with autism, lack some aspects of the theory of mind, and as a result, they sometimes associate meanings to sounds inappropriately (Bloom, 2000). Other children, such as those with *Williams* syndrome, have severe deficits in general intelligence, but an apparently intact theory of mind, and they appear to assign meanings to words much as normal children do. In addition to knowing that other people have private thoughts and wish to convey those thoughts when they speak, children appear to track detailed aspects of other people's mental states and abilities, and use that information when assigning meanings to words. Children can observe where speakers are focusing their attention, and they use that knowledge to infer what objects people are labeling when they speak (Baldwin et al., 1996). However, children do not simply look where the speaker is looking and assume that a new word refers to something at that location. If two objects are visible to the child, but only one of the objects is visible to a speaker, children understand that the speaker can use a novel word to refer to the hidden object, even if the speaker is looking at the visible object (Nurmsoo & Bloom, 2008). Children also pay attention to speakers' general knowledge and reliability as a source of information (Birch & Bloom, 2002; Sabbagh & Baldwin, 2001). Some speakers are more knowledgeable than others, which means that some speakers are more likely to know the meaning of a word. Children capitalize on this to learn new words (Birch, Vauthier, & Bloom, 2008). Children are more likely to believe an adult than a child when the adult produces a name for a novel object. Children also pay more attention to speakers who have been reliable in the past. If children are exposed to an individual who gives the wrong names for familiar objects (objects for which the child already has words), and the individual names a novel object, the child will not reflexively adopt the spoken name as the label for the novel object. All of these effects show that children do not blindly associate sounds with objects. Children engage in sophisticated deduction, and weigh multiple factors when acquiring new vocabulary.[23]

Syntactic bootstrapping

The preceding research indicates that children have a number of tools that they can deploy to figure out noun meanings, but what about verbs? As Cindy Fisher and Leila Gleitman note, young children may have more difficulty learning verb meanings than noun meanings, because verbs convey more complex concepts than nouns. While nouns can refer to concrete, directly observable properties, interpreting a verb requires the child to understand the speaker's perspective on an event (Fisher et al., 1991; Gleitman & Gleitman, 1997). While observing an event involving a duck chasing a rabbit, the speaker could focus on the agent and say *The duck blickets the rabbit*, in which case, *blicket* means "chase." If the speaker focuses on the rabbit, and says *The rabbit blickets the duck*, *blicket* means "flee." The point-and-say method does not explain how children learn the meanings of verbs such as *chase* and *flee*, because the context of the event does not provide enough information, by itself, to specify which perspective the speaker is taking.

Children can take steps toward overcoming this version of the poverty of the stimulus problem by paying attention to syntactic cues to meaning. This hypothesis forms the core of the *syntactic bootstrapping* hypothesis (Brown, 1957; Fisher, 1996; Gleitman, 1990; see Pinker, 1994a, for a dissenting viewpoint). Syntactic characteristics of utterances can support meaning inferences in a number of different ways. First, syntactic properties of utterances could help children figure out whether a new word is a noun or a verb. When children look at a still picture of someone cutting cloth with an unfamiliar tool, and they hear *In this picture, you can see sibbing*, they infer that *sibbing* is a verb and refers to the cutting action.[24] If they hear *Can you see a sib* or *some sib*, they infer that the new word is a noun. The syntactic properties of the utterance in the noun case provide further clues as to what the noun might be. Nouns can be classified as being in the *count noun* category, which is used for items that we view as being individuals (e.g., *I see a cat*, but not **I see a pile of cat*). Nouns can be classified in a different way as belonging to the *mass noun* category, which is used for substances whose components are not treated as individual items (e.g., *I see a pile of dirt*, but not **I see a dirt*). When the new word follows the article *a*, children infer that *sib* refers to a count noun, so they pick out the tool in the picture. When the new words follows the article *some*, they infer that *sib* refers to a mass noun, and they interpret *sib* as being the cloth in the picture. So, syntax can provide cues to word categories.

Children also use syntactic properties of verbs to figure out what verbs mean (Fisher, 2002; Fisher et al., 1991; Göksun, Küntay, & Naigles, 2008; Lee & Naigles, 2008; Song & Fisher, 2005; see Dittmar et al., 2008, for an alternative outlook). In particular, children pay attention to the *subcategorization frame* to home in on a novel verb's meaning (recall from Chapter 4 that *subcategorization* refers to the number and kinds of partners that verbs have in a particular sentence). Consider the following two sentences:

(1) She blicked!

(2) She blicked her!

Even though you do not know the meaning of the verb *blicked* yet, you can draw some conclusions about what the meaning *might* be just by knowing how many arguments (partners) and adjuncts (optional partners) go along with the verb in the sentence. In sentence (1), *blicked* only has a subject argument (*She*). So, in this case, *blicked* is an *intransitive verb*. In sentence (2), *blicked* appears with both a subject and an object argument. So in sentence (2), *blicked* is used as a transitive verb. Children can take information about transitivity into account when they interpret novel verbs. For example, in an experiment by Sylvia Yuan and Cynthia Fisher (2009), children listened to sentences similar to (1) or (2) and then later watched a pair of videos (see Figure 9.3). Children who had heard intransitive

Figure 9.3 Stills from a video depicting a two-participant event (left) and a one-participant event (right) used to test young children's interpretation of the novel verb *blicking* (from Yuan & Fisher, 2009, p. 620)

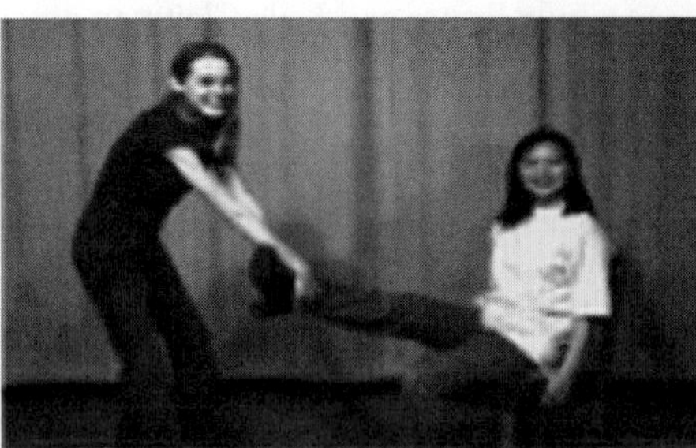

sentences similar to (1) pointed to the right-hand picture when asked to "Find blicking!" Children who had heard the transitive version of the training sentence pointed toward the left-hand picture. Thus, children interpret verbs presented in a transitive frame as actions that relate two different actors, but they interpret verbs presented in an intransitive frame as an action with only a single participant. By combining information gleaned from the syntactic frame (transitive vs. intransitive) with specific information provided by the video, children infer that *blicking* means *waving your arm* or *waving your right arm above your head* in one case, and *pulling someone's leg* in the other case. Note that subcategory information, by itself, is not enough to specify a unique meaning for a verb, because different verbs sometimes have the exact same subcategorization possibilities. However, children *can* figure out verb meanings by combining subcategory information, information from the physical environment, and possibly inferences about the mental state and communicative goals of the speaker as the verb is being spoken.

But how do children figure out these syntactic cues in the first place? Cynthia Fisher and colleagues propose that when children view an event, they develop an organized conceptual representation of that event (Fisher, 2002). When someone describes that event, children associate linguistic units with elements of the (non-linguistic) structured conceptual representation. Consider the left-hand picture in Figure 9.3. In perceiving this event, children will note that someone is initiating the action (the *agent*), someone is being acted upon (the *patient*), as well as details of the action. When children hear a description of the event, such as *She's blicking her*, they map the subject of the sentence (*She*) to the conceptual agent, the object of the sentence (*her*) to the patient, and the verb to the action. Fisher refers to this process of associating words in sentences to concepts in event representations as *alignment.* In her terms (Fisher, 2002, p. 56), "Children might arrive at a structure-sensitive interpretation of a sentence by structurally aligning a representation of a sentence with a structured conceptual representation of a relevant scene." Of course, if the child does not know the difference between *She* and *her*, it will not be possible to do this mapping. But given that infants start to recognize nouns fairly early in development, it is not unreasonable to assume that knowledge of nouns could bootstrap the acquisition of syntactic form. If, for example, the child knows the names of both of the young women in Figure 9.3, and heard a number of sentences describing actions involving those two, they might detect a stable pattern in the linguistic descriptions of the events. That is, that causal agents tend to come before the verb and patients come after.[25] This kind of knowledge would help the child interpret subsequent utterances that mention different sets of actors and actions.[26]

Acquisition of Morphological and Syntactic Knowledge

Every "theory of learning" that is even worth considering incorporates an innateness hypothesis.
NOAM CHOMSKY

There is a special cognitive faculty for learning and using language.
STEVEN PINKER

At around 2 years of age, children begin to create utterances that have more than one word in them. Children's ability to combine words into larger units is often indexed using a simple measure called the *mean length of utterance* (or MLU). This measure counts the number of morphemes or words that the child produces in a single utterance (which is in turn assessed by looking at when the child pauses). Children at about age 2 have MLUs of just over 1, because they continue to express ideas using single-word utterances (*No!*, *More!*, and so on). But as children mature, the mean length of utterance steadily increases and children develop more sophisticated ways to express increasingly complex thoughts. As they acquire skills, children become much more flexible in the way they use language. Instead of repeating snippets of what they hear, children craft utterances that nobody has ever said before. In other words, children become more *productive* in their language use. Many young children's utterances are ungrammatical according to adult language standards (e.g. *I want see my bottle getting fix*, *Mommy I poured you*), but many of them are not (*I'm going to show you where Mr. Lion is*) (Clark, 2009), and production performance gets closer and closer to adult forms. One of the central questions in language development is: How do children acquire the skills they need to form grammatical phrases and sentences? In other words, how do they acquire adult-like knowledge of their native language grammar?

Answering this question requires a detailed analysis of the input that is available to the child learner as well as detailed analysis of the child's production and comprehension skills. This investigation can focus on any number of different types of knowledge and skills. To organize the discussion, let's consider three kinds of grammatical knowledge that children acquire: knowledge of word categories, morphology, and phrase structure. Different languages have different categories of words (for example, some languages lack adjectives; Stoll, Abott-Smith, & Lieven, 2009). So a child learning a language must learn what categories her language has and where specific words fit into the system of categories. In addition, children must learn how those categories of words are expressed within phrases and sentences. Do verbs come before grammatical objects (as in English and Mandarin), after (as in Japanese), or is word order flexible (as in Russian)? The child must also learn how word categories are organized within phrases. In addition to discovering categories and phrase organization, children must also learn aspects of *morphology*—the different forms that a word can take. Morphological marking plays a variety of important roles in language, and different languages have different morphological systems. Some kinds of morphology are used to express different flavors of meaning, such as the difference between present and past tense (e.g., *walk* vs. *walked*; *sing* vs. *sang*). Other aspects of morphology show how words in sentences relate to one another, such as agreement between subjects and verbs (e.g., *The cat<u>s</u> were* … but not **The cat were* …) or between determiners and nouns in languages like French and Spanish (*el burro* but not *la burro*). Morphological marking is also used in many languages to identify a word's *case*, and this helps identify what grammatical and semantic roles a word is playing in a sentence. (English has very little case marking, but other languages, such as Russian, Finnish, and Hindi, make extensive use of case marking. In English, we mark most of our pronouns for case—as in *he* vs. *him*, *she* vs. *her*, *I* vs. *me*—but not other words.) Thus, to learn a language, a child must master its morphological system. Finally, phrase structure knowledge is an important aspect of child language-learning, because there are some ways of combining words that are consistent with the adult grammar, while many ways of combining words in longer expressions are possible but not consistent with the adult grammar.

For about the past two decades, the investigation of child language acquisition has been shaped by two general philosophies and theoretical frameworks. On the one hand, the *nativist approach* has assumed that an innate or instinctual *universal grammar* plays a central role in word category knowledge, as well as the acquisition of morphology and phrase structure knowledge (Chomsky, 1965; Pinker, 1994a; Wexler, 1998). That is, children are born with some of the knowledge that they will need to develop adult language skills already in place. Stephen Crain and his colleagues explain it like this (Crain, Goro, & Thornton, 2006, p. 31, emphasis mine):

> Children are born with a set of universal linguistic principles and a set of parameters *that account for variation among languages ... These innate linguistic parameters define a space of possible human languages—a space that the child explores, influenced by her environment, until she stabilizes on a grammar that is equivalent to that of adults in her linguistic community.*

One advantage of this approach is that it solves the poverty of the stimulus problem as it relates to category knowledge and phrase structure. Scientists working in the nativist tradition have argued that the input available to children is not sufficient for them to rapidly and accurately infer what the adult grammar allows because the language that children hear is full of fragments of phrases and sentences and false starts, which means they are exposed to ungrammatical expressions. Further, even if the input were in perfect agreement with the adult language, nativists argue that the input is consistent with more than one grammar, but that children nonetheless invariably adopt the one grammar on which the language is actually based.

On the other hand, recent developments in psychological research and mathematical modeling have led some scientists to conclude that there is no such thing as a universal grammar (Evans & Levinson, 2009), that children acquire linguistic knowledge gradually and in a piecemeal fashion rather than setting parameters (Theakston et al., 2002), that the input to children is more systematic than had been previously assumed (Huttenlocher, Vasilyeva, Waterfall, Vevea, & Hedges, 2007; Stoll et al., 2009), and that knowledge of word categories, morphology, and phrase structure can be learned by children even when the system is not "seeded" with pre-existing, innate knowledge (Redington & Chater, 1997; Westermann, Ruh, & Plunkett, 2009). These alternative viewpoints and models go by a number of different names—connectionism, subsymbolic computing, statistical learning, usage-based grammar, and so on. Let's keep things simple by lumping them together under the heading *probabilistic learning*, which emphasizes children's opportunistic use of many different sources of information to converge on likely solutions to complex learning problems, including the acquisition of first-language grammar. The following sections contrast the nativist and probabilistic learning approaches to category acquisition, morphology, and phrase structure.

Acquisition of word category knowledge

Language scientists are strongly divided on the question of where a child's knowledge of grammatical categories comes from. On the one hand, scientists following in the nativist tradition believe that knowledge of grammatical categories is innate (Chomsky, 1965;

Pinker, 1996). Specifically, children are born with knowledge of grammatical categories, such as *noun* and *verb*.[27] Exposure to language stimuli causes the child to populate her innate categories with specific words, and children exposed to different languages wind up with different sets of words and, depending on the input, different sets of categories. The categories are populated via a learning process called *semantic bootstrapping*. According to semantic bootstrapping, learning is based on the child's ability to distinguish between physical objects, actors (agents), and actions, independent of any linguistic labels for those concepts. The tricky bit, then, is for the child to line up names referring to different kinds of concepts (e.g., physical objects vs. actions) with different components of the linguistic system (e.g., nouns and verbs). Infants solve the category learning problem, by using "semantic notions as evidence for the presence of grammatical entities in the input" (Pinker, 1996, p. 40). Although this process may lead to the occasional error, the correlation between semantic characteristics and abstract grammatical categories is strong enough in child-directed speech so that a significant fraction of the child's early vocabulary will be assigned to the correct categories. The same learning procedures can cause the infant to acquire knowledge of other grammatical functions, such as which parts of sentences are subjects (e.g. *The baby*), which are argument-taking predicates (e.g., *ate*), which are objects (*the oatmeal*), and which are parts of prepositional phrases (e.g. *with the spoon*).

The chief controversy surrounding the nativist approach to category learning in general, and the semantic bootstrapping hypothesis in particular, is the idea that the infant comes prepackaged with significant amounts of linguistic knowledge. Especially controversial is the idea that the child's knowledge of word categories is essentially the same as the adult's categories. Alternative approaches in the probabilistic learning tradition have challenged the nativist account in two ways. First, they challenge the idea that children have fully abstract, generic categories of words, such as *noun*, before they have substantial experience with the language. As Eve Clark notes (2009, p. 167),

> *we tend to take for granted that [young children] are making use of adult-like word classes. But this assumption is far too strong. Even in such combinations as* hot + X *or* big + X, *where* X *is almost always a noun, this is not because children already have a category "noun" but because the meanings expressed by these patterns call for reference to an entity in the* X *slot.*

If children had an adult-like category of *noun*, then they should be willing and able to replace any noun with any other noun, as long as the resulting substitution leads to a meaningful, plausible sentence. However, in young children's spontaneous speech, they are very selective in the way they combine words. Rather than treating a word like *dog* as a member of a generic *noun* category, and therefore inserting that word in a variety of different appropriate locations, children start by combining such "nouns" with only a small number of verbs denoting a restricted range of actions. Similar effects are found with young children's use of verbs. While they are willing to add inflections to verbs that belong to some semantic classes (e.g., verbs that describe activities such as *run* or *play*), they are not willing to add inflections to verbs belonging to other semantic classes. If young children had a generic category of *verb*, and treated all members as fully interchangeable, then all verbs should be equally likely to be subject to inflections. Thus, it appears as though young children's categories are based more on concrete semantic properties (e.g., *person* vs. *animal*, *activity* vs. *state*) than on abstract grammatical properties (e.g., *X* can replace any other member of the category *X*, regardless of the specific meaning of an individual word; any procedure that can be done with one member of category *X* can be done to all members of category *X*).

Second, probabilistic learning proponents challenge the idea that innate, pre-existing knowledge is necessary for children to develop category knowledge. These accounts propose that the category structure that children develop reflects the kinds of language stimuli that the child is exposed to, and the likelihood of different words appearing in different contexts, rather than on a predetermined category structure (Elman, 1993; MacWhinney, 1998; Onnis, Waterfall, & Edelman, 2008; Waterfall, Sandbank, Onnis, & Edelman, 2010). To support these claims, probabilistic learning advocates have developed connectionist models that take as their input the kinds of simple sentences that are prevalent in child-directed speech. Their outputs vary. In some models, the output is the prediction of the next word in a sentence given a particular sentence fragment. In other models, the existence of grammatical categories is inferred on the basis of similarities between different sentences that contain the same words. An important feature of these models is that they do not need explicit feedback in order to learn the structure of the language that they are being exposed to. Children most often do not receive feedback or correction from caregivers when they make grammatical mistakes, and they typically ignore such correction when it occurs (Pinker, 1996). While it remains a very open question which of the available models, if any, most closely resembles the actual mental process by which young children acquire knowledge of word categories, the existence of such models shows that word categories can be inferred from the kinds of language that infants are exposed to, which undercuts the argument that category knowledge must necessarily be in place prior to the onset of language learning.

Acquisition of morphological knowledge

As noted above, morphology is a central component of a language's grammatical system. To organize the discussion, let's focus on an aspect of inflectional morphology that has received a lot of attention: the acquisition of tense marking on verbs in English. (Acquisition of morphological systems in other languages can be analyzed along the same lines of innate vs. acquired knowledge; e.g., Gerken, Wilson, & Lewis, 2005.) English verbs change from one form to another as tense and aspect change, and the specific form also depends on the person and number of the subject noun phrase. In the present tense, the verb *kick* appears as *kick* with a first-person singular subject noun (*I kick*), but as *kicks* with a third-person singular subject (*He kicks*). Regardless of the person and number of the subject noun, the past tense form is always *kicked* (*I/we/he kicked*). Many English verbs take the same suffix (*-ed*) in the past tense, but some don't. Adult English speakers say *I go*, but not, *I goed*. Instead, they say *I went*. Verbs like *go* are highly frequent in adult and child speech, and their morphological characteristics make them *irregular. Kick*, *block*, *tackle*, and *punt* are regular, because their past tense form is the stem plus the suffix *-ed. Sing*, *ring*, *think*, and *stink*, are irregular because none of them ends in *-ed* in the past tense.

The question is: How do children learn the past tense forms of verbs? One possibility is that they simply memorize the past tense form independently for each verb that they know. This hypothesis runs into trouble immediately on two grounds. First, if children need to hear the past tense form of a verb before they can use it, then they should have trouble coming up with past tense forms for new verbs. However, when children between 4 and 7 years old are given novel verbs, such as *trink*, and are asked to produce the past tense form, they do so easily, most often producing a regular past tense form, such as *trinked*, rather than the irregular analogue to the verb *think*, *trought* (Berko, 1958). Thus, after a certain amount of exposure to English, children appear to acquire a procedure that says: To form the past tense, add *-ed* to the present tense stem. Such productive ability shows that children know more than just memorized forms. The second problem is that, if children are memorizing past tense forms before they use them, then they should almost never make errors, because the language model that they are relying on for input will almost never have the wrong past tense form (i.e., adults speaking would almost never say *ringed* instead of *rang* or *thinked* instead of *thought*). While children in the early parts of the multi-word production stage, beginning around the age of 2, make almost no errors with irregular past tense verbs, over-using the regular form (e.g., saying *thinked* instead of *thought*) emerges during later stages of development (at about 3 years old for some children). Gradually, children learn to differentiate between regular past tense verbs and verbs that require special past tense forms. So, children producing forms that never appear in the input (*thinked, singed, goed*) in addition to producing regular past tense forms for verbs that they have never heard before shows that they are not just memorizing and repeating things that they hear.

To explain children's use of past tense forms, as well as other aspects of morphology (such as plural nouns and possessives), some theorists propose that children acquire a system of *words and rules* (Pinker, 2000). According to this account, infants begin by categorizing words. Early in development, the verb category is sparsely populated and children treat each individual verb as an independent entity. As they are exposed to more and more language, they recognize similarities between different versions of the same verb (*kick* and *kicked, tickle* and *tickled*), and they develop an insight: the past tense can be generated from the present tense form by a rule (add *-ed*). After they have this insight, they apply the rule willy-nilly and all verbs, even the irregular ones, are subjected to the add *-ed* treatment. This over-application of the rule, or *over-regularization*, causes children to make errors until they create a separate list in long-term memory of irregular verb forms. Thus, the mature past tense production system consists of two components. One is a rule-based system that says "look up the present tense stem and add *-ed*." The other is a list of exception words that needs to be searched any time a past tense verb is produced. The list of exception verbs is compiled as children are exposed to a sufficient number of examples of each exception verb. The words-and-rules account explains why children have a "u-shaped" learning curve for past tense morphology. They start out correctly copying independently memorized forms, they make errors once they have sufficient experience to notice and overuse a rule that relates past tense and present tense forms of verbs, and finally they compile a list of past tense verbs that don't play by the rules, eliminating over-regularization errors.

Proponents of the probabilistic learning approach have challenged the words-and-rules formulation on a number of different grounds and this facet of development continues to keep language scientists awake long into the night (Joanisse & Seidenberg, 1999; Seidenberg & Joanisse, 2003). Part of the problem revolves around the description of how, exactly, children behave as they are learning to produce past tense forms for verbs. While the words-and-rules approach argues for the sudden onset of over-regularization, consistent with sudden insight into the existence of a rule, the actual data may not support this claim. First, studies of child language development are often plagued by sparse data problems. That is, very few children are studied, those who are studied are often the children of academic linguists (who have the motivation to keep the necessary detailed records, but who may be subject to certain observational biases), and many studies sample a very small fraction of the child's total language output. Even worse, the context in which the child is speaking often goes unrecorded, as does the overall ambient language that the specific child is exposed to. This problem is particularly acute when the critical question concerns how suddenly a child begins to apply a rule. On that account, the child should go from having a mixture of regular and irregular forms, because production will be based on repeating memorized input, to essentially 100% regular forms once the rule kicks in, after which there should be a gradual decline in the overall proportion of regular forms as the irregular forms once again assert themselves in the child's output. When real children's output is examined, they appear to start out marking only some verbs using the regular past tense, and only gradually increase their use of the regular past tense (McClelland & Patterson, 2002). Probabilistic learning advocates have also noted that, rather than being applied across the board, regularization of past tense verbs occurs more often in some semantic contexts than others, and more often in some phonological contexts than others. All of these phenomena pose problems for the words-and-rules approach. Nonetheless, we might still favor this approach if there were no plausible alternatives. However, as with the development of word category knowledge, proponents of the probabilistic learning framework have developed a number of connectionist models of English past tense morphology (Joanisse & Seidenberg, 1999; McClelland & Patterson, 2002; McClelland & Rumelhart, 1985). These models have the advantage of capturing the u-shaped pattern of acquisition that normally developing children exhibit.. They have the additional advantage of applying over a wider scope than the words-and-rules formulation. For example, implemented connectionist models can be used to predict children's responses to novel verbs in different phonological and semantic contexts as well as explaining morphological errors in selective language impairment (SLI).

Acquisition of phrase structure knowledge

An acquisition theory that faces occasional counterexamples is better than no acquisition theory at all.
STEVEN PINKER

Phrases exist so that components of events can be tied to linguistic elements that convey who did what to whom. Different languages combine words in different ways, and they use different forms to mark agents, patients, instruments, and other role-players in events. A child learning a language must discover the way phrases are organized in order to convey thoughts relating to events. Eve Clark (2009, p. 158), summarizes the challenge infants face in this way:

> *Children who wish to talk about events need to be able to analyze what they observe to decompose scenes into constituent parts relevant to linguistic expressions in the language they happen to be learning. They have to work out ... how to talk about agent versus patient, location versus instrument, or beneficiary versus recipient. They must find out how to mark grammatical relations such as subject and object. And they must also learn how to indicate that the elements in a constituent (a noun phrase or predicate for instance) belong together, through agreement, adjacency, or both, depending on the language.*

As with other aspects of grammar learning, nativist and probabilistic learning approaches make competing claims about how and why children acquire the skills they need to organize words into phrases that conform to the standard imposed by the adult language.

The nativist approach to phrase structure learning argues that the basic knowledge children need to combine words into phrases is present in latent form at birth in the form of *parameters*. Basic word order—whether you produce your subjects before your verbs, or your verbs before your subjects—varies across languages. Thus, there is no pre-existing parameter that says "put your subjects at the beginning of your sentences," but there *is* a pre-existing parameter that says "subjects either come before verbs or after." It is up to the individual infant, armed with this knowledge, to pay attention to the ambient language and figure out how their own particular language relates its subjects to its verbs. Other language characteristics are also argued to be governed by parameters. For example, English requires subjects to be expressed in the verbatim form of a sentence (e.g., *He ate bananas*), even if the subject is a semantically null place-holder (as in *It rained*). Other languages, such as Italian, allow sentences to have an implicit subject. *Ate bananas* would be OK in Italian, as long as context makes it clear who the eater is, but that sentence is not OK in English. The infant learner of Italian sets the "pro-drop" parameter one way; the infant learner of English sets it a different way. According to the nativist theoretician, languages differ from one another because the overall set of parameters takes on different settings for different languages (in addition to arbitrary differences in vocabulary).

One prominent nativist account (Pinker, 1996) proposes that children have considerable knowledge of phrase structure formation very early on, even when they are just beginning to produce utterances that have more than one word in them. Note that the phrase structure rules that children are claimed to possess are essentially identical to the rules that adults have. This claim of equivalence between the child and adult grammars goes by the name the *continuity hypothesis*, which emphasizes the hypothetical similarity of child and adult linguistic knowledge. Examples of this grammatical knowledge are that sentences have subject noun phrases and verbs, that verb phrases consist of a verb and an object noun, and that noun phrases can consist of possessives, adjectives, and quantifying modifiers (e.g., *my shoe*, *big shoe*, and *some shoes*, respectively; other phrase structure rules are also argued to be in place). A grammar that contains rules such as these will be capable of producing the kinds of utterances that are seen early on in the two-word stage, such as *Mommy fix* (sentence = NP + VP), *mama dress* (NP = adjective + noun), and *more milk* (NP = quantifier + noun). One complication for such an account is that, while many utterances produced by young children are grammatical according to the adult grammar, some are not. For instance, young children do not always include the grammatical morpheme *to* when they produce sentences that require it. So, they say **I want hold Postman Pat* instead of *I want <u>to</u> hold Postman Pat* (Kirjavainen, Theakston, Lieven, & Tomasello, 2009). Thus, it is possible that the child version of the relevant phrase structure rule is that V (infinitival) = infinitival verb + noun, rather than VP = <u>to</u> + infinitival verb + noun. Pinker argues that this explanation of the child's production patterns is unsatisfactory because the child will never encounter evidence that this rule is incorrect, and so there should be adults running around saying things like *I want go Denny's*, or *I need talk my lawyer get the charges dropped*.

In contrast with the nativist account of phrase structure knowledge, probabilistic learning theorists contend that learning phrase structure rules, like learning other aspects of language, results from children analyzing the input to which they are exposed. This conclusion is supported by observations that children acquire knowledge of some phrase structure types gradually (parameter-setting predicts sudden onset of phrase structure knowledge) and that children's spontaneous language production mirrors the frequency with which sequences of words occur in language addressed to children (Kirjavainen et al., 2009; Marchman, Bates, Burkhardt, & Good, 1991). For example, verbs that require the grammatical morpheme *to* when they appear in verb-to-verb sequences (e.g., *want to dance*) can often appear in constructions without the word *to* (e.g., *want ice cream*). If children do not have the adult phrase structure rule (infinitival verb = verb + *to* + verb), but instead construct *schemas* by paying attention to what precedes and follows a specific verb, such as *want*, then they will notice that the verb *want* sometimes is followed by *to*, but sometimes is not. The idea that children learn about phrase structure on a verb-by-verb basis predicts that their production patterns should correlate with the way their caregivers talk. In fact, children who make more production errors (e.g., saying *I want hold Postman Pat*) are those children who frequently hear verbs like *want* in sentences that do not have the word *to* in them (e.g., *I want ice cream*, *Polly wants a cracker*). The ease with which children learn to use new verbs and new syntactic structures also corresponds to the frequency with which particular phrase structures appear in the input (Abbot-Smith & Tomasello, 2010; Casenhiser & Goldberg, 2005).

Findings that errors correlate with input have motivated some theorists to favor the *usage-based grammar* account of phrase structure learning (Kidd, Lieven, & Tomasello, 2010; Lany, Gomez, & Gerken, 2007; McClure, Pine, & Lieven, 2006; Tomasello, 2000). According to this account, phrase structure acquisition is closely tied to the acquisition of individual verbs. That is, rather than developing a general phrase structure rule, such as "a verb phrase is a verb plus a noun phrase," young children first learn how individual verbs behave, and only gradually form larger abstract classes of verbs by noticing that different verbs behave in similar ways.[28] Once these larger classes of verbs have been formed, children can then develop the idea that some phrase structure patterns occur repeatedly in the language, and therefore develop a more abstract notion of what phrase structures can look like in the language as a whole. The usage-based account makes a number of predictions that can be evaluated by observing how young children speak. The usage-based grammar hypothesis predicts that, because children are paying attention to how individual verbs behave, they will be conservative in the way they use newly acquired verbs. That is, they will be unlikely to use a verb to express a particular phrase structure unless they have heard somebody else use that verb with that phrase structure. For example, if children hear the sentence *Mommy drank*, which has a subject argument only, they will be unlikely to say *Mommy drank the milk*, which has both a subject and object argument. Lacking a phrase structure rule that says "a verb phrase can be a verb plus a noun phrase," young children are reluctant to add an object noun phrase to *drank* until they have positive evidence that the language allows that to happen. In fact, young children between 2 and 3 years old are conservative in just this way (Lieven, Pine, & Baldwin, 1997). Children in this age range are even willing to violate the general word order that the adult grammar dictates (e.g., subject–verb–object), but only for low-frequency verbs or verbs that they have not been exposed to previously, if an adult speaker models the strange word order (Chan, Meints, Lieven, & Tomasello, 2010). Children are also more likely to correct ungrammatical phrase structures when the ungrammatical phrase structure contains a familiar verb (Matthews, Lieven, Theakston, & Tomasello, 2007). Even complicated phrase structures, such as the embedded sentence structure in *I think Mommy drank the milk* (sentence = sentence + embedded sentence, embedded sentence = noun phrase + verb phrase, verb phrase = verb + noun phrase) depend on the acquisition of specific verbs. In this instance, children's use of the embedded sentence phrase structure is driven almost entirely by their acquisition of the verb *think* (Kidd et al., 2010), which appears very frequently accompanied by an embedded sentence in the language that young children hear. These findings, and others, suggest that young children's knowledge of phrase structure is intimately connected to individual verbs that the child knows, rather than being fully abstract. As with acquisition of word category and morphological knowledge, usage-based theorists have developed mathematical models that acquire phrase structure knowledge as the result of exposure to samples of child-directed speech (Bannard, Lieven, & Tomasello, 2009).

Summary and Conclusions

Language learners face difficult tasks as they try to acquire a first language. They must take a stimulus that comes at them in huge blocks and break it down into manageable chunks. They must learn to associate each bite-sized chunk with some sort of meaning. Neither of these tasks is trivial. Both involve the child deploying a lot of mental firepower to overcome substantial obstacles, such as the segmentation and poverty of the stimulus problems. Fortunately, the child gets an early start, as learning about prosodic features of the native language begins in the third trimester, well before the baby is born. Infants also appear to be endowed with perceptual and representational skills that enable them to tell the difference between different speech sounds from the moment they are born (or at most, within the first 24–48 hours). Knowledge of the prosodic characteristics of utterances represents at least a plausible mechanism for infants to break into the speech stream and start identifying words. Children as young as 2 months old can tell the difference between phonetically identical utterances that have different prosodic qualities. While it may take infants some time to figure out all the details of the prosodic system, infants are capable of using prosodic cues to segment (and remember) words out of fluent utterances by 7½ months old. Characteristics of infant-directed speech appear to be particularly well suited to help infants make use of prosodic cues to word boundaries. Words that are spoken in isolation also appear early on in infants' vocabularies, and so infants may rely to some degree on caregivers doing the segmenting for them some of the time.

Once infants have begun to amass a vocabulary of familiar words, they can use the boundaries of those familiar words to mark out the edges of unfamiliar words. In fact, infants as young as 6 months old appear to use such a "top-down" strategy. Infants also appear to use statistical likelihood information. Infants as young as 6 months old can use the likelihood of one syllable following another to segment word-like units out of a continuous speech stream. We know for sure that infants have a set of tools that is up to the task of segmenting speech; whether language scientists have identified all the tools, or the right set of tools remains an open question.

Infants use another set of tools to assign meanings to words. They need these tools because the environment does not uniquely specify which meanings go with which words. Infants and young children, however, bring to the task a powerful set of perceptual abilities (for example, object recognition comes to the language-learning domain essentially for free) as well as a powerful set of social-cognitive abilities. Point-and-say leverages infants' object recognition abilities. When you point at a rabbit in the grass, you can be certain that the infant will appreciate that the rabbit is a coherent object, separate from its surroundings. Combine the infant's object recognition skills with a bias to interpret new words as whole-object labels, and *gavagai* becomes *rabbit*. But there is much more to word learning than point-and-say. Children appear to understand without being taught that other people have different knowledge and perspectives on events, and that private knowledge and perspectives will affect the way speakers behave. Thus, children can figure out where adults are focusing their attention, and they can flavor their interpretations of utterances accordingly (in Bloom's terms, infants and young children are pretty good mindreaders). But, as with the point-and-say game, children are not slaves to joint attention. Young children (3–4 years old) can view the world from a speaker's perspective, and use inferences about that perspective to assign meanings to novel words. Once children have acquired some basic knowledge about the grammar and syntax of their native language, they can add this knowledge to the toolkit and use it to infer the meanings of novel verbs. As with segmentation, we know that children solve the poverty of the stimulus problem for word meanings. We have some good hypotheses about what those tools are, and research continues to further refine and develop these hypotheses.

Young children begin to string words together into multi-word utterances starting about age 2. To create multi-word utterances that are consistent with adult language standards, children must identify word categories, the morphological markings that go along with different semantic and syntactic functions, and the patterns that govern how words can be put together into phrases and clauses. The nativist approach argues that much of this knowledge is innate. In particular, nativists propose that word category and phrase structure knowledge are in place prior to the onset of language learning. This approach has the advantage of offering a straightforward answer to the poverty of the stimulus problem. Probabilistic learning advocates explicitly deny the existence of innate word category, morphological, and phrase structure knowledge. To support their position, they have presented modeling data showing that word category and morphological knowledge can be acquired as a by-product of unsupervised learning processes. They have also challenged predictions made by the nativist position, specifically that young children will apply phrase structure rules suddenly and broadly once the appropriate parameters are set. When actual children are observed, they appear to master morphological and phrase structure knowledge more gradually than had been previously assumed. In addition, knowledge of phrase structures appears to be closely tied to individual words, especially verbs. Phrase structure knowledge also appears to differ in strength across different verbs, with strength being closely associated with patterns that occur in the language that the child hears.

TEST YOURSELF

1. Explain how prenatal infants can acquire knowledge about language. What aspects of language do they learn and why? How might this knowledge pave the way for postnatal development?
2. Describe a typical HAS experiment. What do the results indicate about infant language skills?
3. What do we know about newborn infants' phonological perception abilities? What role does innate knowledge play? What evidence favors or challenges the idea that infant phonological perception depends on species-specific biological mechanisms?
4. How does an infant's ability to perceive phonological contrasts change as the infant matures? What accounts for these changes?
5. Describe the segmentation problem and explain how children solve it. What role does prosody play? What role does statistical learning play?
6. Describe infant-directed speech and explain how it affects the acquisition of language skills. What happens when an infant's caregiver is depressed? What happens in cultures where adults do not produce infant-directed speech?
7. How do infants and young children learn the meanings of words? What role does "point-and-say" play? How do children overcome the poverty of the stimulus problem? What role do categorization biases play? What role does (non-linguistic) conceptual knowledge play?
8. Describe two competing accounts explaining the acquisition of grammar and the evidence that supports each. Who has the better case, the nativists or the probabilistic learning theorists? Why?

THINK ABOUT IT

1. How is it possible for blind children to acquire vocabulary? How do you think their vocabulary acquisition process compares to sighted children? How do you think it compares to deaf children?
2. Design an experiment to see whether your friends can learn a new language via statistical learning. Hint: You could use Saffran's fake syllable method. Can your friends identify the "words" in your fake language if you expose them to those "words" the way Saffran exposed babies to new "words"?

Notes

1 Although in some experiments, the baby is rewarded for sucking less frequently than baseline (e.g., DeCasper & Fifer, 1980).

2 Steve Pinker has suggested that humans and chinchillas develop categorical perception of speech sounds for different reasons and via different perceptual mechanisms. Human infants demonstrate categorical perception after one or two training trials. Chinchillas and quail can require hundreds or thousands of training trials before they demonstrate similar ability. While this objection may apply to categorical perception in non-human animals, it does not apply to findings of categorical perception in humans of non-speech sounds.

3 To learn about aspiration, hold your hand an inch or so in front of your mouth and say the words *pill* and *spill*. When you say the word *pill*, the /p/ sound is aspirated. You can feel the burst of air right after you start saying *pill*. When you say the word *spill*, there is no aspiration, and you should feel much less air moving after the /p/ sound in *spill*.

4 See Pardo & Remez (2006) for arguments against this proposal.

5 7½-month-olds can also do this trick in reverse. If they are trained on short sentences and later tested on isolated words, they can recognize individual words that were presented as part of the fluent-speech training stimulus (see Jusczyk & Aslin, 1995, Experiment 4).

6 The metaphor is that of "pulling yourself up by your own bootstraps," because babies have to learn how to segment the speech stream all by themselves. No one can teach them how to do it, because you can't take verbal instruction before you know how to identify words. Ignore the fact that pulling yourself up by your own bootstraps is, in fact, physically impossible.

7 Some may object that it is a huge leap to assume that infants could develop such a hypothesis spontaneously (i.e., that babies are dumb). But given the current state of research on infant cognition, we have to at least consider the possibility that babies are smart.

8 This experiment takes advantage of the ERP component called a *mismatch negativity*. In experiments where people are repeatedly exposed to one kind of stimulus (e.g., iambic word) called the *standard*, and are *in*frequently exposed to a different stimulus (e.g., trochaic word) called the *deviant*, the ERP signal shows a negative-going change in voltage measured at the scalp about 200 ms after the onset of the deviant stimulus. Because the ERP wave occurs in response to a stimulus that is different than, or does not match, the more commonly occurring stimulus, researchers call this a mismatch negativity.

9 They *might* want to segment it as *Thisp lace*, though, because some English words do end in /sp/ (as in *clasp*, *grasp*, and *wasp*), and some end in /isp/ (as in *crisp*). So, in this case, phonotactics, by itself, does not lead to one unique, correct segmentation.

10 That is, their output becomes more accurate faster.

11 At least in the industrialized world. Adults in some cultures do not react to babies in this way. Still, the equivalent of infant-direct speech has been observed in China (Mandarin), France, Germany, Italy, Japan, the United Kingdom, and the United States (Cooper & Aslin, 1990).

12 Some would say for the worse.

13 Males also speak motherese to infants, but the name sticks because females still do the bulk of child rearing in places where motherese is spoken.

14 One more reason why mothers with symptoms of postnatal depression should seek professional help.

15 Similar differences in transitional probabilities between phonemes occur within and between syllables. The transitional probability of a /gp/ sequence within a syllable is essentially zero in English. **igp* and **gpi* are both

blocked by phonotactic rules. But the sequence /gp/ can occur in a word, so long as the /g/ sound ends one syllable and the /p/ sound starts the next (as in *pigpen*). In this case, the transitional probability of a phoneme sequence is *higher* between units (syllables) than within units. Thus, the absolute value of a transitional probability need not determine whether people use that information to identify important units of speech. The learner could use higher probability sequences of syllables to group them together, but use higher probability sequences of phonemes to split syllables apart (Seidenberg & McClelland, 1989).

16 The Achilles heel of this approach is what I call the *Superhero* effect. Consider Batman/Bruce Wayne, Superman/Clark Kent, Wonder Woman/Lynda Carter, and Catwoman/Beyoncé Knowles. The two halves of each pair are never seen together, but we know they are the same person (because we saw the movie or read the comic books). A similar situation occurs in language. The /s/ morpheme (as in *cats*) and the /z/ morpheme (as in *dogs*) are in *complementary distribution*: They occur in completely different contexts. But we know that they are the outward manifestations of the same underlying linguistic construct: plural marker. We recognize the similarity (*cats* = more than one cat; *dogs* = more than one dog), even though a straightforward statistical analysis would show that the two forms never co-occur, and therefore should be treated as conceptually separate.

17 A transitional probability of 1.0 means that the first syllable is always followed by the same second syllable. A transitional probability of .33 means that the first syllable is followed by a particular syllable a third of the time.

18 The anthropologists inform us that not all cultures play this game. Apparently, the İKung San do not.

19 There are exceptions to the rule. We individuate familiar people and animals. So if you see a picture of your friend, you don't say *person*, you say *Shelley*. Similarly, if the picture was your pet dog, you wouldn't say, *dog*, you would say *Fido*. This constraint also applies in reverse. If you see a picture of a person and a chair and someone says, *That's Linda*, you assume that the label goes with the person, not the chair. That's why it's funny when George Carlin names his vibrating chair *Linda* in *Scary Movie 3*.

20 Shape bias can be overridden in special circumstances. Children group together objects that have similar functions (are used to accomplish the same goal), whether the two objects are physically similar or not (Kemler-Nelson, 1999).

21 Some instances of apparent overextension may not really be errors. If a child looks at a dog and says *kitty*, it does not mean that the child is mistaking the meaning of the word *kitty* or misidentifying the dog as a cat. The child might simply want us to notice the similarity between dogs and cats, but does not yet have the right vocabulary to express that thought. Babies are smart, so this could really happen.

22 This is somewhat more complicated that it seems. Children develop concepts from directly perceiving the world, in addition to having some innate ideas about how the world works. But languages divide up conceptual space in different ways, and assign words to concepts in different patterns. In English, the word *fit* describes a broad range of containment relations. If one thing goes inside another, we say that they *fit*, regardless of whether it's an arm in a sleeve, a key in a lock, or a peanut in a mason jar. But Korean uses different terms to indicate a loose fit and a tight fit. So, English-speaking and Korean-speaking infants are faced with different perceptual problems. The Korean language learner, but not the English one, has to pay attention to how tightly two objects join to select the right word (Hespos & Spelke, 2004). Further, the Korean speaker may notice relationships between objects that the English speaker does not perceive as a result of needing to select between competing versions of *fit* (see Chapter 1).

23 That does not mean that children *consciously* engage in logical deduction to infer word meanings. But it does mean that the thought process that underlies vocabulary acquisition factors in a variety of sources of information, including those that are made available by the child's theory of mind.

24 This cue can not be sufficient by itself, however, as many nouns also end in *-ing*, and many words are ambiguous between noun and verb meanings, as in *spring* (noun vs. verb; *coiled metal* vs. *jump*) and *stinging* (verb vs. adjective).

25 This could happen because babies are smart.

26 Prosodic cues may also play a role in bootstrapping syntactic knowledge. Prosodic cues such as pauses and particular tone patterns often appear between important syntactic components, such as phrases and clauses (Jusczyk, 1997; Speer & Blodgett, 2006). Although the correspondences are not perfect, they are consistent enough to provide cues to important syntactic boundaries. Research shows that infants are sensitive to these cues, as they will listen longer to fluent speech that has pauses and other prosodic cues inserted between syntactic constituents than to speech where the prosodic cues are misaligned with the syntax (Jusczyk et al., 1992; Jusczyk & Kemler-Nelson, 1996). IDS may enable infants to pick up on syntax–prosody correspondences at an earlier age. For example, 9-month-olds are only sensitive to prosody–syntax correspondences in utterances that have IDS prosody, and do not respond to manipulations of prosody–syntax correspondences in adult-directed speech.

27 The innate component of linguistic knowledge includes more than just word categories. "The child is assumed to know, prior to acquiring a language, the overall structure of the grammar, the formal nature of the different sorts of rules it contains, and the primitives from which those rules may be composed" (Pinker, 1996, p. 31).

28 Artificial grammar learning experiments also support the idea that children start with narrow assumptions about what the language allows, and switch to broader generalizations when positive evidence for such generalizations appears in the input (Gerken, 2006, 2010; Gerken & Bollt, 2008).

References

Abbot-Smith, K., & Tomasello, M. (2010). The influence of frequency and semantic similarity on how children learn grammar. *First Language, 30,* 79–101.

Aguiar, A., & Baillargeon, R. (1999). 2.5 month-old infants' reasoning about when objects should and should not be occluded. *Cognitive Psychology, 39,* 116–157.

Baldwin, D. A., Markman, E. M., Bill, B., Desjardins, R. N., Irwin, R. N., & Tidball, G. (1996). Infants' reliance on a social criterion for establishing word-object relations. *Child Development, 67,* 3135–3153.

Bannard, C., Lieven, E. V. M., & Tomasello, M. (2009). Modeling children's early grammatical knowledge. *Proceedings of the National Academy of Sciences of the United States, 106,* 17284–17289.

Berko, J. (1958). The child's learning of English morphology. *Word, 14,* 150–177.

Birch, S. A. J., & Bloom, P. (2002). Preschoolers are sensitive to the speaker's knowledge when learning proper names. *Child Development, 73,* 434–444.

Birch, S. A. J., Vauthier, S. A., & Bloom, P. (2008). Three- and four-year olds spontaneously use others' past performance to guide their learning. *Cognition, 107,* 1018–1034.

Bloom, P. (2000). *How children learn the meanings of words.* Cambridge, MA: MIT Press.

Bornstein, M. H., Cote, L. R., Maital, S., Painter, K., Park, S., Pascual, L., et al. (2004). Cross-linguistic analysis of vocabulary in young children: Spanish, Dutch, French, Hebrew, Italian, Korean, and American English. *Child Development, 75,* 1115–1139.

Bortfeld, H., Morgan, J. L., Golinkoff, R. M., & Rathbun, K. (2005). Mommy and me: Familiar names help launch babies into speech-stream segmentation. *Psychological Science, 16,* 298–304.

Brent, M. R., & Siskind, J. M. (2001). The role of exposure to isolated words in early vocabulary development. *Cognition, 81,* B33–B44.

Brown, R. W. (1957). Linguistic determinism and the part of speech. *Journal of Abnormal and Social Psychology, 55,* 1–5.

Caselli, C., Casadio, P., & Bates, E. (1999). A comparison of the transition from first words to grammar in English and Italian. *Journal of Child Language, 26,* 69–111.

Casenhiser, D., & Goldberg, A. E. (2005). Fast mapping between a phrasal form and meaning. *Developmental Science, 8,* 500–508.

Chambers, K. E., Onishi, K. H., & Fisher, C. (2003). Infants learn phonotactic regularities from brief auditory experience. *Cognition, 87,* B69–B77.

Chan, A., Meints, K., Lieven, E. V. M., & Tomasello, M. (2010). Young children's comprehension of English SVO word order revisited: Testing the same children in act-out and intermodal preferential looking tasks. *Cognitive Development, 25,* 30–45.

Chomsky, N. (1965). *Aspects of the theory of syntax.* Cambridge, MA: MIT Press.

Chomsky, N. (1981). *Lectures on government and binding.* Berlin, Germany: Mouton de Gruyter.

Christiansen, M. H., Allen, J., & Seidenberg, M. S. (1998). Learning to segment speech using multiple cues: A connectionist model. *Language and Cognitive Processes, 13,* 221–268.

Clark, E. (2009). *First language acquisition* (2nd ed.). Cambridge, England: Cambridge University Press.

Cooper, R. P., & Aslin, R. N. (1990). Preference for infant-directed speech in the first month after birth. *Child Development, 61,* 1584–155.

Cooper, R. P., & Aslin, R. N. (1994). Developmental differences in infant attention to the spectral properties of infant-directed speech. *Child Development, 65,* 1663–1677.

Crain, S., Goro, T., & Thornton, R. (2006). Language acquisition is language change. *Journal of Psycholinguistic Research, 35,* 31–49.

Cutler, A. (1996). Prosody and the word boundary problem. In J. L. Morgan & K. Demuth (Eds.), *Signal to syntax* (pp. 87–100). Mahwah, NJ: Erlbaum.

Cutler, A., & Norris, D. G. (1988). The role of strong syllables in segmentation for lexical access. *Journal of Experimental Psychology: Human Perception and Performance, 14,* 113–121.

Cutting, J. E., & Rosner, B. S. (1974). Categories and boundaries in speech and music. *Perception and Psychophysics, 16,* 564–571.

DeCasper, A. J., & Fifer, W. (1980). Of human bonding: Newborns prefer their mothers' voices. *Science, 208,* 1174–1176.

DeCasper, A. J., Lecanuet, J., Busnel, M., Granier-Deferre, C., & Maugeais, R. (1994). Fetal reactions to recurrent maternal speech. *Infant Behavior and Development, 17,* 159–164.

DeCasper, A. J., & Spence, M. J. (1986). Prenatal maternal speech influences newborns' perception of speech sounds. *Infant Behavior and Development, 9,* 133–150.

Dehaene-Lambertz, G., & Dehaene, S. (1994). Speed and cerebral correlates of syllable discrimination in infants. *Nature, 370,* 292–295.

Dittmar, M., Abbot-Smith, K., Lieven, E., & Tomasello, M. (2008). Young children's early syntactic competence: A preferential looking study. *Developmental Science, 11,* 575–582.

Eimas, P. D., Siqueland, E. R., Jusczyk, P., & Vigorito, J. (1971). Speech perception in infants. *Science, 171,* 303–306.

Elman, J. L. (1993). Learning and development in neural networks: The importance of starting small. *Cognition, 48,* 71–99.

Evans, N., & Levinson, S. C. (2009). With diversity in mind: Freeing the language sciences from Universal Grammar. *Behavioral and Brain Sciences, 32,* 472–484.

Fernald, A., & Hurtado, N. (2006). Names in frames: Infants interpret words in sentence frames faster than words in isolation. *Developmental Science, 9,* F33–F40.

Fernald, A., & Mazzie, C. (1991). Prosody and focus in speech to infants and adults. *Developmental Psychology, 27,* 209–221.

Fernald, A., & Morikawa, H. (1993). Common themes and cultural variations in Japanese and American mothers' speech to infants. *Child Development, 64,* 637–656.

Fernald, A., Perfors, A., & Marchman, V. A. (2006). Picking up speed in understanding: Speech processing efficiency and vocabulary growth across the 2nd year. *Developmental Psychology, 42,* 98–116.

Fernald, A., Swingley, D., & Pinto, J. P. (2001). When half a word is enough: Infants can recognize spoken words using partial phonetic information. *Child Development, 72,* 1003–1015.

Fisher, C. (1996). Structural limits on verb mapping: The role of analogy in children's interpretations of sentences. *Cognitive Psychology, 31,* 41–81.

Fisher, C. (2002). Structural limits on verb mapping: The role of abstract structure in 2.5-year-olds' interpretations of novel verbs. *Developmental Science, 5,* 55–64.

Fisher, C., Gleitman, H., & Gleitman, L. R. (1991). On the semantic content of subcategorization frames. *Cognitive Psychology, 23,* 331–392.

Fisher, C., Hunt, C., & Chambers, K. (2001). Abstraction and specificity in preschoolers' representations of novel spoken words. *Journal of Memory and Language, 45,* 665–687.

Gerken, L. (2006). Decisions, decisions: Infant language learning when multiple generalizations are possible. *Cognition, 98,* B67–B74.

Gerken, L. (2010). Infants use rational decision criteria for choosing among models of their input. *Cognition, 115,* 362–366.

Gerken, L., & Aslin, R. N. (2005). Thirty years of research on infant speech perception: The legacy of Peter W. Jusczyk. *Language Learning and Language Development, 1,* 5–21.

Gerken, L., & Bollt, A. (2008). Three exemplars allow at least some linguistic generalizations: Implications for generalization mechanisms and constraints. *Language Learning and Development, 4,* 228–248.

Gerken, L., Wilson, R., & Lewis, W. (2005). Infants can use distributional cues to form syntactic categories. *Journal of Child Language, 32,* 249–268.

Gleitman, L. R. (1990). The structural sources of verb meanings. *Language Acquisition, 1,* 3–55.

Gleitman, L. R., & Gleitman, H. (1997). What is language made out of? *Lingua, 100,* 29–55.

Göksun, T., Küntay, A. C., & Naigles, L. R. (2008). Turkish children use morphosyntactic bootstrapping in interpreting verb meaning. *Journal of Child Language, 35,* 291–323.

Graf-Estes, K., Evans, J. L., Alibaldi, M. W., & Saffran, J. R. (2007). Can infants map meaning to newly segmented words? *Psychological Science, 18,* 254–260.

Hespos, S. J., Ferry, A. L., & Rips, L. J. (2009). Five-month-old infants have different expectations for solids and liquids. *Psychological Science, 20,* 603–611.

Hespos, S. J., & Spelke, E. S. (2004). Conceptual precursors to language. *Nature, 430,* 453–456.

Hohne, E., & Jusczyk, P. W. (1994). Two-month-old infants' sensitivity to allophonic differences. *Perception and Psychophysics, 56,* 613–623.

Houston, D. M., Jusczyk, P. W., Kuijpers, C., Coolen, R., & Cutler, A. (2000). Cross-language word segmentation by 9-month olds. *Psychonomic Bulletin & Review, 7,* 504–509.

Hurtado, N., Marchman, V. A., & Fernald, A. (2007). Spoken word recognition by Latino children learning Spanish as their first language. *Journal of Child Language, 33,* 227–249.

Huttenlocher, J., Vasilyeva, M., Waterfall, H. R., Vevea, J. L., & Hedges, L. V. (2007). The varieties of speech to young children. *Developmental Psychology, 43,* 1062–1083.

Izard, V., Sann, C., Spelke, E. S., & Streri, A. (2009). Newborn infants perceive abstract numbers. *Proceedings of the National Academy of Sciences, 106,* 10382–10385.

Joanisse, M. F., & Seidenberg, M. S. (1999). Impairments in verb morphology following brain injury: A connectionist model. *Proceedings of the National Academy of Sciences, 96,* 7592–7597.

Jusczyk, P. W. (1997). *The discovery of spoken language.* Cambridge, MA: MIT Press.

Jusczyk, P. W., & Aslin, R. N. (1995). Infants' detection of the sound patterns of words in fluent speech. *Cognitive Psychology, 29,* 1–23.

Jusczyk, P. W., & Bertoncini, J. (1988). Viewing the development of speech perception as an innately guided learning process. *Language and Speech, 31,* 217–238.

Jusczyk, P. W., Friederici, A. D., Wessels, J. M., Svenkerud, V. Y., & Jusczyk, A. M. (1993). Infants' sensitivity to the sound patterns of native language words. *Journal of Memory and Language, 32,* 402–420.

Jusczyk, P. W., Hirsch-Pasek, K., Kemler-Nelson, D. G., Kennedy, L. J., Woodward, A., & Piwoz, J. (1992). Perception of the acoustic correlates of major phrasal units by young infants. *Cognitive Psychology, 24,* 252–293.

Jusczyk, P. W., & Hohne, E. A. (1997). Infants' memory for spoken words. *Science, 277,* 1984–1986.

Jusczyk, P. W., Houston, D. M., & Newsome, M. (1999). The beginnings of word segmentation in English-learning infants. *Cognitive Psychology, 39,* 159–207.

Jusczyk, P. W., & Kemler-Nelson, D. G. (1996). Syntactic units, prosody, and psychological reality during infancy. In J. L. Morgan & K. Demuth (Eds.), *Signal to syntax* (pp. 389–410). Mahwah, NJ: Erlbaum.

Jusczyk, P. W., Luce, P. A., & Charles-Luce, J. (1994). Infants' sensitivity to phonotactic patterns in the native language. *Journal of Memory and Language, 33,* 630–645.

Jusczyk, P. W., Pisoni, D. B., Walley, A. C., & Murray, J. (1980). Discrimination of the relative onset time of two-component tones by infants. *Journal of the Acoustical Society of America, 67,* 262–270.

Jusczyk, P. W., Rosner, B. S., Cutting, J. E., Foard, C. F., & Smith, L. B. (1977). Categorical perception of nonspeech sounds by 2-month old infants. *Perception and Psychophysics, 21,* 50–54.

Kaplan, P. S., Bachorowski, J., Smoski, M. J., & Hudenko, W. J. (2002). Infants of depressed mothers, although competent learners, fail to learn in response to their own mothers' infant-directed speech. *Psychological Science, 13,* 268–271.

Kemler-Nelson, D. G. (1999). Attention to functional properties in toddler's naming and problem-solving. *Cognitive Development, 14,* 77–100.

Kidd, E., Lieven, E. V. M., & Tomasello, M. (2010). Lexical frequency and exemplar-based learning effects in language acquisition: Evidence from sentential complements. *Language Sciences, 32,* 132–142.

Kirjavainen, M., Theakston, A., Lieven, E., & Tomasello, M. (2009). "I want hold Postman Pat": An investigation into the acquisition of the infinitival maker "to." *First Language, 29,* 313–339.

Kluender, K., & Kiefte, M. (2006). Speech perception within a biologically realistic information-theoretic framework. In M. J. Traxler & M. A. Gernsbacher (Eds.), *The handbook of psycholinguistics* (2nd ed., pp. 153–200). Amsterdam, The Netherlands: Elsevier.

Krentz, U. C., & Corina, D. P. (2008). Preference for language in early infancy: The human language bias is not speech specific. *Developmental Science, 11,* 1–9.

Krueger, C., Holditch-Davis, D., Quint, S., & DeCasper, A. (2004). Recurring auditory experience in the 28- to 34-week-old fetus. *Infant Behavior and Development, 27,* 537–543.

Kuhl, P. K., Stevens, E., Hayashi, A., Deguchi, T., Kiritani, S., & Iverson, P. (2006). Infants show a facilitation effect for native language phonetic perception between 6 and 12 months. *Developmental Science, 9,* F13–F21.

Kuhl, P. K., Williams, K. A., Lacerda, F., Stevens, K. N., & Lindblom, B. (1992). Linguistic experience alters phonetic perception in infants by 6 months of age. *Science, 255,* 606–608.

Landau, B., & Gleitman, L. (1985). *Language and experience: Evidence from the blind child.* Cambridge, MA: Harvard University Press.

Lany, J., Gomez, R. L., & Gerken, L. (2007). The role of prior experience in language acquisition. *Cognitive Science, 31,* 481–507.

Lecanuet, J., Granier-Deferre, C., & Busnel, M. (1988). Fetal cardiac and motor responses to octave-band noises as a function of central frequency, intensity, and heartrate variability. *Early Human Development, 18,* 81–93.

Lee, J. N., & Naigles, L. R. (2008). Mandarin learners use syntactic bootstrapping in verb acquisition. *Cognition, 106,* 1028–1037.

Lenneberg, E. H. (1967). *Biological foundations of language.* New York: John Wiley & Sons.

Liberman, A. M., Cooper, F. S., Shankweiler, D. P., & Studdert-Kennedy, M. (1967). Perception of the speech code. *Psychological Review, 74,* 421–461.

Lieven, E. V. M., Pine, J. J., & Baldwin, G. (1997). Lexically-based learning and early grammatical development. *Journal of Child Language, 24,* 187–219.

Liu, H., Kuhl, P. K., & Tsao, F. (2003). An association between mothers' speech clarity and infants' speech discrimination skills. *Developmental Psychology, 6,* F1–F10.

MacWinney, B. (1998). Models of the emergence of language. *Annual Review of Psychology, 49,* 199–227.

Marchman, V. A., Bates, E., Burkhardt, A., & Good, A. B. (1991). Functional constraints of the acquisition of the passive: Toward a model of the competence to perform. *First Language, 11,* 65–92.

Marchman, V. A., & Fernald, A. (2008). Speed of word recognition and vocabulary knowledge in infancy predict cognitive and language outcomes in later childhood. *Developmental Science, 11,* F9–F16.

Markman, E. M., & Hutchinson, J. E. (1984). Children's sensitivity to constraints on word meaning: Taxonomic versus thematic relations. *Cognitive Psychology, 16,* 1–27.

Markman, E. M., & Wachtel, G. F. (1988). Children's use of mutual exclusivity to constrain the meaning of words. *Cognitive Psychology, 20,* 121–157.

Markson, L., & Bloom, P. (1997). Evidence against a dedicated system for word learning in children. *Nature, 385,* 813–815.

Markson, L., Diesendruck, G., & Bloom, P. (2008). The shape of thought. *Developmental Science, 11,* 204–208.

Masur, E. F. (1997). Maternal labeling of novel and familiar objects: Implications for children's development of lexical constraints. *Journal of Child Language, 24,* 427–439.

Matthews. D., Lieven, E. V. M., Theakston, A. L., & Tomasello, M. (2007). French children's use and correction of weird word orders: A constructivist account. *Journal of Child Language, 34,* 381–409.

McClelland, J. L., & Patterson, K. (2002). Rules or connections in past-tense inflections: What does the evidence rule out? *Trends in Cognitive Sciences, 6,* 465–472.

McClelland, J. L., & Rumelhart, D. E. (1985). Distributed memory and the representation of general and specific information. *Journal of Experimental Psychology: General, 114,* 159–188.

McClure, K., Pine, J. M., & Lieven, E. V. M. (2006). Investigating the abstractness of children's early knowledge of argument structure. *Journal of Child Language, 33,* 693–720.

McMurray, B. (2007). Defusing the childhood vocabulary explosion. *Science, 317,* 631.

McMurray, B., & Hollich, G. (2009). Special section: Core computational principles of language acquisition: Can statistical learning do the job? *Developmental Science, 12,* 365–368.

Mehler, J., Jusczyk, P., Labertz, G., & Halsted, N. (1988). A precursor of language acquisition in young infants. *Cognition, 29,* 143–178.

Mills, D. L., Prat, C., Zangl, R., Stager, C. L., Neville, H. J., & Werker, J. F. (2004). Language experience and the organization of brain activity to phonetically similar words: ERP evidence from 14- and 20-month-olds. *Journal of Cognitive Neuroscience, 16,* 1452–1464.

Mirman, D., Magnuson, J. S., Graf-Estes, K., & Dixon, J. A. (2008). The link between statistical segmentation and word learning in adults. *Cognition, 108,* 271–280.

Morgan, J. L., & Demuth, K. (1996). Signal to syntax: An overview. In J. L. Morgan & K. Demuth (Eds.), *Signal to syntax* (pp. 1–24). Mahwah, NJ: Erlbaum.

Nurmsoo, E., & Bloom, P. (2008). Preschooler's perspective taking in word learning. *Psychological Science, 19,* 211–215.

Onnis, L., Waterfall, H. R., & Edelman, S. (2008). Learn locally, act globally: Learning language from variation set cues. *Cognition, 109,* 423–430.

Pan, B. A., Rowe, M. L., Singer, J. D., & Snow, C. E. (2005). Maternal correlates of growth in toddler vocabulary production in low-income families. *Child Development, 76,* 763–782.

Pardo, J. S., & Remez, R. E. (2006). The perception of speech. In M. J. Traxler & M. A. Gernsbacher (Eds.), *The handbook of psycholinguistics* (2nd ed., pp. 201–248). Amsterdam, The Netherlands: Elsevier.

Pelucchi, B., Hay, J. F., & Saffran, J. R. (2009). Statistical learning in a natural language by 8-month-old infants. *Child Development, 80,* 674–685.

Pinker, S. (1984). *Language learnability and language development.* Cambridge, MA: MIT Press.

Pinker, S. (1994a). How could a child use verb syntax to learn verb semantics? *Lingua, 92,* 377–410.

Pinker, S. (1994b). *The language instinct.* New York: Harper.

Pinker, S. (1996). *Language learnability and language development.* Cambridge, MA: Harvard University Press.

Pinker, S. (2000). *Words and rules.* New York: Harper.

Pye, C. (1983). Mayan telegraphese: Intonational determinants of inflectional development in Quiché Mayan. *Language, 59,* 583–604.

Quine, V. O. (1960). *Word and object.* Cambridge, MA: MIT Press.

Redington, M., & Chater, N. (1997). Probabilistic and distributional approaches to language acquisition. *Trends in Cognitive Sciences, 1,* 273–281.

Rosch, E., & Mervis, C. B. (1975). Family resemblances: Studies in the internal structure of categories. *Cognitive Psychology, 7,* 573–605.

Sabbagh, M. A., & Baldwin, D. (2001). Learning words from knowledgeable versus ignorant speakers: Links between preschoolers' theory of mind and semantic development. *Child Development, 72,* 1054–1070.

Saffran, J. R. (2001). Words in a sea of sounds: The output of infant statistical learning. *Cognition, 81,* 149–169.

Saffran, J. R. (2002). Constraints on statistical language learning. *Journal of Memory and Language, 47,* 172–196.

Saffran, J. R. (2003). Statistical language learning: Mechanisms and constraints. *Current Directions in Psychological Science, 12,* 110–114.

Saffran, J. R., Aslin, R. N., & Newport, E. L. (1996). Statistical learning by 8-month-old infants. *Science, 274,* 1926–1928.

Saffran, J. R., Pollak, S. D., Seibel, R. L., & Shkolnik, A. (2007). Dog is a dog is a dog: Infant rule learning is not specific to language. *Cognition, 105,* 669–680.

Saylor, M. M., Sabbagh, M. A., & Baldwin, D. A. (2002). Children use whole–part juxtaposition as a pragmatic cue to word meaning. *Developmental Psychology, 38,* 993–1003.

Seidenberg, M. S., & Joanisse, M. F. (2003). Show us the model. *Trends in Cognitive Sciences, 7,* 106–107.

Seidenberg, M. S., & McClelland, J. L. (1989). A distributed, developmental model of word recognition and naming. *Psychological Review, 96,* 523–568.

Skinner, B. F. (1957). *Verbal behavior.* New York: Appleton.

Song, H., & Fisher, C. (2005). Who's "she?" Discourse prominence influences preschoolers' comprehension of pronouns. *Journal of Memory and Language, 52,* 29–57.

Speer, S., & Blodgett, A. (2006). Prosody. In M. J. Traxler & M. A. Gernsbacher (Eds.), *The handbook of psycholinguistics* (2nd ed., pp. 505–538). Amsterdam, The Netherlands: Elsevier.

Stager, C. L., & Werker, J. F. (1997). Infants listen for more phonetic detail in speech perception than in word-learning tasks. *Nature, 388,* 381–382.

Stoll, S., Abott-Smith, K., & Lieven, E. (2009). Lexically restricted utterances in Russian, German, and English child-directed speech. *Cognitive Science, 33,* 75–103.

Streeter, L. A. (1976). Language perception of 2-month-old infants shows effects of both innate mechanisms and experience. *Nature, 259,* 39–41.

Swingley, D., & Fernald, A. (2002). Recognition of words referring to present and absent objects by 24-month olds. *Journal of Memory and Language, 46,* 39–56.

Swingley, D., Pinto, J. P., & Fernald, A. (1999). Continuous processing in word recognition at 24 months. *Cognition, 71,* 73–108.

Tardif, T., Gelman, S. A., & Xu, F. (1999). Putting the "noun bias" in context: A comparison of English and Mandarin. *Child Development, 70,* 620–635.

Tardif, T., Shatz, M., & Naigles, L. (1997). Caregiver speech and children's use of nouns versus verbs: A comparison of English, Italian, and Mandarin. *Journal of Child Language, 24,* 535–565.

Theakston, A. L., Lieven, E. V. M., Pine, J. M., & Rowland, C. F. (2002). Going, going, gone: The acquisition of the verb "go." *Journal of Child Language, 29,* 783–811.

Thiessen, E. D., Hill, E. A., & Saffran, J. R. (2005). Infant-directed speech facilitates word segmentation. *Infancy, 7,* 53–71.

Thiessen, E. D., & Saffran, J. R. (2003). When cues collide: Use of stress and statistical cues to word boundaries by 7- to 9-month-old infants. *Developmental Psychology, 39,* 706–716.

Tincoff, R., & Jusczyk, P. W. (1999). Some beginnings of word comprehension in 6-month-olds. *Psychological Science, 10,* 172–175.

Tomasello, M. (2000). The item-based nature of children's early syntactic development. *Trends in Cognitive Sciences, 4,* 156–163.

Tsao, F., Liu, H., & Kuhl, P. K. (2004). Speech perception in infancy predicts language development in the second year of life: A longitudinal study. *Child Development, 75,* 1067–1084.

Waterfall, H. R., Sandbank, B., Onnis, L., & Edelman, S. (2010). An empirical generative framework for computational modeling of language acquisition. *Journal of Child Language, 37,* 671–703.

Weber, C., Hahne, A., Friedrich, M., & Friederici, A. D. (2004). Discrimination of word stress in early infant perception: Electrophysiological evidence. *Cognitive Brain Research, 18,* 149–161.

Werker, J. F., Gilbert, J. H. V., Humphrey, K., & Tees, R. C. (1981). Developmental aspects of cross-language speech perception. *Child Development, 52,* 349–355.

Werker, J. F., & McLeod, P. J. (1989). Infant preference for both male and female infant-directed talk: A developmental study of attentional and affective responsiveness. *Canadian Journal of Psychology, 43,* 230–246.

Werker, J. F., & Tees, R. C. (1983). Developmental changes across childhood in the perception of non-native speech sounds. *Canadian Journal of Psychology, 37,* 278–286.

Werker, J. F., & Tees, R. C. (2002). Cross-language speech perception: Evidence for perceptual reorganization during the first year of life. *Infant Behavior & Development, 25,* 121–133.

Westermann, G., Ruh, N., & Plunkett, K. (2009). Connectionist approaches to language learning. *Linguistics, 47,* 413–452.

Wexler, K. (1998). Very early parameter setting and the unique checking constraint: A new explanation of the optional infinitive stage. *Lingua, 106,* 23–79.

Yang, C. (2004). Universal grammar, statistics, or both. *Trends in Cognitive Sciences, 8,* 451–456.

Yuan, S., & Fisher, C. (2009). "Really? She blicked the baby?" Two-year-olds learn combinatorial facts about verbs by listening. *Psychological Science, 20,* 619–626.

Reading

He gets mad because he can't read.

CHICO MARX, DUCK SOUP

Reading is an "unnatural act" that involves the close coordination of motor, visual, and cognitive functions (Gough & Hillinger, 1980). To read efficiently, people need to extract visual information from the environment rapidly, they need to activate stored phonological (sound) and semantic (meaning) representations in the right way, at the right time, and engage simultaneously in higher level integrative and inferencing processes, and plan when and where to move their eyes next. This chapter organizes the discussion of reading into two broad sets of issues: Those involved in the control of eye movements in reading; and higher order cognitive aspects of reading, including how different kinds of writing (different *scripts*) affect the way we extract information from texts, how children learn to read alphabetic script, and why some children and adults have difficulty reading. For starters, let's examine how and why skilled adult readers operate at or near peak efficiency most of the time, which in turn illustrates why speed reading courses are a waste of your time and money.

Speed Reading?

If you type "speed reading" into your favorite web browser, you will uncover lots of websites offering to sell you products that will increase your reading rate, reading comprehension, or both. Sounds like that would be really useful

Introduction to Psycholinguistics: Understanding Language Science, First Edition.
Matthew J. Traxler.

for students who always have too much to read and not enough time. Even universities sometimes offer speed reading as an elective. A very cursory review of published software shows that the asking price for speed reading courses runs from $13 for an Australian product, to $27 for a 16-minute mini-course, to $250 for a super-deluxe version (there may be more expensive versions that did not turn up during my 60-second search). What does your money get you? According to the tubes of the internets, completing a speed reading course can increase your reading speed by 10 times or more above the normal average of about 200 words per minute. As one anonymous authority put it, "Speed readers can read 600 to 2,500 words per minute. Some websites claim speeds of 10,000 words per minute or more." At the top end of that range of speeds, you could read this entire book, including all of the references, the glossary, and the index, in about half an hour. Wow! But hold on a minute. Sometimes things that are published on the internets turn out not to be true. So we need to be careful, because even the purveyors of speed reading courses themselves warn us that some training techniques don't work. One website offers the information that *other* speed reading courses are fraudulent. "Some barely gave the desired results … increased reading speed, improved comprehension, stronger recall and better study results." Some companies even volunteer the information that they have been tested by "independent experts."

Language science can be frustrating in that it is not always clear how basic research findings translate into concrete benefits for the average person. Research on speed reading is a prominent exception to this general rule. The speed reading merchants are correct about one thing: Their methods have been subjected to testing by independent experts. And the independent testing demonstrates quite convincingly that speed reading courses do not have the effects that their proponents claim they do. The main goal of this chapter is to describe well-founded models of what happens when people read texts. These models of reading are based on decades of psychophysical and cognitive research. When you understand the physical and mental processes that go into reading texts, you will understand why a reading rate of 10,000 words per minute (or even a substantial fraction of that) is not possible, and why about 200–250 words per minute is pretty close to the limit of what the cognitive and motor systems involved in reading can handle (unless you are just skimming a text to get the gist of it). Skilled adult readers are already operating at near-peak efficiency, so there's not a lot of tuning up left to do. First, let's review some basic aspects of reading before we return to the research by independent experts—in this case, language scientists who are *not* trying to sell you something—that shows why speed reading courses don't work. On the way, we'll uncover some interesting facts about how the visual system works, how language-processing systems interact when you read, and how that influences the way you move your eyes when you read.

Eye Movement Control and Reading

At a basic level, reading is a behavior. The behavior involves holding a piece of paper in front of your face and pointing your eyes in different directions so that your gaze lands on different parts of the text at different points in time. The end product of this process is a mental representation of the information conveyed by the text. Eye movements in reading are systematically organized so that you start in one location on the page (the upper left-hand corner for English text) and you end up in another location (the lower right-hand corner). Eye movements in general can be classified in two broad categories. *Smooth pursuit movements* involve a continuous, smooth change in the direction of your gaze. This kind of eye movement happens when you track a moving visual target, like a car going by or a clay pigeon at the skeet range, but not when you read. You use another kind of eye movement, *a saccadic eye movement* or *saccade* when you read text (similar eye movements occur when you search a static visual scene looking for a specific stationary object, like in *Where's Waldo* books). Saccadic eye movements occur when there are relatively long periods of time where the eyes are stationary in their orbits[1] (a few hundred milliseconds counts as long in this context), connected by short (7–9 characters on average), very rapid movements (*saccades*). The saccades take about 20 ms (one fiftieth of a second) from start to finish. The purpose of these saccades is to sequentially bring each part of the text into the center of vision, where your ability to detect fine details (your *acuity*) is highest. Deploying the highest acuity areas is critical in reading, because frequently you can only tell the difference between different letters by attending to very small details, like whether there are one or two humps (as in *n* vs. *m*) or whether the vertical line is to the left or the right side of the letter (as in *p* vs. *q*). (Non-alphabetic scripts, like Chinese logographs also differ at this level of very fine detail and require similar processes to read; more about this later.) These very rapid eye movements are also associated with *saccadic suppression*. That is, no visual information is extracted while a saccade is in progress, partly because the visual image on the retina during a saccade consists of a big blur, but also because there is very little time for activity at the retina to send activation to the visual cortex before new visual stimulation from the following stable fixation displaces the visual stimulation that occurred during the saccade. In fact, recent research shows that about 50 ms of stable exposure (about one twentieth of a second) is necessary for the visual system to extract the information it needs to identify individual letters, and hence to identify words (Pollatsek, Reichle, & Rayner, 2006a; Reichle, Pollatsek, & Rayner, 2006). This amount of exposure time is equivalent to the *eye–brain lag*, the amount of time it takes for neural signals at the retina (inside the eyeball) to affect neural signals in the primary visual cortex, *area V1*, at the back of the brain (Clark, Fan, & Hillard, 1995).

When you read English text, most of the saccades that you make move the direction of your gaze further to the right. Eye movements of this kind are called *progressive saccades* (often times just *saccades*) to distinguish them from eye movements that go to the left. These *regressive saccades* or *regressions* take your gaze back to where it has already been. A regression normally occurs when something has gone wrong with the processes involved in interpreting or comprehending the text, and some evidence suggests that regressions are targeted toward parts of the text that are helpful in resolving comprehension problems (Frazier & Rayner, 1982; Meseguer, Carreiras, & Clifton, 2002). The existence of such targeted regressions suggest that readers represent not only the semantic content of the text, but that they also maintain a spatial map that helps them keep track of syntactic choice points and other potentially ambiguous or difficult material.

When skilled adults read, they directly fixate the vast majority of the words on the page. That is, the reader's gaze will land directly on some part of each word, and it will stay there at one position between 250 and 500 ms, on average; or about a quarter to half a second. Some words will be skipped, however. Words that are very highly predictable from the context are skipped more often than words that are less predictable. Very short function words are skipped more often than other kinds of words, but content words that are five or more characters in length are almost always directly fixated.

One of the things that speed reading programs will tell you is that you do not have to fixate each word. According to their theories of reading, you can take in much more than one or two words' worth of information at a time. You can, according to speed reading theory, take in an entire line's worth of text in a single fixation; in fact, you may be able to take in information not just from the line that you are currently fixating, but also information from lines above and below the line you are currently fixating. As a result, instead of fixating nearly every word, you can greatly increase your reading speed by learning to take in an entire line's worth of information, or a collection of lines, in a single fixation. So instead of

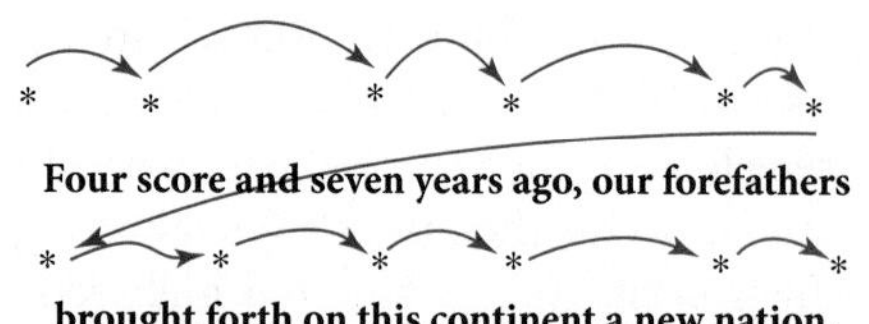

Four score and seven years ago, our forefathers
brought forth on this continent a new nation,

Figure 10.1 A representative pattern of fixations and saccades. The asterisks mark the positions of stable fixations, while the blue arrows mark saccade trajectories

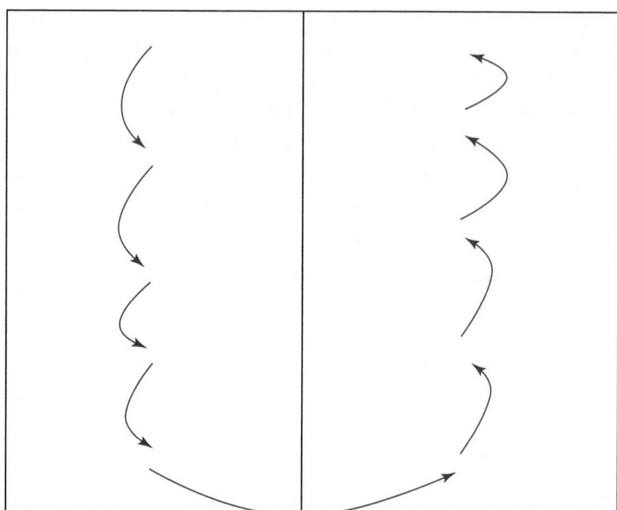

Figure 10.2 How some speed reading courses suggest you should move your eyes in order to increase your reading speed

moving your eyes as a reader normally would (as in Figure 10.1), some speed reading courses encourage you to move your eyes in a series of vertical saccades, jumping several lines each time (as in Figure 10.2).

The problem with this theory is that it is, without question, demonstrably false. At least, no one who has been tested under the appropriate conditions has demonstrated the ability to take in information from multiple lines of text, or even from an entire single line of text, even after successfully completing a speed reading course (Rayner & Pollatsek, 1989). How do we know that this is the case, and why should this be so?

The perceptual span

We know that skilled readers extract information only from the word they are currently looking at and the word immediately to the right on the vast majority of fixations, because 30-plus years of psychophysical research show this to be the case (see Rayner, 1998; Rayner & Pollatsek, 2006; Rayner, Juhasz, & Pollatsek, 2007, for reviews; see Engbert, Nuthmann, Richter, & Kliegl, 2005, below, for a slightly modified viewpoint). The main purpose of this psychophysical research was to find out from what region of text people can extract information on a given fixation. This region of useful vision for reading is known as the *perceptual span*, and it extends from about 4 characters to the left of the currently fixated *letter* to about 15 characters to the right of the currently fixated letter. How do we know that the perceptual span is this size? Much of the research that established this fact was conducted in George McConkie's and Keith Rayner's labs, starting in the 1970s and continuing up through the present. Some of the earliest research was based on the question: How much text does a reader need to see in order to read at a normal speed? And where does that information need to be in the reader's visual field? To find out, McConkie and Rayner systematically manipulated the amount of text that a reader could see at any one time, and they used eye-tracking machines to identify where subjects looked and how long they spent fixating different parts of the text, which told them how fast people could read. Sometimes, the entire text was displayed as it normally appears. Sometimes just the word that subjects were looking at was displayed, and everything else was masked, either with X's or random letters. Sometimes, only a single letter at a time was visible to the subject.

The research that established the existence and the size of the perceptual span in reading involved two related experimental methods. The first is the *moving window* paradigm and the second is the *boundary change* paradigm. In the moving window paradigm (DenBuurman, Boersema, & Gerrisen, 1981; McConkie & Rayner, 1975; Rayner, 1984; Rayner & Bertera, 1979; Rayner, Well, & Pollatsek, 1980; Underwood & McConkie, 1985), part of the text is displayed in the normal way, and part of the text is replaced with something else. This can be done because the visual display can be linked to feedback from an eye-tracking device. The eye-tracker determines where subjects are looking, and the display can be adjusted very quickly accordingly (within milliseconds). So if the normal stimulus looked like this (Dorsey, 2009, p. 72):

> We've been radar-pinged in the "Gimme Three Steps" bar, the most bad-ass honky tonk in all America.

and you were looking at the word *Gimme*, the rest of the text would be replaced by something else, often a series of upper-case X's, like this:

> XXXXX XXXX XXXXXXXXXXXX XX XXX "Gimme XXXXX XXXXXX XXXX XXX XXXX XXXXXXX XXXXX XXXX XX XXX XXXXXXXX

When your eyes started to move to the next word, during the saccade, *"Gimme* would be replaced by X's and the next word would be displayed, like this:

> XXXXX XXXX XXXXXXXXXXXX XX XXX XXXXXX Three XXXXXX XXXX XXX XXXX XXXXXXX XXXXX XXXX XX XXX XXXXXXX

Sometimes, the spaces between the words would be filled with additional X's, and sometimes random letters would be used instead of X's to replace the letters. When only one word is visible at a time, but the location of word boundaries coincide with the position of the X's, reading is about 20% slower than normal. When preview of the next word and word-spacing information are both eliminated by filling the entire line (except for the fixated word) with X's, reading times nearly double. But if the text appears like this, with spacing information intact and the beginning of the next word displayed,

> XXXXX XXXX XXXXXXXXXXXX XX XXX 'Gimme ThrXX XXXXXX XXXX XXX XXXX XXXXXXX XXXXX XXXX XX XXX XXXXXXX

reading rate is just about identical to the normal text. In fact, subjects in this condition often do not realize that there is anything at all unusual about the text.

In boundary-change experiments, an invisible boundary is located somewhere in the text. When the reader's gaze is to the left of the boundary, the critical text is either displayed as normal, or it is distorted in some way. For example, the text to the right of the invisible boundary could be replaced by letters that are similar to the original text, like this:

> We've been radar-pinged in the "Gimme|Fncoo Rhoqd" dov, lfo nedf tol-onn lemfq femt em eff Onomese.

(the "|" marks the invisible boundary, the "|" mark is *not* visible to the subjects)
When the reader's gaze crosses the invisible boundary, the nonsense letters are replaced by the normal letters. So, when you are looking at *"Gimme*, the next bit of text would be *Fncoo*. But when your eyes cross the invisible boundary, *Fncoo* is replaced by *Three*. The purpose of this kind of display is to deny readers accurate *letter preview* information. In normal reading, readers can identify the letters in the word that they are fixating, and they can usually identify the letters that begin the next word to the right. Some recent evidence suggests that readers can also sometimes identify the final letter in the word to the right if the word is five or fewer characters long, because although the image of this letter is blurrier than letters closer to the center of fixation, it suffers less from a kind of visual interference called *lateral masking* from nearby letters (Johnson, Perea, & Rayner, 2007). Being able to identify letters from the word to the right of the fixated word helps readers prepare to process that word at a later point in time, possibly by increasing the activation of phonological (sound) codes associated with the word to the right before that word is directly fixated (Pollatsek, Lesch, Morris, & Rayner, 1992). It does *not* appear to be the case that semantic (meaning) information is activated during parafoveal preview (Rayner & Morris, 1992), however. When parafoveal preview is denied (as described above) reading is slowed down, but is not too terribly disrupted so long as foveal information is preserved (Rayner, Well, Pollatsek, & Bertera, 1982).

Moving-window and boundary-change experiments show that the size of the window matters, in that reading slows down when the window is too small or when a preview of the next word is denied to the reader. But the experiments also show that people do not need an entire normal line of text to read at their normal speed. People's reading speed was affected by how big the window of visible text was, but only up to a certain point. If the window of visible text was too small, reading was severely disrupted. A one-letter window led to the slowest reading times, and people's reading speed increased as the size of the window of visible text increased. But increasing the size of the window beyond about 4 characters to the left of the currently fixated letter and 15 characters to the right did not lead to any further increases in reading speed. Thus, it turned out that people do not need an entire line or even half a line of text in order to read at high speed. All they needed to read at their maximum speed was for the currently fixated word and the beginning of the word to the right of fixation (the first three or four letters) to be visible. Under conditions where only the currently fixated word plus the beginning of the next word is visible, reading speed and comprehension are nearly normal. That is, speed and comprehension for this window size are nearly the same as conditions where an entire page of text is visible (Rayner & Pollatsek, 1989).

The perceptual span is not symmetrical—it is larger on the right-hand side of fixation than the left-hand side (McConkie & Rayner, 1976; Rayner et al., 1980). This does not reflect acuity differences, because acuity is symmetrical around the fovea. Rather, it reflects the fact that, in English orthography (writing), new information usually appears to the right of where you are fixating rather than some other direction.[2] The asymmetric perceptual span is an artifact of learning to read a specific kind of writing system. When people learn to read Hebrew, which is written right-to-left, their perceptual span is asymmetric such that it is bigger on the left than the right (Pollatsek, Bolozky, Well, & Rayner, 1981). When people read languages whose orthography is vertical, their perceptual span is oriented vertically and is larger in the downward than in the upward direction.[3]

Why do we need so little visible text to read normally? Part of the answer is that when we read, we rely heavily on images that are projected onto our *fovea*. The fovea is an area directly in the center of the retina. When we look directly at an object in space, the image of the object is centered on our fovea. This area has terrifically high acuity relative to the rest of the retina, but it occupies only a very small percentage of the total surface area of the retina. Foveal vision extends from the center of vision only out to 1 degree of visual angle in each direction. At normal viewing distances and average text size, this means that only about three or four letters to the right of the current fixation location are imaged in the fovea. So, when people read words that are five to seven characters long, the entire word falls within the fovea, and they can readily identify the individual letters in the word. Normally, people fixate letters just to the left of the middle of the word. This fixation location leads to the fastest reading times, so this point just to the left of a word's center is called the *optimal viewing position*. Sometimes when people read, their gaze will land on the very beginning or the very end of the word, and it will take them a little bit longer than normal to read that word.[4] For words longer than about six or seven letters, part of the word will fall in the *parafovea*. The *parafovea* lies adjacent to the fovea and extends out to about 6 degrees of visual angle from the center of vision (or from the outside edge of the fovea outward about 5 more degrees). Longer words often receive more than one fixation—one toward the beginning of the word and one toward the end—likely because identification the word with certainty requires that all of the letters be imaged in the fovea.

The optimal viewing position provides the visual word-processing system with a stimulus that produces the fastest uptake of the information needed to identify the word. To read at optimal speed, the eye movement planning mechanism should pick the optimal viewing position in the next word as the target for the current saccade. If the saccade successfully lands on the optimal viewing position, lexical access processes have the best possible visual image to work with, and reading speed will be maximized. This is one reason why manipulations that degrade word-length information in the parafovea slow readers down. When word-length information is degraded, the saccade planning mechanism cannot identify and target the optimal viewing position. If the optimal viewing position is not identified, it is likely that the eyes will land somewhere suboptimal. In that case, the reader will either have to put up with a less-than-ideal visual stimulus or else program a corrective saccade, which will take extra time (Morris, Rayner, & Pollatsek, 1990; O'Regan, 1979; Rayner, 1979).

As mentioned previously, the fovea is important because it is very good at discriminating very fine visual details. Acuity (the ability to resolve detail) decreases very rapidly as one moves from the fovea, through the parafovea, out to peripheral vision, where only gross and general characteristics of objects can be identified. When people want to identify the details of an object that is located in their peripheral vision, they reorient their gaze so that the center of the object falls in the center of the visual field—the fovea. So, while people can tell the difference between different letters when a word is imaged in the fovea, and can do this to some degree when letters are in the near-parafovea (the part of the parafovea closest to the fovea), it is physically impossible to tell the difference between different letters that fall toward the edges of the parafovea and on outward into the periphery. It is possible for people to get a reasonably good length estimate for words in the parafovea—because the white space between words is a relatively large target and hence does not require super-high acuity to locate. But people cannot identify individual letters and hence individual words if those words are imaged too far from the center of vision. This fact of physiology immediately falsifies one aspect of speed reading theory—the idea that you can identify all the words on an entire line of text, or even more than one line of text, in a single fixation. There just are not enough visual receptor cells in the parafovea and periphery for the retina to produce a different signal for one letter versus another.

The importance of foveal fixation of words was further emphasized by experiments using a version of the moving-window paradigm where the center of vision was blocked, but parafoveal information was preserved (Rayner & Bertera, 1979). In this condition, if you were fixated on the "*Gimme* part of the Dorsey sentence, your display would look like this:

> We've been radar-pinged in the XXXXXX Three Steps" bar, the most bad-ass honky tonk in all America.

Thus, you would be forced to depend on the parafovea for all of the visual input needed to identify the words in the passage. Under those conditions, reading is very slow and laborious, and readers make many errors identifying the parafoveally displayed words. However, the mistakes they make almost always involve a visual substitution (so *Three* might be mistakenly identified as "Threw" or "Shrek") rather than semantic substitutions (subjects would *not* mistakenly identify *Three* as "Thrice" or "Triple"). That is why language scientists believe that semantic information is (normally) not activated until after words are directly fixated.[5]

Almost all of the words in a passage are directly fixated by skilled readers under normal reading conditions. This is because the perceptual span is only about 20 characters wide, and the subportion of this region that you can use to identify individual letters and words (the *word identification span*) is even smaller. If you want to identify a word, you need to look directly at it. There are some exceptions, to this rule, however. If a word is highly predictable from context, it will be skipped more often than a word that is less predictable from context. Short words are skipped more often than long words. But what is going on here is *not* that the peripheral visual system is producing a sharp image of the word in the parafovea. Rather, readers are combining a degraded peripheral image with top-down information about what the word is likely to be in order to make a sophisticated guess.

Oculomotor and Cognitive Control Theories of Reading

A great deal of theorizing and modeling work has gone into explaining experimental results like those summarized above. All of these models of reading behavior try to explain how the eye movement control system makes two fundamental decisions involved in reading: When should the eyes move and where should the gaze land? There is general consensus that the "where" and "when" decisions are made independently (e.g., Inhoff, Radach, Eiter, & Juhasz, 2003; Kliegl, Nuthmann, & Engbert, 2006; Reichle et al., 2006), but after that it starts to get tricky. In addition to explaining how these basic decisions get made, models of eye movement control in reading need to account for a variety of facts about reading. Why is the beginning of the parafoveal word (the word immediately to the right of the fixated word) so important? Why do readers slow down when parafoveal preview is denied? Why are predictable and short words skipped more often than less predictable and longer words?

In addition to answering questions like these, eye movement control models must also deal with a couple of really important facts about visual information processing and movement planning processes. One crucial fact is that it takes time for visual information to travel from the retina to the visual cortex, and from there to the association areas that are involved in language processing. Another crucial fact is that it takes a relatively long time to plan and execute an eye movement (relative, because in absolute terms, eye movement planning only takes about 100–150 ms). Fixations in reading can be as short as 225 ms (with an average fixation time for a skilled reader between 225 and 300 ms). If it takes 50 ms for visual information to reach the cortex after the beginning of a fixation, and it takes 100–150 ms to plan an eye movement, that leaves a very short amount of time for any linguistic processing to take place before the reader has to start planning the next eye movement. If we subtract planning time and visual information transfer time from the shorter end of the fixation duration range, we would estimate that the language-processing system has as little as 25 ms before it has to start planning the next saccade, which is about the same amount of time it takes for a lecturer's voice to travel from the front of a medium-sized lecture hall to the back. That's fast! Even in language-processing terms, where a lot of mental work gets done routinely in very short amounts of time, 25 ms is just not enough to identify a word, look up its meaning and its grammatical class, figure out what it refers to, and integrate its meaning into the evolving context.

Given what we know about visual processing and eye movement planning, there appears to be very little time for language-related properties tied to individual words to influence when the eyes move when we read. At a minimum, the facts of eye movement planning, the transfer of visual information, and the average fixation time, place severe restrictions on theories of eye movement control in reading. Two classes of model have been proposed to work around these restrictions. The first class, referred to as *oculomotor control* models, argue that language-related information plays no part in eye movement control during reading (O'Regan, 1990, 1992; O'Regan & Lévy-Schoen, 1987; Reilly & O'Regan, 1998; Vitu, O'Regan, Inhoff, & Topolski, 1995; Yang & McConkie, 2001, 2004). These models argue that when we read, eye movements are largely controlled by an internal metronome or stop-watch that signals the eyes to move forward at an average interval of 225–300 ms, regardless of the information content or meaning of the text. Higher level cognitive processes can play a role in triggering regressions (leftward eye movements) or stopping the eyes altogether, but these are exceptions. The vast majority of progressive saccades are controlled by the metronome. The chief advantage of such models is that they can explain why the average fixation is so short (225–300 ms or so). But the major problem with such models is that they do not explain why language-related information—like the frequency with which a word appears in the language, or how well the word fits into its context (how much sense it makes or how predictable it is), or whether the word represents a grammatically legal continuation of the sentence—has a powerful influence on how long people fixate individual words in texts. In short, linguistic properties of words *do* appear to influence when the eyes move during reading. If they do, that would falsify the oculomotor control class of reading theories.

In fact, linguistic properties of words affect how the eyes move even when the words become invisible shortly after readers fixate them (Rayner, Liversedge, & White, 2006). As noted above, it takes about 50 ms for visual information to travel from the retina to the visual cortex. As a result, so long as the visual information extracted from a word is not immediately replaced by another word, reading proceeds essentially undisturbed so long as the words are visible for at least 50–60 ms. This fact was established in a series of experiments that looked at how reading behavior was affected by disappearing text. In these experiments, an eye-tracker monitored where people looked, and the visual display was closely tied to the subject's current gaze location. Using a version of the boundary-change technique, researchers made each word disappear 60 ms after the reader fixated the word. When only the fixated word disappeared, reading was normal, except there were some subtle differences in how likely it was that readers would re-fixate each word (readers were less likely to re-fixate in the disappearing word condition compared to a normal display condition, presumably because there is no point in refixating a word that has already disappeared). Interestingly, the duration of each fixation was closely tied to the frequency of the disappearing word. That is, the words always disappeared after 60 ms, but if the disappearing word was rare, subjects would keep looking at the blank space for a long time (500 ms, say). If the disappearing word was common, subjects would look at the blank space for a much shorter time (250–300 ms, say). These results run strongly counter to the oculomotor control hypothesis, because they show

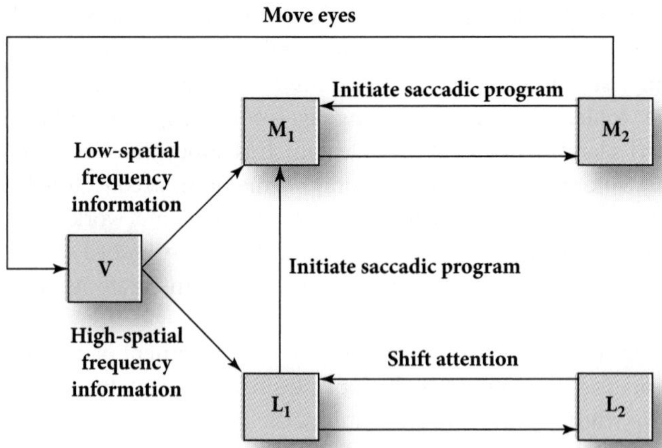

Figure 10.3 Schematic of the E-Z reader model of eye-movement control in reading (from Reichle et al., 2006, p. 6)

that linguistic properties of words (frequency, specifically) strongly influence the decision of when to move the eyes, even when the visual stimulus that leads to word identification is no longer present at the point in time when the eyes start to move.

Because there is now an overwhelming amount of evidence (see Rayner, 1998; Rayner et al., 2007) that shows that linguistic properties of words influence the decision of when to move the eyes, and hence how long individual fixations last, the vast majority of language scientists who study reading subscribe to one of the *cognitive control* theories of eye movement control in reading. As the name implies, cognitive control theories differ from oculomotor theories in that they believe that aspects of higher language processing affect how the eyes move, including influencing decisions about when the eyes should move. This class of theory explicitly denies the claim that eye movements in reading are controlled by an inflexible metronome or deadline mechanism. Cognitive control theories can be further subdivided into models that argue for *serial allocation of attention* or *parallel allocation of attention*. The serial attention models, like *E-Z reader*, argue that we pay attention to, and perform linguistic processing on, one word at a time. Parallel models, such as SWIFT, argue that we pay attention to, and perform linguistic processing on, more than one word at a time.[6] Let's start with a review of the E-Z reader model before briefly looking at SWIFT.

E-Z reader

E-Z reader is a mathematical model that accounts for a number of phenomena that happen when people read texts (Pollatsek, Reichle, & Rayner, 2006b; Reichle, Pollatsek, Fisher, & Rayner, 1998; Reichle et al., 2006; Reichle, Rayner, & Pollatsek, 1999, 2003; Reingold & Rayner, 2006; see also Morrison, 1984; see Figure 10.3 for a schematic). First, the model can account for how language-processing and eye movement planning can all be completed in the relatively short amount of time that passes between the start and the end of a single fixation. To do so, the model assumes that aspects of language processing and aspects of eye movement planning take place simultaneously. That is, the eye movement control system does *not* wait for all of the linguistic processing on a given word to be completed before it starts to plan an eye movement. The sequence of events that take place on an individual fixation goes like this:

1. First 50 ms—visual uptake phase: Visual information travels from the retina to the visual processing areas.
2. Next 75–100 ms—the *L1 stage of lexical access*: Lexical access begins. The L1 stage of the lexical access process produces a rough familiarity check. Essentially, the system judges how often it has seen something like the currently fixated word before. This familiarity check takes less time for frequently encountered words, and more time for rarer and less frequently encountered words. At this point, the word has not been fully identified, its meaning has not been accessed, and it has not been integrated into the evolving context, but the system develops a good idea of whether full lexical access is likely to succeed or not.

As soon as the L1 stage of lexical access is complete, the reader simultaneously engages in steps 3 and 4 (these processes run in parallel):

3. Saccade planning: Begin to plan next saccade.
4. The *L2 phase* of lexical access: Fully identify the specific word, access its meaning, and integrate it into the context.

When the L2 phase of lexical access is complete, the reader shifts her attention to the word to the right of the fixated word and begins the L1 stage of lexical access. When the saccade planning is complete, unless the eye movement plan is canceled, the eyes move and the gaze is directed at the next word in the text.

The E-Z reader model solves the time-crunch problem and allows for linguistic aspects of words to affect fixation durations by adopting a slightly risky eye movement planning strategy. Because the visual processing stage and the L1 stage of lexical access together take about 125 to 150 ms, there is plenty of time to plan the eye movement before the end of the average fixation. Tacking 100 to 150 ms of planning time onto the 125 to 150 ms of visual and L1 processing gives you 225–300 ms total fixation time, which is pretty close to what is usually observed when skilled adults read texts. So far, so good.

Eye movement planning is risky, according to E-Z reader, because it starts before the lexical access mechanism can be certain that it has correctly identified, or will be able to identify, the fixated word. That means that there will sometimes be problems. The eyes may move away from the fixated word before it is identified, which could lead to failures of lexical access. But on the other hand, about 10% of the eye movements in reading are regressions, and those regressions may occur in exactly those cases where the early familiarity check was *not* followed by successful full lexical access. Additionally, lexical access appears to take 250 ms or less from the onset of fixation, which is more than enough time before the next saccade starts, most of the time, so the risk of moving the eyes before lexical access is finished is not too great.[7]

E-Z reader successfully accounts for a number of other reading phenomena as well. For example, word frequency has been shown to account for a substantial percentage of the variability in fixation times. Rare words are fixated longer than more common words. E-Z reader explains this outcome by appealing to the L1 stage of lexical access. More common words lead to a more rapid rise in familiarity than rarer words, so eye movement planning starts sooner for more frequent words than for less frequent words. E-Z reader models predictability effects by assuming a degree of top-down control on saccade target selection. When higher-level language interpretation processes determine that the probability of a specific word appearing next is high, it can prompt the eye movement control mechanism to plan a saccade that jumps over the highly likely word. Thus, E-Z reader can account for both effects of word frequency and predictability and explain why those two factors appear to work independently (specifically, predictability effects are about as big for high-frequency words as they are for low-frequency words; Rayner, Ashby, Pollatsek, and Reichle, 2004).

E-Z reader also accounts for what are called *spillover effects* (Henderson & Ferreira, 1990; Kennison & Clifton, 1995; Rayner & Duffy, 1986). A spillover effect happens when the word *after* a difficult word is fixated for longer than the same word after an easier word. For example, consider sentences (1) and (2).

(1) The intrilligator[8] visited the library this morning.

(2) The investigator visited the library this morning.

Intrilligator is a much rarer word than investigator, and fixation times are much longer on the underlined region in (1) than in (2). But fixation times are also longer on the word *visited* in (1) than in (2). Why should this be? It's the same word in either case, so shouldn't *visited* be just as easy to read in (1) as in (2)? The answer, according to E-Z reader, is that, because *intrilligator* is harder to process than *investigator*, the L1 and L2 stages of lexical access take longer for *intrilligator* than for *investigator*. Because L1 and L2 take longer for *intrilligator*, you have to wait longer to switch your attention to *visited* in (1) than in (2). As a result, you get less time to perform L1 lexical access prior to directly fixating *visited* in (1) than in (2). Essentially, the preview benefit for *visited* is reduced in sentence (1) because the immediately preceding word is hard.

E-Z reader's notion of covert attention shifts prior to direct fixation also helps explain why words are skipped, and why such skipping is more likely to occur for short, frequent words, than for long, infrequent words. Because attention can shift to a word before the eyes directly fixate the word, there is a chance that the L1 and L2 stages of lexical access can be completed before the reader's gaze lands directly on the word in question. If you are looking at a word, and the word to the right can be fully identified before the eyes begin to move, a new saccade can be planned that jumps over the already identified word to the right, which causes that word to be skipped. E-Z reader also successfully simulates skipping that happens when words are highly predictable from the context.

E-Z Reader models word-skipping behavior by assuming an early *labile* stage and a later *non-labile* stage of saccade planning. If the word to the right is identified during the labile stage of saccade planning, the original eye movement plan can be canceled and replaced by the new plan. If the word to the right is identified during the non-labile stage, the original plan will be executed and the word to the right will be directly fixated. Under this second scenario, the fixation on the word to the right will likely be very short, because saccade planning can begin immediately after the original eye movement plan is executed. The assumption of later saccade plans overwriting or replacing earlier saccade plans is based on psychophysical research involving two visual targets that are displayed one after the other at varying stimulus–onset asynchronies (SOAs). If the exposure duration of the first target is short, and the second target is displayed soon after the first, subjects make a single eye movement to the second target. This suggests that the eye movement plan to land on the first target is replaced or overwritten by the eye movement plan to land on the second target. If the first target is displayed for longer and/or the delay between the onset of the first and the second targets is increased, subjects make two separate eye movements, one that lands on the first target and one that lands on the second. In this case, the plan to move to the second target starts too late to cancel the first eye movement plan.[9]

E-Z Reader also explains why parafoveal preview is so important in fast and efficient reading. Parafoveal preview is important because the majority of fixations include time where attention has already shifted one word to the right, which allows you to begin processing the word to the right before you fixate it directly. As Inhoff and colleagues (Inhoff, Eiter, & Radach, 2005, p. 980) explain, "Preview benefits are … common because completion of the two oculomotor stages of saccade programming generally consume more time than completion of L2, so that processing of the next word can commence before it is fixated." Thus, if you read sentence (3) (Dorsey, 2009, p. 304),

(3) She slammed the wooden door behind the screen and ran to call the cops.

part of the time that you spend looking at the word *wooden* would actually involve preprocessing (L1 stage familiarity check) on the following word *door*. If the display were like this while you were reading *wooden*, as in boundary-change experiments:

(3) She slammed the wooden XXXX XXXXXX XXX XXXXXX XXX XXX XX XXXX XXX XXXXX

then when you shifted your attention away from the word *wooden*, you would have nothing useful to work with. In that case, the beginning of the L1 stage familiarity check has to wait until you look directly at the word *door*, which will increase the overall amount of time that it takes to complete the L1 stage of lexical access, which in turn delays beginning to plan the saccade that moves you further to the right.

LIMITATIONS OF THE E-Z READER MODEL

Although E-Z Reader does a very good job modeling many aspects of reading behavior, it will require further development to capture the full range of reading related phenomena. As it is currently configured, E-Z Reader is limited to modeling forward (progressive) saccades. Thus, questions about when and why readers would launch a regressive eye movement are not currently handled by the model.[10] Also, while visual properties of words (e.g., length) and lower level aspects of their linguistic properties (e.g., frequency) are captured in the model, higher level aspects of language processing have not yet been incorporated into the model as sources of variability in fixation durations. As this is an active and ongoing area of research, you can expect future versions of the model to tackle these issues.

Parallel attention models and parafoveal-on-foveal effects

E-Z reader is a prominent example of serial attention models of reading, and SWIFT is a prominent example of parallel attention models of reading (Engbert et al., 2005; Kliegl et al., 2006; Kliegl, Risse, & Laubrock, 2007; see also the GLENMORE model, Inhoff, Connine, Eiter, Radach, & Heller, 2004; Inhoff et al., 2005; Inhoff, Radach, & Eiter, 2006; Radach & Kennedy, 2004; see also Legge's "Mr. Chips" model, Legge, Hooven, Klitz, Mansfield, & Tjan, 2002; Legge, Klitz, & Tjan, 1997).[11] The overall design of the SWIFT reading mechanism is displayed in Figure 10.4. The SWIFT model accounts for many of the same reading phenomena as E-Z reader, such as length and frequency effects on fixation times, spillover effects, and so forth, but it does so using very different processing assumptions.

According to SWIFT, we can attend to and perform lexical access processes on more than one word at a time. Specifically, SWIFT proposes that we process four words simultaneously.[12] The fixated word, the word to its left, and two words to the right. So, although you may be fixating the word *wooden* in sentence (3), you are processing more than just that one word on that fixation. You are also doing some linguistic processing on the preceding word *the* and the following words *door* and *behind*. Although you can attend to and process multiple words in parallel, according to SWIFT, attention is not allocated equally across all of the words in the perceptual span. Instead, there is a *gradient of attention*, such that some words receive more attention than others. In particular, the directly fixated word receives the most attention, words to the right and left of fixation receive less than maximum attention. SWIFT, like oculomotor models, uses a metronome to time progressive saccades, but it is within the cognitive control class of reading models because the operation of the metronome can be perturbed by linguistic aspects of the words within the perceptual span. Specifically, when the foveal word is difficult to process, the execution of the next

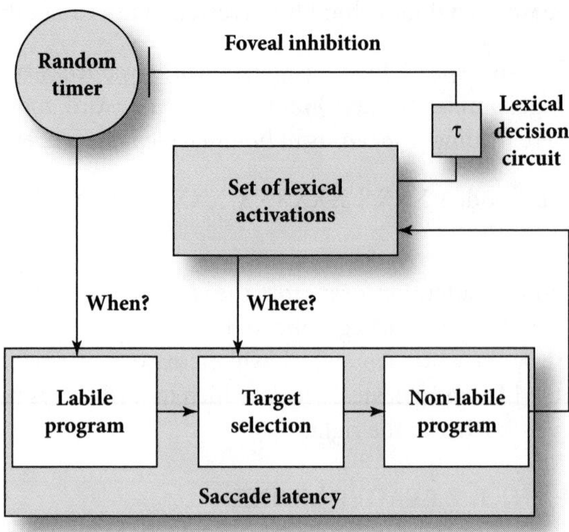

Figure 10.4 Schematic diagram of the SWIFT eye-movement system (from Engbert et al., 2005, p. 788)

saccade can be delayed. However, because the saccade generation system is physically segregated from higher level language processing, there is a time lag between the point in time where the language-processing system decides to delay the next progressive saccade and the point in time where that message reaches the eye movement control system.

SWIFT also differs from E-Z reader in terms of how the target for the next saccade is chosen. In E-Z reader, the target is always the next word, unless the next word has been fully accessed before the saccade is initiated. In SWIFT, an *activation field* is computed which covers the entire perceptual span. Within the perceptual span, different words differ in terms of their relative salience. Salience is affected by both low-level spatial information and higher level language-related information. If a word has already been identified, its salience drops. If a word is far away from the point of fixation, its salience will be less than a word that is nearer to the point of fixation. The target for the next saccade will be the word that has the highest salience in the activation field.

The gradient of attention component of the SWIFT model means that the directly fixated word has the greatest impact on fixation times, but other words can also affect fixation times. As a result, SWIFT predicts that sometimes the word to the right of the fixated word can increase the amount of time that you spend looking at the fixated word. This effect is called a *parafoveal-on-foveal* effect, because the word in the parafovea (the word to the right) affects how much time you spend fixating the word in the fovea (the word you are looking directly at). Because, except for limited circumstances, E-Z reader does *not* predict parafoveal-on-foveal effects, experiments looking for parafoveal-on-foveal effects have provided an important means to try to tell whether readers attend to one word at a time (as in E-Z reader) or more than one word at a time (as in SWIFT). So what evidence is there for parafoveal-on-foveal effects in reading?

Early experiments on parafoveal preview effects suggested that denying preview increased fixation times once the eyes moved from the foveal word to the (non-previewed) parafoveal word, but presence or absence of preview did not affect how long people fixated on the foveal word (e.g., Blanchard, Pollatsek, & Rayner, 1989). More recent research also failed to show parafoveal-on-foveal effects of different preview conditions, and showed no preview benefits for the second word following a fixated word (Rayner, Juhasz, and Brown, 2007; see Rayner, White, Kambe, Miller, & Liversedge, 2003, for a critical review). These results suggest that lexical processing is limited to, at most, the foveal (fixated) and parafoveal word, and give no comfort to proponents of parallel attention models, due to the absence of parafoveal-on-foveal effects. However, more recent studies have begun to turn up evidence that properties of the parafoveal word can influence fixation times on the foveal word (Inhoff, Radach, Starr, & Greenberg, 2000; Inhoff, Starr, & Schindler, 2000; Kliegl et al., 2006; see also Inhoff et al., 2005). For example, a recent experiment by Reinhold Kliegl and colleagues manipulated the preview of a word two words away from the fixated word, so in our example sentence (3) repeated here,

(3) She slammed the *wooden* door *behind* the screen and ran to call the cops.

if you were fixated on the word *wooden* everything would appear as normal, except for the word *behind* (Kliegl et al., 2007). When your eyes crossed an invisible boundary between the word *wooden* and the word *door*, the word *behind* would change from a series of random letters to its normal form. In this experiment, denying people preview of *behind* while they were fixated on *wooden* led to longer reading times when the reader's gaze moved to *door*. Kliegl and his colleagues also manipulated the linguistic properties of the parafoveal word, and they found that this manipulation affected fixation times on the foveal word, as predicted by SWIFT. In another study, Alan Kennedy and Joel Pynte (2005) collected eye movements for 50,000 words of text and found that linguistic properties of the parafoveal word affected fixation times on relatively short fixated words, with somewhat weaker parafoveal-on-foveal effects for relatively long fixated words.

Some further evidence for parallel allocation of attention to multiple words comes from experiments which manipulate the availability of parafoveal preview information. Serial attention models of reading predict that it takes time for your attention to switch from the fixated word to the next word to the right (the *parafoveal word*). Parallel attention models suggest that you start taking up linguistic information about the parafoveal word as soon as you land on the fixated word. According to the serial attention models, if you deny preview of the parafoveal word only very briefly after you land on the fixated word, there should be no problem, because information about the parafoveal word will be available before attention shifts from the fixated word to the parafoveal word. But according to the parallel attention models, information uptake from the parafoveal word starts as soon as your gaze lands on the fixated word, so even a short delay in parafoveal preview should increase reading times. In one such study (Inhoff, et al., 2005),[13] reading was slowed down even when parafoveal preview was denied to subjects only for a short time (140 ms after the foveal word was fixated). In another condition, the parafoveal preview was available immediately, but the preview was eliminated after 140 ms. In this condition, there should have been little preview benefit according to the serial attention model, because attention would have been on the foveal word at the point in time when the parafoveal preview was switched off. This "early" preview, however, provided just as much benefit as a condition where the preview was available only after 140 ms and stayed on until a saccade was initiated, which would have made the preview available after attention had shifted (according to the serial attention model). Thus, these data suggest that linguistic information is extracted from the parafoveal word starting almost immediately after the foveal word is fixated, and this would be more compatible with parallel allocation of attention than serial switching of attention.[14]

The existence, extent, and explanations of parafoveal-on-foveal effects remain controversial, and some data that are cited in favor of the existence of such effects actually appear to support serial accounts (e.g., Morris et al., cited in Inhoff et al., 2005). In Robin Morris and colleagues' experiment, parafoveal preview was either delayed by just a short time (50 ms) or a much longer time (250 ms). If it takes time for attention to shift from the foveal word to the parafoveal word, and processing of the parafoveal word requires attention on that word, then a 50 ms delay of preview information should have little effect on reading times, but longer delays in the onset of the parafoveal preview should be more disruptive (because the longer preview is denied, the more likely it will be that attention has shifted to the parafoveal word before the correct letter information is switched on). Morris and colleagues showed that longer delays in preview onset disrupted reading more than shorter delays in preview onset, consistent with the serial attention hypothesis.

LIMITATIONS OF THE SWIFT MODEL

Like E-Z reader, SWIFT successfully reproduces a number of reading-related behavior patterns, but it does not yet perfectly reproduce the full range of eye movement patterns that human readers produce. For example, SWIFT systematically underestimates the effect of word frequency and overestimates effects of word length (Engbert et al., 2005). There also may be hidden problems related to SWIFT's (and other parallel attention models') assumption of parallel allocation of attention to multiple words simultaneously. It may be that visual processing and object recognition (word recognition in reading, specifically) requires that people pay attention to one visual object at a time.

Why might attention need to be allocated to one word at a time, rather than spread across several words (as in SWIFT and similar models)? One line of reasoning comes out of research on object perception (e.g., Treisman & Gelade, 1980). In these studies, subjects view sets of visual stimuli that are presented for very short durations that are then masked (covered up) with a random visual pattern. Some stimulus sets have a mixture of features, for example, the stimuli could consist of a mixed group of red X's and green O's. If the stimuli are flashed for a very short period of time, sometimes people report seeing a red O, even though all of the O's in the set were green. Treisman explained these mistakes as resulting from *free floating* visual features. When the stimulus is flashed very quickly, it is not possible to allocate attention to all of the stimuli. As a result, the visual system, operating without attentional support, mis-assigns some of the features. It knows it has some X's and O's, it knows it has some green things and some red things, but it creates *illusory conjunctions* by combining the wrong features together. Words are a kind of visual stimulus (albeit a special one), and it is very likely that attention is required to combine the complex set of features (e.g., shapes and positions) to correctly identify individual words. This is another aspect of writing systems that makes speed reading theory unlikely. Even if you could solve the acuity problem, it is not likely that you could simultaneously attend to all of the words on a whole line of text, much less multiple lines.[15]

Finally, "parafoveal-on-foveal" effects can be caused by mislocated fixations (i.e., errors in the saccade execution process), rather than graded attention (Dreighe, Rayner, & Pollatsek, 2008). If the eye movement system misses its target by landing to the left, and attention is actually located at the word to the right of fixation, it will appear as if properties of the parafoveal word are driving fixation times on the foveally fixated word (because they are, but not for the reasons that SWIFT envisions).

Cognitive Processing in Reading I

Different writing systems and scripts

While spoken language has many systematic features that are consistent across different languages, *writing systems* (groups of scripts) and *scripts* (the way individual languages are represented visually) have many idiosyncratic features (Perfetti, Liu, & Tan, 2005; Rayner &

Figure 10.5 An aardvark

Pollatsek, 1989). Thus far, this chapter has been concerned with reading English, which falls into the category of *alphabetic* writing systems. A script in an alphabetic writing system consists of a collection of letters. Individual letters, or small groups of letters (*bigrams* and *trigrams*) correspond to individual speech sounds, or *phonemes*. Alphabetic writing systems contrast with pictographic and logographic writing systems. In a pictographic system, each *character* or symbol looks like the concept that it represents. So in Chinese, the character

looks a bit like a tree and represents the concept "tree." However, Chinese has numerous characters that do *not* physically resemble the concepts that they refer to. For instance, these are the Chinese characters for *aardvark*:

土豚

and Figure 10.5 shows what a real aardvark looks like. Chinese is more properly characterized as an example of a *logographic* writing system. In a logographic writing system, each symbol maps onto a unit of meaning, such as a morpheme or a word, but the symbols do not need to share any physical resemblance to the concepts they denote. Chinese is the only logographic script that is currently in wide use (Rayner & Pollatsek, 1989). Some language scientists suggest that Chinese is more properly characterized as a *morpho-syllabic writing system*, because each symbol represents both a morpheme and a syllable (Perfetti et al., 2007).

The vast majority of characters in Chinese (about 85%) consist of two elements: a *semantic radical*, which gives cues about the character's meaning; and a *phonological radical*, which gives cues about the way the character should be pronounced (Lee et al., 2007). For example, as Lee and colleagues (Lee, Tsai, Huang, Hung, & Tzeng, 2006, p. 151) explain, "the phonetic compound 楓 is pronounced as feng1 (the number represents one of the four tones in Mandarin Chinese) and has the meaning 'maple.' Both its semantic radical 木 (mu4, 'wood') and the phonetic radical 風 (feng1, 'wind') are simple characters with their own meanings and pronunciations."

When Chinese was thought of as a pictographic script, it made sense to think that Chinese script might be processed much differently than English script. But it turns out that there are many similarities in how the two scripts are processed. For one thing, reading both scripts leads to the rapid and automatic activation of phonological (sound) codes. When we read English, we use groups of letters to activate phonological codes automatically (this is one of the sources of the *inner voice* that you often hear when you read). The fact that phonological codes are automatically activated in English reading is shown by experiments involving semantic categorization tasks where people have to judge whether a word is a member of a category. *Heterophonic* (multiple pronunciations) *homographs* (one spelling), such as *wind*, take longer to read than comparably long and frequent regular words, because reading *wind* activates two phonological representations (as in *the wind was blowing* vs. *wind up the clock*) (Folk & Morris, 1995). A related consistency effect involves words that have spelling patterns that have multiple pronunciations. The word *have* contains the letter "a," which in this case is pronounced as a "short" /a/ sound. But most of the time -*ave* is pronounced with the "long" a sound, as in *cave*, and *save*. So, the words *have*, *cave*, and *save*, are said to be *inconsistent* because the same string of letters can have multiple pronunciations. Words of this type take longer to read than words that have entirely consistent letter–pronunciation patterns (Glushko, 1979), and the extra reading time reflects the costs associated with selecting the correct phonological code from a number of automatically activated candidates.

Further evidence for automatic activation of phonological (sound) codes comes from studies involving *heterographic* (multiple spellings) *homophones* (one pronunciation). Words such as *meet* take a long time to reject when a subject is judging whether the word belongs to the category "food." If subjects could go straight from the visual image of *meet* to the meaning of "meet" (to get together), then they would just as easily reject that word as a type of food as an orthographically similar word, like *melt*, that is pronounced very differently. What happens is that the word *meet* activates the sound /meet/, which matches a member of the food category, "meat," and this makes *meet* hard to reject as a kind of food—it has a twin that sounds like a food, and the sound code is activated automatically (Jared & Seidenberg, 1991; Van Orden, 1987, 1991).

It also takes longer to reject a *pseudohomophone*—a string of letters that would be pronounced like a real word, e.g., *brane* (compare to brain), suggesting that looking at the string *brane* activates prestored phonological representations that are associated with a known word, which makes it harder to reject a pseudohomophone than a pronounceable letter string that does not activate a prestored phonological representation (e.g., *brene*) (Coltheart, Davelaar, Jonasson, & Besner, 1977; Rubenstein, Lewis, & Rubenstein, 1971). Similar effects occur in more naturalistic reading tasks. When subjects are asked to find misspelled words in texts, they are more likely to miss a homophone (e.g., *steal* in place of the correct target word *steel*) than a similar looking word that is pronounced differently (e.g., *stale*) (Daneman & Stainton, 1991).[16]

Nothing in a Chinese character maps onto individual phonemes. The entire character represents an entire syllable, and no subpart of the symbol maps onto a subpart of the syllable. Each symbol simultaneously maps onto a morpheme, and most of them map onto a word as well (some words are made up of more than one character, such as aardvark, so there the individual symbols map onto syllables, but not onto words). Because there is a one-to-one mapping between many characters and many morphemes, it is possible that Chinese readers could bypass phonology on their way to accessing character meaning.

If that were the case, then the mental processes used to read Chinese really would be very different from the mental processes used to read English. It turns out, however, that Chinese characters activate phonological representations, just as English words do. Chinese characters can be consistent and inconsistent in ways very similar to English words (Lee et al., 2007). Some Chinese characters have the same phonetic radical, but are pronounced in very different ways. These are *inconsistent characters*. Other Chinese characters have the same phonetic radical, and are pronounced the same. Reading time data and neurophysiological (ERP) data both indicate that inconsistent characters impose greater processing costs than consistent characters, showing that Chinese readers activate phonological representations while reading silently, just as English readers do (Hsu, Tsai, Lee, & Tzeng, 2009; Lee, Tsai, Su, Tzeng, & Hung, 2005; Perfetti et al., 2005; Tsai, Lee, Tzeng, Hung, & Yen, 2004). These studies also indicate that inconsistency costs increase as the frequency of the character decreases (similar to frequency by consistency and frequency by regularity interactions in English reading). Additionally, Chinese characters produce preview benefits when a previewed character shares a phonological code with the target character (Tsai et al., 2004).

Chinese readers even resemble English readers on some characteristics that do not normally appear in Chinese script. In reading English, spacing information is an important aspect of eye movement planning, and reading slows down when spacing information is degraded or denied to the reader. Normally, Chinese script is printed without spaces between the characters. So Chinese readers are used to seeing text where the characters are very close to one another. As a result, you might think that Chinese readers' eye movements are optimized for this spacing pattern, and that their eye movements would be disrupted when confronted with an unusual spacing pattern. However, despite lack of practice with spaced text, Chinese readers had no trouble reading when spaces were placed in the Chinese text between words. These data indicate that words, rather than characters, are the relevant unit that drives eye movements in Chinese, just as they are in English (Bai, Yan, Liversedge, Zang, & Rayner, 2008).

If Chinese script is viewed as "pictures of words," it would make sense that the right hemisphere would be especially crucial, and might entirely control, lexical access in Chinese readers. This assumption is based partly on neurological and neurophysiological studies showing that the right hemisphere plays a prominent role in the processing of visual images and the representation of visuo-spatial information. This critical role of the right hemisphere in processing spatial information results in severe visual information-processing deficits in some patients with right-hemisphere damage, especially right parietal lobe damage (e.g., Rafal & Robertson, 1995), including the phenomenon of *left-hemifield neglect*. Left-hemifield neglect is observed in some right-hemisphere damaged patients. It is characterized by an inability to perceive visual information to the left of the point where the patient is fixating. It turns out, however, that while bilingual Chinese readers have greater right-hemisphere activation while reading Chinese than English, Chinese script activates the same left-lateralized network of brain regions that are activated when English script is read (Fiez, Tranel, Seager-Frerichs, & Damasio, 2006; Jobard, Crivello, & Tzourio-Mazoyer, 2003; Mainy et al., 2008; Perfetti et al., 2007). Figure 10.6 presents a comparison of Chinese and English bilinguals reading English or Chinese script. The figure shows substantial overlap between the two (but some degree of greater activation of right hemisphere by Chinese script).[17] Interestingly, when American college students started to learn to read Chinese, they showed right-hemisphere activation when reading Chinese, but not when reading English (see Figure 10.6, bottom). Chinese bilinguals showed right-hemisphere activation while reading Chinese script and also when reading English script. These data indicate that both the characteristics of the script and individual learning histories affect how the brain responds to different kinds of writing.

Figure 10.6 fMRI data from English (left) and Chinese (right) bilinguals reading English (top) and Chinese (bottom) script (from Perfetti et al., 2007, p. 141). Activations for both nationalities and both scripts include parts of the fusiform gyrus commonly known as the *visual word form area.*

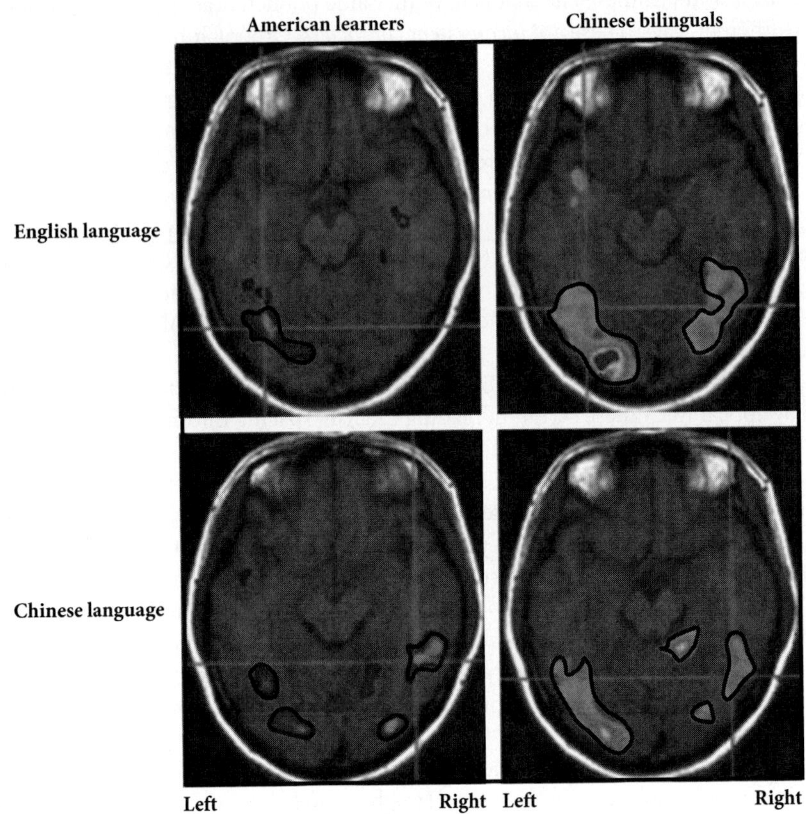

Learning to read

> *Learning to read ... taxes our perceptual abilities to the limit—far more than learning to talk. It requires finer visual, auditory and manual skills than almost anything else most of us learn. A sequence of small, minimally redundant, visual symbols must be discriminated and translated in the phonemic sequence of sounds that comprise each word. (Stein & Walsh, 1997, pp. 147–148)*

On top of that, learning to read is an unnatural task (Gough & Hillinger, 1980). Spoken language is found in every person who is exposed to the appropriate stimuli, and emerges without special training. Writing is a relatively recent invention—it's about 5,500 years old according to Rayner & Pollatsek (1989)—and reading emerges only with special instruction in the vast majority of children. Learning to read an alphabetic script, such as English, involves mastering two related principles. First, children must realize that words are made up of subparts. When children obtain the knowledge that spoken words can be broken down into subparts, they are said to have *phonemic awareness.* Second, children must realize that specific patterns of letters go with specific patterns of speech sounds. When they achieve an understanding of how sets of letters go with sets of speech sounds, they are said to grasp *the alphabetic principle.*

Phonemic awareness is an important precursor of literacy (the ability to read and write). It is thought to play a causal role in reading success, because differences in phonemic awareness can be measured in children who have not yet begun to read. Those prereaders' phonemic awareness test scores then predict how successfully and how quickly they will master reading skills two or three years down the line when they begin to read (Torgesen et al., 1999, 2001; Wagner & Torgesen, 1987; Wagner, Torgesen, & Rashotte, 1994; Wagner et al., 1997; see Wagner, Piasta, & Torgesen, 2006, for a review; but see Castles & Coltheart, 2004, for a different perspective). Phonemic awareness can be assessed in a variety of ways, including the *elision*, *sound categorization*, and *blending* tasks (Torgesen et al., 1999), among others, but the best assessments of phonemic awareness involve multiple measures. In the elision task, children are given a word such as *cat* and asked what it would sound like if you got rid of the /k/ sound. Sound categorization involves listening to sets of words, such as *pin, bun, fun*, and *gun*, and identifying the word "that does not sound like the others" (in this case, *pin*; Torgesen et al., 1999, p. 76). In blending tasks, children hear an onset (word beginning) and a rime (vowel and consonant sound at the end of a syllable), and say what they would sound like when they are put together. Children's composite scores on tests of phonemic awareness are strongly correlated with the development of reading skill at later points in time. Children who are less phonemically aware will experience greater difficulty learning to read, but effective interventions have been developed to enhance children's phonemic awareness, and hence to increase the likelihood that they will acquire reading skill within the normal time frame (Ehri, Nunes, Willows, et al., 2001).[18]

Once children are aware that words are made up of separable speech sounds, they can begin to assign letters and patterns of letters to individual speech sounds and combinations of speech sounds. This process of mapping letters to sounds is complicated for English speakers, because English has a *deep orthography* (as compared to a *shallow orthography*). *Shallow* orthographies have something close to a one-to-one relationship between letters and speech sounds (Spanish and Russian are two languages whose scripts are in the shallow category). So, for example, in Russian, there is no equivalent to the letter "c". When you need the /k/ sound in Russian, you use a "k," as in кошка (pronounced "koe-sh-ka"; *cat*). When you need the /s/ sound, you use the "c" symbol, which is always pronounced like /s/ (as in самовар, pronounced "sam-o-var", *samovar*).[19] English has a deep orthography, because there are multiple mappings between letters and sounds. Sometimes the /s/ sound is spelled with an "s", but sometimes it is spelled with a "c." The "c" sometimes sounds like /s/ (e.g., *ceiling*), but sometimes it sounds like /k/ (e.g., *cat*), sometimes it is silent (e.g., *scene*). English even offers up some very nasty surprises, as in *colonel* and *yacht* (classified as *strange words* in Coltheart's taxonomy).

Why does English have a deep orthography? Why not just spell everything the way it sounds? One reason why English has a deep orthography is that its orthographic system was built to try to do two jobs at once. It tries to convey the sounds that the words make, but it also tries to preserve information about the morphemes that make up the word. So, *sign* really should be spelled *sine* if the goal is to straightforwardly signal the sound of the word using letters. (What's that "g" doing in there? Nothing!) But if *sign* and *signpost* were spelt *sine and sinepost*, then we would lose the visual link to semantically related words that are pronounced differently, like *signal*, and *signature*. So, the orthographic system of English compromises between conveying letter–sound correspondences, which it does much of the time, and preserving morphological relationships between words that are pronounced differently.

English orthography can also be thought of as a *cipher* (Gough & Hillinger, 1980). In a cipher, as opposed to a simple code, there is a complex mapping between different representational elements. In a simple code, one symbol goes with one message. So, if the number 1 always represents "tacos," 2 always represents "rule," then the code "12" represents the message "tacos rule," and "21" would mean "rule tacos." But in a cipher, the meaning assigned to any one symbol is a function of patterns that hold across larger numbers of symbols. In a cipher system, 1 might mean "tacos" when it appears at the beginning of a string and "bacon" when it appears anywhere else; 2 might mean "rule" when it follows 1, but "tasty" when it comes at the beginning of a string. In this cipher system, "12" still means "tacos rule," but "21" means "tasty bacon." So, to know what function a particular symbol (e.g., letter) means, you have to know what context the letter appears in. The function of an individual symbol in one context may be very different than the same symbol in another context (e.g., the letter "c" has at least five different functions, as in *cat*, *ceiling*, *school*, *chunder*, and *scene*).

Given the odd and sometimes apparently random nature of English orthography, it is not particularly surprising that instruction methods involving *systematic phonics*, emphasizing explicit instruction in letter–sound correspondences, and a systematic program starting with simpler letter–sound mappings followed by more complex letter–sound mappings, produce the greatest increases in reading skill when different instruction methods are compared (Ehri, Nunes, Stahl, & Willows, 2001; Ehri, Nunes, Willows, et al., 2002; Stuebing, Barth, Cirino, Francis, & Fletcher, 2008). In other words, even though a multiplicity of variables affect the development of reading skill, including teacher skill, school setting, class size, availability of tutoring, intensity of instruction, and specific student characteristics, phonics instruction still works better than other methods overall.

Systematic phonics is at one end of the instructional spectrum, while *whole-language* methods, which emphasize self-discovery of the alphabetic principle based on immersion in literature, and which provide no explicit phonics instruction, sit at the other end. Other instructional techniques, such as the *whole word* method combine aspects of both phonics and whole-language instruction. The results of a large meta-analysis (a method of combining individual studies into a larger block that provides a more accurate way of assessing how treatments influence performance) showed that some phonics instruction was better than no phonics instruction, and systematic phonics instruction was better than unsystematic phonics instruction. Further, phonics instruction may be especially beneficial to children who have difficulty developing phonemic awareness and grasping the alphabetic principle. As Karla Stuebing and her colleagues explain (2008, p. 124), "some children who are weaker in alphabetic skills may need more explicit phonics instruction … whereas the degree of systematic phonics instruction may be less important for other children with better developed letter–sound knowledge."

This is not to imply that there is no value in other instructional techniques, such as whole-language and whole-word methods. In general, given a random sample of children, systematic phonics instruction will produce the biggest increases in reading skill. But specific individual children can benefit as much from other methods as from phonics.[20] On the other hand, there are children who are at risk of reading failure because they do not have phonemic awareness or have not mastered the alphabetic principle who really do need systematic phonics instruction. So, while there is no inherent, necessary conflict between whole-language and phonics instruction methods, if phonics and whole-language ever go to war, this author will volunteer for Phil Gough's phonics army.

Cognitive Processing in Reading II: Visual Word Processing

The cognitive processes involved in reading words share some of the characteristics of listening to words—both involve taking perceptual input and using it to recognize individual words and access their meanings. However, not all of the principles of auditory word

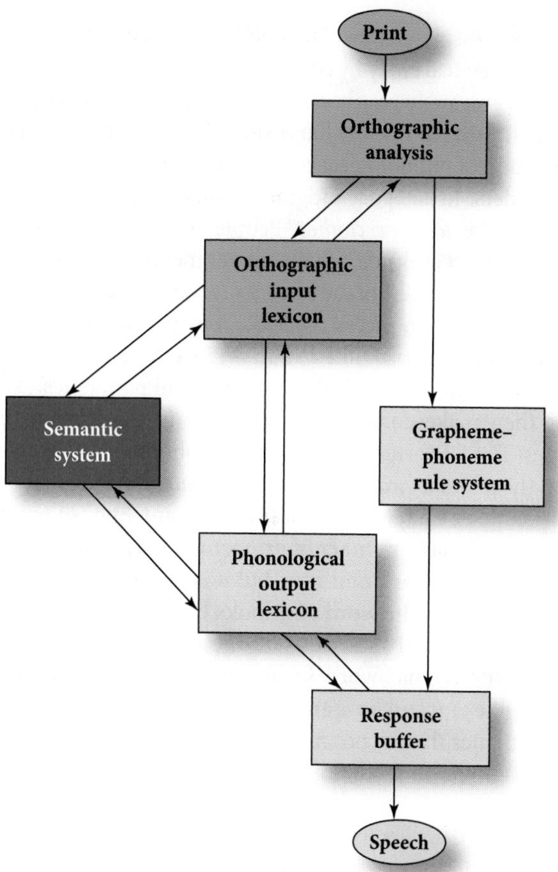

Figure 10.7 The dual-route cascaded (DRC) model of word reading (Coltheart, Rastle, Perry, Langdon, & Ziegler, 2001, p. 213). The model accesses word meanings from print either using a visual code (medium orange shading), via the *orthographic input lexicon*, or an auditory code (light orange shading), via a grapheme-to-phoneme conversion mechanism that maps letters or groups of letters onto speech sounds and uses the speech sounds to activate entries in the semantic (meaning) system

processing apply to visual word processing, or at least they do not necessarily apply in the same way. This section reviews the two major classes of theories that attempt to explain how readers access stored information about words during reading—the *dual-route model* and the *single-route* (sometimes called *triangle*) models, starting with the dual-route model.

Dual-route and DRC models

The *dual-route* and *dual-route cascaded* (DRC) models of visual word recognition and reading aloud (Coltheart, Curtis, Atkins, & Haller, 1993; Coltheart, Rastle, Perry, Langdon, & Ziegler, 2001) are two of the most intensively investigated and highly developed accounts of visual word processing. These models are called *dual*-route or *dual-process* models because they propose that there are two separate ways that people can use visual input to access entries in the mental lexicon. Specifically, readers can "sound out" the word, or they can access the lexicon directly without first activating phonological codes. Figure 10.7 presents a schematic of the DRC processing system. The DRC model says that you can use a sequence of letters to access a word's lexical entry by converting that sequence of letters into a sequence of phonemes. To do this, you apply *grapheme-to-phoneme correspondence* (or GPC) rules on a letter-by-letter basis, starting at the left-hand side of the word and working through it to the right. In fact, activation of phonological codes from word-like letter strings appears to be automatic in skilled readers. In category judgment tasks, people monitor a list of words for members of a category like *food* or *clothes*. People frequently false-alarm to word and pseudo-word stimuli like *meet* and *sute*, which are *not* members of the correct category, but are pronounced the same as members of the category (i.e., *meat* and *suit*; Coltheart, Patterson, & Leahy, 1994). Readers appear to access the lexicon by activating the sounds that go with each letter or cluster of letters (in cases like *ch* and *sh*) in a more-or-less left-to-right fashion. When readers see the word *cat*, they activate its component phonemes, /k/, /a/, and /t/. The activated phonemes then make contact with an entry in the lexicon that has the same sequence of phonemes. The GPC rules are applied by a phonological processing system, and so this route is called the *phonological* or *assembled phonology* route.

The assembled phonology route works just fine for many English words, but it does not work for all of them. English has a number of *orthographically irregular* or *exception* words. The word *have* looks like *gave*, *wave*, and *save*, but it is pronounced with a short /a/ sound rather than the long /ā/ sound. The word *pint* looks like *mint*, *tint*, and *lint*, but it has the long /ī/ sound instead of the usual short /i/ sound. *Colonel* doesn't look like anything else, but is pronounced like the regular word *kernel*, which has a totally unrelated meaning. When exception words like *pint* and *have* are run through the assembled phonology system, it compiles a set of phonemes that do not match any of the entries in the mental lexicon. So assembled phonology can not be used to access stored representations of exception words like *colonel*, *have*, and *pint*.

This does not mean that the assembled phonology route automatically shuts down when readers encounter an exception word. To the contrary, the phonological route stays active and can cause readers to mispronounce exception words. When *pint* is mispronounced with the short /i/ sound, this is called a *regularization error*. Because the phonological route regularizes the pronunciations of exception words, lexical access via assembled phonology fails for those words. DRC solves problems created by the misapplication of GPC rules by proposing that some words can be accessed via a separate system that bypasses the assembled phonology route and contacts the lexicon directly. This alternative route to the lexicon is called the *direct* or *orthographic* route. According to dual-route theory, exception words are accessed via a visual code, and once the matching lexical entry has been activated by the visual input, the lexicon makes the correct pronunciation available. In fact, the behavior of the DRC model on word pronunciation closely matches human performance both on reading under time pressure, where the model makes errors on exception words like *czar*, and *isle*, just like people do, and reading at a slower rate, where the model correctly pronounces 7,980 out of 7,981 words in its vocabulary (with *czar* being the lone exception; Coltheart et al., 2001).

The DRC system therefore allows pronunciation of both regular and exception words. Regular words are accessed via assembled phonology and irregular words are accessed via the direct route.

If the direct route can handle exception words, why not use it for everything? The answer is that we frequently encounter words in writing that we have not seen before, even though we might know what the word means because we have heard it. So, we can have entries in semantic memory and a matching phonological word form, but no experience accessing those entries from print. We can read those words nonetheless by using the assembled phonology mechanism to generate their pronunciations. We can also use the phonological route to generate pronunciations for words that we have never seen before and have not assigned any meaning to (like *mave* or *slood*; see Rastle & Coltheart, 1999a).

According to the DRC model of reading, letters are passed through the grapheme-to-phoneme conversion system starting with the leftmost letter in the word and continuing on through each letter to the right. That is how the mechanism can compile the pronunciation for a word. If letters in words are processed in a serial left-to-right fashion like this, then manipulating the beginning of a word should have an earlier and stronger effect on reading behavior than manipulating the end of a word. This basic prediction has been tested in a variety of ways, and relevant evidence can be found in experiments involving manipulations of the point where a word becomes *irregular* and manipulations of the point where a word becomes uniquely identifiable.

Some work trying to verify whether letters are processed in serial order has focused on the reading of *irregular words*. Some words are *regular*, because they match the normal pattern of letter–sound correspondence in the language. Words like *cat*, *home*, and *trip*, are regular words. Some words are *irregular* or *exception words*. They violate the usual pattern of spelling–sound correspondence in the language. *Yacht*, *colonel*, and *have* are irregular words. The DRC model predicts that exception words should take longer to read on average than regular words, because only the lexical (direct) route supports their pronunciation, while both the lexical and non-lexical routes support the pronunciation of regular words.[21]

The DRC model predicts further that *where* the irregularity appears in the word should affect reading times. Some experimental results show that irregularity appearing early in a word slows reading more than irregularity that appears later in the word (Rastle & Coltheart, 1999b; see Coltheart. Woollams, Kinoshita, & Perry, 1999, and Forster & Davis, 1991, for compatible serial order effects in phonological priming experiments). Words such as *choir* are harder to read than words like *benign*. Both of them are irregular, but irregularity occurs earlier in *choir* than in *benign* (*ch* is usually pronounced as in *chair*, *church*, and *china*; *g* usually makes a noise, as in *signal*, *bagpipes*, and *piglet*).

Similar logic based on serial letter processing leads to the prediction that words with earlier *visual uniqueness points* should be read more quickly than words with later visual uniqueness points. Visual uniqueness points are the written equivalent of the auditory uniqueness points (reviewed in Chapter 3). Some written words have beginnings that are shared with many other words, and some words have beginnings that are shared with very few or perhaps no other words. *Dw-* appears at the beginning of very few words (*dwarf*, *dwell*, and morphological relatives of *dwell*), while *ca-* appears at the beginning of many words. As a result, the visual uniqueness point for *dwarf* occurs at the third letter, while the visual uniqueness point for *carpet* occurs at the final letter (which discriminates it from, e.g., *carpenter*). If words are processed serially, from left to right, then words like *dwarf* should take less time to read than equivalent words that have later uniqueness points. However, when such words are used in a variety of single-word reading experiments (e.g., Radeau, Morais, Mousty, Saerens, & Bertelson, 1992), and naturalistic reading experiments (e.g., Lima & Inhoff, 1985; Miller, Juhasz, & Rayner, 2006; but see Kwantes & Mewhort, 1999), words with early uniqueness points are actually read slower than words with late uniqueness points, contrary to the serial letter encoding hypothesis.[22]

Single-route models

Single-route models of word reading grew out of the parallel distributed processing tradition, as exemplified by models like TRACE and SRN (Elman, 2004; McClelland & Rumelhart, 1981; Harm & Seidenberg, 1999, 2001, 2004; Plaut & McClelland, 1993; Plaut, McClelland, Seidenberg, & Patterson, 1996; Seidenberg & McClelland, 1989, 1990; see Chapter 3). The architecture of a single-route lexical access mechanism is represented in Figure 10.8.

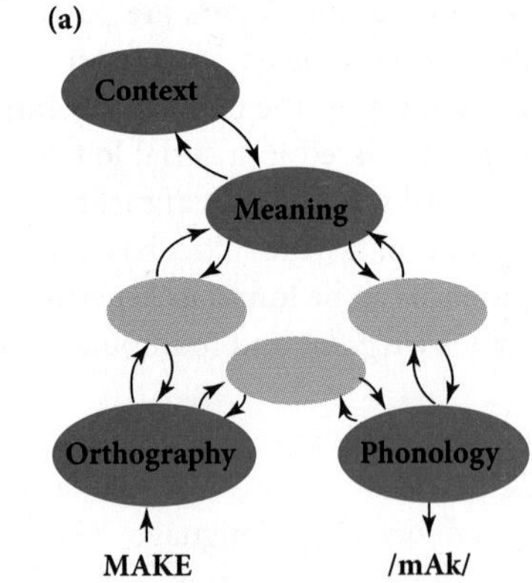

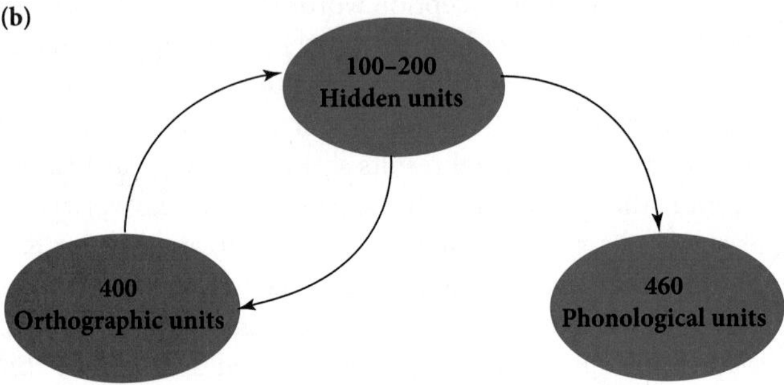

Figure 10.8 A general framework for lexical access (top) and a more specific mechanism for generating pronunciations from visual input (bottom) (from Seidenberg & McClelland, 1989, pp. 526–527)

The single-route mechanism is based on a neural network model containing three groups of processing units. Written input is taken up by a group of processing units, the *orthographic units*, that represent groups of letters. This set of orthographic units is connected both to a group of processing units that represents word meanings and to a set of phonological units that represents word pronunciations. A layer of hidden processing units lies between each group of major processing units. So, visual input leads to a pattern of activity in the orthographic units, that pattern of activity leads to a pattern of activity in the hidden units, and the pattern of activity in the hidden units in turn causes a pattern of activity in the phonology units, which directly govern the naming response.

Every word is represented as a distributed pattern of activation across the entire network. How do these patterns of activation get into the network so that it can respond to visual inputs? As Seidenberg and McClelland explain (1989, p. 525), "Learning … involves modifying the weights through experience in reading and pronouncing words." Each processing unit in the network is connected to other processing units, so that when one unit is activated, it can influence the activation of other units. At the outset, the strengths of the connections, or *connection weights*, between different units are randomized. These connection weights are altered by experience. The experience consists of a number of training trials—about 150,000 trials in the original model. On each trial, a word is presented. This word leads to a pattern of activation across the entire network as activation spreads from unit to unit. After activation has finished spreading through the network, the pattern of activation at the output units, which represent different pronunciations, is compared to the correct output—what the pattern of activation should be if the model is pronouncing the word accurately. At the beginning of training, the output will differ greatly from the correct output. The model gradually becomes more accurate by adjusting the connection weights to minimize the difference between the model's output and the correct pattern in the phonological units. To test how well the model has learned under different training conditions, new words are presented following the training phase (after the connection weights have been fixed or frozen), and the model's accuracy is assessed.

One of the advantages of the single-route architecture is its striking simplicity. As shown at the bottom of Figure 10.8, there are only three sets of processing units, each of which consists of only a few hundred individual units. Nonetheless, with the right kind of training, the model's behavior closely matches human behavior in a number of ways.

One way to assess the model's performance is to look at the difference between the model's output at the phonological units compared with the correct output. This difference produces the *phonological error score*. The phonological error score provides two pieces of information. First, it indicates whether the network's pronunciation matches the correct one, or whether it is pronouncing something other than the appropriate target word. Second, it provides an estimate of how quickly the network responds to a given stimulus—lower error scores indicate faster response times.

After training, the model's error scores were lower when the model's output was compared to the correct target than when the model's output was compared to close possible competitors on about 98% of the test trials. So, the model was highly accurate in pronouncing test words. Second, the model generated lower error scores for words that it was exposed to more often during training. So, just like people, the model responded more quickly to more familiar words. Third, the model also produced regularization errors for low-frequency exception words (such as *brooch*, which the model pronounced as rhyming with *book*; *plaid* was pronounced like *played* instead of as rhyming with *sad*). The model also produced the correct pronunciation for many higher frequency exception words. Fourth, the model produced longer response times for irregular words than for regular words, and this effect was bigger for lower frequency words than for higher frequency words (the so-called *frequency by regularity interaction*; Seidenberg, 1985; Seidenberg, Waters, Barnes, & Tanenhaus, 1984; Taraban & McClelland, 1987; Waters & Seidenberg, 1985). Fifth, the model responded to non-word stimuli similar to the way people respond to the same stimuli. Pseudohomophones (stimuli that are pronounced like words but that are not words) like *brane* caused the model to respond faster than it did when it was exposed to equally long and complex non-words that do not sound like real words. People can name pseudohomophones faster than other non-words, and they have a harder time rejecting pseudohomophones in a lexical decision task (McCann & Besner, 1987). It turns out that pseudohomophones are more similar to real words in their spelling patterns, however, and so the single-route model produces lower error scores for pseudohomophones than other non-words, because it has been trained on many stimuli that are more similar to pseudo-homophones.

Neighborhood effects

Dual-route and single-route models have been in competition as theories of word reading for decades and significant research effort has been invested in trying to determine which kind of model provides a better description and explanation of a variety of reading-related phenomena. Neighborhood effects occur when people read words, and so researchers have tried to find out whether dual-route and single-route models also produce such effects.

The *regularity effect* (regular words are easier to recognize) and the *frequency by regularity interaction* represent represent two kinds of *neighborhood* effects. The term *orthographic neighborhood* refers to the fact that words often come in groups that resemble one another. So, *took*, *book*, *nook*, and *look* are all neighbors because they are all very similar (Coltheart et al., 1977; Glushko, 1979; Yarkoni, Balota, & Yap, 2008). According to *Coltheart's neighborhood metric*, a word's neighborhood consists of all the other words that can be created by changing one letter at one position in the original word. The words *bent*, *tint*, *test*, and *tens*, are all orthographic neighbors of the word *tent*. Different words come in different sized neighborhoods—some words have many neighbors and some only have a few. In word reading, with all other things being equal, the bigger the neighborhood, the faster you respond to a word (Andrews, 1989; Balota, Cortese, Sergent-Marshall, Spieler, & Yap, 2004; Coltheart et al., 1977; Mulatti, Reynolds, & Besner, 2006). This facilitative effect of large neighborhoods may reflect activation fed forward from word-level representations to the phonological representations involved in word pronunciation. Letters that activate large neighborhoods will lead to more units sending activation to the phonological units that are connected to words in that neighborhood.[23]

There are different kinds of neighborhoods, and the kind of neighborhood a word inhabits affects how easy it is to read that word. Different orthographic neighborhoods are described as being *consistent* or *inconsistent*, based on how the different words in the neighborhood are pronounced. If they are all pronounced alike, then the neighborhood is consistent. If some words in the neighborhood are pronounced one way, and others are pronounced another way, then the neighborhood is inconsistent. The neighborhood that *made* inhabits is consistent, because all of the other members of the neighborhood (*wade*, *fade*, etc.) are pronounced with the long /a/ sound. On the other hand, *hint* lives in an *in*consistent neighborhood because some of the neighbors are pronounced with the short /i/ sound (*mint, lint, tint*), but some are pronounced with the long /i/ sound (*pint*). Words from inconsistent neighborhoods take longer to pronounce than words from consistent neighborhoods, and this effect extends to non-words as well (Glushko, 1979; see also Jared, McRae, & Seidenberg, 1990; Seidenberg, Plaut, Petersen, McClelland, & McRae, 1994). So, it takes you less time to say *tade* than it takes you to say *bint*. Why would this be?

Glushko, and the single-route theorists who followed, argued that seeing a string of letters like *tade* or *bint* activates an entire neighborhood of closely matching words (similar effects are predicted by TRACE, as well). In consistent neighborhoods, all of the activated word representations point toward the same pronunciation, long /a/. When a visual stimulus activates possible matches in an inconsistent neighborhood, some of the words point toward one pronunciation, while others point to a different pronunciation. Sorting out this pronunciation conflict takes time, and so words and non-words from inconsistent neighborhoods take longer to pronounce. It turns out, however, that most of the irregular words that we encounter are in the higher frequency end of the familiarity spectrum, and being irregular has only a small effect on how long it takes to recognize and pronounce these words.[24]

The single-route model provides a unified explanation for slow processing of low frequency and irregular words. Specifically, the connection weights that the model needs for accurate performance are adjusted in the right direction more often for both high-frequency and regular words, and less often for both low-frequency and exception words (Seidenberg & McClelland, 1989).

The DRC model also suggests that experience affects performance such that more frequently encountered words are likely to be accessed via the orthographic route, minimizing effects of assembled phonology. Longer access times are posited via the orthographic route for less frequent words, and so regularized pronunciations compiled by the phonological route are able to compete with the pronunciations generated by the orthographic route, which leads to slower response times for less frequent words, especially irregular ones.

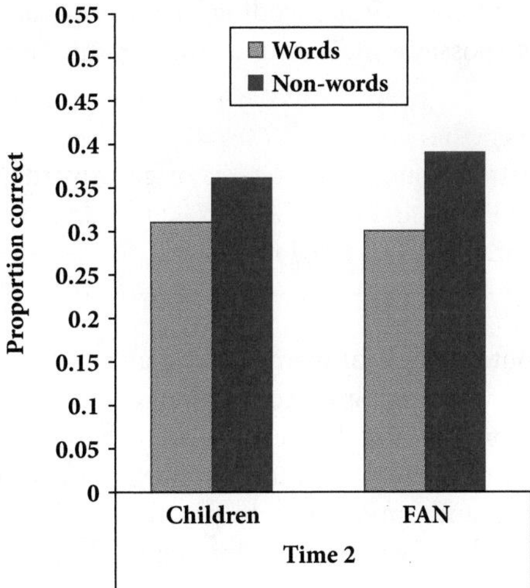

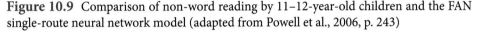

Figure 10.9 Comparison of non-word reading by 11–12-year-old children and the FAN single-route neural network model (adapted from Powell et al., 2006, p. 243)

The single-route models would seem to enjoy a parsimony advantage, since they can produce frequency and regularity effects, as well as their interaction, on the basis of a single mechanism.[25] However, recent studies have indicated that the exact position in a word that leads to inconsistent spelling–sound mappings affects how quickly the word can be read aloud. As noted above, it takes longer to read a word with an inconsistency at the beginning (e.g., *general*, where hard /g/ as in *goat* is more common) than a word with an inconsistency at the end (e.g., *bomb*, where the *b* is silent). This may be more consistent with the DRC serial mapping of letters to sounds than the parallel activation posited by PDP-style single-route models (Coltheart & Rastle, 1994; Cortese, 1998; Rastle & Coltheart, 1999b; Roberts, Rastle, Coltheart, & Besner, 2003).

Non-word pronunciation

Considerable debate between proponents of the dual-route and single-route architectures has focused on the issue of non-word naming. Early versions of the single-route model were less accurate than dual-route models of non-word reading (Besner, 1990; Coltheart et al., 1993). Although the single-route model did well on simpler non-words like *fike*, it did not do nearly as well on more complex non-words like *jinje*. The dual-route model generated pronunciations for words like *jinje* that were similar to what real people produced. However, newer single-route models have been improved in two ways. First, they are trained on letter–sound correspondences. Second, they are exposed to sets of words that are used to teach real children reading skills. When these modifications are made to single-route models, their non-word reading performance rises to the levels observed in beginning readers (see Figure 10.9; Powell, Plaut, & Funnell, 2006).

In addition, recent neuroimaging data show that overlapping brain areas are activated when people read novel words (pseudo-words) compared to real words (see Plate 18, left; Dietz, Jones, Gareau, Zeffiro, & Eden, 2005), which implicates a unified system for reading novel words and familiar words. However, pseudo-words do elicit greater activity than real words in the left inferior frontal gyrus (perhaps implicating greater working memory demands associated with phonological decoding of novel pseudo-words) as well as left posterior fusiform gyrus (possibly indicating a role for this region in the activation of phonological codes).

Dyslexia: Single-Deficit Models

Single-route and dual-route models of word reading also compete to explain why some individuals have difficulty reading. Specifically, they compete to explain how and why some individuals suffer from *dyslexia*. Dyslexia occurs when an individual has a problem reading, even though they are otherwise intellectually and behaviorally normal and have had the proper instruction and opportunity to practice reading. Approximately 15% of males and 5% of females will suffer from developmental dyslexia (Stein & Walsh, 1997). A far smaller proportion of the population will suffer from acquired dyslexia, but among specific types of acquired brain damage, such as semantic dementias associated with syndromes like Alzheimer's and Parkinson's disease, the incidence of dyslexia is very high (Woollams, Lambon Ralph, Plaut, & Patterson, 2007). A great deal of research and theorizing has gone into understanding dyslexia.[26] This section reviews some of the more recent experimental and theoretical work, including a discussion of dual-route and single-route models of dyslexia.

There are some common threads that appear to cut across developmental and acquired dyslexia. First, in both developmental and acquired dyslexia, there are people who have more trouble reading non-words, such as *feen*, than *exception words*—words that look like but sound different than other words, such as *have*. Likewise, there are groups of both developmental and acquired dyslexics who have less trouble reading non-words than reading exception words. When an individual has greater trouble reading non-words than exception words, they are classified as *phonological* (or *deep*) *dyslexics* (Marshall & Newcome, 1973; see also Castles, Bates, Coltheart, Luciano, & Martin, 2006; Joanisse, Manis, Keating, & Seidenberg, 2000; Woollams et al., 2007). When a person has less trouble reading non-words than reading exception words, they are classified as a *surface dyslexic*. It is important to recognize, however, that most dyslexics fall into the *mixed* category. That is, they perform below normal on a variety of reading and reading-related tasks. "Pure" cases of phonological and surface dyslexia are the exception rather than the rule, although "pure" cases have been observed.

One of the continuing controversies in dyslexia research is whether different kinds of dyslexia reflect completely separate underlying deficits or whether different types of dyslexia are caused by variations in the severity of a single underlying problem. One perspective argues that a single deficit in phonological representations gives rise to both surface and phonological dyslexia (Stanovich, 1988; Stanovich & Siegel, 1994; Stanovich, Siegel, & Gottardo, 1997).

Stanovich and colleagues start by rejecting a common classification scheme for dyslexia. Specifically, they reject the requirement that dyslexia diagnosis be reserved for children with normal IQ accompanied by reading problems. Stanovich and colleagues note that this definition implicitly assumes that the reading problems of people with higher intelligence have a different source than the reading problems of people with lower intelligence, and because no direct evidence supports this assumption, they reject the distinction altogether. Instead of investigating a single subset of people with reading problems, Stanovich and colleagues try to identify as many people as possible who share the characteristic of having difficulty reading. Instead of *pre*supposing that different people have different underlying problems that lead to their reading difficulties, they apply sophisticated statistical techniques to find those individual characteristics that best predict why some people have more trouble reading than others. In other words, Stanovich and colleagues try to let their data point them toward underlying causes, rather than using pre-existing ideas to artificially segregate people into "dyslexic, poor reader" and "non-dyslexic, poor reader" groups.

When poor readers were treated as a single group, Stanovich and colleagues (1994; Stanovich, 1988) found that variables that predicted performance in traditionally defined dyslexics also predicted performance in other poor readers, who would not have been considered dyslexic under the traditional definition. Based on how other cognitive variables correlated with reading skill, Stanovich and colleagues concluded that a single problem dealing with phonological information accounted for most of the variability in people's reading skill. As a result, they labeled their approach the *phonological-core variable-difference* model. According to this model, some dyslexic individuals have more degraded phonological representations than others, so they have more severe problems representing and processing phonological information, and those individuals are classified as phonological dyslexics. Their reading behavior, in terms of the kinds of errors they make, greatly differs from younger readers who are matched for overall general reading skill. Other dyslexic individuals have more mildly degraded phonological representations. Their reading behavior in terms of the kinds of errors they make closely matches the pattern displayed by younger readers who have the same overall reading skill.[27] As a result, sometimes researchers call this group of dyslexics *delayed type* rather than *surface* to highlight their similarity to younger, normally developing readers. The reading difficulties exhibited by surface dyslexics, according to this approach, are partly the result of difficulty mapping letters to phonemes, and partly the result of insufficient exposure, training, and practice. The idea is that delayed type dyslexics can catch up to their normally developing peers with more intensive training (although they may always lag somewhat because their phonological representations are not entirely normal).

One problem with the phonological-core variable-difference model is that some dyslexic readers appear to have normal phonological codes. If an individual has degraded phonological codes, they should have some problems processing speech (which of course relies heavily on phonological coding ability). While recent research has identified some subtle speech-processing deficits in groups of phonological dyslexics, about half of the phonological dyslexics who were tested performed the same as a normal control group in various phoneme discrimination tasks (Joanisse et al., 2000; see also Bruno et al., 2007). Thus, contrary to the hypothesis of a single underlying phonological representation deficit, there appear to be significant numbers of phonological dyslexics who have high-fidelity phonological representations.

Other single-deficit accounts of dyslexia focus on the fact that dyslexic readers often times have problems with cognitive tasks such as sequencing (knowing what order things come in, such as knowing that Monday precedes Tuesday), motor control, and spatial information processing (Stein & Walsh, 1997). In light of findings like these, some researchers have looked for a more basic neurological problem that could simultaneously give rise to dyslexia and other cognitive processing problems.

One possible unified deficit theory of dyslexia involves the anatomy and physiology of the neural systems involved in visual word processing. The *magnocellular* theory of dyslexia argues that there is a deficit in one specific part of the visual system: the lateral geniculate nucleus of the thalamus (Borsting et al., 1996; Demb, Boynton, & Heeger, 1997; 1998; Livingstone, Rosen, Drislane, & Galaburda, 1991; Lovegrove, Bowling, Badcock, & Blackwood, 1980; see also Breitmeyer & Ganz, 1976). The lateral geiniculate nucleus is a part of the brain that relays signals from the retina to the visual cortex. It has two kinds of neurons arranged in layers. The *parvocellular* layers are made up of physically small neurons that respond well to differences in color (hue). The *magnocellular layers* are composed of physically larger neurons that respond well to movement and are responsible for dealing with *high temporal frequency information*, visual patterns that change substantially in a relatively small amount of time.

Why might magnocellular abnormalities lead to reading problems? First, the magnocellular layers of the lateral geniculate nucleus are connected to populations of neurons in the parietal lobe that make an important contribution to reading, as evidenced by the fact that damage to these parietal areas can lead to significant impairments in reading ability; and small disturbances in geniculate nucleus function can be magnified in downstream cortical processing areas. Second, magnocellular visual processing contributes to eye movement control, and reading efficiently requires stable, accurately targeted fixations. Reduced magnocellular function may also reduce the ability to target saccades accurately based on peripheral vision (Stein & Walsh, 1997).

The magnocellular hypothesis can explain some patterns of symptoms in some dyslexic readers, but it may not cover the entire spectrum of dyslexic reading problems, and the approach continues to generate new research and new controversies. While some studies (e.g., Galaburda, 1985; Demb et al., 1997, 1998; Eden et al., 1996) found evidence that the physical development or functioning of the magnocellular visual system differs from the norm in dyslexic readers, other studies have failed to find a straightforward connection between magnocellular function and reading disability. For example Anne Sperling and colleagues (Sperling, Lu, Manis, & Seidenberg, 2003) found that dyslexic readers with the greatest difficulty in phonological processing tasks, which are thought to underlie their reading problems, actually had the highest magnocellular function within the dyslexic group. Other studies have found differences in visual processing between skilled readers and phonological dyslexics, but not between skilled readers and surface dyslexics (Borsting et al., 1996). Determining the precise connection between magnocellular function and reading skill will, therefore, require additional research.

Dyslexia: Dual-Route and Single-Route Explanations

Currently, the chief contenders for cognitive theories of word reading, and hence for explaining what goes wrong with reading processes in dyslexia, are the dual-route and single-route models. As a result, considerable research effort has gone into testing whether these models can reproduce behaviors that dyslexic readers exhibit (e.g., Bailey, Manis, Pedersen, & Seidenberg, 2004; Joanisse, et al., 2000; Nickels, Bidermann, Coltheart, Saunders, & Tree, 2008). Developmental dyslexia work has focused on identifying precise patterns of errors produced by different individuals and manipulating aspects of the models to try to reproduce those patterns. Similar logic has been applied to understanding reading deficits following brain damage.

According to the dual-route theory of visual word processing, there are two ways to access a word's pronunciation (Coltheart et al., 2001). The dual-route model therefore suggests that there are two different underlying deficits that give rise to phonological and surface dyslexia (Nickels et al., 2008; see Seidenberg & Plaut, 2006 for a critical review). Damage to the *assembled phonology* route leads to phonological dyslexia, as individuals lose the ability to "sound out" words that they have not seen before. Damage to the direct route leads to surface dyslexia, as individuals are compelled to "sound out" all words, even words like *have*, *pint*, and *yacht* that cannot be "sounded out."

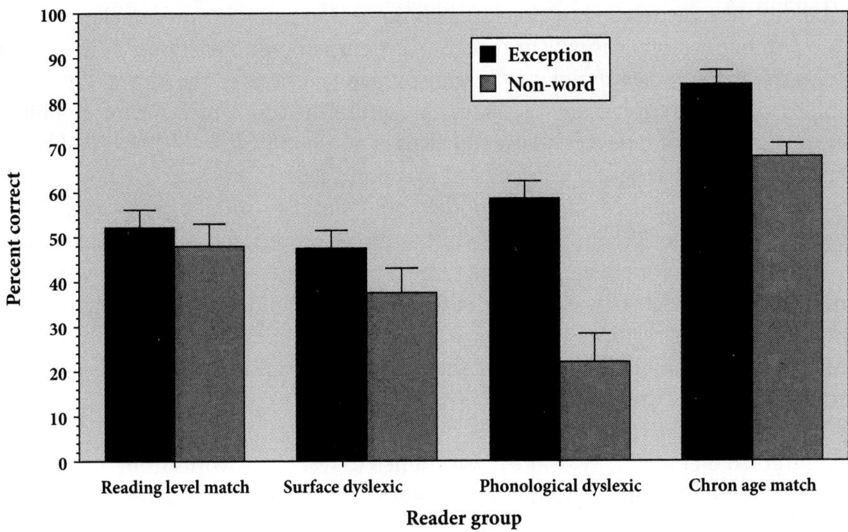

Figure 10.10 Accuracy at reading exception words (e.g., *have, pint*) and non-words (e.g., *bint, tade*) for surface and phonological dyslexics compared to reading level (left) and age-matched controls (right) (from Bailey et al., 2004, p. 141). Notice that surface dyslexics are about equally impaired on exception and non-words, while phonological (deep) dyslexics are far more impaired at reading non-words than familiar exception words. Both groups of dyslexics are impaired on both kinds of targets compared to age-matched controls

Single-route models of reading view word reading as resulting from the operation of a unified neural network, with different kinds of impairment resulting from different types of damage within the system (Harm & Seidenberg, 2004; Woollams et al., 2007; Plaut et al., 1996; Seidenberg & McClelland, 1989; see Nickels et al., 2008 for a critical review). Phonological dyslexia can be modeled within this framework as resulting from damage to units that represent the phonological (sound) codes needed to pronounce words. Surface dyslexia can result from changes to other aspects of the model, such as the number of processing units available to the system (which can be thought of as the amount of processing resources that the system can dedicate to the task), or the rate at which the system can learn from feedback. So, while single-route models view non-word and exception-word reading as being governed by the same sets of representational units running the same processes, different kinds of dyslexia reflect different underlying deficits, as different kinds of damage to the system produce different patterns of behavior.

Figure 10.10 shows representative data on non-word and exception-word reading for surface and phonological dyslexics, as well as age-matched and reading ability-matched control subjects. The DRC model straightforwardly explains these different forms of dyslexia by proposing that different components of the DRC access system are damaged in surface and deep dyslexia (Bailey et al., 2004; Castles & Coltheart, 1993; Manis, Seidenberg, Doi, McBride-Chang, & Petersen, 1996). Surface dyslexia reflects a problem using the direct route to access word meanings, coupled with an intact assembled phonology route. The intact assembled phonology route enables surface dyslexics to pronounce regularly spelled words and novel words, but they regularize exception words. According to the dual-route model, deep dyslexia is caused by a problem in the assembled phonology route, coupled with an intact direct route. If the deep dyslexic has seen a word before, the word's meaning and pronunciation can be accessed via the direct route. If the deep dyslexic has *not* seen the word before, the assembled phonology route is not able to compile a pronunciation, and the resulting pronunciation is usually unrelated to the correct pronunciation.[28] When the DRC model is used to simulate dyslexic symptoms, separate lesions in the direct route and the assembled phonology route are necessary to capture the kinds of behavior exhibited by patients with different types of dyslexia (Nickels et al., 2008).

Single-route models have also been used to capture aspects of dyslexia. For example, the original Seidenberg and McClelland model could simulate some aspects of poor word reading. When half of the hidden units in the model were removed, its error scores for high-frequency words were at about the same level as the error scores for low-frequency words in the full model. This reduction in the number of hidden units had a greater effect for irregular than for regular words, which suggests that a greater number of hidden units is necessary for the model to represent the item-specific information that is required to pronounce exception words accurately.

A subsequent model adopted a more complex system of phonological representations and was trained on phonology before it was trained to recognize words from print (Harm & Seidenberg, 1999). When the phonological representations in this model were degraded in different ways, different patterns of reading performance emerged. *Mild* damage to the network was imposed by limiting the degree to which representations of different phonemes differed from one another. *Moderate* damage was simulated by eliminating one subcomponent of the phonological system and reducing the number of connections by half in the remaining units, on top of the mild form of damage. In the mild damage condition, the model had no trouble with exception words, but did have mild problems with non-words (the pattern observed in deep dyslexia). *Severe* damage was simulated by adding random noise to the pattern of activity within the phonological units. Severe damage to the network produced deficits in both exception-word and non-word reading, which is the pattern observed in surface dyslexia. These simulations provide an existence proof for the single-route architecture: Different patterns of word-reading deficits that are observed in different kinds of dyslexia can be produced by a computational mechanism that has a single set of connections between visual input and word pronunciations.

Which modeling technique provides a better account of dyslexia, dual-route or single-route? The only concise statement that can characterize this immense body of research is something like the following: There is no consensus as to the causes of developmental and acquired dyslexia. Max Coltheart recently claimed that the field *has* reached consensus on one thing. Specifically (Coltheart, 2006, p. 124), "reading theorists have reached unanimity concerning the existence in the skilled reading system of two separate procedures for reading aloud, i.e., two routes from print to speech … Route A can yield a correct response when the stimulus to be read is a word familiar to the reader … Route B is the route that is essential for correct reading aloud of nonwords." However, my own personal survey research suggests that this claim is premature.

LET'S HVAE SMOE FUN CONRER: INTERNET HOAX ROCKS LANUGAGE SCEINCE WOLRD

A few years ago, many people received e-mails that reported a finding from "A Cambridge University Researcher." According to the mass e-mail, the researcher had discovered an amazing fact about English:

> It deosn't mttaer in waht oredr the ltteers in a wrod are, the olny iprmoetnt tihng is taht the frist and lsat ltteer be at the rghit pclae.

Most people find that reading the previous sentence is not too hard, even though most of the letters are in the wrong place. If you're having trouble, here's the spoiler:

> It doesn't matter in what order the letters in a word are, the only important thing is that the first and last letter be at the right place.

If this were true, if it really did not matter where the letters in a word are, that would really challenge the idea that readers identify words by assigning sounds to letters from left to right. It turns out that the claim that letter order doesn't matter at all is wrong, but there is a grain of truth in the claim that reading is sometimes easy even when the letters are scrambled up. It does matter what order the letters in a word are, but it really is true that some letter positions are more important than others, and people really can read texts with scrambled up letters.

We know that letter order does matter because reading speed depends on whether the letters are in their normal or a scrambled up order (Johnson et al., 2007; Rayner, White, Johnson, & Liversedge, 2006; White, Johnson, Liversedge, & Rayner, 2008; see also Christianson, Johnson, & Rayner, 2005, for possible morphology effects; see also Velan & Frost, 2007, who showed that letter reversal had dramatic effects in people reading Hebrew). In general, reversing the order of letters in words does slow reading down, so you will read *matter* faster than *mttaer*. But swapping out letters is worse than reversing them, *moffer* will be harder to handle than *mttaer*. Further, the place in the word where the distortion takes place matters a lot. Distorting the beginning or end of a word disrupts reading more than distorting the middle of the word does, which is partially consistent both with the internet claim and the DRC assumption of serial letter encoding. However, the fact that letter reversal in the middle of a word is minimally disruptive suggests that people do not tightly bind letters to the central serial positions in their mental representations of words. Preview experiments and priming experiments also support this conclusion.

Denying accurate preview of middle letters of words is less disruptive than denying preview of the beginnings or ends of words (Johnson et al., 2007; White et al., 2008). When used as prime words, transposed-letter non-words, such as *jugde*, speed up the processing of words that are semantically related to the unscrambled version (e.g., the target word *court*, which is related to *judge*); and those facilitative effects also depend on where in the prime word the letter reversal occurred (Perea & Lupker, 2003). All of these findings argue against the strict serial processing of letters in words. If letters were processed in a strict left-to-right fashion, or if the lexicon were searched based on a strict left-to-right matching of letters and lexical entries, then reversed letters in the middle of a word should be just as problematic as reversed letters at the beginning of a word.

On the other hand, results from letter-reversal experiments do support the idea that intact word beginnings are especially important in accessing lexical representations in reading, just as they are in spoken language processing. A recent pseudo-word reading study reinforces this conclusion (Mulatti, Peressotti, & Job, 2007). In this study, subjects read five-letter Italian words that had their second or fourth letters replaced so that the result was a pronounceable non-word (if it had been done in English, they could have changed *table* into *toble* or *tabre*). Changing the second letter was more disruptive than changing the fourth letter. These results, like the letter reversal result, might suggest that the lexicon is normally accessed in reading using a cohort-like process (see Chapter 3), under which phonological or orthographic codes extracted from the beginning of the word activate a set of onset-matching candidates from the lexicon (see also Briihl & Inhoff, 1995).

Other research also points away from strictly serial letter encoding. This research shows that consonants have an earlier effect on word identification than vowels do (Lee,

Rayner, & Pollatsek, 2001). In these studies, boundary-change methods were combined with different letter previews to see how much different previews would affect reading times. In some cases, consonants were displayed right away, while vowels were displayed after a short delay. In other cases, vowels were displayed before consonants were. Reading times were longer when consonant information was withheld than when vowel information was withheld, suggesting that readers pay more attention to consonants than vowels while accessing the lexicon, although a given vowel might be in a more leftward position than a given consonant (see also Berent & Perfetti, 1995).

Summary and Conclusions

This chapter has reviewed the mental processes involved in eye movement control and reading. Currently, all theories of eye movement control in reading incorporate the existence of the *perceptual span*, and a smaller *word identification span*. These theories differ in that some assume the serial allocation of attention across words, while others assume that the current window of attention captures as many as four words at a time. Serial attention accounts capture a wide variety of reading-related phenomena, including length and frequency effects, spillover effects, and preview effects. Parafoveal-on-foveal effects are less compatible with serial than parallel attention accounts, but additional empirical work is needed to firmly establish the existence of such effects and to rule out oculomotor (landing position) error as the source of parafoveal-on-foveal effects. Additional research shows that different kinds of scripts (e.g., Chinese vs. English) evoke broadly similar, left-lateralized mental processes, but there are subtle differences in the way different scripts activate phonological information, which influences when competition effects emerge during reading. In addition, phonemic awareness appears to be more critical for learning to read alphabetic scripts than logographic scripts. The reading problems observed in different types of dyslexia are not currently attributable to any single underlying cause, and a large and lively field of research continues to provide evidence in favor of a variety of theoretical approaches, including the single- and dual-route models of reading, as well as a variety of potential underlying neural deficits in dyslexic readers.

TEST YOURSELF

1. How are eye movements controlled during reading? What kinds of eye movements are involved? How much of the text do readers fixate? Why? Describe the perceptual span, how we know it exists, and explain how it affects eye movements during reading. How do the physical limits of the eye affect eye movements in reading?
2. Compare and contrast oculomotor and cognitive control accounts of reading. Why might the reading system incorporate a deadline? What evidence suggests that eye movements in reading are under cognitive control?
3. Compare and contrast the E-Z Reader and SWIFT models of raeding. Describe some of the evidence that supports each model.

4. What's the difference between a writing system, a script, and an alphabet? What effects do different writing systems have on cognitive processing during reading? How do readers of Chinese compare to readers of English?
5. How do children learn to read? Which instruction method works best?
6. How does the dual-route cascaded (DRC) model compare to the single-route model of reading? Which results might be inconsistent with the DRC model? Which results might be inconsistent with the single-route model? What kinds of results are most compatible with each model? Which model do you prefer and why?
7. What is dyslexia? What are the different subtypes? What causes them?

THINK ABOUT IT

1. Sponsor a speed reading contest. Pick a newspaper article or part of a textbook. Give different people different amounts of time (e.g., 10, 15, 30 seconds, 1 minute, 5 minutes, ...) to read the material. Make up some comprehension questions and test people. Plot comprehension accuracy versus time. What do you think will happen? What do your results say about speed reading?

Notes

1 Not counting very tiny vibratory eye movements called *visual nystagmus* and very, very small smooth eye movements called *drift*, and very tiny systematic movements called *microsaccades*. Nystagmus helps prevent the visual system from adapting to a stimulus, which reduces the neural response and hence degrades our perception of the stimulus. Drift is the result of very small errors in muscle control. Microsaccades may move the eyes to locations where the uptake of visual information better suits the needs of cognitive processes, such as lexical access.

2 The exception is when you reach the end of a line, when a *return sweep* takes you leftward and downward to new information.

3 Chinese used to be written this way, but apparently is converting to a horizontal script, Tzeng, personal communication.

4 With the exception being the *reverse landing position effect*. In the reverse landing position effect, sometimes fixation times are shorter when the eye lands on the very end of a word than when the eye lands in the middle of the word. This effect probably reflects oculomotor error. The reader is most likely actually encoding the following word, but saccade error has fixated the eye just to the left of the target.

5 Major exceptions involve cases of word-skipping, where lexical access appears to be completed during fixations on the word to the left or to the right of the target.

6 There are a number of other models of eye movement control in reading that could be profitably reviewed, including Legge's "Mr. Chips" model and SERIOL, among others. Space limitations preclude detailed treatment. Interested readers should consult Legge et al., 1997; Legge et al., 2002; Whitney, 2001; Whitney & Cornelissen, 2008.

7 The rapid completion of lexical access is supported by the fact that ERP signals are modulated by lexicality (whether a stimulus is a word or not) within 100 ms of fixation onset, by frequency information within about 160 ms, and by regularity (whether the word is pronounced like other words with the same spelling pattern or not) within 200 ms of fixation onset (Sereno, Rayner, & Posner, 1998; see also Inhoff & Rayner, 1986, for early frequency effects in reading).

8 Latin for "book binder."

9 At some intermediate exposure durations and SOAs, only one eye movement is executed and it lands in between the first and second target.

10 It may be difficult for any model to fully capture factors that trigger regressions, as they are the most randomly varying eye movement behavior involved in reading (Traxler, Williams, Blozis, & Morris, 2005).

11 Legge explicitly denies that his model is meant to be taken as a theory of how people read (see, e.g., Legge et al., 2002, but Mr. Chips is often included as a possible analog to the human reading system because it successfully captures a number of landing position and optimal viewing position effects. The current version of the GLENMORE model assumes temporally overlapping but not fully parallel processing of words within the perceptual span (Inhoff, et al., 2006). Hence, it may be viewed as an intermediate position between serial attention models, such as E-Z reader and fully parallel models, such as SWIFT.

12 The latest published version of SWIFT includes a set of parameters that can change the gradient of attention so that the model performs more like a serial processing system, but the default version of the model includes parallel activation and a window of attention that takes in more than one word at a time (Engbert et al., 2005).

13 See Pollatsek et al. (2006b), for a different perspective.

14 Inhoff et al. (2005) suggest that there may be a short lag before linguistic information starts to accrue from the parafoveal word; but that estimate is based on an experiment involving alternating case, and so may not be representative of more common reading situations involving regular fonts. Other experiments that manipulated font found that difficult fonts slowed the overall reading rate, but font difficulty did not interact with linguistic properties of words, such as word frequency (Rayner, Reichle, Stroud, Williams, & Pollatsek, 2006).

15 It is just barely possible that some hyper-efficient chunking strategy could allow a reader to pay attention to an entire line of text during a single fixation, but that still ignores the fact that acuity limitations mean that the reader can only identify letters in the fixated word and the next word to the right. So, speed reading would have to involve massive guessing based on contextual information, gross word shape information for parafoveal words, and huge, steaming piles of luck.

16 Some theorists argue that phonological codes are activated more slowly than orthographic codes when people read English (e.g., Daneman & Reingold, 1993; Rastle & Coltheart, 1999a).

17 A recent ERP study provided some evidence that orthographic neighborhood effects may work somewhat differently for Chinese script as compared to English (Huang et al., 2006). These data suggested that bigger orthographic neighborhoods had an early facilitative effect on the activation of phonological codes associated with a character, but later increased competition when lexical selection required the suppression or deactivation of larger numbers of possible competing representations.

18 Phonemic awareness plays a less dramatic role in the acquisition of reading skill in logographic scripts, such as Chinese. Skilled monolingual readers of Chinese tend to be less aware than their English counterparts of the individual phonemes that make up Chinese words (O. J. L. Tzeng, personal communication).

19 A kind of fancy tea kettle.

20 The trouble is that, given the current state of the art, it is impossible to tell ahead of time which children will benefit most from non-phonics instruction.

21 Additional important work has involved testing whether dual-route and single-route models can reproduce neighborhood consistency effects—the extent to which a single spelling pattern has a unique pronunciation. *-ank* is entirely consistent, because all words ending in *-ank* are pronounced to rhyme with *sank*. *-ave* is inconsistent, because some words ending in *-ave* rhyme with *save*, but there are exceptions, like *have*. Some recent work suggests that the DRC is more successful at reproducing regularity effects than consistency effects, and that changes to the model that are necessary to produce consistency effects negatively affect its ability to simultaneously reproduce other well-established reading phenomena (e.g., Jared, 2002).

22 These "inverse uniqueness point" effects are most likely actually bigram or trigram familiarity effects. Words like *dwarf* contain rare sequences of letters, which slows down word recognition (see also Gernsbacher, 1984).

23 Some theorists propose that neighborhood effects really reflect phonological similarity rather than orthographic similarity (Mulatti et al., 2006; Yates, Locker, & Simpson, 2004), because when orthographic similarity is controlled, phonological similarity still affects lexical decision times.

24 Seidenberg (1985) also showed individual differences in the response to irregular words. Highly skilled college-age readers were essentially unaffected by irregular words.

25 Although dual-route models have been implemented using localized representations of words and algorithmic or rule-based conceptualizations of orthography-to-phonology mappings, it is possible to implement a dual-route style model that incorporates parallel distributed processing representational and learning assumptions (e.g., Harm & Seidenberg, 2004; Perry, Ziegler, & Zorzi, 2007; Zorzi, Houghton, & Butterworth, 1998), and such models can simulate a wide variety of word-processing effects, such as the frequency by regularity interaction and the effects of semantic properties like imageability.

26 A recent literature search turned up over 4,000 articles on dyslexia in the PyscInfo database, over half of which were published since 2001.

27 Other researchers also advocate delays in skill acquisition as the cause of dyslexia in some individuals. Because the pattern of non-word and exception-word performance in surface dyslexia closely resembles the pattern observed in younger, less experienced readers, Harm and Seidenberg (1999) suggest that the term *reading delayed* better captures the essence of the problem in people typically labeled as *surface dyslexic*. However, phonological (deep) dyslexics display a pattern of reading that is not observed at any point in normal reading development.

28 Deep dyslexics also make semantic and morphological errors while reading familiar words (Coltheart et al., 2001).

References

Andrews, S. (1989). Frequency and neighborhood effects on lexical access: Activation or search? *Journal of Experimental Psychology: Learning, Memory, and Cognition, 15,* 802–814.

Bai, X., Yan, G., Liversedge, S. P. Zang, C., & Rayner, K. (2008). Reading spaced and unspaced Chinese text: Evidence from eye movements. *Journal of Experimental Psychology: Human Perception and Performance, 34,* 1277–1287.

Bailey, C. E., Manis, F. R., Pedersen, W. C., & Seidenberg, M. S. (2004). Variation among developmental dyslexics: Evidence from a printed-word-learning task. *Journal of Experimental Child Psychology, 87,* 125–154.

Balota, D. A., Cortese, M. J., Sergent-Marshall, S. D., Spieler, D. H., & Yap, M. J. (2004). Visual word recognition of single-syllable words. *Journal of Experimental Psychology: General, 133,* 283–316.

Berent, I., & Perfetti, C. A. (1995). A rose is a REEZ: The two-cycles model of phonology assembly in reading English. *Psychological Review, 102,* 146–184.

Besner, D. (1990). Orthographies and their phonologies: A hypothesis. *Bulletin of the Psychonomic Society, 28,* 395–396.

Blanchard, H. E., Pollatsek, A., & Rayner, K. (1989). Parafoveal processing during eye fixations in reading. *Perception and Psychophysics, 46,* 85–94.

Borsting, E., Ridder, W. H., Dudeck, K., Kelley, C., Matsui, L., & Motoyama, J. (1996). The presence of a magnocellular defect depends on the type of dyslexia. *Vision Research, 36,* 1047–1053.

Breitmeyer, B. G., & Ganz, L. (1976). Implications of sustained and transient channels for theories of visual pattern masking, saccadic suppression, and information processing. *Psychological Review, 83,* 1–36.

Briihl, D., & Inhoff, A.W. (1995). Integrating information across fixations during reading: The use of orthographic bodies and of exterior letters. *Journal of Experimental Psychology: Learning, Memory, and Cognition, 21,* 55–67.

Bruno, J. L., Manis, F. R., Keating, P., Sperling, A. J., Nakamoto, J., & Seidenberg, M. S. (2007). Auditory word identification in dyslexic and normally achieving readers. *Journal of Experimental Child Psychology, 97,* 183–204.

Castles, A., Bates, T., Coltheart, M., Luciano, M., & Martin, N. G. (2006). Cognitive modelling and the behaviour genetics of reading. *Journal of Research in Reading, 29,* 92–103.

Castles, A., & Coltheart, M. (1993). Varieties of developmental dyslexia. *Cognition, 47,* 149–180.

Castles, A., & Coltheart, M. (2004). Is there a causal link from phonological awareness to success in learning to read? *Cognition, 91,* 77–111.

Christianson, K., Johnson, R. L., & Rayner, K. (2005). Letter transpositions within and across morphemes. *Journal of Experimental Psychology: Learning, Memory, and Cognition, 31,* 1327–1339.

Clark, V. P., Fan, S., & Hillard, S. A. (1995). Identification of early visual evoked potential generators by retinotopic and topographic analyses. *Human Brain Mapping, 2,* 170–187.

Coltheart, M. (2006). The genetics of learning to read. *Journal of Research in Reading, 29,* 124–132.

Coltheart, M., Curtis, B., Atkins, P., & Haller, M. (1993). Models of reading aloud: Dual-route and parallel-distributed processing approaches. *Psychological Review, 100,* 589–608.

Coltheart, M., Davelaar, E., Jonasson, J. T., & Besner, D. (1977). Access to the internal lexicon. In S. Dornic (Ed.), *Attention and performance 4.* London, England: Academic Press.

Coltheart, V., Patterson, K., & Leahy, J. (1994). When a ROWS is a ROSE: Phonological effects in written word comprehension. *The Quarterly Journal of Experimental Psychology, 47A,* 917–955.

Coltheart, M., & Rastle, K. (1994). Serial processing in reading aloud: Evidence for dual-route models of reading. *Journal of Experimental Psychology: Human Perception and Performance, 20,* 1197–1211.

Coltheart, M., Rastle, K., Perry, C., Langdon, R., & Ziegler, J. (2001). DRC: A dual route cascaded model of visual word recognition and reading aloud. *Psychological Review, 108,* 204–256.

Coltheart, M., Woollams, A., Kinoshita, S., & Perry, C. (1999). A position sensitive Stroop effect: Further evidence for a left-to-right component in print-to-speech. *Psychonomic Bulletin & Review, 6,* 456–463.

Cortese, M. J. (1998). Revisiting serial position effects in reading. *Journal of Memory and Language, 39,* 652–665.

Daneman, M., & Reingold, E. (1993). What eye fixations tell us about phonological recoding during reading. *Canadian Journal of Experimental Psychology, 47,* 153–178.

Daneman, M., & Stainton, M. (1991). Phonological recoding in silent reading. *Journal of Experimental Psychology: Learning, Memory, and Cognition, 17,* 618–632.

Demb, J. B., Boynton, G. M., & Heeger, D. J. (1997). Brain activity in visual cortex predicts individual differences in reading performance. *Proceedings of the National Academy of Sciences of the United States of America, 94,* 13363–13366.

Demb, J. B., Boynton, G. M., & Heeger, D. J. (1998). Functional magnetic resonance imaging of early visual pathways in dyslexia. *Journal of Neuroscience, 18,* 6939–6951.

DenBuurman, R., Boersema, T., & Gerrisen, J. F. (1981). Eye movements and the perceptual span in reading. *Reading Research Quarterly, 16,* 227–235.

Dietz, N. A. E., Jones, K. M., Gareau, L., Zeffiro, T. A., & Eden, G. F. (2005). Phonological decoding involves left posterior fusiform gyrus. *Human Brain Mapping, 26,* 81–93.

Dorsey, T. (2009). *Nuclear jellyfish.* New York: Harper Luxe.

Dreighe, D., Rayner, K., & Pollatsek, A. (2008). Mislocated fixations can account for parafoveal-on-foveal effects in eye movements during reading. *The Quarterly Journal of Experimental Psychology, 61,* 1239–1249.

Eden, G. F., Vanmeter, J., Rumsey, J., Maisog, J., Woods, R., & Zeffiro, T. (1996). Abnormal processing of visual motion in dyslexia revealed by functional brain imaging. *Nature, 382,* 66–69.

Ehri, L. C., Nunes, S. R., Stahl, S. A., & Willows, D. M. (2001). Systematic phonics instruction helps students learn to read: Evidence from the national reading panel's meta-analysis. *Review of Educational Research, 71,* 393–447.

Ehri, L. C., Nunes, S. R., Willows, D. M., Schuster, B. V., Yaghoub-Zadeh, Z., & Shanahan, T. (2001). Phonemic awareness instruction helps children learn to read: Evidence from the national reading panel's meta-analysis. *Reading Research Quarterly, 36,* 250–287.

Elman, J.L. (2004). An alternative view of the mental lexicon. *Trends in Cognitive Sciences, 8,* 301–306.

Engbert, R., Longtin, A., & Kliegl, R. (2002). A dynamical model of saccade generation in reading based on spatially distributed lexical processing. *Vision Research, 42,* 621–636.

Engbert, R., Nuthmann, A., Richter, E. M., & Kliegl, R. (2005). SWIFT: A dynamical model of saccade generation during reading. *Psychological Review, 112,* 777–813.

Fiez, J., Tranel, D., Seager-Frerichs, D., & Damasio, H. (2006). Specific reading and phonological processing deficits are associated with damage to left frontal operculum. *Cortex, 42,* 624–643.

Folk, J. R., & Morris, R. K. (1995). Multiple lexical codes in reading: Evidence from eye movements, naming time, and oral reading. *Journal of Experimental Psychology: Learning, Memory, and Cognition, 21,* 1412–1429.

Forster, K. I., & Davis, C. (1991). The density constraint on form priming in the naming task: Interference effects from a masked prime. *Journal of Memory and Language, 30,* 1–25.

Frazier, L., & Rayner, K. (1982). Making and correcting errors during sentence comprehension: Eye movements in the analysis of structurally ambiguous sentences. *Cognitive Psychology, 14,* 178–210.

Galaburda, A. M. (1985). Developmental dyslexia: A review of biological interactions. *Annals of Dyslexia, 35,* 21–33.

Gernsbacher, M. A. (1984). Resolving 20 years of inconsistent interactions between lexical familiarity and orthography, concreteness, and polysemy. *Journal of Experimental Psychology: General, 113,* 256–281.

Glushko, R. J. (1979). The organization and activation of orthographic knowledge in reading aloud. *Journal of Experimental Psychology: Human Perception and Performance, 5,* 674–691.

Gough, P. B., & Hillinger, M. L. (1980). Learning to read: An unnatural act. *Bulletin of the Orton Society, 30,* 179–196.

Harm, M. W., & Seidenberg, M. S. (1999). Phonology, reading acquisition, and dyslexia: Insights from connectionist models. *Psychological Review, 106,* 491–528.

Harm, M. W., & Seidenberg, M. S. (2001). Are there orthographic impairments in phonological dyslexia? *Cognitive Neuropsychology, 18,* 71–92.

Harm, M. W., & Seidenberg, M. S. (2004). Computing the meanings of words in reading: Cooperative division of labor between visual and phonological processes. *Psychological Review, 111,* 662–720.

Henderson, J. M., & Ferreira, F. (1990). Effects of foveal processing difficulty on the perceptual span in reading: Implications for attention and eye movement control. *Journal of Experimental Psychology: Learning, Memory, and Cognition, 16,* 417–429.

Hsu, C., Tsai, J., Lee, C., & Tzeng, O. J. L. (2009). Orthographic combinability and phonological consistency effects in reading Chinese phonograms: An event-related potential study. *Brain & Language, 108,* 56–66.

Huang, H., Lee, C., Tsai, J., Lee, C., Hung, D. L., & Tzeng, O. J. L. (2006). Orthographic neighborhood effects in reading Chinese two-character words. *NeuroReport, 17,* 1061–1065.

Inhoff, A. W., Connine, C., Eiter, B., Radach, R., & Heller, D. (2004). Phonological representation of words in working memory during sentence reading. *Psychonomic Bulletin & Review, 11,* 320–325.

Inhoff, A. W., Eiter, B. M., & Radach, R. (2005). Time course of linguistic information extraction from consecutive words during eye fixations in reading. *Journal of Experimental Psychology: Human Perception and Performance, 31,* 979–995.

Inhoff, A. W., Radach, R., & Eiter, B. (2006). Temporal overlap in the linguistic processing of successive words in reading: Reply to Pollatsek, Reichle, and Rayner (2006a). *Journal of Experimental Psychology: Human Perception and Performance, 32,* 1490–1495.

Inhoff, A. W., Radach, R., & Eiter, B., & Juhasz, B. (2003). Distinct subsystems for the parafoveal processing of spatial and linguistic information during eye fixations in reading. *The Quarterly Journal of Experimental Psychology, 56A,* 803–827.

Inhoff, A. W., Radach, R., Starr, M., & Greenberg, S. (2000). Allocation of visuo-spatial attention and saccade programming during reading. In A. Kennedy, R. Radach, D. Heller, & J. Pynte (Eds.), *Reading as a perceptual process* (pp. 221–246). Oxford, England: Elsevier.

Inhoff, A. W., & Rayner, K. (1986). Parafoveal word processing during eye fixations in reading: Effects of word frequency. *Perception and Psychophysics, 40,* 431–439.

Inhoff, A., Starr, M., & Schindler, K. (2000). Is the processing of words during eye fixations in reading strictly serial? *Perception and Psychophysics, 62,* 1474–1484.

Jared, D. (2002). Spelling–sound consistency and regularity effects in word naming. *Journal of Memory and Language, 46,* 723–750.

Jared, D., McRae, K., & Seidenberg, M. S. (1990). The basis of consistency effects in word naming. *Journal of Memory and Language, 29,* 687–715.

Jared, D., & Seidenberg, M. S. (1991). Does word identification, *120,* proceed from spelling to sound to meaning? *Journal of Experimental Psychology: General,* 358–394.

Joanisse, M. F., Manis, F. R., Keating, P., & Seidenberg, M. S. (2000). Language deficits in dyslexic children: Speech perception, phonology, and morphology. *Journal of Experimental Child Psychology, 77,* 30–60.

Jobard, G., Crivello, F., & Tzourio-Mazoyer, N. (2003). Evaluation of the dual route theory of reading: A metanalysis of 35 neuroimaging studies. *Neuroimage, 20,* 693–712.

Johnson, R. L., Perea, M., & Rayner, K. (2007). Transposed-letter effects in reading: Evidence from eye-movements and parafoveal preview. *Journal of Experimental Psychology: Human Perception and Performance, 33,* 209–229.

Kennedy, A., & Pynte, J. (2005). Parafoveal-on-foveal effects in normal reading. *Vision Research, 45,* 153–168.

Kennison, S., & Clifton, C., Jr. (1995). Determinants of parafoveal preview benefit in high and low working memory capacity readers: Implications for eye movement control. *Journal of Experimental Psychology: Learning, Memory, and Cognition, 21,* 68–81.

Kliegl, R., Nuthmann, A., & Engbert, R. (2006). Tracking the mind during reading: The influence of past, present, and future words on fixation durations. *Journal of Experimental Psychology: General, 135,* 12–35.

Kliegl, R., Risse, S., & Laubrock, J. (2007). Preview benefit and parafoveal-on-foveal effects from word n + 2. *Journal of Experimental Psychology: Human Perception and Performance, 33,* 125–1255.

Kwantes, P. J., & Mewhort, D. J. K. (1999). Evidence for sequential processing in visual word recognition. *Journal of Experimental Psychology: Human Perception and Performance, 25,* 376–381.

Lee, H., Rayner, K., & Pollatsek, A. (2001). The relative contribution of consonants and vowels to word identification during reading. *Journal of Memory and Language, 44,* 189–205.

Lee, C., Tsai, J., Chan, W., Hsu, C., Hung, D. L., & Tzeng, O. J. L. (2007). Temporal dynamics of the consistency effect in reading Chinese: An event-related potentials study. *NeuroReport, 18,* 147–151.

Lee, C., Tsai, J., Huang, W., Hung, D. L., & Tzeng, O. J. L. (2006). The temporal signatures of semantic and phonological activations for Chinese sublexical processing: An event-related potential study. *Brain Research, 1121,* 150–159.

Lee, C.-Y., Tsai, J.-L., Su, E. C.-I., Tzeng, O. J. L., & Hung, D. L. (2005). Consistency, regularity and frequency effects in naming Chinese characters. *Language and Linguistics, 6,* 75–107.

Legge, G. E., Hooven, T. A., Klitz, T. S., Mansfield, J. S., & Tjan, B. S. (2002). Mr. Chips 2002: New insights from an ideal-observer model of reading. *Vision Research, 42,* 2219–2234.

Legge, G. E., Klitz, T. S., & Tjan, B. S. (1997). Mr. Chips: An ideal observer model of reading. *Psychological Review, 104,* 524–553.

Lima, S. D., & Inhoff, A. W. (1985). Lexical access during eye fixations in reading: Effects of word-initial letter sequence. *Journal of Experimental Psychology: Human Perception and Performance, 11,* 272–285.

Livingstone, M. S., Rosen, G. D., Drislane, F. W., & Galaburda, A. M. (1991). Physiological and anatomical evidence for a magnocellular defect in developmental dyslexia. *Proceedings of the National Academy of Sciences of the United States of America, 88,* 7943–7947.

Lovegrove, W. J., Bowling, A., Badcock, D., & Blackwood, M. (1980). Specific reading disability: Difference in contrast sensitivity as a function of spatial frequency. *Science, 210,* 439–440.

Mainy, N., Jung, J., Baciu, M., Kahane, P., Schoendorff, B., Minotti, L., Hoffman, D., Bertrand, O., & Lachaux, J. (2008). Cortical dynamics of word recognition. *Human Brain Mapping, 29,* 1215–1230.

Manis, F. R., Seidenberg, M. S., Doi, L. M., McBride-Chang, C., & Petersen, A. (1996). On the bases of two subtypes of development dyslexia. *Cognition, 58,* 157–195.

Marshall, J. C., & Newcombe, F. (1973). Patterns of paralexia: A psycholinguistic approach. *Journal of Psycholinguistic Research, 2,* 175–199.

McCann, R. S., & Besner, D. (1987). Reading pseudohomophones: Implications for models of pronunciation assembly and the locus of word-frequency effects in naming. *Journal of Experimental Psychology: Human Perception and Performance, 13,* 14–24.

McClelland, J. L., & Rumelhart, D. E. (1981). An interactive activation model of context effects in letter perception: I. An account of basic findings. *Psychological Review, 88,* 375–407.

McConkie, G. W., & Rayner, K. (1975). The span of the effective stimulus during a fixation in reading. *Perception and Psychophysics, 17,* 578–586.

McConkie, G. W., & Rayner, K. (1976). Asymmetry of the perceptual span in reading. *Bulletin of the Psychonomic Society, 8,* 365–368.

Meseguer, E., Carreiras, M., & Clifton, C., Jr. (2002). Overt reanalysis strategies and eye movements during the reading of mild garden path sentences. *Memory & Cognition, 30,* 551–561.

Miller, B., Juhasz, B. J., & Rayner, K. (2006). The orthographic uniqueness point and eye movements during reading. *British Journal of Psychology, 97,* 191–216.

Morris, R. K., Rayner, K., & Pollatsek, A. (1990). Eye movement guidance in reading: The role of parafoveal letter and space information. *Journal of Experimental Psychology: Human Perception and Performance, 16,* 268–281.

Morrison, R. E. (1984). Manipulation of stimulus onset delay in reading: Evidence for parallel programming of saccades. *Journal of Experimental Psychology: Human Perception and Performance, 10,* 667–682.

Mulatti, C., Peressotti, F., & Job, R. (2007). Zeading and reazing: Which is faster? The position of the diverging letter in a pseudoword determines reading time. *The Quarterly Journal of Experimental Psychology, 60,* 1005–1014.

Mulatti, C., Reynolds, M. G., & Besner, D. (2006). Neighborhood effects in reading aloud: New findings and new challenges for computational models. Journal of *Experimental Psychology: Human Perception and Performance, 32,* 799–810.

Nickels, L., Bidermann, B., Coltheart, M., Saunders, S., & Tree, J. J. (2008). Computational modelling of phonological dyslexia: How does the DRC model fare? *Cognitive Neuropsychology, 25,* 165–193.

O'Regan, J. K. (1979). Eye guidance in reading: Evidence for the linguistic control hypothesis. *Perception and Psychophysics, 25,* 501–509.

O'Regan, J. K. (1990). Eye movements and reading. In E. Kowler (Ed.), *Eye movements and their role in visual and cognitive processes* (pp. 395–453). Amsterdam, The Netherlands: Elsevier.

O'Regan, J. K. (1992). Optimal viewing position in words and the strategy–tactics theory of eye movements in reading. In K. Rayner (Ed.), *Eye movements and visual cognition: Scene perception and reading* (pp. 333–354). Berlin, Germany: Springer-Verlag.

O'Regan, J. K., & Lévy-Schoen, A. (1987). Eye movement strategy and tactics in word recognition and reading. In M. Coltheart (Ed.), *Attention and performance 12: The psychology of reading* (pp. 363–383). Hillsdale, NJ: Erlbaum.

Perea, M., & Lupker, S. J. (2003). Does *jugde* activate *court*? Transposed-letter similarity effects in masked associative priming. *Memory & Cognition, 31,* 829–841.

Perfetti, C. A., Liu, Y., Fiez, J., Nelson, J., Bolger, D. J., & Tan, L. (2007). Reading in two writing systems: Accommodation and assimilation of the brain's reading network. *Bilingualism: Language and Cognition, 10,* 131–146.

Perfetti, C. A., Liu, Y., & Tan, L. H. (2005). The lexical constituency model: Some implications of research on Chinese for general theories of reading. *Psychological Review, 112,* 43–59.

Perry, C., Ziegler, J. C., & Zorzi, M. (2007). Nested incremental modeling in the development of computational theories: The CDP+ model of reading aloud. *Psychological Review, 114,* 273–315.

Plaut, D. C., & McClelland, J. L. (1993). Generalization with componential attractors: Word and nonword reading in an attractor network. *Proceedings of the 15th Annual Conference of the Cognitive Science Society* (pp. 824–829). Mahwah, NJ: Erlbaum.

Plaut, D. C., McClelland, J. L., Seidenberg, M. S., & Patterson, K. (1996). Understanding normal and impaired word reading: Computational principles in quasi-regular domains. *Psychological Review, 103,* 56–115.

Pollatsek, A., Bolozky, S., Well, A. D., & Rayner, K. (1981). Asymmetries in the perceptual span for Israeli readers. *Brain & Language, 14,* 174–180.

Pollatsek, A., Lesch, M., Morris, R. K., & Rayner, K. (1992). Phonological codes are used in integrating information across saccades in word identification and reading. *Journal of Experimental Psychology: Human Perception and Performance, 18,* 148–162.

Pollatsek, A., Reichle, E., & Rayner, K. (2006a). Serial processing is consistent with the time course of linguistic information extraction from consecutive words during eye fixations in reading: A response to Inhoff, Eiter, and Radach (2005). *Journal of Experimental Psychology: Human Perception and Performance, 32,* 1485–1489.

Pollatsek, A., Reichle, E. D., & Rayner, K. (2006b). Tests of the E-Z reader model: Exploring the interface between cognition and eye-movement control. *Cognitive Psychology, 52,* 1–56.

Powell, D., Plaut, D., & Funnell, E. (2006). Does the PMSP connectionist model of single word reading learn to read in the same way as a child? *Journal of Research in Reading, 29,* 229–250.

Radach, R., & Kennedy, A. (2004). Theoretical perspectives on eye movements in reading: Past controversies, current issues, and an agenda for future research. *European Journal of Cognitive Psychology, 16,* 3–26.

Radeau, M., Morais, J., Mousty, P., Saerens, M., & Bertelson, P. (1992). A listener's investigation of printed word processing. *Journal of Experimental Psychology: Human Perception and Performance, 18,* 861–871.

Rafal, R., & Robertson, L. (1995). The neurology of visual attention. In M. Gazzaniga (Ed.), *The cognitive neurosciences* (pp. 625–648). Cambridge, MA: MIT Press.

Rastle, K., & Coltheart, M. (1999a). Lexical and nonlexical phonological priming in reading aloud. *Journal of Experimental Psychology: Human Perception and Performance, 25,* 461–481.

Rastle, K., & Coltheart, M. (1999b). Serial and strategic effects in reading aloud. *Journal of Experimental Psychology: Human Perception and Performance, 25,* 482–503.

Rayner, K. (1979). Eye guidance in reading: Fixation locations within words. *Perception, 8,* 21–30.

Rayner, K. (1984). Visual selection in reading, picture perception, and visual search: A tutorial review. In H. Bouma & D. Bouwhuis (Eds.), *Attention and performance 10* (pp. 67–96). Hillsdale, NJ: Erlbaum.

Rayner, K. (1998). Eye movements in reading and information processing: 20 years of research. *Psychological Bulletin, 124,* 372–422.

Rayner, K., Ashby, J. Pollatsek, A., & Reichle, E. D. (2004). The effects of frequency and predictability on eye fixations in reading: Implications for the E-Z Reader model. *Journal of Experimental Psychology: Human Perception and Performance, 30,* 720–732.

Rayner, K., & Bertera, J.H. (1979). Reading without a fovea. *Science, 206,* 468–469.

Rayner, K., & Duffy, S. A. (1986). Lexical ambiguity and fixation times in reading: Effects of word frequency, verb complexity, and lexical ambiguity. *Memory & Cognition, 14,* 191–201.

Rayner, K., Juhasz, B. J., & Brown, S. J. (2007). Do readers obtain preview benefit from word n + 2? A test of serial attention shift versus distributed lexical processing models of eye movement control in reading. *Journal of Experimental Psychology: Human Perception and Performance, 35,* 230–245.

Rayner, K., Juhasz, B. J., & Pollatsek, A. (2007). Eye movements during reading. In M. J. Snowling & C. Hulme, *The science of reading: A handbook* (pp. 79–98). London, England: Blackwell.

Rayner, K., Liversedge, S. P., & White, S. J. (2006). Eye movements when reading disappearing text: The importance of the word to the right of fixation. *Vision Research, 46,* 310–323.

Rayner, K., & Morris, R. (1992). Eye movement control in reading: Evidence against semantic preprocessing. *Journal of Experimental Psychology: Human Perception and Performance, 18,* 163–172.

Rayner, K., & Pollatsek, A. (1989). *The psychology of reading.* Englewood Cliffs, NJ: Prentice Hall.

Rayner, K., & Pollatsek, A. (2006). Eye-movement control in reading. In M. J. Traxler & M. A. Gernsbacher (Eds.), *The handbook of psycholinguistics* (2nd ed., pp. 613–658). Amsterdam, The Netherlands: Elsevier.

Rayner, K., Reichle, E. D., Stroud, M. J., Williams, C. C., & Pollatsek, A. (2006). The effect of word frequency, word predictability, and font difficulty on the eye movements of young and older readers. *Psychology and Aging, 21,* 448–465.

Rayner, K., Well, A. D., & Pollatsek, A. (1980). Asymmetry of the effective visual field in reading. *Brain & Language, 14,* 174–180.

Rayner, K., Well, A. D., Pollatsek, A., & Bertera, J.H. (1982). The availability of useful information to the right of fixation in reading. *Perception and Psychophysics, 31,* 537–550.

Rayner, K., White, S. J., Johnson, R. L., & Liversedge, S. P. (2006). Raeding wrods with jubmled lettres. There is a cost. *Psychological Science, 17,* 192–193.

Rayner, K., White, S. J., Kambe, G., Miller, B., & Liversedge, S. P. (2003). On the processing of meaning from parafoveal vision during eye fixations in reading. In J. Hyöna, R. Radach, & H. Deubel (Eds.), *The mind's eye: Cognitive and applied aspects of eye movement research* (pp. 213–234). Amsterdam, The Netherlands: Elsevier.

Reichle, E. D., Pollatsek, A., Fisher, D. L., & Rayner, K. (1998). Toward a model of eye movement control in reading. *Psychological Review, 105,* 125–157.

Reichle, E. D., Pollatsek, A., & Rayner, K. (2006). E-Z Reader: A cognitive-control, serial-attention model of eye-movement behavior during reading. *Cognitive Systems Research, 7,* 4–22.

Reichle, E. D., Rayner, K., & Pollatsek, A. (1999). Eye movements control in reading: Accounting for initial fixation locations and refixations within the E-Z Reader model. *Vision Research, 39,* 4403–4411.

Reichle, E. D., Rayner, K., & Pollatsek, A. (2003). The E-Z Reader model of eye movement control in reading: Comparisons to other models. *Behavioral and Brain Sciences, 26,* 446–526.

Reilly, R., & O'Regan, J. K. (1998). Eye movement control in reading: A simulation of some word-targeting strategies. *Vision Research, 38,* 303–317.

Reingold, E. M, & Rayner, K. (2006). Examining the word identification stages hypothesized by the E-Z reader model. *Psychological Science, 17,* 742–746.

Roberts, M. A., Rastle, K., Coltheart, M., & Besner, D. (2003). When parallel processing in visual word recognition is not enough: New evidence from naming. *Psychonomic Bulletin & Review, 10,* 405–414.

Rubenstein, H., Lewis, S. S., & Rubenstein, M. H. (1971). Evidence for phonemic recoding in visual word recognition. *Journal of Verbal Learning and Verbal Behavior, 10,* 645–647.

Seidenberg, M. (1985). Constraining models of word recognition. *Cognition, 20,* 169–190.

Seidenberg, M. S., & McClelland, J. L. (1989). A distributed, developmental model of word recognition and naming. *Psychological Review, 96,* 523–568.

Seidenberg, M., & McClelland, J. L. (1990). More words but still no lexicon: Reply to Besner et al. (1990). *Psychological Review, 97,* 447–452.

Seidenberg, M. S., & Plaut, D. (2006). Progress in understanding word reading: Data fitting versus theory building. In S. Andrews (Ed.), *From inkmarks to ideas: Current issues in lexical processing.* Hove, United Kingdom: Psychology Press.

Seidenberg, M. S., Plaut, D. C., Petersen, A. S., McClelland, J. L., & McRae, K. (1994). Nonword pronunciation and models of word recognition. *Journal of Experimental Psychology: Human Perception and Performance, 20,* 1177–1196.

Seidenberg, M., Waters, G. S., Barnes, M. A., & Tanenhaus, M. K. (1984). When does irregular spelling or pronunciation influence word recognition? *Journal of Verbal Learning and Verbal Behavior, 23,* 383–404.

Sereno, S. C., Rayner, K., & Posner, M. I. (1998). Establishing a time-line of word recognition: Evidence from eye movements and event-related potentials. *NeuroReport, 9,* 2195–2200.

Sperling, A. J., Lu, Z., Manis, F. R., & Seidenberg, M. S. (2003). Selective magnocellular deficits in dyslexia: A "phantom contour" study. *Neuropsychologia, 41,* 1422–1429.

Stanovich, K. (1988). Explaining the differences between the dyslexic and the garden-variety poor reader: The phonological-core variable-difference model. *Journal of Learning Disabilities, 21,* 590–604.

Stanovich, K., & Siegel, L. S. (1994). Phenotypic performance profile of children with reading disabilities: A regression-based test of the phonological-core variable-difference model. *Journal of Educational Psychology, 86,* 24–53.

Stanovich, K., Siegel, L. S., & Gottardo, A. (1997). Converging evidence for phonological and surface subtypes of reading disability. *Journal of Educational Psychology, 89,* 114–127.

Stein, J., & Walsh, V. (1997). To see but not to read: The magnocellular theory of dyslexia. *Trends in Neurosciences, 20,* 147–152.

Stuebing, K. K., Barth, A. E., Cirino, P. T., Francis, D. J., & Fletcher, J. M. (2008). A response to recent reanalyses of the national reading panel report: Effects of systematic phonics instruction are practically significant. *Journal of Educational Psychology, 100,* 123–134.

Taraban, R., & McClelland, J. L. (1987). Conspiracy effects in word pronunciation. *Journal of Memory and Language, 26,* 608–631.

Torgesen, J. K., Alexander, A. W., Wagner, R. K., Rashotte, C. A., Voeller, K. K. S., & Conway, T. (2001). Intensive remedial instruction for children with severe reading disabilities: Two instructional approaches. *Journal of Learning Disabilities, 34,* 33–58, 78.

Torgesen, J. K., Wagner, R. K., Rashotte, C. A., Rose, E., Lindamood, P., Conway, T., et al. (1999). Preventing reading failure in young children with phonological processing disabilities: Group and individual responses to instruction. *Journal of Educational Psychology, 91,* 579–593.

Traxler, M. J., Williams, R. S., Blozis, S. A., & Morris, R. K. (2005). Working memory, animacy, and verb class in the processing of relative clauses. *Journal of Memory and Language, 53,* 204–224.

Treisman, A. M., & Gelade, G. (1980). A feature-integration theory of attention. *Cognitive Psychology, 12,* 97–136.

Tsai, J., Lee, C., Tzeng, O. J. L., Hung, D. L., & Yen, N. (2004). Use of phonological codes for Chinese characters: Evidence from processing of parafoveal preview when reading sentences. *Brain & Language, 91,* 235–244.

Underwood, N. R., & McConkie, G. W. (1985). Perceptual span for letter distinctions during reading. *Reading Research Quarterly, 20,* 153–162.

Van Orden, G. C. (1987). A ROWS is a ROSE: Spelling, sound, and reading. *Memory & Cognition, 15,* 181–198.

Van Orden, G. C. (1991). Phonologic mediation is fundamental to reading. In D. Besner & G. W. Humphreys (Eds.), *Basic processes in reading: Visual word recognition* (pp. 77–103). Hillsdale, NJ: Erlbaum.

Velan, H., & Frost, R. (2007). Cambridge University versus Hebrew University: The impact of letter transposition on reading English and Hebrew. *Psychonomic Bulletin & Review, 14,* 913–918.

Vitu, F., O'Regan, J. K., Inhoff, A. W., & Topolski, R. (1995). Mindless reading: Eye movement characteristics are similar in scanning letter strings and reading texts. *Perception and Psychophysics, 57,* 352–364.

Wagner, R. K., Piasta, S. B., & Torgesen, J. K. (2006). Learning to Read. In M. J. Traxler & M. A. Gernsbacher (Eds.), *The handbook of psycholinguistics* (2nd ed., pp. 1111–1142). Amsterdam, The Netherlands: Elsevier.

Wagner, R. K., & Torgesen, J. K. (1987). The nature of phonological processing and its causal role in the acquisition of reading skills. *Psychological Bulletin, 101,* 192–212.

Wagner, R. K., Torgesen, J. K., & Rashotte, C. A. (1994). Development of reading-related phonological processing abilities: New evidence of bidirectional causality from a latent variable longitudinal study. *Developmental Psychology, 30,* 73–87.

Wagner, R. K., Torgesen, J. K., Rashotte, C. A., Hecht, S. A., Barker, T. A., Burgess, S. R., et al. (1997). Changing relations between phonological processing abilities and word-level reading as children develop from beginning to skilled readers: A 5-year longitudinal study. *Developmental Psychology, 33,* 468–479.

Waters, G. S., & Seidenberg, M. (1985). Spelling–sound effects in reading: Time course and decision criteria. *Memory & Cognition, 13,* 557–572.

White, S. J., Johnson, R. L., Liversedge, S. P., & Rayner, K. (2008). Eye movements when reading transposed text: The importance of word-beginning letters. *Journal of Experimental Psychology: Human Perception and Performance, 34,* 1261–1276.

Whitney, C. (2001). How the brain encodes the order of letters in a printed word: The SERIOL model and selective literature review. *Psychonomic Bulletin & Review, 8,* 221–243.

Whitney, C., & Cornelissen, P. (2008). SERIOL reading. *Language and Cognitive Processes, 23,* 143–164.

Woollams, A. M., Lambon Ralph, M. A., Plaut, D. C., & Patterson, K. (2007). SD-Squared: On the association between semantic dementia and surface dyslexia. *Psychological Review, 114,* 316–339.

Yang, S.-N., & McConkie, G. W. (2001). Eye movements during reading: A theory of saccade initiation time. *Vision Research, 41,* 3567–3585.

Yang, S.-N., & McConkie, G. W. (2004). Saccade generation during reading: Are words necessary? *European Journal of Cognitive Psychology, 16,* 226–261.

Yarkoni, T., Balota, D., & Yap, M. (2008). Moving beyond Coltheart's N: A new measure of orthographic similarity. *Psychonomic Bulletin & Review, 15,* 971–979.

Yates, M., Locker, L., & Simpson, G. B. (2004). The influence of phonological neighborhood on visual word perception. *Psychonomic Bulletin & Review, 11,* 452–457.

Zorzi, M., Houghton, G., & Butterworth, B. (1998). Two routes or one in reading aloud? A connectionist dual-process model. *Journal of Experimental Psychology: Human Perception and Performance, 24,* 1131–1161.

Bilingual Language Processing

Q: What do you call someone who speaks multiple languages?

A: Multi-lingual.

Q: What do you call someone who speaks one language?

A: American.

L. N. VAN DER HOEF,[1] FORMER CHANCELLOR OF UC DAVIS

Bilinguals know and use two languages on a regular basis. The majority of people in the United States are *monolingual*, and know and use only a single language. However, most people in the world are bilingual. For example, the majority of the people who live in Europe are bilingual (Lemhöfer et al., 2008). In The Netherlands, nearly everyone, about 90% of the population, is bilingual. What does it mean to be bilingual and how do bilinguals differ from monolinguals? Being bilingual is not the same as having "two monolinguals in the same body" (Grosjean, 1989; Kroll, 2006). People do not partition their brains the way you can partition the hard drive on your computer, storing one language in one physical location and the other language in another physical location. People do not create an entirely separate set of input and output processes for each of the languages they know. As a result, we cannot assume that the theories we use to understand monolinguals will work just as well for bilinguals. For starters, a bilingual speaker must have ways to recognize which language she is hearing and ways to control which language gets control when she speaks. Bilinguals have two distinct labels for things, which complicates

Introduction to Psycholinguistics: Understanding Language Science, First Edition.
Matthew J. Traxler.

lexical access in both comprehension and speech production, consequently bilinguals name pictures and recognize non-words slower than monolingual speakers do (van Heuven, Dijkstra, & Grainger, 1998).

Much of the research in bilingual language processing over the past two decades has focused on the degree to which two languages share mental resources, such as storage space in long-term memory and speech-production processes, how the two languages are associated with one another in long-term memory, and how competition between the two languages is managed when both languages are activated at the same time. This chapter focuses on similar issues, especially sources of competition between languages in bilinguals and how that competition is resolved, and the surprising mental benefits that flow from learning a second language. In addition, the chapter reviews some methods for teaching second languages and specific individual characteristics that make it easier to learn a second language. Finally, the chapter takes a look at how learning a second language affects the neural systems that support language functions.

Mary Potter and the Secrets of Bilingualism[2]

One fundamental issue in bilingual research involves the question of how bilingual speakers represent knowledge about words. Recall that *lexical knowledge* (stored information about words) can be subdivided into different components relating to word meanings (concepts), and phonological form (sounds). Most theories of bilingualism propose that learning a second language does not entail learning an entirely new set of concepts, but does obviously involve learning an entirely new set of phonological forms or labels for concepts.[3] Having two labels for a given concept creates the possibility of translating from one label (*cat*, say) to the other (*koshka*, if you speak Russian). But how are the two sets of labels related to one another in memory, and what processes do you undertake to translate from one to the other? The modern study of lexical representation in bilingual speakers and the process of translation traces its roots to a study by Mary Potter and her colleagues (Potter, So, Von Eckardt, & Feldman, 1984). In that study, the process of translating from a person's first language (L1) to a second language (L2) was compared to the process of naming pictures in the L2. The researchers were testing two ideas about how words in the L1 relate to words in the L2. According to the *word association model* (WAM), language learners directly associate L1 labels with L2 labels (illustrated in the left panel of Figure 11.1). When people study a foreign language, they often use rote memorization strategies, such as flash-cards with the labels from the two different languages printed on either side. This kind of rote memorization can create a direct link in long-term memory between the visual image of the words or the sound of the words in the two languages, and need not involve meaning or concepts at all. If so, thinking of the sound of the L1 word should bring to mind the sound of the L2 word without necessarily activating the meaning of either word. Potter and colleagues contrasted the WAM with the *concept mediation* (CM) hypothesis (as in the right-hand panel of Figure 11.1). According to the concept mediation hypothesis, translating from L1 to L2 involves accessing the concept that goes with the L1 label, and then following the link from the concept to the L2 label. Thus, L1-to-L2 translation is referred to as being *concept mediated*, because you start at the L1 lexical (label) representation, and you must pass through the conceptual representation before you can access the L2 label.

Potter and colleagues (1984) used picture naming and translation because the WAM and the CM hypothesis make different predictions about how long it should take to do the two different tasks. According to the WAM, it should take more time to name a picture in the L2 than to translate from L1 to L2. Consider the left-hand side of Figure 11.1, which illustrates

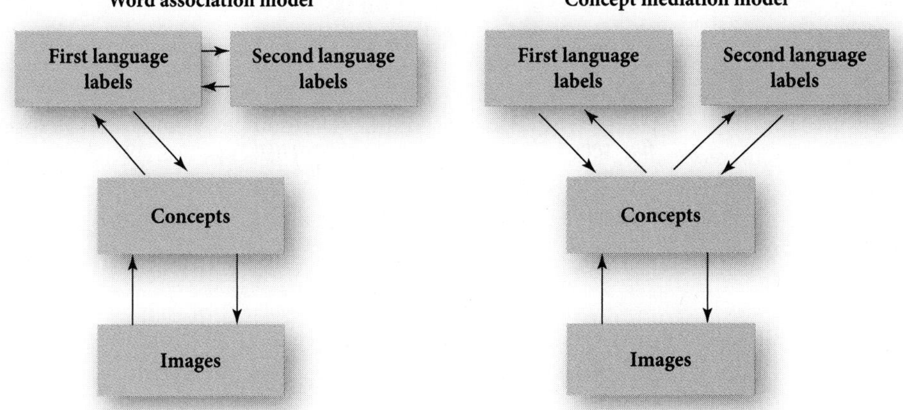

Figure 11.1 The word association (WAM) and concept mediation (CM) models of L1–L2 links

how picture naming and translation are accomplished according to the WAM. To name a picture in L2, you start by recognizing the picture and activating a matching conceptual representation. Then, the conceptual representation activates the L1 label (note that the concept does *not* directly activate the L2 label, because there are *no* direct connections between the concept and the L2 label). Only after activating the L1 label can you gain access to the L2 label. According to the WAM, translation is much easier. You just look at the L1 word, you activate the matching sounds (the label), and then the activated L1 label activates the associated L2 label. According to the WAM, translating from L1 to L2 involves fewer processing events than naming a picture in L2, which means that translation should take less time than picture naming.

Now consider the right side of Figure 11.1, which illustrates picture naming and translation according to the CM hypothesis. In L2 picture naming, you start with the picture, which activates a matching conceptual representation, which activates an L2 label (because there are direct connections between concepts and L2 labels). Translation requires the same number of processing steps (two), because you start with the L1 label, that activates a concept (much as the picture does and at roughly the same speed), which activates the L2 label.

To contrast the WAM and the CM hypothesis, Potter and her colleagues (1984) had Chinese-English[4] bilinguals name pictures in their L2 (English) and translate matching Chinese words for the same concepts. This group of speakers was highly skilled at speaking English, and so were considered *proficient* bilinguals. In a separate experiment, English-French novice bilinguals (American high school students studying French) performed the same two tasks, only the response language was French instead of English. Both groups produced the same pattern of results. Translating L1 words into L2 words took the same amount of time as naming a picture using a word from the L2. These results showed that the WAM was wrong. Bilingual speakers did not, regardless of how skilled they were, go directly from the L1 label to the L2 label when translating from L1 to L2. Instead, bilingual speakers appeared to activate concepts (meanings) associated with the L1 labels and used connections between the activated concepts and the L2 labels to complete the translation task.

Potter and colleagues' (1984) ideas about how concepts and labels are related to one another, and how labels in different languages are related to one another indirectly via concepts, have been characterized as being a *hierarchical model*, because knowledge related

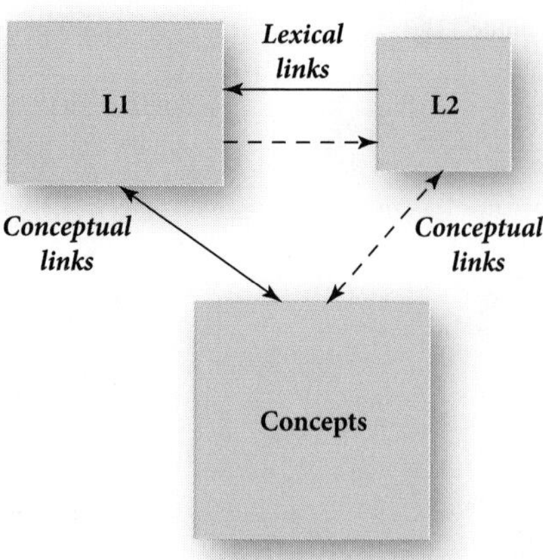

Figure 11.2 The revised hierarchical model (RHM) (from Kroll & Stewart, 1994, p. 158)

to words is distributed across different subcomponent systems, L1 labels, L2 labels, and concepts (Kroll, 2006, 2008a, b, c; Kroll & Stewart, 1994; Schwartz & Kroll, 2006b; Sholl, Sankaranarayanan, & Kroll, 1995). Research conducted after Potter and colleagues' groundbreaking experiments on the way bilingual speakers organize knowledge about words in their two languages showed that life is somewhat more complicated than the CM hypothesis proposed. For one thing, bilinguals are able to translate in both directions. *Forward translation* involves starting with L1 and speaking in L2. *Backward translation* involves starting with an L2 word and speaking the L1 equivalent. The CM hypothesis says that L1-to-L2 and L2-to-L1 translation are both *concept mediated* (because you access a concept to complete the path from the L1 label to the L2 label and from the L2 label to the L1 label). Kroll and her colleagues proposed a new version of the hierarchical model, which is known as the *revised hierarchical model* (or RHM). According to the revised hierarchical model, L1 labels connect directly to L2 labels (as in Figure 11.2), but those connections are weaker in the L1–L2 direction than in the L2–L1 direction. As a result, it should be possible to translate from L2 into L1 without passing through the store of conceptual representations. However, going in the other direction, from L1 to L2, should still work like the CM hypothesis says it does. In fact, across a range of different degrees of proficiency and fluency in L2, bilingual speakers generally translate from their L2 into their L1 faster than they translate from their L1 into their L2 (as the RHM predicts).

Additional evidence for the RHM comes from experiments that investigate whether semantic (meaning) factors influence translation in different directions (Altarriba & Mathis, 1997; Caramazza & Brones, 1979, 1980; De Groot, Dannenburg, & van Hell, 1994; Kroll & Stewart, 1994; Sholl et al., 1995; see also Heredia, 1997; Schoonbaert, Duyck, Brysbaert, & Hartsuiker, 2009).[5] Recall that the CM hypothesis suggests that L1 to L2 translation involves activating conceptual (semantic) representations. According to the RHM, L2 to L1 translation is different, because the conceptual representations are bypassed due to the existence of direct L2–L1 *lexical* connections. Because of the asymmetry between L1–L2 connections and L2–L1 connections, coming up with a word in your L2 should be more affected by semantic (meaning) factors than should translating from your L2 into your L1. That is because getting to L2 from L1 involves a detour through the concept (semantic) system, but you can go straight from L2 to L1 via direct lexical connections.

This hypothesis has been tested in different ways. In one kind of experiment, subjects are given lists of words to translate. Sometimes the words are in their L1, sometimes they are in their L2. Sometimes, a block of words all comes from the same semantic category (like *fruits*). Sometimes a block of words switches back and forth between different categories (like *fruits* and types of *furniture*). Because different examples of fruits are associated with one another, activating the concept for *banana* will also activate related concepts, such as *apple*, *orange*, and *pear*. This creates the possibility of semantic interference, as the different concepts compete to be expressed. The possibility for this kind of competition would be lessened if you could bypass the conceptual memory system in which that semantic competition takes place. The RHM predicts that you will get more semantic interference in forward translation (L1–L2) than in backward translation (L2–L1), because forward translation leads to activation of conceptual memory more than backward translation does. In fact, presenting a whole list of fruits as a block slowed bilinguals down when they were translating from L1 to L2 (compared to the condition where different categories were intermixed). When bilinguals performed backward translation, they were just as fast when the list of words-to-be-translated was presented with all the fruits together as when the fruits were interwoven with other categories of things.

A different type of experiment involving semantic priming and picture naming also provided evidence for the RHM. In these experiments, participants switch back and forth between naming pictures and translating words from one language to another. Naming pictures involves accessing the conceptual store (Potter et al., 1984), as does forward translation. Backward translation does not involve activating conceptual information as much as either picture naming or forward translation. Because both forward translation and picture naming involve activating conceptual information (according to the CM hypothesis and the RHM), forward translation should happen faster if the conceptual representation you need is already activated (i.e., if it has been semantically primed). In fact, subjects performed forward translation faster if they had recently named a picture in their L1 that represented the concept that went with the L2 label. Naming the picture activated the conceptual representation, and having that conceptual representation activated helped subjects complete forward translation involving that concept. By contrast, L2–L1 translation is unaffected by recent picture naming. Backward translation is completed just as quickly whether or not the relevant concept has recently been activated by picture naming (see also Lee & Williams, 2001). These results suggest that forward translation involves accessing concepts (because pre-activating the appropriate concepts helps) and backward translation does not involve accessing concepts, because pre-activating a matching concept did not affect backward translation.

Languages Are Simultaneously Active During Comprehension and Production

The first rule of bilingualism is that the two languages compete. When bilinguals listen to speech, lexical entries and their corresponding semantic representations compete for activation and selection. When bilinguals speak, words from the two languages compete to gain control of the output mechanisms (the speech apparatus). Despite the conflict between the two languages and the accompanying possibilities for confusion, fluent bilinguals generally do not have any inkling that different lexical entries are simultaneously active (the same way monolingual speakers are rarely aware that semantically ambiguous words such as *bank* have more than one meaning) and they rarely use a word from the "wrong" language by mistake. Such mistakes do occur, however, especially when the bilingual speaker is under stress or is experiencing strong emotions (see Figure 11.3). Such mistakes are also more

Figure 11.3 When this black bear (*Ursus Americanus*) walked through a parking lot at Yellowstone National Park in 2008, a German tourist told the author, in German, that the bear was limping. The German tourist switched to English right away because the author's German is nicht so gut
Note: The bear was eating grass. Bears will eat anything

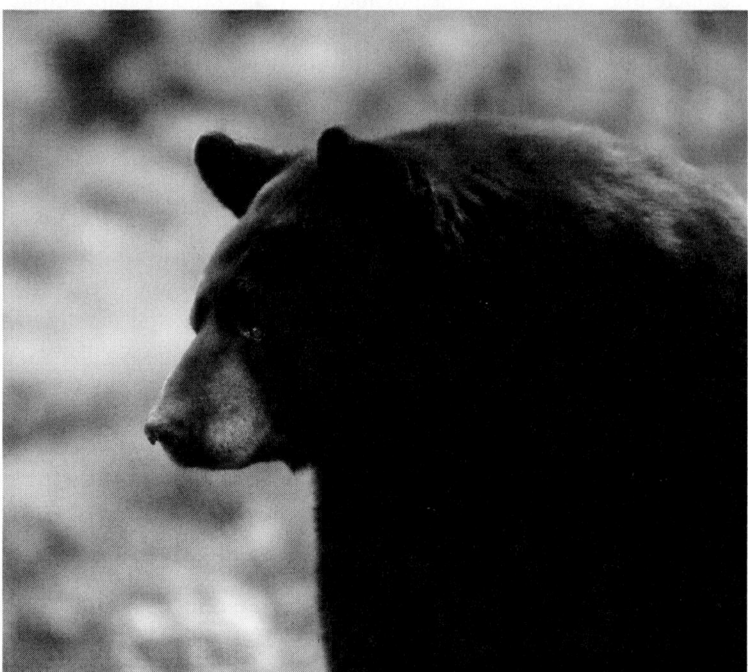

common when the bilingual is speaking in her less-dominant or well-practiced language (Poulisse & Bongaerts, 1994). Given that bilinguals are usually unaware that their languages are in conflict and rarely make cross-language errors in production, is it possible that knowledge about their two languages really is stored in different, separate components of long-term memory? Why should we believe that the languages are in competition if subjective experience and overt behavior normally show no trace of such competition? Despite the apparent ease of access to context-appropriate language representations, at least among proficient bilinguals, laboratory research indicates that a bilingual's two languages really do compete both during language comprehension and speech production. Let's consider each of these in turn.

What evidence suggests that both of a bilingual's languages are simultaneously activated during listening and comprehension? Some evidence comes from the *cognate advantage*. A *cognate* is a word in one language that has a counterpart in another language that is spelled or pronounced identically (or nearly so), and that has the same meaning. For example, the Spanish word *piano* is a cognate of the English word *piano*—they look alike, they sound alike, and they mean the same thing. In picture naming and translation, bilinguals (but not monolinguals) respond to cognates faster than non-cognates. Also, the N400 component of the ERP wave form is smaller for cognates than non-cognates (Christoffels, Firk, & Schiller, 2007; see note 5 in Chapter 3), whether the cognate is presented in the bilingual participant's L1 or L2. The *cognate advantage* occurs when the bilingual speaker is operating under monolingual task conditions where only one of the two languages is obviously relevant to the task, and when the bilingual speaker is operating under task conditions where responses in either language may be required (*bilingual mode*), whether the bilingual is responding in her stronger or weaker language. The cognate advantage is strongest when the two versions have the same orthography (spelling) and phonology (pronunciation); the advantage shrinks as the simlarity in pronunciation across the two languages diminishes (Costa, Caramazza, & Sebastian-Galles, 2000; Lemhöfer et al., 2008; Schwartz, Kroll, & Diaz, 2007; Soares & Grosjean, 1984; van Hell & Dijkstra, 2002).[6] Bilingual speakers are also less likely to experience tip-of-the tongue states for cognates than other kinds of words (Gollan & Acenas, 2004), suggesting that having two simultaneously activated lexical representations boosts the activation of the phonological codes that go with the cognate. The cognate advantage shows that both of the bilingual speaker's languages are active at the same time. If the bilingual could completely switch off the task-irrelevant language, cognate effects would not appear when the task requires only one of the two languages (but cognates are processed faster than non-cognates even when the bilingual thinks that the task involves only one language).

Further evidence for simultaneous activation and language competition comes from effects of *interlingual homographs* (Dijkstra, Grainger, & van Heuven, 1999; Kroll, 2006). Interlingual homographs are words that look alike and sound alike, but that mean different things in different languages. They look and sound like cognates, but they are not cognates. Because they look and sound similar, but mean different things (and may be pronounced somewhat differently as well), such words are sometimes called *false friends*. For instance, the German word *chef*, meaning *boss*, looks and sounds like the English word *chef*, meaning *skilled food cooker*. When bilingual speakers read or hear interlingual homographs, they respond to them slower than words that appear in only one of their languages. That is, interlingual homographs behave like (monolingual) semantically ambiguous words, and likely for the same reasons. For monolingual speakers of English, balanced ambiguous words take longer to read and name than unambiguous words, because the visual form of the word automatically activates multiple meanings, and competition between activated meanings slows selection and integration of a single meaning. Interlingual homograph effects show that the orthographic (spelling) and phonological (sound) form is shared between languages (to the extent that they have a similar script or a similar phonological system), and that hearing or seeing a given form automatically activates whatever semantic information is associated with that form.

Although language production provides clear opportunities for competition across languages, because the bilingual speaker has to choose which label to apply to a given concept, language input might selectively activate only a single language at a time. That is, the prosodic and phonological patterns of different languages can be quite distinct. Given that the input in the bilingual's L1 can sound very different from their L2, it might be reasonable to think that less conflict would occur in listening than in production. Recent research, however, suggests that when bilinguals listen to words, matching candidates from both of their languages become activated, and accessing the context-appropriate meaning requires them to select from among the set of activated candidates. Further, activation does not respect the distinction between the two languages. Listening to L1 words activates L2 candidates, and listening to L2 words activates L1 candidates (Marian, Spivey, & Hirsch, 2003; Spivey & Marian, 1999). Mike Spivey and Viorica Marian tested whether spoken input activated one language only, or whether such input activated both the L1 and L2 lexicon. To do so, they presented Russian-English bilinguals with short instructions in Russian or English (e.g., *Click on the marker*) while they were looking at a set of pictures on a computer screen. The bilinguals carried out the instructions using a mouse to move the cursor over the appropriate target. Unbeknownst to the participants, some of the pictures on the screen had similar names in both English and Russian. For example, the Russian word for *stamp* is *marka*, which is pronounced similarly to the English word *marker*. These objects were labeled *distractors*, because the similarity in pronunciation might cause people to look at the wrong object (the stamp instead of the marker), *if* the phonological (sound) information activated the inappropriate language. If participants were able to switch off Russian while carrying out English instructions (or vice versa), they should avoid looking at the distractor objects. Monolingual English speakers almost never look at a picture of a stamp while hearing the word *marker*, because *stamp* shares very little phonology with *marker*, and so serves as a very weak competitor. If Russian-English bilinguals can selectively activate English labels for objects, without activating Russian labels, they too should rarely look at the distractor (*stamp*/*marka*) while listening to *marker*. In fact, Russian-English bilinguals were far more likely to look at the stamp (*marka* in Russian) when the instruction said *Click on the marker*, compared to objects with totally unrelated names. Similarly, if the instructions were given in Russian (*Polozhi marku*, "put the stamp …"), participants frequently looked at the object with the same-sounding English name (the marker). This result shows that, while comprehending speech, whether operating in the stronger or weaker language, mental representations from a bilingual's two languages are simultaneously activated and influence their behavior.

These results are also compatible with theories of mental representation that propose that lexical representations from the bilingual's two languages share space in long-term memory. That is, rather than being neatly partitioned into "Russian" and "English" bins, that are searched separately when a bilingual is listening to one versus the other language, looking at a picture of a stamp while hearing the word *marker*, shows that the phonological information is activating representations of meaning based on both phonology-to-L1 lexicon and phonology-to-L2 lexicon mappings. The data show that activation reaches all the way into the semantic (meaning) representations, and that activation of those meanings exceeds the minimum required to control behavior before the entire acoustic stimulus has been processed. (If bilinguals waited to do a complete analysis of the acoustic stimulus, they would never look at the stamp because the phonological codes for *marker* do not fully match the stored codes for *marku*). Thus, bilinguals, like monolinguals, undertake a radical form of *incremental processing* when processing speech, as proposed by models like COHORT (see Chapter 3; Gaskell & Marslen-Wilson, 1997; Marslen-Wilson, 1973). That is, they begin to activate stored representations that encode different meanings immediately after they start to hear the beginning of a word, regardless of which of their languages is being spoken at the moment. So *mar-* activates two associated meanings from two different languages because there are two words, *marker* and *marka*, that have partially overlapping phonological representations, and the lexical access system does not switch off one language or filter out meanings that come from the "wrong" language. This does not mean that words in the two languages have identical phonological or lexical representations (if they did, a bilingual would not be able to tell the difference between Russian and English), and in fact neuroimaging data (Marian et al., 2003) show that Russian and English are associated with subtle differences in neural activity in Russian-English bilinguals. Specifically, Russian and English activated overlapping areas of Broca's and Wernicke's areas, but the point in the brain representing the *center of mass* (the spatial mid-point of the set of activated voxels) differed between Russian and English.[7]

These cohort-like effects that cross language boundaries are also reflected in cross-language neighborhood effects. In *progressive de-masking* experiments, a target word is displayed for a short time (about 10 ms) followed by a pattern that covers up the place where the target word appeared. Gradually, the exposure time for the target word increases, and the exposure time for the pattern mask decreases, until the subject is able to identify the target word. For bilinguals, target-word identification time depends on characteristics of the target word itself, such as how long and frequent it is in its own language, but it also depends on how many neighbors the target word has in the bilingual's other language (van Heuven et al., 1998). Response times are especially slow when the target word is in the bilingual's L2, and the orthographic neighbors—words that look like the target word—are from the bilingual's L1, and when the L1 neighbors occur more frequently or are more familiar than the L2 target word.

Further evidence for shared phonological and semantic representations comes from studies involving *pseudohomophones*. Pseudohomophones are words that are spelled like real words, but are not real words. *Tode* is a pseudohomophone of *toad*, and in monolingual readers, reading *tode* will prime the response to the word *frog* (which is associated with the word *toad*). Pseudohomophone priming effects also occur between a bilingual's two languages. For example, the Dutch word for rope is *touw*. In a masked priming experiment, Dutch-English bilinguals responded faster to *touw* when it was preceded by the English pseudohomophone *roap*, which has the same phonological representation as *rope*, and which activates the Dutch word with the same meaning, *touw* (Duyck, 2005). If phonological activations were restricted to the target language (Dutch), *roap* would have no effect on behavior, because there is no word in Dutch that matches *roap*. The fact that *roap* speeds up the response to *touw* shows that English phonology is active while Dutch is being processed, and that English phonology makes contact with shared semantic representations (perhaps the concept representations in the CM and RHM accounts), which in turn facilitates processing of Dutch target words (see also van Wijnendaele & Brysbaert, 2002).

Although a bilingual's two languages are simultaneously activated during a variety of language comprehension tasks, the two languages are not necessarily equally activated all the time. Most of the time, the dominant (usually the L1) is the more active of the two, and so the dominant language is more immune to influences coming from the L2 than vice versa (Jared & Kroll, 2001; Jared & Szucs, 2002). To demonstrate the relative immunity of L1 lexical access to interference from a weaker L2, English-French bilinguals named English words that had French *enemies* (French words that look like the English target words but are pronounced differently) or control words that had no French enemies. The existence of French enemies did not affect how long it took English-French bilinguals to name the target words. Then, participants named a group of French words. Naming the French words presumably increased the activity of French spelling–sound patterns. After naming a bunch of French words, participants named another group of English words. This time, having a French enemy made a huge difference and response times were much slower. These results suggest that the L2 orthographic and phonological representations are normally less activated and may not substantially affect L1 function unless something happens that boosts the activation of the L2 representations (like saying a large number of words in the L2). Weaker L2 representations can affect performance in a stronger L1, but perhaps only when bilingual speakers have recently switched from their L2 back into their L1.

Competition in production

Many models of bilingual language production use a modified version of the production models reviewed in Chapter 2, such as Levelt's production model that assumes a strict serial process in message formulation, or Dell's production model that assumes cascading activation and interaction between different levels of representation (e.g., Dell, 1986). According to both of these production models, message formulation begins with activation of non-linguistic conceptual representations (ideas), proceeds to the *lemma* level, which contains abstract representations that encode the meanings and syntactic properties that words possess, and ultimately to a set of phonological representations that the speaker uses to generate a plan to move the muscles controlling the speech apparatus. For the bilingual speaker, most theories assume that the conceptual representations are shared between the two languages, at least for concrete objects. However, most theories assume that lemmas are not shared. So, to say anything at all, the bilingual must have some means of activating the language-appropriate (L1 or L2) lemmas, while deactivating or suppressing inappropriate lemmas that are tied to the same concepts.

According to Roelofs' (1992) model, in bilingual language production, the correct lemma must be selected before activation spreads to the associated phonological (sound) representations. According to other models, activation spreads automatically throughout the network of associated lemma and phonological representations as soon as the conceptual representations become activated (e.g., Hernandez, Li, & MacWhinney, 2005). Thus, even if the bilingual speaker quickly selects the language-appropriate lemma, there may be some activation in the phonological representations for the other language. So, if a Dutch-English speaker is trying to say *mountain* in English, there may be some activation for the phonological representations associated with the Dutch lemma for that same concept (i.e., *berg*). In Roelofs' serial selection model, the problem for the bilingual speaker is to select the correct lemma. Once this has been done, production proceeds in a fairly straightforward manner. Thus, there should be very little activation of language-inappropriate phonological representations (i.e., trying to say *mountain* should not activate the Dutch lemma and the corresponding phonological representation, *berg*). To summarize, because language production in general involves conceptual, lemma, and phonological representations, and the connections between them, competition and interference may occur at any of the three levels of representation; and specific patterns of interference depend on whether you assume that concept selection, lemma selection, and phonological encoding take place in a serial order, with concept selection preceding lemma selection preceding phonological encoding, or in a cascaded fashion, with lemmas becoming activated before concept selection is complete, and phonological encoding beginning before lemma selection is complete.

To find out whether lemma and phonological representations compete during speech production in bilinguals, researchers have used tasks that require bilinguals to pay attention to one stimulus, such as a picture, while trying to ignore a simultaneously presented distractor stimulus, such as a spoken word (this task is similar to the *picture–word interference* task that we reviewed in Chapter 2; Costa & Caramazza, 1999; Hermans, Bongaerts, de Bot, and Schreuder, 1998; La Heij et al., 1990). By manipulating characteristics of the spoken-word distractor, such as its semantic and phonological relationship to the picture, researchers can determine whether that additional information helps the bilingual speaker access the appropriate lemma and phonological representation, or whether the spoken stimulus interferes with producing the word that reflects the meaning of the picture. Further, researchers can give the interfering stimulus a head start by speaking the distractor before showing the picture, they can present the picture and the distractor stimulus simultaneously, or they can give picture naming a head start by presenting the picture before the distracting stimulus is spoken. In one such study, Dutch-English bilinguals tried to name pictures using the English names for the pictures (e.g., *mountain*) while listening to distractor stimuli that were either related to phonology or the semantic representations that went with the picture name. The distractors could be presented either in English or Dutch. Sometimes the distractors sounded like the target name. The English word *mouth* sounds like the target word *mountain*, because they share word onsets. The Dutch word *mouw* (meaning "sleeve"), also shares a phonological onset with the target word. Sometimes, the distractors were semantic competitors for the target concept, as in the English word *valley* or the Dutch word *dal* (meaning "valley"). The bilingual speakers named the target picture (*mountain*) faster when the distracting stimulus had a similar phonological form (*mouth* and *mouw* both helped), but they were slower when the distractor stimulus had a meaning that was associated with, but different from, the target word (*valley* and *dal* both slowed down the naming response for the picture of a mountain). The phonological facilitation and semantic interference effects were about the same size when the distractor was in the same language as the target name (English) or when the distractor came from a different language from the target name (Dutch).[8] These results indicate that bilinguals cannot shut off or ignore their L1 while speaking words in their L2. If they could, hearing a word from the L1 that is phonologically related to the target word (it sounds similar) would not help the bilingual say the name of the target picture in the L2. Similarly, if the L1 was switched off, distractor words like *dal* that have no meaning in the L2 would be treated as completely unrelated to the target. Instead, hearing *dal* causes the bilingual to think of the concept *valley*, and that makes it harder to name the target concept *mountain*. Other experiments (e.g., Lee & Williams 2001) also showed semantic interference between languages in picture naming, but suggested that such interference effects might occur only in one direction—with L1 distractors having a powerful effect on L2 targets, but little effect of L2 distractors on L1 targets.[9]

Additional evidence for cross-language interference comes from the kinds of errors that bilinguals make when performing word production in the face of distracting stimuli (Miller & Kroll, 2002). In a set of experiments where the target and distractor stimuli were presented in written form, and the task was to translate the target word into the other language (L2 if the target word was printed in L1; L1 if the target word was presented in L2). Sometimes, the distractors were presented in the language that the response was supposed to be in. If the subject saw the word *cat*, they were supposed to translate that into Spanish and say *gato*. Sometimes the distractor would be in the *output language* (*perro*), and sometimes it would be in the input language (*dog*). When the distractors were in the output language, phonologically similar distractor words speeded up the translation process and semantically related distractor words slowed it down (just like in the picture-naming experiments). The distractor effects were weaker when the distractors were in the input language (*dog* had less of an effect on the *gato* response than *perro* did). These results show that semantic interference effects in the translation task are a bit different than semantic interference effects in picture naming. Miller and Kroll suggest that bilingual speakers boost the activation of the target (response) language and decrease the activation of the source language very quickly when performing translation, in part because the to-be-translated word provides information about which representations are needed (in ways that pictures do not). Thus, while there is still evidence for cross-language influences on translation (e.g., having shared phonology across representations in the two languages helps; having semantic competitors hurts), that competition may be resolved more quickly in translation tasks than other tasks that bilinguals can perform.

Effects of fluency, balance, and language similarity on competition

While many studies of bilinguals provide evidence of "inappropriate" activation of semantic and phonological representations from the non-target language, some studies produce little or no evidence of interference between a bilingual's two languages. Interference appears to be minimized when the bilingual individual is highly fluent and about equally proficient in both languages, and when the two languages are highly similar (Costa & Caramazza, 1999; Costa, Miozzo, & Caramazza, 1999; Costa & Santesteban, 2004). Spanish and Catalan have very similar grammars and vocabularies (about 75% of the words are cognates). In parts of Spain where Catalan is spoken, a large fraction of the population also speaks Spanish, and bilingual speakers have plenty of opportunities to use each of their two languages. This situation is not true for all bilinguals, and so we might expect to see some differences between the usual pattern and that displayed by Catalan-Spanish bilinguals. In fact, when such bilinguals perform the picture–word interference task, they experience facilitation, rather than competition, under conditions that produce interference in other groups of bilinguals. For example, Catalan-Spanish bilinguals might be asked to name a picture of a table in Catalan, for which the correct response is *taula*. Simultaneously, they might see or hear the Spanish word *mesa*. Normally, activating the Spanish phonology (*mesa*) would make it more difficult to activate and use the Catalan phonology (*taula*). However, in this case, hearing or seeing *mesa* made it easier for the Catalan-Spanish bilingual to say *taula*. Based on results like these, Costa and colleagues argue that, although seeing a picture of a table activates both the Spanish phonology (*mesa*) and the Catalan phonology (*taula*), selection for speech production occurs in a *language-specific* way (see Colomé, 2001, for additional evidence of simultaneous activation of Spanish and Catalan phonological representations in Catalan-Spanish bilinguals). Despite simultaneous activation of two sets of phonological representations, Catalan-Spanish bilinguals appear to restrict their search for output phonology representations to the target language. Hearing or seeing *mesa* reinforces activation of the semantic information that goes with the picture of a table, which causes the Catalan phonology to be more strongly activated than normal, but simultaneous activation of the Spanish phonology does not lead to interference (because the Spanish phonological representations are never searched and so never have a chance to compete for control of the speech planning process). If phonological search and selection encompassed both the Catalan and Spanish phonological systems, *mesa* would compete with *taula*, and interference (as evidenced by slow response times) would result.

Catalan-Spanish bilinguals also appear to perform differently than other kinds of bilnguals on language-switching tasks. Other groups of bilinguals that have been studied slow down when switching from speaking their L2 to speaking their L1 (Meuter & Allport, 1989). Highly fluent Catalan-Spanish bilinguals do experience a switch cost, but that cost is just as big no matter which direction they switch. In fact, Catalan-Spanish-English trilinguals, who are very fluent in Catalan and Spanish, but much less fluent in English, have symmetrical switch costs even when they change into and out of a weaker third language (English). Thus, in this group of language users, switching languages appears to reflect changing out a global task set or goal, but does not appear to involve suppressing one language to enable access to another, weaker language. These results could be explained by a theory that says bilinguals develop the ability to control access to different sets of language representations without using a suppression mechanism. This would explain why Catalan-Spanish bilinguals do not experience competition in picture–word interference tasks and why they have symmetrical language-switching costs. However, before we conclude that learning a second language to a high degree of proficiency endows the learner with the mental equivalent of a language "on/off" switch, further research is needed to sort out what effect similarity between the two languages has on the degree to which they compete, and what effect different degrees of second language skill have on the ability to control access to one language at a time (and see Grosjean, Li, Münte, & Rodriguez-Fornells, 2003, for a further commentary and critique of the Spanish-Catalan research; see Kroll, Bobb, Misra, & Guo, 2008, and Kroll, Bobb, & Wodniecka, 2006, for recent reviews of language selection studies; see Costa, Santesteban, & Ivanova, 2006, for evidence that proficiency, rather than language similarity, can lead to selective access).

Shared syntactic structure representations

The preceding section suggested that orthographic and phonological forms are shared across a bilingual's two languages, and that this shared phonology can lead to semantic interference in those cases where different meanings in the two languages share aspects of orthographic or phonological representation. Work on sentence production suggests that syntactic structure representations are also shared across a bilingual speaker's two languages when the two languages use similar syntactic structures to convey meaning. For example, Spanish and English passive voice sentences resemble one another. Compare the following two sentences (from Hartsuiker, Pickering, & Veltkamp, 2004, p. 411):

(1) The truck is chased by the taxi.
(2) El camión es perseguido por el taxi.

Like English, the Spanish passive voice reverses the normal order of the thematic agent and patient, and places the agent within a prepositional phrase (*by the taxi*, *por el taxi*). Because the same types of words appear in the same order (determiner, noun, verb, preposition, determiner, noun) in both Spanish and English, Spanish-English and English-Spanish bilinguals might use the same syntactic representations to support the parsing and interpretation of both languages, at least for structures that are as similar to one another as the passive. The *shared syntax account* proposes that bilinguals re-use as much of the syntax of their L1 as possible when learning and using an L2. For example, instead of creating an entirely new mental representation to encode the English passive, a native Spanish speaker could simply associate English words that can appear in passives with the syntactic representation that they acquired for the passive when they first learned the Spanish structure. Doing so could make English easier to learn—new vocabulary could be associated with well-known components of the L1 grammatical system—and could make English sentences easier to comprehend.

If syntactic structure representations are shared across languages, then processing a sentence in one language should have an effect on processing syntactically similar sentences in another language, even if the two sentences have very different meanings. This hypothesis has been tested in a variety of experiments involving *syntactic priming* (Hartsuiker et al., 2004; Hartsuiker & Pickering, 2008; Loebell & Bock, 2003; Salamoura & Williams, 2006). *Syntactic priming* occurs when producing one syntactic structure for one sentence makes it more likely that you will produce the same structure for a subsequent sentence. Syntactic priming can also occur between comprehension and production. People who hear one syntactic structure, such as the passive form in *The church was struck by lightning*, are more likely to produce a passive form to describe a picture that follows right away (Bock, 1986). Syntactic priming is thought to occur because listening to or producing one sentence activates syntactic structure representations that determine the order in which words should be produced as well as the specific forms that the words should take. Reactivating the same syntactic structure representation is easier than activating an entirely new representation, which leads speakers to repeat the same structures more often than chance dictates and makes it easier for comprehenders to process consecutive sentences that have the same syntactic structure (Tooley, Traxler, & Swaab, 2009; Traxler, 2008). If, as the shared syntax hypothesis asserts, syntactic structure representations are shared across a bilingual's two languages, then producing or comprehending one syntactic structure in one language should lead to a similar structure being produced in the other language. In fact, bilinguals who hear a syntactic structure in one language are more likely to produce the same syntactic structure when responding in their other language. Further, syntactic priming effects are just as large when the bilingual switches between languages as when they produce consecutive utterances in the same language. The effects also persist across brief lags, as bilinguals are likely to recall previously studied sentences using the same syntactic form as a sentence they have recently comprehended (Meijer & Fox Tree, 2003).

One recent study also demonstrated cross-language syntactic priming in comprehension (Weber & Indefrey, 2009). German-English bilingual readers processed English sentences faster after they read German sentences with the same syntactic structure. This facilitated comprehension process due to syntactic priming also produced a reduction of neural activity when two consecutive sentences had the same structure in regions of the brain that are commonly implicated in language comprehension (left middle temporal gyrus and left inferior frontal lobe). Reductions in neural activity are often observed when tasks are more practiced or are easier to carry out. So reduced neural activity for target sentences preceded by a prime sentence with a similar syntactic structure suggests that reading the related prime sentence helped readers interpret the target sentence, possibly because the syntactic representations activated by the prime sentence were also used to comprehend the target sentence.

Although syntactic priming occurs across languages that have similar syntactic structures (like the English and Spanish passives) it may occur less strongly when subcomponents of the syntactic structure differ across languages. Consistent word order appears to be the crucial factor that determines whether syntactic representations are shared across languages, and therefore whether syntactic priming will occur.[10] In German passives, the verb appears at the end of the sentence, as in sentence (3) (from Bernolet, Hartsuiker, & Pickering, 2007, p. 933):

(3) Der Fluss wurde von dem chemischen Abfall vergiftet.

"The river was by the chemical waste poisoned."[11]

In English passives, the verb appears in the middle of the verb phrase, next to the auxiliary verb *was*. However, other syntactic structures, such as the double-object/prepositional dative (*I gave him a letter* versus I gave a letter to him) have the same types of words in the same order in both German and English. German and English passives do not appear to prime one another. German-English bilinguals are no more likely to use the passive form in English after hearing a German passive than they are after hearing other syntactic forms in German (and vice versa; Loebell & Bock, 2003). However, Germans are more likely to produce a double-object dative in English (*I gave him a letter*) after hearing a double-object dative in German (*Der kleine Junge schrieb einen Brief an seinen Brieffreund*; Bernolet et al., 2007, p. 933). Thus, while some syntactic representations appear to be shared across languages, others may be used for only one of a bilingual's two languages. Specifically, syntactic structures that use the same types of words in the same order in both languages appear to become activated when either language is used, while structures that use different types of words or different serial ordering of words are less affected by activation of related syntactic structures from the other language. On the other hand, precise matching across the two languages may not be necessary for syntactic forms in one language to be active while the other language is being produced. For example, facial gestures that convey syntactic information in sign language are produced when sign language-spoken language bilinguals talk to non-signers, which suggests that syntactic/grammatical form information is activated even when a bilingual's two languages are expressed in completely different modalities (i.e., manual gesture versus speech; Pyers & Emmorey, 2008).

Shared syntactic representations across languages has been proposed as a mechanism that contributes to language change over time as migration and language contact changes the kind of input that language learners and adult speakers hear (Loebell & Bock, 2003). Children who are being raised in bilingual environments provide opportunities to study what happens to language patterns as children are being exposed to different syntactic structure patterns in two different languages. For example, English and French differ in the placements of adjectives within phrases. English adjectives nearly always appear before the nouns that they modify (*grape juice* rather than *juice grape*), and this prototypical placement affects how monolingual English children interpret novel two-word strings like *balloon clown* (a kind of clown, most likely) and *clown balloon* (a kind of balloon; Nicoladis, 2006). Some French adjectives do sometimes appear in front of the nouns that they modify, but this is restricted to specific adjective–noun combinations. *Grand dame* (important woman) appears more often than *dame grand* (woman important). French grammar therefore permits both noun–adjective and adjective–noun order, noun–adjective is the default pattern, and French-speaking children have to learn which adjective–noun pairs go against the dominant pattern. This task is complicated when the child is simultaneously exposed to English, because meaning can no longer be used as a reliable cue to word order. In fact, children raised in French-English bilingual environments are more likely to violate the adjective–noun word order pattern while speaking both French and English (compared to monolingual children from either language group). Word order violations are more common in French, which does have two word order possibilities, than English, which rarely uses the noun–adjective ordering. These results indicate that the two grammatical systems are simultaneously active in bilingual language learners, and that bilingual children are more willing than monolingual children to violate predominant grammatical patterns, especially when the grammar does not completely rule out a less common pattern.

Models of Language Control in Bilingual Speakers

Theories of bilingualism differ in the details of how word meanings are accessed and how bilingual speakers choose to express concepts in one of their languages, but there is general consensus that under all but the most extraordinary circumstances, both languages are active simultaneously and representations from the two languages frequently compete to control access to meaning (during comprehension) or access to phonological output processes in speech production. Nonetheless, bilingual speakers rarely mistakenly use a word from the wrong language.[12] Therefore, they must possess some powerful cognitive tools that enable them to select the appropriate labels (or suppress inappropriate labels) while they are speaking and ignore words (and their accompanying meanings) from the non-target language while they are listening to speech or reading. A substantial body of research focuses on the question of how bilinguals are able to respond in the intended language and avoid mistakenly responding in a contextually inappropriate way. How is that done?

Early theories (and Costa and colleagues' revival of *selective access* models) proposed that bilingual speakers possessed the mental equivalent of a light switch that can be set to activate or deactivate individual languages at will. According to the *language switch hypothesis*, a German-English bilingual could avoid mistakenly misinterpreting *chef* as *boss* when listening to English because the individual could simply deactivate or switch off her knowledge of German while listening to English. Similarly, while speaking English, the German-English bilingual would avoid using German terms to convey concepts because access to the German lexicon would be blocked by the conscious intention to speak English. But is such an extraordinary degree of control possible? If so, changing from speaking one language to the other should be as simple as setting the language switch to the right position. If bilinguals possess a language switch, we might expect to see similar patterns of behavior when a bilingual speaker changes from her L1 to her L2 compared to when she switches from her L2 to her L1.

A number of experiments have investigated what happens when bilinguals speak in one of their languages and then need to change to their other language. Because words themselves provide cues that can affect activation levels of the bilingual's two languages, these studies have often used Arabic numerals (numbers) as stimuli (e.g., Meuter & Allport, 1989). Arabic numerals are the same regardless of what language context bilinguals come from and so serve as a kind of universal script. They are therefore ideal stimuli when the experimental questions require the experimenter to isolate the effects of switching from one language to another from other potential influences on participants' behavior. Typically, the background behind the number appears in different colors to tell the bilingual participant which language to respond in. For example, if the background is green, the bilingual should speak in her L1. If the background is red, she should speak in her L2. Sometimes, two or more trials in a row have the same color background, and so the bilingual participant responds in the same language over multiple trials. However, on some critical trials, a change in the background color tells the bilingual participant to change from one language to the other (these are called *switch* trials). Sometimes she switches from her L1 (stronger) to her L2 (weaker). Sometimes she switches from her L2 to her L1. The question is, relative to continuing in the same language, how does switching languages affect the bilingual participant's behavior? Is it just as easy to switch from the L1 to the L2 as from the L2 to the L1 (as the language switch hypothesis would predict)? Or do different kinds of language switches lead to different patterns of behavior? The answer is that, for many bilinguals, switching from the L2 back into the L1 (stronger) language leads to slower responses than switching in the other direction. This asymmetric pattern of *switch costs* is sometimes referred to as being *paradoxical.* The L1 is supposed to be stronger, so why should it be harder to *stop* speaking the L2 in order to start speaking in the (stronger) L1?

Meuter and Allport (1989) proposed that paradoxical switch costs were caused by *involuntary persistence* of a *task set* (e.g., p. 26). Bilinguals, when faced with stimuli like pictures and numerals have a choice of responses. They can use the L1 label or the L2 label. However, for the vast majority of bilinguals, the salience and accessibility of the two sets of labels is not the same. For most bilinguals, the L1 will be stronger than the L2 because it was acquired earlier and practiced more than the L2 (although for some bilinguals who spend the majority of their time operating in the context of the language acquired second, the L2 is actually stronger than their L1). Because the L1 is stronger than the L2, the bilingual speaker must suppress the L1 lexicon in order to boost the relative activation of the L2 labels. (This is similar to what happens in monolingual speakers when confronted with a contextually inappropriate but dominant meaning of an ambiguous word.) Because the L2 is weaker than the L1, bilinguals do not need to suppress the L2 when speaking words in the L1. This asymmetric need for suppression creates the asymmetric switch costs. When speaking the L2, the L1 must be strongly inhibited or suppressed, otherwise the stronger L1 labels would sieze control of the output process and the "wrong" names would come out. When speaking the L1, little or no inhibition or suppression is applied to L2 labels, which are more weakly activated by the visual stimulus. When switching from the L2 into the L1, it takes time for the suppressed L1 labels to regain the activation levels necessary for them to be used to plan the motor movements involved in speech production. Based on asymmetric switch costs, some theories of bilingual language production explain the absence of unintended language intrusions as reflecting two factors. First, L2 labels are normally too weakly activated to compete with L1 labels for expression during speech. Second, when speaking in the L2, a strong general suppression mechanism reduces the activation of L1 labels to the point where they do not prevent L2 phonological representations from controlling the speech output process.

BIA+

The BIA+ model (Dijkstra & van Heuven, 1998) represents a modified form of the familiar TRACE model of lexical access. In addition to feature, letter (or phoneme), and word nodes, the BIA+ model incorporates a level of representation that encodes which language is most activated at a given point in time. So, for a Dutch-English bilingual when listening to Dutch, top-down excitation and inhibition help keep the Dutch lexical and phonological representations more activated than possible English competitors. This architecture does not completely preclude greater activation accruing for an individual lexical representation in the non-target (e.g., English) representations, and so bilingual speakers can switch from one language to the other and they can recognize when a word has been slipped in from the non-target language (as when a speaker uses an English word, such as *check*, rather than the Dutch version, such as *rekening*). Thus, the BIA+ model assumes a largely unified phonological and lexical system whose component representations are influenced by higher level control structures that keep track of which language is being heard at the moment.

The BIA+ model therefore predicts, based on TRACE processing assumptions (see Chapter 3), that any particular input to the system will activate multiple potential matching candidates, and that partially activated lexical representations will compete with one another for selection. This competition can take place within a single language (as when *cat* competes with *car*, *cap*, and *can*), but it can also take place across languages (Sunderman & Kroll, 2006). For example, imagine that a bilingual subject is trying to judge whether two words from different languages mean the same thing (the *translation judgment task*). The Spanish word *cara* might activate the English word *card*, because they look and sound similar—they are related in *form*. The Spanish word *cara* might activate the English word *head*, because *cara* means *face*, and *face* is associated with *head*—a kind of semantic relation. In fact, when Spanish-English bilinguals judge whether two words are *translation equivalents* (have the same meaning), they false-alarm to both form-related and semantically related distractors. So, rather than neatly activating just the English translation equivalent, the Spanish word activates a set of English candidates that are related to the Spanish word both by virtue of looking and sounding like it (a kind of orthographic or phonological neighborhood effect) or by virtue of having a similar meaning (a kind of semantic neighborhood effect). Thus, we can use the same principles that we used to understand monolingual lexical access to understand bilingual lexical access. Both involve simultaneous activation of multiple candidates followed by competition and selection of the best matching candidate.

Inhibitory control

The *inhibitory control* model of bilingual language processing proposes that a set of language-specific processes and general cognitive skills determines how the bilingual speaker responds in a variety of language tasks (Green, 1998). The inhibitory control system includes a goal-monitoring mechanism and a supervisory attention system that interact with language-specific systems that carry out the current task. (Is the bilingual trying to translate a word? or is she just trying to repeat it out loud?) All of these systems interact with lemma (abstract word) and lexeme (phonological code) representations that reflect knowledge of L1 and L2 components (see Figure 11.4). According to the inhibitory control model, language switch costs can be incurred because of changes in the status of the *goal* or *language task schema* components. Different kinds of errors, such as unwanted intrusions from the context-inappropriate language can occur if the supervisory attention system

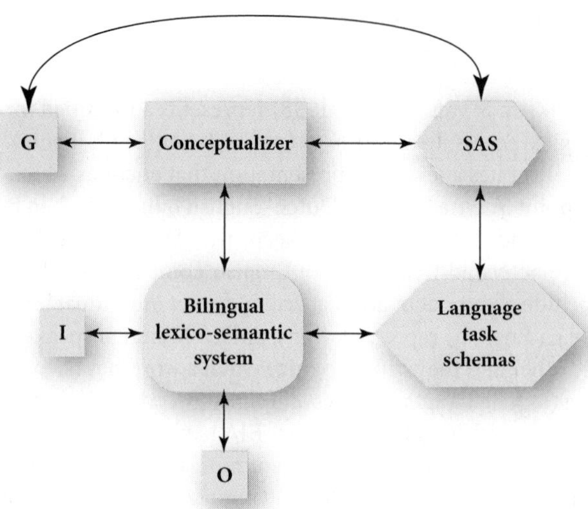

Figure 11.4 A schematic of Green's (1998, p. 69) *inhibitory control* model. G represents the system's current *goal*. The *conceptualizer* represents non-linguistic semantic representations or concepts. *SAS* stands for Supervisory Attention System that monitors the current goal and the current language task schema. A *language task schema* is a set of mental processes that can satisfy the current goal (such as *translate from L2 to L1; make a lexical decision, encode a concept in your second language*). The *lexico-semantic system* contains the lemma and lexeme representations that the bilingual speaker needs to express or decipher meanings in the two languages. I stands for *input*. O stands for *output*

wavers, causing an inadvertent change in the current task schema. The supervisory attention system is also involved in voluntary, consciously willed changes in language task, such as switching from speaking the L2 to speaking the L1, and in fact brain regions that are associated with executive control and attention (frontal lobes) show different degrees of activation when speakers switch from one language to the other (Abutalebi & Green, 2007). One advantage of the inhibitory control model is that it shows how bilinguals can perform different tasks with a given set of language inputs, and it helps explain phenomena like switch costs, unwanted language intrusions, and selective loss of language abilities (such as temporary inability to translate in a particular direction) following brain damage or transcranial magnetic stimulation. The inhibitory control model also helps explain why adult L2 learners tend to master lexical semantics (meaning) better than L2 syntax and grammar (Kotz & Elston-Güttler, 2004; Weber-Fox & Neville, 1996). Learning new word meanings is like learning other kinds of facts, and is well supported by the declarative memory system. Learning syntax and grammar involve learning procedures, like figuring out which of a number of possible suffixes is needed for a word appearing in a particular syntactic position.

Context effects and the zooming in hypothesis

The author's informal survey of Dutch-English and Spanish-English bilinguals found that even highly fluent and practiced bilingual speakers are less comfortable functioning in a mixed L1–L2 context than operating in a context where only their L2 is required. That is, if the bilingual speaker is holding a three-way conversation with a monolingual L1 speaker and a monolingual L2 speaker, they find themselves expending more mental effort and being more careful about their choice of words. According to these informants, the context of language use affects their process of production in noticeable ways. Is it possible that language control depends on contextual factors? Is language control easier in some situations than in others? Anecdotal reports are backed by laboratory research showing that recent experience can affect the way bilingual speakers access the lexicon (Elson-Güttler, Gunter, & Kotz, 2005). German-English bilinguals performed a lexical decision task after reading interlingual homographs (e.g., *gift*, which means "poison" in German) that were presented at the end of English sentences. The target words could be related to either the English meaning (e.g., *present*) or the German meaning (e.g., *death*). Interlingual homographs normally produce interference in naming and other lexical tasks, as meanings from the two languages become simultaneously active. However, if the German-English bilinguals watched a 20-minute movie that was narrated in English, there was no evidence that the L1 meaning (poison) had any effect on L2 (English) lexical decisions after about 15 minutes of performing the L2 lexical decision task. Brain wave (ERP) recordings also failed to show any difference between the brain's response to interlingual homographs and monolingual English control words after the first 15 minutes of the lexical decision task. These results indicate that providing substantial contextual support, in the form of a film with English narration and English sentences, appears to reduce or eliminate the competition from the un-necessary language, even when the un-necessary language is the bilinguals' dominant and native one.[13]

Context also appears to reduce the influence of the non-appropriate language during language comprehension as well. Experiments on L2 reading and mixed reading-and-naming tasks also show that context can have an effect on cross-language lexical activations. These experiments showed that in contexts that are highly constraining, and in which a specific word is highly likely to appear, the normal cognate advantage disappears (Schwartz & Kroll, 2006a). Similar effects of context occur in naturalistic reading (Altarriba, Kroll, Sholl, & Rayner, 1996; see also Duyck, Van Assche, Drieghe, & Hartsuiker, 2007; Schwartz & Fontes, 2008). These experiments involved target words that were presented in either highly constraining sentences or weakly constraining sentences. If someone told you *I went down to the bank and deposited all my* ..., you would be highly confident that the next word would be *money*, and you would be right most of the time. If someone told you *I would like to have some* ..., you would be less likely to guess *money*, so that sentence context is less constraining. Highly constraining sentences produce specific expectancies for specific words to appear. So, even though, *I went down to the bank and deposited all my dinero* makes perfect sense to a Spanish-English bilingual, the normal effects of word frequency do not appear in mixed-language sentences like this one. Instead, high-frequency Spanish words behave more like low-frequency Spanish words. This makes sense if you consider that the meanings of *money* and *dinero* relate to the context, but only one of the two words will be appropriate in a given context. *Dinero* will be more appropriate than *money* in the context of a Spanish sentence (and vice versa in English sentences). The fact that *dinero* acts like a low-frequency word in the context of a highly constraining English sentence context suggests that, when Spanish-English bilinguals read the context *I went down to the bank and deposited* ..., *dinero* has been deactivated or suppressed due to the pre-activation or high expectation that the specific word *money* will appear soon. Thus, as per the *zooming in* hypothesis, context may increase the activation of some stored representations and decrease the activation of others, thereby modulating the degree of cross-language competition at different points in time.

Bilingualism and Executive Control

Learning a second language and using it regularly confers substantial benefits beyond the obvious one of being able to communicate with a larger number of people. Wider cognitive benefits include enhanced attentional skills and the ability to respond efficiently in situations where different sources of information point toward different responses (Bialystok, Craik, Klein, and Viswanathan, 2004; Bialystok, Craik, & Luk, 2008). Specifically, bilinguals outperform monolinguals in tasks that require an individual to ignore task-irrelevant information that could lead to the wrong response. This ability to perform *interference suppression* (ignoring distracting information;) supports the ability to perform *response inhibition* (bypassing a stronger but incorrect response in order to execute a weaker but correct response; Bialystok et al., 2008, p. 869). Interference suppression and response inhibition are two components of what is called *executive control*, the set of skills that allows us to manage our thought processes effectively. Executive control, like other thinking skills, can be improved through practice. Being bilingual helps people improve their executive control skills by giving them practice at managing conflicting information. For example, if you want to describe the picture in Figure 11.3, and you speak English and Spanish, you have a choice of saying *bear* or *oso*. Further, when bilinguals think of the concept "bear," labels in both of their languages become activated and compete for selection (although greater conflict likely occurs when an individual speaks in the weaker language). This is similar to the conflict that occurs for monolinguals when two words are very closely related in meaning and both are equally good labels for a concept (e.g., *couch* and *sofa*; *dinner* and *supper* if you come from the midwestern part of the United States). The difference between monolinguals and bilinguals, however, is that while a few words are near-synonyms for the monolingual, nearly every single word in the L2 has an equally good label, equivalent to a synonym, in the L1. Thus, bilinguals get a great deal of practice in the interference suppression component of executive control. But does this practice in executive control actually lead to greater skill? Are bilinguals really better able to manage conflicting information than monolinguals?

The answer appears to be a resounding "yes," based on experiments involving the *Simon* and *ANT* tasks (Bialystok et al., 2004, 2008; Costa, Hernández, & Sebastián-Gallés, 2008). In the Simon task, participants press one key for one stimulus and another key for a different stimulus. For example, you might press a key with your left hand for green-colored objects, and another key with your right hand for red-colored objects. Sometimes, the stimulus appears on the left-hand side of the screen, sometimes in the middle, and sometimes on the right. Generally speaking, it is easier to press the left-hand key when the green stimulus is on the left-hand side of the screen. The spatial location of the stimulus and the response are *congruent*, so these are called *congruent* trials. Participants have more difficulty pressing the left-hand key when the green stimulus appears on the right-hand side of the screen. The spatial location of the stimulus and the response are *incongruent*, and these are *incongruent* trials. The difference in response time and accuracy between congruent and incongruent trials gives an estimate of how much difficulty participants have resolving the conflict between color and spatial location. A bigger difference between congruent and incongruent trials indicates more difficulty managing the conflict. The ANT task is a variant of the widely-used *flanker task*. The participant's task is to indicate whether an arrow points toward the left or the right. The target arrow is surrounded by arrows that either point in the same direction as the target (on congruent trials) or in a different direction (on incongruent trials).

In both the Simon and ANT tasks, bilinguals are a little bit faster than monolinguals on congruent trials (suggesting that they are better at paying attention and remembering

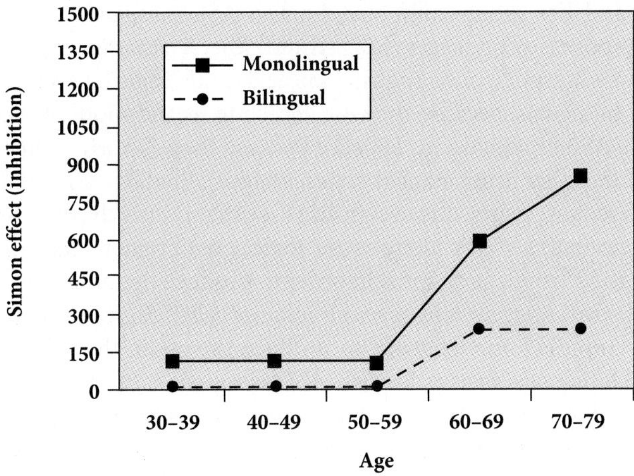

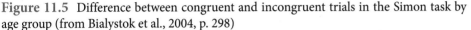

Figure 11.5 Difference between congruent and incongruent trials in the Simon task by age group (from Bialystok et al., 2004, p. 298)

what they are supposed to be doing), but bilinguals really shine on incongruent trials. On incongruent trials, bilinguals are much less affected by conflict between spatial and color information than monolinguals. Bilingual children as young as three years old show superior ability to ignore task-irrelevant information relative to their monolingual peers (Bialystok, 1999).[14] The bilingual advantage gets larger the older people get (Bialystok et al., 2004; see Figure 11.5). While it is not possible to rule out entirely the idea that people with better executive control are more likely to become bilingual (rather than that bilingualism and the accompanying practice in managing conflict give you better executive control skills), the fact that the bilingual advantage appears in even very young bilinguals, who are generally bilingual by virtue of environmental factors and not by choice, suggests that causality runs from being bilingual to enhanced executive control.

Perhaps bilinguals are better at executive control simply because they have superior thinking skills across the board. In fact, this does not appear to be the case. For example, you might think that continual exposure to and use of two phonological systems would make bilinguals better than their monolingual peers in tasks that require them to discriminate between different phonemes and other tasks that require phonological awareness. While some bilinguals are better at some phonological tasks than monolinguals, this advantage does not appear consistently across groups of bilingual speakers (Bialystok, Majumder, & Martin, 2003). Spanish-English bilingual children are better than English monolingual speakers on *phoneme segmentation* (take a word like *cat* and say how many different sounds it has), but they are not better on other tasks involving phonological knowledge (such as *rhyme judgment*, does *dog* sound like *puppy* or *log*?) and *phoneme substitution* (what word do you get when you take the /k/ out of *kind* and replace it with the /m/ sound from *mat*?). Chinese-English bilinguals are worse than English monolingual children on a wide variety of phonological awareness tasks.[15] Thus, being bilingual does not by itself lead to superior knowledge and performance across all language-related skills.

In fact, not all bilinguals have superior executive control when compared to monolinguals. Karen Emmorey and her colleagues (Emmorey, Luk, Pyers, & Bialystok, 2008) studied English-American Sign Language (ASL) bilinguals' performance on a version of the ANT task. Emmorey and her group compared English-ASL bilinguals to a mixed group of participants who spoke two languages (English and either Vietnamese, Cantonese, or Italian) and a third group who spoke only English. She called the English-Vietnamese/Cantonese/Italian *unimodal* bilinguals, because they use speech to express both of their languages. By contrast, English-ASL bilinguals are *bimodal* because they express one of their languages using speech and the other using manual gestures (signs). English-ASL bilinguals sometimes produce two different messages, one in sign and the other in speech (sometimes on purpose, sometimes inadvertently). Thus, there is no logical requirement that they suppress the output of one of their language systems in order to produce the other. By contrast, it is not possible to speak two different languages simultaneously.[16] So, while unimodal bilinguals must necessarily suppress one language to produce the other, that requirement does not hold for bimodal bilinguals, such as English-ASL bilinguals, and so bimodal bilinguals may not have the same kind of practice managing response conflict or suppressing interfering information. In fact, bimodal bilinguals' (English-ASL speakers) responses on the ANT task were identical to monolingual speakers', while unimodal bilinguals showed the usual advantage on both congruent and incongruent trials. Thus, the bilinguals' advantage in executive control does not flow simply from knowing two languages. Those two languages must be expressed in the same modality (e.g., speech), which creates the conditions for interlanguage competition and the need to suppress one response in favor of another.

Teaching Techniques and Individual Differences in Second Language Learning

Studying bilingual language processing can help us understand how individuals improve their L2 skills, which can in turn help teachers design better ways to teach people an L2. This is especially important for adults who begin to learn an L2 post-puberty, as their outcomes are generally poorer than for people who learn an L2 in childhood (Kotz & Elston-Güttler, 2004; Kroll, 2006; Weber-Fox & Neville, 1996; but see Kotz, Holcomb, & Osterhout, 2008). A number of theories have been offered to explain why adults have more trouble acquiring an L2. Greater difficulty acquiring an L2 in adults compared to children may be the result of a genetically determined *critical period* or *sensitive phase* for language acquisition. The genetically determined critical period may occur because *implicit learning* or *procedural memory* systems that we need to carry out lexical access and syntactic parsing processes are more *plastic*, or changeable, early in life, but become more static or fixed later in life (Ullman, 2001). If procedural memory systems (the memory systems that you use to carry out automatic skills like walking, tying your shoes, or riding a bike) cannot be modified to accommodate new L2 functions, those new L2 functions must be carried out using *declarative memory* systems (the memory systems that you use to keep track of factual knowledge), and declarative memory systems are poorly suited to the rapid and automatic execution of language-interpretation and production processes. Alternatively, adults may have trouble learning L2s because acquiring an L2 requires modification of an L1 processing system that has become fixed or entrenched (Hernandez et al., 2005). Whichever of these theories ultimately proves to be correct (and there may be grains of truth in all of them), adult language learners need effective teaching and learning strategies to maximize their chances of mastering an L2.

Research on teaching and learning L2s reflects different trains of thought and different tactics pursued in different laboratories. Some research uses basic-science findings that provide insights into the mental processes that occur as learners acquire knowledge about their L2 to develop new teaching techniques, while other research investigates established teaching methods. An example of the former is an application of the revised hierarchical model to language learning (Kroll, Michael, & Sankaranarayanan, 1998). Because the L1 is more dominant than the L2, learners may have a hard time ignoring or suppressing L1 responses in order to respond more appropriately in the L2. As L2 learners acquire proficiency in their L2, they progress from translating L2 terms into their L1 equivalents to accessing conceptual representations directly from the L2 terms (bypassing L1 lexical representations; Talamas, Kroll, & Dufour, 1999). Teaching techniques that minimize the activation of L1 representations as L2 representations and processes are being acquired may facilitate learning the L2 by speeding up the transition from looking up the L1 label to accessing concepts directly from L2 labels. As indicated previously, reading or hearing a word in the L2 tends to automatically activate L1 translation equivalents (as per the RHM), which reinforces the connection between the L1 term and the conceptual store without having much effect on the direct connection between the L2 term and the conceptual store. One way to bypass this automatic response is to present L2 terms in the context of pictures that reflect unusual visual perspectives of the object. For example, you might show a picture of the underside of a cat while simultaneously exposing the L2 learner to the L2 name for *cat*. This manipulation slows down access to the L1 label for the pictured item and gives the L2 learner a visual cue that is very specifically associated with the L2 label.

Teaching an L2 is different than teaching other subjects, because L2s may not be used in the student's daily activities outside the classroom. Thus, the context of L2 use is normally quite different than the context of L2 study. *Immersion* techniques offer one way to bring language study and language use contexts into closer contact. In language immersion programs, student-teacher interactions, including L2 instruction, occur in the L2. *Study abroad* programs offer a form of immersion that intermixes formal instruction on vocabulary and grammar in the L1 with significant direct exposure to the L2 and culture outside of the classroom. Study abroad and immersion provide greater opportunities for students to practice their L2 skills, and so it is not surprising that, for many L2 skills, immersion and study abroad appear to produce outcomes superior to stay-at-home instruction provided in the L1 (Collentine & Freed, 2004; Segalowitz & Freed, 2004). In particular, study abroad experience appears to lead to greater average gains in *fluency*—the ability to speak the L2 in larger chunks with fewer false-starts, hesitations, and filled pauses. However, L2 learning involves multiple component skills, and some of these benefit more from immersion and study abroad than others. Comprehension processes, such as the speed of lexical access from L2 words, seem to be more similar across people who study at home and those who study abroad. Also, L2 learners vary with respect to the general cognitive skills, degree of L2 proficiency, and attitudes that they bring to the language-learning context, and these individual difference variables influence how much individual learners benefit from different language contexts.

Individual differences in cognitive skills such as verbal working memory capacity and phonological memory ability both influence how rapidly people can acquire an L2 and how much they benefit from immersion. People who have better phonological memory abilities, as evidenced by greater ability to discriminate between different sequences of non-word consonant–vowel–consonant syllables, make greater gains in L2 speaking fluency than people with weaker phonological memory ability (O'Brien, Segalowitz, Freed, & Collentine, 2007; Papagno, Valentine, & Baddeley, 1991). This correlation likely reflects the requirement for L2 learners to maintain L2 phonological representations in an activated form as they learn to segment and classify components of L2 spoken input. People who have weaker phonological coding and memory skills may require greater practice and at-home instruction before they can benefit maximally from study abroad or immersion techniques. This latter conclusion is supported by data showing that students with lower working-memory skills who studied abroad had outcomes similar to students with higher working-memory skills who studied at home (Sunderman & Kroll, 2007). The biggest L2 gains were made by students with high working-memory capacity who were immersed in a study-abroad program. Thus, while immersion generally produces better outcomes than stay-at-home classroom instructions, this is not true for all learners at all levels of L2 proficiency. Thus, the exact fit between the language learner and instructional methods appears to determine how quickly the language learner can acquire new skills. As Collentine and Freed (2004, p. 164) note, "(there is no evidence that) one context of learning is uniformly superior to another for all students."

The Neural Bases of Bilingualism

The neurophysiological and neuroimaging approach to understanding bilingualism is still in its infancy, but such studies have already produced substantial advances in our understanding of bilingualism. Such studies demonstrate that the brain reorganizes itself as it acquires skill in the L2, and that such reorganization begins almost immediately after people begin to learn an L2. Neurophysiological (ERP) experiments show that the brain's response to the meaning and syntax of the L2 changes very quickly, even before the learner's behavior shows any trace of having acquired new knowledge. ERP researchers studied native English speakers who were beginning to learn French in college classes (McLaughlin, Osterhout, & Kim, 2004). The participants' task was to say whether strings of letters were real words in French or not (i.e., they made *lexical decisions*). After an average of 14 hours of classroom instruction (and as little as 5), participants' brain wave activity differed when they were reading real French words compared to when they were reading strings of letters that were not words in French (or English). However, their overt judgment performance was at chance level. So, even though some part of learners' brains knew the difference between a real French word and a fake French word (or *pseudoword*), they were not consciously aware of the difference, and that newly acquired knowledge did not yet affect their overt behavior. A similar study used *grammaticality judgment* (Is this sentence OK in the target language or not?) on native English speakers who were learning Spanish. As in the lexical decision study, people who were learning Spanish were at chance on the overt grammaticality judgment task. Nonetheless, their brain wave activity was different when the sentences were grammatical in Spanish compared to when they were ungrammatical (Tokowicz & MacWhinney, 2005).

Quite a bit of neuroimaging research has been directed toward finding out whether two languages share space in the brain or whether the each language occupies its own territory. These studies can also help to test whether the same interpretative processes are carried out in the same way by native speakers of a language and by non-native speakers. *Late bilinguals*, people who begin to learn an L2 in adulthood (compare to *early bilinguals*, who begin to learn an L2 in infancy or childhood) tend to have difficulty with some aspects of the syntax of their L2, especially more complex features of non-native syntax, such as passivization and long-distance dependencies (Clahsen & Felser, 2006; Yokoyama et al., 2006). However, fMRI data from bilinguals show that brain regions normally associated with language processing (such as middle and superior temporal lobes, Wernicke's and Broca's areas) tend to be activated whether the bilingual individual is processing their L1 or their L2. Even late bilinguals show considerable overlap with native speakers in the gross regions of the brain that are activated during language comprehension tasks (Yokoyama et al., 2006).

Other imaging studies have investigated how the brain responds to conflict between representations in the bilingual's L1 and L2. One study that focused on processing of interlingual homographs (compared to non-conflicting control words) showed that interlingual homographs caused greater activation in parts of the brain that are typically associated with executive control and monitoring for conflicting information (i.e., inferior frontal lobe and anterior cingulate cortex; Van Heuven, Schriefers, Dijkstra, & Hagoort, 2008). Different patterns of brain activity occur when bilinguals look at pictures and carry out a phonological judgment task (Rodriguez-Fornells et al., 2005). For example, you might be asked to press a key when the picture name contained the phoneme /t/. If you were a Catalan-English bilingual, you would press the button when you saw a picture of a table (*taula* in Catalan), whether you were responding based on your L1 or L2, so these are called *consistent* trials. However, if you were a Spanish-Catalan bilingual, your response would depend on which language you were supposed to be judging (*t* does not appear in *mesa*, the Spanish word for *table*). So, these are called *conflict* trials. Both ERP and fMRI showed differences between consistent and conflict trials in bilinguals, but not in monolingual control subjects. In the fMRI experiment, the anterior cingulate was more activated by conflict trials than by consistent trials, similar to the interlingual homograph results.

Conflict and competition initiated by language switches also trigger different patterns of activation in the brain compared to tasks where multiple responses are made in the same language (Abutalebi et al., 2007; Wang, Xue, Chen, Xue, & Dong, 2007). Notably, in more than one fMRI study, greater bilateral brain activation occurred when bilinguals switched from L1 to L2 than when they switched from L2 to L1. In behavioral experiments, bilinguals experience greater difficulty switching from L2 back to L1, so greater activity in the opposite direction may reflect the mental effort required to suppress the L1 in order to access the L2.

Some studies do find subtle differences in the regions that are activated by L1 and L2, especially when complex syntactic structures appear in the L2 stimuli (as in Marian et al., 2003). Results like these reinforce neurophysiological results (e.g., Weber-Fox & Neville, 1996) showing that even highly proficient bilinguals may have brain responses that are subtly different from native speakers. However, it is not clear that these differences in brain activity between L1 and L2 processing reflect language-specific processes (e.g., that one brain region handles lexical access or syntax for L2, and another region does the same job for L1 stimuli). It may be that differences in patterns of activation across L1 and L2 tasks reflect differences in difficulty processing the two languages. Most bilinguals are *unbalanced* (which does not mean that they are unstable, it just means that they have an easier time functioning in their dominant language; *balanced* bilinguals are equally comfortable operating in different language environments). Thus, differences in brain activity between L1 and L2 could simply reflect the fact that producing and understanding the L1 is easier than producing and understanding the L2. In fact, when task difficulty is taken into account when contrasting neural activity in response to L1 and L2 stimuli, the pattern of brain activity is nearly identical across the two languages (Hasegawa, Carpenter, & Just, 2002). While the question certainly remains open, it is important when interpreting behavioral, neurophysiological, and neuroimaging results to consider the possibility that some effects may occur simply because doing a task in one language may be more difficult than doing the task in another language.

Summary and Conclusions

The majority of the world's language users are bilingual, and so it is appropriate that we spend some time getting to understand how their circumstances relate to monolinguals'. In this chapter, you have learned that bilinguals access both L1 lexical representations and language-external conceptual representations when they encounter words in their L2.

The strength of connections between L2 labels and L1 labels, and between L2 labels and concepts, changes as the L2 learner increases her proficiency in the L2. However, even highly proficient bilinguals have representations from both of their languages activated simultaneously. Although proficiency and language dominance modulate the degree of competition between the two languages, bilinguals must develop powerful mental mechanisms to make sure that they activate the appropriate representations at the appropriate times to accomplish their current goals. While it is unlikely that bilinguals possess the mental equivalent of a light switch, language scientists have not nailed down the precise nature of the mental processes that give proficient bilinguals such exquisite control over their production and comprehension processes. Neurophysiological and neuroimaging research indicates that a bilingual's two languages share space in the brain, although subtly different patterns of activation occur for the L1 and L2, and differences appear as well when bilinguals switch languages, depending on whether the switch is from the more dominant to the less dominant language or vice versa. The brain's response to semantic information carried by L2 stimuli can be very similar to the brain's response to L1 semantic information, but late learners appear to be permanently disadvantaged when dealing with more complex aspects of L2 syntax and grammar. These disadvantages can be minimized by teaching methods, including study abroad and immersion, so long as those teaching techniques are well matched with the cognitive resources available to the L2 learner and the learner's degree of proficiency in the L2. Regardless, bilinguals enjoy certain advantages over monolinguals. Aside from being twice as likely than monolinguals to find someone to talk to,[17] bilinguals are especially advantaged in the area of cognitive control and executive function.

TEST YOURSELF

1. Compare and contrast the word association and the concept mediation models of bilingual language organization. Compare each of them to the revised hierarchical model. Why have language scientists largely abandoned the word association and concept mediation models in favor of the revised hierarchical model?
2. What has the study of cognates contributed to the understanding of bilingualism? How about interlingual homographs?
3. How do we know that bilinguals' two languages compete and interfere with one another? Why can't they stop it?
4. What has the study of Catalan-Spanish bilinguals and trilinguals contributed to our understanding of bilingualism?
5. Describe studies suggesting that syntactic structure representations are shared across languages in bilinguals.
6. What happens when a bilingual switches between her two languages?
7. Describe some of the benefits of being bilingual (besides the obvious one of being able to talk to more people). How do bilingual brains differ from monolingual brains?

THINK ABOUT IT

1. Do you think it's easier to become trilingual than it is to become bilingual? If so, what makes it easier to become trilingual? Do you know anyone who is trilingual? Ask them about their experience learning new languages.
2. Some computer programs can translate words and phrases from one language into another. How do you think these programs work? Will computers ever replace human translators?

Notes

1 Which means "of the foot" in Dutch.

2 With apologies to Mary Potter, who has made numerous significant contributions to language science research, and J. K. Rowling, who writes books.

3 Exceptions to this general principle include complex concepts like *schadenfreude* from German which does not have a simple equivalent in English. It means something like, "the feeling of pleasant superiority that you get when you see someone else suffering." Abstract, difficult-to-define concepts such as "freedom" and "justice" may also have subtly different meanings in different languages. Nonetheless, for concrete objects, such as *house*, *tree*, and *man*, for example, theorists generally assume that the underlying concepts are identical or nearly so across speakers of different languages and have a single, unified representation in bilinguals.

4 This chapter follows the convention of listing the bilingual speaker's first or more dominant (better known) language first, and their second or less dominant language second.

5 And see Ruiz, Paredes, Macizo, & Bajo (2008) for evidence of direct lexical–lexical L1–L2 and L2–L1 links in highly skilled professional translators.

6 It appears that not all language combinations have symmetrical cognate effects. Gollan and colleagues' (Gollan, Forster, & Frost, 1997) masked-priming studies involving Hebrew-English bilinguals indicated that L2 targets were primed by L1 cognates more strongly than L1 targets were primed by L2 cognates. Gollan and colleagues concluded that having a shared orthography or script was an important factor that mediates cross-language cognate effects (Hebrew is written in a different script and has an even deeper orthography than English, as information about vowels is usually left implicit in Hebrew). Cognate effects are at least partially independent of script, however, as both Hebrew-English and Japanese-English bilinguals (Hoshino & Kroll, 2008) show a cognate advantage when processing L2 targets. These results suggest that shared or unified phonological and semantic representations, rather than shared orthography, produce the cognate advantage.

7 Results like these need to be interpreted cautiously. Deciding whether a given voxel is activated or not is a complex function involving the sensitivity of the MRI machine, the number of trials, and other factors associated with signal-to-noise ratios, and depends on arbitrarily defined thresholds for deciding what counts as being activated. It is certainly possible that one could find a reasonable set of imaging parameters that would produce greater spatial dissociations between L1 and L2 activity; and fully overlapping, indistinguishable patterns of activity could occur with different levels of precision in the imaging technique and differently defined thresholds.

8 However, if the picture-naming process is given enough of a head start (i.e,. the picture appears a few hundred ms before the distractor), the semantic distractor has no effect. This latter result suggests that, if concept activation and lemma selection are completed before the semantic distractor appears, the semantic distractor does not have a chance to interfere with activating the phonemes you need to speak the target name.

9 As predicted by the RHM.

10 But see Weber and Indefrey (2009) for German-to-English passive priming in self-paced reading.

11 Master Yoda sometimes uses similar constructions for active voice sentences, as in "Mind what you have learned. Save you it can."

12 The author's informal survey of Spanish-English, English-Spanish, and Dutch-English bilinguals turned up no individuals who made such mistakes more than once a week (based on self-report), and most of the interviewees said that they rarely (a few times a year) or never made such mistakes. They also reported that, on the rare occasions when they did make such an error, it was because they could not retrieve the appropriate word in their weaker language.

13 Note, however, that in a follow-on study using similar methods (including a film-context induction and ERP recording), the same group failed to replicate some of the critical effects from the original study (Paulmann, Elston-Güttler, Gunter, & Kotz, 2006). However, this latter experiment involved single-word lexical decision without sentence contexts. So, the combination of contextual induction and immediate language context (in the form of sentences) may be required before access becomes selective.

14 These findings are based on card-sort and act-out tasks, rather than the Simon task, which is way too boring to be used with young children.

15 That is not particularly surprising in light of theories that tie phonological awareness to proto-literacy skills, given that the Chinese logographic writing system is based on syllables rather than phonemes (see Chapter 10).

16 At least, no one has figured out yet how to say *cat* and *gato* at the same time. The same way you can't say *cat* and *dog* at precisely the same time.

17 Apologies to Woody Allen.

References

Abutalebi, J., Brambati, S. M., Annoni, J., Moro, A., Cappa, S. F., & Perani, D. (2007). The neural cost of the auditory perception of language switches: An event-related functional magnetic resonance imaging study in bilinguals. *Journal of Neuroscience, 27,* 13762–13769.

Abutalebi, J., & Green, D. (2007). Bilingual language production: The neurocognition of language representation and control. *Journal of Neurolinguistics, 20,* 242–275.

Altarriba, J., Kroll, J. F., Sholl, A., & Rayner, K. (1996). The influence of lexical and conceptual constraints on reading mixed-language sentences: Evidence from eye fixations and naming times. *Memory & Cognition, 24,* 477–492.

Altarriba, J., & Mathis, K. M. (1997). Conceptual and lexical development in second language acquisition. *Journal of Memory and Language, 36,* 550–568.

Bernolet, S., Hartsuiker, R. J., & Pickering, M. J. (2007). Shared syntactic representations in bilinguals: Evidence for the role of word-order repetition. *Journal of Experimental Psychology: Learning, Memory, and Cognition, 33,* 931–949.

Bialystok, E. (1999). Cognitive complexity and attentional control in the bilingual mind. *Child Development, 70,* 636–644.

Bialystok, E., Craik, F. I. M., Klein, R., & Viswanathan, M. (2004). Bilingualism, aging, and cognitive control: Evidence from the Simon task. *Psychology and Aging, 19,* 290–303.

Bialystok, E., Craik, F., & Luk, G. (2008). Cognitive control and lexical access in younger and older bilinguals. *Journal of Experimental Psychology: Learning, Memory, and Cognition, 34,* 859–873.

Bialystok, E., Majumder, S., & Martin, M. M. (2003). Developing phonological awareness: Is there a bilingual advantage? *Applied Psycholinguistics, 24,* 27–44.

Bock, J. K. (1986). Syntactic persistence in language production. *Cognitive Psychology, 18,* 355–387.

Caramazza, A., & Brones, I. (1979). Lexical access in bilinguals. *Bulletin of the Psychonomic Society, 13,* 212–214.

Caramazza, A., & Brones, I. (1980). Semantic classification by bilinguals. *Canadian Journal of Psychology, 34,* 77–81.

Christoffels, I. K., Firk, C., & Schiller, N. O. (2007). Bilingual language control: An event-related brain potential study. *Brain Research, 1147,* 192–208.

Clahsen, H., & Felser, C. (2006). How native-like is non-native language processing? *Trends in Cognitive Sciences, 10,* 564–570.

Collentine, J., & Freed, B. F. (2004). Learning context and its effects on second language acquisition: Introduction. *Studies in Second Language Acquisition, 26,* 153–171.

Colomé, À. (2001). Lexical activation in bilinguals' speech production: Language-specific or language-independent? *Journal of Memory and Language, 45,* 721–736.

Costa, A., & Caramazza, A. (1999). Is lexical selection in bilingual speech production language-specific? Further evidence from Spanish-English and English-Spanish bilinguals. *Bilingualism: Language and Cognition, 2,* 231–244.

Costa, A., Caramazza, A., & Sebastian-Galles, N. (2000). The cognate facilitation effect: Implications for models of lexical access. *Journal of Experimental Psychology: Learning, Memory, and Cognition, 26,* 1283–1296.

Costa, A., Hernández, M., & Sebastián-Gallés, N. (2008). Bilingualism aids conflict resolution: Evidence from the ANT task. *Cognition, 106,* 59–86.

Costa, A., Miozzo, M., & Caramazza, A. (1999). Lexical selection in bilinguals: Do words in the bilingual's two lexicons compete for selection? *Journal of Memory and Language, 41,* 365–397.

Costa, A., & Santesteban, M. (2004). Bilingual word perception and production: Two sides of the same coin? *Trends in Cognitive Sciences, 8,* p. 253

Costa, A., Santesteban, M., & Ivanova, I. (2006). How do highly proficient bilinguals control their lexicalization process? Inhibitory and language-specific selection mechanisms are both functional. *Journal of Experimental Psychology: Learning, Memory, and Cognition, 32,* 1057–1074.

De Groot, A. M. B., Dannenburg, L., & van Hell, J. G. (1994). Forward and backward translation by bilinguals. *Journal of Memory and Language, 33,* 600–629.

Dell, G. S. (1986). A spreading activation model of retrieval in sentence production. *Psychological Review, 93,* 283–321.

Dijkstra, T., Grainger, J., & van Heuven, W. J. B. (1999). Recognition of cognates and interlingual homographs: The neglected role of phonology. *Journal of Memory and Language, 41,* 496–518.

Dijkstra, T., & van Heuven, W. J. B. (1998). The BIA model and bilingual word recognition. In J. Grainger & A. M. Jacobs (Eds.), *Localist connectionist approaches to human cognition* (pp. 189–225). Mahwah, NJ: Erlbaum.

Duyck, W. (2005). Translation and associative priming with cross–lingual pseudohomophones: Evidence for nonselective phonological activation in bilinguals. *Journal of Experimental Psychology: Learning, Memory, and Cognition, 31,* 1340–1359.

Duyck, W., Van Assche, E., Drieghe, D., & Hartsuiker, R. J. (2007). Visual word recognition by bilinguals in a sentence context: Evidence for nonselective lexical access. *Journal of Experimental Psychology: Learning, Memory, and Cognition, 33,* 663–679.

Elson-Güttler, K. E., Gunter, T. C., & Kotz, S. A. (2005). Zooming into L2: Global language context and adjustment affect processing of interlingual homographs in sentences. *Cognitive Brain Research, 25,* 57–70.

Emmorey, K., Luk, G., Pyers, J. E., & Bialystok, E. (2008). The source of enhanced cognitive control in bilinguals. *Psychological Science, 19,* 1201–1206.

Gaskell, M. G., & Marslen-Wilson, W. D. (1997). Integrating form and meaning: A distributed model of speech perception. *Language and Cognitive Processes, 12,* 613–656.

Gollan, T. H., & Acenas, L. R. (2004). Cognate and translation effects on tip-of-the-tongue states in Spanish-English and Tagalog-English bilinguals. *Journal of Experimental Psychology: Learning, Memory, and Cognition, 30,* 246–269.

Gollan, T. H., Forster, K. I., & Frost, R. (1997). Translation priming with different scripts: Masked priming with cognates and noncognates in Hebrew-English bilinguals. *Journal of Experimental Psychology: Learning, Memory, and Cognition, 23,* 1122–1139.

Green, D. W. (1998). Mental control of the bilingual lexico-semantic system. *Bilingualism: Language and Cognition, 1,* 67–81.

Grosjean, F. (1989). Neurolinguists, beware: The bilingual is not two monolinguals in one person. *Brain & Language, 36,* 3–15.

Grosjean, F., Li, P., Münte, T. F., & Rodriguez-Fornells, A. (2003). Imaging bilinguals: When the neurosciences meet the language sciences. *Bilingualism: Language and Cognition, 6,* 159–165.

Hartsuiker, R. J., & Pickering, M. J. (2008). Language integration in bilingual sentence production. *Acta Psychologica, 128,* 479–489.

Hartsuiker, R. J., Pickering, M. J., & Veltkamp, E. (2004). Is syntax separate or shared between languages? *Psychological Science, 15,* 409–414.

Hasegawa, M., Carpenter, P. A., & Just, M. A. (2002). An fMRI study of bilingual sentence comprehension and workload. *Neuroimage, 15,* 647–660.

Heredia, R. R. (1997). Bilingual memory and hierarchical models: A case for language dominance. *Current Directions in Psychological Science, 6,* 34–39.

Hermans, D., Bongaerts, T., de Bot, K., & Schreuder, R. (1998). Producing words in a foreign language: Can speakers prevent interference from their first language? *Bilingualism: Language and Cognition, 1,* 213–229.

Hernandez, A., Li, P., & MacWhinney, B. (2005). The emergence of competing modules in bilingualism. *Trends in Cognitive Sciences, 9,* 220–225.

Hoshino, N., & Kroll, J. F. (2008). Cognate effects in picture naming: Does cross-language activation survive a change of script? *Cognition, 106,* 501–511.

Jared, D., & Kroll, J. F. (2001). Do bilinguals activate phonological representations in one or both of their languages when naming words? *Journal of Memory and Language, 44,* 2–31.

Jared, D., & Szucs, C. (2002). Phonological activation in bilinguals: Evidence from interlingual homograph naming. *Bilingualism: Language and Cognition, 5,* 225–239.

Kotz, S. A., & Elston-Güttler, K. (2004). The role of proficiency on processing categorical and associative information in the L2 as revealed by reaction times and event-related brain potentials. *Journal of Neurolinguistics, 17,* 215–235.

Kotz, S. A., Holcomb, P. J., & Osterhout, L. (2008). ERPs reveal comparable syntactic sentence processing in native and non-native readers of English. *Acta Psychologica, 128,* 514–527.

Kroll, J. F. (2006). Adult bilingualism and bilingual development. In E. Hoff & P. McCardle (Eds.), *Childhood bilingualism* (pp. 125–134). Clevedon, England: Multilingual Matters.

Kroll, J. F. (2008a). Adult second language acquisition: A cognitive science perspective. In J. J. Blascovitch & C. R. Hartel (Eds.). *Human behavior in military contexts* (pp. 106–126). Washington, DC: The National Academies Press.

Kroll, J. F. (2008b). Juggling two languages in one mind. *Psychological Science Agenda*, American Psychological Association, *22*. Retrieved April 1, 2010, from http://www.apa.org/science/psa/kroll.html.

Kroll, J. F. (2008c). *Teaching about Bilingualism in Introductory Cognitive Science Courses.* Website developed by the Pomona College Department of Linguistics and Cognitive Science. Retrieved April 1, 2010, from http://www.lsc.pomona.edu/HewlettCognitiveScience/index.html.

Kroll, J. F., Bobb, S. C., Misra, M., & Guo, T. (2008). Language selection in bilingual speech: Evidence for inhibitory processes. *Acta Psychologica, 128,* 416–430.

Kroll, J. F., Bobb, S. C., & Wodniecka, Z. (2006). Language selectivity is the exception, not the rule: Arguments against a fixed locus of language selection in bilingual speech. *Bilingualism: Language and Cognition, 9,* 119–135.

Kroll, J. F., Michael, E., & Sankaranarayanan, A. (1998). A model of bilingual representation and its implications for second language acquisition. In A. F. Healy & L. E. Bourne (Eds.), *Foreign language learning: Psycholinguistic experiments on training and retention* (pp. 365–395). Mahwah, NJ: Erlbaum.

Kroll, J. F., & Stewart, E. (1994). Category interference in translation and picture naming: Evidence for asymmetric connections between bilingual memory representations. *Journal of Memory and Language, 33,* 149–174.

La Heij, W., de Bruyn, E., Elens, E., Hartsuiker, R., Helaha, D., & van Schelven, L. (1990). Orthographic facilitation and categorical interference in a word-translation variant of the Stroop task. *Canadian Journal of Psychology, 44,* 76–83.

Lee, M-W., & Williams, J. N. (2001). Lexical access in spoken word production in bilinguals: Evidence from the semantic competitor priming paradigm. *Bilingualism: Language and Cognition, 4,* 233–248.

Lemhöfer, K., Dijkstra, T., Schriefers, H., Baayen, R. H., Grainger, J., & Zwitserlood, P. (2008). Native language influences on word recognition in a second language: A megastudy. *Journal of Experimental Psychology: Learning, Memory, and Cognition, 34,* 12–31.

Loebell, H., & Bock, K. (2003). Structural priming across languages. *Linguistics, 41,* 791–824.

Marian, V., Spivey, M., & Hirsch, J. (2003). Shared and separate systems in bilingual language processing: Converging evidence from eyetracking and brain imaging. *Brain & Language, 86,* 70–82.

Marslen-Wilson, W. D. (1973). Linguistic structure and speech shadowing at very short latencies. *Nature, 244,* 522–523.

McLaughlin, J., Osterhout, L., & Kim, A. (2004). Neural correlates of second-language word learning: Minimal instruction produces rapid change. *Nature Neuroscience, 7,* 703–704.

Meijer, P. J. A., & Fox Tree, J. E. (2003). Building syntactic structures in speaking: A bilingual exploration. *Experimental Psychology, 50,* 184–195.

Meuter, R. F. I, & Allport, A. (1989). Bilingual language switching in naming: Asymmetrical costs of language selection. *Journal of Memory and Language, 40,* 25–40.

Miller, N. A., & Kroll, J. F. (2002). Stroop effects in bilingual translation. *Memory & Cognition, 30,* 614–628.

Nicoladis, E. (2006). Cross-linguistic transfer in adjective-noun strings by preschool bilingual children. *Bilingualism: Language and Cognition, 9,* 15–32.

O'Brien, I., Segalowitz, N., Freed, B., & Collentine, J. (2007). Phonological memory predicts second language oral fluency gains in adults. *Studies in Second Language Acquisition, 29,* 557–582.

Papagno, C., Valentine, T., & Baddeley, A. D. (1991). Phonological short-term memory and foreign language vocabulary learning. *Journal of Memory and Language, 30,* 331–347.

Paulmann, S., Elston-Güttler, K. E., Gunter, T. C., & Kotz, S. A. (2006). Is bilingual lexical access influenced by language context? *NeuroReport, 17,* 727–731.

Perani, D., Abutalebi, J., Paulesu, E., Brambati, S., Scifo, P., Cappa, S. F., et al. (2003). The role of age of acquisition and language usage in early, high-proficient bilinguals: An fMRI study during verbal fluency. *Human Brain Mapping, 19,* 170–182.

Potter, M. C., So, K-F. S., Von Eckardt, B., & Feldman, L. B. (1984). Lexical and conceptual representation in beginning and proficient bilinguals. *Journal of Verbal Learning and Verbal Behavior, 23,* 23–38.

Poulisse, N., & Bongaerts, T. (1994). First language use in second language production. *Applied Linguistics, 15,* 36–57.

Pyers, J. E., & Emmorey, K. (2008). The face of bimodal bilingualism: Grammatical markers in American Sign Language are produced when bilinguals speak to English monolinguals. *Psychological Science, 19,* 531–536.

Rodriguez-Fornells, A., van der Lugt, A., Rotte, M., Britti, B., Heinz, H., & Münte, T. F. (2005). Second language interferes with word production in fluent bilinguals: Brain potential and functional imaging evidence. *Journal of Cognitive Neuroscience, 17,* 422–433.

Roelofs, A. (1992). A spreading-activation theory of lemma retrieval in speaking. *Cognition, 42,* 107–142.

Ruiz, C., Paredes, N., Macizo, P., & Bajo, M. T. (2008). Activation of lexical and syntactic target language properties in translation. *Acta Psychologica, 128,* 490–500.

Salamoura, A., & Williams, J. N. (2006). Lexical activation of cross-language syntactic priming. *Bilingualism: Language and Cognition, 9,* 299–307.

Schoonbaert, S., Duyck, W., Brysbaert, M., & Hartsuiker, R. J. (2009). Semantic and translation priming from a first language to a second and back: Making sense of the findings. *Memory & Cognition, 37,* 569–586.

Schwartz, A. I., & Fontes, A. B. A. D. L. (2008). Cross-language mediated priming: Effects of context and lexical relationship. *Bilingualism: Language and Cognition, 11,* 95–110.

Schwartz, A. I., & Kroll, J. F. (2006a). Bilingual lexical activation in sentence context. *Journal of Memory and Language, 55,* 197–212.

Schwartz, A. I., & Kroll, J. F. (2006b). Language processing in bilingual speakers. In M. J. Traxler & M. A. Gernsbacher (Eds.), *The handbook of psycholinguistics* (2nd ed., pp. 967–1000). Amsterdam, The Netherlands: Elsevier.

Schwartz, A. I., Kroll, J. F., & Diaz, M. (2007). Reading words in Spanish and English: Mapping orthography to phonology in two languages. *Language and Cognitive Processes, 22,* 106–129.

Segalowitz, N., & Freed, B. F. (2004). Context, contact, and cognition in oral fluency acquisition: Learning Spanish in at home and study abroad contexts. *Studies in Second Language Acquisition, 26,* 173–199.

Sholl, A., Sankaranarayanan, A., & Kroll, J. F. (1995). Transfer between picture naming and translation. *Psychological Science, 6,* 45–49.

Soares, C., & Grosjean, F. (1984). Bilinguals in a monolingual and a bilingual speech mode: The effect on lexical access. *Memory & Cognition, 12,* 380–386.

Spivey, M. J., & Marian, V. (1999). Cross talk between native and second languages: Partial activation of an irrelevant lexicon. *Psychological Science, 10,* 281–284.

Sunderman, G., & Kroll, J. F. (2006). First language activation during second language lexical processing: An investigation of lexical form, meaning, and grammatical class. *Studies in Second Language Acquisition, 28,* 387–422.

Sunderman, G., & Kroll, J. F. (2007). When study-abroad experience fails to deliver: The internal resources threshold effect. *Applied Psycholinguistics, 30,* 79–99.

Talamas, A., Kroll, J. F., & Dufour, R. (1999). From form to meaning: Stages in the acquisition of second-language vocabulary. *Bilingualism: Language and Cognition, 2,* 45–58.

Tokowicz, N., & MacWhinney, B. (2005). Implicit and explicit measures of sensitivity to violations in second language grammar. *Studies in Second Language Acquisition, 27,* 173–204.

Tooley, K. M., Traxler, M. J., & Swaab, T. Y. (2009). Electrophysiological and behavioral evidence of syntactic priming in sentence comprehension. *Journal of Experimental Psychology: Learning, Memory, and Cognition, 35,* 19–45.

Traxler, M. J. (2008). Structural priming among prepositional phrases: Evidence from eye-movements. *Memory & Cognition, 36,* 659–674.

Ullman, M. T. (2001). The neural basis of lexicon and grammar in first and second language: The declarative/procedural model. *Bilingualism: Language and Cognition, 4,* 105–122.

Van Hell, J. G., & Dijkstra, T. (2002). Foreign language knowledge can influence native language performance in exclusively native contexts. *Psychonomic Bulletin & Review, 9,* 780–789.

Van Heuven, W. J. B., Dijkstra, T., & Grainger, J. (1998). Orthographic neighborhood effects in bilingual word recognition. *Journal of Memory and Language, 39,* 458–483.

Van Heuven, W. J. B., Schriefers, H., Dijkstra, T., & Hagoort, P. (2008). Language conflict and the brain. *Cerebral Cortex, 18,* 2706–2716.

Van Wijnendaele, I., & Brysbaert, M. (2002). Visual word recognition in bilinguals: Phonological priming from the second to the first language. *Journal of Experimental Psychology: Human Perception and Performance, 28,* 616–627.

Wang, Y., Xue, G., Chen, C., Xue, F., & Dong, Q. (2007). Neural bases of asymmetric language switching in second-language learners: An ER-fMRI study. *Neuroimage, 35,* 862–870.

Weber, K., & Indefrey, P. (2009). Syntactic priming in German-English bilinguals during sentence comprehension. *Neuroimage, 46,* 1164–1172.

Weber-Fox, C., & Neville, H. J. (1996). Maturational constraints on functional specializations for language processing: ERP and behavioral evidence in bilingual speakers. *Journal of Cognitive Neuroscience, 8,* 231–256.

Yokoyama, S., Okamoto, H., Miyamoto, T., Yoshimoto, K., Kim, J., Iwata, K., et al. (2006). Cortical activation in the processing of passive sentences in L1 and L2: An fMRI study. *Neuroimage, 30,* 570–579.

Sign Language

The vast majority of people use spoken language to communicate, but significant numbers of deaf individuals around the world use signed languages instead. Approximately 300,000 people in the United States use sign language as their primary means of communication (Emmorey, 2002). On the surface, signed languages appear to differ radically from spoken languages. Most obviously, spoken languages make use of auditory channels, while signed languages make use of visual channels. But this difference in form between signed and spoken languages disguises substantial similarities between the two types of language. In fact, signed languages have all of the fundamental properties of spoken languages (e.g., phonology, morphology, grammar and syntax). Signed languages combine meaningless sublexical units into larger components that do carry meaning, the same way spoken languages combine meaningless phonetic features, phonemes, and syllables into meaningful expressions. Signed languages, just like spoken languages, have grammatical principles that determine how units of the language can combine. In both signed and spoken languages, the store of sublexical units could produce an infinite set of combinations, but only a subset of these combinations occurs. In English, we do not say *Down spoon put Sharon big the*, because the grammar imposes constraints on production. Similarly, in sign language, although it is physically possible to include leg movements as part of a sign, and although it would be physically possible to gesture below the knees, sign language grammar imposes constraints that prevent this from happening. Similarly, signed languages have systems of reference so that speakers and listeners can track the actions of characters over time in extended narratives, they express complex meanings, and they have their own poetics. Because signed languages share the

Introduction to Psycholinguistics: Understanding Language Science, First Edition.
Matthew J. Traxler.

fundamental characteristics of spoken languages, but express them in a different set of physical forms, researchers can use the contrast between the two language types to investigate which aspects of language processing occur regardless of modality (visual vs. auditory), and which are determined by the specific manner in which the language conveys meaning.

This chapter will introduce you to the characteristics of signed languages, describe similarities and differences in the way signed and spoken languages are produced and comprehended, describe how the study of signed languages has led to new insights about language function in general, and especially how the brain is organized to support language functions (the *neural basis* of language). The chapter also explores how deafness, using sign language, and speech reading affect how the brain is organized to process language. Much of the research cited in this chapter was based on American Sign Language (ASL) and British Sign Language (BSL), because these are the most widely studied sign languages. However, *typological studies* (studies that compare and contrast different languages) show that many of the same factors that influence the form and processing of ASL and BSL also apply to other signed languages (for example the use of head position and facial gesture to inflect verbs or discriminate between statements and questions; Zeshan, 2004). You should recognize, however, that the details of specific gestures differ across different languages, and so monolingual users of one sign language (e.g., ASL) do not understand users of another sign language (e.g., BSL).[1]

Characteristics of Signed Languages

At an abstract level of description, signed languages work just like spoken languages (Corina & Knapp, 2006; Corina & Sandler, 1993; Emmorey, 2002). Signed and spoken languages combine separately stored meaningless subcomponents to express complex meanings (Thompson, Emmorey, & Gollan, 2005). A grammar governs how the subcomponents can be combined to produce meaningful expressions. Sign languages have gestures that are the equivalent of root morphemes in spoken languages, and the collection of gestures in sign language comprises a lexicon. The sign language lexicon is divided into subcomponents that reflect different sign classes, such as noun and verb. Some signs are produced with one hand, and some are produced with both, but for one-handed signs, the meaning remains the same no matter which hand is used.

This categorical organization of signs in the sign language lexicon is one of the aspects of signed languages that distinguishes them from non-language gestural systems, such as pantomime. While both signed languages and pantomime make use of manual gestures, and people can use pantomime to express a subset of the things that they could express using sign language, the gestures in pantomime do not have the categorical organization that is present in signed languages.[2] Nothing in pantomime differentiates between "verb" gestures and "noun" gestures, for example. Pantomime also lacks the means to express fine-grained aspects of meaning, such as tense and aspect. When Marcel Marceau takes his invisible poodle for a walk, his gesturing does not indicate whether were are supposed to interpret the action as taking place now, some time in the future, some time in the recent past, or some time in the distant past. Likewise, he is not telling us whether the action happened once, more than once, or constantly. By contrast, signed languages use tense and aspectual morphemes to express precisely those details of the intended meaning (unless the speaker purposefully leaves that information unspecified). Finally, pantomime and sign language production and comprehension are *neurally dissociable* functions. Sign language can be impaired while pantomime is relatively intact, and vice versa (Kegl & Poizner, 1997;

Rönnberg, Söderfeldt, & Risberg, 2000). Some deaf signers with brain damage cannot produce grammatical sentences in sign language, but can copy non-linguistic pantomime gestures (the opposite pattern has not yet been observed). Sign language also has a syllabic structure, because signs must incorporate an aspect of movement to be well-formed, and this characteristic is lacking in pantomime.

Sign language is not a complex form of pantomime, but how are sign language gestures formed and how do they express meaning? The modern study of signed languages traces its origins to William Stokoe's research in the 1960s (Stokoe, 1976, 1978, 2005a, b). Stokoe suggested that sign language gestures could be broken down into three basic components or *parameters*: *hand shape* (or *hand configuration*), *location*, and *movement* (or *path*). (Later on, other researchers suggested that a fourth parameter, *orientation* should be added.) Let's consider each of these in turn.

Hand shape (or *hand configuration*) reflects the way the fingers and thumb are held in relation to the rest of the hand and how the hand is oriented toward the rest of the arm. You may be familiar with the hand shapes that are used in the ASL *finger-spelling alphabet* (see Figure 12.1). Finger-spelling is often used when ASL does not have a sign for a specific concept. This occurs frequently for proper names and technical terms, as well as for some types of animals (e.g., ASL has a sign for *elephant*, but it does not have a sign for *bee*). Hand shape is considered a *phonological feature*,[3] because the meanings of different signs can be differentiated on the basis of hand shape. For example, if you spread your fingers and thumb apart and hold them out straight (sometimes called the "five" hand shape), then touch your thumb to your head near your temple, you have just made the ASL sign for *father*. If you change the shape of your hand to the ASL finger-spelling "Y" hand configuration, and touch your thumb to the same spot, you have just made the ASL sign for *cow*. The "five" and "Y" handshapes in ASL represent a kind of *minimal pair*. The minimal change that differentiates between *father* and *cow* in ASL should remind you of the minimal differences between speech sounds (phonemes) that similarly differentiate between spoken words (as in *pat* and *bat*).[4]

Many phonemes in spoken language are perceived categorically, and so are the phonological components in sign language (Emmorey, McCullough, & Brentari, 2003). Sign forms, like phonetic forms, can vary along some dimensions continuously, and some parts of that variation in form have a greater effect on perception than others. Sign language has allophones, just as spoken language does, when small variations in form do not lead to differences in the way a sign is categorized. For example, Emmorey and colleagues describe the open–closed dimension of hand shape (fingers straight versus fingers curled up) as *aperture*. Aperture varies from very open (fingers straight out) to very closed (fingers very curled up). Some signs can be differentiated by aperture value alone, such as the distinction between the ASL sign for "say" and the sign for "to" (see Figure 12.2). Some changes in aperture value are treated as *allophonic* because the change in aperture does not lead to a change in perceived meaning. Other changes of equal magnitude are perceived as changing meaning. To find out how perceived meaning changes with changes in aperture values, Karen Emmorey and her colleagues had deaf signers and hearing non-signers view pairs of pictures (taken from continuously changing sets of stimuli like those in Figure 12.2). The participants' task was to say whether the two pictures were identical or different (*discrimination task*) or whether the two pictures belonged to the same category or not (*categorization task*). Their results showed that signers tended to lump pictures together into distinct categories. So, for example, the pictures from the top row in Figure 12.2 would be perceived as being the same and grouped together into one category, and the pictures in the bottom row would be perceived as being the same (and different from pictures from the top row) and belonging to a separate category. These results closely align with the results from perception of spoken language and suggest that signed language phonological components are mentally represented similarly to spoken

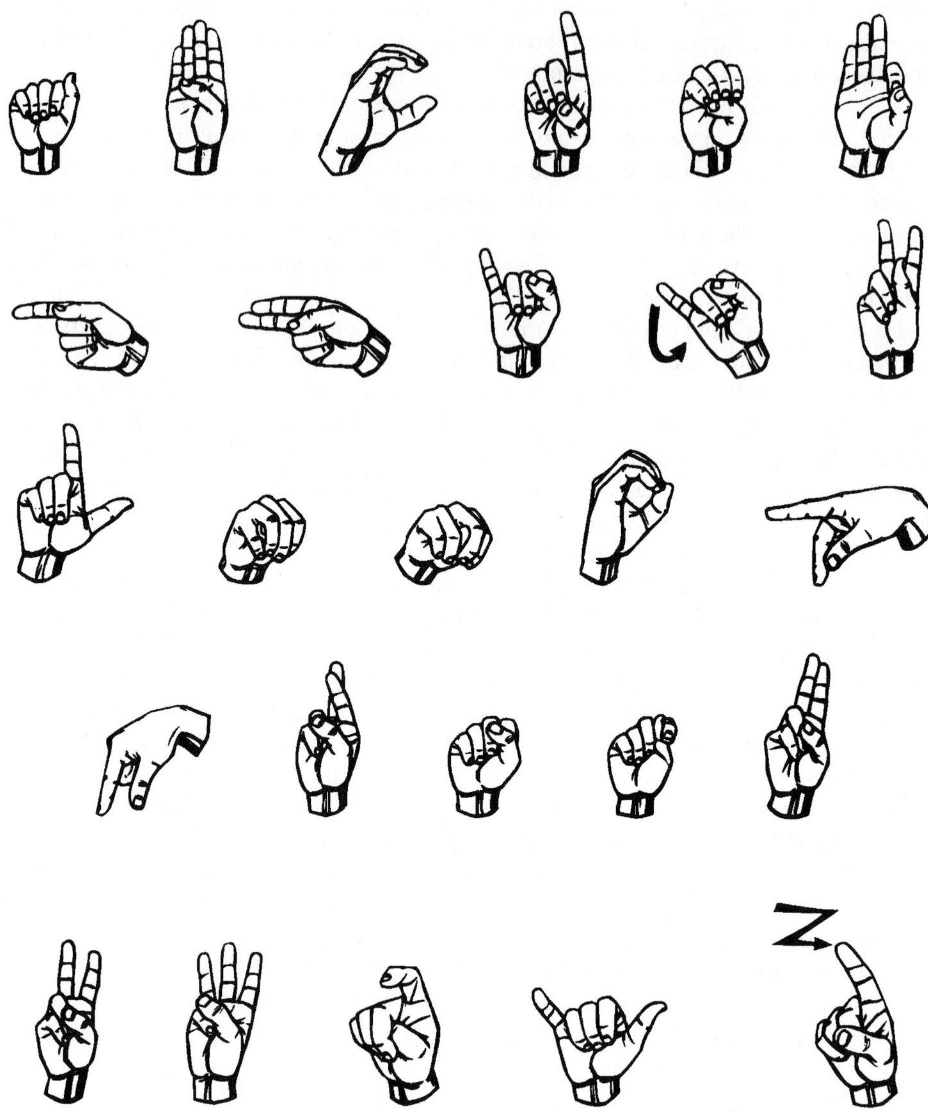

Figure 12.1 The ASL manual (finger-spelling) alphabet (© 2007, William Vicars, sign language resources at Lifeprint.com)

language phonological components. Because discrimination and categorization for hand shape were different between signers and non-signers, the categorical perception of hand configuration appears to result from experience with the language, not from some fundamental property of the hand shapes or visual processing in general.

Location refers to the place in space where the sign is articulated. *Signing space* includes the region in close proximity to the upper body and face. Members of minimal pairs of signs can be distinguished by where in space they are articulated. Eye level and chin level are two locations where signs can be articulated. If a particular hand shape and pattern of movement are articulated at eye level, the corresponding sign means "summer." If the hand shape and

Figure 12.2 Continuous change in hand shape from the ASL sign for "say" (upper left) to the ASL sign for "to" (lower right) (from Emmorey et al., 2003, p. 27)

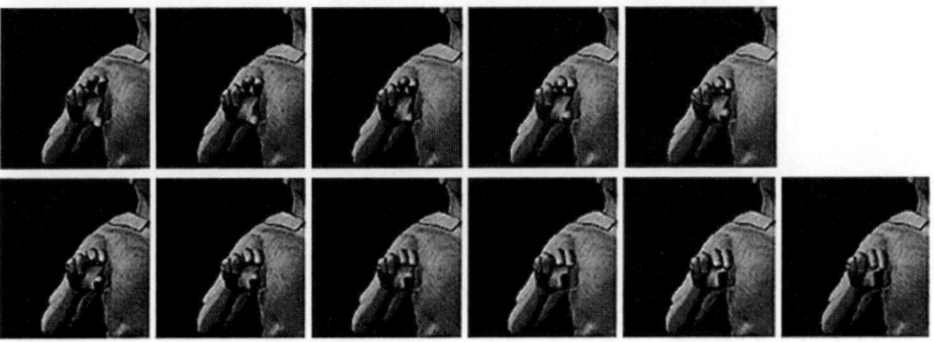

pattern of movement remain the same, but the sign is articulated lower in the vicinity of the chin, the corresponding sign means "dry." Thus, location is a characteristic that produces minimal pairs and hence qualifies as a phonological feature in ASL.

Movement qualifies as a phonological feature because it, too, participates in minimal pairs, but movement also serves morphological and syntactic functions as well. One commonly cited example of morphological function involves the verb "give" (Corina, Kritchevsky, & Bellugi, 1996; see Figure 12.3). The hand shape for the base (stem) uninflected form of the verb "give" is formed by turning the palm upward, holding all the fingers parallel to one another, and touching the tip of the index finger with the tip of the thumb. The motion of the base form starts near the signer's shoulder and proceeds in the direction away from the body. To change from the base form to a different form, such as *give to each*, the hand shape stays the same, and the motion occurs in the same plane as the base form, but the trajectory of the movement changes. Instead of being a simple linear motion, the signer makes a series of back-and-forth movements, starting at one side of the plane and progressing horizontally toward the other. To change from the base form to a different inflected form, a different pattern of motion can be used. To express "give continually," a circular motion along the vertical axis is added to the base form. The motion begins in the same place, but the hand drops down as it circles back after the outward part of the movement. Notably, the two forms of motion can be combined and recombined to produce even more complex meanings, such as "give to each in turn repeatedly." Native signers can identify these patterns of movement and indicate their implications for meaning even under conditions where hand shape and location information have been deleted from the signal (Bellugi, Poizner, & Klima, 1989). Thus, movement really does represent a separate and independent layer of representation in sign language.

Movement is also used in verb agreement. In spoken languages such as English, verbs agree with their subjects in number and not much else. Other languages, such as French and Spanish, have more complex systems of agreement, including gender. Russian has an even more complex system of agreement involving number, gender, and case. In all of these systems, the form of the verb changes (from *give* to *gives* for example) as the characteristics of the subject noun change. In ASL, verbs agree with their subject and object nouns spatially, and some verbs agree with the semantic category of the argument nouns. As the pioneering educator of the deaf, Frederick Barnard (1835/2000, p. 204) describes it, (italics and parentheses in original):

> *Suppose I wish actually to paint a proposition of this simplicity: "A man kicks a dog." I must first make the* sign *of the dog, and assign to it a location. I must then make the sign of*

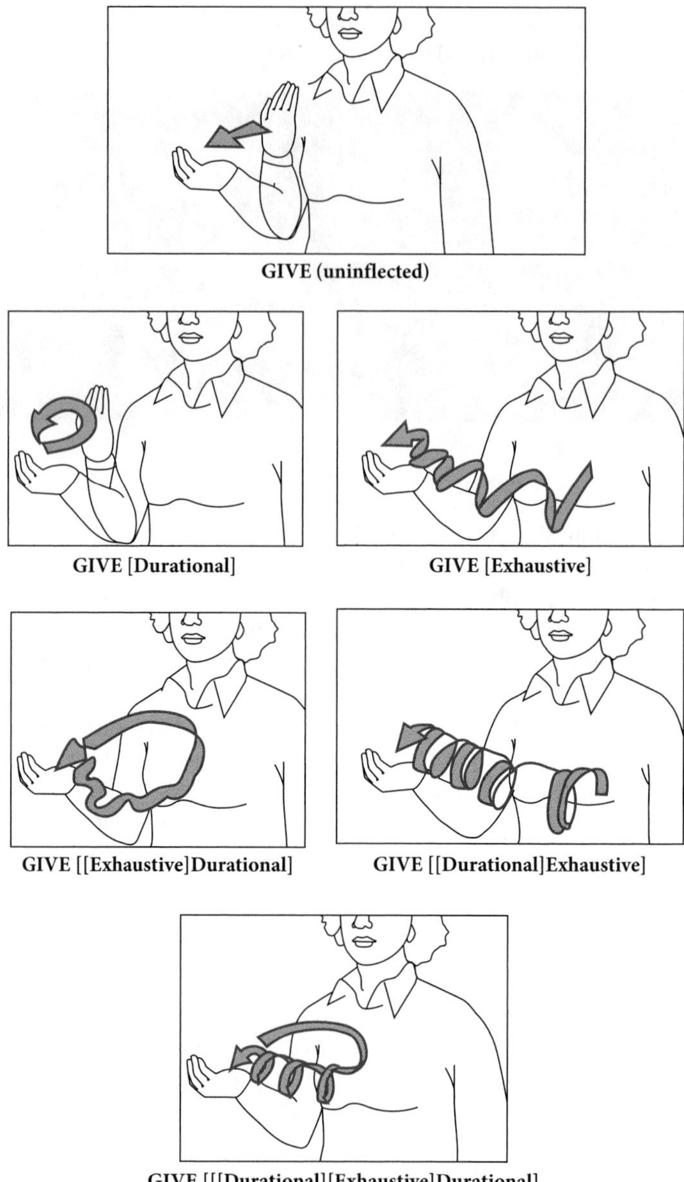

Figure 12.3 Different forms of the verb "give" showing how different motion trajectories represent different inflectional morphemes (from Corina et al., 1996, p. 332)

> *a man, giving it also a suitable location, and finally represent the action (by actually performing it) as passing in the proper direction between the two.*

Verbs of motion are especially morphologically complex in ASL and can include seven or more morphemes, all of which are produced at the same time (Singleton & Newport, 2004). To express the idea that Susan gave something to Bill, the signer would make the sign for Susan and indicate a particular place in space, make the sign for Bill and indicate a different place. Then, the articulation of "give" would start at the same place where Susan was signed and proceed to the place where Bill was signed. Eye gaze may also be used to mark some kinds of arguments for some types of verbs (locatives, specifically), but does not appear to be a general feature of all verbs in ASL (Thompson, Emmorey, & Kluender, 2006).

Sign language morphology

ASL signs have a morphological structure, just as spoken words do, and signers represent different components of signs separately. Recall from Chapter 2 that spoken words are often made up of more than one morpheme and that the *stem* or *root morpheme* plays an important role in lexical representation and lexical access. To interpret morphologically complex words like *wanted*, comprehenders identify the root morpheme (*want*) and separately interpret the past tense inflectional morpheme *-ed*. In production, the independence of the two morphemes is reflected in *stranding errors*. When speakers mistakenly move a word into the wrong position, they often produce the past tense inflectional morpheme in the correct position (as in **booked the want* instead of *wanted the book*). As Figure 12.4 illustrates, ASL also combines roots and inflections to produce morphologically complex signs. Unlike spoken language, ASL root and inflectional morphemes are produced simultaneously. The hand shape and the movement contour overlap in time. As a result, ASL users might represent morphologically complex signs as an unanalyzed whole, keeping all of the different parts tightly connected in memory. Alternatively, signers could represent component morphemes of complex signs separately, just as speakers separately represent the component morphemes of complex words.

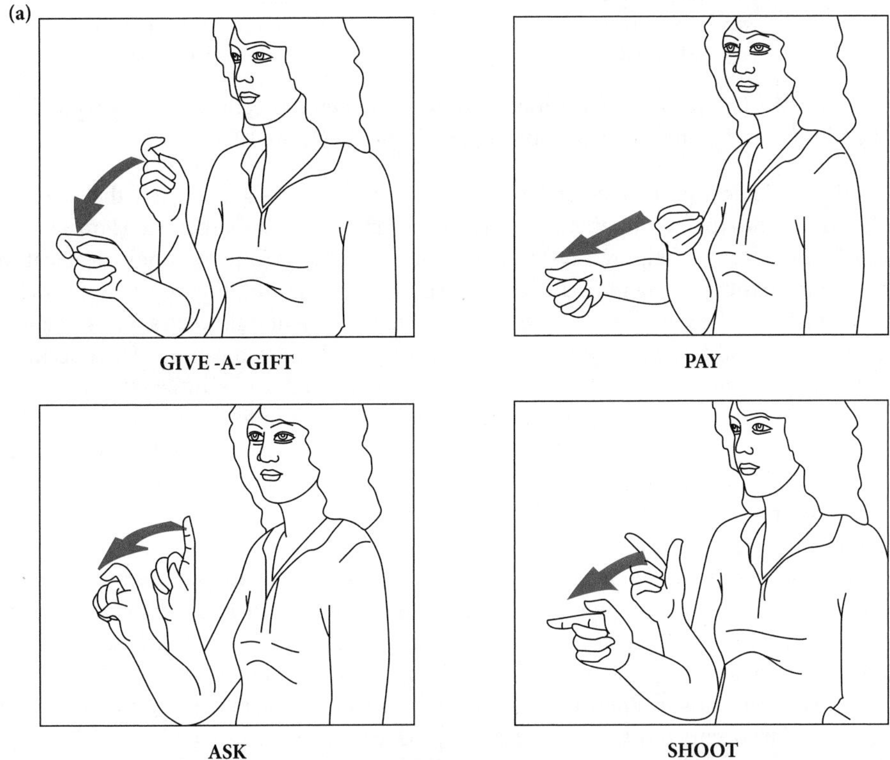

Figure 12.4a Four ASL verbs with different hand configurations but the same motion parameter (from Poizner, Newkirk, Bellugi, & Klima, 1981, pp. 123 and 124)

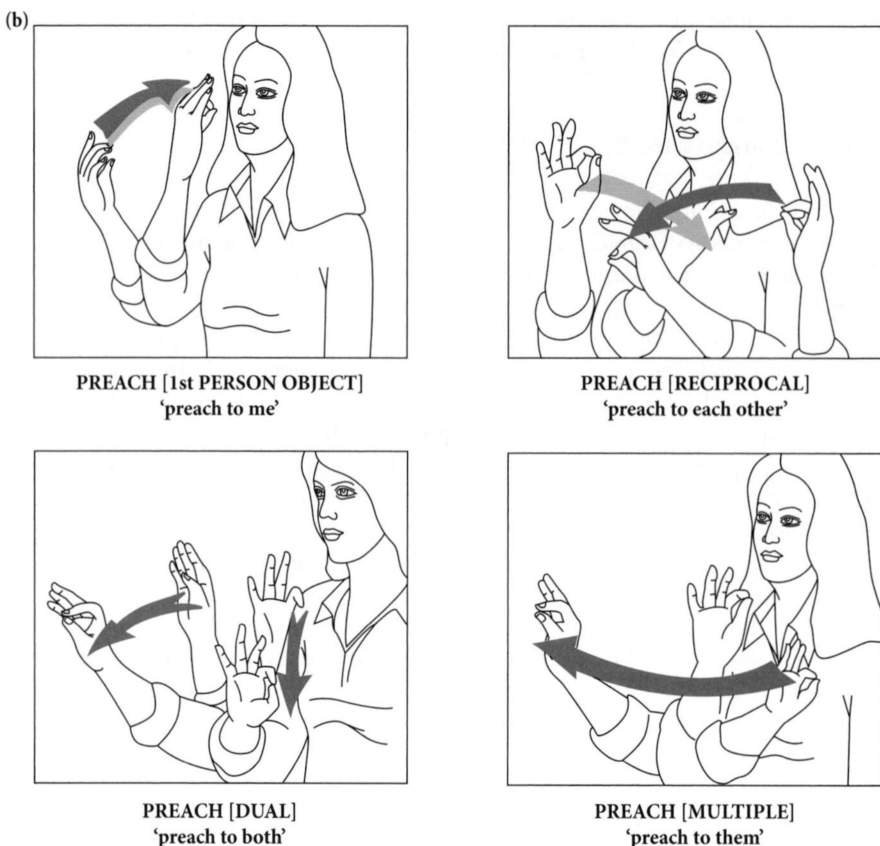

Figure 12.4b The verb "preach" with different movement trajectories signifying different inflections (from Poizner, Newkirk, Bellugi, & Klima, 1981, pp. 123 and 124)

Studies of lexical processing and short-term memory for signs suggest that signs are broken down into their component features as they are being comprehended (Poizner et al., 1981). The four signs in Figure 12.4a use different hand shapes (one morphological feature) but the same basic movement (a different morphological feature). Figure 12.4b shows four signs that all have the same hand shape, but different movement trajectories. Thus, changing one morphological feature (hand shape or movement) changes meaning. The question is whether signers remember each of the signs as an unanalyzed whole, or whether they break the signs down into their components and store hand shape information separately from movement information. If they store each sign as an unanalyzed whole, then they should remember the entire sign every time they successfully remember one component of the sign. By contrast, if they store the components separately, then they may recall only part of the sign without recalling the whole thing.

The available evidence points toward the latter hypothesis—analysis, decomposition, and separate storage of sign components. One piece of evidence is that signers experience the equivalent of the tip-of-the tongue phenomenon—which is called the *tip-of-the-fingers* phenomenon by sign language researchers (Thompson et al., 2005). Signers often have the subjective feeling that they know the sign for a particular concept, but are currently unable to produce it. This occurs most often for less frequently occurring signs, and especially proper names. Signers can often times correctly produce one component of the sign, such as its location or movement, without being able to produce the whole thing. A second line of evidence comes from short-term memory for signs. When signers are asked to watch and later recall a sequence of morphologically complex signs (like those in Figure 12.4b), they often times recall the correct motion or the correct hand shape for a sign, but combine those correct components with morphemes from other signs in the list. So, "preach to one another," might be recalled as "preach repeatedly," "give to each" might be recalled as "give to each other," and so forth. Such mismatching of morphemes between signs in the to-be-recalled list could not occur if each sign were stored as an individual episodic memory or an unanalyzed whole. A third line of research involves assessing whether components of signs are recognized separately and at different times, or whether different parts of signs are perceived simultaneously, indicating that they are treated as perceptual wholes (Emmorey & Corina, 1990). This line of research shows that sign comprehenders perceive sign location first, followed by hand shape, followed by movement. Finally, studies of brain-damaged signers show that some characteristics of signs are more vulnerable to damage than others (Corina, 1998; Corina & McBurney, 2001). For example, hand shape errors are more frequently observed following brain damage than other kinds of errors. As a result, brain-damaged patients often produce a sign in the correct location with the correct movement trajectory, but with the wrong hand shape. Thus, producing and perceiving signs involves keeping track of the component features of signs. These individual components are combined into complex gestures during production; and complex gestures are broken down into more basic components during comprehension and are stored separately in long-term memory.

In addition to manual gestures, signed languages make use of facial expressions to signify both emotional tone (which also occurs in spoken languages) and to convey grammatical information, such as how an action was carried out and whether a given expression is to be taken as a statement of fact or a question (Emmorey, Thompson, & Colvin, 2008; McCullough, Emmorey, & Sereno, 2005; Zeshan, 2004).[5] When linguistic facial expressions are used, their timing is quite precise. They start and end almost exactly at the same time as the accompanying manual gestures (hand and arm movements) start and end. Linguistic facial gestures can mark questions, topics, if–then statements (*conditionals*), relative clauses, and adverbial expressions. For example, the *MM facial gesture* (which is made by pressing the lips together and pushing them outward) indicates that the concurrently articulated verb action was completed effortlessly by the agent. The *TH* facial gesture, which is made with the tongue slightly protruding from the lips, means that the accompanying action was done carelessly. McCullough and colleagues' (2005) fMRI data suggest that the brain response of deaf and hearing individuals differs for both emotional and linguistic prosody. Hearing individuals show a right-lateralized response when looking at pictures of emotional faces, but deaf individuals show a more balanced (left vs. right) pattern of activity. By contrast, the response to pictures of linguistic facial gestures is strongly left lateralized in signers, but not in hearing individuals.

Lexical Access in Sign Language

The study of on-line sign language processing is in its infancy, and so very few studies have investigated lexical access in sign language. As a result, language scientists do not yet know how well standard models of lexical access, such as FOBS, COHORT, and TRACE apply to sign language comprehension. Even basic questions like whether frequent signs are easier to comprehend than rare signs or whether signs from dense neighborhoods are easier to comprehend than signs from sparse neighborhoods have not yet been settled. One recent study represents an initial attempt to start filling in these gaps in our knowledge (Carreiras, Gutiérrez-Sigut, Baquero, & Corina, 2008). Phonological neighborhoods in sign language consist of sets of signs that share location, hand shape, or movement. Like spoken words, some signs come from denser neighborhoods than others. Models of lexical access that were developed on the basis of spoken languages suggest that members of a neighborhood compete with one another for selection during lexical access. To determine whether similar effects occur in sign language, Manuel Carreiras and his colleagues measured reaction times for signs from densely populated neighborhoods and compared them to signs from sparsely populated neighborhoods. Studies of spoken language recognition show that neighborhood density interacts with word frequency or subjective familiarity. Low-frequency words are harder to process when they have higher frequency neighbors, but high-frequency words are less affected by the presence of neighbors. Carreiras and his research team asked signers to rate how familiar they were with different signs, and they tested whether the effects of neighborhood density depended on familiarity. They found a general effect of familiarity, with more familiar signs being easier to recognize than less familiar signs.[6] Familiarity also interacted with neighborhood density, but in different ways for different sign parameters. Unfamiliar signs were harder to process than familiar signs when they came from dense neighborhoods, when the neighborhood was defined by location, but unfamiliar signs were *easier* to process when neighborhood was defined by hand shape. Thus, while familiarity effects in sign language are consistent with results from spoken and written word processing, some of the neighborhood effects are not. As a result, theories of lexical access built from studies of spoken languages may not be straightforwardly extended to sign language. Instead, theories of lexical access in sign language may have to take into account the unique properties of signs. Assuming that future research confirms that location and hand shape neighborhoods produce different effects, lexical access theories for sign language will have to explain why representing multiple signs with the same location feature slows down comprehenders, but representing multiple signs with the same hand shape feature speeds them up. (These effects contrast with phonological overlap effects in spoken language. Words that have shared sounds tend to facilitate each other during lexical access of spoken words.)

Sign Language Acquisition and Language Evolution

Children are the fastest language learners. They acquire new words at an amazing rate after the first 18 months or so and are able to determine the complex features of their native language's grammar and syntax without any formal instruction at all. Phenomena like these have persuaded some language scientists that humans are specially adapted for language learning and are born with a *language bioprogram* that includes a genetically installed *language acquisition device* (see Chapters 1 and 9). The language bioprogram hypothesis was built chiefly on the basis of studying hearing and speaking children, but to show that a human characteristic is truly universal, the language bioprogram hypothesis needs to work equally well for deaf children learning sign language. Language scientists have therefore begun to study sign language in an attempt to gather new evidence about universal characteristics of language acquisition. Such studies show that the acquisition of signed languages in infancy closely resembles the acquisition of spoken languages. Some studies suggest that signing children may acquire their first 10 signs faster than hearing infants acquire their first 10 words, but the differences in timing of the one-word, two-word, and multi-word stages are about the same in both groups (Corina & Sandler, 1993; Meier & Newport, 1990).

Additionally, signed language acquisition appears to be constrained by critical or sensitive periods, just like spoken language (Newman, Bavelier, Corina, Jezzard, & Neville, 2002; Singleton & Newport, 2004). A minority of signers learn the language from birth, while many are exposed to standard ASL only after reaching school age or beyond. In fact, only 3–7% of

ASL users are native signers (Jordan & Karchmer, 1986). Even though deaf signers who are raised in a hearing environment will tend to communicate with their hearing parents and siblings using self-generated systems of signs, called *home sign*, those home sign systems generally lack complex morphology and syntax, and so do not qualify as full-blown languages. One outcome of this state of affairs is that many deaf children experience language delay and lack of communication during infancy and early childhood. However, deaf children are not normally otherwise deprived or abused, which distinguishes them from other cases of language input delay, such as "Genie" and *feral children* (Curtiss, 1977). Therefore, language outcomes for non-native deaf signers reflect the delayed onset of learning, rather than deprivation or other physical and cognitive deficits that result from neglect and abuse. By studying deaf signers who begin to learn sign language at different ages, researchers can test the critical period hypothesis without worrying too much about factors other than age of acquisition.

Such studies support the conclusion that at least some aspects of language are subject to critical or sensitive phases (Lenneberg, 1967; Mayberry & Fischer, 1989; Neville & Bavelier, 1998; Newport, 1990), because individuals who begin learning the language before the end of the critical period develop normal language skills, but individuals who begin learning the language later do not. Studies of sign language learners indicate that different aspects of the language are subject to different critical periods. The acquisition of the meaning of signs appears to occur normally throughout the lifespan, which is similar to the pattern that holds for spoken languages. Although some aspects of grammar, such as word order conventions, also appear to develop fairly normally regardless of when people begin to use sign language, other aspects of ASL grammar suffer when learning starts after puberty. The morphological structure of ASL presents much greater challenges to older learners, and is mastered to the highest levels of accuracy only by native signers who begin to learn sign language in infancy or early childhood. As in spoken language learning, people who begin to learn the language early tend to make grammatical errors that preserve the meaning of the intended utterance, while late learners tend to make errors that preserve the physical form of the intended utterance, even though those errors lead to substantial changes in intended meaning. Further, differences in the control of ASL grammar remain even after the effects of experience are taken into account, which suggests that age, rather than total amount of practice using the language, determines how proficient an individual will become. Groups of signers who have an equal number of years using the language still differ in proficiency when one group started learning the language younger than the other group.

Why are younger children better learners than older children and adults? Some theorists suggest that younger children lack the working-memory capacity necessary to retain large amounts of uninterpreted information (Newport, 1990). As a result, younger children may need to rapidly break down complex stimuli into their component parts to get at the essence of the intended message, which can then be retained in a more stable form. Older individuals may instead store morphologically complex signs as unanalyzed wholes and therefore may not recognize that complex signs can be broken down into subcomponents, and that those subcomponents can recombine in regular ways to compose new messages. Alternatively, the language bioprogram may require specific kinds of inputs at specific developmental stages for learning to progress along the normal path. According to this hypothesis, infants and young children are attuned to the linguistic environment, and can glean cues from that environment to figure out how their native language works, but only for so long. Researchers who favor the bioprogram hypothesis point to critical period phenomena to support the time limit aspect of the theory, and they point to other kinds of data to support the idea that infants are attuned to linguistic input.

Such support can be found in studies showing that infants prefer speech over other complex auditory stimuli. The fact that infants prefer speech suggests that humans are adapted to acquire language, but is that preference universal and is it driven by the physical characteristics of speech, or is it instead driven by more abstract properties of language?

Investigating how infants respond to sign language is one way to answer these questions. A recent study of sign language shows that infants would rather look at someone making real ASL signs than someone making equally complex manual gestures that do not convey any linguistic information (Krentz & Corina, 2008). Therefore, infants' preference for language does not appear to be driven by the acoustic characteristics of speech. Rather, infants like to receive language input, no matter how that input is conveyed. Theories of language acquisition need to explain what it is about language, not what it is about sound or gesture, that babies really like and why they really like that more than other things. One candidate is that language ability plays a vital role in survival and reproduction, such that over time individuals who prefer language, however transmitted, have survived and reproduced at higher rates than individuals who prefer other kinds of stimuli, as per the language bioprogram hypothesis. Another alternative is suggested by Stokoe (2005b), who argues that manual gestures are evolutionarily older than speech, that manual gestures were the first human communication system, and that communicative processes that support sign language were later adapted for speech. On this account, infants' preference for speech could be a by-product of a preference for communicative gestures.

Children's innate drive to learn language can also be seen in the creation and development of new languages. Nicaraguan Sign Language (LSN) provides a case study of the formation of a new language (Emmorey, 2002; Pinker, 1994). Before the Sandinista movement took control of Nicaragua in the 1980s, there was no formal system of education for deaf Nicaraguans, and they tended to be isolated from one another. Shortly after the Sandinistas took over the government, they established a school for the deaf in the capital, Managua. Deaf students from around the country came to this school and started to communicate with each other for the first time. In the early days of the school, the sign language that was used in the school most closely resembled a *pidgin*. Children in the school spontaneously adopted the same signs for common objects and actions, but their signing lacked grammatical features, such as tense and aspect marking on verbs, and agreement between subjects and verbs, that appear in full-blown languages such as ASL. However, within a few years, and without being exposed to other sign languages, the children themselves introduced complex grammatical features, and NSL is now recognized as a language on par with ASL, BSL, English, and so forth.

The LSN studies point toward a special role of children in the creation and development of new languages. Bringing deaf children into contact led to a sign language pidgin, which in turn led to a spontaneous increase in the regularization of sign language forms and the introduction of more complex morphology and syntax. LSN provides a documented case of children spontaneously inventing the language forms that they need to communicate complex ideas when the language environment did not naturally provide those forms. This outcome demonstrates that children learning language are not like parrots. They do not merely repeat the forms that they see and so their language output goes beyond the input they are given. This phenomenon of active transformation can also be observed in individual children. As noted previously, the vast majority of children who learn sign language do so in an academic setting, as the vast majority of their parents do not use sign language. In a very small minority of instances, a deaf child will be raised from birth in a home where sign language is used, but where the sign language differs from the standard form. This can happen when the parents are non-native signers. This situation gives researchers the opportunity to test what happens when an individual child learns sign language from birth the way a native signer does, but where the sign language in the home provides a highly variable and sometimes ungrammatical model for the child. The question, then, is whether the child will grow up signing exactly like his parents, with the same degree of variability and the same kinds of grammatical errors, or whether the child will end up signing more like a native signer who learned from other native signers. The deaf child "Simon" provides just such a case study (Singleton & Newport, 2004).

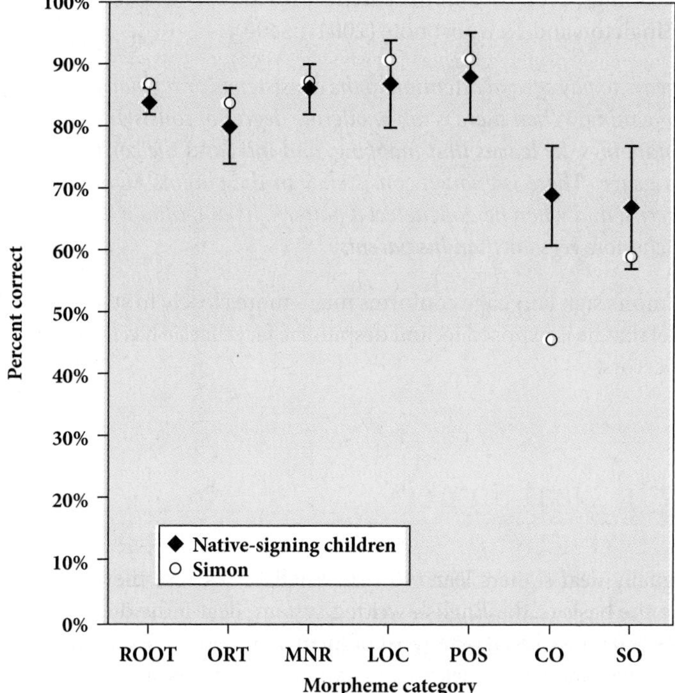

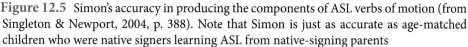

Figure 12.5 Simon's accuracy in producing the components of ASL verbs of motion (from Singleton & Newport, 2004, p. 388). Note that Simon is just as accurate as age-matched children who were native signers learning ASL from native-signing parents

Singleton and Newport (2004) studied the production of verbs of motion in Simon and his parents, because these verbs are especially tricky due to their morphological complexity. The form of a verb of motion in ASL is determined by the combination of the path of motion (*root*), the orientation or direction of motion (*orientation*), how the object moves (*manner*), the relative locations of different objects involved in the movement (*location* and *position*), and the handshapes that are used to express the semantic categories of the different objects (*central* and *secondary object hand shape*; Singleton & Newport, 2004, p. 378).[7] Simon's parents produce verbs of motion correctly much less consistently than native signers do and their degree of accuracy differs across the different components of the verbs. For instance, they are more accurate for location and motion, and less accurate for hand shape. Because Simon's chief source of sign language input is his parents, if he simply copies the patterns that his parents use, then he should be similarly inaccurate and variable when producing verbs of motion. Surprisingly, Simon's performance is nearly identical to age-matched native signers who were learning sign language from parents who were native signers. Figure 12.5 shows Simon's performance on the seven morpheme types that go into a verb of motion in ASL. Simon's performance is at or above the average of his age-matched native-signing peers on six out of seven morpheme categories. He scored relatively poorly on central object hand shape because his parents used idiosyncratic signs for some of the objects tested, not because he has poor control over ASL hand shape. Notably, Simon's performance on the set of verbs tested is substantially higher than the people he was learning sign language from—his parents.

Thus, like the Nicaraguan children who developed NSL, Simon does not merely copy the forms that he sees and does not reproduce patterns at the same frequency they occur in the input. Instead, he detects patterns and relationships between sign language forms and underlying meanings, even though his parents present him with shifting and inconsistent patterns. As Singleton and Newport note (2004, p. 400),

> *Simon appears to pay special attention to the consistency or regularity of mappings between form and meaning. When there is any moderate degree of consistency in his parents' form–meaning mappings, he learns that mapping, and increases the consistency of the mapping in his own usage. There is enough consistency in the parents' signing to enable Simon to detect patterns, and when he does detect a pattern, he amplifies it, thereby making his own output much more regular than his parents'.*

As a result, Simon's sign language conforms much more closely to standard ASL, despite the variable model that he is exposed to, and despite the fact that he has numerous opportunities to reproduce errors.

Reading in Deaf Signers

Many prelingually deaf signers learn to read English. Because they lack the phonological codes that are the basis of the English writing system, deaf individuals typically experience great difficulty learning to read, and most of them attain only a rudimentary level of reading skill. Median performance in hearing impaired students is about the same as median performance of hearing third graders (Allen, 1986). Deaf signers also show a different neurophysiological (ERP) response while reading English words when compared to hearing individuals. First, the lateralization of the brain's response to reading words differs between deaf and hearing individuals (Neville, Kutas, & Schmidt, 1980). Signers show greater ERP activity over the right hemisphere while reading than do hearing individuals. Second, groups of deaf and hearing individuals respond differently to words, depending on whether the words are open-class or closed-class (Neville, Mills, & Lawson, 1992). Deaf signers' N400 response to open-class words is indistinguishable from hearing individuals, suggesting that both groups respond about the same way to the meanings of words. However, deaf signers do not produce two ERP components that hearing individuals produce when they read closed-class words (the N280 and a late negative shift starting about 400 ms after the word appears). Thus, deaf signers' response to words that carry syntactic structure information appears to differ from the norm.[8] They may therefore not analyze the syntax of English sentences to the depth necessary to extract the intended meaning, despite knowing the meanings of the content words that the sentences convey. If so, more in-depth instruction in English grammar and syntax at earlier ages may help improve the English reading skills of deaf signers.

The Neural Basis of Sign Language: Left-Hemisphere Contributions to Production and Comprehension

Signed languages activate left-hemisphere regions that are also involved in spoken-language tasks, such as word perception, sentence processing, semantic categorization, and discourse comprehension (Bavelier et al., 1998; Corina, Vaid, & Bellugi, 1992; MacSweeney et al., 2006; McGuire et al., 1997; Neville et al., 1998; Petitto et al., 2000; Rönnberg, Söderfeldt,

& Risberg, 1998; Sadato et al., 2005; Söderfeldt, Rönnberg, & Risberg, 1994). The areas activated by signed language production and comprehension include posterior (rearward) *perisylvian* cortical areas and the classically defined Wernicke's area, the temporal lobes, and anterior (frontward) areas including the left inferior frontal gyrus (LIFG), which encompasses the classically defined Broca's area. Left posterior areas are associated with phonological and lexical processes in spoken language processing. Comprehension of single signs activates these posterior areas and the LIFG as well (Neville et al., 1998).

The pattern of brain activity in the left hemisphere during sign language production also resembles the pattern observed during spoken language production. Recall from Chapter 3 that the temporal lobes appear to have a posterior-to-anterior organization for different aspects of meaning, with more complex combinations of features activating more anterior parts of the temporal lobes. PET data from deaf signers also show this posterior–anterior organization (Emmorey, Grabowski, et al., 2003; José-Robertson, Corina, Ackerman, Guillemin, & Braun, 2004; see also Braun, Guillemin, Hosey, & Varga, 2001). In one PET study, signers were asked to covertly sign the names of the images that appeared on the screen. Some of the images were generic types (like badgers and elephants), and some were unique entities (like Barbara Streisand). Covertly signing the names for these images activated left- and right-hemisphere temporal lobe regions, comparable to effects that occur in spoken language production, and covert naming of unique entities was associated with more anterior (frontward) temporal lobe activity, while generic nouns produced more posterior (rearward) activity. Like spoken language production, ASL production also activates areas of the LIFG. LIFG becomes active during both single-sign production and sentence production (McGuire et al., 1997; Neville et al., 1998; Petitto et al., 2000).

Similar patterns of activation in the left hemisphere in deaf and hearing individuals point toward some interesting commonalities and differences between the two groups (Neville et al., 1998; Petitto et al., 2000). Both groups activate the superior (upper) temporal lobes while perceiving language, but the stimulus that drives this common neural activity is different for deaf and hearing individuals. In deaf individuals, the superior temporal lobe activity is being driven by visual stimulation rather than auditory input (while the opposite is true for the hearing individuals). In deaf individuals, the superior temporal lobes become activated when deaf people see meaningful signs or when they engage in speech-reading. In hearing individuals, fMRI data show that posterior superior temporal lobes on both sides of the brain become activated when hearing subjects watch someone make mouth and face movements that look as though the person is speaking (Calvert et al., 1997). Thus, the critical factor that drives superior temporal lobe activity does not appear to be sound (acoustic stimuli), but rather stimuli that occur when people produce language, whether that language is spoken or signed.

In hearing individuals who do not know sign language, the superior temporal lobes will not respond to sign language gestures. In deaf signers, these same regions respond robustly to sign. What accounts for this difference? Does the temporal lobe respond specifically to language in deaf people? Or will it respond to any visual stimulus? If the former, then the temporal lobe seems to be specifically tuned to language. If the latter, then the visual system appears to move in and occupy parts of the temporal lobes in deaf people that are used for auditory processing in hearing individuals. One way to test these hypotheses is to present visual stimuli to deaf individuals that do not transmit language-related information (Finney, Fine, & Dobkins, 2001). If the superior temporal lobes respond only to language-related stimuli, then non-language visual stimuli should have no effect on this area. When *congenitally deaf* subjects (people who have been deaf from birth) viewed a very basic moving visual stimulus (called a *sine-wave grating*), they showed increased neural activity in superior temporal lobe regions that are activated by auditory stimuli in hearing individuals. Additional fMRI studies confirmed the finding that superior temporal regions classically defined as auditory association cortex respond to non-language visual stimuli in congenitally deaf subjects (Finney, Clementz, Hickok, & Dobkins, 2003). Thus, it appears that visual processes do move into superior temporal lobe regions that are not needed for auditory processing in deaf individuals. However, these superior temporal lobe regions do still appear to respond more strongly to language than other kinds of visual stimuli. fMRI data show that the left temporal lobes of deaf signers respond more strongly to sign language than other equally complex visual stimuli (Sadato et al., 2005). So, while the superior temporal lobes of congenitally deaf individuals respond to visual stimuli in general, the left superior temporal lobe still appears to prefer language-related input more than other complex visual stimuli. On the whole, the way the brain is organized depends in part on the specific sensory input that the brain receives, but also on "hard-wired" preferences, in this case for language.

Does the Right Hemisphere Play a Special Role in Sign Language?

The left hemisphere responds to sign language much the same way it responds to spoken language. But what does the right hemisphere do? The right hemisphere plays a vital role in the processing of visuospatial information. People who experience right-hemisphere brain damage often perceive space differently than other people. For example, right-hemisphere brain damage can lead to *hemifield neglect*, a disorder in which people appear to be unaware of the left side of the visual world. Because sign languages depend on visuospatial perception, and because the right hemisphere is heavily involved in visuospatial perception, some theorists have suggested that the right hemisphere is more heavily involved in sign language than in spoken language. However, the idea that signed languages activate right-hemisphere regions that do not normally participate in spoken language processing remains controversial (e.g., Hickok, Bellugi, & Klima, 1998b; MacSweeney et al., 2002; Neville et al., 1997, 1998; Rönnberg et al., 2000).

Helen Neville and her research team were the first to apply neuroimaging techniques to the study of sign language processing. Her research suggested that deaf and hearing native signers make use of right hemisphere regions that are not involved in the processing of spoken or written language. Plate 19 shows the neural response measured by fMRI to ASL sentences compared to meaningless sign-like gestures. The data come from two groups of native signers, one of which was deaf and one of which was hearing (Neville et al., 1998). An additional group of hearing non-signers was also tested as a control. As Plate 19 indicates, people who did not know sign language showed the same neural response to meaningful signs as they showed to meaningless signs. By contrast, both groups of native signers showed greater brain activity in both the left and right hemispheres in response to meaningful ASL sentences than meaningless gestures (see the red and yellow areas of Plate 19). These activations were observed in classically defined language areas, such as the occipital-temporal-parietal junction and inferior frontal lobes in the left hemisphere (including Wernicke's and Broca's areas). However, both groups of signers also showed activation in right-hemisphere areas that are the counterparts (*homologues*) of left-hemisphere language areas. The right-hemisphere response was remarkably similar across deaf and hearing native signers, although deaf native signers showed greater right inferior frontal lobe activity than hearing native signers. Neville and colleagues viewed the right-hemisphere response to ASL as reflecting the pairing of right-hemisphere visuospatial processing abilities with the visuospatial properties of the signed language. In their words

(p. 928), "the specific nature and structure of ASL results in the recruitment of the right hemisphere into the language system."

Additional studies also indicated that some regions of the right hemisphere respond to sign language but not to written language. Rönnberg and colleagues (1998) asked deaf signers and hearing subjects to memorize words for a later recognition test in one task (the *episodic memory* task) and to semantically categorize words in another (the *semantic judgment* task). They measured cerebral blood flow using PET scan methods and found that the semantic judgment task activated primarily left-hemisphere regions in both signers and hearing subjects. By contrast, the episodic memory task led to significant right-hemisphere activity in the deaf signers (but not in the hearing subjects), in an area near the junction of the parietal and occipital lobes. When hearing non-signers perceive meaningful gestures, they activate regions of the left hemisphere, rather than the right occipito-parietal regions activated by sign language in deaf signers (Decety et al., 1997). Thus, the right-hemisphere occipito-parietal response to gesture appears to occur only when those gestures are an established part of a signed language.

People who acquire sign language at different ages may use different brain mechanisms to process sign, and this complicates the search for right-hemisphere brain regions that respond specifically to sign language, and not other kinds of visuospatial stimuli. Brain organization in native signers may differ from non-native signers and hearing people because native signers start learning sign language earlier, because they have greater practice using sign, because native signers tend to be deaf, or some combination of these factors. The recruitment of some right-hemisphere regions for sign language processing may occur only if the onset of sign language learning occurs prior to the end of some critical period. Functional imaging (fMRI) data show that parts of the neural response to meaningful signs differ across native and non-native signers (Newman et al., 2002; just as Neville et al., 1998, showed that part of the neural response in native signers depended on whether the native signers could hear or were deaf). In hearing native signers, right-hemisphere regions were more activated during viewing of meaningful ASL signs than during viewing of non-language manual gestures. By contrast, a matched group of hearing signers who started to learn sign language after puberty showed only left-hemisphere response to meaningful signs. These data imply three things about right-hemisphere involvement in sign language processing: First, because the right hemisphere was activated by signs in hearing signers, right-hemisphere involvement does not depend on the individual being deaf. Second, because meaningful signs lead to greater right-hemisphere activity in native signers than non-native signers, some right-hemisphere regions may participate in sign language processing only if the individual begins to learn sign during some early critical period. Finally, because both hearing and deaf native signers activated right-hemisphere regions to a greater extent while viewing meaningful signs than viewing non-meaningful sign-like gestures, some of the right-hemisphere response seems to be specifically tied to the linguistic content of the signs, rather than reflecting emotional or visuospatial information signaled by the visual presentation of a human in motion.

Other researchers propose that greater right-hemisphere response to sign language in the preceding studies is the result of low-level display properties, possible emotional information conveyed by video-taped speakers, or other non-linguistic factors, (Hickok et al., 1998b). Studies that have attempted to control these factors have presented video-taped stimuli to groups of deaf signers and groups of hearing non-signers (MacSweeney et al., 2002; Söderfeldt et al., 1994). The idea is to present both groups with stimuli that show a person producing language. The signers watch videos of a signer producing sentences in sign, while the hearing subjects watch videos of a speaker speaking the same sentences. When neural activity in the signers and speakers was compared, both showed the same amount of right- and left-hemisphere activity. Further, Hickok and colleagues noted that while left-hemisphere damage leads to greater linguistic deficits than right-hemisphere damage, brain damage in the right hemisphere also leads to decreases in language-processing ability when right-hemisphere damaged patients are compared to intact age-matched control subjects. Thus, reductions in language-processing ability following right-hemisphere damage may reflect the general effects of brain damage, rather than the specific impairment of some language-related process.

Further, although hearing native signers show right-hemisphere activation in the posterior temporal lobes when watching a signer produce meaningful signs, the degree of activation is similar across the right and left temporal lobes (Söderfeldt et al., 1994). In addition, right hemisphere activity also occurs when hearing native signers watch and listen to someone talking. Results such as these provide no support for a special role of the right hemisphere in sign language processing. Instead, they may indicate that signed and spoken languages are processed in a similar way by primarily left-hemisphere mechanisms.

To sum up, the evidence for a special role of the right hemisphere in processing sign language appears to be mixed and further studies will be necessary to show definitively that the right hemisphere participates in sign language in ways that it does not participate in the processing of spoken language and to determine what specific sign language functions need right-hemisphere support.

Why is language left lateralized?

However the right-hemisphere-in-sign-language controversy is ultimately resolved, there is no question that basic functions in both sign and spoken language are strongly left lateralized. Why should this be? Some theorists argue that the left hemisphere is structured to handle fast-changing patterns, while the right hemisphere specializes in tracking and assessing more slowly changing stimuli. In speech, acoustic energy changes very rapidly, and very small timing differences can change the way the acoustic signal is perceived. So, if the left hemisphere is specialized for fast-changing stimuli, and the right hemisphere is not, then it would make sense that speech and language functions would be left lateralized. Studying signed languages offers one means to test this hypothesis. Some estimates of sign language articulation suggest that the shortest phonological segments in sign take about 200 ms to articulate (Hickok, Bellugi, & Klima, 1998a). This is approximately an order of magnitude longer than comparable articulation processes in spoken language. So, if the left hemisphere specializes in fast change, and the right hemisphere specializes in slow change, we would expect speech functions to be strongly left lateralized and sign functions to be strongly right lateralized.

We have already seen that native signers, whether hearing or deaf, do activate right-hemisphere regions while processing sign (Neville et al., 1997, 1998), but these right-hemisphere regions do not appear to be absolutely necessary for sign language comprehension. Instead, data from brain-damaged signers shows that aphasic symptoms follow left-hemisphere brain damage in signers just as they do in speakers (Hickok, Bellugi, & Klima, 1996, 1998a; Pickell et al., 2005).[9] Left-hemisphere damage leads to phonological and morphological errors in sign, for example using the wrong hand shape, the wrong location, or the wrong movement (see Figure 12.6). Sign language aphasias include non-fluent and fluent types that resemble the same types in spoken language aphasia. As in spoken non-fluent aphasia, non-fluent sign aphasics have halting, effortful production, without obvious deficits in sign language comprehension. Fluent aphasics produce sequences of signs in rapid succession, but their signing is characterized by phonological and grammatical errors.[10] By contrast, right-hemisphere damage can lead to difficulties with reference and other discourse functions, such as maintaining a coherent topic, providing the

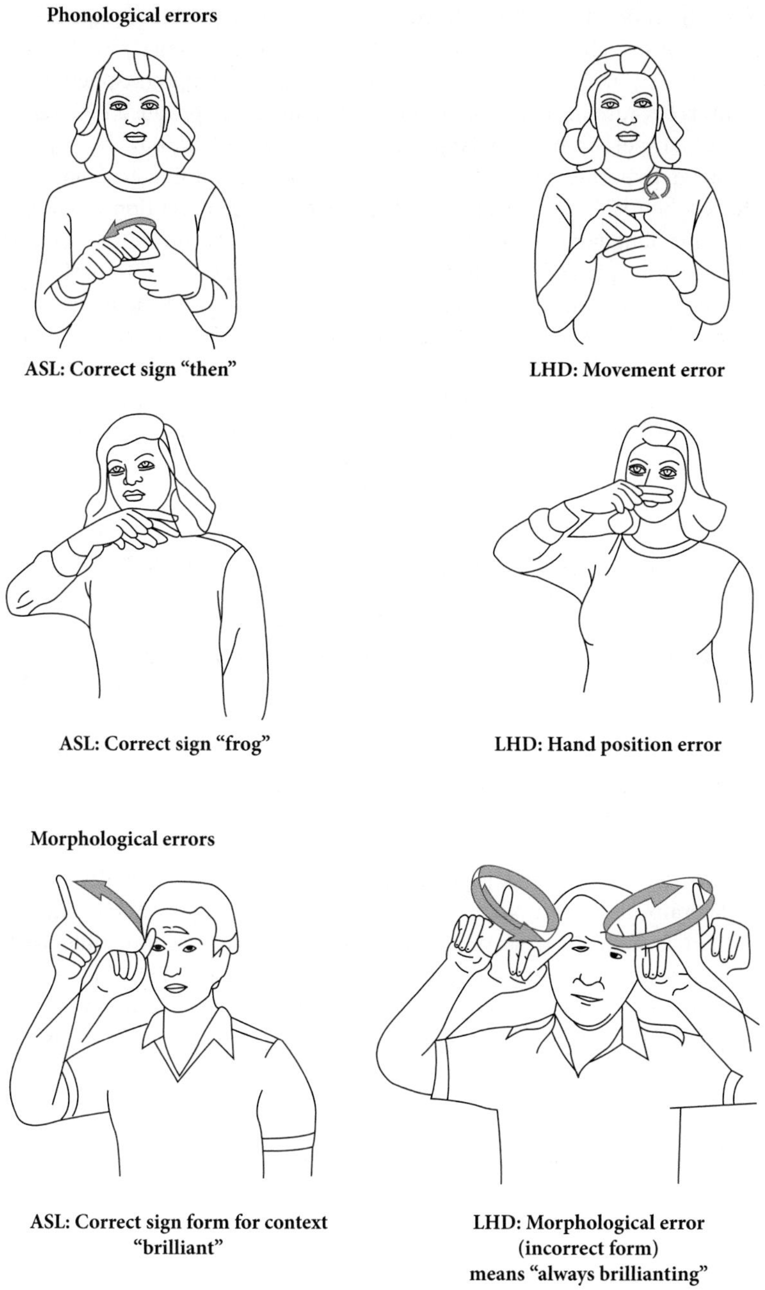

Phonological errors

ASL: Correct sign "then"

LHD: Movement error

ASL: Correct sign "frog"

LHD: Hand position error

Morphological errors

ASL: Correct sign form for context "brilliant"

LHD: Morphological error (incorrect form) means "always brillianting"

Figure 12.6 Examples of errors in the production of aphasic signers (from Hickok et al., 1998a, p. 132)

appropriate level of detail in a narrative, and avoiding *confabulation*, including information in a narrative that has no basis in fact (viz, making stuff up; Hickok et al., 1998a, 1999).

The general conclusion, then, is that left-hemisphere brain regions are critical to the basic sign language functions involved in comprehending and producing meaningful expressions (Hickok, Love-Geffen, & Klima, 2002). When the left hemisphere is damaged, these functions can be severely degraded. While right-hemisphere regions may participate in sign comprehension, they do not appear to play a necessary role for sentence-length and shorter expressions.[11] These findings call into question the theory that language is left lateralized because it involves rapid pattern changes that the left hemisphere is specialized to detect. This is because the components of sign languages are produced at a relatively slow rate (compared to speech), but sign language is left lateralized anyway.

An alternative hypothesis says that the left hemisphere dominates language functions because the left hemisphere specializes in the planning and execution of complex motor movements and language involves the planning and execution of complex motor movements. Most people are right-handed, and use their right hand to perform tasks that require fine motor control. Controlling the speech apparatus and the manual articulators involved in sign language both require exquisite levels of fine motor control and planning of sequences of motions. However, research on sign language aphasia shows that the control of non-linguistic gestures can be impaired while control of linguistic gestures remains relatively intact (Corina, 1999; Hickok et al., 1998a).[12] Some patients are not able to copy complex gestures that are not part of the ASL repertoire of movements, but they are able to copy and spontaneously produce equally complex gestures that are part of the sign language repertoire. Thus, planning of complex movements and control of linguistic gestures appear to be independent, and so left lateralization of language does not appear to occur because the left hemisphere specializes in complex motor control.

Because the neural response to language in both signers and speakers is primarily left lateralized, and because the breakdown of language functions in signers and speakers with brain damage follows the same patterns, we can safely conclude that specific physical features of language do not determine how the brain is organized to process language. Lexical and syntactic processes take place primarily in the left hemisphere whether the language is spoken and transmitted via auditory channels or signed and transmitted via visual channels. Supplementary right-hemisphere processing may take place in the case of signed languages, because it depends in part on visuospatial functions that are right lateralized. Neither the fast-change nor the motor sequencing hypotheses explain this pattern of lateralization, as both would predict stronger right lateralization of signed languages than is actually observed. One hypothesis that *is* compatible with the left lateralization of both signed and spoken languages is that the left hemisphere is specifically adapted for abstract grammatical processing, including phonology and syntax, regardless of the specific physical means by which phonological and syntactic information is transmitted.

The Effects of Deafness and Learning Sign Language on Cognitive Processing

Some people believe that when you lose one of your five senses, your other senses compensate by becoming more sensitive. If so, deaf people should have better vision than hearing people. Studies of visual thresholds in deaf people show that basic visual processes are about equally sensitive in deaf and hearing people (Bavelier, Dye, & Hauser, 2006; Bosworth & Dobkins, 1999; Neville & Lawson, 1987), so hearing people are just as able as deaf individuals to detect visual stimuli. However, there are differences in the way deaf and hearing people respond to some kinds of visual stimuli. In particular, deaf individuals detect peripheral visual stimuli faster and more accurately than hearing individuals, especially when the visual task requires the allocation of attention to the visual periphery (Neville & Lawson, 1987; Neville, Schmidt, & Kutas, 1983). This greater ability to detect peripheral visual targets is accompanied by a difference in the brain's response to those targets. ERP data show that peripheral visual targets produce changes in neural activity faster in deaf than in hearing individuals. Faster reaction to peripheral targets does not indicate better vision overall in deaf subjects, because, when visual targets were presented to the center of the visual field (the fovea), the ERP wave forms for deaf and hearing individuals looked very similar to one another, and reaction times for the two groups were the same. So, deaf and hearing individuals have the same ability to detect centrally presented visual stimuli, but deaf signers have better perception of visual stimuli in the periphery than the central visual field, and that advantage is affected by attention.

Functional imaging experiments indicate that being deaf and learning a sign language early both affect the way the brain responds to central and peripheral visual stimuli (Bavelier et al., 2000, 2001). In one fMRI study, two groups of *early signers*, people who had learned sign language in early childhood, viewed visual displays consisting of moving dots. One of the groups consisted of deaf people, while the other contained hearing individuals. Motion either occurred in the center of the visual field or the periphery. Deaf people showed a greater neural response in parts of the visual system that process motion compared to hearing individuals, but both groups of subjects responded to centrally presented motion about the same. Thus, the peripheral processing advantage does not occur in hearing native signers, and that means that the advantage results from being deaf, not from knowing sign language.

Deaf signers also appear to be left lateralized for visual processing (Neville et al., 1983; Neville & Lawson, 1987). In particular, their visual thresholds for motion detection are lower in the right visual field (left hemisphere). However, this left-hemisphere lateralization of visual processing appears to be a function of learning sign language at an early age, as it also occurs in hearing native signers. One study tested congenitally deaf early signers, hearing early signers, and hearing non-signers. They responded to central and peripheral visual targets, which were sometimes presented after a cue that told the participants where to focus their attention. This study confirmed that deaf individuals show greater activity than hearing individuals in parts of the brain that respond to visual motion. In addition, both deaf and hearing native signers showed a leftward shift of neural activity in visual processing brain regions (see also Bosworth & Dobkins, 1999, 2002). Thus, being deaf appears to enhance the brain's response to peripheral visual targets. Learning sign language early appears to enhance the left hemisphere's response to visual motion, perhaps because left-hemisphere language systems depend heavily on the analysis of visual motion to comprehend sign.[13] Finally, the left-hemisphere advantage occurs in native signers whether or not they are paying attention to the right visual field. This finding shows that the effect is perceptual—the visual systems of signers are more sensitive to those RVF targets independent of where their focus of attention is at any given moment.

Why are deaf people better at perceiving the visual periphery? And why are both deaf and hearing signers better at perceiving visual targets in the right than in the left visual field? Perceptual effects that occur in deaf (but not hearing) signers probably reflect both physical changes in the brain that result from being deaf and changes in the strategies that deaf people use to process perceptual stimuli as the result of using sign language. The chief physical difference between the brains of deaf individuals and hearing individuals lies in the inputs to the primary and secondary auditory cortices, located in the upper portion of the middle and posterior temporal lobes. Age at onset of deafness and experience with sign language and speech-reading influences how these brain regions change in response to the experience of being deaf. Children who are deaf from birth or shortly thereafter, sometimes called *prelingual deaf*, have no experience with spoken language, and they experience profound changes in the way different parts of the brain communicate with one another (Bavelier et al., 2006). In particular, parts of the temporal lobes (secondary auditory cortex) that would normally respond to sound respond instead to visual (and possibly tactile) stimulation.

One major strategic difference between deaf and hearing individuals reflects the means they have available to monitor the environment for opportunities and threats. While hearing individuals are able to use their ears to monitor the peripheral environment, including the environment behind them, deaf individuals must use vision both for processing focally attended information and to check the surrounding environment. As a result, deaf individuals perform worse than matched hearing individuals on tasks that require vigilant focus on central targets. For example, when deaf individuals are asked to monitor visually presented numbers for a two-number sequence, they have longer response times and make more errors than matched hearing individuals do (Quittner, Smith, Osberger, Mitchell, & Katz, 1994).

Perspective taking and sign language

Learning sign language appears to affect the way visual stimuli are processed, and it affects other cognitive processes as well. Sign languages require comprehenders to manipulate mental space and to consider things from multiple perspectives, not just their own. These requirements appear to change the way deaf people think. Sign language comprehenders need to routinely mentally rearrange visual space in order to see things from their conversation partner's perspective. Signers typically describe physical space from their own visual perspective, so sign comprehenders need to understand that when the signer places one object on the right and another on the left, the relative positions of those objects need to be reversed in the comprehender's mind to accurately represent the actual layout of the scene. In fact, sign comprehenders have more trouble dealing with spatial arrays when they are described from the comprehenders' *own* perspective (which is unusual in sign language communication) and find it easier to deal with spatial arrays described from someone else's perspective (which occurs more commonly in sign language; Emmorey, Klima, & Hickok, 1998). Signers therefore get a lot of practice in mentally rearranging space. This practice leads to superior spatial abilities in signers compared to non-signers. Signers are better able to generate mental images of complicated arrangements of objects, and they are faster and more accurate at determining whether two visual stimuli are mirror images of one another, no matter how differently the two stimuli are oriented in space relative to one another (Emmorey, Kosslyn, & Bellugi, 1993).

Some expressions in sign language require the comprehender to subdivide space and manipulate spatial relationships in order to keep track of multiple characters' perspectives. As Courtin (2000, p. 267) notes,

> *some verbs require dividing the linguistic space into subspaces, each one referring to a single item … that will be part of the scene. This linguistic process is called "spatial mapping" … the frame of reference in sign language discourse is sometimes shifted in space when the signing is done from the viewpoint of one of the protagonists … these features force the addressee to understand multiple visual perspectives of the same entity. In other words, sign-language expression requires a certain understanding of the relativity of perspectives.*

Practice in manipulating mental space leads to the previously mentioned advanced skills in spatial cognition, but it may have additional benefits as well. Tracking the events in a story by "seeing" the events unfold from different characters' visual perspectives provides practice in thinking about other people's perceptions and knowledge, which is a critical component of *theory of mind* (thinking about what other people perceive, feel, and believe). Native signers outperform their hearing peers on tests requiring theory of mind skills (Courtin, 2000; Rönnberg et al., 2000). In particular, native signers do better on *false belief* tests. In a false belief test, subjects view a scene with two characters. One of the characters places an object and then leaves. Another character moves the object to a different location. The first character then re-enters the scene and the subject needs to say where the first character will look for the object. The first character should look in the place where they left the object, not its actual new location. Native signers are more likely to correctly indicate where the character will look, and this ability emerges at younger ages in native signers than in other groups of people.

Cochlear Implants

A cochlear implant (CI) is a prosthetic device that can be placed in close proximity to the auditory nerve. The cochlear implant is an electronic device that has a number of electrodes that can produce low-grade electrical current in response to the pattern of sound energy in the environment and, in essence, partially replaces the output of auditory receptor cells (see Goldstein, 2002; Kandel & Schwartz, 2000). As a result, the CI gives the wearer information about the relative mix of low-, mid-, and high-frequency sounds in the speech envelope. Cochlear implants may be considered when an individual is profoundly deaf, has not benefited from a hearing aid, and has intact primary auditory and auditory association cortices. Many cochlear implant users report significant improvement in their ability to comprehend speech either in a quiet situation or in background noise, but not everyone benefits from cochlear implants. People who are deaf for shorter amounts of time and who have less total hearing loss tend to benefit more (van Dijk et al., 1999). Children who receive implants before 2½ to 3½ years old develop better auditory perception with the implant than children who receive implants later (Sharma & Nash, 2009). The timing of implantation matters because, if the brain does not receive auditory input early in life, it will not establish connections between primary auditory cortex and the surrounding auditory association areas that participate in the analysis of complex stimuli, including speech. Further, restoring hearing with a cochlear implant will not result in the normal neural response to sound if cortical reorganization is complete prior to implantation (Gilley, Sharma, & Dorman, 2008; Sharma, Nash, & Dorman, 2009). In fact, if minimal auditory function is not restored before a person reaches adulthood, a cochlear implant will not allow them to understand speech (Doucet, Bergeron, Lassonde, Perron, & Lepore, 2006).

The degree of success that CI users experience following the procedure depends on factors related to the reorganization of neural systems caused by deafness. The auditory system is organized such that sensory signals are registered in the primary auditory receiving area on the upper surface of the temporal lobe. This area is closely connected to a band of surrounding neural tissue, variously known as area A2 or auditory association cortex. In hearing individuals, the primary auditory receiving area (area A1) processes sounds, whatever their source and whatever their information content. Auditory association cortex (area A2) analyzes more complex aspects of the acoustic signal, including aspects that are present in speech. But in addition to processing auditory information, the auditory association cortices are commonly involved in *multisensory integration.* That is, they respond to inputs from both hearing and vision, as indicated by differential neural response in these regions under different audio-visual presentation conditions, such as those that occur in the McGurk effect (see Chapter 2). Because the auditory association cortices connect to parts of the brain that undertake visual processing, the neural reorganization that takes place in this region in deaf individuals involves increased response to visual signals.[14] Thus, neural plasticity and the way auditory association cortex is connected to visual areas prior to the onset of deafness supports retasking of these areas after the onset of deafness. In fact, in deaf signers, the auditory association cortex (area A2) responds robustly when deaf signers watch someone produce signs or phonologically regular non-signs, and when they engage in speech-reading (Capek, MacSweeney et al., 2008; Capek, Waters et al., 2008). Notably, the primary auditory cortex, area A1, does not respond to visual stimulation as people watch signs (Lee et al., 2001). In effect, hypo-metabolism (less than normal levels of neural activity) in the auditory association cortex serves as a signal for visual functions to "colonize" the under-utilized brain tissue. This colonization can take place in younger and older children as well as adults.

Outcomes for CI users

How long does it take for the CI to work? Once the implant is switched on, input to the primary auditory receiving area is restored immediately. However, that does not mean that normal hearing is restored right away. CI users experience a period of increasing auditory function over the first year or so after surgery. Why does it take so long for the implant to work?

In congenitally deaf individuals, the primary auditory cortex will have never received input from the auditory pathway,[15] and it takes some time for the brain to adjust to the new inputs. In addition, cochlear implants provide much coarser input to the auditory nerve than does normal cochlear tissue. There are tens of thousands of auditory receptor cells on the intact basilar membrane. Cochlear implants have two dozen electrodes at most.[16] As a result, "Cochlear implants produce patterns of auditory nerve activation that differ markedly from those produced normally by the cochlea" (Schorr, Fox, van Wassenhove, & Knudsen, 2005, p. 18748). Because cochlear implants provide many fewer inputs to the auditory nerve than the intact natural tissue would, the auditory information generated by the implant does not allow the CI user to differentiate between highly similar sounding words (such as *take* and *cake*; Giraud, Price, Graham, Truy, & Frackowiak, 2001). However, experienced CI users can reliably identify a large percentage of the words they hear by combining auditory information provided by the cochlear implant and visual information that the speaker provides while pronouncing different words.

After implantation, CI users may continue to rely on visual processes to help them identify words in speech (Giraud et al., 2001). CI users are much less accurate than matched controls when listening to purely auditory speech information. However, when hearing control subjects are presented with degraded speech that leads to the same accuracy as the CI users, and then disambiguating visual information is added to the test items, experienced CI users are much more accurate at identifying the content of the speech (Rouger et al., 2007). Thus, deafness causes people to rely more on visual cues to recognize words, and they continue to do so well after receiving a CI. In this group, "Comprehension of fine details in speech such as consonants therefore relies on enhanced coupling between specific sounds and specific visual events such as mouth movements" (Giraud et al., 2001, p. 661). People with normal hearing also combine auditory and visual information when perceiving speech, but CI users are thought to rely on visual information to a greater degree (Doucet et al., 2006). This relatively greater attention to, and reliance on, visual information provides CI users with numerous opportunities to practice integrating visual and auditory information during speech perception. Some theorists argue that such practice turns CI users into better multisensory integrators than hearing people.

CI users rely more on visual cues to identify phonemes and words in part because deafness changes the way the brain is organized. In particular, after an extended period of deafness, parts of the auditory association cortex that normally handle complex speech-perception functions may be colonized by visual processes and rendered incapable of dealing with auditory inputs even after hearing is restored (Giraud, et al., 2001). When deaf individuals learn sign language, watching someone produce signs activates parts of the auditory cortex (area A2) that are normally activated only by complex sounds, including speech (Lee et al., 2001). A similar pattern holds for those who learn to speech-read. Watching sign or speech-reading does not influence activity in the primary auditory receiving area of the cortex (area A1), however. The longer an individual remains deaf, the more likely it is that auditory association cortex will be taken over by visual processes, including sign perception, but this takeover apparently does not extend into the primary auditory cortex (area A1).

In congenitally deaf individuals, a CI does not produce activity in the auditory association cortex. However, in people who go deaf later in life, after learning a spoken language, the CI will create neural activity in both the primary receiving area and auditory association cortex (Nishimura et al., 1999). These differences in brain activity reflect the different learning histories of the two groups. Auditory association area (A2) in congenitally deaf individuals never receives coherent input from A1, and so other sensory inputs dominate neural activity in A2. Auditory association area in postlingually deaf individuals is tuned to speech and other complex sounds before deafness occurs, and so re-establishing the connection with the outside world can reactivate A2's response to A1 activity.

Although CI users normally combine auditory and visual cues to identify words, many CI users experience substantial improvement in their ability to understand words based solely on the auditory input. What is the basis of this improvement in auditory performance? One candidate is reorganization of the neural response to sound, in particular, reorganization of parts of the brain that normally respond to visual information (Giraud et al., 2001). CI users who have good word-identification ability from auditory input show a distinct pattern of neural response to speech sounds. Specifically, parts of the visual cortex respond to purely auditory stimulation.[17] The visual cortex in CI users does not respond to all auditory stimulation, but it does respond to words, phonetically legal syllables, and "potentially meaningful" environmental sounds. The degree of visual cortex activation to sounds is strongly related to cross-modal speech perception abilities. Those individuals who can best use visual information to identify words, the best speech-readers that is, have the strongest visual cortex response to auditorily presented speech.

In addition to being able to hear and understand speech, cochlear implants can lead to enhanced focal attention as CI users learn to adjust their attentional strategies following restoration of some hearing function. Cross-sectional studies evaluate different individuals who have different levels of an independent variable, and in such studies where time since cochlear implantation serves as the independent variable, greater experience with the CI is associated with greater hearing function and with more success on focal attention tasks (Quittner et al., 1994). This is true for both school-aged children up through the teen years and for infants and toddlers (Quittner et al., 2007). Longitudinal studies, which involve monitoring specific individuals over an extended period of time, also show that focal attention improves as individuals have greater experience with the cochlear implant, and that it generally takes a year or more post-implantation for performance to near its maximum level. Notably, improvements in attention can occur sooner than improvements in the ability to understand speech.

Differences in neural organization between CI users and hearing individuals also produce differences in the way the two groups integrate information from auditory and visual channels (Schorr et al., 2005). In the McGurk effect, there is a conflict between the information in the visual channel and information in the auditory channel. For normal hearing individuals, the conflict between the two channels can lead to a percept that is not present in either channel (i.e., you integrate the sound of /ba/ with the sight of /ga/ and you perceive /da/). Sometimes, hearing individuals fail to integrate (or *fuse*) information from the two channels. In those cases, hearing individuals' perception will be dominated by the auditory information (e.g., they will perceive the McGurk stimulus as /ba/). CI users also vary in their ability to fuse the auditory and visual signals, and that ability to fuse generally increases with increased experience with the CI. It normally takes about 30 months of experience before CI users start to show the usual McGurk effect. Those CI users who fail to fuse the two channels typically perceive the speech sound that corresponds to the visual channel (they perceive /ga/). In people with cochlear implants, there may be greater consistency in the mappings between visual information and lexical entries (words) than in the mappings between auditory perception and lexical entries, and deaf individuals may have spent considerable time and effort learning how to recognize words from oral gestures. Because the experience of deafness has led to atypical organization of the auditory and visual areas of the brain, and because deaf individuals are in general more dependent upon vision even for non-language tasks, it makes sense that this general pattern would persist following the restoration of hearing.

Part of CI users' recovery of function may be caused by new associations between vision and sound formed in visual cortices, but the retraining of auditory association cortex may play a role as well (Nishimura et al., 2000). In particular, competition between visual and auditory input for space in the auditory association cortex may prevent these areas from responding to auditory input until this area is retrained after surgery. Evidence for these claims comes from groups of CI users who have had different amounts of experience with the implant. Short-term users of CIs do not show any increased activity in superior temporal cortex when an auditory signal is added to a visual signal. That is, their auditory cortex does not appear to recognize when it has an auditory signal to deal with if a visual stimulus is presented simultaneously (Champoux, Lepore, Gagné, & Théoret, 2009). Their auditory areas will respond to auditory signals that are presented by themselves (without concurrent visual stimulation), but that response is dampened when the visual stimulus overlaps in time with the auditory stimulus. By comparison, auditory processing regions in long-term users of CIs show a greater response to simultaneous auditory and visual stimulation, when compared to purely auditory stimulation, which suggests that the presence of a visual stimulus does not extinguish the response to the simultaneously presented auditory stimulus.

Summary and Conclusions

Sign language has all of the properties of spoken language except the noise. Sign languages differ from one another in the specific forms that they use, but they all have well-organized systems of phonology, morphology, grammar, and syntax, and they all take meaningless subunits and combine them into meaningful complex forms. Because sign language makes use of visual channels, rather than auditory channels, it provides a vital means to test our theories about language in general.

Direct comparisons of sign language and spoken language show substantial commonalities, but also some important differences. Studying sign language also helps us understand language acquisition in general, and there are striking similarities between the way sign language and spoken language are learned. In particular, children progress through similar stages of learning at about the same time whether they are learning sign language or spoken language; and learners of both types of language can produce output that differs greatly from the model that they are exposed to. Basic sign language processes appear to be left lateralized, and the patterns of language breakdown in sign language following brain damage closely resembles the patterns of breakdown in spoken languages when people suffer damage to comparable parts of the brain. Neuroimaging research also finds substantial overlap in brain areas that respond to signs (or words) and sentences, whether they are presented in sign language or speech. The contrast between signed and spoken languages helps us understand why basic language functions are left lateralized. The research reviewed above suggests that neither the fast change nor the complex motor planning hypotheses are compatible with the pattern of deficits that follow from brain damage. Thus, the left hemisphere appears to be specifically adapted to processing abstract characteristics of language, such as phonology, morphology, and syntax.

However, there appear to be some important differences between deaf people and sign language users when compared to hearing speakers. First, specific aspects of sign language phonology appear to affect how lexical access proceeds. While some sign parameters appear to produce the same kinds of neighborhood effects that are observed in spoken languages, others do not. Additionally, deaf individuals appear to allocate attention differently than hearing individuals, and as a result are more sensitive to the visual periphery. Signers, whether deaf or hearing, also appear to have a left-hemisphere bias in the perception of visual stimuli, and especially visual movement. Signers also appear to be better able to manipulate mental space than non-signers, most likely as a result of processing language forms that require spatial transformations. Finally, being deaf and learning sign language can change the way the brain, and especially the auditory association cortex, respond to visual stimulation. This cortical reorganization in turn affects how people respond to cochlear implants.

TEST YOURSELF

1. How do signed languages compare to spoken languages? In what ways are they similar or identical? In what ways are they different? Why do language scientists reject classifying signed languages as a form of pantomime?
2. Describe the sign language equivalent of spoken language phonology. How does the perception of sign language and spoken language phonology compare?
3. What role does movement play in sign language phonology and syntax?
4. Describe evidence suggesting that signers undertake morphological decomposition when comprehending signs. What role do facial expressions play in sign language morphology?
5. What have studies of deaf signers contributed to our understanding of critical periods and the biological basis of language acquisition?
6. What do studies of deaf signers indicate about the way the brain is organized for language?
7. How does deafness affect attention, spatial information processing, and other aspects of cognition? What effects does knowing a sign language have? What negative effects does it have on cognitive abilities?
8. What happens to the brain when a child receives a cochlear implant?

THINK ABOUT IT

1. Some hearing parents of deaf children insist that their children learn to speak and speech-read, rather than sign. Some members of the deaf community object to cochlear implants, because they feel that the deaf child is losing his or her cultural identity. What's your view? Should deaf children be taught to sign or speak? Should they receive cochlear implants?

Notes

1 That should come as no surprise. We do not expect monolingual French speakers to understand Japanese, and vice versa.

2 Some signs may begin their careers as part of a non-linguistic pantomime-like gesture (Lang & Stokoe, 2000). However, sign-language signs are the result of a process of refinement and *reduction*, whereby an arbitrary part of a more complex pantomime-like gesture comes to represent the whole concept. Thus, many signs retain iconic features (they look like some aspect of the concept they represent), but that iconicity is also essentially arbitrary, because different iconic features can be used in different signed languages to represent the same concept, as in the ASL, Danish, and Chinese Sign Language signs for "tree," which are very different from one another (Thompson, Vinson, & Vigliocco, 2009).

3 Stokoe called it a *cheiremic* parameter, from the Greek word for *hand* (*cheir*). But most contemporary authors use the word *phoneme* when describing sublexical features of signs to highlight the conceptual similarity between the sign language lexical system and the spoken lexical system. See Corina and Sandler (1993) for a variety of linguistic analyses of sign language phonology.

4 Differences in the way different groups of signers form hand shapes can produce the sign language equivalent of a foreign accent (Bellugi et al., 1989).

5 ASL-English bilingual individuals produce grammatical ASL facial gestures even when they are speaking to non-signers (Pyers & Emmorey, 2008).

6 In the first experiment in Carreiras et al. (2008), this effect of familiarity only occurred in non-native signers.

7 Producing ASL verbs is like playing 3-d chess. By contrast, English verb agreement looks like tic-tac-toe.

8 Note that deaf signers show different responses to open- and closed-class ASL signs which convey semantic and grammatical information in comparable ways to spoken words (Neville et al., 1997). Deaf signers therefore do show differential neurophysiological response to open- and closed-class lexical items, so the results for the English reading task do not reflect a general lack of response to closed-class forms.

9 Pickell and colleagues (2005) report a case of non-fluent aphasia following right-hemisphere damage, but because the individual was left-handed this case most likely reflects a reversal of the usual language lateralization pattern rather than a case of crossed aphasia.

10 A cortical stimulation study on an awake deaf signer who was undergoing preparation for neurosurgery to treat epilepsy also supports the non-fluent/fluent symptom distinction (Corina, et al., 1999). This patient produced effortful, slow signs with lax articulation after frontal stimulation, while posterior stimulation led to semantic substitution errors followed by attempts to correct the form and eventual approximation of the correct sign.

11 Hickok and colleagues (2002) do present evidence that right-hemisphere damage leads to a 25% decrease in sentence-level comprehension, but this is still less than the deficits exhibited by left-hemisphere damaged signers, and the deficit following right-hemisphere damage could reflect the general effects of brain damage, rather than a language-specific effect.

12 Similarly, some right-hemisphere damaged patients have substantial spatial perception deficits, but are able to correctly perceive and produce complex spatial relationships involved in sign language. That is, they appear to perceive signing space just as accurately as neurologically intact control subjects (Corina et al., 1996). The fact that some signers can perceive linguistically meaningful gestures while simultaneously having trouble perceiving non-linguistic gestures (and vice versa) shows that their problems are not at the level of basic visual perception. That is, their optics and neural processing of basic visual information (shape, color, and movement) are intact. Rather, in the case of sign language aphasia, the problem arises when basic visual processes attempt to make contact with stored linguistic representations.

13 Emmorey and McCullough (2009; see also Corina, 1989) report that the perception of facial expression is left lateralized in deaf signers, but not in hearing signers. Hence, the effects of deafness and signing do not appear to be identical for visual motion processing (where signing appears to cause a general leftward shift, with

deafness enhancing this effect) and facial expression processing (where only deafness appears to cause a leftward shift).

14 A complementary reorganization takes place in blind individuals. There, classically defined vision areas can be reconfigured to respond to auditory or tactile inputs.

15 Superior olivary nucleus, inferior colliculus, and the medial geniculate nucleus of the thalamus (Goldstein, 2002).

16 Because of the physical properties of the basilar membrane, hair cells never fire individually in response to environmental sound. Nonetheless, the intact inner ear provides much finer detail than even the most advanced cochlear implant.

17 Giraud et al. (2001) identify the calcarine cortex and the lingual gyrus in the occipital lobes as being sites that respond to auditory information following substantial experience with a cochlear implant.

References

Allen, T. E. (1986). Patterns of academic achievement among hearing impaired students: 1974 and 1983. In A. N. Schildroth & M. A. Karchmer (Eds.), *Deaf children in America* (pp. 161–206). San Diego, CA: College-Hill Press.

Barnard, F. A. P. (1835/2000). Existing state of the art of instructing the deaf and dumb. *Journal of Deaf Studies and Deaf Education, 5,* 200–216.

Bavelier, D., Brozinsky, C., Tomann, A., Mitchell, T., Neville, H., & Liu, G. (2001). Impact of early deafness and early exposure to sign language on the cerebral organization for motion processing. *The Journal of Neuroscience, 21,* 8931–8942.

Bavelier, D., Corina, D., Jezzard, P., Clark, V., Karni, A., Lalwani, A., et al. (1998). Hemispheric specialization for English and ASL: Left invariance-right variability. *NeuroReport, 9,* 1537–1542.

Bavelier, D., Dye, M. W. G., & Hauser, P. C. (2006). Do deaf individuals see better? *Trends in Cognitive Sciences, 10,* 512–518.

Bavelier, D., Tomann, A., Hutton, C., Mitchell, T., Corina, D., Liu, G., et al. (2000). Visual attention to the periphery is enhanced in congenitally deaf individuals. *The Journal of Neuroscience, 20,* 1–6.

Bellugi, U., Poizner, H., & Klima, E. S. (1989). Language, modality, and the brain. *Trends in Neuroscience, 12,* 380–388.

Bosworth, R. G., & Dobkins, K. R. (1999). Left-hemisphere dominance for motion processing in deaf signers. *Psychological Science, 10,* 256–262.

Bosworth, R. G., & Dobkins, K. R. (2002). Visual field asymmetries for motion processing in deaf and hearing signers. *Brain and Cognition, 49,* 170–181.

Braun, A. R., Guillemin, A., Hosey, L., & Varga, M. (2001). The neural organization of discourse: An $H_2{}^{15}O$-PET study of narrative production in English and American Sign Language. *Brain, 124,* 2028–2044.

Calvert, G. A., Bullmore, E. T., Brammer, M. J., Campbell, R., Williams, S. C. R., McGuire, P. K., et al. (1997). Activation of auditory cortex during silent lipreading. *Science, 276,* 593–596.

Capek, C. M., MacSweeney, M., Woll, B., Waters, D., McGuire, P. K., David, A. S., et al. (2008). Cortical circuits for silent speechreading in deaf and hearing people. *Neuropsychologia, 46,* 1233–1241.

Capek, C. M., Waters, D., Woll, B., MacSweeney, M., Brammer, M. J., McGuire, P. K., et al. (2008). Hand and mouth: Cortical correlates of lexical processing in British Sign Language and Speechreading English. *Journal of Cognitive Neuroscience, 20,* 1220–1234.

Carreiras, M., Gutiérrez-Sigut, E., Baquero, S., & Corina, D. (2008). Lexical processing in Spanish Sign Language (LSE). *Journal of Memory and Language, 58,* 100–122.

Champoux, F., Lepore, F., Gagné, J., & Théoret, H. (2009). Visual stimuli can impair auditory processing in cochlear implant users. *Neuropschologia, 47,* 17–22.

Corina, D. P. (1989). Recognition of affective and noncanonical linguistic facial expressions in hearing and deaf subjects. *Brain and Cognition, 9,* 227–237.

Corina, D. P. (1998). Studies of neural processing in deaf signers: Toward a neurocognitive model of language processing in the deaf. *Journal of Deaf Studies and Deaf Education, 3,* 35–48.

Corina, D. P. (1999). On the nature of left hemisphere specialization for signed language. *Brain & Language, 69,* 230–240.

Corina, D. P., & Knapp, H. P. (2006). Psycholinguistic and neurolinguistic perspectives on sign languages. In M. J. Traxler & M. A. Gernsbacher (Eds.), *The handbook of psycholinguistics* (2nd ed., pp. 1001–1024). Amsterdam, The Netherlands: Elsevier.

Corina, D. P., Kritchevsky, M., & Bellugi, U. (1996). Visual language processing and unilateral neglect: Evidence from American Sign Language. *Cognitive Neuropsychology, 13,* 321–356.

Corina, D. P., & McBurney, S. L. (2001). The neural representation of language in users of American Sign Language. *Journal of Communication Disorders, 34,* 455–471.

Corina, D. P., McBurney, S. L., Dodrill, C., Hinshaw, K., Brinkley, J., & Ojemann, G. (1999). Functional roles of Broca's area and SMG: Evidence from cortical stimulation mapping in a deaf signer. *Neuroimage, 10,* 570–581.

Corina, D. P., & Sandler, W. (1993). On the nature of phonological structure in sign language. *Phonology, 10,* 165–207.

Corina, D. P., Vaid, J., & Bellugi, U. (1992). The linguistic basis of left hemisphere specialization. *Science, 255,* 1258–1260.

Courtin, C. (2000). The impact of sign language on the cognitive development of deaf children: The case of theories of mind. *Journal of Deaf Studies and Deaf Education, 5,* 266–276.

Curtiss, S. (1977). *Genie: A psycholinguistic study of a modern day "wild child."* San Diego, CA: Academic Press.

Decety, J., Grèzes, J., Costes, N., Perani, D., Jeannerod, M., Procyk, E. et al. (1997). Brain activity during observation of actions: Influence of action content and subject's strategy. *Brain, 120,* 1763–1777.

Doucet, M. E., Bergeron, F., Lassonde, M., Perron, P., & Lepore, F. (2006). Cross-modal reorganization and speech perception in cochlear implant users. *Brain, 129,* 3376–3383.

Emmorey, K. (2002). *Language, cognition, and the brain: Insights from sign language research.* Mahwah, NJ: Erlbaum.

Emmorey, K., & Corina, D. (1990). Lexical recognition in sign language: Effects of phonetic structure and morphology. *Perceptual and Motor Skills, 71,* 1227–1252.

Emmorey, K., Grabowski, T., McCullough, S., Damasio, H., Ponto, L. L. B., Hichwa, et al. (2003). Neural systems underlying lexical retrieval for sign language. *Neuropsychologia, 41,* 83–95.

Emmorey, K., Klima, E., & Hickok, G. (1998). Mental rotation within linguistic and non-linguistic domains in users of American sign language. *Cognition, 68,* 221–246.

Emmorey, K., Kosslyn, S. M., & Bellugi, U. (1993). Visual imagery and visual-spatial language: Enhanced imagery abilities in deaf and hearing ASL signers. *Cognition, 46,* 139–181.

Emmorey, K. & McCullough, S. (2009). The bilingual brain: Effects of sign language experience. *Brain & Language, 109,* 124–132.

Emmorey, K., McCullough, S., & Brentari, D. (2003). Categorical perception in American Sign Language. *Language and Cognitive Processes, 18,* 21–45.

Emmorey, K., Thompson, R., & Colvin, R. (2008). Eye gaze during comprehension of American Sign Language by native and beginning signers. *Journal of Deaf Studies and Deaf Education, 14,* 237–243.

Finney, E. M., Clementz, B. A., Hickok, G., & Dobkins, K. R. (2003). Visual stimuli activate auditory cortex in deaf subjects: Evidence from MEG. *NeuroReport, 14,* 1425–1427.

Finney, E. M., Fine, I., & Dobkins, K. R. (2001). Visual stimuli activate auditory cortex in the deaf. *Nature Neuroscience, 4,* 1171–1173.

Gilley, P. M., Sharma, A., & Dorman, M. F. (2008). Cortical reorganization in children with cochlear implants. *Brain Research, 1239,* 56–65.

Giraud, A., Price, C. J., Graham, J. M., Truy, E., & Frackowiak, R. S. J. (2001). Cross-modal plasticity underpins language recovery after cochlear implantation. *Neuron, 30,* 657–663.

Goldstein, E. B. (2002). *Sensation and perception.* New York: Wadsworth.

Hickok, G., Bellugi, U., & Klima, E. S. (1996). The neurobiology of sign language and its implications for the neural basis of language. *Nature, 381,* 699–702.

Hickok, G., Bellugi, U., & Klima, E. S. (1998a). The neural organization of language: Evidence from sign language aphasia. *Trends in Cognitive Sciences, 2,* 129–136.

Hickok, G., Bellugi, U., & Klima, E. S. (1998b). What's right about the neural organization of sign language? A perspective on recent neuroimaging results. *Trends in Cognitive Sciences, 2,* 465–468.

Hickok, G., Love-Geffen, T., & Klima, E. S. (2002). Role of the left hemisphere in sign language comprehension. *Brain & Language, 82,* 167–178.

Hickok, G., Wilson, M., Clark, K., Klima, E. S., Kritchevsky, M., & Bellugi, U. (1999). Discourse deficits following right-hemisphere damage in deaf signers. *Brain & Language, 66,* 233–248.

Jordan, I. K., & Karchmer, M. A. (1986). Patterns of sign use among hearing impaired students. In A. Schildroth & M. Karchmer (Eds.), *Deaf children in America* (pp. 125–138). San Diego, CA: College-Hill Press.

José-Robertson, L. S., Corina, D. P., Ackerman, D., Guillemin, A., & Braun, A. R., (2004). Neural systems for sign language production: Mechanisms supporting lexical selection, phonological encoding, and articulation. *Human Brain Mapping, 23,* 156–167.

Kandel, E. R., & Schwartz, J. H. (2000). *Principles of neural science.* New York: McGraw-Hill.

Kegl, J., & Poizner, H. (1997). Crosslinguistic/crossmodal syntactic consequences of left hemisphere damage: Evidence from an aphasic signer and his identical twin. *Aphasiology, 11,* 1–37.

Krentz, U. C., & Corina, D. P. (2008). Preference for language in early infancy: The human language bias is not speech specific. *Developmental Science, 11,* 1–9.

Lang, H. G., & Stokoe, W. C., Jr. (2000). A treatise on signed and spoken language in early 19th century deaf education in America. *Journal of Deaf Studies and Deaf Education, 5,* 196–199.

Lee, D. S., Lee, J. S., Oh, S. H., Kim, S., Kim, J., Chung, J., et al. (2001). Cross-modal plasticity and cochlear implants. *Nature, 409,* 149–150.

Lenneberg, E. (1967). *Biological foundations of language.* New York: John Wiley & Sons, Inc.

MacSweeney, M., Campbell, R., Woll, B., Brammer, M. J., Giampietro, V., David, A. S., et al. (2006). Lexical and sentential processing in British Sign Language. *Human Brain Mapping, 27,* 63–76.

MacSweeney, M., Woll, B., Campbell, R., McGuire, P. K., David, A. S., Williams, S. C. R., et al. (2002). Neural systems underlying British sign language and audio-visual English processing in native users. *Brain, 125,* 1583–1593.

Mayberry, R. I., & Fischer, S. D. (1989). Looking through phonological shape to lexical meaning: The bottleneck of non-native sign language processing. *Memory & Cognition, 17,* 740–754.

McCullough, S., Emmorey, K., & Sereno, M. (2005). Neural organization for recognition of grammatical and emotional facial expressions in deaf ASL signers and hearing nonsigners. *Cognitive Brain Research, 22,* 193–203.

McGuire, P. K., Robertson, D., Thacker, A., David, A. S., Frackowiak, R. S. J., & Frith, C. D. (1997). Neural correlates of thinking in sign language. *NeuroReport, 8,* 695–698.

Meier, R. P., & Newport, E. L. (1990). Out of the hands of babes: On a possible sign advantage in language acquisition. *Language, 66,* 1–23.

Neville, H. J., & Bavelier, D. (1998). Neural organization and plasticity of language. *Current Opinion in Neurobiology, 8,* 254–248.

Neville, H. J., Bavelier, D., Corina, D., Rauschecker, J., Karni, A., Lalwani, A., et al. (1998). Cerebral organization for language in deaf and hearing subjects: Biological constraints and effects of experience. *Proceedings of the National Academy of Sciences of the United States of America, 95,* 922–929.

Neville, H. J., Coffey, S. A., Lawson, D. S., Fischer, A., Emmorey, K., & Bellugi, U. (1997). Neural systems mediating American sign language: Effects of sensory experience and age of acquisition. *Brain & Language, 57,* 285–308.

Neville, H. J., Kutas, M., & Schmidt, A. (1980). Event-related potential studies of cerebral specialization during reading. *Annals of the New York Academy of Sciences, 425,* 370–376.

Neville, H. J., & Lawson, D. (1987). Attention to central and peripheral visual space in a movement detection task: An event-related potential and behavioral study. II: Congenitally deaf adults. *Brain Research, 405,* 268–283.

Neville, H. J., Mills, D. L., & Lawson, D. S. (1992). Fractionating language: Different neural subsystems with different sensitive periods. *Cerebral Cortex, 2,* 244–258.

Neville, H. J., Schmidt, A., & Kutas, M. (1983). Altered visual evoked potentials in congenitally deaf adults. *Brain Research, 266,* 127–132.

Newman, A. J., Bavelier, D., Corina, D., Jezzard, P., & Neville, H. J. (2002). A critical period for right hemisphere recruitment in American Sign Language Processing. *Nature Neuroscience, 5,* 76–80.

Newport, E. L. (1990). Maturational constraints on language learning. *Cognitive Science, 14,* 11–28.

Nishimura, H., Doi, K., Iwaki, T., Hashikawa, K., Oku, N., Teratani, T., et al. (2000). Neural plasticity detected in short- and long-term cochlear implant users using PET. *NeuroReport, 4,* 811–815.

Nishimura, H., Hashikawa, K., Doi, K., Iwaki, T., Watanabe, Y., Kusuoka, H., et al. (1999). Sign language "heard" in the auditory cortex. *Science, 397,* 116.

Petitto, L. A., Zatorre, R. J., Gauna, K., Nikelski, E. J., Dostie, D., & Evans, A. C. (2000). Speech-like cerebral activity in profoundly deaf people processing signed languages: Implications for the neural basis of human language. *Proceedings of the National Academy of Sciences of the United States of America, 97,* 13961–13966.

Pickell, H., Klima, E., Love, T., Kritchevsky, M., Bellugi, U., Hickok, G. (2005). Sign language aphasia following *right* hemisphere damage in a left-hander: A case of reversed cerebral dominance in a deaf signer? *Neurocase, 11,* 194–203.

Pinker, S. (1994). *The language instinct.* New York: Harper.

Poizner, H., Newkirk, D., Bellugi, U., & Klima, E. S. (1981). Representation of inflected signs from American Sign Language in short-term memory. *Memory & Cognition, 9,* 121–131.

Pyers, J. E., & Emmorey, K. (2008). The face of bimodal bilingualism: Grammatical markers in American Sign Language are produced when bilinguals speak to English monolinguals. *Psychological Science, 19,* 531–536.

Quittner, A. L., Barker, D. H., Snell, C., Cruz, I., McDonald, L., Grimley, M. E., et al. (2007). Improvements in visual attention in deaf infants and toddlers after cochlear implantation. *Audiological Medicine, 5,* 242–249.

Quittner, A. L., Smith, L. B., Osberger, M. J., Mitchell, T. V., & Katz, D. B. (1994). The impact of audition on the development of visual attention. *Psychological Science, 5,* 347–353.

Rönnberg, J., Söderfeldt, B., & Risberg, J. (1998). Regional cerebral blood flow during signed and heard episodic and semantic memory tasks. *Applied Neuropsychology, 5,* 132–138.

Rönnberg, J., Söderfeldt, B., & Risberg, J. (2000). The cognitive neuroscience of signed language. *Acta Psychologica, 105,* 237–254.

Rouger, J., Lagleyre, S., Fraysse, B., Deneve, S., Deguine, O., & Barone, P. (2007). Evidence that cochlear-implanted deaf patients are better multisensory integrators. *Proceeding of the National Academy of Sciences, 10,* 7295–7300.

Sadato, N., Okada, T., Honda, M., Matsuki, K., Yoshida, M., Kashikura, K., et al. (2005). Cross-modal integration and plastic changes revealed by lip movement, random-dot motion and sign languages in the hearing and deaf. *Cerebral Cortex, 15,* 1113–1122.

Schorr, E. A., Fox, N. A., van Wassenhove, V., & Knudsen, E. I. (2005). Auditory-visual fusion in speech perception in children with cochlear implants. *Proceedings of the National Academy of Sciences of the United States of America, 102,* 18748–18750.

Sharma, A., & Nash, A. (2009). Brain maturation in children with cochlear implants. *The ASHA Leader, 14,* 14–17.

Sharma, A., Nash, A., & Dorman, M. (2009). Cortical development, plasticity, and re-organization in children with cochlear implants. *Journal of Communication Disorders, 42,* 272–279.

Singleton, J. L., & Newport, E. L. (2004). When learners surpass their models: The acquisition of American Sign Language from inconsistent input. *Cognitive Psychology, 49,* 370–407.

Söderfeldt, B., Rönnberg, J., & Risberg, J. (1994). Regional cerebral blood flow in sign language users. *Brain & Language, 46,* 59–68.

Stokoe, W. C., Jr. (1976). The study and use of sign language. *Sign Language Studies, 10,* 1–36.

Stokoe, W. C., Jr. (1978). Sign language versus spoken language. *Sign Language Studies, 18,* 69–90.

Stokoe, W. C., Jr. (2005a). Sign language structure: An outline of the visual communication systems of the American deaf. *Journal of Deaf Studies and Deaf Education, 10,* 3–37.

Stokoe, W. C., Jr. (2005b). Visible verbs become spoken. *Sign Language Studies, 5,* 152–169.

Thompson, R., Emmorey, K., & Gollan, T. H. (2005). "Tip of the fingers" experience by deaf signers. *Psychological Science, 16,* 856–860.

Thompson, R., Emmorey, K., & Kluender, R. (2006). The relationship between eye gaze and verb agreement in American sign language: An eye-tracking study. *Natural Language and Linguistic Theory, 24,* 571–604.

Thompson, R., Vinson, D. P., & Vigliocco, G. (2009). The link between form and meaning in American Sign Language: Lexical processing effects. *Journal of Experimental Psychology: Learning, Memory, and Cognition, 35,* 550–557.

Van Dijk, J. E., van Olphen, A. F., Langereis, M. C., Mens, L. H. M., Brokx, J. P. L., & Smoorenburg, G. F. (1999). Predictors of cochlear implant performance. *Audiology, 38,* 109–116.

Zeshan, U. (2004). Interrogative constructions in signed languages: Crosslinguistic perspectives. *Language, 80,* 7–39.

Aphasia

Because language processes are carried out by networks of neurons in the brain, it makes sense to ask how, exactly, are those processes organized? Are different parts of the brain specialized to undertake specific language-processing tasks? If so, which bits do which jobs? How do the different parts of the brain share information? Are all people's brains organized the same way for language? Language scientists use two chief methods to investigate the relationship between language-processing ability and the brain. As we have seen elsewhere, neurophysiological and brain-imaging methods like ERP, magnetoencepalography (MEG), and fMRI have provided important insights into how different parts of the brain work together to support language production and comprehension. The other main way to investigate brain–language relationships is to look at what happens to language-processing abilities when the brain is damaged or disabled. In both kinds of research, scientists are interested in discovering the *neural underpinnings* of language—they want to know which parts of the brain participate in which language production and comprehension processes.

Investigating the neural underpinnings of language can be done at different levels of specificity. Individual patients can be studied in detail to see how particular *lesions* (areas of brain damage) in particular places relate to particular patterns of symptoms (we will see a number of examples later). We can also look at much larger combinations of brain regions. For example, we can even look at entire cerebral hemispheres to learn something about how the brain supports language. Studying hemispheric function has taught us that the left hemisphere plays a dominant role in speech and language comprehension in the vast majority of right-handers (~96%) and a substantial majority of left-handers (~70%; Rasmussen & Milner, 1977). This conclusion

Introduction to Psycholinguistics: Understanding Language Science, First Edition.
Matthew J. Traxler.

is supported by patients who have taken the WADA test (Wada & Rasmussen, 1960). In the WADA test, an anesthetic, usually sodium amobarbitol, is injected into an artery that leads either to the left hemisphere or the right hemisphere. In effect, one half of the brain is put to sleep, while the other half functions as it normally does, except that it does not receive normal input from the other hemisphere. While one half of the brain is anesthetized, patients are asked to name familiar objects. For most people, anesthetizing the left hemisphere causes them to become mute, and they also have trouble understanding language. Anesthetizing the right hemisphere has minimal effects on language production and comprehension (but we will see in the next chapter that some language-processing functions do seem to depend on the right hemisphere).

Conclusions about language function derived from the results of the WADA test are also consistent with studies of patients with left-hemisphere brain damage. The most dramatic and obvious language-related symptoms show up following damage to the left hemisphere, and that will be our focus in this chapter. In this chapter, we will see that distinct patterns of language disorder can result from strokes, tumors, and other events that damage brain tissue in the language-dominant (usually left) hemisphere.[1] We will also explore whether brain damage in particular parts of the left hemisphere is associated with specific symptoms or patterns of language disorder.

Aphasiology: What Happens to Language When the Brain Is Damaged?

Before modern brain-imaging techniques such as PET and fMRI were developed, scientists based many of their inferences about how language-processing functions are implemented in the brain by studying language disorders resulting from brain damage (Dronkers, Plaisant, Iba-Zizen, & Cabanis, 2007; Finger, 2001; Selnes & Hillis, 2000). Philosophers have speculated about where the language centers reside for centuries (Prins & Bastiaanse, 2006),[2] and the earliest direct tests of the *localization hypothesis*—the idea that specific parts of the brain perform specific language functions—date from the early 1800s. For example, the French physician Simon Aubertin provided early evidence that the left frontal lobe was involved in speech production. Aubertin was treating a patient who had shot off a chunk of his skull in a failed suicide attempt, leaving a large part of his left frontal lobe exposed. Aubertin found that when he pressed on his patient's left-hemisphere frontal lobe with a spatula, the patient immediately stopped talking (Finger, 2001; Woodill & Le Normand, 1996). Aubertin viewed this result as being incompatible with the *equipotentiality hypothesis*—the notion that intellectual abilities, including language, result from the mass action of the entire brain. He reasoned that, if the processes supporting speech were widely dispersed throughout the brain, then interfering with a small portion of the brain (via the spatula treatment) should have little or no effect on speech. Because there was such a dramatic change in language performance when frontal lobe function was temporarily disrupted, Aubertin concluded that normal frontal lobe function was a necessary component of speech production.

Aphasiology, the scientific study of language disorders resulting from brain damage, began in earnest in the second half of the 1800s when Paul Broca published the case history of a patient named Leborgne.[3] Paul Broca was a surgeon working in Paris, France who was consulted about Leborgne. Upon examination, Broca found that Leborgne could only say one thing, the syllable *tan*, and then only with great difficulty. (Leborgne would also produce the occasional swearword when he thought he was not being understood.) Shortly after

Figure 13.1 The left hemisphere of Leborgne and Lelong's brains. Closeup of Broca's area appears in the right-hand pictures. (From Dronkers et al., 2007)

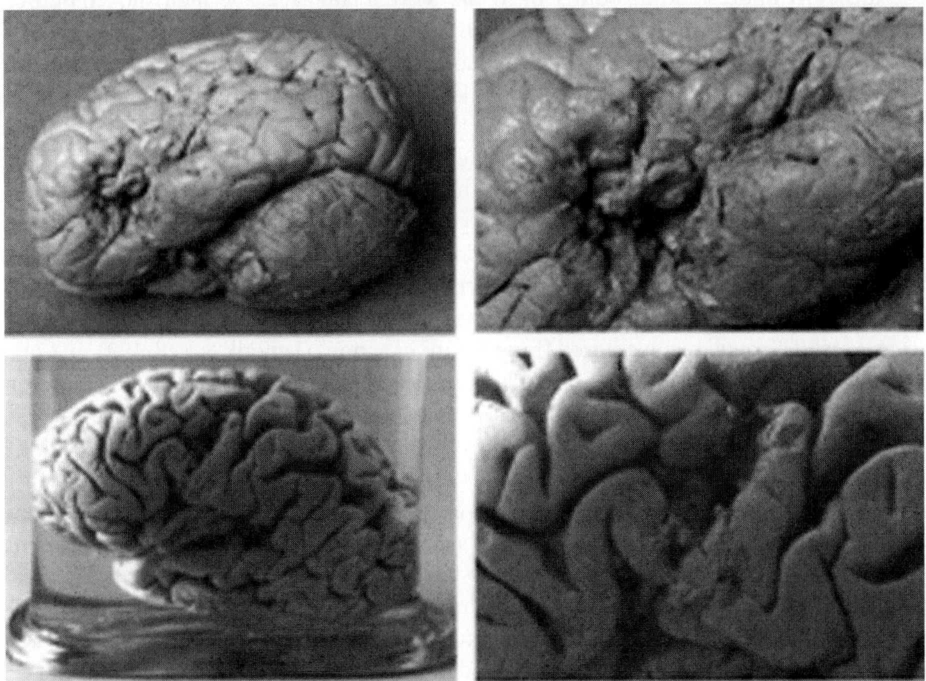

examining Leborgne, Broca encountered a second patient named Lelong, who had a similar pattern of symptoms. Lelong could say five words, and he had the same trouble speaking as Leborgne. After the two men died, Broca studied their brains to see whether they had anything in common. At the time, *phrenologists* had already advanced the claim that language was governed by the frontal lobes (Lanczik & Keil, 1991; Prins & Bastiaanse, 2006). Following Franz Gall, phrenologists studied the shape of people's heads because they believed that head shape was determined by the shape of the underlying brain, and the shape of the underlying brain determined various personality and mental characteristics. Other contemporary philosophers argued that language could not be pinned to any specific brain region and was instead produced by the cooperative action of a wide variety of brain regions. When Broca autopsied the two patients, he found that they both had substantial brain damage in the frontal lobe of the left hemisphere. Amazingly, instead of dissecting their brains, Broca preserved them so that future generations of scientists could study them. Figure 13.1 shows a photograph of the left hemisphere of Leborgne's and Lelong's brains. In both brains, you can clearly see a large area of missing tissue in the inferior (bottom) part of the left frontal lobes. Broca sided with the phrenologists, and with Aubertin, and concluded that a particular part of the frontal lobes (an area that would subsequently be named *Broca's area*) was necessary for fluent, meaningful speech in normal individuals. This conclusion is based on a fundamental tenet of aphasiology: If part of the brain is damaged, and a person subsequently is unable to do some task (like speak or understand sentences), then the part of the brain that was damaged must have participated in the performance of that task. If a group of people all have the same symptoms, and all have brain damage in the same place, then that part of the brain is necessary for the successful performance of the task.

A few years after Broca published his studies of the patients Leborgne and Lelong, Carl Wernicke[4] described a different language syndrome, based on two patients, Susanne

Adam and Susanne Rother, who had a pattern of symptoms much different than those exhibited by Broca's patients (Eling, 2006).[5] These patients could speak and hear, but they had difficulty understanding both spoken and written language, and their spoken output was also marked by the use of *neologisms* (new, made-up words) and by semantic anomalies. One of the two patients appeared to understand "absolutely nothing" (Mathews, Obler, & Albert, 1994, p. 447). This latter patient was autopsied after she died, and she was found to have a lesion in the posterior (rear) portions of her brain, near the place where the temporal, parietal, and occipital lobes meet. She also had widespread loss of tissue in her cerebral cortices. No information about the existence or location of a lesion is available for the other patient.

After reviewing Susanne Rother's lesion location and both patients' patterns of comprehension and speech output, Wernicke formulated his theory of "sensory" and "motor" aphasia. Wernicke proposed that posterior regions of the brain stored "remembered images," while frontal regions stored "impressions of action" (Lanczik & Keil, 1991, p. 174). Wernicke proposed that there are two kinds of "remembered images" that are critical for language comprehension. One set of "images" reflects the phonological (sound) information associated with words, while the other reflects the conceptual/semantic (meaning) information. Hence, Wernicke viewed Broca's aphasia as reflecting a failure of the (motor) movement system (hence, *motor* aphasia), while patients with posterior damage suffered from dysfunction in the perceptual-memory system (hence, *sensory* aphasia). More specifically, they suffered from an inability to retrieve a trace of the "sound image" in their attempts to comprehend language. As such, the patients' problems did not reflect an overall reduction in intellect or the ability to think. Rather, aphasia reflected brain damage interfering with language comprehension and production processes; and brain damage in the language centers did not adversely affect patients' ability to think.[6]

The classic WLG model

The Wernicke–Lichtheim–Geschwind (WLG) model of neural organization for language is probably the best known account of language organization in the brain (Geschwind, 1965; see also Martin, 2003; Shallice, 1988). One of the fundamental tenets of this model involves the claim that perception and motor (movement) processes are undertaken by separate neural systems in the brain. Perceptual processes are assumed to be undertaken by posterior (rear) portions of the brain. Motor processes are assumed to be undertaken by anterior (frontward) portions of the brain. Thus, receptive language processes involved in comprehension take place in posterior temporal and parietal lobe regions, while production processes take place in the frontal lobes. In particular, the parts of association cortex that lie just in front of the parts of the motor strip that control mouth and tongue movements store the patterns of movements involved in speech.

According to the WLG model, three cortical structures in the left hemisphere are responsible for core processes in language production and comprehension. *Wernicke's area* consists of a set of brain regions at the junction of the parietal and temporal cortices, including the superior temporal lobe and the angular gyrus. This area is just posterior of the area of temporal cortex that is responsible for the basic acoustic analysis of auditory stimuli. The angular gyrus, an area just behind and slightly higher than Wernicke's area, is also thought to be involved in language processing, especially during analysis of visual input (Corina & McBurney, 2001; Newman, Bavelier, Corina, Jezzard, & Neville, 2002). A second brain region, *Broca's area*, consists of a portion of the left inferior (bottom) part of the left frontal lobe. A third brain structure, called the *arcuate fasciculus*, is a bundle of white matter (myelinated axons of neurons) that was thought to convey information from Wernicke's area to Broca's area. Plate 20 shows a model of the arcuate fasciculus and related fiber tracts generated from *diffusion tensor imaging* (DTI), a form of MRI (Catani, Jones, and ffytche, 2005). The portions of the language-processing region that occupy parts of the cerebral cortex are collectively identified as being the *perisylvian region*, because the way the fissures and gyri are laid out looks a bit like a tree (hence *sylvian*). The fissure between the temporal and frontal lobes is the trunk of the tree, and the branches are the gyri (bulges in the cortex) that extend from the lateral sulcus or fissure toward the rear of the brain.

According to the WLG model, these three areas together are responsible for the cognitive processes that yield a basic semantic and syntactic analysis of an utterance in comprehension. They are also responsible for producing fluent, meaningful speech. According to the model, Wernicke's area is responsible for storing conceptual, semantic (meaning) representations, as well as other lexical information, including part of speech, subcategorization (for verbs), argument structure (also for verbs), and *thematic role* information (what roles different words normally play in expressing meaning). This area is also thought to be responsible for storing the phonological (sound-based) codes that are used in identifying words during speech comprehension. The model proposes that Broca's area is involved in constructing grammatical sequences of words and planning motor movements in production. The arcuate fasciculus is thought to relay semantic and lexical information about words from the conceptual and phonological representations in Wernicke's area to Broca's area during speech and written language production.

According to the WLG model, these three brain structures work together to support language production. As articulated by Caplan and Hildebrandt (1988, p. 297), "Concepts access the phonological representations of words in Wernicke's area, which are then transmitted to the motor-programming areas for speech in Broca's area. Simultaneously … the concept center activates Broca's area. The proper execution of the speech act depends on Broca's area receiving input from both these different cortical areas." Because specific language functions are located in particular parts of the brain, the posterior (rear) and anterior (front) parts of the language system can function to some degree independently. Thus, some language abilities can be degraded or destroyed while other abilities are spared. Comprehension can be degraded without damage to the ability to speak, and the ability to speak can be degraded without impairment in the ability to understand speech. So, damage to different regions of the brain can lead to different types of underlying language dysfunction and different patterns of symptoms.

The classic WLG model identifies three main types of language disorders and ties each of them to one of the structures described above. Damage to Wernicke's area should lead to problems with the perceptual processing of speech. More specifically, damage in this area should lead to problems accessing the phonological (sound) and lexical (meaning) information that goes along with words, which directly causes problems in comprehension

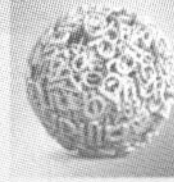

SAMPLE OF SPEECH FROM A FLUENT APHASIC PATIENT (FROM DICK ET AL., 2001).

(In response to a question about the episode in which he suffered his stroke):
It just suddenly had a feffort and all the feffort had gone with it. It even stepped my horn. They took them from earth you know. They make my favorite nine to severed and now I'm a been habed by the uh stam of fortment of my annulment which is now forever.

and knock-on effects in production. In comprehension, the inability to use speech to access the conceptual store interferes with semantic interpretation. In production, the inability of the speech planning centers to access the appropriate phonological codes leads to speech that is essentially meaningless. Damage to Broca's area should interfere with the processes necessary for the construction of syntactically well-formed utterances and with planning and executing the motor movements necessary for speech, leading to *apraxia of speech* (labored, halting, "telegraphic" output). Damage to the arcuate fasciculus should sever communication between the posterior language-processing areas and Broca's area, leading to problems repeating the verbatim input, but sparing the ability to understand language and the ability to produce meaningful speech. These three kinds of language disorders are referred to as *Wernicke's*, *Broca's*, and *conduction aphasia*, respectively. In the next section, we will explore each of these disorders in more detail.

WERNICKE'S APHASIA

Wernicke's aphasia (also known as *fluent* aphasia) is characterized by fluent but largely meaningless speech and difficulty comprehending spoken and written input. The box on p. 483 provides a sample of the kind of speech produced by a patient with Wernicke's aphasia. You can see video of a patient with Wernicke's aphasia here: http://www.youtube.com/watch?v=aVhYN7NTIKU. The primary problem in Wernicke's aphasia seems to be in mapping (non-linguistic) conceptual representations of word meanings onto the phonological codes that allow speakers to express meaning using words and that allow listeners to use words to access conceptual representations.[7] There are a number of notable aspects of the sample of speech in Wernicke's aphasia given in the box. First, count the number of *neologisms*—made-up words. There are several. One possible explanation is that the phonological codes that go with the concepts the speaker wanted to convey were not available to the speech planning mechanism, so the mechanism used whatever phonological information was active and available at the time the utterance was planned. Second, note that the sentences are largely grammatically sound (e.g., they have a subject and a predicate) and one, the last one, has a fairly complex syntactic structure.

According to the WLG model, the conceptual representations still make contact with Broca's area, and the output planning mechanisms are still intact in patients with Wernicke's aphasia. As a result, such patients can still speak fluently. But because the phonological (sound) codes are not matched to the conceptual information by posterior processes, the output of the frontal system is meaningless. In addition, Wernicke's aphasics may lack some of the self-monitoring abilities that normally allow us to determine whether what we say matches up with the meaning we are trying to convey. That is, Wernicke's aphasics have as much trouble understanding their own speech as they have understanding other people's speech. Wernicke's aphasia is related to a separate disorder known as *anomia*, because it entails the inability to retrieve the names of objects and actions, even though conceptual understanding of those objects and actions remains intact. In general, although Wernicke's aphasics perform better on some tasks when they are given visual input (i.e., text) rather than auditory input, they tend to perform well below average on comprehension tasks with both auditory and visual input.

BROCA'S APHASIA

Broca's aphasia (sometimes referred to as *agrammatic* or *non-fluent* aphasia) is characterized by halting, effortful speech that is meaningful, but that is largely devoid of grammatical structure. As articulated by Bates and colleagues (Bates, Friederici, & Wulfeck, 1987, p. 21), "Broca's aphasia involves a central grammatical deficit, demonstrated in both receptive and expressive processing, with its primary effects on the

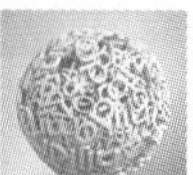

SAMPLE OF SPEECH FROM A NON-FLUENT APHASIC PATIENT (FROM SAFFRAN, BERNDT, & SCHWARTZ, 1989)

a mother ... three kids ... bad mother ... one kid beautiful ... rich ... Italian ... mother ... stepmother ... talk about Cinderella ... Cinderella ... clean my house ... you Cinderella. close the door ... Cinderella like jail ... mother ... three kids ... I love mother ... Cinderella walk ball ... people ball ... rich people ... man and Cinderella dance dance dance party ... one ... dance dance dance ... dance every time ... ball beautiful people ... people watched Cinderella ... Cinderella ... beautiful clothes ... and ... garments ... twelve o'clock night ... Cinderella ... oh no ... oh no ... I'm sorry ... I'm sorry people ... I love you baby ... walk walk ... tumble ... one shoe ... bye-bye ... Cinderella ... pumpkin cab ... oh shoe ... oh please ... oh well ... walk pumpkin car.

retrieval and/or interpretation of closed class elements (words like *of, the, and, because*), free-standing grammatical function words and bound grammatical morphemes (like the *ed* in *kicked*, or the *es*, in *classes*)." One of the common tests for aphasia involves asking patients to retell well-known stories, like Cinderella. To make the task a bit easier, the clinician shows the patient pictures that go with the story (this minimizes the demands on the patient's long-term memory). The box above presents an example of the speech that a Broca's aphasic produced under these task conditions. (If you have access to the tubes of the Internets, have a look at this video of a patient with Broca's aphasia: http://www.youtube.com/watch?v=f2IiMEbMnPM.) Compare this box to the output of the patient with Wernicke's aphasia on p. 483. They are really very different. This is why neurologists and psycholinguists view the disorders as being distinct and reflecting different underlying deficits.

As you can see in both the box above and the video, patients with Broca's aphasia have a great deal of difficulty speaking, and the string of words is mostly unstructured, but the patient has provided quite a lot of semantic information related to the story. S/he includes all of the major characters—Cinderella, the Evil Stepmother and Step-sisters, and the Prince. S/he also includes information about setting and all the main details of the plot—including the critical point that the Prince falls in love with Cinderella. S/he even manages to work in the detail about the carriage made from a pumpkin. What is lacking in the patient's response on the task is the smooth output that a normal individual would provide. Further, grammatical markers, such as auxiliary verbs, tense and number agreement morphemes are almost entirely absent.

This absence of the normal range of grammatical forms and grammatical cues is the defining characteristic of Broca's aphasia. It is important to recognize, however, that the severity of speech problems can vary widely among patients diagnosed with Broca's aphasia. At the most extreme end of the spectrum are patients with *apraxia of speech* (such as that in the sample), which is also described as being *agrammatic*. According to Caramazza and Berndt (1978, p. 911), "Agrammatic speech has a strikingly telegrammatic form in which syntax seems to be restricted to a single declarative form, function words are infrequently present, and verbs, when used, are most often uninflected" (by *uninflected*, they mean that the verbs do not have the usual suffixes, like *-ed*, and *-ing*). A less severe form of speech disorder occurs in Broca's patients who have *paragrammatic speech*. Again, as described by Caramazza and Berndt (p. 912),

> *Paragrammatic speech seems to involve not so much a restriction of syntactic organization as the inappropriate juxtaposition of lexical items. [For example], indefinite noun phrases are often substituted for an appropriate noun, and when a noun of specific reference is chosen it is often the wrong one … [This] often results in serious grammatical distortions, such as category violations (e.g., the use of a noun in a verb or adjective position) and selectional restriction violations (e.g., the use of an animate noun in a sentence that requires an inanimate noun). Nevertheless, the speech of these patients generally gives the appearance of being syntactically well structured.*"[8]

Could this halting, effortful speech occur simply because Broca's aphasics have trouble retrieving the names of words when they speak? This does not appear to be the case. For example, as part of diagnostic testing procedures, stroke patients are often asked to complete a *confrontation naming test* (which is a subpart of larger tests of language abilities such as the *Boston diagnostic aphasia examination* and the *Western aphasia battery*). In the confrontation naming test, patients are shown pictures of commonly encountered objects and are asked to come up with the appropriate name. Although they sometimes have difficulty retrieving and articulating individual words on the confrontation naming test, Broca's aphasics are generally able to correctly label commonly encountered objects. The fact that many Broca's aphasics can respond to requests (e.g., *Tell me the Cinderella story*, and *Tell me what happened to your leg*) and provide meaningful responses in conversation led early researchers to view their disorder as being largely or entirely confined to speech production. They believed that language comprehension in Broca's aphasia was essentially fully intact.

CONDUCTION APHASIA

Conduction aphasia is characterized by an intact ability to understand spoken and written language, intact ability to produce fluent, grammatical speech, but a marked inability to repeat the verbatim form of phrases and sentences. Repetition of individual words appears to be intact, however. Conduction aphasics appear to have difficulty repeating phrases and sentences because the phonological information they need to perform the task does not remain in an active state for very long. Although they rapidly lose the phonological information associated with the speech input, conduction aphasics do retain semantic information from spoken input over an extended period of time. This is confirmed by tasks that ask conduction aphasics to repeat utterances. For example, when a conduction aphasic was asked to repeat *The pastry cook was elated*, the patient responded by saying, *Something about a happy baker* (Dronkers, Redfern, & Ludy, 1998).

Conduction aphasics' problems maintaining phonological information in an active state are also demonstrated by their performance on recognition tasks. Such tasks minimize the cognitive load involved in retaining information over a short period of time. One study involving a recognition task tested immediate sentence recognition in 14 patients with conduction aphasia (Baldo, Klostermann, & Dronkers, 2008). The patients heard a sentence like *The van was dirty*. Then, right away, they were shown a card that had three sentences printed on it. One was the sentence they had just heard. Two of the sentences on the test card were distractors in which one of the original words was replaced by a very close semantic alternative, such as *truck*, or *car* in the place of *van*. On some trials, one word in the distractor sentence was replaced by a word with a completely unrelated meaning, such as *The apple was dirty*. Conduction aphasics were almost never fooled by the distractors when the distractors had completely different meanings than the target, which shows that they were able to retain semantic information about the input sentence over a very short delay. However, when the distractors and the target sentence were closely related in meaning, conduction aphasics performed nearly at chance levels. That is, they were unable to remember, even for a few seconds, whether the original sentence said *car*, *truck*, or *van*. You will recall from the chapter on discourse processing that this is how normal participants behave when a lot of time and lots of distractions occur between the original sentence and the test period (see Chapter 5, "Three turtles sat on a log and a fish swam beneath them/it" experiments by Bransford, Barclay, & Franks).

Conduction aphasics lack the ability to maintain phonological information even for a very short period of time, but the fact that they can remember the meaning of the sentences they hear shows that they can use phonological information to access the conceptual store. So, while they can't remember the exact form that an utterance took, even a few seconds after they heard it, they are able to use the phonological information to activate semantic information from long-term memory, and this activated semantic information from long-term memory is more stable. As a result, conduction aphasics can use semantic information to support understanding and production. The semantic information allows them to paraphrase sentences, but phonological information decays too fast for them to successfully repeat what they hear.[9]

Problems with the classic WLG model

Carl Wernicke developed ideas about conduction aphasia (difficulty with repetition independent of major comprehension or production difficulties) based on his clinical study of patients with posterior (rearward) brain damage and his physiological study of human brain anatomy. Later studies confirmed the existence of conduction aphasia and provided further evidence about the relationship between conduction aphasia and neuro-anatomy. However, many contemporary neurologists, linguists, and psycholinguists view the classic WLG model as providing an inadequate description of the neural mechanisms involved in language processing. Why is this the case?

One of the main criticisms of the classic model is that it does not accurately describe the brain areas that are involved in language processing. For example, Broca (and subsequent followers of Broca) claimed that non-fluent aphasia resulted from damage to the cerebral cortex (the top layers of the brain) in a particular subregion of the inferior frontal lobes. In particular, Broca claimed that expressive language disorder resulted from damage to two adjacent parts of the inferior frontal lobe, *pars triangularis* and *pars opercularis* (see Figure 13.2). This was based on his examination of the brains of his patients, especially Leborgne and Lelong. However, it is fairly uncommon that a stroke or a tumor damages one or both of these cortical regions without damaging a lot of other brain tissue as well. In fact, although Leborgne and Lelong's lesions did include the cortical areas that comprise Broca's area, they included much more than that. In the recent past, computerized axial tomography (CT) and MRI scanning have been used to image Leborgne and Lelong's brains on two occasions. Both sets of scans indicated that brain damage in both cases extended significantly into subcortical structures (parts of the brain that lie below the *neo-cortex*, or top layers of the brain), including fiber tracts that connect the rear part of the cortex to the frontal lobes (Dronkers et al., 2007; Signoret, Castaigne, Lehrmitte, Abelanet, & Lavorel, 1984; see also Amici, Gorno-Tempini, Ogar, Dronkers, & Miller, 2006). Hence, the severe speech disturbance that occurred in Leborgne's and Lelong's cases could have been the result of damage to areas other than Broca's area. In fact, when lesions occur that are restricted to the classically described Broca's area (pars opercularis and pars triangularis), such lesions lead to relatively short-lived speech problems, but not the long-lasting, dramatic production disorders that occurred in the cases of Leborgne and Lelong (Brunner, Kornhuber, Seemüller, Suger, & Wallesch, 1982; Mohr et al., 1978; Penfield & Roberts, 1959).

Figure 13.2 *Pars triangularis* and *pars opercularis* (adapted from Dronkers et al., 2007)

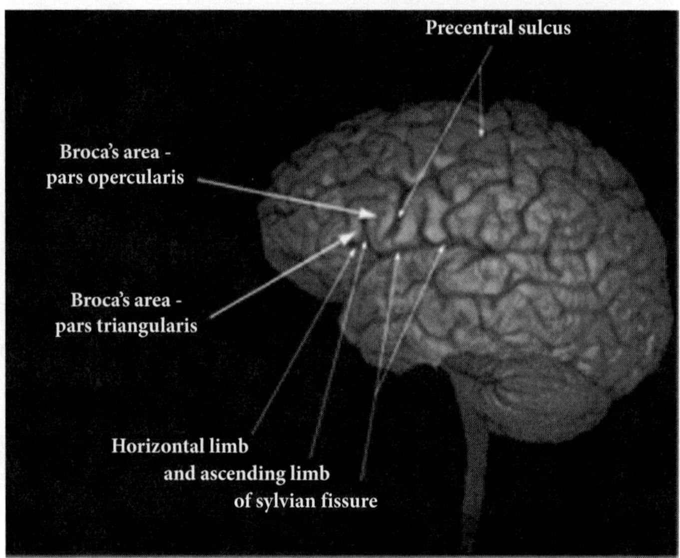

In the case of Wernicke's area and Wernicke's aphasia, the first problem is that Wernicke's classification of his patients was probably faulty (Mathews et al., 1994). For example, one of Wernicke's original patients' symptoms were most likely caused by dementia. In fact, Wernicke only classified her as aphasic *after* he found a lesion in her left temporal lobe. That is, he deduced that because she had a lesion in the right place, she must have the disorder that is caused by a lesion in that place. Another problem is that different neurologists don't agree about where, exactly, Wernicke's area is and how big it is (see Martin, 2003, for a review of this debate). Further, contrary to Wernicke's assumptions, damage to Wernicke's area and Wernicke's aphasia do not always go together. Wernicke's aphasia symptoms can appear without damage to Wernicke's area; and damage to Wernicke's area does not always cause symptoms of Wernicke's aphasia to appear. As Martin (2003, p. 57) indicates, "Assuming the most common definition—the posterior third of the superior temporal gyrus—there is evidence that a lesion restricted to this area does not give rise to … Wernicke's aphasia and that a wider lesion is needed." (As we just saw, the same thing applies to Broca's area and Broca's aphasia.) Further, Wernicke's aphasia symptoms typically associated with *focal* brain damage (brain damage restricted to a particular part of the brain) can also occur in patients with dementia caused by *multifocal* or *diffuse lesions* (in which brain damage is widespread) that do not necessarily include the classically defined Wernicke's area (Mathews et al., 1994).

A number of other studies also suggest that areas other than the classic trio play substantial roles in language comprehension and production. For example, damage to a region of the brain known as the *basal ganglia* (see Figure 13.3) has been shown to determine the pattern of symptoms in Broca's aphasia (Brunner et al., 1982). In Brunner and colleagues' study, 40 patients' brains were imaged using CT scanning methods. The patients' patterns of language disorder were assessed by looking at their spontaneous speech and a variety of structured language production tasks. Patients were categorized as having Broca's or Wernicke's aphasia (among other types), and the degree of speech impairment was also measured. One of the main findings of this study is that patients with damage to Broca's area did not have the classic major disruption of speech (apraxia plus repetitive speech) unless they also had damage to the basal ganglia. Another part of the frontal cortex, the

Figure 13.3 The basal ganglia

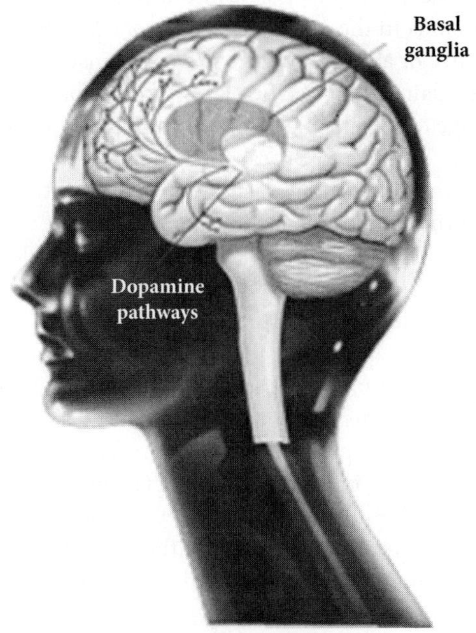

Figure 13.4 The insula

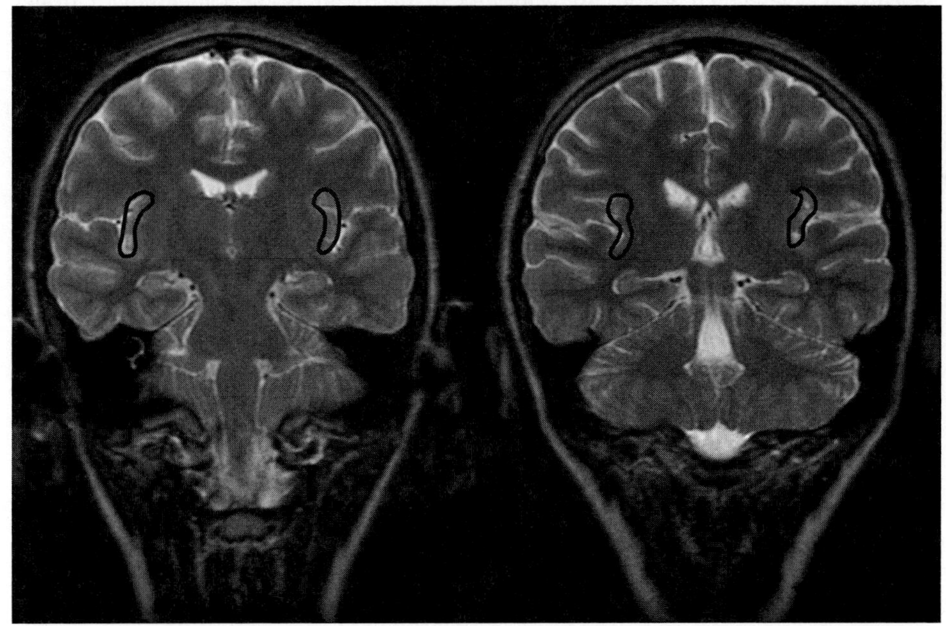

insula (see Figure 13.4) also appears to be critical in speech production, and it is damage or sparing of this area that seems to determine whether the most dramatic speech disruption, *apraxia of speech*, will appear following a stroke or tumor (Dronkers, 1996). This conclusion is based on a study by Nina Dronkers, who used CT and MRI methods to identify the location of lesions in a sample of 25 patients with apraxia of speech. When lesion locations were compared, all 25 patients had damage in the insula. A further 19 patients were identified who had aphasia symptoms but who did not have apraxia of speech. None of these 19 patients had lesions in the insula. Thus, the one brain area whose fate correlated perfectly with the presence or absence of apraxia was the insula.

The WLG model also claims that specific patterns of language-related symptoms should follow from brain damage to specific parts of the brain. Damage to Wernicke's area should cause Wernicke's aphasia. Damage to Broca's area should cause Broca's aphasia. However, research over the past two decades has cast significant doubt on these claims. A broad survey of patients with different patterns of language disorders and lesions of different sizes in different parts of the brain shows that there is no clear correlation between symptoms and lesion location, contrary to the predictions of the WLG model. For Broca's aphasia, many patients have lesions that are outside Broca's area (Caplan, 2006b; Vanier & Caplan, 1990).

Based on their observations of a large sample of patients who had brain damage and language comprehension problems, the neurologists David Caplan and Nancy Hildebrandt (1988) argue that clear lesion–symptom correlations are hard to find. They used a statistical technique that organizes patients into subgroups that resemble one another and differ from other subgroups. Caplan and Hildebrandt tried to use lesion location and size to predict which groups their patients would end up in and the kinds of symptoms those groups of patients would have in common. According to the WLG model, patients with posterior lesions should group together on the basis of generalized comprehension problems. Patients with frontal lesions should group together on the basis of specific problems understanding grammatically complex sentences. Contrary to this prediction, Caplan and Hildebrandt found that patients' performance on a battery of sentence comprehension tasks did not depend on where their lesions were located in the brain. Some patients with frontal lobe lesions did just fine on tasks involving grammatically complex sentences, while some patients with posterior lesions did poorly. What *did* predict patients' performance was the size of their lesions. Patients with large lesions, regardless of location, tended to perform poorly. Patients with smaller lesions, again regardless of location, tended to score higher on the comprehension tests.

The lack of correlation between lesion location and pattern of symptoms has also been found in a number of other studies. In Brunner and colleagues' (1982) study, only one out of four patients with damage to Wernicke's area showed symptoms of Wernicke's aphasia. The rest were classified as Broca's aphasics. Of five patients with damage to both Wernicke's area and subcortical tissue, only one was classified as having Wernicke's aphasia. Of three patients with damage restricted to Broca's area, two had short-term speech problems that cleared up. One did not have any apparent speech disturbance at all. However, two patients who had damage to Broca's area and underlying subcortical tissue both were classified as Broca's aphasics based on significant, long-lasting speech production problems. Other studies show that patients with damage to Wernicke's area make numerous grammatical errors when they produce sentences, in addition to producing semantically inappropriate or content-less words and neologisms. This is especially apparent in languages that make use of a wider variety of grammatical markers than English does (Bates et al., 1987; English relies heavily on word order to assign semantic roles to individual words and phrases). Amici and colleagues (2006) conducted an imaging study of 42 aphasia patients and found Broca's-like symptoms in patients with posterior lesions as well as patients with frontal lobe lesions, although they speculated that the two sets of patients might have different underlying reasons for having speech production and grammatical comprehension difficulties. Murdoch (1988) used neurological examination and behavioral assessment to classify a sample of aphasic patients. In their sample, two patients showed the classic production profile associated with Wernicke's aphasia, but neither patient had damage in Wernicke's area. One had bilateral lesions (lesions in both hemispheres) in the parietal-occipital region. The other Wernicke's patient had a lesion restricted to subcortical areas below the frontal and temporal cortices.

The WLG model also predicts that patients with brain damage outside the classic language areas (Wernicke's, Broca's, and arcuate fasciculus) should *not* have problems comprehending or producing language. For example, damage to the right hemisphere should not affect syntactic parsing and assignment of words to semantic roles. However, in tasks that require patients to use grammatical cues, like word order and number agreement, to assign meaning to strings of words such as *The horse the dog kicked*, surgical patients without brain damage and patients with damage outside the classic language areas both paid less attention to grammatical information (number and case marking on verbs and nouns) than did control subjects (Bates et al., 1987; Dick et al., 2001). Thus, according to Bates and her colleagues, the kinds of brain damage that lead to production difficulties do so, not because syntactic processors are selectively damaged, but rather because brain damage reduces the amount of general-purpose resources that are necessary for a variety of complex thought processes, including language. Because using and being sensitive to grammatical cues requires general-purpose processing resources, and because dealing with pain and coping with injuries occupy those resources, grammatical cues that are weak or inconsistent (like case marking in English or word order in German) have less of an influence on the way patients interpret language, even for patients who have not suffered damage in the classically defined language areas. Bates and colleagues' approach therefore resembles Caplan, Waters, and their colleagues' interpretation of their patients' symptoms. However, Caplan and Waters' team argues that brain damage to the perisylvian language-processing regions reduces a pool of processing resources that is dedicated solely and specifically to language interpretation and production (Caplan & Hildebrandt, 1988; Caplan & Waters, 2006; Waters & Caplan, 1996).

If the location of a patient's lesion does not predict what kind of symptoms the patient will have, what can we conclude about the relationship between brain structures and language processing? Is the organization of the brain for language processing random? Are the concepts of *mass action* (that higher level cognitive processes evenly distributed throughout huge areas of the brain) and *equipotentiality* (the idea that any part of the brain can undertake any kind of mental process) right? The fact that patterns of lesion–deficit correlations are complex does not necessarily mean that equipotentiality is correct. One possible alternative solution is to hypothesize that language depends on a variety of brain regions, at both the cortical and subcortical level, but that the way brain regions are organized for language in general, and syntactic processing specifically, differs across different individuals (Caplan & Hildebrandt, 1988). This approach can explain why two different people with lesions in different locations can both have the same pattern of language dysfunction. It can also explain why two different people with lesions in roughly the same place can have different sets of symptoms. (Word of caution: Because no two brains are identical, and because no two lesions are ever identical, no two cases are ever 100% comparable.)

The fact that there could be variability in localization of language function across individuals does not mean that there is absolutely zero consistency in the way language-processing functions are implemented in the brain. If we had enough people in a sample, and if we had good data on the location of people's lesions and their pattern of performance on a variety of language-processing tasks, we might be able to discover some degree of consistent organization of language functions across the population. *Voxel-based lesion-symptom mapping* (VLSM) is a research technique that can potentially uncover such relationships (Bates et al., 2003; Dronkers, Wilkins, Van Valin, Redfern, & Jaeger, 2004; Wilson & Saygin, 2004).

VLSM starts with the collection of data from a large sample of patients with focal lesions. The data include scan information that shows the location and size of each person's lesion(s). Each scan is divided into a number of *voxels*, or cubic regions of brain (voxels are the three-dimensional equivalent of *pixels*—your computer display is made up of an array of pixels). Then, each voxel in each patient is classified as either being intact or damaged. Next, all of the patients are tested on a variety of language-processing tasks. Finally, each voxel across the entire group of patients is examined. All of the patients with damage in that voxel are put into one group. All of the patients where that same voxel is healthy are put into another group. If that voxel plays an important role in a language function, then the group with damage in that voxel should score lower on the test than the other (healthy voxel) group.

Plate 21 represents the results of this kind of analysis (from Dronkers et al., 2004). Left-hemisphere regions are plotted on the left side of the figure. The graph relates the degree to which individual voxels contribute to performance on the CYCLE-R test, which measures how well patients are able to understand a variety of sentence types. The gray regions represent areas where performance does not depend on having intact brain tissue. The blue regions represent areas where brain damage leads to slightly worse performance. The red regions represent areas where brain damage leads to big reductions in performance on the CYCLE-R test. As you can see, a wide range of both anterior and posterior brain regions appear to contribute to sentence understanding. These regions did not include the classically defined Broca's and Wernicke's areas (although damage to brain regions very close to the standard Broca's and Wernicke's areas did correlate with performance on the CYCLE-R test). Notably, the VLSM analysis identified large areas of brain tissue outside the classically defined language areas as well, including large parts of the temporal lobe that had not previously been viewed as contributing to sentence understanding.

One final problem with the classic WLG model is its assumption of a posterior–anterior division of labor, with receptive language residing in the posterior regions of the brain and language production residing in the anterior portions. This characterization of the neural basis of language predicts that frontal lobe damage and/or apraxia of speech will not correlate with comprehension difficulty either because speech functions are localized in the language production areas or, if the localization assumptions are relaxed, because language production processes are still undertaken by brain regions distinct from those that undertake language comprehension processes. There were no hard data to contradict these assumptions until more detailed assessment of Broca's aphasics starting in the 1970s revealed that those patients did have some difficulty understanding some aspects of language. We turn to this body of research next.

Broca's Aphasia, Wernicke's Aphasia, and Syntactic Parsing

Overt behavioral differences in speech production are the primary means of distinguishing between Wernicke's and Broca's aphasias, but more subtle differences can also be observed under the right conditions. It turns out that, while Wernicke's aphasics have considerable difficulty across the board understanding language, Broca's aphasics have their own set of problems in comprehending spoken and written language. For example, Broca's aphasics appear to have significant problems understanding sentences in the passive voice, such as sentence (1) (Caplan, 2006a; Caramazza & Zurif, 1976; Goodglass & Baker, 1976; Schwartz, Saffran, & Marin, 1980):

(1) The girl was kissed by the boy.

Sentences like (1) are called *reversible passives* because both of the nouns in the sentence, *girl* and *boy*, are equally capable of initiating the action (*kissing*) described by the verb; and they are equally capable of being the theme or recipient of that action, so you can switch the actors around and still have a good sentence, as in *The boy was kissed by the girl*. In *sentence–picture matching* experiments, Broca's aphasics listen to *reversible* (like 1) and *non-reversible* passives (like 2):[10]

(2) The cheese was eaten by the mouse.

While Broca's aphasics have little difficulty choosing a picture that expresses the meaning of non-reversible passives like (2), they generally perform much worse on reversible passives like (1) (when compared to their own performance on non-reversible passives, their performance on the active-voice counterparts to passives, and the performance of non-brain-damaged, age- and education-matched control subjects). We can infer from this that Broca's aphasics are able to access semantic information tied to individual words and use that information to figure out who did what to whom as long as the semantic information tied to individual words makes their roles clear (e.g., cheese can be eaten, but it can't eat anything; mice are good eaters but bad recipients of the eating action, especially if the eater is a piece of cheese). So the Broca's aphasia patient does not need to do any syntactic structure-building operations to figure out what sentences like (2) mean. By contrast, the aphasic patient does need to parse sentences like (1) to figure out what they mean, because lexical (word-based) information by itself does not indicate who did the kissing and who got kissed. Thus, there appears to be something wrong with the way Broca's aphasics parse sentences.

But what, exactly, goes wrong when Broca's aphasics try to parse sentences? Are they completely incapable of discovering relationships between words in sentences when there are no semantic (meaning) cues to help them out? This *global parsing failure* hypothesis was proposed by Caramazza and Berndt (1978) to explain why Broca's aphasics have trouble with reversible passives like (1) (see also Berndt & Caramazza, 1980, 1982). Because Broca's aphasics in their studies appeared to have problems both with the production of syntactically well-structured sentences and comprehension of reversible passive sentences, Caramazza and Berndt proposed that both the production and comprehension symptoms were tied to a single underlying functional deficit. Specifically, they proposed that the same underlying system was involved in syntactic processing operations in both comprehension and production in *agrammatic aphasia*. Thus, if a patient has agrammatic or paragrammatic speech, the hypothesis that they have a single fundamental problem with syntax explains why they also have trouble parsing and interpreting sentences in comprehension. The global parsing failure hypothesis also predicts that patients who have agrammatic or paragrammatic speech will also show deficits in other areas where knowledge of grammar and syntax is critical for the performance of complex language skills. For example, we might expect an agrammatic patient to have greater problems reading grammatical function words (e.g., *of*, *some*, *how*) than reading semantically "heavier" content words (e.g., *rectangle*, *follow*). Just such a case was reported recently by Druks and Froud (2002).

Further evidence that parsing processes necessary for sentence comprehension are disrupted in Broca's or agrammatic aphasia comes from studies of gap-filling syntactic processes. These studies included a number of agrammatic aphasics (as indicated by agrammatic or paragrammatic speech), as well as samples of Wernicke's aphasics (chosen on the basis of their fluent, but semantically impoverished spoken output). In a set of lexical decision and priming experiments, Edgar Zurif and his colleagues (Caramazza, Berndt, Basili, & Koller, 1981; Zurif, Swinney, Prather, Solomon, & Bushell, 1993) asked Wernicke's and Broca's aphasics to process sentences with long-distance dependencies (see Chapter 4) and react to probe words at critical points in the sentences. In one study, Broca's and Wernicke's aphasics listened to sentences like (3)

(3) The people liked the waiter from the small town *1* who *2* served the drinks.

(The *1* and *2* marks indicate points in the sentence where target words were presented during the experiment.) Sentences like (3) are called *subject relatives* because the filler noun phrase *the waiter* serves as the subject of the relative clause *who served the drinks*. That is, the relative clause could be paraphrased as saying *the waiter served the drinks*. Thus, the sentence has a long-distance dependency (*the waiter* is the subject of the verb *served*, but *waiter* is a long way away from *served* in the actual sentence). To understand the sentence, then, people need to keep the filler phrase *the waiter* active in a working memory buffer as they process the material that comes between *the waiter* and the verb *served*. The parser needs to assign a subject to the verb *served*, the parser knows that *waiter* can be a subject, and so a long-distance dependency can be (and is) formed at this point. According to the *gaps-and-traces* hypothesis, the connection between *waiter* and *served* is formed immediately after the relative pronoun *who*, which is where the *gap* site is located.

Zurif and his colleagues tested whether Wernicke's and Broca's aphasics could form a dependency between *waiter* and *who* by testing the aphasics' reactions to words that were presented just before and just after the relative pronoun (Zurif et al., 1993). Two different kinds of probe words appeared in this experiment. The *related* target words were semantically associated with *waiter* (this might be a word like *menu*). The *control* words were unrelated to the filler noun. By testing just before and just after the relative pronoun *who*, the experimenters could tell whether the aphasics were doing something special with the filler noun *waiter*. According to the gaps-and-traces hypothesis, listeners should place the filler noun in a working memory buffer (and ignore it temporarily) while they are processing the material in the sentence that follows the filler noun. When they reach the gap site immediately after *who*, listeners should re-activate the filler noun in order to complete the long-distance dependency. If this process takes place as the theory claims, words related to *waiter* should be processed more rapidly than unrelated control words at the gap site, but not before. If participants are asked to make a lexical decision to the target words, differences in reaction times between the related and control probe words should show up after the relative pronoun *who*.

When Zurif and his colleagues tested this hypothesis, aphasic subjects' responses to the probe words (e.g., *menu*) were the same, whether the probe words were presented before or after the gap site (Zurif et al., 1993). Wernicke's aphasics, however, did respond differently before and after the gap site. Before the gap site, Wernicke's aphasics responded to control words and words related to the filler phrase in the same way. That is, there was no priming effect when the target words were presented before the gap site. Just after the gap site, Wernicke's aphasics reacted faster to the related target words than the control target words, indicating that they had formed the long-distance dependency. The pattern of results for Broca's and Wernicke's aphasics show that the Broca's aphasics were not able to assign the filler noun *waiter* a role within the relative clause. This pattern of results makes sense if you recall that Broca's aphasics are thought to have difficulty performing syntactic processes. They understand individual words quite well, but they have a hard time figuring out the relationships between words. And while Wernicke's aphasics have some difficulty understanding the meaning of what they hear, they apparently have some intact intra-lexical spreading activation processes (these can account for their faster responses to the related target words) and they are able to complete syntactic processes, such as those processes involved in the formation of long-distance dependencies. The same pattern of effects—significant priming for Wernicke's aphasics, no priming for Broca's aphasics—is observed when *object relative* sentences are tested (Zurif, Swinney, Prather, & Love, 1994). So, Wernicke's aphasics show priming after the verb *kissed*, but Broca's aphasics do not, in the sentence *The girl that the boy kissed ran away.*

Other studies also point toward a specific problem with grammatical/syntactic information processing in Broca's aphasics. For example, *determiners* (function words like *a*, *the*, *an*, and *this*) normally play a pretty subtle role in the meanings that sentences express. We normally use the determiner *the* to refer to concepts already introduced into the discourse. We normally use the corresponding determiner *a/an* to refer to concepts that are new to the discourse. However, sometimes the placement of a determiner makes a big difference in the way a sentence should be interpreted. For example, sentences (4) and (5) have very different meanings, but they are almost identical and differ only in the order of two words (*the baby* vs. *baby the*):

(4) Jane showed her the baby pictures.
(5) Jane showed her baby the pictures.

Normally, people have no trouble figuring out that sentence (4) involves showing someone some pictures of a baby (maybe more than one baby). Likewise, sentence (5) means that some baby got to see some pictures (and the pictures were not necessarily of babies). However, Broca's aphasics have difficulty interpreting sentences like (4) and (5). In one study, they were nearly at chance when their understanding was assessed using the sentence–picture matching test (Heilman & Scholes, 1976).

Difficulty distinguishing the meaning of sentences like (4) and (5) could suggest that non-fluent aphasics have a general problem with *function words*, including determiners. However, results like Heilman and Scholes' could just show that non-fluent aphasics have trouble processing determiners. However, additional data do suggest that the problem that non-fluent aphasics have extends to more than just determiners. Another study looked at the processing of a broad range of *function words* by Wernicke's and Broca's aphasics (and normal control subjects; Friederici, 1988). Words in a language can be divided into two general classes: *content* words and *function* words (sometimes referred to as *open class* and *closed class*). Content words refer to concepts like things (nouns, usually), actions (verbs), and properties (adjectives). Although precise estimates vary (because, e.g., many technical jargon words are spoken only by very small subsets of speakers), there are about 100,000 content words in English, of which about 50,000 are used with any regularity. New content words are being introduced all the time as new objects are invented, or as people discover new ways to talk about old concepts. (Content words are called open-class words because this class of words can have new members.) Function words play a different role. They are largely empty of semantic content and their job is to signal syntactic relationships between words and phrases and to indicate abstract semantic content. For example, the connective *because* typically indicates that what follows is the cause of the event that was just mentioned (as in *Tim fell over because Jane pushed him*; Traxler, Bybee, & Pickering, 1997). The determiner *this* is used in place of other determiners, like *a*, *the*, or *that*, often times because the noun that follows plays an important or focal role in the discourse. There is a relatively small number of function words that occur with any frequency in English (about 300), and it is highly unusual for a new one to be added to the language.[11]

Most people have less difficulty accessing closed-class function words than open-class content words. For example, function words are read faster and skipped more often than equally long content words (Rayner & Pollatsek, 1989). However, because function words typically serve to signal grammatical relations, rather than specific concepts, they may cause particular difficulty for Broca's aphasics, because function words signal grammatical relationships that Broca's aphasics may have difficulty constructing or retrieving from memory. When Wernicke's aphasics are asked to make lexical decisions to content and function words, their performance mirrors that of normal control subjects (Friederici, 1988). Although they are slower than age-matched normal individuals overall, Wernicke's aphasics react more quickly to function words than to content words. Broca's aphasics show the opposite pattern. They react more slowly to function words. We can conclude, therefore, that Broca's aphasics are troubled not just when they have to figure out how words in sentences relate to one another. They also have difficulty dealing with single words when those words are tied to abstract grammatical information (let's return to this topic later when we review the evidence for the *slowed lexical access* hypothesis).

This study also provides insight into the question of whether working-memory restrictions cause degraded sentence-processing performance in Broca's aphasics. The working-memory demands involved in making lexical decisions to single words are very small, and so slow and error-prone performance on this task is unlikely to be the result of working-memory problems. It is always possible, of course, that single-word-processing difficulty and sentence-processing difficulty are caused by different underlying impairments, but a more parsimonious theory would tie difficulty accessing grammatical information and difficulty building syntactic structures for sentences to the same underlying deficit.

The trace deletion hypothesis

The global parsing failure hypothesis explains why non-fluent aphasics produce telegraphic speech and have a variety of comprehension problems, including trouble understanding reversible passives, other forms of filler-gap dependencies, and function words. But, and this is a big "but," the global parsing failure hypothesis does not match all of the typical non-fluent aphasic's behavior. For example, the global parsing failure hypothesis suggests that non-fluent aphasics have lost access to the grammatical knowledge necessary to parse strings of words. If so, they should have problems across the board on tasks that require the use of grammatical knowledge, or tasks that require them to build syntactic structures for sentences, and this is not the case (Caplan, DeDe, & Michaud, 2006; Caplan & Hildebrandt, 1988; Caramazza, Capitani, Rey, & Berndt, 2001; Grodzinsky, 1995; Linebarger, 1995).

First, while non-fluent aphasics often perform poorly on tasks that test their comprehension of passive sentences and sentences that involve displaced elements (filler-gap sentences), they are capable of performing very well on tests that require them to judge whether those same sentences are grammatical or not. They perform at a high level even when the grammatical relationships that they are being asked to judge are very complicated. Consider the ungrammatical question (6) (from Linebarger, 1995):

(6) *Was the girl enjoy the show?

This question is ungrammatical because the form of the verb *enjoy* does not match the form of the displaced auxiliary verb *was*. (*Did the girl enjoy the show?* would be OK.) If aphasics are just generally incapable of parsing sentences, they should not notice that the auxiliary verb has the wrong form, because it only has the wrong form when compared to a word that is separated from it in the verbatim form of the sentence. You have to be able to parse sentence (6) in order to recognize that there is a relationship between *Was* and *enjoy*, and to realize that one of the two separated elements is not in its proper form. Despite the tricky nature of the sentence, non-fluent aphasics, on the average, correctly judged sentences like (6) to be ungrammatical over 85% of the time, far above chance. Likewise, if non-fluent aphasics are generally insensitive to grammatical function words, they should perform poorly on ungrammatical sentences like (7) (again, from Linebarger, 1995):

(7) *The photograph my mother was nice.

Here again, non-fluent aphasics were very accurate at rejecting (7) as being a proper sentence. Linebarger also tested non-fluent aphasics on a number of other kinds of sentences, and their ability to tell which sentences were grammatical and which were not was really very good, far above chance on all the types she tested. Non-fluent aphasics' preserved ability to accurately judge the grammaticality of a wide variety of sentence types shows that they retain a significant amount of grammatical knowledge, and so we cannot attribute their production and comprehension difficulties to a general parsing failure, or a general lack of knowledge about syntax and grammar. Instead, it is pretty clear that non-fluent aphasics can access and use grammatical knowledge under the right conditions. Their grammatical knowledge has *not* been lost.

If grammatical knowledge is preserved in non-fluent aphasia, and non-fluent aphasics still have trouble understanding some kinds of sentences, what is the problem? The *trace deletion* hypothesis represents one possible answer to this question (Drai & Grodzinsky, 2006; Drai, Grodzinsky, & Zurif, 2001; Grodzinsky, 1986, 1995; Grodzinsky, Piñango, Zurif, & Drai, 1999; Mauner, Fromkin, & Cornell, 1993, propose a similar theory). The trace deletion hypothesis proposes that the mental operations involved in filler-gap processing are localized in Broca's area. When Broca's area is damaged, the aphasic patient loses the ability to discover long-distance relationships. Consider, for example, sentence (8):

(8) It was the girl that the boy kissed.

A filler-gap analysis of (8) would yield a description like (9):

(9) It was <u>the girl</u> [filler] that the boy kissed [gap].

The trace deletion hypothesis says that, in non-fluent aphasia, elements in the syntactic representation of a sentence that do not take an overt phonological form (they are not spoken out loud) are deleted. In that case, there will be no indication that the filler phrase *the girl* goes together with the verb *kissed*. More specifically, there will be no indication that *the girl* is the grammatical object of the verb *kissed*, and so it will not be clear that *the girl* is the recipient of the action of kissing.

A similar analysis applies to the processing of sentences that have passive voice. If we marked the filler and gap positions, the resulting sentence would look like (10):

(10) *The girl* [filler] was kissed [gap] by the boy.

Why do passives involve fillers and gaps? According to some linguistic theories (Chomsky, 1981; Grodzinsky, 1986), passive sentences also involve a co-indexation operation that links up a filler with a gap site. According to these accounts, in the underlying representation of (10), *girl* would appear in its normal position following the verb *kissed*, as in (11):

(11) was [[kissed] *the girl*]

However, this D-structure cannot be directly expressed as a sentence, because it lacks a subject (every sentence must have a subject and a predicate). To correct this deficiency, a mental operation is undertaken to move *the girl* to subject position, which results in the passive *The girl was kissed*. When *the girl* moves out of its canonical position, it is marked as a filler, and the place it moved out of is marked as a gap site, as in (12):

(12) *The girl* [filler] was [kissed [gap]].

If we want to include an explicit statement of who did the kissing, we need to add a prepositional phrase following the gap site. Doing so yields sentence (10), above.

So, the trace deletion hypothesis predicts that non-fluent aphasics will have trouble with passives for the same reason that they have trouble with other sentences that involve fillers and gaps. The non-fluent aphasic's representation would not include a special marker that identifies *the girl* as a filler, and it would not include a gap marker following the verb *kissed*. As a result, the non-fluent aphasic would not recognize that the verb *kissed* governs the noun *the girl* by assigning the semantic role *patient* or *experiencer* to *the girl*. Lacking this understanding of the structural relations, the non-fluent aphasic is likely to mistakenly treat *girl* as something other than the recipient of the kissing action.

What happens when the syntactic representation of the sentence does not provide the framework needed to assign semantic roles to elements of the sentence? Non-fluent aphasics do assign meanings to sentences like (9), and (10), so they do not simply fail to interpret them. One other possibility is that non-fluent aphasics apply a *heuristic* (a quick-and-dirty decision-making strategy) to assign semantic roles to the nouns in sentences like (9) and (10). Specifically, they might apply a general "first noun is the agent" strategy. In that case, non-fluent aphasics should consistently treat the first noun in the sentence as the initiator of the action in the sentence. If so, they will consistently interpret sentences like (9) and (10) as if they said *The girl kissed the boy*, when they really mean the opposite. However, this does not seem to be the case. In fact, when non-fluent aphasics are asked to interpret sentences like (9) and (10), they treat *girl* as the agent only about half the time. Thus, it does not seem to be the case that non-fluent aphasics consistently use the "first noun is the agent" interpretation strategy.

Non-fluent aphasics do not consistently treat the first noun of passive sentences and sentences with other forms of long-distance dependencies as the agent of the action described by the sentence. As a result, Grodzinsky and colleagues propose that, when faulty representations fail to specify unambiguously who did what to whom, non-fluent aphasics basically just guess. So, if there are two nouns in a passive sentence, non-fluent aphasics will treat the first one as the agent about half the time; and they will treat the second noun as the agent about half the time. In active-voice sentences, no fillers or gaps are involved, so trace deletion does not apply, and non-fluent aphasics should be very highly accurate in figuring out who the agent is and who the patient is. In one sample of 42 non-fluent aphasic patients, this prediction (50% correct on passives and other filler-gap sentences, 100% correct on active voice and other *canonical* forms) was very consistent with the overall pattern of performance when picture matching was used to assess understanding. Figure 13.5 represents the data from this study. Percent correct appears on the *x*-axis. The *y*-axis represents the number of patients performing at different degrees of accuracy. The solid line represents performance on active-voice sentences. The dashed line represents performance on passives. Note that performance on passives is lower than performance on actives, and is centered around the 50% correct mark.

Data like these motivated Grodzinsky and colleagues to propose that the process that goes wrong in non-fluent aphasia is precisely the one that links up filler phrases with their canonical locations. He proposed that this highly specific language interpretation function is carried out in intact brains inside Broca's area (*pars opercularis* and *pars triangularis*) (Drai et al., 2001; Drai & Grodzinsky, 2006; Grodzinsky, 1986, 1995; Grodzinsky et al., 1999). This area is also responsible for speech planning processes, and so damage to Broca's area leads simultaneously to apraxia of speech. Hence, all patients with damage in Broca's area should have trouble connecting filler phrases and gap sites in addition to speech production problems; and patients without damage in Broca's area should be able to fill gaps (whether or not they have speech production problems). Regardless, because fillers and gaps play no role in the representation of active-voice sentences and other canonical forms, non-fluent aphasics should have no problem processing those kinds of sentences.

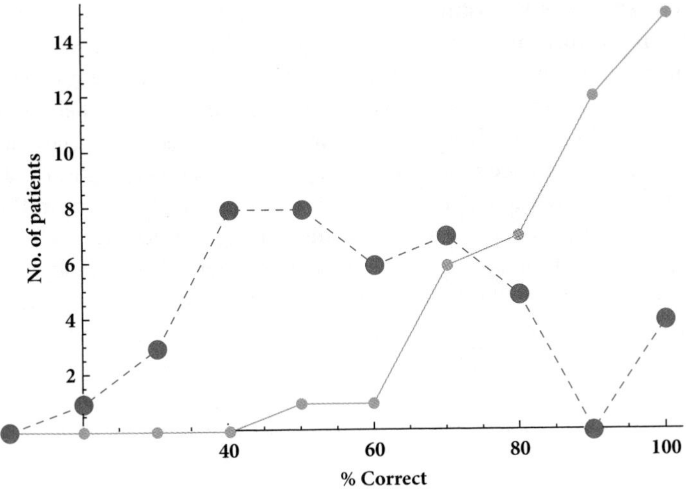

Figure 13.5 Number of patients vs. performance level in actives (full line) and passives (dashed); scores are for 42 patients (6–48 trials each) (from Grodzinsky et al., 1999)

Evidence against the trace deletion hypothesis

One potential problem with the trace deletion hypothesis is that its assumption that agrammatic aphasics have no problem processing active voice and other kinds of *canonical* sentences appears to be unsupported.[12] Recall that Zurif and his colleagues found that agrammatic aphasics showed abnormal patterns of priming in sentences with *subject relative* clauses (Zurif et al., 1993). This indicates that the formation of grammatical dependencies is impaired in agrammatic aphasics even when the elements appear in their normal, canonical order. Other canonical sentence forms also appear to cause problems for agrammatic aphasics. For example, Schwartz and colleagues (Schwartz et al., 1980) tested five agrammatic aphasics on sentences like (13):

(13) The box is in the cage.

Sentence (13) has two role-players, *box* and *cage*, that appear in the usual order for English (in English, *locative adjunct* modifiers, like *in the cage*, normally appear after the nouns that they modify). Schwartz and colleagues used sentence–picture matching to assess patients' understanding of canonical sentences like (13). Surprisingly, their five agrammatic aphasic patients made numerous errors in interpreting canonical sentences like (13). Even on simple, active sentences like (14), the patients were accurate only 75% of the time, which is above chance, but nowhere near 100% accurate.

(14) The dancer applauds the actor.

Gregory Hickok and colleagues (Hickok, Zurif, & Canseco-Gonzalez, 1993) provide further evidence that comprehension of canonical forms is impaired in non-fluent aphasia (see also Sherman & Schweikert, 1989). They tested a non-fluent aphasic patient's understanding of sentences like (15):

(15) The tiger that chases the lion is big.

This sentence expresses two distinct propositions (*the tiger is big* and *the tiger chases the lion*), but does not involve any constituents being out of their normal positions. The syntax of the sentence is not completely straightforward, however, as the comprehender needs to determine that *the lion* is part of a relative clause (*that chases the lion*) and is not directly a part of the subject of the main clause. That is, the sentence does *not* mean *the lion is big*, even though the end of the sentence says *the lion is big*. Because sentences like (15) do not involve any fillers or gaps, the trace deletion principle does not apply, and non-fluent aphasics should be able to understand them with a high degree of accuracy. However, when a non-fluent aphasic was tested using picture matching and truth-value judgment tasks,[13] his performance on sentences like (15) was at the same low level as his performance on sentences with long-distance dependencies (right at chance performance, i.e., he was guessing at the meaning), although his performance on other sentences without long-distance dependencies was very good (100% correct in one experiment, 88% correct in another experiment with *subject cleft* test sentences like *It was the horse that chased the cow*).

Next, the trace deletion hypothesis predicts that non-fluent aphasics will show a clear pattern of comprehension performance. Comprehension of passive and object relative sentences will be impaired, because representing the syntax of those sentences involves fillers and gaps. Comprehension of sentences in the active voice will be intact, because such sentences do not involve fillers and gaps. However, the empirical record of comprehension performance in non-fluent aphasia shows that this neat dichotomy does not accurately describe the way non-fluent aphasics respond to different kinds of sentences (e.g., Caplan et al., 2006). Some non-fluent aphasics are highly accurate in their comprehension of filler-gap sentences; some are highly inaccurate in their comprehension of canonical sentences (Caramazza et al., 2001; but see Grodzinsky et al., 1999 for a robust defense of the trace deletion hypothesis).

Another problem for the trace deletion hypothesis is that it predicts a fairly neat pattern of performance across different tasks. That is, because the deficit in non-fluent aphasia is the inability to compute long-distance dependencies, non-fluent aphasics should have trouble with any task that involves long-distance dependencies, and this does not appear to be the case. One kind of dissociation of task performance in non-fluent aphasia is the difference between comprehension tasks and grammaticality judgment tasks. Non-fluent aphasics look dysfunctional on a lot of comprehension tasks, but do very well on the same sentence types in grammaticality judgment (Caplan & Hildebrandt, 1988; Grodzinsky, 1995; Linebarger, 1995; Linebarger, Schwartz, & Saffran, 1983a). Further, within the comprehension domain, various tasks can be used to assess non-fluent aphasics' understanding (including picture-matching, truth-judgment, and *act-out* tasks in which patients listen to sentences and then move little figurines around to portray the meaning expressed by the test sentences). These different tasks could impose different loads on a variety of general cognitive resources, including attention and working memory, as well as language-specific components such as phonological short-term memory and gap-filling processes. It is not surprising, therefore, that non-fluent aphasics' accuracy varies depending on which kind of comprehension test is used to assess their degree of understanding (Caplan, 2006b; Caplan, Waters, & Hildebrandt, 1997; Cupples & Inglis, 1993). For example, Caplan and colleagues (2006) tested a group of 42 aphasic patients, none of whom had severe problems understanding the meaning of individual words. Hence, none of the patients would be classified as Wernicke's aphasics. All of them were right-handed and had focal lesions somewhere in the left hemisphere. If agrammatic aphasia is characterized by a general inability to deal with long-distance dependencies (as in the trace deletion hypothesis), then patients who show problems with passives or object relative clauses on one task (say, picture matching) should also have problems with the same sentences on other tasks (e.g., act-out or grammaticality judgment). This would represent a *task-independent* deficit. Because, according to the trace deletion hypothesis, the processing problem should occur only for some kinds of sentences, trace deletion predicts that agrammatic aphasics will show evidence of a *task-independent, structure-dependent* deficit. That is, they should have trouble with some kinds of sentences, no matter how you test them. They should interpret other kinds of sentences just like normal people do, again no matter how you test them. However, across the 42 patients that they tested, Caplan and his colleagues found only 2 who had a task-independent, structure-dependent deficit. Of those 2, only 1 had the pattern predicted by the trace deletion hypothesis—trouble with both passives and object relative clauses across multiple tasks, good performance on other sentence types across multiple tasks. Thus, the vast majority (over 90%) of this fairly large sample of patients had patterns of performance that do not fit into the trace deletion framework.

Finally, the trace deletion hypothesis predicts a very tight correlation between lesion location and pattern of comprehension deficit. Patients with lesions in Broca's area should have trouble understanding sentences that involve filler-gap dependencies, but should understand other kinds of sentences just fine. Patients with lesions outside Broca's area should be very accurate in understanding sentences with filler-gap dependencies. This neat pattern does not exist in the available data (Caplan, 2006b; and others; Dronkers et al., 2004).

The trace deletion hypothesis does not appear to do a very good job predicting the pattern of deficits that appear in agrammatic aphasics. It also does not seem to square very well with the imaging data that show that agrammatic symptoms appear in patients with lesions in various parts of the perisylvian regions of the left hemisphere outside of Broca's area. The next section reviews a number of alternative frameworks that have been developed to try to capture what goes wrong in agrammatic aphasia. It is important to recognize that none of these proposals has ironclad evidence in its favor. They are included because they are important proposals in the field of aphasiology.

The mapping hypothesis

The mapping hypothesis starts with the twin observations that agrammatic aphasics have intact syntactic representations and some ability to parse sentences, as evidenced by their ability to judge the grammaticality of various kinds of sentences combined with lack of ability to correctly interpret passives and various kinds of long-distance dependencies (see above). Thus, there is an apparent dissociation between performance in one domain (grammaticality judgment) and another domain (semantic interpretation). What is the problem? According to the mapping hypothesis (Linebarger, 1995; Linebarger, Schwartz, & Saffran, 1983a, 1983b; Schwartz et al., 1980), the problem is that agrammatic aphasics are unable to used structured representations to assign semantic roles to elements of sentences. As Marcia Linebarger and her colleagues explain (1983a, p. 387, emphasis theirs), "the problem agrammatic listeners have is not in *constructing* syntactic representations but in *exploiting* them in semantic interpretation." So, when non-fluent aphasic patients hear sentences, they do parse them, fill gaps, and compute other grammatical relations, but they are not able to use those structured representations to determine who did what to whom. This hypothesis has the primary advantage of being able to explain different patterns of performance on grammaticality judgment and interpretive tasks. Its primary disadvantage is that it is essentially a redescription of the data. Non-fluent aphasics do well on grammaticality judgment, they do poorly on interpretation, therefore their problem has to do with interpretation. This should not be read as minimizing the contribution, however. Clearly, the mapping hypothesis is both important and a clean departure from previous theorizing. It is certainly well worth knowing that access to intact grammatical knowledge is preserved to some degree in non-fluent aphasia.

The resource restriction hypothesis

If non-fluent aphasics can parse sentences, why can't they go ahead and use those syntactic structure representations to assign the appropriate meaning to the sentences? One possibility is that both building syntactic structures and assigning meaning to structured representations requires "resources." In normal individuals, there are enough resources to support both kinds of operations simultaneously. However, brain-damaged individuals suffer a reduction in resources, such that less demanding and more reflexive processes (like parsing) continue to be carried out, but more demanding and less reflexive processes (like using syntactic structures to assign thematic roles) fall by the wayside. Although this proposal is somewhat vague—we don't have particularly good independent methods to measure "resources"—there may in fact be data to support this position. For one, recall that one of the basic findings of the Caplan and Hildebrandt (1988) large-scale study was that knowing the amount of brain damage, rather than knowing lesion location, gave you the best chance at predicting how aphasics would perform on a variety of sentence types across a number of different language tasks. If there is a more or less straight line relationship between amount of intact brain tissue and "resources," then it makes sense that lesion size would relate to patients' accuracy and speed on various sentence interpretation tasks. This approach can also explain why an individual patient's performance can be very good on one task, but very poor on another task, when both tasks involve the same kind of sentence. It is probably safe to assume that the sentence itself imposes a constant burden on whatever processing resources are available, but there is no particularly good reason to believe that different tasks (e.g., picture matching and grammaticality judgment, for example) impose equal burdens on the available cognitive resources. If we assume that the total resource demand is an additive or multiplicative function of the sentence itself and the task that the patient is asked to undertake, then the resource limitation hypothesis would predict good performance only if the total resource demand was below the amount available. So, performance for a given sentence type might look normal if the comprehension task imposed few demands on the available resources, but performance on the exact same sentence type would look abnormal if the comprehension task imposed higher demands on the available resources.[14]

The slowed syntax hypothesis

The slowed syntax hypothesis posits that non-fluent aphasics' primary deficit is that they build syntactic structures slower than normal. This slowing could result from a reduction in the resources necessary to parse sentences (a reduction in the "syntactic workspace"; Caplan & Hildebrandt, 1988; Waters & Caplan, 1996). It could also occur because non-fluent aphasics cannot activate information associated with individual words fast enough to keep pace with other processes necessary to interpret sentences (slowed lexical access). In a way, this formulation bridges the mapping and resource restriction hypotheses. Slowed lexical access and slowed parsing could be the result of restricted resources and slowed parsing could, in turn, cause a failure to use syntactic representations to assign meaning. If the information from the lexicon is not available at the point in time where the syntactic structure has been built, then no thematic assignment will be possible. Conversely, if the syntactic structure has not been completed at the point when activated lexical information starts to decay, the aphasic patient will fail to connect individual lexical items to positions in a syntactic tree that determine what semantic roles they should play. This approach is summarized by Marcia Linebarger and her colleagues (1983a, p. 388): "Agrammatic aphasics are simply less efficient parsers than normal listeners; … they are capable of carrying out all of the necessary operations to achieve a full parse of input sentences, but at greater effort and computational expense than is normally the case." In addition to potentially unifying the resource restriction and mapping hypotheses, the slowed lexical access hypothesis may also be able to incorporate findings related to non-fluent aphasics' response to function words. Linebarger and her colleagues continue (p. 388), "the lack of special access routines for the closed class vocabulary slows down parsing, (but) it does not necessarily prevent it from happening."

Recently, researchers have subjected the slowed lexical access hypothesis to more direct testing. Recall that previous research (Caramazza et al., 1981; Zurif et al., 1993) suggested that non-fluent aphasics were incapable of performing gap-filling operations. That is, when probe words were presented immediately after gap sites, non-fluent aphasics did not show priming effects for target words that were semantically related to the filler phrase. Does that mean that non-fluent aphasics are totally incapable of filling gaps? Possibly. But what if their syntactic structure-building processes were just slow? If so, aphasics would be capable of filling gaps, they would just do so more slowly than normal. If non-fluent aphasics are slow, but can fill gaps, then priming effects should occur, just later than normal.

To test this prediction, Petra Burkhardt and her colleagues (Burkhardt, Piñango, & Wong, 2003) tested a group of non-fluent aphasic patients using the cross-modal lexical priming method that had been previously used to assesses gap-filling processes in aphasics and normal individuals. In the experiment, three non-fluent aphasics listened to sentences with object relative clauses, like (16):

(16) The kid loved *the cheese* [filler] which the brand new *1* microwave melted [gap] *2* yesterday afternoon *3* while the entire family was watching TV.

(*1*, *2*, and *3* mark the three points where probe words were presented.) Burkhardt and her colleagues tested the non-fluent aphasics' response to target words that were semantically related to the filler phrase (such as *cheddar*). Aphasics' responses were tested at three different points in the sentence (marked with asterisks in the example, above). One was before the gap, one was right at the gap, and one was a little over half a second after the gap site. Just as in previous experiments, non-fluent aphasics did not show any evidence of priming at the gap site (point *2*). But they did show priming at the later test point (point *3*). When tested about a half a second after the gap site, non-fluent aphasics responded faster to the semantically related target words (e.g., *cheddar*) than they did to control words that were unrelated to the filler phrase. Tracy Love and her colleagues (Love, Swinney, Walenski, & Zurif, 2008; Love, Swinney, & Zurif, 2001) tested a further eight non-fluent aphasics on very similar sentences, and found the same result—priming effects appeared about a half second after the gap site, but not at the gap site itself. Other studies also provided evidence that non-fluent aphasics are slower than normal at interpreting *reflexive pronouns* (like *himself* and *herself*), and processing other kinds of moved constituents (Burkhardt et al., 2003; Piñango and Burkhardt, 2001). These results suggest that parsing processes in non-fluent aphasia are not as reflexive and automatic as they are in normal individuals.[15] Whether this loss of automaticity is a cause or consequence of resource reduction or effortful lexical access is a question that needs further study.

Treatment and Recovery from Aphasia

Perhaps the best reason to study aphasia is that understanding the way language processing breaks down can lead to insights that help clinicians design better treatment methods to improve language function in aphasic patients. Can people who develop aphasia after brain damage get better and recover their ability to comprehend and produce language? One piece of good news about aphasia is that many patients recover a considerable amount of language function after suffering a stroke or tumor. Most patients with aphasia suffer the condition as the result of a stroke or a head injury. These conditions are non-progressive, meaning that once the initial episode is over, the brain does not experience further damage. In those kinds of cases, most patients experience improvements in language function starting as soon as a few days after the injury. Improvements in language function can occur over a span of several months to several years (Cappa & Vallar, 1992). In fact, one of Carl Wernicke's original patients, Susanne Adam, showed marked improvement in the production of grammatical forms within two weeks of the appearance of her aphasic symptoms, although she still had major difficulty understanding simple requests (Mathews et al., 1994). A little over three weeks after she first fell ill, Susanne Adam understood almost everything that she heard, she was able to detect and correct errors in her own spontaneous speech, as well as repeat sentences on demand. Her speech was not entirely normal, but it was greatly improved from when she was first examined. Her most significant long-lasting symptom was an inability to write spontaneously or to write down things she was told. So, suffering from aphasia is not a permanent condition in all cases—many patients recover significant language functions after they get over their original trauma. But what determines whether someone will recover from aphasia? What kinds of treatments are available for aphasic patients and are they effective?

Recovery of function may reflect the return of physical functioning of neurons in the damaged hemisphere outside the parts of the brain that were destroyed, it may reflect the reorganization of functions in the brain to circumvent the damaged area, or it could reflect a change in lateralization, such that the non-damaged right hemisphere takes over some of the functions that were previously dominated by left-hemisphere structures (Cardebat et al., 2004; Crinion & Price, 2005; Duffau et al., 2003; Stein, Rosen, & Butters, 1974; Weiller et al., 1995). Some researchers believe that aphasic symptoms following left-hemisphere damage occur because the right hemisphere is relatively over-active (Belin et al., 1996; Martin et al., 2004). That is, aphasics' symptoms are the result of the right hemisphere muscling in and displacing functions previously performed by the now weakened left hemisphere. These researchers have used *transcranial magnetic stimulation* (TMS) to interfere with neural functioning in the intact right-hemisphere regions in stroke patients. TMS involves applying a very strong magnetic field right next to someone's scalp. This induces low-grade current flow in the brain, which in turn causes neurons to depolarize and fire. When TMS was applied repeatedly (10 times) over the right hemisphere of a group of non-fluent aphasics, their ability to name novel pictures was improved.

Right-hemisphere regions may be recruited following left-hemisphere brain damage because the left-hemisphere areas are unable to function. So, rather than being a cause of poor language function, an "over-active" right hemisphere might be the result of left-hemisphere damage. That is, less efficient right-hemisphere mechanisms take over because the left hemisphere can't do the job. If so, we would expect to see increasing amounts of right-hemisphere activity in patients who show lesser language abilities following a stroke. This possibility has been investigated using functional imaging techniques (Cao, Vikingstad, George, Johnson, & Welch, 1999). fMRI was used to assess language-related activity in both hemispheres in a group of non-fluent aphasic patients. Some of the patients showed more bilateral activation in response to picture-naming and verb-generation tasks,[16] and some showed predominantly right-sided activation. Patients who had more bilateral activation had better performance on the language tasks than patients whose activation was greater in the right hemisphere. These results may indicate that the right hemisphere makes relatively larger contributions to language functions as left-hemisphere function is more degraded.

There appear to be physical constraints on the extent to which patients can recover language function following brain damage. First, the size of the lesion appears to matter quite a bit. The amount of brain tissue in the posterior perisylvian region that is destroyed by stroke correlates with language function in both the immediate post-stroke period (two to four weeks) as well as the longer term (a year or more post-stroke).[17] As was noted previously, small focal lesions located within the classically defined Broca's area are associated with short-lived speech and comprehension problems. Larger focal lesions, especially those that include subcortical white-matter tracts and the basal ganglia are associated with more severe forms of non-fluent aphasia. One reason why larger focal lesions lead to more severe and long-lasting symptoms may be because brain regions bordering those areas that are normally involved in language-processing functions are similar enough at the level of individual neurons that they are able to take over some language-processing functions that they would not normally participate in. In a sample of 22 Wernicke's aphasics, those with damage to supramarginal and angular gyrus had poorer long-term outcomes than patients without damage to those regions (Kertesz, Lau, & Polk, 1993). Finally, the kind of injury that the patient sustained also correlates with the degree of dysfunction. In general, head injury patients do better over the long term than stroke patients.

Treatment options for aphasia include pharmacological therapy (drugs) and various forms of speech therapy.[18] Let's review pharmacological therapy before turning to speech therapy. One of the main problems that happens following strokes is that damage to the blood vessels in the brain reduces the blood flow to perisylvian brain regions, and *hypometabolism*—less than normal activity—in those regions likely contributes to aphasic symptoms. Therefore, some pharmacological treatments focus on increasing the blood supply to the brain, and those treatments have been shown to be effective in some studies (Kessler, Thiel, Karbe, & Heiss, 2001). The period immediately following the stroke appears to be critical in terms of intervening to preserve function. For example, aphasia symptoms can be alleviated by drugs that increase blood pressure if they are administered very rapidly when the stroke occurs (Wise, Sutter, & Burkholder, 1972). During this period, aphasic symptoms will reappear if blood pressure is allowed to fall, even if the patient's blood pressure is not abnormally low. In later stages of recovery, blood pressure can be reduced without causing the aphasic symptoms to reappear. Other treatment options capitalize on the fact that the brain has some ability to reorganize itself following an injury (this ability is called *neural plasticity*). It turns out that stimulant drugs, including amphetamines, appear to magnify or boost brain reorganization. When stimulants are taken in the period immediately following a stroke, and patients are also given speech-language therapy, their language function improves more than control patients who receive speech-language therapy and a placebo in the six months after their strokes (Walker-Batson et al., 2001).

Behavioral speech therapies normally supplement physical, pharmacological treatments for aphasia, and the good news is that a range of effective therapies is available. A review involving over 800 cases showed that intense therapy can improve both comprehension and production outcomes in aphasia (Bhogal, Teasell, & Speechley, 2003), and the more therapy an individual patient receives, the better their outcomes are. Further, intense therapy provided over a shorter span of time proved to be more effective than less intensive therapy provided over a more extended period. So, it's better to receive eight or more hours of therapy per week for a few weeks than it is to give two hours of therapy a week for several months. The bad news is that it is not always clear which therapy will work best for an individual patient (Nickels & Best, 1996).

Some speech therapy techniques are designed to exploit both neural plasticity of the damaged hemisphere and the recruitment of intact homologous (*same region*) brain areas in the opposite hemisphere. *Melodic intonation therapy* (MIT) represents one such technique (Albert, Sparks, & Helm, 1973; Schlaug, Marchina, & Norton, 2008; Sparks, Helm, & Albert, 1974; Sparks & Holland, 1976). In this form of therapy, melodic musical patterns are overlaid onto short phrases. The treatment program begins with the therapist humming short melodic phrases and having the patient hum along and tap the beat as well. The next step is to introduce words and have the patient sing along. Next, a short delay is inserted before the patient responds. Finally, the musical aspects of the phrases are gradually reduced until the output sounds more like normal speech. The idea behind MIT is to recruit intact right-hemisphere regions that normally play a role in singing or producing prosodic features during regular speaking. Although there are not a lot of outcome studies to prove that MIT is generally effective, some data do suggest that non-fluent aphasic patients benefit from this kind of therapy, and that exposure to this kind of therapy changes the way their brains respond to spoken language. For example, Belin and colleagues (1996) used PET imaging to study seven non-fluent aphasics who had undergone between one month and nine years of MIT. The patients' tasks in the experiment were to listen passively to words spoken and to repeat words with and without MIT contours. Greater left-hemisphere frontal lobe activation was observed in the MIT conditions, and there was also a reduction in "inappropriate" activations in the right-hemisphere homologue of Wernicke's area.

Other forms of therapy are designed to help patients improve their ability to successfully activate the lexical representations of words, which could help both fluent and non-fluent aphasics. Non-fluent aphasics could benefit from increasing their ability to activate the appropriate phonological information to express the concepts that they wish to convey. Non-fluent aphasics may benefit from improved lexical access if we assume that part of their problem is that lexical access is not keeping pace with other language comprehension and production processes. Different treatment techniques have been developed that target phrase- and sentence-level grammatical processes (e.g., Thompson, Shapiro, Tait, Jacobs, & Schneider, 1996).

One way to try to enhance lexical access involves *intensive semantic training* (IST; Davis, Harrington, & Baynes, 2006).[19] In IST, the interventions ask patients to judge various aspects of words and sentences but they do *not* make the patient say the words and sentences out loud. The idea is to allow patients the opportunity to practice retrieving or constructing various aspects of the speech input, without compelling them to practice making errors (see also Warriner & Humphreys, 2008). In IST, patients are presented with pictures of common objects and they are asked to think of various properties of the names of those objects, such as how many syllables it has, what sound it begins with, what the name rhymes with and so forth. After sufficient practice, patients are able to name the pictured objects at a greater degree of accuracy than before treatment.

In one Wernicke's aphasic patient who received IST, fMRI data showed increases in activation in left inferior frontal gyrus after IST (Davis et al., 2006). This patient's accuracy on naming also improved. One critical test of any treatment method is whether the improvement in performance transfers to non-practiced items. In this case, the patient included more content nouns in his spontaneous speech after treatment than before, suggesting that the IST effects did generalize beyond the concepts targeted directly by the treatment.

Similar principles have been applied to boost phonological access processes in a non-fluent aphasic patient (Davis, Farias, & Baynes, 2009). In the phonological form of the treatment, the patient is given a written word and is then played a series of words, one of which matches the written word. The patient is asked to indicate which of the samples matches the written word, but is discouraged from overtly naming the written word during the training phase. The purpose of this exercise is to increase the patient's awareness of phonological contrasts, again without giving the patient the opportunity to practice making errors. As in IST, this kind of phonological awareness intervention helped improve the intelligibility of the patient's speech, and the benefits extended to words outside the training set.[20]

A related treatment method, *phonological components analysis* (PCA; Leonard, Rochon, & Laird, 2008) also gives patients the opportunity to practice activating components of target items without overtly naming the pictured object. If the patient can successfully supply five phonological features of the target word, the patient is then asked to name the object. If the patient is not able to supply any of the characteristics of the name (how many syllables it has, what it starts with, what it ends with, and so forth), the clinician provides the patient with a number of options and asks the patient to choose one. If the patient is really stuck, the clinician provides the answer and asks the patient to repeat it. Carol Leonard and her colleagues treated 10 patients, 9 of whom had a form of non-fluent aphasia and 1 of whom had Wernicke's aphasia, using PCA. Out of the 10 patients, 7 showed improvement in naming ability after treatment, and improvements extended beyond the set of trained words. The 3 patients who did not show significant improvement were among the most disabled prior to the treatment phase of the study.

One reason why treatments like IST and PCA are effective is that they give patients the opportunity to choose between different competing representations. The intervention assumes that when patients look at a picture, information related to the pictured concept will be activated, but so will information that competes with the pictured concept (as proposed by various interactive accounts of lexical processing, see Chapter 3, and discourse processing, see Chapter 5). Thus, to correctly name the object in the picture, aphasics must successfully ignore or suppress activated but irrelevant information. Having patients produce information associated with the target concept, without overtly naming it, gives them the chance to practice ignoring or inhibiting irrelevant information and prevents them from strengthening any tendency to say the wrong thing.

Summary and Conclusions

To conclude, let's return to the questions that motivated this chapter in the first place.

(1) *Are different parts of the brain specialized to undertake specific language-processing tasks?* There is considerable evidence from the imaging of intact brains that some parts of the brain do consistently participate in some language functions in different individuals (e.g., Stromswold, Caplan, Alpert, & Rauch, 1996). Some evidence from studies of brain-damaged patients also points towards the critical contribution of specific brain areas to specific language functions. In particular, the insula seems to play a vital role in speech production (e.g., Dronkers, 1996; Dronkers et al., 2004; Shafto, Stamatakis, Tam, & Tyler, 2008).

(2) *If so, which bits do which jobs?* This question is harder to answer. Producing and understanding language requires the action of both classically described sensory (posterior) brain regions and classically described motor (anterior) brain regions. Although some researchers argue that specific tasks, like the construction of syntactic *traces*, takes place in specific brain regions (i.e., Broca's area in the left inferior frontal gyrus), neuroanatomical and behavioral studies have cast substantial doubt on these claims. Outside individual case studies, there does not appear to be consistent evidence that damaging specific regions of the neocortex interferes with only a small subset of the processes necessary to produce and understand language. Thus, there is no clear evidence that specific language functions are localized to small, well-defined regions of the brain.

(3) *Are all people's brains organized the same way for language?* As we have seen, we can learn a lot about language by studying the way language processing breaks down when different parts of the brain are damaged. If the same brain areas are involved in the same language-processing tasks in all people, then different individuals with brain damage in the same areas should show the same pattern of deficits. However, one frustrating fact for theories that link specific language functions to specific places in the brain is that no two brains are identical and, when people experience brain damage, no two lesions are ever in exactly comparable places. In fact, the pattern of language-processing deficits varies substantially across different people who have damage to comparable regions in the brain. Some people who have lesions in the left frontal lobe in what is classically considered *Broca's* area do not show the characteristic halting, agrammatic speech with spared comprehension typically associated with *Broca's aphasia*. While others who have damage in other parts of the frontal

lobes do have the symptoms characteristic of that disorder (Caplan & Waters, 2006). Thus, it is *not* safe to conclude either that particular language functions are completely localized to particular brain regions or that everyone's brains are organized the same way. It is more likely that even basic language functions, like producing a sentence, require the coordinated action of a broad network of brain regions. How, exactly, this activity is coordinated remains to be described and explained. So, to close this chapter, I want to leave you with a homework assignment based on a question raised by Mathews and colleagues (1994, p. 461) years ago: "How is it possible that diffuse lesions can give rise to a pattern of language deficit, virtually identical to that of a focal lesion?" Answering this question is a task that the current generation of language scientists will pass to the next generation of language scientists.

TEST YOURSELF

1. Describe the WADA test. What has WADA testing revealed about the neural underpinnings of language?
2. Compare and contrast the localizationist and equipotentiality hypotheses. Describe evidence that favors each approach.
3. Describe Wernicke's theory of "sensory" and "motor" aphasias. To what did he attribute each kind of deficit? What did Geschwind add to Wernicke's ideas (and why) to produce the "classic"/WLG model of aphasia?
4. Compare and contrast Broca's/non-fluent, Wernicke's/fluent, and conduction aphasias.
5. What evidence suggests that the WLG model is inaccurate? What should replace the WLG model?
6. What kinds of syntactic parsing problems do Broca's and Wernicke's aphasics experience? How well does the trace deletion hypothesis explain these problems? What evidence challenges the trace deletion hypothesis. Describe results suggesting that grammatical knowledge is preserved in fluent and non-fluent aphasias.
7. Compare and contrast the mapping, resource restriction, and slowed syntax hypotheses.
8. What treatments are available for aphasia? Which are the most effective?

THINK ABOUT IT

1. Language scientists are deeply divided about what Broca's area does. Some believe that it performs highly specific language computations (like forming traces). Others believe that Broca's area contributes to language processing by supplying working memory resources. Still others think that the area is involved in planning or sequencing speech movements. What is your view? What do you think Broca's area does?

1 Although rare, the right hemisphere is sometimes the dominant language hemisphere in right-handed people. Evidence for this conclusion comes from cases of *crossed aphasia*, disturbance of normal language function that occurs in the same hemisphere that controls the dominant hand (right hemisphere in right-handers). Because left-handers tend to have variable dominance for language, *crossed aphasia* is normally diagnosed only for right-handed patients (Hartman & Goodsett, 2003). Crossed aphasia is usually accompanied by visual neglect, functional blindness to objects in the left hemifield (i.e., the patient is effectively blind to all objects that are to the left of where the patient is looking). Although non-fluent (Broca's or agrammatic) crossed aphasia is the most common form of crossed aphasia, crossed versions of Wernicke's (or fluent) aphasia have been reported (Mansur, Radanovic, Penha, de Mendonça, & Adda, 2006).

2 Prins and Bastiaanse (2006, p. 763) write, "The first reference to aphasic phenomena that we know of comes from the so-called 'Surgical papyrus of Edwin Smith,' which was discovered in 1862 in the Egyptian city of Luxor. This was written about 1700 BC (although the original text is thought to have been written several centuries earlier)."

3 Precursors to Broca include Jean-Baptiste Buillaud, who described eight patients with speech production problems and frontal lobe damage contrasted with six patients without speech disorder who had intact frontal lobes, and Marc Dax, who argued for left-hemisphere language dominance on the basis of a set of patients with speech problems and right-sided *hemiparesis* (paralysis of half of the body).

4 Caspari (2005) reports that Carl Wernicke was killed in a traffic accident involving an ox cart. If so, he is probably the only neurologist in history to be killed by a farm animal. If you know of any other examples, please contact the author.

5 Some authors believe that Wernicke's mentor, Theodor Meynert, actually deserves credit for discovering fluent aphasia (Eling, 2006). Meynert appears to have described a case of fluent aphasia as early as 1866. Wernicke's book about aphasia was published in 1874.

6 Language disturbances do occur following forms of brain damage that result in general declines in intellectual ability. For example, aphasia symptoms can occur in patients with Alzheimer's dementia, a brain disorder that is associated with a general atrophy (reduction) in brain tissue and the accumulation of "plaques and tangles" on the surface of the cerebral cortex. However, dementia involves significant behavior and emotional changes, plus mental confusion, that are not normally observable in patients with "pure" language disorders (Mathews et al., 1994).

7 Sometimes Wernicke's aphasia is described as primarily the inability to understand speech and written language. Some clinicians (D. Caplan, personal communication) see evidence in the spoken output of Wernicke's aphasics that they do understand some of the input they receive, and recognize that their own output does not express their intended meaning. For example, in the video referenced above, the patient with Wernicke's aphasia makes a contextually appropriate attempt to describe how many years he had been a dentist, even though he produces a variety of numbers, none of which appear to express an accurate estimate of how long he was a dentist.

8 Patients most often show a mixture of agrammatic and paragrammatic speech (Caplan, 2006a; De Bleser, 1987).

9 One way to interpret this pattern of performance is to relate it to Baddeley's model of working memory. Conduction aphasia would seem to be a fairly straightforward failure of the articulatory loop component of the working-memory system described in Baddeley's model (Baddeley, 1986; Baddeley & Hitch, 1974).

10 One thing that complicates the interpretation of these findings is that, in the picture-matching task, the pictures that go along with the "correct" meaning of sentences like (2) depict events that could not possibly happen in the real world (you have a picture of a piece of cheese eating a mouse). Thus, a person could do really well on the task even if she did not understand the sentence at all, just by pointing to the picture of an event that could happen in the real world.

11 Although they do come and go slowly over time. For example, modern English is gradually losing the relative pronoun *whom*. Its functions are being taken over by the word *who*.

12 Remember that *canonical* sentences are those sentences where the verbatim (or surface) form is the simplest and most straightforward way to express the meaning conveyed by the sentence.

13 In truth-value judgment tasks, patients hear a sentence and then see a single picture. They are asked to judge whether the picture expresses the same meaning as the sentence they just heard.

14 But see MacDonald and Christiansen (2002) for a strong and well-reasoned critique of the resource limitation hypothesis.

15 Michael Walsh Dickey studied gap-filling processes in aphasics using the visual world paradigm, focusing on processing of *wh*-questions, like *Who did the boy kiss that day at school?* and object relatives like *Point to who the bride was tickling at the mall* (Walsh Dickey, Choy, & Thompson, 2007; Walsh Dickey and Thompson, 2006). Non-fluent aphasics made rapid eye movements to the appropriate visual target (a picture of a girl right after the word *kiss*; the patient of the tickling action right after the verb *tickling*). Dickey and his colleagues

argue that gap-filling processes are still essentially reflexive and automatic in non-fluent aphasia. If so, slowed or delayed priming effects in the cross-modal lexical priming paradigm may reflect the load imposed by the task, rather than being a pure measure of gap-filling processes.

16 In the verb-generation task, patients are shown a picture of an object (like a knife) and asked to produce a verb that goes along with that object (like *cut*).

17 The degree to which brain tissue is destroyed, and therefore the degree of function that is preserved, is strongly affected by how long treatment is delayed after a stroke starts. So, it is important to begin treatment as soon as possible. Here are some of the warning signs of stroke:

- Sudden numbness or weakness of the face, arm or leg, especially on one side of the body
- Sudden confusion, trouble speaking or understanding
- Sudden trouble seeing in one or both eyes
- Sudden trouble walking, dizziness, loss of balance or coordination
- Sudden, severe headache with no known cause

If someone you know experiences any of these warning signs, seek medical help immediately.

18 And the aforementioned experimental TMS therapy.

19 Many thanks to Dr. Kathy Baynes for bringing this therapy technique to my attention. May her successful treatment efforts continue to confound medical staff everywhere.

20 And subjectively, patients report enjoying IST and the phonological training version a lot (K. Baynes, personal communication).

References

Albert, M. L., Sparks, R. W., & Helm, N.A. (1973). Melodic intonation therapy for aphasia. *Archives of Neurology, 29,* 130–131.

Amici, S., Gorno-Tempini, M. L., Ogar, J. M., Dronkers, N. F., & Miller, B. L. (2006). An overview of primary progressive aphasia and its variants. *Behavioral Neurology, 17,* 77–87.

Baddeley, A. D. (1986). *Working memory.* Oxford, England: Oxford University Press.

Baddeley, A. D., & Hitch, G. J. (1974). Working memory. In G. A. Bower (Ed.), *The psychology of learning and motivation: Vol. 8. Advances in Research and Theory* (pp. 47–89). San Diego, CA: Academic Press.

Baldo, J. V., Klostermann, E. C., & Dronkers, N. F. (2008). It's either a cook or a baker: Patients with conduction aphasia get the gist but lose the trace. *Brain & Language, 105,* 134–140.

Bates, E., Friederici, A., & Wulfeck, B. (1987). Grammatical morphology in aphasia: Evidence from three languages. *Cortex, 23,* 545–574.

Bates, E., Wilson, S. M., Saygin, A. P., Dick, F., Sereno, M. I., Knight, R. T. et al. (2003). Voxel-based lesion–symptom mapping. *Nature Neuroscience, 6,* 448–450.

Belin, P., Van Eeckhout, P., Zilbovicius, M., Remy, P., Françoise, C., Guillaume, S., et al. (1996). Recovery from nonfluent aphasia after melodic intonation therapy: A PET study. *Neurology, 47,* 1504–1511.

Berndt, R., & Caramazza, A. (1980). A redefinition of the syndrome of Broca's aphasia. *Applied Psycholinguistics, 1,* 225–278.

Berndt, R. S., & Caramazza, A. (1982). Phrase comprehension after brain damage. *Applied Psycholinguistics, 3,* 263–278.

Bhogal, S. K., Teasell, R., & Speechley, M. (2003). Intensity of aphasia therapy, impact on recovery. *Stroke, 34,* 987–993.

Brunner, R. J., Kornhuber, H. H., Seemüller, E., Suger, G., & Wallesch, C. W. (1982). Basal ganglia participation in language pathology. *Brain & Language, 16,* 281–299.

Burkhardt, P., Piñango, M. M., & Wong, K. (2003). The role of anterior left hemisphere in real-time sentence comprehension: Evidence from split intransitivity. *Brain & Language, 86,* 9–22.

Cao, Y., Vikingstad, E. M., George, K. P., Johnson, A. F., & Welch, K. M. A. (1999). Cortical language activation in stroke patients recovering from aphasia with functional MRI. *Stroke, 30,* 23313–2340.

Caplan, D. (2006a). Aphasic deficits in syntactic processing. *Cortex, 42,* 797–804.

Caplan, D. (2006b). Why is Broca's area involved in syntax? *Cortex, 42,* 469–471.

Caplan, D., DeDe, G., & Michaud, J. (2006). Task-independent and task-specific syntactic deficits in aphasic comprehension. *Aphasiology, 20,* 893–920.

Caplan, D., & Hildebrandt, N. (1988). *Disorders of syntactic comprehension*. Cambridge, MA: MIT Press.
Caplan, D., & Waters, G. (2006). Comprehension disorders in aphasia: The case of sentences that require syntactic analysis. In M. A. Gernsbacher & M. J. Traxler (Eds.), *The handbook of psycholinguistics* (2nd ed., pp. 939–966). San Diego, CA: Elsevier.
Caplan, D., Waters, G. S., & Hildebrandt, N. (1997). Determinants of sentence comprehension in aphasic patients in sentence-picture matching tasks. *Journal of Speech, Language, and Hearing Research, 40,* 542–555.
Cappa, S. F., & Vallar, G. (1992). The role of the left and right hemispheres in recovery from aphasia. *Aphasiology, 6,* 359–372.
Caramazza, A., & Berndt, R. S. (1978). Semantic and syntactic processes in aphasia: A review of the literature. *Psychological Bulletin, 85,* 898–918.
Caramazza, A., Berndt, R. S., Basili, A. G., & Koller, J. J. (1981). Syntactic processing deficits in aphasia. *Cortex, 17,* 333–348.
Caramazza, A., Capitani, E., Rey, A., & Berndt, R. S. (2001). Agrammatic Broca's aphasia is not associated with a single pattern of comprehension performance. *Brain and Language, 76,* 158–184.
Caramazza, A., & Zurif, E. B. (1976). Dissociation of algorithmic and heuristic processes in language comprehension: Evidence from aphasia. *Brain & Language, 3,* 572–582.
Cardebat, D., Demonet, J. F., de Boissezon, X., Marie, N., Marié, R. M., Lambert, J., et al. (2004). Behavioral and neurofunctional changes over time in healthy and aphasic subjects: A PET language activation study. *Stroke, 34,* 2900–2906.
Caspari, I. (2005). Wernicke's Aphasia. In L. Lapointe (Ed.), *Aphasia and related neurogenic language disorders* (3rd ed., pp. 152–154). New York: Thieme.
Catani, M., Jones, D. K., and ffytche, D. H. (2005). Perisylvian language networks of the human brain. *Annals of Neurology, 57,* 8–16.
Chomsky, N. (1981). *Lectures on government and binding*. Dordrecht, Holland: Foris.
Corina, D., & McBurney, S. L. (2001). The neural representation of language in users of American Sign Language. *Journal of Communication Disorders, 34,* 455–471.
Crinion, J., & Price, C. J. (2005). Right anterior superior temporal activation predicts auditory sentence comprehension following aphasic stroke. *Brain, 128,* 2858–2871.
Cupples, L., & Inglis, A. L. (1993). When task demands induce "asyntactic" comprehension: A study of sentence interpretation in aphasia. *Cognitive Neuropsychology, 10,* 201–234.
Davis, C., Farias, D., & Baynes, K. (2009). Implicit phoneme manipulation for the treatment of apraxia of speech and co-occurring aphasia. *Aphasiology, 23,* 503–528.
Davis, C. H., Harrington, G., and Baynes, K. (2006). Intensive semantic intervention in fluent aphasia: A case study. *Aphasiology, 20,* 59–83.
De Bleser, R. (1987). From agrammatism to paragrammatisms: German aphasiological traditions and grammatical disturbances. *Cognitive Neuropsychology, 4,* 187–256.
Dick, F., Bates, E., Wulfeck, B., Utman, J. A., Dronkers, N., & Gernsbacher, M. A. (2001). Language deficits, localization and grammar: Evidence for a distributive model of language breakdown in aphasic patients and neurologically intact individuals. *Psychological Review, 108,* 759–788.
Drai, D., & Grodzinsky, Y. (2006). A new empirical angle on the variability debate: Quantitative neurosyntactic analyses of a large data set from Broca's Aphasia. *Brain & Language, 96,* 117–128.
Drai, D., Grodzinsky, Y., & Zurif, E. (2001). Broca's aphasia is associated with a single pattern of comprehension performance: A reply. *Brain & Language, 76,* 185–192.
Dronkers, N. F. (1996). A new brain region for coordinating speech articulation. *Nature, 384,* 159–161.
Dronkers, N. F., Plaisant, O., Iba-Zizen, M. T., & Cabanis, E. A. (2007). Paul Broca's historic cases: High resolution MR imaging of the brains of Leborgne and Lelong. *Brain, 130,* 1432–1441.
Dronkers, N. F., Redfern, B. B., & Ludy, C. (1998). Brain regions associated with conduction aphasia and echoic rehearsal. *Journal of the International Neuropsychological Society, 4,* 23–24.
Dronkers, N. F., Wilkins D. P., Van Valin, R. D., Redfern B. B., & Jaeger, J. J. (2004). Lesion analysis of the brain areas involved in language comprehension. *Cognition, 92,* 145–77.
Druks, J., & Froud, K. (2002). The syntax of single words: Evidence from a patient with a selective function word reading deficit. *Cognitive Neuropsychology, 19,* 207–244.

Duffau, H., Capelle, L., Denvil, D., Sichez, N., Gatignoal, P., & Lopes, M. (2003). Functional recovery after surgical resection of low grade gliomas in eloquent brain: Hypothesis of brain compensation. *Journal of Neurology, Neurosurgery, & Psychiatry, 74,* 901–907.

Eling, P. (2006). Meynert on Wernicke's aphasia. *Cortex, 42,* 811–816.

Finger, S. (2001). *Origins of neuroscience: A history of explorations into brain function.* Oxford, England: Oxford University Press.

Friederici, A. (1988). Autonomy and automaticity: Accessing *function words* during sentence comprehension. In G. Denes, C. Semenaz, & P. Bisiacchi (Eds.), *Perspectives on cognitive neurophsychology* (pp. 115–133). Hillsdale, NJ: Erlbaum.

Geschwind, N. (1965). Disconnection syndromes in animals and man. *Brain, 88,* 237–294.

Goodglass, H., & Baker, E. (1976). Semantic field, naming, and auditory comprehension in aphasia. *Brain & Language, 3,* 359–374.

Grodzinsky, Y. (1986). Language deficits and the theory of syntax. *Brain & Language, 27,* 135–159.

Grodzinsky, Y. (1995). A restrictive theory of agrammatic comprehension. *Brain & Language, 50,* 27–51.

Grodzinsky, Y., Piñango, M. M., Zurif, E., & Drai, D. (1999). The critical role of group studies in neuropsychology: Comprehension regularities in Broca's aphasia. *Brain & Language, 67,* 134–147.

Hartman, D. E., & Goodsett, M. (2003). A case of crossed aphasia. *Gunderson Lutheran Medical Journal, 2,* 43–46.

Heilman, K. M., & Scholes, R. J. (1976). The nature of comprehension errors in Broca's, conduction, and Wernicke's aphasics. *Cortex, 12,* 258–265.

Hickok, G., Zurif, E., & Canseco-Gonzalez, E. (1993). Structural description of agrammatic comprehension. *Brain & Language, 45,* 371–395.

Kertesz, A., Lau, W. K., & Polk, M. (1993). The structural determinants of recovery in Wernicke's aphasia. *Brain & Language, 44,* 153–164.

Kessler, J., Thiel, A., Karbe, H., & Heiss, W. D. (2001). Piracetam improves activated blood flow and facilitates rehabilitation of poststroke aphasic patients. *Stroke, 31,* 2112–2116.

Lanczik, M., & Keil, G. (1991). Carl Wernicke's localization theory and its significance for the development of scientific psychiatry. *History of Psychiatry, 2,* 171–180.

Leonard, C., Rochon, E., & Laird, L. (2008). Treating naming impairments in aphasia: Findings from a phonological components analysis treatment. *Aphasiology, 22,* 923–947.

Linebarger, M. C. (1995). Agrammatism as evidence about grammar. *Brain & Language, 50,* 52–91.

Linebarger, M. C., Schwartz, M., & Saffran, E. (1983a). Sensitivity to grammatical structure in so-called agrammatic aphasics. *Cognition, 13,* 361–392.

Linebarger, M. C., Schwartz, M., & Saffran, E. (1983b). Syntactic processing in agrammatism: A reply to Zurif and Grodzinsky. *Cognition, 15,* 215–225.

Love, T., Swinney, D., Walenski, M., & Zurif, E. (2008). How left inferior frontal cortex participates in syntactic processing: Evidence from aphasia. *Brain & Language, 107,* 203–219.

Love, T., Swinney, D., & Zurif, E. (2001). Aphasia and the time-course of processing long distance dependencies. *Brain & Language, 79,* 169–171.

MacDonald, M. C., & Christiansen, M. H. (2002). Reassessing working memory: Comment on Just and Carpenter (1992) and Waters and Caplan (1996). *Psychological Review, 109,* 35–54.

Mansur, L. L., Radanovic, M., Penha, S. S., de Mendonça, L. I. Z., & Adda, C. C. (2006). Language and visuospatial impairment in a case of crossed aphasia. *Laterality, 11,* 525–539.

Martin, P. I., Naeser, M. A., Theoret, H., Tormos, J. M., Nicholas, M., Kurland, J., et al. (2004). Transcranial magnetic stimulation as a complementary treatment for aphasia. *Seminars in Speech and Language, 25,* 181–191.

Martin, R. C. (2003). Language processing: Functional organization and neuroanatomical basis. *Annual Review of Psychology, 54,* 55–89.

Mathews, P. J., Obler, L. K., & Albert, M. L. (1994). Wernicke and Alzheimer on the language disturbances of dementia and aphasia. *Brain & Language, 46,* 439–462.

Mauner, G., Fromkin, V., & Cornell, T. (1993). Comprehension and acceptability judgments in agrammatism: Disruption in the syntax of referential dependency. *Brain & Language, 45,* 340–370.

Mohr, J. P., Pessin, M. S., Finkelstein, S., Funkenstein, H. H., Duncan, G. W., & Davis, K. R. (1978). Broca's aphasia: Pathologic and clinical. *Neurology, 28,* 311–324.

Murdoch, B. E. (1988). Computerized tomographic scanning: Its contributions to the understanding of the neuroanatomical basis of aphasia. *Aphasiology, 2,* 437–462.

Newman, A. J., Bavelier, D., Corina, D., Jezzard, P., & Neville, H. J. (2002). A critical period for right hemisphere recruitment in American Sign Language processing. *Nature Neuroscience, 5,* 76–80.

Nickels, L., & Best, W. (1996). Therapy for naming disorders (Part I): Principles, puzzles, and progress. *Aphasiology, 10,* 21–47.

Penfield, W., & Roberts, L. (1959). *Speech and brain mechanisms.* Princeton, NJ: Princeton University Press.

Piñango, M. M., & Burkhardt, P. (2001). Pronominals in Broca's aphasia comprehension: The consequences of syntactic delay. *Brain & Language, 79,* 167–168.

Prins, R., & Bastiaanse, R. (2006). The early history of aphasiology: From the Egyptian surgeons (c. 1700 BC) to Broca (1861). *Aphasiology, 20,* 762–791.

Rasmussen, T., & Milner, B. (1977). The role of early left brain injury in determining lateralization of cerebral speech functions. *Annals of the New York Academy of Sciences, 299,* 355–369.

Rayner, K., & Pollatsek, A. (1989). *The psychology of reading.* Hillsdale, NJ: Erlbaum.

Saffran, E. M., Berndt, R. S., & Schwartz, M. F. (1989). The quantitative analysis of agrammatic production: Procedure and data. *Brain & Language, 37,* 440–479.

Schlaug, G., Marchina, S., & Norton, A. (2008). From singing to speaking: Why singing may lead to recovery of expressive language function in patients with Broca's aphasia. *Music Perception, 25,* 315–323.

Schwartz, M., Saffran, E., & Marin, O. (1980). The word order problem in agrammatism: I. Comprehension. *Brain & Language, 10,* 249–262.

Selnes, O. A., & Hillis, A. (2000). Patient Tan revisited: A case of atypical global aphasia. *Journal of the History of the Neurosciences, 9,* pp. 233–237.

Shafto, M. A., Stamatakis, E. A., Tam, P. P., & Tyler, L. K. (2008, September). *Senior moments and the brain: Convergent measures and an aging network.* Paper presented to the Architectures and Mechanisms for Language Processing Conference. Cambridge, England.

Shallice, T. (1988). *From neuropsychology to mental structure.* Cambridge, England: Cambridge University Press.

Sherman, J. C., & Schweickert, J. (1989). Syntactic and semantic contributions to sentence comprehension in agrammatism. *Brain & Language, 37,* 419–439.

Signoret, J., Castaigne, P., Lehrmitte, F., Abalanet, R., & Lavorel, P. (1984). Rediscovery of Leborgne's brain: anatomical description with CT scan. *Brain & Language, 22,* 303–319.

Sparks, R. W., Helm, N., & Albert, M. (1974). Aphasia rehabilitation resulting from melodic intonation therapy. *Cortex, 10,* 303–313.

Sparks, R. W., & Holland, A. L. (1976). Method: Melodic Intonation therapy for aphasia. *Journal of Speech and Hearing Disorders, 41,* 287–297.

Stein, D., Rosen, J. J., & Butters, N. (1974). *Plasticity and recovery of function in the central nervous system.* New York: Academic Press.

Stromswold, K., Caplan, D., Alpert, N., & Rauch, S. (1996). Localization of syntactic comprehension by positron emission tomography. *Brain & Language, 52,* 452–473.

Thompson, C. K., Shapiro, L. P., Tait, M. E., Jacobs, B. J., & Schneider, S. L. (1996). Training *wh*-question production in agrammatic aphasia: Analysis of argument and adjunct movement. *Brain & Language, 52,* 175–228.

Traxler, M. J., Bybee, M. D., & Pickering, M. J. (1997). Influence of connectives on language comprehension: Eye-tracking evidence for incremental interpretation. *Quarterly Journal of Experimental Psychology A, 50,* 481–497.

Vanier, M., & Caplan, D. (1990). CT scan correlates of agrammatism. In L. Menn & L. Obler (Eds.), *Agrammatic aphasia* (pp. 97–114). Amsterdam, The Netherlands: Benjamin.

Wada, J., & Rasmussen, T. (1960). Intracarotid injections of sodium amytal for the lateralization of cerebral speech dominance. *Journal of Neurosurgery, 17,* 266–282.

Walker-Batson, D., Curtis, S., Rajeshwari, N., Ford, J., Dronkers, N., Salmeron, E., et al. (2001). A double-blind, placebo-controlled study of the use of amphetamine in the treatment of aphasia. *Stroke, 32,* 2093–2098.

Walsh Dickey, M., Choy, J. W. J., & Thompson, C. K. (2007). Real-time comprehension of wh-movement in aphasia: Evidence from eye-tracking while listening. *Brain & Language, 100,* 1–22.

Walsh Dickey, M., & Thompson, C. K. (2006). Automatic processing of wh- and NP-movement in agrammatic aphasia: Evidence from eyetracking. *Brain & Language, 99,* 73–74.

Warriner, A. B., & Humphreys, K. (2008). Learning to fail: Reoccurring tip-of-the-tongue states. *The Quarterly Journal of Experimental Psychology, 61,* 535–542.

Waters, G. S., & Caplan, D. (1996). The capacity theory of sentence comprehension: Critique of Just and Carpenter (1992). *Psychological Review, 103,* 761–772.

Weiller, C., Isensee, C., Rijntes, M., Huber, W., Müller, S., Bier, D., et al. (1995). Recovery from Wernicke's aphasia: A positron emission tomographic study. *Annals of Neurology, 37,* 723–732.

Wilson, S. M., & Saygin, A. P. (2004). Grammaticality judgment in aphasia: Deficits are not specific to syntactic structures, aphasic syndromes or lesion sites. *Journal of Cognitive Neuroscience, 16,* 238–252.

Wise, G. W., Sutter, R., & Burkholder, J. (1972). The treatment of brain ischemia with vasopressor drugs. *Stroke, 3,* 135–140.

Woodill, G., & Le Normand, M. T. (1996). Broca's "discovery" of brain localization in aphasia. *Journal of Developmental Disabilities, 4,* 50–72.

Zurif, E., Swinney, D., Prather, P., & Love, T. (1994). Functional localization in the brain with respect to syntactic processing. *Journal of Psycholinguistic Research, 23,* 487–497.

Zurif, E., Swinney, D., Prather, P., Solomon, J., & Bushell, C. (1993). An on-line analysis of syntactic processing in Wernicke's aphasia. *Brain & Language, 45,* 448–464.

Right-Hemisphere Language Function

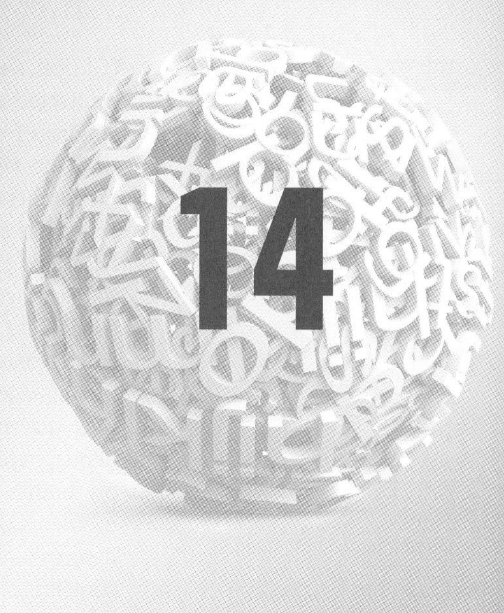

The *interhemispheric* or *longitudinal fissure* divides the brain in half from front to back, separating the two *cerebral hemispheres*, one on the left, one on the right. A band of nerve fibers called the *corpus callosum* connects the two hemispheres and enables signals generated in one hemisphere to cross over and affect the activity in the other hemisphere. Communication between the two hemispheres allows them to cooperate on a variety of information-processing tasks. But do they always do so? Or does each hemisphere act independently? For about the first century of research on language and the brain, scientists generally believed that language was completely *lateralized* and was governed by the left hemisphere of the brain acting on its own. Complete *lateralization* would mean that all of the necessary representations and processes for producing and understanding language would be housed in the left hemisphere. The right hemisphere would not participate in language production and interpretation at all. The basis for this conclusion was that serious language deficits, including loss of the ability to speak, were commonly observed following *left-hemisphere brain damage* (LHD), but similar serious deficits were rarely observed following *right-hemisphere brain damage* (RHD). When serious language production or comprehension deficits occur following RHD, this is called *crossed aphasia*, and that condition accounts for a tiny fraction of the total number of cases of aphasia (Marien, Paghera, De Deyn, & Vignolo, 2004).

Starting in the first half of the twentieth century, physicians began to find cases of right-handed children who suffered from aphasia-like symptoms following RHD (Basser, 1962). Findings like these suggested to researchers that left lateralization of language emerged over time as children mature, and did not represent an inevitable aspect of the human cognitive architecture

Introduction to Psycholinguistics: Understanding Language Science, First Edition.
Matthew J. Traxler.

(Chiron, Jambaque, Nabbout, Lounes, Syrota, & Dulac, 1997). Hence, researchers were motivated to take a closer look at how laterality changes with development and to look for language functions in the right hemisphere in adults. More recent research has demonstrated that the right hemisphere does play a role in a variety of language production and comprehension tasks. So, rather than being completely left lateralized, language-related activity is present in both hemispheres in the vast majority of people. Although language functions can appear fairly normal even when only one hemisphere is processing language, under normal circumstances both hemispheres respond to language input, and both participate in producing language output. Given that both hemispheres participate in language, researchers would like to know how, exactly, different parts of the brain respond to language input, what information is stored in long-term memory in each hemisphere, how that information is used to understand and produce language, and how the two hemispheres cooperate to carry out different language-processing tasks. Because the preceding chapter focused primarily on left-hemisphere language functions and the problems that occur after left-hemisphere brain damage, this chapter will focus on right-hemisphere language functions. In particular, it will explore how the right hemisphere contributes to speech production and comprehension, word processing, and discourse representation and processing.[1]

Speech Perception and Production

The left hemisphere provides the text while the right hemisphere plays the accompaniment.
FRANK MERREWETHER AND MURRAY ALPERT

Speech production is controlled by the left hemisphere in the vast majority of people, whether they are right-handed or left-handed. Over 90% of right-handers are left lateralized for speech, as are over 70% of left-handers (the rest of the left-handers are either right lateralized for speech or are able to produce speech with either hemisphere; Snyder, Novelly, & Harris, 1990; Wada & Rasmussen, 1960; but see Knecht et al., 2000). To determine which hemisphere controls speech, researchers sometimes use the *WADA* test. In the WADA test, a drug (amobarbital or sodium amytal) is injected into the carotid artery on either the patient's left or right side. Because the artery on each side supplies blood to only one hemisphere, one half of the brain can be anesthetized without affecting the other half. The patient's response on a given task therefore reflects only the functioning of the alert, non-drugged hemisphere. If patients can name pictures of common objects during the WADA test, then the non-drugged hemisphere must be capable of controlling speech. If the left hemisphere controls speech in most people, what does the right hemisphere contribute to speech processing? One major contribution of the right hemisphere is the production and interpretation of *prosody*.

Prosody is that part of the speech signal that is left over after all of the information that identifies individual words has been removed. It consists of the pattern of tones, pauses, tempo, and changes in loudness (*accent*) that people produce as they speak. Prosody can be broken down into two general types, *linguistic* (or *syntactic*) and *emotional* (or *affective*). Linguistic prosody adds information that colors the meaning of an utterance or helps listeners to package words into phrases (among other functions; see Chapter 4; see also Speer & Blodgett, 2006). An example of a feature of linguistic prosody that colors meaning is *emphatic stress*. This feature is present when a word or words in an utterance are pronounced more loudly than other words in the same utterance. Stress is often used to distinguish new information from old. For example, if someone asked *Who went to the store?*, it would be odd to emphasize the word *store* in the answer, as in *Kenny went to the* ***STORE***. (Try it!) Instead, one would emphasize the word *Kenny*, because that is the new information that the questioner is seeking. Pauses in the speech stream are a form of linguistic prosody that can help listeners place words in the correct phrases. Similarly, differences in the pattern of pitch or tone across the length of an utterance can signal the difference between a statement of fact (pronounced with a falling tone at the end in English) and a question (pronounced with a rising tone at the end). Further, the pattern of tones and the duration of words in an utterance depend on the position of those words in a syntactic structure. A word is pronounced for a longer duration and with a different pattern of tones when it appears at the end of a syntactic phrase than when it appears in other positions within a syntactic phrase. The relationship between aspects of linguistic prosody and aspects of syntactic structure and meaning allow listeners to use prosodic cues to help decide how to assign structure and meaning to utterances that they hear. Emotional prosody cues appear in the speech signal because the speaker's emotional state can change the way an utterance is produced. Excited speakers will usually speed up. Frightened speakers will speed up and use higher than average loudness and pitch. Sad speakers will slow down and speak with flattened pitch and lower volume. Even the act of smiling while talking changes acoustic aspects of speech. As a result, the speech signal contains numerous prosodic cues to the speaker's emotional state.

Language scientists have investigated the ways that the left and right hemispheres contribute to the production of linguistic and emotional prosody, and the degree to which the two hemispheres are sensitive to different prosodic cues in the speech signal. Research in the past three decades has shown that the right hemisphere plays a role in the production and comprehension of prosody, but controversy remains on a number of topics, including whether there is a clear differentiation between right- and left-hemisphere contributions to prosody (whether the two hemispheres handle different aspects of prosody), whether specific aspects of prosody are localized to particular brain regions, whether prosodic deficits can be separated from more general cognitive deficits, and whether clinical studies or brain imaging studies provide better evidence for or against particular accounts of the neural underpinnings of prosody (see, e.g., Baum & Pell, 1999; Bryan, 1989; Kinsbourne, 1986; Lebrun, Lessinnes, De Vresse, & Leleux, 1985; Ross & Monnot, 2010; Van Lancker-Sidtis, Pachana, Cummings, & Sidtis, 2006).

One theory of hemispheric contributions to speech production and perception views the right hemisphere as analyzing the speech signal for its prosodic information, while the left hemisphere extracts the words, the syntax, and the standard meaning (Ross, 1981; 1984; Ross & Monnot, 2008, p. 51). According to Ross' *right-hemisphere prosody* account, the right hemisphere is organized to handle linguistic and affective prosody in a manner analogous to the way the left hemisphere is organized to handle the propositional and syntactic aspects of language. As a result, prosody is "a dominant and lateralized function of the right hemisphere" (Ross & Monnot, 2010, p. 1). To be a *dominant* function of a cerebral hemisphere, brain damage limited to one side of the brain must produce a deficit in performance of that function. For example, syntax is a dominant function of the left hemisphere, because damage within the left hemisphere can impair a person's ability to produce grammatical speech and to understand speech when syntax plays a key role in assigning semantic roles to constituents in the sentence (e.g., Zurif, Swinney, Prather, Solomon, & Bushell, 1993). To be a *lateralized* function, the function must remain largely unchanged when the opposite hemisphere is damaged. Syntax is therefore a *dominant* and *lateralized* function of the left hemisphere.

When the *right-hemisphere prosody* account proposes that prosody is a dominant and lateralized function of the right hemisphere, it predicts two basic outcomes: (a) *unilateral* damage to the right hemisphere (damage that leaves the opposite hemisphere completely intact) should impair production and comprehension of prosody; and (b) unilateral damage to the left hemisphere (that leaves the right hemisphere completely intact) should leave production and comprehension of prosody essentially unchanged. Prediction (a) is slightly complicated because different prosodic functions may be localized within different areas of the right hemisphere, with receptive or comprehension functions proposed to be controlled by posterior regions near the temporo-parietal junction, and expressive (output or production) functions being controlled by anterior regions within the right frontal lobe. This proposed spatial arrangement of different prosodic functions leads to a third prediction, namely that production and comprehension of prosody should dissociate. There should be patients who can understand prosody but not be able to produce it; and there should be patients who can produce prosody but not be able to understand it. Because the right-hemisphere prosody account makes predictions about how brain damage should affect the perception and production of prosody based on which part of the brain is damaged, much of the research in this area involves testing patients who have suffered some kind of brain injury (similar to much of the research on *aphasia* reviewed in the previous chapter). In fact, theorists such as Ross view the loss of prosodic processing ability as being the right-hemisphere equivalent of speech production and comprehension problems that follow from left-hemisphere damage (i.e., *aphasias*). To highlight this connection, Ross uses the term *aprosodia* to describe problems perceiving or producing prosodic information.

The first prediction from the right-hemisphere prosody account, that unilateral right-hemisphere damage will lead to aprosodia, is amply supported by the empirical record. Right-hemisphere damage in adults does frequently lead to impairments in the comprehension and production of affective aspects of prosody (e.g., Charbonneau, Scherzer, Aspirot, & Cohen, 2003; Heilman, Scholes, & Watson, 1975; Kucharska-Pietura, Phillips, Gernand, & David, 2003; Pell, 1998, 2007; Ross, 1981; Rymarczyk & Grabowska, 2007; Tompkins & Mateer, 1985; see also Bell, Davis, Morgan-Fisher, & Ross, 1990 and Cohen, Branch, & Hynd, 1994, for studies involving children). Recent neuroimaging studies also show that the right hemisphere responds more strongly than the left hemisphere when affective prosody is manipulated (Wildgruber, Pihan, Ackermann, Erb, & Grodd, 2002). Further, some patient and imaging studies suggest regional differences in responses to affective prosody such that, for example, some brain areas respond more strongly to happy intonation than angry intonation (Johnstone, van Reekum, Oakes, & Davidson, 2006; Rymarczyk & Grabowska, 2007). Functional imaging studies have also shown greater left-hemisphere activity for contentful speech and greater right-hemisphere activation for *degraded speech* (speech that has been altered by having information that identifies individual words removed), indicating relatively greater right-hemisphere response to prosodic cues (Ischebeck, Friederici, & Alter, 2008; Meyer, Alter, & Friederici, 2003; Plante, Creusere, & Sabin, 2002).

Right lateralization of response to prosodic features appears very early, as children as young as 4 months old show a right-lateralized neural response to prosodic manipulations (Homae, Watanabe, Nakano, Asakawa, & Taga, 2006; see also Wartenburger et al., 2007 for a study involving older children). Homae and colleagues used *near-infrared optical topography* to study 3-month-old infants' responses to prosodic aspects of speech. Near-infrared optical topography is a brain imaging technique that uses wavelengths of light that are capable of penetrating the skull and the top layers of brain tissue. The amount of light that is reflected from the brain depends on its oxygenation level (similar to the way the radio signals generated in MRI scanning depend on blood-oxygen levels). Homae and colleagues played samples of normal and *flattened* speech to 3-month-old infants while they were asleep (the infants, not the research team). They made the flattened speech by taking normal speech and smoothing out the changes in *fundamental frequency* (F_0) (fundamental frequency is a measure of the lowest tones in the speech signal—the "bass" tones). Figure 14.1 represents

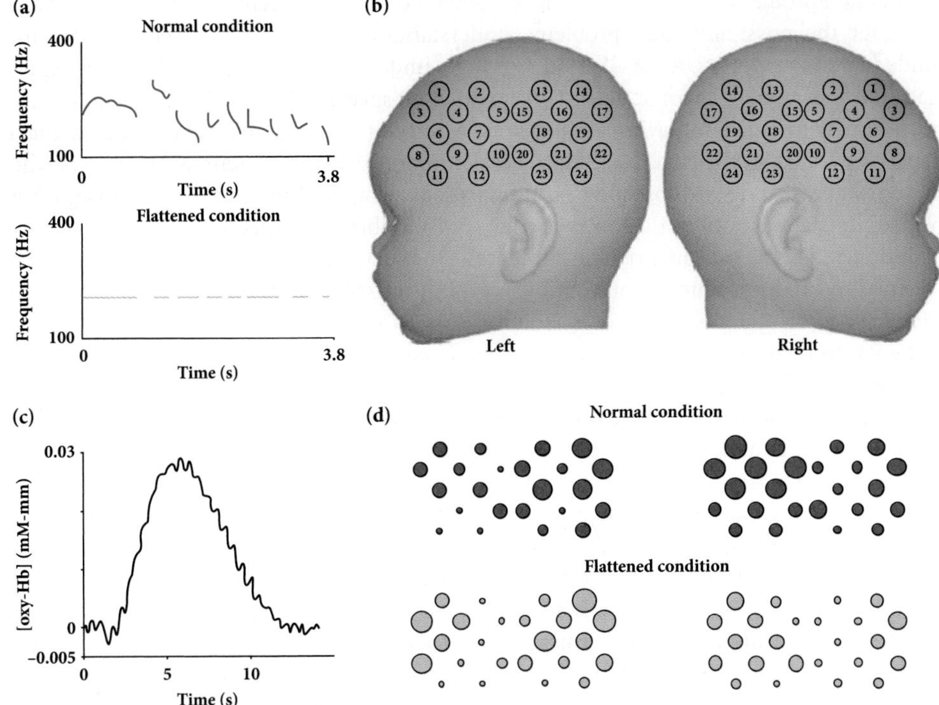

Figure 14.1 Prosodic contours (left) and neural response (right) in 3-month-old sleeping infants (from Homae et al., 2006, p. 277)

the oxygen levels in different parts of the sleeping infants' brains as normal (top) or flattened speech (bottom) was played. Both hemispheres responded to both kinds of speech, but as you can see by comparing the top and bottom parts of panel (d), the left hemisphere responded the same way whether the speech was normal or flattened. This shows that these infants' left hemispheres did not respond to changes in prosody. Now look at the right half of panel (d). This part of the graph shows that the infants' right hemispheres responded much more to normal speech than to flattened speech. Thus, even at 3 months old, and even in their sleep, infants' right hemispheres are responding to prosody. A follow-up study on 10-month-old children using the same technique showed that bilateral frontal regions respond more strongly to flattened prosody than normal speech, suggesting that babies have a good understanding of what their native language prosodic pattern is by 10 months old (Homae, Watanabe, Nakano, & Taga, 2007).

Further evidence for right lateralization of prosody comes from adult patients undergoing WADA testing. In a group of adult subjects who underwent the WADA procedure, production of emotional prosody was impaired when the right hemisphere was anesthetized (compared to the same individuals prior to the injection of the anesthetic; Ross, Edmondson, Seibert, & Homan, 1988). Although some patients with right-hemisphere brain damage appear to comprehend and produce prosody as well as non-brain-damaged control subjects, a substantial body of evidence from both healthy and brain-injured people supports the claim that right-hemisphere damage can and often does lead to disruption in the production or comprehension of prosody (e.g., Pell & Baum, 1997a, b).[2]

Before we can conclude that right-hemisphere brain damage causes a deficit in prosodic comprehension or production, and therefore that the damaged regions are necessary for prosody functions, we have to consider the possibility that the comprehension and production problems are caused by a more general disability. Specifically, we have to try to rule out the possibility that problems understanding prosody really reflect problems understanding emotion. After all, if you no longer understand the difference between happy, sad, and angry, you will not be able to match different speech patterns to different emotions, as occurs sometimes following right-hemisphere brain damage. Fortunately, researchers have conducted studies that look for general emotion perception deficits in patients who have trouble dealing with prosody. Finding patients who have problems with prosody but who understand emotions the same way that control subjects do effectively rules out general emotion deficits as the cause of their problems. One such study showed that individuals can be impaired in the production of emotional prosody but still understand speakers' emotional states based on the way their voices sound (Ross & Monnot, 2008). This means that the patients' problems may be limited to the mental systems that handle prosodic information, and do *not* reflect a general problem understanding other people's emotional states. Some patients have also been described who are able to imitate the emotional tone of a model, although their spontaneous speech is largely devoid of emotional prosodic features (Ross, 1981). Successful imitation in people whose spontaneous speech lacks emotional prosody may indicate that *planning* of the prosodic contour itself is impaired, but the mechanisms that actually program the motor movements to execute the plan are intact. Wertz and colleagues (Wertz, Henschel, Auther, Ashford, & Kirshner, 1998) also found that prosodic comprehension ability was relatively spared when compared to the spontaneous production of prosody in a sample of right-hemisphere-damaged patients. Perception and production of prosody have been shown to be impaired in patients with otherwise well-functioning emotional perception (Heilman et al., 1975). These outcomes indicate that aspects of prosodic information processing can be selectively impaired, leaving other aspects intact, and without corresponding impairments in the understanding of emotions. General problems perceiving emotions does not cause aprosodia.

The right-hemisphere prosody hypothesis suggests that prosodic output and input functions are controlled by different parts of the brain. Evidence in favor of regional specialization for particular prosodic functions comes from the correlation of symptoms with particular right-hemisphere brain regions (similar to the VLSM technique reviewed in the previous chapter). For example, Ross and Monnot (2008) assessed whether patients could spontaneously produce affective prosody versus imitate the prosody of another speaker. Patients with damage to right frontal regions were impaired in the spontaneous production of emotional prosody, while patients with damage to right temporal/parietal regions showed poor ability to understand affective prosody. This group of patients also included individuals with intact comprehension and poor production of prosody as well as individuals with the opposite pattern. In Bryan's (1989) study, patients with right temporal lobe damage were more impaired than patients with damage in other areas on tasks that required them to tell the difference between pairs of sentences based on their prosodic features (see also Heilman, Leon, & Rosenbek, 2004). These patterns of prosodic disturbances are argued to be analogs of Broca's and Wernicke's aphasia, respectively, and the right-hemisphere regions are roughly analogous to the left-hemisphere structures that are classically associated with non-fluent (Broca's) and fluent (Wernicke's) aphasias (but see the preceding chapter for a critique of the classic view).

If emotional prosody is a lateralized function of the right hemisphere, then left-sided brain damage should leave the production and comprehension of emotional prosody intact. However, some studies have shown deficits in either the production or understanding of emotional prosody in patients with left-hemisphere brain damage (e.g., Kucharska-Pietura et al., 2003). In Pell and Baum's (1997a, 1997b; see also Pell, 1998) studies, patients with (left-hemisphere damage (LHD) and right-hemisphere damage (RHD) listened to sentences composed of fake content words (e.g., *Jodah eezeth aram pazing*). (Can you think of a reason why they would use nonsense words instead of real words in this study?) These sentences were recorded by an actor who spoke them in a number of different emotional tones, such as angry, happy, and sad. The patients performed several tasks related to the sentences. In a *discrimination* task, they tried to tell whether two consecutive sentences were spoken in the same or different emotional tones. In an *identification* task, they pointed to pictures to indicate which emotion the speaker was trying to express. While both RHD and LHD groups performed more poorly than non-brain-damaged (NBD) control subjects on the identification task, both groups performed at the same level as NBD controls on the discrimination task. Bryan's (1989) study also showed deficits in prosodic perception following left-hemisphere damage.[3] Some neuroimaging (fMRI) data also show left-hemisphere activity during tasks that require subjects to identify emotions from prosodic information (Adolphs, Damasio, & Tranel, 2002). These findings support a couple of important conclusions. First, they show that the perception of the acoustic (sound) properties that make up prosodic features is different from the ability to use those acoustic properties. Patients were able to tell when two sentences were spoken with different prosodic contours, but they were unable to connect those prosodic contours with particular emotions. Perhaps more important, the fact that the LHD group was as impaired as the RHD group on the identification task calls into question whether comprehension of emotional prosody is lateralized to the right hemisphere, which would refute Ross' hypothesis about the neural underpinnings of linguistic and emotional aspects of language processing.

Ross and Monnot's (2008) response to results like these is to suggest that, although LHD and RHD groups may both be impaired on emotional prosody, they might be impaired for different reasons. RHD patients might be impaired because the right hemisphere houses the machinery that identifies the acoustic cues for emotional prosody and the representations that are activated by particular patterns of emotional prosody. LHD patients might be impaired because the left hemisphere takes right-hemisphere input via the corpus callosum and integrates the emotional prosody pattern with the syntactic and semantic analyses generated by left-hemisphere mechanisms (see also Poeppel, 2003). If so, losing the integrative functions housed in the left hemisphere could be as debilitating as losing the analytical machinery in the right hemisphere for some language tasks. Pell (1998; see also Baum & Dwivedi, 2003; Pell, 2006) also reported results suggesting that specific prosodic cues, such as duration (how long it takes to say a word or phrase), have different effects on LHD patients than they have on RHD patients, which would support Ross's claim that RHD and LHD prosodic dysfunctions result from different mechanisms.

Some recent research on healthy adults employing dichotic listening tasks also supports the *callosal transfer* hypothesis—the idea that prosodic perception takes place in the right hemisphere, and that the outcome of these perceptual processes is then transmitted to the left hemisphere (Erhan, Borod, Tenke, & Bruder, 1998; Grimshaw, Kwasny, Covell, & Johnson, 2003). In dichotic listening experiments, different speech signals are presented to the two ears. For example, a subject might hear the word *shirt* in her left ear, and the word *house* in her right ear. The subject's task is to monitor the meaning of the words. She is supposed to press a button when she hears a word that represents a kind of building, for instance (this would be a *semantic categorization task* version of the experiment). Subjects respond faster when a word is presented to the right ear, because the left hemisphere is more efficient at activating specific word meanings (and right-ear signals affect the left hemisphere more than the right).[4] If the two test words were spoken with different emotional tones, let's say happy versus sad, and subjects were asked to press a button when they heard a sad tone of voice, they would be faster when the "sad" word was played to their left ear, indicating that the right hemisphere is more efficient than the left at detecting emotional prosody. By testing to see how quickly subjects can respond to different test items played to different ears using either the left or the right hand, experimenters can tell whether the two hemispheres normally share information, or whether a given task is normally carried out by one hemisphere acting alone. If people respond just as quickly no matter what hand they respond with, this indicates that information is normally transmitted from the non-dominant hemisphere to the dominant hemisphere for processing (rather than being processed in whichever hemisphere the signal originally starts in). When the emotional stimulus is played to the right ear (and goes to the left hemisphere), it does not matter much whether the response is made with the right hand (controlled by the left hemisphere) or the left hand (controlled by the right hemisphere). This suggests that the acoustic information that identifies emotional tone is normally transferred to the right hemisphere for processing, rather than being analyzed by the left hemisphere. If so, this would be consistent with the right-hemisphere prosody hypothesis and Ross' ideas about callosal transfer. However, further research is required to determine whether both left- and right-hemisphere structures are involved in building representations encoding emotional prosody, or whether LHD impairments on emotional prosody tasks reflect a breakdown of communication between the two hemispheres.

However the emotional prosody debate is ultimately settled, it may be that some aspects of prosody are dominant and lateralized functions of the left hemisphere rather than the right. The *functional hypothesis* proposes that emotional prosody and linguistic prosody can be neatly differentiated and that they are processed differently by the two cerebral hemispheres (Behrens, 1985; see also Kaan & Swaab, 2002). According to this theory, the acoustic information that makes up the prosodic signal is available to both hemispheres. The left hemisphere extracts those features that are involved in lexical disambiguation (e.g., the stress pattern that discriminates ***green****house* from *green* ***house***), phrase packaging, and type of speech (e.g., *declarative* statements of fact vs. *interrogative* questions vs. *command* requests or orders). According to the functional hypothesis, the right hemisphere specializes in those aspects of prosody that provide indirect information about the speaker's state of mind. Neuroimaging studies that have contrasted normal and degraded speech have found that normal speech leads to a left-lateralized pattern of activation, while degraded speech produces the opposite pattern (Plante et al., 2002).[5] The clinical literature also supports differential response to linguistic prosody features by the right and left hemispheres. Some studies show that RHD patients are largely normal in the recognition and use of features of linguistic prosody while being impaired in the recognition and use of features of emotional prosody (Hoyte, Brownell, Vesely, & Wingfield, 2006; Shah, Baum, & Dwivedi, 2006). Patients tested with reaction-time tasks have also produced evidence for left-lateralized representation of linguistic prosody (Walker, Fongemie, & Daigle, 2001). In one experiment, RHD patients were faster to say that they understood spoken "garden path" sentences than LHD patients, suggesting that the left hemisphere is normally involved in analyzing prosodic cues that correlate with phrase boundaries. In a further experiment where patients listened to garden path sentences and simultaneously responded to visually presented words, RHD patients also showed evidence of faster syntactic disambiguation. Note, however, that at least one study (Baum, Pell, Leonard, & Gordon, 2001), has failed to find deficits in production of linguistic prosody cues in either LHD or RHD groups.[6]

One further complication is that, before we reach an accurate understanding of the relationship between prosodic processes and hemispheric specialization, prosodic processing must be separated from both lower-level acoustic processing and more general cognitive faculties, such as general emotional processing, working-memory capacity, motor control, self-monitoring, and so forth. For example, recognizing the prosodic features that accompany happiness or excitement requires the acoustic system to recognize changes in fundamental frequency (F_0) and loudness over time. If the acoustic system is not capable of providing this information, then an intact prosodic system will still fail to recognize the appropriate emotion. Some authors have suggested that the two hemispheres are specialized for different aspects of low-level acoustic information, with the left hemisphere processing the acoustic stream for short-term changes (such as the formant transitions that correspond to different phonemes) and the right hemisphere processing the acoustic stream for longer-term changes, on the order of several seconds, that correspond to emotional prosodic features (e.g., Poeppel, 2003; Robin, Tranel, & Damasio, 1990). In fact, prosodic deficits are sometimes correlated with other acoustic processing problems (e.g., Nicholson et al., 2003). If prosodic deficits were purely a function of lower-level acoustic processing deficits, then we would expect patients with prosodic problems to have problems with other tasks that involve the modulation of pitch or temporal (time) information. However, prosodic and other acoustic deficits have been shown to dissociate in some patients (e.g., Bryan, 1989). A correlation of deficits in visual and auditory emotion processing is also sometimes found (e.g., Charbonneau et al., 2003; Pell, 1999). However, in other patients, emotional processing problems are seen only in one perceptual modality, with vision and hearing showing different patterns of performance (Habib, 1986). Thus, as with the relationship between prosody and emotion perception, prosodic deficits are not always a by-product of a general auditory processing problem. It seems safe to say, then, that prosodic processing resides among a suite of other social and cognitive capacities and depends upon those capacities for input and feedback, but that prosody represents a separable dimension of cognitive performance that operates under its own set of principles and that can break down independent of the other cognitive systems that support it.

While right-hemisphere cortical structures play a critical role in the production and understanding of linguistic and emotional prosody, subcortical structures also participate in prosodic processing. Emotional responses are mediated by subcortical structures such as the hypothalamus and the amygdala. For example, surgical lesioning of parts of the hypothalamus in cats can lead them to behave as though they are enraged. It should not be surprising, then, that damage to subcortical structures in humans can also lead to deficits in the production and comprehension of emotional prosody. One case study described two people whose injuries were limited to subcortical structures, while the cerebral cortices were spared (Van Lancker-Sidtis et al., 2006). In both cases, the patients showed good comprehension of emotional prosody on a variety of tasks, but both patients were significantly impaired in either the expression or control of emotional prosody. In both cases, the patients spoke largely in a monotone. In one case, the patient adopted a "more aggressive conversational style" post-injury. In a similar vein, Brownell & Stringfellow (1999) note that conversational style following RHD may be more terse and blunt, characteristics they attribute to these patients' failure to support spoken requests with explanatory material. Case studies like these provide further evidence that receptive and expressive prosodic functions are dissociable. Most importantly, they indicate that a network of both cortical and subcortical brain regions is involved in formulating prosodic aspects of speech.

Word Processing

Given that dramatic speech production and comprehension deficits are rarely observed in patients with right-hemisphere brain damage, it would be tempting to conclude that the right hemisphere either lacks word-level representations, or has them but does not participate in lexical processing unless something terrible happens to the left hemisphere. Nothing could be farther from the truth (Peck, 1962). Detailed study of both intact and brain-damaged individuals suggests that the right hemisphere does contain lexical representations and that it does participate in a variety of word-level processes, including lexical access and lexical ambiguity resolution (e.g., Beeman, 1993; Burgess & Simpson, 1988). The influence of right-hemisphere lexical processing during word recognition processes in normal readers can be demonstrated by experiments involving *lateralized presentation* of words (e.g., Long & Baynes, 2002). To test whether the two hemispheres cooperate, or if one hemisphere processes words all by itself, researchers have studied what happens when the same word is presented to both hemispheres simultaneously compared to what happens when one word is presented to the left hemisphere, and a different word is presented to the right hemisphere. If the two hemispheres normally cooperate during word identification, then presenting the same word to both hemispheres should help; and presenting different words to the two hemispheres should cause interference. If only one hemisphere normally participates in word identification, then the subject's response should be the same whether the same or different words are presented to the two hemispheres (because the subject's response depends only on the dominant hemisphere).

A word can be presented to one hemisphere without the other hemisphere being directly stimulated by the word because of the way the visual system is configured. The left half of each retina in the eye sends signals only to the right side of the brain; and the right side of the retina sends signals only to the left half of the brain. As a result, stimuli in the *left visual field* (or LVF) will be processed first by the right side of the brain; and anything that appears in the *right visual field* (or RVF) will be processed first by the left half of the brain. The LVF includes everything to the left of the *fixation point*, the point in space that you are looking at. The RVF includes everything to the right of the fixation point. Of course, the two hemispheres normally share information via the corpus callosum, but visual information is divided between the two halves of the brain and there is some noise in the process of transferring information between the two hemispheres. As a result, the directly stimulated hemisphere gets a head start on processing the stimulus, and it has a more accurate, higher quality picture to work with (Zaidel, Clarke, & Suyenobu, 1990). In *divided visual field* experiments, stimuli are presented either to the left of fixation, to the right of fixation, or in both locations simultaneously. (Sometimes, stimuli are presented at the fixation point as a control condition.) Results of divided visual field experiments show that people respond faster when the same word is displayed simultaneously to the right and left of fixation, and they respond slower when different words are displayed on each side of the fixation point (Eviatar & Ibrahim, 2007; Henderson, Barca, & Ellis, 2007; Mohr, Pulvermüller, & Zaidel, 1994). Thus, the right hemisphere contributes to word processing (if it didn't, response times and accuracy would not differ depending on whether the LVF and RVF have the same or different stimuli). But what, exactly does the right hemisphere do? Is it just a pale imitation of the left hemisphere? Or does something qualitatively different happen there?

One way to address these questions is to study patients who have undergone a surgical procedure called *callosotomy* (Gazzaniga, 1983, 1984; Gazzaniga, Smylie, Baynes, Hirst, & McCleary, 1984; Gazzaniga & Sperry, 1967). Callosotomy disconnects the two hemispheres and can prevent the transfer of visual information between the two. The surgery is used when people have life-threatening epilepsy that does not respond well to seizure-controlling medication. After patients have recovered from the surgery, the way each hemisphere responds to language can be assessed. When such patients are asked to name common objects that are presented either visually or manually (the patients handle the object with either the right or left hand), the vast majority of patients are able to name objects shown in the RVF (or objects that they hold in their right hands), but are unable to name objects shown to the LVF (or held in the left hand). These results match up well with other studies showing left-hemisphere dominance for speech. Patients in these studies are also unable to make judgments about the sounds of words when those words are presented in the LVF (and are processed by the right hemisphere). They are not able to say whether two words rhyme, nor can they judge whether two consonant–vowel sounds played in their left ear are the same or different. Therefore, the right hemisphere does not appear to either house or have access to the phonological (sound) information associated with individual words.

One might conclude on the basis of these results that the right hemisphere has no word-related knowledge at all. However, some of the patients who could not make phonological judgments using their right hemispheres could make semantic judgments using the same right hemisphere. For instance, these patients could judge whether a visually presented word matched a visually presented picture, where both of the stimuli were presented in the LVF. These patients could also make semantic (meaning) judgments for two words presented in the LVF (which project to the right hemisphere). They could judge whether two words in the LVF were synonyms, whether a word and a picture in the LVF referred to the same thing (for nouns denoting objects as well as verbs denoting actions), and whether an individual word belonged to a semantic category, such as animals or man-made objects. The right hemisphere, independent of the left, does appear to have knowledge about words. Specifically, it has some sense of word meanings, at least in some people. (Only a small minority of patients could perform *any* language-related tasks following callosotomy for stimuli presented to the right hemisphere.)

On the basis of his studies with callosotomy patients, Gazzaniga argues quite forcefully that right-hemisphere language processing is the exception rather than the rule. He states (1983, p. 531), "Of the 44 split-brain patients living in the United States, only … 5 have shown clear evidence of language processes in the right hemisphere, the quality and extent of which ranges from rudimentary naming skills to language skills essentially identical to left hemisphere processes." And (p. 525), "Most split-brain patients do not possess right hemisphere language of any kind." He suggests further that the presence of right-hemisphere language abilities is the result of reorganization forced on the brain by damage caused by epilepsy (p. 527, "When [language is] present, it can be attributed in almost every case to the presence of early left hemisphere brain damage"). If this hypothesis is correct, then the divided visual field experiments described above must be tapping some non-linguistic (perhaps visual) processing advantage, rather than reflecting lexical or semantic processing of words by the right hemisphere. Other researchers have also interpreted Gazzaniga's data not as showing right-hemisphere language function, but as reflecting some residual ability for the right hemisphere to communicate with the left hemisphere. However, this latter possibility is strongly ruled out by the fact that, while some of the callosotomy patients could do picture–word matching for stimuli in either visual field, they were not able to tell whether two stimuli presented to opposite hemispheres were the same or different. If their two hemispheres were still capable of communicating with one another, then they should have been able to tell when both hemispheres were looking at the same stimulus and when they were looking at two different stimuli.

But is it correct to say that the right hemisphere lacks word processing ability (unless left-hemisphere damage forces the brain to reorganize)? A growing body of evidence suggests that the right hemisphere does possess word knowledge, and does use its knowledge to support left-hemisphere language functions. In addition to the divided visual field experiments mentioned previously, additional evidence for right-hemisphere word knowledge comes from functional imaging (fMRI) studies and semantic priming studies. The neuroimaging data show that, in healthy adult subjects, both hemispheres (and temporal lobes, especially) respond to words presented both visually and auditorily. Right-hemisphere activation should not occur if the right hemisphere lacks word knowledge. Semantic priming studies using divided visual field methods also provide evidence for semantic representations residing in the right hemisphere (e.g., Beeman et al., 1994; Burgess & Simpson, 1988). These priming studies reveal some intriguing differences between word processing in the two hemispheres, and they are well worth a closer look, so let's turn to them next.

The coarse coding hypothesis

Although neuroimaging data show that the right hemisphere responds to words, those studies do not by themselves tell us what knowledge the right hemisphere houses or how it accesses and uses that knowledge to support comprehension. What we need are some more detailed ideas about how words are represented, and how relationships between different words are organized. The *coarse coding* hypothesis provides a more detailed explanation of how word knowledge is organized in the two hemispheres (Beeman, 1998; 2005; Beeman & Chiarello, 1998; Beeman et al., 1994). According to the coarse coding hypothesis, lexical (word) knowledge is organized differently in the two hemispheres. In addition to differences in phonological processing (the left hemisphere has the phonological codes; the right hemisphere is "silent"), the left and right hemispheres organize semantic knowledge differently. The left hemisphere has sharply and neatly differentiated semantic representations. This enables people to make very fine semantic distinctions between closely related words. Take for example, the words *encourage* and *compel*. People know that the words *encourage* and *compel* have overlapping but not identical meanings (they both involve one person motivating another person to act, but *compel* has an aspect of coercion that *encourage* lacks). According to the coarse coding hypothesis, the left hemisphere is more likely than the right to recognize the distinction in meaning between *encourage* and *compel*. Further, when activation spreads between different lexical representations in the left hemisphere, it does so very quickly, but activation does not spread very far. As a result, semantic activation in the left hemisphere tends to be tightly focused on a small number of very closely related concepts. A different pattern occurs in the right hemisphere. In the right hemisphere, semantic representations are less cleanly differentiated. Functionally, the right hemisphere has a greater tendency to lump related concepts together. According to the coarse coding hypothesis, activation in the right hemisphere is more "diffuse"—concepts are overall less strongly activated in the right hemisphere, and activation is spread over a broader range of concepts than in the left hemisphere. As a result, activation increases more slowly in the right hemisphere than the left, and more distantly related concepts can influence each other as activation spreads further in the right-hemisphere lexical-semantic network. While both hemispheres store information about words, the qualities of the lexical representations are quite different in the two hemispheres, and the way different lexical representations affect one another via the spread of activation is also quite different. What evidence is there that left- and right-hemisphere lexical representations are different? And what evidence supports the idea that signaling between lexical representations is different in the right hemisphere than the left hemisphere?

To address these questions, Mark Beeman and others have combined semantic priming techniques with the divided visual field experimental method (Beeman, 1993; 1998; 2005; Beeman et al., 1994; see also Faust & Lavidor, 2003). Some of these experiments have used strongly associated prime–target pairs (such as *doctor–nurse* or *lunch–break*). Priming is assessed by comparing response times to the target words for strongly associated prime-target pairs (such as *doctor–nurse*) and unassociated pairs (such as *farmer–nurse*). When strongly associated pairs are presented in the RVF (to the left hemisphere), priming occurs very quickly and target words like *nurse* are responded to much faster following the associated prime word (*doctor*) than the unassociated control word (*farmer*). People are slower overall when the primes and targets are presented in the LVF (to the right hemisphere), and the amount of priming between the strongly associated pairs is much smaller than the amount of priming that occurs when the same prime-target pairs are presented to the left hemisphere. Results like these show that the left and right hemispheres respond differently to words (the left hemisphere is faster) and they also respond differently to prime–target pairs. The left hemisphere responds more quickly to a strong association between a prime and a target word; the right hemisphere does not respond as strongly. Both of these findings are consistent with the coarse coding hypothesis in that activation appears to occur more quickly overall in the left hemisphere, and activation appears to spread strongly between words that are strongly associated with one another.

Based on the preceding results, one might conclude that the right hemisphere is just a weak mirror image of the left when it comes to word processing. Perhaps the associated words had less of an effect on the right hemisphere because it is just more feeble than the left at activating word meanings. However, additional experiments show that the right hemisphere does show priming effects under the right conditions. Remember that the coarse coding hypothesis says that the lexical representations in the right hemisphere have less distinct boundaries and that activation can spread between more distantly or weakly related concepts in the right hemisphere than in the left. To test these claims, some experiments tested for effects of *summation priming*. In priming experiments like those just described, each target word is preceded by a single prime word (or a single control word). In summation priming experiments, each target word is preceded by more than one prime word. Each of the prime words in summation priming may be weakly related to the target word, but when you add the prime words together, they strongly suggest a specific target word. If you saw the prime words *glass*, *foot*, and *cry*, you would likely think of the target word *cut*. This is true even though none of the individual prime words is strongly associated with the word *cut*. (If you ask people to list words that come to mind when they hear *glass*, or *foot*, or *cry*, they almost never say the word *cut*.) Beeman and colleagues conducted reaction-time experiments using summation priming stimuli. In these experiments, subjects responded to target words like *cut* following a set of primes that *converge* on the target (e.g., the prime words were *glass*, *foot*, and *cry*) or a set of control primes (e.g., *glass*, *bacon*, and *cry*). When the target words were lateralized to the LVF (i.e., they were presented to the right hemisphere), subjects responded faster in the summation priming condition than the control condition. When the target stimuli were presented in the RVF (to the left hemisphere), no priming was observed in the summation condition relative to the control condition. (So the right hemisphere *is* better than the left at something!)

These results are important for a couple of reasons. First, they show that the right hemisphere is not just the weaker partner to the left. If it were, the right hemisphere should always perform worse than the left on any word-processing task; but in this case, the right hemisphere performed better. Second, the results are fully consistent with the coarse coding hypothesis' claims about the spread of activation in the two hemispheres. One reason why the right hemisphere would produce priming in the summation condition is that activation spreads between concepts that are more distantly related, and the target word thereby gets a little bit of a boost from all of the summation primes. If spread of activation were more tightly focused in the left hemisphere, *cut* would not have its activation boosted even by multiple weakly associated primes, and so summation priming has no effect when the target word is presented to the left hemisphere.

Coarse coding contends that word meanings are organized differently in the left and right hemispheres. If so, different kinds of prime words should have different effects on target words when the primes and targets are presented to the left and right hemispheres. Some experiments therefore have looked at priming based on *associative* relations (two words occur together, or one word comes to mind easily when another is heard) versus *categorical* relations (Bouaffre & Faïta-Ainseba, 2007; Chiarello, Burgess, Richards, & Pollock, 1990; Chiarello & Richards, 1992; but see Deacon et al., 2004; Grose-Fifer & Deacon, 2004). Categorical relations are based on whether two words belong to the same superordinate category. *Duck* and *crow* share a categorical relation because they both belong to the category *bird*. Some researchers believe that associative and categorical relations are processed differently in the two hemispheres, because word meanings are organized differently in the two hemispheres. The left hemisphere maintains links between strongly associated words, while the right hemisphere maintains categorical links between words whether they are strongly associated or not. To tell whether categorical relations are treated differently than associative relations, we need to find words that are associatively but not categorically related, and we need to find words that are categorically but not associatively related. Finding words from different categories that are associated is pretty easy—*bird–brain*, *school–teacher*, and *cop–car* all have members from different semantic categories that are nonetheless highly associated. Doing the opposite, finding category members that are *un*-associated is a little tougher, but it can be done. *Couch–lamp* both come from the category *furniture*, but people rarely produce *lamp* as an associate of *couch*, and vice versa. In divided visual field experiments, associative prime–target pairs (e.g., *cop–car*) produce robust priming effects when presented to the left hemisphere, and sometimes produce priming when presented to the right hemisphere. (*Un*-associated) category prime–target pairs, by contrast, are much more likely to produce priming effects when presented to the right hemisphere than when presented to the left hemisphere. Thus, it appears that the right hemisphere organizes word meanings differently than the left. Specifically, the right hemisphere is more likely to recognize that two words share a category relationship, while the left hemisphere bases its semantic organization more on pure association.

The coarse coding hypothesis also receives support from experiments on lexical disambiguation. Recall from Chapter 3 that some words have more than one meaning, and that when we hear or see such words, we reflexively activate all of the meanings that are associated with a particular word (Duffy, Henderson, & Morris, 1989; Seidenberg, Tanenhaus, Leiman, & Bienkowski, 1982; Swinney, 1979). If the lexical representations in the two hemispheres have different qualities and are organized differently, do the two hemispheres also respond differently to ambiguous words? Some evidence suggests that they do respond differently. Curt Burgess and Greg Simpson (1988) used priming techniques to assess whether the two hemispheres respond the same way to target words associated with the dominant (more frequent) or subordinate (less frequent) meanings of ambiguous words (see also Chiarello, Maxfield, & Kahan, 1995; Faust, Ben-Artzi, & Harel, 2008; Faust & Chiarello, 1998; Meyer & Federmeier, 2008).[7] Ambiguous words, such as *pitcher*, can have a highly frequent meaning (e.g., "person who throws a baseball") and an infrequent meaning (e.g., "thing that you use to pour water into a glass"). Because the word and its dominant meaning are more closely associated, coarse coding predicts that the left hemisphere will activate the dominant meaning more quickly and more strongly than the subordinate meaning (which may not be activated at all in the left hemisphere). Because the right hemisphere, relatively speaking, favors more distantly associated meanings, it is more likely to activate subordinate meanings of ambiguous words. To test these hypotheses, Burgess and Simpson presented ambiguous prime words and lateralized presentation of target words related to the dominant meaning (e.g., *baseball*) and subordinate meanings (e.g., *water*). They also manipulated *stimulus offset asynchrony* (SOA), the amount of time that elapses between presentation of the prime word and presentation of the target, to see how quickly different meanings became activated in the two hemispheres.

As shown in Figure 14.2, both the left (top) and right (bottom) hemispheres showed priming for the dominant meaning at a very short SOA. The left hemisphere continued to show activation of the dominant meaning even after a relatively long delay intervened between presentation of the prime word and presentation of the target. Now take a look at activation of the subordinate meanings. Compare how activation changes over time in the left hemisphere (activation of subordinate meanings decreases) versus the right hemisphere (activation of subordinate meanings increases). In other words, the two hemispheres have opposite responses to subordinate meanings. The left hemisphere deactivates

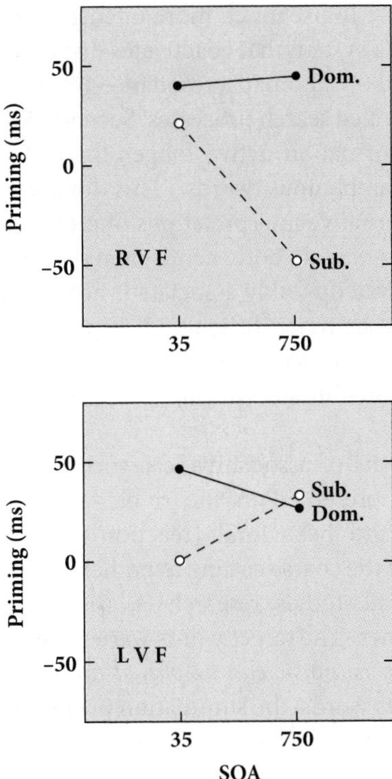

Figure 14.2 Priming results for *dominant* (solid line) and *subordinate* (dashed line) meanings for the left hemisphere (top) and right hemisphere (bottom), and short SOAs (left) and long SOAs (right) (from Burgess & Simpson, 1988, p. 96)

subordinate meanings, but the right hemisphere increases them over time. This pattern of results is consistent with coarse coding's claims about the narrowness of left-hemisphere semantic activations (in this case the left hemisphere primed only the ambiguous word's most strongly associated meaning), that weaker associates will be activated in the right hemisphere, and that the amount of time it takes for activation to accrue in the two hemispheres should differ.

A substantial body of evidence from different types of priming experiments suggests that word representations are organized differently in the right and left hemispheres. But what purpose is served by having two different stores of word-related knowledge and different patterns of connections between different lexical entries? Having a carbon copy of the left hemisphere lexicon in the right hemisphere and duplicate input and output processes would have the advantages conveyed by redundancy. It's always good to have a spare of anything important, which is why people pay good money to have a copy of their computer hard drives even if they never have to recover their files. But research over the past 20 years shows that the right hemisphere is *not* a carbon copy of the left. We can conclude, therefore, that the brain is sacrificing the advantages of redundancy in favor of something else, but what is this something else? Coarse coded lexical representations could convey two advantages that might be more beneficial than straight redundancy. First, a substantial part of discourse comprehension and dialogue involves drawing inferences (see Chapter 5). Beeman and others suggest that having a right-hemisphere semantic system that can detect relationships between distantly associated concepts makes drawing inferences easier (we'll review some of the evidence for right-hemisphere contributions to inference in the next section). If spreading activation activated only highly similar or strongly associated concepts, then we would have to use much more intensive, controlled mental processes to generate inferences. Having a system that coactivates distantly related concepts means that more inferences can be based on automatic, resonance-like processes, which should require less mental effort than controlled search processes. Second, the right hemisphere appears to keep weakly associated information active longer than the left hemisphere, including subordinate meanings of ambiguous words. This longer-lasting activation may help comprehenders develop alternative interpretations of utterances if an initial interpretation proves to be faulty in some way. If both hemispheres purged subordinate meanings of ambiguous words, or deactivated weakly associated meanings, then replacing a dominant but incorrect meaning could be more difficult. Of course, keeping subordinate meanings and weakly associated information active could make the process of selecting an appropriate meaning in the first place more difficult (due to increased competition), but apparently the game is worth the candle.

Although different patterns of associative, categorical, and summation priming have been observed for stimuli presented in the right versus left visual hemifield, recent neurophysiological (ERP) and behavioral (reaction-time) experiments have failed to confirm some predictions of the coarse coding hypothesis (Kandhadai & Federmeier, 2007, 2008). In two nearly identical studies, researchers looked for hemispheric differences in response to summation primes. The target words were either ambiguous, such as *organ* (as in *your left lung is an organ* vs. *music can be played on an organ*) or unambiguous, such as *tiger*. For the *un*ambiguous words, the summation primes were both related to the target (as in *lion*, *stripes*, *tiger*). For the ambiguous words, the summation primes pointed to different meanings; one of the primes was associated with one meaning, and the other prime was associated with a different meaning (as in *kidney*, *piano*, *organ*). In both sets of experiments, subjects made lexical (word, non-word) decisions or else they explicitly judged whether the meanings of the prime words were related to the meanings of the target words. Both the prime words and the target words were presented either in the left or right visual field. The coarse coding hypothesis predicts more priming in the right hemisphere than the left hemisphere for the ambiguous target words (because the right hemisphere is good at keeping more than one meaning of an ambiguous word active). The degree of priming for the unambiguous targets depends on how closely the two primes are to the target word. In the first set of experiments, no differences in the pattern of priming were detected for left versus right-lateralized presentations. Targets were equally primed or un-primed whether the stimuli were presented to the left hemisphere or to the right hemisphere. In the follow-up study, the ERP response was the same whether the stimuli were presented in the LVF or the RVF. Based on these results, one might be tempted to say that the right and left hemispheres are responding to the prime–target triplets in the same way.

There are a number of reasons why this conclusion may not be valid. First, there was a substantial lag (800 ms) between presentation of the last prime stimulus and the onset of the target word. Other studies, going back to Burgess and Simpson (1988), show that patterns of priming change as the amount of time between a prime and a target word changes (see also Traxler & Foss, 2000). Second, interpreting these results as being problematic for coarse coding requires us to "accept the null hypothesis"; that is, we need to believe that the experiments failed to find a difference between right- and left-hemisphere processing because for these stimuli there is no difference to be found. Absence of evidence is not the same thing as evidence of absence, however. Because experiments sometimes fail to detect differences that really are there, we have to be cautious drawing conclusions from null results. Third, in the context of the medical patient data and other experimental and imaging data on normal subjects, we really do need a theory that predicts and explains differences in lexical processing between the two hemispheres. Aphasia follows left-hemisphere damage but not right (except in a tiny, tiny proportion of cases). Lateralized presentation of prime–target pairs frequently (but not always) produces different patterns of behavior on a variety of tasks. Any theory that says the right hemisphere is functioning the same as the left has no way to explain any of these outcomes. So, at this stage, we should keep open the possibility that null results reflect insensitivity to left–right differences in processing, rather than showing that the left and right hemispheres are equivalent.

Right-Hemisphere Contributions to Discourse Comprehension and Production

Chapter 5 reviewed some of the neuroimaging studies that indicate that the right hemisphere responds to changes in discourse coherence (e.g., Kuperberg, Lakshamanan, Caplan, & Holcomb, 2006; Robertson et al., 2000; St. George, Kutas, Martinez, & Sereno, 1999; see Johns, Tooley, & Traxler, 2008, for a review). Neuroimaging studies indicate that the right hemisphere is sensitive to the qualities of a discourse and that it may play a role in building the situation model when extended discourse is comprehended. This section reviews some of the research on patients with right-hemisphere brain damage as well as recent studies on healthy adults that provides further evidence about the right hemisphere's role in discourse processing. More specifically, research on right-hemisphere function suggests that the right hemisphere participates in processes that establish a representation of the *macrostructure* of the discourse and processes that generate inferences.

To understand discourse, comprehenders must build a *macrostructure* that connects different sections of a discourse together by finding causal or referential connections between the different parts of a story. This contrasts with building *microstructure* representations for individual text elements, such as individual sentences. Neuroimaging and neurological studies show that the right hemisphere plays a role in comprehending the macrostructure of a discourse. When subjects are asked to monitor a conversation for change in its main topic or theme, changes in neural activity are observed in the right hemisphere (based on fMRI imaging, Dapretto, Lee, & Caplan, 2005). Some studies of patients with RHD show that such patients are less able to connect different parts of a discourse together in a coherent way (Delis, Wapner, Gardner, & Moses, 1983; Schneiderman, Murasagi, & Saddy, 1992). One study tested for right-hemisphere involvement in building macrostructure representations. In this study, patients who had suffered RHD received information about the theme of a paragraph and were then asked to organize a series of five other prewritten sentences to make a coherent paragraph about the given theme. Patients with RHD were less able to perform this task than age-matched healthy control subjects. Patients with RHD also have trouble identifying the main idea or theme of a story (Rehak et al., 1992). Narrative production can also be impaired following RHD. When patients are asked to retell well-known stories (e.g., *Cinderella*), patients with RHD omit more important ideas than patients with LHD (Bartels-Tobin & Hinckley, 2005; but see Marini, Carlomagno, Caltagirone, & Nocentini, 2005).[8] Discourse comprehension and production problems following RHD appear to be fairly stable over time, at least from 1 month to 6 months following the brain injury, although some patients do show improvements in discourse comprehension and production in the first year following the traumatic event (Brady, Armstrong, & Mackenzie, 2006; Mackenzie, Brady, Begg, & Lees, 2001). Thus, deficits in the processes that build macrostructures are not likely a by-product of acute problems caused by the traumatic event. Based on these results, the right hemisphere appears to play a vital role in keeping track of the main idea or theme of a story as well as using the theme to organize the various subcomponents of the story into a coherent macrostructure.

Comprehenders must also draw inferences to understand discourse (see Chapter 5), and inferencing skills can be degraded when the right hemisphere is damaged. In one large-scale study, patients with RHD and LHD were compared to age-matched healthy controls (Ferstl, Walther, Guthke, & von Cramon, 2005). While the RHD patients performed just as well as the other groups in answering questions about explicitly stated information, they had more difficulty answering questions about information that was implied by the story, but was not explicitly stated. Patients with RHD also seem to be less able to use context to infer the meanings of unfamiliar words (Keil, Baldo, Kaplan, Kramer, & Delis, 2005). Patients with frontal lobe damage were asked to read stories with made-up words (e.g., *prifa*). The contexts provided information that you could use to deduce the meaning of the made-up word (e.g., *My prifa is sore from sitting on this hard wooden chair all morning*). Patients with RHD were compared to patients with LHD. Both groups had trouble inferring the meanings of the novel words, but RHD patients performed worse than LHD patients on this task.

While the preceding evidence favors a right-hemisphere contribution to inference generation, that does not mean that inferencing is completely right lateralized. Left-hemisphere contributions to inferencing are suggested by studies showing that RHD patients can draw even sophisticated predictive inferences if context strongly supports the target inference, but even these patients do not appear to be able to maintain the inference over time or incorporate it into a durable representation of the story (Lehman-Blake & Tompkins, 2001). RHD patients are also able to make referential inferences. They can figure out what a pronoun refers to, even when the pronoun could refer to more than one previously introduced referent (Leonard, Waters, & Caplan, 1997a, 1997b). Left-hemisphere damage or bilateral damage in the frontal lobes may also affect people's ability to draw inferences, and these findings are compatible with recent neuroimaging experiments that indicate that the left hemisphere increases its neural activity when inferences are drawn (Ferstl, Guthke, & von Cramon, 2002; Kuperberg et al., 2006). Taken together, these results indicate that the left hemisphere also participates in inference generation. We might conclude therefore that both hemispheres cooperate to draw inferences, and that problems can result when either hemisphere is disabled. Some theorists claim the hemispheres divide their labor, with each taking on a particular kind of inference. Based on the outcomes of divided-field priming studies and neurological data, Beeman and colleagues suggest that the left hemisphere handles coherence inferences, while the right hemisphere handles predictive inferences (Beeman, Bowden, & Gernsbacher, 2000; see Shears et al., 2008, for a similar claim with respect to causal versus "planning" inferences). This position, however, like the arguments against coarse coding, relies on us believing a null result (no significant priming for predictive-inference-related words presented in the RVF), and so we should treat it just as cautiously as other null results.

The right hemisphere appears to participate in macrostructure building and inferencing in discourse production and comprehension, but some discourse functions appear to be largely or completely left lateralized. Building a microstructure while comprehending a discourse involves extracting the *propositions* represented by the contents of individual sentences (propositions reflect the relationships between participants in events; see Chapter 5). Propositional representations appear to be built and maintained largely or completely in the left hemisphere. This conclusion is supported by a series of studies by Debra Long and colleagues involving divided visual field methods (Long & Baynes, 2002; Long, Baynes, & Prat, 2005; Prat, Long, & Baynes, 2007). In these experiments, healthy adult participants read stories that were built around a central theme, such as *earthquake*. The stories contained sentences that had more than one proposition, such as:

(1) The townspeople were amazed to find that all of the buildings had collapsed except the mint.

Each story consisted of two related sentences, so sentence (2) would follow sentence (1):

(2) Obviously, the architect had foreseen the danger because the structure withstood the natural disaster.

To see whether people organize representations in long-term memory around the propositions in the sentences, prime–target pairs were selected that either came from the same proposition (e.g., *amazed* and *townspeople*), different propositions in the same sentence (e.g., *townspeople and buildings*), or different sentences (e.g., *townspeople* and *architect*). If participants' representations in memory reflect the propositions, then prime–target pairs from the same proposition should lead to better recognition and faster responses than prime–target pairs where the two words come from different propositions (this is what normally happens; see Chapter 5). To find out whether the two hemispheres have the same or different representations, prime–target pairs were either presented in the LVF or the RVF. When the target words appeared in the RVF (i.e., were presented to the left hemisphere), prime–target pairs from the same proposition produced bigger priming effects than prime–target pairs from different propositions in the same sentence, which in turn produced bigger priming effects than prime–target pairs with words drawn from different sentences. When the same prime–target pairs were presented in the LVF (to the right hemisphere), none of these priming effects was significant. The only difference the right hemisphere recognized was between prime–target pairs drawn from the same story and prime–target pairs where the two words came from different stories. So, while the right hemisphere knew which concepts came from which stories, there was apparently no organization below the level of the story.

Long and her colleagues also tested whether the right and left hemispheres created inferences about the theme or topic of the story by presenting target words that were related to a topic inference. If you read sentences (1) and (2), you would likely infer that *danger* and *natural disaster* both referred to an earthquake. If you draw this inference, you should respond faster to the word *earthquake* and/or have a harder time rejecting it as a word that you saw when you read sentences (1) and (2). *Earthquake* never appears in the story, but if you infer that the topic is *earthquake*, you might falsely remember it as being a part of the story. When the target word *earthquake* was presented in either the RVF or LVF, healthy adults were more likely to remember it as being part of the story (even though it was not), which indicates that both hemispheres drew the inference that the story was about an earthquake. These results suggest an account under which the left hemisphere does detailed microstructure processing and keeps track of the propositions that a discourse contains, but the right hemisphere keeps track only of the gist of a story, and does not recognize fine distinctions between the different propositions that go together to make up the gist.

Right-Hemisphere Contributions to Non-Literal Language Understanding

Non-literal language processing may draw on right-hemisphere resources, perhaps because the right hemisphere maintains activation of meanings that are more weakly associated with particular words. Both of these capabilities could be useful in the understanding of metaphors, because understanding metaphors often requires looking beyond an obvious literal meaning to a less obvious or more subtle metaphoric meaning (see Chapter 7). Indeed, some patients with RHD appear to be selectively impaired on tasks that require them to come up with metaphoric meanings. One study looked at differences between (right-handed) aphasic patients who had damage to their left hemisphere and non-aphasic patients who had damage to their right hemisphere (Brownell, Simpson, Bihrle, Potter, & Gardner, 1990). These patients were tested on adjectives like *warm* that have a primary literal meaning (e.g., temperature) and a secondary metaphoric meaning (e.g., being a loving person). The patients were shown a set of adjectives and were asked to choose which of two other words were closest in meaning. If brain damage leads to a general inability to access secondary meanings, both aphasic and non-aphasic patients should have difficulty performing the task. If, by contrast, brain damage can selectively interfere with metaphoric meanings, then some patients should have greater difficulty doing the meaning judgment task than others. In fact, patients with RHD were less able to find the secondary metaphoric meaning than aphasic patients with LHD. The patient data suggest, therefore, that an intact right hemisphere supports the construction or recovery of metaphoric meanings. Healthy adults also sometimes show greater activation of metaphorical meanings in the right hemisphere and greater activation for literal meanings in the left hemisphere (Anaki, Faust, & Kravetz, 1997). Direct manipulation of the healthy adult brain using TMS also produces evidence that the right hemisphere contributes to the understanding of novel metaphors (Pobric, Mashal, Faust, & Lavidor, 2008). When right-hemisphere function was disturbed by the application of a high-intensity magnetic field next to the scalp, healthy adults were slower and less accurate when judging whether a pair of words shared a literal versus metaphoric relation.

However, as we saw in Chapter 7, not all studies show a left–right difference in response to literal and metaphor meanings (Faust & Weisper, 2000; Kacinik & Chiarello, 2007; but see Faust & Kravetz, 1998). Experiments involving lateralized presentation of literal and metaphor-related word meanings (compare *she has a cold drink* vs. *she has a cold personality*) sometimes show equivalent priming effects when the target words are presented in the left or right visual field. fMRI results show bilateral frontal activation for metaphoric meanings (Eviatar & Just, 2006; see also Bottini et al., 1994; Rapp, Leube, Erb, Grodd, & Kircher, 2004), as do ERP experiments (Coulson & Van Petten, 2002). Further, when different kinds of metaphoric statements are compared, fMRI results suggest that left–right asymmetries in priming tasks may result from differences in the relative salience, frequency, or novelty of the different meanings, rather than reflecting simpler literal versus non-literal distinctions (Mashal, Faust, & Hendler, 2005). All of these results cast doubt on strict right lateralization of metaphor processing. Therefore, there appears to be a clash between two sources of information: The patient data show substantial deficits in metaphor processing following RHD; but the behavioral, neuroimaging, and neurophysiological studies on healthy adults suggest that both hemispheres respond to metaphoric statements. As sometimes happens, contradictory results like these call for additional research to clarify each hemisphere's role in comprehending non-literal language.

What You Can Do with One Hemisphere

Most adults are strongly left lateralized for speech and syntax, with prosodic processing abilities being the best and perhaps only candidate for a strongly right-lateralized language process. Infants are born with some ability to recognize the prosody of their native language, but everything else gets added on later (Jusczyk, 1997). Thus, infants do not start out with language strongly represented in the left hemisphere. In fact, if anything, word processing during early child development (0–3 years) is more strongly represented in the right hemisphere than the left (Chiron et al., 1997), and is definitely represented more strongly in the right hemisphere compared to later stages of development (Mills, Coffey-Corina,

& Neville, 1997). In the first year and a half, the ERP response between words that children know versus words that they don't know differ over both the left and the right hemisphere. But by 20 months old, those differences no longer appear over the right hemisphere, suggesting a leftward shift in the brain's response to familiar words. However, children as old as 5 or 6 years can experience aphasic symptoms (halting, effortful or loss of speech) following RHD (Basser, 1962), which suggests that at least up to 5 or 6 years old, children are not yet left lateralized for speech. The presence of aphasia in children with RHD motivated some to believe that children, when they are born, are able to develop language skills to equally high levels of skill in either hemisphere. This *equipotentiality* hypothesis has been the focus of a great deal of research on child language development. Besides the presence of aphasia in children with RHD, what evidence favors equipotentiality?

Children who have undergone a surgical procedure called *hemispherectomy* (or the somewhat less complete procedure called *temporal lobectomy*) have been studied to test the equipotentiality hypothesis. Specifically, researchers wish to know whether both hemispheres are capable of developing language to the same extent (e.g., Basser, 1962; Mayor-Dubois, Maeder-Ingvar, Deonna, & Roulet-Perez, 2008). In the hemispherectomy procedure, all, or nearly all, of the cerebral cortex on one side of the brain is removed. In the temporal lobectomy procedure, one of the temporal lobes of the brain is removed, but other cortical tissue in the affected hemisphere is left in place. Radical procedures like hemispherectomy and temporal lobectomy carry substantial risks for the patient, and so they are carried out as a last resort and usually only after significant brain damage has occurred. In many cases, epileptic seizures will be the immediate problem. Children experience brain damage as the result of seizures, and if medication fails to control those seizures, surgery may be the only viable option. The great majority of children who undergo hemispherectomy experience reduced seizure activity, and some are able to stop taking anti-seizure medication (over 80% success was reported in one large sample; Wilson, 1970, see also Basser, 1962; Stark, Bleile, Brandt, Freeman, & Vining, 1995). Although the majority of hemispherectomy patients have below average intelligence, this is largely due to brain damage caused by their seizures, and the surgery does not normally lead to further declines in intelligence. (Hemispherectomy patients represent a cross-section of intellectual ability, and some develop superior intelligence, go on to graduate from college, and have successful professional careers.) Some patients actually experience mild increases in intellectual functioning following the surgery, probably because the healthier hemisphere no longer suffers from interference from the more damaged hemisphere. The vast majority of children who undergo hemispherectomy develop speech production and perception abilities in the normal range, regardless of which hemisphere remains following the surgery, with normal or near normal understanding of even complex language components, such as metaphors and idioms (Kempler, Van Lancker, Marchman, & Bates, 1999).[9] Thus, as with some of Gazzaniga's patients who had speech- and word-processing abilities in the right hemisphere, children whose left hemispheres were removed were eventually able to function at a high level, both speaking and understanding speech, using just the right hemisphere. Thus, it appeared that both hemispheres can develop sophisticated language abilities, as per the equipotentiality hypothesis.

How is it possible that children can develop sophisticated language abilities when the hemisphere that is normally dominant for many language functions (the left) is removed? Equipotentiality offers an explanation: Language organization is a function of developmental processes that normally result in left-hemisphere language (perhaps because the left hemisphere is better designed to handle rapidly changing stimuli). But if those developmental processes are disturbed, the right hemisphere, due to its *plasticity* (its ability to reorganize based on experience), can develop functions that the left hemisphere would normally carry out. However, there is a time limit on this ability to reorganize, and correlational studies show that right lateralization of language occurs more often in children who start experiencing neurological problems early; while left lateralization or bilateral organization is more common in children whose neurological problems start later (Satz, Strauss, Wada, & Orsini, 1988).

The ability to use right-hemisphere resources for language also comes with a cost, however, as the presence of "extra" language functions in the right hemisphere occupies neural tissue that would normally be used for other functions, such as spatial processing. The *crowding hypothesis* says that, if the right hemisphere takes over language functions from a damaged left hemisphere, it will be less able to carry out spatial perception tasks (because the usual right hemisphere spatial functions are "crowded out" by interloping language functions). When patients with early onset of neurological symptoms were tested for language laterality, there was a strong negative correlation between right-hemisphere control of speech and performance on tests of spatial ability. As indices of right-lateralized speech increased, scores on tests of spatial ability decreased (Strauss, Satz, & Wada, 1990).

The existence of crowding of right-hemisphere spatial function by speech processes might indicate that the right hemisphere has some trouble accommodating displaced left-hemisphere language processes. And so, following early reports of successful language development following hemispherectomy, researchers began taking a closer look at language function following hemispherectomy, and they found that language outcomes were not the same following left and right hemispherectomy (Day & Ulatowska, 1979; Dennis & Kohn, 1975; Dennis & Whitaker, 1976). To investigate language processing functions in more detail, researchers looked at the comprehension of syntax by children who had undergone right vs. left hemispherectomy. Syntax is generally viewed as being a left-lateralized function in most healthy adults. Syntactic comprehension and production problems are far more common following LHD than RHD, and neuroimaging studies show greater left than right hemisphere response when syntactic structure is manipulated. It might be that way for a reason. Perhaps the left hemisphere is just better than the right hemisphere at processing syntactic structure information.

To try to find out, Maureen Dennis and her colleagues performed a number of tests that required children to use their knowledge of syntax. In some tests, children were presented with sentences, and were asked to judge whether the sentences were "acceptable" or "unacceptable." Children were also asked to correct the sentence when they detected a problem. The sentences had problems with various aspects of syntax. Some of the sentences violated the normal word order that occurs in English sentences. For example (Dennis & Whitaker, 1976, p. 416), *Cash shouldn't send people through the mail* (although a non-syntactic agent-first semantic strategy might cause people to judge this sentence as being "unacceptable" even if they lacked normal syntactic processing abilities). Other sentences included number agreement violations (p. 417, *The best cars in Canada is a Ford and some Datsun*). Children who had their left hemisphere removed detected fewer syntactic errors than children who had their right hemisphere removed.[10] Children without a left hemisphere also performed at a lower level than right-hemidecorticate children on a task that required them to repeat a sentence verbatim, and they were less able to produce utterances that required movement of a syntactic constituent from its canonical location in the sentence (Dennis & Kohn, 1975). Children were also tested for speech perception and production abilities, as well as individual word comprehension and production. Including these latter tests helps to rule out a theory under which left-hemisphere patients perform worse than right-hemisphere patients because they know less about words or have trouble understanding speech. Additional testing involved matching of auditory sentences to pictures that could be described using either active (*The girl pushed the boy*), passive (*The boy was pushed by the girl*), or *negated passive* form (*The girl was not pushed by the boy*). Left-hemidecorticate children had difficulty comprehending the negated passives (but not the actives or the simple passives), when compared to age- and intelligence-matched right-hemidecorticate children. In addition, some left-hemidecorticate children have trouble with inflections, and so are unable to detect problems with sentences such as *He ated his breakfast* (Day & Ulatowska, 1979). These syntactic processing problems cannot be blamed on a general lack of intelligence, because even very high-functioning people have problems with some aspects of syntax following left hemispherectomy (Van Lancker-Sidtis, 2004). One patient with a college degree showed subtle problems comprehending linguistic prosody and passive sentences. Syntactic problems can therefore occur in highly intelligent people who have had ample opportunity to learn. Based on the syntactic processing deficits that follow left but not right hemispherectomy, Dennis and Whitaker conclude (1976, p. 404), "Language development in an isolated right hemisphere, even under seizure-free conditions, results in incomplete language acquisition." Thus, equipotentiality does not appear to be an accurate description for spoken language development.

But what about writing and reading? Children are capable of learning to read regardless of which hemisphere is removed, but at least some studies suggest that different forms of dyslexia follow depending on which hemisphere is removed (Ogden, 1996; Patterson, Vargha-Khadem, & Polkey, 1989). Thus, the two hemispheres do not appear to be equipotential for reading, in that different reading problems appear to follow when damage occurs to the right versus the left hemisphere. On the whole, then, different outcomes are likely for both spoken and written language processing following left versus right hemispherectomy, with lower overall performance being more common after left hemispherectomy than right hemispherectomy (remember, though, that regardless of which side is operated on, children typically develop language skills that are more than adequate to serve their communication needs). Thus, equipotentiality does not appear to accurately describe language development and the capabilities of the two hemispheres.

Why Lateralization?

Having provided evidence that the right hemisphere participates in some language tasks, the left hemisphere still appears to be more critical for basic language production (i.e., speech) and comprehension processes (e.g., syntax). On the whole, people tend to function better with a disabled right hemisphere than a disabled left hemisphere. Given this asymmetry, how did the brain get to be that way and why? One possible answer to the why question is based on balancing the spatial abilities of the right hemisphere and its ability to integrate information over longer time scales (e.g., Poeppel, 2003) with the fast-change-detection abilities of the left hemisphere that are necessary for phonemic processing and speech. Under this view, relatively recent (in evoluationary terms) language skills take advantage of older, pre-existing perceptual abilities, which already differed between the two hemispheres when language emerged. If both hemispheres had high spatial and low verbal ability, then people would enjoy fewer benefits of cooperative action and knowledge transmission conveyed by language. On the other hand, if both hemispheres had high verbal ability at the cost of spatial abilities, people might not have sufficient pattern-recognition skills to detect threats and opportunities in the environment. You can't talk if you've been eaten by a tiger. So, at some point in history, there may have been lots of people who had strong speech and syntactic abilities in both hemispheres, but they may have been selected against due to their lesser spatial abilities.

Summary and Conclusions

This chapter has reviewed studies that focus on right-hemisphere language function. The evidence comes in a variety of forms, including a large number of studies of patients with brain damage, neuroimaging and neurophysiological experiments, and behavioral investigations of laterality, many of which involve the divided visual field technique or other forms of lateralized stimulus presentation. On the whole, the current consensus appears to be that prosodic processing functions are lateralized to the right hemisphere, although those aspects of prosody that are important in identifying syntactic boundaries or disambiguating lexical (word) identity may be lateralized to the left hemisphere. Loss of prosodic processing ability following LHD may mean that the left hemisphere is normally involved in analyzing speech to extract prosodic information, but it could also reflect loss of processes that integrate prosody (supplied by the right hemisphere) with other cues to meaning. Research on lexical processing suggests differences in semantic representations and patterns of activation in the two hemispheres, with the coarse coding hypothesis currently enjoying the greatest degree of support in the research record. The right hemisphere appears to play a role in inference generation during discourse comprehension, although the left hemisphere also appears to participate in those functions, possibly to a greater degree depending on what kind of inference is required. The right hemisphere responds to non-literal meanings, but because data from medical patients and healthy adults do not neatly align, further research is needed to clarify how non-literal language affects each hemisphere. Finally, research on children who have undergone hemispherectomy demonstrates that two hemispheres are not strictly necessary for language skills to develop, although somewhat better outcomes are associated with an intact left hemisphere.

TEST YOURSELF

1. Describe different kinds of prosody and the purposes each one serves. What roles do the two cerebral hemispheres play in producing and responding to prosody?
2. What is the *right-hemisphere* prosody account? What evidence supports it? What evidence suggests that it may not be correct?
3. What's the difference between a dominant function and a lateralized function?
4. Describe an experiment that used near-infrared optical topography. What does the experiment contribute to the study of prosody?
5. Present the case for and against right-hemisphere lateralization of affective prosody.
6. Contrast the right-hemisphere prosody account with the "functional" hypothesis. Which one do you favor and why?
7. How does the right hemisphere respond to spoken and written words? How do these responses differ from the left hemisphere's response? What explains these differences? What are the strengths and weaknesses of the coarse coding hypothesis?

8. How does the right hemisphere respond to semantically ambiguous words? Describe experiments that reveal what the right hemisphere does with an ambiguous word.
9. What does the right hemisphere contribute to discourse processing? Describe evidence suggesting that the right hemisphere plays a special role in generating inferences. Describe evidence suggesting that the left and right hemispheres build different text-base representations.
10. Describe the right-hemisphere contribution to non-literal language understanding.
11. What happens when one hemisphere is removed to prevent fatal progressive brain damage? What happens when the left hemisphere is removed compared to what happens when the right hemisphere is removed?

THINK ABOUT IT

1. Popular psychology would have us believe that there are "left-brained" people and "right-brained" people. Do you think the same thing could apply to language? What would a right-brained language producer sound like? Children who lose an entire cerebral hemisphere can appear to have a fully intact brain when it comes to their language abilities. What implications does this have for nativists?

Notes

Drs. Kristen Tooley and Clint Johns contributed to the literature review for this chapter and helped compose the sections on non-literal language and inferencing. The author is deeply grateful for their assistance.

1 Some neuroimaging studies suggest that parts of the right hemisphere respond to syntactic and sentence-level manipulations (e.g., Grodzinsky & Friederici, 2006; Grodzinsky & Santi, 2008; Meyer, Friederici, & von Cramon, 2000), but syntactic processing dysfunction following right-hemisphere brain damage is exceedingly rare in people who are left lateralized for speech and the contribution of the right hemisphere to syntactic parsing, if any, is poorly understood at present. Hence, this chapter will not review right-hemisphere contributions to sentence-level syntactic processes.

2 Failures to find deficits in prosody comprehension or production following right-sided brain damage are no more surprising than failures to find aphasia in all patients with left-hemisphere brain damage. Such failures to find prosodic deficits in right-brain-damaged patients may reflect the sparing of those brain regions that are involved in prosodic processing, atypical lateralization of prosodic functions (analogous to atypical lateralization of speech in right-handed people), residual function in undamaged portions of the affected hemisphere, or intrahemispheric transfer of function from damaged to undamaged regions.

3 BUT: Bryan's (1989) patients were aphasic at the time of testing, and so direct comparisons to non-aphasic right-hemisphere patients may not be appropriate.

4 Gazzaniga (1983) criticizes his own, and by extension everyone else's, research on laterality in spoken language comprehension, because the inputs to each hemisphere from the ears are not as neatly segregated as visual inputs are. However, if input from a given ear projected equally to each hemisphere, and if the two hemispheres undertook the same processes simultaneously, we should never observe a processing advantage based on which ear a stimulus was presented to. So, while caution is certainly advisable in interpreting the outcomes of

dichotic listening experiments, the fact that ear advantages are observed suggests that different processes are taking place in the different hemispheres.

5 Degraded speech also tends to activate regions of left-hemisphere frontal lobes (Ischebeck et al., 2008; Kotz, Frisch, von Cramon, & Friederici, 2003; Meyer et al., 2000; Meyer, Alter, Friederici, Lohmann, & von Cramon, 2002), but probably does so for reasons related to strategic comprehension monitoring or executive control, rather than reflecting left-hemisphere participation in analyzing the prosodic contour.

6 But again, it is difficult to know what to make of failures to find effects. It could be that the researchers were looking at the wrong kinds of patients or used stimuli that could be processed by intact areas of the damaged hemisphere, or that they lacked sufficient experimental power to detect the relevant effects.

7 Rodd and colleagues' (Rodd, Davis, & Johnsrude, 2005) fMRI data also suggest a role for right frontal cortex in resolving semantic ambiguity.

8 Marini and colleagues' (2005) study showed that RHD patients could successfully retell a story that they had previously read, but they had difficulty making up a new story to go along with a series of pictures. Thus, these patients appear to have trouble with planning processes, as opposed to problems with macrostructure in general. It is also possible that intact memory processes allowed the patients to retell the story essentially as a list of episodes, without having a coherent macrostructure representation.

9 Notable exceptions involve cases where intellectual functioning was severely impaired prior to surgery, and removal of one hemisphere may have reduced computational power below the minimum necessary to support speech (Wilson, 1970).

10 One of the children in the Dennis & Whitaker (1976) study spontaneously corrected some of the sentences for which she had not consciously detected a grammatical error. This may indicate that her implicit knowledge of syntactic form was intact, while her ability to apply that knowledge in an explicit judgment task was impaired. This would represent the opposite of the pattern seen in some Broca's aphasics, who are sometimes able to accurately judge grammaticality when they are unable to produce the same grammatical structure themselves.

References

Adolphs, R., Damasio, H., & Tranel, D. (2002). Neural systems for recognition of emotional prosody: A 3-D lesion study. *Emotion, 2,* 23–51.

Anaki, D., Faust, M., & Kravetz, S. (1997). Cerebral hemispheric asymmetries in processing lexical metaphors. *Neuropsychologia, 36,* 691–700.

Bartels-Tobin, L. R., & Hinckley, J. J. (2005). Cognition and discourse production in right hemisphere disorder. *Journal of Neurolinguistics, 18,* 461–477.

Basser, L. S. (1962). Hemiplegia of early onset and the faculty of speech with special reference to the effects of hemispherectomy. *Brain, 85,* 427–460.

Baum, S. R., & Dwivedi, V. D. (2003). Sensitivity to prosodic structure in left- and right-hemisphere damaged individuals. *Brain & Language, 87,* 278–289.

Baum, S. R., & Pell, M. D. (1999). The neural bases of prosody: Insights from lesion studies and neuroimaging. *Aphasiology, 13,* 581–608.

Baum, S. R., Pell, M. D., Leonard, C. L., & Gordon, J. K. (2001). Using prosody to resolve temporary syntactic ambiguities in speech production: Acoustic data on brain-damaged speakers. *Clinical Linguistics and Phonetics, 15,* 441–456.

Beeman, M. (1993). Semantic processing in the right hemisphere may contribute to drawing inferences from discourse. *Brain & Language, 44,* 80–120.

Beeman, M. (1998). Coarse semantic coding and discourse comprehension. In M. Beeman & C. Chiarello (Eds.) *Right hemisphere language comprehension: Perspectives from cognitive neuroscience* (pp. 51–78). Mahwah, NJ: Erlbaum.

Beeman, M. J. (2005). Bilateral brain processes for comprehending natural language. *Trends in Cognitive Sciences, 9,* 512–518.

Beeman, M. J., Bowden, E. M., & Gernsbacher, M. A. (2000). Right and left hemisphere cooperation for drawing predictive and coherence inferences during normal story comprehension. *Brain & Language, 71,* 310–336.

Beeman, M. J., & Chiarello, C. (1998). Complementary right- and left-hemisphere language comprehension. *Current Directions in Psychological Science, 7,* 2–8.

Beeman, M., Friedman, R. B., Grafman, J., Perez, E., Diamond, S., & Lindsay, M. B. (1994). Summation priming and coarse coding in the right hemisphere. *Journal of Cognitive Neuroscience, 6,* 26–45.

Behrens, S. J. (1985). The perception of stress and lateralization of prosody. *Brain & Language, 26,* 332–348.

Bell, W. L., Davis, D. L., Morgan-Fisher, A., & Ross, E. D. (1990). Acquired aprosodia in children. *Journal of Child Neurology, 5,* 19–26.

Bottini, G., Corcoran, R., Sterzi, R., Paulesu, E., Schenone, P., Scarpa, P., et al. (1994). The role of the right hemisphere in the interpretation of figurative aspects of language: A positron emission tomography activation study. *Brain, 117,* 1241–1253.

Bouaffre, S., & Faïta-Ainseba, F. (2007). Hemispheric differences in the time-course of semantic priming processes: Evidence from event-related potentials (ERPs). *Brain and Cognition, 63,* 123–135.

Brady, M., Armstrong, L., & Mackenzie, C. (2006). An examination over time of language and discourse production abilities following right hemisphere brain damage. *Journal of Neurolinguistics, 19,* 291–310.

Brownell, H. H., Simpson, T. L., Bihrle, A. M., Potter, H. H., & Gardner, H. (1990). Appreciation of metaphoric alternative word meanings by left and right brain-damaged patients. *Neuropsychologia, 28,* 375–383.

Brownell, H. H., & Stringfellow, A. (1999). Making requests: Illustrations of how right-hemisphere brain damage can affect discourse production. *Brain & Language, 68,* 442–465.

Bryan, K. L. (1989). Language prosody and the right hemisphere. *Aphasiology, 3,* 285–299.

Burgess, C., & Simpson, G. B. (1988). Cerebral hemispheric mechanisms in the retrieval of ambiguous word meanings. *Brain & Language, 33,* 86–103.

Charbonneau, S., Scherzer, B. P., Aspirot, D., & Cohen, H. (2003). Perception and production of facial and prosodic emotions by chronic CVA patients. *Neuropsychologia, 41,* 605–613.

Chiarello, C., Burgess, C., Richards, L., & Pollock, A. (1990). Semantic and associative priming in the cerebral hemispheres: Some words do, some words don't ... sometimes, some places. *Brain & Language, 38,* 75–104.

Chiarello, C., Maxfield, L., & Kahan, T. (1995). Initial right hemisphere activation of subordinate word meanings is not due to homotopic callosal inhibition. *Psychonomic Bulletin & Review, 2,* 375–380.

Chiarello, C., & Richards, L. (1992). Another look at categorical priming in the cerebral hemispheres. *Neuropsychologia, 30,* 381–392.

Chiron, C., Jambaque, I., Nabbout, R., Lounes, R., Syrota, A., & Dulac, O. (1997). The right brain hemisphere is dominant in human infants. Brain, *120,* 1057–1065.

Cohen, M. J., Branch, W. B., & Hynd, G. W. (1994). Receptive prosody in children with left or right hemisphere dysfunction. *Brain & Language, 47,* 171–181.

Coulson, S., & Van Petten, C. (2002). Conceptual integration and metaphor: An ERP study. *Memory & Cognition, 30,* 958–968.

Dapretto, M., Lee, S. S., & Caplan, R. (2005). A functional magnetic resonance imaging study of discourse coherence in typically developing children. *NeuroReport, 16,* 1661–1665.

Day, P. S., & Ulatowska, H. K. (1979). Perceptual, cognitive, and linguistic development after early hemispherectomy: Two case studies. *Brain & Language, 7,* 17–33.

Deacon, D., Grose-Fifer, J., Yang, C-M., Stanick, V., Hewitt, S., & Dynowska, A. (2004). Evidence for a new conceptualization of semantic representation in the left and right cerebral hemispheres. *Cortex, 40,* 467–478.

Delis, D. C., Wapner, W., Gardner, H., & Moses, J. A. (1983). The contribution of the right hemisphere to the organization of paragraphs. *Cortex, 19,* 43–50.

Dennis, M., & Kohn, B. (1975). Comprehension of syntax in infantile hemiplegics after cerebral hemidecortication: Left-hemisphere superiority. *Brain & Language, 2,* 472–482.

Dennis, M., & Whitaker, H. A. (1976). Language acquisition following hemidecortication: Linguistic superiority of the left over the right hemisphere. *Brain & Language, 3,* 404–433.

Duffy, S. A., Henderson, J. M., & Morris, R. K. (1989). Semantic facilitation of lexical access during sentence processing. *Journal of Experimental Psychology: Learning, Memory, and Cognition, 15,* 791–801.

Erhan, H., Borod, J. C., Tenke, C. E., & Bruder, G. E. (1998). Identification of emotion in a dichotic listening task: Event-related brain potential and behavioral findings. *Brain and Cognition, 37,* 286–307.

Eviatar, Z., & Ibrahim, R. (2007). Morphological structure and hemispheric functioning: The contribution of the right hemisphere to reading in different languages. *Neuropsychology, 21,* 470–484.

Eviatar, Z., & Just, M. A. (2006). Brain correlates of discourse processing: An fMRI investigation of irony and conventional metaphor comprehension. *Neuropsychologia, 44,* 2348–2359.

Faust, M., Ben-Artzi, E., & Harel, I. (2008). Hemispheric asymmetries in semantic processing: Evidence from false memories for ambiguous words. *Brain & Language, 105,* 220–228.

Faust, M., & Chiarello, C. (1998). Sentence context and lexical ambiguity resolution by the two hemispheres. *Neuropsychologia, 36,* 827–835.

Faust, M., & Kravetz, S. (1998). Levels of sentence constraint and lexical decision in the two hemispheres. *Brain & Language, 62,* 149–162.

Faust, M., & Lavidor, M. (2003). Semantically convergent and semantically divergent priming in the cerebral hemispheres: Lexical decision and semantic judgment. *Cognitive Brain Research, 17,* 585–597.

Faust, M., & Weisper, S. (2000). Understanding metaphoric sentences in the two cerebral hemispheres. *Brain and Cognition, 43,* 186–191.

Ferstl, E. C., Guthke, T., & von Cramon, D. Y. (2002). Text comprehension after brain injury: Left prefrontal lesions affect inference processes. *Neuropsychology, 16,* 292–308.

Ferstl, E. C., Walther, K.; Guthke, T., & von Cramon, D. Y. (2005). Assessment of story comprehension deficits after brain damage. *Journal of Clinical and Experimental Neuropsychology, 273,* 367–384.

Gazzaniga, M. S. (1983). Right hemisphere language following bisection. *American Psychologist, 38,* 525–537.

Gazzaniga, M. S. (1984). Right hemisphere language: Remaining problems. *American Psychologist, 39,* 1494–1496.

Gazzaniga, M. S., Smylie, C. S., Baynes, K., Hirst, W., & McCleary, C. (1984). Profiles of right hemisphere language and speech following brain bisection. *Brain & Language, 22,* 206–220.

Gazzaniga, M. S., & Sperry, R. W. (1967). Language after section of the cerebral commisures. *Brain, 90,* 131–148.

Grimshaw, G. M., Kwasny, K. M., Covell, E., & Johnson, R. A. (2003). The dynamic nature of language lateralization: Effects of lexical and prosodic factors. *Neuropsychologia, 41,* 1008–1019.

Grodzinsky, Y., & Friederici, A. D. (2006). Neuroimaging of syntax and syntactic processing. *Current Opinion in Neurobiology, 16,* 240–246.

Grodzinsky, Y., & Santi, A. (2008). The battle for Broca's region. *Trends in Cognitive Sciences, 12,* 474–480.

Grose-Fifer, J., & Deacon, D. (2004). Priming by natural category membership in the left and right cerebral hemispheres. *Neuropsychologia, 42,* 1948–1960.

Habib, M. (1986). Visual hypoemotionality and prosopagnosia associated with right temporal lobe isolation. *Neuropsychologia, 24,* 577–582.

Heilman, K. M., Leon, S. A., & Rosenbek, J. C. (2004). Affective aprosodia from a medial stroke. *Brain & Language, 89,* 411–416.

Heilman, K. M., Scholes, R., & Watson, R. T. (1975). Auditory affective agnosia. Disturbed comprehension of affective speech. *Journal of Neurology, Neurosurgery, & Psychiatry, 38,* 69–72.

Henderson, L., Barca, L., & Ellis, A. W. (2007). Interhemispheric cooperation and non-cooperation during word recognition: Evidence for callosal transfer dysfunction in dyslexic adults. *Brain & Language, 103,* 276–291.

Homae, F., Watanabe, H., Nakano, T., Asakawa, K., & Taga, G. (2006). The right hemisphere of sleeping infant perceives sentential prosody. *Neuroscience Research, 54,* 276–280.

Homae, F., Watanabe, H., Nakano, T., & Taga, G. (2007). Prosodic processing in the developing brain. *Neuroscience Research, 59,* 29–39.

Hoyte, K. J., Brownell, H., Vesely, L., & Wingfield, A. (2006). Decomposing prosody: Use of prosodic features for detection of syntactic structure and speech affect by patients with right hemisphere lesions. *Brain & Language, 99,* 44–46.

Ischebeck, A. K., Friederici, A. D., & Alter, K. (2008). Processing prosodic boundaries in natural and hummed speech: An fMRI study. *Cerebral Cortex, 18,* 541–552.

Johns, C. L., Tooley, K. M., & Traxler, M. J. (2008). Discourse impairments following right hemisphere brain damage: A critical review. *Language and Linguistics Compass, 2,* 1038–1062.

Johnstone, T., van Reekum, C. M., Oakes, T. R., & Davidson, R. J. (2006). The voice of emotion: An fMRI study of neural responses to angry and happy vocal expressions. *Scan, 1,* 242–249.

Jusczyk, P. (1997). *The discovery of spoken language*. Cambridge, MA: MIT Press.

Kaan, E., & Swaab, T. Y. (2002). The brain circuitry of syntactic comprehension. *Trends in Cognitive Sciences, 6,* 350–356.

Kacinik, N. A., & Chiarello, C. (2007). Understanding metaphors: Is the right hemisphere uniquely involved? *Brain & Language, 100,* 188–207.

Kandhadai, P., & Federmeier, K. D. (2007). Multiple priming of lexically ambiguous and unambiguous targets in the cerebral hemispheres: The coarse coding hypothesis revisited. *Brain Research, 1153,* 144–157.

Kandhadai, P., & Federmeier, K. D. (2008). Summing it up: Semantic activation processes in the two hemispheres as revealed by event-related potentials. *Brain Research, 1233,* 146–159.

Keil, K., Baldo, J., Kaplan, E., Kramer, J., & Delis, C. (2005). Role of frontal cortex in inferential reasoning: Evidence from the word context test. *Journal of the International Neuropsychological Society, 11,* 426–433.

Kempler, D., Van Lancker, D., Marchman, V., & Bates, E. (1999). Idiom comprehension in children and adults with unilateral brain damage. *Developmental Neuropsychology, 15,* 327–349.

Kinsbourne, M. (1986). Cerebral representation of language in left and right hemispheres. *Journal of Neurolinguistics, 2,* 371–381.

Knecht, S., Deppe, M., Dräger, B., Bobe, L., Lohmann, H., Ringlestein, E.-B., et al. (2000). Language lateralization in healthy right-handers. *Brain, 123,* 74–81.

Kotz, S. A., Frisch, S., von Cramon, D. Y., & Friederici, A. D. (2003). Syntactic language processing: ERP lesion data on the role of the basal ganglia. *Journal of the International Neuropsychological Society, 9,* 1053–1060.

Kucharska-Pietura, K., Phillips, M. L., Gernand, W., & David, A. S. (2003). Perceptions of emotions from faces and voices following unilateral brain damage. *Neuropsychologia, 41,* 1082–1090.

Kuperberg, G. R., Lakshmanan, B. M., Caplan, D. N., & Holcomb, P. J. (2006). Making sense of discourse: An fMRI study of causal inferencing across sentences. *Neuroimage, 33,* 343–361.

Lebrun, Y., Lessinnes, A., De Vresse, L., & Leleux, C. (1985). Dysprosody and the non-dominant hemisphere. *Language Sciences, 7,* 41–52.

Lehman-Blake, M. T. & Tompkins, C. A. (2001). Predictive inferencing in adults with right hemisphere brain damage. *Journal of Speech, Language and Hearing Research, 44,* 639–654.

Leonard, C. L., Waters, G. S., & Caplan, D. (1997a). The use of contextual information by right brain-damaged individuals in the resolution of ambiguous pronouns. *Brain & Language,* 57, 309–342.

Leonard, C. L., Waters, G. S., & Caplan, D. (1997b). The use of contextual information related to general world knowledge by right brain-damaged individuals in pronoun resolution. *Brain & Language, 57,* 343–359.

Long, D. L. & Baynes, K. (2002). Discourse representation in the two cerebral hemispheres. *Journal of Cognitive Neuroscience, 14,* 228–242.

Long, D. L., Baynes, K., & Prat, C. S. (2005). The propositional structure of discourse in the two cerebral hemispheres. *Brain & Language, 95,* 383–394.

Mackenzie, C., Brady, M., Begg, T., & Lees, K. R. (2001). Communication ability following right hemisphere brain damage: The family perspective. *Advances in Speech-Language Pathology, 3,* 81–95.

Marien, P., Paghera, D., De Deyn, P. P., & Vignolo, L. A. (2004). Adult crossed aphasia in dextrals revisited. *Cortex, 40,* 41–74.

Marini, A., Carlomagno, S., Caltagirone, C., & Nocentini, U. (2005). The role played by the right hemisphere in the organization of complex textual structures. *Brain & Language, 93,* 46–54.

Mashal, N., Faust, M., & Hendler, T. (2005). The role of the right hemisphere in processing nonsalient metaphorical meanings: Application of principal components analysis to fMRI data. *Neuropsychologia, 43,* 2084–2100.

Mayor-Dubois, C., Maeder-Ingvar, M., Deonna, T., & Roulet-Perez, E. (2008). The role of epilepsy in early language development in a child with a congenital lesion in the right hemisphere. *Developmental Medicine & Child Neurology, 50,* 870–875.

Merrewether, F. C., & Alpert, M. (1990). The components and neuroanatomic bases of prosody. *Journal of Communication Disorders, 23,* 325–336.

Meyer, A. M., & Federmeier, K. D. (2008). The divided visual world paradigm: Eye tracking reveals hemispheric asymmetries in lexical ambiguity resolution. *Brain Research, 1222,* 166–183.

Meyer, M., Alter, K., & Friederici, A. (2003). Functional MR imaging exposes differential brain responses to syntax and prosody during auditory sentence comprehension. *Journal of Neurolinguistics, 16,* 277–300.

Meyer, M., Alter, K., Friederici, A. D., Lohmann, G., & von Cramon, D. Y. (2002). FMRI reveals brain regions mediating slow prosodic modulations in spoken sentences. *Human Brain Mapping, 17,* 73–88.

Meyer, M., Friederici, A. D., & von Cramon, D. Y. (2000). Neurocognition of auditory sentence comprehension: Event related fMRI reveals sensitivity to syntactic violations and task demands. *Cognitive Brain Research, 9,* 19–33.

Mills, D. L., Coffey-Corina, S., & Neville, H. J. (1997). Language comprehension and cerebral specialization from 13 to 20 months. *Developmental Neuropsychology, 13,* 397–445.

Mohr, B., Pulvermüller, F., & Zaidel, E. (1994). Lexical decision after left, right and bilateral presentation of function words, content words and non-words: Evidence for interhemispheric interaction. *Neuropsychologia, 32,* 105–124.

Nicholson, K. G., Baum, S., Kilgour, A., Koh, C. K., Munhall, K. G., & Cuddy, L. L. (2003). Impaired processing of prosodic and musical patterns after right hemisphere damage. *Brain and Cognition, 52,* 382–389.

Ogden, J. A. (1996). Phonological dyslexia and phonological dysgraphia following left and right hemispherectomy. *Neuropsychologia, 34,* 905–918.

Patterson, K., Vargha-Khadem, F., & Polkey, C. E. (1989). Reading with one hemisphere. *Brain, 112,* 39–63.

Peck, R. N. (1962). *The happy sadist.* Garden City, NJ: Doubleday.

Pell, M. D. (1998). Recognition of prosody following unilateral brain lesion: Influence of functional and structural attributes of prosodic contours. *Neuropsychologia, 36,* 701–715.

Pell, M. D. (1999). Fundamental frequency encoding of linguistic and emotional prosody by right hemisphere damaged speakers. *Brain & Language, 69,* 161–192.

Pell, M. D. (2006). Cerebral mechanisms for understanding emotional prosody in speech. *Brain & Language, 96,* 221–234.

Pell, M. D. (2007). Reduced sensitivity to prosodic attitudes in adults with focal right hemisphere brain damage. *Brain & Language, 101,* 64–79.

Pell, M. D., & Baum, S. R. (1997a). The ability to perceive and comprehend intonation in linguistic and affective context by brain-damaged adults. *Brain & Language, 57,* 80–99.

Pell, M. D., & Baum, S. R. (1997b). Unilateral brain damage, prosodic comprehension deficits, and the acoustic cues to prosody. *Brain & Language, 57,* 195–214.

Plante, E., Creusere, M., & Sabin, C. (2002). Dissociating sentential prosody from sentence processing: Activation interacts with task demands. *Neuroimage, 17,* 401–410.

Pobric, G., Mashal, N., Faust, M., & Lavidor, M. (2008). The role of the right cerebral hemisphere in processing novel metaphoric expressions: A transcranial magnetic stimulation study. *Journal of Cognitive Neuroscience, 20,* 170–181.

Poeppel, D. (2003). The analysis of speech in different temporal integration windows: Cerebral lateralization as "asymmetric sampling in time." *Speech Communication, 41,* 245–255.

Prat, C. S., Long, D. L., & Baynes, K. (2007). The representation of discourse in the two hemispheres: An individual differences investigation. *Brain & Language, 100,* 283–294.

Rapp, A., Leube, D., Erb, M., Grodd, W., & Kircher, T. (2004). Neural correlates of metaphor processing. *Cognitive Brain Research, 20,* 395–402.

Rehak, A., Kaplan, J. A., Weylman, S. T., Kelly, B., Brownell, H. H., & Gardner, H. (1992). Story processing in right-hemisphere brain-damaged patients. *Brain & Language, 42,* 320–336.

Robertson, D. A., Gernsbacher, M. A., Guidotti, S. J., Robertson, R. R. W., Irwin, W., Mock, B.J., et al. (2000). Functional neuroanatomy of the cognitive process of mapping during discourse processing. *Psychological Science, 11,* 255–260.

Robin, D. A., Tranel, D., & Damasio, H. (1990). Auditory perception of temporal and spectral events in patients with focal left and right cerebral lesions. *Brain & Language, 39,* 539–555.

Rodd, J. M., Davis, M. H., & Johnsrude, I. S. (2005). The neural mechanisms of speech comprehension: fMRI studies of semantic ambiguity. *Cerebral Cortex, 15,* 1261–1269.

Ross, E.D. (1981). The aprosodias: Functional-anatomic organization of the affective components of language in the right hemisphere. *Archives of Neurology, 38,* 561–569.

Ross, E. D. (1984). Right hemisphere's role in language, affective behavior and emotion. *Trends in Neuroscience, 7,* 342–346.

Ross, E. D., Edmondson, J. A., Seibert, G. B., & Homan, R. W. (1988). Acoustic analysis of affective prosody during right-sided Wada Test: A within-subjects verification of the right hemisphere's role in language. *Brain & Language, 33,* 128–145.

Ross, E. D., & Monnot, M. (2008). Neurology of affective prosody and its functional-anatomic organization in right hemisphere. *Brain & Language, 104,* 51–74.

Ross, E. D., & Monnot, M. (2010). Affective prosody: What do comprehension errors tell us about hemispheric lateralization of emotions, sex and aging effects, and the role of cognitive appraisal. *Neuropsychologia, 49,* 866–877.

Rymarczyk, K., & Grabowska, A. (2007). Sex differences in brain control of prosody. *Neuropsychologia, 45,* 921–930.

Satz, P., Strauss, E., Wada, J., & Orsini, D. L. (1988). Some correlates of intra- and interhemispheric speech organization after left focal brain injury. *Neuropsychologia, 26,* 345–350.

Schneiderman, E. I., Murasagi, K. G., & Saddy, J. D. (1992). Story arrangement ability in right brain-damaged patients. *Brain & Language, 43,* 107–120.

Seidenberg, M. S., Tanenhaus, M. K., Leiman, J. M., & Bienkowski, M. (1982). =Automatic access of the meanings of ambiguous words: Evidence from priming and eye fixations. *Memory and Cognition, 28,* 1098–1108.

Shah, A. P., Baum, S. R, & Dwivedi, V. D. (2006). Neural substrates of linguistic prosody: Evidence from syntactic disambiguation in the productions of brain-damaged patients. *Brain & Language, 96,* 78–89.

Shears, C., Hawkins, A., Varner, A., Lewis, L., Heatley, J., & Twachtmann, L. (2008). Knowledge-based inference across the hemispheres: Domain makes a difference. *Neuropsychologia, 46,* 2563–2568.

Snyder, P. J., Novelly, R. A., & Harris, L. J. (1990). Mixed speech dominance in the intracarotid sodium amytal procedure: Validity and criteria issues. *Journal of Clinical and Experimental Neuropsychology, 12,* 629–643.

Speer, S., & Blodgett, A. (2006). Prosody. In M. J. Traxler & M. A. Gernsbacher (Eds.), *The handbook of psycholinguistics* (2nd ed., pp. 505–538). Amsterdam, The Netherlands: Elsevier.

Stark, R. E., Bleile, K., Brandt, J., Freeman, J., & Vining, E. P. (1995). Speech-language outcomes of hemispherectomy in children and young adults. *Brain & Language, 51,* 406–421.

St. George, M., Kutas, M., Martinez, A., & Sereno, M. I. (1999). Semantic integration in reading: Engagement of the right hemisphere during discourse processing. *Brain, 122,* 1317–1325.

Strauss, E., Satz, P., & Wada, J. (1990). An examination of the crowding hypothesis in epileptic patients who have undergone the carotid amytal test. *Neuropsychologia, 28,* 1221–1227.

Swinney, D. A. (1979). Lexical access during sentence comprehension: (Re)consideration of context effects. *Journal of Verbal Learning and Verbal Behavior, 18,* 645–659.

Tompkins, C. A., & Mateer, C. A. (1985). Right hemisphere appreciation of prosodic and linguistic indications of implicit attitude. *Brain & Language, 24,* 185–203.

Traxler, M. J., & Foss, D. J. (2000). Effects of sentence constraint on priming in natural language comprehension. *Journal of Experimental Psychology: Learning, Memory, and Cognition, 26,* 1266–1282.

Van Lancker-Sidtis, D. (2004). When only the right hemisphere is left: Studies in language and communication. *Brain & Language, 91,* 199–211.

Van Lancker-Sidtis, D., Pachana, N., Cummings, J. L., & Sidtis, J. J. (2006). Dysprosodic speech following basal ganglia insult: Toward a conceptual framework for the study of the cerebral representation of prosody. *Brain & Language, 97,* 135–153.

Wada, J., & Rasmussen, T. (1960). Intracarotid injection of sodium amytal for the lateralization of cerebral speech dominance. Experimental and clinical observations. *Journal of Neurosurgery, 17,* 266–282.

Walker, J. P., Fongemie, K., & Daigle, T. (2001). Prosodic facilitation in the resolution of syntactic ambiguities in subjects with left and right hemisphere damage. *Brain & Language, 78,* 169–196.

Wartenberger, I., Steinbrink, J., Telkemeyer, S., Friedrich, M., Friederici, A. D., & Obrig, H. (2007). The processing of prosody: Evidence of interhemispheric specialization at the age of four. *Neuroimage, 34,* 416–425.

Wertz, R. T., Henschel, C. R., Auther, L. L., Ashford, J. R., & Kirshner, H. S. (1998). Affective prosodic disturbance subsequent to right hemisphere stroke: A clinical application. *Journal of Neurolinguistics, 11,* 89–102.

Wildgruber, D., Pihan, D., Ackermann, H., Erb, M., & Grodd, W. (2002). Dynamic brain activation during processing of emotional intonation: Influence of acoustic parameters, emotional valence, and sex. *Neuroimage, 15,* 856–869.

Wilson, P. J. E. (1970). Cerebral hemispherectomy for infantile hemiplegia: A report of 50 cases. *Brain, 93,* 147–180.

Zaidel, E., Clarke, J. M., & Suyenobu, N. (1990). Hemispheric independence: A case paradigm for cognitive neuroscience. In A. B. Scheibel & A. F. Wechsler (Eds.), *Neurobiology of higher cognitive function* (pp. 297–355). New York: Guilford.

Zurif, E., Swinney, D., Prather, P., Solomon, J., & Bushell, C. (1993). An on-line analysis of syntactic processing in Broca's and Wernicke's aphasia. *Brain & Language, 45,* 448–464.

NAME INDEX

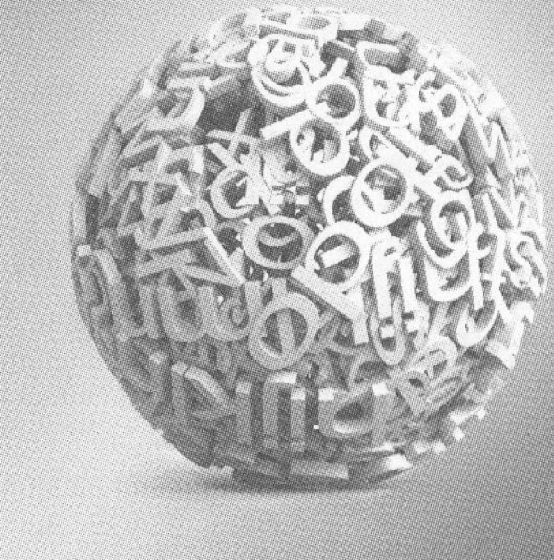

References to notes and figures are entered as (respectively) 21n or 21f. Plates are entered as Plate 1, Plate 2, etc. and are listed at the end of each entry after all other references.

Introduction to Psycholinguistics: Understanding Language Science, First Edition.
Matthew J. Traxler.

SUBJECT INDEX

References to notes and figures are entered as (respectively) 21n or 21f. Plates are entered as Plate 1, Plate 2 etc., and are listed at the end of each entry after all other references.

Introduction to Psycholinguistics: Understanding Language Science, First Edition.
Matthew J. Traxler.